CONTEMPORARY SOCIOLOGY

CONTEMPORARY
SOCIOLOGY

Edited by

JOSEPH S. ROUCEK

University of Bridgeport

PHILOSOPHICAL LIBRARY

New York

Printed in the United States of America

DEDICATED TO

Mae and Emil Kabella

Preface

The present work is indeed a labor of love since the leading specialists in the various fields of sociology in the United States and abroad have paused in their specialized researches to give us a synthesis of the various trends in the most prominent fields. One could argue what should or could also have been covered. But every effort has been made to cover the most prominent branches of sociology in America and its developments in Europe, Russia and her satellites, Asia, Africa and South America.

Only those specialists who have edited works of this type can probably appreciate the endless hours and aggravations needed to bring such a planned book to a fruition. Fortunately, the editor has been encouraged to complete the task by Dr. Dagobert D. Runes, Editor of the Philosophical Library, and helped by Salvatore Signore of the University of Bridgeport. Hence, if the work will make its contribution to man's collective knowledge, the editor will be amply compensated for his editorial efforts.

JOSEPH S. ROUCEK
University of Bridgeport
Bridgeport, Conn.

Table of Contents

I. FRAMEWORK

II. TRENDS IN THE UNITED STATES

III. SOME APPLICATIONS OF SOCIOLOGY

V. SOME CRITICAL COMMENTS

I.

FRAMEWORK

CONTEMPORARY TRENDS IN SOCIOLOGY IN AMERICA AND ABROAD

Carle C. Zimmerman
Harvard University

Sociology, as it is known in the United States, developed originally as an expansion of Western social thinking under the guidance of Europeans such as August Comte, Herbert Spencer, and many others.[1] It came to the United States largely due to the teaching and writing activities of a small group of men, notably Lester F. Ward, Franklin H. Giddings, Albion W. Small, Charles H. Cooley, Charles A. Ellwood, William Graham Sumner, E. A. Ross and W. I. Thomas.[2] In the United States it has particularly flowered as a research and teaching discipline due to the rapid growth of higher education here and our emergence from a polyglot settlement of all "races and creeds" to a unified nation and a world leader. Membership in the American Sociological society increased from 1242 in 1945 to 4350 in 1954 and more than five thousand today. In spite of the enhanced situation of sociology in the United States, its development and course in Europe, Asia, South America, Japan, Mexico and Russia, specifically, has been about the same as in the United States.

Nearly every country of advancing literacy teaches sociology in its main universities, has its own textbooks, its own professional sociological societies, its journals and researchers in the field. The sociological writings in these diverse countries cite about the same authorities and deal with about the same subjects. Consequently, in the remainder of this chapter trends in sociology in general will be discussed without regard to country or continent.

NINETEENTH CENTURY SOCIOLOGY

The early sociology, from the first independent sociological work by Comte, shortly after 1830, down to the beginning of World War I in this country, was largely a theory or theories concerning social

3

change. The last big popular work of this type was somewhat of an anomaly, being published with somewhat rosy linear predictions in 1933, when the world was already embarked definitely, as we can see now, upon the ensuing debacles of depression, fascism, communism, World War II, communist dictatorship, cold war and the birth pains of the atomic age.[3]

The sociologists of this earlier period knew very well the difference between social statics, or structure, and social dynamics, or change, but considered social change the main problem of society. It is true they developed an inadequate theory of change, the "linear evolutionary hypothesis" but at least they tried to solve the major problem of social dynamics. These sophisticated and learned men, but a step or so removed from the Middle Ages, and working in the midst of the developing Industrial Revolution, could not even imagine any approach to a study of the structure of society except for the purpose of understanding change.[4]

The main intellectual difficulty of these Ninetenth Century sociologists was not their choice of a theory of social change as the *pièce de resistance* of the new science, but the unfortunate and one-sided nature of the particular hypotheses they first formulated. Since the days of the early Greeks the great and remembered philosophers of western society had considered *Change and its Control* as the major social problem.[5]

The Nineteenth Century Sociologists followed a hypothesis that the succession of events in time was mostly ruled by law and in orderly sequence and, in general, that the process was not unique. They lived in a Newtonian world which believed in an orderly nature of things, ruled by an ever present, always the same, *immanent* cause. This "cause idea" was a universal groping for something ideal in civilization. The ideal varied with the authors, from Hegel's "freedom of the spirit" to Sumner's "what worked best."[6]

So the Nineteenth Century Sociologists departed from the claims of the professional historians, that the succession of events in time was very complicated and each happening was largely unique, and sought a grand theory of society and its changes like the *Principles* emphasized by Newton in his theories of mechanics. This, they thought, would unite and integrate the social sciences and make understandable the course of man.[7] As we show later, it did that for all practical purposes.

In this situation, the early sociologists developed this main theory of social change which postulated men as advancing steadily in time. Of course, they noted some hesitations and difficulties in this course, but "man's rugged road" had, on the whole, been forward. This is the main idea now known as " linear (or stair-steps) evolutionism." There were numerous explanations of this theory, depending upon whether the sociologist followed more closely the idealism of Hegel or the materialism of Marx, or straddled both, but all these theories of constant progress or development were closely related. All of them used a sort of semi-organic analogy between society and a constantly growing body to explain their theories.

The trouble with their theories was that they did not fit the "facts of history" and were largely analogies. As a result of this the hypothesis exploded in the difficulties of the second decade of the Twentieth Century and most scientists lost complete faith in the evolutionary ideas.

This leads up to the "contemporary trends in sociology" and is their necessary background. In defense of the older theories, even though considerably erroneous, it must be said that they were eminently satisfactory as philosophies and "field theories" for the time. All the great changes of modern society of the industrial revolution period could find a background, an apparently satisfactory explanation and a justification, in these evolutionary theories. Every major social movement of our present time, which is grounded in the philosophy of the Nineteenth Century, took off from a variety of this grand evolutionary theory.

As a corollary, we might also point out that Newton's "laws" of force and friction in relation to mass and movement are only valid in a very work-a-day area, but, in spite of this, they guided the world towards its great industrial development.

The reasons for the decay of these older theories of social change, and their vocal rejection by sociologists about 1920, were both factual and intellectual. They failed to explain the "facts" of social change as these began to unroll and develop in the wars, revolutions, and turmoil of the second decade of the Twentieth Century. Thinkers began to ask how such a theory of social change could explain the greatest war in history of that time. The sociologists began to feel that the evolutionary school had gotten too far away from the facts of historical experience.

The wars and revolutions thus blew up the material or factual situation. The world-wide acceptance of Oswald Spengler's gloomy

Decline of the West, a book which claimed that societies always went through "time unrelated" cycles of "immanent growth and decay" put the finish to the intellectual ideas of steady development. Spengler's philosophy of pointlessness and despair helped to replace the former optimistic frame of steady growth and development. Spengler extended the analogy of the earlier group to make society a growing organic body to senility and to decay.

THE SEARCH FOR NEW INTEGRATION

Any particular grand phase of a culture, such as a new era in a physical or a social science, seems that it has to have an integrating philosophy. The above parallel between the social functions of the principles of Newton in the physical sciences, and the evolutionary idea of social change in the social sciences, was not happenstance. As physical science moved early in this century past the middle or ordinary events of life, into the study of the opposites of the infinitesimal (very small) and the macroscopic (very large) universes, it had to have something in addition to Newtonianism. This it got, at least temporarily, in the relativity formulas of Einstein and others. But sociology has as yet not attained or at least accepted a new social formulation for the atomic age. As a result of this search, the struggles of competing groups to find and establish a satisfactory new integrating formula, is the major story of contemporary trends in sociology. Details have been many, but these may be consolidated into a few major trends.

One of the first hypotheses building a school in this new search was marked by the turning from a study of society in time—social change—to a study of the forms and processes of society—social statics. In a large degree this is encompassed in the phrase—"sociology studies primarily the relation between the individual and society or various aspects of the larger whole." This involved not only the psychological, but also the physical and class aspects of modern society.

THE STUDY OF COMMUNITY AND ECOLOGY

As a prelude to this, it may be noted that numerous writers of the older school of sociology had begun to break over into these newer phases of the field. Albion Small, followed by C. J. Galpin and, more lately, numerous other sociologists, began to try to understand the relation of the individual to the larger group through analysis of local community of origin—the village or town or primary group. This type of study enlarged and built upon the earlier thoughts of F. Tönnies upon the "gemeinschaft" or familiar community, and the "mechanical social organization" of E. Durkheim. Durkheim thought that "mechanical social organization" was an apt title for those social forms emphasizing similarities of the "conscience collective" or group aspects of the mind. C. H. Cooley had also pointed out earlier in great detail the importance of the differentiation of the primary, or face-to-face groups as opposed to the secondary or anonymous groups.

Out of this interest developed much of the modern ecological interest in sociological studies. This may be noted by the popularity of studies of the morphology and ecology of the city by the University of Chicago groups around R. E. Park and E. A. Burgess in the nineteen-twenties. This ecology interest developed, and later, joined hands with the study of the small group's psychological forms of interrelation. This gave rise to Sociometry. Sociometry is a very intimate study of the inner structure of social relations and applies particularly to the influence of these upon the development of personality and character. More recently the studies of this type have reappeared under another name "Sociology of small groups."

RISE OF STATIC SOCIOLOGY

Along with this development came the rise of interest in the "psychological aspects" of the relation between the individual and the group or of groups to each other. Many of the earlier sociologists had also had a particular interest in this approach as illustrated by the emphasis upon imitation by G. Tarde and E. A. Ross. Further, W. I. Thomas and F. Znaniecki had attracted wide attention by their use of the words "attitudes" and "values" as analytical tools and their classification of the "four wishes" in an attempt to integrate the psychological approach to sociological structure. Many others had contributed also to this.

Among these others may be noted especially the work of Vilfredo Pareto of Italy and Switzerland whose *General Treatise on Sociology* (1915) (Translated as *Mind and Society*) spanned all four fields. He kept a fair amount of the idea of orderly change, supplied a more exact history, but added relations between groups and classes and supplied the psychological attributes under a classification of what he called "residues and derivations" or instincts and sentiments.

SIMMELISM, PSEUDO-WEBERISM, AND PARSONIANISM

However the great break into the psychological aspect of the relation of the individual to the group, particularly among sociologists in America, came through the influence of R. E. Park, Ellsworth Faris and others around Chicago in the early twenties. Faris began to enlarge upon the ideas of W. I. Thomas and to blend into them some of his interpretations of George Mead and John Dewey. The greatest change, came, however, when Park introduced the "formal sociology" of the Germans, particularly Simmel, into a rather large treatise turned out by him with Burgess. This reduced nearly all theoretical sociology into a study of the psychological forms of social interaction, such as conflict, subordination, socialization and other mental process forms.

For a decade or more this school dominated American sociology and then gradually dropped quietly out of circulation as a recognizable entity. However due to its influence, other European and, particularly German, classificatory sociologists became popular, and succeeded it with somewhat different names. Among these was the introduction of Weberian sociology into America. Max Weber (1864-1920) was a sort of abridgment of the Nineteenth Century School of Germany. He emphasized social change in his theory of gradual movement from *kurwille* to *freiwille* but paid a great deal of attention to forms and processes of social interaction at any particular time. However, due to the influence of Talcott Parsons and others, Weber's English translations have become synthesized into the formal, structural and static sociologies which have risen to the highest vogue among many Americans and English sociologists.

All of these psychological-structural sociologies are primarily classificatory, and describe relative static conditions. They hypothecate understanding only stable societies and not the living reality. Their dealings almost solely are with the nexus between the individual and the social order.

Their basic idea may be illustrated by the Parsonian conception of "social action" which is the current most popular expression of this static sociology as formalism was in the Twenties and Sociometry in the Thirties. " Social action" is the act of relating the "Actor" to the "Situation." By this the person gets a place in the "institution." "Institutionalization" is regarded by Parsons as the integrative mechanism of the social system. First the actor gets a place in the structure known as a "status" and this status has an expectation inherent in it, a "role." These roles become organized into recurrent complexes called "institutions." Out of this process, and other subsidiary deviations, we get the "social system," the "personality system" and the "cultural system."

This shows that much of contemporary sociology has abandoned the major study of social change. It has done so by making "structure," not the time-course of society, the major problem of sociology. According to these existentialist postulates, change is only a minor sociological preoccupation. Parsons recognizes this in his denial that an adequate study of social change is possible now and "most probably never."

Thus in the field of most popular hypotheses and theory, contemporary sociology is at the complete antithesis with the earlier group. Comte and Hegel primarily studied change seeking to understand order. Now, by hiding our heads in the sand, we try to preclude the study of change. When we do remark on change, it is interpreted by reference to some plausible but overthrown assumptions of the earlier Marxist school.[8]

THE RISE OF NEO-POSITIVISTIC EMPIRICISM

Man has always used two basic methods of search for proof of new truths. One is deduction, or the approach from previous accepted ideas to specific new details, and the other induction, or the study of specific particular facts culminating in a generalized truth. Ordinarily the greatest thinkers have recognized both methods as valid and have attempted to use all methods in their search. Their procedure has been to start with accepted ideas, to make a theoretical extension of these and then to test that new tendril of thought by its agreement with empirical experience.[9]

Outstandingly twice in the history of social thought this generalized approach has been wholly denied in favor of quantitativism and empiricism alone, first in the theoretical pronouncements by Francis Bacon (1561-1626) and second in the sociological neo-positivist school since 1920.

The older school of sociology generally started with a theory, as for instance the ideas of movement of social systems in time, and then collected great numbers of concrete cases to bear out and "prove" the extenuation of this idea. Much of the newer school of empirical positivism sublimates any theories they may have and attempts sociological investigation seemingly solely upon the collection of "facts."

This new approach, the lop-sidedly quantitative, takes off in large part from the acceptance of many hypotheses in Karl Pearson's *Grammar of Science* as well as earlier similar circumlocutions by Hume and Comte. It is claimed to be a close following of the "natural science approach" for sociology. That is, according to the general claims of the upper echelon of this school, all of the physical sciences are experimental and quantitative.[10] Since, according to many of them, it is difficult to experiment with human beings—human life being considered sacred and not to be tampered with as in the case of the Pavlovian experiment with dogs—mathematical manipulations of a quantitative sort may be substituted for the "experiment." This led to the movement to substitute varieties of multiple and partial correlation for experiment in sociology.

The theory of this school is that we can not know *cause* but only *probability* and how things operate. Really they are denying both timeless cause and probability and seeking only partial (i.e. material) cause. Multiple correlation is a statistical device for comparing a number of associated events, according to their prevalence, with the event under study and to attempt to find what proportion and how the total of the studied event moves with increases and decreases of the associated others. For instance if broken homes, working mothers, slum dwellings and lack of guided social clubs are supposed to affect the rates for juvenile delinquency, the multiple correlation seeks to find how large a proportion of this juvenile situation is related to these four combined. An argument exists as to whether the multiple coefficient (R) means "proportion" in all its ranges, but for the purposes of simplification it is assumed so here. Partial correlation, on the other hand, is a device supposed to eliminate changes in the matter studied, due to any particular factor. Thus juvenile delinquency, for an illustration, may be studied in relation to any one variable, when others are "held constant."

This new kind of empiricism, with ramifications, has swept much modern sociology. In other countries it is gaining headway due to American influence. It is associated with a certain amount of amateurishness in metaphysics and in mathematical reasoning, but these difficulties are remediable. The positivists, even their most rabid leaders, reason like everyone else, including the housewife who seeks to cook a new dish like an older one which it resembles, but they claim not to do so.

Of most importance in this development comes the denial of the possibility of finding at least some approach to "cause," or a variety of cause other than the "material," in the field of sociology. The decay of metaphysical theory has been associated with decline in understanding of the nature of logic and proof.[11] As a result the sublimated older theories, as illustrated by the change explanations in the Static-Structural school, always reappear in an inadequate, disguised, and often discarded form.

Since a careful study of genetic, or historical development of present sociological problems has been neglected, the experience of the past, with the same problems, or varieties of them, exists largely in folk beliefs or inadequate forms. These are accepted without critical re-examination. This has led to a separation of empirical sociology from theory. Our contemporary theory is little subject to critical empirical examination. So now we have considerable confusion in the ranks of sociologists.[12]

SOME GOOD ASPECTS OF NEO-POSITIVISTIC FUMBLING

However devastating this series of inadequacies due to the rabid growth of the new empiricism as the "soul and body" of contemporary sociology, it has not all been detrimental. Its first good point has been the preparation of social thinkers to move to a new era, of thought and analysis, fitted to the Atomic Age, with few hangovers from the past to impede it. Such happened in Eighteenth Century rationalism preceding the great Industrial Revolution. Now men can, and will, rename many of the older ideas, still valid though temporarily discredited, or portions of them, and find ready acceptance for them.

A second is that it gives much sociological investigation, by sympathy and association, a considerable amount of the aura now shedding itself onto physical science and science generally because of the mysteries of the recent developments in the field of the microscopic and macroscopic worlds.

The third gain is that it abandons the arm chair and puts the sociologists in close contact with the actual world. Many great ideas have been discovered by accident, without hypotheses. Enthusiastic probing cannot all go wrong. An illustration is the accidental discovery of the Wonder Drugs. Many sociologists plowing ahead in concrete investigations have found new and helpful ideas and this may enlarge itself. Nevertheless, a new revived theory, particularly in the field of social change and its processes, will be necessary for any full fruition of our present blundering toward creativity. The greater thinkers in our present ranks are pointing this out, even though they as yet have small audiences.

Finally, since men reason the same no matter what they claim to do, the search for certitude in such an important field as sociology can not help but grow as a result of this enthusiasm for a "new model" in the type of study.

RISE OF NEO-DYNAMIC SOCIOLOGY

The third great trend in contemporary sociology has been the revival of interest in social change theory as in the Nineteenth Century. This "neo-dynamic sociology" seems to be seeking to retain the older school's good points and to correct its "bad" ones. Its good points were the recognition of social change as the major problem of sociology; the search for principles; the genetic or historical approach; the use of a rounded causal analysis in the search for certitude; and the recognition that human beings tend to recreate social systems about some basic "humanistic" formula in each new order of events.

The "bad points" of the Nineteenth Century sociology lay in its "Western provinciality"; its neglect of the "facts" of history; its failure to acknowledge the existence of grand crisis periods when new fruitions demanded an adjustment of course; and its neglect of the "intellect" as a factor in social control and change. This "immanent causation" thing which blinded that century of social theory simply meant that Topsy, and only our Topsy, "naturally" grew up and went to college. She never was supposed to have any growth or adolescent pains or crises, and never had to think about "new ideals" and "make up her mind" to go to college. Furthermore, it took no account of the fact that, as time passed on, college entrance examinations would appear, and these, due to increasing competition, would become more and more difficult and rigid.

It was not difficult for Oswald Spengler to overthrow the old field of evolutionary change, as we have noted earlier, and to institute his theories of ending and unrelated cycles in history. He was a close student of the writings of Heraclitus, who about 500 B.C. in Greece had developed a similar "dark" philosophy. Further Spengler merely increased the "organic analogy" commonly used by the earlier sociologists, and added two phases to the early analogy of creation and growth of cultures, those of maturity and decay, and inevitable death, of any social system. Thus in the psychological depression brought about by World War I, he pursued "immanent causation" and "organic analogy" to their ultimate logical ends.

He had had numerous predecessors who challenged the nineteenth century ideas of change, notably Goethe and Nietzsche in Germany, Le Play in France, Brooks Adams in the United States, Corrado Gini in Italy, W. E. Flinders-Petrie in England, and, to some extent, Danilevsky in Russia.

Spengler made two positive contributions. One was his demolition of the old optimistic school, a thing which the historians could not do because sociologists either did not take specious criticism by historians seriously, or minded more the "grand theory of sociology" than they did the "aberrant facts" of history. His second positive contribution was the stimulus he gave to two other men to try to meet the criticism of the older idea and to rectify it to create a neo-dynamic sociology. These two were independent scientists, neither acquainted with the other until both became famous, Arnold Toynbee, British historian, and Pitirim Sorokin, Russian-American sociologist.

ARNOLD TOYNBEE AND THE NEO-DYNAMIC SOCIOLOGY

Toynbee, although a historian by training, becomes a sociologist by interest and by the fact that his ideas on social change have captured the lay sociological audience in the world which, in an earlier generation, would have read Comte, Spencer and Sumner.

In contrast to the only one flow of civilization idea, characteristic of the XIX Century writers, and also to the pronouncement of the eight "cultures" theory of Spengler, he finds more than thirty "civilizations" for his study. He commences his work by an elaborate and logical proof that primitive, and non-literate, non-historical civilizations (or cultures) are different species from the great historical aggregates which have left their records available for us to study. The primitive cultures he terms "rabbits." These he says are or have been small in size, many in number, short in life, meager in influence, and of no epoch-making importance in the course of man. The historical ones, circa thirty in number, he terms as "elephants," and characterizes them as large in size, few in number, long in life, great in influence, and important to the life of men. Toynbee's work concerns only the elephants, because the Western society in which we live and wish to understand is an "elephant."

With this differentiation in mind, Toynbee finds that twenty-one of his elephants (great civilizations) have run their natural and complete, or almost complete, life. In addition he notes that five other civilizations have taken an "abortive" course. In a large degree, Toynbee's numerous volumes are an attempt to find the dynamic patterns in the twenty-one great civilizations which already have largely lived a full span. Thus, in this sense, Toynbee is more of an organicist than his predecessors because he recognizes different species—primitive and historical—and also of failures in his great species—those with arrested and abortive ends.

Following this analysis, Toynbee divides his *civilizations* or "intelligible and essential fields of historical study" into two classes. These are five "originals" which have emerged and flowered, and a remainder (about sixteen) which are affiliated, in the sense that they grew out of the embers and traditions of the earlier original. His five originals are Egyptian, Sumerian, Chinese, Mayan, and Indic. These five original civilizations could have some of Spengler's alleged general traits of independent and non-related separate organic realities, but the others—the related civilizations—certainly had organic connections with their predecessors as well as with their contemporaries.

With this approach, Toynbee finds that civilizations (with exceptions for the "abortive" and arrested and with later exceptions in the breakdown periods which he speaks of as "petrified") have certain standard patterns of organic change. They emerge, grow, reach a peak, flower, and die away. Their course is fairly uniform, and, in a large degree, pre-determined by the inner nature of their species.

All through the life cycle of a civilization is a constant process, challenge-response. This is similar to the biological characteristics of wasting-away and replacement of tissues. In the early biological years, replacement is more rapid than wasting away, and in later years, the process reverses itself. In the early periods of a civilization, response is adequate to, and greater than, challenge, so there is growth and fulfillment. In later civilization periods, response is inadequate to challenge, and the social organism dies—slowly in the cases of petrified civilizations but more rapidly in others.

The challenge idea is used essentially by Toynbee to mean two things. First there are the challenges in the environment, such as climate or warlike neighbors, which if successfully met, make for the initial emergence of a civilization. Once the civilization is under-way, its major challenge is largely from a difference in ideology between the proletariat, or masses, and the elite, or creative minority. These differ as to the response to be given to a situation. As long as the elite have the better answers (judged by the longevity of the civilization) and can carry the masses with them (right response) the civilization prospers.

When the elite become demoralized, or are incapable of leadership, the internal proletariat are alienated from their leaders and join forces with the external proletariat of barbarians. The weight of these two groups together enable the masses to destroy the civilization simply—to put it in non-Toynbean words—because they live illog-ically for the moment and do not have the foresight to see the longtime implications of their acts. Theoretically, petrified civiliza-tions are those of such low challenge that mediocre response holds them together, or even an opposite case of a civilization with high challenge, but equally high response. However his examples of petri-fied civilizations, if they were such, were ones which some may now consider as of relatively low challenge—Hellenic, Sumerian and Minoan.

Toynbee's numerous scholarly volumes contain a great many de-tails illustrating the mechanism of grand social change. He describes in detail the typical process of decay which, according to his theories, concerns most of the incidents of history. In each of his civilizations he finds some fateful step taken at an early age, from which there is no recovery, and which eventually causes the death of the civilization. This constant living in perdition, or inescapable damnation, rather than purgatory, or state of expiatory hope, is a carryover in Toynbee of the "immanent determination" of the XIX Century sociological school plus the pessimism of the Spenglerian group.

However Toynbee is not at all times an unequivocal pessimist—in the sense that he feels that all cultures are damned at all times, includ-ing our own world. In *Civilization on Trial* he presents an essay in which he indicates a belief that the real progress is in religion. Each of the civilizations, in dying, creates a Universal Church, as he had already claimed to show in his first volumes on history. This above attitude of progress is said to be in religious values, from one universal development similar to Hegel's unfolding of the "spirit." *(Geist)*

We may close these remarks on the social change theory of Toynbee with a few observations which are believed to be pertinent to the field of sociology. As soon as the major thesis of XIX Century general sociology, the attempt to understand social change, began to be blighted and replaced by existentialist meanderings, new figures from out of sociology took up this traditional theme. These outsiders were rejected by their fields of origin but, while not accepted by sociologists proper, captured the lay sociological public.

SOROKIN AND NEO-DYNAMIC SOCIOLOGY

The third of the great figures contributing a major social change theory during the first half of the XX Century was a sociologist by profession. The emergence of Sorokin in this field restores a certain amount of dignity and sanity to the field of study of social change in the sense that social change in sociology is its purest essence. If Sorokin had not emerged we would have to admit that the inner professional field on the science had given up its main problem and turned its solution over to amateurs—or at least to new and inadvertent converts.

The second important consequence of the emergence of Sorokin in this field is that the standard terminology of sociologists, as well as their subordinate theories of social action, hinged fundamentally in the long run to an adequate theory of social change, as known to Sorokin as a professional sociologist. This means that his analysis of social change, where it differs from preceding theories in the field, will also be of influence in helping to change and renovate the subordinate sociological theories.

Sorokin is a former Russian sociologist who was exiled by the Communists in 1922—after reprieve from a death sentence. He spent two years in Czechoslovakia. Here he met the son of E. A. Ross, who told his father about Sorokin and eventually led to his migration to the United States. From 1924 to 1930 he was at the University of Minnesota and then came to Harvard where he has been since. Until established in America his work dealt largely with criminal law, crime and revolution. From 1924 to 1930 he preoccupied himself with sociological theory, including rural sociology as well. Between 1930 and

1945 his main work was in social change and dynamics. After 1945 he has been investigating the sociological background of personality, with particular reference to altruism. Thus his work on social change was his mature effort.

Sorokin considers that society is the result of the interaction of persons and that the results or products of this interaction, other than the groups of men in society, is culture. Consequently a society is always integrated, or integrating, into a real or semi-real group, something more than the sum of the individuals. The methods of integration are logically according to Sorokin *mechanical adjacency, constraint, causal-functional* relations and *logico-meaningful* systematization. In a sense this list of methods of integration is one moving from almost pure nominalism toward almost pure realism.

A group of persons in a new land would be largely mechanically adjacent. Force of circumstances would, in a large degree, constrain them to remain mechanically adjacent. The establishment of a social system with any exchange or interchange would make them into a causal-functional reality. In this causal functional relation every person is both a cause and a function of every other one. All the ordinary social relations are causal-functional, as husband-wife, parent-child, employer and workman, ruler and subject, and so on.

However the higher degree of organization comes in the logical-meaningful integration. Sorokin uses the device of the picture puzzle to illustrate this. In a picture puzzle, the parts fit together according to the meaning of the picture, and only that way. Thus the ruler and subject do not fit together the same under a dictatorship as under a free democracy. In one, a change of rulers means a struggle and a bloody purge of opponents. In the other, it is an election, with the losers following the Machiavellian technique of adopting the policies with which the successful group has taken over power. Then the "outs" seek to regain power by appealing to the ruled.

Thus a social system, according to Sorokin's analysis, has an *élan vital*. It is a moving thing, always changing. This immediately leads Sorokin to ask what are the principals which guide and direct this change. In this analysis Sorokin comes to the cyclical and rhythmical movements of a society, and thus gives us one of the most unique and satisfactory leads in the field of social change which Western man has developed to the present.

Sorokin accepts the main tenet of all good sociology in that he sees that change is inherent in society. He does not have to explain why there is change, but what kind of change exists, and how it varies from time to time. In doing this he introduces a number of concepts which are helpful. The basic of these are *society, culture* and *personality*. The meaningful interaction of individuals makes personality. Culture is the totality of these meanings, values, norms which are possessed by the persons and the vehicles which aid in this interaction. Society is the totality of interacting personalities. These three processes are always moving and always changing because society is always an unstable equilibrium in which a movement of one thing makes it necessary for everything else to change.

In order to understand the directions of movement at any one time Sorokin measured various phases of Western culture from the time of the early Greeks to date, a period of about four thousand years. This put him into the field of actual historical data for his theory of change.

From these measurements Sorokin found fundamental changes in all branches of culture, painting, art, music, conceptions of finding truth, government and so on. However he also noted a tendency toward recurrence of the same general types at different times. This led him to a typing of kinds of cultures and to a consideration of what may be called the *sociological thory of limits.*

The *sociological theory of limits* is basic to Sorokin's ideas on social change. It is an old idea, certainly fundamental to Aristotle's idea of the *mean.* But for Sorokin it is a principle of more general validity, to be found in the phenomena of all science, as well as in social affairs. According to Sorokin, nothing ever proceeds endlessly in one direction. As time goes on the forces pushing the matter to one direction tend to satiate themselves and to weaken and the opposite forces feel more and more constrained and grow stronger.

Thus he makes this principle of limits a grand set of guides for historical social change in the West. He recognizes that some social change is at all times non-repetitive and purely historical. He also sees the new combinations of the old as varying because each is in a new historical situation. But his fundamental theories concern repetitive social change.

He sets up two polarized concepts, *sensate* and *ideational* culture. The differences between these two concepts are similar to the modern idea of Epicurean, on the one hand, and Stoic on the other. In sensate culture the main outlook of the individual is for extra-person stimuli, for articles which appeal to the ordinary untrained tastes, such as is seen in a quantity consumption culture. Ideational, on the other hand, is the opposite. Here the individual withdraws from a large number of outside objects and finds his pleasure more within. It is difficult to define these concepts of Sorokin except that in the one men accept the truth of sense impressions and in the other one of faith or a deeper reality behind sense impressions.

Now the problem arises, considering many facets of a culture, how it is that there can be ideational and sensate periods in the *totality*. This is where Sorokin's logico-meaningful integration comes into play. Things fit together with similar meanings. If peace and prosperity are related to each other, and war and poverty or chaos, then ordinarily the opposites do not cross over and mix greatly. A sensate culture would ordinarily color most of the objects and values of society of its period by sensatism, and the ideational the opposite.

SUMMARY AND CONCLUSIONS

Any analysis of sociology in a few pages necessarily can only summarize a few important matters and these very inadequately. But from the analysis here one can see that sociology is on the march. Its main new hypotheses since the decay of its Newtonian period have been in three fields, static-structural study, neo-positivism, and neo-dynamism. There are other incidental trends, but these are of the major intellectual sort. This total search is an attempt to find a new orientation fitted to the atomic age.

However in passing, in addition to our previous criticisms, several other major difficulties should be pointed out. One of these is the control of disposable research and training funds almost entirely by the neo-positivist empiricists. In this respect they almost dominate the field.[13] This group has set a pattern of short, natural-science like, papers for publication, many of which deal with meticulous issues in sociology. The papers are filled with empirical data and statistical formulae. They have a particular fondness for measures of variation about the mean, thus giving a semblance of fair sampling of their universes, although the real universes they study are rather hazily stated, or are nominalistic. Such terms as "lower-middle-class-Protestant" dominate the descriptions of universes whether these exist as important fields or not. Back of many of these studies are many intrinsic, but sublimated, theories of the earlier sociologies never clearly brought to the forefront.

A second difficulty lies in the limited facilities for publication, particularly of theoretical studies, genetic studies, new hypotheses, monographic works and definitive treatises in particular fields. The larger book publishing companies are brutally frank in their rejection of almost any books of more profound intellectual significance than elementary texts. These are designed, according to the study by A. H. Hobbs, from other similar "mass-appeal" works and seldom cross into the field of explicit sociological theory, static-structural systems or neodynamic developments. Text writing in sociology has developed into a specific trade, little related to the field as a whole. Whatever advanced works the publishers do pick are most often written not by men known for their accomplishments in the field, but for their capacity at plausible cogency of a simple nature.

One retiring editor of a large publishing house boasted in public at a society meeting that his "success" was due to the fact that he never accepted a work called "a definite treatise," "a monograph" or "a contribution." The university presses, outside of subsidized publications, or popular appeal works, are also largely avoiding creative publication partly because of lack of funds and partly in imitation of the private publishers. The smaller firms have limited funds and resources and tend to be dominated by presently popular cliques such as the structural-static sociologists. This arrogance tends to give a "publishing house" dictated science, seemingly as if God, by revelation, gave them unusual insight.[14]

If prototypes of Durkheim, Tönnies, Max Weber and Sumner were to appear with comparable monographs and treatises today, four out of five would have extreme, if not insurmountable, difficulty in bringing their ideas before the public. An eminent Swiss economist and sociologist, Wilhelm Roepke, came to Emory University the summer of 1956 and delivered a series of lectures in sociology. Upon his return to Switzerland he wrote in an American journal the comment that he could get his works published easily in Switzerland, with its less than five millions of people, but this was practically impossible in the United States with its one hundred and sixty millions. Many publishing contracts for social sciences in America today he noted were one-sided and unethical—even illegal and inequitable.

A third problem is the rise of existentialism, or philosophy of detachment of the science from the main body and culture of the society and of confining the intellectual horizons of existence of the sociologist purely within the cult. Signs of this are the feelings of detachment of sociologists from the major struggles of society, the development of very abstruse and wordy sociologies, understandable, if at all, only by other sociologists or devotees of the particular cult, and the constant reification of mathematical formulas and "models".

The distinguished Italian philosopher, Norberto Bobbio, noted this sociological after effect of this non-involvement thought facade somewhat earlier.[15] Its ramifications in the upper echelons of American (and of considerable European) sociology has been particularly great since the beginning of World War II. The situation is implemented in a considerable part by the excesses of certain members of the academic set who have risen temporarily to public attention as leaders in lay matters during this generation. The first title given these men two decades ago, "brain trusters", was one of some respect, but the later derogation, "egg-head," is one of mistrust and antagonism. Roepke, mentioned earlier, was amazed at this feeling of antagonism and fear between the general public and social scientists he found among the two score brilliant and leading young sociologists at Emory University in the summer of 1956.

A fourth problem is the intermixing and bracketing of psychology and sociology in various departments under the assumption that the basic hypotheses and approaches of these two sciences are identical and need not be separated. This means that one or the other has to dominate the field, and since psychology has greater membership, more prestige, and a wider audience, it dominates and tends to control the methods used in sociology.[16] Psychology deals with the individual and the "inner man." Sociology, on the other hand, deals with the culture, the group, the "conscience collective" and the whole man. Both are necessary sciences, and their main hypotheses should be working tools for every student of society. However, obviously one does not go to the well with a spoon or to the coffee canister with a bull dozer.

However all these problems are remediable, and will be corrected in time by natural curative processes, if not taken up sooner in a voluntaristic manner. Sociology *is* on the march, but it could travel more rapidly—and on the main paths of culture—if more thought and attention were given to its main metaphysical problems.

SELECTED BIBLIOGRAPHY

E. F. Dakin, Ed., *Today and Destiny* (New York: A. A . Knopf, 1940). Consists of an explanation of Spengler's views on Social Change largely made up of excerpts from the *Decline of the West* by Spengler.

M. C. Elmer, *Contemporary Social Thought* (Pittsburgh University Press, 1956). Elmer, now 70, knew personally nearly all the great men among American sociologists, and from time to time gathered their comments on the development of the field; while the book is not critical, it does tell the story as the sociologists have seen their struggle.

Alwin W. Gouldner, "Some Observations on Systematic Theory, 1945-1955," pp. 34-42, in Hans L. Zetterberg, Ed., *Sociology in the United States of America* (Paris: UNESCO, 1956).

E. Kilzer and E. A. Ross, *Western Social Thought* (Milwaukee: The Bruce Publishing Company, 1954). Chapters XIII through XX take up the development of modern sociology since the Eighteenth Century and carry it down to date, annotated in reference to American sociologists, now living.

Clement S. Mihanovich, (Ed.) *Social Theorists* (Milwaukee: Bruce 1953). This whole volume devoted to contemporary trends in sociology is organized about the points of view of eighty important social theorists. It contains a valuable appendix "Who's Who in Social Theory." Opinions on various points of about six hundred other writers are given. This scholarly work has its individual advantages in coverage.

P. A. Sorokin, *Social Philosophies in an Age of Crisis* (Boston: Beacon Press, 1950). Sorokin explains his own theories of social change, and contrasts them with those of Spengler, Toynbee and many others who have written on the subject in the past quarter century.

A. J. Toynbee, *A Study of History* (New York: Oxford University Press, 1947). A one volume abridgment of the first six volumes of Toynbee's study by D. C. Somervell, and gives an interpretation of his views (with Toynbee's blessing); *Ibid. Civilization on Trial,* (New York, Oxford University Press, 1949). This essentially summarizes Toynbee's later views on social change, altered after his first six volumes of *A Study of History.*

For other works, look up those of Howard Becker, George Ludberg, R. K. Merton, Talcott Parsons, S. A. Stouffer, Florian Znaniecki in Gouldner, *op.cit.* Since World War II, most countries have sought to reassess their sociology. UNESCO has implemented this kind of work. Space being limited in this document we can not mention all these studies. For France, however, see especially the writings of Georges Gurvitch, Armand Cuvillier and others. For Germany note particularly the recent writings of the venerable Leopold von Wiese and a capable monograph by a German-American, Helmut Schoeck of Emory University. Similar developments have taken place in Italy, England and the United States. For India see the recent developments inspired by G. S. Ghurye and Radhakamal Mukerjee in particular. Sterling work has been done by Lucio Mendietta y Nuñez in Mexico and by Manuel Fraga Iribarren at the Instituto Balmes, Madrid.

Carle C. Zimmerman (1897–) was born a son of a school teacher in Cass County (Missouri); took his Ph.D. in Sociology and Economics at Minnesota in 1925 after attending the Universities of Missouri, North Carolina State, and Chicago; has carried on extensive field sociological investigations in four American states, in Siam, Cuba, Canada, England, Germany and Italy; taught sociology at Minnesota from 1923-30 and at Harvard since 1931, when he returned from a year as adviser to the Royal Government of Siam. In addition to service in two wars he has served on commissions for the United States government and for Cuba and Canada. His books and monographs were in the field of Rural Sociology to 1934. After that they were in studies of standards of living and community studies until 1940. Since then he has published a number on family sociology, including *Family and Civilization* (New York: Harpers, 1948) and part of *Marriage and the Family* (Chicago: Regnery, 1956); his most recent work is in the field of *Social Change and Social Theory*.

In 1954-55 he was Visiting Research Professor at the University of Rome. He is a Fellow of the AAAS and a Councillor of the American Academy of Arts and Sciences. His position on sociological development, as one may see from the preceding chapter, is one that sees theory of no value unless followed by empirical study and empiricism as of no value unless growing out of theory. Consequently he is, always has been, and will remain impatient with anything else that claims to be sociology.

He has an M.A. *(honoris causa)* from Harvard and a Doctor of Science *(honoris causa)* from North Carolina State.

NOTES

1. Among other earlier Europeans who profoundly influenced Sociology were G. W. F. Hegel, the philosopher, who wrote on social change and Frederic Le Play who fathered the case study and family budget method. The ideology of Karl Marx, the follower of Hegelianism, but the economic materialist, has permeated much of Western thought since his time. In the latter part of the Nineteenth century, the great influence in European sociology was split about even between F. Tönnies of Germany and Emile Durkheim of France. Georg Simmel influenced the Parke-Burgess school at the University of Chicago, and Gabriel Tarde contributed to the ideas of E. A. Ross. The Russians maintain that Nicholas Danilevsky was their stellar non-linear sociologist in the latter part of the century.

2. Ward taught at Brown University in his later years. Small was at Chicago, as was Thomas. Giddings taught at Columbia, Cooley at Michigan, Ellwood at Missouri, Ross at Wisconsin and Sumner at Yale. Ellwood later went to Duke.

3. Various authors, *Recent Social Trends in the United States* (New York: McGraw-Hill Book Co. Inc., 1933). Many non-sociologists contributed to this work as members of the President's Research Committee, but it was directed by two sociologists, W. F. Ogburn and Howard W. Odum.

4. Concerning this see Carle C. Zimmerman, *Patterns of Social Change* (Annals of American Sociology, Washington, D. C., Public Affairs Press, 1956).

5. Frederic Le Play emphasized change, but was a cyclicalist. Danilevsky was also of an exception. Tönnies and Durkheim slightly abridged the evolutionary school. Gabriel Tarde centered mostly in the role of imitation in society. In America, Ross followed Tarde's influence but Cooley and Thomas paid more attention to group, and to attitude-value theories. Thomas rejected the evolutionary doctrine early in his career.

6. All the later prominent philosophers (after the Fourteenth Century) read repeatedly the poem by Lucretius (first century B.C.) *De Rerum Natura* (On the Nature of Things). Isaac Newton (1642-1727) outlined and stated the principles for a regular, law-controlled universe in his *Principia*. An astonishing basic similarity exists between Nineteenth Century sociologists and Newtonian principles.

7. See here Kenneth E. Bock, *The Acceptance of Histories* (Berkeley, The University of California Press, 1956); Carle C. Zimmerman and Joseph B. Ford, *Social Change and Control* (Norman, Okla., The University of Oklahoma Press, 1957).

8. On this whole matter see Alvin W. Gouldner in *Sociology in the United States of America* (Paris, UNESCO, 1956, Ed. H. L. Zetterberg, 34-42).

9. See Felix Kaufman, *Methodology of the Social Sciences* (New York: Oxford University Press, 1944); P. H. Furfey, *The Scope and Methodology of Sociology* (New York: Harper & Brothers, 1953) Ch. III.

10. Many natural sciences are almost purely observational such as geology and astronomy. Observation plays a large part in all of them. Einstein's theoretical formulas were an extension of theories with repeated observation to see if they explain all cases. On this problem see N. S. Timasheff, *Sociological Theory*, (Garden City, L. I.: Doubleday & Co., Inc. 1955), Chapter XV; Max Born, *Natural Philosophy of Cause and Chance*, (Oxford: Clarendon Press, 1949) Chs. I, II, & VII; Carle C. Zimmerman in *Ghurye Felicitation Volume* (Popular Book Depot: Bombay, India, 1954), Ch. III.

11. R. M. MacIver points this out in *Social Causation* (Boston, Ginn 1942); See Furfey, *op. cit.,* Ch. 3 for numerous other references.

12. See A. H. Hobbs, *The Claims of Sociology* (Harrisburg, Pa.: Stackpole 1951), Ch. I; On this Gouldner, *op. cit.,* fn. 8, p, 41, says "It almost seems as if two sets of books are being kept, one for . . . equilibrium and another for . . . change"; Merton recognizes it and asks for a new body of theory, that of the "middle range" separate from the "systems"; Furfey, *op. cit.,* fn. 9, Ch. I, wants a new science called "metasociology" to remedy this difficulty; Sorokin in *Fads and Foibles in Modern Sociology,* (Chicago, Regnery, 1956) attacks it savagely under the title "Amnesia and the Discoverer's Complex." Bock, *op. cit.* fn 7. says "We can be reduced to the idiot's approach to life, where each succeeding instant is new and without precedent . . ." (p. 125) and says . . . it is a last resort for men who have failed to cope rationally with the problems of social living . . ." (p 130).

13. See Peter H. Rossi in *Sociology in the USA, op. cit.,* fn. 8, 21-34. Rossi points out (p 33) that "researchers" and "teachers" are separating, neither well acquainted with the activities of the other.

14. See on this a competent analysis by Hans Zetterberg in *Sociology in the USA, op. cit.,* fn 9, 14 *et passim.*

15. See Nordberto Bobbio, *Philosophy of Decadentism, a Study in Existentialism* (Tr. by David Moore) (Oxford: B. Blackwell, 1948). See here also Hans Zeisel in *Sociology in the USA, op. cit.,* fn. 8, p 56.

16. For instance James Byrnes, former Justice of the US Supreme Court and then Governor of South Carolina, in discussing the segregation issue, refers to works done by numerous sociologists on race problems. In his eight references to them, he calls them "social scientists" once and "psychologists" seven times. At no time did he call them "sociologists" although one of them, E. Franklin Frazier, is a former president of the American Sociological Society. The whole group under criticism, as for instance those who worked with Myrdal, were practically all sociologists. Thus what sociologists have done in this important field was considered entirely "psychological." See *US News and World Report,* May 18, 1956, 53-4.

II.

TRENDS IN THE UNITED STATES

THE COMMUNITY

John E. Owen
Florida Southern College

Since all social research emerges from, and interacts with, the external social reality that it essays to describe and explain, an understanding of the genesis and development of community study necessitates an appreciation of the trends and changes that have occurred in American communities themselves. Viewed on a long-term basis, the following changes in American life can be discerned: rapid population growth; the transition from a primarily rural to an increasingly urban economy, with the problems attendant upon industrialization, urbanization, and immigration; the modification of old norms, values, controls, and behavior-patterns in a world of rapid cultural transition; the rise of community welfare services of increasingly comprehensive scope; the establishment and growth of many voluntary bodies for the improvement of community living, especially in the fields of health, welfare, education, and recreation; official concern and action on a local-state-federal basis for community well-being; the professionalization of social work; the growth of the "community-centered" school and an adult education program, the latter reaching over thirty million persons; a community organization movement aiming at "community strategy" and concerted attack upon local problems; and, since World War II, rising interest in and concern with local and regional planning, by virtue of the problems accruing from population increase and social mobility; and the recognition of the new field of gerontology. For these and many other reasons, "community consciousness" has been heightened and sensitized, both among professional sociologists and lay citizens. Within this social setting of community study, the growth of relevant research will now be reviewed.

29

HISTORICAL BACKGROUND OF COMMUNITY RESEARCH

Scientific social surveys in Europe can be traced back to the work of Frederick Le Play in the middle of the nineteenth century. In the subsequent decades, the Rowntree survey of York, England, and Charles Booth's work, *Life and Labor of the People of London* (1892-97), were important landmarks. In America, the work of Jacob Riis, the "muckrakers," *The Hull House Maps and Papers* (1895), and the Russell Sage Foundation's *Pittsburgh Survey* (1914) were noteworthy. Pioneer students of community theory included Ferdinand Tönnies, and later R. M. MacIver, whose *Community: a Sociological Study* (1917) was an early classic. Community research in the 1920s and immediately afterwards was engaged in by J. F. Steiner, Nels Anderson, Arthur E. Wood, Edmund de S. Brunner, Louis Wirth, Niles Carpenter, B. A. McClenahan, C. C. North, C. C. Zimmerman, A. E. Morgan, R. D. McKenzie, M. C. Elmer, Read Bain, and Luther Fry, among others. At Columbia University a dozen or more of Franklin Giddings' earlier postgraduate students prepared their Ph.D. dissertations in the area of community research.

August B. Hollingshead claims that the growth of research in the American community began about the year 1895 and that for two decades thereafter the predominant feature was an interest in the city and its problems, regarded in a normative and reformist framework. This was followed by a more analytical trend during World War I, associated with the research of C. J. Galpin and Robert E. Park's ecological emphasis. Rural surveys multiplied during this period, while Park's graduate students at Chicago produced several well-known studies of urban areas and community facets, e.g., the gang, delinquency areas, the hobo, the ghetto, the taxi-dance hall, and the slum. A new research era began with the Lynds' *Middletown,* and since about 1933 community research can be classified as ecological, structural, and typological, with increasing attention paid to the latter two areas. The typological approach observes a community in terms of its culture, external relations, geographic-economic base, population-composition, and size, in order to ascertain the configuration of these elements and their relationship to community functioning. Hollingshead sees this approach exemplified in Carle C. Zimmerman's *The Changing Community* (1938) and in the research of C. C. Taylor, Charles P. Loomis, Robert C. Angell, and Louis Wirth;[1] he concludes that ". . . students of the community have amassed a greater store of facts about American life, as it is lived in specific places in our era, than any other group of social scientists."[2]

CURRENT LITERATURE AND TRENDS

A long-term trend has been the movement away from philosophical writing about the community or "society as a whole" to the study of specific communities, viz., delimited research of manageable proportions. This has been part of a larger trend in American sociology generally, in the direction of empiricism, more careful research, emphasis upon actual techniques of investigation, formulation of problems, hypothesis-testing, and fact-finding.

Current areas of research in the community include comparative studies, in addition to the analysis of structured relationships and institutions. Social action studies *per se* have tended to enjoy less popularity than research dealing with the social structure of present-day communities. The dynamics of social behavior and the instrumentalities of community control over individual conduct have received relatively little attention from community researchers.

Another recently discernible trend (since about 1945) has been a change of emphasis from the former sharp line of demarcation between urban and rural sociology to greater interest in the community *per se,* typified by the appearance of at least one text by a rural and an urban sociologist in collaboration (e.g., Brunner and Hallenbeck) together with the publication of college texts specifically treating the community, notably by Kinneman, Bernard, and Mercer.

John A. Kinneman's *The Community in American Society* was the outcome of an early interdisciplinary social science teaching program that emphasized rural-urban interdependence and interrelationships, itself the portent of a new trend to offer a sociology or social science course dealing with the community as a central point of interest and departure. Almost every aspect of community life is reviewed by Kinneman, with the help of a judicious use of concrete data, graphs, maps, and tables. A useful introduction to community study, his volume centers around the themes of population, structure, institutions, function, and organization. Jessie Bernard's *American Community Behavior* was typical of the texts that treat national problems from the vantage-point of the local community. Blaine E. Mercer's *The American Community,* like Kinneman's volume, had the integrated social science approach and manifested its author's awareness of the sociologist's dual role and responsibility as scientist and citizen, this latter being indicative of a gradually emergent trend in the profession generally. Utilizing the structural-functional approach, Mercer furnished an introductory analysis of the patterns of community change, community and personality, role and status, conflict and cooperative processes, institutions, and planning.[3]

A needed pioneering work with a framework which gives evidence of establishing a potential new trend is Floyd Hunter's *Community Power Structure* (1953), an objective analysis of political power written from a sociological orientation.

Probably the best work of analysis of the American social system itself was Robin M. Williams' *American Society: A Sociological Interpretation.* An especially competent study of American values, it combined the Parsonian structural-functional analysis with research data and gave attention to the structural aspects of family and economic life, education, religion, and stratification.

The dislocation and unrest produced by the aftermath of World War II coincided with a growing body of books and articles around the theme that modern man is alienated from his old roots, has lost a sense of community, and that it is difficult if not impossible in an industrialized "mass-society" to embody the primary group values of the older and less depersonalized community. An outstanding work was Robert A. Nisbet's *The Quest for Community.* It revolved around the thesis that local groups such as the family and church have been disorganized by the centralizing forces of the state-power, with the consequence that the social solidarity and sense of cohesion and ethical certainty of the past have disintegrated. This study is an excellent analysis of the values inherent in small communities. Exceptionally well-written, and combining historical with sociological data, it may almost be said to have established a trend in itself, or certainly to have clarified in explicit form modern political tendencies of which many social scientists had been aware. For a grasp of the widespread changes in community life in Western culture, Nisbet's volume is essential reading. Its value is enhanced by an informed historical approach that puts community studies in better perspective. The structural disorganization in community life today is interpreted in the light of a conflict between the centralized state and the functional authority of the church, family, and small neighborhood. Nisbet claims that " . . . the concern for community, its values, properties, and means of access, is the major intellectual fact of the present age."[4] But the smaller human associations are no longer functionally relevant to the larger economic and political decisions that affect the life of modern man.

Dean Nisbet's work is an insightful and incisive analysis of the problem of liberal values in the post-medieval Western world. In every sense a learned study, *The Quest for Community* manifests a knowledge of literature, moral philosophy, history, and political theory rare among sociologists. It is a major contribution to social theory and to the theme of "the community" in its larger context.

Among studies of specific communities, a definitive work recently appeared. A comprehensive and competent survey, *The Doukhobors of British Columbia,* was concerned with a small religious community whose norms deviate from those of the larger society of western Canada. It is distinctive by virtue of being the result of a request by a government body for the aid of social scientists in policy formulation. Canadian and American scholars from several humanistic disciplines worked as a team on this project, and exemplified the possibilities of a combined cooperative approach. The editor of the completed work, Harry B. Hawthorn, also made a contribution to community theory by indicating a need to qualify, as well as to extend, Simmel's views on the conditions of survival of a secret community.[5]

METHODOLOGICAL CONSIDERATIONS

The growing stress upon empirical research in sociology has caused attention to be given increasingly to problems of *method* in studying the community, this being one aspect of a wider trend in the profession. One problem which has plagued students has been that of defining the meaning of the term. Community study was hindered in the past by the fact that "community" and "society" were wellnigh indistinguishable concepts, particularly when applied to primitive groupings. The term "community" continues to refer to a heterogeneous variety of social groups, large and small. Definitions have centered around the idea of a group's territory, combined with its shared culture, bond of union, tradition, and other elements of moral order. The term can also be used to refer to the felt sense of coherence in a group, the total complex of attitudes, values, and sentiments that binds its members together in *a* community.

Although community studies currently comprise a sizable segment of the growing literature of American sociology, the concept still remains somewhat imprecise and partly on that account the progress of rigorously refined research tends to be retarded. The writer concurs in Hollingshead's judgment that although generalizing constructs explaining observed data have been formulated, areas in which slower advancement has occurred include clarity of terminology, precision of concepts, formulation of hypotheses, and congruity of theoretical statements with empirical data. Hollingshead sees three definitions of "community" in current sociology. It is used to denote group solidarity, cohesion, and common interests; it can refer to a geographic area with spatial boundaries; or it can imply a socio-geographic structure embodying the ideas of the first two. Hollingshead further claims that community study stands in need of a coherent theoretical framework rather than an accumulation of facts for their own sake,[6] a contention that could validly apply to areas of sociology outside community analysis.

Other writers have expressed a similar recognition of the desirability of strengthening the partnership in a scientific division of labor between empirical research and theoretical analysis. In some stimulating reflections on the logic of sociological method in community study, (The Little Community, 1955) Robert Redfield has portrayed some of the dilemmas of community analysis. Redfield distinguishes between scientific analysis and holistic synthesis and demonstrates that sympathetic insight and understanding are as necessary in social study as in constructive citizenship. His small volume inquires into the possibility of a science of human wholes, surveys the potential roads to studying the community, and is a reminder that the sociologist's point of view determines the view.

The myth of the possibility of a thorough-going "objectivity" by virtue of the social scientist's posing as a non-participating and non-involved spectator dies hard. In a thought-provoking article that has significant implications for the methodology of community analysis Alfred McClung Lee notes that "practical" men, actively engaged in community affairs as business, governmental, and civic specialists, are in reality clinical students of society, and that their method of research and analysis has contributed to sociology more than it has received in recognition. Students of the community could, Lee avers, learn from clinical studies in three ways: first, by submitting their theories to the rigors of clinical discussions where the findings of practical students are brought to bear upon the results of orthodox research techniques; second by gaining access to clinical records of ethnic and racial defense agencies (e.g., the American Jewish Committee, and the N.A.A.C.P. Legal and Defense Fund), trade associations, and trade unions; and third, by making clinical studies on college campuses and in professional societies.

Lee defines this clinical study of society as "the critical accumulation of sociological wisdom based upon concerned and intimate observation and therapeutic manipulation of social groups which have problems" or, more briefly, "the study of society through first-hand experience with group responses to therapeutic efforts." On this view, a mine of experience in the mental processes and records of community organization workers, political strategists, and social group workers lies untapped. Clinical study is a procedure which has given depth of insight to some of the greatest sociologists of the past, but Lee sees it as being currently ignored though "practical" men use it constantly.[7]

This article has been cited because to the present writer its argument is thoroughly sound. Both in community study and related fields, there is still the need for what Cooley termed "dramatic knowledge." And for community inquiries in particular the relevant research implications and potential gains of this "clinical study" could prove highly impressive. At the time of writing, however, Lee's suggestion is too recent to have been acted upon extensively.

But community analysis is now one of the recognized modes of social inquiry, and has been greatly aided and improved by up-to-date techniques of description, such as participant observation, interviews and questionnaires, attitude surveys, field observations, statistics, case-histories, and content analysis of community records and documents, all of which have been utilized to supplement the older surveys. The community, the concrete grouping of individuals sharing a common territory and culture, has come to be regarded as a useful laboratory for the study of societal problems and phenomena. The newer research theories can be tested, and the modern techniques put to work, in small community settings. This approach patently lends itself to interdisciplinary teamwork, embracing synthetic rather than "single-tool" methodological procedure. In this connection a new technique which should be of appreciable benefit is represented by the cross-cultural references of the Human Relations Area Files at Yale University, which make accurate comparative studies possible with a remarkable facility not previously attained.

Both survey method and community study originated, at least in part, in anthropology. Community study has been termed "anthropology's chief contribution to area research" by Julian Steward, who has given an evaluation of the anthropological approach to community studies, emphasizing their significance in providing a cultural or ethnographic orientation. This approach is also historical and comparative. There is the disadvantage, though, that it does not relate community analysis to a larger framework (e.g., the national culture) and too many surveys in the past have been merely "snapshots of a community" rather than "moving-pictures of a region." Community study lacks an explicit exposition of its methodology. Arensberg speaks of the "crippling failure of sociological sense" in the semantic confusion between community as organization and as a person's maximum range of face to face acquaintance, pointing up the conceptual problem previously cited. The basic question, says Arensberg, is " the comparison of the organizational forms of animal life and human culture," and to answer it will necessitate a clarifying of the concepts of community study, with further exploration, experiment, and model-building.[8]

As may be surmised from the foregoing, the condition of theoretical formulations in community research is in need of revision, though structural-functional analysis has proved to be a promising framework. This approach is favored by Gordon W. Blackwell, who defines it as "operational study of institutional patterns, social differentiation, and social stratification of the community as these elements interact with each other to define the status and beliefs of individuals and become dynamic through the basic functions of the social systems comprising a community as accomplished by role fulfilment by individuals."[9]

Three other trends in method and theory are worthy of note. The first has been a tendency to interpret community leadership situations in terms of sociometry, and to seek empirical data on neighborhood behavior by means of interaction scales and designs. As in other approaches to community study, the state of theory involved has tended to be insufficiently developed. A second trend, also an expression of broader influences in sociology, has centered around the growing recognition accorded to values as data in social research.[10] The view that values can be objectively studied has come to be more widely appreciated since about 1945. There is a greater interest in the functional significance of values and this interest has shown itself in community study, which now gives attention to attitudes and systems of belief. Surveys and social action programs are less inclined to ignore the prevailing sentiments, responses, opinions, prejudices, and intellectual climate of the community under analysis. It may be reasonably expected that this postwar concern with social values will be expressed with greater scientific rigor as the newer tools of research are employed to make more precise the normative insights of the past.

A third area of interest centers around the "folk" concept and the folk-urban continuum. The folk concept was formulated experimentally by Robert Redfield in 1930 in his work, *Tepoztlan*. Later, in Yucatan, Redfield was occupied in field research with a series of communities in order to examine the hypothesis that a breakdown of isolation and an increase in heterogeneity are causal elements in secularization and disorganization. The term, "folk society," is an ideal type, and in attempting to evaluate the term, Horace Miner indicates three general areas of criticism. First, there is a problem of "lack of fit" between the empirical data on specific societies and the nature of those societies that might be expected from the ideal type construct. Second, there is the problem of defining the traits and characteristics of the ideal types, and third, the limitations of the folk-urban continuum in affording theoretical insight. A re-evaluation of Redfield's 1930 book was attempted by Oscar Lewis. He placed less stress on the folk hypothesis, and rejected the folk-urban continuum. This anthropological analysis of a community was typical of investigations based on much detailed research and manifesting a grasp of the complexity of theoretical and methodological issues.[11]

CLASS STRUCTURE AND STRATIFICATION

A rising interest in class structure and class consciousness has been a feature of American sociology for the last two decades. This review will concentrate on stratification analyses of specific communities and on problems of method that apply to this area, as depicted in recent research.

Following the famous landmark set by the Lynd study, *Middletown*, (1929) and the new "participant observation" method it employed, several community studies oriented more specifically to social class have appeared. James West's *Plainsville, USA,* analyzed a small midwestern farming community between 1939 and 1941 to observe its status-system, cultural changes, and socialization process. The methodology included participant observation, notebook and informal interviews, life-histories, and records. As with *Middletown* and *Middletown in Transition,* there was noted a contradiction between systems of belief and the actual behavior of the local residents. Plainsville did have a status-system, though the inhabitants denied its existence.

The year 1949 saw the publication of two surveys of community class-structure. Hollingshead's *Elmtown's Youth* dealt with adolescence in a small Illinois town and the effect of class upon behavior patterns. Its author's thesis was that adolescent behavior bears a functional relationship to parental status in the community. The local belief that class-structure and status-awareness were absent from such a town was clearly revealed to be a myth. Hollingshead found five classes in Elmtown and concluded that in the lives of young people and their families status was operationally significant. The methodology was comparable in scope to the preceding studies. Another 1949 work was *Under the Elms,* by David and Mary Hatch, an analysis of a New England community utilizing structural-functional theory applied to class structure.

The most imposing stratification research up to the time of writing is W. Lloyd Warner's "Yankee City" series, originally involving the work of thirty social scientists for a five-year period (1930-34). Newburyport, Massachusetts, and a Southern city were selected for class-structure analysis. A punch-card method enabled Warner to obtain detailed data on the population which was found to comprise six classes as seen by the local inhabitants themselves.

Warner's hypotheses were given in his 1949 manual of operations for the measurement of social status, *Social Class in America.* His method is termed "evaluated participation" (E. P.) and consists of six techniques, namely, matched agreements, status reputation, institutional membership, comparison, symbolic placement, and simple assignment.

Whether Warner's social classes actually exist or have been merely reified is a point on which no general agreement obtains. There has also been some question as to how accurately the prestige-system of communities is actually portrayed by his scheme. But despite these criticisms, without the work of Warner and his followers, American stratification research would be unquestionably impoverished.[12]

"Class" continues to be an imprecise concept, with no appreciable consensus as to the meaning of class lines. Some studies stress the external marks of class, while other research has been grounded in class-awareness. Among the latter, Richard Centers' *Psychology of Social Classes* (1949) concentrated upon an individual's personal attitude regarding his status in the community. Centers examined the significance of occupational status, role, and common loyalties in determining the conceptions that individuals entertain about themselves. Basing his attitude-research on a sample of 1100 white males, he viewed class in an essentially psychological framework rather than a structural orientation.

Throughout the study of class, there has been an awareness on the sociologist's part of the methodological hazards involved, of which the problem on definition and criteria of class is long-standing. Hollingshead has noted three categories of sociological writing on the topic of stratification, namely, theoretical formulations, empirical inquiries in specific communities and "mass society," and speculation as to the trends of stratification. Sociologists are not in any essential agreement on this last issue, though few if any would uphold the thesis that America is a nonstratified society. Whether social classes are becoming more rigid is not a settled issue; data on social levels in past decades is not to be had. [13]

At mid-century the field of stratification had become so popular that a special issue of the *American Journal of Sociology* (January, 1953) was devoted to it and contained a bibliography of 333 items. The following year saw the publication of the first textbook in this specialty, Cuber and Kenkel's *Social Stratification in the United States,* which gave a semantic, theoretical, and research approach to the literature, followed by an evaluation of significant community studies and a discussion of theoretical issues, among them being the problem of unidimensional and multidimensional qualities of class, the continuum versus categorical theories, and the question of functionalism. That these and other issues are unresolved and will necessitate further patient research is made very apparent by Cuber and Kenkel. While undeniable progress has been made in stratification research, the state of both research and theory is currently fluid, dynamic, and developmental, a condition that renders summarization difficult but augurs well for future advances in this area.

CONCLUSION

From a long history rooted in anthropology and the early survey movement, American community analysis has broadened in scope, popularity, and application. During the years following World War II, awareness of the community as a field of study has appreciably increased, partly on account of the rising recognition of the community as a setting for societal interaction and the changes that have occurred in American life in the last two decades. College and university courses in "The Community" as distinct from urban and rural sociology or ecology, have been introduced into several sociology and social science curricula.

Research techniques and procedures have been sharpened in sophistication and precision. A marked emphasis on methodology has been noticeable, though the realm of community theory has not shown a comparable advance. Unsuspected benefits might accrue from more active participation in "clinical studies" that could be utilized for the testing of current theories and the gaining of new hypotheses for research. Similarly, cross-fertilization of social science approaches would seem appropriate for community analysis. Structural-functional theory has furnished the framework for several recent studies. Although many methodological problems stand in need of clarification, the growing attention given by students of the community to research procedures and scientific canons may be legitimately regarded as the necessary first step toward their solution. Class and stratification research is currently in vogue, as is the literature of modern man's alienation from mass-society.

Community action programs have developed both in number and scope since the prewar years, partly owing to the disruptions and transitions occasioned by the war and the consequent readjustment. A "community strategy" has made itself evident in many localities. Sociologists have shown a new interest in values in contrast to the sterile "objectivism" of the past.

With the ever-growing complexity of American society and the problems posed by mid-century culture, community organization and planning have assumed a new significance, and several manuals of operation for community surveys have been published since World War II. Though the problems on which the sociologist seeks valid knowledge are grave and complex, a combination of the scientific attitude with enlightened concern and intelligent action may be expected to effect their eventual alleviation and enhance the interactive tone of community life.

SELECTED BIBLIOGRAPHY

John F. Cuber and William Kenkel, *Social Stratification in the United States* (New York: Appleton-Century-Crofts, 1954). A critical review of recent literature on class and stratification.

Harry B. Hawthorn, Ed., *The Doukhobors of British Columbia* (Vancouver: The University of British Columbia and J. M. Dent and Sons, Ltd., 1955). A comprehensive survey of a small religious community.

Wayland Hayes, *The Small Community Looks Ahead* (New York: York: Harcourt, Brace 1947). A plea for planning in small communities.

E. T. Hiller, "The Community as a Social Group," *American Sociological Review*, VI (April, 1941), 189-202. A theoretical contribution to community analysis.

Arthur Hillman, *Community Organization and Planning* (New York: The Macmillan Company, 1950). An integrated treatment of two significant recent movements.

August B. Hollingshead, "Community Research: Development and Present Condition," *American Sociological Review* XIII (April, 1948), 136-156. Critical summary of recent literature.

Floyd Hunter, *Community Power Structure: A Study of Decision Makers* (Chapel Hill: University of North Carolina Press, 1953). A sociological approach to the study of political power.

John A. Kinneman, *The Community in American Society* (New York: Appleton-Century-Crofts, 1947). An interdisciplinary approach to the community, stressing rural-urban interdependence.

Blaine E. Mercer, *The American Community* (New York: Random House, 1956). A useful text based on the structural-functional approach.

Robert A. Nisbet, *The Quest for Community, A Study in the Ethics of Order and Freedom* (New York: Oxford University Press, 1953). A noteworthy study of the influence of state power upon the community.

John E. Owen, "Sociology at Mid-Century," *The Western Humanities Review*, VIII (Winter, 1954), 33-40. Critical review of recent trends.

Robert Redfield, *The Little Community* (The University of Chicago Press, 1955). Stimulating reflections on possible approaches to the little community.

Herbert H. Stroup, *Community Welfare Organization* (New York: Harper, 1952). A comprehensive recent text.

W. Lloyd Warner, Marchia Meeker, and Kenneth Eels, *Social Class in America: A Manual of Procedure for the Measurement of Social Status* (Chicago: Science Research Associates, 1949). A handbook of investigative techniques in social stratification.

Roland L. Warren, *Studying Your Community* (New York: Russell Sage Foundation, 1955). A working manual for community study and survey-making.

John E. Owen (b. Manchester, England, 1919) A. B. Duke University (1943); Boston University (1944); Tufts University; (1944); University of Southern California, M.A. (1946); Ph.D. *ibid.* (1949); University of London (1952). Assistant Professor of Sociology, Ohio University, (1949-51); Visiting Professor of Sociology, Smith-Mundt grant (Department of State), University of Helsinki, Finland (1951-52); Lecturer, University of Maryland Overseas Program, United Kingdom, 1952-53; Associate Professor, Florida Southern College (since 1953); Professor and Chairman of Sociology Department since 1956; Visiting Professor, summers, Stephen F. Austin State College, Texas (1951); University of Alberta, Canada (1955); Appalachian State College, (1957). Author: Some sixty articles in academic journals in America, Canada, Britain, France, Finland, India, Ceylon, Japan, and the Philippines; chapter, "The Agencies of Social Control," in Bossard, *et al, Introduction to Sociology* (1952); chapter, "The Role of Valuation in Sociology," in *The Frontiers of Social Science, Essays in Honor of Radhakamal Mukerjee* (Lucknow University, India, 1956). Membership: Phi Beta Kappa, American Sociological Society, Southern Sociological Society.

NOTES

1. August B. Hollingshead, "Community Research: Development and Present Condition," *American Sociological Review,* (April, 1948), 136-139, 144.

2. *Ibid.,* 145. Howard W. Odum regards the area of community study as very appropriate for research and theoretical development in the frame of reference of social change. "In all probability, if a single area of sociological structure were to be sought out for the measurement of greatest social change, it would be in the realm of community, from the early simple primary relationships of rural, religious, kinship groups to the complex, urban, industrial society toward which advanced state civilization tends to move." *American Sociology, The Story of Sociology in the United States Through 1950* (New York: Longmans, Green, 1951), 291. Odum sees four areas of sociological specialization as having emerged, namely, community structure, organization, and behavior; rural society; urban society; and industrial society. Since the last three have become recognized as distinct and delimited areas of research, this chapter will concentrate on the first of the four fields.

3. John A. Kinneman, *The Community in American Society* (New York: Appleton-Century-Crofts, 1947); Jessie Bernard, *American Community Behavior* (New York: The Dryden Press, 1949); Edmund de S. Brunner and W. C. Hallenbeck, *American Society: urban and rural patterns* (New York: Harper, 1955); Blaine E. Mercer, *The American Community,* (New York: Random House, 1956).

4. Robert A. Nisbet, *The Quest for Community, A Study in the Ethics of Order and Freedom* (New York: Oxford University Press, 1953), 30.

5. Harry B. Hawthorn, *The Doukhobors of British Columbia* (Vancouver: The University of British Columbia and J. M. Dent and Sons, Ltd., 1955); see also: Harry B. Hawthorn, "A Test of Simmel on the Secret Society: The Doukhobors of British Columbia," *American Journal of Sociology*, LXII (July, 1956), 1-7.

6. Hollingshead, *op. cit..*, 145.

7. Alfred McClung Lee, "The Clinical Study of Society," *American Sociological Review*, (December, 1955), 650, 653.

8. Julian Steward, *Area Research, Theory and Practice* (New York: Social Science Research Council Bulletin 63, 1950), 22,23; see also Conrad M. Arensberg, "The Community-Study Method," *American Journal of Sociology*, LX (September, 1954), 119, 124.

9. Gordon W. Blackwell, "A Theoretical Framework for Sociologican Research in Community Organization," *Social Forces*, XXXIII (October, 1954), 62. Blackwell has furnished in this article a useful list of suggested hypotheses for community research in terms of structural-functional theory.

10. As an example of a study that points out very clearly the role of local values and the significance of value-differences for the analysis of communities, see Irwin T. Sanders, *Making Good Communities Better* (Lexington: University of Kentucky Press, rev. ed., 1953). The significance of value-orientations in shaping community action was portrayed in Evon Z. Vogt and Thomas F. O'Dea's "A Comparative Study of the Role of Values in Social Action in Two Southwestern Communities," *American Sociological Review*, XVIII (December, 1953), 645-654.

11. See Redfield's *Tepoztlan, A Mexican Village* (The University of Chicago Press, 1930) also Oscar Lewis, *Life in a Mexican Village: Tepoztlan Restudied* (Urbana: University of Illinois Press, 1951); and Horace Miner, "The Folk-Urban Continuum," *American Sociological Review*, XVII (October, 1952), 535.

12. W. Lloyd Warner and Paul S. Lunt, *The Social Life of a Modern Community* (New Haven: Yale University Press, 1941), & *The Status System of a Modern Community* (New Haven: Yale University Press, 1942); see also Harold W. Pfautz and Otis D. Duncan, "A Critical Evaluation of Warner's Work in Community Stratification," *American Sociological Review*, XV (April, 1950), 205-215.

13. August B. Hollingshead, "Trends in Social Stratification: A Case Study," *American Sociological Review*, XVII (December, 1952), 679-686; see also Kingsley Davis and Wilbert Moore, "Some Principles of Stratification," *American Sociological Review*, X (April, 1945), 242-249, and the consequent criticism by Melvin M. Tumin, rejoinder by Davis, and comment by Moore. Chapter VII of Talcott Parsons, *Essays in Sociological Theory Pure and Applied* (Glencoe: The Free Press, 1949) is also pertinent here.

PERSONALITY

Svend Riemer

University of California (Los Angeles)

The personality has changed with the viewpoint of those who observed it. Personality has always been important as a determinant of social behavior. But there have been changes in the opinion of what this determinant is. The personality of man has been considered a physical determinant and later an environmental one manipulated by education.

Originally, personality was looked upon as entirely inherited. A close connection was assumed to exist between the inheritance of man and his physical constitution. Consequently, some link joined those schools of thought according to which man's social behavior was inherited and those according to which the individual had a certain constitution which made him behave in a certain manner. In other words, the inheritance was directly given credit for man's social behavior, or his social behavior was related to his constitution and assumed to be partly inherited.

This line of thought connects such different men as Cesare Lombroso and William Sheldon. The former lived from 1836 to 1909 in Italy,[1] while the latter (born in 1899) is still teaching at Harvard University.[2] Lombroso, to be sure, emphasized the influence of inheritance upon the individual and what he did, while Sheldon emphasized a close relationship between the physical characteristics of an individual and his social behavior.

All in all, the personality of man has been conceived in different ways. Three main changes have occurred in the view on personality: (1) The influence of inheritance and constitution has been replaced by the influence of education and environmental conditioning. (2) Influences of the environment have changed from very obvious to very subtle ones. (3) Environmental influences have been tied closely to the culture of the individual.

Sociologists have been aware of these changes and they have tried

44

to express them by the use of different words for the personality as understood once upon a time and today.[3] They talked about the *individual* if only biological factors of a person were involved. They talked about the *personality*, on the other hand, if they also considered the influences of man's environmental experiences upon behavior in his social environment.

Recently, the persistent behavior of an individual has been described as a result of environmental influences. Some steps have been taken in discriminating between behavior in general and behavior with social significance. Only behavior with social significance, of course, is of interest to the sociologist.

We also talk about the "human personality" in general, and the "social personality" in particular. In the same manner, we have shifted our discussion from behavior to social behavior. It is hard to imagine, of course, any behavior without social ramifications. At the end of scientific developments, personality was discussed as social personality, and our concern has been devoted mainly to social behavior although asocial behavior hardly exists. If it does exist, it exists as an abstraction, as a borderline concept only.

THE HEREDITARIANISTS

Once, all social behavior was looked upon as the result of a biological organism inherited by individual man. All behavior was considered determined by man's constitution, and his constitution— in turn—was thought of as inherited from his ancestors. These claims go back even to times before Cesare Lombroso when man's thinking about personality was in its infancy.

Early in the 19th century, scientific presentation had to get along without photography or similar reproductions of the human physique. At that time, the silhouette sufficed as a means of storing up man and physical characteristics in memory for purposes of scientific generalization.[4]

At this time, early attempts allocated behavior to definite parts of the human brain where they were assumed to manifest themselves by protrusions of the skull. To this time, in fact, we owe all interests in "bumps on the head" often made by charlatans. They were assumed to correspond to different aptitudes. They were thought of as indicating certain abilities that had been inherited.

Cesare Lombroso made even more definite claims about criminal behavior. In Milan he claimed to be able to detect the actual criminal from a number of suspects by observing their physical characteristics. He considered the criminal as distinguished by long arms and legs. His pronounced extremities were accompanied, furthermore, by a fleeing forehead and a receding chin. There were bumps behind the ears of the criminal, and other signs of "atavism" occurred in this throw-back to prehistorical days. In his search for criminal types, Lombroso even used photography. He came to the conclusion that criminals were born so. They could not escape behavior to which they were doomed because they had inherited it.

To Lombroso we owe the beginning of empirical scientific methods. We owe to him precise empirical observation and careful generalizations; but he missed out in the use of one tool applied as a matter of course in all investigations today. He did not use a control group.

From Lombroso, a direct line of intellectual development leads to men like Kretschmer and Sheldon. They took no stand with regard to the difficult question of what behavior tendencies were inherited and what were not; but their whole life work was concerned with the demonstration of correspondences between physical characteristics and inclinations to behave in a predetermined manner.

They were not quite as specific as Lombroso, who did not only think that general tendencies toward crime could be inherited, but even felt that an embezzler inherited his delight in embezzlement, just as a thief was bound to have inherited his inclination toward thievery. It took such specific claims to make useful the life histories of criminals in one and the same family where the same crime was committed again and again.

Lombroso himself desisted in later years from a theory of personality which gave credit to inheritance as a determinant of human behavior. He ended by correlating all sorts of physical factors with crime—such as blue eyes or the origin from a Northern region—without questioning the underlying cause-and-effect relationship. It might have been that the vendetta in Sicily and its extinction in other parts of Italy influenced his correlations; still, Lombroso was finally interested in causes only where they established a high correlation between physical factors and the tendency to commit crime. Causal relationships were hinted at but never clearly asserted.

Still, Kretschmer[5] came up later with an ingenious hypothesis, and William Sheldon gave final empirical proof[6] to the idea that a close association existed between the physical constitution of man and his tendency to socially significant behavior. While both scientists arrived at more or less the same findings, their nomenclature was very different.

The systematic scheme in the following refers to Kretschmer's as well as Sheldon's terminology. Behavior tendencies, in either case, were given in terms of abnormal psychology. Still, physical attributes and behavior tendencies were associated with each other:

Asthenic body type (Kretschmer's terminology)—schizoid behavior—ectomorph (Sheldon's terminology)
Pyknic body type—cycloid behavior—endomorph
Athletic body type—paranoid behavior—mesomorph

To use plain language, the assumption was that a slender person would be inclined to schizoid reactions in his behavior, while fat deposits were more readily expected in a person inclined to cycloid behavior; a muscular person, on the other hand, was more likely to be a paranoid, i.e. querulent or—in more serious cases of insanity—characterized by delusions of grandeur and ideas of persecution.

Some mutual relationship between body type and social behavior was undoubtedly demonstrated. Slenderness or fat or a muscular physique could, however, be the result instead of the cause of the conditions which inclined an individual to certain social behavior. In other words, we cannot find out from these studies whether the behavior is really shaped by the physique of a personality, or whether this physique does not influence acting in either one way or another.

OF SCEPTICS AND CRITICS

Heredity was accepted for a long time as a determinant of social behavior. Even today, many people are convinced—without relying on scientific proof—that the hereditarianists are right. A somewhat undecided position was taken by those engaged in twin research, which was ready to give credit to either hereditarianists or environmentalists.

Charles Goring was the first scientist who became a critic of Lombroso[7] and his claims that heredity determined all future social behavior. The simple application of a scientific tool today used in many studies led him to a refutation of Lombroso. He did not investigate criminals alone, but made use of a control group to see whether his investigation of criminal personalities had not uncovered attributes found in any group of people. In addition to criminals, he investigated an equal number of university students for comparison.

In his book, *The English Prison Convict,* Charles Goring published the results of his study. He was not amazed to find that, by and large, criminals did not show different attributes from the general population. According to exact measurements, the students he investigated were somewhat heavier and taller than the criminal population. But the quality of "atavism" which Lombroso considered important as a cause for crime was present among the students just as in the criminal population. It could be assumed, in fact, that this quality would be found among all people and was, therefore, not typical for the rather peculiar group of criminals.

Thus, Goring devalidated the theory that all criminals were born so because they had inherited a propensity toward criminal behavior. By using a control group, he showed that criminals were much alike to a group selected at random from the student body and, therefore, probably representative for any population group. If this were true, Lombroso had no right to speak of the typical criminal at all.

Another sceptic of the claims made by the hereditarianists was L. L. Bernard.[8] He wrote a book refuting the instinct-theory. Now, this theory had supported the claims of the hereditarianists because it assumed that the behavior of all men resulted from innate instincts. He demonstrated that the instinct-theory often had to reason in a circle. It knew about the instinct only from previous persistent behavior, and then laid the blame for all ensuing behavior on the threshold of previously discovered instincts. In other words, this theory drew conclusions about an instinct from certain behavior, and then explained all behavior from the instinct it had proven in the first place.

L. L. Bernard put an end to the use of this approach which had reached the height of its influence with the help of a good scholar such as McDougall[9] who explained most behavior in terms of instincts inherited and inherent in the constitution of men. Today, nobody uses the instinct-theory anymore for an explanation of human behavior.

Some further criticism of the trust in hereditarianism came from the use of twin-studies in research on human personality. These twin-studies had the advantage, of course, of holding one factor constant. If identical twins were made the object of such a study, heredity did not vary between these twins. Any differences of social behavior found in a pair of identical twins, therefore, had to be due to different environmental experiences.

More or less descriptive and unprecise in the use of case study methods, early twin-research often demonstrated that two identical twins—as if forced by destiny—did the same things at the same time or suffered from similar diseases at the same time, although now living in different social environments.[10]

Needless to say, these early twin-studies were often used without rigid discipline in the case study method. They proved whatever the author wanted to prove. Not infrequently, they were made to prove that an individual had inherited the tendency to behave in a certain manner by inheriting the corresponding type of personality.

These twin-studies, however, raised some doubt about the importance of heredity in personality formation. It became obvious that even identical twins sometimes developed different personalities and behaved in different manners. This could only be due to different environmental experiences. It demonstrated that the environment was an active force in the formation of personality and the future behavior of the individual.

THE ENVIRONMENTALISTS

The importance of environment and its influence on personality and social behavior was discovered in two ways. First, John Dewey emphasized empirical research and wanted a treatment of children according to which they remained true to different phases of childhood development.[11] Second, from the earliest sociologists on, there has been more emphasis on environmental influences upon personality and the social behavior of men.

Through Dewey, the school life in the United States has adopted the environmental theory of personality. Education was optimistic about the molding of personality and behavior tendencies. If personality and behavior tendencies, on the other hand, were too firmly determined by inheritance, then no parent or teacher could do much in shaping the personality of a small child. The hereditarianists could only recommend different kind of institutionalization if the child behaved worse than hoped for. A more optimistic slant was promoted by a theory of personality which admitted the possibility that the personality of children could be changed after birth.

Sociology advanced slowly—like most other sciences—from deductive reasoning to empirical research and, finally, became one of the many scientific disciplines in teaching and research. Through these different stages, however, sociology emphasized the possibility of environmental influence on the personality of men.

This was expressed in the writings of Sumner[12] to whom we owe the understanding of folkways in a society which produced different personalities and different social behavior. Different types of environment were analyzed by a man like Charles Horton Cooley who discussed the primary and the secondary group and the different social controls inherent in them. Means of social control had even earlier been discussed by E. A. Ross.[13]

According to conditioning psychology, an individual was apt to behave like his social environment expected him to behave. Rewards and punishments originated in the social environment itself and tended to form the kind of personality best fitted into this self-same social environment.

Later, W. I. Thomas observed the clash between personality and social environment when he matched social attitudes (the individual's) and social values (the social environment's). To better accomplish this constant comparison between environmental expectations of behavior and the individual propensities to behave in a certain manner, he talked about the four wishes of the individual to which counterparts could be found in the social environment, thus making a good social adjustment possible.[14]

Some refinement in the approximation of personality and environment was, furthermore, achieved by George Mead at the University of Chicago. He discussed the combination of social attitudes rather than isolated ones when discussing social roles. In his *Mind, Self, and Society,* this thinker called attention to the circumstances that the individual internalized not only his own behavior but also that of his partner in the action he shared with him. This made it possible for the individual to switch from one action pattern to the opposing one in the social environment where he participates through active behavior.[15]

THE CULTURE-PERSONALITY APPROACH

In the middle of the twentieth century, the culture-personality approach wielded great influence in the field of personality studies by either sociology or anthropology. Social anthropology, as a matter of fact, is often based on the assumption that early childhood experiences color the personality of man later on, and that these childhood experiences are more or less the same in all families of the same culture. Much research has been carried out with this approach, and most teaching in social anthropology follows this approach important to us because it sees the person as a result of environmental experiences. To be sure, at this juncture we do not make use in either sociology or anthropology anymore of conditioning psychology where reward and punishment for desirable or undesirable behavior are inherent in the environment itself. The relationship between the social environment and the personality produced by it is now somewhat more indirect.

It is assumed that early frustrations of the libido cause personality traits later in the adult and carry various tendencies toward behavior according to the time when a free expression of the libido has been interrupted. There are oral personalities in some cultures because in many families some repression is exerted when the child wants to be fed from the mother. But there are anal personalities, also, if the child suffers inhibition because it is not allowed in his family to express freely the urge to enjoy excretory processes. Narcissistic traits are believed to ensue if the child is not allowed to explore his own body. If so inhibited, he may come to adore his own self later on in life.

The relationship between childhood and later personality traits is established through the subconscious of the individual. This gets hold of frustrated drives if the instinctual force of the libido cannot express itself freely. The subconscious makes two alternative consequences possible. It can lead to either neurosis or distinct personality traits.

Neurotic behavior ensues if the individual suffers intensively and wants to see a doctor to alleviate the symptoms which follow his culturally caused inhibitions. It ensues, also, if the person—due to these cultural inhibitions—begins to function without efficiency as an adult in this same culture. There is no other than a functional definition of neurosis. It is either due to suffering or due to inefficiency. These are the only reasons for outright neurotic behavior.

Anything less than neurotic behavior has no other consequences than social behavior with certain characteristics that stand out in the culture without leading to suffering of inefficiency. The personality traits of every individual in every culture are seen in this light. They are seen as next to neurotic behavior. They place their own stamp upon the adult personality which typically exists in this culture.

All personality traits which prevail in a given culture are due to repression of instinctual urges into the subconscious where they never come to rest, but continue to make the individual neurotic or at least endow him with characteristic traits of persistent behavior. It is always a question, therefore, of repression of some kind of instinctual force. This instinctual force appears in the form of the libido.

The recent investigations of human personality which are here under discussion stem, of course, from psycho-analytical thought.[16] In orthodox psycho-analysis, however, some kind of instinct is assumed to exist far and wide in all cultures. This instinct is not as specific as instincts under the auspices of so-called instinct-theory. Nevertheless, the energy for all human action is thought to be anchored in the libido present in all cultures. Certainly, its gradual transformation from a force urging the individual to seek nourishment from his mother to an individual enjoying excretion, to one that explores his own body or is prone to handle his private parts, to one experimenting in homo-sexual interests, this sequence is assumed by the orthodox analyst to be present in more or less the same fashion in all cultures.

The libido, however, has also been conceived differently. Some have thought of it as sex while others had shied away from such specific ideas about the energy source used by all human beings. They have thought of the libido as a general life force to reach the hetero-sexual state only late in its development. But whether sex or life force in general, some instinctual force was assumed to support all activity of human beings.[17]

In the exploration of human personality as well as analytical therapy, the underlying system of thought has undergone incisive changes. Today, there is less emphasis upon early childhood experiences. There has been a gradual change from orthodox (strictly Freudian) to neo-orthodox analysis as practiced by many followers of Freud. Among these Karen Horney and Erich Fromm are prominent.[18] They have in common the assumption that traumatic experiences of the individual may occur even late in life. With regard to psychotherapy, they have developed the further notion that the process of transference might be unnecessary whereby anxieties of early childhood are first directed against the psycho-analyst before they are dissolved and the individual cured when suffering of a neurosis. In other words, the neo-analysts believe that self-analysis is possible.

The neo-analysts will call attention to those cultures where typical experiences of the individual occur relatively late in life. There are many cultures, for example, where prevailing institutions cause the people to be differently inclined than elsewhere because certain institutions shape the puberty rites in distinctive fashion. Or they may be given relative freedom with regard to hetero-sexual expression at this time and, thus, they may be different from the people which result wherever the culture represses such hetero-sexual behavior in adolescence or young adulthood. Some cultures have different adolescents and, therefore, different adults.

The culture-personality approach has even gone further. Any kind of institutional setting existing in a particular culture is investigated with the question in mind of what consequences these institutions might have for the adult personality that prevails in this culture.

A variety of different cultures have been investigated in this manner —always with interest in the connection between the impact of a culture-wide institution upon the personality and the most frequent personality and his behavior. Best known are the various investigations by Margaret Mead who studied not only the childhood training in some primitive cultures but also the practices of adolescents in others.[19] Gregory Bateson contributed through his pictorial account of Bali. Geoffrey Gorer wrote about the American character, and West did the same thing while generalizing from the investigation of a Western community in the United States.[20]

In the meantime, many critical writings have also been published. The culture-personality approach has been criticized theoretically;[21] it has been condemned because of lack of empirical evidence,[22] and a sociologist has gone out to study childhood training methods and to see whether different training would possibly effect the adult personality.[23] Unfortunately, the latter came out with predominantly negative findings. The positive evidence, however, seems to outweigh the negative criticism by far.

THE COMBINED APPROACH OF ENVIRONMENTALISTS
AND HEREDITARIANS

At present, human personality and social behavior are neither expected to be wholly hereditarian or environmentalist. We owe it to painstaking twin-research that personality has been broken down into different attributes and that we are now putting numerical rather than absolute questions to our empirical materials.[24] We want to know to what extent one attribute or the other is shaped by either environment or heredity and constitution—thus making a scientific problem of one that has so far been treated on a metaphysical basis. The days are gone when either hereditarianists of environmentalists could claim to know all about the determination of social behavior. We now ask for an answer to the question of how much either heredity or environment have contributed to the molding of different personality traits.

We call this the synthetic approach to human personality and its social behavior. All people possess a body, as well as an id and a social personality. Surely, different sciences deal with different aspects of personality. A similar notion is inherent in the following discussion of bio-genic, psycho-genic, and socio-genic traits.[25]

At present, human personality has to be considered in its different parts. It cannot be considered heredity or environment anymore which shape personality and, thereby, determine social behavior. We must look upon human personality with the different facets of its composition in mind.

BIO-GENIC TRAITS

Bio-genic traits are part of the constitution of a person. They are innate to his biological organism. In fact, biological organism and constitution are synonymous terms. Both refer to the body as it stands before us.

We may inherit the tendency to grow tall or small. We may grow strong and athletic or weak and not very robust due to a heritage bestowed upon us by the parents who gave us birth. Through heredity, we have blond hair or black, we have blue eyes or brown, we are susceptible to some diseases but not to others. Our inheritance gives us an idea about our potential.

In addition to inheritance, however, the physical environment may influence the manner in which we behave. It does so by influencing our physical constitution, and this, in turn, may influence our behavior.

We may suffer of iodine deficiency if we live in a region where all vegetables have a low iodine content. This may affect us through the thyroid glands. If they are stimulated too much, our behavior is likely to be nervous and very intense. If, on the other hand, our thyroid glands are not stimulated very much by the iodine available in the region in which we live, rather apathetic behavior may well be the consequence. Medical doctors can do various things about such deficiency or overabundance. They may operate to eliminate too much stimulation of the thyroid glands. To make up for startling deficiencies, on the other hand, we may use iodized salt. In this manner, the availability of iodine in the natural foods of a region may be manipulated.[26]

Constant use of alcohol may also affect the constitution of the drinker. It may change the brain cells of the individual so that even a complete cessation of drinking will not counteract the consequences of previous drinking habits.

In these two examples, the behavior of the individual and his social personality is changed due to influences of the physical environment which change his constitution. The bio-genic traits of the individual are changed by changes in his physical environment.

PSYCHO-GENIC TRAITS

Our knowledge about psycho-genic traits is the most doubtful but also the most challenging. Every individual has a characteristic manner to approach different social situations. We may go to church and school, study at the university or join the army. In every social situation, we are recognized due to the manner in which we approach it. We may act aggressively or submissively; we may act with keen interest or in a very apathetic manner; we may act as introverts or extroverts. In other words, our form of behavior is always colored in a very particular manner that has nothing to do with the content of the social behavior required in the social situation at hand. About the content of such behavior we learn more when talking about socio-genic traits. Psycho-genic traits, however, color the form of behavior with which an individual indulges in all social situations in which he participates.

On the basis of clinical observation and case studies, it is now assumed that these psycho-genic traits are formed early in life. Psycho-analytical thought suggests that these traits result from early frustrations of a person's libido. If this happens, the psycho-genic traits will be repressed by the individual into the subconscious and cause later neurosis or personality traits.

These psycho-genic traits are even intermingled with socio-genic traits. They are not only important because of repressions into the subconscious. They are important, also, because they happen to be the first experiences altogether. Mainly, such traits are formed within the intimate circle of family living, but they may also occur in inter-action with other individuals who come into contact with the family. The truth of the matter is that these traits formed at the beginning of the life history of an individual are particularly important because they tend to be cumulative. If a person begins by acting in a certain manner, his social environment may later expect that he or she will continue to act in this same manner. Thus, the behavior of a person once started in early childhood is reinforced in the course of his life time.

Neurotic behavior, of course, ensues only in few cases. Whether we want to call a person neurotic or not depends, as stated already, entirely upon his inclination to look for the help of a medical doctor. We may call a person neurotic if he suffers so much from his predicament of suppressed urges that he asks for help from a medical doctor. Or his inefficiency in occupational activities may lead to a search for help.

The neurotic, however, is not most important to us. More important are those borderline cases of repression where the personality of the individual becomes colored by distinctive personality traits. It is interesting to know that early childhood experiences affect the adult personality later on. Adult personality traits are influenced forever because an individual underwent educational experiences in early infancy.

In this manner, early childhood and adult personality are linked to each other. Their personality type is determined which prevails in a certain culture.[27] The culture determines the prevailing educational experiences of all individuals by determining what the family will do for the child. Indirectly, then, culture and personality are bound to each other by influencing the family or being influenced by it.

SOCIO-GENIC TRAITS

In contrast to psycho-genic traits, socio-genic traits are learned in the social situation to which they are applied. No psycho-analytical thought is necessary to account for them. Reward and punishment through which the individual may be either praised or blamed by other participants in the social situation are enough explanation. He conforms to the type of behavior expected from all members of the social group. Conditioning psychology and a direct connection between stimulus and response may explain why the individual assimilates certain socio-genic traits and makes them part of his social personality.

Socio-genic traits range from isolated attitudes to integrated social roles and configurations of attitudes in well-rounded personalities. First, it was W. I. Thomas[28] who mentioned social attitudes in the book he had written together with Florian Znaniecki. He matched them with social values which related to the manner in which the social group expected the individual to behave. Both social attitudes and social values were assumed to express themselves in a behavior pattern which could make either fits or misfits of the individuals.

A more integrated conception of the attitudes held by the individual comes from George Mead[29] who mentioned not only social roles but also the internalization of entire interaction patterns. Prior to George Mead, of course, sociologists were concerned with the combination of social attitudes in the social personality of the individual. The earliest writers of sociology, already, mentioned the model accepted by the individual as an integrated unit of the social personality and social behavior. Today, it is more customary to talk about social roles and the internalization of the entire interaction system which makes the switching of social roles easily possible. A submissive daughter or housewife may react to a father or husband who is fairly aggressive. But it will often be observed that after the death of the partner in interaction either daughter or wife easily switch over to the social role previously accepted by father or husband.

Socio-genic traits have often been phrased in the form of wishes. We know of four fundamental wishes, namely those for security, new experience, response, and recognition. It is to be understood, however, that these wishes have nothing to do with instincts. They only represent practical ways in which the sociologist analyzes his empirical materials. They were first developed by W. I. Thomas in his book on the *Unadjusted Girl*,[30] the wayward girl in Chicago who was analyzed and compared with her social environment with the help of a profile containing the four wishes in various admixtures. Both the social environment and the individual, again, were described in terms of the four wishes.

It is important to mention, though, that W. I. Thomas was not dogmatic about those four wishes. He did not consider them inherent in the biological organism of the individual, albeit by way of inheritance or influences of the physical environment. The four wishes were only convenient manners in which to describe both the individual and his social environment and discuss their fitness to each other. Although still present in the minds of people, the instinct-theory had been laid aside by the time W. I. Thomas developed his theory of sociology.[31]

RECENT DEVELOPMENTS IN THE SOCIOLOGICAL THEORY OF PERSONALITY

At present, sociology is mainly concerned with the relationship of individual socialization to the background of an individual's cultural environment.[32] This has taken, most often, the form of the culture-personality-approach which was mentioned above. The individual was expected to be educated in families of his own culture, and how he was educated depended upon the manner in which his culture regulated childhood education. Through the mechanism of libido repression in a culturally typical fashion, then, the adult personality of that culture was assumed to take on certain personality traits resembling the neurotic behavior to which the same individual was inclined through the effects of culture.

While the culture-personality approach is most used and dominates the field of social anthropology,[33] it would be wrong to overlook other developments of equal importance. One of these is tied to the notion of functionalism which sees different aspects of a culture as interdependant upon each other.[34] The adult personality of this culture is tacitly assumed to fit well into the subdivisions of this culture. Cultural functionalism, then, is assumed to be matched by a corresponding spread of personality traits. Where such an adaptation is not achieved with ease, we talk about manifest and latent functions. The individual assimilates both although in the case of latent functions the interpretation of the individual case is not easy.

Psychological theories of personality, of course, have also accompanied the course of sociological theories of personality. Of these the work of the Swiss psychologist, Jean Piaget, is perhaps most important to the social scientist.[35] He tries to show with the help of exacting empirical studies that every child develops from extreme egotism to an identification with the social roles of others. In other words, the child develops moral judgment in close contact with the demands of his culture. Social scientists will never fail to consider child psychology according to which man's identification with his own cultural environment repeats itself in every individual case.

A further development in the sociological theory of personality is owed to Talcott Parsons.[36] He discusses the prerequisites of cultural integration and comes to the conclusion that a twofold measure of integration is necessary. Not only must the culture itself be capable of perpetuating itself; it is necessary, also, that the individual finds sufficient gratification within his culture to leave the cultural system intact. This, furthermore, illustrates the point that modern sociological theory about personality is mainly concerned with the fitness of the individual to his own culture, and the manner in which every culture depends upon its adult personalities.

SELECTED BIBLIOGRAPHY

Herbert Blumer, *An Appraisal of Thomas and Znaniecki's The Polish Peasant in Europe and America* (New York: Social Science Research Council, 1939). A recent attempt to re-evaluate the classical study of the Polish Peasant in the light of modern methodological thought.

James H. Bossard, *The Sociology of Child Development* (New York: Harper, 1948). A comprehensive presentation of modern childhood which discusses the process of the socialization of the child from different viewpoints.

John Dewey, *Intelligence in the Modern World* (New York: The Modern Library, 1939). This publication contains a collection of the writings of the famous pragmatic American philosopher. Students unfamiliar with his work find an opportunity here to become acquainted with it.

Erik H. Erikson, *Childhood and Society* (New York: W. W. Norton, 1950). A systematic account of Freudian psycho-analysis and its application to the evaluation of modern society.

Sigmund Freud, *The Basic Writings* (New York: The Modern Lirary, 1938). A selection from the writings by this famous author. It offers a fairly good approach to the student who may have become impatient with many secondary sources. The basic mechanism of the formation of neuroses and less distinct personality traits is made obvious.

Erich Fromm, *Escape from Freedom,* (New York: Farrar and Rinehart, 1941). This publication is of interest both for the sociologist and the psychologist. It gives a psychological interpretation of the recent history of Western Civilization, thereby emphasizing man's willingness to expose the responsibility which an age of individualism has placed upon him.

Charles B. Goring, *The English Convict* (London: H. M. Stationary Office, 1913). The official and generally known refutation of Lombroso's claim about the importance of heredity as a determinant of human behavior is contained in this publication.

John J. Honigman, *Cuture and Personality* (New York: Harpers and Brothers, 1954). A late collection of most of the work that has been done in this field of study. In addition to a good and complete bibliography, the book contains an outline of principles followed at the present time by most writers.

Karen Horney, *The Neurotic Personality of Our Time* (New York: W. W. Norton, 1937). The most well-known publication of the author. she tries to show here how certain neurotic tendencies are typically brought about through the institutions of life in our modern society.

Karen Horney, *New Ways in Psycho- Analysis* (New York: W. W. Norton, 1939). This book shows where the author and many other neo-analysts are inclined to approach the problem of neuroses differently from the orthodox analyst who follows Sigmund Freud.

Abram Kardiner and others *The Psychological Frontiers of Society* (New York: Columbia University Press, 1945). An early publication about the culture-personality approach; the student will also find an early outline of what the culture-personality approach is trying to do in its empirical studies.

Cesare Lombroso, and Gina Ferrero, *Criminal Man* (New York: G. B. Putnam's Sons, 1911). This is the earliest conception of crime as visualized by Lombroso. Here, crime appears as the result of "atavism." The book should be read by everybody with historical interest, and certainly by those who want to defend the position that it is heredity that causes people to react as they do.

George H. Mead, *Mind, Self, and Society* (University of Chicago Press, 1934). A post-humous work of the stimulating lecturer, this classical work develops all important facets of the theory of the social role of the individual through which he gains his social personality. At one time or another, every sociology student must read this book which contains most aspects of personality formation as offered by the sociologist.

Horatio H. Newman, Frank N. Freeman, and Karl Hozinger, *Twins: A Study of Heredity and Environment* (University of Chicago Press, 1937). A biologist, a psychologist and a statistician join in a model-study of twins in which the question of heredity and environment as factors influencing the social behavior of human beings are clearly assessed with regard to their relative importance. Contrary to more absolutistic previous studies, the empirical material is now asked to what extent different attributes of the individual are affected by either heredity or environment.

Jean Piaget, *The Moral Judgment of the Child* (Glencoe, Ill.: The Free Press, 1948). Perhaps the most characteristic empirical study of the author who here shows how, in the game of marbles, the moral judgment of the child gradually emerges from a mainly egocentric attitude in earlier childhood years.

Svend Riemer, born in Berlin (1905), studied at the Universities of Berlin and Heidelberg; Ph.D., Heidelberg (1930); also studied on a scholarship at the London School of Economics (1929-1930). Lectured at the Universities of Kiel and Stockholm. Came to U.S. in 1938; after spending a scholarship year at Columbia University and at the University of Chicago, taught at the University of Minnesota, University of Washington, Cornell University, University of Wisconsin, and University of California (Los Angeles), and in the summer schools of New York University and the University of Chicago. Is now Assistant Professor of Sociology, University of California (Los Angeles).

NOTES

1. Cesare Lombroso and Gina Ferrero, *Criminal Man* (New York: G. P. Putnam's Sons, 1911) and Cesare Lombroso, *Crime: Its Causes and Remedies,* (trans. by Henry P. Horton, Boston: Little Brown, 1918).

2. William H. Sheldon & S. S. Stevens & W. B. Tucker, *The Varieties of Human Physique* (New York: Harper, 1942).

3. More popularly people talked earlier about character and temperament when discussing the persistent aspects of human behavior; present discussions are more concerned with different forms of personality.

4. Johann Caspar Lavater, *Essays on Physiognomy* (Boston: William Spotswood & David West, 1794).

5. Ernst Kretschmer, *Koerperbau und Charakter* (Berlin: Springer, 1921), or trans. by W. I. H. Sprott (London: Kegan Paul, Trench & Trubner, 1925).

6. Sheldon, *op. cit.*

7. Charles Goring, *The English Prison Convict* (London: H. M. Stationary Office. 1913).

8. L. L. Bernard, *Instinct: A Study in Social Psychology* (New York: Henry Holt 1924).

9. William McDougall, *An Introduction to Social Psychology* (London: Methuen & Company, 1908).

10. Johannes Lange, *Crime and Destiny* (New York: Bond, 1930).

11. John Dewey, *Intelligence in the Modern World* (New York: The Modern Library, 1939).

12. William Graham Sumner, *Folkways* (Boston: Ginn & Company, 1906).

13. Charles Horton Cooley, *Human Nature and the Social Order* (New York: Charles Scribners Sons, 1902); Edward A. Ross, *Social Control* (New York: The MacMillan Company, 1901).

14. W. I. Thomas & Florian Znaniecki, *The Polish Peasant in Europe and America,* (New York: A. A. Knopf, 1927), and W. I. Thomas, *The Unadjusted Girl,* (Boston: Little Brown & Company, 1923).

15. George H. Mead, *Mind, Self, and Society* (University of Chicago Press, 1934).

16. Sigmund Freud, *The Basic Writings* (New York: The Modern Library, 1938).

17. For a rather complete statement by an orthodox psycho-analyst, see Erik H. Erikson, *Childhood and Society* (New York: W. W. Norton & Company, 1950).

18. Karen Horney, *The Neurotic Personality of Our Time* (New York: W. W. Norton & Company, 1937), *New Ways in Psycho-Analysis* (New York: W. W. Norton & Company, 1939); *Self-Analysis* (New York: W. W. Norton & Company, 1941); Erich Fromm, *Escape from Freedom* (New York: Farrar & Rinehart, Inc., 1941).

19. Margaret Mead, *Growing Up in New Guinea* (New York: William Morrow & Company, 1930); *And Keep Your Powder Dry,* (New York: William Morrow & Company, 1942). These, of course, are only examples of the writings about many different cultures by Margaret Mead.

20. For an early collection of culture-anthropology writings, see Abram Kardiner and Others, *The Psychological Frontiers of Society* (New York: Columbia University Press, 1945).

21. A. R. Lindesmith & A. L. Strauss, "Critique of Culture-Personality Writings," *American Sociological Review,* XV (1950), 587-600.

22. Harold Orlanski, "Infant Care and Personality," *Psychological Bulletin,* XIX (1949), 1-48.

23. William H. Sewell, "Infant Training and the Personality of the Child," "The Functional Prerequisites of Social Systems," *The American Journal of Sociology,* LVII (1952), 150-159.

24. Horatio H. Newman, Frank N. Freeman & Karl J. Holzinger, *Twins: A Study of Heredity and Environment* (University of Chicago Press, 1937)

25. Ernest W. Burgess & Harvey J. Locke, *The Family* (New York: The American Book Co., 1953).

26. William F. Ogburn & Meyer F. Nimkoff *Sociology* (Boston: Houghton Mifflin Company, 1950), 2nd edition, Chap. XI "Constitutional Factors in Personality," 195-215.

27. Walter Goldschmidt, "Values and the Field of Comparative Sociology," *American Sociological Review,* XVIII (June 1953), 287-293.

28. W. I. Thomas & Florian Znaniecki, *op. cit.*

29. George Mead, *op. cit.*

30. W. I. Thomas, *op. cit.*

31. L. L. Bernard, *Instincts: A Study in Social Psychology* (New York: Henry Holt, 1924).

32. For a good study of contemporary socialization, see James H. Bossard, *The Sociology of Child Development* (New York: Harper & Brothers, 1948).

33. James West, *Plainville U.S.A.* (New York: Columbia University Press, 1945); Geoffrey Gorer, *The American People* (New York: W. W. Norton, 1948); John J. Honigman, *Culture and Personality* (New York: Harper, 1954).

34. Ruth Benedict, *Patterns of Culture* (New York: Penguin Books, 1946); Robert K. Merton, *Social Theory and Social Structure* (Glencoe, Ill: The Free Press, 1948), Part I: Sociological Theory, 21-41.

35. Jean Piaget, *The Moral Judgment of the Child* (Glencoe, Ill.: The Free Press, 1948).

36. Talcott Parsons, *The Social System* (Glencoe, Ill.: The Free Press, 1951),

INSTITUTIONS

Robert C. Hanson
Michigan State University

The meaning of the concept institution as it has been defined and used in social science texts in the last twelve years is presented in the first part of this paper. In the second part, the dominant textbook explanation of the appearance and persistence of institutions is critically examined. Finally, current research problem areas in the field are surveyed.

The Concept "Institution" in Contemporary Social Science. A list was made of all text books in sociology, social psychology, social or cultural anthropology, and general social science that were reviewed in the *American Sociological Review* from February 1945 through December 1956.[1] The compilation resulted in 84 titles. Approximately 40 per cent of these have been systematically analyzed for the definitions and actual usages of the term institution. While the selection of books to be analyzed has been based solely on their convenient availability, it is probable that any significant trends appearing in this period would be found in the sample.

The Importance of the Concept. Over 85 percent of the texts analyzed included a listing of the term institution in the index and presented a formal definition, or used the term as a technical concept in the text. It was a central concept in some 70 percent of the texts in that it provided the basis for the division of the text into chapters, e.g., political, economic, religious institutions, or was given special treatment as a concept of theoretical importance for the work as a whole. Only in a few social psychology and cultural anthropology books was the term not utilized as a concept, neither appearing in the index nor in the text except incidentally.

The Variety of Definitions. Despite the explicitly stated importance of the concept and the widespread use of the term institution in the literature, it is apparent that no single definition can command universal acceptance at the present time. The most frequent type of definition found in the works analyzed emphasizes the culturally patterned behavioral aspect of institutions. An institution is defined as a complex of norms or rules regulating activity, or as a set of behavioral patterns, a code of behavior, or a standardized group-reaction pattern. As N. S. Timasheff and P. W. Facey define it, "An institution is a closely knit set of rules which imposes a relatively permanent way of satisfying the specific needs prevalent in society."[2]

Somewhat less frequently an institution is regarded as the same as a social group, as a unit of social organization. J. S. Slotkin defines institutions as "groups in which the social interaction between the members is regulated by custom,"[3] and P. A. Sorokin seems to use the terms institution, social system, and organized group interchangeably in distinguishing organized interaction from other types of interaction.[4]

A third common type of definition refers to institutions as systems or complexes of roles. For example, C. A. Dawson and W. E. Gettys state that "the established roles which are linked in systems of social expectations are called social institutions."[5]

Finally, some authors phrase their definitions in ways indicating that an institution incorporates several diverse kinds of referents into a single cultural configuration or system. J. O. Hertzler's definition is typical of this eclectic type:

> Social institutions are purposive, regulatory and consequently primary cultural configurations, formed, unconsciously and/or deliberately, to satisfy individual wants and social needs bound up with the efficient operation of any plurality of persons. They consist of codes, rules and ideologies, unwritten and written, and essential symbolic organizational and material implementations.[6]

Most of the definitions of institutions found in the works analyzed were classified into one of the four types exemplified above. Other variations exist but these were not numerically significant.[7]

Phenomena Labelled Institutions, and their Common Elements. The survey of the text book literature indicates that there is more agreement on what phenomena are to be called institutions than on how the concept should be defined.

What are called institutions may at first seem to be different *phenomena* if we decide only on the basis of a superficial interpretation of one common meaning of the words labelling the phenomena. However, further analysis of the phenomena brings the realization that besides a "dominant" meaning of a word, other meanings are implied or are less frequently thought of in connecting the word to phenomena. In the following partial list of institutions, institutions are classified according to one common or dominant meaning.[8] The later analysis attempts to show that all three kinds of referents are denoted by any named institution.

First, organized social groups appear to be the most obvious referent of some phenomena named institutions: families, clans, castes, classes, cults, sects, political parties, corporations, labor unions, clubs, a Town Council, The Royal Society for the Prevention of Cruelty to Animals, etc.

Second, complex behavior patterns are the obvious referents of other phenomena called institutions: marriage, exogamy, levirate, dowry, courtship, concubinage, prostitution, witchcraft, ancestor worship, chieftainship, trial by jury, municipal government, markets, land tenure, slavery, peonage, games, dances, etc. Special types of complex behavior patterns in which the primary aspect has a periodic or ceremonial character are also called institutions: reunions, initiations, graduations, funerals, coronations, harvest festivals, county fairs, Mother's Day, Sabbath, Christmas, Independence Day, Memorial Day, May Day, etc.

Third, physical culture complexes appear as the dominant referents of some phenomena labelled institutions: prisons, stores, factories, banks, hotels, property, money, restaurants, playgrounds, theatres, gymnasiums, hospitals, churches, universities, art galleries, etc.

When sociocultural phenomena of the kind listed above are subjected to analysis, elements common to all these phenomena called institutions can be identified, despite the differences in dominant referential aspects.

1. The first element common to all institutions is a *culturally defined pattern of social structure*. It is not the group itself—the interacting persons making up the family, or a church or university, or a labor union, or the participants in an initiation ceremony—that makes such groupings institutions; the membership may change but the institution persists. Rather it is the pattern of positions or statuses —the social structure—that can be and is transmitted from one set of members to others, from one generation to another, that is institutionalized. It is the *pattern of organization* that is cultural, transmissible, and capable of institutionalization.

2. The second element common to all institutions is a complex of

culturally defined norms which regulate the role behavior of persons holding the various positions in the social structure of the institution. Each role carries with it appropriate values, attitudes, and behavior prescriptions that are expressed or implied in the norms for that role. The behavior of a person acting in a given role will vary in accordance with norms defining obligatory or other appropriate behaviors in relation to both the social and physical objects in the situation.[9] Like social structures, norms are cultural, transmissible, and capable of institutionalization.

3. The third element common to all institutions is the *cultural definition of physical objects* connected with an institution. Buildings, equipment, symbolic objects and other kinds of physical culture traits and complexes are given their meaning and significance in terms of the activities of the institution. The same building might serve as a school, a store, a church, or a house. Which "meaning" the building has depends on its place in a particular institutional context. A wedding ring has a different significance than other kinds of rings because of its connection with marriage. Obviously, the meanings of physical objects can be transmitted from one set of members of an organized group to the new members or the next generation.

These three elements of institutions are tied together in a single sociocultural complex. It was observed that the institutional element of organized groups was the social structure. Behavior in the group is guided by norms for each role. If we look at the behavior patterns called institutions, such as marriage or communion, analysis again brings us to a social structure. The observable behavior is patterned and persistent because institutionalized norms regulate behavior, and the roles reflect a social structure—a patterning of social positions. Thus the marriage of persons means that their behavior now will be regulated by norms defining their relationship in the roles of wife and husband; a market implies norms regulating the behavior of buyers and sellers; slavery implies owner and slave roles, and so on. Both the normative patterns guiding role behavior and the culturally defined pattern of positions can be transmitted. Similarly, the behavior of participants in ceremonies or in other periodic behavior patterns is guided by norms appropriate for a given position or status. Observable behavior remains essentially the same in initiation ceremonies, at periodic festivals, or celebrations despite changes in group membership, because—*if* these ceremonies or occasions are institutions

of a group—the role structure and normative patterns guiding role
behavior are cultural patterns that have been transmitted to new
members of the group.

Finally, if we analyze the sociocultural phenomena involved in universities, factories, prisons, hospitals and other institutions where a
dominant aspect is the material culture complex, we again discern
a social structure and a set of norms regulating behavior. A series of
statuses, each with distinguishable rights and duties, persists despite
changes in personnel. The behavior of persons holding the various
positions is regulated by norms appropriate for each role. In any
given situation, the norms for a given role define the meaning of, and
the person's relation to, other social objects and the physical objects
connected with the institution.

In summary, the common elements of all institutions are brought
together in the concept *role*. Role implies a position or status in a
social structure; it implies a *set of norms* regulating behavior; it implies a situational analysis in which *relations to physical objects are
defined* as well as relations to social objects by the norms for the role
in that situation. But the actual existence of an institution depends
not only on the existence of elements but also on their organization
into a single system of *social* and cultural phenomena. In other words,
the fact that institutionalization has occurred means that socialization
and social control processes which account for the maintenance of
the institution are present in the actions of the existing membership
of the social system.

The Identification of Institutions. An institution may be distinguished from other types of sociocultural phenomena by the kind
of complexity of organization it involves and by the presence of
built-in persistence mechanisms. What is called an institution varies
with the system level of the analysis. Thus we speak of international
legal institutions like the International Court of Justice, or national
legal institutions like the Supreme Court, or of state, county and
local courts as legal institutions. Taking the United States as the
concrete social system under analysis, "the university" as an abstraction of many particular institutions may be examined as one of the
educational institutions of our culture. If a particular university were
the social system under analysis, then the graduation ceremony, the
Academic Senate, and the student government would be examples of
institutions of that university.

Once the social system level has been determined, an institution stands as a meaningful unit of analysis of intermediate complexity between role units on the one hand and a social system on the other. A plurality of roles are united in a single institution, while a single social system may maintain a whole series of institutions.[10]

Thus, the institution provides the context within which single social positions, single normative patterns, or single physical culture traits gain meaning and significance; it unites cultural patterns of social structure, behavior and material culture into a single meaningful unit of analysis. But the analysis of institutions requires their own placement within a context—an institution is always tied to an operating social system by which it is maintained and through which it may be transmitted to new members or to other groups.

Institutions persist when new members learn the structure, norms and values of the institution through interaction with persons within authority roles of the institution, and when sanctions operate to assure behavioral conformity with existing normative patterns. As socialization proceeds, the new members internalize the cultural norms defining their roles. In their relations with the significant others already enacting institutional roles, new members' behavior consistent with "expected" behavior in his role receives positive sanctions and inconsistent behavior receives negative sanctions. Hence, persons are motivated to enact their imputed roles within the present social structure according to the existing normative pattern defined for these roles. While other "protective" mechanisms might be isolated as contributing to persistence,[11] socialization and social control processes are crucial as identifying criteria in the designation of institutions. Such processes account for the observation that human behavior may be patterned and persistent despite changes in the membership of the organized social group.

THE POVERTY OF NEED THEORY IN THE STUDY OF INSTITUTIONS

In his survey of the field of social organization and social institutions in 1945,[12] Florian Znaniecki interpreted the "terminological chaos" he found as a sign of "rapid and many-sided development of scientific problematization" inherent in a period of transition from one coherent system of sociological theory then breaking down toward another emerging system of theory. Herbert Spencer's theory of social organization and institutions, which had guided subsequent theorizing and research well into the twentieth century, had rested on the methodological assumption that the elementary systems of sociological analysis were "societies," in which the specialized parts were institutions functioning to maintain the existence of the whole. Znaniecki noted that although this and related assumptions had proved inadequate for directing further fruitful research, "the essential nucleus of Spencer's theory of society is still being transmitted to most college students . . ."[13]

According to Znaniecki, the emerging system of theory, which had dropped the geographically delimited "society" as the unit system of analysis as well as other assumptions, carried with it implications and consequences for the field which were incompletely realized, hence the observable state of confusion.

Znaniecki's assessment of theoretical trends in the field seems reasonable and sound, and applies to the contemporary situation. For example, in the forefront of modern structural functionalism, in Talcott Parson's *The Social System,* society is no longer *the* unit of sociological analysis. Social systems become the focus of sociological theory and society then is but one type of social system, one that is in principle self-subsistent.[14]

Robert Merton's analysis of three basic postulates of traditional functionalism— the functional unity of society, universal functionalism, and indispensability—led him to conclude that such postulates "have proved to be debatable and unnecessary to the functional orientation."[15]

It appears, then, that leading exponents of contemporary sociological theory are altering basic methodological assumptions that had been lodged in the structural-functional tradition. However, the situation now is still the same as observed by Znaniecki—the old assumptions still dominate the textbooks—society is still the basic unit of analysis and institutions are the indispensable parts which are functionally integrated in providing for the needs of persons or for the maintenance of the society as a whole. Whether these theoretical assumptions (which are here designated "need theory") are still being postulated in discussions of advanced theory or are ever used as heuristic guides in contemporary research on institutions is debatable, but the evidence that they are still being transmitted to college students in the text book literature is undeniable. Nearly eighty per cent of the authors of the books analyzed either included the need satisfying properties of institutions in their definition of an institution, and/or they explained their existence in terms of their relation to biological or societal needs. In view of this pattern of acceptance, it seems worthwhile to bring together the critical arguments of minority positions, and to expand the criticism to additional issues.[16]

The most extensive treatment of institutions to appear in the twelve year period under discussion is J. O. Hertzler's *Social Institutions*. While his work will be used as a reference for need theory postulates and difficulties, the same pattern may be found repeatedly in the text-book literature.

The Empirical Inadequacy of Need Theory. The appearance and persistence of institutions are accounted for in need theory by two interdependent postulates—the functional integration of institutions as parts contributing to the maintenance of a total society, and the indispensability of institutions as means of satisfying biological and societal needs. Both of these postulates prove to be empirically untenable when other observations of the same author are compared with the theoretical assumptions. In discussing the functional relationships of institutions, Hertzler states:

> Not only are institutions interdependent, but they are bound together in sequences of development. *The full development and effective functioning of a society depends on the successful co-operation and coherence of the various institutions and other elements of the social order.* All must be consistent with each other . . . At the same time it must be remembered that *there is a fundamental functional division of labor among institutions.* . . In a well-organized and properly functioning society all the parts must each perform their appropriate functions.
>
> If, for any of many reasons, the institutions—perhaps only those which at the moment are key institutions—fail to function properly, the society as a whole may be sick; it may be disorganized or even deteriorating. . . . In a "normal" society, the basic institutions form an efficient, interlaced and interdependent operating system.[17] (Hertzler's emphasis.)

But in other sections of the work, Hertzler has observed:

> It is equally true that all the institutions of a given people at a given time are *not* at a uniform stage of development. . . . Finally the fact is not to be ignored that institutions have *never developed logically and harmoniously, or in proper sequence* even though a general life-cycle may be discerned. The parts of a given institution, in many cases, have not developed con-

temporaneously. The development is invariably disjointed and jerky; different institutions or parts of institutions are *out of gear with each other*. Hence the maladjustments that exist in *every* society.[18] ((My emphasis.)

In the section on changes of institutions, Hertzler again points out facts that fail to correspond with his postulates:

> There are no isolated, untouched societies, secure and comfortable in the purity of their culture and the invariability of their institutions. Today all over the world we note the impact of highly organized modern cultures upon each other as well as upon primitive groups. . . . .
> All such contacts result in great change in the cultures in general and the institutions in particular of the contacting societies. . . . No culture is in a state of quietude and equilibrium.[19]

Thus, according to theory, every culture is composed of institutions integrated with each other and each performing functions necessary for the maintenance of the society. In fact, existing cultures and institutions are observed to have changed as peoples come into contact with each other. Today, then, "societies" *are maintained* despite disequilibrium and lack of integration of their institutions (which is theoretically impossible); institutions are "out of gear" in every society, but this is theoretically *not* true of the "normal" society.

With regard to the indispensability of institutions, Hertzler states:

> Most institutions are more or less permanent, universal, and regularized means of satisfying the common and basic needs of human beings in their respective natural and social environments. They insure continuous and satisfactory human existence. . . . They serve a *vital and indispensable* function in their respective groups.[20] (My emphasis.)

Later, in discussing the different rates of change of institutions, and consequently the lag of some institutions, Hertzler observes:

> This lagging of some institutions results in them being not only out of date but also "off their guard." Men are not inactive in the meantime; they do not conveniently go to sleep until the institutional practices have been adjusted to the needs of the present. *They go right on satisfying their basic needs in whatever ways they can.*[21] (My emphasis.)

Obviously, then, the appearance and persistence of institutions cannot be explained by assuming that they are indispensable for the satisfaction of needs if at the same time it is observed that men go on satisfying basic needs (that existing institutions are *not* satisfying) in whatever ways they can.

Note that under the functional unity assumption, neither the dysfunction of an institution, nor the disintegration of a society could be empirically possible states of an existing group of people.

According to the postulates of the theory, the functions performed by institutions are *necessary* for the maintenance of the society; if an institution fails to function, an essential need is not being met, the society supposedly disintegrates and the people will not survive. Any recognition of dysfunction among the institutions of a people then implies either that the supposed system is in a state of disintegration in which case "the society" is not the unified, coherent unit presupposed by functional theory; or, it implies that the function of the institution was not necessary for the maintenance of the society after all in which case the postulate is unnecessary and empirically untenable. You cannot have both possibilities—functionally integrated institutions as a necessary condition for the existence of a society *and* the recognition of *dys*function of an institution in an *existing* society— and have a logically consistent empirically relevant theory.

Suppose the condition "disintegration" is taken to be a sign of a changing society. Then further theoretical difficulties appear. If people survive as a group although their institutions are changing, i.e., disintegrating, the postulate that institutions must necessarily be integrated for the maintenance of a society is obviously contradictory to the observed condition. If the term society is to be limited to refer only to those peoples whose institutions *are* in a state of "functional integration," then contemporary usage of the term society to designate the people living together in civilizations, modern national states, or in non-literate groups who have come into continuous acculturative contact with modern states, would be inconsistent since such people's institutions have unquestionably changed while an identifiable group of people have survived. In short, the postulate that an institution performs a "necessary" function in a necessarily integrated set of institutions in every society is simply inconsistent with the fact that people may persist as a group while their institutions change.

The Methodological Inadequacy of Need Theory. It is an important methodological rule that variation cannot be explained by an appeal to a constant, or to relate the rule to the present context, variation and change of institutions cannot be explained by reference to constant, universal needs or prerequisites. Yet, without seeming to be aware of the methodological fallacy, some need theorists attempt to explain both wide variations within institutions—e.g., various kinds of marriage patterns—and, *changes* of institutions by reference to the same constant needs or functions. If the needs of men are constant, and are *causally* responsible for a set of institutions which function to meet those needs, then the institutions of any concrete society should never change, the need being constant. Yet, if we look at the histories of cultures, we observe that institutions have changed. Therefore, the constant and causal aspects of need theory are incompatible. At least one is wrong. Observations must be directed to variables that correlate with changes in institutions. On the other hand, for an author to explain changes in institutions by proposing new needs or changing specific needs is to perform with a theory like a magician pulling rabbits out of his hat.[22] A post-facto "explanation" can always be proposed, but such speculation utilizing empirically empty concepts provides no basis for directing inquiry to classes of objectively determinable facts.

Need theory is inadequate methodologically not because it explains too little, but because, like instinct theory, it explains everything. As a consequence a particular need satisfaction explanation has little heuristic value—it is typically incapable of test against observable facts which would clearly confirm or refute the proposed explanation. Under these circumstances investigation is not initiated and theory cannot advance. If we take any particular institutional role it is easy to assign dozens of needs of the person that are met in the performance of the role in different situations. It is just as easy to propose a number of social functions for a given institution. But what kinds of facts would refute a reasonable explanation? For example, in an institutionalized religious feast, is it the satisfaction of hunger, or the need of sociability, or a need for periodic expressions of member statuses, that is being met? Or is the feast really part of the exchange pattern of the economic system? Is it the need for the development of group solidarity, or some other need that is being satisfied and therefore accounts for the existence of the institution?[23]

It can be argued that:

> Property is an institution in the sense that there is a system of rules fixing the way that men satisfy their need for the possession of material things. Marriage is an institution in that there

is a coherent set of rules establishing the way that men satisfy the linked needs for sexual union and for the procreation of children. . . . Democracy is an institution, a system of rules imposing a way of satisfying a need for government.[24]

Then, by the same kind of reasoning we may conclude that slavery is a system of rules fixing the way that men satisfy their need for the possession of other human beings, concentration camps exist as institutions because they provide a coherent set of rules that establish the way that men satisfy their need to torture and murder each other; institutionalized suicide exists because it satisfies the need for death, and so on.

The Widespread Disagreement among Need Theorists. Taking a society—a group of people sharing a common culture and territory—as the unit of analysis, the need theorists of concern here seem to agree on two general propositions: (1) some needs are universal; therefore, if any society is to exist or is existing, there are certain basic biological and social needs (or functional prerequisites) that must be or are being met; (2) institutions satisfy these needs (or fulfill the necessary functions) so institutions, as such, are universal.

Beyond this level of agreement, one finds little except confusion and disagreement in the literature taking the need satisfaction approach to the study of institutions.[25] Specifically, (1) there is disagreement as to *which* needs are to be regarded as basic or universal. (2) There is confusion as to whether the term institution should refer to what might be called otherwise a universal category or sector of culture corresponding to a "basic need," e.g., "*the* economic institution," or should refer to sociocultural complexes *within* such a category, e.g., economic institutions like banks, corporations, and the market. (3) There is disagreement as to *which* categories or institutions are basic, primary, major or universal. The number ranges from one—either the family or marriage—to twelve or more. (4) There is disagreement on what the primary *function* of any particular institution is. (5) There is disagreement on whether the institutions of any particular society are explained by reference to *universal* needs or functions or are to be explained in terms of *specific* needs and *specific* functions necessary for the maintenance of the particular society in question.

The Dispensability of Need Theory. The persistence of institutions can be accounted for without reference to needs. In the first place, in the experience of any individual, institutions are existing when he is born into the group. What wants, needs, and values that individual will develop and how they are to be fulfilled will depend on his socialization experiences in relation to persons acting out roles within the institutional framework of the group. The obligatory norms imposed by the institutions of the group in which he is a member may be explicitly contradictory to "basic biological needs," as in cases of institutionalized patterns of suicide, fasting, celibacy, torture, infanticide and old-age murder, and so on. In an analysis of the behavior of any group and the institutions maintained by that group, we lose conceptual power if we explain the persistence of the institutions by starting with the needs of individuals. Rather, we account for the behavior of group members (in so far as it is patterned and repetitive role behavior) in terms of norms prescribed by existing institutions. Since the persistence of institutions can be accounted for by linking their transmission in time to observable social processes—recurrent because they are built into institutional roles, giving causal significance to needs is unnecessary. The socialization of new members and social control or sanction systems are processes carried out by the present membership of the group through which behavioral conformity and cultural continuity beyond the present membership is attained, hence, the persistence of the institution.

The appearance and change of institutions can be accounted for without reference to needs. Despite lip service to the theory that "needs of the present" cause adjustments in old institutions or the appearance of new ones, Hertzler and other need theorists, in actually analyzing change, do not usually stop with a need satisfaction explanation. They often cite events which have an observable effect or impact on given institutions. Such events include catastrophic natural events such as floods, epidemics or droughts; population movements—emigration, migration; crises—panics, depressions, invasions, wars, and revolutions.[26] Such events would likely disrupt the performance of roles through which the typical socialization and control of new members had been achieved, thus introducing the possibility that changes in the institution through the diffusion or invention of different elements will occur.

Thus a focus on social processes rather than on need satisfaction provides content to the study of institutions. The imputation of needs to a social system in accounting for the *presence* of institutions is unnecessary and fruitless when processes can be described that account for the persistence of these institutions. In the analysis of how *changes* in institutions occur, the focus is properly on how external impacting events or conditions affect the socialization and social control processes in the then existing set of institutions, how different elements are introduced through diffusion or invention especially in periods when social control processes have been disrupted, and how the induced changes guide emergent normative cultural patterns toward a particular structure within a limited range of structural possibilities for that system level. To argue that changed needs caused a change in the institution is to introduce objectively unverifiable explanatory concepts which closes off inquiry into processes of persistence and change. On the other hand, propositions about processes invite inquiry into what actually has occurred and is occurring. Inquiry is directed to sets of objectively determinable facts which confirm or refute proposed hypotheses, and our theories and knowledge about institutions can advance.

RESEARCH TRENDS AND PROBLEM AREAS

Since other reports in this book cover developments in specific institutional fields, there is no attempt here to document in notes specific researches in particular areas. The problem has been to determine what, if anything, has been common in research trends in a number of institutional fields in order to identify trends for "research in institutions in general." Also, current problems in specific fields are placed within a general problem area framework. The problem areas are then presented abstractly so that they are applicable in principle to any institution and may be rephrased into specific research problems for a particular institution.[27]

Considering institutions in general for signs of trends, the large number of empirical studies in which the concept role is the central theoretical tool appears as the most impressive development in the last decade, judging from summary accounts and abstracts of recent research.[28] These studies seem significant in two respects. First, they have appeared in practically every traditional subject area of sociology. There have been studies of labor leaders, managers, military officers, state legislators, county sheriffs, teachers, salesmen, retired, ministers, chaplains, scientists, doctors, and many other professions and occupations. Second, there is some evidence that a kind of fusion of a number of social sciences is occurring around the role concept.[29] It provides a conceptual link between the person, the interactive process, and institutionalized cultural patterns. Questions regarding the relation of social structure and personality have been raised in increasing numbers of studies via the role concept.[30] Operational distinctions between role expectations, role behavior or enactment, role-taking, and the self have been successfully employed in a number of experimental and quasi-experimental studies.[31] Studies employing Parsons' pattern variables in the research design have become increasingly frequent in the 1950's; some of these have been part of the growing literature on role conflict.

Aside from the common ground in role-oriented studies, current problem areas vary from one institutional field to another, so that what is the subject of intensive investigation in one area has not even been considered as a relevant research problem in some other institutional field. Yet a little reflection brings the realization that many such problems are not inherently tied to a particular area, but are problems common to institutions in whatever traditional category they may be classed. Consequently, hypotheses and operational tools developed in one field may be fruitfully applied to other institutional areas with the prospect that the ranges of variation and types of relationships in institutional structures and processes may more readily become apparent. In short, it appears that there is room for a great deal of crossfertilization within research sections of sociology itself. For example, it seems probable that hypotheses proved useful in political sociology in the study of bureaucracy and the formal organization of unions, government agencies, and corporations could provide leading hypotheses for the investigation of the large-scale organization of hospitals, churches, and universities. The insight into personal motivation and the nature of social controls contributing to efficient role performance that have been derived from morale and unit effectiveness studies in military sociology could be merged with the propositions developed in the work satisfaction and productivity studies in industrial sociology. Hypotheses could be tested further against other types of "work-units" where variations in "output" are evident and comparative studies are feasible, e.g., in police units, athletic teams, and many other types of units in local, state, and national government, in reformatories, hospitals, universities and so on. The processes involved and the problems created in the succession of the top administrator of an organization is another problem area that cuts across traditional subject division lines, but has hardly been touched except in industrial sociology. Similarly, the field of cross-cultural studies of institutions is wide open for investigation. In comparative cross-cultural studies, the study of kinship systems is by far the most advanced. G. P. Murdock's *Social Structure*[32] provides a model of theoretical and methodological rigor in dealing with large masses of data that may well be followed by students working on cross-cultural studies of other types of institutions.

Many of the current problem areas listed below have been raised in isolated instances in highly limited contexts. It is to be hoped that the abstraction of general problem areas from these particular contexts will stimulate new kinds of researches into old subject areas and encourage the cross-fertilization of insights and knowledge originally gained through disciplined research in particular institutional areas.

A. Current problem areas in which the primary focus is on role:

1. Role descriptions—union leader, minister, business executive, etc.

2. Recruitment and selection—background characteristics of persons in the role; extent to which selection is not based on achieved or universalistic characteristics; career patterns; status and "style of life" in the community.

3. Socialization processes—the transmission and acquisition of knowledge and skills required for the role; the institutionalization of attitudes and values.

4. Ideology and values—degree of class consciousness and identification; characterization of value patterns; prejudice in roles.

5. Role and personality studies—differential role performance and—motivation, levels of aspiration and frustration, individual adjustment, mental sickness; causes and consequences of marginal roles; morale (e.g., work satisfaction) and performance (e.g., productivity); relation of motivational factors to horizontal and upward mobility, and to intra-institutional informal structures; role conflict and its consequences.

6. Decision making in a role—relation to lines of authority, communication networks, consensus processes, extra-institutional pressures; relative influence of formal and informal structures.

7. Social control—formal and informal patterns; problems of deviation from rules (e.g., variations as due to differences in the organizational structure.)

8. Social perception—of the institution (or parts of it) by the person in the role; the public image of the role, what the public "expectations" are, and how these have evolved.

B. Current problem areas in which the primary focus is on an institution, or institutions:

1. Differential structures as a problem area:

a. descriptive studies (e.g., of a union, plant, a particular communication industry, a military organization; or role relationships—client-professional, manager-union leader, teacher-superintendent, etc.)

b. the extent of bureaucracy as a function of size; measuring the degree of specialization (e.g., when is a "specialty" an autonomous position, or a profession?)

c. organizational structure related to domination by a particular kind of elite (e.g., in a professional society.)

d. variation in role patterns and the success, efficiency or productivity of units (e.g., marriage, military, work units)

e. the institution and the organization of its material culture (e.g., family and housing).

2. The persistence of norms and structures as a problem area—maintenance processes and problems:

a. formal patterns of control compared with other internal control systems (e.g., elite domination, informal cliques as important controls).

b. social control and deviation problems as a function of structural variation (e.g., voluntary commitment organizations like political parties vs. obligatory commitment type organizations such as government agencies); consequences of various structures for democratic processes; degree of deviation from norms as a function of status.

c. the impact of existing institutional values on the value systems of new personnel; the impact of a bureaucratic organization on the role of a participant "professional."

d. intra-institutional conflict situations and settlement processes (e.g., strikes, mediation, grievance procedures, bargaining process).

e. problems of succession, and of horizontal and vertical personnel mobility—selective processes determining who moves which way and under what instigating conditions.

f. inter-institutional relations and/or the relation of an institution to its maintenance social system (e.g., how outside values and pressures affect inside conduct and decisions—in a plant, school system, etc.).

3. The change of institutions as a problem area.

a. descriptive histories or generalized event sequences (e.g., the history of a union movement; stages in the U.S. family life-cycle).

b. innovation and/or differential acceptance of change (e.g., new farm practices) as a function of status and related factors—motivation, ideology, marginality, etc.; as a problem of the communication of information; as a function of total social systems.

c. processes of institutionalization and role differentiation (e.g., what beginning elements and processes account for the emergence of a profession?)

d. crisis situations (e.g., the impact of a catastrophic event such as the depression; assessment of resources to cope with a crisis).

e. impact of other institutions or institutional sectors as a determinant of change—e.g., effect of technological changes; change in size or significance relative to other institutions; change in the character of an institution (e.g., the structure of corporations) as a function of a change in that institutional sector (e.g., a change in the nature of economic organization in the U.S.)

C. Current problem areas in which the primary focus is comparative institutions, within a culture or cross-cultural:

1. Cross-cultural variations in the structure and processes within a given class of institutions (e.g., variations in kinship systems, economic and political organizations).

2. The relation of various institutional sectors to each other in the same culture (e.g., religion, or science, or the family and the state, economic order, educational system, etc.)

3. The relation of institutional sectors to the class system (e.g., social class and education, religion, economic organization, etc.)

4. Elites and power structures (e.g., which institutional elites have the most power in the society? how has this changed in time? in which institutional sphere is there the most rapid upward mobility? to what extent is there conflict or consensus among elites—how are decisions of one group communicated to others and what determines acceptance and rejection?)

5. The problem of how end social effects in an institutional sector are determined when institutionalized individual expectations are

non-purposive with respect to the end result (e.g., the operation of the price system in a free economy).

D. International institutions.

Although the trend reports often cite the need for more comparative research and especially cross-cultural studies of institutions, there is not evident a similar demand for studies of *international* institutions. Yet international institutions occur in most of the commonly recognized institutional categories. There are religious institutions that are international, such as the Roman Catholic Church. International political institutions such as the World Court, the League of Nations, the U.N. and the Communist Party are easily recognized. There are business companies, labor unions and banks that are international and international institutions in recreation and in the arts and sciences also exist, such as the Olympics, and international professional societies. But traditional structure-function theory which takes a society as its unit of analysis cannot account for the existence of international institutions since, according to the theory, institutions exist as integrated parts of a coherent whole, maintaining the society in which they function. It is obvious that existing international institutions are not part of an integrated system, nor have their functions been "necessary" for the maintenance of "world society." The study of the establishment, persistence, and dissolution of international institutions, then, is a logical further step in the research program sketched above. The results of such research should prove to have significant consequences for contemporary sociological theory.

SELECTED BIBLIOGRAPHY

Hans Gerth and C. Wright Mills, *Character and Social Structure: The Psychology of Social Institutions* (New York: Harcourt, Brace, 1953). Relations between political, economic, military, religious, and kinship institutions and character and personality are explored demonstrating the fruitfulness of the role concept.

J. O. Hertzler, *Social Institutions* (Lincoln: University of Nebraska Press, 1946). This work represents the most extensive treatment of institutions in general to appear in the last twelve years.

E. T. Hiller, *Social Relations and Structure: A Study in Principles of Sociology* (New York: Harper, 1947). One of the best analyses of institutions as culture complexes of norms of social relations is presented in this book.

Everett C. Hughes, "Institutions," in Alfred McClung Lee (ed.), *New Outline of the Principles of Sociology* (New York: Barnes and Noble, Inc., 1946), 223-281. A concise treatment of institutions in general by a leading authority in the field.

Werner S. Landecker, "Institutions and Social Integration," *Papers of the Michigan Academy of Science, Arts and Letters*, XXXIX (1954), 477-493. In this attempt to increase the research utility of the concept institution, Landecker describes variables to be used in research on institutions and develops ten illustrative hypotheses relating the variables and types of institutions.

Robert H. Lowie, *Social Organization* (New York: Rinehart and Co., 1948. A most impressive characteristic of Lowie's book is the large number of clearly described institutions collected from societies all over the world and throughout human history.

Bronislaw Malinowski, *A Scientific Theory of Culture and Other Essays* (Chapel Hill: The University of North Carolina Press, 1944). Institutions are grounded in human needs by a highly regarded and influential exponent of functionalism.

Don Martindale and Elio D. Monachesi, *Elements of Sociology* (New York: Harper and Brothers, 1951). These writers, influenced by Chapin, present one of the best text book discussions of institutions, including a criticism of need theory.

George Peter Murdock, *Social Structure* (New York: The Mac-Millan Co., 1949). The theoretical and methodological rigor which characterizes this research on kinship systems provides a high standard to guide other researchers on comparative institutions.

Talcott Parsons, *The Social System* (Glencoe, Ill.: The Free Press, 1951). Institutions are central in this basic theoretical work by the leading exponent of modern structural functionalism.

A. R. Radcliffe-Brown, *Structure and Function in Primitive Society* (Glencoe, Ill.: The Free Press, 1952). Institutions function to maintain the total social structure according to this influential sociologistic functionalist whose important essays and addresses are collected in this volume.

Ragnar Rommetveit, *Social Norms and Roles* (Minneapolis: University of Minnesota Press; Oslo: Akademisk Forlag, 1954). Rommetveit presents a semi-formalized social psychological theory of norms and roles and shows how hypotheses were tested against data on religious attitudes and sex roles of adolescents in Norway.

Theodore R. Sarbin, "Role Theory," *in* Garner Lindzey (ed.), *Handbook of Social Psychology* (Cambridge: Addison-Wesley Publishing Co., Inc., 1954), 223-258. Sarbin discusses recent research involving the role concept and includes an extensive bibliography on role theory and research.

Pitirim A. Sorokin, *Society, Culture, and Personality: Their Structure and Dynamics* (New York and London: Harper and Brothers, 1947) 70-91. Sorokin draws a distinction between law norms and other types in this concise analysis.

Florian Znaniecki, "Social Organization and Institutions," *in* Georges Gurvitch and Wilbert E. Moore (eds.), *Twentieth Century Sociology* (New York: The Philosophical Library, 1945), 172-217. Trends in the field into the 1940's are described, certain theoretical positions are critically examined, and some heuristic concepts to replace inadequate ones in the field are suggested in this summary report by Znaniecki.

Robert C. Hanson (1926-   ), received his B.A. in Psychology at the University of California (1949) and the M.A. in Sociology and Social Institutions from the same institution (1951); while studying at Harvard University in the Department of Social Relations (1951-52) was also Research Assistant in the Research Center in Creative Altruism; while Teaching Assistant in the Department of Sociology and Social Institutions, University of California, received the Ph.D. (1955). Today is Assistant Professor in the Department of Social Science, Michigan State University.

NOTES

1. Some basic theoretical works were included in the list, such as B. Malinowski, *The Dynamics of Culture Change;* T. Parsons, *The Social System* and E. E. Evans-Pritchard, *Social Anthropology.* Collections of readings were not included.

2. *Sociology: An Introduction to Sociological Analysis* (Milwaukee: The Bruce Publishing Co., 1949) , 279.
Cf. also, Arnold W. Green, *Sociology: An Analysis of Life in Modern Society* (New York, etc.: McGraw-Hill, 1952) , 79, and Harry Holbert Turney-High, *General Anthropology* (New York: Thomas Y. Crowell, 1949) , 575.

3. *Social Anthropology. The Science of Human Society and Culture* (New York: The Macmillan Co., 1950) , 25.

4. P. A. Sorokin, *Society, Culture, and Personality: Their Structure and Dynamics* (New York and London: Harper, 1947) , 70-91; cf. also, Hubert Bonner, *Social Psychology, An Interdisciplinary Approach* (New York: American Book Co., 1953) , 319-320.

5. C. A. Dawson & W. E. Gettys, *An Introduction to Sociology* (New York: The Ronald Press, 1948) , 249; cf. also, Talcott Parsons, *The Social System* (Glencoe, Ill.: The Free Press, 1951) , and Ronald Freedman, Amos H. Hawley, Werner S. Landecker, and Horace M. Miner, with a chapter by Guy E. Swanson, *Principles of Sociology: A Text with Readings* (New York: Henry Holt, 1952) , 173.

6. *Social Institutions* (Lincoln: University of Nebraska Press, 1946) , 4; cf. also, John Lewis Gillin & John Philip Gillin, *Cultural Sociology* (New York: The Macmillan Co., 1948) , 315; and George A. Lundberg, Clarence C. Schrag, and Otto N. Larsen, *Sociology* (New York: Harper & Brothers, 1954) , 194.

7. The extremes of variation may be indicated by two examples: Marion Levy, Jr. uses the term "institution" to refer to a particular type of normative pattern, examples being "not passing a red traffic light" and "not killing those who oppose one's views." The latter "institution" is more highly institutionalized than the

former in terms of conformity and sanction aspects. At the other extreme, James Feibleman uses the term "institution" to refer to what many other social scientists would call "categories," "sectors," or "aspects" of culture. Thus, for Feibleman, "economics" is an institution, "politics" is another, "ethics" another. Cf. Marion J. Levy, Jr. *The Structure of Society* (Princeton University Press, 1952), 102-104, and James Feibleman, *The Theory of Human Culture* (New York: Duell, Sloan & Pearce, 1946), 103-104.

8. While institutions in the following list are classified according to only one referent, it will be obvious that other meanings of the terms suggest other kinds of referents. Thus "market" can mean the coming together of people for buying and selling (normative behavior), or it may refer to the people organized to buy or sell (role structure), or to a place where goods are for sale (physical culture complex). Other terms here classified under one heading have the same triple significance.

9. Space limitations prohibit a discussion of the classification of norms. For a concise analysis, see P. A. Sorokin, *op. cit.*, 71-85, and the classification scheme of Clyde Kluckhohn in his "Patterning in Navaho Culture," in Leslie Spier (ed.) *Language, Culture, and Personality* (Menasha, Wis.: Sapir Memorial Publication Fund, 1941), 109-130, cited in Ralph L. Beals and Harry Hoijer, *An Introduction to Anthropology* (New York: The Macmillan Co., 1953), 213. See also Talcott Parsons, *op. cit.*, 58-112, for a classification of the pattern variables of role definition. On the possibility of developing a formal logic for norms, see Ragnar Rommetveit, *Social Norms and Roles* (Minneapolis: University of Minnesota Press, 1954), and Alan Ross Anderson & Omar Khayyam Moore, "The Formal Analysis of Normative Concepts, "*American Sociological Review*, XXII (February, 1957), 9-17

10. Cf. Parsons, *op. cit.*, 39-40.

11. For example, collectivity orientation in authority roles, a high degree of morale among members, mutually supporting ties with other institutional groups, and "vested" interests.

12. "Social Organization and Institutions," *in* Georges Gurvitch & Wilbert F. Moore, Eds., *Twentieth Century Sociology* (New York: The Philosophical Library, 1945), 172-217.

13. *Ibid.*, 178.

14. Parsons, *op. cit.*, 19, 101, 113.

15. *Social Theory and Social Structure. Toward the Codification of Theory and Research* (Glencoe, Ill.: The Free Press, 1949), 27.

16. A number of authors have been critical of the need theory postulates. Some specific arguments of the following authors have been incorporated in this analysis: Znaniecki, *op. cit.*, 192 ff.; E. T. Hiller, "Institutions and Institutional Groups," *Social Forces*, XX (March, 1942), 302 ff.; Leslie A. White, *The Science of Culture* (New York: Farrar, Straus & Co., 1949), 124 ff., 338-339; Raymond Firth, *Elements of Social Organization* (London: Watts & Co., 1951), 33-34; Don Martindale & Elio D. Monachesi, *Elements of Sociology* (New York: Harper, 1951), 388-394.

17. Hertzler, *op. cit.*, 206-7; 260-61.

18. *Ibid.*, 87.

19. *Ibid.*, 280-281.

20. *Ibid.*, 41-42.

21. *Ibid.*, 254.

22. Cf. Pitirim Sorokin's criticisms of instinct theories in his *Contemporary Sociological Theories* (New York and London: Harper, 1928), 603-617.

23. Cf. Firth, *op. cit.*, 34.

24. Timasheff & Facey, *op. cit.*, 279.

25. Due to space limitations, these points cannot be documented here although the evidence showing wide disagreement is ample.

26. Hertzler, *op. cit.*, 261 ff.

27. For example, while the decision-making of judges and government officers has been recently studied as problems in the fields "sociology of law" and "political sociology," decision-making evidently has not been raised as a problem area in other fields where its study would be equally relevant and significant, e.g., in the sociology of religion.

28. The primary sources for these summary views have been *Sociological Abstracts* and Hans L. Zetterberg, (ed.), *Sociology in the United States of America, A Trend Report* (Paris: UNESCO, 1956), 156 pp.

29. Cf. Howard W. Odum, *American Sociology. The Story of Sociology in the United States through 1950* (New York: Longmans, Green & Co., 1951), 450 ff. See also, Talcott Parsons & Edward A. Shils, (eds.), *Toward a General Theory of Action* (Cambridge: Harvard University Press, 1951), 5-29.

30. See especially, Hans Gerth & C. Wright Mills, *Character and Social Structure. The Psychology of Social Institutions* (New York: Harcourt, Brace & Co., 1953).

31. Cf. Theodore R. Sarbin's summary analysis and bibliography in his "Role Theory," in Gardner Lindzey (ed.), *The Handbook of Social Psychology* (Cambridge: Addison-Wesley, 1954), 223-258. See also the attempt to develop and test a semi-formalized social psychological theoretical system in which role is central by Ragnar Rommetveit, *op. cit.*

32. G. P. Murdock, *Social Structure* (New York: The Macmillan Company, 1949).

THE FAMILY

Carle C. Zimmerman
Harvard University

Family sociology is the oldest organized intellectual discipline. This is due to several reasons. Any primitive form of society depends in a large degree upon the extended family system—the clan, gens or genos—for its local and civil rule and as the responsible collective unit for the support of more extensive, or overhead, forms of government. Consequently, all beginning folk or social literature of importance—such as the Heroic Documents or the beginning of codified law—is fundamentally a theory of family control. This aims to systematize the "common law" and to enroll the people directly into the legal codes of the expanding society. The growth of sovereignty, and of domestic civil peace and order, hinges upon the subordination of the clan and the transfer of the control of the nuclear family directly to public law and regulation.

Hence no civilized period of our society has been without its family sociology. It is true that only in the last century and a half have these ideas been labelled sociology as such. However under other labels similar ideas as found in modern family sociology have existed and must be considered family theory.

All of this advanced movement of subordinating the nuclear family directly to the larger society first took place early in Western history before the Sixth Century B.C. It fell away however in the anarchy of the Dark Age which crept over Europe between the Sixth and Tenth Centuries A.D. Then the same civilizing movement concerning the family was repeated in an almost identical general manner. By the end of the Twelfth Century the foundation elements of the modern nuclear family of the West were in existence.

From then until the Nineteenth Century, when the separate discipline of modern scientific sociology came into being, the main controversy in family theory was between the Church doctrine of the Twelfth Century and the public law doctrine of secular control which developed in the ensuing centuries. The Church wished to keep the family as a religious unity and under Canon law control whereas the States wished to dominate it under public law and control. By the commencement of the Nineteenth Century the States had the family legally, but the Church, both Protestant and Catholic branches, had it informally, religiously and ceremonially. Both forms of rule, the religious and the secular, are now important in the family.

MODERN FAMILY SOCIOLOGY: ITS THREE PERIODS

This leads up to the Nineteenth Century and the rise of modern family sociology. Fundamentally, modern domestic theory falls into three great periods of thought. The first period may be called the Nineteenth Century doctrine, which covers the period from the French Revolution to the onset of World War I in 1914. The French Revolution seriously disturbed the family ideology of Europe both by experiments in France itself and by the spread of many new family ideas all over Europe through the Napoleonic law codes.

The second period of modern sociology is equated with extreme family reforms following World War I. These reforms differed in their extremity and perpetuation by country but fundamentally they were alike in essentials—whether under Communism, Fascism or movements toward democratic totalitarianism. This will be shown further.

The third period began at about the end of World War II and is still in existence. In essence it is a recovery or reaction to the social disorganization brought to a peak by the extreme family changes in the second period.

Theoretically an analysis such as this is supposed to be limited to the trends in family sociology, and its various branches, in law, in politics, in social work and in religious doctrine. However in the real world a doctrine in any branch of family sociology is always related rather closely to the changes in the family. Consequently in the ensuing analysis we summarize changes in the family along with the variations in the themes and doctrines of the various branches of family sociology.

Family sociology is not by any means the sole proprietorship of the professional text writer in the field. From the logical and cultural points of view, the political, the juristic, the religious and the special family sociologies have been separated as disciplines during the past generation and each has paid little attention to the others. Nevertheless, in spite of this segmentation and separation of philosophy, there has been considerable agreement among the various fields concerned with the family. They all study a common unity—the family—and its changes have made the separate doctrines a unity.

THE NINETEENTH CENTURY SCHOOL

Nineteenth Century sociology made "the family" a time-section in the theory of a constantly changing "domestic unit." According to all the popularly accepted theories the nuclear family unit was an historical development and would pass away with the newer organization of society which would follow.

In all of the major theories of society of this period, the family was included and, increasingly, each step hypothecated the domestic unit as becoming more and more a "nominalistic," man-made, temporary, ever-changing-in-one-direction, time-limited unit. This means that fundamentally, family sociology from its Pre-Comtean origin to World War I considered *the society of similar individuals* as the only perpetual realism and the nuclear domestic family a dated creation of it. The family was considered to have an historical beginning and eventually a similar temporal decay and replacement by some other domestic arrangement more adapted to the modern mass world then beginning to emerge.

This philosophical position of Nineteenth Century sociology did not arise unexpectedly and out of the blue. It was an end position, within the theory of limits, taking off from the complete naturalism of society, and all its major manifestations, as codified in the *Summa* of Thomas Aquinas. This work expressed the most advanced social thought of the West toward the end of the Thirteenth Century. The steps toward the complete nominalist conception of the family were gradual but ever onward. By 1500 dominant philosophers concerning the nature of society had yielded to nominalism all its parts except the state and the family. The family began to be considered very much nominalistic only after 1750. The pure nominalist conception of the family became a cardinal tenet of Marxist philosophy after 1850.

The great practical attempts at "factual" or nominalist organization of large segments of the Western family system came in the decades between World War I and II spearheaded by legal measures in Russia and Germany but followed sympathetically in a psychological fashion certain other Western countries, including the USA.[1]

THE EARLY TWENTIETH CENTURY SCHOOL

The main difference between the earlier Nominalist position regarding the family in most Nineteenth Century sociology and the extreme views of the early Twentieth Century lay in the widespread later theory that the state had the "right," and in some respect the "duty" to extinguish the family as a "natural" social institution. The reason given for this need to break up the family as a legal group was to make the individual directly responsible to the political agency, not as beforehand through the family. Various phases of this philosophy appeared in many fields. In the United States it was widely held that the primary responsibility for the individual would change over to a new community form replacing the family. Social workers began to multiply in numbers and power and to deal more directly with the individual. This trend regarding the individual reached its high point at about the onset of the depression of the Thirties after which it had to recede on account of the tremendous growth in the numbers needing help and supervision.[2]

In the field of law during this period, the greatest influence or change was not in the field of family law but arose in jurisprudence incidental to other legal changes. However, it became conventional for courses formerly called "family law" to be described as simply "domestic relations."

In the religious field during this period the older dogma of family virtue came up against the desertion, divorce, birth control and other denouncements of the "jazz" age of the Twenties. Frankly the religious were confused by the changes in the mores and considerable divergence of views began to develop.

THE VARIOUS ATTEMPTS TO EXTINGUISH
FAMILY REALISM

In political views on the family, Russia first after 1917, later Germany and Italy (for a short while) began steady movements toward the new "right" and "duty"—the attempt to extinguish the family by abrogation of all older family law—except with retention of a slight deference to incest. This is what is called in legal terminology the rise of the "factual family" as opposed to the older "ethical family" consideration.[3] The "factual" family is one that considers living together "marriage" and living apart (not a cause of but) divorce. In such a social system marriage and family have no legal consequences—or at least very few. The Communists did it to get rid of the state, (so they claimed) and the Fascists did it to make the state, totalitarian (so they claimed). But both did it in a similar fashion.

In the United States during this period the conception of family responsibilities began to shrink. The change was achieved mostly by legal fictions, such as the widespread acceptance of separate jurisdictions for divorce alone—the rise of migratory divorce. The one and two child families began to be emphasized as most desirable. A philosophy of "eat, drink, and be merry" took over. "Puritanism" began to be called "a system of repressions" as if the idea of individual restraint was thwarting human life. F. Scott Fitzgerald epitomized much of this and its consequences in his *The Beautiful and the Damned* and Sinclair Lewis' *Main Street* expresses a good deal of the same feeling. This theory cropped up later, in the "mammalian right" theory of the sexological school, even after the family had begun to reverse itself towards more solidarity.

THE CLIMAX OF NOMINALIST FAMILY SOCIOLOGY

American fiction and drama began to desert the older theme of divorce as a tragedy and to present it as a necessary and even an ennobling experience.[4]

In the field of family sociology the older evolutionary teachings began to give away, in part, and to change otherwise. The changes were manifested by the rise of the first books of a new kind of family sociology which is now still popular, though changed considerably, the "functional" approach. Probably the first of this new type of work was the book *Marriage* by Ernest R. Groves (1933) which appeared just five years after the last of the important of the older evolutionary texts *Problems of the Family* by Willistine Goodsell, (1928). Thus again did Athenaeus succeed caducary law.

The chief characteristic of this kind of work is the inherent implication that the family is not a natural process of life but should be made existentialist. That is if one chooses a family, through marriage, the text becomes a sort of "Emily Post guide to family happiness." At no place in these works is the alternative—passing out of the social system by not becoming an integral part of "the chain of being" presented clearly, even though it is admitted that the important people marry and reproduce within family units. In other words, the functional works tend to present an unreal view of the living social life to persons just at the verge of becoming irreversably committed to that life.

A second phase of the change in family sociology during this period was the rise of the "functionless, affection only, school" of family sociology. Although preceded by a number of other studies, the work by William F. Ogburn in *Recent Social Trends in the United States,* 1933, *op. cit.* gave it its great, and still continued, popularity in American sociology. In this development the Marxian version of the older Nineteenth Century school of social change is used as a plausible intellectual foil to misinterpret some meaningless statistics. According to this version, all functions of the family except affection, and possibly reproduction, have been taken over by other agencies as, for illustration, it is claimed:

> Schools have taken over "education."
> Policemen have taken over "protection."
> Churches have taken over "religious instruction."
> Waiters and restaurants—feeding."
> Chain stores have taken over "economic activities of the home."
> Working away from home for wages or salary has taken over the former concrete "support activities" of the parent.

The weakness, invalidity and logical phantasy of these claims have been analyzed elsewhere.[5] Suffice to say they gave one branch of the existentialist school of family sociology a plausible grounding in sociological theory and allowed the general philosophy of existentialism to take over.

The "functionless" and the "functional" schools of family sociology are sisters, in that one has to grow up to replace the other. Their children, from the philosophical point of view, have to take on a very moral "amoral" view of life as illustrated by Sartre, Simone de Beauvoir and the pleadings of the Kinsey reports.

CHANGES WITHIN THE FAMILY SYSTEM ITSELF

However during the early Twentieth Century, commencing before 1920 and culminating in vaster developments after 1950, the family system of Europe and America began some changes of its own without regard to the directives, or their lack, furnished by the major family disciplines. These changes may be described first as independent movements of the family systems, or key portions thereof, at self-discipline and a gradual turn toward "natural unitism and realism." Secondly, since the change included only a portion of the families, and not all, some followed the older course and some the new, so that a polarization of good and bad, or old and new, family types began and have widened.

At first this polarization or separation of the older and newer family types was only minor and unnoticeable; later about 1950 it became violent. Thus it happened that after 1950 the Western world witnessed the most violent contrast of two family types, one semi-factual and one semi-ethical, it had seen for some centuries. For instance since 1950 in the United States we have seen the following contrasts.

THE ANTI-SOCIAL POLARIZATION

1. From the factual family system we have the highest level of real divorces (excluding immediate post war fluctuations from hasty marriages) ever seen in Western society since rates of such have been recorded. This rapid rise began among the civilian population sometime in 1942, thus violating and reversing the older alleged principle that wars and their resultant increases in social solidarity were associated with reduced divorce rates. After the war there were high peaks of divorces due to the returned soldiers, and then the situation settled down in its regular form with higher rates than before World War II.

2. From the factual family system we have also the highest rates for desertions and quasi-desertions of families that we have ever had. A quasi-desertion is an avoidance of the paying of alimony and support moneys legally due a deserted or divorced woman and the children. This is accomplished in the United States by rapid change of legal jurisdictions by the former husbands or deserting wage earners so that the state and federal funds for Aid to Dependent Women and Children must provide the funds for support. The courts cannot keep up with the quasi-deserters. (In England and Wales alone these matters cost the public directly thirty millions of pounds in 1955.)

3. Also from the factual family system (assisted by war breakages) we have reaped a harvest of juvenile delinquency which is outstanding

and probably only equalled by conditions resulting from the Revolutions in France after 1798 (and its family demoralization) and that in Russia after 1917.

THE PRO-SOCIAL POLARIZATION

Contrasted with this, and on the good side, the family made certain gains in the increasing power in the opposite group, the ethical family system. This is measured by the following important facts.

1. For the first time in the history of a free, urban and rationalized family system, a vast and long-continued decline in the real birth rate is arrested and a steadily increasing number of our families have moved from the one and two-child types into the three-or-more-child, or socially-reproductive, types. This alone has junked all previous predictions as to the growth and size of the population of the United States of America.

2. This ethical family system has isolated itself away from the "factual" families and surrounded itself with other good families of similar ethical views. Out of this pocketed situation it has been able to control its children to follow its views. By doing this it has been able to push the children upwards in the social system, so that now we have higher proportions of high school graduates and students in colleges and professional schools than any other time in our history. As a result the proportions of technically trained persons in our social system is greater than at any previous point in history and the proportions of unskilled laborers in the country is now down near ten percent, the lowest proportion in history.

3. Finally, on the good side, is the fact that matching our high juvenile delinquency rates are the rates for unusually creative youth. More young persons now are doing more good and creative things than ever before in our history.

Thus the changes within the family system itself have been a movement toward a gradual reversal of the trend toward a nominalist and fragile, non-social, family type toward a stronger socially creative unit. Some have continued the older way and others have moved progressively towards a newer adaptation. This has been true not only in the United States of America but also in many important segments of the European community. We now have to show this, and to explain it, and to point out its influence on the subject of family sociology.

REVERSAL OF TREND IN THE WESTERN FAMILY SYSTEM

This change of course in important phases of the American family system was a subtle elusive thing, as yet little understood. It had something to do with the environment of persons born betwen 1915 and 1920 and still continues. It should be said at the beginning that the mores of a culture move slowly, like a giant pendulum, but also very ponderously. For some generations up to the period 1910-1915, the Americans born each year moved slowly but surely toward a lower birth-rate. By the period 1910-1915, each "cohort" of 1000 typical American women reached its all time low of reproduction. Then gradually after 1915, each 1000 female children born began to have at a given comparable age more children than their immediate preceding year's cohort at the same age.

As a result of this change in reproduction, all previous estimates of the size of the American population for the latter half of the Twentieth Century had to be revised radically upward. Between 1920 and 1940 the American population began to dip in the slant of its growth curve as if it were reaching a peak and would shortly stabilize or turn downward. The direction was reversed after 1940 as if it were moving toward a newer and higher peak.[6]

A second aspect of this trend toward family revival as indicated earlier was marked by its conspicuous regrouping in the cities so that environment control helped direct the motivation of the teen-agers toward creativity.[7] In essence "good families" now surround themselves with similar families and the world of the child seems "good."

However this is not the whole story. Conspicuous changes of a rational nature took place in such important European countries as Italy, France, Germany and Russia not to mention others. In Italy the totalitarian movement toward "factual familism" inherent in Fascism, had to be given up early because of the great influence of the Catholic Church. However that country is rapidly reducing its birth-rate to meet the challenge of overpopulation facing its culture and the movement is not directed by either a political power or a religion—that is it is in the "private" mores.[8]

France, its neighbor, but one with a very low birth-rate for nearly a century, has reversed the trend during this same period. Germany a country very completely dominated by the factual family ideology of Nazism has shown a remarkable recovery toward ethical concepts.

The binding story however is in Russia which has not had a military defeat and has had the same political regime of Communism since 1917. By 1928 its family system as a legal and social arrangement had been almost completely shattered. The change towards ethical familism under the legal fiction of "for the good of the community" began in 1936. All factual aspects of the family system were completely abolished by the family laws of 1944. In all practical aspects divorce, abortion, and the other evidences of the so called "legal right and duty of family extinction" were abolished then. The new code was so rigid that it had to be corrected slightly toward more freedom in the legal changes of 1949.[9]

These changes are not all, nor do they refer to all countries, but they do include five of the more prominent and most populous of the West and concerned families of more than a half billion persons in 1950. Nor were the changes all alike in the empirical sense. It showed as a decrease in the birth-rate in Italy, and an increase in France and in the U.S.A. It showed similar changes in family attitudes in Russia with the same political regime continuing, and in Germany with the changes of regimes. The point is that the changes only become important from the family point of view if we view them collectively as a renascence of family realism, or ethicalism, in relation to the cultures as opposed to the older trends toward factualism, nominalism and cultural irresponsibility.

MAIN CAUSES OF THE TREND
FOR MORE FAMILY SOLIDARITY

Sociology is a search for certitudes, first of all, and after that it looks for "causes" and generalizations. We have pointed out what seems to be a certitude, signs of change in the movement of the Western family system from a nòminalist position more toward a realist one, and from factual organization toward more "ethical" organization. If this is a certitude, how may it be explained causally? If it has a definite recognizable cause, this increases the probability that it is a "certitude."

Conjecturally several reasons may be pointed out. First of all, it should be indicated that the family is what may be called a dual-field type of organization. It is not only a private sexual relation, or an institution insuring a certain amount of private social expression to the individual, but it is also a collective or cultural organization, the basic structural cell of society. While society makes family law, within limits, it also largely reserves the interior regulation of the family to private action by the members—unless specified otherwise.

Then our first principle in searching for a cause of a reversal of family type would be to seek something in the nature of our culture, or our private needs, or both, which has arisen in the past century which would cause the reversal in family movement. This makes our problem clearer. What is there in the relation between modern culture and the family, or modern conditions and the private life of the individual, or both, which would condition people to turn their backs on a broad trend of the past toward nominalistic conditions within the family?[10]

One of the first aspects of highly integrated modern cultures is that the individual is buffeted by every great world change. We only have to go back a century before modern communication began and then no such conditions existed. Now a disturbance in Berlin, Egypt, Korea or any one of a thousand other areas immediately stirs a billion persons. In such a situation as this people who wish a certain amount of peace and containment within their lives have to seek it in the family circles.

This reformation of the family as a stronger private agency when the individual is constantly buffeted by a disturbed world is explanatory of a number of phenomena. Lately we have noted the revolt of youth in the Iron Curtain countries, particularly Poland and Hungary and even Russia itself in spite of the fact that these very youth have been the group most subject to Communist educational attempts and, they themselves have never known anything else but Communism as a form of government and control. Somehow or other within their families the older traditions of freedom had been remembered and taught cautiously to the children.

Then again we have the phenomenon of the complete reversal of the factual family in Russia proper after long discussion at party meetings up to 1944. At that time the older ethical family system had not been outlined in Russian public law since 1917, twenty eight years before. Somehow or other within the families, in spite of Communist education, the older ideal of the family had been preserved.

In Germany, in spite of the turmoil of Fascist engagements against the family, the destructive war, the dismemberment of the country, the occupation (with its sexual let down) we find the solidarity of the family reasserting itself.

A case study of this has been made for West Germany by Helmuth Schelsky based upon about fifteen studies made by Schelsky or under the guidance of Wiese and others. None of these scholars were Nazis. The German family first had totalitarian rule, then the war, and finally the after-war conditions. After the war, 9,100,000 East German exiles were forced upon them by the Soviets; 2,500,000 family heads were degraded by denazification and demilitarization; 2,500,000 spouses were lost in the war; 2,000,000 prisoners were kept in Russia in slave labor camps a long time before returning them; 1,500,000 mutilated persons had lost arms, legs or major senses; and, finally, 4,500,000 had ordinary wounds from war or bombing. In total this affected 22,000,000 persons, but since some categories overlapped, the war destruction alone affected severely between a third and a half of the families.

ADEQUATE RESPONSE TO CHALLENGE

According to these scientists the difficulties, which would be expected to weaken the family system, rather strengthened it considerably. "At the time when the state and the economic organization were destroyed, and when almost every citizen was exposed to immediate dangers and terrible losses, marriage and the family offered protection and natural support and the domestic institutions were recognized as the last form of social security . . . When the outer world failed, and the individual was isolated *(Ohne Uns)* the family strengthened its effort *(Mit Uns)* . . . and this was even accompanied by a decline in eroticism *(Abbau der Erotic)*." (This above passage is freely translated from Schelsky's report in *Colloques Internationaux* for which see the full title in the bibliography. References upon which the statements are based cover about fifteen titles in the work.)

This buffeting has taken place also in the United States. In the Twenties it was reflected in the revolt against Puritanism. In the Thirties the great depression struck at the wage earners, salaried persons, business men and investors alike. Then in the Forties came the warring period of World War II, with its absentee husbands and fathers, its blackouts and food restrictions. After that has been the artificial shortages, or at least high prices, for food, the Cold War, the Korean episode and higher and higher taxes for armament and help to other countries, then inflation.

In such a situation as this it became a time, in many senses, of "every (family) for itself." The families were forced to draw closer together and to lead an inner life most privately their own.

A second "cause" which makes the reactivation of family realism and solidarity more a certitude, is the increased demands of modern cultures upon the family to produce a new and more expensive type of human product. Time was, and not so long ago, when a child could withdraw from schooling in the early teens and help his family. Now with most of our children in high-school, college or professional institutions, even up to twenty-five years of age, more strain is put upon the family requiring them to do things in a family way greater than before. This is reflected in the ever increasing body of law concerning the obligations and duties of parents to children.[11]

The other Western countries have done the same. In wartime they regiment the family and demand more from it in work, sacrifice, munitions, soldiers, and so on. In peacetime they expect each unit to give its children more and more education, the expenses of which are paid very largely by the families in the absence of help from the children and more financial aid given to them. The most spectacular growth has been in Russia, but of course the other Western nations had more compulsory education at the commencement of the period.[12]

Without pursuing this line of inquiry further, it is evident that in the modern social systems, with their technical developments, the demands upon the family are greater than ever before. As a result the pressure for more family unity or sacrifice and "realism" makes the probability of its increase more and more a certitude. It is obvious and can not be escaped. The family system has been buffeted, inspired and forced to a renewed movement toward realism.

FAMILY CHANGE AND FAMILY SOCIOLOGY

Social change of this type is slow and ponderous. It is achieved largely by use of plausibilities, rationalizations and fictions. When the factual family system of Soviet Russia became increasingly unfitted to the new militaristic state, the Russians did not say "Communist family ideology is wrong." Rather they hedged, rationalized, and gradually came round to the new position. First they "fumigated" the public mind by contending Lenin's views on the family and his personal behavior were puritanical. Then instead of saying that they rejected Communistic family ideology for the Victorian, they accepted

the older view as "improved Communism." They forbade all semblance of factual marriage views under the slogan that such changes
were "good for the community."

In family sociology we now witness the same ponderous turning of
the family system in the whole Western world. This is marked in
sociological works by several intellectual changes. One is the disappearance of knowledge and use of the older books or of newly printed
versions of the older doctrine, or even anything resembling it. Second,
is the appearance of a new doctrine, with plausible, but generally
false contentions of relations to the older one. This new type of doctrine claims that it is the "old," but factually the only connection
between the two is merely spacious and plausible. Third, is the
appearance of new kinds of books about the family, only a few of
which even attempt to be creative. However all of them begin sub-
stituting for the older works so that the "new knowledge" of the
family is gained from them. Fourth, then, are latent changes of
opinion beginning. Many of the leading intellectuals, those who deserted the old views for the half-way new, begin to recognize the
really new and to swing over towards it.

Fifth, and finally, historical and genetic studies (types of the old
school) disappear until such a time as the doctrines associated with
them are forgotten and can re-emerge as new. A portion of this disappearance is achieved by the rise of another existentialist form of
sociology, one which denies the past as even relevant to the present
or which plays endlessly with abstruse and pointless theories of the
family as if seeking to gain a sort of synthetic fatigue. All five of
these movements are to be found simultaneously in our current family
sociology. Some authors represent only one of the changes, but others
show traces of several.

Any complete proof of these five changes is beyond the possibilities
of this chapter. However the eight most widely used family texts were
examined. These are not the functional, or "how to do it" types
but written in "fundamental theory." They include five thousand
pages of reading and two and a half million words. The texts were
analyzed as to reference to the four great theorists and scholars of
the older school, August Bebel, Marxian theorist, Arthur W. Calhoun,
historian of the American family system, C. E. Howard, historian of
the Western family system since the Dark Ages, and E. A. Westermarck,
the great scholar and theorist of human marriage. If these men were
well reported in these books the sociological connections between

the older and the newer schools would be well established in the same sense that modern physical science knows the relation of its new ideas to the older Newtonian.

These eight books had 33 references to the names of these four great scholars, but only 8 were "substantive" (that is they gave the conclusions on a particular subject reached by the earlier scholar). The ideas of Bebel were not reported at all in any even for purposes of criticism. Calhoun, possibly because he wrote purely on the American scene, had six good substantive analyses, and one other, a statistic from the 1860 census culled via Calhoun's report of it.

Howard and Westermarck, the two greatest earlier scholars in the sense of dealing with the total family scene (not the American or the Communist ideology alone but general history and theory), each were given one minor substantive reference.

In spite of this lack of reference to the earlier scholars most of the texts go over the same ground, thus giving a certain historical and evolutionary change plausibility to their works. They claim to be a constructive development of the older theory but they are not.

One of the most common but fatal hypotheses in these works unknowingly really reverses the major scientific result achieved by the great Westermarck. At the end of his fourth volume on *Human Marriage* he carefully points out that marriage is founded *in the family* and not the *family in marriage*. By this he meant that the former practice of interpreting the family based upon a study of marriage practice alone had failed signally to see that marriage is a custom and a rite which could, and did, have endless variations within the same general family type. Yet the modern school endlessly emphasizes *marriage over family*.[13] As J. H. S. Bossard has said "they teach the young about marriage but little is said on what to do the next forty or fifty years of family life."

FUNCTIONAL FAMILY SOCIOLOGY

In 1900 family sociology was scarcely taught as an independent subject. Now it is rapidly becoming the most important second course. As new marriage and family courses are added, not requiring previous sociological study, classes on the domestic institution may shortly enroll more students than all other sociology courses combined. This rapid growth has made it a big money-maker for the text trade. As a result movements to capture the market have produced the "functional" or "do-it-yourself" types of marriage guidance works. These are now unique to the United States although Israel and England have started in this manner.

The first "functional" texts were somewhat amateurish sociologically and many ideas proposed were more plausible and "daring" than sound. Gradually, however, as family mores began to move back toward realism, some of the texts began to change and to improve. While the situation is not corrected as yet, the more recent works or "revisions" of earlier ones have improved.

Many of the weaknesses of the functional-existential works would have been eliminated earlier if the modern theorists or general sociologists, with only a half-dozen exceptions, had not completely neglected the field of the family. This is also an unfortunate situation for sociology generally because humans from the cradle to the grave spend more than ninety-five percent of their time in, around, and for their families. The family has been, is, and grows increasingly as man's common denominator. No institution has been as significant in man's rugged course as the family and its changes.

The growing significance of family sociology, in the absence of interest, knowledge or concern with the field by the self-denominated "general theorists" has led to two other results. Family sociologists have struck out on their own and, working without much guidance, have repeated many mistakes of the older intellectual courses. They give advice in fields in which they are not equipped such as sex, legal matters, and the full significance of the impingement of culture upon the individual. In one very prominent case an author, obviously reporting upon the important decision in *North Carolina vs. Williams* knew neither the name of the cases nor the significance of this series of Supreme Court decisions.

For instance, in general the handling of the matter of estrangement between spouses is done in such a way as to imply that the settlement by separation is a simple matter like changing your grocer or getting a new job. There are warnings, of course, such as "the cure may hurt more than the disease," but in most works the situation is handled in a very surface manner.

Thus divorces are unconsciously implemented, children are left in custody of mothers who are incapable alone of handling them successfully (90-95 per cent of custodies are with the mothers) and hundreds of thousands of husbands and fathers avoid not only physical but economic duties to their wives and children. "Quasi-desertions" or moving from one jurisdiction to another to avoid support and alimony payments are becoming a national scandal. Present data showing a close sympathy between divorce and juvenile delinquency rates (with about a dozen years lag between the rises) points up the seriousness of this matter.

In many of them sex (copula) is handled inadequately, amateurishly, mis-informationally and with lack of taste. The intrusion of the book publishers into the field is really serious. Science gets into the hands of non-scientists. Public relations take over and honesty or truth if heavy, unpopular, or unpleasant gets nowhere. It would be interesting to see a new Westermarck come into the field now with plans to publish four or five original volumes on the family. Under such a situation we would not have had either a George Elliot Howard or an Arthur W. Calhoun.

There are a few conspicuous exceptions to these remarks but space does not afford the details.

EXISTENTIAL FAMILY SOCIOLOGY (the Abstruse School)

The second phase of the existential movement, or that unconstructive portion of modern sociology which is marking time by verbosity, obscurity, excessive reiteration of structural analyses and long spun-out meaningless empiricism, has also shared a place (though not valorous or creative) in modern family sociology. This so-called "scholarly" group has not been particularly damaging because the nature of the great clientele for family sociology (young minds on the college level) will not brook very much of such meaningless mental discursements.

One of the shibboleths of this extistentialist group is that "all cultures are alike" in that they have a recognizable nuclear family system supposedly consisting of husband and wife, parents and children, more or less as an autonomous or private social system, disengaged in part from the other social unities. This is partly true and partly untrue. Its major untruth lies in its relevancy now when our main concern is with the fragility of the relations between husband and wife, parent and child, and the outer culture and the home. It also has a "tranquilizing" influence upon the "functionalists" and "functionless" groups because these works are the major content of the "broader study" of the authors.

Human beings being bisexual and generic-disjunctive have generally mated in pairs and produced young by recognizable parents. Since others ordinarily can't or won't (or both) raise these young the parents are forced to do so and this has given them the nuclear family. Whatever the pre-literates may or may not have done, history of the great cultures from Homer, Genesis, pre-Hammurabic codes, Vedic hymns and Confucius indicates the perennial necessity and prevalence of this semi-autonomous social unit among all the high or literate cultures of the world to date.

In a general period of family upheaval and change of course, the major problems of family sociology rest in the relations between the major culture and the nuclear unit. It is a matter of ideals, duties, obligations, and privileges. Changes in these, or the willingness of the family to support the culture and the willingness of the culture to leave the family alone are what is important.

The existentialist school, in all its phases, has given a disservice by diverting attention from this key facet of the present family situation—relation between family and culture—over to domestic internal affairs. The totality of cultural history has shown that if external-internal relations of the family are adjusted to the needs of the time, the other is largely self-regulatory.[14]

CONCLUSIONS

This chapter points out that family sociology is a very ancient intellectual subject. The great and growing public interest in it now is due to the fact that we are entering a new "era" of social time. Any great change like the decay of Greece, the birth of the Roman Empire, the rise of the Christian movement at the end of that empire, the end of the Dark Age or beginning of the Renaissance and the Reformation has seen similar movements in family sociology because of disturbances between the external cultural world and the family.

The modern family has moved slowly toward conceptions of nominalist relations between the outer culture and the inner organization. This movement reached an extreme peak between World Wars I and II. Then the family began a slow turning movement toward a realist relation with the new culture of the new Atomic Age.

This nominalism had as its most typological doctrine that of no need for responsibility and consonance between family motives and outer cultural motives. On the reverse, the realist doctrine is a need for consonance between family and cultural objectives.

The three modern schools of family sociology, the Nineteenth Century, the early Twentieth, and the Contemporary Functional-Functionless have not been related to each other as ideas, like the steady flow of knowledge and its increasing verification in a physical science, but more or less mechanically because each was fitted to a changing segment of a moving family system. Otherwise the three schools of thought are separate doctrines. Imagine Westermarck, Bebel and the writer of one of the modern functional-functionless best sellers having luncheon together at a faculty club today! Each of the three had communicated a family doctrine to millions in a short space of time, the past century. But these doctrines are so different that they could not communicate with each other.

Above and beyond all this there is, however, the fundamental problem, *the need for the growth of family sociology as an interconnected scientific doctrine.* The failure of this to grow as it should may be charged in a large part directly to the naïveté and ephemeralness of most sociological theorists and "general practitioners" of the art. Family sociology will remain and grow after the current ephemeral doctrines are dead and forgotten. But we need now, more than anything else in sociology, a carefully thought out and valid system of family sociology.[15]

SELECTED BIBLIOGRAPHY

J. H. S. Bossard, *Marriage and the Child* (Philadelphia: University of Pennsylvania Press, 1940); Bossard & E. S. Boll, *Family Situations* (Philadelphia: University of Pennsylvania Press, 1943); Bossard, *The Sociology of Child Development* (New York: Harper, 1948); Bossard & Boll, *Ritual in Family Living* (Philadelphia: University of Pennsylvania Press, 1950.) These authors at the University of Pennsylvania have conceived and published a series of valuable studies dealing with the whole family situation. See particularly: Bossard & Boll, *The Large Family* (Philadelphia: University of Pennsylvania Press, 1956).

E. Franklin Frazier, *The Negro Family in the United States* (Chicago: the University of Chicago Press, latest revision 1957). Recognized as a very good study of the family system of the fifteen millions of Negroes in the United States.

Anna Freud and Dorothy T. Burlingham, *War and Children, Infants without Families.* (New York: International University Press,

1943). The daughter of Sigmund Freud prepared an analysis about English children orphaned temporarily or completely during World War II; this very careful study made over a number of years merits attention to the conclusions of the authors. The two women are the world's outstanding child psychologists and the data concern 20,000 children.

Reuben Hill, *Families under Stress* (New York: Harper & Brothers, 1949). A study of 820 Iowa families which documents in detail how modern culture buffets the family system by its periodic crises; it deals with the families during World War II and their reunion after the war.

Earl L. Koos, *Families in Trouble* (New York: Kings Press, 1946). A study of the influence of trouble upon tenement families in New York City which emphasizes the use of friends and increasing family responsibility in crises; the author has a more recent family study, just now going to print, which should be consulted.

Arthur Phillips, (Ed.),*Survey of African Marriage and Family Life* (New York: Oxford University Press, 1953). This book by the International African Institute is one of the most scholarly, profound and important publications in the modern study of the family; it deals with the impact of modern industrial society and the Christian religion upon the family system of the seventy six major tribal units of the entire continent of Africa. It illustrates the thesis of nominalism and realism, and its impact upon the relations between the nuclear family and the external culture, made in this chapter, except in the reverse. In Africa under modernization, the nominalism of general social relations is up against an old-time family realism of primitive "trustee" nature. The result of new and old in conflict is very demoralizing, but also very instructive from the standpoint of those who wish to learn "family sociology."

Eliot Slater and Moya Woodside, *Patterns of Marriage* (London: Cassell and Co., 1951). A very careful study of the English working and middle-class urban families made in London between 1943 and 1946; its authors are a medical doctor and a psychiatrist. A very interesting and valuable book based upon a careful study of 200 cases and a knowledge of much of the pertinent English literature on the subject.

John L. Thomas, S. J., *The American Catholic Family* (Englewood Cliffs, N. J.: Prentice-Hall, 1956). A creative and much needed work concerns the theoretical and actual family system among the more than thirty millions of American Catholics; the author is a member of the Catholic Institute of Social Order and of the faculty of Sociology at Saint Louis University and well known as a scholar in the field of family sociology. Here one can find out about the difficulties of the Catholic family system in America.

The Association of American Law Schools, *Selected Essays on Family Law* (Brooklyn: Foundation Press, 1950). A collective work by a committee of "selection" as well as "authors," with 1122 pages, and

67 chapters by 43 outstanding jurists; the sociology consists of 7 pages only, a partial reprint of Ogburn's contention that the modern family has lost most of its functions. The value of the book is that it shows that legal sociology of the family is even more complicated than formal family sociology; this is because the law has to deal eventually with the whole situation, the right, the duty, and the after-effects on plaintiff, defendant and public at large. This is one of the very few (if not the only) modern works in English which recognized family law as an entity and not a series of domestic relations; it also goes back into the canon and Roman Law backgrounds of our family system and hence gives a perspective seldom found in modern family study.

Colloques Internationaux du Centre National de la Recherche Scientifique, *Sociologie Comparée de la Famille Contemporaine* (Paris: Editions du Centre National de la Recherche Scientifique, 1955). Includes the papers and discussions in the field of family sociology for France, Germany, England and Italy. The Colloquium was organized by the National Research center in Paris because, in the opinion of this research organization, family sociology had had the least development in France and was most needed there; it consists of 10 papers, which are original contributions summarizing family conditions in the four countries, a synthesis and concluding chapter, and four good bibliographies, one for each language. Those for France and England are the most lengthy and best developed. The work on the German family shows how the very heavy pressure of the disrupted social system has brought about a new sort of inward turning, an increase of family solidarity (family realism as pointed out earlier in this chapter). This kind of work written by thoughtful scholars who are general sociologists, *per se,* indicates what we need in the United States.

(For Zimmerman's *curriculum vitae,* see p. 23.)

NOTES

1. For this development see Carle C. Zimmerman, *Family and Civilization* (New York: Harper, 1947), chaps 19-22; Otto von Gierke, *Natural Law and the Theory of Society, 1500-1800* (Tr. by Ernest Barker) (Cambridge, England: The University Press, 1934).

2. On this matter see *Recent Trends in the United States* (New York: McGraw-Hill, 1933), chaps XIII-XV and XXIII, XXIV; Frederick Lewis Allen, *The Big Change—America Transforms Itself, 1900-1950* (New York: Harper, 1952) chapts 5-10.

3. See the Association of American Law Schools, *Selected Essays on Family Law* (Brooklyn: The Foundation Press, 1950) all of Section 3, Part IV, especially, 907 937.

4. James Barnett, *Divorce and the American Divorce Novel, 1858-1937* (Philadelphia: The University of Pennsylvania Press 1939) ; D. M. Koster, *The Theme of Divorce in American Drama 1871-1939* (Philadelphia: University of Pennsylvania Press, 1942) .

5. Carle C. Zimmerman & L. F. Cervantes, *Marriage and the Family* (Chicago: Henry Regnery, 1956) , 64-91.

6. Demographic figures are complicated and can not be introduced here. Proofs of the statements in the above two paragraphs are given in W. S. & E. S. Wotinsky, *World Population and Production* (New York: The Twentieth Century Fund, 1953) , 44 ff.; United Nations, *Proceedings of the World Population Conference, 1954* (NewYork: UNESCO, 1956) , Volume I, Meeting 6; P. K. Whelpton, *Cohort Fertility: Native White Women in the United States* (Princeton University Press 1954).

7. Proofs of this for Los Angeles are given in Zimmerman, Cervantes, *op. cit.* fn. above, no. 5; verification for other cities (Boston, New Orleans, St. Louis, Omaha and Denver) will be published by the same authors in a forthcoming volume.

8. Carle C. Zimmerman, "American Roots in an Italian Village" in *Genus*, XI, No. 1-4, (Rome, 1955) .

9. P. A. Sorokin, *The American Sex Revolution* (Boston: Porter Sargent, 1956) , ch. V; R. Schlesinger, *Changing Attitudes in Soviet Russia: the Family* (London: Routledge & K. Paul, 1949) .

10. This analysis of cause is not absolute but temporal. It seeks the functional relations between contemporary family and culture which demands, in a sense of fulfillment, or requires, in a sense of blocking the older trend, a new family arrangement. Phases of this causal analysis are discussed in detail in Zimmerman, *op. cit.,* fn. 1, chapters XXVIII-XXIX.

11. On this see White House Conference on the Family, *The American Family* (Washington, D. C., A special Bureau Publication, 1948) , chapter VI.

12. Harry Schwartz, in New York Times, Dec. 31, 1956, page C7 analyzes the situation in Russia based upon a 1956 statistical report by the Communist Government entitled *Cultural Construction in the U.S.S.R.*

13. A. H. Hobbs, *The Claims of Sociology* (Harrisburg, Pennsylvania: The Telegraph Press, 1951) , chapter 7 where this is documented in detail for 83 texts used in 551 colleges and universities.

14. Roscoe Pound in *Selected Essays on Family Law, op. cit.* fn. 3, p. 3. The idea has been documented in detail in Zimmerman, *op. cit.,* fn. 1, and Zimmerman-Cervantes, *op. cit.,* fn. 5, supra.

15. This chapter has not referred to the dozens of texts in family sociology by name because these are very numerous. A most competent bibliography is by W. L. Ludlow, *A Syllabus and Bibliography on Marriage and the Family* (New Concord, Ohio; Radcliffe Press, 1951) . A few may be mentioned with the thought, however, that invidious distinction should not be made with the unmentioned. E. W. Burgess & H. J. Locke, *The Family From Institution to Companionship* (New York, American Book Co., 1957 2nd Ed.) has great prestige. It combines a pseudo-evolutionary attachment to the older school with analysis of current families and great emphasis upon empirical tests of mate selection. M. F. Nimkoff, *Marriage and the Family* (Boston, Houghton Mifflin Co., 1947) is similar to Burgess & Locke except its pseudo-attachment to the Nineteenth Century doctrine is more flagrantly documented as for instance to animal sociology—the major rational gimmick which eventually led to the current variety of the "mammalian hypothesis of sex. J. T. & M. G. Landis, *Building a Successful Marriage* (Englewood Cliffs

N. J.: Prentice Hall, 1953) (2nd. Ed.) is outstanding in the "do-it-yourself" field. Other books are by Joseph K. Folsom, E. M. Duvall, Clifford Kirkpatrick, Reuben Hill, R. S. Cavan, Robert Winch, Robert Foster, Howard Becker and numerous writers. T. Parsons & R. F. Bales, *The Family: Socialization and Inter-action Process* (Glencoe, Ill.: The Free Press, 1955) is best representative of the abstruse school of existentialism. Zimmerman-Cervantes, *op. cit.,* gives more than 500 selected works in their bibliography

People generally in America, Mexico and Western Europe are worried about the current family situation and will subscribe generally to any work predicating the "happy family" no matter how thin it may be as sociology if it seems plausible. This has led to a great deal of family counselling and an institute for accreditation known as the American Institute of Marriage Counsellors, Inc., 270 Park Avenue, Room C., 701, New York, 17, New York. Standards in this field should be carefully supervised, as in medicine, because definite indications of quackery, exploitation and social harm have appeared under this guise and are widespread in some sections of the country.

SOCIAL CONTROL

Kurt H. Wolff

Ohio State University

This chapter is concerned with explicit conceptions of "social control" used or developed in the United States since 1945. It does not consider (1) postwar studies of what on some grounds may, and on some others might not, be argued to be the "workings" of "social controls," especially in contemporary American society;[1] and (2) trends and undertakings in postwar sociology which could profitably be analyzed with reference to conceptions of "social control" that are contained in them or exemplified by them.[2]

I. TRADITIONAL USES OF "SOCIAL CONTROL"

A third type of literature—studies of rather miscellaneous matters designated as "social controls"—is as voluminous as the application of the term has been prolific and variegated ever since Edward Alsworth Ross introduced it in the 1890's.[3] While likewise tangential to this chapter, it serves to highlight its focus, and will therefore be quickly surveyed.

The sixty-odd years during which the concept of social control has been in use show, almost of necessity, some modifications and shifts in accent; yet, the bulk of the literature even of the last decade can hardly be argued to transcend Ross or other "founders" of American sociology, notably Cooley and Sumner, either in removing confusions and ambiguities inherent in the early treatments or in proposing new conceptions. To suggest its nature and scope and to show its traditional character, it will briefly be indicated as it appears in sociological journals, in introductory, and in social-control textbooks.

(1) *Periodical Literature.* Aside from a few general considerations of "social control" problems (and two "nontraditional" papers reserved for Part II of this chapter), the concept of social control or rough

equivalents have been applied to many different subject matters which are no more related to one another than are any portions of the field of sociology. Among them (in alphabetical order) are communication, community, drug addiction, economy (including industry and labor), fashion, humor, law, the mentally ill, military life, nonliterate peoples, philanthropy, political apathy, race relations, religion, small colleges, social types, and war, particularly World War II.[4]

(2) *Introductory-Sociology Textbooks.* Some of these, as well as several readers in introductory and general sociology, present no, or only an incidental, treatment of "social control." Their authors apparently find it possible to give an overview of sociology or its principles, of social science, social life, society, or social relations without, or only casually, using the concept of social control. Instead, they operate with such ideas as norms, normative integration, integration, social order and sanctions, order in society, social organization; or treat social control in discussing group life, deviant behavior, or roles, social relations, culture, political organization, types of society, etc.[5]

Other textbooks, notably those (in chronological order) by Lee, MacIver-Page, Roucek-Warren, Bogardus, Biesanz, Hertzler, Broom-Selznick, Burma-DePoister, Queen-Chambers-Winston, Rose, Sutherland-Woodward-Maxwell, and Koenig-Hopper-Gross,[6] give the concept more or less conspicuous treatment, and most of them define it. For MacIver-Page (137), it is "the way in which the entire social order coheres and maintains itself—how it operates as a whole, as a changing equilibrium"; Roucek-Warren (163, 263) mean by it "all processes by which society and its component groups influence the behavior of individual members toward conformity"; Biesanz (64), "the means by which society establishes and maintains order"; Hertzler (306), "the way social power and social influence *function* to regulate, direct, adjust, and organize the social conduct of individuals and groups"; Queen *et al.* (28), "the regulation of the behavior of an individual by a group"; Rose (58), "the ways in which people, as members of a society, influence one another" and (567) "any means, or the sum total of means, by which a group influences or directs its individual members"; and Sutherland *et al.* (369) identify a "form of social control" as "any social attitude, custom, or institution which modifies behavior in the direction of group unity."[7]

(3) *Social-Control Textbooks.* It took almost a quarter of a century following Ross for another textbook on social control to appear (Frederick E. Lumley, *Means of Social Control,* 1925). Three more were

published in the 1930's (Jerome Dowd, *Control in Human Societies,* 1936; L. L. Bernard, *Social Control in Its Sociological Aspects,* 1939; and Landis, *Social Control: Social Organization and Disorganization in Process,* 1939), and one each in the 40's (Roucek) and 50's to date (LaPiere); the present decade also saw the revision of Landis and Roucek (both in 1956.) The postwar textbook literature thus consists of four books—the two Roucek editions, the Landis revision, and LaPiere.

Roucek's original work,[8] written by 27 contributors, has 30 chapters in five Parts: Foundations, Institutions, Means and Techniques, Social Control and Public Opinion, and Contemporary Problems of Social Control. Despite minor changes and a strong topical orientation, the 1956 edition has not caught up with Stalin's death, altogether contains little on the Soviet Union, and shows only slight revisions in the treatment of the atomic bomb.

Landis's first edition was analyzed by Gurvitch in his critical survey of the field up to 1945.[9] Although much more revised than Roucek's book, the basic outlook remains the same: a social-problems approach, if somewhat intensified, and the diagnosis that no substitute for the primary group has been found. The reiterated belief "that social control is the major problem of our time" (v) and the topical interest which this text shares with others, nonetheless have failed to result in the discussion of such "topics" as automation, the atom bomb, totalitarianism, or genocide.

Richard T. LaPiere, *A Theory of Social Control* (New York: McGraw-Hill, 1954), introduces a conception which would account for behavior that cannot be understood by reference to either socialization or the actor's situation. This "third dimension of behavior" (64-65), "social control," operates "on the basis of the individual's desire for social status, induces him to conform to group standards of conduct whatever his personal inclinations or situational temptations" (325). Regard for status is universal. Its locus is the primary group, even where the larger group is a *Gesellschaft* (19-24),[10] for the "status [-granting] group" exercises the more control over an individual member, all other factors remaining equal, the smaller it is, the longer it lasts, and the more often the members associate with each other (101-106). "Status groups cannot be defined in categorical terms" (106), but some groupings—population categories, aggregations, assemblages, publics, institutional organizations—may safely be excluded. Despite their modern great variety, they fall into the few categories of work, community, recreational, and peer groups and the many different methods by which their members try "to bring a deviant member into conformity to the group norms" are based on "a few universal principles or more properly, techniques" (220), namely physical, economic, psychological, and ideological. A conceptual supplement to "social control" is "countercontrol," which "results from the efforts, continually being made but rarely successful, of an individual to gain ascendancy over the other members of the group," or of a group or organization over another (325). It would have helped if "control" and "countercontrol" had been compared with Ross's distinction between social and individual ascendancy (for Ross "social control," it may be recalled, was one of two subdivisions of the former) and with various definitions of "social control," among them several quoted in this chapter, which resemble his concept of "countercontrol." The means of gaining individual ascendancy are force or intimidation, and inducement or seduction or trickery (classed together as "autocratic control"), and conviction, persuasion, and conversion ("democratic control"); "conquest," that is, organizational ascendancy, may similarly be military, economic, or cultural. (In these discussions of "countercontrol," "counter" is usually dropped.) The final chapter, "Social Crisis, Demoralization, and Control," is written on the recognition that a "theory of social control would be incomplete without at least some acknowledgment of the fact that upon occasion the complex system of social control operating in any society may be disrupted and, indeed, temporarily suspended" (523).

(4) *A Comment on the Intellectual Status of "Social Control."* This rapid survey suggests that like many other sociological concepts, "social control" has neither a standardized area of application[11] nor a standardized referent. This range of its extension reflects decisions on, or between, dichotomies (such as intentional or conscious vs. spontaneous or unconscious; or personal vs. impersonal, commented upon by Gurvitch in respect to the pre-1945 literature[12]), as well as a variety of approaches, notably that which sees social control as a problem of social integration (positive; order, normative order, cohesion, etc.) as against one of constraint (negative; control of deviance).[13] The confusions and uncertainties can be found in Ross's original treatment,[14] which, along with their persistence, suggests the unexamined influence of extratheoretical factors on the field. Among these there may be the attractiveness of the word "control" against the feeling that it jars, at least semantically, with the tradition and profession of democracy;

the faith in the automaticity of the order of our society against fears lest it be not secure but in need of controls to be enacted; the survival of trust in a *laissez-faire* harmony against temptation by planning, organizing, manipulating. At any rate, the largely nontheoretical, nontechnical nature of the concept may be related to the absence of "social control" from two more theoretical and technical types of presentations of sociology: histories of social thought, social philosophy, and sociology itself[15] (except for its occasional treatment in reference to particular thinkers), including the UNESCO survey of postwar American sociology[16] and two recent and important assessments of the social and behavioral sciences[17]; and the annual reports of the American Sociological Society on "Current Sociological Research."

II. NEWER APPROACHES TO "SOCIAL CONTROL"

The work to be presented in this section differs from the writings surveyed thus far in being less tied to tradition, whether Ross's or Cooley's or a more diffuse one. It consists of studies (in chronological order) by Gurvitch, Homans, Parsons, Skinner, Nadel, and Nett.

(1) *Gurvitch.*[18] Gurvitch claims that a viable theory of social control must rid itself of the restrictions imposed on it by 19th-century sociology. That is, it must realize that social control is universal, not a matter of evolution or progress; that it advocates neither "order" nor "progress," neither "society" nor the "individual"; and that "kinds" of social control are cultural phenomena, chief among them religion (and magic), morality, law, art, knowledge, and education, and must be distinguished from "agencies," which are social phenomena, namely social bonds (forms of sociability), groups, and inclusive societies. "Social control" is the whole of cultural patterns, social symbols, collective spiritual meanings, values, ideas and ideals, as well as acts and processes directly connected with them, whereby inclusive society, every particular group, and every participating individual member overcome tensions and conflicts within themselves through temporary equilibria and take steps for new creative efforts (291; original in italics).

Gurvitch anticipates the objection that thus defined, the study of "social control" is identical with the sociology of culture; he counters it by arguing that while the subject matters of the two disciplines are indeed the same, their approaches differ. "Social control" focuses on the interrelations among kinds, forms (of which presently), and agencies of social control, whereas the sociology of culture ("sociology of human spirit") explores the "functional relationship of the ideational elements with the social conjunctures" (292-293).[19] The "forms" of social control, then, are depth-levels or strata within each "kind," namely (1) routine forms (cultural usages, patterns, rules, symbols, often organized, that is, standardized and stereotyped, and hence exercising constraint and losing touch with the more spontaneous forms); (2) the more spontaneous control through values, ideas, ideals; and (3) "the even more spontaneous social control through direct collective experiences, aspirations, and creations, including revolts and revolutions" (294; original in italics). Finally, "means" (or "techniques" or "instruments") are numerous, variable, and not typically associated with kinds, forms, or agencies.

Gurvitch's conceptual scheme gains in clarity by acquaintance with some of his other work in sociology.[20] Whether for lack of such acquaintance, or because the tradition out of which Gurvitch's sociology develops is French rather than American,[21] or because of weaknesses intrinsic to his conception of social control, it has not, as far as could be ascertained, been analyzed in the American literature in the field.[22] The theoretically most relevant reason for this failure could be advanced as the argument that Gurvitch has actually laid out a scheme for the sociology of culture, if not for general sociology, and has merely called it one for social control; and there is good evidence (cf. n. 19 above) that he has done so. If so, it may suggest that "social control" was considered an acceptable or necessary topic in a survey of 20th-century sociology as it was undertaken in 1945; and the observations reported at the end of the preceding section may indicate that such a view has since changed. Aside from these "extrinsic" comments, an intrinsic analysis of Gurvitch's conception of social control might well show that his "social control" has no part in his "sociology of culture."

(2) *Homans.*[23] The task Homans has set for himself in *The Human Group* is the development of a theory of small groups. He proceeds by collating observations made by "a few able students of social behavior" (442)[24] and deriving from them systems of interrelated, generalizing, analytical hypotheses. One of these systems emerges upon such questions as "What makes custom customary?" (311), "Why does structure persist?" (282), "How and why do the members of a group comply with the group norms or obey the orders of the group leader"

(281)? The answer is what Homans proposes to mean by "social control."

> 1. Control is the process by which, if a man departs from his existing degree of obedience to a norm, his behavior is brought back toward that degree, or would be brought back if he did depart. The remaining statements hold for both actual and virtual departures.
> 2. There is nothing new about control, no separate element that we have not already found coming into social organization (301).

In other words, "social control" and "social organization" are not different subject matters; rather, the former is an aspect which emerges if the latter is approached with the above questions.

> 3. The separate controls [that is, the relations between a man's disobedience to a norm and the various consequences of that disobedience (295)] are nothing more than the old relations of mutual dependence [among norms, activities, sentiments, and interaction (288)] taken differentially.
> 4. Control as a whole is effective in so far as an individual's departure from an existing degree of obedience to a norm activates not one but many separate controls (301). The effects are, so to speak, out of proportion to the cause. A departure from the existing level of activity may have consequences for a man's material gains . . . for his interaction with others, and for his social rank, because his activity is related to all of these things and not one only (449).
> 5. That is, any departure activates the system of relations so as to reduce future departures.
> 6. Punishment does not necessarily produce control [but may vindicate the violated norm and bring the group to the point where the offense occurred; cf. 308-311]. The state of a social system in which control is effective [in which, e.g., punishment produces control] we shall call a state of equilibrium of a system (301). [That is, a state in which] not all conceivable states of the system can be actual states (312).

The control inherent in the "external system"—the state of the elements of group behavior (sentiment, activity, interaction) and of their interrelations considered from the standpoint of the group's survival in its environment (cf. 90)—is based on individual self-interest, and is thus "automatic" (286); but there is also control based on sentiment; and control constituted by "the mutual dependence between social rank and performance in a certain activity" (288). Control may be described "in the language of reward and punishment" or of "distribution of goods," tangible and intangible (cf. 294). Further, there is the distinction between "formal" or "external control," by which Homans seems to refer to control exercised by agencies other than the actor, and "informal" or "internal" control, which appears to denote internalized controls (cf. 284). This distinction is related to similar dichotomies found in social-control literature (cf. some of the authors mentioned in Part I, Section 2, above), including "law" vs "mos." "Authority," in Homans' scheme, is limited to a relation between group leader and member, namely the member's acceptance of an order given by the leader (418).

Homans' theory of social control is systematic not only in the sense of being developed in an orderly procession of self-conscious methodological steps but also in the very different sense of undertaking the construction of a social system from its elements, their interrelations, and, to some extent, the interaction between the system and its environment. In Homans' own view, the greatest weakness of his theory in general is that it has not yet reached the stage where values can be assigned to its variables (cf. 444 ff). Yet in respect to "social control," and perhaps other concepts as well, a conceptual analysis may be necessary before such a quantifying phase can be aimed at. For it could be that "social control" is not a necessary element in Homans' conceptual scheme. If this should turn out to be the case, "social control" would have to be reformulated as such an element, or it would have to be shown why it should stay what it wholly or in part seems to be at the present stage of development, namely more an adjunct pragmatically justified on methodological and substantive grounds than an element arrived at by logical or empirical explication of the other elements of the system. Such an analysis might be made both through logical and methodological investigations and through inquiry into the sociological and historical nature of Homans' undertaking.

(3) *Parsons*.[25] Parsons' major treatment of social control is found in *The Social System*. The concept complements that of deviance. From the standpoint of the actor, deviance is behavior in violation of a norm; social control, the actor's (and his interactor's) motivation to counteract such behavior. From the standpoint of the interactive system, deviance is disequilibrating behavior, and social control the complex of forces resulting in reequilibration. Ego (an actor in an

interactive system) is motivated to deviant behavior when alter (with whom ego interacts) frustrates ego's expectation of him. This results in various solutions constituting either re-equilibration through a change in the system, restoration of its former state, or "compromise." "Compromise" refers to an ambivalence in ego's attitudes ("need-dispositions"), affects ("cathexis"), or value orientation. It has a negative ("alienative") and a positive ("conformative") component. The domination of the latter over the former results in compulsive conformity; inversely, in compulsive alienation. But deviant orientation must also be differentiated in regard to "activity" (the actor's taking more "initiative" than he is expected to) and "passivity" (taking less). A third differentiation is between ego's orientation toward alter as a person (social object) as against his orientation toward the normative pattern. These three differentiations result in an eightfold typology of deviant behavior (*ibid.*, 259, Table 4). The discussion of their "social structure" follows the analysis of deviance from the standpoint of the foci of strain inhering in the normative patterns of the social system, from the angle of the sanctions connected with this, and from that of role conflict in relation to deviance (a disturbance in the order of allocations of ego's roles resulting from ego's deviant motivation or from conflicting role expectations in the social system itself).

Social control, with its preventive and re-equilibrating aspects, begins in socialization and displays its "most fundamental mechanisms . . . in the normal processes of interaction" (301), "in the institutional integration of motivation and the reciprocal reinforcement of the attitudes and actions of the different individual actors involved in an institutionalized social structure" (302). Only the breakdown of ordinary social controls calls for more specialized and elaborate mechanisms, among which Parsons discusses two, ritual and "secondary institutions." Ritual, conspicuous in the fields of religion and magic, health and bereavement, is characterized by permissiveness, the opportunity to "act out" tensions accompanying strains, and by support, emphasizing the concern of the group with the situation. The "American youth culture," Parsons' example of a "secondary institution," also exhibits permissiveness, functions as a "safety valve," shows its own integration with major institutional structures (especially through formal education), and is "self-liquidating" (youths becoming adults). "Secondary institutions" raise the question of the functional significance to society of certain instances of malintegration which make for such phenomena as religious toleration, limitations on formal controls and status rankings, "tact," anonymity, and the segregation of activities and population elements. They gain this functional significance from two processes that are at work in them: "insulation" and "isolation." The former localizes potentially conflicting elements; the latter forestalls the structuring the spread of which insulation would check—reaction to illnes roughly illustrates the first; reaction to criminality, the second. The analysis of illness, particularly the physician's role, applies to that of the mechanisms of social control generally. They exhibit support (by which some characteristics of deviance can be reconnected with institutionalized values), permissiveness (e.g., encouraging "confession," channeling the expression of grievances, guaranteeing anonymity), and the refusal to reciprocate deviant expectations.[26]

It can hardly be doubted that Parsons' treatment of "social control" is the most comprehensive and systematic (in both senses of the term used in the comment on Homans) that has been achieved so far. Despite its importance, however, it raises serious problems. Only one complex of these can be mentioned here. It may be introduced by pointing to the unclarity of the relationship between two types of social control, the first inherent in the social system, the other (social controls) appearing when the first breaks down. Inasmuch as the first develops in the process of socialization, its failure must result from socialization that is inadequate, especially in respect to its forestalling or preventive features. The implication seems to be that adequate socialization would obviate the need for social controls. On this view, Parsons appears to postulate, by implication, an adjustive individual,[27] or to have a conception that is dominated by the image of this type of individual at the neglect of society[28] and culture (which, along with personality, are the three "systems" he has set himself the task to connect in a unified theory). To say this may be to specify Clark's contention that his theory is psychological rather than sociological,[29] for which comment it is further relevant to note that neither power nor force (coercion) figure in Parsons' treatment of social control: power is not mentioned at all; force is twice, once emphatically as a psychological concept (277-278), the other time, in discussing the treatment of the criminal, clearly as a matter that has no corresponding element in his conceptual scheme (312). Coser[30] has called attention to the relative absence of a third pre-eminently sociological concept, that is, conflict, from Parsons' work as a whole; he characterizes this work as "an extended commentary on the Hobbesian question: How is social

order possible?"[31] Conflict tends to be replaced by (such psychologically
oriented terms as) "tension," "strain," "sickness,"[32] and the increasing
importance of the therapeutic paradigm in the Parsonian treatment
of social control itself has been noted. It could be that Parsons exhibits a tendency, characteristic of recent Western, particularly American, culture generally, namely to find the examination of the individual more acceptable than that of society. Among many manifestations
of this tendency is the widespread interest in psychology, especially
psychoanalysis, as against the "insulated" status (to borrow one of
Parsons' terms) of the "sociology of knowledge" with its analysis of
society.[33]

(4) *Skinner.*[34] Skinner's discussion of control is part of his attempt
at outlining a "science of human behavior." It is developed in two
stages. The first, an analysis of "controlling agencies" (government and
law, religion, psychotherapy, economic control, and education), is
introduced by a short chapter on "group control" and leads to the
second, the crux of the matter, the control of human behavior on the
whole. Much more explicitly than the three authors previously discussed in this section, Skinner conceives of his undertaking in its
relevance to our time (cf. esp. Ch. I, "Can Science Help?")[35] and thus
is pushed beyond analysis into advocacy and is faced with such problems as the possibility of scientific value judgments (428-430), of a
scientific ethic (328-329), of a scientific answer to the question what
culture should be "designed" (426-428), and "who should control"
(445-446). His answer to these questions is in terms of "survival," an
evolutionary practice only recently, and in an important sense mis-
leadingly, formulated as a "value" (433). If this is accepted—whereby
Skinner himself insists on the difficulties of assessing the survival value
of cultural practices (434-436)—the question "Who should control?"
becomes "Who *will* control in the group which does survive?" (446),
and the answer to it is the probability that "the most reliable estimates [made by a science of behavior] of the survival value of cultural
practices" furnish the basis for "the most effective control." This does
not mean, however, that the scientists will be the controllers; only that
science can "supply a description of the kind of process of which it
itself is an example" (*ibid.*).

> If a science of behavior can discover those conditions of life
> which make for the ultimate strength of men, it may provide a
> set of "moral values" which, because they are independent of the
> history and culture of any group, may be generally accepted (445).

We thus envisage "a possible safeguard against despotism" (443). For instead of condemning a government that slaughters or enslaves a captured population as wrong or contrary to the dignity of man (thus acting on notions not "independent of the history and culture of any group"), it is possible to condemn it as eventually weakening the government itself and reducing the effectiveness of the enslaved (444-445). Yet again, science is not justified in setting up group or state over individual, or vice versa, for these are "segments in a continuous series of events," and scientific interpretation "must eventually apply" "to the whole series" (449).

Only a commitment to ignore the valuational character of such a position and not to examine its consequences permits one to call it, as Skinner does, the result of scientific analysis, and to anticipate its distastefulness "to most of those who have been strongly affected by democratic philosophies" *(ibid.).* This anticipation is one of the consequences of his position which Skinner has selected for emphasis on no plausible theoretical grounds but rather on the basis on which his whole book is built, namely, relevance to our time (including people, among them those commented upon). Yet this time disappears before an evolutionary and allegedly scientific "ultimate" ("survival value," 449; "strength of man," 445), and "science" becomes formalistic, loses its subject matter, turns into scientism.

(5) *Nadel.*[36] As the title of Nadel's paper indicates, its major emphasis is the distinction between "social control" and "self-regulation." This distinction is suggested by the fact that a society may keep its orderliness and culture even though such specific controls as legal sanctions, procedures of enforcement, and formalized apportionments of rewards and punishments are weakened. It is thus seen to be, in some measure, self-sustaining. Indeed, if it were not, it would need controls in an infinite regression—controls of legal sanctions, controls of these controls, etc.[37] Instead, there are true elements of self-regulation, namely the conditions under which traditional behavior (in Max Weber's sense) is desirable, good, and a safe and known routine. And we do find that in primitive societies it is the most important behaviors that have the weakest specific controls: those which are observed to occupy a focal position in an "instrumental nexus" and are stated to be "most important" by the actors (who attach "value" to them).[38] "Instrumentality" in respect to an action refers to the appropriateness of means to ends; and an appropriate means to an end not only tends to become routinized but, in primitive more than in other societies,

thereby to be sanctified as well. Since socially approved behavior thus
is at once instrumental and valuable, deviation from it provokes
"penalization" (demonstrable failure and irreparable guilt over the
violation of the internalized norm) rather than "punishment" (following a redeemable "sin"). Instrumentality and value ("value" referring
to classes of "ideologically founded" objects held to be intrinsically
worthwhile) tend to differentiate with the separation of social roles,
the specialization of offices and tasks, and, indirectly, the size of the
group, that is, with increasing civilization.

Every act that follows a prescribed norm demonstrates the norm's
validity as much as explicit assertion or teaching does.[39] This "circu-
larity" parallels the "feedback" in physical systems: "output," that is,
conduct in accordance with a norm, is partly returned as "input,"
or "information sustaining further action of that character" (273).[40]
On the other hand, unorthodox conduct which fails to carry its own
penalty also weakens the underlying values, and this possibility makes
any social system vulnerable and, if actualized, results in its breakdown or refashioning. Nadel mentions only one way in which such
actualization may occur: "when rulers, judges, legislators or, for that
matter, teachers and moralists apply or preach a doctrine in which
they themselves do not believe . . . [thus standing] outside the value
system they wish to maintain" *(ibid.)*. This situation raises the question
of the controls of the controls—the answer is self-interest and political
expediency. "And here, if you like, we touch upon social controls in
purest form, exercised from outside and unobscured as well as unaided
by any self-regulation" *(ibid.)*.

Nadel thus distinguishes, in effect, between Parsons' "social control"
and "social controls," and his functional approach makes the connection between the two clearer than does Parsons' more psychological
orientation. Yet it is precisely in regard to the latter that Nadel's
theory falls short; and it would greatly be strengthened by the incorporation of a typology of "orientations to social controls" such as is
developed by Merton and used in Gerth and Mills's treatment of the
problem (cf. n. 7 above). Nadel's analysis has the great merit, among
others, of exhibiting the advantages of a functional approach and
thus, beyond the observation just made, inviting comparison with
other approaches, thereby helping to "codify" social-control theory
and make it more tenable.

(6) *Nett.*[41] Nett begins his paper with a critical historical survey
of "social control" in American sociology. The earliest writers, es-

pecially Sumner and Cooley—involuntarily—established society as something for the individual to conform with. Park and Burgess made "social control" into a science of strategy; but in leaving much of the discussion of the rational to political scientists, they set a precedent for subsequent scant attention to its rational and strategic aspects, which neglect may perhaps be explained by the fact that "the level of human behavior at which rationality occurs is less easily stereotyped than are the levels of human behavior which are irrationally determined" (43). Following Lumley, Landis, and Bernard, "unified theories" of social control have receded behind examinations of specific aspects treated under such headings as "structure and function," "collective behavior," "role and status"—all of them underlining "conformity tendencies of man" (40).[42]

On the whole, "social control" has characteristically been seen as the problem of how society "orders, conditions, and controls its membership" (41). But it may equally well be formulated as the task of regulating a society so as "to tap, organize, and adapt its creative strength" (ibid.).[43] The first view stresses conformity as a product of social organization; the second, deviance as engendering "continuous social organization" (ibid.):"instead of asking how society orders and controls the individual, students of social control might ask how society takes its organization and momentum from its behaving individuals" (43). Evidence in favor of such a view lies in the observation that conformers, rather than deviators, "bring society to ruin" (42). In the first place, it takes masses of the former to support the latter before any revolutionary ideas can become effective; and indeed there is "an assumption among political realists that most demagogues simply play the known areas of conformity and do not reckon truly with social deviators at all" (ibid.). In the second place, historical experience shows society to lose its vitality in periods of domination by conformers. Yet there is frequent hostility toward innovators. The reason is their refusal to choose among the prescribed alternatives of action (whereas the violation of an accepted alternative merely demonstrates its excellence [cf. n. 39 above]). The more accepted alternatives there are, the less dangerous is the deviator, and an ideal democratic society would not keep him in a marginal position, would thus substitute a "smooth change continuum" (43) for radical change, and gain a maximum chance of survival. (Compare this assessment of a projected type of society with Skinner's.)

Nett's analysis is distinguished by bringing at least some elements of a sociological perspective to bear on the American treatment of "social control" and hence arguing an alternative approach on the strength of its empirical plausibility. His comments on rationality, however, need expansion and clarification, including the analysis of the relevance of "rationality" (as against commonsense, perhaps) in American history and culture in light of which the sociological treatment of social control seems to be viewed; and a similar and related explication appears to be called for in respect to his hypothetical democratic society and its maximum survival chance.

(7) *The Intellectual Status of "Social Control": Temporarily Concluded.* If it is significant to locate the literature surveyed in the first part of this chapter in the tradition launched by Ross, it may be no less significant to call the writings treated in Part II essentially traditional as well, although in line with several and newer traditions. Gurvitch aside, chief among them, appearing as more or less important elements in these writings, are (in chronological order) a Pareto-influenced, sober attempt at building a theory (Homans), an effort toward interdisciplinary integration (Parsons), scientism (Skinner), a Weberian and cultural-anthropological functional analysis (Nadel), and dissatisfaction with the limitations imposed by a traditional view (Nett)—but the latter may well be grounded as an "accepted alternative." To point out such traditional elements is not to ignore or slight the importance of the intrinsic development of a science. It calls attention to the fact that the writings surveyed (like many others) show no trace of asking whether the social sciences are sciences for which intrinsic development has the same meaning it has for physics, or whether, on the contrary, they are mixed concerns for which such a development, and its being taken for granted, also depend on the existence of an orderly society (rather than a panicky-resigned one[44]) —and if the latter, whether we live in such a society. The traditions named as elements in these writings can themselves in part be understood as reactions to "disorder." Thus it may be argued that the current fascination with interdisciplinary studies is, among other things, a variant of scientism, itself an anxious embrace (rather than a scientific analysis) of secularization and its concomitants and consequences; and Homans' and Nadel's treatments of social control are traditional more generally than in the senses indicated above simply by virtue of not raising the question whether the concept is as purely theoretical, sociologically and historically as neutral, as they assume in employing it. The textbooks referred to in Part I fall short in

their treatment of totalitarianism, death camps and slave camps, the administered nature of life in the West, atomic energy, automation, and other novelties of our time which may be seen to have changed and to be further changing individual, society, freedom, choice, privacy alternatives, and other fundamental phenomena and their meanings, all of which is in need of sociological analysis; and the works discussed in Part II appear to exemplify, rather than confront, this need. If it were to be confronted, the concept of social control would probably be transformed beyond recognition, and the recent uses of it surveyed here would reveal their historical nature with incomparably greater clarity than this cursory analysis has been able to achieve.[45]

SELECTED BIBLIOGRAPHY

Sebastian DeGrazia, *The Political Community: A Study of Anomie* (Chicago: University of Chicago Press, 1948). A conception of social control (without using the term) from the standpoint of "ruler" (in a very broad sense of the word) and belief systems as ordering society, and with special emphasis on "simple" and "acute" anomie.

Carl J. Friedrich, ed., *Totalitarianism* (Cambridge: Harvard University Press, 1954). A collection of conference papers designed to illuminate the nature and various aspects of totalitarianism.

Georges Gurvitch, "Social Control," in Gurvitch and Wilbert E. Moore, eds., *Twentieth Century Sociology* (New York: Philosophical Library, 1945), 267-296. A survey of major American conceptions of "social control," from Ross to Landis, and a presentation of Gurvitch's own.

A. B. Hollingshead, "The Concept of Social Control," *American Sociological Review*, VI (1941), 217-224. A history of the concept, with attention to precursors of Ross and to its dual source (Ross and Cooley) in American sociology, and a presentation of Hollingshead's own position.

George C. Homans, *The Human Group* (New York: Harcourt, Brace, 1950), esp. Ch. 11, "Social Control," 281-312. A clear and important presentation of the emergence of the concept of social control in the process of developing a theory of small groups.

Richard T. LaPiere, *A Theory of Social Control* (New York: McGraw-Hill, 1954). An attempt to formulate a theory of social control on the basis of the key concepts of desire for status, status groups, and countercontrol; also a textbook.

Edwin M. Lemert, "The Folkways and Social Control," *American Sociological Review*, VII (1942), 394-399. A critique of Hollingshead's paper and a counterproposal of a conception of social control stressing process and group structure.

C. Wright Mills, *The New Men of Power: America's Labor Leaders* (New York Harcourt, Brace, 1948); *White Collar: The American Middle Class* (New York: Oxford University Press, 1951); *The Power Elite (ibid.*, 1956). Studies of three important strata of American society, containing much enlightening material on the structure of contemporary organization and stratification, and hence on social control.

S. F. Nadel, "Social Control and Self-Regulation," *Social Forces,* XXXI (1953), 265-273. A theoretical functional analysis of society as a self-regulating mechanism.

Roger Nett, "Conformity-Deviation and the Social Control Concept," *Ethics,* LXIV (1953), 38-45. Proposing a conception of "social control" oriented toward creativity, rather than order and conformity.

Talcott Parsons, *The Social System* (Glencoe, Ill.: Free Press, 1951), esp. Ch. VII, "Deviant Behavior and the Mechanisms of Social Control," 249-325. Being based on Parsons' comprehensive theory of social systems, this is the most systematic attempt at a theory of social control.

Joseph S. Roucek and associates, *Social Control,* second edition (New York: Van Nostrand, 1956) A useful textbook which introduces the reader to a wide variety of areas in contemporary life studied from the standpoint of "social control."

B. F. Skinner, *Science and Human Behavior* (New York: Macmillan, 1953), esp. Ch. XXIX, "The Problem of Control," 437-449. Application of Skinner's view of science to the problems of controlling society, present and future.

Hans Speier, "The Social Determination of Ideas," *Social Research,* V (1938), 182-205, and Talcott Parsons, "The Role of Ideas in Social Action," *American Sociological Review,* III (1938), 652-664. Two supplementary essays, suited to show the connection between theoretical concerns with "social control" and certain trends in the "sociology of knowledge."

William H. Whyte, Jr., *The Organization Man* (New York: Simon and Schuster, 1956). In type of analysis resembling Mills's, this perceptive study of the various facets of the "organization man" offers much for the development of a historically more realistic conception and theory of social control.

Kurt H. Wolff, born Darmstadt, Germany, studied at Universities of Frankfurt, Munich, and Florence; Ph. D., Florence; taught at Southern Methodist University, Earlham College, and Ohio State, where he has been an Associate Professor of Sociology since 1952; taught summers at College of the Pacific and New School for Social Research; SSRC fellow, Viking Fund grantee; U. S . Specialist, Department of State; faculty fellow, Fund for the Advancement of Education; ed., transl.,*The Sociology of Georg Simmel;* transl. Simmel, *Conflict;* contributor to scientific and other journals.

NOTES

1. The reader is invited to consult a number of chapters in the present volume for their relevance to the understanding of social control, notably those on Political Sociology, the Sociology of Bureaucracy and Professions, the Sociology of Economic Organization, Public Opinion and Propaganda, and Military and Industrial Sociology.

2. Particularly the concerns in three, otherwise rather disparate, areas of study: "group dynamics," totalitarianism, and certain emphases in the "sociology of knowledge." On the first, see the chapters on Sociometry and on Role Theory and Sociodrama in this volume; on totalitarianism, note, most recently, Carl J. Friedrich and Zbigniew K. Brzezinski, *Totalitarian Dictatorship and Autocracy* (Cambridge: Harvard University Press, 1956); and on the "sociololgy of knowledge," cf. the relevant chapter in this volume.

3. In a series of 20 articles published in *The American Journal of Sociology,* Vols. I (1895-96) to III, V and VI (1900-01), and worked into his famous text, *Social Control: A Survey of the Foundations of Order* (New York: Macmillan, 1901). For predecessors of Ross and the dual source of "social control" in American sociology (Ross and Cooley), see A. B. Hollingshead, "The Concept of Social Control," *American Sociological Review,* VI (1941), 217-224.

4. Space limitations forbid the listing of references. A briefly annotated bibliography may be obtained on request from the author.

5. Again, space limitations do not permit bibliographical specification, available on request.

6. Alfred McClung Lee, *New Outline of the Principles of Sociology* (New York: Barnes and Noble, 1946), Ch. XXIX, "Social Control," by Everett Cherrington Hughes; R. M. MacIver and Charles H. Page, *Society: An Introductory Analysis* (New York: Rinehart, 1949), Ch. 7, "The Mores and Social Control"; Joseph S. Roucek and Roland L. Warren, *Sociology: An Introduction* (Ames, Iowa: Littlefield, Adams, 1951), Ch. 19, "Social Control"; Emory S. Bogardus, *Sociology,* fourth edition (New York: Macmillan, 1954), Ch. 13, "Group Controls"; John and Mavis Biesanz and others, *Modern Society: An Introduction to Social Science* (New York: Prentice-Hall, 1954) Ch. 25, "Social Control through Government" (also in connection with the discussion of the "functions of culture" and of social change); Joyce O. Hertzler, *Society in Action: A Study of Basic Social Processes* (New York: Dryden Press, 1954), Ch. XIX, "Social Order and Social Control"; Leonard Broom and Philip Selznick, *Sociology: A Text with Adapted Readings* (Evanston, Ill.: Row, Peterson, 1955), Adaptation 1, "Group Behavior and Social Control," by Ronald Lippitt (also in connection with the discussion of sentiments and the structure of group, association, and family); John H. Burma and W. Marshon Ch. 8, 'Social Control"; Stuart A. Queen, William N. Chambers and Charles M. DePoister, *Workbook in Introductory Sociology* (New York: Prentice-Hall, 1955); Winston, *The American Social System: Social Control, Personal Choice, and Public Decision* (Boston: Houghton Mifflin, 1956), *passim;* Arnold M. Rose, *Sociology: The Study of Human Relations* (New York: Alfred A. Knopf, 1956), Ch. 3, "Social Control"; Robert L. Sutherland, Julian L. Woodward, and Milton A. Maxwell, *Introductory Sociology,* fifth edition (Chicago: J. B. Lippincott, 1956), Ch. 28, "Social Reorganization and Social Control" (also in connection with the discussion of government); Samuel Koenig, Rex D. Hopper, and Feliks Gross, *Sociology: A Book of Readings* (New York: Prentice-Hall, 1953), Ch. 21, "Social Control" (H. C. Brearley, "Nature of Social Control," *Sociology and Social Research,* XXVIII

[1943], Harold D. Lasswell, "The Garrison State," *American Journal of Sociology*, XLVI [1941], and Simon Marcson, "Control of Ethnic Conflict," *Social Forces*, XXIV [1945]).

7. "Social control" is hardly, if at all, discussed in textbooks on social psychology (although Ross conceived of it as one of its fundamental subdivisions). It is all the more interesting to note its central place in Hans Gerth's and C. Wright Mills's *Character and Social Structure: The Psychology of Social Institutions* (New York: Harcourt, Brace, 1953); cf. Chs. VIII and IX, "Institutional Orders and Social Controls." In regard to "types of social control," the authors acknowledge their indebtedness to Karl Mannheim and Max Weber (256, n. 24). Under "Orientation to Social Controls," they follow Robert K. Merton's fourfold typology (developed in "Discrimination and the American Creed," in R. M. MacIver, ed., *Discrimination and National Welfare* [New York: Institute for Religious and Social Studies, 1948], 99-126) of verbal plus behavioral affirmation; expediency and fear of sanctions; verbal affirmation plus behavioral deviation; and verbal plus behavioral deviation.

8. Joseph S. Roucek and associates, *Social Control* (New York: Van Nostrand, 1947). The second edition, 1956, is likewise written by 27 contributors, of whom two are replacements.

9. Paul H. Landis, *Social Control: Social Organization and Disorganization in Process* (Chicago: Lippincott, 1939); Georges Gurvitch, "Social Control," in Gurvitch and Wilbert E. Moore, eds., *Twentieth Century Sociology* (New York: Philosophical Library, 1945), 267-269; in Landis, 183-284.

10. This section, "Rediscovery of the Primary Group," may profitably be collated with "Primary Group Relationships in Modern Society" by Harry C. Harnsworth (*Sociology and Social Research*, XXXI [1947], 291-296), to stimulate, possibly, inquiry into the relation between theoretical concern with primary groups, on the one hand (cf. especially Edward A. Shils, "The Study of the Primary Group," in Daniel Lerner and Harold D. Lasswell, eds., *The Policy Sciences*, Stanford: Stanford University Press, 1951, 44-69), and inclination toward the primary group as an attitude found in American sociology, on the other (cf., e.g., C. Wright Mills, "The Professional Ideology of Social Pathologists," *American Journal of Sociology*, XLIX [1943], 165-180; Roscoe C. Hinkle, Jr., and Gisela J. Hinkle, *The Development of Modern Sociology: Its Nature and Growth in the United States* [Garden City, N. Y.: Doubleday, 1954], 3-4).

11. Cf. especially the periodical literature mentioned above; also the use of the term "control" in such a title as *Controls from Within: Techniques for the Treatment of the Aggressive Child,* by Fritz Redl and David Wineman (Glencoe, Ill.: Free Press, 1952).

12. Gurvitch, *op. cit.,* 267-285, *passim.* For an older but still very useful survey and critique of different conceptions of "social control," see Earl Edward Eubank, *The Concepts of Sociology* (Boston: Heath, 1932), Ch. XI, "Concepts Pertaining to Societary Control," especially 215-220.

13. Here the above-cited literature on introductory and social-control texts is perhaps more instructive than that found in the magazines. For an analysis of "social controls" treated in some 70 introductory, social-problems, and family textbooks, see A. H. Hobbs, *The Claims of Sociology: A Critique of Textbooks* (Harrisburg, Pa.: Stackpole, 1951), 125-135. Cf. Gurvitch, *op. cit.;* Eubank, *op. cit.;* Hollingshead, *op. cit.* (n. 3 above); but also Edwin M. Lemert, "The Folkways and Social Control," *American Sociological Review,* VII (1942), 394-399.

14. Cf. Gurvitch, *op. cit.,* 271-273, and some of the sources cited in the preceding note.

15. Also in Florian Znaniecki's profound *Cultural Sciences: Their Origin and Development* (Urbana: University of Illinois Press, 1952), although the whole approach of this analysis centers on the idea of order in its several distinct meanings. The non-treatment in some of the texts and readers cited in ns. 6 and 7 also may reflect the nontheoretical, nontechnical nature of "social control."

16. Hans L. Zetterberg, ed., *Sociology in the United States: A Trend Report* (Paris: UNESCO, 1956).

17. Leonard D. White, ed. *The State of the Social Sciences* (Chicago: University of Chicago Press, 1956), and Roy K. Grinker, ed., with the assistance of Helen MacGill Hughes, *Toward a Unified Theory of Human Behavior* (New York: Basic Books, 1956).

18. Gurvitch, *op. cit.*

19. This not altogether satisfactory attempt at distinguishing between the "sociology of human spirit" and the study of "social control" can probably be disregarded, as far as Gurvitch is concerned, inasmuch as he himself disposes of it as purely terminological in at least two places, where he says that the "sociology of human spirit" is what "American sociologists" call "social control": *La Vocation actuelle de la Sociologie: Vers une Sociologie différentielle* (Paris: Presses Universitaires de France, 1950), 339, 411.

20. Little of it available in English. On the "sociology of human spirit," see, however, Gurvitch, *Sociology of Law* (New York: Philosophical Library, 1942), 42 ff.; on "microsociology" (the study of forms of sociability), "Microsociology and Sociometry," in Gurvitch, ed., *Sociometry in France and the United States* (New York: Beacon House, 1950), 1-31. Gurvitch's main work in sociology proper is *Vocation actuelle* cited in preceding note, esp. Part I (1-348); for a brief exposition, see my review in *American Sociological Review*, XVI (1951), 119-121. Also cf. René Toulement, *Sociologie et Pluralisme dialectique: introduction a l'oeuvre de Georges Gurvitch* (Louvain: Editions Nauwelaerts; Paris: Béatrice-Nauwelaerts, 1955), an analysis of the whole of Gurvitch's work to date (briefly reviewed by me in *American Journal of Sociology*, LXII [1957], 430).

21. This may be relevant despite the fact, noted by Hollingshead (*op. cit.*, 217), that "social control" is a Comtean notion: it was developed in America.

22. Among the postwar textbooks on social control, Landis and Roucek cite it; the works to be discussed in the remainder of this chapter do not.

23. George C. Homans, *The Human Group* (New York: Harcourt, Brace, 1950), esp. Ch. 11, "Social Control," 281-312. Two circumstances have left their characteristic imprint on this work: L. J. Henderson's influence on Homans' conception of science and scientific method (cf. Robert K. Merton, "Introduction" to *The Human Group*, xix, and Homans' "Preface," xxv) and Homans' own longstanding study of Pareto (cf. Homans and Charles P. Curtis, Jr., *An Introduction to Pareto: His Sociology*, New York: Alfred A. Knopf, 1934).

24. Reported chiefly in the Hawthorne studies (E. Mayo, T. N. Whitehead, F. J. Roethlisberger and W. J. Dickson), in *Street Corner Society* (William F. Whyte), and in work on the Tikopia (Raymond Firth).

25. Talcott Parsons, *The Social System* (Glencoe, Ill.: Free Press, 1951), esp. Ch. VII, "Deviant Behavior and the Mechanisms of Social Control," 249-325.

26. The therapeutic situation is introduced before (*ibid.*, 301) and is further developed as a paradigm in an Appendix to the chapter, 321-325, which adds "the manipulation of reward" to permissiveness, support, and the denial of reciprocity as the control functions of therapy. These are seen to be identical with the phases through which task-oriented groups studied by Robert F. Bales tend to go, in

Talcott Parsons and Robert F. Bales, *Family, Socialization and Interaction Process* (Glencoe, Ill.: Free Press, 1955) , 38-41. For additional developments beyond *The Social System* (largely a further elaboration of the therapeutic paradigm) see Parsons and Bales, *op. cit.,* 36, 58, 156. For earlier phases of Parsons' theory of social control, cf. *The Structure of Social Action* (New York and London: McGraw-Hill, 1937) , especially on Durkheim's theory of social control (376-408, 435-441, 463-465) ; "Propaganda and Social Control" (1942) in *Essays in Sociological Theory, loc. cit.,* Ch. XIII, (Ch. VIII, rev. ed.) ; and Parsons, Edward A. Shils, with the assistance of James Olds, "Values, Motives, and Systems of Action," in Parsons and Shils, eds., *Toward a General Theory of Action* (Cambridge: Harvard University Press, 1951) , 227-230 (almost contemporaneous with *The Social System* but much less worked out given the context of the book in which these pages appear) . Elaboration and new application of Parsons' social system theory later than Parsons and Bales, *op. cit.,* contains nothing on social control (Parsons' contributions to Grinker, ed., *op. cit.* (n. 17 above) , and Parsons and Neil J. Smelser, *Economy and Society: A Study in the Integration of Economic and Social Theory* [Glencoe, Ill.: Free Press, 1956]) .

27. This, it is perhaps needless to say, has nothing to do with Parsons' recent insistence on the interpretation and interdependence of social systems and personality systems and their resulting in uneven degrees of internalization in the participants in an interactive system and in uneven degrees of internalization of the roles in the same individual. Cf. Parsons in Grinker, ed., *op. cit.,* 331.

28. Which for Parsons is an empirically self-subsistent (*The Social System,* 19) or the most inclusive type of social system (Grinker, ed., *op. cit.,* 327) . The latter term resembles Gurvitch's (cf. mention above) but Parsons' and Gurvitch's "conceptual histories," and hence the meanings of this term, are quite different.

29. S. D. Clark, review of *The Social System, American Journal of Sociology,* LVIII (1952) , 103-104. "This is perhaps most evident in his [Parsons'] chapter on deviant behavior . . ." (103b) . I cannot agree with several of Clark's other contentions regarding Parsons' book.

30. Lewis A. Coser, *The Functions of Social Conflict* (Glencoe, Ill.: Free Press, 1956) , esp. 21-23, 34, 161, n. 6.

31. *Ibid.,* 21.

32. *Ibid.,* esp. 22.

33. Among the writers on social control treated in this chapter, Gerth and Mills (n. 7 above) contrast most with Parsons. Their outlook is predominantly Weberian, whereas Parsons, though "one of the foremost Weberian scholars in this country and . . . deeply influenced by Weber's thought," seems in his peripheral interest in social change and conflict "more directly related to the Durkheimian quest for social cohesion . . ." (Coser, *op. cit.,* 21) .

34. B. F. Skinner, *Science and Human Behavior* (New York: Macmillan, 1953) , esp. Ch. XXIX, "The Problem of Control," 437-449.

35. In this respect, though hardly in any other, his resemblance is greater to Mannheim than to Gurvitch, Homans, and Parsons. Cf. Karl Mannheim's discussion of social control in *Man and Society in an Age of Reconstruction* (New York: Harcourt, Brace, 1941) , Part V, III-VI, 265-366; also *Freedom, Power, and Democratic Planning* (New York: Oxford University Press, 1950) , *passim.*

36. S. F. Nadel, "Social Control and Self-Regulation," *Social Forces,* XXXI (1953) , 265-273.

37. Cf. Homans' questions, "What makes custom customary, why does structure

persist?" In his answers, however, Homans does not distinguish between Nadel's "self-regulation" and "social control," which latter is for Homans the same as "social organization" (roughly corresponding to Nadel's "self-regulation"), differently looked at. Cf. comments on Homans at the end of Section 2 above.

38. This distinction between *zweckrational* and *wertrational* (Max Weber; cf. Nadel, *The Foundations of Social Anthropology*, Glencoe, Ill.: Free Press, 1951, 31) pervades Parsons' analysis of action and has entered, as an ingredient transformed, his scheme of "pattern variables" (cf. Parsons, Shils, Olds, *op. cit.*, [n. 26 above], 48 and Chapter 1; Parsons, *The Social System, loc. cit.*, Chapter II, esp. 58-67).

39. Cf. Ronald Freedman *et al., Principles of Sociology: A Text with Readings,* revised edition (New York: Henry Holt, 1956), 187: ". . . strong normative integration exerts pressure toward its own maintenance. A high degree of normative integration generates intense indignation as a typical reaction to nonconformist behavior. In turn, the occurrence of this response has a restraining effect on potential nonconformists and thus tends to preserve a high level of normative integration." Nadel does not explicitly analyze this "cohesive function" of the breach of norms, which was earlier developed by Durkheim and Simmel. Cf. Coser, *op cit.*, esp. "Propositions" 1, 2, 8, 9, 13, 16; and Nett below.

40. Among the authors discussed in this chapter, only Parsons operates with input-output concepts, though unlike Nadel, not in conjunction with the concept of "social control." Cf. Parsons and Bales, *op. cit.*, 174-178; Parsons and Smelser, *op. cit.*, 296, 307 and *passim.*

41. Roger Nett, "Conformity-Deviation and the Social Control Concept." *Ethics,* LXIV (1953), 38-45.

42. As examples, Nett cites Herbert Blumer in Alfred McClung Lee, *op. cit.* (n. 6 above); Richard T. LaPiere, *Collective Behavior*; Robert K. Merton, *Social Theory and Social Structure;* Ralph Linton, *The Study of Man;* George Peter Murdock, *Social Structure.*

43. A similar line is taken by Melvin M. Tumin in respect to "creativity" in his "Obstacles to Creativity," *Etc.,* XI (1954), 261-271, and to "stratification," in "Some Principles of Stratification: A Critical Analysis," *American Sociological Review,* XVIII (1953), 387-394.

44. A society characterized by "acute anomie" (Sebastian DeGrazia, *The Political Community: A Study of Anomie* [Chicago: University of Chicago Press, 1948]) or by "disequilibrium" (Godfrey and Monica Wilson. *The Analysis of Social Change* [Cambridge: University Press, 1945]) and, on the other hand, by "apathy," "passivity," "conformity," etc. One of the symptoms of these features is the "moral dilemma" of the "organization man," keenly analyzed (along with a criticism of Erich Fromm's *The Sane Society*) by William H. Whyte, Jr., in *The Organization Man* (New York: Simon and Schuster, 1956), esp. 357-362.

45. A fuller but still far from satisfactory critique of sociology in relation to our time may be found in Kurt H. Wolff, "Before and After Sociology," *Transactions of the Third World Congress of Sociology* (1956), Vol. VII, 151-160.

SOCIAL ORGANIZATION
AND DISORGANIZATION

Theodore I. Lenn
Teachers College (New Britain, Conn.)

The concepts *social organization* and *social disorganization* may be viewed as typical of those theoretical formulations with which sociologists have not been too happy, if lack of concensus amongst the many might be construed as professional discontentment.

Over a decade ago, when Znaniecki was called upon to deal with the topic of *social organization* in a symposium similar to the present one, he freely admitted that, "A malicious critic of sociology could hardly find a better way of rousing scepticism about its scientific status than by collecting the definitions given by sociologists of 'social organization,' . . ."[1]"We have decided, therefore," he continued, "to consider existing definitions as purely heuristic devices which symbolize preliminary attempts to circumscribe a field of research with reference to certain theoretic problems that sociologists have been trying to solve."[2]

The present writer can report little change in the situation since Znaniecki's study. Nevertheless, the concept of *social organization* has brought forth less controversy than has the concept of *social disorganization*. Because of this, we shall devote less time in this chapter to the treatment of the organization concept, whereas our major attention will focus on the *disorganization* frame of reference and its use in current sociological analysis.

SOME LEADS FROM ANTHROPOLOGY

For a definitive inquiry into the nature of social organization, one is prompted to explore the literature of anthropology. Anthropologists have tended to study total societal organizations, whereas sociologists have devoted their major efforts to the study of the segments of society, viz., the behavior of selected groups, community structures and social institutions. As Firth has stated, "Most social anthropologists have worked at one time or another among communities of small scale. This has led them to see how closely different aspects of social activity are related (i.e., *organized*), institutionally and in the personal behavior of individuals."[3]

> Social anthropology . . . studies . . . social behavior, generally in institutionalized forms, such as the family, kinship systems, political organization, legal procedures, religious cults, and the like, *and the relations between such institutions*; . . .
>
> So, whereas some custom of a people . . . is of interest for the ethnologist as evidence of an ethnic movement, of a cultural drift, or of past contact between peoples, it is of interest to the social anthropologist as part of the *whole social life of the people at the present time.*[4]

According to Murdock, however, the theoretical formulations of anthropologists, both in America and Europe, have not produced, as yet, any singular systematic exposition to explain the evolution of social organization.[5] But social and cultural theorists have prodded at great length in this area and have produced much fruit. ". . . It is not chance," states Herskovits, "that the field of social organization has been one of the aspects of culture most assiduously studied; out of this has come a great body of data, and some of the most widely discussed hypotheses bearing on human behavior and human relationships."[6]

Social organization: Sociological concept.

In dealing with the concept of *social organization*, sociologists have concerned themselves basically with the following six allied concepts.

1. Social group
2. Association
3. Social institution
4. Social system
5. Social structure
6. Society

The lack of consensus concerning the use of the *organization* concept as an analytical tool is readily identifiable from the variable references to human clusters encompassing the aforementioned categories, ranging from two-person groups to total complex societies.

Znaniecki found it necessary to deal with several of these categories when he was called upon to write on the subject in the aforementioned symposium.[7]

As of now, it does not appear that there is any way in which to prevent this multiple use of the organization concept. Moreover, there seems to be no strong reason why it should not be used as it is, so long as a *single ingredient* in each of the six concepts can be called upon to serve as a consistent common denominator within the basic meaning of the overall *social organization* concept.

G. P. Murdock has employed the concept almost synonymously with the concept of society when he gives it as "the organization of a society into sub-groups . . ."[8] Hertzler has also tended to equate the concept with society. "Members of a society," he states, "are societally organized. They belong to . . . numerous groups (centered) around common needs and commonly held interests. . . . Hence the over-all organization of the society is that of a cooperative entity of innumerable groups with varied functions and varied degrees of organization."[9] Rose defines social organization as "the structure of common meanings and values of a society. Since meanings and values are often structured into institutions, the social organization is the totality of institutions."[10] Carr views the concept somewhat synonymously with association. He states, ". . . an organization can be defined as a form of association created to accomplish a specific purpose by coordinating the activities of selected individuals toward a common end through division of labor under authoritative direction. . . . Social organizations range from an *ad hoc* picnic party committee to . . . the United States Government."[11] Broom and Selznick tell us, "The student of social organization is interested in groups and activities that are interdependent, that form unified 'social systems.'"[12] Mercer appears to favor the term *social structure* but uses it almost in the same sense. The "arrangement of individuals in patterns of interrelationship, defined and controlled by a complexity of standards, values, norms, beliefs, customs, mores, habits, myths, and the more concrete facts of technology and material things they share, is what we mean by *social structure.*"[13]

What then constitutes the central core of the six allied concepts that permit them to be used almost interchangeably with the concept of social organization? Williams possibly provides us with this common denominator when he states:

. . . it is that state of interaction in which the actions of any one participant are to an appreciable degree determined by his orientation to the behavior of other participants. Organization may be quite temporary—as in the patterned interaction of a street crowd —or relatively permanent, as in religious, political, or familial groupings. The patterning of action may be formal, rigid and explicit, or it may be flexible, vague, and implicit. . . . The generic quality . . . (is) *recurrence*; the fact that interactions become predictable, that is, patterned, through participants' becoming aware of each other's behavior. Organization in this sense operates quite as clearly in a friendship as in an industrial corporation.[14]

Thus far, the writer has merely tried to establish that the concept of social organization, rather than being restrictive, and concerned only with some specific human grouping, has been used, instead, as a sociological tool for designating any and all of the different human groupings whose "identifying mark is that participants come to act in regularized ways through meaningful apprehension of what others have done, are doing, and are likely to do."[15]

SOCIAL ORGANIZATION: NORMATIVE OR DE FACTO?

But now a second concern beckons. The concept *social organization* has been used by some writers to designate a *normative* phenomenon, while others have treated the concept in a *de facto* or *operational* context. Still others have not been completely clear in differentiating, and seem to have employed the concept almost in a dual-role framework simultaneously.

Parsons' *Social System* concentrates on the *normative* elements of social structure and process.[16] Parsons openly admits to this by pointedly stating "if theory is *good theory*, there is no reason whatever to believe that it will not be *equally* applicable to the problems of change and to those of process within a stabilized system."[17] Lockwood has stated that "the non-normative elements of social action . . . constitute a set of variables which Parsons has ignored by concentrating on the normative elements of social structure and process."[18]

MacIver and Page,[19] in their appraisal of the components of social organization reveal a view of the total social organization as being basically a functional system. ". . . the different constituents of the

social structure— . . . community, . . . class . . . group . . . associations
. . . are particular adaptations of one to another. . . . These we
shall call functional systems."[20] Another view of organization in a
functional context is expressed by Carr, who states, "The persistence
of social structures . . . implies some functional relationship. . . .
It implies a constant process of adjustment and readjustment by
functionaries . . ."[21]

ORGANIZATION/DISORGANIZATION: STRUCTURAL-
FUNCTIONAL ANALYSIS

This manipulation of the organization concept in terms of normative and/or *de facto* contexts leads us into structural-functional analysis.[22] Although it is not intended at this point to deal with this latter
development at any great length, some clarification properly needs to
be introduced, because it is by way of structural-functional analysis
that *organization* and *disorganization* come into their proper juxtaposition.

Mercer's cogent statement provides a concise overview:

> Structural-functional analysis in sociology is the attempt to
> learn empirically (1) what structures (uniformities) are involved
> in human interrelationships, (2) what positive and negative con-
> tributions to its persistence and ordered change (that is, functions
> and dysfunctions) are associated with a structure, and (3) what
> specific functions and dysfunctions are associated with what par-
> ticular aspects or segments of a social structure.[23]

Social disorganization.

The data of *disorganization* are to be found in this same structural-
functional frame of reference, particularly in those references that
bespeak of *"negative contributions"* and *"dysfunctions"* that are involved in the "persistence and ordered change" of particular segments
(human relationships) of a social structure.

To demonstrate the above assumption, it will be necessary once
again to wade through a mass of disarray. An examination of present-
day sociological writing in the field of "social problem" analysis, points
up some sharp differences of opinion almost immediately with regard
to *approach*.[24] The very titles of some of the more recent textbooks
that are devoted to "negative contributions" and "dysfunctions" is

enough for an eye-opener. These include such labels as *Social Dis-organization, Social Pathology, Disorganization: Personal and Social, The Sociology of Social Problems, Problems of American Society: Values in Conflict, Social Policies in the Making,* and *Analysis of Social Problems.* From the authors of each of these works comes a strong prefatory statement, ranging from pages to chapters, designed to point up the specific approach of the book and its uniqueness and outright difference from all other approaches. Some writers writing under the same title do not fully agree in their respective approaches.

These differences in professional agreement are not here condemned. Possibly we have here an index of good health and vigor in a discipline that refuses to "settle down" to absolutes. Nevertheless it is not an easy chore to systematize from such raw data as these.

Not only do the approaches show much variability but the very selection of the subject matter that is treated between the covers of each volume also reveals wide disparity. Although the social data that are selected for analytical treatment represent persistent social issues ("problems"), that currently confront our society, and as such, *constitute integral segments of our social organization,* the variations in *choice* of "problems" are very wide indeed. Possibly there is strong significance to the fact that no two basic works show complete agreement in their very choice of "problems" for consideration. "Values may be and are properly and necessarily applied in the preliminary selection of 'significant,' and 'important' problems for research." [25]

We shall probe the field of *social disorganization,* both as a theoretical construct and as an operational tool, by observing its use in present-day textbooks on the subject of "social problems."

Almost arbitrarily, we shall select two widely used books. These are by Faris,[26] and by Elliott and Merrill.[27]

In their opening theoretical statements, the authors of both texts are very much in agreement.

DISORGANIZATION: THEORETICAL CONSIDERATIONS

The following half-dozen paired statements serve not only to point up reasonable consensus between the authors of both books, but also to demonstrate admirably well the typical present-day meaning that is given to the *disorganization* frame of reference by those who use it analytically:

  E & M: "The primary concern of this volume is with those basic processes that are to some extent the fundamental causes of . . . 'social problems.'"[28]

1. *Faris*: *"Social Disorganization* . . . is an attempt to study problems from the standpoint of the social processes which bring them about. It is . . . a study of the genesis of anti-social attitudes . . . and of the conflict between these attitudes and those held by the larger defining group."[29]

2. *Faris*: "Social disorganization is the weakening or destruction of the relationships which hold together a social organization."[30]

  E & M: "Social disorganization occurs when there is . . . a breakdown of the social structure . . ." There is brought about "the dissolution of institutional relationship and behavior patterns . . ."[31]

3. *Faris*: "Social disorganization can occur in varying degrees, from a very slight amount . . . to complete dissolution of the organization."[32]

  E & M: "There may be all degrees of social disorganization . . ."[33]

4. *Faris*: "The disruption of roles and the failure of functions (constitute) . . . the essential conditions of disorganization . . ."[34]

  E & M: The group "assigns the statuses and roles to the individual. When these statuses and roles are clear . . ., a society is relatively well organized. When the reverse is true, social disorganization is present."[35]

5. *Faris*: "Social disorganization may occur in systems of any size."[36]

  E & M: ". . . we shall consider it (social disorganization), in terms of its manifestations, in the person, the family, the local community, the nation, and the world of nations."[37]

6. *Faris*: "The association between rapidly changing conditions and a certain amount of . . . disorganization in a society has long been recognized."[38]

  E & M: "Social disorganization is part of the price of social change."[39]

Although Faris as well as Elliott and Merrill have provided a well-rounded view of the *social-disorganization* format, there are some additional points that help to fill out the picture that sociologists have of this concept.

Horton and Leslie include in their explanation of social disorganization the fact that "order and predictability of former days are replaced by confusion and chaos."[40] Ebersole views it as "institutional integration."[41] Sutherland *et al.*, have also viewed it similarly, having described *disorganization* as the "emergence of conflicts between the mores and the institutions."[42] It is Rose who reminds us that disorganization is "as natural to societies as are stability and mutual adjustment of parts."[43]

DISORGANIZATION AND VALUES

With regard to the role of *values*, however, and to the views that the different authors hold regarding values in their respective writings, some differences soon appear.

Faris forthrightly proclaims, "The concept is meant to be employed objectively, that is, the determination of whether or not a condition of disorganization exists should be independent of whether or not the observer approves or disapproves."[44] This position is representative of those writers who make no compromise in the recognition of anything but true scientific assessment. Yet, a careful reading of the Faris book, betrays some break in faith with this principle at several different points. While the author does not directly engage in evaluative discussion, there are value-laden terms that do come up from time to time. It is quite likely that many a student infers clear-cut values. Faris speaks of ". . . interests and abilities that lead toward *normal* social life . . .,"[45] of the "failure of the *normal* mechanisms of social control,"[46] and at another point he tells us that ". . . early attitudes may still be found today in *conservative areas*."[47] These and many others like these are truly "harmless" statements, but the fact remains that words like *normal* and *conservative* are value terms that imply *selected* criteria on the part of the writer.

Unlike Faris, Elliott and Merrill do not make the point that the disorganization concept is intended to be entirely objective. They state, "Social values constitute the major defining factors in behavior and determine whether or not a given situation constitutes a social problem."[48] They go on to say, "Social values are thus important and legitimate concerns of the sociologist."[49]

The authors conclude their recognition of the role of values, by stating that, "The contemporary conflict in social values reflects perhaps the most widespread social disorganization . . ."[50] Under careful scrutiny, this position is really not too different from the point made by Faris, when he categorically proclaims that, "We organize for what we want and need, and the organization is the instrument for achieving the wants."[51]

Yet, despite the strong recognition that values are at the core of the "social problem," the authors of both these volumes take vigorous issue with a sociological analysis that would employ anything like a "conflict in values" format as a frame of reference. Elliott and Merrill are strong in their opinion that prior to the social disorganization approach, "there has seldom been any attempt to integrate the subject matter" (of "social problems"), within a scheme of systematic sociology,"[52] while Faris speaks out quite bluntly of the "social problems" approach thus, "It clearly is involved with value connotations and is therefore not an objective concept."[53] He labors the point that there is no consensus in the literature of social problems on what the major social problems are. But neither is there much more agreement between his own selection of problems with those selected by Elliott and Merrill, both writing under the same title and ostensibly employing the same conceptual approach.

DISORGANIZATION: SOME CRITICAL REMARKS

Many sociologists have taken the "social disorganization" approach to task, not so much as a theoretical construct, but more specifically they have criticized its shortcomings as an operational technique for analytical assessment of social problems.

Herman[54] has said in fewer words what others have taken longer to say. "The approach," he states, "has not lived up to its original intention of giving adequate consideration to the process which brings problems about. After a brief excursion into the difficult task of exploring the process, practically all books styling themselves 'social disorganization' pass quickly to a review of problems."[55] According to Herman and others, the view is strongly maintained that those who employ the *social disorganization* approach as a tool for "problem" analysis are merely asserting that social problems are an outgrowth of social disorganization, and that "more is necessary than to assert that this is so."[56]

Lemert,[57] although favoring the *social disorganization* approach "over the concept of social problems," nevertheless joins in the opposition:

Its supporters have been somewhat less open advocates of a particular type of moral order, but nevertheless value-judgments inhere in the varying definitions and usages of the term. Reliance upon concepts of "process," "interaction," and "cultural lag" without giving detailed meaning to the terms has left the larger term "social disorganization" vague and difficult to demonstrate. In this connection it is especially important to note down the blurring and lack of sharp distinction between social disorganization and personal disorganization.[58]

From what we have observed thus far, it becomes obvious that many differences prevail among sociologists today, as it did when Znaniecki wrote of the concept of social organization. It could be said that the situation is even somewhat less clear with regard to the disorganization concept. Yet the situation is not so dark that we cannot see some trends with clarity.

What was so succinctly stated by two behavior scientists only a half dozen years ago obtains even with greater significance today.

Although it is true to some extent among all students of society and social behavior, it is especially true among sociologists that they can look back a few short years to the time when their field was dominated by persons whose attitudes toward social behavior were essentially subjective in nature. They were, first of all, reformers who "knew" about the world and were bent upon getting others to conform to their way of thinking. Their viewpoints were strongly ethnocentric, prejudiced, and frequently very unrealistic. Their "social problems" approach to the study of society and social behavior was provincially oriented and devoid of objectivity.[59]

If the social disorganizationists have succeeded in doing nothing more than to attempt to demonstrate that Durkheim's (and later Merton's) *Anomie,* and Thomas and Znaniecki's *Polish Peasant* contributions provide us with a conceptual tool that can lead us away from that period of reformism, as noted above, then there is much for which sociology, as a scientific discipline, can be appreciative.

It appears, moreover, that the disorganizationists have also probed deeper than was ever done before to demonstrate what was mere hypothesis over a quarter of a century ago, *viz.,* "All the problems of social life are thus problems of the individual; and all problems of the individual are at the same time problems of the group."[60]

However, it does not appear that the social disorganizationists have as yet produced an operational tool for sociological analysis that can claim wide acceptance by the sociological fraternity. Almost conspicuous by its total absence is the area of measurement related to disorganization.

Even if great strides have been made to minimize ethnocentric evaluation of social problems, this, in itself, cannot be equated with objective measurement of those segments of the total organization that have been isolated and identified as *disorganization*. With respect to this factor, are we really much further along from the original "cultural lag" thesis?

Is it possible that in their efforts to renounce that early reformist period that present-day sociologists have gone "overboard" in their *quantitative* exercises?

If the experiences of sociologists have been limited with regard to analytical investigations of *total* societal organizations, then are sociologists the ones, as of now, to unravel the "defects" of *total* societal organizations?

Warner's comments seem appropriate:

> The (sociological) approach—the study of the part rather than the whole—cannot tell us much about the nature of our total society; . . . the statistical and general one, gives us some understanding of the whole but provides insufficient knowledge about most of the vital human detail which anthropologists believe is the most important kind of evidence for understanding the social life of man.[61]

ORGANIZATION/DISORGANIZATION:
AN ARITHMETICAL SUMMARY

At the risk of oversimplification and other unforeseeable sins of omission or commission, we will now try to reduce the theoretical framework of organization/disorganization to an all-time irreducible minimum. The objective will be an attempt to isolate and identify the grist that constitutes the subject matter of the social disorganizationists.

A fundamental assumption is that social organization and social disorganization are concepts that are so akin as to make it impossible to treat one without the other. Implied in the concept *organization* are norms. Indeed these norms *are* the value-system of a given societal organization. Specifically this means that all group, community and institutional behavior patterns that make up a given society constitute the very structure or *organization* of that society.[62]

The status of a given social organization, at any given time, can be *described* in terms of those *normative criteria that designate the kind of society toward which we aim*. The total configuration of normative criteria, *because of its very existence,* is viewed by the mass society (more specifically by its power-structure spokesmen), as desirable, proper and good. This part of the social organization is here labelled *NORMATIVE.*

At any given time, moreover, a certain amount of this *normative* pattern is actually practiced by the mass society. This latter network of behavior we shall designate as *DE FACTO—1.* Thus, in American society, a belief in God and in the basic values of religion, and a belief in our codes of government constitute the *NORMATIVE.* To the extent that the mass society actually practices and abides by these norms, this network of behavior (mostly overt) is here labelled *DE FACTO—1.*

We will now indulge in some very simple arithmetic.

Let us assume that all the goals and standards which are embodied in a given social organization, *viz.,* its total *NORMATIVE* to equal 100 units. Let us assume further that the mass society *practices* only 60 units of this NORMATIVE arrangement. We are then left with 40 units of behavior that remains to be identified. These 40 units are also of a *de facto* nature, and will be assigned to *DE FACTO—2 and DE FACTO—3. DE FACTO—2* is usually that part of the NORMA-TIVE which the mass society "tolerates" in a passive way. It represents those norms to which we make no objection, nor do we actually violate them. This "tolerative" behavior may be observed with regard to community chest or Red Cross campaigns to raise money. A segment of a given social organization may not contribute to a community campaign nor actively support it in any other way. At the same time this population segment may do nothing to prevent its existence and operation. This social behavior must still be labelled *de facto,* in the sense that inaction is, in itself, a form of action. Let us return to our arithmetic, and assume that the amount of behavior that can be described as *DE FACTO—2* ("tolerative" behavior) constitutes 10 units.

We shall identify the residue of 30 units of social behavior as *DE FACTO—3.* This behavior reprsents active, overt behavior that deviates from the normative codes to such an extent as to be in direct violation with them. Inasmuch as this behavior is contrary to the *NORMATIVE* (it will be recalled that the NORMATIVE, by its very *existence*, was assumed to be the proper and desirable objectives of social behavior), then logic dictates that *DE FACTO—3* behavior is unacceptable and undesirable to the mass society. Thus we have a web of group, community and institutional behavior that prevails within the society but is adjudged by that same society to be undesirable and detrimental to it. This *DE FACTO—3* behavior we shall label as *social disorganization*.

Thus our arithmetical exercise would run as follows:

I. *NORMATIVE*:	Those ideals / goals / values which a society identifies as the standards of behavior toward which it aims. (Basically derived from religious and legal foundations of the past.)	100 units
II. *DE FACTO—1*:	This represents that part of the normative which the mass society accepts, not only attitudinally, but actually practices.	—60 units
	Balance.	40 units
III. *DE FACTO—2*:	"Tolerative" behavior.	—10 units
IV. *DE FACTO—3*:	SOCIAL DISORGANIZATION. ("Social problems")	30 units

If that "residue" of the total social organization which is designated in the above scheme as social disorganization is to be subjected to scientific assessment, then we are immediately faced with a primary question. Specifically, what is the scientific methodology to be for identifying the "disorganized" areas that are to be analyzed? As of now, it is immediately obvious that the subject matter designated as *disorganization* has been selected on the basis of *indices* of behavior patterns that show a "relative lack of unanimity existing in a given society."[63] These indices cover a wide range. They include such "problems" based on statistics on juvenile delinquency, prostitution, illegitimate births, divorce, literacy rates, as well as rates of mobility, corruption, vice and crime.

Organization/Disorganization: Values reconsidered.

But why and on what bases were these indices accumulated in the first place? Answers to questions of this type are all too obvious. The indices represent quantitative identifications of *de facto* social behavior patterns that are contrary to our normative codes. In short they are a quantitative reflection of *values in conflict* in a given social organization. And when certain of these indices, and not others, are selected to comprise a textbook under the label, *Social Disorganization,* is it not possible, even very probable, that the selector's own values are indeed showing.[64]

Social disorganizationists must still face the basic problem of what constitutes the "good society." We have previously alluded to values in connection with social organization. If organization and disorganization represent reverse aspects of the same functioning society, then the discussion of values begs to be reconsidered.

When a writer presents a few introductory theoretical remarks on the role of values, and then goes on to deal with selected "social problems," allowing only for a minimum of attention to the values, *per se,* that underlie these same "problems," we have a practice that does not seem to be acceptable to many present-day sociologists. The scientific attitude in modern sociology makes no compromise with Max Weber's intonement that, "Criticism is not to be suspended in the presence of value-judgments."[65] But this principle seems to be more of a normative attitude than a *de facto* analytical practice, according to some who view the *results* of the social disorganization approach.

One of the strongest statements imputing value orientations to the social disorganization approach comes from the pages of Cuber, Harper and Kenkel:

> The usefulness of social disorganization as an interpretative concept is seriously limited by the fact that specific value judgments underlie its application to any social situation. The term implies disapproval and abnormality, temporary undesirability, a trend which (if unchecked) will lead to institutional dissolution. The use of the social disorganization hypothesis seems often to serve as a shroud for moralizing rather than as a tool for analysis.[66]

SUMMARY

Modern sociologists, disorganizations or not, will all agree with Lundberg that "no science tells us *what to do* with knowledge that

constitutes the science. Science only provides the car and a chauffeur
for us. It does not directly tell us where to drive."[67]
But the label of "scientist" does not make one so. Indeed such
doings only delay scientific development. As of now, it appears that
sociologists, in company with their fellow behavior scientists, must
await an operational scientific methodology for dealing with the
measurement and assessment of *values,* before their task for dealing
with the alleged "defects" in a given social organization will become
subjective to objective assessment.

> The recording of symbolic materials as found in life settings
> . . . provide the analyst only with raw materials. Inspection of
> such materials may lead a sensitive person to certain insights and
> conclusions, and these may be, in a certain sense, "correct." But,
> in the long run, both scientific and practical progress require
> more than sensitive insight. . . . To the extent that investigators
> cannot communicate to others how their insights are accom-
> plished, the ability to achieve them is retained as private property
> of individuals. These conditions would produce, at best, experts
> and not a body of knowledge.[68]

SELECTED BIBLIOGRAPHY

Bernard Barber, "Structural-Functional Analysis," *American Sociological Rev*iew, XXI (April, 1956), 129-135. A well-formulated statement of "structural-functional analysis" in contemporary sociology,
providing provocative theoretical insights to organization/disorganiza-
tion problems of conceptualization.

Morris G. Caldwell and Laurence Foster (Editors), *Analysis of Social
Problems* (Harrisburg, Pa.: Stackpole, 1954) Ch. 1. "Nature of and
Approaches to Social Problems," provides a "pro and con" coverage
of the varied approaches to the study of "social problems." Its bibliography, including periodical references on the subject is commendable.

J. F. Cuber, R. A. Harper and W. F. Kenkel, *Problems of American
Society: Values in Conflict* (New York: Holt, 1956, 3rd edition). An
analysis of selected social problems in terms of social values, and how
these impinge on the formulation, causation and solution of problems.
The book takes a strong position that "the sociologist is better suited
to the role of *interpreter of values* than to the role of *value advocate.*"
Especially recommended is Chapter 22, "The Social Disorganization
Concept Re-examined."

Luke Ebersole, *American Society* (New York McGraw-Hill, 1955).
An elementary textbook devoted to an analysis of American social
organization. Not as rigorous as the Williams book (see below), but

unique in the fact that it and the Williams book are the only two recent systematic sociological assessments of overall American society.

Mabel A. Elliott and Francis E. Merrill, *Social Disorganization* (New York, 1950, 3rd edition). A popular textbook employing the social disorganization approach in the analysis of a very wide range of "social problems" under the headings of "Individual Disorganization," "Community and National Disorganization," and "International Disorganization."

Robert E. L. Faris, *Social Disorganization* (New York: Ronald, 1955, 2nd edition). A good account of the concepts of social organization, social disorganization, as well as personal disorganization. Discusses selected areas of disorganization in terms of "those basic processes that are to some extent the fundamental causes of many of the troubles studied under the terms of 'social problems' and 'social pathology.'"

Erich Fromm, *The Sane Society* (New York: Rinehart, 1955). A social psychiatric assessment of the broad areas of social behavior in American culture. The author's theme of "normative humanism" will be of strong interest to students of social organization and disorganization.

Joyce O. Hertzler, *Society in Action* (New York: Dryden, 1954). Especially recommended are Part 4, "Societal Structuralization and Functionalization," and Part 5, "Destructuralization and Defunctionalization."

Edwin M. Lemert, *Social Pathology: A Systematic Approach to the Theory of Sociopathic Behavior* (New York: McGraw-Hill, 1951). For the somewhat advanced student with some background in sociology and psychology, this textbook, employing the "pathological approach," provides considerable insight to personal and social deviations. The author denies to the "social disorganization" approach, its right to be considered "a body of concepts which can be called 'systematic theory.'"

C. Wright Mills, "The Professional Ideology of Social Pathologists," *American Journal of Sociology*, XXXXIX (September, 1943), 165-180. A forthright statement of some background highlights of social pathologists, especially the earlier writers. This is developed to demonstrate their injection of moral judgments into many of their writings.

F. S. C. Northrop, *The Logic of the Sciences and the Humanities* (New York: Macmillan, 1948). Especially recommended is Chapter XXI, "The Scientific Method for Determining the Normative Social Theory of the Ends of Human Action."

W. Lloyd Warner, *American Life: Dream and Reality* (University of Chicago, 1953). An example of the anthropological approach to the study of social organization. The underlying theme focuses on "the facts of social class and color caste." The American community is used "as a laboratory for research on contemporary American life."

Robin M. Williams, *American Society* (New York: Knopf, 1951). A first-rate sociological analysis of American social organization. One of the first concise, yet comprehensive sociological treatments of overall American social organization. Included is a basic consideration of "group relations and the harmony and conflict that characterize them," as well as an assessment of values and the integration of society.

Florian Znaniecki, "Social Organization and Institutions," in G. Gurvitch and W. E. Moore, *Twentieth Century Sociology* (New York: Philosophical Library, 1945), 172-217. An excellent theoretical account of social organization, especially "with reference to particular 'social groups,' or 'associations,' instead of with reference to a 'society.' "

Theodore I. Lenn, A.B., M.A., Ph.D., New York University, is Associate Professor of Sociology, Teachers College of Connecticut (New Britain); has served as a member of the summer session faculties at New York University, Trinity College (Hartford, Conn.), and the University of Maine; is the author of several articles and book reviews, as well as *Workbook and Readings in Sociology* (1956).

NOTES

1. Florian Znaniecki, "Social Organization and Institutions," in G. Gurvitch and W. E. Moore, *Twentieth Century Sociology* (New York: Philosophical Library, 1945), 172.

2. *Ibid.,* 173.

3. Raymond Firth, *Elements of Social Organization* (New York: Philosophical Library), 5.

4. E. E. Evans-Pitchard, *Social Anthropology* (Glencoe, Ill.: Free Press), 5-6.

5. George P. Murdoch, *Social Structure* (New York: Macmillan, 1949), Ch. 8.

6. Melville J. Herskovits, *Man And His Works* (New York: Knopf, 1948), 290.

7. Znaniecki, *loc. cit.*

8. In Henry Pratt Fairchild *et al., Dictionary of Sociology* (New York: Philosophical Library, 1944), 287.

9. Joyce O. Hertzler, *Society in Action* (New York: Dryden, 1954), 19.

10. Arnold M. Rose, *Sociology: The Study of Human Relations* (New York: Knopf, 1956), 567.

11. Lowell J. Carr, *Analytical Sociology* (New York: Harper, 1955), 28.

12. Leonard Broom and Philip Selznick, *Sociology* (White Plains, N. Y.: Row, Peterson, 1955), 12.

13. Blaine E. Mercer, *The American Community* (New York: Random House, 1956), 4.

14. Robin M. Williams, *American Society* (New York: Knopf, 1951), 444-445.

15. *Loc. cit.*

16. Talcott Parsons, *The Social System* (Glencoe, Ill.: Free Press, 1952.)

17. Parsons, *op. cit.,* 535.

18. David Lockwood, "Some Remarks on 'The Social System,'" *The British Journal of Sociology,* VII (June, 1956), 134.

19. R. M. MacIver and C. H. Page, *Society: An Introductory Analysis* New York: Rinehart, 1949), Chs. 21-23.

20. *Ibid.,* 494.

21. Carr, *op. cit.,* 357.

22. See Talcott Parsons, *Essays in Sociological Theory* (Glencoe, Illinois: Free Press, 1954, 2nd edition), Ch. XI; Robert K. Merton, *Social Theory and Social Structure* (Glencoe, Illinois: Free Press, 1949), Ch. I; Bernard Barber, "Structural-Functional Analysis," *American Sociological Review,* XXI (April, 1956), 129-135.

23. Mercer, *op. cit.,* 15.

24. For a concise survey of these varied approaches, see Morris G. Caldwell and Laurence Foster (Editors), *Analysis of Social Problems* (Harrisburg, Pa.: Stackpole, 1954), Ch. 1.

25. Robert S. Lynd, *Knowledge for What?* (Princeton University, 1939), 183.

26. Robert E. L. Faris, *Social Disorganization* (New York: Ronald, 1955, 2nd edition).

27. Mabel A. Elliott and Francis E. Merrill, *Social Disorganization* (New York: Harper, 1950, 3rd edition).

28. Faris, *op cit.,* iii.

29. Elliott and Merrill, *op. cit.,* xi.

30. Faris, *op. cit.,* 81.

31. Elliott and Merrill, *op cit.,* 20.

32. Faris, *op. cit.,* 34.

33. Elliott and Merrill, *op. cit.,* 20.

34. Faris, *op. cit.,* 63.

35. Elliott and Merrill, *op. cit.,* 22.

36. Faris, *op. cit.,* 38.

37. Elliott and Merrill, *op. cit.,* 21.

38. Faris, *op. cit.,* 39.

39. Elliott and Merrill, *op. cit.,* 25.

40. Paul B. Horton and Gerald R. Leslie, *The Sociology of Social Problems* (New York: Appleton-Century-Crofts, 1955), 28.

41. Luke Ebersole, *American Society* (New York: McGraw-Hill, 1955), 308.

42. R. L. Sutherland, J. L. Woodward, M. A. Maxwell, *Introductory Sociology* (Philadelphia: Lippincott, 1956), 509.

43. Rose, *op. cit.,* 148.

44. Faris, *op. cit.,* 81.

45. *Ibid.,* 288.

46. *Ibid.,* 246.

47. *Ibid.,* 403.

48. Elliott and Merrill, *op. cit.,* 28.

49. *Loc. cit.*

50. Elliott and Merrill, *op. cit.,* 30.

51. Faris, *op. cit.,* 36.

52. Elliott and Merrill, *op. cit.,* xi.

53. Faris, *op. cit.,* 36.

54. Abbott P. Herman, *An Approach to Social Problems* (Boston: Ginn, 1949).

55. *Ibid.,* 22.

56. *Ibid.*, 23.

57. Edwin M. Lemert, *Social Pathology: A Systematic Approach to the Theory of Sociopathic Behavior* (New York: McGraw-Hill, 1951) .

58. *Ibid.*, 15.

59. Richard Dewey and W. J. Humber, *The Development of Human Behavior* (New York: Macmillan, 1951) , 712.

60. E. W. Burgess and R. E. Park, *Introduction to the Science of Sociology* (Chicago: University of Chicago, 1924) , 55. See especially E. R. Mowrer, *Disorganization: Personal and Social* (Philadelphia: Lippincott, 1942) .

61. W. Lloyd Warner, *American Life: Dream and Reality* (University of Chicago, 1953) , 32.

62. The historical record very poignantly insists that basic and dominant over the entire network of "rules and regulations" that prescribe any given social organization are those norms (values) that are implicitly and allegedly or explicitly rooted in religion and/or government.

63. Elliott and Merrill, *op. cit.*, 32.

64. See C. Wright Mills, "The Professional Ideology of Social Pathologists," *American Journal of Sociology*, XLIX (September, 1943) , 165-180.

65. Max Weber, *The Methodology of the Social Sciences* (Glencoe, Ill.: Free Press, 1949, first published in 1904) , 52.

66. J. F. Cuber, R. A. Harper and W. F. Kenkel, *Problems of American Society: Values in Conflict* (New York: Holt, 1956, 3rd edition) , 475.

67. George A. Lundberg, *Can Science Save Us?* (New York: Longmans, Green, 1947) , 31.

68. Leon Festinger and Daniel Katz, *Research Methods in the Behavorial Sciences* (New York: Dryden, 1953) , 434-435.

METHODOLOGY AND RESEARCH

E. A. Tiryakian
Princeton University

To preface this discussion, one may contrast the development of methodology and that of research methods by using as an analogy Ogburn's familiar thesis of cultural lag: research methods, viewed as the material aspect of sociological culture, have shown a tremendous advancement in size and scope since World War II, whereas methodology, an "adaptive" or non-material element, has tended to lag behind.[1]

We shall bifurcate our review by first treating trends in methodology and then considering those that have taken place in sociological research. Unfortunately, the space limitation of this article makes it necessary for the writer to select only certain salient aspects of research activity.

METHODOLOGY

Just what is or constitutes methodology is still somewhat of an equivocal matter among American sociologists. One sector seems to view it as dealing with field techniques, and research articles frequently have a section headed "methodology" which is no more than a *description* of the research procedures used in the course of the investigation. On the other hand, methodology has been termed "the logic of science,"[2] "the logic of scientific procedure,"[3] and "the consideration of the general grounds for the validity of scientific propositions and systems of them."[4]

We should like to suggest that methodology is concerned with the explication and evaluation of the interdependent processes constituting scientific inquiry. It is not confined to research procedures (of observation and measurement) only but also covers in its scope the processes of concept formation and theory construction. Any science may be said to have the purpose of describing in as few logically interrelated propositions as possible the nature of its subject matter; to achieve this, scientific inquiry attempts to develop propositions about the relationships between concepts capable of empirical verification. Methodology critically surveys every step involved along the way: making explicit the assumptions contained in various parts of the inquiry (assumptions underlying the concepts or propositions to be tested, the measuring instruments, the interpretation and analysis of the data observed, etc.), evaluating which procedures will be the most efficient, considering the grounds upon which a proposition has been validated or invalidated by means of the selected procedures, and finally, seeing in what way do the obtained data affect the existing corpus of that science.

Methodology, in other words, attempts to make clear both what is considered as the "given" and the "problematical" in scientific inquiry; it also attempts to evaluate the procedures by which the "problematical" is thought to be solved. Any aspect of scientific inquiry is subject to methodological analysis; methodology performs the function of relating the body of theoretical propositions to the empirical setting of a given discipline and vice versa. From theory to research and from research back to theory lie a great number of decisions; methodology seeks to evaluate the grounds upon which these decisions are made.

Although methodology is still considered in some sociological circles as somewhat of a philosophical Trojan horse or else as a hoary remain of a paleolithic age of armchair speculation, there is indication that this is becoming a minority view. A small but notable number of methodological works appeared during the post-war period, and interest in methodology quickened.

A major trend in methodology has been the awareness of the pressing need of sociology to develop formalization: "the observance of a conventional set of rules in order to make explicit the logic of scientific proof." [5] To bring this about, Furfey[6] suggested that there be established for sociology criteria of relevance and criteria of scientific quality: standards for determining whether a given proposition does or does not fall within the scope of sociology, and standards for determining whether a given proposition shall be incorporated into the body of propositions constituting sociology.

Another approach to formalization has come from a growing concern with the use and development of models.[7] Of course, the use of models is not a recent innovation in sociology, even though the term itself has become fashionable in relatively recent times.[8] However, in recent years a distinctively new species of models is beginning to make its entrance into the sociological arena: the mathematical model. Already, a recent volume edited by Lazarsfeld[9] contains models pertaining to attitudes, imitative behavior, distribution of social status, and norms of behavior; other mathematical models have been constructed dealing with social interaction among group members.[10] Although it is still too early to evaluate the contributions of these models, one can at least sympathize with the attempt to substitute the open fields of mathematical thinking in place of the semantic jungles which continue to plague sociology. Indubitably, a meaningful application of mathematics to sociological thinking and research areas will lead to important methodological and concrete developments.

A major trend in the methodological thinking of the post-war era has been a renewed concern over the use of concepts and definitions.[11] The methodological difficulties facing sociology in seeking to formulate propositions capable of rigorous testing stem partly from the varied usage given to basic concepts and the indiscriminate borrowing of concepts from other disciplines; examples of current concepts used with a variety of meanings and for the most part with little precision are "structure," "institutionalization," "dynamic (or static) equilibrium," and "function."[12]

Herbert Blumer has gone so far as to say that the equivocal aspect of sociological concepts is "the basic deficiency in social theory . . . and for that matter of our discipline."[13] Rather than focus our attention upon *definitive concepts* (i.e., those giving the "real" definition or the essential attributes of a class of objects), Blumer suggested that we give greater emphasis to *sensitizing* concepts, those acting as indicators of where to direct investigations. They have the advantage that they can be tested, improved, and refined; moreover, "their validity can be assayed through careful study of empirical instances which they are presumed to cover."[14]

Underlying the methodological concern with concepts is the growing awareness among sociologists that for sociological inquiry to become truly scientific a body of concepts must be developed which will have both empirical relevance and theoretical significance. Of great pertinence in this context is the succinct and comprehensive monograph by the philosopher Carl Hempel, *Fundamentals of Concept Formation in Empirical Science*.[15] In his discussion of methods and types of concept formation, Hempel explains that definitions are one of a number of possible ways of forming concepts. His analysis is an important methodological contribution which is highly welcome.

Along with a growing concern over concepts and the importance of concepts in research design as well as theory construction is a related trend in sociology to bring about a closer integration between theory and research. The schism betwen these two branches in the past has had the unfortunate consequence that theory construction has contributed little to the researchers and that the results of the latter have been of little significance for theoretical development. Moreover, large numbers of empirical studies are completely divorced from one another and much of sociological research shows the absence of some continuity. Parsons has attributed the failure of sociological research to be cumulative as stemming from a "lack of an adequate working theoretical tradition."[16] On the other hand, the empiricist faction decries that too much sociological theory has little relation to existing conditions and that its propositions are incapable of verification.

To bridge this gap, Merton[17] has presented a thoughtful discussion of the interdependence of theoretical and research activity and the contributions each make to the other. He has championed the use of "middle-range" rather than systematic or general theories since the former are more immediately fruitful for research purposes. This appeal met with support from many quarters. An extension of Merton's proposal is to be found in the work of Zetterberg,[18] who has proposed the development of axiomatic or deductive-type theories; these are also middle-range (or "miniature") in contrast to more sweeping "inclusive" ones. Although this approach is still inchoate, it might make valuable methodological contributions in the future.

METHODOLOGICAL CRITIQUES

One of the significant trends in methodological writing in recent years has been the increased number of sophisticated research critiques. Indeed, this constitutes one of the bright spots in the development of sociological methodology.

A major methodological criticism to which sociological research is vulnerable is that of overgeneralization. In treating this problem at length, Arnold Rose[19] found prevalent three different types: (1) overgeneralization of research findings, (2) overgeneralization in using a technique developed to investigate one set of problems in another context and without proper modification, (3) overgeneralization in the employment of statistical methods. One of the remedies he advocated was to increase the number of replicative studies. The methodological functions of replicative studies are the verification of the generalizations of the original study and the setting of limits under which the generalizations are valid. At present there are relatively few replicative studies, the replication has not been systematically conducted, and the results are for the most part contradictory or inconclusive.

An important trend has been the number of excellent critiques of specific research projects and research instruments. At the beginning of the period under review, Angell presented a comprehensive methodological evaluation of the personal document and of the studies which may have employed it.[20] In the middle of this post-war period were published the initial works of a series entitled *Continuities in Social Research;* the first two volumes assayed studies which though not primarily sociological have nevertheless made their imprint upon the soil of sociological research. The first critique[21] was the collaborative efforts of several social scientists to evaluate the voluminous *American Soldier* studies of Samuel Stouffer and his associates.[22] As has been pointed out,[23] this evaluation has led to important considerations for the study of primary groups, reference group theory and survey analysis. The second volume[24] contained a number of papers which appraised a much-discussed psychological tome, *The Authoritarian Personality.*[25] Among these may be singled out the one by Hyman and Sheatsley, "'The Authoritarian Personality'—A Methodological Critique," which is a comprehensive and sophisticated critique of the whole study from its conceptual framework through its data analysis; this methodological analysis is extremely germane to sociological research.

The most recent methodological critique to be mentioned is also one of the most outstanding ones written in the social sciences: Pitirim A. Sorokin's *Fads and Foibles in Modern Sociology and Related Sciences.*[26] With a precise methodological scalpel, Sorokin dissects the pathological aspects of most of the contemporary methods and techniques of research. Believing that there is a significant difference in the phenomena studied by the social and the natural sciences, Sorokin finds that "most of the defects of modern psychosocial science are due to a clumsy imitation of the physical sciences."[27] He exposes serious methodological deficiencies in the application of analogues taken from physical sciences, in small group research, as well as in the use of quantitative methods, statistics, and mathematical models.

In concluding this section one can only voice the hope that this new activity in methodological thinking will have salutary consequences for sociological research, to which we now turn our attention.

RESEARCH DESIGN

In the wake of the greatly accelerated pace of sociological research in recent years has come an increased interest in research design: "the entire process of conducting a research study."[28] Research design is basic to scientific inquiry: it is a set of blueprints covering all the stages of research from the deduction of hypotheses to the analysis and evaluation of the data.

Of growing importance in research design has been the sampling plan of a study, which involves at least three facets: (1) the definition of the population or universe to be sampled, (2) the size of the sample, and (3) the representativeness of the sample. If any or all of these are faulty, this will tend to vitiate the generalizations stemming from the empirical results of the study. Sampling procedures have become greatly refined and more precise in the endeavor to increase the efficiency of the design; there has been a trend away from "judgment" and "quota" sampling towards forms of sampling less susceptible to a biased selection of elements, e.g., random, probability, stratified, area and cluster sampling.

Another important feature of the design is that it should be capable of specifying the controls used during the course of research. Stouffer[29] presented the classical model of the controlled experiment (two groups matched in all respects observed before and after the introduction of the experimental variable into one group) as an ideal to keep in mind although in actuality sociological research has to settle for less rigorous designs. Since these latter "study" designs constitute the overwhelming majority of current sociological research, it is important to be aware of their limitations. If the observations are limited to one group studied at only one time, it is dubious to speak of experimentation at all and difficult to state anything significant about the variables under consideration. Because equating groups of individuals is so difficult in the social sciences, Stouffer suggested the variable to be studied should be stated precisely and that there be as few of them as possible (so as to have enough observations in any one cell). The desiderata for a hypothesis are that it may be adequately testable and that if demonstrable it be of some significance.

Another treatise in this context was the one of Chapin,[30] who described three types of experimental designs: (1) *cross-sectional,* i.e., observing two matched groups at the same time, (2) *projected,* i.e., observing two matched groups prior to the administration of a treatment upon the experimental group, and (3) *ex-post-facto,* i.e., seeking to discover the antecedents of a treatment after the effect has occurred. Also of importance has been the development of the *longitudinal* design in which repeated observations at various times are made on the same group. Several studies of opinion formation have been conducted following this plan (called in this context the "panel study") which enables one to see not only the direction of opinion or attitude change but also *who* does the changing under what influences.[31]

A final aspect of this growing emphasis upon research design has been the appearance in recent years of a number of fine research manuals which stress the interdependence of the processes composing scientific inquiry. As an example one may cite Ackoff's *The Design of Social Research,*[32] which stresses the importance of methodologically designed research, i.e., research planned beforehand whose procedures and decisions can be evaluated.

TRENDS IN RESEARCH

Alongside continued interest in established sociological fields of research such as demography and ecology, there has been a phenomenal growth in studies devoted to small groups: groups of limited size, usually ranging from 2-20 members, and characterized by face-to-face interaction.[33] Needless to say, the study and description of group behavior belongs to a long established sociological tradition, but it is only in the contemporary period that so much concentrated effort has gone into the *experimental* study of small groups inside research laboratories. At the same time, one must add, there has been continuing interest of groups in "naturalistic" surroundings such as industry groups, play groups, etc.

Diffuse as has the experimental research of small groups become, nevertheless, it is possible to delineate the main schools which stimulated the growth of this field (1) the socio-psychological "field theory" group of Kurt Lewin and his followers (Lippitt, Cartwright, Zander, Festinger, etc.), which has loosely come to be known as the "group dynamics" approach, (2) the sociological school headed by R. F. Bales which treats small groups as social systems, and (3) the group associated with the name of sociometry under the leadership of Moreno.[34]

A paramount concern of small group research has been the development of a reliable method of observing the interaction taking place between group members. Various methods of "systematic observation" have been devised; of central importance for these has been the construction of a classificatory scheme for the recording of interaction. Some systems of classification are designed to record specific aspects of the interaction or are geared for a particular type of group. Bales[35] has constructed a 12-category scheme of general applicability with the property that any verbal or non-verbal behavior of group members may be registered in one (and only one) of the categories by trained observers. The scoring is done by means of an "interaction recorder" which enables the researcher to have a permanent record of scores in their original sequence. By finding out the type of interaction between various members at different times and the different problems faced by the group, Bales has been able to make a number of generalizations concerning the role differentiation and the system processes that occur at succeeding stages of the group's existence.

Small group studies have not only uncovered a number of empirical findings concerning various aspects of interaction (communication patterns, power structure, group productivity, group cohesion, etc.), they have also brought a new rapprochement between theory and research. For example, the empirical findings of Bales have given support to some of the theoretical propositions of Talcott Parsons and the latter have stimulated further empirical research on the part of Bales.[36] Another illustration is that Simmel's well-known observations regarding the power structure of a three-member group have been empirically tested in small group research.[37] If this trend continues, the small group may well become in the near future the proving grounds of much of sociological theory, just as the fruit fly became an indispensable research agent of genetics.

Sociometry, especially designed by Moreno to measure patterns of attraction and repulsion between group members, has become a widely utilized approach to small group research; much of its terminology (e.g., "role playing," "sociometric star," "isolate," "group therapy," "sociogram," etc.) has become an accepted part of the sociological vocabulary. Its original techniques have been retained, but there has been a pronounced shift away from Moreno's emphasis on sociometry as a therapeutic method of reducing interpersonal conflict. An extension of sociometric measurement has come from "relational analysis"[38] whereby the individual is asked to state how the other group members perceive him in terms of acceptance and rejection. Perhaps the most important trend in sociometric research is the development of new techniques for the analysis and tabulation of choice-rejection data: in addition to earlier graphic and index analyses, new approaches have been made by use of statistical methods (e.g., the development of a probabilistic model), matrix analysis, and even factor analysis.[39]

Post-war research has not been limited to small groups but has also continued an earlier interest in large communal groups, observed in a naturalistic rather than in a laboratory setting. The generic term for this type of research (involving the use of several techniques such as participant observation, interviewing, etc.) may be called the "community study" method.[40]

A main emphasis in community studies has been uncovering the stratification system relating members to one another. William L. Warner and his associates published a detailed guide of the procedures they used to measure social prestige in the community called "Jonesville."[41] The assignment of individuals to their respective social class positions is dependent upon two separate methods. The first, Evaluated Participation (E.P.), is a composite of six rating techniques by which informants evaluate the social participation of the members of the community; it is essentially a subjective method of social class placement. The other method is the Index of Status Characteristics (I.S.C.), which is an index of four socioeconomic factors (occupation, source of income, house type, dwelling area); it constitutes an "objective" approach which translates into socioeconomic terms social class concepts, and conversely. Warner has claimed that his methods (and findings) are applicable to the whole of the United States; however, this has not met with uniform agreement on the part of other sociologists.[42]

Another type of community study of social stratification was that reported by A. B. Hollingshead,[43] who tested the hypothesis that the behavior of adolescents is related to the position of their families in the social structure. To delineate the class structure in the community he studied, Hollingshead used a rating procedure whereby judges rated the families of adolescents against a control list of 20 families. His results were on the whole comparable to those of Warner.

To avoid the limitations of community studies, research of stratification was extended to the national level by means of a list of occupational roles which may be easily ranked or scored by a representative sample of the population. Such studies of occupational stratification have shown a great consistency in the prestige ranking of occupations, both at home and abroad;[44] however, these studies have been mainly descriptive and have not been related to more general aspects of social stratification.

A main trend in sociological research has been the increased use and methodological refinement of the "social survey" method, a composite of quantitative and non-quantitative techniques, which taken together form a powerful device for obtaining and analyzing data on almost any subject of inquiry.[45] The main techniques of the major types of surveys (descriptive and explanatory) include sampling, questionnaire construction, interviewing, and statistical techniques of data analysis. Although none of these are innovations, it must be pointed out that there has been a new level of sophistication used in their application and that greater methodological attention has been paid to each technique.

The questionnaire as an instrument designed to elicit some desired information from respondents has replaced in popularity other forms of personal records such as diaries, memoirs, and life-story documents; it certainly is not a new technique, but it has greatly benefited from a greater degree of refinement in the construction of questions, their ordering, and other facets which if uncontrolled may lead to distortions in the validity of results.

The interview as a technique (some would call it an art) of data collection has become "the favored digging tool of a large army of sociologists."[46] It has been widely utilized and cross-fertilized by a variety of disciplines including anthropology, clinical and social psychology, and of course, sociology. Depending upon the flexibility allowed the interviewer in the way and the order in which he asks the questions, the interview may be "structured" or "unstructured" (or "non-directive"), "standardized" or "unstandardized." A new type developed was the "focused" interview which seeks information from a group of persons who have been exposed to the same stimulus or situation.[47] Since the instrument which records the data is a person, the interview situation itself constitutes social interaction. The factors which affect the role relationship between interviewer and interviewee have been studied so as to become aware of sources of error occurring in survey research as a result of using this technique. A comprehensive methodological appraisal of the interview, which makes an intensive examination of the sources of interviewer error and their control, has been published by Hyman.[48]

Recent mathematical developments in techniques of measurement and analysis have come into sociological research by way of social psychology, particularly from the field of attitude measurement. Theoretical models of ordered structures or scales dealing with qualitative data were advanced by Guttman[49] and Lazarsfeld,[49] respectively. The Guttman approach to scaling, "scale analysis" (involving "scalogram" and "intensity" analysis), is a unidimensional model relating the scale items to a single continuum. In a "perfect" scale of internal consistency the items have a cumulative property so that from a respondent's scale score one may reproduce his response to the individual items comprising the scale. The approach of Lazarsfeld, "latent structure analysis," is an extension and amplificaton of earlier methods of factor analyis developed by Thurstone and others. Whereas in the Guttman method the distribution of responses to scalable items is an operational definition of the attitude, the Lazarsfeld model seeks to relate items not in terms of their manifest relationship, but rather by means of an inferred latent continuum. Both of these models and their techniques have won among some sociologists a great deal of admiration for their usefulness in handling a variety of qualitative data. The Guttman approach to scaling, in particular, has been extensively used with certain improvements which have made it more facile to administer; furthermore, there has been an endeavor to adapt it to group (rather than individual) data, which would make it more sociologically relevant.[50]

CONCLUSION

We must reiterate that because of space limitation this survey of methodology and research in the post-war period has had to confine itself to some of the more salient developments in these respective fields. We should like to conclude with a few generalizations.

1. Although still lagging behind research developments, there has been an increased interest in methodology, especially in methodology as a nexus between research and theory.

2. Sociological research has greatly increased in scope and in the variety of approaches comprising it. Furthermore, it has benefited from contributions of other social sciences and has developed an eclectic, "interdisciplinary" status.

3. The emphasis in research has been the elaboration and refinement of quantitative methods. However, it is the personal feeling of the writer that present research must guard against an overconcern with reliability at the detriment of validity. We have reached a stage where we can observe and measure data with greater precision and accuracy than in previous periods; what is essential now is the codification of research findings and the incorporation of *meaningful* data into the body of propositions constituting sociological theory.

SELECTED BIBLIOGRAPHY

Russell, L. Ackoff, *The Design of Social Research* (Chicago: University of Chicago Press, 1953). A methodologically organized text of social research. Discussion of problem formulation, ideal research model, and practical research model.

John T. Doby, ed., *An Introduction to Social Research* (Harrisburg: The Stackpole Company, 1954). A manual of scientific research stressing general methodological considerations as well as specific methods such as scaling, constructive typology, participant observation and interviewing.

Wm. J. Goode, and Paul K. Hatt, *Methods in Social Research* (New York: McGraw-Hill, 1952). A manual of research discussing in step-by-step fashion various procedures of inquiry.

Marie Jahoda; Morton Deutsch; and Stuart W. Cook, *Research Methods in Social Relations*, 2 vols. (New York: The Dryden Press, 1951). The first volume discusses basic processes of research problem formulation, measurement, data collection, analysis and interpretation. The second covers selected techniques such as sampling, content analysis, panel study, etc.

Felix Kaufman, *Methodology of the Social Sciences* (New York: Oxford University Press, 1944). A general treatise on methodology, stressing the processes of verification, invalidation and falsification in scientific procedures.

Paul F. Lazarsfeld, and Morris Rosenberg, *The Language of Social Research* (Glencoe: The Free Press, 1955). A reader in methodology and research papers, mostly the latter.

Marion J. Levy, Jr., "Some Basic Methodological Difficulties in Social Science," *Philosophy of Science,* XVII (October, 1950) 287-301.

A concise review of basic methodological problems facing social scientists.

Gardener Lindzey, ed., *Handbook of Social Psychology*, v. I Part 3 contains lengthy articles surveying developments of research methods used in social research sociometric measurement, attitude measurement, the interview, systematic observational techniques and others.

Mildred Parten, *Surveys, Polls and Samples* (New York: Harper, 1950). A detailed exposition of the survey method including questionnaire construction, sampling field administration, etc. Contains an exhaustive bibliography.

Pitirim A. Sorokin, *Fads and Foibles in Modern Sociology and Related Sciences* (Chicago: Henry Regnery, 1956). A comprehensive methodological critique of recent research developments showing the pitfalls of pseudoscientific thinking.

Edward A. Tiryakian (1929–), A.B. Princeton (1952). Ph. D. Harvard (1956), is Instructor in Economics and Sociology, Princeton University; Fullbright Scholar in the Philippines and Visiting Lecturer in the University of Philippines (1954-1955); currently engaged in writing on methodology and occupational stratification.

NOTES

1. As an illustration, a recent reader in the methodology of social research, originally planned to be divided equally between methodological and research papers, is devoted for the most part to examples of research because the editors found "the number of studies making use of sophisticated research practices is far greater than the number of papers which articulate or codify or discuss the procedures themselves." P. F. Lazarsfeld and M. Rosenberg, eds., *The Language of Social Research* (Glencoe: The Free Press, 1955) , 4.

2. Felix Kaufmann, *Methodology of the Social Sciences* (New York: Oxford University Press, 1944) , 230.

3. Robert K. Merton, *Social Theory and Social Structure* (Glencoe: The Free Press, 1949) , 84.

4. Talcott Parsons, *The Structure of Social Action,* 2nd ed. (Glencoe: The Free Press, 1949) , 24.

5. P. H. Furfey, "The Formalization of Sociology," *American Sociological Review,* XIX (October, 1954) , 525-8.

6. *Ibid.* Furfey calls the science which would develop these two sets of criteria "metasociology"; this term seems superfluous since this task falls within the realm of methodology.

7. In a technical sense, a model is a set of assumptions, axioms, or fundamental premises which focuses the direction of subsequent research by pointing to the immediately relevant aspects of the phenomena under scrutiny. The model itself is not a composite of statements of fact, hence cannot be directly validated or invalidated; from the model one deduces propositions regarding existing conditions

and it is these that are subject to empirical verification. See, for example, Svend Riemer, "Premises in Sociological Inquiry," *American Journal of Sociology*, LIX (May, 1954), 551-5; Paul Meadows, "Models, Systems and Science," *American Sociological Review*, XXII (February, 1957), 3-9; M. M. Beshers, "Models and Theory Construction," *American Sociological Review*, XXII (February, 1957), 32-8.

8. For a thorough coverage of earlier models (biological, mechanical, etc), see Pitirim A. Sorokin, *Contemporary Sociological Theories* (New York: Harper, 1928).

9. P. H. Lazarsfeld, ed., *Mathematical Thinking in the Social Sciences* (Glencoe: The Free Press, 1954).

10. H. A. Simon, "A Formal Theory of Interaction in Social Groups," *American Sociological Review*, XVII (April, 1952), 202-11; F. F. Stephan and E. G. Mishler, "Participation in Small Groups," *American Sociological Review*, XVII (October, 1952), 599-608.

11. Timasheff has discussed four types of definitions pertaining to basic concepts: (1) etymological or verbal, (2) inductive, (3) imposed, and (4) operational. "Definitions in the Social Sciences," *American Journal of Sociology*, LIII (November, 1947), 201-9.

12. For an exposition of the varied ways in which "function" has been used, see R. K. Merton, *Social Theory and Social Structure* (Glencoe: The Free Press, 1949), 22-7.

13. "What is Wrong with Social Theory?," *American Sociological Review*, XIX (February, 1954), 5.

14. *Ibid.*, 8.

15. Carl Hempel, *International Encyclopedia of Unified Science*, v. II, no. 7 (Chicago: University of Chicago Press, 1952).

16. T. Parsons, *Essays in Sociological Theory*, rev. ed. (Glencoe: The Free Press, 1954), 350.

17. Merton, *op. cit.*, 83-111.

18. H. L. Zetterberg, *On Theory and Verification in Sociology* (New York: The Tressler Press, 1954).

19. Arnold Rose, *Theory and Method in the Social Sciences* (Minneapolis: University of Minnesota Press, 1954).

20. Robert C. Angell, "A Critical Review of the Development of the Personal Document Method in Sociology 1920-1940," in L. Gottschalk, C. Kluckhohn, and R. Angell, *The Use of Personal Documents in History, Anthropology, and Sociology* (New York: Social Science Research Council, 1945), 177-232.

21. R. K. Merton and P. F. Lazarsfeld, eds., *Studies in the Scope and Method of "The American Soldier"* (Glencoe: The Free Press, 1950).

22. *Studies in Social Psychology in World War II* (Princeton University Press, 1949).

23. Peter H. Rossi, "Methods of Social Research 1945-55," in H. L. Zetterberg, ed., *Sociology in the United States of America* (Paris: UNESCO, 1956), 26.

24. R. Christie and M. Jahoda, eds., *Studies in the Scope and Method of "The Authoritarian Personality"* (Glencoe: The Free Press, 1954).

25. T. W. Adorno, *et al.*, *The Authoritarian Personality* (New York: Harpers, 1950).

26. Pitirim A. Sorokin, *Fads and Foibles in Modern Sociology and Related Sciences* (Chicago: Henry Regnery, 1956).

27. *Ibid.*, 174.

28. Edw. A. Suchman, "The Principles of Research Design," in J. T. Doby, ed., *An Introduction to Social Research* (Harrisburg: The Stackpole Company, 1954), 253.

29. S. A. Stouffer, "Some Observations on Study Design," *American Journal of Sociology*, LV (January, 1950), 355-61.

30. S. A. Chapin, *Experimental Designs in Sociological Research* (New York: Harper, 1947).

31. P. F. Lazarsfeld, B. Berelson, H. Gaudet, *The People's Choice* (New York: Columbia University Press, 1948); B. Berelson, P. F. Lazarsfeld, Wm. N. McPhee, *Voting* (University of Chicago, 1954).

32. R. L. Ackoff, *The Design of Social Research* (University of Chicago Press, 1953).

33. For a cross-section of small group researches, see D. Cartwright and A. Zander, eds., *Group Dynamics: Research and Theory* (Evanston: Row, Peterson and Co., 1953); *American Sociological Review*, XIX (December, 1954); for a bibliography which surveys the field, see F. L. Strodbeck and A. P. Hare, "Bibliography of Small Group Research, 1900-1953," *Sociometry*, XVII (May, 1954), 107-78.

34. J. L. Moreno, *Who Shall Survive?* rev. ed. (Beacon, N. Y.: Beacon House, Inc., 1953).

35. R. F. Bales, *Interaction Process Analysis* (Cambridge, Mass: Addison-Wesley 1950).

36. T. Parsons, R. F . Bales, E. A. Shils, *Working Papers in the Theory of Action* (Glencoe: The Free Press, 1953).

37. T. M. Mills, "Power Relations in Three-Person Groups," in Cartwright and Zander, *op. cit.*, 428-42; F. L. Strodtbeck, "The Family as a Three Person Group," *American Sociological Review*, XIX (February, 1954), 23-9.

38. R. Tagiuri, "Relational Analysis: An Extension of Sociometric Method Upon Social Perception," *Sociometry*, XV (February-May, 1952), 91-104.

39. See G. Lindzey and E. F. Borgatta, "Sociometric Measurement," in G. Lindzey, ed., *Handbook of Social Psychology*, vol. 1 (Cambridge, Mass: Addison-Wesley Publishing Co., 1954), 405-48.

40. For a general description of this method, see C. M. Arensberg, "The Community-Study Method," *American Journal of Sociology*, LX (September, 1954), 109-24.

41. Wm. L. Warner, M. Meeker, K. Eells, *Social Class in America* (Chicago: Science Research Associates, 1949).

42. For a detailed criticism of the methods of the Warner school, see R. Kornhauser, "Warner's Approach to Social Stratification," in R. Bendix and S. M. Lipset, *Class, Status and Power* (Glencoe: The Free Press, 1953), 224-55.

43. *Elmtown's Youth* (New York: John Wiley, 1949).

44. Alex Inkeles and Peter Rossi, "National Comparisons of Occupational Prestige," *American Journal of Sociology*, LXI (January, 1956), 329-39.

45. H. Hyman, *Survey Design and Analysis: Principles, Cases and Procedures* (Glencoe: The Free Press, 1955).

46. M. Benney and E. C. Hughes, "Of Sociology and the Interview," *American Journal of Sociology*, LXII (September, 1956), 137.

47. R. K. Merton, M. Fiske, P. L. Kendall, *The Focused Interview: A Manual of Problems and Procedures* (Glencoe: The Free Press, 1956).

48. H. Hyman, *et al., Interviewing in Social Research* (Chicago: University of Chicago Press, 1954).

49. S. Stouffer, *et al., Measurement and Prediction* (Princeton: Princeton University Press, 1950); P. F. Lazarsfeld, ed., *Mathematical Thinking in the Social Sciences* (Glencoe: The Free Press, 1954).

50. J. W. Riley Jr., M. W. Riley, J. Toby, *Sociological Studies in Scale Analysis: Applications, Theory, Procedures* (New Brunswick: Rutgers University Press, 1954).

CRIMINOLOGY

Samuel Koenig
Brooklyn College

The study of crime has gradually evolved from speculative thought to a science of criminal behavior. Since behavior violating the rules of society and punishable by it has undoubtedly existed from the dawn of organized human group life, it has always been the subject of some attention in all societies. It was not, however, until the rise of large heterogeneous societies with complex social systems that disregard of the social codes by their members became frequent enough to be considered in some of these societies as a problem to which thought had to be given.

Interpretations of the nature of crime and the criminal varied with the prevailing *Weltanschauung,* or outlook upon life, as well as with the state of knowledge in a particular society. Since a strictly empirical approach to an understanding of phenomena, particularly of social phenomena, is of a relatively recent origin, views regarding the nature of the criminal, up to recent years, have been based upon speculation which was sometimes weird and mystical. It was only with the advance of knowledge based upon systematic investigation of social phenomena that criminal behavior began to be investigated empirically.

BIOLOGICAL THEORIES OF CRIMINAL BEHAVIOR

Since it was in the study of physical and natural phenomena that truly scientific advances were first made, early attempts at getting an understanding of the causes of criminality were influenced by biological doctrines and resulted in theories maintaining that the source of criminal behavior is to be found primarily in the physical makeup of individuals. Early criminologists were impressed by the possibilities of connecting the discoveries in biology and anthropology with criminal behavior, and, hence, actually brought forth what seemed to them incontrovertible proof of the biological nature of criminality.

Thus, under the impact of the theories of Darwin, Mendel, and others, on the one hand, and of the accounts of anthropologists, especially those of Herbert Spencer, on the other, there appeared, in the last quarter of the past century, the so-called Positive School of Criminology, of which the Italian physician Cesare Lombroso was the chief exponent. Employing empirical, or "positivistic," methods, which have susequently been shown to suffer from serious flaws and to be based on *a priori* concepts, Lombroso, in his *L'Uomo Delinquente*, published in 1890, found that the criminal was a born type, having inherited criminal traits, and that he was characterized by distinct anomalies, or stigmata, of body and mind, sometimes showing a reversion (atavism) to what were presumably characteristics of primitive man. Lombroso's theory gained wide acceptance at the time and, for a while, was thought to be the answer to the age-old question of who the criminal was. It could not, however, stand up for long against close scrutiny and was gradually abandoned or radically modified by those who did not give it up entirely. Perhaps the first to challenge it was the English statistician Charles Goring. Through a painstaking statistical study, involving 3,000 convicts and noncriminal control groups, Goring proved the fallaciousness of the claim of the existence of a criminal type.

While the positivist position with regard to the cause of criminality has been entirely discredited in the United States, some European criminologists, particularly on the continent, are still impressed by the theory. In the United States an attempt at a biological interpretation of criminality has been made in the 1930's by the late Harvard anthropologist E. A. Hooton in his book *Crime and the Man*. Subjecting some 14,000 prisoners and inmates of mental institutions to minute measurements and comparing them with control groups consisting of normal and insane non-criminals, Hooton arrived at the conclusion that criminals, while not possessing physical stigmata such as described by Lombroso, are biologically inferior to non-criminals and that different racial groups tend to engage in certain types of crimes. Hooton's study has encountered widespread criticism. Students in the field have pointed to his failure to match correctly the sample of criminals and non-criminal control groups, his disregard of sociological and psychological factors, and the making of unwarranted inferences regarding behavior from physical characteristics.

Hence, few criminologists were impressed with the evidence, most of them considering the study as far from offering proof of a biological determination of criminal behavior.

As intimated above, the theory that criminality is largely biologically determined and has an hereditary basis has not been discarded entirely by European criminologists. Some of the exponents of this theory maintain a moderate view. Thus, the Austrian criminologist Adolf Lenz maintains that one inherits a predisposition to maladjustment, including criminal behavior, unless the environment in which the individual finds himself is extremely favorable, in which case he might escape his destiny, so to speak. Similarly, Louis Vervaeck, a Belgian criminologist, contends that criminals, at least the hardened or habitual offenders, suffer from constitutional defects, largely transmitted through heredity, which prevent them from adjusting properly to life. It is, however, chiefly the Italian criminologists who still cling to the Lombrosian theory. Eli D. Monachesi points out that Italian criminologists have hardly modified the proposition laid down originally by Lombroso. Perhaps, he remarks, this may be accounted for by the fact that most of the Italian criminologists are medical men.[1]

PSYCHOLOGICAL THEORIES

With the decline of Lombroso's morphological theory of criminality, there appeared attempts at proving the belief that criminal behavior was due primarily to inherited mental defects, among which low intelligence, or feeble-mindedness, was considered to be the most important. Already in the 1880's the Italian criminologist Raffaele Garofalo, while accepting Lombroso's claims, maintained that the criminal is psychologically or morally deficient. Goring, although disproving Lombroso's theory, arrived at the conclusion, which was hardly based on reliable sources, that "weak-mindedness" was the primary cause of criminality.

A number of other psychologists came up with similar theories. In the United States Henry H. Goddard became the chief exponent of the school, flourishing in the first two decades of this century, maintaining that mental deficiency was underlying as a main cause of delinquent and criminal behavior. The contentions of Goddard and similar ones by other psychologists, found little support in subsequent studies on the mental capacities of prisoners. The chief blow to the contention that criminals tend to have inferior intelligence was dealt by the psychologist Carl Murchison. In his study,[2] involving the administering of the Alpha Test, given to American soldiers during World War I, to criminals in prisons in several states, he found that the criminals ranked higher than soldiers in the draft army, i.e., that criminals included a larger proportion of individuals of high intelligence than civilians. Although some flaws have been discovered in Murchison's study, the conclusion has been found to be on the whole valid. Other studies confirmed these conclusions. Few, if any, American criminologists at present consider intelligence as a factor of importance in precipitating crime.

Various attempts have been made also at connecting neuroses, psychoses, and psychopathy with criminality in a cause-and-effect relationship. Numerous studies, involving psychiatric tests of all kinds and comparisons of criminals and noncriminals, have sought to demonstrate that one or another type of mental illness or emotional disturbance was underlying criminal behavior. However, the conclusions of nearly all of these studies have been questioned or found to be entirely lacking in validity. Most of these studies have been found to suffer from questionable diagnoses, subjective interpretations, unwarranted inferences, and, in general, conclusions which lend themselves to different, sometimes opposite, interpretations. These shortcomings are thought to be due to the lack of a precise definition or agreement among psychologists and psychiatrists as to the origin, symptoms, classification, and effects of mental illness. Consequently, the findings of different investigators as to the prevalence of mental illness among criminals vary enormously. Moreover, the existence of a psychosis in the case of a criminal does not *ipso facto* mean that it was the psychosis that is responsible for the criminal behavior.

Even less acceptable to the majority of criminologists has been the conclusion of some psychiatrists that psychopathy played a major role in the etiology of criminality. The conclusion of these psychiatrists have been found by students to be entirely unreliable as psychopathy is a disorder that is ill-defined. There is a lack of agreement as to the origin and symptoms of this illness as well as to the methods of diagnosis. Criminality, as E. H. Sutherland points out, is frequently considered by these psychiatrists to be proof of the existence of a psychopathic state; then psychopathy is looked upon as the cause of criminality, which represents reasoning in a circle.[3]

Some psychiatrists and psychoanalysts have advanced a theory maintaining that the cause of criminal and delinquent behavior is to be found in emotional disturbances, originating in difficult family situations, which prevent an individual from seeking ego-satisfaction through approved channels, or result in his failure to tame successfully his id, i.e., his instinctual impulses. These claims, if considered as sole explanations of the origin of criminality, namely, if factors of the social environment are not taken into consideration, have also been rejected overwhelmingly by criminologists. The grounds for their rejecting them are many, but the chief ones are the lack of agreement among psychiatrists and psychoanalysts as to the interpretation of data and the difficulty of studying empirically the variables involved and of proving the contentions. Moreover, psychiatrists and psychoanalysts tend to study the unusual, the extreme, or bizarre, cases, most of whom are likely to be mentally or emotionally ill individuals, but who constitute a minute fraction of the total criminal population. Their conclusions, even if true, could therefore hardly be applied to explaining criminal behavior in general, which they purport to do.

Psychiatrists and psychoanalysts have, nevertheless, made basic contributions to our understanding of criminal behavior. This is especially true of those who have recognized the importance of the social environment and included it in their explanations. Oustanding among these are the psychiatrists, William Healy, Franz Alexander and Augusta F. Bronner.[4] Healy and his collaborators found that delinquency was the result of an individual's attempt to seek release from inner tensions and of desires to satisfy such urges as new experience, security, acceptance, recognition, and status. He concluded that delinquency and crime signify an individual's adjustment to life in socially disapproved ways, when prevented from doing so in socially acceptable ways. While finding that criminal behavior has its roots in the inner world of the individual, Healy and others adhering to this theory, maintain that the social environment provides the patterns and examples for such behavior. The factors involved are thus viewed to be both of a psychogenic and sociogenic nature.

The findings of Healy and his collaborators exerted a stimulating influence on criminological research. They not only added considerably to our understanding of the nature of criminal behavior, but called attention to its being a result of a variety of factors rather than of any single one, as implied in the theories discussed above.

The idea that criminal behavior involves a combination of factors and cannot be explained on the basis of any particular one was recognized already by some nineteenth century criminologists. It was not, however, until the second decade of this century that the multiple-factor approach was given substantiation and developed —primarily by sociologists.

THE SOCIOLOGICAL APPPROACH IN CRIMINOLOGY

Socio-Psychological Theories. It may be said that at present the predominant view in criminology is that criminal behavior is a result of a process indistinguishable from that involved in behavior in general. Criminal behavior, like other behavior, is thus considered to be due to learning—the learning of anti-social ways—from others. In other words, criminality, from the sociological point of view, is acquired by an individual from his environment, if that environment contains in it elements conducive to such behavior. By environment here is meant the immediate surroundings, such as family, neighborhood, and friends, and the remoter ones, namely, the community and the culture as a whole. However, only few criminologists of this school of thought limit their explanation to environmental factors alone. Most contend that while the environmental forces are basic, the personality traits of the individual and even his biological make-up play a role. Put differently, it is in the interaction of personality and environment, or in the impact of environment upon personality, that explanations must be sought.

This theory may therefore be referred to as the socio-psychological, and represents a kind of a synthesis of the contentions of sociologists and psychiatrists as well as psychoanalysts. While sociologists have recognized the importance of personality in their attempts to explain criminality, psychiatrists and psychoanalysts, with the exception of extremists, are increasingly taking into consideration the environment and culture in their interpretations of criminal behavior. At present a certain rapprochement among the representatives of the behavioral disciplines is being reached, at least among the moderates, the main difference being one of emphasis.

The view that the social environment and culture are the major factors involved in criminal behavior is also not a recent one. Already the nineteenth century Belgian statistician Adolphe Quetelet and his followers maintained that society itself is the source of crime. And the Italian criminologist Enrico Ferri, although a disciple of Lombroso, in his work, significantly titled *Criminal Sociology* and published in 1896, dwells upon the importance of the social environment, particularly the economic conditions, in producing crime. Two decades later the Dutch criminologist, William A. Bonger, in his *Criminality And Conditions,* propounded the theory that criminal behavior is almost entirely a product of the environment and is specifically caused by the abuses and pressures of the capitalistic system. However, evidence, based upon carefully collected data, showing how the interaction of the social environment and personality results in criminal behavior and the multiplicity of factors involved in it, was not presented until the 1930's.

In the early thirties a number of studies appeared which confirmed ideas only vaguely expressed heretofore and furthered what came to be known as the sociological approach to the phenomenon of crime— an approach which received its greatest development in the United States. These were the ecological studies made by C. R. Shaw and his collaborators as well as by others, which demonstrated the adverse effect of deteriorated neighborhoods upon the behavior of individuals living in them. In some of these studies, Shaw and associates employ the life-history method, designed to bring out the interaction of personality and environment. In England, an important study by Cyril L. Burt, *The Young Delinquent,* in which comparison is made of delinquents and nondelinquents, also disclosed the deleterious effects of bad family and social conditions upon children.

At the same time other highly significant research was done, particularly by Sheldon and Eleanor T. Glueck. Their research, involving comparisons of physical, mental, and emotional traits, family relationships and other environmental factors of delinquents and nondelinquents, resulted not only in further refinements of methods and techniques of study but in highly revealing data on the etiology and nature of delinquency and criminality.

Perhaps the most significant contribution of the Gluecks is the attempt at predicting criminal behavior. Even though their predictive scales await further refinements and validation, it is conceded that their research represents a definite advance in the study of delinquent behavior and its treatment. Aside from the Gluecks, a number of other efforts have been made at discovering personality traits suspected of being related to delinquent and nondelinquent behavior, which shed further light on the problem. Among these, the Minnesota Multiphasic Personality Inventory (MMPI) and the New York State Youth Commission's study are particularly important.[5]

The point of view holding that criminal behavior is a result of the interaction of environment and personality, as already intimated, is perhaps the most widely accepted approach at present. This is very clearly expressed in a formula by W. C. Reckless.[6] Crime, he writes, is a result of

$$\frac{\text{S or Situation.}}{\text{I or Individual}}$$

By "situation" (S) he means primarily the pressures and disorganizing forces in a society, and by "individual" (I) he means either the inherited or acquired personality traits. These may be strengths, such as a strong moral sense, feelings of security, etc., which enable an individual to withstand those pressures or disorganizing forces surrounding him, or they may be weaknesses, such as a weak ego structure, high suggestibility, inadequacy, instability, etc. Whether or not a person becomes a criminal, or anti- social in other ways, will depend on the degree of pressures and strength of demoralizing forces present as well as upon the extent to which the individual is able to offer resistance. "Somewhere in the concatenation of weaknesses and strengths of the individual (the internal components)," writes Reckless, "the impact of the confronting situation, and the inability of the surrounding social order to absorb this impact for the individual, lies the riddle of crime and delinquency causation. The *S* needs an *I* and the *I* an *S*. Those who overemphasize the one to the exclusion of the other are probably myopic. As a matter of fact we do not know what *I* really is without the *S,* and we do not know what the *S* is without the *I.*"[7]

The Concept of Culture Conflict and Social Disorganization as Causes of Crime. A more purely sociological theory is the one maintaining that criminal behavior is a result of culture conflict. By this is meant the conflict in conduct norms, arising out of contact between different value systems, prevalent in most parts of the United States. Clashes in these norms result in conflicting views regarding law and moral standards, and, hence, in attitudes of disregard toward them. Exponents of this theory, however, consider an investigation not only of the conflict situation, but of the individual in whom this conflict of values becomes internalized, as essential to a full understanding of the process leading to criminal behavior.

Another aspect of this situation is the occurrence of a weakening of force of the mores upon members of a society—or social disorganization. The result is confusion, uncertainty, or ambivalence with regard to ethical standards and morality. When coupled with materialistic values, such a state, it is held, has the effect of driving individuals, particularly those who are emotionally unstable, neurotic, or frustrated in meeting their needs, to anti-social or criminal behavior. This view is explained by D. R. Taft, one of its principal exponents, as follows:

Assume "a culture dynamic, complex, materialistic, admiring the successful in a competitive struggle but permitting many to fall short of success. . . . Destroy in such a culture primary group controls which prevent serious departure from approved traditional patterns. Develop in such a culture, through the process of social change, a confusion of tongues in definitions of morality, hypocritical rationalizations as to contrasts between the criminal and the noncriminal, the dangerous and nondangerous. . . . Give prestige and important pattern-setting roles in that society to groups with rather unsocially oriented values which not infrequently are exploitative"—and "there will be considerable conflict, often taking the form of crime."[8]

Although, concludes Taft, such a situation impinges differently upon different individuals, depending upon the personality traits and peculiar circumstances under which they live and function, such a culture is bound to produce a high incidence of crime and delinquency, which is an outgrowth of its inherent character.

Sociologists consider not only the present-day cultural situation of a society with its conflicts and disorganization a source of criminality, but regard certain cultural patterns of the past as significantly affecting the present state. Mabel A. Elliott, among others, has pointed out that the American frontier with its pattern of lawlessness continues to influence powerfully Americans' attitudes towards law and ethical standards.[9] The forces at work in producing criminality in our society are thus conceived of as far from being entirely of a contemporary nature. Neither is the high incidence of crime in America to be attributed primarily to the large numbers of immigrants, as is still popularly believed. Although, owing to the admittedly disorganizing effects upon society of large waves of immigrants who arrived in this country, the crime rate undoubtedly has been adversely affected, the foreign-born have been found to have a comparatively low crime rate. It is only second-generation individuals (those born here of foreign-born parents) who have been found to have a crime rate somewhat higher than natives of native parentage, which is believed to be due to their being particularly subject to culture conflict and to their position of cultural marginality.

The Theory of Differential Association. While, as pointed out above, most criminologists view criminal behavior as a result of a variety and multiplicity of factors, both psychogenic and sociogenic, the search for unitary causes, is going on. Outstanding among the more recent theories propounding a unitary explanation of the etiology of crime is that advanced by Edwin H. Sutherland, known as the "differential-association" theory.

According to this theory, which resembles that of the French criminologist Gabriel Tarde, who held crime to be due to imitation and suggestion, criminal behavior may be explained by the process of learning which is, basically, the same as that leading to a person's becoming, say, a lawyer, doctor, teacher, or banker. Criminal behavior, maintains Sutherland, is acquired by an individual through association with criminals. A person does not invent criminal behavior, but learns it from others. The likelihood that an individual will become a criminal is greatest when his contact with criminal elements is intimate and direct. Indirect influences, such as movies or newspapers, are relatively unimportant in producing criminal behavior. A person becomes a criminal "because of an excess of definitions favorable to violation of law over definitions unfavorable to violation of law,"[10] Whether an individual living among criminal elements becomes a criminal depends upon the "frequency, duration, priority, and intensity" of contact. In other words, whether a person will engage in criminal activities or not will depend upon which pattern, the criminal or anti-criminal, both of which are present, is stronger, or exerts greater pressure.

Sutherland discounts entirely the theories deriving criminal behavior from frustrations, drives, values, status seeking, etc., on the ground that these explain equally as well law-abiding and criminal behavior. What does explain criminal behavior, states Sutherland, is the presence of criminal elements in an environment which an individual has been forced, so to speak, to associate with. By way of elucidation Sutherland gives the following example: If a boy who is by nature sociable and active and, at the same time, lives in a deteriorated neighborhood with a high crime and delinquency rate, he is most likely to learn, through contact, delinquent behavior from delinquent boys in the area and later to acquire criminal ways. The unsociable, introverted boy, however, may not be brought into contact with them and thus avoid becoming a delinquent. Under different conditions e.g., in a neighborhood relatively free of delinquency, the sociable, active youngster may join, say, a scout troop and thus avoid engaging in delinquent activities. Thus, he concludes, an individual's "associations are determined in a general context of social organization." [11]

While believed to possess a great deal of plausibility, Sutherland's theory has also encountered considerable criticism. The criticism is based chiefly on the claim that, like Tarde's imitation theory, it fails to explain satisfactorily why one "chooses" to associate with either criminal or law-abiding elements. This may be due to the fact that the process by which individuals learn in general is as yet not clear. It is also being pointed out that Sutherland relegates the psychological and biological factors, considered to be very significant, to relative unimportance, thus offering at best only a partial explanation of why persons become criminals.

White Collar Criminality. A significant contribution to criminological thought in recent years, is the concept of white-collar criminality introduced by Sutherland in 1940.[12] Although others, notably Albert Morris, in his *Criminology,* have called attention to this form of crime, it was Sutherland who elaborated and refined the concept.[13] According to Sutherland, white-collar crime is the commission of criminal acts by persons in business, industry, and the professions in the course of transacting their business or practicing their professions. These are usually respected people who because of class bias, leniency shown to upper-class people in the courts, power, and the ineffectiveness of the law, rarely are committed to prisons and, hence, avoid being considered criminals. It is only the lower-class people, engaging in conventional and comparatively trivial crimes, who are caught, convicted, and imprisoned. Yet the damage inflicted by white-collar criminals is infinitely greater than that done by the lower-class offenders. Moreover, he holds, white-collar criminality is not only costly in monetary terms, but in a social sense. It affects adversely general morality in that it increases feelings of distrust, cynicism, and is thus productive of a state of social disorganization, whereas the effect of other types of crime on social institutions is relatively small.

An important conclusion Sutherland arrives at from his research on the phenomenon of white-collar crime is that the picture we have formed of the contemporary criminal is necessarily a distorted one. Our knowledge of the criminal is based on individuals who are in prison, and these are hardly typical of the vast and very important number of criminals who hardly ever get there. In other words, the picture is derived from a biased sample and is therefore incorrect. A consideration of white-collar crime, he asserts, will show that the theories connecting crime primarily with the lower classes, with poverty, low intelligence, psychopathy, etc., are erroneous, and, hence, that the remedies suggested are doomed to be ineffective.

Sutherland's concept of the white-collar criminal has been criticized by some criminologists on the ground that it misuses the term criminal. "Criminal," say these criminologists, is a legal term and should be applied only to a person who has been found by a court guilty of a crime and not to unproved cases, not to individuals engaging in unethical practices, as Sutherland seems to imply, even though they may be considered as highly harmful to society and considered as criminals by many people. Sutherland and his followers insist, however, that to make conviction by a court the only criterion of criminality might be acceptable *legally* but certainly not *sociologically,* and that the objections raised are largely of a semantic nature.

Another phenomenon considered of great significance in understanding the contemporary problem of crime is the fact that it is increasingly carried on in a highly organized form and in an efficient and a business-like manner. Indeed, it often cannot be differentiated from ordinary, legitimate business and not infrequently merges with it. This was graphically brought out in the investigations of the Kefauver Crime Investigating Committee. Perhaps the most significant fact disclosed by the Committee is the extent of involvement of big business, respected business men, and high ranking municipal and state officials.

The fact that crime in contemporary society tends to be organized has been brought out in a number of studies years before the investigations of the Kefauver Committee. Organized crime, as H. E. Barnes and N. K. Teeters point out, marks a real revolution in criminal activity in the United States. These two authors find that twentieth century crime in America passed through three distinct phases, namely: (1) the period prior to World War I, during which crime tended to be of the traditional type, i.e., robbery, burglary, theft, forgery, etc.; (2) "big crime," principally in the form of racketeering, which flourished between World Wars I and II; and (3) the tremendous growth of "big crime", particularly in the form of gambling.[14]

TREATMENT OF THE CRIMINAL

The almost universally shared view among criminologists at present is that the criminal is a product—a product of both the forces within the individuals as well as of those of the external world, the environment. In other words, the criminal as such is not by his own making, because he choses to be anti-social, or of his own free will. Consequently, criminal behavior is looked upon as being the result of the failure of society to meet properly the needs of certain individuals, who, therefore, adopt disapproved ways of satisfying them. Society, according to this view, allows the existence of conditions which are conducive to criminal behavior—especially on the part of those who by virtue of their personality traits readily succumb to those conditions. Society is thus considered to a very large extent, responsible for the prevalence of criminality. At the same time, it is being more and more realized that one cannot speak of criminal behavior, or criminals, in general, but rather of different kinds of crime and different kinds of criminals.

This point of view forces a departure from the conventional belief that criminals alone are responsible for being what they are and that the duty of the community is to impose punishment upon them so that they will learn their lesson and become law-abiding. It also implies that while the criminal, obviously, must be held accountable, the community must assume the responsibility of creating conditions under which the risk for individuals' becoming criminals will be reduced. It, furthermore, means that conventional punishment, having proved to be ineffective, rehabilitation, the use of positive, scientifically based, methods must be employed to deal effectively with prisoners. Finally, since it has become quite apparent that individuals become criminals for different reasons and that criminals vary as much among themselves as ordinary individuals, treatment must be individualized.

These views are incorporated in what came to be known as the New Penology, which is gradually being adopted, in various degrees, by the prison systems throughout the civilized world. The New Penology requires a well-equipped plant, an enlightened, efficient, and competent administration, and a trained staff which includes, aside from regular physicians, psychologists, psychiatrists, and social workers. Rehabilitative work is undertaken by following scientifically discovered facts regarding human behavior in general and particularly the kind called criminal. Progress along these lines, in the United States, admittedly, has been most pronounced in the federal prison system, while most of the state and municipal institutions are sadly lagging behind.

Despite the fact that the new penal philosophy is far from having been universally adopted, and that, wherever it has found a place, many of its principles have not been put into practice, advances are taking place. Great strides have been made in the system of classifying criminals. This makes possible the individualization of treatment, which, as pointed out above, is essential to the effective rehabilitation of criminals. Through measures such as education, vocational training, recreation, and medical and psychiatric treatment, including group therapy, more and more prisoners are helped to start a law-abiding existence. Probation as a means of treatment is becoming more and more accepted. Probation has been found to be one of the most effective ways of preventing individuals from further pursuing their criminal ways. As one authority states, probation "has accomplished more in restoring American offenders to a law-abiding status than all the other types of penal treatment combined."[15]

Prevention of crime has, of course, been recognized as the goal to strive for. But prevention presents vastly greater difficulties of achievement than rehabilitation or reform, for it presupposes that the symptoms are definitely known and readily detectable, which is still far from having been attained. Nevertheless, some advances have been made here, primarily on the juvenile level. Some of the attempts made at prediction have been mentioned above; others are being made, and the results are encouraging. Since certain social and cultural conditions have been found to be productive of criminal behavior, it is obvious that these must be dealt with, if effective measures are to be taken in combatting it. Also in this direction some progress may be noted.

Crime and delinquency, particularly certain aspects of it, are being recognized more and more as an international, rather than a local, problem, and, hence, as necessitating a concerted attack on the part of all nations. Knowledge regarding crime and delinquency in its multifarious forms and expressions, as well as effective ways of dealing with the problem, it is believed, can be best obtained through cooperative studies and surveys of situations in various parts of the world and through an interchange of findings among students in different countries. Consequently, in recent years, the problem of crime has become one of the concerns of the United Nations. This concern expressed itself in the formation of a number of organizations entrusted with the task of studying, on a comparative basis, the various aspects of the problem. Among the organizations thus formed may be mentioned the International Association of Penal Law, the International Society of Criminology, the International Penal and Penitentiary Commission, and the Howard League of Penal Reform.

More specifically, the above-named organizations aim at establishing international penal policies, at devising effective means of crime prevention, at agreement on a humanitarian treatment of prisoners, at sharing among nations of one another's experience in dealing with crime problems. Among the other goals of these organizations are research on the problems of crime, the results of which are made available to all. This is sought by means of international conferences and the issuing of journals and other publications.

Thus, while our understanding of the whole complex of criminal behavior is still very incomplete and the effective control of it still far from attainment, we are coming into the possession of an ever greater knowledge and are acquiring ever better techniques and ways of dealing with one of the major problems of our times.

SELECTED BIBLIOGRAPHY

Harry E. Barnes, *The Story of Punishment* (Boston:Stratford Co., 1930). An Account of punishment throughout the ages.

Walter Bromberg, *Crime and the Mind* (Philadelphia: J. B. Lippincott Co., 1948). A sociologically oriented psychiatrist investigates the emotional factors in crime.

Caryl Chessman, *Cell 2455: Death Row* (New York: Prentice-Hall, 1954). An extremely interesting autobiographical account of a convict fighting for his life from death row in San Quentin prison.

Sheldon Glueck, & Eleanor T., *Delinquents in the Making: Paths to Prevention* (New York: Harper, 1952). A statistical study, comparing the traits and social backgrounds of 500 delinquent with 500 nondelinquent boys.

Estes Kefauver, *Crime in America* (Garden City: Doubleday, 1951). Report of the Senate Crime Investigation Committee.

Lewis E. Lawes, *Twenty Thousand Years in Sing Sing* (New York: Long and Smith, 1932). The late warden of Sing Sing Prison gives enlightening account of his experience with prisoners.

Morris Ploscowe, *Crime and Criminal Law* (New York: Collier, 1939). A discussion of the development and function of criminal law.

Otto Pollack, *The Criminality of Women* (Philadelphia: University of Pennsylvania Press, 1950). A study of the involvement of women in crime; explodes the idea that women are less criminal than men.

Roscoe Pound, *Criminal Justice in America* (Cambridge: Harvard University Press, 1945). A penetrating analysis of criminal justice by the eminent Harvard jurist.

Kenyon D. Scudder, *Prisoners are People* (Garden City: Doubleday, 1952). An account of the methods used in a minimum security prison.

Clifford R. Shaw, H. D. McKay, & H. B. Hanson, *Brothers in Crime* (University of Chicago Press,1938). The story of five Brothers, tracing their behavior from juvenile delinquency to adult crime.

Bruce Smith, *Police Systems in the United States* (New York: Harper, 1949). An authoritative account of the workings of the police system and its problems.

Edwin H. Sutherland, *White Collar Crime* (New York: The Dryden Press, 1949). A study of criminal activities among large industrial and commercial establishments in the United States.

Clyde B. Vedder, Samuel Koenig, & Robert E. Clark, Eds., *Criminology: A Book of Readings* (New York: The Dryden Press, 1953). A comprehensive collection of articles by various authorities on the different aspects of crime.

Pauline V. Young, *Social Treatment in Probation and Delinquency* (New York: McGraw-Hill, 1952). An analysis, with case studies, of the various aspects and problems of probation.

Samuel Koenig, who received his Ph.D. degree from Yale University, is Associate Professor of Sociology and Anthropology at Brooklyn College of the City of New York; did extensive research on ethnic groups in Connecticut, resulting in a number of publications; in 1950-51 he made a study of the emerging culture patterns in Israel, on a grant from the Social Science Research Council, the findings having appeared in a series of articles in learned periodicals. Served as Research Associate on the Committee for the Study of Recent Immigration from Europe, (1944-46), as a member of the Editorial Board of the *Slavonic Encyclopedia* (1947-48), and as Book Review Editor of *Social Problems* (1953-56). Is the author, co-author, or co-editor of a number of books; *Immigrant Settlements in Connecticut, Studies in the Science of Society, Jews in a Gentile World, One America, The Refugees Are Now Americans, Criminology: A Book of Readings,* and *Sociology: A Book of Readings;* his most recent book is *Man and Society: The Basic Teachings of Sociology* (1957).

NOTES

1. "Trends in Criminological Research in Italy," *American Sociological Review,* I (1936) , 398-404.

2. Carl Murchison, *Criminal Intelligence* (Worcester, Mass.: Clark University, 1926).

3. E. H. Sutherland, Revised by R. D. Cressey, *Principles of Criminology* (Philadelphia: J. B. Lippincott, 1955) , 1935.

4. See particularly: William Healy & A. F. Bronner, *New Light on Delinquency and Its Treatment* (New Haven: Yale University Press, 1936); Franz Alexander & William Healy, *Roots of Crime* (New York: A. A. Knopf, 1935).

5. Cf. S. H. Hathaway & E. D. Monachesi, *Analyzing and Predicting Juvenile Delinquency with the MMPI* (Minneapolis: University of Minnesota Press, 1935); *Reducing Juvenile Delinquency* (Albany, 1952).

6. W. C. Reckless, *The Crime Problem* (New York: Appleton-Century-Crofts, 1955), 79.

7. *Ibid.,* 80.

8. D. R. Taft *Criminology* (New York: The Macmillan Co., 1956), 341-342.

9. Mabel A. Elliott, *Crime in Modern Society* (New York: Harper, 1952), 259ff.

10. Sutherland, *op. cit.,* 78.

11. *Ibid.,* 79.

12. "White-Collar Criminality," *American Sociological Review,* V (February, 1940) 1-12.

13. Cf. his *White Collar Crime* (New York: The Dryden Press, 1949).

14. Harry E. Barnes & N. K. Teeters, *New Horizons in Criminology* (New York: Prentice-Hall, 1951), 4.

15. M. A. Elliott, *op. cit.,* 809.

RACE AND INTERGROUP RELATIONS

H. H. Smythe
Brooklyn College

Intergroup relations is a part of the overall field of human relations and human behavior,[1] but the scope of this paper is concerned mainly with those relationships growing out of functional association of what are called and understood as minority peoples and dominant groups, although reference is made here also to group relations in general; race is not used here in its purely scientific anthropological sense but in its more realistic implications referring to those thought to be different in some physical, cultural, religious or other aspect, hence the meaning implied here is rather a sociological conceptualization of race as it is used in the modern world. The significance of these relationships, long studied in sociology, has taken on new dimensions of importance since the end of the Second World War,[2] and currently no other problem, in one way or another, seems so important as that of intergroup relations for sociologists, psychologists, political scientists, and practitioners in the field of race relations. The validity of this belief is attested by the numerous and varied types of research being continually projected and carried on.[3]

RESEARCH

An analysis of such journals as the *American Sociological Review, Sociology and Social Research, American Journal of Sociology, Phylon, Social Forces, Journal of Social Issues, Journal of Human Relations, Journal of Educational Sociology, Journal of Negro Education Sociological Abstracts* and others up through 1956 and a sampling of books published in recent years indicate some idea of the range and kinds of research now underway in intergroup relations. The Negro is still the most widely studied group,[4] and attention is heavily concentrated around problems related to desegregation and his integration into the overall society. The Japanese[5] have begun to receive

184

wider treatment, while increasing attention is being given to research concerned with Puerto Ricans, Mexicans, other Spanish-speaking groups, refugees, and Indians. Other minorities, such as Chinese, Jews, and Filipinos, have not been neglected but the work being done on them is more limited in extent and different in nature from that for the aforementioned groups.[6] Aside from domestic minorities, studies are being made of peoples abroad in terms of problems arising from intergroup relationships, of the Eta and Korean in Japan, the Yemenite and North African Jews in Israel, groups in Mexico, selected groups in Africa, the South African apartheid problem, and social change in Egypt, India, Greece, Lebanon, and other areas.[7]

Social distance testing continues to occupy a prominent place[8] with the Bogardus scale and variations of it still being the most popular measuring tool. Some indication of how world developments have intruded here is to be found in the increasing number of studies being made of groups abroad such as Arab-Jew, and groups in Israel, Mexico, Japan, among others. Likewise, interest in attitudes continues to hold attention with Negro-white studies being predominant. An increasing trend here also is the attempt to connect attitudes with results from the field of perception research. Work is also being done on various aspects of human relations in general, integration, intercultural education, and analyses of labor relations and discriminatory policies and practices within unions.[9]

A noticeable shift has taken place in the field of racial research. In the past major effort was focused on studies combatting racist doctrine and to point out the many errors in both methodology and interpretation, all invalidating attempts to establish groups on a biologically distant, fixed, unchangeable hierarchy resting on "innate intelligence." Following the accumulation of a considerable body of data revealing the impossibility of demonstrating differences on a racial basis, that the evidence on etiology is too meager to be conclusive, and the recognition of the significant role of environmental factors, interest here has declined and studies of "race" per se are almost nonexistent. Rather, emphasis has turned to an analysis of prejudice[10] and its ramifications with students concentrating on stereotypes. the reduction of tension, influence of prejudice on personality and its role in discriminatory and segregatory practices.[11]

Perhaps because of difficulty inherent in collecting data work in the field of intermarriage research is still very limited; few studies have been made or are being made. The few that have been undertaken have tended to refute many of the old beliefs long held concerning cross-group marital configurations, especially as regards socio-economic levels of mating and family action patterns.[12]

Under the impact of social changes emanating from the aftermath of war a noticeable positive change has developed as regards inter-disciplinary research activities in intergroup relations. The vastness of the dimensions of the problem itself forced recognition of the necessity of collaborative effort and currently it is common practice to arrange conferences, hold seminars, conduct periodic meetings in which social scientists other than sociologists, natural scientists, as well as representatives of policy makers discuss up-and-down-the-range of intergroup affairs. It is unfortunate, however, that so far the line in which this cross-disciplinary approach is moving is not in the direction of integration of materials, ideas, and approaches and the segmentation of individual points of view continue along traditional dichotomized paths of one approach versus the other.[13]

It is well understood by sociologists that in the final analysis the test of the validity of their findings lies in the field of action, a trying out of their results in the actuality of ongoing events in intergroup relations. Although the findings of sociologists and other social scientists have had considerable effect upon action in the field of intergroup relations, a considerable block yet remains on this level of operation. The practitioner still finds it difficult generally to discover practical application of some of the conclusions of sociological research, to find real relevance of sociological findings to his daily activties, and he continues to be bewildered by the results of research which are inconclusive or conflicting.[14]

However, the trend here seems to be turning in the right direction and those having the responsibility to effect positive improvement in the action field have found some useful aids from sociologists and other social scientists[15] such as in the use of discussion groups to affect attitudes of individuals, emphasis on the equality of status in bringing diverse groups together to promote understanding, encouragement of intercultural educational practices in the schools at a much lower grade level than previously, the employment of group dynamics and the socio-drama at local levels of operation and in workshops, the utilization of the Rumor Clinic device, the application of human relations techniques in police training, and an increasing awareness on the use and understanding of the concept of the "reference group" in the conduct of intergroup relations work.

One of the most significant recent developments has been the recognition of the role of power as an important and influential factor in the study of minorities and a concept of basic value in the understanding and solution to problems in the intergroup field. Sociologists have traditionally centered their attention on the constant and even features of society more than on the dynamic and irregular aspects, but there are developing indications that point to an increasing recognition of the importance of the power concept as a significant tool in the study of intergroup relations problems and in creating programs for social action. Bierstedt, Lasswell, Hunter, Roucek, Schermerhorn, among others, understanding the implications of the theory of power from the foundations laid by political scientists, have gone ahead from their preliminary research to project the possiblities available here in the use of the concept of power for intergroup relations research.

Sociologists are also now giving more consideration to the implications of personality study for intergroup relations work. Largely confined to psychological investigations previously, the monumental work of Stouffer and his associates on the American soldier opened the way and encouraged further research which has seen steady growth since the publication of Stouffer's study.[17]

The series of United States Supreme Court decisions in 1954 negating the legality of racially separate school systems affected the whole field of race and intergroup relations and opened up a number of research opportunities. Studies have been and are being carried on exploring the processes of desegregation, community structure and stratification, relation between prejudice and discrimination, strategies and tactics in reducing racial tension, evaluation of legislation to eliminate restrictions and friction between groups, educational problems, and so on.[18]

The use of factor analysis and analysis of variance is moving ahead in research of intergroup relations, although most work has and is still being done by psychometrists and workers in psychology and allied fields here. Lazarsfeld and his associates,[19] however, have pointed up avenues for analyses and opportunities for use. The traditional approaches to group relations, such as the racist approach, leader-follower relations, human nature, and national character analysis, animal behavior, and human relations and others continue to be examined and reexamined, but receive less attention than in the past. For students of intergroup relations are ever mindful that in order to attain an approach of inclusiveness and validity one must understand the limitations of historically important concepts and trends and that the elimination of their negative influence is a necessary preliminary step.

In addition to the research pointed out above in more detail a measurable quantity of work is also being carried out that is concerned with relations between labor and employer groups, relations between majority and minority groups, and between political groups. International bodies like UNESCO and other United Nations affiliates, have organized programs for the scientific study of groups and their problems with the view of eliminating friction and tension, and research of lesser dimension continues.[20] The field of intergroup relations is so vast in scope, and so intricate and complex in nature that the studies that must be made are literally never-ending. All of this, of course, aside from helping to create the growth of an intergroup relations profession, gives rise to a considerable number of problems, some new, some old.[21]

Some of these problems and the areas in which further research is needed are how to use mass media in intergroup relations activity; the limitations and validity of the use of knowledge to promote understanding and acceptance; the effectiveness and use of legislation and litigation; the study of reactions of minority groups both internally and externally; how to handle incidents of prejudice and discrimination; interrelationship of the school and community with focus upon intergroup relationships; reanalysis of the use and value of community self-surveys; the role of power and the power structure in effecting social change; the reconciliation of persuasive techniques with democratic processes; questions of status and role, of solidarity and morale; and methods of making research findings available so that they will have direct application to meaningful practice.

In addition, sociologists need to delve more deeply into the use of sociometric techniques and their application for intergroup study; refinement and clarification of concepts; the testing, assessment, and development of theory; leadership in both small and large groups with special emphasis on position and role in group structure; interminority relationships; leaderless groups and situations of intergroup significance; delineation of approaches and conceptions in the study of race and intergroup problems; the assessment of multivariate design and its place in the field of intergroup research and action; the interrelationships of legal structure, power relations, and their relation to economic elements and conditions; interdisciplinary integration of knowledge; personal involvement in intergroup situations; and hypothesis formation and policy formulation. Basic to everything is the tremendous need for the formulation of a comprehensive and adequate theory of intergroup relations and the synthesis and integration of the various approaches used in their study and analysis.

COURSE OFFERINGS

The departments of sociology or combined ones of sociology and anthropology offer a wide range of courses concerned specifically with race and intergroup relations, or offerings which can be related directly to their study. The information here is based upon an examination of courses found in the catalogs of Virginia, Wisconsin, Roosevelt, Harvard, Columbia, Princeton, Indiana, Kansas, Missouri, New Mexico, West Virginia, Fisk, Kentucky, Louisville, Minnesota, Rutgers, Oklahoma, Washington, Maryland, Notre Dame, Michigan State, Ohio State, Northwestern, Alabama, Arizona, Stanford, Southern California, Denver, Florida, Hawaii, Tulane, Georgia, Illinois, Vermont, Chicago, Mississippi, California, Howard, Iowa, American, North Carolina, Atlanta, Georgetown, Yale, Texas, Connecticut, Arkansas, and Catholic universities, as well as the University of California at Los Angeles and Bates, Brooklyn, and South Carolina State colleges.

Although the general courses on race relations and minority groups were offered in most of these institutions, some of them apparently did not feel the importance of race and intergroup relations required a separate course offering in the subject and had none listed. It was significant that such large institutions as Columbia, Harvard, Princeton, Minnesota, Washington, Notre Dame, Denver, Vermont, Chicago, Georgetown, and Yale gave no basic course in either minority groups or race relations. Institutions in the South, such as Florida, Georgia, and Oklahoma likewise neglected to list offerings in these fields; and of the southern institutions examined, on the whole they were found to offer very few courses in any respect that dealt with the general field of intergroup relations.

There is a trend, however, towards interest in peoples in selected parts of the world for a significant number of these institutions offered courses dealing with peoples and conditions in Asia, Africa, and the

Pacific, but the sample here indicated a lessening of interest in the peoples of Europe. Very few had any listing at all on the Middle East; and likewise, almost no attention is being paid to intergroup relations in the Caribbean.[22] Courses on race were insignificant in quantity, but a growing number of schools are focusing on Latin America. A surprisingly large percentage still single out the Negro for specific course treatment or use the Negro as the core of their basic course on minorities or race relations, while a sizeable group is giving courses on the American Indian or Indian in Latin America. A few institutions have set up research centers, as well as added courses for the study of various phases of intergroup relations.

BOOKS

American sociologists in the field of race and intergroup relations are still largely circumscribed in their approach to problems. Attention in courses is still focused largely around questions concerned with minorities in the United States and analyses of processes relating to them. This, however, is due mainly to the lack of wider training and breadth of vision; but more so to the fact that few sociologists in institutions of learning, and especially those handling the work on race and intergroup relations have traveled or studied abroad and observed conditions and peoples first-hand. They, like the majority of Americans, have not yet realized that Asia and Africa are becoming of increasing significance on the world scene, and that the problems of race and intergroup relations are intimately interwoven with the larger issues of nationalism, cultural rejuvenation, and political developments leading toward independence. This myopic tendency has carried over to the textbook and general work field, so that although textbooks and other volumes on race and intergroup relations continue to be written in significant numbers and every year publishers continue to carry new ones or new editions of older listings, the current trend continues to be an emphasis on books dealing largely with the American scene, rather than race and intergroup relations from a world view.[23]

Paul A. F. Walter, Jr., and more recently E. Franklin Frazier have tried to remedy this deficiency for a text with a wider framework and encompassing peoples and group relations outside the confines of the United States;[24] but a textbook that deals with minorities and minority problems in the world in general yet remains to be written. Awareness of this lack, however, is becoming evident and a useful volume to help fill this lacuna developed from the Conference on Race Relations in World Perspective held in Honolulu in 1954, with the publication the following year by the University of Hawaii of *Race Relations in World Perspective,* under the editorship of Andrew W. Lind. The book, however, does not lend itself for use as a text since it is a collection of papers presented at the conference and not an integrated, systematized synthesis of materials; and its companion volume by Melvin Conant, *Race Issues on the World Scene,* published also in 1955, is simply a summary of the discussions and papers that were delivered at the meeting.

The books in general on race and intergroup relations continue to focus around specific groups and their problems in terms of a national or a regional emphasis. However, the movement onto the world scene of formerly subordinate peoples has seen interest awakened in other parts of the world on the part of sociologists and others abroad and they are bringing out studies dealing with intergroup relations, specific minorities, and problems of race relations,[25] all of which provide good source and reference materials and extend the horizons of sociologists and others here in the United States teaching and investigating in race and intergroup relations.

ORGANIZATIONS AND JOURNALS

Although there is no specific society in the United States that is composed solely of sociologists working in the field of race and intergroup relations, there are several national organizations the membership of which is largely made up of sociologists, and, of course, the overall body, the American Sociological Society. It and its regional affiliates, and such nationwide groups as the Society for the Psychological Study of Social Issues and the Society for the Study of Social Problems all whose memberships contain a sizable group of sociologists, give a prominent place on the programs of their annual meetings to race and intergroup relations.

There are a number of organizations, largely localized on a city, state, or regional basis, whose basic membership is made up mainly of practitioners in the field but to which some sociologists belong and take an active part in their affairs. And a sort of parent body of these, the National Association of Intergroup Relations Officials (NAIRO), always has in attendance at its meetings and functioning actively in its work a number of sociologists whose work is either directly or indirectly related to race and intergroup matters. A world group, the International Society for the Scientific Study of Race Relations, with headquarters offices at Boston University and Howard University in Washington, D. C., was organized in 1955. The major organizations just mentioned, except the international body at this writing, all publish some kind of journal which is issued at regular intervals. These and the other professional sociological periodicals (see page 184 this chapter for listings) in almost every issue carry some articles growing out of research being done in the field of race relations, intergroup problems, and allied areas.

TRAINING AND EMPLOYMENT

Sociologists who work in the race and intergroup field are still trained basically as professional sociologists: they usually major in sociology as undergraduates but begin to give a greater emphasis to work on the graduate level that prepares them to become more specialized in this area of study and research.[26] As yet in the United States there is no institution that has organized a specific program as a part of its fundamental curriculum to train a sociologist purely as a specialist in race and intergroup relations and give a degree in this definite area of study. However, two institutions, Tulane University and Springfield College in Massachusetts, have special programs on the graduate level in the field of human relations that are oriented heavily towards the field of race and intergroup relations. It is not unusual for some students interested in this work to emphasize sociology on either the undergraduate or graduate level, then enter the field of social work and take training leading to specialization in the intergroup field.

Generally, those planning to make this area of activity either a major or minor part of their work-career continue to concentrate on courses dealing with minority problems, race relations, human relations, study of race, group analysis, and take some work in other social sciences, especially psychology and anthropology. As part of their informal training they may either voluntarily contribute their services or work part-time with some agency concerned with minorities or

race relations activity to get some practical experience. Upon graduation most individuals continue to carry on their work in race and
intergroup relations usually in teaching or research as a member of
some college or university faculty. However, a growing number of
sociologists with a background of training in race and intergroup
relations is going into nonacademic jobs with either public or private
agencies.

The agencies concerned with race and intergroup relations are far
too numerous to mention in a chapter of this kind, but almost every
minority group has one or more representative bodies in the intergroup field.[27] In the United States many of them have and continue
to employ on their staffs, either as full or part-time workers, sociologists, and it is common practice for them to utilize the services of
sociologists and other social scientists on a consulting basis for special
projects, to formulate programs, supervise and direct research, and
to write and publish reports of findings growing out of field investigations. The increasing emphasis that is given to race and intergroup
relations work has developed a trend towards a greater expansion on
this level, so that more and more professional sociologists connected
largely with educational institutions and teaching as a basic occupation are devoting time to such activity.

Each year sees an increasing number of workshops, seminars, and
special institutes centering about race and intergroup relations as a
basic theme. Sociologists not only help to organize, direct, conduct,
and to speak as specialists at these, but some attend them as participating students. Also, some foundations, interested in promoting work
in intergroup relations, set up special study groups to which is sent
a selected number of sociologists, along with representatives from
other social sciences, professions, and action organizations. There is,
too, a growing trend for more sociologists to seek overseas opportunities through Fulbright fellowship grants, other governmental and
private exchange programs to teach, work, study, and carry on research concerned with problems of race and intergroup relations
abroad.[28]

INTERNATIONAL ASPECTS

This increasing interest in going abroad and the encouragement of
overseas visitors to come to America has opened up a new trend in
intergroup relations. This is the idea that foreign relations are more

than military, commercial, and political; rather these are fundamentally human relations. This international concept of human relations is simply an extension deriving from the movement of tourists who in their travels carried on informally interpersonal and intercultural exchange. The postwar period with its increasing tensions on the world front, however, has pushed to the fore the need for an organized approach to human relations on this broader plane of activity, one involving the development of a scientific point of view slanted towards the improvement of human relations on this level. As a consequence research in intergroup relations on an international basis has been moving ahead and the number of projects is gradually expanding.[29]

Institutions and agencies have abetted this ever-widening range of the international concept of intergroup relations and social scientists, students, and individuals from other walks of life have been aided. These bodies are too numerous to mention but a sampling of voluntary agencies engaged in the promotion of international understanding can be mentioned. Foundations that bear the names of Rockefeller, Whitey, Guggenheim, Rhodes, Ford, Carnegie, Rotary International, American Association of University Women, World Student Service Fund, and the Institute of International Education have helped individuals to go abroad as well as come to the United States. The American Friends Service Committee has worked long in the intergroup field abroad, as well as at home, through its activities of work camps, international seminars, friendship centers, peace caravans, and the like. The Brethren Service Commission, National Catholic Welfare Conference, Church World Service, American Jewish Joint Distri'ution Committee, and the National Conference of Christians and Jews and other such organizatons have and continue to sponsor programs directly related to the international concept of intergroup relations; and the work of governmental agencies along similar lines has already been mentioned.

In concluding it should be pointed out that world problems in a larger sense will continue to make the problems of race and intergroup relations ever crucial in the formation and alteration of attitudes of a person, in his integration or lack of it as a personality, and in molding the general trends of his interpersonal and intergroup outlooks; while other aspects of human relations are colored so diffusively by his social and cultural background that study and research in the intergroup relations field are going to remain in the foreground for a long time to come. Sociology, as well as other disciplines, has a responsibility to keep probing into this still unsettled and unstable setting, recognizing that the perplexing problems in the field must be handled adequately; and approached with the knowledge that projects must be formulated on sufficient grounds with some understanding of the implication of results. And we must continue to examine the group setting, realizing that the action occurring is intrinsically related to the functional aspects of intergroup relations.

SELECTED BIBLIOGRAPHY

Gordon W. Allport, *The Nature of Prejudice* (Cambridge, Mass.: Addison-Wesley Publishing Co., 1954). A comprehensive and systematic survey of group prejudice emphasizing social, legal, and economic aspects and the psychological causes of hatred and conflict.

Gordon W. Allport, *The Resolution of Intergroup Tensions* (New York: The National Conference of Christian and Jews, 1952). Evaluation of the author's own research and a summary of that of other social scienticists on various methods of reducing intergroup tension.

F. K. Berrien, *Comments and Cases in Human Relations* (New York: Harper & Brothers, 1951). Deals with conditions and circumstances affecting interpersonal relations, using material from sociology, psychology and anthropology, with case histories of disturbances in interpersonal relations typical of those one might be called upon to meet.

Lloyd Allen Cook and Elaine Forsyth, *Intergroup Education* (New York: McGraw-Hill Book Co., 1954). Concerned with intercultural educational developments.

Community Relations Service, *The Pen is Mightier* (New York: Community Relations Service Publications, American Jewish Committee, 386-4th Avenue, 1954). A comprehensive bibliography of materials on civil and human rights, discrimination and prejudice, relations among church, state, and schools, and on combatting prejudice.

John P. Dean and Alex Rosen, *A Manual of Intergroup Relations* (Chicago: University of Chicago Press, 1955). A working manual of solutions to problems of intergroup communication, staff and leadership training, minority group participation, and suggestions for the use of tactics in negotiating and fostering better intergroup relationships.

E. Franklin Frazier, *Race and Culture Contacts in the Modern World* (New York: Alfred A. Knopf, Inc., 1957). A global treatment of the racial problem in the modern world in terms of the cultured problems created by the expansion overseas of European civilization.

Oscar Handlin, *Race and Nationality in American Life* (Boston: Atlantic, Little, Brown & Co., 1957). A socio-historical analysis of prejudice and hatred as they affect races, religions, and nationalities in the U. S., including treatment of postwar refugees.

Marie Jahoda, Morton Deutsch and Stuart W. Cook, *Research Methods in Social Relations* (New York: The Dryden Press, 1951). A volume on the introductory level of research methods with special reference to prejudice, dealing with basic processes, selected techniques, and the application of methodology to the solution of practical problems in social relations.

Harold D. Lasswell, Charles E. Merriam ,and T. V. Smith, *A Study of Power* (Glencoe, Ill.: The Free Press, 1951). An analysis of power concept in the contemporary world.

M. F. Ashley Montagu, *Man's Most Dangerous Myth: The Fallacy of Race* (New York: Columbia University Press, 1952). An examination of contemporary aspects of "race" theory with a discussion of some remedies for the social disease of racism.

F. S. C. Northrop, *The Taming of the Nations* (New York: The Macmillan Co., 1953). A study discussing the cultural basis of international policy.

Muzafer Sherif and Carolyn W. Sherif, *Groups in Harmony and Tension: An Integration of Studies on Intergroup Relations* (New York: Harper & Brothers, 1953). An analysis combining fundamental features of works on race relations and collective behavior concerned with relations both within and between groups, and discussing influences creating harmony and tension in these settings.

Barbara M. Solomon, *Ancestors and Immigrants* (Cambridge, Mass., Harvard University Press, 1956). A socio-historical analysis of the ideas which produced a rationale for immigration restriction, using New England as a locale of study.

Vanderbilt University School of Law, *Race Relations Law Reporter* (Nashville, Tennessee: published six times a year). Only journal of its kind and dealing with race relations material in all fields where the issue of race or color is presented as having legal consequence.

Jacques Vernant, *Refugee in the Post-War World* (New York: 1953). A treatment of the problems of the displaced persons of World War II.

Hugh H. Smythe, a member of the Sociology-Anthropology Departmental faculty, Brooklyn College in New York, holds degrees in social science, sociology, and anthropology, including a Ph. D. from Northwestern University emphasizing research on Africa and the Caribbean; has had wide experience in research and teaching with both institutions and organizations, both here and abroad. Following World War II army service, he did graduate work at Columbia University's East Asian Institute, then went to Japan under a United States government program serving for two years as a Visiting Professor at Yamaguchi National University, during which time he did considerable research, traveling, writing, and speaking. In a trip around the world, subsequent to his Japanese experience, studied racial, cultural, religious, intergroup, and international relations in Asia and Europe, has published extensively in publications in Europe, Asia, America, and Australia; his activities have brought him election to membership in several scientific honor societies as well as biographic inclusion in *American Men of Science, Who Knows and What,* and *Leaders in American Science.* The holder of several fellowships, scholarships, and grants-in-aid, he is an editor of *Sociological Abstracts, Africa Today,* the *Journal of Human Relations,* and special reporter for *Eastern World* published in London; among other projects, is currently engaged in research of intergroup relations and minority problems on an international basis.

NOTES

1. A source illustrating the overall interrelationships involved in intergroup relations is Muzafer Sherif and Carolyn W. Sherif, *Groups in Harmony and Tension* (New York: Harper, 1953.)

2. Howard K. Smith, Columbia Broadcasting System commentator, broadcasting from London on May 10, 1953, on events in North Africa, emphasized the urgency involved in human relations today when he said: "As the threat of military attack from Communism appears to diminish, it becomes ever clearer that the main threat to Western civilization in our time may be our failure so far to find a new friendly relationship to the underdeveloped two-thirds of the world. The colored peoples' resentment of us grows with the passing months." Quoted in Stewart G. Cole and Mildred Wiese Cole, *Minorities and the American Promise* (New York: Harper, 1954), 256.

3. Some idea of the extent and types of research either now underway or already completed may be obtained from Muzafer Sherif and M. O. Wilson, *Group Relations at the rossroads* (New York: Harper, 1953) and from the annual reports and directors of research in such agencies as the American Jewish Committee, Race Relations Department of the National Council of Churches, the Anti-Defamation League, National Council of Christians and Jews, National Urban League, Catholic Interracial Council, and others.

4. The Ford Foundation through its Fund for the Advancement of Education underwrote and sponsored a series of studies relating especially to desegregation and school integration, among them being, Harry S. Ashmore, *The Negro and the Schools* (Chapel Hill: The University of North Carolina Press, 1954); Robin Williams, editor, *Community as Studies of Educational Integration*; Truman Pierce *et al, Public Education in the South Today,* all published by the University of North Carolina Press during 1954-1955. In addition individual studies such as Hylan Lewis, *Blackways of Kent,* 1955, same publisher; Eli Ginzberg, *The Negro Potential* (New York: Columbia University Press, 1956), and other work of the Conservation of Human Resources Project at Columbia University also studies of the National Planning Association Committee of the South, Selected Studies of Negro Employment in the South (Washington, D. C.: NPA, 1955), and the work done for the NPA by Donald Dewey, *Four Studies of Negro Employment in the Upper South* (Washington, D. C.: NPA, 1953); work has been done also by the Cornell Social Science Research Center, especially noteworthy being the Cornell University Intergroup Relations Study. These are but a few samples of the voluminous materials and numerous studies done and being done on the Negro.

5. Most studies on the Japanese have been reported in journals, for as yet there is no definitive work available of Japanese-Americans; although a useful source is the three-volume study, *Japanese-American Evacuation and Resettlement* (Berkeley: University of California Press, 1946-1954).

6. For the Chinese see Rose Hum Lee, *The City* (Philadelphia: J. B. Lippincott, 1955) and her "The Chinese Abroad," *Phylon,* XVII (3rd quarter, 1956); like the Japanese, there is no definitive work available on the Chinese in the United States, but the journals are beginning to carry reports of developing studies of Chinese life in America; some insights are gained from F. W. Riggs, *Pressures on Congress: A Study of the Repeal of Chinese Exclusion* (New York: King's Crown Press, 1951). C. B. Embry, *America's Concentration Camps: The Facts About our Indian Reservations Today* (New York: McKay, 1956), and Helen B. Shaffer, "Changing Status of American Indians," *Editorial Research Reports* (May 26, 1954), are examples of work on Indians. The material on Puerto Ricans continues to pour forth, examples being Bureau of Applied Social Research, *Puerto Rican Population of New York City* (New York: Columbia University, 1954), series of papers edited by A. J. Jaffe and Clarence Senior, "Migration to the Mainland," *Monthly Labor Review* (December, 1955). For Filipinos, Puerto Ricans, Mexicans and other Spanish-speaking peoples a good example is John H. Burma, *Spanish-Speaking Groups in the United States* (Durham, N. C.: Duke University Press, 1954). For listings on the Jew, see bibliography, *Civil Liberties and Civil Rights in the United States Today* (American Jewish Committee, 1956), 21-22.

7. For studies on groups other than Africans see Vols. XXV-XLI of *Sociology and Social Research, passim* (1950-1956); the material on Africa is voluminous, a few helpful sources serving as examples are: C. Grove Haines, Ed., *Africa Today* (Baltimore: Johns Hopkins University Press, 1955); Calvin W. Stillman, Ed., *Africa in the Modern World* (Chicago: University of Chicago Press, 1955); special issues of *The Annals,* "Contemporary Africa: Trends and Issues," CCXCVIII (March, 1955), and "Africa and the Western World," CCVI (July, 1956).

8. Mozell Hill, "Some Problems of Social Distance in Intergroup Relations," in Muzafer Sherif and M. O. Wilson, *Group Relations at the Crossroads* (New York: Harper & Brothers, 1953). The journals especially *Sociology and Social Research* since 1950, contain pertinent data on the social distance developments.

9. For examples of work being done here consult Sherif and Wilson, *op. cit.,* passim; "Segregation and Integration in College Fraternities," special issue of *Social Problems,* II (January, 1955); the summer yearbook numbers of the *Journal of Negro Education* 1953 to 1956 (Vols. XXII-XXV); and Kenneth B. Clark, *Prejudice and Your Child* (Boston: The Beacon Press, 1955); G. Roheim, "Fairy Tales and Dreams," in *Psychoanalytic Study of the Child* (New York: International University Press, VIII, 1953); Joseph B. Gittler, *Understanding Minority Groups* (New York: John Wiley & Sons, 1956).

10. An outstanding example here is Gordon W. Allport, *The Nature of Prejudice* (Cambridge, Mass.: Addison-Wesley Publishing Co., 1954).

11. Among numerous studies made and still being made the UNESCO series, "The Race Question in Modern Science," "The Race Question in Modern Thought," and "Race and Society" (Paris: UNESCO), containing a number of individually authored monographs is noteworthy; these appeared during the period 1951-1954 and other data will be found in almost all of the journals listed at the beginning of this section.

12. See Joseph Golden, "Patterns of Negro-white Intermarriage," *American Sociological Review,* XIX, 2 (April, 1954).

13. Sherif and Wilson, *op cit.*, and Muzafer Sherif and Carolyn Sherif, *Groups in Harmony and Tension* (New York: Harper, 1953), especially 5-8, "Interdisciplinary Research Activities and Levels of Approach."

14. For a competent analysis here consult Oscar Cohen, "Social Research and Intergroup Relations," *Social Problems,* II, 1 (July, 1954).

15. For a report on this development see John P. Dean and Alex Rosen, *A Manual of Intergroup Relations* (Unversity of Chicago Press, 1955); also Lewis M. Killian, "The Social Scientist's Role in the Preparation of the Florida Desegregation Brief," *Social Problems,* III, 4 (April, 1956).

16. H. D. Lasswell and A. Kaplan, *Power and Society* (New Haven: Yale University Press, 1950); Robert Bierstedt, "An Analysis of Social Power," *American Sociological Review, XV* (December, 1950); Floyd Hunter, *Community Power Structure* (Chapel Hill: University of North Carolina Press, 1953); R. A. Schermerhorn, "Power as A Primary Concept in the Study of Minorities," *Social Forces,* XXV, 1 (October, 1956); Joseph S. Roucek, "Minority-Majority Relations in their Power Aspects," *Phylon,* XVII, 1 (1956); Morris Rosenberg, "Power and Desegregation," *Social Problems,* III, 4 (April, 1956).

17. S. A. Stouffer, E. A. Suchman, L. C. DeVinney, S. A. Star, and R. M. Williams, Jr., *The American Soldier: Adjustment During Army Life. Studies in Social Psychology During World War II,* Vol I (Princeton University Press, 1949); Martin Grossack, "Psychological Research and the Negro," *Phylon,* XVII, 1; James W. Prothro and Charles U. Smith, "The Psychic Cost of Segregation," *Phylon,* XV, 4 (1954); Kenneth B. Clark, *op. cit.*

18. Examples are Guy B. Johnson, "A Sociologist Looks at Racial Desegregation in the South," *Social Forces,* XXXIII, 1 (October, 1954); James M. Nabrit, "Desegregation and Reason," *Phylon* XVII, 3 (1956); special issue of *Social Problems,* Ed. by Kenneth B. Clark, on "Desegregation in the Public Schools," II, 4 (April, 1955); special issue of *The Annals,* "Racial Desegregation and Integration," Ed. by Ira de A. Reid, CCCIV (March, 1956). The series of study projects financed by the Ford Foundation and results published by the University of North Carolina Press, 1954-1955, have been mentioned above. Other studies completed or now in progress may be reviewed through a check of any of the major sociological journals listed above, or through contact with major intergroup relations agencies listed above in footnote No. 3, or through communication with such foundations as Ford, Rockefeller, Carnegie, Whitney and so on. Likewise, another source of information is the department of sociology or anthropology, or the special human or social relations centers in various higher institutions of learning.

19. See Paul F. Lazarsfeld and Morris Rosenberg, *The Language of Social Research* (Glencoe, Ill.: The Free Press, 1955).

20. Everett C. Hughes and Helen M. Hughes, *When Peoples Meet: Racial and Ethnic Frontiers* (Glencoe, Ill.: The Free Press, 1952); Inis L. Claude, Jr., *National Minorities: An International Problem* (Cambridge: Harvard University Press, 1955); *UNESCO Courier,* a monthly bulletin, contains a regular account of its diversified activities, as well as a list of publications of studies it has sponsored or is sponsoring. For work of U. N. agencies, work completed or in progress, see United Nations *Reporter* (August, 1953), and subsequent issues for later releases.

21. Helen E. Amerman, "Is Intergroup Relations a Profession?" *Journal of Human Relations,* IV, 1 (Autumn, 1955); Willard Johnson, "Social Science Research and Intergroup Relations Agencies," *Journal of Human Relations,* V, 1 (Autumn, 1956); Warren G. Bennis, "Some Barriers to Teamwork in Social Research," *Social Probelms,* III, 4 (April, 1956).

22. Although the Caribbean is ignored, major school libraries subscribe to the journal *Social and Economic Studies,* published by the Institute of Social and Economic Research, University College of the West Indies, Jamaica, BWI, and issued quarterly; it contains material pertinent to the study of intergroup relations in that part of the world, among other data.

23. Examples of recent publications are Sister Francis Jerome Woods, *Cultural Values of American Ethnic Groups* (New York: Harper, 1956); Oscar Handlin, *Race and Nationality in American Life* (Boston: Little, Brown, 1957); and Stewart G. Cole and Mildred Wiese Cole, *Minorities and the American Promise* (New York: Harper, 1954).

24. Paul A. F. Walter, Jr., *Race and Culture Relations* (New York: McGraw-Hill Book Co., Inc., 1952); E. Franklin Frazier, *Race and Culture Contacts in the Modern World* (New York: Alfred A. Knopf, 1957).

25. Examples of the type of volumes being published include Anthony H. Richmond, *Color Prejudice in Britain* (London: Routledge & Kegan Paul, 1954, or New York: Grove Press); Virginia Thompson and Richard Adloff, *Minority Problems in Southeast Asia* (Stanford University Press, 1955); Marvin Harris, *Town and Country in Brazil* (New York: Columbia University Press, 1956); and John and Mavix Biesanz, *The People of Panama* (New York: Columbia University Press, 1955).

26. See Calvin F. Schmid and Mildred Giblin, "Needs and Standards in Training Sociologists," *Sociology and Social Research,* XXXIX, 5 (May-June, 1955).

27. Some idea of the multiplicity of such agencies belonging simply to one segment and functioning in the intergroup relations field may be obtained from a check of the affiliated bodies of the National Community Relations Advisory Council with offices in New York City. This group alone comprises more than forty affiliates, of both national and local structure.

28. Information concerning the developing trend here is obtainable from reports of the Institute of International Education, New York City, or the International Exchange of Persons office of Department of State in Washington, D. C.

29. Harold E. Snyder has outlined some of this work on the international level in his *When Peoples Speak to Peoples* (Washington, D.C., 1953), especially 15-21; individual example is seen in the International Social Science Bulletin, published quarterly by the United Nations Educational, Scientific and Cultural Organization, Paris, VIII, 1, on "Cultural Assimiliation and Tensions in a Country of Large-Scale Immigration: Israel;" also *Phylon,* special issue on "Colored Peoples on the World Political Scene," XVI, 4 (1955).

POLITICAL SOCIOLOGY

Feliks Gross
Brooklyn College

AMERICAN AND EUROPEAN SOCIOLOGY OF POLITICS

The sociology of politics had a counterpart in a social reality—the great European mass movements, their problems and their goals. The former grew as a part of general theory of those movements—or supplied the broad field of observation and reflexions for sociologists, historians and philosophers. The American sociology of politics took its impetus, theories and even interest from the European forerunners. Soon however, the focus and the research were influenced by the American political scene, sociological method and interest. Differences between American and European political movements had their impact on the field, and those differences are significant.

The European mass movements were visionary,—while American politics were pragmatic. The former appealed to the masses through broad social images, visions-social myths: the "ideologies and utopias" of sociology students. Visions—even blueprints of perfect socialist or nationalist societies were thrown before the masses and motivated the people. The American political movements had its visionary period in the 18th century—in times of the Revolution—but pragmatism was and is its main quality.

For an American man of politics—the relevant issue is whether an idea works or does not work. Ideas by themselves do not carry this significance as they do in Europe. For a European the ideas and elaborated ideologies have a value for themselves; for some they are even more important than the reality. An American does not solve all the problems at once—according to a vision, a master plan or a blue-print. He tries to meet a situation, to solve—and move step by step to another one. He does not believe in great visions—only in practical solutions.

The theoreticians of European mass movements emphasized the institutions. Improvement of institutions—they believed—will make a better society. The American idealist put his faith rather in the individual—in improvement and change of human relations he saw the hope for mankind. Thus the individual became the key point of social change. Perhaps America is a mass society, but the emphasis is on the individual not on the mass. It is not an accident that the great contribution of American social science is rather in education than in sociology. The former had a revolutionary impact all over the world, it has attacked the very basis—the medieval and renaissance tradition of the school. An idea of a new school was advanced—a school geared rather to the future than to the past, a school which emphasized the individual instead of the status quo system. This approach in school systems did create numerous problems difficult to answer, but it was revolutionary.

The American political theoreticians were of course interested in institutions—but in a different manner than most of the Europeans. The 18th century political philosophers were a kind of political engineer who studied and built a workable mechanism of the constitution, they constructed a system of checks and balances which could harness a dangerous force—political power. They were pragmatic. The Europeans searched for an ideal—a model, a theoretical structure. The American experimenters were interested in institutions which really work.

The differences extend further. A significant area of the sociology of politics is the study of the modes of operation of political movements or collective behavior. Certain European political movements developed techniques of mass operations, such as mass meetings, political parades and such manifestations. Political rituals, symbols, party songs, party uniforms, even architectural devices were used to control and manipulate the masses. Neither the British nor the Americans fancy this type of behavior to the degree found in parts of Europe. Hitler rallied easily fifty or even a hundred thousand listeners, submissive and uninformed at one place for a mass meeting. Mass excitement was produced by horns, trumpets, drums and bands, which flared up in well chosen moments, between the speeches which in turn were also interrupted by rhythmical exclamation or slogans. The American political movements are rather a-ritualistic. The parades were festive in their quality—less political; with rare exceptions they were rather national celebrations and much less party propositions. (Elections belong to such exceptions.)

The pattern of collective behavior could be roughly divided into excitatory and inhibitory. The excitatory mass movements operate through overt patterns such as rituals and mass manifestations, a typical example we may find in the Nazi, Communist, Fascist or Falangist movements. Through physical expressions of the excitatory operation outlets were created for emotional stress, and irrational behavior was formalized, channeled and manipulated. The excitatory type of operation grows in times of crisis, and to a certain degree it could be observed even in well working democracies. The fact remains, that acute crisis produced in Germany—strongly excitatory type of movements, like Nazism—while in similar situation, such movements did not succeed in Great Britain. Neither uniforms nor regimented patterns of behavior had appealed to the British. The American political movements have inhibitory tendencies—certain European movements had the excitatory one. At present, in Western Europe the excitatory type of political behavior is in strong decline, it survived however in the Soviet sphere, and the tendencies did not disappear entirely in other countries either.

European politics was not homogeneous. The British, Scandinavians and the Swiss were more inhibitory in their political behavior, and far less visionary and much more pragmatic than most of the countries of the Continent.

The Americans were rather inhibitory and pragmatic in their political behavior—while many of the European nations were excitatory and visionary. In times of crisis the pragmatic and inhibitory group of nations did not produce Hitler, Franco, Mussolini and although the behavior had a tendency toward the other pattern, it never became as extreme as for instance in Italy or Germany.

The visionary and excitatory groups of Europe with their extensive party organizations, strategies and tactics, ideologies, variety of collective behavior offered a more visible and dramatic field of study than the inhibitory and pragmatic.

American sociology of politics—which took its roots from earlier European studies—inherited its directions from the general political climate of the United States. It is strongly pragmatic and in a sense a practical discipline. In addition it follows the dominant trend of American sociology, the quantitative and the method-centered orientation, with strong bent toward "scientism." The theoretically oriented group plows ahead, with less support and recognition.

QUANTITATIVE METHOD

Polls and Study of Political Attitudes. Interest in public opinion has been for many years traditional in American scholarship as evidenced by the contributions of such individuals as Lowell, Lippmann, Santayana and Bryce. In the second quarter of the 20th century it grew rapidly and new quantitative methods were devised and the research activities grew to the proportions of a major national industry. This type of study corresponded also to the pragmatic, practical even utilitarian attitudes of contemporary American sociology and its quest for recognition as a science. Hypotheses could be tested in a dispassionate way and the computing machines supplied the impressive mechanical regalia, a visual aspect of a true laboratory work. The polling method is the key of this type of quantitative political attitude research. It gained wide popularity, and public opinion columns were carried by great daily papers, like the *New York Herald Tribune,* while *Fortune* Magazine gauged public opinion frequently and carefully.

In a great library of books and articles we can mention only a few examples—selected partially as representative of the field, partially at random. George Gallup's *Guide to Public Opinion* and Paul E. Lazarsfeld's *People's Choice* are representative of this field.[1] Methods were carefully selected and the emphasis was put on sampling. According to Gallup, the crucial issue is the proper selection of a "cross-section." The latter permits the use of only a small sample which accurately represents a large universe of voters. The number of voters interviewed by the American Institute of Public Opinion run from 3000 to 5000 (depending on the problem) with 600 field representatives situated in all parts of the country conducting the sampling. The samples were originally tested with respect to six factors: (1) representation by states, (2) sex, (3) urban and rural areas, (4) age, (5) income, (6) partisanship. Here are some of the typical questions which were asked: "Do you favor a third term for Roosevelt?," "Would you favor a constitutional amendment for any president to run for a third term?"[2] The Literary Digest poll,[3] which forecasted wrongly Landon's victory over Roosevelt, had an impact on methods and in consequence new techniques were introduced. The polls had their appeal to young sociologists and to business.[4]

The quantitative school was enthusiastic about the whole approach. Gallup assured, that thanks to the new methods, public opinion can be ascertained at all times, and heralded a new stage in the development of democratic government.[5]

Impressive as the results of the quantitative school are, the method contains a number of shortcomings. Symbols are taken out of context. Such norms as democracy or socialism mean different things for different persons and in different situations. In poll techniques, they must necessarily be presented out of such context. The questions are often devised "a priori" by the Institute. They are not always spontaneous expression of a dynamic public opinion. Usually, the answers can be given in definite terms— "yes," "no," "I do not know," in extreme colors—red or green, with no alternatives for more subtle explanations. Not every political problem is a clear-cut proposition which lends itself to quantitative study. The students of quantitative approach were open to criticism and continued to improve their methods.[6]

Strong criticism of the whole field came from a minority of political scientists and sociologists. Lindsay Rogers, in his sharp and witty criticism, emphasized the complex quality of political opinion. He quotes Tom Harrison (Mass Observation) and argues that there is a vast difference between what people really "think, say and do." Sections of the public have no information in political matters, and opinion in some matters might be limited solely to certain groups. Even a democratic government at times runs its business without an outspoken public opinion, since most of the people have neither time nor interest to study them. Some of the problems are technical to a point, that only some segments of a nation take an interest in, and make an effort to study them.[7]

The content analysis is another technique in the study of politics. Content analysis can be made quantitatively. But in such an approach symbols, which are counted (for instance repetition of a name of a candidate in a newspaper) are taken out of context. Alfred McClung Lee, in his study of Father Coughlin's anti-semitic program, applied an imaginative and original non-quantitative method. Comparing a number of speeches, Lee found a specific technique of the propagandists which he called "Tricks of the Trade" such as a testimonial, plain folk talk, transfer. He designed for each of these techniques a symbol similar to punctuation. He put this symbol wherever the "gimmick" was used by the propagandist. Furthermore, he compared speeches of Coughlin with those of Goebbels and indicated similarities. By use of such a method, the reader can understand the purposes of the propaganda, the ways of operation, its techniques and appeal. The polling method cannot offer full understanding of the phenomenon, it supplies only statistical results. In such a sense, methods based upon observations, interviews, content analysis—oriented toward understanding and explanation represent a superior approach.[8]

The statistical method in political attitudes research won strong support in powerful academic centers. A number of interesting studies in the area of political attitudes indicate its significance.[9] But this is not the crucial area of political sociology—it is rather an ancillary one. The fundamental problems of politics are not statistical. Statistics can only offer illustration and some verification to theories and hypothesis. No one of the great theories in the field of sociology, medicine or physics were achieved via computing machines and most of them did not need any statistics for verification. To quote Engels—Sadi Carnot, established his findings in thermodynamics because he studied and understood the working of one steam-machine; one thousand engines would not contribute any more. Statistics supplies data—it helps, suggests to understand the phenomena—and in certain areas (population) it is basic. Understanding of phenomena is not identical however with statistical figures.

Political Ecology. The study of spatial distribution of political attitudes and behavior—the political ecology—is pragmatic and practical. The interest in this area corresponds to the practical needs of a working democracy as well as to the dominant trends in American sociology.[10]

Before the First World War, André Siegfried, a French political geographer, advanced a thesis on spatial distribution of political attitudes in France. According to Siegfried, the distribution of votes and party preferences follows in France the old historical division into *pays*, not the administrative divisions which were established by the Revolution. His study was based on extensive research and fact finding which embraced such factors as geographical configurations, land holdings, class structures. In his multi-causal approach, Siegfried has shown the persistence of political attitudes and values, and their interdependence with social, economic and geographical factors.[11] Later, Siegfried re-stated his thesis, that the French political life has permanent traits and that by the 18th century the basic political attitudes were fully formed.[12]

Students of American political ecology found similar relationships and comparable persistence of political patterns. Voting behavior in the United States also corresponds to certain traditional regions. Distribution of voting behavior in certain rural areas seems to have a relationship with geographical configuration, geological structure of the area, rainfall, forms of land tenure, in addition to other factors. The natural environment influences the selection of crops—for instance corn or wheat. A wheat farmer is much more subject to economic fluctuations than a corn grower. The prosperous corn growing counties in certain states constitute, according to Heberle, a region of conservatism. The wheat growing farmers are much more subject to economic insecurity, than the much more diversified corn growers. Their votes, according to Rice and Heberle, are much more subject to fluctuations than those of the corn growers.[13] The study of the natural environment and its impact on the voting behavior is probably the most impressive area of political ecology. The research was not limited to a single-cause approach—other factors—were carefully considered: class structure, political and economic factors, traditional preferences—such as Populism or the LaFolette Progressive Movement in Wisconsin.

Heberle in his studies emphasizes the relationship between the natural environment, class structure and spatial distribution of voting behavior. In the study of Schlesvig-Holstein, in Germany, between 1932-34, he found that the strength of the Nazis was in the rural areas. A careful analysis of the agrarian population indicated that the farmers were far from being homogeneous. The support of the Nazis came from the small independent family farms, much less from the owners of large estates or large farms. The former sub-class had a tendency to vote for Nazis, who had an appeal to them, due to economic situation. In this area the Nazis won 51% of the vote in 1932, while immediately before and after the First World War, this was a stronghold of Social Democrats. Heberle's suggestion was that the change in voting behavior occurred in this area in a specific sub-class, due to specific economic conditions.[14] Of course, the case of Schlesvig-Holstein does not and cannot explain the phenomenon of Nazism—it gives only a limited insight into a specific area. The operation of the Nazi movement was far more complex and powerful. Heberle's main thesis was, however, that the class structure has a direct impact on voting behavior. He did not overlook other factors, such as religion, indicating for instance the relationship between religious distribution and voting behavior in Franconia. Similar methods were applied in his study of gubernatorial primaries in Louisiana. Here the hypothesis was focussed on rural areas, class structure and traditional ideological trends. Heberle and Bertrand found the Huey Long faction won in areas where only half a century before, Populism was strong in the small farm areas. Long's influence moved on the tracks of a radical democratic movement.[15]

Since in any working democracy, voting behavior is a continuous and repetitive phenomenon, the ecological studies of this type have a practical significance and potentialities of continuous research. The non-dogmatic, multi-factor approach offers flexibility to interpretation and method.

Political Parties. In any working democracy, the study of political parties is of a practical significance. The party system forms the essential part of the entire mechanism. In America—historians and political scientists share this large field. In theoretical studies, the strong relationship between class, economic interest and political behavior was stressed without customary invocation to Marx, by scholars of repute such as Charles A. Beard. The Americans were not afraid, nor did they dodge the issue. Sometimes it was overemphasized as in Charles Beard's famous study of the American constitution. Economic interests and political attitudes were also explored in various areas of the country as shown in the study by Holcombe.[16] Nor was the American scholar and newspaperman afraid to present to the young readers and students the full picture of corruption or the manipulation of machine politics, as exemplified in the works of Lincoln Steffens, Jacob Riis, and others. The students of American politics were less theoretical than the Europeans. They were more devoted to facts. They developed a great skill in their presentation with courage and faith in the truth—even a very ugly truth.

In times of threat and danger parties were studied which were hostile to what is called the "American way of life." The interest was pragmatic and practical: to understand the movements that the democracies had to cope with. Such was the case with Nazism, Fascism, and Communism. Autobiographies of rank and file Nazis, supplied a basis for Abel's well known study[17] (although the veracity of those autobiographies might sometimes be open to question). Becker studied the German youth movement and propaganda. Ebenstein and Franc Neuman investigated ideologies. Hanna Arendt supplied a general theory and elucidation of the whole phenonemon of totalitarianism (more on the philosophical side), while Fromm gave a social and psychological explanation.[18]

When Soviet expansion and Stalin's strategy endangered Europe and indirectly the United States, the whole field of Communism and Soviet Russia began to flourish. Powerful institutes were organized, courses appeared in university buletins, and research in this area was generously supported. Vast amounts of literature appeared in the field on Communist parties, their structure, organization, propaganda techniques, the elite and history. Every detail was carefully studied, over studied and even duplicated.[19] The practical significance of this issue created the interest. At the same time, while it was not difficult to publish a study of the Polish or Czechoslovakia communist elite, it was and it still is very hard to find support for publicaion of a history of a Czechoslovakian Social-Democratic Party or a Bulgarian Peasant Party. Institutes on the Soviet Union and Communism were not paralleled by similarly extensive research on ailing democratic parties or new, emerging ones. Of course, studies did appear[20]—but support for such studies could not compare with the other field.

Sometimes the college fraternity overlooked the earlier studies on the Communist movement. Long before Soviet studies became a fad, liberally oriented labor theoreticians and students of Soviet affairs published books and articles in which the Communist party, and their leaders were analyzed. Politics were realistically and not naively anticipated. Prominent in this group were D. Dallin, W. H. Chamberlain, B. Nikolayevsky, S. Schwarz, Bertram Wolfe, Sol Levitas and many others who gathered around the Socialist weekly *New Leader*. In turn, a few sociologists wrote rather naive articles about the Soviet system even after a visit to the Soviet Union.

Interest in the social-democratic movement has had its ups and downs in the United States. In America, as in France, the trade unions were seperated from political movements. Whenever this happened, the social-democratic party declined, while the unions were either captured by the Communists or remained temporarily politically indifferent, transformed into a business organization. Similarly the field of labor economics, was separated from other academic disciplines; it became so strong in America that extensive studies developed in leading universities and departments were created such as the School of Industrial Relations at Cornell University, and offerings in Labor Econonmics at the University of Wisconsin, under the leadership of Professor Selig Pearlman. The interest in the social democratic movement had never disappeared. Texts were published such as the informative and comprehensive volume by Harry Laidler, *Social Economic Movements* (Crowell, 1944) and recent publications[21] were additional evidence of this interest. Books, articles and monographs appeared on Canadian, French, Austrian and Polish socialist movements.[22] The field is so extensive and needs a far broader evaluation. This is only an indication of the area.

American interest in social movements cannot and is not limited solely to American and European phenomena. Situated between Asia and Europe, it has a vital interest in the future development in the latter continent. The interest is again pragmatic and scholarly. The Asiatic and African continents are in a state of revolution, new political and social movements appeared, old hopes were frustrated and new ones raised. This development had an impact on American scholarly interest and studies on Asiatic cultures as well as political movements have appeared lately.[23]

It is not easy to separate purely sociological studies of political parties from the other disciplines. Generally, it may be said that specific interest, such as ideological appeal of the parties, elite, power and structure could be indicated as fields of specific sociological interest.

Ideologies. European movements supplied an extensive body of political theory. The ideologies in Europe were born of dilemmas and misery. Political parties in Europe have their party theoreticians. Neither the Republican or the Democratic Parties can make such a claim. Adlai Stevenson tried and lost his election. Some of the political experts argue that he was too intellectual. Brogan, in his *American Character* speaks about American dislike for abstract theory and this dislike is not conducive to an advancement of elaborate political ideologies. American politics being pragmatic is based largely on practical plans for immediate action, whereas in Europe it is an elaborate image of a perfect society or an entirely new society. In a time of the Second Industrial Revolution of atomic energy and automation, with workers receiving the highest salaries in the history of mankind, in times of general prosperity, America did not produce a new ideology or a vision of a new society. Pragmatic political philosophy is one of the factors. European ideologies grew in times of misery and dissatisfaction of the masses. Can a society of satisfied masses with the highest standard of living in human history, produce a new dynamic ideology? This question still awaits an answer. The Constitution and the political system is another factor. It works and this in a pragmatic society is the supreme test. The Constitution is generally accepted as a fundamental institution and a value system. If one looks for universally shared American values, the Constitution is the place to look. Consequently the Constitution supplies the elements of stability and continuity. Many of the European Continental Constitutions were changed from time to time. The traditional, written text (its core) of the American constitution does not change, although it undergoes reinterpretation. It is a somewhat similar symbol as the British Crown; in a sense it is a modern and democratic expression of the same principle and function: continuity, tradition and integration.

The literature on ideologies is, however, extensive. European ideological movements are taught in classrooms and seminars. American Socialism is studied, rather, as part of an interesting and different past. Probably, the most active ideologists, are those of the modern pragmatic, and in a sense, liberal conservative persuasions.[24] A number of important studies have been published in the field of theory of democracy. Robery MacIver in *Web of Government* gives a synthesis of what may be called a sociology of government. Robert Dahl examines social and political conditions under which a populist democracy, rule by majority, can operate.[25]

The concept of ideologies has been too often reduced to a concept of a social myth—something unreal and impractical. In addition the dominant empirical-inductive approach to sociology is not conducive to ideological-theoretical discussions. To sociologists of the dominant position, the study of society should deal with reality which exists, not with what ought to be. A scientist in physics tries to develop models which did not exist before. He smashes the atom. The medical scientist attempts to develop new drugs and methods of treating dread diseases. They are studying "what should and what ought to be done." The "what ought to be" approach of the physical and biological scientists is the key for the future betterment of mankind. Great Britain and the continental theoreticians supplied plans for model societies. American political thinking did so in the 18th century with *The Constitution* as a model, before it began to operate. Europe has been a great experimental laboratory for the modern United States. Social Security and Public Housing are examples of the successful experimentation adapted here. The European social scientists outlined models of new types of societies, sometimes such models were

purely theoretical propositions, otherwise, they had practical significance. Such models are related to ideological systems with broad social
images, which is quite foreign to the American type of thinking.

The normative field of ideologies must be separated from empirical
study. The former is based upon value judgments, the latter on description of facts and inferences. The latter would be recognized by
most as the proper domain of sociology. Its purpose is to study the
origin of political idea systems, their impact on society, the relationship between the former and the latter, and their ideological appeals.
This field borders at least partially, on that of the sociology of knowledge. Mannheim's volume on *Ideology and Utopia* produced an interest which was great enough to justify an inexpensive paper-back
edition. Weber's famous work on Protestant ethics is regularly quoted
in American sociology classes. Tawney's book on *Religion and Rise
of Capitalism* can be purchased for thirty five cents in many drug
stores. These authors have made fundamental contributions in this
field. Karl Mannheim's fundamental problem concerns the relationship between society and political ideology (ideas actually held) and
utopias (ideas projected into the future). Ideologies, according to
Mannheim, are idea systems of the prevailing social order, while utopias are of a desired future. Political ideologies are similar to thought
processes and are a result of social interaction and are social facts.
In this sense, Mannheim is not distant from Durkheim's concept of
collective representation. The ideas, and here Tawney, Weber and
Mannheim agree, correspond to a certain interest. Only then, if
they correspond to economic interests, Marx said, do they capture the
masses. The interests however are not necessarily purely economic
ones. Max Weber, in his essay on Protestant Ethics indicated that it
is the idea system which has an impact on the economic system.
Werner Sombart in his voluminous study of modern capitalism, indicated the significance of values in economic development, while
Tawney's contributions are methodological. Tawney's masterly analysis
of the mutual interpendence between religious values and economic
change, his re-interpretation of Weber, tightening his frame of reference, showed how closely related the problems of economic interest
and political ideology are. American political ecologists have also
studied this problem from an empirical and statistical standpoint.

Charles A. Beard, one of the greatest American historians, analyzed
the close relationship between economic interest and political ideologies in America.[26] He presented a general theory, based upon careful

consideration of facts. Beard's work is as much in the realm of sociology as is that of Weber. The former are sociological contributions by an historian and the latter, historical contributions by a sociologist. Beard emphasized the role of economic interest and its impact on political movements. In a sense his ideas are closer to Marx than to Weber.

Symbols and values form a fundamental part of political ideologies. The entire architecture of idea-systems rests on values, while symbols supply important tools of ideological appeal. How and why certain political ideas appeal—the problem of selection and preference— became an important area for sociological study.[27] Lasswell and his school advanced the study of political symbolism.[28] The value approach gained a strong interest among anthropologists and social scientists as might be indicated by the work of Charles Morris in the field of personality and value choice.[29] The study of the structure of political ideologies is a field that should be mentioned.[30]

STUDY OF REVOLUTIONS

The interest in this field is great enough to justify the excellently equipped library and institute, The Hoover Library on War, Peace and Revolutions at Stanford University, California. Many important books in this field originated in this institution.[31]

Theoretical sociological interest in revolutions was mainly centered on the study of revolutionary types, processes, and patterns of action. G. S. Pettee, Crane Brinton and L. P. Edwards are representatives of American scholarship in this field.[32] Pettee attempted to establish the major types of revolution and analyze the processes, Edwards and later Brinton studied the revolutionary process by way of the comparative approach. Brinton compared the English, American, French and Russian revolutions and indicated similarities, stages which were repetitive in all four revolutions (rule of the moderates, accession of the extremists, reigns of terror and virtue, Thermidor). Brinton emphasized the role of the intelligentsia. Although the role of intellectuals in the revolutions is paramount, he seemed to overestimate them while he underestimated the masses and social economic conditions. Studies were also made of patterns of action, revolutionary strategies and tactics.[33] From the earlier works on revolutions, Tocqueville seems to be far more popular than studies by Marx and Engels, although the

214 TRENDS IN THE UNITED STATES

latter were penetrating in their analysis of revolutionary processes, especially of 1848 and 1871.

CONCEPTUAL APPROACH AND THEORY

It would be a mistake to suggest that American political science and sociology is entirely dominated by the quantitative and pragmatic schools. A number of scholars and independent theoreticians advanced the field of general theory and suggested conceptual schemes and approaches.

Essential in sociology of politics is a general theoretical concept, a frame of reference, an approach which could be applied to a variety of systems and thus permit a comparative study of political institutions and behavior in different societies. Such a frame of reference was advanced by Adolf A. Berle, Jr., who suggested the concept of political force in terms of ideology and apparatus. These two elements form the key to a theory which resembles Durkheim's approach.

Durkheim, in his study of *Origin of Religious Beliefs,* made a distinction between the religion as a system of beliefs and the church—the institutional frame, the organization. The religion—the idea—in Durkheim's theory is the collective representation which integrates the group. The function of the ideology and apparatus in a political movement is similarly defined in Berle's *Natural Selection of Political Forces* (Kansas University Press 1950), but there is no direct influence or link between Durkheim and the latter. Berle arrived at his extensive study of contemporary political movements—both totalitarian and democratic. His basic contention is that the broad universalistic ideology has not only a wider appeal than the narrow totalitarian and nationalistic, but also a more lasting one. Berle's theory is a dynamic one. He thinks in terms of political appeals and movements. In consequence a third link seems relevant in this theory—the study of patterns of action (political strategy and tactics). The field of sociology of politics might be centered around these three interrelated and interdependent concepts: ideology (and value systems), party (political organization) and patterns of action. This type of a conceptual frame of reference supplies a focus and suggests a limited field. It permits comparative study of political sociology in various societies. Such frame of reference should supply only an orientation which permits far wider theoretical ramifications.

Similar efforts were made by political scientists, especially in the study of comparative government. New methods were discussed in 1944 by a committee of the American Political Science Association, and more recently by the Social Science Research Council. A frame of reference was suggested by Macridis based on the study of decision making, power, ideology and institutions.[34] Lasswell originated the psychological approach in political science and the field was soon extended to personality and culture concepts.[35] Theories varied from the extreme partisans of Freud, to the moderate followers of Adler. Some theories were far fetched. The Oedipus complex was advanced in studies of political personality and the application of the quasi-Freudian "swaddling theories" met with strong criticism. According to the latter, Soviet dictatorship was explained by early childhood training (swaddling). Some of these theories, intellectually hazardous, were evidence of the imaginative attempts which were far from reality and truth.

The study of elite and power is another area which has attracted a great deal of interest. The concepts are not new. Mosca, sixty years ago, and Pareto, later, advanced their theories along these lines. Pareto, in his writing, reflected the general interest which the French historians had in this field. Half a century ago, Roberto Michels, in his studies of political parties, analyzed the movements from the vantage point of oligarchies, the political elite. Interestingly enough, a Polish Russian socialist theoretician, Vatslav Machajski, had some influence in America. Machajski, in his *Intellectual Worker,* published at the turn of the century, suggested that the evolution of the capitalistic system or possibly the future socialist system, may establish a monopoly of power by the educated elite (the know-how) over the working class. Machajski anticipated the dictatorship of bureaucracy and the military. Machajski's theories were further advanced and revised by Max Nomad.[36] Recent studies of the elite show a growing interest in this field. C. Wright Mills, in his *Power Elite,* applied the idea of circulation of elite to the American scene. In this book, written in a Veblenian spirit, Mills suggests that power circulated in the United States within the same class. Lasswell originated extensive studies of the Soviet, satellite and Nazi elites. Whether such detailed and concentrated study has practical and theoretical significance, raises a question.[37]

THE QUEST FOR INTEGRATION

Charles A. Beard, in his presidential address in 1947, warned against the overdepartmentalization of the social sciences, which in consequence may lead to sterility. Political sociology faces both the issues of departmentalization and integration. What are the relations of political science, history, international relations-personality studies to political sociology? Sociology is a generalizing discipline. As such, should it embrace such a vast area? What are the limits? On the other hand practical needs, scholastic and educational interest, requires broad integration of the social sciences.

The field of international relations and the new "policy sciences" brings into focus this problem. Is there any specific field of international relations? C. A. W. Manning, in his UNESCO study[38] indicates the broad ramifications of the discipline, and points to certain sociological areas. Grayson Kirk found the inherent difficulties of this field which requires an extensive encyclopedic knowledge of the social sciences; the various disciplines, including sociology, fall within the study of international relations.[39] The syllabus of Professor Manning of the University of London, contains the study of the structure of International Society, Sociology of International Law to mention a few subjects, which are within the area of sociology.[40] Processes of conflict, cooperation or neutrality are definitely basic to international relations, they are also social, sociological relations. A distinction can be made between relations between governments (inter-political) and between peoples (inter-cultural, or international *sense stricto*). The study of such relations is part of the sociological approach.[41]

Another field are the policy sciences. This discipline represents an effort to apply or integrate social sciences with the field of government and politics.[42] A Victorian forerunner in this direction was Walter Bagehot in his famous treatise *Physics and Politics*. Manning rightly indicates that one of the functions of the policy sciences is to determine "for whom and how" and "for what objectives." In consequence, they cannot be isolated from ethical, normative, and political judgments. This implies even a broader integration, an integration of political philosophy and the social sciences. The sociologists who insist on "scientism" and "purity" may find sooner or later that separation of sociology from ethical judgment means either sterility or rationalization. Scientific research (as much as it is possible) should be free of value judgment, it should be independent and objective, but it can hardly remain divorced from ethical considerations. The research stage should be value-free. Once the research is finished we should ask the question—what is the objective of our research? Maybe this question should be asked at the beginning.[43]

Political sociology faces the conflicting issue of specialization and integration. It is vital for a discipline to establish limits, explore and develop definite methods, in the field. On the other hand, understanding of world politics, search for solutions, research and even college curricula, suggest integration. Probably there is no perfect answer.

Political sociology, under a variety of titles, appears today in many universities in the college curriculum. The paramount role which great political movements have played and will play in the future, the increasing international responsibilities of the United States suggests that political sociology will grow in its significance.

SELECTED BIBLIOGRAPHY

Walter Bagehot, *Physics and Politics* (Boston: Beacon Press, 1956 ed.). The paperback reprint of this Victorian classic indicates its timeliness; Bagehot was among the first to apply modern social sciences, above all sociology and anthropology to the field of politics.

B. R. Berelson, Paul F. Lazarsfeld, & W. N. McPhee, *Voting: A Study of Opinion Formation in a Presidential Campaign* (University of Chicago Press, 1954). A quantitative study of the voting behavior in the 1948 Presidential election as seen through a sample of Elmira citizens.

A. A. Berle, Jr., *Natural Selection of Political Forces* (University of Kansas Press, 1950). Develops a theory of social forces (ideology and apparatus); suggests a theory of ideological preferences.

Crane Brinton, *Anatomy of Revolution* (New York: Prentice-Hall, 1950). A well-known comparative study of revolutions and their stages.

Karl W. Deutsch, *Nationalism and Social Communication* (Boston: nationalism, based on concepts of communication and on quantitative Mass. Institute of Technology, 1953). A new approach to study of methods.

Heinz Eulau; Samuel J. Elersveld; & Morris Janowitz, *Political Behavior: A Reader in Theory and Research* (Glencoe, Ill.: The Free Press, 1956). A reader collecting important writings in theory, empirical research, from the point of view of the behavioral sciences.

George Gallup and Saul R. Rae, *The Pulse of Democracy, The Public Opinion Poll and How It Worked* (New York: Simon and

Schuster, 1940). A well known account of the quantitative study of political attitudes.

Harold F. Gosnell, *Grass Roots Politics, National Voting Behavior of Typical States* (Washington: American Council on Public Affairs 1942). Analysis of political behavior based on evaluation of a variety factor.

Feliks Gross (ed.), *European Ideologies* (New York: Philosophical Library 1948). Discussion of patterns of actions (strategy and tactics), structure and function of political ideologies. Survey of European ideologies; *Seizure of Political Power* (New York: Philosophical Library, 1958). A sociological study of violent transfer of power. Comparative study of revolutions and underground movements.

Rudolph Heberle, *Social Movements, An Introduction to Political Sociology* (New York: Appleton, Century Crofts; 1951) A textbook in political sociology, based on American and European data.

Karl Mannheim, *Ideology and Utopia* (New York: Harvest Books, originally published in 1936). A study of social origin of political ideas (ideologies and utopias).

Roberto Michels, *Political Parties* (Glencoe: Free Press, 1949 ed.). A classic study of political oligarchies.

Robert M. MacIver, *The Web of Government* (New York: Macmillan, 1947). A clear presentation of the fundamental problems of sociology of government, regarded as a classic in its field.

Harold D. Lasswell, Charles Merriam, T. V. Smith, *A Study of Power* (Glencoe: Free Press, 1950). Different approaches to the problem of power.

Harold D. Lasswell, *The Political Writings* (Glencoe: Free Press, 1951). Contains *Psychopathology and Politics*. Lasswell represents a particular psychoanalytical approach, indicative of Freudian trends in political science and sociology of politics.

Stuart A. Rice. *Quantitative Methods in Politics* (New York; Knopf, 1927). An attempt to devise quantitative method, which could secure value-free data on political behavior.

Samuel A. Stouffer, *Communism, Conformity and Civil Liberties; A Cross-section of the Nation Speaks Its Mind* (New York: Doubleday, 1955). A quantitative study of political attitudes toward non-conformists. The sample embraced more than 6000 persons, interviewed by 500 skilled interviewers.

Feliks Gross received his Doctor's degree (1931) from the Faculty of Law and Government, University of Cracow (Poland); Professor of Sociology and Anthropology, Brooklyn College and Adjunct Professor, The Graduate School of Arts and Sciences, Department of Government, New York University; was Visiting Professor of Foreign Policy, University of Virginia (1950, 1952, 1954, 1956); also Visiting Professor of Political Science and Director of the Institution of International Affairs, University of Wyoming; lectured at the University of Illinois, Michigan, Pittsburgh, Wayne, Indiana, Texas and other universities. Is the author of: *Nomadism* (Warsaw: Kasa Mianowskiego, 1936), published on the recommendation of the Polish Academy of Sciences and with the introduction by Bronislaw Malinowski; *Proletariat i Kultura* (Warsaw, 1938); edited (with Z. Myslakowski) biographies of Polish workers: *Robotnicy Pisza* (Warsaw, 1938); author of numerous works: *The Polish Worker* (New York: Roy, 1945); *Crossroads of Two Continents* (New York: Columbia University Press, 1945); *Foreign Policy Analysis* (New York: Philosophical Library, 1954); editor of: *European Ideologies* (New York: Philosophical Library, 1948); co-editor: *Struggle for Tomorrow: Political Ideologies of the Jewish People* (New York: Arts, 1954); Associate Editor: *Slavonic Encyclopaedia* (New York: Philosophical Library, 1949; Co-author of: *Central-Eastern Europe: Crucible of World Wars* (New York: Prentice-Hall, 1945). edited by Joseph S. Roucek; etc. Editor of *New Europe and World Reconstruction* (1941-1945), a monthly on international affairs and Secretary General of Central & Eastern European Planning Board (of Czechoslovakia, Greece, Yugoslavia and Poland); also Advisor, the Polish Government in Exile. Since 1950, Consultant, the Free Europe Committee and Research Adviser, the Mid-European Studies Center.

NOTES

1. George H. Gallup, *A Guide to Public Opinion Polls* (Princeton University Press, 1948) ; also George H. Gallup and Saul F. Rae, *The Pulse of Democracy, The Public Opinion Poll and How It Works* (New York: Simon and Schuster Inc., 1940.)

2. George H. Gallup and Claude Robinson, "American Institute of Public Opinion—Surveys, 1935-1938," *The Public Opinion Quarterly,* II (July 1938) , 373 ff.

3. Archibald M. Crossley, "Straw Polls in 1936," *The Public Opinion Quarterly,* I (January, 1937) , 24 ff.; George H. Gallup, "The Future Direction of Election Polling," *The Public Opinion Quarterly,* XVII (Summer, 1953) , 202 ff., introduced a new type of sampling, the "pin point" method of sampling by precincts. Among earlier studies see Paul Lazarsfeld as quoted above. E. Pendleton Herring, "How Does the Voter Make Up His Mind?," *The Public Opinion Quarterly,* II (January, 1938) , 24 ff.; Harold F. Gosnell "How Accurate Were the Polls?," *The Public Opinion Quarterly,* I (January, 1937) , 97 ff. The quantitative method was also extended to studying the effect of television on voting behavior. For an example of this see G. D. Wiebe, "Responses to the Televised Kefauver Hearings: Some Social Psychological Implications," *The Public Opinion Quarterly,* XVI (Summer, 1952, 179 ff. A question put before 260 respondents was: "The Kefauver hearings were about six weeks ago. As you think back to that time, how did you feel about the conditions that were brought to light?"

4. See A. M. Crossley, *op. cit.,* p. 28.

5. George H. Gallup, *A Guide to Public Opinion Polls* (Princeton University Press, 1948) , 4 ff.

6. Hadley Cantril, *Gauging Public Opinion* (Princeton University Press, 1944) .

7. Lindsay Rogers, *The Pollsters; Public Opinion, Politics, and Democratic Leadership* (New York: Alfred A. Knopf, 1949).

8. Alfred McClung Lee and Elizabeth Bryant Lee, *The Fine Art of Propaganda* (New York: Harcourt, Brace, 1939). Another example of content analysis is Marver Bernstein, "Political Ideas of Selected American Business Journals," *The Public Opinion Quarterly*, XVII (1953), 259 ff.

9. Samuel A. Stouffer, in *Communism, Conformity, and Civil Liberties; A Cross Section of the Nation Speaks Its Minds* (New York: Doubleday, 1955) has shown that there is a fear of symbols and concepts among certain strata of the population while Karl Deutsch's *Nationalism and Social Communication* (New York: John Wiley & Sons), and the Technology Press of the Massachusetts Institute of Technology, 1953, attempted to apply new, precise, and largely quantitative methods to the study of nationalism. Paul Lazarsfeld and Allen Barton, *Anti-Democratic Beliefs Among American Workers: Qualitative Survey Analysis and a Methodological Introduction* (Glencoe, Ill.: The Free Press, 1953), is also pertinent. For an example of the extension of public opinion study to the field of foreign policy see Thomas A. Bailey, *The Man in the Street; The Impact of American Public Opinion on Foreign Policy* (New York: The Macmillan Co., 1948).

10. For an excellent survey of the field see Rudolf Heberle, *Social Movements: An Introduction to Political Sociology* (New York: Appleton-Century-Crofts, 1951), 218 ff.

11. André Siegfried, *Tableau Politique de la France de l'ouest sous la Troisième Republique* (Paris: Colin, 1913).

12. Siegfried, *Tableau de Partis en France* (Paris: Grasset, 1930).

13. Rudolf Heberle, *op. cit.*, 244 ff.; Stuart A. Rice, *Quantitative Methods in Politics* (New York: Alfred A. Knopf, 1928), and Harold F. Gosnell in his *Grass Roots Politics; National Voting Behavior of Typical States* (Washington, D. C.: American Council on Public Affairs, 1942) explained the political voting behavior in particular areas. Heberle, in interpreting his work, indicates how Wisconsin's speedy agricultural recovery influenced the vote; see Heberle, *op. cit.*, p. 249.

14. Rudolf Heberle, *From Democracy to Nazism, A Regional Case Study of Political Parties in Germany* (Baton Rouge, La.: Louisiana State University Press, 1945).

15. Rudolf Heberle and Alfred L. Bertand, "Factors Motivating Voting Behavior in a One Party State," *Social Forces*, XXVII, (May 1949); also V. O. Key, *Southern Politics* quoted by Heberle, *op. cit.*, 251 ff.

16. Arthur N. Holcombe, *The Political Parties of Today; A Study in Republican and Democratic Politics* (New York: Harper, 1924); Charles A. Beard and William Beard, *American Government and Politics* (New York: The Macmillan Co., 1949); see also: T. W. Cousens, *Politics and Political Organizations in America* (New York: The Macmillan Co., 1942); Harold F. Gosnell, *Machine Politics: Chicago Model* (University of Chicago Press, 1937); V. O. Key, *Politics, Parties and Pressure Groups* (New York: T. Y. Crowell Co., 1942.)

17. Theodore F. Abel, *Why Hitler Came to Power* (New York: Prentice-Hall Inc., 1948). Also Howard Becker, *German Youth: Bond or Free* (New York: Oxford University Press, 1946. Konrad Heiden, *Der Fuhrer* (Boston: Houghton Mifflin Co. 1944), and the same author's *History of National Socialism* (New York: Alfred A. Knopf Inc., 1948); Raymond E. Murphy and Associates, *National Socialism*, Division of European Affairs, Department of State 1943.

18. Erich Fromm, *Escape From Freedom* (New York: Rinehart & Co., 1941).

19. Philip Selznick, *The Organizational Weapon, A Study of Bolshevik Strategy and Tactics* (New York: McGraw Hill, 1952) also see: Nathan Leites' *A Study of Bolshevism* (Glencoe, Ill.: The Free Press, 1953) ; Margaret Mead, *Soviet Attitudes Toward Authority* (New York: McGraw Hill, 1951) ; in addition to these sources a library of books on communism was published by the Harvard University Press: Alex Inkeles, *Public Opinion in Soviet Russia,* Merle Feinsod, *How Russia is Ruled;* Raymond Bauer, *The New Man in Soviet Psychology;* Adam Ulam, *Titoism;* Benjamin I. Schwartz, *Chinese Communism and the Rise of Mao;* Barrington Moore, Jr., *Soviet Politics; The Dilemma of Power,* Ruth Fischer, *Stalin and German Communism.* For an excellent analysis and personality study of the leaders of the Russian Revolution see Bertram Wolfe's *Three Who Made a Revolution* (Boston: Beacon Press, 1948) ; Gabriel A. Almond and Associates, *The Appeals of Communism* (Princeton University Press, 1954) .

20. Studies of non-communist movements also form a part of the curriculum. For example, see: Sigmund Neumann, *Modern Political Parties: Approaches to Comparative Politics* (University of Chicago Press, 1956) ; Paul Duverger, *Les Partis Politiques* (Paris: Colin, 1954) also (in English translation) : Robert A. Brady, *Crisis in Britain, Plans and Achievements of the Labour Government* (Berkeley, Calif.: University of California Press, 1950) ; Feliks Gross, *European Ideologies* (New York: Philosophical Library, 1948) , gives a general survey of political ideologies.

21. Donald D. Egbert & Stow Persons, Eds., *Socialism and American Life* (Princeton University Press, 1952) ; Walter Galenson, *Comparative Labor Movements* (New York: Prentice-Hall, 1952) ; this field is quite extensive and a special chapter could be offered to provide a separate bibliography, such as: S. M. Lipset, *Agraraian Socialism, A Study of the Cooperative Commonwealth Federation in Saskatchewan* (Berkeley, Calif.: University of California Press, 1950) ; Dean E. McHenry, *The Third Force in Canada* (Berkeley, Calif.: University of California Press, 1950) ; Gross, *The Polish Worker, A Study of a Social Stratum* (New York: Roy, 1945) .

22. A number of studies appeared in *The Annals* of the The American Academy of Political Science; also in *The Political Science Quarterly;* in the publication of the Institute of Pacific Relations. The interest in his area is growing and the literature is becoming extensive, for example see: Cora Dubois' *Social Forces in Southeast Asia* (Minneapolis, Minn.: University of Minnesota Press, 1949) ; Lin Mou shêng, *Men and Ideas; An Informal History of Chinese Political Ideas* (New York: John Day, 1942) ; Erich H. Jacoby, *Agrarian Unrest in Southeast Asia* (New York: Columbia University Press, 1949) ; F. S. C. Northrop, *Meeting of East and West; An Inquiry Concerning World Understanding* (New York: The Macmillan Co., 1946) ; also see: his *Ideological Differences and World Order* (New Haven: Yale University Press, 1949) . Karl Wittfogel, on the other hand, suggested a theory largely opposed to the views of Northrop, indicating that despotism originated among certain Oriental societies; for further elaboration of his position see his *Oriental Despotism and Hydraulic Society* (New Haven, Yale University Press, 1956) .

23. Clinton Rossiter, *Conservatism in America* (New York: A. A. Knopf, 1955) ; Russell Kirk, *Conservative Mind* (Chicago: Regnery, 1954) ; Peter Viereck, *Conservatism Revisited* (New York: Scribner's, 1949) .

24. Robert M. MacIver, *The Web of Government* (New York: The Macmillan Co., 1954) ; Robert A. Dahl, *A Preface to Democratic Theory* (University of Chicago Press, 1956) .

25. Charles A. Beard, *The Economic Basis of Politics* (New York: Vintage Books 1957) .

222 TRENDS IN THE UNITED STATES

26. Gabriel A. Almond & Associates, *The Appeals of Communism* (Princeton University Press, 1954), may serve as an example; this study is based on four years of extensive interviewing with former American, British, French, and Italian communists.

27. Harold D. Lasswell, Daniel Lerner, and Itheil Pool, *The Comparative Study of Symbols* (Stanford University Press, 1952); also: Itheil Pool & others, *Symbols of Internationalism* (Stanford University Press, 1951).

28. Charles Morris, *Varieties of Human Values* (University of Chicago Press, 1956); and his: *Signs, Language, and Behavior* (New York: Prentice-Hall, 1946).

29. Feliks Gross, Ed., *European Ideologies* (New York: Philosophical Library, 1948), especially Chapter I, "Mechanics of European Politics."

30. Stanford University Press and the Hoover Institute (Stanford University) published a number of important studies in the field of history and the sociology of revolution. Typical of these is: James Bunyan & H. H. Fisher, *The Bolshevik Revolution, 1917-1918, Documents and Materials* (Stanford University Press, 1934); also there are numerous studies which have been frequently mentioned in this chapter.

31. George S. Pettee, *The Process of Revolution* (New York: Harper, 1938); L. P. Edwards, *The Natural History of Revolution* (University of Chicago Press, 1927); Crane Brinton, *The Anatomy of Revolution* (New York: W. W. Norton, 1938); Pitirim A. Sorokin, *The Sociology of Revolution* (Philadelphia: Lippincott, 1925) Red D. Hopper, "The Revolutionary Process," *Social Forces*, XXVII (1950).

32. Feliks Gross, *Seizure of Political Power* (New York: Philosophical Library, 1957).

33. R. C. Macridis, *The Study of Comparative Government* (New York: Doubleday, 1956).

34. Harold D. Lasswell, *Power and Personality* (New York: W. W. Norton, 1948). The study of political power is an important area of research; for further works, see: Lasswell, *World Politics and Personal Security*; Charles E. Merriam, *Political Power*; T. V. Smith, *Power and Conscience*, these three works are published, collectively, as: *A Study of Power* (Glencoe, Ill., The Free Press, 1950). Smith's approach is a philosophical one, while Merriam's is that of a political scientist; Lasswell views this problem in terms of a psychological point of view (which is Freudian to a great extent); the latter's writing is neither clear nor easy to comprehend. Lasswell's work can be accepted as a general hypothesis capable of being interpreted in a variety of ways. Space limitations does not permit a more extensive bibliography; however, one further work is important to mention: G. M. Gilbert's *The Psychology of Dictatorship* (New York: The Ronald Press, 1950); this book represents a first hand study of the leaders of Nazi Germany during the Nuremberg trials, and is probably the best study of this type.

35. Roberto Michels, *Political Parties* (Translated by Eden and Cedar Paul, Glencoe, Ill.: The Free Press, 1949); see also: excerpts from Machajski's writings and Max Nomad's "Masters—Old and New," in V. F. Calverton, editor, *The Making of Society* (New York: Modern Library, 1937).

36. Harold D. Lasswell & C. Easton Rothwell, *The Comparative Study of Elites; An Introduction and Bibliography*, George Schueller, *The Politburo*, Daniel Lerner & others, *The Nazi Elite*; Max Knight, *The German Executive, 1890-1933*; & Robert C. North, *Kuomintang and Chinese Communist Elites* (all published as the Hoover Institute Studies).

37. C. A. W. Manning, *The University Teaching of Social Sciences, International Relations* (Paris: UNESCO, 1954). Joseph S. Roucek "The Sociology of Violence,"

Journal of Human Relations, V. 3 (Spring, 1957), 9-21, and bibliographical references, 19-21.

38. Quincy Wright, in his *Study of International Relations* (New York: Appleton-Century-Crofts, 1955), attempts to integrate social science; see also his *Problems of Stability and Progress in International Relations* (Berkeley: University of California Press, 1954); Grayson Kirk in his *Study of International Relations in American Colleges and universities* (New York: Council of Foreign Relations), indicates that th is discipline covers almost every field of the social sciences.

39. Manning, *op.cit., 95-96.*

40. Donald R. Taft applied a sociological approach to the study of international conflicts in his *Preliminary Introduction to the Sociology of International Conflict,* Urbana, Ill.) Feliks Gross tried to develop a sociological and integrated frame of reference to the study of foreign policy as a pattern of social action in his *Foreign Policy Analysis* (New York: Philosophical Library, 1954); Pitirim Sorokin's research is oriented toward pacification study, a sociological study of the building of international cooperation; the Princeton University group, headed by Professor Richard Snyder, has advanced sociological concepts in the study of decision making in international relations.

41. Daniel Lerner and Harold D. Lasswell, *The Policy Sciences* (Stanford University Press, 1951), has chapters on personality, primary groups, national character, culture, world organization, research procedures and policy integration.

42. Feliks Gross, "Soziologie und Ethik," *Kölner Zeitschrift für Soziologie* (1953/4), Heft 2, 59ff.

POPULATION

Harry R. Doby
Central Michigan College

American sociologists in general have manifested considerable interest in demography since the close of World War II.[1] But this interest for the most part has been indirect and incidental, stemming from their chief concern with various other topics. For example, it would be impossible to make a thorough study of human ecology, rural sociology, and the Negro family without consulting data of a demographic nature, and the same is true of many other related topics. Statistics pertaining to population are deemed essential if analyses of social institutions and social problems are to be made on a quantitative basis. As a result, sociologists engaged both in research and teaching find that an understanding of population trends is necessary not only for descriptive purposes but for demonstrating the existence of significant relationships between factors which have a bearing on given social problems.

In contrast to the traditional economic and biological orientation of so many of the older population studies, the current trend is in the direction of greater emphasis on cultural, social and psychological factors. This means that social scientists tend to regard the data of the statisticians as a point of departure in their efforts to find explanations for demographic phenomena in terms of social-psychological factors. Fortunately, the current trend toward greater integration of the social sciences—and away from compartmentalization—has contributed substantially to the development of a common core of knowledge in relation to population which can serve these different disciplines equally well. Since social scientists are mainly interested in people and their problems, the field of population is their common meeting ground.

American sociologists seem inclined to devote much more attention to the practical than to the theoretical aspects of population study. Among the factors responsible for this tendency are the following:

(1) the need for reasonably accurate population data for use in connection with various phases of social planning; (2) the close relationship betwen demography and social problems, especially in urban-industrial areas; (3) growing interest in the dynamics of population, resulting from wartime dislocations on an international scale and from internal migration of record proportions; (4) the many requests for investigations of the social, economic, and political significance of movements of urban populations to the suburbs; (5) the practical implications of differential fertility in terms of socio-economic status, geographic area, religious background, etc.; (6) economic and social aspects of changes in the age and sex composition of the population; and (7) speculation concerning the need for a population "policy" on a national scale, a policy calling for the maintenance of a balance between population and natural resources on a regional basis throughout the country.

Data pertaining to the quantity, distribution, and composition of our population are especially necessary if modern experiments in social planning are to be effective. The personnel requirements of defense industries during and after World War II called for an orderly influx of competent workers into areas where new factories could be built and adequate housing provided. Measures designed to safeguard civilians in the event of an atomic war would be useless without a thorough knowledge of urban demography to serve as their foundation. Perhaps no better example of the need for population studies can be found than in the case of projected programs for building new schools and for recruiting new teachers to meet the demands of our rapidly expanding school population. A similar situation exists with reference to other social institutions and agencies, such as churches, settlement houses, and welfare departments, which try to modify their plans in accordance with changing demographic conditions in urban areas. Bureaus of social research of federations of social agencies and research departments of metropolitan planning commissions, for example, would be unable to function if they did not have access to detailed population data or if they ignored the significance of population shifts.

Population studies motivated chiefly by practical considerations, therefore, continue to serve many useful social purposes. In certain social-problem situations population analysis is a necessary first step that is preliminary to all other approaches, judging by current American practices.

TRENDS IN POPULATION RESEARCH

In spite of the fact that the great majority of American sociologists do not engage in population research as one of their primary areas of interest, the total number of projects pertaining to demography which are reported in a typical year compares favorably with the total number reported for most other fields of sociology. In 1954, the Census of Research of the American Sociological Society reported 44 projects in Population, 50 projects in Marriage & Family, and 42 projects in Social Psychology—and these were the leaders. In 1953 there were 49 projects in Population and 61 projects in Social Psychology.

The proportions of all projects devoted to population research during selected years, according to the report issued in 1954, were as follows: 1946, 7%; 1947, 9%; 1948, 11%; 1949, 6%; 1951, 6%; 1952, 7%; 1953, 8%; 1954, 8%. Over a span of 16 years, which began in the 1930's, only one field, Social Psychology, reported a higher ratio of research projects than did Population, although Rural Sociology ranked almost as high as the latter.[2]

One index of the increasing interest in the field of population for the period of 1945-1955 is the number of doctoral dissertations where the *main emphasis* was on population. Listed by year, they are as follows: 1945, 2; 1946, 6; 1947, 4; 1948, 4; 1949, 4; 1950, 9; 1951, 9; 1952, 9; 1953, 10; 1954, 6; 1955, 12. This listing shows a total of 75 dissertations in the area of population, or an average of 6.8 per year. Chicago led with 12. Louisiana State and North Carolina came next in order with 10 and 7 respectively. In general, there has been an *upward trend* in the number of dissertations on Population completed in the period 1945 to 1955. Of the 75 Ph.D. dissertations completed during the period, 20 dealt with Migration, 19 with Population proper, 31 with Fertility Differentials, and 5 with Vital Statistics. Included in these totals are studies devoted to research methods.

Another significant index of interest in research is the list of articles published in the *American Sociological Review*, the official journal of the American Sociological Society. In 1956, for example, a total of 7 articles were devoted to various aspects of population studies, or 9.3 per cent of all the articles published in the journal during that year. Corresponding figures for preceding years were as follows: 1955, 5; 1954, 3; 1953, 4; 1952, 5; 1951, 1; 1950, 4; 1949, 2; 1948, 7; 1947, 2; 1946, 4; 1945, 4. While the percentage of articles pertaining to popu-

lation research usually is not large in the aggregate, it does compare
favorably with the figures for other fields.

The *Index to the American Sociological Review,* published in 1956,
covers all issues of the journal which appeared during the period
extending from 1936 through 1955, and it is an excellent source of
information concerning researches in the field of population. Persons
using the *Index* must bear in mind that some articles are cross-refer-
ences under two or more headings and that it is not always easy
to determine in what area of research a particular study belongs.
Nevertheless, the *Index* affords a fair picture of the types of researches
conducted and of the kinds of articles published since the *Review*
was first issued.

According to the classifications used in the *Index,* nearly all articles
in the *Review* which pertain to "population" were listed under one
or more of these headings: Population, Fertility, Census, and Birth
Rate.[3] During the period extending from 1945 through 1950 there
were 13 articles on Population, 4 articles on Fertility, 4 articles on
the Census, and 2 articles on the Birth Rate. From 1951 through
1956 there were 14 articles on Population, 10 articles on Fertility, 2
articles on the Census, and none on the Birth Rate. Thus, with the
figures for 1956 added to those covered by the *Index,* it will be noted
that a total of 27 articles on Population, 14 articles on Fertility, 6
articles on the Census, and 2 articles on the Birth Rate were published during the period 1945-1956, or 49 articles in all which dealt
with the topic of population in one form or another. In addition,
perhaps as many as a dozen other articles in borderline areas might
be included under one or more of the preceding headings. For the
purpose of this discussion what seems most significant in regard to
the foregoing is the unmistakable evidence of sustained interest in
research on population among American sociologists, especially since
the number of articles listed compares favorably with the totals
compiled for other fields of research. It might be well to note also
that the population of some 20 articles on internal migration during
the period 1945-1956 reflected a developing interest in the dynamics
of population growth in a nation where geographic mobility effected
changes of demographic significance.

IMPROVING THE CENSUS

Human ecologists and demographers have frequently criticized
government statistics for being reported for political units of area

rather than those areas which would be better suited to the problems which they intend to study with the data. The Census Bureau has responded to this need by designing new units of area such as Metropolitan Districts, Census Tracts, and Industrial Areas. A new development in this direction, sponsored by the Committee on Statistical Areas in the Census Bureau is the establishment of a new set of areas called "Economic Areas." Two types of areas have been recognized: (a) Metropolitan Economic Areas and (b) Non-metropolitan Economic Areas. A Metropolitan Economic Area consists of a central city of 50,000 or more inhabitants and its county plus adjacent counties, provided those adjacent counties and the central city have a combined population of 100,000 or more. The Non-metropolitan Economic Area is composed of counties having a similar pattern of social and economic traits related to its mode of gaining its livelihood. About 441 Economic Areas have been established, 148 of them being Metropolitan and 293 Non-Metropolitan. It is hoped that these units will be genuinely "functional" and in addition to permitting the easy assemblage of a great many different kinds of statistical data, will lend themselves to such research as (a) Administrative Planning, (b) Sampling, (c) Multiple-variable Cross-tabulation, (d) the Measurement of Inter-relationships, and (e) the study of Variation. This introduction of the Economic Area will be of great help in getting a simple and comprehensive description of the environment and thus aid in the formal testing of hypotheses concerning the relationships between behavior and the environment, and the relationships between variables under varying environmental conditions.

Other changes are being introduced by the Census Bureau. With reference to the 1950 census, for the first time data are being published for small areas such as counties and census tracts so that the proportion of migrants will be known for thousands of small areas and can be related to other characteristics of these areas. Also the origin and destination of migrants will be tabulated in terms of state and economic areas.

Revision of some intercensal estimates and the initial calculation of others has made possible the publication of many new or improved vital rates. Changes in the population schedule give us new kinds of information about marital status. Characteristics of persons married less than one year, or divorces less than one year are obtainable for the country as a whole. Social security programs will have available useful tabulations of widows by age, duration of widowhood, number of children, and income. Distinctions are now made between such units as households, married couples, primary families, secondary families, subfamilies, and unrelated individuals. A source of statistics on "doubling up" has been provided in the 1950 census and for the first time since 1930, statistics on families and on marital status will be published for counties and other small areas. The Census Bureau of Agricultural Economics are undertaking the collation of a national sample of Population, Housing, and Agriculture Schedules. Examples such as these impress us with the facts that the Census Bureau is making available many new kinds of data which can be used by sociologists as source materials for fruitful studies into the ever-increasing complexities of our social order.

To promote still further the usability of census data, a check on the accuracy of census results was made on the 1950 Census in the form of a Post-enumeration Survey. This had two major purposes: The first was to provide a measure of accuracy of the results of the Census in order to aid the consumer of Census data in avoiding the drawing of inferences that would be unwarranted by the accuracy of the data. The second purpose was to find the sources of the errors and the size of the error associated with each source. The study resulted in some changes in the philosophy of the staff of the Bureau of the Census. Formerly, the goal was thought of in terms of perfection in the attempt to get the most accurate measure possible for what was being measured. The new philosophy is not built around the principle of highest possible accuracy, but substitutes the principle of determining the level of accuracy that is optimum by balancing the losses due to errors against the costs of greater accuracy. Already, considerable modification in some of the methods of Census work has been undertaken. The Bureau has, by design, reduced the accuracy of compilation, where errors are subject to close control and were on a near zero basis. Higher error tolerances have been introduced in processing work, controlled at specified levels through quality control or sample verification and other techniques. Economics that are achieved in this way make it possible to take measures to improve the quality of the field work where error levels are considerably higher.

One of the more important recent contributions to information on the composition and characteristics of our population has been the refinement of census procedures in obtaining data on such critical characteristics as employment and unemployment, family composition, education, mobility, and income. The wealth and accuracy of such data now available to the demographer is of quite different order from that provided 20 years ago. This must be credited in part to the competence of the census staff, but in part it must be attributed to the force of interests in legislative circles. Fortunately economic, social, and hygienic data are also demographic data. Therefore, the volume of information on the "characteristics" of populations rises with the growth and diversification of technology and social interests.

1950 WORLD CENSUS OF AGRICULTURE

Of interest to sociologists are the research possibilities in the 1950 World Census of Agriculture. Data will be available on the volume of production of all important agricultural products, number of livestock, number of agricultural holdings and their principal characteristics, number and characteristics of the people who secure their livelihood from agriculture, and areas under crops. Over half of the world's population is represented in this Census. Demographers will be interested in the attempt of FAO to (a) improve statistical methods and the training of technical personnel so that the results will be reasonably accurate, (b) the setting up of classification and conversion schemes for tabulation and presentation of the data so that the statistics will be additive, (c) the development of a basic list of items to be investigated in all countries, with appropriate provision for variation in the agricultural patterns for the various countries, so that the data will give an adequate account of the world's agriculture, (d) the development of precise definitions and concepts with reference to these items so that the data will be comparable. This program has been the outcome of experience and advice from all parts of the world and points to the making of considerable progress in this field.

WORLD POPULATION TRENDS AND FUTURE RESOURCES

Although the growth of population which came with the growth of Western technology has not constituted, in itself, a problem, we are more than ever concerned today about the future of the world's people. There is a growing fear that natural resources are approaching the limits of their exploitation. Many think that the rate at which production from natural resources is likely to increase will be slower than present rates of population growth. According to J. Russell Whittaker, "we must have either an expansion of land resources or increased production of present resources if the population of the foreseeable future is to be fed at even minimum levels of adequacy." [4]

The scope of the problem is indicated by the projections of world population prepared by the staff of the United Nations. The projections of the United Nations consist of calculations of a hypothetical 1980 population for the world. The calculations are based on the assumption of birth and death rates continuing at observed 1946-48 levels. If we accept this assumption, the population of the world may be estimated at 3,523 million for 1980. Projections have been made which are based on three sets of assumptions—high, low, and medium —taking into account differential trends and the stage of each medium in the demographic revolution. From these, we may conclude that the population of the world will increase at least five hundred million by 1980 and under favorable conditions, as much as 1,200 million.

These projections of world population document the assertion that there must be a great increase in the world's productivity even if present levels of living as they now exist in various parts of the world, are to be maintained. Philip M. Hauser[5] thinks the fantastic rate of growth of population cannot possibly be sustained. We must control fertility! Yet, no new means for rapidly modifying value systems and human motivation have been developed. Neither have we found means to produce adequate incentives in mass populations to increase productivity. Thus the Gordian knot of the "population problem" threatens to be more formidable than the various economic development programs can cope with, and even threatens the maintenance of world peace and order.

QUALITATIVE ASPECTS OF POPULATION

There is a growing recognition that demographers have special responsibility for investigating the influence of population changes on the characteristics of populations. This responsibility is referred to in the statutes of the Population Association of America and in the statutes of the International Union for the Scientific Study of Population which discusses the *qualitative aspects* of population. Interest in the relation of population trends to genetic characteristics, for example, is the joint province of demographers and geneticists, as their studies bear on the special field of eugenics. This subject merits special emphasis because of its profound importance for the future of mankind and the absence of support by any special interest groups. Qualitative population studies made on the relation of differential production to the distribution of intelligence (survey of eleven-year-old children in Scotland in 1947, as a sequel to a comparable survey in 1932) and Glick's analysis of the changes in the life cycle of families are of interest. Glick's study indicates the need for more effective rapport between students of the family and students of population trends, in the planning of research.

We seem to be moving toward complex problems involving demography, sociology, psychology—problems such as the relation of population trends to attitude formation, values, and behavior—including special problems in political behavior, delinquency, and mental disease.

Some authorities believe that the qualitative aspects of population changes are now more important and interesting than questions relating to the trend of the total number.

METHODOLOGY

The field of population is on the whole in good shape as regards methodology. A considerable portion of the research energy of population students has been devoted to devising methods of "correcting," "adjusting," or "refining" the data so as to improve the quality and precision of the measurements used. The methods available to the research student today are, in fact, superior to the data with which he must work, and more than a small part of the methods used have been devised to deal with inadequate data.

Since fertility, mortality and other vital phenomena are greatly affected by the structure of a population, particularly by its age and sex composition, methodological developments have taken the direction of producing measurements which in a scientific sense permit control of these variant structural characteristics. Thus, to control the age and sex composition of a population so as to study, let us say, the impact of economic or cultural factors on fertility and mortality, various methods of standardization have been devised to reveal differentials which crude rates tend to distort or obscure.

Other important methodological developments lie in the "projection" of populations, which under stipulated assumptions, tell us what the numbers and composition of future populations would be. However, there is still some confusion about the meaning and usefulness of such projections which are all too frequently confused with predictions.

Of considerable interest, is the development of efficient procedures for sampling human populations. The possibility of obtaining basic "core" population and vital statistics with precision and timeliness has been greatly extended. Moreover, these methods have greatly increased the feasibility of intensive investigations to get at psychological and cultural factors in population dynamics.

But the demographer, too, must look to methodological developments in other fields for help. The relatively recent attention devoted to psychological and social-psychological aspects of population dynamics has made it clear that the population student, like his colleagues in other social sciences, is dependent on the development of better psychometric and other techniques designed to get at basic attitudes and motivation in human behavior.

THEORY

A look at the whole of the area of population study today convinces one that research in the field shows a predominantly empirical and practical orientation. Theoretical inquiry for the most part takes the form of concern with techniques and procedures for analyzing quantitative data. Probably the major contribution of sociologists to population theory to date is an indirect one, and consists largely in placing emphasis on cultural and institutional factors as opposed to biological and genetic factors in dealing with the problem of quality in population.

There is a growing awareness among students of population of the errors incident to too direct application of stable population functions to empirical populations—especially in the case of inferences based on observations at a particular point in time. Man as an animal is both mobile and social. The age and sex composition of many human populations deviates appreciably from a biological structure, due to the effects of migration. Also, human behavior is influenced by changing social conditions. The uncritical application of stable population theory to real populations can, therefore, lead to irrational conclusions. This points to the need for caution in the application of analytical theory and the necessity for refining and adding to the available theoretical constructs.

Some developments toward the kind of integrated theory that might serve as a guide for the interpretation of demography's diverse and particularized findings have taken place. An adequate theory has been defined as a dynamic theory, that would take a multi-science approach and take account of demographic interrelations as between countries and groups within nations.

According to Rupert B. Vance,[6] the framework for one such theory is now emerging. This theory is based on the realization that the transition from high-level deaths and births to the new equilibrium at a low level of vital rates furnishes the population dynamics for the last 300 years of the Western world. The line of succession runs from Dr. Walter Willcox whose studies of world population growth opened up this whole field to Dr. Frank Notestein who has done so much to clinch the analysis. The Demographic Revolution unfolds in a manner reminiscent of the Industrial Revolution. Different countries reach different stages of this transition in terms of (1) a time sequence in the West and (2) in terms of culture contacts and time states as regards non-Western countries.

The marked increase in the population of Europe is seen as due to the demographic gap which emerged as fertility remained high for 100 years and more after deaths took a sharp decline. Differential fertility emerged in the initial stage of the great decline in birth rates. Outside the West no countries now appear to have the demographic slack which new continents and untapped industrial markets once offered Europe. Demographic movements in succeeding countries, however, are to be judged by economic stages and cultural diffusion as well as the resistance to change within each culture. Such an overall view can give meaning to the many descriptive population studies now made country by country. If this transition proceeds in orderly sequence it will be the function of demographic studies to classify populations by stage and sequence.

Although this development in theory, as outlined by Rupert S. Vance seems encouraging, the present status of population theory is best summed up in the following statement of Warren S. Thompson: "Population study in the United States has not greatly concerned itself with theory as such but has rather used statistical methods to discover and interpret the facts in particular problems, leaving the theory to take care of itself." [7]

OUTLOOK FOR THE FUTURE

This brief survey of current trends in population study might be concluded by attempting to answer briefly the following questions: What are the areas of population that need improvement? What are the important frontiers of research? What is the outlook for the field of population?

In the field of vital statistics the greatest need without question is the need for improving the completeness of birth and death registration. There is also need for greater detail in the cross-classification of birth and death tabulations which, in their present form, although valuable, obscure many important relationships. There is particularly need for the introduction of such items as duration of marriage, parity, characteristics of the father, and indexes of social-economic and cultural level as basic controls in the tabulation of births. Similarly there is need for the introduction of various indexes of social-economic and cultural status and of occupation in the tabulation of deaths. Perhaps the most conspicuous need in this area, however, lies in the need for comprehensive coverage in marriage and divorce statistics.

More research is needed to obtain knowledge concerning actual causal relationships, sequences of behavior, basic attitudes, and human motivations that enter into the patterns we can describe in relatively precise quantitative terms. One badly needed and important type of research activity in this area is that which would explore specific problems of the acceptability and utilization of contraception and other means of voluntary population control. We must attempt to answer the question: How can the areas of the world containing impoverished masses of people and constituting over half of the world's total population be subjected to the influences of modern science and technology without producing population increases that would make the social and economic problems we face today even more difficult?

It is apparent that the research interests of the student of population cut across the interests of the conventionally organized social and natural science disciplines, including medical men, economists, sociologists, biologists, geneticists, geographers, statisticians, and even physicists. Population as a field for research is a kind of melting pot for a variety of scientists, on the one hand, and engineers or practitioners on the other. As a focal area for the intermingling of diverse interests, the field of population affords a relatively unique opportunity for the cross-fertilization of theory and methods and for the pursuit of interdisciplinary researches.

SELECTED BIBLIOGRAPHY

A. M. Carr-Saunders, *World Population: Growth and Present Trends* (Oxford: Clarendon Press, 1936). One of the best introductions to the problem of world population.

Robert C. Cook, *Human Fertility: The Modern Dilemma* (New York: William Sloane Associates, 1951). A basic introduction to the problem.

Walter Firey, "Review of Current Research in Demography and Human Ecology," *American Sociological Review*, XVII (April, 1952).

Imre Ferenczi and Walter F. Wilcox, *International Migrations* (New York: National Bureau of Economic Research, 1929). Although outdated, good on international migration data; the other volumes contain interesting articles by competent population specialists.

N. H. Hansen, W. N. Hurwitz and Leon Pritzker, "The Accuracy of Census Results," *American Sociological Review*, XVIII (August, 1953), 416-423.

Paul K. Hatt, Ed., *World Population and Future Resources* (New York: American Book Co., 1952). Contains several valuable studies.

P. M. Hauser, "Present Status and Prospects of Research in Population," *American Sociological Review*, XIII, 4 (August, 1948).

Harry Jerome, *Migration and the Business Cycle* (New York: National Bureau of Economic Research, 1926). Propounds the theory that in migration in the United States the pull is greater than the push.

C. V. Kiser and P. K. Whelpton, "Fertility Planning and Rates by Socio-Economic Status," *The Milbank Memorial Fund Quarterly*, XXVII (April, 1949), 61-94.

Paul H. Landis and Paul K. Hatt, *Population Problems* (New York: American Book Co., 1954). A substantial textbook.

Milbank Memorial Fund, *Demographic Studies of Selected Areas of Rapid Growth* (Proceedings of the Twenty-Second Annual Conference, April 12-13, 1944, New York, 1944).

Report of the Committee on Research, *American Sociological Review*, XX (February, 1955), 97-100.

T. Lynn Smith, *Population Analysis* (New York: McGraw-Hill, 1948). One of the best introductory statements.

Joseph L. Spengler and Otis Dudley Duncan, Eds., *Demographic Analysis* (Glencoe, Ill.: The Free Press, 1956). The best available collection of papers exemplifying historical, regional, topical, and methodological approaches to population and demographic problems.

Warren Thompson, *Population Problems* (New York: McGraw-Hill Book Co., 1953). A straight-forward presentation.

Rupert D. Vance, "Is Theory for Demographers?" *Social Forces,* XXXI, 1 (October, 1952).

Walter P. Willcox, *Studies in American Demography* (Ithaca, N. Y.: Cornell University Press, 1940), chapter 20.

Harry R. Doby, Assistant Professor of Sociology, Central Michigan College (Mt. Pleasant, Mich.), is the author of articles in professional publications and joint editor (with Bernard N. Meltzer and Philip M. Smith) of the forthcoming *Readings in Educational Sociology* (to be published by Thomas Y. Crowell Company in 1958).

NOTES

1. The writer is indebted to Dr. Sherman Ricards for his generous loan of materials for this study.

2. Report of the Committee on Research, *American Sociological Review,* XX February, 1955), 97-100.

3. *Index to the American Sociological Review,* Volumes 1-20, 1936-1955, Leonard Broom, editor (published by the American Sociological Society, New York University, Washington Square, New York, N. Y., 1956).

4. *World Population and Future Resources,* Edited by Paul K. Hatt (New York: American Book Co., 1952), 75.

5. Philip M. Hauser, "World Population Trends," *Sociology and Social Research* (November-December, 1954), 79.

6. Rupert H. Vance, "Is Theory for Demographers?" *Social Forces,* XXXI, No. 1 (Oct., 1952).

7. Warren S. Thompson, "Population Studies," *American Journal of Sociology,* I, No. 6 (May, 1945), 437.

HISTORICAL SOCIOLOGY

Harry Elmer Barnes
Malibu (California)

THE NATURE OF HISTORICAL SOCIOLOGY

It is not to easy to define the nature and province of historical sociology. Despite the fact that many of the early sociologists were more interested in the history of human society than any other phase of their subject, there does not exist in any language a comprehensive work covering the development of human society from primitive origins to the atomic age. Interest in historical sociology has sharply declined among sociologists during the preceding half-century, and especially since the first World War. Hence, one cannot readily refer a reader or student to a book which clearly illustrates the nature of this field of sociological study. It should not be confused with the more general and descriptive history of civilization, although there are many relationships between these two approaches to the development of human activities and institutions. In a broad way, it would not be misleading to say that historical sociology is made up mainly of the theories, generalizations, and laws that may be derived from the history of civilization.

It is probable that we can best delineate the scope and purpose of historical sociology by indicating the main problems with which it deals. It seeks to describe and explain the origins of associated life among human beings, relying mainly upon the data assembled by anthropogeography, human ecology, biology and psychology. It traces the development of social organization, structures and institutions. It recounts the social beliefs and attitudes which have influenced and shaped social activities and social changes during the course of history. It examines the validity of the theory of specific and universal stages in the growth of social life and organization. It endeavors to discover whether there are valid laws or trends in social evolution which apply to all humanity. It sets forth the historical basis of

238

social maladjustment, laying special stress on cultural lag in treating the period since the rise of modern mechanical technology. In so doing it not only points out the disparity between machines and institutions but also the differences in the relative rate of development among the various types of human institutions.[1]

The main purpose of all this is to provide a broad and genetic perspective which will enable us better to understand social relations today and help to plan a more rational, secure and prosperous society in days to come. Unfortunately, sociologists have tended to spurn, disparage or ignore this invaluable perspective just about in proportion to the extent to which better historical data have been placed at their disposal in recent years.

SOME REMOTE ORIGINS OF HISTORICAL SOCIOLOGY

It is understandable that historical sociology developed rather late in man's intellectual experience.[2] Until the rise of the doctrine of evolution and the establishment of so-called prehistoric archeology, there was little substantial information to give man any true conception of a long human past on the planet. The thoughts of primitive man on the subject could only have run back a few generations, and all customs and material culture were regarded as the work of supernatural forces. Primitive creation myths were carried over into the early historical period in such well-known examples as the Osiris Myth, the Gilgamesh Epic, and the Book of Genesis. Everything was attributed to the gods, and the work of the latter was regarded as relatively recent. Perhaps the first real perception of the enormity of the human part is to be found in Book III of Plato's *Laws,* where he observes that "Every man should understand that the human race either had no beginning at all, and will never have an end, or that it began an immense while ago." Many of the Greek and Roman writers held that man originally lived in a wild and unregulated state of nature, which came to an end when orderly society was established, either by force or sociability.

A very common belief in ancient times was that there had been a marked decline in human felicity with the progress of civilization, thus anticipating some of the ideas of Rousseau. The Hebrews pictured a Garden of Eden and a subsequent "fall of man." The Greeks and Romans widely believed that there had been an original Golden Age. This was notably the view of the Roman philosopher, Seneca (3 B.C.-A.D. 65). The early Christian Fathers merged Seneca's hypothesis of a primordial Golden Age with the Hebrew myth of the Garden of Eden, and Seneca's idea of a subsequent decline of human well-being with the Hebrew tale of the "fall of man" after the expulsion from Eden. The following period of misery, confusion and disorder was mitigated by the rise of orderly social relations as a result of the establishment of political society or the state. The Christian Fathers added to the pagan views of the past and current state of society, the idea, drawn from the Persians, that all earthly experience was merely a preparation for the bliss of saved souls in the world to come. These views, best synthesized by St. Augustine in his *City of God*, were passed on to the medieval theologians and social philosophers, and constituted the main dogmas of historical sociology during the Middle Ages.

The two most substantial contributions to historical sociology in classical antiquity came from an historian, Polybius (203-121 B.C.), and a poet, Lucretius (99-55 B.C.). In his *History of Rome,* Polybius attributed the origins of associated life to primitive man's sense of weakness in isolation, to reflective sympathy, and to a perception of likeness (similar to Giddings' later notion of "consciousness of kind"). Political society originated in force, but was made permanent and improved as a result of a perception of its utility to society. Polybius' interpretation of the origins and nature of customs and morals anticipated the views of William Graham Sumner.

It is probable that Epicurus (c. 342-270 B.C.) made the most impressive contribution to historical sociology of all ancient writers. Since, however, virtually all of his writings have been lost, we have to rely for the views of the Epicureans upon the Roman poet, Lucretius (96-55 B.C.) who acknowledged that his statement was far briefer and much inferior to the presentation made by Epicurus. In his great philosophical poem, *On the Nature of Things,* Lucretius produced a theory of social evolution which was far superior as a general statement to anything else presented until the time of the late eighteenth-century social philosophers. The struggle for existence; the survival of the fittest; the modes of living among primitive peoples; the origin of fire, language, industry, religion, domestic relations, and the arts of pleasure; the sequence of the main culture ages; and the development of economic relations were set forth with amazing clearness and accuracy. It required nearly two thousand years for social and historical thought in Christian lands to catch up again with his perspective and interpretations.

The medieval Christians produced no realistic writer on historical sociology, but one of great ability and insight, for a person of that period, appeared in the Muslim scholar and statesman, Ibn Khaldun (1332-1406), author of the notable *Prolegomena to Universal History*. He founded the philosophy of history, provided a brilliant description of tribal society, traced in some detail the stages in the evolution of human society, and emphasized the unity and continuity of the historical process. The first approximation to historical sociology in Christian Europe was contained in the works of the French political philosopher Jean Bodin (1530-96), author of two notable books: *Six Books concerning a Commonwealth*, and *A Method for Easily Understanding History*. Bodin followed Aristotle and anticipated David Hume and modern sociologists in holding that society came into being as a result of the natural sociability of man, founded on reflective sympathy. He foreshadowed Adam Ferguson, Gumplowicz and the social Darwinists in contending that the state was set up through force. His work on history was the foremost Christian contribution to the philosophy of history down to that time. The Spanish Jesuit philosopher, Juan de Mariana (1536-1624), in his work on *Royalty and its Establishment*, not only anticipated Rousseau's alluring picture of primitive society in the state of nature, but also John Fiske's idea that human society is mainly a product of the unique prolongation of human infancy. He believed that political society arose from the sense of its utility and was established through a social contract.

The most influential contribution to historical sociology during the early modern period was the idea that human society arose from deliberative action, resulting in a social contract to live together in an orderly fashion. The idea was vaguely anticipated by some of the classical social philosophers, and was first clearly set forth by the able Christian social philosopher, Aeneas Sylvius (later Pope Sylvester II) (1405-64). The fully developed conception of the social contract was first elaborated by an English churchman, Richard Hooker, (1552-1600), in his *Laws of an Ecclesiastical Polity*. It was further expanded by a notable group of writers, mainly Thomas Hobbes, (1588-1679); Algernon Sidney (1622-83); John Locke (1632-1704); Baruch Spinoza (1632-77); Jean Jacques Rousseau (1712-78); and Immanuel Kant (1724-1804).

In a broad and general way, the social contract theory ran as follows: men originally lived happily in a state of nature, but the rise of property produced envy, quarrels and disorder until life became unendurable—as Hobbes expressed it, a life that was "poor, nasty, brutish and short." To escape from such a situation it was decided to set up orderly social relations through a contract to live peacefully, one with another. But, to assure this condition, it was necessary to establish political society or the state, and this was done by a second or governmental contract. Some of these social contract philosophers believed that this doctrine was a true history of the origins of society and the state; others, notably Hobbes, Spinoza and Kant, regarded it chiefly as a philosophical assumption, or what sociologists today call a "social construct."

The social contract theory was devastatingly attacked by the British philospher, David Hume (1711-76), from the logical, psychological, and historical points of view. Logically and psychologically, Hume condemned the social contract theory as implying knowledge prior to experience—that men could have realized the value of orderly social relations before ever living under such conditions. Historically, he held that there was no record of a society being thus created. Hume held that society arose through a social instinct based on reflective sympathy, while the state came into being through force and coercion. Hume's views were followed and systematized in the *History of Civil Society* by Adam Ferguson (1723-1816), a Scotch philosopher who is regarded by many as the real founder of historical sociology.

Another important contribution to the field of historical sociology in this stage was the emergence of the theory of progress, which reversed the classical and Christian idea of social and cultural decline from pristine paradise.[3] The idea of human progress was first set forth by the English scholar, Francis Bacon (1561-1626), especially in his *New Atlantis*. He denied that the ancients were superior to moderns in wisdom and knowledge, and held that a social utopia might be brought about through a better application of science and technology to human problems. The doctrine of progress was further developed by Bernard de Fontenelle (1657-1757), in his *Dialogues of the Dead,* and *Disgression on the Ancients and the Moderns,* and by Charles Perrault (1628-1703), in his *Parallel of the Ancients and Moderns.* These writers contended that there has been no biological progress during the course of history and that achievements in the field of aesthetic endeavor provide no evidence of progress. But in the realm of material culture there has been vast progress since ancient times. This is essentially the view still held by historical sociologists and cultural historians.

The theory of progress was given more systematic and precise statement by the English political philosopher, William Godwin (1756-1836), in his *Inquiry Concerning Political Justice,* and by the French writer, the Marquis de Condorcet (1743-94), in his *Sketch of the Intellectual Progress of Mankind.* The first contention that progress might be assured and made permanent by actual social planning was embodied in the work of the French writer, Abbé de Saint-Pierre (1658-1753), in his *Discourse on the Polysynodie.* He thus anticipated the dynamic teleological views of Auguste Comte and Lester F. Ward.

Another important addition to the equipment of historical students of society arose as a result of the expansion of Europe and the explorations, discoveries and colonial enterprise that followed the voyages of Columbus and Vasco da Gama.[4] The explorers brought back a large body of new information bearing on the life of both primitive and modern men that had been hitherto little known to Europeans. This emphasized the great variety of customs and attitudes exhibited by mankind relative to all phases of human activities, and tended to break down the sociological provincialism of European writers. The best early summary of such information was embodied in the *Travels into Persia and the East Indies* by Jean Chardin (1643-1715). Reflection on the significance of such material led to the *Spirit of Laws* by the Baron de Montesquieu (1689-1755), and to the *Customs of American Savages Compared with the Customs of Early Times* by Joseph François Lafiteau (1681-1746). This line of thought and writing led to such important later phases of historical sociology as William Graham Sumner's *Folkways,* and the comparative cultural anthropology of men like Julius Lippert (1839-1909), who profoundly influenced Sumner.

Comparative sociology and the new knowledge of manners and customs exerted a powerful influence on the rise of the history of civilization in the writings of Voltaire (1697-1778) and his successors. Voltaire's *Essay on the Manners and Spirit of the Nations* (1756) is rather generally regarded as the first impressive work on the history of civilization, a field closely related to historical sociology and a chief source of information for the latter. Also contributing much to a broad perspective on the human past was the rise of the philosophy of history in the works of Johann Gottfried Herder (1744-1803) and his successors. The most suggestive and stimulating of all the books in this field was Herder's volume, *Ideas for the Philosophy of the History of Mankind.*

The final contribution to the formative period of historical sociology which we shall mention here is associated with the rise of geology and prehistoric archeology in the eighteenth century.[5] These destroyed the restricted conception of the human past which had come down from the ancient creation tales. The Hebrew chronology, which had been adopted by the Christians, had held that mankind was created, a few days after the earth took form, about 4000 years before Christ. After the establishment of scientific geology and the first impressive discoveries by archeologists dealing with the stone ages, any such limited conception of terrestrial and human time was rendered completely absurd. Historical sociology was now provided with a temporal perspective on a substantial scientific foundation, such as Plato had only intuitively perceived.

The establishment of scientific geology, which gave a true idea of the vast age of the earth, is associated with the work of John Mitchell (1724-1793), Abraham Werner (1749-1817), James Hutton (1726-1797), and Charles Lyell (1797-1875). The first great classic was Lyell's *Principles of Geology* (1830-33).

Geology provided the background and foundation for significant work in prehistoric archeology. It revealed the total age of the earth and that of strata of rocks near the surface. When the first students of the stone ages found human skeletal remains and artifacts in rock formations tens of thousands of years old, it was quite evident that man and his works dated from a period long anterior to 4004 B.C. The leading pioneers in prehistoric archeology were John Frere, William Buckland, C. J. Thomsen and, above all, the able Frenchman, Jacques Boucher de Perthes (1788-1868). While these men were putting archeology on its feet to analyze the significance of ancient human artifacts, men like Friedrich Blumenbach (1752-1840) were founding physical anthropology to enable scholars to interpret the nature and meaning of human bones found in geological formations of relatively great antiquity.

Archeology, physical anthropology, and the ethnological discoveries of explorers stimulated scholars to draw a parallel between primitive men and existing savages and to launch the study of comparative anthropology even before the rise of Darwinian biology.

Leaders here were such men as Gustav Klemm and Franz Theodor Waitz (1821-1864). But the full flower of historical sociology could not appear until the exposition of Herbert Spencer's doctrine of cosmic evolution and the Darwinian theory of biological evolution. To these and their impact on historical sociology we may now turn our attention.

EVOLUTIONARY THEORY AND SOCIOLOGY

The most important single contribution to the establishment of historical sociology on the firm foundation of scientific method was the introduction of the doctrine of evolution, applied to society and its institutions.[6]

It is commonly believed that this was almost wholly due to the work of Charles Darwin. But the formulation of a general theory of evolution, cosmic as well as social, was overwhelmingly the result of the writings of Herbert Spencer (1820-1903). Spencer worked out a conception of evolution on a universal basis, interpreted in terms of physical processes. As he expressed it: "Evolution is an integration of matter and a concomitant dissipation of motion, during which matter passes from a relatively indefinite, incoherent homogeneity to a relatively coherent heterogeneity and during which the retained motion undergoes a parallel transformation." In short, it consists in an integration of matter and a differentiation of form and function.

Spencer promulgated this theory in the second half of his germinal work, *First Principles*, published in 1863, and subsequently applied it to all phases of organic development, psychological growth, and social evolution. By so doing, he provided a broad panorama of the course of cosmic, terrestrial, biological and social evolution, all founded upon a secular and scientific approach. Many details of his doctrine and interpretations have been modified or entirely discarded, but the evolutionary perspective and the scientific method have remained the cornerstone of all subsequent work in the field of historical sociology. Spencer's own specific effort to expound the course of social evolution was a rather extreme, weak and naïve, if comprehensive, application of the methods and concepts of the evolutionary anthropologists, and is now rarely investigated or remembered, save by students of the history of sociological and anthropological theory. But, more than any other writer, Spencer made the evolutionary doctrine basic in all subsequent sociological thought and scholarly work.

The work of Charles Robert Darwin (1809-1882), culminating in his justly famous *Origin of Species* (1859), was limited chiefly to the field of biological evolution and rested upon such processes and factors as the struggle for existence, the survival of the fittest, variation, selection, transmission and adaptation. While he amply proved their validity when limited to the realm of biological development, he never pretended that they could be taken over literally and applied to the evolution of human society. But precisely this carry-over of Darwinian biological concepts to the social field was executed by a group of writers, generally known as "Social Darwinists." The leading members of this group were Ludwig Gumplowicz (1838-1909); Gustav Ratzenhofer (1842-1904); and Franz Oppenheimer (1864-1943). These writers stressed the idea that war and social conflict represent the social analogue of the struggle for existence in the biological realm, and constitute the mainspring of social development, just as the struggle for existence in the biological world brings about the survival of the fittest organisms.

Gumplowicz was chiefly concerned with showing how the conflicts and struggles of social groups create the state, and ultimately produce class conflicts within the state. His notion that the state, or political society, was produced and has grown chiefly as the result of wars and related conflicts is generally accepted by sociologists and political scientists, although other sociologists, such as Jacques Novicow (1849-1912), have contended that Gomplowicz overlooked many non-military factors that notably helped on the origins and development of political institutions. Ratzenhofer was more concerned with the conflicts between social classes and interest-groups within the state than he was with the earlier warfare and struggles which brought the state into being. His work in this field was of great significance for the later development of sociological theory, for upon it was based the conception of a social process as developed by Albion W. Small and his disciples. The views of Oppenheimer upon social and political origins closely resembled those of Gumplowicz and Ratzenhofer, but his work in the field of social and political evolution was more deeply involved with what he regarded as the great social evil through the ages, namely, land monopoly, which had been a product of past conquests. The views of these European writers were essentially accepted in the United States by Lester Frank Ward (1841-1913), especially in his later works, such as *Pure Sociology* (1903).

A more discriminating and acceptable application of Darwinian theories to social evolution was made by William Graham Sumner (1840-1910), and his disciple, Albert Galloway Keller (1874-   ), especially in the latter's *Societal Evolution*. Keller believed that the "mores," as presented and analyzed by Sumner, could be substituted for germ cells and embryos in the organic world, and that the Darwinian processes of variation, selection, transmission and adaptation could legitimately be applied to the development and operations of the mores. Another aspect of applying Darwinism to social evolution was to be seen in the rise and temporary popularity of the doctrine of a definite analogy between the biological organism and society. The development of society was comparable to the growth of an organism. This approach was voluminously expounded by such writers as Spencer, Paul von Lilienfeld (1829-1903); Albert Schaeffle (1831-1903), and René Worms (1869-1926). But the most influential impact of the Darwinian impulse upon historical sociology consisted in the rise of evolutionary and comparative anthropology.

THE EVOLUTIONARY AND COMPARATIVE METHOD IN ANTHROPOLOGY

So far as dealing with the actual course of social development is concerned, there is little doubt that the most fruitful innovation growing out of evolutionary thought was the rise of comparative, or evolutionary, anthropology. Although it was mainly concerned with social and political origins, it still colored the methods and conclusions of historical sociology for more than a half-century after the heyday of Spencer and Darwin.[7]

Those who adhered to this approach to social origins held that there are universal organic laws of development in the growth of social institutions. It was believed that there had been orderly and gradual social growth and change, much the same the world over, and in general proceeding from the simple to the complex. The universality and similarity of social development among all peoples were predicated upon the unity of the human mind and similarities in the geographical environment. This would inevitably produce parallelisms in institutional and cultural evolution among peoples widely separated in geographic distribution. The course of social evolution was assumed in advance, and to validate the predetermined scheme isolated examples of all types of culture, drawn from the most diverse regions and periods of time, were linked together. The most voluminous contributors to this school of thought were Charles J. M. Letourneau (1831-1904), Sir James George Frazer (1854-1941), and by far the most substantial, Lewis Henry Morgan (1818-1881).

Letourneau wrote extensively and uncritically upon the evolution of many institutions and phases of social life, such as property, political institutions, law, morals, and the changing status of women. He summarized his theories and findings in a work on *Sociology Based on Ethnology* (1892). Frazer wrote equally voluminously, mainly on various phases of religious origins and comparative religion. His most widely read book was *The Golden Bough,* which was first published in 1900, and frequently enlarged and reprinted. Frazer wrote eloquently and was easily the most popular of all the writers of the evolutionary school. While he made many mistakes in detail, no other author has done as much to relate religion to its secular, anthropological background.

Morgan was a more careful and reliable writer than either Letourneau or Frazer. Unlike Letourneau or Frazer, Morgan spent considerable time in the field and studied primitive life at first hand with much astuteness. His earliest contribution to social evolution was his *Systems of Consanguinity and Affinity of the Human Family,* which appeared in 1870. Although his theory of the evolution of the family has been rather completely discredited by subsequent zoölogical and anthropological research, it was a real *tour de force* for the time when it was published. Much more important was his *Ancient Society* which was published in 1877. Here, he traced the evolution of social institutions from the most rudimentary savagery to the establishment of civilization with the rise of political society in the ancient Near East. He associated the successive stages of social evolution with related advances in technology. No other book ever published in the field of social science exerted as great an influence upon sociological conceptions of the course of social evolution in primitive times. For more than a generation it was the veritable bible of anthropologists and those sociologists who were interested in the history of the human society. While many of Morgan's views were challenged by later anthropologists, notably by Robert H. Lowie in his *Primitive Society* (1920), his *Ancient Society* is, historically speaking, probably the most important and influential single book which has appeared in the course of the development of historical sociology. By the time its content was seriously challenged, most sociologists had ceased to show much interest in historical sociology, aside from the work of men like Alfred Vierkandt, William F. Ogburn, C. A. Ellwood, F. S. Chapin, and M. M. Willey, who were mainly influenced by the more critical anthropology of Franz Boas, R. R. Marett and P. M. Ehrenreich. They gave their attention chiefly to theories of cultural change.

MORE CRITICAL TRENDS IN ANTHROPOLOGY AND HISTORICAL SOCIOLOGY

While the general evolutionary approach continued to dominate anthropology and sociology long after the days of the early and more extreme school, research was conducted in more precise and discriminating fashion and the results of such work were less open to challenge by later discoveries[3].

The outstanding figure in this transitional period was the eminent English anthropologist, Sir Edward Burnett Tylor, (1832-1917) who dominated the English scene as fully as Morgan did the American. His outstanding work was *Primitive Culture* (1871), in which he developed his famous theory of Animism as the earliest stage of religious life. He summarized his views in a brief book, *Anthropology* (1881), and it is a tribute to his work that the book remains today the most illuminating introduction to primitive life, unmarred by serious errors. He rejected the dogma of primitive promiscuity, accepted the idea of the diffusion of culture, as well as independent origins, anticipated the conception that historical sociology is chiefly a study of cultural change by means of a science of culturology, and introduced the technique of studying primitive life on a statistical basis, a method applied much later by his English successors, L. T. Hobhouse, G. C. Wheeler and Morris Ginsberg.

While he adhered essentially to the methods and ideas of the older evolutionary school, the Finnish anthropologist, Edward A. Westermarck (1882-1939), was saved from earlier mistakes chiefly through the fact that he checked his original assumptions and somewhat uncritical methods of library research by spending much time in actual field work, especially in Morocco. His most famous work was his classic, *History of Human Marriage,* which was first published in 1891 and was enlarged and reprinted many times thereafter. He rejected the then popular view of the evolution of the family from an alleged primitive promiscuity, and established the fact that monogamy has been the prevailing type of human family from the earliest times to the present day. Later, he applied a discriminating use of evolutionary theory to the development of moral ideas and practices. Westermarck's conclusions on the history of the family were about the only departure from the dogmas of the evolutionary school which was widely heeded at the time by sociologists concerned with social evolution.

A voluminous return to the evolutionary methods appeared with the publication of Robert Briffault's three-volume work on *The Mothers,* which came out in 1927. But even Briffault did not contend that there had ever been any universal period of a primitive matriarchate, as had been maintained by J. J. Bachofen—a period in which women actually ruled society. But, accepting John Fiske's theory of the importance of the prolongation of human infancy, Briffault did hold that in primitive society the role and influence of females were predominant in creating group sentiments, the social mind, and the early institutions of the human race. In other words, women first socialized the race. While his methods were open to the same criticism as those of the early exponents of the evolutionary theory, Briffault's notions of the role of women in primitive society cannot be laughed out of court and constitute an important contribution to historical sociology, if accepted with some discrimination and restraint.

The German scholar most comparable to Tylor in England was Julius Lippert (1839-1909). He wrote widely on many phases of primitive life and cultural history, and summarized most of his views in his book on *The Cultural History of Mankind* (1887). While accepting in a broad and general way the basic assumptions of the evolutionary school, he rejected many of its dogmas, such as inevitable unilateral evolution and parallel cultural development, universal patterns of institutional and cultural growth, and invariable stages of institutional evolution. He held that the chief fact of historical sociology is cultural evolution, maintained that culture is superorganic, and stressed the importance of cultural diffusion as well as independent development of cultural traits. He was an important link between evolutionary anthropology and contemporary culturology. Lippert exerted a considerable influence upon American historical sociology, since his writings were a main source upon which Sumner and Keller drew for Sumner's work on *Folkways* and the Sumner-Keller, *Science of Society.*

No writer of the transitional school more fully reflected the conflicting trends than the able Russian social historian and anthropologist, Maksim Kovalevsky (1851-1916). He adhered to the general framework of the evolutionary or comparative school, but like Westermarck spent a considerable amount of time in actual field work. He conceded that social evolution is clearly to be differentiated from biological evolution and that social development does not slavishly follow the laws of organic growth. He repudiated the "slips-of-paper" research methods of Spencer, Frazer, Westermarck and Briffault and held that evidence must not be torn from its context in the total culture of the group. Comparisons can only be made in connection with truly comparable stages and types of cultural development. He emphasized the dangers in universal generalizations, and stressed the importance of studying variations as well as identities in social evolution. These qualification on extreme evolutionism appeared mainly in Kovalevsky's later work. If he had lived to finish his *Sociology,* it is possible that he would have developed into a member of the more critical school of anthropologists and culturologists.

The full repudiation of the untenable dogmas of the evolutionary and comparative school of anthropologists appeared in the work of men like P. M. Ehrenreich in Germany; Richard R. Marett in England; and, above all, Franz Boas (1885-1942) and his disciples in the United States. The Boas school did not reject the possibility of social and cultural evolution, but they did completely repudiate the methods by which evolutionary writers reached their conclusions, such as the "slips-of-paper" research technique and the tearing of validating items from the total cultural complex. They held that a far greater amount of field work is necessary before any general picture of the evolutionary process can be produced. In doing this field work, they insisted that the anthropologist must concentrate upon what they call a *culture area,* namely a geographical region where the life and institutions of the primitive peoples to be studied represent an essentially unified, although not necessarily unique, complex. They contended that the main purpose of such intensive field work is to provide valid empirical evidence for subsequent generalizations as to possible laws or trends in social evolution. They only sounded a salutary word of caution about generalizations concerning social evolution in advance of adequate research and reliable data. What they totally rejected was the formulation of *a priori* and preconceived schemes of social evolution, and then seeking to validate them by indiscriminate gathering of often irrelevant or inadmissible evidence. Unfortunately, a few members of this critical school have gone over to such an extreme repudiation of evolutionary doctrines that their position is as untenable as the dogmas of the earlier evolutionists.

It might be useful at this time to refer briefly to the American scene with respect to the changes in methods and attitudes relative to anthropology and historical sociology. We have already noted that Lewis Henry Morgan was the main American example of the methods and conclusions of the evolutionary or comparative school—probably the ablest member of this group. The Westermarck stage was well represented by the historian and sociologist, George Elliot Howard, whose main interest also lay in the history of the family. He produced a monumental *History of Matrimonial Institutions*. The attitudes of Lippert were mirrored in the work of Sumner and Keller, who were Lippert's chief American admirers. W. I. Thomas's *Source Book for Social Origins* (1909) represented much the same ethnographic interests. The dualism between the old and the new, as illustrated by Kovalevsky, was reflected in the able work of Hutton Webster, whose rigorous training as an historian protected him against serious pitfalls in his discriminating use of the comparative method. We have already indicated that Boas and his disciple represented the full culmination of the critical school and the rejection of the main dogmas and methods of the evolutionary and comparative group. William F. Ogburn, Charles A. Ellwood, and F. Stuart Chapin were representative sociologists who exploited these new critical trends. Leslie A. White has been the most vigorous advocate of a new science of culturology, which will be founded on the ideas of Tylor, Lippert, Vierkandt, Kroeber and others, to the effect that culture is a unique, super-organic product.

THEORIES OF CULTURAL EVOLUTION

With the rise of critical anthropology and its impact on historical sociology, interest tended to center on culture as the raw material for study, and attention was turned to theories of cultural change rather than to the laws of unilateral evolution which had absorbed the evolutionary and comparative school. The latter had held to the doctrine of the independent origins and evolution of culture and institutions, a process which had been the same the world over.[9]

Beginning in a moderate degree with Tylor and Lippert, and encouraged by the eminent anthropogeographer, Friedrich Ratzel, a revolt arose against this view on the part of writers who went to the opposite extreme and contended that the independent origin of a cultural trait or institution was relatively rare. Human inventiveness in this field was held to be very limited. The observed similarity of cultural traits and institutions over the planet was alleged to be due mainly to their diffusion through contacts made between the peoples involved. The outstanding exponents of this rejection of the theory of independent development were Leo Frobenius, Fritz Graebner, G. Elliot Smith, and W. J. Perry. The latter went to the extreme of contending that the pyramid culture of Yucatan must have been brought from Egypt.

More moderate and critical scholars have tended to reject both of these extreme stands and to adopt a more scientific historical and analytical procedure. This has been promoted chiefly by Felix von Luschan and P. M. Ehrenreich in Germany; Marett in England; and Boas and his followers in the United States. They contended that many alleged parallelisms are only superficially identical and are not such in their deeper psychic or cultural content. Again, real similarities may have developed from quite different origins through what they call the process of "convergence." One of the leading theoreticians of the Boas School, Alexander A. Goldenweiser, made the telling point that, due to the biopsychic nature of man, the unity of the human mind, and the similarities in geographic surroundings, the varieties of material culture, social institutions, and group beliefs are inevitably limited. Hence, we may expect to find many similarities in culture without any contacts whatever between the peoples involved.

Another recent effort to solve the problem of cultural orgins, diversities and similarities is what is known as the functional analysis, most comprehensively stated by Bronislaw Malinowski (1884-1942), in his *A Scientific Theory of Culture* (1944), and also followed in discriminating fashion by Richard Thurnwald and A. R. Radcliffe-Brown. These writers contend that cultural phenomena do not arise and develop primarily as a result of easy and widespread inventiveness or from imitation through cultural contacts and borrowing (diffusion). They are an inevitable product of the human organism in its geographical and social setting. The universal functional needs of man, expressing themselves in different habitats and social settings, suffice quite adequately to explain the origins, the similarities, and the diversities in the social evolution of mankind.

With the rise of the critical school of anthropologists, the emergence of the concept of culture as the center of anthropological interest, and the controversy over the interpretations of cultural development, anthropologists tended to shift their concern from evolution to cultural change. Since those sociologists who have shown any real interest in the history of society have always tended to rely upon the teachings of anthropologists, they soon transferred their interest from grandiose schemes and formulae of social evolution to a more intensive study of culture and cultural change. As Professor Howard Becker has well observed, they have mainly shifted their allegiance from Morgan and Frazer to Boas and his school, Marett, and other critical students of cultural origins and changes. This has been well illustrated by the sociological writings of William F. Ogburn and his followers, C. A. Ellwood, F. S. Chapin, W. D. Wallis, and others, all of whom were directly and decisively influenced by Boas, Marett, or both. Lamentably, however, by the time that critical anthropology and the intensive study of cultural traits had arrived on the scene, most sociologists had lost all interest whatever in the history of society and the genetic approach to sociological topics. They are today as ignorant of critical anthropology and culturology as they are of the work of the old evolutionary school. Such contact as they have with this field relates mainly to the debate over the relative validity of the theory of cultural lag in accounting for contemporary social problems. The American sociologist who has given most attention to the cultural approach to sociology and social science as a whole is Florian Znaniecki (1882-1958), in his *Cultural Reality* and *Cultural Sciences*. But he made no serious effort to apply this technique of analysis to social evolution as a whole.

SOCIOLOGISTS, SOCIAL EVOLUTION AND CULTURAL CHANGE

We have already made it clear that professional sociologists have rarely undertaken any independent investigation of the evolution of human society. While in the days of the earlier, systematic sociologists there was much interest in the subject of social evolution, they relied for their information and pattern of exposition upon the work of anthropologists and ethnologists, especially the comparative or evolutionary school. It may be fruitful here briefly to summarize the nature of the interest in historical sociology which has been manifested by such sociologists as have shown any serious concern over this field.[10]

August Comte (1798-1857) wrote before there had been much serious study of primitive society. Hence, his interest in the history of society was chiefly limited to the historic period, to which he gave extensive attention in his *Principles of a Positive Polity*. He postulated three main stages in the evolution of society since early historic times: (1) Theological-Military, covering mainly the ancient Near Orient; (2) Metaphysical-Legal, chiefly the classical and medieval period; and (3) the modern Scientific-Industrial Era. He provided elaborate subdivisions for each of these. This historic panorama played a vital role in Comte's sociological system. Herbert Spencer gave much attention to social evolution, following as we have seen, the methods and tenets of the evolutionary school. He believed that the outstanding trend in social evolution was the gradual transition from a social system organized primarily for warfare to one oriented chiefly for industrial purposes. He forecast the possibility of a later era in which ethical considerations would be dominant. In treating historical matters in his earlier books, Lester F. Ward was greatly influenced by Comte; in his later writings he followed Gumplowicz.

No sociologist gave more attention to social evolution and historical sociology than did Franklin Henry Giddings (1855-1931) in his early days at Columbia. Indeed, the chair he held was one of "Sociology and the History of Civilization." He was much influenced by Morgan and Comte. He divided social evolution into three successive stages: Zoögenic, or animal society; Anthropogenic, or the period of transition from animal to human society; Demogenic, or the historical period. The latter, he divided into three periods, almost identical with the Comtian scheme: the Military-religious, or ancient oriental society and the early Middle Ages; the Liberal-legal, Greece and Rome and early modern history; and the Economic-ethical, the era since the Industrial Revolution. In his later years, Giddings diverted his attention mainly into problems of psychological and statistical sociology. The Sumner-Keller activity in the ethnographic aspects of historical sociology has already been mentioned several times.

We have already pointed out that W. I. Thomas in his earlier period followed roughly the Lippert-Sumner interest in ethnography in his *Source-Book for Social Origins* (1909), although even here he stressed socio-psychological factors in evolution. In his later *Primitive Behavior* (1937), he reflected the Boas influence in shifting emphasis to the cultural approach to primitive society. He never made any attempt to fill in the gap between his work on primitive society and his many psychological studies of contemporary society and its problems. Émile Durkheim's chief contribution to historical sociology was an intensive case study of religious origins in Australia, which we shall mention later on. In other works, he viewed social evolution as essentially the transition from a social system based upon a mechanical and constraining solidarity, produced by group repression of individuality, to one founded upon organic and voluntary solidarity that arises from the social division of labor and the functional organization of society. Jacques Novicow (1849-1912) looked upon social evolution as a process whereby lower forms of conflict were transmuted into higher manifestations, the sequence being: economic, political and finally intellectual. Kovalevsky gave much attention to social evolution, dividing it into these stages: (1) the horde and matrilineal society; (2) the era of the gens and the transition to the paternal family; (3) patriarchal nomadism; (4) feudalism; and (5) democracy. Hobhouse provided a statistical study of primitive life and institutions, and interpreted social and political evolution as a sequence of stages in which kinship, authority, and citizenship have furnished the basis of social cohesion and political organization. The ablest English contribution to historical sociology was Hobhouse's *Morals in Evolution*, a book far broader in scope than its title indicates.

The eminent German sociologist, Max Weber, applied the case-study approach to historical sociology in works on ancient agrarian societies, the interrelation of religion and capitalism in early modern European society and the Far East, and the growth of rationalism. His younger brother, Alfred Weber, applied the same method in working out the interrelations between cultural history and cultural sociology. Franz Müller-Lyer produced an ingenious, if not too critical, synthesis of Spencerian evolutionism, comparative anthropology, cultural analysis, and economic determinism in tracing the process of social evolution. Like Morgan before him and Ogburn, later, he stressed the importance of technological advances in promoting institutional changes. Even more emphatic in advocating the cultural approach to historical sociology was Alfred Vierkandt (1867-   ), who held that historical sociology should be devoted primarily to a study of cultural evolution. He rejected the idea of the evolutionary and comparative anthropologists that there are any universal and inevitable trends and stages in social evolution similar the world over, and questioned the likelihood of diffusion unless a group was culturally prepared to receive any given contribution. He anticipated W. F. Ogburn by more than a decade in stressing the importance of cultural lag for history and the current social scene.

The chief American contributors to the cultural approach to historical sociology were William F. Ogburn (1886-   ) and his disciples, notably Malcolm M. Willey and Joseph Folsom, F. Stuart Chapin, Wilson D. Wallis and Charles A. Ellwood. Ogburn's basic book here was his *Social Change* (1922). He laid special stress on the relation between technology and social changes and did more than any other American sociologist to make the idea of cultural lag a vital item in all consideration of social evolution and current social problems. He was more influenced in his cultural approach by Boas and Goldenweiser than by Giddings. F. Stuart Chapin, another leading student of Giddings' contributed one of the more substantial works in the cultural approach to social evolution in his *Cultural Change,* in which he also revealed the Boas influence. He also preserved in part Giddings' famous lectures on the history of civilization and social evolution in his *Historical Introduction to the Study of Social Evolution,* and his *Historical Introduction to Social Economy.* Chapin's longtime colleague at the University of Minnesota, Wilson D. Wallis, made a worthy contribution to the field in his *Cuture and Progress.* While Charles A. Ellwood (1873-1946) is usually regarded as mainly a contributor to the psychological analysis of society, later in his life he turned to an interest in the cultural approach to sociology and social evolution, primarily due to the influence of Robert R. Marett and Morris Ginsberg. His *Cultural Evolution* is one of the more important American contributions to the field.

Several other American contributions to this field should be mentioned. In Part II of his *The Function of Socialization in Social Evolution,* Ernest W. Burgess presented the best epitome of historical sociology ever produced in the United States. The most erudite of American students of strictly historical sociology is W. Christie Mc Leod, an opinion which the writer of this chapter bases upon a careful examination of a vast unpublished manuscript by Dr.

McLeod. His knowledge and facility in a special sector of this field was revealed by his *Origin and History of Politics*. While Howard Becker has not contributed notably to the writing of historical sociology, his knowledge of the literature, principles and theories involved is unrivalled here or abroad. The most extended work by an American sociologist dealing with historical matters, that of Pitirim A. Sorokin, will be dealt with in treating the philosophy of history, where it most properly belongs. It is also worthy of note that one of the most important contributions to historical sociology came from the pen of a professional historian, Frederick J. Teggart, and was embodied in his *Prologomena to History; The Processes of History;* and the *Theory of History*. While these works suffered from Teggart's lack of knowledge of theoretical sociology, they are notable for stressing the contention that the migration of peoples and the growth of communication between them is the most dynamic factor in social evolution.

The preceding rather casual summary of some of the main contributions made to historical sociology by sociologists leads to several cogent conclusions. Sociologists have made important fragmentary and peripheral contributions to historical sociology, but this was done mainly by the earlier sociologists. No sociologist has written and published a comprehensive work covering the whole field of social evolution, in amazing contrast to the mass of books sociologists have produced in every other special field of their subject. Even such space as was given to social evolution by sociologists has been filled mainly by taking over the contributions made to the subject by anthropologists and social historians. There has never been any real "school" of historical sociology, such as there has been in biological, psychological, cultural, theoretical and statistical sociology. While the earlier sociologists gave some attention to historical sociology, their work and interests were altogether inadequate and unoriginal, and even this all but disappeared after the first quarter of the present century. At mid-century, sociologists have even tended to regard the historical treatment of sociological topics as literally a waste of time and space. E. C. Hayes' *Introduction to the Study of Sociology*, published in 1915, was the last textbook in the field to give any serious attention to historical factors, save only for the textbook edited by the present writer and Jerome Davis, and the former arbitrarily demanded the inclusion of such a section, which met with no enthusiastic response from sociologists. Many omitted this introductory historical section entirely when they used the book as a text. Moreover, the present writer has always regarded himself as professionally an historian.

SOME IMPORTANT CONTRIBUTIONS OF SOCIOLOGISTS TO METHODOLOGY IN THE FIELD OF HISTORICAL SOCIOLOGY

Although, as we have seen, sociologists have tended to minimize or ignore the importance of the history of human society, a few have made some important contributions to methodology in this field, even if their work has been mainly wasted effort.[11]

The earlier sociologists who gave most attention to historical sociology had no method of their own; they simply followed the uncritical methods of the evolutionary anthropologists. When the more critical cultural approach to historical sociology was provided by men like Boas, Marett, Ehrenreich and the like, it came too late, for sociologists were then shedding even their former inadequate attention to the subject, although Vierkandt, Ogburn, Ellwood, Chapin, and a few others, paid their passing respect to this new and helpful development.

Émile Durkheim (1858-1917) was the outstanding sociologist who launched a substantial direct attack upon the methods and tenets of the evolutionary anthropologists. He rejected the procedure of this school in their attempt to derive universal laws of social evolution from the study of many institutions as they have appeared in the most diverse regions and periods of time. He contended that any valid conclusions must rest upon the results of many intensive studies, each devoted to a single institution in a definite culture area. For this purpose, he chose the origins and development of religion, especially totemism, in Australia. To this theme he devoted an imposing work, *Elementary Forms of Religious Life* (1912). While Durkheim's motives were admirable and his general assumptions usually sound, the results of his work have not been highly esteemed by experts in the field. He did no field work and relied mainly upon printed sources which were often unreliable and inadequate for his purposes. But he showed great psychological acumen and thoroughly established the fact of the social origins and basis of religious life and its accompanying ceremony and ritual.

More influential was the work of Max Weber (1864-1920), regarded by many as the ablest of German sociologists. He was the most prominent sociological exponent of the case-study approach to historical sociology, akin in general to the methods followed by Durkheim in his study of Australian religious life. Weber's use of this method was what he called the "Ideal-Typical" procedure. He proposed the initial formulation of an ideal social construct or type—an arbitrary assumed form of personality reaction, social attitude, social process, or social structure—which could be empirically established, intellectually isolated, and then studied in detail in a given area or topic. After thus being tested, its further relevance and validity could be established or refuted by applying the results of the original study to conditions in other times and places. Weber's main utilization of this method was in his studies of the relation between religious and ethical ideals, on the one hand, and economic development, on the other. His most famous work was *Protestant Ethic and the Spirit of Capitalism* (1905). He applied the results reached in this study to the same general problems in India and China. While Weber's name gained much respect, sociologists made little use of his methodology in the field of historical sociology. An exception was the work of his brother Alfred, who claimed that this method was the only valid one by which to confirm or refute generalizations relative to social evolution. Weber's fame was spread in the United States chiefly as a result of the valiant work of his disciple, Talcott Parsons, who translated the famous *Protestant Ethic*. But, since by this time American sociologists had no interest in historical sociology, Weber's ideal-typical method was not widely used in the study of social evolution here.

A very specialized contribution to methodology in the field of historical sociology was what is known as the life-history and personal documentation technique, which was worked out by William I. Thomas (1863-1947), aided by Florian Znaniecki, in the methodological introduction to his *The Polish Peasant in America,* and elaborated by Znaniecki in his *Method of Sociology.* Valuable as it may be for the purpose for which it was formulated, this method has very limited utility in the broad field of social evolution. As we have noted above, Znaniecki has been the leading sociologist anywhere in dealing with the general cultural approach to sociology and the social sciences.

A final technique which sociologists have applied to the study of the history of society has been the statistical. It had been suggested in able fashion by Tylor away back in 1889, but little was done to put his suggestion into practical application, although the idea had been briefly approved and applied by J. Mazzarella and S. R. Stein-metz. The main excursion in this field was conducted by the distinguished English sociologist, Leonard T. Hobhouse (1864-1929) and his colleagues, G. C. Wheeler and Morris Ginsberg, and embodied in their *Material Culture and Social Institutions of the Simpler Peoples* (1915). While impressive as a collection of information, this work is no more highly esteemed by experts than Durkheim's study of Australian religion. Specialists declare that the results obtained were self-evident at the outset—that it was to be expected that more complex and highly developed institutions would be correlated with more advanced technology—the very basis of Morgan's classification in his *Ancient Society*. Further, their selection of the "tribe" as the unit of statistical study inevitably made the investigation loose and uncertain, and imperfect anthropological sources were too often relied upon. But the authors did establish the fact that sex mores, marriage and the family are less affected by technological advances than other institutions, save for religion. This book is not in the same class as a contribution to social evolution with Hobhouse's masterly volume on *Morals in Evolution*. The use of statistics by Pitirim A. Sorokin in his monumental *Social and Cultural Dynamics* has been condemned by Hans Speier and others as even less critical than the adventure of Hobhouse, Wheeler and Ginsberg.

THE PHILOSOPHY OF HISTORY AND HISTORICAL SOCIOLOGY

The most imposing books dealing with social evolution as a whole have been the works on the philosophy of history which were so popular in the first half of the nineteenth century and have been ably summarized by Robert Flint—the volumes from Herder to Hegel and his successors. They had the broad sweep that would have been appropriate to historical sociology but they were written mainly on the basis of religious assumptions, had a predetermined thesis to prove, and were composed more in the spirit of subjective philosophical dogmatism than in accord with the scientific methods of sociology and the established facts of history. The able German scholar, Paul Barth (1859-1922), made a very constructive suggestion in his *Philosophy of History as Sociology* (1897), namely, that historical sociology should supplant the philosophy of history by adopting its broad sweep and perspective, while abandoning its subjectivity and its carelessness about facts, especially those which ran contrary to the subjectivity and dogmas of the author. In other words, historical sociology would place the philosophy of history on the firm foundation of scientific method and historical accuracy. But Barth's appeal received almost no response from sociologists, save a benedictory pronouncement by Albion W. Small. The only sociologist who ever heeded the exhortation, Sorokin, based his immense work on as extreme subjectivity as any of the classic philosophers of history. Due to the paucity of works on historical sociology in our time, we may well make passing references to the leading works on the philosophy of history in our day.[12]

The first important book was Brooks Adams' *The Law of Civilization and Decay* which appeared two years before that of Barth. Like his brother Henry, Brooks was profoundly affected by the alleged relation between thermodynamics and human development. He held that the evolution of society is, in the most profound sense, the human manifestation of cosmic energy. The actions and destinies of all societies are refined and secondary expressions of solar energy. The trend of social evolution, determined mainly by economic factors and processes, is a never ending cycle which begins in Barbarism, develops into Civilization, and then, due to corruption and exploitation, returns to Barbarism.

Far more complex and sophisticated was the philosophy of history set forth by Oswald Spengler (1880-1936) in his widely read and highly controversial work on *The Decline of the West* (1921). Spengler advanced the same idea of inevitable and recurring cycles in social development that Adams expounded, but it was a more complicated and dramatic conception of the cyclical theory of history. According to Spengler, all great historic cultures pass through the inevitable stages in the life cycle of any organism: birth, youth, maturity, and old age. In a more dramatic manner, Spengler often varied the phraseology to that of spring, summer, autumn and winter. All cultures wind up in the stage of civilization, which is the final and decadent period of the culture—the winter era. There have thus far been six great historic cultures: Egyptian, Old Chinese, Classical, Indian, the Arabian and the Western (Europe and America). The Western is the latest, has long since reached the stage of civilization, and is now doomed to extinction, to be replaced in all probability by a new Far Eastern culture.

The great interest which Spengler's work provoked after the first World War was even exceeded by that centered on the massive work of Arnold Toynbee (1889-   ) on *A Study of History* which appeared in installments between 1933 and 1954. Toynbee was not a sociologist but an able historical expert on the Near East, especially Greece and Turkey. This interest and training are basic in his philosophy of history for, although he does not admit it, his whole system is an effort to apply a philosophical interpretation, based on the actual rise and fall of classical civilization, to all the world civilizations of the historical period—some twenty-one, in Toynbee's calculation.

According to Toynbee, civilization arises from what he calls "challenge and response," mainly man's reaction to the challenge of the physical environment. Leadership resides in a creative minority which the masses follow readily because of admiration and respect. When civilization has been fully attained, the creative minority always lose their spiritual creativeness and become what he calls a dominant minority. This brings about a "time of troubles," taking the form of class struggles and parochial wars within the culture, of external wars, and schisms in the souls of the citizens. The dominant minority seeks to correct the situation by creating a world state to curb internal and external wars. To counter this, the discontented internal proletariat create a universal church which in time the dominant minority accept. Then follows the effort of an external proletariat, the barbarians at the gate, to get admitted and introduce their manners and customs. When this finally succeeds, the culture is on the high road to inevitable disintegration, although it may still have centuries of fictitious "Golden Age" prosperity and glory (the Indian Summer period) before complete collapse. All except some seven of the twenty-one civilizations have already collapsed, and of these six are surely doomed. Even our Western civilization has little chance of survival save in a Second Coming of Our Lord under Anglican auspices. For this reason, Joseph Hergesheimer well epitomized Toynbee's philosophy of history in his remark that "Toynbee buries the universe in an Anglican churchyard." In his latest volumes, Toynbee seems to have some doubt that even an Anglican revival can save Western culture.

It hardly needs to be pointed out that such a work is not historical sociology; it is hardly a true philosophy of history. It is really what Howard Becker calls it—"a Theodicy," namely, a theological vindication of divine justice in permitting evil to exist in the world.

Nevertheless, the book is vastly erudite and presents much information which would be of great value, should some able and energetic historical sociologist rise from the dead in future days.

Almost equally subjective is the four-volume *Social and Cultural Dynamics* of Pitirim A. Sorokin (1889-   ), the only prominent sociologist of our day who has given serious attention to the history of society. Sorokin rejects the idea of unilateral, or even any real, progress in social evolution, and also Spengler's notion of cycles of history. He finds only fluctuations from era to era—fluctuations that will never cease so long as the human race exists. All good societies are ideational, namely, those that are based on faith and spiritual values; all bad ones are sensate, those which are secular, empirical and hedonistic. Between them in historical fluctuations we usually find an idealistic compromise. Societies tend to fluctuate from ideational to sensate to idealistic, and then back to ideational. Western culture is now in a base or sensate period, but there are signs of a coming idealistic compromise, heralded by men like Toynbee and Sorokin himself. He noted with pride that the author of this chapter once designated him as a modern St. Augustine. As Hans Speier has well summarized his view of the historic process: "There is no final doomsday, there is only a condition, a prophecy of recurring doomsdays alternating with recurring days of a more fortunate [ideational] lot of mankind."

SOME APPLICATIONS OF HISTORICAL SOCIOLOGY

Historical sociology might be of great value to contemporary social science by providing a broad perspective on the problems of our age, revealing the achievements and mistakes of the past, and recommending a repetition of the former and avoidance of the latter. Enlightening laws of social development might be discovered and elucidated. But all this has had little exploitation by contemporary sociologists. As we have stated several times earlier, the former sociologists who had some interest in historical sociology espoused erroneous notions with respect to social evolution, although they gained some salutary temporal and factual orientation. By the time more accurate material had been provided, sociologists had turned their back on the past.

Probably the most important contribution that historical sociology has made to sociology is the conception of cultural lag, which goes back to Francis Bacon's emphasis on the power of worship of the past, intellectual inertia, and the lag between science and institutions. This idea was developed far more fully by Müller-Lyer, Vierkandt, Ogburn and others. Another phase of cultural lag has been the differential rate of change in social institutions themselves, best dealt with in Keller's *Societal Evolution*. The combination of these leads to social disorganization, which is the main source of contemporary problems. This idea was contributed chiefly by W. I. Thomas. A phase of this which was anticipated by Charles H. Cooley and has been elaborated mainly by writers on social work and community organization is the rapid disintegration of the older primary groups as a result of the growth of urban life. All three of these phases of cultural lag have been most completely synthesized by the writer of this chapter in his books on *Social Institutions* and *Society in Transition*. But even this broad conception of cultural lag came to be abandoned by sociologists about as soon as it was established, on the grounds that, being well established and invaluable for sociological analysis, it should be forthwith abandoned so that sociologists could devote their attention to theoretical obfuscation and "gobbledook," to use Maury Maverick's illuminating and cogent term, and to quantitative mysticism and legerdemain. This trend is about as logical as it would have been had physicists abandoned the law of gravitation as soon as Newton had fully validated it.

A final contribution of historical sociology, on the pessimistic side, has been the substitution of the idea of social change for the notion of undoubted and unilateral progress. It was long believed that the progress of science and technology would bring better days—even utopia—to human society, and the theory of progress annunciated by the writers of pre-Industrial Revolution days seemed to be fully vindicated. This optimism reached its height in the writings of such emancipated novelists as Edward Bellamy and H. G. Wells. But this rosy prospect is no longer espoused by thoughtful sociologists. If the ultimate destruction of civilization through wars and social chaos, brought about by the abuse of the very technology which Bellamy and Wells regarded as the main foundation of progress, now seems to be the very probable outcome of the historic process, it is no longer possible dogmatically to defend the idea of progress. But social change can be demonstrated. Even the destruction of civilization through the technological facilities of the electronic age will be social change, even if the last in the series. The most cogent book underlining the pessimistic realism of our time is George Orwell's *Nineteen Eighty-four* (1948) in which he portrays modern society as tied invincibly to cold and phony warfare until such day as the cold war is transmuted into a hot war of final destruction.

As to the outlook for historical sociology, it would only be the use of badly needed space in this book to repeat what has already been said earlier.[13] The outlook for historical sociology is not unlike the outlook for snakes after St. Patrick's traditional visit to Ireland— there is none. It is now dead, and the trends are all against any prospect of its revival. Even if by some miracle interest in it should reappear, there is every probability that its content would be a liability to integrity and scholarship, for its writing would pass under the scrutiny, if not the direction, of the various "Ministries of Truth" throughout the world. Indeed, this lamentable trend has already set in on an impressive scale.

The writer may document this dolorous view of the outlook for historical sociology by a personal note, set down with no bitterness, since his own professional interests no longer gravitate around social history or historical sociology. When the publishers of *Society in Transition* contemplated a new edition, they wisely sought the opinion of a wide sampling of the more distinguished American sociologists. The only point on which virtually all of them agreed was that the portion of the original book which could best be spared was the succinct historical introduction to each chapter or part of the book. Some of the commentators even suggested that these portions should be thrown out, even though the space were not needed for other topics. Historical sociology appeared to them to be something worse than useless.

SELECTED BIBLIOGRAPHY

Harry E. Barnes, *Historical Sociology: Origins and Development* (New York: Philosophical Library, 1948). Brief historical survey of the literature and materials dealing with the rise, achievements and fall of historical sociology; the only extant guide to the subject.

Harry Elmer Barnes *et al.*, *Introduction to the History of Sociology* University of Chicago Press, 1947). Contains authoritative chapters on many of the leading historical sociologists. The best reference on the subject-matter of this chapter.

Harry E. Barnes and Howard Becker, *Social Thought from Lore to Science* (2 vols., Washington: Harren Press, 1952). The most complete history of sociological thought from ancient times to the present day. Covers the main contributions to historical sociology from *Genesis* to Toynbee.

Harry E. Barnes, Howard Becker, *et. al. Contemporary Social Theory* (New York: Appleton-Century, 1940). Symposium which constitutes the most comprehensive work on contemporary sociology, social thought and its applications. Contains much material on recent trends in sociological work in the historical field.

L. L. Bernard *et al., The Field and Methods of Sociology* (New York: Macmillan, 1940). Symposium covering all main fields of sociology with an authoritative chapter on historical sociology by Howard Becker.

E. S. Bogardus, *A History of Social Thought* (Los Angeles: Miller, 1928). Broad general survey of the whole history of sociological thought and writings.

L. M. Bristol, *Social Adaptation* (Cambridge: Harvard University Press, 1915). Book is broader than its title. Good summary of social thought at the time, especially its presentation of Social Darwinism and criticism thereof.

Robert Flint, *The Philosophy of History in France and Germany* (New York: Scribner, 1874). The classic work on the older philosophy of history.

Alexander Goldenweiser, *History, Psychology and Culture* (New York: Knopf, 1933). Valuable for its critical essays on theories of cultural development and social evolution.

A. C. Haddon, *History of Anthropology* (New York: Putnam, 1910). Brief but authoritative book on the development of anthropology, archeology and historical sociology as they stood a half-century ago.

F. N. House, *The Range of Social Theory* (New York: Holt, 1929). Topical review of sociological theories, covering much of historical sociology; *The Development of Sociology* (New York: McGraw-Hill, 1936). Readable survey and appraisal of sociological theories, including those dealing with social evolution.

R. H. Lowie, *The History of Ethnological Theory* (New York: Farrar and Rinehart, 1937). An invaluable book for the development of historical sociology, since most of the latter has been taken over from anthropology and ethnology.

G. A. Lundberg, Read Bain, Nels Anderson, *et. al., Trends in American Sociology* (New York: Harpers, 1929). Symposium especially valuable for chapters on cultural sociology.

H. W. Odum, *American Sociology* (New York: Longmans, Green, 1951). Comprehensive and highly factual survey of American sociology to 1950. Mentions such work as has been done by American sociologists in the historical field.

W. F. Ogburn, Alexander Goldenweiser *et al., The Social Sciences* (Boston: Houghton Mifflin, 1927). Symposium which contains valuable chapters on history, anthropology and sociology.

A. W. Small, *Origins of Sociology* (Chicago: University of Chicago

Press, 1924). Valuable for its treatment of the relation of history and historiography to the rise of sociology.

B. J. Stern, *Lewis Henry Morgan: Social Evolutionist* (Chicago: University of Chicago Press, 1931). Brief survey of the life and work of the most important figure in the rise of historical sociology. Should be compared with the chapter on Morgan by L. A. White in Barnes, *Introduction to the History of Sociology*.

Leslie A. White, *The Science of Culture* (New York: Farrar and Strauss, 1949). The most competent account of the cultural interpretation of social evolution, and the best prospectus of the emergent science of culturology.

Harry Elmer Barnes (1889-   ), B.A., summa cum laude, Syracuse (1913), M.A. (1914), Ph.D., Columbia University (1918). Lecturer in History, Columbia University (1917); Professor of History, Clark University (1920); Professor of Historical Sociology, Smith College (1923) and also Professor of Economics and Sociology *ad interim,* Amherst College (1923-1925); Lecturer in Education, Teachers College, Columbia University (1937-1938); resigned his Professorship at Smith College and entered the editorial department of the Scripps-Howard newspapers (1929-1940); Visiting Professor at Temple University (1946); University of Indiana (1951); Washington State College (1945-1955). His *History of Western Civilization* (2 vols., 1935) was called "unquestionably the masterpiece of the New History." It was followed by his monumental *Intellectual and Cultural History of the Western World.* One of the most prolific writers of our times, has authored numerous studies in the fields of cultural history, criminology, penology and the history of sociology, including Howard Becker and Harry Elmer Barnes, *Social Thought from Lore to Science* (Washington, D. C.: Harren Press, 1952), 2 vols.; Barnes, Ed., *An Introduction to the History of Sociology* (University of Chicago Press, 1948); etc.

1. On the nature of historical sociology, see Howard Becker in H. E. Barnes and Howard Becker, *Contemporary Social Theory* (New York: Appleton-Century, 1940), Chap. 15..

2. For an account of contributions to historical sociology from ancient times to 1800, consult H. E. Barnes and Howard Becker, *Social Thought from Lore to Science* (Washington: Harren Press, 2 Vols., 1952), Vol. I, Chaps. I-XIII.; and, more briefly, H. E. Barnes *et al.; Introduction to the History of Sociology* (Chicago: University of Chicago Press, 1947), Chaps. I-II.

3. J. B. Bury, *The Idea of Progress* (New York: MacMillan, 1932).

4. Barnes and Becker, *Social Thought from Lore to Science,* Vol. I, Chaps. VIII-IX; and H. E. Barnes, *A History of Historical Writing* (Norman: University of Oklahoma Press, 1937), Chap. VII.

5. A. C. Haddon, *History of Anthropology* (New York: Putnam, 1910); and H. E. Barnes, in Barnes and Becker, *Contemporary Social Theory*, Chaps., 9, 16.

6. Barnes, *Introduction to the History of Sociology*, Chaps. IV-VIII, XVI, XIX, XXII.

7. Alexander Goldenweiser, in Barnes and Becker, *Contemporary Social Theory*, Chap. 14; and in H. E. Barnes, *History and Prospects of the Social Sciences* (New York: Knopf, 1925), Chap. V; Leslie A. White, in Barnes, *Introduction to the History of Sociology*, Chap. V; and B. J. Stern, *Lewis Henry Morgan: Social Evolutionist* (Chicago: University of Chicago Press, 1931).

8. Goldenweiser, *loc. cit.*, and R. H. Lowie, *The History of Ethnological Theory* (New York: Farrar and Rinehart, 1937); Barnes, *Introduction to the History of Sociology*, Chaps. VI, XXIII, XXXIII-XXXIV.

9. On theories of cultural evolution, see Lowie and Goldenweiser as cited above.

10. Becker, in Barnes and Becker, *Contemporary Social Theory*, Chap. 15; Barnes and Becker, *Social Thought from Lore to Science*, Vol. I, Chaps. XV, XX; Vol: II, *passim* Barnes, *Introduction to the History of Sociology*, Chaps. III, VIII, XIII, XVII, XXII, XXIII, XXXVIII, XL, XXVII, XXXII, XLIV, XLVI.

11. Barnes, *Introduction to the History of Sociology*, Chaps. XIII, XVII, XXXII, XL.

12. Robert Flint, *The Philosophy of History in France and Germany* (New York: Scribner, 1874); Barnes, *Introduction to the History of Sociology*, Chaps. XXXVII, XLVI; H. E. Barnes, *Historical Sociology; Origins and Development* (New York: Philosophical Library, 1948), Chap. VII; and J. T. Shotwell, "Spengler: A Poetic Interpreter of History," *Current History*, May, 1929, pp. 283-287.

13. Barnes, *Historical Sociology: Origins and Development*, Chap. IX.

SOCIAL PSYCHOLOGY

Robert M. Frumkin

Oswego State Teachers College (New York)

Without a doubt social psychology has become the most popular field interest and center of research activity among American sociologists. A cursory examination of the 1956 *Directory of Members of the American Sociological Society* indicates that about 75 per cent of the members list social psychology *per se* or a social psychological subfield as one of their major fields of competence. Further evidence for this dominance of social psychology is shown by the fact that in the American Sociological Society *Research Census Reports* social psychology (and /or its subfields) has, since 1949, led in number of social research projects engaged in by Society members. And Leonard S. Cottrell, Jr., in his 1950 presidential address read before the Society, ended that address by suggesting that with the solution of some neglected problems a matured social psychology will "undertake its obligations and responsibilities as the basic social science." [1]

Why is it that social psychology is so popular in America? And why have American sociologists found so much interest in a field which psychologists claim is but another subfield of general psychology? What is the historical background of American social psychology? What have been its conceptions of man and society? How do these conceptions of man and society relate to current basic issues and research methods in the field of social psychology? What are current needs and future possibilities of this field? As suggested by Cottrell, will social psychology become *the* basic social science? It is the purpose of this chapter to attempt to answer the above questions especially in the light of the developments in the field of social psychology since World War II.

HISTORICAL BACKGROUND

Modern social psychology is a distinctive product of western civilization. To Plato and Aristotle we owe our gratitude for having aroused

270

interest in the social nature of man. To western thought we are indebted for the development of science, a method which is the *sine qua non* for the study of the social nature of man.[2] But it is to the unique history and development of the United States of America to which we must seek explanation for the interest in and development of modern social psychology.

America was developed by people under the dominance of a Protestant, especially Calvinist, ethic. This ethic, it has been suggested, paved the way for the development of mature capitalism and modern science, it provided the orientation that prompted individuals to seek success as a means of finding out whether or not they were predestined for salvation.[3] This, however, is not the whole story. For it was the fact that America was a vast, undeveloped frontier in which that ethic could be fully tested that accounted for the development of that characteristic American rugged individualism which has become a sacred and integral part of the American ethos.

Darwin's *Origin of Species* (1859) and its biological evolutionism was reinterpreted by social theorists such as Herbert Spencer and William Graham Sumner to mean that there was scientific evidence for the *laissez faire* principle, a principle highly compatible with the Protestant ethic as it found expression in the development of capitalism. It is not thus surprising to find that especially in the latter part of the 19th century and the beginning of the 20th century that intellectual works were characterized by what the Hinkles refer to as *voluntaristic nominalism*,[4] the view that social phenomena ultimately derive from the actions of individuals. In fact this point of view persists today largely through the continuing impact of Freudian psychoanalysis and behaviorism. One might almost venture to suggest that the opposing view, *sociological realism,* the standpoint that social phenomena are the prior conditions of human action, is actually in disfavor. For even the most profound theories of action today are essentially nominalistic. And even though biological determinism is essentially passé among sociologists, psychobiologistic or voluntaristic nominalistic theories seem to lead in popularity over truly sociological realistic theories. At times, in a very real sense, it seems as if man in his understanding of himself and society, at the middle of the 20th century, is still in what Comte called the metaphysical stage of development. However, since World War II, social scientists have gained respect for aiding the armed forces solve practical problems in human relations which required some understanding of the social psycho-

logical nature of man. Today social scientists are employed in public
and private agencies and enterprises as researchers, consultants, and
advisers on social psychological problems. Also, undergraduates preparing for many professions are finding that majoring in sociology
provides the kind of preparation needed to be successful in the complex society we live in. And, perhaps, the best sign that social science
has come of age is the fact that in important matters of social policy
social scientists are now being called in as expert witnesses, as for
example, in the current civil rights litigations in connection with
public school segregation in the U.S.[5]

In retrospect, one can see that the voluntaristic nominalism which
has been so characteristic of American thinking shows favorable
signs of being reconstructed in a way in which sociological realism
will be of equal and, perhaps, superior significance in the determination of social policy and of aiding men to understand themselves and
society better.[6]

THE CONCEPTIONS OF MAN AND SOCIETY IN AMERICAN
SOCIAL PSYCHOLOGY

There are four principal conceptions of man and society in American social psychology, and most reflect, as previously suggested, the
predominance of the voluntaristic nominalistic point of view. They
are as follows: (1) the behavioristic conception; (2) the Freudian
conception; (3) the sociological conception; and (4) the interactionist
conception.

1. *The Behavioristic Conception.* The proponents of this point
of view stress whatever man is and whatever he makes of society is
biologically determined. That is, through trial and error, through
reward and punishment, through primary need gratification man
becomes what he becomes, that social processes, such as cooperation
and accommodation, are but means of primary need gratification, that
human values are but elaborations of particular biological needs.
Thus, for example, religious goals would in behavioristic terms be
interpreted as means of satisfaction of biological needs.[7]

2. *The Freudian Conception.* Much like behaviorism, the Freudian conception of man and society is essentially irrationalistic and
biologistic. For it claims that human personality is the end result
of the way man satisfies his blind instinctual needs in conflict with a

society which is in a sense a super-rationalization constructed by man in order to suppress and control these needs.[8] It further claims that character is molded in early childhood by the ways in which parents repress and transform instincts to meet the demands of society, a claim which has been seriously questioned in recent years.[9]

3. *The Sociological Conception.* In contrast to the behavioristic and Freudian conceptions, the proponents of this view see man as essentially the same biologically. Therefore, man's social nature and character are primarily determined by the culture practiced by the society in which man grows up. Thus, man's nature as distinguished from that of nonhumans is socially determined. Furthermore, social phenomena have an existence of their own and cannot be reduced to the level of the individual phenomena.[10]

4. *The Interactionst Conception.* Perhaps the most promising and one of the most popular conceptions of man today is that known as the *Interactionist* conception as developed by the so-called Chicago School consisting of Charles H. Cooley, John Dewey, George H. Mead, and William I. Thomas. The interactionists reject both the biological determinism of behaviorism and Freudianism as well as sociological determinism. Instead they agreed that personality and society are both the products of social interaction. In this way they take into account both the biological realities of man as well as the social realities of society. The key concept here is that of *role* which is fast becoming the conceptual bridge between psychology and sociology in their attempts to gain a common understanding of the social nature of man.[11]

Summary. The behavioristic and Freudian conceptions of man and society are essentially those of a biological determinist cast, while the sociological conception is essentially one representing a social determinist point of view. The most popular and promising conception today is that known as the interactionist, a conception which rejects biological and social determinism in favor of a theory of social interaction which involves at once a consideration of both individual and social organization as they relate to the concept of role.

SOME BASIC PROBLEM AREAS IN SOCIAL PSYCHOLOGY

When one attempts to explain the popularity of social psychology one is tempted to state, with some justification, that this popularity is due to the fact that social psychology is close to life, it deals with a vital and fascinating phenomenon—the social nature of man. A survey of some of the basic problem areas with which social psychologists are concerned provides evidence for the above assertion.

1. *The Development of a Mature Conception of Man.* Recently Asch suggested that students of man have too often drawn " a caricature rather than a portrait of man." [12] That is, they have not looked at the whole man, they have not examined some of his most characteristic features. What is needed is a conception of man which takes into account both his irrationalism and rationalism, a conception which takes into account at once both the psychological and sociological organization of human behavior. As indicated previously, the interactionist conception is promising in this regard but much is still wanting. At any rate serious attempts are now being made to paint a portrait rather than a caricature of man.[13]

2. *The Dynamics of the Socialization Process.* The way in which the human animal becomes a social being has been an ever present concern. Much light on this process has been shed by the Chicago School, discussed previously, especially by George H. Mead.[14] Illuminating also have been the accounts of social isolation and of feral children and men.[15] J. H. S. Bossard has given an excellent account of early socialization[16] and John E. Horrocks of adolescent socialization.[17] Helpful also have been the studies by anthropologists on the comparative aspects of socialization in different cultures.[18] Although much valuable research has been done in this area there still remain many interesting and crucial problems that warrant attention.[19]

3. *The Dynamics of Social Interaction.* The new focus in social psychology seems to be centering on the study of the dynamics of social interaction. The concept of role takes a dominant position in this orientation and many worthy studies have resulted from it.[20] Also gaining in interest is the study of social processes, of cooperation and competition, conflict, and accommodation.[21] Interaction theory has furthermore been utilized by many educational sociologists as, for example, Florence Grenhoe Robbins.[22] Such theory has likewise contributed much to applied social psychology, especially in recent family counseling practices.[23] The study of the dynamics of social interaction therefore has become significant in terms of theory and method as well as the application of social psychology.

4. *The Dynamics of Communication.* This lively and active field includes the study of the communicator, the communicant, the content and effects of the communication.[24] It includes the study of

verbal and nonverbal communication[25], public opinion and propaganda,[26] and the study of mass media of communication and their effects.[27]

5. *The Dynamics of the Teaching-Learning Process.* A keen interest has also been shown in the dynamics of the teaching learning process following the classic studies of Waller and Lewin.[28] Nathaniel Cantor has applied current theory to his own teaching and reported his findings in two readable and fascinating works.[29] This area should offer promising opportunities for research at the present time as well as in the future.

6. *The Analysis of Individual and Group Differences.* Under this heading would be included the differential effects of heredity and environment on the personality of the individual, the relation of such factors as home training, formal education, occupation, sex, ethnic and religious background, social class, etc., on the character of individuals and the relation of such factors to group differences.[30]

7. *The Study of Social Pathology.* The application of social psychology to the study of social problems has gained new impetus in recent years by the creation of the Society for the Study of Social Problems. Among the social pathological problems it studies are those of crime, group conflict, delinquency, family disorganization, mental illness, prejudice, etc. The Society's first and second sponsored publications indicate that social psychological theory has special relevance for those interested in understanding and solving social problems.[31]

8. *The Dynamics of Family Adjustment.* In the study of the dynamics of family adjustment social psychological theory has found numerous followers. Recently, for example, LaForge and Suczek developed an *Interpersonal Check List* which makes it possible to describe the degree of concordance and discrepancies in reciprocal role perceptions and expectations.[32] Clifford Kirkpatrick's *Scale of Family Interests* has also been found helpful in the assessment of marital adjustment.[33] Role theory in particular has been found to be a family research orientation with many possibilities.[34]

9. *The Study of Prejudice.* Social psychological literature is replete with studies on prejudice. Among the investigators in this area have been such outstanding scholars as Gordon W. Allport, Emory S. Bogardus, John Dollard, Eugene L. Hartley, Gunnar Myrdal, and Arnold M. Rose.[35]

10. *The Study of Interpersonal Competence.* The social psychology of interpersonal competence is now receiving new attention under

the impact of what has been popularly called the problem of human relations. Public and private agencies have been making increasing use of the social psychologist as an expert in human relations.[36] A recent and noteworthy work on interpersonal competence has been published by Foote and Cottrell.[37] The concept of interpersonal competence would seem to indicate a fruitful tool for applied social psychological research.

11. *The Study of Group Formation and Development.* The study of the formation and development of the group, sometimes called small group research or group dynamics, according to recent reports, is among the most popular research areas in existence in American social psychology. Although there have been some severe criticisms of this area, that is, that it has been dysfunctional for the development of a mature social science, small group research has helped to win the respect of the managerial elites of American society and has therefore had very practical consequences which are highly functional.[38]

12. *The Study of Social Perception.* The role of cognitive factors in social interaction has received considerable attention from Gestaltists, phenomenonologists, and cultural determinists such as Asch, Krech and Crutchfield, and Sherif.[39] In any mature conception of man, and, therefore, in any mature social psychological theory, the role of cognitive factors in social interaction will have to be taken into account.

13. *The Dynamics of the Leader-Follower Relationship.* The selection of leaders in the armed forces and for important positions in industry has led to another growing field often called that of leadership. While early studies concentrated on the characteristics of leaders, recent studies are concerned more with the dynamics of the leader-follower relationship.[40]

RESEARCH METHODS AND RESEARCH TRAINING
A. RESEARCH METHODS

1. *Testing and Scaling.* The primary aim of testing and scaling has been to transform qualitative material into quantitative data. Outstanding work in this area has been done under the rubric of attitude measurement, for example, the work, among others, of Thurstone,[41] Sletto,[42] and Guttman.[43] Sletto has pointed out that the next

steps in the advancement of social measurement will occur when there is a greater integration of measurement and theory and when a combination of techniques developed in human ecology, sociometry, and scale construction, shall be applied to critical social problems.[44]

2. *Sociometric Measurements.* Sociometric measurements refer to the ways in which social psychologists measure, in particular, the dynamics of interaction in groups. Although sociometry has generally been associated with the work of Moreno, most methodologists, including Moreno, suggest that the term should be used to refer to all attempts to measure social behavior.[45]

3. *Statistical and Mathematical Techniques.* Statistical and mathematical techniques developed in the past quarter of this century have been of great value in making it possible, among other things, to have precise measurements of variables, to measure the relations between them, to assess their reliability and validity.[46] Of recent importance is the development of nonparametric methods which avoid stringent assumptions generally held in conventional methods.[47]

4. *Content Analysis.* A fascinating research method is that known as content analysis, a method by which the manifest content of communication can be described objectively, systematically, and quantitatively.[48] The method has been especially useful in studying propaganda[49] and literature as a reflection of cultural values.[50]

5. *Cross-Cultural Method.* In this method researchers collect data on various peoples to test hypotheses concerning human behavior.[51] The most notable recent work using this method has been done by Murdock[52] and Whiting and Child.[53] This method should prove useful in the development of social psychology as the basic social science by helping social psychologists to discard hypotheses about human behavior which is a result of their ethnocentrism.

6. *Experimental Methods.* The control and manipulation of the variables involved in human behavior in such a way that they might be separated and observed or measured is known as the experimental method.[54] Chapin and his associates have done important work in designing experiments and using experimental methods.[55] Such methods are indispensable for the development of a science of social psychology.

7. *Sociobiography.* An important but sometimes neglected method is that known variously as the case method, life-history method, or sociobiography. The value of the intensive study of the individual was first illustrated by the famous work of Thomas and Znaniecki[56] and later by Allport on the use of personal documents in research.[57]

Goldhamer suggests in his recent critique of social psychological studies that the urgent need is for the investigator to simply spend more time with the subjects he is studying.[58] There is no quarreling with this point.

B. RESEARCH TRENDS

Since World War II the most significant research trends have been as follows: (1) Convergence of sociological, anthropological, and psychological approaches, that is, efforts toward an interdisciplinary approach; (2) The establishment of large scale research organizations which engage in interdisciplinary research projects of considerable magnitude and scope; (3) The increase in research trained social scientists, technical facilities, and financial resources available for social psychological research; (4) Expansion of research in public and private agencies; (5) The increase in the application of social psychological theory and method to the solution of social problems and in determining social policy; (6) The recognition of social psychology as a profession (for example, the fact that the New York State Civil Service Commission has positions for "Social Psychologists" with substantial salaries which indicate the high value placed on social psychology as a profession); (7) The increase in interest in social psychological theory and research which has made it the most popular field of concentration among American sociologists.[59]

CURRENT NEEDS AND FUTURE POSSIBILITIES

The current needs and future possibilities of social psychology have been well stated by Cottrell. He points out by way of criticism that: (1) Social psychological terminology is rather fuzzy; (2) Hypotheses advanced lack rigorous formulation; and (3) Methods are not well adapted for operationally testing and validating hypotheses set forth, and, therefore, as with every science, basic conceptual tools and research methods must be clarified and refined for the tasks at hand. He acknowledges the fact that some consensus has been reached on, for example, the concepts of role, self, situation, and field, but these concepts, at present, lack precision and rigor in their conceptualization and applicability in research.

Cottrell believes that systematic attention to and study of emphatic responses; the self, especially relative to identification models; the situation, particularly its cognitive aspects; and motivation, in terms of a situational approach; attention to these problems and solution of them will help social psychology become the basic social science.[60]

It is the feeling of S. E. Asch, and of this writer, that the future possibilities of social psychology could be great indeed if only social psychologists recognized the productive forces in man, if only they would find out how the interests and curiosity, the intelligence, imagination, and creativity of man relate to his behavior and the social phenomena he is both cause and consequence of. That is to say, man is not only what he is but also what he thinks and dreams and hopes he should and could be. Why not investigate such productive aspects of man to see how they relate to what he actually is? To the writer's knowledge Kurt H. Wolff is the only student of man who has done any serious thinking and research in this vein in recent years.[61] The present conception of man seems too often to hold, I am afraid, the notion that man is the hopeless slave of biological, psychological, and sociological forces beyond his control. Too little attention is paid to the fact that man is also a rational, intelligent being capable of planning and controlling his own destiny.[62]

SUMMARY

Social psychology in America spent its childhood in an atmosphere which favored biological and psychological determinism as embodied in the behavioristic and the Freudian conceptions of man which have been called collectively by some *voluntaristic nominalism*. At the turn of the 20th century and up and until a little after World War I it was not therefore surprising that its early adolescence was dominated by instinct theories propounded by the English influential psychologist McDougall instead of the sociological realistic theories of Durkheim. Only in the late twenties and throughout the thirties, through the impact of anthropology and the study of social problems did the full relevance of the social factors in behavior gain real attention. During World War II and since that time American social psychology has passed its middle adolescence and is almost, but not quite, through with late adolescence. That is to say, American social psychology, through convergences in psychology, anthropology, sociology, psychology, and psychiatry, in terms of both developments in its theory and research methods, has stepped from Comte's metaphysical stage of development to the doorstep of the positivistic stage of development, social psychology is becoming mature. What is needed is a conception of man which takes into account man's biological, psychological, and sociological nature simultaneously without neglecting such unique attributes of his nature as those of curiosity, creativity, imagination, that is, the productive forces in man. With such a conception of man is also needed precisely and rigorously defined conceptual tools and research techniques to test hypotheses concerning man's social nature. Within the next two or three decades American social psychology should have reached full maturity, it should be well into its positivistic stage of development and able to take the responsibilities that go with that status.

SELECTED BIBLIOGRAPHY

Allport, Floyd H.,*Social Psychology* (Boston: Houghton-Mifflin, 19-24). A classic social psychological textbook from the behavioristic point of view.

Asch, Solomon E., *Social Psychology* (New York: Prentice-Hall, 1952). A scholarly text from the point of view of Gestalt psychology.

Foote, Nelson N. and Leonard S. Cottrell, *Identity and Interpersonal Competence* (Chicago: University of Chicago Press, 1955). Suggests a fairly mature social psychological framework for family research with the idea of interpersonal competence as the key concept.

Gillin, John (Editor), *For a Science of Social Man* (New York: Macmillan, 1954). Represents an attempt on the part of mature scholars from anthropology; psychology, and sociology to formulate an integral conception of man for the development of a science of social man.

Karpf, Fay B., *American Social Psychology* (New York: McGraw-Hill, 1932). A comprehensive history of American social psychology.

Klineberg, Otto, *Social Psychology* (New York: Holt, 1954). A textbook with a comparative approach to social psychology with extensive use of anthropological and sociological as well as psychological materials.

Kluckhohn, Clyde and Henry A. Murray, Eds., *Personality in Nature, Society, and Culture* (New York: Knopf, 1948). A collection of studies which attempt to bridge the frontiers of biology, psychology, sociology, anthropology, and psychiatry in the study of personality.

Krech, David and Richard S. Crutchfield, *Theory and Problems of Social Psychology* (New York: McGraw-Hill, 1948). A textbook with a phenomenological approach to social psychology.

Lindesmith, Alfred R. and Anselm L. Strauss, *Social Psychology* (New York: Dryden, 1956). A textbook in the sociological tradition of the interactionist school of thought.

Lindzey, Gardner, Ed., *Handbook of Social Psychology* (Reading, Mass.: Addison-Wesley, 1954). A comprehensive review of the field of social psychology by leaders in every important subfield. Volume I deals with theory and method. Volume II deals with special fields and applications.

Newcomb, Theodore M., *Social Psychology* (New York: Dryden, 19-50). A textbook which gives equal recognition to the psychological and sociological organization of human behavior.

Parsons, Talcott and Edward A. Shils (Editors), *Toward A General Theory of Action* (Cambridge, Mass.: Harvard University Press, 1954). An attempt by mature scholars from psychology, anthropology, and sociology to formulate a general theory of action for the social sciences.

Rohrer, John H. and Muzafer Sherif (Editors), *Social Psychology at the Crossroads* (New York: Harper, 1951). A collection of 17 lectures on social psychology by eminent scholars from psychology, sociology, and anthropology.

Sherif, Muzafer and Carolyn W. Sherif, *An Outline of Social Psychology* (New York: Harper, 1956). A textbook which is an able combination of individualistic and sociologistic approaches to the study of human behavior.

Swanson, Guy E., Newcomb, Theodore M., and Eugene L. Hartley (Editors), *Readings in Social Psychology* (New York: Holt, 1952). An excellent collection of social psychological studies representative of American social psychology.

Robert M. Frumkin did his undergraduate work at Upsala College and his graduate work at the New School for Social Research and the Ohio State University, taught Sociology and Psychology at the Hampton Institute, was a Social Research Analyst in Social Psychiatry for the Ohio State Department of Mental Hygiene and Correction; taught at the University of Buffalo; is now Assistant Professor of Social Studies, Oswego Teachers College, Oswego, New York; member of Alpha Kappa Delta (the national honorary sociology fraternity) and Psi Chi (the national honorary psychology fraternity. Author of *The Measurement of Marriage Adjustment, The Meaning of Sociology, The Patient as a Human Being, Hospital Nursing: A Sociological Interpretation,* and *The Nurse as a Human Being,* has published numerous articles in social science, medical, nursing, and educational journals. Recipient of the John Ericsson Society of New York Fellowship in Science (1945-1946).

NOTES

1. "Some Neglected Problems in Social Psychology," *American Sociological Review,* XV (December, 1950) , 705-712.

2. William Dampier, *A History of Science* (New York: Macmillan, 1949) .

3. Max Weber, *The Protestant Ethic and the Spirit of Capitalism* (London:

Allen & Unwin, 1930); Robert K. Merton, *Science, Technology and Society in 17th Century England* (Bruges; Belgium: St. Catherine Press, 1938).

4. R. C. Hinkle & G. J. Hinkle, *The Development of Modern Sociology* (New York: Doubleday, 1954).

5. Kenneth B. Clark, "The Social Scientist as an Expert Witness in Civil Rights Litigation," *Social Problems,* I (June, 1953), 5-10.

6. Since space in which to deal in broader perspective with the historical background of modern social psychology was extremely limited, those interested in seeking more detailed and less sketchy accounts should consult *inter alia* some of the following: Fay B. Karpf, *American Social Psychology* (New York: McGraw-Hill, 1932); James W. Woodard, "Social Psychology," in G. Gurvitch & W. E. Moore (Editors), *Twentieth Century Sociology* (New York: Philosophical Library, 1945); and Gordon W. Allport," The Historical Background of Modern Social Psychology," in Gardner Lindzey (Editor), *Handbook of Social Psychology* (Cambridge, Mass.: Addison-Wesley, 1954), Volume I.

7. See *inter alia,* Floyd H. Allport, *Social Psychology* (Boston: Houghton-Mifflin, 1924); John B. Watson, *Behaviorism* (New York: Norton, 1930).

8. A. A. Brill, Ed., *The Basic Writings of Sigmund Freud* (New York: Random House, 1938).

9. William H. Sewell, "Infant Training and the Personality of the Child," *American Journal of Sociology,* LVIII (1952), 150-159.

10. The most orthodox scholar in the sociological tradition is Emile Durkheim; see his *The Rules of Sociological Method* (University of Chicago Press, 1938). A recent text strongly sociologistic is the writer's *The Meaning of Sociology* (Buffalo: University of Buffalo Bookstore, 1956, Second Edition).

11. A notable attempt in the development of interactionist theory is exemplified by the work of Theodore M. Newcomb. See especially his "Social Psychological Theory," in J. H. Rohrer & M. Sherif, Ed., *Social Psychology at the Crossroads* (New York: Harper, 1951).

12. Solomon E. Asch, *Social Psychology* (New York: Prentice-Hall, 1952), 24.

13. See *inter alia,* John Gillin, Ed., *For a Science of Social Man* (New York: Macmillan, 1954); Talcott Parsons & Edward A. Shils, Ed., *Toward a General Theory of Action* (Cambridge, Mass.: Harvard University Press, 1954); Theodore M. Newcomb, "Social Psychological Theory," *op. cit.*

14. See his posthumous classic *Mind, Self, and Society* (University of Chicago Press, 1934).

15. See *inter alia,* Kingsley Davis," Final Note on a Case of Extreme Isolation," *American Journal of Sociology,* LII (March, 1947), 432-437; J. A. L. Singh & R. M. Zingg, *Wolf Children and Feral Men* (New York: Harper, 1939); and Clarence Leuba, *The Natural Man* (New York: Doubleday, 1954).

16. See his *Sociology of Child Development* (New York: Harper, 1948).

17. See his *Psychology of Adolescence* (Boston: Houghton-Mifflin, 1951).

18. See *inter alia,* Ruth Benedict, *Patterns of Culture* (Boston: Houghton-Mifflin, 1934); Ralph Linton, *The Cultural Background of Personality* (New York: Appleton-Century-Crofts, 1945); and Margaret Mead, *From the South Seas* (New York: Morrow, 1939).

19. For a comprehensive review of developments in this area see Irvin L. Child, *"Socialization,"* in Gardner Lindzey, Ed., *op. cit.,* Volume II.

20. For a review of developments in role theory see Theodore R. Sarbin, "Role

Theory," in Gardner Lindzey, Ed., *op. cit.*, I; see also Kurt H. Wolff, Ed., *The Sociology of Georg Simmel* (Glencoe, Ill.: Free Press, 1950).

21. See *inter alia*, M. A. May & L. W. Doob, *Competition and Cooperation* (New York: Social Science Research Council, 1937); Margaret Mead, Ed., *Competition Cooperation among Primitive Peoples* (New York: McGraw-Hill, 1937); S. A. Stouffer, et. al., *The American Soldier* (Princeton University Press, 1949).

22. See *Educational Sociology* (New York: Holt, 1953); *The Sociology of Play, Recreation, and Leisure Time* (Dubuque, Iowa: W. C. Brown, 1955).

23. A. R. Mangus, "Integration of Theory, Research, and Family Counseling Practice," *Marriage and Family Living*, XIX (February, 1957), 81-85.

24. For an excellent general account of communication see E. L. Hartley & R. E. Hartley, *Fundamentals of Social Psychology* (New York: Knopf, 1952), Part I.

25. On nonverbal communication see *inter alia*, Ray L. Birdwhistell, *Introduction to Kinesics* (Louisville: University of Louisville Press, 1953); Jurgen Ruesch & Weldon Kees, *Nonverbal Communication* (Berkeley: University of California Press, 1956).

26. See *inter alia*, Daniel Katz et al., Eds., *Public Opinion and Propaganda* (New York: Dryden, 1954).

27. For a review of studies in this area see Carl I. Hovland, "Effects of the Mass Media of Communication," in Gardner Lindzey, Ed., *op. cit.*, Volume II.

28. See *inter alia*, Willard Waller, *The Sociology of Teaching* (New York: Wiley, 1932); Kurt Lewin et al., "Patterns of Aggressive Behavior in Experimentally Created 'Social Climates'," *Journal of Social Psychology*, X (May, 1939), 271-299; and more recently, Florence Greenhoe Robbins, "The Impact of Three Social Climates upon a College Class," *School Review*, LX (May, 1952), 275-284.

29. See Cantor's works entitled *The Dynamics of Learning* (Buffalo: Henry Stewart, 1956); *The Teaching-Learning Process* (New York: Dryden, 1953).

30. See *inter alia*, C. Kluckhohn & H. A. Murray, Eds., *Personality in Nature, Society, and Culture* (New York: Knopf, 1953); David Riesman et al., *The Lonely Crowd* (New Haven: Yale University Press, 1950).

31. Arnold M. Rose, Ed., *Mental Health and Mental Disorder* (New York: Norton, 1955); Jerome Himelhock & Sylvia F. Fava, Eds., *Sexual Behavior in American Society* (New York: Norton, 1955); see also Edwin M. Lemert, *Social Pathology* (New York: McGraw-Hill, 1951); Paul B. Horton & Gerald R. Leslie, *The Sociology of Social Problems* (New York: Appleton-Century-Crofts, 1955).

32. Rolf LaForge and Robert F. Suczek, ". . . An Interpersonal Check List," *Journal of Personality*, XXIV (September, 1955), 94-112.

33. Robert M. Frumkin, *The Measurement of Marriage Adjustment* (Washington, D.C.: Public Affairs Press, 1954).

34. A. R. Mangus, *op. cit.*

35. For an excellent review of this active area of study see John Harding et al., "Prejudice and Ethnic Relations," in Gardner Lindzey, Ed., *op. cit.*, Volume II.

36. See *inter alia*, F. K. Berrien & W. H. Bash, *Human Relations* (New York: Harper, 1957); George C. Homans, *The Human Group* (New York: Harcourt, Brace, 1950).

37. Nelson N. Foote & Leonard S. Cottrell, Jr., *Identity and Interpersonal Competence* (University of Chicago Press, 1955).

38. A. Paul Hare et al., Eds., *Small Groups* (New York: Knopf, 1955); George A.

Theodorson, "Elements in the Progressive Development of Small Groups," *Social Forces,* XXXI (1953), 311-320.

39. Solomon E. Asch, *Social Psychology* (New York: Prentice-Hall, 1952); D. Krech & R. S. Crutchfield, *Theory and Problems of Social Psychology* (New York: McGraw-Hill, 1948); M. Sherif & C. W. Sherif, *An Outline of Social Psychology* (New York: Harper, 1956).

40. See *inter alia,* Alvin W. Gouldner, Ed., *Studies in Leadership* (New York: Harper, 1950); Melvin Seeman & Richard T. Morris, *A Status Approach to Leadership* (Columbus: Ohio State University Research Foundation, 1950). For a review of the leadership field see Cecil A. Gibb, "Leadership," in Gardner Lindzey, Ed., *op. cit.,* Volume II.

41. Louis L. Thurstone & E. J. Chave, *The Measurement of Attitudes* (University of Chicago Press, 1929).

42. Raymond F. Sletto, *Construction of Personality Scales by the Criterion of Internal Consistency* (Minneapolis: Sociological Press, 1937).

43. Louis Guttman, "A Basis for Scaling Qualitative Data," *American Sociological Review,* IX (1944), 139-150.

44. Raymond F. Sletto, "Next Steps in Social Measurements," *Sociometry,* X (1947), 354-362; Bert F. Green, "Attitude Measurement," in Gardner Lindzey, Ed., *op. cit.,* Volume I.

45. For a review of these research methods see Gardner Lindzey & Edgar F. Borgatta, "Sociometric Measurement," in Gardner Lindzey, Ed., *op. cit.,* Volume I.

46. Frederick Mosteller and Robert R. Bush, "Selected Quantitative Techniques," in Gardner Lindzey, Ed., *op. cit.,* Volume I.

47. L. E. Moses, "Nonparametric Statistics for Psychological Research," *Psychological Bulletin,* XLIX (1952), 122-143.

48. Bernard Berelson, "Content Analysis," in Gardner Lindzey, *op. cit.,* Volume I.

49. A. M. Lee & E. B. Lee, *The Fine Art of Propaganda* (New York: Harcourt, Brace, 1939).

50. Milton C. Albrecht, "Does Literature Reflect Common Values?" *American Sociological Review,* XXI (December, 1956), 722-729.

51. John W. Whiting, "The Cross-Cultural Method," in Lindzey, *op. cit.,* Volume I.

52. George P. Murdock, *Social Structure* (New York: Macmillan, 1949).

53. John W. Whiting & Irvin L. Child, *Child Training and Personality* (New Haven: Yale University Press, 1953).

54. Allen L. Edwards, "Experiments: Their Planning and Execution," in Lindzey, *op. cit.,* Volume I.

55. F. S. Chapin, *Experimental Designs in Sociological Research* (New York: Harper, 1947).

56. W. I. Thomas & F. Znaniecki, *The Polish Peasant in Europe and America* (New York: Knopf, 1927), 2 Volumes.

57. Gordon W. Allport, *The Use of Personal Documents in Psychological Science* (New York: Social Science Research Council, 1942), Bulletin 49.

58. Herbert Goldhamer, "Recent Developments in Personality Studies," *American Sociological Review,* XIII (October, 1948), 555-565.

59. John Useem, "Sociology: Recent Trends," *Social Education,* XIV (March, 1950), 102-104.

60. Leonard S. Cottrell, Jr., "Some Neglected Problems in Social Psychology," *op. cit.*

61. Wolff's work is still in progress and is tentatively entitled *Loma Culture Change: A Contribution to the Study of Man.*

62. Karl Mannheim, *Freedom, Power, and Democratic Planning* (New York: Oxford University Press, 1950); Erich Fromm, *The Sane Society* (New York: Rinehart, 1955).

THE SOCIOLOGY OF KNOWLEDGE

Leo P. Chall

Brooklyn College

To speak of trends in the sociology of knowledge since World War II is a difficult if not impossible task. Only the barest outlines can be made, partly because ideas, like men, age, and with age, change their appearance, lose some of their original vigor and become less meaningful. Social research has created a new *lingua franca* in which problems traditionally identified as those within the sociology of knowledge have gained little impetus and development. That sociologists publish little sociology of knowledge in their journals becomes obvious when one peruses *Sociological Abstracts*. On the other hand, honor and votive deference is paid the sociology of knowledge in dissertations and M.A. theses which seldom see the printers ink. The sociology of knowledge appears to function as a maintainer of enthusiasm on the part of the graduate student for sociology as a field. As an academician and professional sociologist teaching courses at institutions of higher learning, he soon channels his energy and interest in other directions.

The dissatisfaction with the language of the sociology of knowledge may even be seen by the desire of a number of scholars to change its name. Thus Louis Wirth thought "it should rather be called the sociology of intellectual life," [1] and John W. Bennett, in Kurt H. Wolff's seminar on the sociology of knowledge, suggested the term "sociology of intellectual behavior." [2] In part this may be a desire to dissociate the sociology of knowledge from philosophy generally and epistemology specifically. *Der Streit um die Wissenssoziologie* of the 1920's in Germany and a decade later in the United States is for practical purposes a dead letter. Nonetheless, discussions of whether the sociology of knowledge is possible, whether it trespasses epistemology, and whether relativity of knowledge is admissible as a framework linger on. From time to time problems in this area are revived and lengthy discussions result. [3]

Such discussions, frequently models of logical and philosophic anal-

286

ysis,[4] have not helped the sociology of knowledge become a systematic field, building a theory "of the middle range." Theories of vast generality with the quality of finality have appeared. None have, however, withstood the test of time, and at present appear to be mere items in human intellectual history.

What is it about the sociology of knowledge that has prevented it from flowering in the past decade? First, the time is perhaps not now ripe for it. Merton suggests that a sociology of knowledge develops when

> conflicting perspectives and interpretations within . . . [a] society [lead] to an active and reciprocal *distrust* between groups. Within a context of distrust, one no longer inquires into the content of beliefs and assertions to determine whether they are valid or not, one no longer confronts the assertions with relevant evidence, but introduces an entirely new question: how does it happen that these views are maintained?[5]

The United States of the 1930's may indeed be characterized as a society of "conflicting perspectives and interpretations" and we know historically of the entrance of the sociology of knowledge with the translation of Mannheim and the great interest and many discussions and study of ideologies, philosophies, points of view, etc. But the last decade in the United States (1945-54) has also shown itself to be full of "conflicting perspectives and interpretations," and little sociology of knowledge has been practiced. Perhaps Merton's hypothesis needs be modified to read: The sociology of knowledge flowers when conflicting perspectives and interpretations occur in a society, and when such a society is economically inactive.[6]

The second answer may lie in the different concerns and language of social researchers. The philosophic problems, such as that of "imputation" and *Seinsverbundenheit* do not concern the social researchers. As scientists they make only those assumptions necessary to solve problems arising from data secured on the basis of the empiricist theory of knowledge. Imputation, in the empirical sense, is the unraveling of 'causes' by manipulating the variables defined in the research problem. Survey analysis has made it possible to make some causal statements through the technique of 'elaboration'[7] which may, as a start, be used to solve the problem of 'imputation' empirically. Sociologists of knowledge have not as yet appropriated survey techniques and secondary analysis into their methodology.

This lack of synchronization of substantive problem areas with methodological developments in empirical research leads us to the third hypothesis as to why the sociology of knowledge is not blooming. It is exemplified by Merton in his discussion of the difference between European and American sociology of knowledge.

> ... the European variant being concerned with knowledge, comes to deal with the intellectual elite; the American variant, concerned with widely held opinion, deals with the masses. The one centers on the esoteric doctrines of the few, the other on the exoteric beliefs of the many.[8]

Merton suggests that communication and public opinion research is the American variant if not the equivalent of the sociology of knowledge. He goes on to say that European sociology of knowledge has studied the theories and rationalizations of intellectuals and other elite groups—these theories and rationalizations existing decades prior to the time of their study. The American variant has, on the other hand, plumbed the depth of mass attitudes, beliefs, levels of information, and opinions with the focus on the here-and-now of these beliefs.

One of the early preoccupations of the American variant has been the study of propaganda.[9] Propaganda analysis focussed upon identifying techniques of imparting 'false knowledge,' and 'ideology' for purposes of persuasion, and tended to de-emphasize the study of social mechanisms whereby certain people become propagandists and others students of them. Thus the American variant is only in part a sociology of knowledge. Though it relates attitudes to sociological variables and to other attitude patterns (conservativism-radicalism, authoritarianism-egalitarianism, nationalism-internationalism, etc.) little attempt has been made to link these attitudes to those social as distinct from psychological mechanisms making for their acceptance or rejection, and identifying the individuals and groups instrumental in manipulating attitude patterns. Nor is it within the scope of public opinion studies to do so. It has been communications research that has developed the experimental study of such mechanisms.

Public opinion and communications researchers have thus not joined together, but pursue their independent interests. This leads to compartmentalizing and the carrying on of partial 'sociologies of knowledge' without completing the circuit and creating a *full* sociology of knowledge.[10]

The basic thought of the sociology of knowledge—that a symmetric relationship between 'knowledge' (attitudes, information, beliefs, opinions) and 'society' (groups, social levels, communities, classes) exists—has diffused itself among the academic disciplines. Each has taken one or two links from the long concatenated chain that constitutes the sociology of knowledge on the conceptual level, and absorbed it into its own framework.[11] In totality, the sociology of knowledge is sparingly pursued by sociologists, though it is still traditionally and linguistically coupled to our field. The sociology of knowledge has in large part become the latent frame of reference of the sciences of man.

RECENT CONTRIBUTIONS

It is not possible within the limited space allotted to classify and discuss the relevant work of innumerable authors and fully document the above suggestion. We shall select freely from the rich harvest of studies and published materials. Lest the reader feel some bias in the selection, let him be assured that the selections are used for illustrative purposes and do not necessarily represent the extant or very best writings on the subject. We have selected the fields of psychology, the study of language, and criticism in the social sciences as areas of intellectual endeavor to exemplify our point of the diffusion of the sociology of knowledge into other disciplines and its absorption as a latent frame of reference. Psychology has been selected because it has captured the popular imagination and made deep inroads into the bureaucratic and administrative facets of the American social structure. Language, because it is the medium through which science creates its conceptual apparatus; through which the layman and serious student receive their knowledge of science, and who, through their own unique use of language, create an independent image of it. Criticism in the social sciences has been selected because it exemplifies the mechanisms through which acceptance or rejection of new ideas proceed, and because it offers the best opportunity to isolate extra-intellectual factors in intellectual behavior.

For extensive bibliographies and excellent summary statements of the sociology of knowledge in its full sense, the reader is referred to Kurt H. Wolff's mimeographed seminar notes;[12] H. Otto Dahlke's discussion; [13] Robert K. Merton's paradigm of the sociology of knowledge;[14] H. D. Duncan's interpretation of literature, rhetoric and the flow of ideas between an audience and an author;[15] Franz Adler's recent summary of the sociology of knowledge since 1918;[16] and, Bernard Barber's review of the sociology of knowledge and science in the past decade, 1945-1955. The latter makes a point similar to ours and discusses the way in which history, political science and the sociology of science has contributed to the sociology of knowledge.[17]

IN PSYCHOLOGY

It was, I believe, Bertrand Russell who, with caustic humor, observed that rats used by American psychologists seem to be busily and actively running around their mazes, whereas their relatives in Germany sit down and think the maze through. This observation is pregnant with the hypothesis of the sociology of knowledge, though no one as yet has attempted to research and identify the mechanisms that might prove or disprove the assertion.

What has been of much greater interest to psychologists is the apparent fertility of the American cultural ground to Freudian intellectual seeds. Why is psychoanalysis as a technique of therapy so widespread in America as compared to other countries of the Western World?

No significant sociological explanation has yet been offered. An interesting hypothesis on a related matter, is suggested by Adelson in a recent paper.[18] He suggests that

> Freud's mode of thought, . . . his way of viewing the human situation, runs counter to attitudes deeply entrenched in the American disposition. . . . the antithesis [postulated] . . . is this: between Freud's view, which emphasizes the limitations imposed on man by his nature, and the American vision, an optimistic one, which is captured by the idea of infinite possibility.[19]

Why then is psychoanalysis widespread in America? Adelson goes on

> The [American] interpersonal emphasis leads us to look at the ego in its relationship to other egos; . . . the [Freudian] idea of a complicated psychical structure implies the existence of relatively stable response dispositions, which may violate the American emphasis on a free and flexible ego. . . . The American systems stress the self concept, or nuances of character, . . . the peripheral facets . . . , that which is in consciousness, or easily accessible to observation.[20]

The intellectual tradition of G. H. Mead, C. H. Cooley, John Dewey and the pragmatism so characteristically American, predisposes us to reject the theory of the libido and psychosexuality and those aspects of Freud's theories which offer a bleak and hopeless image of man.

New orientations develop (Horney, Fromm, Sullivan, Rank, Reich, Rogers, clinical psychology) [21] and it appears that a

> relationship between the degree of complexity we attribute to the organism and the attitudes we take concerning the prospects, limitations, and necessary duration of the therapeutic process[22]

exists, over and above the cultural theme which predisposes us to reject certain aspects of Freud because it does not fit our image of man.

The American cultural framework facilitates the acceptance of ideas and methods harmonious with it, and inhibits the acceptance of theories contradicting it. Gardner Murphy echoes this point in a more rhetoric way:

> My point is that the great insights regarding the unconscious were actively resisted; that the concept of sexuality, particularly infantile sexuality, had obviously occasioned horror in the hands of other therapists; that the conception of ego functions as needing constantly to keep a powerful control over instinctual tendencies was alien to the whole way of thinking which was associated with enlightened leaders like James, Dewey, and Cooley . . . ; and that the conception of conscience as derivative partly from dark forces of hostility of parents toward children and the fear of children for parents was patently one which the thoughtful and liberal world . . . rejected. I can only say . . . that those who have not begun to utilize such conceptions are those fortunate or unfortunate persons whose lives are cast in such lines as to make it unnecessary for them to deal with the tangled skein of personal maladjustment.[23]

We see the sociology of knowledge hypothesis incorporated as a frame of reference both by Adelson and Murphy. What their interpretation misses is the identification of those chains that forge a link between the absorption of the American theme of 'possibility' by specific individuals or groups on the one hand, and on the other, the identification of the characteristics of the individuals who make the theme part of their professional armament. The questions begging answers from a sociology of knowledge framework are: Who are the people or groups that tend to absorb such optimistic themes of American culture? What are their social, ethnic, religious origins? What have been the dynamics of their family of orientation and of procreation? What identifications, and with whom, have led them into the profession of psychoanalysis, psychiatry, and/or psychology?

That some relationship exists between personality structure and the milieu wherein psychologists develop, even the man on the street appears to maintain. In an unrandom sample from New York, Pennsylvania, New Jersey, and Illinois, 38% of respondents perceived psychologists as 'queer.'[24] This may well be interpreted as a belief by the man in the street that people having problems become problem solvers!

What leads to what, the direction of the cause in the process of the acceptance or rejection of ideas, is again exemplified by Pastore in a study of the ideological concomitants of the nature-nurture controversy. Inspecting the writings of 24 scientists active in the nature-nurture controversy, Pastore isolated statements relevant to their sociopolitical orientations. He found that "varying nature-nurture emphases were significantly related to particular socio-political orientations. Those emphasizing environmental factors tended toward liberalism or radicalism; those emphasizing hereditary factors tended toward conservatism."[25] But there was no one-to-one relationship, and to interpret a causal relationship was difficult. Pastore suggested the following possibilities: (1) Hereditary factors determine attitudinal predispositions, hence socio-political attitudes derive from the predispositions. (2) The bias of the subject matter in which the scientist operates is accepted, and if not, the scientist denies "the validity of his subject matter."[26] (3) The nature-nurture position conditions the socio-political outlook. (4) The socio-political outlook determines the scientific position. (5) " . . . since the study was confined to the written

> expressions of [the] individuals, a selective error [was] thereby introduced. Many individuals with a definite point of view with regard to nature-nurture questions did not express themselves on socio-political issues. Conceivably this may be due to the fact that such individuals sensed a contradiction between their scientific and political outlooks, and consequently refrained from expressing themselves politically. Thus the relationship between [attitudes and scientific position] could have been accidental."[27]

We see again the penetration of the idea of the sociology of knowledge, but the results indicate that only a part of the necessary data were collected to make the research a full fledged sociology of knowledge study. Instead, the findings are interesting but inconclusive.

With the above presentation of two instances of research conducted by psychologists in their area, the sociology of knowledge hypothesis has been kept in mind, and it seems very likely that more and more such research will appeal to psychologists in their attempts to understand the development and objectification of their science.

IN LINGUISTICS

Since all information, knowledge, attitudes, and opinions possessed by a person or group are received through some "communicative act," the manner in which the communicative act is structured is pertinent to the sociology of knowledge. One aspect of the communicative act, whatever conceptual framework one might take,[28] concerns the symbols used and the extent of the subvention of their meanings.

What has largely remained unexplored is the Whorfean hypothesis that the individual is

> constrained to certain modes of interpretation even while he thinks himself most free. . . . All observers are not led by the same physical evidence to the same picture of the universe, unless their linguistic backgrounds are similar, or can in some way be calibrated. . . .[29] . . . we cut up and organize the spread and flow of events as we do largely because, through our mother tongue, we are parties to an agreement to do so, not because nature itself is segmented in exactly that way for all to see. Languages differ not only in how they build their sentences, but in how they break down nature to secure the elements to put in those sentences.[30]

A concerted effort is being made by linguists to conceptualize the Whorfean hypothesis and make it researchable. In a recent symposium Hockett,[31] writing on the problem of translatability as exemplified by Chinese versus English, suggests

> it is not so much . . . what *can* be said in [different languages], but rather as to what it is *relatively easy* to say. . . . the history of Western logic and science, from Aristotle down, constitutes not so much the story of scholars hemmed in and misled by the nature of their specific languages as the story of a long and successful struggle against inherited linguistic limitations.[32]

Wright, in another symposium notes that, in

> . . . the highly ritualized social life of traditional China, such distinctions as that between right and left have accumulated a vast number of symbolic associations. The left is east, the rising sun, . . . the place of honor. What . . . happened—under the influence of this group of symbols—to the meaning of the statement in the New Testament that Jesus is seated on the

right hand of God? . . . And what was a Chinese to make of the
passage in Chapter 25 of Matthew where the left is specified as
the place of dishonor, whose occupants were to depart "into the
eternal fire which God prepared for the devil and his angels?" . . .
[or] in the history of Marxist ideas whose terminology and meta-
phor were developed in an urban and industrialized Europe
and had, in China, to be communicated to a predominantly agricultural people.[32]

These examples do not portray merely the difficulty of translation
from one language to another, but indicate the constraint language-
habits have upon innovative thought. To this extent, the sociology of
knowledge is interested in delimiting those linguistic mechanisms
which hinder or facilitate the acceptance and communication of ideas.

Also worthy of study is the recent penetration of economic and
physical terminology into non-economic disciplines. Riesman, discussing Freud's attack upon narcissism states

> narcissism is, so to speak, the last refuge of the individual from
> his *creditors* (italics ours) social and personal. And yet . . .
> [Freud] was the inventor of a therapy designed to lift from the
> individual his oppressive *mortgage,* or at least to provide for a
> *stay of foreclosure* and *a remission of payments* long since due.[34]

Or view Sorokin, rebutting Moreno's theory of spontaneity-creativity,
suggesting that creativity is not passive and petrified, but "radio-
active".[35] W. J. H. Sprott, in his Josiah Mason Lectures, speaking of
Lewin's topological psychology through an example of a child entering a room which has a sweet on a mantlepiece, topologizes:

> The forces are symbolized in a very professional way. . . .It looks
> significant; it looks scientific; it is, in fact, bogus. If we could
> measure the forces *before* the child moves there might be some-
> thing in it; . . . The interpretation is all *ex post facto*: "there
> must have been a strong vector here, a weak one there", and so
> on. We are merely invited to use force terminology as a trans-
> lation of perfectly adequate psychological terminology. . . .Since
> one has no means of measuring the forces, the symbolic apparatus
> really gives a false impression of scientific accuracy.[36]

Note the linguistic structure wherein the *Crestwood Heights* ideology
and its circulation is placed as it is discussed by the researchers:

> . . . the process by which beliefs are *produced* and, as it were,
> *consumed* . . . cannot be understood by attending narrowly to
> Crestwood Heights itself. Just as the Crestwood family is pri-
> marily a consumption unit for material goods which are pro-
> duced in specialized units elsewhere, so . . . is Crestwood Heights

> . . . a *consumption unit* for ideas, views, theories, opinions that
> are *produced elsewhere,* also by a core of persons *specialized for
> such production.* . . .Crestwood Heights affects what is *produced*
> for the idea or belief or opinion or attitude *market.*[37] (italics
> ours)

We need not point to the prevalence of such terms in psychology
as 'human engineering', 'conservation of human resources', etc., which
seem to structure man in a relatively inanimate caste. Separate disciplines such as psychoanalysis, psychology, economics, etc., have distinct linguistic meaning-structures arrived at through their own historic
development. What mechanisms in our intellectual and academic life
operate to make translatability of different linguistic structures desirable[38] and what accounts for the current habit of discussing ideas
with the aid of borrowed concepts foreign to the subject matter of the
idea discussed? If analogies are as dangerous for precise communication as logicians claim, because the language structures 'what is meant';
are not intellectuals parties to 'disenchanting', 'dehumanizing', 'de-
contextualizing' man, intellectual fields, or theoretic formulations? Or
are the above examples an attempt to 'naturalize' or 'economicize'
the *Geisteswissenschaften?* Perhaps the above is merely indicative of
the desire to use concepts having higher status value than the subject
matter under discussion; thus lending one's own subject a high chance
of acceptability? Perhaps, this is in part the Simmelian suggestion
come to roost, that as capitalism advances, its counting and mensu-
rating pattern permeates the intellectual and scientific terminologies?[39]

Clearly the Whorfean hypothesis here borders upon the hypothesis
of the sociology of knowledge. The use of language becomes the lens
through which particular groups interpret reality, both as given to
them through their professional socialization, and as they henceforth
'freely' perceive through their own innovative creativity. The beginning of the study of language from the sociology of knowledge
viewpoint has been made. Will sociologists be challenged to pursue it?

CRITICISM

From time to time the discovery is made that the content of criticism does not invalidate that which is criticized, because the content
of criticism is a function of the critic's identification with a particular
school-of-thought (and therefore also its language), the type of institution wherein his loyalties are anchored, and, the people he considers

his intellectual peers, betters, or friends. Criticism thus contains many extra-scientific or extra-intellectual factors which are amenable to study. The content of criticism may well contribute to the sociology of knowledge and to greater understanding of the mechanisms through which the social sciences develop.[40]

It is not usual to criticize books extensively in the social sciences, and only when a research or work of commanding importance appears, is it possible to accumulate reviews in sufficient quantities and from a variety of sources to make a study of them profitable. Among the many works of commanding importance in the past decade, two have received close study: *The American Soldier,*[41] and the *Kinsey Report.*[42]

Cochran-Mosteller-Tukey[43] content analyzed six 'important' reviews of the Kinsey Report to distill those criticisms uniformly noted by the reviewers. The assumption was that such agreement lends the criticism 'validity.' This quantifying of opinions and thereby establishing validity rather than reliability of 'attitudes' towards the use of 'research-methods', may be questioned, and is again only a partial sociology of knowledge. For the study to have been a full sociology of knowledge, it would be necessary to cross-tabulate the list of methodological and statistical misdemeanors attributed to Kinsey with the substantive findings these errors invalidate. If the errors invalidate those items which may be identified as major values to which our culture explicitly adheres to, the stage is set for the investigation of the question: are the methodological and statistical discussions undertaken to invalidate findings inimical to the values of the criticizing group? We pose this question for two reasons. First, because Cochran-Mosteller-Tukey in summary have this to say about the criticisms of the first volume of the Kinsey Report:

> . . . many of the most interesting statements [by Kinsey] in the book are not based on the tabular material in the book and it is not made . . . clear . . . on what evidence the statements are based. . . . That . . . the conclusions are often stated too boldly and confidently, . . . much of the writing in the book falls below the level of good scientific writing. . . . On the other hand, [Kinsey does] a fairly competent job of summarizing what the data appear to show. In the case of stability of sexual patterns, our doubts about their conclusions arise from wondering whether the older and younger generations are comparable, and from doubts about the reliability of any comparison involving recent recall versus quite remote recall. In the case of homosexuality, we

are chiefly concerned about possible bias in the sample. . . . With vertical mobility . . . memory of events may be distorted by changes in social level since the time at which the events occurred. . . . the extent to which Kinsey's averages really represent average behavior is a matter of judgment.[44]

Clearly, the language of the Kinsey Report was unacceptable to the critics. Yet, Kinsey is also praised that he "fairly competently summarized what the data show." Findings on the stability of sexual patterns, homosexuality, and vertical mobility are questioned due to the memory factor. Has anyone questioned the validity of the data reported in Hollingshead's *Elmstown's Youth*, also in large part based on recalled information, or the numerous other studies of communities? Is there an extra-intellectual factor at work?

Hyman and Sheatsly seem also to feel that there are grounds for searching for extra-intellectual factors:

The content analysis . . . provides a rare, perhaps unique, opportunity to see what elements of subjectivity or idiosyncrasy characterize present-day technical standards of research. . . . in some places our present principles fall short. . . . The principles either provide no clear standard as to correct practice or they point to a technical problem demanding solution, without being able to point the direction of that solution. . . .[45]

In such twilight situations the hypothesis of the sociology of knowledge takes on imperative dimensions. Is the critic to dismiss behavior studies whose conclusions may not fit his notion of what actual behavior consists of by citing faulty technique used, or that techniques not yet developed have not been used?

That criticism is also a function of the critics' presumed relation to ideas has also been shown by using 275 reviews and articles of the Kinsey Report. Creating a typology of 'intellectuals' on the basis of their presumed relation to ideas,[46] Chall found Producers of Ideas were most favorable to the Kinsey Report (64%), Adapters (51%) and Communicators of Ideas were least favorable (41%). Toward the much discussed definition of 'normality' and the 'ideal-real dichotomy' themes, 59% of the Producers, 33% of Adapters, and 28% of Communicators of Ideas lent their support. As time proceeded, however, unfavorable reviews tended to increase, within all three groups. It was therefore hypothecated, that criticism depends upon the relationship of the critic toward ideas. If he primarily creates them, he tends to be favorable to new ideas; if he primarily

adapts them, he sieves them through an *a priori* frame of reference
and then decides whether he will accept the new idea or not; if he
primarily communicates, he reacts to the idea with that attitude
he perceives is held by the milieu to which his communication is
sent. It was further suggested, that criticism is sensitive to a general
attitude-opinion constellation, and as an attitude pattern crystallizes,
critics tend to approach a 'norm.'

The above two studies are a challenge to a substantive field which
so far has been plagued by normative orientations and ethical tight-
rope-walking. Studies analyzing Kinsey or reviews of research done
in sexual behavior contain most useful data as yet not fully explored.
Such exploration can greatly contribute to the sociology of knowledge,
because this substantive area is imbued with emotional and extra-
intellectual factors, which, when isolated, will better map the geography of the cauldron wherein both 'ideologies' [47] and 'knowledge'
are fashioned.

Lerner presents a content analysis of comments and commentators
on *The American Soldier* and creates a most interesting typology
of them.[48] The 'intellectuals' are divided into friendly and hostile,
each in turn divided into high brow, middle brow, and low brow.
The resultant two by three table issues six cells. The friendly-high-
brows labeled "Paternal-Benedictory," the friendly-middlebrow "Fra-
ternal-Missionary," and the friendly-lowbrow, "Filial-Pietistic." The
hostile-highbrow becomes "Oedipedic-Imprecatory," the hostile-middlebrow, "Rivalrous-Diabolic," and the hostile-lowbrow is arrestingly
termed "Juvenile-Delinquent." The classification by commentators
and reviewers is even more enlightening. Theodore Ropp is classed
a friendly-highbrow; A. M. Schlesinger a hostile-highbrow; C. I. Hovland and P. F. Lazarsfeld are friendly-middlebrows; and Nathan
Glazer and Herbert Blumer are relegated to the hostile-middlebrow
cell. The friendly and unfriendly lowbrows consist of the military
representatives of the American defense establishment.

Lerner's role-attitude categories appear to be significant more by
what they betray than by what they describe. Is this perchance the
working out of the hypothesis of the sociology of knowledge, showing
that sociologists most active in the creation of *The American Soldier*
are friendly-middlebrows? We cannot withstand the beckoning of a
good joke, and must cite that the Juvenile-Delinquents are, of course,
the journalist(ic) book critics who pretend "to know more (or understand better) about the subject of the book under review than its

author" [49] Whether this is true or not (and most likely it is) is not the question, but the generalization is frequently made that only the "intellectual intelligentsia" may criticize a book written by an "intellectual." At worst, the "intellectual" demands first to criticize it before the unenlightened lay-journalist misunderstands the finer print of the *American Soldier,* and communicates the findings to those on an 'intellectually' lower and more naive level than his peers.

Similarly with the publication of the second volume of the Kinsey Report, the author has observed that the scientific journals did not publish their reviews for months, to perhaps permit the mass media turmoil to subside before publishing their comments.

Studies of reviews and comments on books of monumental importance to the socal sciences could greatly contribute to empiricizing the sociology of knowledge. Who are reviewers? Where do they write? Do they evaluate a book the same when writing in their own professional media and differently when writing to other professionals and laymen? Does the status of the reviewer in his own academic discipline affect the manner in which new ideas are accepted? Do the older members of the profession tend to be more receptive and younger members more scrutinizing and keep more firmly to the rigid methodological requirements of scientific research? Answers to any or all of the above questions will solidify the sociology of knowledge. Perhaps studies such as this will be made of the reviews between 1918 and 1925 of Freud's writings in the medical journals of Austria and Germany; of the reviews of *The American Dilemma* in the regional historic journals of the United States; and of the discussion of *The Polish Peasant in Europe and America* on both sides of the Atlantic. Accumulated studies such as these will provide the basic datum from which the intellectual's mechanisms to accept or reject ideas will be isolated, and permit one to assess when faulty use of methodological techniques is called upon to invalidate empirical findings, and when and under what condition ideas percolate down or capillate up.

The identification and specification of the critic's role in the social and behavior sciences is slowly progressing, and is a most urgent task for the sociology of knowledge to take under its wing. As defender of society or the purity of his chosen field of study, the criteria for criticism a critic selects may be invalid and thus produce a critique unworthy of serious scientific consideration, yet it may be seriously considered and gain a wide circle of adherents. If he defends an idea which by scientific criteria is quite valid, though the subject matter is perceived as boding ill for social values much adhered to, the critic runs the risk of at worst being criticized for poor judgment, and at best being ignored. Though review writing has in the past decades become a declining art, creating controversy through a review may frequently result in gaining fame, but may just as frequently lead to scholarly oblivion.

We have shown how the sociology of knowledge has penetrated psychology, linguistics and social science criticism. Surveys of the field of political science and history will reaffirm the major thesis of this paper, that the field of the sociology of knowledge has lost its original language and has become a latent part of the entire range of the behavioral sciences.

SELECTED BIBLIOGRAPHY

Reinhard Bendix, *Work and Authority in Industry: Ideologies of Management in the Course of Industrialization* (New York: John Wiley, 1956). A recent work on the development of the managerial ideology in the U.S. and Eastern Germany.

Theodore Geiger, *Aufgaben and Stellung der Intelligenz in der Gesellschaft (Function and Position of Intellectuals in Society)* (Stuttgart: F. Enke Verlag, 1944). An analysis of the status of intellectuals in European society, delimiting their role, accomplishment, and limitations.

Karl Mannheim, *Ideology and Utopia* New York: Harcourt, Brace, 1936); *Essays on the Sociology of Knowledge* (New York: Oxford University Press, 1952); *Essays on Sociology and Social Psychology* (New York: Oxford University Press, 1953); *Essays on Sociology and Culture* (New York: Oxford University Press, 1956). The first volume was translated by L. Wirth & E. Shils; the last volumes were translated and edited by P. Keckemeti—and the second also by Ernst Mannheim; these works make available in English Mannheim's major contribution to the field known as the sociology of knowledge.

J. J. Marquet, *The Sociology of Knowledge* (Boston: The Beacon Press, 1951). A discussion and analysis of Mannheim's and Sorokin's theories of the sociology of knowledge.

Robert K. Merton, *Social Theory and Social Structure* (Glencoe, Ill.: The Free Press, 1949). A significant discussion of the sociology of knowledge, with a schematic analytic-synthetic scheme known as the "paradigm in the sociology of knowledge."

Pitirim A. Sorokin, *Social and Cultural Dynamics* (New York: American Book Co., 1937-41). A monumental four volume interpretation of the sociology of knowledge presenting a typology of societies and the kind of knowledge extant in them.

H. L. Wilensky, *Intellectuals in Labor Unions: Organizational Pressures on Professional Roles* (Glencoe, Ill.: The Free Press, 1956). An analysis of the position óf the intellectual and professional in a labor union and the identification of the pressures, roles and statuses, determining and influencing them.

Leo P. Chall is a Lecturer in the Department of Anthropology and Sociology, Brooklyn College and Editor of *Sociological Abstracts.*

NOTES

1. Quoted in Howard W. Odum, *American Sociology* (New York: Longmans, Green, 1951), 231.

2. Kurt H. Wolff, *The Sociology of Intellectual Behavior* (Seminar Notes, Mimeographed Columbus, Ohio: Ohio State University, 1947 & 1949); also: "The Unique and the General: Toward a Philosophy of Sociology," *Philosophy of Science,* XV, 3 (1948), 203.

3. Virgil G. Hinshaw, Jr., "Epistemological Relativism and the Sociology of Knowledge," *Philosophy of Science,* XV, 1 (1948), 4-10 see also: Thelma Z. Lavine, "Naturalism and the Sociological Analysis of Knowledge," in Y. H. Krikorian, Ed., *Naturalism and the Human Spirit* (New York: Columbia University Press, 1944), 183-209.

4. Alexander von Schelting, review of Mannheim's *Ideology and Utopia,* in *The American Sociological Review,* I (1936), 664-674.

5. Robert K. Merton, "The Sociology of Knowledge," in Georges Gurvitch & Wilbert E. Moore, Eds., *Twentieth Century Sociology* (New York: The Philosophical Library, 1945), 368; see also his: *Social Theory and Social Structure* (Glencoe, Ill.: The Free Press, 1949), 199-264.

6. There are four possibilities when two dichomotized variables are cross-tabulated: Economic activity high or low, distrust high or low thus

Economic Activity

	+	−
+	1	2
−	4	3

(Distrust)

Cell 1 is characteristic of a society with high economic activity and a relatively high incidence of distrust. Such a society may be the United States in the last decade. We hypothecate that in a society such as this no sociology of knowledge will be practiced, or it will 'go underground,' i.e., permeate other fields of intellectual activity. Cell 2 characterized by low economic activity and a high incidence of distrust, is exemplified by Germany in the 1920's and the United States in the 1930's. In such a situation a sociology of knowledge is possible and has historically occurred. Cell 3 describes a society with low economic activity and a low incidence of inter- and intra-group distrust. Such are the characteristics of homogeneous preliterate or primitive societies. Cell 4 with high economic activity and a similar low incidence or level of distrust is characteristic of the United States during World War II, a time when the sociology of knowledge was little practiced while public opinion, propaganda, and communications studies, the closest neighbors of the sociology of knowledge, were pursued, as the rest of the introductory section of this paper will illustrate. This scheme is in no sense a final one, for many more than two variables enter into the situation.

7.   Elaboration as a technique is the process of cross-tabulating two variables and introducing a third one as a test variable. The resultant partial relationships may frequently be interpreted in a causal framework. See Patricia L. Kendall and Paul F. Lazarsfeld, "Problems of Survey Analysis," in Robert K. Merton and Paul F. Lazarsfeld, Eds., *Continuities in Social Research* (Glencoe, Ill.: The Free Press, 1950), 133-196; H. H. Hyman, *Survey Design and Analysis* (Glencoe, Ill.: The Free Press, 1955), Chapter VII; see also the Preface by P. F. Lazarsfeld which may be viewed as a statement of the sociology of education if not a sociology of knowledge. Paul F. Lazarsfeld & Morris Rosenberg, Eds., *The Language of Social Research* (Glencoe, Ill.: The Free Press, 1955), especially Chapters I, 19-39, 83, 106; Chapter III, 206-259; Chapter V, 449-468; Chapter VI, 498-518 & 554-564.

8.   Merton, *Social Theory and Social Structure*, 201.

9.   Alfred McClung Lee & Elizabeth B. Lee, *The Fine Art of Propaganda* (New York: Harcourt, Brace, 1939).

10.   Merton, *op. cit.*, 201.

11.   See: Carl I. Hovland, Irving L. Janis, & H. H. Kelley, Eds., *Communication and Persuasion* (Yale University Press, 1953), and many studies in *Human Relations, Public Opinion Quarterly, a*nd other periodicals; for references see:*Psychological Abstracts* and *Sociological Abstracts*.

12.   Wolff, *op. cit.* See also his forthcoming "Social Theory & Sociology of Knowledge," in L. Gross' symposium (to be published by Row, Peterson & Co.).

13.   H. Otto Dahlke, "The Sociology of Knowledge," in H. E. Barnes & Howard Becker, Eds., *Contemporary Social Theory* (New York: Appleton-Century, 1940), 64-89.

14.   Merton, *op. cit.*

15.   Hugh D. Duncan, *Language and Literature in Society* (University of Chicago Press, 1953), the bibliography is of herculean proportions.

16.   Franz Adler, "The Sociology of Knowledge Since 1918,"*The Midwest Sociologist*, XII, 1 (1955), 3-12, and "The Range of Sociology of Knowledge," Chapter 13, in Howard Becker & Alvin Boskoff, *Modern Sociological Theory* (New York: The Dryden Press, 1957).

17.   Bernard Barber, "Sociology of Knowledge & Science 1945-1955," in Hans L. Zetterberg, Ed.,*Sociology in the United States of America: A Trend Report* (Paris: UNESCO, 1956), 68-70.

18.   Joseph Adelson, "Freud in America: Some Observations," *The American Psychologist,* XI (1956), 467-470.

19.   Adelson, *op. cit.*, 467, 468.

20.   Adelson, *op. cit.*, 469.

21.   It is of interest to note that the orthodox American Psychoanalytic Association lists 672 accredited members, and the American Psychiatric Association about 12,000 members.

22.   Adelson, *op. cit.*, 469.

23.   Gardner Murphy, "The Current Impact of Freud Upon Psychology," *The American Psychologist,* XI 12 (1956), 669.

24.   Lester Guest, "The Public's Attitude Toward Psychologists," *The American Psychologist,* III, 4 (1948), 139.

25.   Nicholas Pastore, *The Nature-Nurture Controversy* (New York: Columbia University Press, 1949), 176.

26.   Pastore, *op. cit.*, p. 179.

27.   Pastore, *op. cit.*, 181.

28.   See: Hovland, Janes & Kelley, *op. cit.*, Jurgen Ruesch, M.D. & Gregory Batson,

Communication: The Social Matrix of Psychiatry (New York: W. W. Norton, 1951) ; C. E. Shannon & W. Weaver, *The Mathematical Theory of Communication* (Urbana: University of Illinois Press, 1949) ; Colin Cherry, *On Human Communication: A Review, Survey, and a Criticism* (New York: John Wiley, 1957), and many others.

29. Benjamin L. Whorf, *Collected Papers in Metalinguistics* (Washington, D. C.: Department of State, 1932), 5, 21.

30. *Ibid.*, 21.

31. Charles F. Hockett, "Chinese Versus English: An Exploration of the Whorfian Theses," in Harry Hoijer, Editor, *Language in Culture* (Chicago: University of Chicago Press, 1954).

32. Hockett, *op. cit.*, p. 122.

33. Arthur F. Wright, "The Chinese Language and Foreign Ideas," in Arthur F. Wright, Editor, *Studies in Chinese Thought* (Chicago: University of Chicago Press, 1953), pp. 300-301.

34. David Riesman, *Individualism Reconsidered* (Glencoe, Ill: The Free Press, 1954) p. 337.

35. Pitrim A. Sorokin, "Remarks on J. L. Moreno's 'Theory of Spontaneity-Creativity,'" *Sociometry*, 18, 4, (1955), p. 380.

36. W. J. H. Sprott, *Science and Social Action* (Glencoe, Ill: The Free Press, 1954) p. 70 and 71.

37. John R. Seeley, R. Alexander Sim, and Elizabeth W. Loosley, *Crestwood Heights* (New York: Basic Books, 1956), p. 343.

38. See the various strains towards 'interdisciplinarianship,' on the one hand, and the serious attempts on the other, towards 'unified theories of human behavior. Noteworthy are such works as Talcott Parsons and Edward A. Shils, Editors, *Toward a General Theory of Action* (Cambridge: Harvard University Press, 1951), Roy R. Grinker. MD, Editor, *Toward a Unified Theory of Human Relations* (New York: Basic Books, 1956), the annual Conference Transactions in *Cybernetics* (as of 1949), *Group Process* (as of 1954) (New York: Josiah Macy, Jr. Foundation), and many others. The trend is fully affirmed with the publication of a new journal *Behaviorial Science* founded in 1956.

39. George Simmel, *Die Philosophie des Geldes* (München: Dunker und Humblot 1900).

40. Kurt H. Wolff, "The Sociology of Knowledge: Emphasis on an Empirical Attitude," *Philosophy of Science*, 10, 3, (1943), p. 123.

41. Daniel Lerner, "The *American Soldier* and the Public," in Robert K. Merton and Paul F. Lazarsfeld, Editors, *Continuities in Social Research* (Glencoe, Ill: The Free Press, 1950), pp. 212-251.

42. Leo P. Chall, "The Reception of the Kinsey Report in the Periodicals of the United States: 1947-1949," in Jerome Himelhoch and Sylvia Fleis Fava, Editors, *Sexual Behavior in American Society* (New York: W. W. Norton, 1955), pp. 364-378.

43. William G. Cochran, Frederick Mosteller, and John W. Tukey with the assistance of W. O. Jenkins, *Statistical Problems of the Kinsey Report on Sexual Behavior in the Human Male* (Washington, D. C.: The American Statistical Association, 1954).

44. Cochran-Mosteller-Tukey, *op. cit.*, p. 150 (the analysis is based on six major reviews of the Kinsey Report).

45. Herbert H. Hyman and Paul Sheatsley, "Comment" in "The Cochran-Mosteller-Tukey Report on the Kinsey Study: A Symposium," *The Journal of the American Association*, 50, 271, (1955), p. 815.

46. Chall, *op. cit.*, pp. 371-373.

47. David Greenwood, "The Ideology of Dr. Alfred Kinsey" in his *Essays in Human Relations*, (Washington, D. C.: Public Affairs Press, 1956) pp. 1-10, wherein it is asserted within Mannheim's frame of reference that, "in most respects his [Kinsey's] ideology is progressive, in a few respects conservative but hardly, in the strict sense, utopian." (p. 5)

48. Lerner, *op. cit.*, pp. 224-230.

49. Lerner, *op. cit.*, p. 228.

SOCIOLOGY AND AMERICAN CATHOLICS

Paul Mundy
Loyola University

Almost twenty years ago a prominent American sociologist commented on the need to consider sociological developments among American Catholics in these words:

> "For forty years or more there has been growing up in the United States a school of Roman Catholic sociological theorists. For the most part their work has been ignored by the great mass of American sociologists. It is a comment upon our civilization that a separate school of social theorists could exist for so long and receive so little attention. It is pretty conclusive evidence that in-group and out-group attitudes not only prevail among American sociologists, but frequently inhibit critical attention and thinking.[1]

These words of mixed interest and concern were undoubtedly influenced by the research efforts of Melvin J. Williams, who had recently completed the writing of his doctoral dissertation under the direction of Ellwood.[2] As if anticipating that his comments were likely to be brushed aside by his colleagues, the late Professor Ellwood went on to say:

> . . . "Catholic sociological theorists can claim . . . that they are no more guilty of making use of metaphysical postulates than the rest of us; indeed, that from one point of view they are less guilty, since they proceed with full consciousness of their metaphysical postulates, which is not always the case with non- Catholic sociological thinkers . . .
> It is certainly to be hoped that the lack of attention by non-Catholic American sociologists to the sociology which is taught in Roman Catholic institutions and which is producing a rich and voluminous sociological literature will soon be a thing of the past."[3]

Like so many bravely launched ships bearing express sociological hopes, this one has not had the fully smooth sailing wished for it by Ellwood; nevertheless, it must be recognized that the work of American Catholic sociologists is more widely known and respected today. In part, it must be noted, this change has been produced by an increasing maturity and competence among Catholic sociologists themselves; in part, it has come about by a greater friendliness and objectivity among other professional sociologists—more and more aware, as Ellwood asserted, that the rejection of *one* system of values does not assure a value-free system as a logical consequence. In the introduction to his forthcoming book, Zahn makes the point in these words:

> "The awarenes of the relationship between human social behavior and moral value standards does not so dominate the activities of the Catholic social scientist that he is unable to meet the accepted canons of competent scholarship. The Catholic who accepts a value system in which divorce is recognized as a moral evil and, therefore, a "social problem" will use the same sources and probably the same methods in analyzing and describing this social phenomenon as will his non-Catholic colleague. He will differ only at the level of interpretation; and who is to say that the non-Catholic sociologist who regards a high divorce rate as being a healthy sign of flexibility in marital adjustment is any more "value-free" in his sociology than the Catholic who regards the same high rate as a moral evil which expectedly endangers the common good by weakening the most crucial social institution.[4]

Accompanying and reinforcing this change of outlook were two significant developments: first, a more critical estimate of the basic assumptions of positivism; second, within the sphere of Catholic education, an increasing acceptance of sociology in the curricula. As one trenchant critic observed, positivists

> "share a strong common *faith in certain articles of belief* such as determinism, the non-existence of moral absolutes, and the impossibility of revealed religion. These beliefs, obviously, are not conclusions resulting from scientific sociological research. They are *propositions of the philosophical and theeological order* accepted by the positivistic sociologists and *woven into their systems of sociological thought.*"[5]

The importance of the second factor is suggested by L. L. Bernard's judgment that "the change of Catholic educational policy in the matter of naming courses with sociological content and listing them in a separate department of sociology is one of the outstanding trends in the teaching of sociology."[6] It will be well to consider this educational emphasis briefly at this time.

SOCIOLOGY IN CATHOLIC EDUCATION

An early interest in sociology among American Catholic educators is demonstrated by the fact that The Catholic University of America established the subject on a departmental basis in 1894. While sociology had been taught as a separate course offering at Yale as early as 1873, the University of Chicago set up what is commonly considered to be the first such department in the United States in 1893. The history of the early years of growth at Catholic University mirrors an uncertainty as to the place of sociology in the educational picture—an uncertainty not unique to Catholic circles. The originally separate department came shortly to be known as ethics-sociology; administratively, it was moved from the Faculty of Law to the School of Philosophy. Social welfare and social work emphases developed, starting with the 1908 course listings, and continued until 1924. Anthropology was the next discipline to be closely associated with sociology. From 1934 on, and particularly after 1937, the separate departmental basis was established once again. The first doctorate in sociology at Catholic University was awarded in 1904. From its inception through 1955, Catholic Univeristy's Department of Sociology conferred 95 Ph.D.'s and 398 Master's degrees, with majors in sociology.[7]

Numerous other Catholic universities and colleges added sociology to their program of studies in the present century, although usually at the undergraduate level. At present, in addition to Catholic University, rather comprehensive graduate programs are offered by Fordham, Loyola (of Chicago), Notre Dame, and St. Louis universities.

Of 911 doctorates in sociology conferred by American institutions during the period 1936-1950, 84 (9.2 per cent) were conferred by Catholic universities.[8] The Catholic University of America, with 65 Ph.D. degrees, ranked fourth among fifty-eight universities listed as granting the doctoral degree in sociology.

In 1955 a rather comprehensive questionnaire survey was made concerning the teaching of sociology in more than fifteen hundred Catholic institutions—high schools, seminaries, colleges, and universities. An over-all response of fifty-five per cent disclosed, it was reported, that sociology courses were being taught to the following extent among the responding institutions: high schools, 73 per cent; major (advanced training) seminaries, 75 per cent; minor (preliminary training) seminaries, 30 per cent; college and universities, over 80 per cent. with about half of these offering a major program of concentration in the field.[9]

The summary section of the Report includes the following remarks, which in part, perhaps, have a relevance outside Catholic institutions:

> "There is a widespread feeling at all levels of the survey that sociology lacks status. All three sub-committees received comments indicating that an atmosphere beclouded with apathy, doubt, confusion and even hostility surrounds their field in the attitude of students, colleagues and particularly administrators . . . sociology has yet to attain a *sine qua non* status in the curricula of Catholic education . . . an acceptable dichotomy between "pure" sociology and Catholic thought is yet to be drawn."[10]

APPROACHES TO SOCIOLOGY

As is indicated by the quotation above, Catholic sociologists are in some disagreement as to the nature and scope of their discipline. There are a variety of viewpoints regarding what is "sociological" among these sociologists, despite their unity of religious belief. One commentator has noted "Through a basic misconception, the sociological thought of Catholics has been widely regarded as a monolithic product of authoritarian dictation . . . historical facts render invalid a further description of sociology among Catholics as something by nature alien to non-Catholic thinking on social relationships." [11]

Whatever the variety, two dominant points of view are in real, if sometimes quiet, conflict. One group holds that sociology is an autonomous social science, inherently distinct, analytical, "pure"; the other group asserts that sociology is synthetic, sociophilosophical, socioethical. The first group does not always deny the legitimacy of utilizing the relevant postulates of other disciplines, whether these be statistical, anthropological, psychological, philosophical, theological; it simply insists that the lines of scientific demarcation constitute a genuine specialization and separation, as reflected in the distinct formal object (point of view) of sociology in dealing with its material object (subject matter). The second group does not reject the necessity of logical distinction; it simply asserts that there is an

inevitable and inherent involvement of sociophilosophical and socioethical principles when *man, men in society, social relationships, social
institutions,* etc., are studied, rendering impossible a valid and meaningful separation of sociology, *in toto,* from these other disciplines.
The dispute has not been altogether wasteful; a vigorous examination
of basic matter has served to clarify the positions taken. The sharp-
ness of the disagreement has become somewhat dulled in recent years,
and there is declining interest in maintaining the semantic battle
lines today.[12] In part, this is traceable to some reasoned appeals for
reconciliation and to some actual shifting of ground by the leaders.[13]
There has gradually come to pass the rather general acceptance of
the idea that there are *Catholic sociologists* but, strictly speaking, not
a Catholic sociology, just as there is no Methodist or Jewish sociology.
How, then, explain the American Catholic Sociological Society and its
Review?

THE AMERICAN CATHOLIC SOCIOLOGICAL SOCIETY

A letter from the Reverend Ralph A. Gallagher, S.J., Loyola University (Chicago), was sent out to "all the Catholic Universities and
colleges of the Mid-west" to found "a Mid-west Conference of Catholic
Sociology" in February 1938. Father Gallagher, recognized as the
founder of the American Catholic Sociological Society, explained that
he was carrying out the wish of "a few representatives of Catholic
colleges of the Middle West" expressed at the American Sociological
Society meeting the previous December. One respondent suggested
a change in name for the organization "because I do not think there
is a Catholic sociology any more than there is a Catholic algebra."
That the organizational meeting on March 26, 1938, was favorably
regarded by the American Sociological Society is evident from the
telegram received from H. A. Phelps, secretary of the Society: "Best
wishes of the officers and members of the American Sociological Society to the Mid-west Conference of The Catholic Sociological Society
during its first annual meeting and the years to come."[14]

Thirty-one delegates, including one non-Catholic, from thirty midwestern colleges and universities attended the organizational meeting
at Loyola University. Despite the geographical concentration of the
persons attending this meeting, the present name of the Society was
adopted. As a statement of purpose the group expectedly made recom-

mendations along both sociological and religious lines, urging serious study, research and professional responsibility, at the same time hoping for a sense of unity and some exploration of the sociological implications of Catholic thought.[15] These recommendations served as the basis for Article II (Statement of Purpose) of the Society's Constitution.

Since the developments among American Catholic sociologists are especially reflected in the changing emphases and trends taking place within the American Catholic Sociological Society, it is necessary to give some special attention to the Society during the twenty years of its existence. Both strands of growth are inextricably woven together.

The Early Years of the Society. As if to allay the fears of separatism on the part of some of those in attendance at the first convention in December 1938, Father Gallagher, in the first presidential address, stated: "We have no intention of becoming intellectual isolates. We are affiliated with the American Sociological Society."[16] Although this intent was clear, the precise nature of the affiliation apparently became less distinct to both societies and gradually ended with the passing of time.

The Society's second president, the Rev. Raymond W. Murray, C.S.C., of Notre Dame, attempted to make clear another aspect of the relationship of the Society's members to other sociologists: "We do not deny the right of our non-Catholic confreres to hold a social philosophy of their own choosing . . . you cannot, even if you wish to do so, avoid being philosophical when you deal with man . . . We claim to use the inductive method, but always in conformity with what we believe to be a sound philosophy."[17] Thus he asked for a general recognition of the fact that philosophical orientations for sociology exist inside *and outside* the Society—that Catholic sociologists, to repeat Ellwood's remark, "are no more guilty of making use of metaphysical postulates than the rest of us." The real difference between Catholic and non-Catholic sociologists, at times, President Murray pointed out, seems to lie in the degree of awareness that non-sociological postulates are incorporated in one's sociological thought and the willingness to grant to others the same academic freedom of expression that one claims for one's self.[19]

While fully mindful of the legitimacy of such orientation, the fourth president in his address expressed some concern that this not become a dominant factor. He called for a clarification of position among Catholic sociologists to avoid becoming social philosophers or social reformers. "We have not sufficiently differentiated social philosophy proper and these two from social reconstruction or action. Much of our so-called Catholic sociology has been social philosophy and more particularly *social ethics*."[19]

This situation persisted for several years after that expression of concern had been directed to Catholic sociologists in 1941. An examination of more than two hundred titles of papers and discussions at the first nine conventions disclosed that about three-fourths of the topics treated seemed more philosophical-religious than sociological. Topical analysis of article titles appearing in *The American Catholic Sociological Review* from March 1940 through March 1948 again showed the philosophical-religious emphasis dominant over the sociological one by a ratio of approximately two to one.[20]

After World War II this orientation shifted in a striking manner. Callahan, in his study of the *Review,* found that in the six-year period 1940-1945 the *Review* carried 72 articles predominantly philosophical-religious and 55 in the sociological "study and research" category; in the next nine-year period, 1946-1954, he placed 19 in the philosophical-religious area and 109 in the more strictly sociological one. He noted that "there is a progressively greater number of item-entries and articles generally under this [study and research] category."[21]

The Recent Years of the Society. As for the present decade, the presidential addresses show a shift in thinking from subject-definition to self-definition, reflecting the change of problem-interest throughout the entire membership. Topics being treated now concern the Catholic sociologist as scientist, his changing status and role, his relationship to other sociologists, his involvement with his co-religionists and the greater community, his concern for more adequate research opportunities. This represents a maturing and critical self-analysis; it is neither ego-gratifying nor morbidly self-conscious. One is entitled to predict that as this stage has replaced the former one of concern for hammering out a thoughtful and precise definition of sociology as a field of specialization, this will be succeeded in turn by an expanding preoccupation with scholarly endeavor and achievement in a widening variety of subdivisions of sociology. It is inevitable that increasingly the Catholic sociologist will find himself allied with his non-Catholic colleague as educator and researcher in a combination of mutual advantage as two-sided chilling fears and suspicions disappear in the warm light of knowledge and understanding.

Indicative of this emergent emphasis is the 1951 report by Father

Thomas J. Harte, C.Ss.R., on the proportions of lay and religious sociologists teaching in Catholic institutions of higher learning. Of 111 educator-respondents, 32 (28.8 per cent) were members of the laity, prompting the comment, "The 'clericalism' of the sociology personnel in Catholic schools probably results from sheer economic necessity rather than any systematic effort to baptize the science." [22] After listing some acomplishments he identified as liabilities "a penchant, in teaching and writing, for the easier course of over-emphasis on the 'what-ought-to-be' to the neglect of the patient analysis of 'what is;' smug satisfaction with what is, not infrequently, second-rate scholarship for ourselves and our students; and, finally, professional inertia and apathy towards social research." [23]

Using an intentionally provocative approach to an examination of the status of Catholic sociologists, John J. Kane observed, "To date no Catholic has been president nor held high office in the officially recognized professional sociologist's group in this country, the American Sociological Society . . . a distinguished non-Catholic sociologist . . . expressed amazement that a Catholic could be a sociologist." [24]

The following year Father Joseph P. Fitzpatrick, S. J., suggested that the work of the Catholic sociologist is frequently misunderstood and undervalued by many Catholics, in part because of their lack of comprehension of social problems and their apathetic attitude toward the scientific knowledge of society. He warned that the "zeal for knowledge must not be looked upon simply as a practical instrument for the work of the Church. It must be a genuine love and respect for knowledge for its own sake." [25]

In reference to non-Catholics, he stated:

> ". . . Catholic scholars [should] . . . put themselves again intimately in touch with the men in whom these [scientific] ideas and values are at work, in touch with the non-Catholic scholar . . . the non-Catholic social scientist.
> ". . . It will never be done by locking ourselves within the gates of our own isolated world.
> ". . . we may both advance, Catholic and non-Catholic alike, to cooperate as scholars in gaining a knowledge of the world God has made." (Pp. 395-396.)

A penetrating discussion of the preëminent position that must be accorded research in Catholic higher education was set forth by C.J. Nuesse, now Dean of the School of Social Science at The Catholic University of America. He asserted:

"Most disturbing is the seeming lack of a genuine corporate concern on the part of American Catholic agencies and institutions for the support of social research.

". . . the academic history of sociology only reflects the larger far-reaching conflict between the qualitative demands of scholarship and the popular demand for education at the collegiate and even at the graduate level as an instrument of social mobility.

". . . decisions on present and future [educational policy] problems must be made to a greater extent than in the past with awareness that scholarship has a first claim on protection and continuous investment." [26]

Sister Mary Jeanine [Gruesser], O.S.F., first sister to be elected president of the Society, reminded the members that they could more fully turn their attention to the "sociological implications of the Catholic thought-pattern." In suggesting an increased interest in the sociological study of Catholicism, she urged no narrow focus: "The sociologist must learn how, and to what extent, the sense of community influences the ways in which Catholics relate to members of the human family of whatever class, race, or nationality . . . ." [27]

The most recent address by Brother D. Augustine [McCaffrey], F.S.C., was largely concerned with some lingering hostility between Catholic and non-Catholic sociologists, as shown at times by the "casual and uncritical imputation of authoritarianism levelled against scientific Catholic sociologists," or the stated or implied assumption that there is a conflict between science and religion, or the type of sophistication in writing to show that the author is "in line" with one particular set of metaphysical value judgments. [28]

> "It is not sufficient to learn the skills of interviewing, schedule making, titration, or microchemistry. It is also necessary to learn the "proper" style for reporting research and to learn whom and what to respect among other scientists and their doctrines."

Members, Officers, and Activities of the Society. Over the years the Society has had a moderate but regular growth. On June 15, 1938, the first membership report showed 26 constitutent and 7 institutional memberships. At the close of 1956 the eighteenth annual convention was informed that there were 406 constituent, 56 student, and 53 institutional memberships; subscriptions to the *Review* totaled 575, including 62 in foreign countries. Three listings of the members have been made in the postwar period, of which the first two gave some data on background, fields of interest, and publications of the members. [29]

The highest elective office in the Society, the presidency, has been held by nine members of the laity, eight priests, two Brothers, and one Sister. The list of presidents follows:

Rev. Ralph A. Gallagher, S.J. 1938
Rev. Raymond W. Murray, C.S.C. 1939
Paul J. Mundie 1940
Rev. Francis J. Friedel, S.M. 1941
Walter L. Willigan 1942
Eva J. Ross 1943
Rev. Paul Hanly Furfey 1944
Brother Gerald J. Schnepp, S.M. 1945
Alphonse H. Clemens 1946
Rev. Leo Robinson, S.J. 1947
Franz Mueller 1948
Rt. Rev. Robert B. Navin 1949
Clement S. Mihanovich 1950
Rev. Thomas J. Harte, C.Ss.R. 1951
John J. Kane 1952
Rev. Joseph P. Fitzpatrick, S.J. 1953
C. Joseph Nuesse 1954
Sister Mary Jeanine (Gruesser), O.S.F. 1955
Brother D. Augustine (McCaffrey), F.S.C. 1956
Allen Spitzer 1957

The names of those elected to the Executive Council and appointed to the Editorial Board of the *Review* are to be found on the inside front cover of the *Review*.

Since 1952 the Society has awarded an anual prize of one hundred dollars to the member contributing the most outstanding piece of published research between October 15 of one year and October 14 of the next. These members have been designated for this honor:

1952-1953 Paul Hanly Furfey, *The Scope and Method of Sociology* (New York: Harper, 1953).

1953-1954 No award.

1954-1955 Joseph H. Fichter, S. J., *Social Relations in the Urban Parish* (Chicago: University of Chicago, 1954). Honorable Mention: John J. Kane, *Catholic-Protestant Conflicts in America* (Chicago: Regnery, 1955); Nicholas S. Timasheff, *Sociological Theory* (Garden City, N. Y.: Doubleday, 1955).

1955-1956 John L. Thomas, S.J., *The American Catholic Family* (Englewood Cliffs, N. J.: Prentice Hall, 1956). Honorable Mention: Sister Frances Jerome Woods,

C.D.P. *Cultural Values of American Ethnic Groups* (New York: Harper, 1956); Carle C. Zimmerman and Lucius F. Cervantes, S.J., *Marriage and the Family* (Chicago: Regnery, 1956).

Through the establishment of local chapters and a variety of committees within the parent body, the Society has endeavored to add to the professional growth of the members. From the outset, the Society's journal has been an important aspect of this activity.

THE AMERICAN CATHOLIC SOCIOLOGICAL REVIEW

In March 1940 the *Review* was launched as a quarterly open to members and non-members. It is now (1957) in its eighteenth year of publication. Original articles are solicited. Like most other such journals, the *Review* is unable to pay an honorarium for material used. By the end of 1956 a total of 283 articles had appeared in the first 68 issues.

A fairly comprehensive study of the *Review* through 1954 examined these articles for changing content,[30] as previously noted, and authorship. Concerning the writers, Callahan said:

> " . . . of the 148 contributors of the 255 articles to the *ACSR* in its first fifteen-year period of existence, one hundred nineteen were men and the other twenty-nine were women. The majority (sixty-two) of the men contributors were laymen, but not necessarily Catholics, and fifty-seven . . . Catholic clergy . . . The majority (seventeen) of the twenty-nine women contributors were members of Catholic religious orders of women and twelve were laywomen, but not all Catholics."[31]

From its founding, the *Review* has had its editorial and business offices at Loyola University, Chicago. For fifteen years, it was edited by the Rev. Ralph A. Gallagher, S.J.; since 1956, the present writer has served as editor.

There are, apart from the *Review*, many avenues of publication open to Catholic, sociologists.[32] Yet the attention devoted to the Society and the *Review* rest on the reasonable assumption that these constitute the major sources of information on the patterns of sociological thought among American Catholics. Happily, the comprehensive and objective study of Catholic sociologists to 1950 by Williams in his

Catholic Social Thought, as previously noted, eases the burden for anyone called upon to discuss trends in this area of sociological development.

CONCLUSION

For many obvious reasons, the writer cannot attempt to evaluate the mounting volume of articles and books published by American Catholic sociologists. Space limitations, the diversity and specialization of output, the need for greater perspective in time, the fact that some detailed analyses have already been made in certain areas—all these render this additionally needed discussion of broad fields and individual contributors inopportune here and now.

It is hoped, however, that this examination of the undulating trends among American Catholics working in the field of sociology suggests the seriousness of purpose and commitment to scientific endeavor of these sociologists. There is certainly a widening interest and a deepening maturity indicative of increasingly significant scholarly accomplishment, which in the past and present commends itself to the attention of any fair-minded sociologist. Religion, it is apparent, is becoming an increasingly irrelevant criterion of professional differentiation—and, consequently, of acceptance or rejection.

This is simply to say that the American Catholic sociologist at times merits attention for reasons other than that of religious affiliation—unfortunately often judged to be a basic note of distinction by himself and others. To be worthy of attention, of course, he must have something of importance to say in his discipline; otherwise, but only then, he deserves to be ignored. He wholeheartedly accepts the criteria of academic achievement: intelligence, imagination, objectivity, competence, rigor of method, honesty. These ingredients of scholarship are neither the automatic prizes nor the inevitable losses of holding one variety or another of intellectual conviction in non-sociological matters.

SELECTED BIBLIOGRAPHY

F. Gilbert Callahan, A Descriptive Analysis of *The American Catholic Sociological Review, 1940-1954,* Unpublished Master's thesis (Loyola University, Chicago, 1956). Treats the first fifteen years of the *Review's* history, development, editorial board; gives summary and analysis of contents.

Donald Campion, S.J., "Sociology of Catholics in America," in *Social Theorists,* edited by Clement S. Mihanovich (Milwaukee: Bruce, 1953), 343-368. Article devoted to a very general survey of Catholic social movements, theories, and leaders, with passing mention of sociology; bibliography, 364-368.

John D. Donovan, "American Catholic Sociologists and the Sociology of Religion," in special issue (devoted to the sociology of religion and edited by Thomas J. Harte, C.Ss.R.) of *The American Catholic Sociological Review,* XV (June, 1954), 104-114. A highly critical estimate of the work of Catholics in this field; bibliography, 112-114.

Charles A. Ellwood, "Roman Catholic Sociology," *Sociology and Social Research,* XXVI (November-December, 1941), 114-116. A brief comment on the general unfamiliarity of American sociologists with the work of Catholics in sociology.

Joseph P. Fitzpatrick, S.J., "Catholic Responsibilities in Sociology," *Thought,* XXVI (Autumn, 1951), 384-396. An appeal for Catholic sociologists to join with others in scholarly study of social life; "Catholics and the Scientific Knowledge of Society," *The American Catholic Sociological Review,* XV (March, 1954), 2-8. Brief examination of the factors in the general Catholic population creating an apathy for scientific study of society.

Paul Hanly Furfey, "The Sociologist and Scientific Objectivity," *The American Catholic Sociological Review,* VI (March, 1945), 3-12. A provocative discussion of some evidences of folk thinking and unconscious biases among professional sociologists; "Value-Judgments in Sociology," *The American Catholic Sociological Review,* VII (June, 1946), 83-95. A presentation of the case for a "narrow" and a 'broad" definition of sociology and a recognition of metasociological value judgments; *The Scope and Method of Sociology* (New York: Harper, 1953). A highly imaginative and stimulating treatment of the basic elements of a genuinely scientific sociology by outstanding Catholic sociologist.

Sister Mary Jeanine [Gruesser], O.S.F., "The Catholic Sociologist and the Catholic Mind," *The American Catholic Sociological Review,* XVII (March, 1955), 2-9. Suggests approaches for the study of the sociological implications of the Catholic thought-pattern.

Thomas J. Harte, C.Ss.R., "Catholics as Sociologists," *The American Catholic Sociological Review,* XIII (March, 1952), 2-9. Report on a survey among 159 American sociologist-respondents, including 111 teaching in the field.

John J. Kane, "Are Catholic Sociologists a Minority Group?" *The American Catholic Sociological Review,* XIV (March, 1953), 2-12. Mixing wit and concern, the writer examines the status and role of the American Catholic sociologist briefly.

Brother D. Augustine [McCaffrey], F.S.C., "The Scientific Catholic Sociologist," *The American Catholic Sociological Review,* XVIII (March, 1957), 2-9. Some bases for lingering hostility among sociologists today are noted.

Clement S. Mihanovich, compiler, "Who's Who Among Catholic Sociologists," *The American Catholic Sociological Review,* VII (October, 1946), 174-199; XII (December, 1951), 265-276. Contains data on background, publications, fields of specialization. [See also the *Review's* "List of Members," XV (December, 1954), 372-381.]

Bernard G. Mulvaney, S.S.V., "The Department of Sociology of The Catholic University of America, 1894-1955," *The American Catholic Sociological Review,* XVI (December, 1955), 266-274. Short history of the oldest department under Catholic auspices, followed by a compilation of degree holders with topics, from 1904 to 1955, 275-309.

C. J. Nuesse, "Sociology in Catholic Education: Prospect for Capital Development," *The American Catholic Sociological Review, XVI* (March, 1955), 2-11. A strong assertion of the need to stress research in sociological planning of Catholic institutions.

"Report of the Committee on the Teaching of Sociology in High Schools, Seminaries, Colleges and Universities," *The American Catholic Sociological Review,* XVII (March, 1956), 37-42. A survey based on 860 questionnaire returns, showing that about three-fourths of the responding high schools, major seminaries, colleges and universities have sociological offerings.

Richard M. Rosenfelder, S.J., *A History of the American Catholic Sociological Society from 1938 to 1948,* Unpublished Master's thesis (Loyola University, Chicago, 1948). An attempt to reconstruct the early years of the Society from the written records of the time.

Melvin J. Williams, "The Need for the Study of Roman Catholic Sociological Theory," *Sociology and Social Research,* XXVI (November-December, 1941), 116-118. Statement in support of Ellwood's position noted above; "Catholic Sociological Theory—A Review and Prospectus," *The American Catholic Sociological Review,* IV (October, 1943), 137-143. Abstract of doctoral dissertation completed at Duke in 1941, *A Survey of Roman Catholic Sociological Theory in the United States Since 1900; Catholic Social Thought* (New York: Ronald, 1950). A comprehensive scholarly, and objective work by a non-Catholic sociologist; to Williams, a "Catholic thinker" is a person "who was or is a member of the Catholic Church and who has shown sympathy for some or all Catholic social teachings." Of special relevance to this subject are chapters 4, 5, 11-13, 15; bibliography, 495-530.

Paul Mundy, Associate Professor of Sociology, Loyola University (Chicago), has been the editor of *The American Catholic Sociological Review* (1955-   ), after serving as Assistant to the Editor (1951-1954); is current Chairman of the Committee on Teaching Sociology, the American Catholic Sociological Society. Received his B.A. degree *magna cum laude* from the University of Scranton; was a Sellew Scholar and a Knights of Columbus Fellow at the Catholic University of America, where he received the M.A. degree (1948) and the Ph.D. with distinction (1951). Was research assistant at the Princeton University Office of Population Research (Library of Congress) and editorial assistant on *Population Index* (1946-1950); Lecturer and Instructor, The Catholic University of America (1948-1951); Assistant Professor, Loyola University (1951-1957). He assisted in the research for the United Nations' Population Division report, *The Population of Tanganyika* (Lake Success, N. Y.: United Nations, 1949) and numerous other demographic studies directed by Dr. Irene B. Taeuber of the Office of Population Research, Princeton University; his work has appeared in *Population Index,* the *Journal of Negro Education, The American Catholic Sociological Review,* and other periodicals. At present, he is directing research in the Institute of Social and Industrial Relations of Loyola University.

NOTES

1. Charles A. Ellwood, "Roman Catholic Sociology," *Sociology and Social Research,* XXV (November-December, 1941), 114.

2. M. J. Williams, *A Survey of Roman Catholic Sociological Theory in the United States Since 1900* (Durham, N. C.: Duke University, 1941). Williams appended a note of his own to Ellwood's remarks noted above in "The Need for the Study of Roman Catholic Sociological Theory," *loc. cit.,* 116-118.

3. *Ibid.,* 115, 116.

4. Gordon C. Zahn, *Readings in Introductory Sociology* (Westminster, Md.: Newman, in press). This comment of Zahn is also noted in a discussion of this matter by Brother D. Augustine, F.S.C., "The Scientific Catholic Sociologist," *The American Catholic Sociological Review,* XVIII (March, 1957), 2-9. This was the presidential address to the American Catholic Sociological Society, December 27, 1956, at its eighteenth annual convention.

5. Paul Hanly Furfey, "The Sociologist and Scientific Objectivity," *The American Catholic Sociological Review,* VI (March, 1945), 8-9. (Italics added).

6. "The Teaching of Sociology in the United States in the Last Fifty Years," *The American Journal of Sociology,* L (May, 1945), 542.

7. Bernard G. Mulvaney, C.S.V., "The Department of Sociology of the Catholic University of America, 1894-1955," *The American Catholic Sociological Review,* XVI (December, 1955) 266-274; this article is followed by a compilation of Catholic University's advanced degrees in sociology, by year, name of recipient, and dissertation topic, from 1904 through 1955, 275-309. See also: Paul Hanly Furfey, "Sociology at The Catholic University," *The Catholic University of America Bulletin,* XXIII (January, 1956), 1-2; this utilizes much of the Mulvaney findings in presenting a brief account effectively.

8. Office of Scientific Personnel, National Academy of Sciences—National Research Council, *The Baccalaureate Origins of Doctorates in the Arts, Humanities and Social Sciences Awarded in the United States from 1936 to 1950 Inclusive* (Publication 460; Washington, D. C., 1956).

9. "Report of the Committee on the Teaching of Sociology in [Catholic] High Schools, Seminaries, Colleges and Universities" (Prepared by Wm. Jarrett, under the direction of Clement S. Mihanovich, Committee Chairman, December, 1955), *The American Catholic Sociological Review,* XVII (March, 1956), 37-42.

10. *Ibid.*, 41.

11. Donald Campion, S. J., "Sociology of Catholics in America" in *Social Theorists,* edited by Clement S. Mihanovich (Milwaukee: Bruce, 1953) , 362; despite the title of the chapter, this is actually a broad historical account of American Catholic social movements, leaders, and theories, rather than sociology as such.

12. A detailed treatment of the controversy appears in Melvin J. Williams, *Catholic Social Thought* (New York: Ronald, 1950) , especially chapters 4, 5, 15. A short account is presented in the same author's abstract of his doctoral dissertation: "Catholic Sociological Theory—A Review and Prospectus," *The American Catholic Sociological Review,* IV (October, 1943) , 137-143. Early issues of *The American Catholic Sociological Review* also reflect the disagreement.

13. Two articles by Paul Hanly Furfey in *The American Catholic Sociological Review* are of note in expressing some cautions about extremism: "The Sociologist and Scientific Objectivity," cited in footnote 5; "Value—Judgments in Sociology," VII (June, 1946) , 83-95. Williams, *Catholic Social Thought,* 91, 95, notes the shifting of the leaders.

14. Cf. Richard M. Rosenfelder, S. J., *A History of the American Catholic Sociological Society from 1938 to 1948* (Unpublished Master's thesis, Loyola University, Chicago, 1948) .

15. *Ibid.*, chapter II.

16. *Report of the American Catholic Sociological Society, 1938,* 62. Rosenfelder, *op. cit.*, chapter III, discusses the indeterminate status of the new organization with respect to the American Sociological Society.

17. "Presidential Address—1939," *The American Catholic Sociological Review,* I (March, 1940) , 41.

18. This somewhat unconscious tendency to introduce one's philosophy into sociology, as mentioned by Ellwood and Murray, has been treated at some length by Furfey in *The Scope and Method of Sociology* (New York: Harper, 1953) , 183-185, 192-193, 217-228, 491-509; for a more general consideration of the problem, see also chapters 1-10, 20. The same author has explored this topic in the following as well: "The Social Philosophy of Social Pathologists," *Social Problems,* II (October, 1954) , 71-75; "The Humanitarian Philosophy and the Acceptance of Sociological Generalizations," *The American Catholic Sociological Review,* XV (June, 1952) , 117-122, and the articles cited in footnote 13.

19. Francis J. Friedel, S. M., "Are We Accepting the Challenge?" *The American Catholic Sociological Review,* III (March, 1942) , 4.

20. Rosenfelder, *op. cit.*, chapter II; also Table III gives data on the first nine conventions, which were held at irregular intervals: none in 1943 and 1944 due to wartime travel regulations, but two in 1946.

21. F. Gilbert Callahan, *A Descriptive Analysis of The American Catholic Sociological Review, 1940-1954,* Unpublished Master's thesis (Loyola University, Chicago, 1956) , 48-49.

22. "Catholics as Sociologists," *The American Catholic Sociological Review,* XIII (March, 1952) , 5.

23. *Ibid.*, 9.

24. "Are Catholic Sociologists a Minority Group?" *The American Catholic Sociological Review,* XIV (March, 1953) , 5.

25. "Catholics and the Scientific Knowledge of Society, *The American Catholic Sociological Review,* XV (March, 1954) , 5. The same author had previously ex-

amined in some detail "Catholic Responsibilities in Sociology," *Thought*, XXVI (Autumn, 1951), 384-396.

26. "Sociology in Catholic Education: Prospect for Capital Development," *The American Catholic Sociological Review*, XVI (March, 1955), 4, 7, 8.

27. "The Catholic Sociologist and the Catholic Mind," *The American Catholic Sociological Review*, XVII (March, 1956), 7.

28. Brother D. Augustine McCaffrey, *op. cit.* On the last mentioned point of writing style, the author calls attention to this ingenuous admission in William J. Goode and Paul K. Hatt, *Methods in Social Research* (New York: McGraw-Hill, 1952), 23:

> "It is not sufficient to learn the skills of interviewing, schedule making, titration, or microchemistry. It is also necessary to learn the "proper" style for reporting research and to learn whom and what to respect among other scientists and their doctrines."

29. C. S. Mihanovich compiled two fairly detailed summations titled "Who's Who Among [American] Catholic Sociologists" for *The American Catholic Sociological Review*, VII (October, 1946), 174-199; XII (December, 1951), 265-276. A simple "List of Members" also appealed in *ibid.*, XV (December, 1954), 372-381.

30. Callahan, *op. cit.*, 50-59, 90-91, also makes a classification patterned after the sixteen subject categories used by Ethel Shanas in her analysis of "The 'American Journal of Sociology' through Fifty Years," L (May, 1945), 524.

31. *Ibid.*, 59.

32. Cf. Callahan, *op. cit.*, Appendix IV, where he attempts to trace the work of writers for the *Review* published elsewhere.

URBAN SOCIOLOGY

Mel J. Ravitz

Wayne State University

This chapter on Trends in Urban Sociology is intended neither as an historical review of the research activities of those sociologists who sport the prefix "urban," nor is it meant to be a compendium of all recent research about urban phenomena. This chapter seeks simply to do three main things: a) to indicate some of the chief characteristics of our changing urban centers since the end of World War II; b) to note some major books and articles, both specifically sociological and non-sociological, that have appeared during this period of time and that bear on urban living; and c) to raise or re-raise some of the key issues that occupy (or ought to) the current attention of those sociologists, planners and citizens interested in contemporary urban life. More briefly, this chapter aims at revealing some of the physical and social characteristics of the living American city, exposing some of its basic problems, and considering what is being done and what can be done to resolve these problems.

Insofar as the emphasis is as indicated, this chapter will necessarily deal with a number of pressing practical problems. Lest some, however, gain the erroneous impression that this chapter recommends sociologists to become urban planners and seek solutions to the many practical problems raised, let it be understood at the outset that the distinction between the sociologist and the urban planner is clearly recognized throughout. The one is chiefly concerned with understanding the general structure and functions of human society in order to add to the storehouse of human knowledge; the latter is chiefly interested in planning a better city. Though there is a relationship between these two roles, they are not the same. Increasingly, however, the urban planner as well as the citizen, the politician, and the administrator have come to realize that the sociologist has knowledge to contribute.

Indeed, the sociologist with his focus on understanding human behavior and with his training in scientific method can contribute a most important element to analysing urban life: an interest in conducting and an ability to conduct scientific research as over against mere project research. This latter type of research, widely conducted currently in planning offices and most governmental and business agencies, is geared to the solution of practical and immediate problems or even long-range problems. It seeks the accumulation of sufficient information on which to base a probable estimate or on which to make some practical decision. Such research is useful, but its usefulness is limited usually to the immediate project. It is in the conduct of scientific research in the urban area that the sociologist can be of greatest value not only to his own field but also in the solution of some of these practical problems. The scientific research approach involves the utilization of hypotheses, of objective and repeated observation or of experimentation, and of careful generalization based on warranted evidence. The essence of this approach lies in its cumulative and developmental character. Only scientific research concerns itself with rigorously testing hypotheses; thus, only this type of research possesses the possibility of adding generalizations to the general fund of knowledge. This latter type of research is genuinely efficient inquiry; it seeks to build knowledge upon knowledge.

While it would be undesirable for sociologists to cease their investigation of society and human behavior for its own sake, surely sociologists who are interested in the urban community will want to learn to communicate better what they have discovered about urban living so that it will be understood and utilized by the urban planner. To refuse to do this is to ignore that a social scientist is also a citizen of the community in which he lives; to fail to do this is to concede that sociologists are able only to communicate with each other and that their knowledge must remain divorced from the real world.

On the other hand, a responsibility rests with the urban planner to clarify for the sociologist the nature of the practical problems he confronts and to encourage the sociologist to conduct his research into social behavior and society within the urban context. Certainly our cities are rich mines of relevant human behavior, and scientific knowledge of such urban behavior may aid in the solution of many practical problems.

What is suggested here is that the sociologist and the urban planner continue their respective professional orientations, but that there be some improved exchange of problems and knowledge between them. Sociologists already know much about human behavior in the urban setting which urban planners are either unaware of, or if they are aware, are unable readily to comprehend or apply. An important area of inqiury for both the sociologist and the urban planner in the years ahead will be their relationships with each other.

RURAL-URBAN DIFFERENCES

If the concept is correct that rural and urban are but points on the same continuum and not two separate, discontinuous realms, then it follows that the two fields of rural and urban sociology are no longer discrete. Actually, it is quaint to speak of URBAN sociology in a day when virtually the entire country has been urbanized and the few surviving vestiges of ruralism can be found only in isolated geographic pockets or in the exaggerations of the dude ranch or the television program. This is not to suggest that urban uniformity has descended on the society and leveled all before it; it is simply to note that the city's influence on the hinterland is, has been, and doubtless will continue to be enormous. Indeed, so great has this influence been that it seems inappropriate any longer to speak of a separate urban sociology applicable presumably to urban places and a rural sociology applicable presumably to rural places. This no longer represents conditions in American society. This present society may be most perceptively viewed as a mass society; its residents, whether they live in metropolitan centers of a million or more population or in the cross roads towns, are attuned alike to the same mass instruments of social control: the police, the law, the courts, the prisons; they are subject—all of them—to the same mass media of communication: T.V., radio, the movies, newspapers, magazines, billboards; the people of this society, regardless where in the country they live or what their personal characteristics, respond to the same mass symbols of aspiration and achievement: a new car, a good house in an attractive neighborhood, quality clothes for oneself and one's family, a job promotion, a pay raise, the respect of friends, neighbors, colleagues, opportunity to send one's children off to college, etc.

The point is this: today's American society is most accurately seen as a mass society within which there are very few important social dividing lines separating rural dweller and city dweller. Because our society is increasingly undifferentiated between a distinctly rural and a distinctly urban realm, so too our sociology ought to become increasingly undifferentiated. This rural-urban distinction preoccupied sociologists of the pre-World-War II days; as a consequence urban sociologists were interested in all phenomena that occurred within the city; whatever took place in the rural areas came within the purview of the rural sociologist. This division occurred despite the fact that oftimes the same kinds of behavior happened in both places. This desire to carve out the proper realm of the two sociologies: rural and urban, was perhaps an appropriate approach for an earlier day that permitted each of the two fields to take unto itself a variety of topics that belonged to neither or to both: the family, intergroup relations, crime, delinquency, mental illness, etc. Much of the past study of rural and urban sociology was devoted to a comparison of the varying characteristics of these two different locales. Much necessary descriptive work was thereby done in a society that was actually divided. To continue to treat these differences in any but a historical fashion will be to continue to play with concepts that have outlived the reality that suggested them. Such frivolity is not uncommon among sociologists. All too frequently we have kept our eye on the concept and not on its underlying social reality.

RECENT URBAN CHARACTERISTICS: POPULATION

Two chief characteristics of the American city since the end of World War II are: a) the immense increase and remarkable redistribution of population and, b) the gradually accelerating urban renewal movement.

World War II brought large populations to our industrial cities. The 1950 Census shows a population increase in urban places of about twenty two millions over 1940. Not all of these people, however, migrated to the city. Part of this population, at least—perhaps as much as a third—was considered urban in 1950 because of a redefinition of the concept "urban,"[1] the other two-thirds moved from rural to urban places. Even with this qualification, it is clear that a vast wave of people moved into cities during this single decade; more have moved there since 1950.

While cities generally have increased in population during these recent years, it has been the metropolitan area and particularly the suburban portions that have reported the amazing growth. Hawley[2] has sought to document this shift to the suburbs as he emphasizes that the city is no longer a suitable matrix within which to consider our large concentrations of people; he prefers to speak of the expanded metropolitan community. Others refer to it as the metropolitan complex. Detroit population trends suggest, for example, that by 1960 there will actually be more people residing outside the corporate limits of the city than inside. This characteristic of growth, expansion, and redistribution of population poses such basic questions for the student of urban living as these: where does this swarm of suburbanites come from? Do they tend first to pass through the central city and then move out to the suburbs in quest of amenities they do not find inside? Or, do they tend to move directly to these suburbs from the other parts of the country whence they came? Put more generally, where and why do American families move?

RECENT URBAN CHARACTERISTICS: URBAN RENEWAL

It is not expected that the populations of our cities will level off in the near future. Projections to 1970 suggest that these populations will continue to grow. This population growth and redistribution is directly related to a second major characteristic of the modern urban community: the emphasis on physical planning and replanning. Although it would be incorrect to state that urban planning came into existence with the recent growth of population, it is true that concern with planning has stimulated a concern with population growth; moreover, we may note that population growth since World War II certainly has helped reinforce the contention of the planners that physical renewal and planning are essential. It would, of course, be possible to have population growth and redistribution without urban renewal; indeed this is the situation in many places; on the other hand, it is less likely that cities would undergo renewal without considerable population growth and change. Physical planning as an academic discipline and as an operating activity seeks to discover and recommend the most desirable relationships between people and land. An expanding population obviously challenges the ingenuity of the planner to meet the greater needs for residential land, utilities, economic and social service activities, recreational facilities, etc.

Altough it is possible that urban renewal would have become a

significant aspect of modern urban life even had there been no surge
of urban population during the past fifteen years, this surge of population has made more urgent this vast task of remaking our urban
centers. Throughout America we are overwhelmed by the fact that
in the past several years our large cities have come of age, have filled
up to their limits, and indeed have spilled over into the suburbs;
these cities or rather, these metropolitan complexes, are now beginning
to undertake the gigantic job of renewal. To this renewal of our urban
centers sociologists have a vital contribution to make. Redevelopment
of the older core area of these centers, conservation of the middle
aged, still livable neighborhoods, and guidance and development of
the new growth areas constitute realms of challenge for the sociologist.

URBAN LAND USE

As our metropolitan areas continue to grow and as our cities move
more determinedly in the direction of reconstruction for improved
human uses, we come to recognize that urban land has not always
been wisely used. The land use of many of our largest metropolitan
centers is quite cluttered and chaotic as a result of uncontrolled development over a period of many decades. Differing quantities of land
have accumulated in residential, industrial, recreational, agricultural
uses without any over all management of its economic efficiency or its
aesthetic quality. The present pattern of settlement and development
of these metropolitan areas is not always promising of greater order,
efficiency or harmony. These cities sprawl in all directions without
apparent coordination and with the new growth areas widely scattered
and difficult to service.

In addition to the problem imposed by the indiscriminate and
uncontrolled growth of these metropolitan areas, it is anticipated that
they will continue to increase in population, thereby exerting additional pressure on the several local governments and on the planners.
Ultimately we shall have to provide for the many needs of an enlarged
population in these places. To meet these needs satisfactorily we shall
have to assign the necessary quantity of land for the various essential
types of land use. As we attempt to peer and plan ahead some questions planners and sociologists alike have a stake in answering are
these: what should be the pattern of regional land use toward which
we should strive? Should this pattern be permitted to continue in
the direction of further sprawl which is the simpler thing to do in-

asmuch as it is what we are permitting in large part now? Should we, in other words, continue the established trends of land use development with the usual functions of the various parts of the city remaining what they have always been? Or should we, at some point, seek to establish community nuclei surrounding the central city? What should be the size and population of these smaller community settlements? Where in the region should they be located? At what distance from each other? How shall they be joined by transportation? Should each community be economically self-sufficient? And if so, how do we rearrange the functions of the various other parts of the city, especially the central city which is undergoing considerable strain and tension as it endeavors to expand services and yet is losing its tax base to all of the surrounding area? More concisely, can sociologists help suggest some preferred way to organize the use of regional land so as to avoid the errors of earlier unplanned development and so as to facilitate and improve modern urban living?

More specifically, there are particular problems of concern to the sociologist in each of several institutional spheres: housing, economic, religious, educational, recreational, political. In sections that follow we shall attempt to consider some of these institutional spheres and also some recent related research.

From one perspective, the American city may be seen to consist essentially of three broad types of areas: an area of old housing, an area of middle aged housing, and an area of new housing built by and large since the end of World War II.

PROBLEMS OF THE OLD CITY

Within the old core of the city lies its worn-out dilapidated neighborhoods. Here have lived wave upon wave of new migrants to the city. It is here that many American cities are currently undertaking programs of redevelopment—clearance and rebuilding. Since 1949 and the passage of the Federal Housing Act of that year there has been some impetus provided to clear the slums. A generous Federal subsidy of two-thirds the cost of such activity is slowly serving to move our communities in the direction of redevelopment. It is expected that this program of redevelopment will continue into the next half century or more; hopefully the same mistakes allowed before as the city grew haphazardly will not be made.

One important consequence of this redevelopment apart from the obvious removal of the slums will be the necessity to rethink the whole question of appropriate and preferred land use. What should be put on the cleared land? Houses for residential use? What kind of houses? Commercial establishments, industrial development? What should stand on this newly cleared land? If not the former uses, where should these then be established? What shall be done with the many people to be displaced by clearance? Where will they go? Particularly is this latter problem acute inasmuch as the population ultimately to be relocated in so many of our cities will be large and much of it will be Negro. This is an especially pertinent problem for the sociologist because it raises the value question of the kind of heterogeneity our cities are to have: segregated or integrated? Are these Negro families who have been long over-crowded in the oldest and most dilapidated portions of the city to be forced into new segregated neighborhoods, perhaps in the middle segments of the city or are they to be permitted freely to move where their financial ability permits and their preference indicates? Abrams[3] explores this whole problem of changing neighborhoods with sharp insight. Others have dealt with particular aspects of this problem, with the reactions of people in these changing neighborhoods, with the fluctuations of economic values, with the intergroup attitudes, with action suggestions to guide residents of these neighborhoods.[4]

Large scale public housing provides one possible answer to the problem of human displacement and relocation. Our cities since the late 1930's have been constructing some public housing under Federal Acts. But never has there been enough such public housing to meet the full need. Opponents of public housing have effectively cut the number of proposed starts and even those agreed upon have not always been built. Aside from the political issue of whether to have public housing or not, there are basic qusetions that even its proponents raise: should future public housing projects be of the same huge character as these built so far? What should be the maximum size of public housing projects? How can they best be related to the several recreational, school, social service needs of their occupants? What are some of the social psychological consequences of the new homogeneity of family type now seemingly clustered in these projects? Dunham and Grundstein[5] have written of these housing projects becoming reservoirs of public assistance receiving families, many without fathers. Apparently this situation is in part at least the consequence of economic inflation and a failure to raise the maximum income standards for admittance to public housing; this effectively excludes most families with working fathers. Relevant questions to be considered are: how should the rental scale for admittance to public housing be determined? What ends are sought through public housing and how can they most efficiently be realized? Merton[6] has written an interesting essay on public housing in which he investigated the way in which residents develop friendships and acquaintanceships and with whom. Propinquity seemed to be an important factor in determining who associated with whom.

The study by Deutsch and Collins[7] must also be noted in this consideration of public housing. They too were interested in the nature and frequency of contacts, although their chief focus was on a comparison of integrated and segregated housing projects.

Mumford[8] has an excellent short essay on New York's Stuyvesant Town Housing Project in which he makes some critical observations of customary public housing developments from the vantage point of the planner, the architect, and the human beings who must live in them and use their facilities.

Private housing provides another possible answer to the problem of human displacement and relocation. Here, however, the problem is to create housing within the price range of the people displaced, who, generally speaking, have lower incomes than persons living elsewhere in the city. Moreover, the question of kind of private housing is also relevant. What kind of housing best meets the needs of the various types of modern American families, urban and suburban? How should the internal space of a modern house be most satisfactorily organized to meet the needs of the changed American family? These are questions which have come to receive the attention of a number of writers.[9] Usually, however, this attention is directed to the elementary question of the number of rooms various types of families prefer. This is but the merest beginning of a necessary analysis of the relationship of family living patterns and spatial arrangements, both inside the home and outside.

PROBLEMS OF MIDDLE AGED CITY

Outside the old core of the American city lies a ring of middle aged neighborhoods. Blight will attack these neighborhods next unless the people who live there cooperate with the municipal government to prevent it. Here, the housing is beginning to show signs of decay.

Here the plan of a growing number of American cities is to attempt to break through apparent citizen indifference to activate and organize the residents of these areas on a block and neighborhood-wide basis in order to encourage them to help rejuvenate their area and improve it. Improvement of their private property together with necessary improvements of public property by the city with financial subsidy by the Federal government are expected to conserve these middle-aged neighborhoods.

These blight prevention activities beginning to take place in the American city likewise raise some interesting questions that are relevant for sociologists: what is the nature of the apathy that seems to grip many residents of the modern metropolis? How can this apathy be overcome on the block and neighborhood level in order to induce citizens to develop grass roots leadership and organization to help replan their own areas? How, in short, do we develop a sense of moral integration within the vast, impersonal city? Angell's[10] excellent study of moral integration of the American city stands as a first step in understanding and measuring urban cohesion. Here Angell seeks to analyse the possible factors which contribute to and which obstruct such cohesion.

Related to this matter of integration is the fact that in many of these middle aged neighborhoods where physical deterioration is at the point of beginning, racial change is also beginning to occur. One problem becomes that of encouraging both Negroes and whites to cooperate to concern themselves with the common physical problems of maintenance and improvement. Some suggestions along this line and a consideration of ensuing intergroup relations may be found in a recent article by Ravitz.[11]

The middle aged area of the city provides a fascinating challenge for the sociologists; here exist the various points of contact between Negro and white populations especially. In one sense, this constitutes a frontier in the study of intergroup relations. Not only interracial relationships, but interclass and interreligious relationships as well. To name but two institutional areas of contact and also of conflict we may mention the school and the church. Both of these institutional agencies are confronting considerable pressure at the moment in a great many American neighborhoods that are undergoing change. The schools in many of these neighborhoods are facing the issue of how adequately to teach together students who have had adequate educational preparation and home incentive and students who are new to the neighborhood and who are perhaps deficient in educational preparation and sometimes educational incentive. Related to this specific problem is the more general one of how to help prepare the children and teachers in schools that will soon become racially integrated. This is a basic problem in the realm of educational sociology that requires exploration. Doubtless there are a number of possible solutions some of which have already been tried in different localities. These might well be reviewed and analysed for generalizable suggestions elsewhere.

Another institutional agency undergoing pressure at the moment is the church of these changing neighborhoods, especially the Protestant denominations. Many of these churches are facing the issue whether to stay and strive to serve the residents of the neighborhood, many of whom are now Negroes, or whether to move away to the fringes or suburbs in order to try to catch up with members of their congregation who have moved, some because of racial prejudice. The decision to this issue is not an easy one and many church boards could use assistance in aligning practice with principle of brotherhood.

PROBLEMS OF THE NEW GROWTH AREAS

The new growth areas of the metropolitan city have been developing at an almost geometric rate. Hawley[12] has recently recorded this growth by decades for the United States. The likelihood is strong that this suburban growth especially, will continue indefinitely in both time and space. These suburbs are the new residential portions of the metropolitan area. The question arises as to whether and how these new residential suburbs can be best related to the rest of the community? This touches closely on another, more fundamental questions: what shall be the function of the suburbs in contrast to the function of the central city? Are there new functions each should assume? Not only is this question appropriate for the residential suburb but for the industrial ones as well. There has developed in many metropolitan areas a new growth of industry moving out from the central city where the tax rate was high and where the need for parking and expansion space could not easily be met. It is likely that this industrial growth and relocation will continue and alternately precede and parallel residential development. Whatever it does in this regard, however, it does raise again the question of whether the central city or the suburbs or both in some new functional arrangement shall serve as the industrial center of the emerging metropolitan city. The new pattern of our cities will depend on a careful study of these problems by the scociologist and the planner working together.

COMMUNITY

A persistent problem for the sociologist in any era but especially since the recent rapid explosion into the suburban hinterland has been clarification of the concept "community." What is a community? How do we define it in social terms? In physical terms? Should plans for land use be developed in relationship to the community unit or some other? What considerations are important when planning for communities, especially new communities in the area surrounding the central city?

Some of the characteristics of communities as they appear to some planners and sociologists and some of the specific problems emerging from these characteristics are those that relate to transportation, to the job, to shopping, to schools, to churches, to recreation.

Indispensable to any community is its system of transportation to move both goods and people. Particularly is this important as the community expands in both population and size. As the press of population expansion has mounted and as these communities have pushed out miles from the central business district, many of our cities have begun to develop modern systems of major highways and throughways to try to facilitate traffic flow to and from place of residence and place of work. Other cities have argued that expressways move cars and not people; therefore they have moved in the direction of some form or other of mass transit. The issue is not yet resolved as our traffic congestion increases and as we run the risk of choking ourselves to death in our mad scramble to assert our individuality in our private vehicles. Certainly this is one of the social problems relating particularly to the journey to and from work. There are other problems too. What do people want in terms of proximity to work? How far are people willing to travel? How can we tie residence more closely to place of work, if that is the preferred solution? We might note that we are only beginning to enter into the sociological study of urban transportation; hitherto we have made the rash assumption that the problems of this realm were chiefly engineering and planning problems. We are at last aware that it is people who are redistributing themselves in the metropolitan community, that it is people who make decisions to use some streets rather than others, and that it is people with their attitudes, behavior patterns, and customs who must be correctly understood if we are to be able to build streets and highways that people will use. One of the most penetrating studies of the problems of urban transportation is a series of three short essays by Mumford[13] in which he suggests that through superior physical planning and a willingness to control the private use of the auto-mobile it would be possible to create cities fit for modern human living. A number of empirically designed studies have been done in which traffic and transportation in the city have been the major points of attention. These include some of the origin and destination studies of recent years.[14]

Not only do people travel to work; they also travel to their shopping. The days of the corner grocery stores are long since past. Shopping is done increasingly in a different pattern from formerly all across the country. Since the end of World War II we have seen the rapid growth around each metropolitan area of a number of regional shopping centers, each seeking to serve a particular segment of the enlarged area and each incidently putting pressure on the downtown business district. A debate rages among students of the urban economy as to whether the downtown business center can survive and what it will have to do in order to survive. Moreover, the question is posed as to whether the developing pattern of dispersed shopping centers throughout the region will meet the needs of residents of these newly established residential fringes and suburbs? Is there any preferable plan for dividing and redistributing functions within the community? What are the criteria for measuring the social adequacy of shopping centers?

Other elements of the community include the school, the church and recreation space and facilities. All of these are being provided as our metropolitan communities expand; however, there is serious question as to whether they are being adequately and intelligently provided. Some questions relating to all three of these facilities are: how to locate them most advantageously to best serve the residents of neighborhoods and communities; how to build schools and recreation centers to be of maximum service to children during the day and to adults in the evening? How, in an anonymous society which has already surrendered many functions to the experts, to maintain a maximum of citizen control over school policy without interfering with technical decisions? With regard to recreation, what are the real recreation needs of the changed and changing modern American family; how can these needs best be met?

CITIZEN PARTICIPATION AND CONTROL

As our metropolitan cities have grown in population and size, many small villages, townships, cities have sprung up in the area surrounding the central city. We are confronted at present with each of these metropolitan areas containing a welter of political subdivisions. Hawley[15] states that the average number of such political units within these metropolitan areas is 96. This is almost fantastic; such multiplicity of autonomous political units presents overwhelming problems of administration and control. How do we meet problems of taxation in such a politically splintered situation, especially as the central city is losing population and expanding public services? How do we adequately coordinate necessary regional planning activities such as water supply, sewage, transportation, industrial development? How do we overcome this tremendous cultural lag imposed by the fact that population has increased and redistributed itself faster than the political means of administration and control over the region have been able to develop? As sociologists and political scientists probe this realm of study we are brought face to face with some of the basic issues of sociology: what are the stages in the process of disintegration? How do we integrate a large community? What feeling of belonging and identification can we provide for people at the grass roots? How can we secure citizen participation in the affairs of government? How do we develop capable leadership on the grass roots level, whether in the urban neighborhood or the suburban community?

A number of studies have sought to gain answers to these questions: Angell's[16] study probed the various factors contributing to or hindering normative integration of the large American city. Freedman and Axelrod[17] sought to investigate the group ties of the urbanite in somewhat the same fashion that Komarovsky[18] did. Both studies suggest that the urban dweller is not so totally isolated and non-participative as previously thought; both also emphasize the differential participation of various segments of the community. A few other studies may be noted in passing inasmuch as they relate closely to this general basic sphere of community involvement.[19]

A larger study that deals, at least by implication, with this fundamental area of the social fabric of the community is by Homans.[20]
In his analysis of the elements of the human group, Homans offers
the following cogent suggestion:

> At the level of the small group, society has always been able to
> cohere. We infer therefore that if civilization is to stand it must
> maintain, in the relation between the groups that make up soci-
> ety and the central direction of society, some of the features of
> the small group itself.[21]

How can we manage to retain some of these features in the large and
emerging larger metropolitan community is one of the most significant
aspects of the entire problem of citizen participation.

SUMMARY

In this overview of the sociology of the city since the end of World
War II, we have concentrated on some of the important studies that
have been done. The intention was to raise questions, some of which
can be immediately answered by our available knowledge; this points
the way into that future where we shall have to spend the rest of our
lives. Not all of our available knowledge of the city has been gathered
by those who bear the professional label "sociologist"; much of this
knowledge has been contributed by planners, architects, social workers,
political scientists. No attempt was made here to restrict the chapter
to an exclusive concern with the findings of the profesional sociologist;
the approach was to examine the changing city and the work of all
who had something relevant to say about it.

As our populations in the metropolitan centers continue to increase
and redistribute themselves and as the process of urban planning and
renewal proceeds, as indeed they will for the next half century, sociologists have opportunity to help create a metropolitan community
that suits human needs. To the extent that the task of understanding,
and building and rebuilding our metropolitan centers concerns human
values, attitudes and needs, as it basically does, the challenge is thrown
to the sociologist to utilize his concepts and skills to provide satisfactory, meaningful knowledge which the planner, the politician and
the people can use. The livability of our cities today and tomorrow
depends on whether and how well sociologists meet this challenge.

SELECTED BIBLIOGRAPHY

Charles Abrams, *Forbidden Neighbors:* A Study of Prejudice in Housing (New York: Harper, 1955). A recent analysis of the many problems inherent in our racially and religiously changing neighbors in metropolitan America. The author is an expert in the area of intergroup housing.

Robert Cooley Angell, *The Moral Integration of American Cities,* Part II of the *American Journal of Sociology* (July, 1951). A pioneering effort to investigate the relationship of both negative and positive factors to the normative cohesion of the American city.

Donald Bogue, *The Structure of the Metropolitan Community;* A Study of Dominance and Subdominance (Ann Arbor: University of Michigan Press, 1949). One of the best analyses of the relationship of the central city to the surrounding countryside.

Miles L. Colean, *Renewing Our Cities,* (New York: The Twentieth Century Fund, 1953). A brief but penetrating examination of the concept of urban renewal and what it is beginning to mean to the future of our cities.

Wilma Donahue (ed.), *Housing the Aged* (Ann Arbor: University of Michigan Press, 1954). A symposium of experts on the increasingly relevant problem of our cities: where and how to best house and rehouse our senior citizens. The author herself is an authority in the rapidly developing sphere of geriatrics.

Walter Fiery, *Land Use in Central Boston* (Cambridge: Harvard University Press, 1947). A basic technical study of land use in Boston and the patterning of the city; stresses the cultural factor as more important than the classical ecologists had suggested.

Robert Moore Fisher, *The Metropolis in Modern Life* (New York: Doubleday and Co., 1955). Considers the basic forces manifest in the newly emerging modern metropolis. Report of conference held in 1954 in connection with Columbia University Bicentennial; many illustrious experts on the problems of the modern city and life within it.

Arthur B. Gallion, *The Urban Pattern* (New York: D. Van Nostrand Co., 1950). A sophisticated critical review of the process of city building and planning; emphasizes the responsibility of the citizen in this process. Contains an excellent bibliography.

Paul K. Hatt and Albert Reiss (eds.), *Reader in Urban Sociology* (Glencoe, Ill., The Free Press, 1951). An anthology of articles dealing with the various aspects of urban life: population, stratification, mobility, housing, etc. Many excellent readings.

Amos H. Hawley, *The Changing Shape of Metropolitan America; Deconcentration Since 1920* (Glencoe, Ill., The Free Press, 1956). A brief but comprehensive review of the population data of American cities with an effort to evaluate the changed and changing shape of the emerging metropolitan community.

Arthur Hillman, *Community Organization and Planning* (New York:

The Macmillan Company, 1950). Consideration of the community and community organization as the central foci for modern urban planning, both social and physical.

Floyd Hunter, *Community Power Structure* (Chapel Hill: University of North Carolina Press, 1952). A good study of the power structure of a large southern city, Regional City. Consideration of the concentration of power and the nature of decision-making in the community.

Lewis Mumford, *From the Ground Up* (New York: Harcourt, Brace and Co., 1956). The best of Mumford's corner in the New Yorker over the past several years. Splendid insights into urban living as only the author of *Culture of Cities* could develop.

Robert Weaver, *The Negro Ghetto* (New York: Harcourt, Brace and Co., 1948). An analysis of the factors shaping the pattern of segregation in American cities. A sound review of relevant forces by one who knows the problems of the ghetto first hand.

Coleman Woodbury (ed.), *The Future of Cities and Urban Redevelopment* (University of Chicago Press, 1953). Probably the most comprehensive volume (two volumes with its companion piece: *Urban Redevelopment: Problems and Practices*), dealing with the physical and social dimensions of urban renewal, particularly redevelopment. Several contributing authors, but the whole bearing the imprint of the editor.

Mel J. Ravitz, Ph. D., University of Michigan (1955); Instructor in Sociology, Wayne State University (1949); Sociologist on the staff of the Detroit City Plan Commission (1953); Assistant Professor of Sociology, Wayne State University (1956–), while serving on a part-time basis with the Plan Commission. His publications include: "The Role of the Sociologist in an Urban Planning Agency," "Some Critical Roadblocks to Urban Renewal," "Integration of Nurses: A Latent Function of Hospital Discrimination," "Some Socio-Demographic Considerations in Settlement House Relocation," etc.

NOTES

1. Donald J. Bogue, "Urbanism in the United States, 1950" *The American Journal of Sociology*, LX (March, 1955), 471-486.

2. Amos H. Hawley, *The Changing Shape of Metropolitan America* (Glencoe, Illinois: The Free Press, 1956).

3. Charles Abrams, *Forbidden Neighbors: A Study of Prejudice in Housing* (New York: Harpers, 1955).

4. See, for example: Morton Deutsch and Mary Evans Collins, *Intergroup Relations in Interracial Housing: A Study of the Socio-Psychological Effects of Occu-*

pancy *Pattern* (Research Center for Human Relations, New York University, Washington Square, New York, Mimeographed draft of report), later published as *Interracial Housing—A Psychological Evaluation of a Social Experiment* (University of Minnesota Press, 1951); Clifton R. Jones, "Invasion and Racial Attitudes," *Social Forces,* XXVII (March, 1949); Arnold Rose, F. L. Atelsek, and L. R. McDonald, "Neighborhood Reactions to Isolated Negro Residents: An Alternative to Invasion and Succession," *American Sociological Review,* XVIII (October, 1953), 497-07; E. F. Schietinger, "Racial Succession and the Value of Small Residential Properties," *American Sociological Review,* XVI (December, 1951), 832-35; S. Joseph Fauman and Joseph B. Robinson, *Guide to Changing Neighborhoods* (National Community Relations Advisory Council, 1956).

5. H. Warren Dunham and Nathan D. Grundstein, "The Impact of a Confusion of Social Objectives on Public Housing: A Preliminary Analysis," *Marriage and Family Living,* XVII, No. 2 (May, 1955), 103-12.

6. Robert K. Merton, "The Social Psychology of Housing," an essay in Wayne Dennis (ed.), *Current Trends in Social Psychology* (University of Pittsburgh Press, 1948).

7. Deutsch and Collins, *op. cit., passim.*

8. Lewis Mumford, *From the Ground Up* (New York: Harcourt, Brace, 1956), Ch. 13, "Prefabricated Blight."

9. See for example: Frederick Gutheim, *Houses for Family Living* (New York: The Woman's Foundation, 1948); Svend Riemer, "Maladjustment to the Family Home," *American Sociological Review,* X (October, 1945), 642-48; Lewis Mumford, *op. cit.,* especially Chapters 1, 2, 13, and 21.

10. Robert Cooley Angell, *The Moral Integration of American Cities,* Part II of the *American Journal of Sociology,* LVII, No. 1, (July, 1951).

11. Mel Jerome Ravitz, "Block That Blight," *Adult Leadership,* V 1, (May, 1956), 4-5 27-29.

12. Hawley, *op. cit.,* Chapter I.

13. Mumford, *op cit.,* 199-229.

14. J. Douglas Carroll, Jr., "Some Aspects of the Home-Work Relationships of Industrial Workers," *Land Economics* (November, 1949), 414-22; Kate K. Liepmann, *The Journey to Work—Its Significance for Industrial and Community Life* (New York: Oxford University Press, 1944).

15. Amos H. Hawley, in a telecast over Station WDTR, "Our Sprawling Cities," October 23, 1956.

16. Angell, *op. cit., passim.*

17. Ronald Freedman and Morris Axelrod, "Who Belongs to What in the Great Metropolis?" *Adult Leadership,* I (November, 1951).

18. Mirra Komarovsky, "The Voluntary Associations of Urban Dwellers," *American Sociological Review,* XI (December, 1946), 686-98.

19. Theodore Caplow and Robert Forman, "Neighborhood Interaction in a Homogeneous Community," *American Sociological Review,* XV (June, 1950), 357-66; Alvin H. Scaff, "The Effect of Commuting on Participation in Community Organizations," *Ibid.,* XVII (April, 1952), 215-20; Mel Jerome Ravitz and Adelaide Dinwoodie, "Detroit Social Workers Mobilize Citizen Aid for Urban Renewal," *Journal of Housing,* XIII (July, 1956), 232-34.

20. George C. Homans, *The Human Group* (New York: Harcourt, Brace, 1950).

21. *Ibid.,* 468.

HUMAN ECOLOGY
AND HUMAN GEOGRAPHY

George A. Theodorson
Pennsylvania State University

Both human ecology and human geography have traditionally focused on the relationship between man and his environment. Human ecology, however, has emphasized the interrelationships among men, the structure of community organization, and the spatial distributions of social activities under various environmental conditions. The emphasis of human geography has been on the direct relationship between man and a physical environment, the effects of local topography and climate upon man, and man's modifications of his physical habitat. Thus it may be said that human ecology emphasizes the relationships among men in an environmental setting, while human geography emphasizes the physical environment itself and man's reciprocal relationship with that environment.

HUMAN GEOGRAPHY

Human geography developed in the late nineteenth and early twentieth centuries from the study of general geography, largely through the efforts of Friedrich Ratzel, Ellen Semple, Paul Vidal de la Blanche, and Jean Brunhes. Human geography was considered a branch of sociology through the 1929's, and may be regarded as a predecessor of human ecology. It contributed to the latter such concepts as migration, mobility, segregation, natural areas, etc.[1] With the development of human ecology, emphasizing the relationships among men, sociologists turned their attention from human geography. A distinction was drawn between the two fields, with sociologists concentrating their attention on human ecology. Today human geography is not considered a branch of sociology, but rather the province of geographers. The major portion of this chapter, therefore, will be devoted to human ecology.

"CLASSICAL" HUMAN ECOLOGY

The term "human ecology" was introduced by Park and Burgess in 1921. The conception of human ecology was based largely on earlier studies of plant and animal ecology. A body of ecological theory was developed in the 1920's and '30's to form what may be called the "classical" ecological position.

According to this "classical" position, as stated by Park, the basic process in human relationships is competition, largely involving a struggle for space. However, because of the high degree of inter-dependence and division of labor among humans, competition must always involve an automatic and unplanned degree of cooperation, forming what is called competitive-cooperation. As a result of com-petitive-cooperation men form relationships of unplanned interde-pendence called symbiotic relationships. Human society is seen as organized on two levels: the biotic and the cultural. The biotic level involves basic, non-thoughtful adjustments made in the struggle for existence. The biotic level is regarded as sub-social, and is based on the organization of symbiotic relationships. The struggle for existence, based on competitive-cooperation, and resulting in the organization of the biotic level of society, also determines the spatial distribution of persons. The spatial distribution is therefore seen as reflecting the organization of the biotic level of society. The cultural level of society, whose basic process is communication and consensus, is seen as a superstructure resting upon the biotic level. The biotic level of society was regarded as the proper field of investigation for human ecology, and therefore cultural factors were excluded from ecological investigations.[2]

The "classical" position also held that the organization of the biotic community is based on the dominance of the central business district, with variations in naturally formed areas of homogeneous population and land use occurring because of distance from and varying degrees of influence of the central business district. This conception was expressed, for example, in Burgess' theory of con-centric zones.[3] It also was reflected in the study of gradients, or vari-ables which increase or decrease regularly with distance from the central business district (such as rate of suicide). Dominance together with competition and human mobility were seen as resulting in the processes of centralization of services, and concentration, segregation, invasion, and succession of populations.[4] Most of the empirical investigations of the "classical" ecologists were of large American cities, particularly Chicago.

In addition to Park and Burgess, the "classical" position was represented by MacKenzie,[5] Wirth,[6] and others.

Starting in the late thirties and continuing into the forties the "classical" position was subjected to severe criticism. In 1937 Davie reported that Burgess' concentric zone hypothesis did not apply to New Haven.[7] The following year Alihan severely attacked the basic position of the "classical" ecologists, particularly criticizing their distinction between the biotic and cultural levels of society.[8] During the period from 1945 to 1950 criticism of the "classical" position mounted. In 1945 Llewellyn and Hawthorn criticized ecological theory for not taking sufficient account of cultural factors, for the lack of clarity of its concepts, and for the insufficient substantiation of theory with empirical facts.[9] In 1946 Hatt reported that the concept of natural areas did not apply to the section of Seattle that he studied. He felt that the concept was of value if the researcher defined it by criteria relevant to his specific research project, rather than looking for *the* natural areas of a city. He accused ecologists of a tendency toward reification of their concepts.[10] Hollingshead, in 1947, criticized ecological theory for not taking cultural factors into account.[11] The same year Firey attempted to demonstrate that traditional ecological theory was limited to a certain, historically unique value context associated with modern capitalism and industrialism.[12] Shevky and Williams, in 1949, criticized the "classical" ecologists for the descriptive, non-experimental nature of their method, as well as for limiting themselves to the large, modern American city.[13] Thus by 1950 the "classical" position, having been subjected to more than a decade of sharp criticism was thoroughly undermined, and, in its original form, is virtually without proponents today. Since 1950 criticisms of traditional ecology primarily have been confined to questions relating to the ecological distribution of particular variables, such as mental illness.[14]

RECENT TRENDS IN HUMAN ECOLOGY

Growing Emphasis on Cultural Factors

The distinction between the biotic and cultural levels of society is no longer made by human ecologists. The impossibility of excluding cultural factors from ecological investigations is well recognized today. Ecologists, however, are not agreed on the extent to which culture may be a valuable and primary explanatory concept in ecological theory. Those who place primary emphasis on culture have been referred to as "sociocultural" ecologists. Two leading proponents of this position are Firey and Hollingshead. Firey has maintained that space may have symbolic value and should not always be regarded as having only cost-imposing qualities. He has emphasized that space takes on meaning for man through cultural definition, and that at every point cultural values intervene between the physical environment and the human community.[15] Hollingshead has stressed the sociocultural framework within which human activities occur, and the regulation of competition by cultural values.[16] Other writers also have emphasized the importance of sociocultural factors in understanding ecological structure. For example, Heberle has emphasized that human ecology deals with value-oriented relationships between men and value-oriented adjustments of men to their environment.[17] Still others, such as Isard, Kavesh, and Kuenne, have noted the limiting and modifying influences of social values, although they are primarily concerned with economic structure.[18]

Several research studies have presented evidence to support the "sociocultural" position. Firey, in studying land use patterns in central Boston, found that the maintenance of Beacon Hill as an upper class residential district could only be explained by symbolic values. He also found symbolic values the only adequate explanation of what he called "space fetishes," such as the common, three cemeteries, old churches, old meeting houses, etc., in the central business district despite their serious economic dysfunctions. Patterns of land use and community structure in Back Bay, the North End, and the South End were also explained in terms of cultural values.[19] Jonassen studied the Norwegian community in New York City, and concluded that the movement of this community could not be understood without taking their modified rural values into account.[20] Myer's study of the residential movement and distribution of New Haven Italians also supported the "sociocultural" point of view. He found that their movement could only be understood in terms of the degree of their integration into the dominant social system.[21] Kobrin found that the failure of some boys to behave delinquently in areas of high delinquency could be explained by the duality of conduct norms in the area.[22] Vogt and O'Dea in studying two New Mexican communities found that while the geographic situaton set certain limits for the development of each, differences in community organization could only be explained in terms of individualistic versus cooperative values.[23]

Not all human ecologists at present support the "sociocultural" position. Another current ecological position may be referred to as "neo-orthodox." Closer to traditional ecology, it rejects culture or values as a primary explanatory concept in ecological theory, but it does not accept many of the assumptions of "classical" ecology. Two leading representatives of this position are Quinn and Hawley. Neither Quinn nor Hawley regards motivations and attitudes as the proper primary focus of human ecology. However, both reject the "classical" distinction between a cultural and a biotic level of society. Both men further agree that human ecology should not be concerned with spatial distributions in and of themselves, but only as they reflect patterns of community structure. Despite these similarities, there are important differences between the positions of Quinn and Hawley. Quinn maintains a distinction between a social and a sub-social level of interaction. The social level involves mental awareness and communication through the use of symbols, while the sub-social level involves the utilization of limited resources or limited space. The sub-social level is seen by Quinn as the proper focus for human ecology. He does not, however, equate this with the "classical" biotic level since he insists that the sub-social level involves a cultural context and cannot be understood except in terms of it. While the two levels are regarded as aspects of a unified areal whole, the social level is considered peripheral to the major focus of human ecology. In the process of sub-social interaction units become spatially distributed. The main principle governing this distribution is seen as the principle of minimum costs, including social as well as economic costs.[24] Quinn's position is closer to that of the "classical" ecologists than is Hawley's. Hawley rejects Quinn's distinction between a social and a sub-social level of interaction, and sees it as a carryover from the earlier distinction between a biotic and a cultural level. He regards all human interrelationships as social. Hawley sees the main task of human ecology as the analysis of community structure, which he sees primarily in terms of the division of labor. Community structure from the ecological point of view is seen as the organization of sustenance activities, the way a population organizes itself for survival. This organization of sustenance activities results in a spatial distribution. Those activities least able to withstand the time and energy costs of more distant locations and with a maximum need for accessibility will tend toward a central location. Hawley's orientation to human ecology may be regarded as basically economic. He feels that economic data are readily available, and are often indices of socal phenomena. Hawley also feels that culture has become too inclusive a concept to be of any real explanatory value.[25]

A number of research studies in human ecology conducted in the past decade have not dealt with the theoretical issues discussed above. Rather, they have been concerned with specific, empirical problems. Firey, after a survey of research in human ecology and demography being conducted in 1950 and the first half of 1951, reported that research during this period showed a predominantly empirical and practical orientation, with theoretical inquiry limited primarily to techniques and procedures for analyzing quantitive data.[26] This failure to explicitly state their theoretical framework does not mean that these studies do not have implications of theoretical value. They reflect, in general, a "neo-orthodox" orientation, since they tend toward a more traditional type of ecological investigation, while not implying an acceptance of the basic "classical" assumptions. Their primary emphasis is not on cultural values, but they do not exclude values from their investigations. If one accepts the "sociocultural" position these studies may still be regarded as useful in analyzing predominant trends in community structure within the sociocultural framework of urban, industrial, American society.

Several studies have dealt with traditional, gradient type, ecological distributions of particular variables. Duncan and Duncan reported a study of social stratification through ecological distribution in Chicago. They found a residential distribution of occupational status, and a corresponding distribution of socioeconomic status, with centralization inversely related to status.[27] Schmid and Van Arsdol, in a study of Seattle, found that the highest rates both of occurrence and residence of suicides and attempted suicides were in the central business district and adjacent areas, and the lowest rates were in the outlying residential areas.[28] In a study of illegitimate birth rates in Honolulu, reported by Schmitt, a classical ecological distribution was found with rates following a gradient and tending to correlate with housing, health, and social variables.[29]

Other studies have been concerned with questions relating to residential segregation. For example, Bell in 1953, using an index of segregation devised by Shevky and Williams, compared patterns of segregation in San Francisco with those of Los Angeles.[30] In a study reported in 1951 of areas segregated on the basis of type of dwelling units and living patterns, Cohen contrasted the characteristics of upper and lower class rooming house districts in Los Angeles.[31] Dealing with the related question of invasion, Brussat, in 1951, reported that in Milwaukee Negro expansion was not following the traditional pattern of invading adjacent areas, but had skipped over a large area to invade a deteriorated area some distance away.[32] In the same year in a study of Negro invasion in a section of Chicago, Schietinger reported that invasion was accompanied by an increase in the price of properties sold to Negroes, a decrease in the price of properties sold to whites, and a decline in assessed valuations. A decline in prices was found to accompany long term Negro occupancy.[33]

A third group of studies has involved economically oriented ecological investigations. Foley and Breese in a book and a series of articles published from 1949 to 1954 have been concerned with the daytime movement of population into the central business districts of American cities. They have presented data comparing different size cities and showing trends in this daily movement of population.[34] Interest in city size also was shown by Clark, who, in 1945, attempted to determine an optimum city size for the provision of services,[35] and by Schnore and Varley, who, in 1955, contrasted the characteristics of smaller and larger cities.[36] Reeder in 1953 reported in a study of industrial location in Chicago that large firms employing over one hundred employees, and particularly those receiving and shipping a large amount of tonnage by rail, tend to be located near rail lines, while small firms do not.[37] In an article published in 1950, and based on a study of twenty-three American cities, Schmid presented a series of generalizations largely typical of the findings of studies made of modern, American cities, within an implicitly "neoorthodox" framework. Schmid found that large American cities have a definite and pervasive ecological structure, with a regular pattern of distribution of such variables as sex, age, race, nativity, income, education, occupation, and fertility.[38]

Growth of Comparative Human Ecology

Acompanying the growing emphasis upon cultural factors in human ecology, and perhaps in part responsible for that development, has been an increasing number of studies of ecological structure in cultural settings other than that of the United States. The "socio-cultural" ecologists' contention that the "classical" ecological pattern which tends to prevail in American cities is due to a certain cultural milieu and not intrinsic to all communities is supported by these studies. A number of studies have dealt with the ecological structure of Latin-American cities and have found a traditional Spanish pattern very different from that of cities in the United States. As early as 1934, Hansen studied the ecology of Merida in Yucatan. He found a traditional pattern which had existed from the sixteenth to the late nineteenth century, in which the plaza was the center of the city and the center of the area of highest prestige. The cathedral and government buildings adjoined the plaza. Nearby was the retail business district, and in an adjacent area were the homes of the upper class. As one proceded from the center of the city outward socioeconomic level declined, the reverse of the "classical" ecological pattern of cities in the United States. The area surrounding the center of the city was divided into five barrios, semi-autonomous districts with considerable community cohesion and organization. Each barrio had its own plaza. This pattern has been changing in Merida and it has been becoming more like the typical pattern found in the United States. This change has accompanied growing outside contact and industrialization.[39] A similar pattern in Mexico City was reported by Hayner in 1945. For six hundred years Mexico City grew slowly, and therefore had no zone of transition near the central business district. As in the case of Merida residential desirability declined with distance from the central plaza. In recent years with the growth of population, industry, and transportation the pattern has been shifting to one like that found in the United States. Hayner reported, however, that in the town of Oaxaca, which had been fairly inaccessible until recently, the traditional Latin-American pattern still prevailed.[40] Essentially the same situation was reported by Hawthorn and Hawthorn in 1948 for Sucre, Bolivia. The traditional pattern placed the upper class around a central plaza, but there too recent changes have been taking place. However, in Sucre the new pattern had not yet completely prevailed, and a mixed pattern was found with lower class families residing on almost every block in the city.[41] In a study of Guatemala City Caplow found the traditional ecological pattern followed the typical Latin-American plan. As in the other cities he found certain recent changes had occurred, mainly resulting in the decline of the barrios. However, other traditional patterns were found to have a strong tenacity. Many wealthy families, especially the older upper class families, had maintained a central location. Crime was found to increase with distance from the center of the city, and no process of invasion and succession was found due to a marked tendency to maintain traditional land use patterns.[42] Thus throughout Latin-America there existed a traditional ecological pattern very different from that found in the United States. This pattern was not due, however, to any intrinsic features of the environmental setting of Latin-American cities, but rather to a definite Spanish colonial policy. This may be demonstrated by the differences between Spanish and Indian towns. McBride, in a study of Guatemala, found that when a sizable number of Ladinos (mixed Indian and Spanish group, considering themselves Spanish) is present a settlement will take the form of a centralized town, while without many Ladinos an even larger population aggregate will form only an agricultural settlement.[43] Stanislawski studied eleven towns in the state of Michoacán in Mexico. He found a striking difference between Hispanic and Indian towns. The Hispanic towns followed the pattern described above. Stanislawski reported an additional interesting spatial distribution based on occupational prestige. High prestige occupations, such as retail merchants, mule drivers, and leather workers tended toward central locations on main arteries, while low prestige occupations, such as non-leather crafts, were in peripheral locations or in blind alleys. In the Indian towns, in contrast, the plaza was unimportant and no spatial distribution of prestige was found.[44]

Several studies also have appeared of the ecological structure of communities outside of the Americas. Caplow in 1952 published a study of urban structure in France. Caplow found a number of ways in which the French city differs from the typical pattern of the United States, including: less centralization, no increase in centralization with increased city size, a different pattern of daily population movement—no convergence at a central point, no conspicuous pattern of invasion and succession, no regular association of social class with spatial distribution, no uniform tendency for density of population to decrease toward the periphery of the city, and the maintenance of quartiers—local communities with strong identification and distinct customs—in both large and small cities. Caplow also found, as Firey did in Boston, that land values were not all-important in determining urban patterns, but that historic parks, palaces, etc. were able to resist commercial pressures.[45] Sipes in 1954 studied the ecology of eight non-literate communities, and found that kinship was important in influencing community structure, while economic factors were of much less significance than in American communities.[46] In an analysis of the preindustrial city (present day cities of North Africa and certain parts of Asia as well as medieval European cities) Sjoberg emphasized ecological differences between these cities and modern, American industrial cities. The preindustrial cities are characterized by well defined neighborhoods often based on differences between social classes, ethnic, or occupational groups, and characterized by primary relationships. These sections of the city are sometimes separated by walls that are locked at night. There tends to be no specialization of land use in that the same building commonly serves as a residence and workshop. The business district is not the center of dominance. In medieval Europe, for example, the cathedral was the focal point of the city.[47]

These studies together with the findings of the "sociocultural" ecologists presented above indicate that the ecological structure found in studies of Chicago and other large American cities (e.g. the distribution of gradients, the importance of economic factors in determining land use) are the characteristics of unplanned, industrial cities where economic values are foremost, and possibly also are limited to capitalist societies where private property and competition prevail. One study, however, contradicts the conclusion that the traditional American ecological pattern is limited to industrial cities. Comhaire has reported that Leopoldville in the Belgian Congo and Brazzaville in French Equatorial Africa have ecological patterns very similar to those prevalent in American cities.[48] No explanation for this is given by the author. Since this ecological pattern can no longer be considered universal and automatic, its presence in a non-industrial setting requires investigation and explanation, so that the circumstances under which this pattern arises may be accurately determined. This suggests the importance of a theoretical framework if specific empirical studies are to make a meaningful contribution.

Studies made of cities devastated during World War II have indicated a tendency to restore pre-war ecological patterns. This tendency was found by Iklé in a study of western European cities in 1949 and 1950,[49] and confirmed by Grebler in 1956.[50] Hawley found the same tendency in Okayama, Japan, and further reported that the ecological pattern of Okayama was similar to that of American cities.[51]

Growing Interest in a Broader Area than the Limits of the Large City.

The earlier ecological studies were concerned primarily with the structure of the large city. In recent years interest has spread beyond the limits of the city itself. A number of ecologists have turned their attention to the metropolitan community. Community structure has been accepted as the basic concern of human ecology by Hawley,[52] Firey,[53] Quinn,[54] and others. Although no clear-cut agreement has been reached for delimiting the boundary of a community, and different criteria result in different boundaries, ecologists agree that the community extends beyond the political boundaries of a city, and includes, at a minimum, the surrounding suburbs.

A study of metropolitan communities by Isard and Whitney revealed the differentiation of function that has occurred between central and outlying cities. They found that the main loss of retail trade to central cities was felt by outlying cities within a twenty mile radius of the central cities, with little loss beyond that radius.[55] An extensive study of the structure of the metropolitan community has been made by Bogue. He hypothesized that technologically advanced societies are dominated by metropolises, and thus the United States has become divided into a series of metropolitan communities, each dominated by a metropolis. Within the metropolitan community, Bogue regards the metropolis itself as a dominant, smaller cities as subdominants, rural non-farm communities as influents, and rural farm communities as subinfluents. The smaller communities are distributed about the dominant city, forming a definite pattern characteristic of metropolitan communities. However, Bogue does not regard this pattern as inevitable or unchangeable.[56]

One section of the metropolitan community that has been the subject of growing interest is the area outside the limits of the central city and the surrounding smaller cities, or the rural-urban fringe. A considerable number of studies have been concerned with this area. Firey studied the fringe as a marginal, problem area in 1946, before recent suburban patterns developed.[57] Andrews, in 1945, and Dewey, in 1948, were concerned with motivations for moving to the fringe.[58] Differences between rural and urban migrants to the fringe were studied by Rodehaver.[59] Blizzard and Anderson have emphasized the dual rural-urban nature of the fringe and the presence of both rural and urban problems.[60] Whitney has pointed out that the growth of rural non-farm population is due to the develop-ment of the fringe and therefore is a phase of urban growth.[61] Other investigators have been concerned with the social structure of fringe areas—changes that occur in a community becoming a fringe,[62] pat-terns of participation of fringe residents in organizations,[63] and patterns of social relations among fringe residents.[64] In addition, Martin has studied factors associated with adjustment to fringe resi-dence.[65] Differentiation within the fringe area also has received attention. Kish distinguished between inner and outer suburban zones, and found greater differentiation in the inner zones in terms of such factors as occupation, rents, and political alignment.[66] Schnore distinguished between industrial and residential suburbs, and studied the characteristics of each.[67]

Growing Concern with Refinement of Methodological Techniques

A large number of studies in the past decade have been concerned with methodological techniques to be used in ecological investiga-tions. One of the most important articles written in this area was a criticism of ecological correlations by Robinson in 1950. Robinson demonstrated that ecological correlations cannot validly be substi-tuted for individual correlations.[68] For example, if it were found that areas with a high percentage of Negroes were the ones with a high rate of illiteracy, it could not validly be assumed that Negroes have a higher rate of illiteracy than whites. This type of assumption was fairly common in ecological investigations in the past. This left the problem of what to do when only ecological data are available and the investigator is interested in the behavior of individuals. A partial solution to this problem was proposed by Goodman who offered a method for inferring the behavior of individuals from eco-logical data, but only under very special circumstances.[69] Duncan and Davis have presented a method by which individual correlations may be approximated from ecological data. This method will not yield a specific correlation, but a range within which it is known that the correlation falls. The extent of this range will vary under different circumstances.[70]

A number of writers have been concerned with indexes of segre-gation, which have been the subject of considerable controversy. A number of writers have proposed different indexes of segregation and criticized those proposed by others.[71] Duncan and Duncan in

1955 criticized as inadequate all the indexes of segregation proposed thus far, and emphasized that adequate indexes cannot be devised without dealing with theoretical issues.[72]

Other investigators have been concerned with methods for: delimiting areas of various sizes,[73] measuring the economic structure of an area,[74] and measuring the economic interrelationships between areas.[75]

CONCLUSIONS AND PROSPECTS

It seems clear that "classical" human ecology essentially is a thing of the past, and therefore the attacks on the "classical" position, which were so prevalent in the late forties, have served their function and it may be expected that they will cease. It may be hoped that the next phase in the development of human ecology will consist of a merging of the "neo-orthodox" and "sociocultural" positions. Both Hawley[76] and Firey[77] have indicated that much of the difference between the two positions may be verbal rather than real. The development of human ecology would certainly be helped if those conducting specific empirical investigations would make explicit the theoretical framework within which their investigations are being conducted, and the theoretical implications of their results.

The period since 1945 has seen in large measure the maturation of human ecology from a field of descriptive studies limited to one cultural context and burdened with many a priori assumptions to an emerging science of community structure.

SELECTED BIBLIOGRAPHY

Milla A. Alihan, *Social Ecology* (New York: Columbia University Press, 1938). Presents a devastating criticism of the "classical" ecological distinction between biotic and cultural levels of society, from which "classical" ecology never recovered.

Don J. Bogue, *The Structure of the Metropolitan Community* (Ann Arbor, Michigan: Horace H. Rackham School of Graduate Studies, University of Michigan, 1949). Attempts to demonstrate that the metropolis is a true dominant; the organization of American Society is seen as a series of communities, each dominated by a metropolis.

Theodore Caplow, "The Social Ecology of Guatemala City," *Social Forces*, XXVIII (December, 1949), 113-127. A summary of research on the ecology of the Spanish-American city is presented, together with the author's study of Guatemala City.

Theodore Caplow, "Urban Structure in France," *American Sociological Review*, XVII (October, 1952), 544-549. Shows how the ecology of the French city differs from that of the American city, giving reasons for these differences.

Otis D. Duncan and Beverly Duncan, "A Methodological Analysis of Segregation Indexes," *American Sociological Review*, XX (April, 1955), 210-217. Analyzes the mathematical and conceptual inadequacies of segregation indexes presented to date, and suggests in general what is needed in this area.

Walter Firey, *Land Use in Central Boston* (Cambridge: Harvard University Press, 1947). Attempts to demonstrate that traditional ecology cannot adequately explain land use patterns in Boston; explains these patterns in terms of prevailing values.

Amos H. Hawley, *Human Ecology* (New York: The Ronald Press Co., 1950). Discusses the development and scope of human ecology; analyzes community structure, emphasizing the organization of sustenance activities and the effects of developments in transportation and communication.

A. B. Hollingshead, "Community Research: Development and Present Condition," *American Sociological Review*, XIII (April, 1948), 140-141, 146-148, and 152-156. A summary of criticism of "classical" ecology and questions facing ecological theory in 1948; Quinn, Firey, and Hawley attempt to answer the questions raised by Hollingshead, in discussions at the end of the article.

Christen Jonassen, "Cultural Variables in the Ecology of an Ethnic Group," *American Sociological Review*, XIV (February, 1949), 32-41. The movement of the Norwegian community in New York City is analyzed in terms of the prevalence of certain traditional values.

Emma Llewellyn & Audrey Hawthorn, "Human Ecology," in Georges Gurvitch and Wilbert Moore (editors), *Twentieth Century Sociology* (New York: Philosophical Library, 1945), 466-499. Reviews human ecology up to 1945; essentially a summary and criticism of the "classical" ecological position.

Robert E. Park, *Human Communities* (Glencoe, Illinois: The Free Press, 1952). Presents the "classical" ecological position.

James A. Quinn, *Human Ecology* (New York: Prentice-Hall, 1950). Discusses the scope of human ecology, its techniques of investigation and its methods of presenting data; also summarizes research findings. The theoretical emphasis is on the sub-social level of interaction.

W. S. Robinson, "Ecological Correlations and the Behavior of Individuals," *American Sociological Review*, XV (June, 1950), 351-357. Demonstrates that ecological correlations may not validly be used to infer the behavior of individuals.

Calvin Schmid, "Generalizations Concerning the Ecology of the American City," *American Sociological Review*, XV (April, 1950), 264-281. A typical ecological pattern is found to characterize the twenty-three American cities studied; the cities show a consistent pattern of distribution of a number of variables.

Eshref Shevky and Marilyn Williams, *The Social Areas of Los Angeles* (Berkeley: University of California Press, 1949). A typology is presented for the comparative study of cities, in which cities are divided into areas based on degree of urbanization and socio-economic level.

George A. Theodorson, Assistant Professor of Sociology at the Pennsylvania State University, received his B.A., M.A., and Ph.D. (1954) degrees from Cornell University. From 1953-54 conducted small group research at the Univerity of Chicago; from 1954-56 an Assistant Professor at the University of Buffalo; has publications in the *American Sociological Review; Social Forces,* and *The American Journal of Sociology.*

NOTES

1. Floyd N. House, *The Development of Sociology* (New York: McGraw-Hill Book Co., 1936), 132-138.

2. Robert E. Park, *Human Communities* (Glencoe, Illinois: The Free Press, 1952); See also: Emma Llewellyn and Audrey Hawthorn, "Human Ecology," in Georges Gurvitch and Wilbert Moore (editors), *Twentieth Century Sociology* (New York: Philosophical Library, 1945), 466-499.

3. Ernest W. Burgess, "The Growth of a City: an Introduction to a Research Project," in Robert Park, Ernest Burgess, and R. D. McKenzie (editors), *The City* (Chicago: University of Chicago Press, 1925), 47-62.

4. Llewellyn and Hawthorn. *op. cit..* 492-493.

5. R. D. McKenzie, *The Metropolitan Community* (New York: McGraw-Hill Book Co., 1933).

6. Louis Wirth, "Human Ecology," *The American Journal of Sociology*, L (May, 1945), 483-488.

7. Maurice Davie, "The Pattern of Urban Growth," in George P. Murdock (editor), *Studies in the Science of Society* (New Haven: Yale University Press, 1937), 133-161.

8. Milla A. Alihan, *Social Ecology* (New York: Columbia University Press, 1938).

9. Llewellyn and Hawthorn, *op. cit.,* 493-494.

10. Paul Hatt, "The Concept of Natural Areas," *American Sociological Review* X, (August, 1946), 423-427.

11. A. B. Hollingshead, "A Re-examination of Ecological Theory," *Sociology and Social Research*, XXXI (January-February, 1947), 194-204.

12. Walter Firey, *Land Use in Central Boston* (Cambridge: Harvard University Press, 1947).

13. Eshref Shevky and Marilyn Williams, *The Social Areas of Los Angeles* (Berkeley: University of California Press, 1949), 1.

14. D. L. Gerard and L. G. Houston, "Family Setting and the Social Ecology of Schizophrenia," *The Psychiatric Quarterly*, XXVII (January, 1953), 90-101; J. A. Clausen and M. L. Kohn, "The Ecological Approach in Social Psychiatry," *American Journal of Sociology*, LX (Sept., 1954), 140-149.

15. Firey, *op. cit.*, 32-33; See also: Walter Firey, "Sentiment and Symbolism as Ecological Variables," *American Sociological Review*, X (April, 1945), 140-148; Walter Firey, "Discussion," of A. B. Hollingshead, "Community Research: Development and Present Condition," *American Sociological Review*, XIII (April, 1948), 152-**153.**

16. Hollingshead, "A Re-examination of Ecological Theory," *op. cit.*

17. Rudolph Heberle, "On Political Ecology," *Social Forces*, XXXI (October, 1952), 1-9.

18. Walter Isard, Robert Kavesh, and Robert Kuenne, "The Economic Base and Structure of the Urban-Metropolitan Region," *American Sociological Review*, XVIII (June, 1953), 317-321.

19. Firey, *Land Use in Central Boston, op. cit.*

20. Christen T. Jonassen, "Cultural Variables in the Ecology of an Ethnic Group," *American Sociological Review*, XIV (February, 1949), 32-41.

21. Jerome K. Myers, "Assimilation to the Ecological and Social Systems of a Community," *American Sociological Review*, XV (June, 1950), 367-372.

22. Solomon Kobrin, "The Conflict of Values in Delinquency Areas," *Ibid.*, XVI (June, 1951), 653-661.

23. Evon Z. Vogt and Thomas F. O'Dea, "A Comparative Study of the Role of Values in Social Action in Two Southwestern Communities," *Ibid.*, XVIII (December, 1953), 645-654.

24. James A. Quinn, *Human Ecology* (New York: Prentice-Hall, 1950); See also James A. Quinn, "Discussion," of A. B. Hollingshead, "Community Research: Development and Present Condition," *op. cit.,* 146-148.

25. Amos H. Hawley, *Human Ecology* (New York: The Ronald Press, 1950); See also Amos H. Hawley, "Discussion," of A. B. Hollingshead, "Community Research: Development and Present Condition," *op. cit.*, 153-156.

26. Walter Firey, "Review of Current Research in Demography and Human Ecology," *American Sociological Review*, XVII (April, 1952), 212-215.

27. Otis D. Duncan and Beverly Duncan, "Residential Distribution and Occupational Stratification," *Ibid.*, LX (March, 1955), 493-503.

28. Calvin F. Schmid and Maurice D. Van Arsdol, Jr., "Completed and Attempted Suicides: A Comparative Analysis," *Ibid.*, XX (June, 1955), 273-283.

29. Robert C. Schmitt, "Illegitimate Birth Rates in an Atypical Community," *Ibid.*, LXI (March, 1956), 476-477.

30. Wendell Bell, "The Social Areas of the San Francisco Bay Region," *Ibid.*, XVIII (February, 1953), 39-47.

31. Lillian Cohen, "Los Angeles Rooming-House Kaleidoscope," *Ibid.*, XVI (June, 1951), 316-326.

32. William K. Brussat, "Incidental Findings on Urban Invasion," *American Sociological Review*, XVI (February, 1951), 94-96.

33. E. F. Schietinger "Racial Succession and Value of Small Residential Properties," *Ibid.*, XVI (December, 1951), 832-835.

34. Gerald W. Breese, *The Daytime Population of the Central Business District of Chicago* (Chicago: University of Chicago Press, 1949); Donald L. Foley, "The Daily Movement of Population into Central Business Districts," *American Sociological Review*, XVII (October, 1952), 538-543; Donald L. Foley, "Urban Daytime Population: A Field for Demographic-Ecological Analysis," *Social Forces*, XXXII (May, 1954), 323-330.

35. Colin Clark, "The Economic Functions of a City in Relation to Its Size," *Econometrica*, XIII (April, 1945), 97-113.

36. Leo F. Schnore and David W. Varley, "Some Concomitants of Metropolitan Size," *American Sociological Review*, XX (August,1955), 408-414.

37. Leo G. Reeder, "A Note on the Burgess-Davie, Firey Differences Regarding Industrial Location," *American Sociological Review*, XVIII (April, 1953), 189-191.

38. Calvin F. Schmid, "Generalizations Concerning the Ecology of the American City," *Ibid.*, XV (April, 1950), 264-281.

39. Asael T. Hansen, "The Ecology of a Latin American City," in E. B. Reuter (editor), *Race and Culture Contacts* (New York: McGraw-Hill Book Co., 1934), 124-142.

40. Norman S. Hayner, "Mexico City: Its Growth and Configuration," *The American Journal of Sociology*, L (January, 1945), 295-304.

41. Harry B. Hawthorn and Audrey E. Hawthorn, "The Shape of a City, Some Observations on Sucre, Bolivia," *Sociology and Social Research*, XXXIII (November-December, 1948), 87-91.

42. Theodore Caplow, "The Social Ecology of Guatemala City," *Social Forces*, XXVIII (December, 1949), 116-127.

43. Felix W. McBride, *Cultural and Historical Geography of Southwest Guatemala*, Smithsonian Institution, Institute of Social Anthropology, Publication No. 4 (Washington, D. C.: United States Government Printing Office, 1947), 85.

44. Dan Stanislawski, "The Anatomy of Eleven Towns in Michoacán," *Latin-American Studies*, X (Austin: University of Texas Press, 1950).

45. Theodore Caplow, "Urban Structure in France," *American Sociological Review*, XVII (October, 1952), 544-549.

46. Richard Sipes, *The Ecology of the Primitive Community*, unpublished Master's dissertation, Pennsylvania State University, 1954.

47. Gideon Sjoberg, "The Preindustrial City," *The American Journal of Sociology*, LX (March, 1955), 438-445.

48. J. Comhaire, "Some Aspects of Urbanization in the Belgian Congo," *The American Journal of Sociology*, LXII (July, 1956), 8-13.

49. Fred C. Iklé, "The Effect of War Destruction Upon the Ecology of Cities," *Social Forces, XXIX* (May, 1951), 383-391.

50. Leo Grebler, "Continuity in the Rebuilding of Bombed Cities in Western Europe," *The American Journal of Sociology*, LXI (March, 1956), 463-469.

51. Amos H. Hawley, "Land Value Patterns in Okayama, Japan, 1940 and 1952," *Ibid.*, LX (March, 1955), 487-492.

52. Hawley, "Discussion," *op. cit.*

53. Firey, "Discussion," *op. cit.*

54. Quinn, "Discussion," *op. cit.*

55. Walter Isard and Vincent Whitney, "Metropolitan Site Selection," *Social Forces*, XXVII (March, 1949), 263-269.

56. Don J. Bogue, *The Structure of the Metropolitan Community,* (Ann Arbor, Michigan: Horace H. Rackham School of Graduate Studies, University of Michigan, 1949).

57. Walter Firey, *Social Aspects to Land Use Planning in the Country-City Fringe: The Case of Flint, Michigan,* Special Bulletin 339 (East Lansing, Michigan: Michigan State College Agricultural Experiment Station, June 1946); Walter Firey, "Ecological Considerations in Planning for Urban Fringes," *American Sociological Review,* XI (August 1946), 411-421.

58. Richard B. Andrews, "Urban Fringe Studies of Two Wisconsin Cities, A Summary," *Journal of Land and Public Utility Economics,* XXI (November, 1945), 375-382; Richard Dewey, "Peripheral Expansion in Milwaukee County," *The American Journal of Sociology,* LIV (September, 1948), 118-125.

59. Myles W. Rodehaver, "Fringe Settlement as a Two-Directional Movement," *Rural Sociology,* XII (March, 1947), 49-57.

60. Samuel W. Blizzard and William F. Anderson II, *Problems in Rural-Urban Fringe Research: Conceptualization and Delineation,* Progress Report No. 89 (State College, Pennsylvania: Agricultural Experiment Station, Pennsylvania State University, November, 1952).

61. Vincent H. Whitney, "Rural-Urban People," *The American Journal of Sociology,* LIV (July, 1948), 48-54.

62. Solon T. Kimball, *The New Social Frontier: The Fringe,* Special Bulletin 360 (East Lansing, Michigan: Agricultural Experiment Station, Michigan State College, June 1949).

63. Alvin H. Scaff, "The Effect of Commuting on Participation in Community Organizations," *American Sociological Review,* XVII (April, 1952), 215-220; Walter T. Martin, "A Consideration of Differences in the Extent and Location of the Formal Associational Activities of Rural-Urban Fringe Residents," *American Sociological Review,* XVII (December, 1952), 687-694.

64. Walter T. Martin, "The Structuring of Social Relationships Engendered by Suburban Residence," *American Sociological Review,* XXI (August, 1956), 446-453.

65. Walter T. Martin, "Some Socio-Psychological Aspects of Adjustment to Residence in the Rural-Urban Fringe," *American Sociological Review,* XVIII (June, 1953), 248-253.

66. Leslie Kish, "Differentiation in Metropolitan Areas," *Ibid.,* XIX (August, 1954), 388-398.

67. Leo F. Schnore, "The Functions of Metropolitan Suburbs," *The American Journal of Sociology,* LXI (March, 1956), 453-458.

68. W. S. Robinson, "Ecological Correlations and the Behavior of Individuals," *American Sociological Review,* XV (June, 1950), 351-357.

69. Leo A. Goodman, "Ecological Regressions and Behavior of Individuals," *American Sociological Review,* XVIII (December, 1953), 663-664.

70. Otis D. Duncan & Beverley Davis, "An Alternative to Ecological Correlation," *Ibid.,* 665-666.

71. Julius Jahn, Calvin Schmid & Clarence Schrag, "The Measurement of Ecological Segregation," *Ibid.,* XII (June, 1947), 293-303; Richard Hornseth, "A Note on 'The Measurement of Ecological Segregation,' by Julius Jahn, Calvin Schmid & Clarence Schrag," *Ibid.,* XII (October, 1947), 603-604; Julius Jahn, Calvin Schmid & Clarence Schrag, "Rejoinder to Dr. Hornseth's Note on 'The Measurement of

Ecological Segregation,' " *Ibid.*, XIII (April, 1948), 216-217; Josephine Williams, "Another Commentary on So-Called Segregation Indices," *Ibid.*, XIII (June, 1948), 298-304; Shevky & Williams, *op. cit.*, 33-35; Donald O. Cowgill & Mary S. Cowgill, "An Index of Segregation Based on Block Statistics," *Ibid.*, XVI (December, 1951), 825-831; Bell, *op. cit.*

72. Otis D. Duncan and Beverly Duncan, "A Methodological Analysis of Segregation Indexes," *American Sociological Review*, XX (April, 1955), 210-217.

73. Joel Smith, "A Method for the Classification of Areas on the Basis of Demographically Homogeneous Populations," *Ibid.*, XIX (April, 1954) 201-207; William H. Form, Joel Smith, Gregory P. Stone, and James Cowhig, "The Compatibility of Alternative Approaches to the Delimitation of Urban Sub-Areas," *Ibid.*, XIX (August, 1954), 434-440; Donald J. Bogue, "An Outline of the Complete System of Economic Areas," *The American Journal of Sociology*, LX (September, 1954), 136-139.

74. Isard, Kavesh, and Kuenne, *op. cit.*; George K. Zipf, "The Hypothesis of the Minimum Equation as a Unifying Social Principle: with Attempted Synthesis," *American Sociological Review*, XII (December, 1947), 627-650.

75. Walter Isard and Robert Kavesh, "Economic Structural Interrelations of Metropolitan Regions," *The American Journal of Sociology*, LX (September, 1954), 152-162; George K. Zipf, "The P_1P_2/D Hypothesis: On the Intercity Movement of Persons," *American Sociological Review*, XI (December, 1946), 677-686.

76. Hawley, "Discussion," *op. cit.*, 156.

77. Walter Firey, "Residential Sectors Re-examined," *The Appraisal Journal*, XVIII (October, 1950), 453.

RURAL SOCIOLOGY

J. Allan Beegle
and
Charles P. Loomis
Michigan State University

The growth of rural sociology as a distinct branch of the parent discipline in the United States is scarcely a half century old. Sociological observations concerning rural phenomena have been made from the viewpoint of numerous non-sociological disciplines and many scholars have made substantial contributions to rural sociology who are not considered primarily rural sociologists. *The Systematic Source Book in Rural Sociology,* for example, supplies ample evidence of interest in peculiarly rural problems throughout recorded history. Max Weber,[1] to cite an illustration, made contributions to the analysis of rural phenomena, especially in his studies of feudalism, Polish minorities, rural Russian social structure and the German, Scotch and Celtic Village Communities, but he is now remembered primarily for his work in other areas.

Rural sociology, as it has developed in many parts of the world, is more properly a "Rural-Urban Sociology." That is, one segment or the other, is used as a base-line of comparison against which deviations may be measured. Some of the generalizations made by Ibn-Khaldun, the Arabian historian, such as, "Nomadic and rural people are more healthy, more sound, more brave, more resourceful, more self-reliant, more independent, and more stern, less immoral, less degenerate, than the urban people,"[2] exemplify the point being made. The methods, techniques and principles of rural sociology are derived from the parent discipline. However, the special problems of interest on the part of rural sociologists in different countries and at different periods of time are extremely diverse.

DEVELOPMENT OF RURAL SOCIOLOGY IN THE U. S.

The growth of rural sociology in the United States is closely related to the so-called Land-Grant College movement and is a logical part of the philosophy from which this movement came. The Land-Grant colleges were established through the Morrill Act of 1862 and today number 69 institutions. The purpose of this Act was to set aside public lands for the establishment or support of colleges and universities "to teach such branches of learning as are related to agriculture and the mechanic arts." Further federal legislation established the Agricultural Experiment Stations and the Cooperative Extension Service, thus creating the three major functions of teaching, research, and extension. Rural sociologists may be found today performing one or all of these functions in most of the Nation's Land-Grant colleges.

The human side of agriculture received little attention until 1908 when President Theodore Roosevelt appointed a Country Life Commission. The report of this Commission dealt with rural living standards, needs and desires of farm people, and marks the original outlines of the domain of investigation of rural sociology. C. J. Galpin, appointed to the faculty of the University of Wisconsin in 1911, is generally conceded to be the first rural sociologist attached to a university. His research into the social organization of Walworth County and published under the title, "The Anatomy of the Rural Community" in 1915, represents one of the original research investigations in rural sociology. Sufficient interest in rural life was manifest to warrant the establishment of the section on rural sociology in the American Sociological Society in 1917.

In 1919, shortly after World War I, the Bureau of Agricultural Economics of the United States Department of Agriculture, was created. One of the Bureau's units, the Farm Life Studies Division, headed by C. J. Galpin, represented the federal organization interested in rural sociological research. The financial implementation of rural sociological research in the states, however, awaited the passage of the Purnell Act in 1925. In this Act, monies were set aside for research in home economics, agricultural economics, marketing, and rural sociology.

Rural sociology, the review "devoted to the scientific study of rural life," was established in 1936. Shortly thereafter the Rural Sociological Society was formed. In addition to performing teaching, research and extension functions, rural sociologists, particularly in the last decade, have been employed as specialists in rural life abroad.

RURAL SOCIAL SYSTEMS AND CONSTITUENT ELEMENTS[3]

The subject matter of rural sociology consists of the investigation and analysis of rural social systems and of the elements of which these systems are composed. A concrete social system is an interactive social structure such as a family, a *kibbutz,* an *ejido,* or a farmers' coopera-tive. Members of such structures interact more with members than non-members when that structure is operating to meet its objectives. Thus, the concrete social system is a functioning, interactive entity composed of inter-related parts or elements. Social systems may also be regarded as abstract units, or ones in which patterns of interactive relationship prevail from generation to generation and from area to area.

In any interactive social system, the following elements may legit-imately be the concern of the rural sociologists: (1) ends or objectives, (2) norms, (3) status-roles, (4) power, (5) social rank, (6) sanctions (7) facilities and (8) territoriality.

Ends or Objectives. Whether or not ends or objectives are explicitly stated, all social systems possess such goals. Ends and objectives may be regarded as those changes (or perhaps the maintenance of the *status quo*) which members of the system expect to acomplish through the operation of the system. Clearly, ends and objectives are closely inter-related with other elements of social systems. The ends and objectives of a farmers' cooperative, for example, may be that of performing services that would be impossible for an individual and that of maxi-mizing monetary returns.

Norms. The rules or guiding principles which prescribe that which is acceptable or unacceptable may be regarded as the norms of a system. Norms may be considered the rules governing the operation of a social system, and thus establish the expectancy patterns in a social system. Not only are written rules, regulations, laws, and con-stitutions sources of norms, but also the unwritten standards deter-mining that which is right and acceptable in given situations. In a rural baseball club, for example, the norms include those rules of conduct prescribed by the rule-book as well as commonly accepted rules constituting "fair play."

Status-roles. By status-role is meant that which is expected in a given status or position. This concept stresses the expectancy patterns of a position, divorced as completely as possible from the personality or psychological character of the occupant of that position. As a part of the father's status-role in most rural areas of the United States, for example, he is expected to perform the heavy work in the fields, take care of the machinery, and make needed repairs around the farm. The mother's status-role includes the preparation of meals, canning and preserving, and the primary care of young children. In most rural areas in America, extreme surprise would be evoked if these status-roles were to be regularly reversed. Community norms define these expectancy patterns and sanctions are applied in instances of continuous violation.

Power. Power, an element of all social systems, may be regarded as control over others. At least two components may be segregated, namely authority and influence. Authority may be regarded as the right to control others as bestowed by the members of a social system. Thus, authority may be considered that form of power emanating from a given social-role. Influence, on the other hand, may be regarded as the right to control others based upon non-authoritative sources, such as human relations skills, wealth, superior knowledge, and other special abilities. The Grange, one of the major American farm organizations, viewed as a social system, is organized into a complete and specified set of status-roles, including "master" and "lecturer." The master, by virtue of his status-role exercises authority in the form of conducting meetings and appointing committees. The lecturer, exercises authority in the form of organizing and conducting educational programs. Influence and the degree of influence exerted by the master or lecturer depend upon personal abilities, human relations skills, and a whole host of related factors.

Social Rank. Within social systems, social rank refers to the relative ranking or position of members, based upon consensus as to what is to be rated high or low. In most concrete situations, the social rank of an individual is not unrelated to his power both in and outside the system as well as such attributes as wealth, personal appearance and morals. In James West's study of Plainville,[4] a rural community located between the Corn and Cotton Belts, the following were found to be most useful in determining social rank: (1) Location, that is, residence in hilly or prairie lands; (2) Technology, that is, the extent of mech-

anization; (3) Lineage, or relationship to the early settlers as opposed
to newcomers; (4) Wealth; and (5) Morals and manners.

Sanctions. Sanctions are considered those satisfactions giving or depriving mechanisms at the disposal of a social system. They represent
the rewards and punishments available to the system which induce
compliance with the ends and norms of the system. The embodiment
of the ends and norms on the part of an individual member of a
given social system often leads to rewards in the form of prestige,
immunity from authority, election to esteemed position and wealth.
Violation of the ends and norms of the system brings penalties of
varying intensity. To the Amish boy who surreptitiously attends a
motion picture, only mild sanctions may be invoked by the community, to the adult Amish farmer who purchases a truck, tractor and
electrifies his home, however, powerful sanctions, shunning or even
banishment from the community, will be brought to bear.

Facilities. Facilities are to be regarded as those means utilized by
a social system in order to attain its ends. Facilities may consist of
material properties and equipment but they may also comprise ideas,
skills, symbols, and trademarks. The farm home, barns and other
real estate involved in the farm operations, the livestock and those
items used by the family in achieving its objectives, illustrate facilities.
The academic discipline of Farm Management specializes in the analyses of the application of facilities in the achievement of productive
goals. Facilities are important for rural sociology especially as they
are included in the level of living of the farmer and as they affect
social rank.

Territoriality. Finally, the spatial arrangements and requirements
of a social system are considered territoriality. All social systems
possess spatial attributes which can play an important part in the
functioning of the system. Numerous studies, for example, have shown
the close connection of success of action programs in rural areas
and the choice of meeting place in relation to rural locality group
structure.

No claim is made by the writers, that the categories listed above
are mutually exclusive, nor that they represent a complete identification of the significant elements of social systems. The writers, however,
believe that they are essential to at least an elementary understanding
of social systems. Furthermore, in themselves they constitute categories
for investigation by those interested in sociology and rural sociology.

We now turn to the subject matter with which rural sociologists concern themselves. The writers have arbitrarily chosen to organize the content of the field of rural sociology around selected rural social systems. These may be categorized as follows: (1) Rural Family Systems; (2) Rural Informal Systems; (3) Rural Ecological Systems; (4) Rural Hierarchical Systems; and (5) Rural Systems Centering upon Religion, Education, and Government.

RURAL FAMILY SYSTEMS

As one of the most primary of groups and structures, rural sociologists have shown enormous interest in the rural family, its structure, function and value orientation. Although the family unit is given great importance in social sciences generally, family interaction, family structure, and other relationships bearing upon the family system is central to many rural sociological researches. That the rural family is a "work unit," generally more isolated and more solitary than the non-rural family, in part at least, is responsible for the rural sociologists' interest. The form of the family is highly variable despite its universality. The status roles, power, and social rank attached to the roles, on the part of family members not only change with time but are specific to a particular rural culture. The status roles of the children, although more often defined to include work in rural than in non-rural families, are by no means identical in all rural cultures. The norms governing acceptable relationships between family members, who should marry, sex composition of the parental core, and size of family are all specific to a particular rural culture. The most universal of the norms is the incest taboo which is closely related to the integration of the family.

Growing from such variations in the form of the rural family are a series of classifications and typologies utilized by rural sociologists.

One such typology—polygyny, polyandry, and monogamy—categorizes families in regard to the composition of the adult members and the nature of the norms prescribing who may marry. Another illustration is Le Play's classification of families[5] into: (1) the patriarchial family (2) the stem family and (3) the unstable family. The patriarchal type is characteristic of rural areas. It is characterized by stability, adherence to tradition, and "extended" in that married children are established either as a part of the parental household or in the immediate vicinity. The unstable family possesses little attachment to the parental household and provides little resistance to change. This family comes into existence with the marriage tie, increases in size as children are born, decreases in size when the children leave home, and finally passes out of existence when the original pair dies. The stem type possesses attributes of the other two types, and is characteristic of areas in which rural-urban migration is extensive and where primogeniture is common. Some elements of patriarchal type families are preserved through the transfer of property to a portion of the family. The remainder of the family members must seek employment elsewhere, often in the urban areas, and they may remain in more or less close contact with relatives living on the family lands.

Consanguine and conjugal family types[6] is another classification of family systems utilized by rural sociologists. The consanguine type, consisting of a number of blood relatives surrounded by a number of married persons and their children, is often used to describe features of some rural cultures. The conjugal type, a family form consisting of married persons and their children, is often used to describe features of some urban cultures. In the first type, authority and relatively high rank is more often vested in a line of succession; while in the latter, authority is vested in the conjugal pair.

The nature of family functions, the extent to which these functions are fulfilled and the extent of differences with urban families are common themes in the work of rural sociologists. There is widespread consensus in the literature that the rural family performs its functions more effectively than the urban family.[7] In regard to the functions of reproduction, differentials between rural and urban areas, and size and composition of rural households, a large literature has developed. Other family functions, such as the care and protection of young and aged, and recreation, are thoroughly treated by rural sociologists.

The functions of providing an arena for socialization and the preparation for the status-roles and social rank of the general society, however, are newer ideas and are now beginning to command attention in research. In most cultures and perhaps more so in primarily rural cultures, the family is the most important source of affection and love for the child. Such relations appear to provide an ideal atmosphere in which all learning may occur, particularly the internalization of the culture, the constituent social systems, and elements such as status-roles, norms, ends and objectives.

In the studies made by rural sociologists abroad the family system has rarely been ignored. At least a general description of the rural family is to be found in such works as those concerning rural Argentina, Mexico, Brazil, Cuba, and Bolivia.[8] In the Rural Life Studies,[9] among the most representative work of rural sociologists in the United States, analysis of the farm family situation is prominent. Illustrative of the attention paid the family system is the following quotation from Leonard and Loomis:

> The role of the woman has always been a subordinate one in the Spanish culture. Her role is definite, and despite its subordinate nature is one of extreme importance in the stability and integration of the group. It is a much more restricted one than that of the man. A woman is expected to be faithful to the teachings and practices of the church. In doing this she may make up for some of the negligence of the husband. Her principal function is to produce children. Her interests are centered in the family and the home. She receives neither encouragement nor appreciation for participation outside this limited sphere. If she follows these rules of conduct she will have been successful in her role in the village. Failing in any one she will have incurred the serious displeasure of the group. It is rarely that she dares risk stepping out of the role prescribed for her. To do so might mean ostracism from the social life of the women folk. This is no easy punishment to bear when visiting and conversation with other women offer the only release from the drab routine of housework and child care.[10]

Four major interests or themes related to the rural family system, particularly by American rural sociologists, seem dominant. These are: family description as a part of rural community studies; rural family levels of living; rural family size and composition; and rural family life cycle analysis in relation to economic correlates.

The rural community studies published by the Agricultural Experiment Stations almost invariably represent an attempt to describe social life, including family life, in a selected area. Such purely descriptive studies are becoming increasingly rare.

Historically, one of the chief concerns of rural sociologists in America has been the improvement of the material level of living of farm families. Studies of living levels and the creation of indexes of level of living are still important interests, although the orientation of improvement no longer looms large. Recently, problems of low income farmers and farm areas are gaining the attention of rural sociologists.

A major special interest relating to the family system, is in differential fertility and mortality, population change, migration, family size and composition. Evidence of the demographic emphasis by rural sociologists is found in an examination of the *Rural Sociology* journal as well as in the textbooks in the field.

Family life cycle analysis, epecially as related to economic well-being of rural families is notable in the literature of rural sociologists relating to the family. The relation of life cycle to interaction patterns and family solidarity, to expansion and contraction of the enterprise, and to urban life cycle stages are important emphases.

RURAL INFORMAL SYSTEMS

Rural sociologists were late in recognizing the reality and important function of informal groups. In isolating units of observation, rural sociologists characteristically viewed the family as the most primary, solitary, and elemental, with the locality group—the neighborhood or village—as ranking nearest the family in these respects. Regardless of the reason for their neglect until recently, rural sociologists are now recognizing the role of the informal group, particularly with respect to success and failure of action programs and in the process of diffusion of new ideas.

Among the functions of informal systems, rural sociologists generally concede the following to be the most significant. First, since the informal group ranks next to the family in degree of intimacy, it is an important agency of socialization and attitude formation. Second, the network of informal relations represents a system of communication through which news and information passes readily. Finally, decision-making powers often reside in small, informal groups rather than in the formal structures.

The most frequently used method of determining informal groupings is through a questionnaire known as the "sociometric test." The population being studied is asked to respond to questions designed to reveal its interaction patterns. Informants may, for instance, list other persons with whom they visit most frequently. Certain control information such as age, sex, income, etc., is also secured. These data are then analyzed and eventually depicted visually in a "sociogram."

Rural sociologists are becoming increasingly interested in informal systems in relation to the problems faced by action agents in rural areas. Those interested in the analysis of power almost inevitably became concerned with informal networks of interrelations. Furthermore, in the problem of communication and diffusion of new ideas (a classic problem for the Agricultural Extension Service in the U. S.), recent research points to the crucial role played by informal groups of friends and neighbors in the decision to accept new practices.[11]

RURAL ECOLOGICAL SYSTEMS

Among the oldest and most persistent interests of rural sociologists is in questions concerning the mode of distribution of farmers on the land. Interest in rural ecological systems may be categorized into those concerned with: (1) patterns of settlement on the land; (2) "natural" groupings, including the rural community; and (3) systems of land division.

Patterns of Settlement on the Land. Investigations concerning patterns of settlement, particularly in France, England, and Germany,[12] represent the most basic work done in this area. Basically, there are two types of settlement patterns, with a number of special cases falling under each type. These types are: group settlement, usually referred to as the village pattern; and dispersed settlement, in which rural families are separated spatially from one another. Demangeon[13] further classifies grouped settlements into the following: (1) The village with rotation of fields (of ancient origin); (2) the village with contiguous fields (of most recent origin associated with colonization of lands); and (3) the village separated from its fields. He further classifies dispersed settlements into four types differentiated essentially by the date of colonization or of agricultural evolution in which they appeared.

In America, settlement patterns on the land are considered by rural sociologists to be of three types. According to Smith and others,[14] these types include the village form, the single farmstead form, and the line village form. The latter, it must be noted, is simply a special case of the village type. While a discussion of the advantages and disadvantages of the various forms of settlement is almost invariably allotted space in the textbooks on rural sociology, only a few research investigations in this area have been undertaken, at least in the United States. The explanation is probably to be found in the fact that American rural areas, except for some of the Mormon areas and for areas in which the French and Spanish influence have been felt, are characterized by the dispersed, or single farmstead form of settlement.

There is some evidence from American research studies that dispersed settlement, maximized by Homestead laws and land surveys, is in the process of weakening. There is a tendency for farmsteads to be located near to main roads and crossroads, within reasonable distance of neighbors. Contrariwise the Mormon, French and Spanish village communities seem to be dispersing. Other research concerning patterns of settlement has been concerned primarily with cost of providing various types of services under different settlement forms.

Natural Groupings, including the Rural Community. Rural sociological literature in this country is replete with studies of the following categories of rural locality groups: neighborhoods; communities; and regions and other homogeneous areas. The neighborhood, the smallest of the locality groups, is generally regarded to be a clustering of families in restricted space and in which frequent interaction, usually described by local participants as "neighboring," occurs. The community, a larger spatial group, is generally considered that unit within which members carry on most of their day to day activities in meeting common needs. A common distinction, in addition to that of size, is that rural neighborhoods possess incomplete services while rural communities possess relatively complete services. Regions or homogeneous areas are generally considered to be those large geographic areas characterized by a degree of homogenity with respect to a series of indexes. Thus, cultural areas, economic areas, type-of-farming areas are common in the literature.

Several methods of delineating the boundaries of communities[15] have developed by rural sociologists. The best example is the "trade and service center" method which involves an identification of the geographic limits outside a center for a series of services.

In America, there is considerable evidence that the neighborhood as a meaningful and influential group in the lives of rural people is disappearing. Various mutual-aid activities such as the exchange of work, cooperative butchering, and local apple butter boils, have virtually disappeared. With increasing commercialization, specialization and improved transportation, the larger trade-centered community appears to be commanding the allegiance of farm people. Such phenomena as the cross-roads store, the open-country church, and other foci of local identification are disappearing from the neighborhood and rapidly becoming a part of the services of larger centers.

Three types of regions or homogeneous areas have been of special utility to rural sociologists. These include cultural areas, type of farming areas and rural problem areas. In most homogeneous area delineations, nationally distributed variables for county units are utilized and the social reality of the areas derived is open to serious question. Following the work of Lively, for example, Mangus[16] used the following variables in his rural cultural delineation of the United States: (1) plane of living index; (2) fertility ratio; (3) percent of farms producing less than $1000 gross income; (4) percent of tenancy; (5) land value per capita of farm population; (6) percent of rural families residing on farms; and (7) percent of farm produce consumed on farms. Type-of-farming areas,[17] delineated in much the same way, are widely used in analyses made by rural sociologists. Problem areas,[18] usually defined in terms of low-income and level-of-living, have recently commanded the attention of rural sociologists. These areas, defined ordinarily in terms of groupings of counties, possess little or accidental status as social systems.

Sytems of Land Division. Closely related to patterns of settlement as well as locality groupings in rural areas is the mode of dividing and distributing farm lands. Due to the belief that the mode of dividing lands has an impact upon ecological and social relations, interest is evidenced in this area by rural sociologists.[19] Except for theoretical alternatives, the major systems of land division are: (1) the indiscriminate location system with natural objects such as trees, rivers, and rocks used in demarcating boundaries; (2) river-front system, with rivers and streams furnishing the base of survey; and (3) the rectangular system, based upon the meridians. The indiscriminate location system, generally without plan, has the disadvantage of being both indeterminate and impermanent. In these respects, the river-front system is an improvement while the rectangular system is both permanent and determinant. The rectangular system, as applied in the United States, however, fostered the dispersed form of land settlement.

RURAL HIERARCHIAL SYSTEMS

In all rural societies, differences in social rank or standing is exhibited by the constituent groups and individuals. Such differences are based upon standards that have their roots in the values of a given society. These standards form the basis for evaluation and for the hierarchial system into which various social groups find their places. Numerous factors are important in the determination of social rank but the following seem to be of special significance: (1) the possession of wealth or property; (2) relation to a family; (3) possession of power; (4) personal abilities and achievement; and (5) acceptance of the values of the social system.

Rural sociologists have a long-standing and continuous interest in questions related to social rank in rural areas. Among the dominant problems of concern to rural sociologists are the following: Tenancy as related to hierarchical differences; size of land holdings as related to hierarchial arrangements; and the description and analysis of social classes in rural areas.

Tenancy and Hierarchial Arrangements. The nature and extent of property rights in land have been exceedingly variable in time and space. The greater the rights in land and the greater the decision-making power over how that land may be used, however, the greater is prestige and social-rank likely to be. Particularly in peasant cultures and in the western nations generally, owners probably possess higher social rank than tenants while hired workers possess lower social rank than the owners or tenants.

For the United States, Smith proposes a classification of farmers according to tenure, based chiefly upon a separation of farm operators from farm laborers. Hence, his classification represents an attempt to set up groups according to the extent to which the farmer is able to exercise entrepreneurial functions. Smith's classification follows:[20]

I. Farm Operators
   a. Owners and part owners
   b. Managers
   c. Renters
      1. Cash
      2. Standing
      3. Share
II. Farm Laborers
   a. "Share Tenants"
   b. Sharecroppers
   c. Wage hands
   d. Unpaid family laborers

The farm operators, or those exercising the entrepreneurial functions, are of three main types. First, are the farm owners and part-owners, or those who retain title to the land farmed. Second, are the managers or those employed for the purpose of exercising managerial functions. Obviously, absentee landlords, whether they are individuals, corporations, industries, banks or other owners, represent the main users of the services of farm managers. Third are the renters, or those who contract with the owner for the right to use land. Within this group of renters, three types are distinguished. The cash renter is one who exchanges cash for the right to use land; the standing renter is one who pays a specified part of the crop. The laborer classes include "share tenants," sharecroppers, wage hands and unpaid family workers. In addition to the last two categories of farm laborers which are self-explanatory, Smith distinguishes the "share tenant" who receives a larger share of the crop due to his contribution of some machinery and horsepower over and above his personal labor, from the sharecropper who does not make this extra contribution.

While the classification just outlined has special relevance to the American tenure conditions, it is not without applicability in other parts of the world. The fundamental types of land proprietorship as outlined in the *Source Book in Rural Sociology*[21] are more encompassing in space and time. In this scheme owners are distinguished from non-owners. Owners are either individual (or family) and collective (village community or any corporate body). Non-owners, in turn, are either tenants or laborers and employees. Each of these groups may possess either an individual or a collective landlord.

While an extensive literature concerning these types and their social concomitants exists,[22] relatively little has been the work of rural sociologists. Rural sociologists in the United States have been concerned almost exclusively with tenant groups and often find themselves advocating the small, family-sized, family-owned farm as the ideal.

Size and Hierarchial Arrangements. Size of farm enterprise coupled with tenancy as related to class structure is an interest of long-standing on the part of rural sociologists. Despite an enormous range existing between countries, type of farming areas and stage of social and economic development, typologies in use generally attempt to distinguish three size categories, representing "small," "medium," and "large." The small size class, sometimes referred to as "minifundia" includes farms large enough to provide bare subsistence or less for the occupant family. The medium size class, well exemplified by the "family-sized" farm[23] in the United States, includes those farms large enough to occupy family members fully at farm work, with the possibility of hiring some labor during peak work seasons. The large size class, referred to as latifundia, corporation farmers, plantations, *haciendas*, etc., is a type requiring the labor of many.

Rural Social Classes. The delineation and description of broad classes or estates in rural areas is increasingly basic to the work of rural sociologists. The more recent literature contains many examples of rural social class studies. Two examples of observation and research into rural social classes will be cited. The first is a study of social class in Atirro, a large-estate community and in San Juan Sur, a small farm community in Costa Rica;[24] the second is a description of social class in Mylly, Finland.[25]

Although the investigators had other objectives, the writers will emphasize the approach, the methods, and results of the comparison of social status in the two Costa Rican communities. Atirro, a hacienda or large-estate community consisted of some 65 families; San Juan Sur, a line village of small farm owners, comprised approximately 75 families.

The investigators regard social status structure to be a hierarchial arrangement of members of a social system, the basis of which is consensus on the part of members of the system. The characteristics to be rated high or low, and the relative weights of various characteristics, are rooted in the values of the system.

"Judges" selected from the different status levels and who knew all members of the community were interviewed. Each judge was asked to rank all heads of households "on the basis of the importance of the person to the community." In this manner an average rank score was obtained for the head of each household. In addition, visiting patterns were obtained for all families. The question asked to reveal the interaction patterns was simply: "which families do you visit most frequently?" Thus, an index of "prestige" as well as interaction as evidenced by visiting were obtained by the investigators.

In their observations concerning the bases of social status, the investigators enumerate four: (1) authority and power; (2) kinship relationship; (3) property holdings and wealth; and (4) personal attributes and achievements such as age, sex, beauty, skill and ability. In Atirro, the owner of the hacienda derived his social status largely from the first three criteria; in San Juan Sur, the leader of the small farm community possessed human relations skills and was a good speaker. Hence, his position came largely from the last criterion.

Based upon clusterings of ranks supplied by "judges" and cleavages in interaction, three classes were distinguished. An owner or "proprie-tory" class, consisting of four families, was distinguished from the "skilled-supervisory" class primarily because of primary identification outside Atirro. The "skilled-supervisory" class, consisting of fourteen families, is involved with management of the hacienda. In addition, the chauffeur, carpenters, and stone masons identify with and form a part of this class. The "labor" class, made up largely of unskilled workers, is the largest class present in Atirro. Interaction as reflected by visiting occurs largely within the class lines described.

While the investigators found differences in status in San Juan Sur, stratification of the type found in Atirro did not exist. The differences in rank were attributable largely to the amount of land owned and the ownership of land itself. Since the family was the central and most important social system and since most of the landless persons were related by kinship to owners in the community of San Juan Sur, no cleavages in interaction could be detected. Hence, while the in-vestigators were able to make distinctions on the basis of prestige scores, visiting relations revealed no cleavage and no strata forming classes, estates or castes.

Mylly, a commune located in south-central Finland, consists of a central village, several cross-road hamlets, and surrounding open coun-try farmers. The commune contained over 500 farms but nearly half were "nominal" farms with less than five acres of cultivated fields. As in many parts of Finland, agriculture centered around the production of hay and grain in support of dairying combined with forest work in the winter.

In present-day Mylly, social class differentiation is minimal. Amer-icans acquainted with the rural south or with the specialty-crop areas of the West Coast would certainly be impressed with the relatively slight social class distinctions found not only in Mylly but also in most areas of rural Finland. Wealth, it appears, accounts for part of the differences in social class, but it is of markedly less significance in determining class position than in rural America. Ideological con-siderations and voting behavior figure more prominently in social stratification in Mylly than in rural areas of the United States or Costa Rica.

As already pointed out, some residents of Mylly are employed out-side of agriculture. In addition, there are teachers, shopkeepers, a few professionals, the minister, and others who provide services for the farmers. Within agriculture, there are farm owners, tenants, and farm laborers. The tenant group is exceedingly small, and the distinctions among owners are not great.

The hierarchy of prestige in Mylly today appears something as follows: at the top is a small group including the minister, certain public officials, bank and factory managers, and some owners of large, old estates. Just below this group come the shopkeepers and the farmers who own substantial holdings and have resided in the commune for a considerable period. Next in order come the small and nominal farmers, and finally the farm laborers.

The prestige of the minister is still very great in Mylly, although the position bears less authority than formerly. His judgment is sought on innumerable problems, and he is repeatedly shown deference. The chairman of the commune board, by virtue of his authority in civic matters, possesses much prestige throughout the commune. Among the group of bank and factory managers, one should be mentioned in particular—the manager of the small textile factory. His prestige derives from the fact that he is an employer and that a group of displaced Karelian textile workers have looked to him for leadership. Aside from the fact that the large estates possess much land, they have long histories and are often genuine museums. If any "aristocrats" exist in Mylly, they are the owners of the large estates. Few professional persons reside in the village. The doctor, for example, lives in an adjacent commune and makes weekly trips to the village. The teachers potentially have great prestige, but it varies with length of service, age, and sex. Within the farmer group, size of holdings, length of residence, and ownership appear to be important in imparting social rank. Small farmers, part-time farmers, and farm laborers are more insecure and possess fewer amenities.

In the not too distant past, the Mylly region, as well as Finland generally, consisted of large estates (*Kartano*) and villages containing small farmers and independent workers. The large estates, reminiscent of the feudal manor, had a complex social organization. In broad outline, it was something as follows: the owner of the estate, of course, was the chief authority, but direct supervision was delegated to an overseer. There were, then, regular tenants who farmed sections of the estate and usually paid rental in the form of work on the estate and a share of the crop. Of somewhat lower status were the farm hands (*muonamies*) who were paid partly in kind for work on the estate. On most estates, there were also servants, both young boys and maids (*rengit ja piiat*). These servants were paid a yearly wage, partly in kind. Shortly before the turn of the century, it is reported servant boys received 100 marks and servant girls 50 marks a year (less than one dollar at current rate of exchange). In addition to the money wages, which today sound infinitesimally small, the boys received two coarse cotton shirts, one linen shirt, a half-wool suit, summer and winter boots, two pairs of socks, and two pairs of mittens. The maids received 15 ells of coarse cotton and 10 of linen, suit material, two pairs of leather shoes, two pounds of wool for stockings and mittens, and one-half peck of flax for their own planting. Sometimes the servant boys also had a flax field. In addition to the social groups mentioned, independent workers might live on the land of an estate, in return for which they often worked on the estate. Such craftsmen as shoemakers and tailors, although not a permanent part of the *kartano*, migrated from estate to estate. Evidence of their prestige is found in the fact that they occupied special quarters while at work on a given estate.

The villages, made up primarily of the smaller farmers, were the centers of conservatism in which the old customs and traditions were kept alive. An essential feature on the small farm even to a greater extent than on the *kartano*, were the servants, that is *rengit* and *piiat*. To a large extent, the servants were subject to the will and whim of the master, or *isanta*. As might be expected, the servants moved about from farm to farm seeking better conditions. Hiring day was in the fall at the church, and at this time contracts for the coming year were made.

Except for a few large estates, and these are much smaller today than formerly, little remains of the former social organization of Mylly. The social groups of an earlier day are remembered vividly by Mylly residents who themselves were once *rengit* or *piiat*, but otherwise, they have disappeared as elements of the social life of rural areas.

Rural Systems Centering upon Religion, Education, Occupation and Government[26]

The roles, functions, inter-relations with other rural systems, and trends with respect to rural religion, rural education, occupational organization, and rural government have always been and continue as major interests of rural sociologists. Very often the research interests in these systems, especially in America, are either rather exclusively descriptive or problem oriented. As pointed out previously, since rural sociologists often are interested in the total community, these systems necessarily enter into the analysis.

With the declining farm population and expanding size of the farmer's community in the United States, for example, rural sociologists have shown interest in the disappearance of the open-country church. They have also become interested in plans for consolidation and cooperation among denominations as means of meeting the problem. In addition, rural sociologists, often evaluate the role of religion in rural as over and against urban population.

A great deal of energy has been expended in observation and study of rural school problems. Problems of the open-country one-room school, training and salaries of rural teachers, ecological problems associated with consolidation, and curriculum as related to migration from rural areas all come within the purview of rural sociological interests.

The development of large farmers' organizations has likewise been a focus for research for rural sociology. The whole farmers' movement in the United States has brought the farmer into power politics and the arenas of organized economic action. The farmers' movement as an attempt on the part of farmers to adjust to the ever increasing dependency upon the price and market regime is a focus of study of rural sociology.[27] Likewise the activities of farmers' organizations as adult education agencies have been studied.[28] The influence of the Farm Bureau, Grange, Farmers' Union and the cooperatives through the National Council of Farmers' Cooperatives has increased over the decades.

Power relations among governmental units, the number and duplication of governmental units, and the relation of geographical units to sociological groupings are all questions that have captivated rural sociologists in America. This area of interest, at least in the United States, has not been a dominant research concern of rural sociologists. More concern has been centered upon changes in locality groupings, rural religion, education, occupational organizations and rural services generally as these are brought about by mechanization, commercialization, professionalization, specialization and improved transportation.

Territorial Changes. As the trade center or community was enlarged from that based upon the convenient "team haul" of a few dirt-road miles to the larger and more impersonal trade center community based upon the paved road and the automobile, older neighborhoods, many one- and two-room rural schools, smaller country churches, rural organization halls and smaller service units of all kinds became outmoded. If population decrease, common in many of the outlying areas, was a concomitant factor to which all these systems must adjust, they were caught between the two blades of scissors-like action: lack of members on the one hand and the trend of the larger centers to absorb the smaller.[29]

Mass Media. Not only did the improved roads and vehicles of transportation lessen the farmer's dependence upon neighborhood services but modern mass media has brought the metropolitan centers into his home. Many rural sociological studies deal with the influence of these phenomena.[30] In fact there is evidence that willingness to tolerate liberal and radical ideologies is positively correlated with the extent of travel and contact of farmers and others with the large centers. Likewise the greater the progress of farmers in the educational systems, the greater the willingness to be tolerant.[31]

Mechanization and Commercialization. Just as large-scale commercialization and industrialization have revolutionized urban life, so have the same processes changed rural life. Rural sociologists have constantly studied the changes brought about by these forces. Likewise the "explosion" of cities into the countryside and the development of the rural-urban "fringe" has received the attention of a considerable number of rural sociologists.[32]

These processes have led to a great heterogeneity of the rural populations in the newly industrialized regions. As a partial consequence of this heterogeneity rural sociologists are finding for the first time that rural suicide rates may equal or even be higher than urban rates.[33] Likewise other indices indicate that the organizations and rural social systems are undergoing important changes. More and more farmers are working at least part time in cities. Even in the last 20 years the increase in this phenomenon has been great—in 1920 approximately one eighth of all farm operators reported having worked 100 or more days off their farms—a considerable portion of which was in urban centers. By 1949 the proportion had more than doubled.

Professionalization and Specialization. Rural sociologists are concerning themselves more and more with the proliferation of agricultural specialists and agencies found throughout rural life today. The many federal and state agencies which affect the income and operation of farming are increasing. Likewise the farmer today purchases services from veterinarians, medical doctors, farm managers, lawyers and many other professionals which were not as readily available at an earlier date. Moreover, farmers are more organized and often more specialized than formerly. Various breed associations, special product organizations, are important organizations and in some instances enter the economic arena to determine price. More frequently they exert pressure on the legislature for increased support of agricultural research and extension. These special organizations in some states may be as influential as the larger general farmers' organizations.

Farmers are better trained for their farming operations than formerly. The number of students of vocational agriculture in the high schools of the United States increased from 31,000 in 1920 to 765,000 in 1950. Whereas there were only 2,405 students enrolled in colleges of agriculture in 1903, in 1951 slightly more than 10,400 bachelor's degrees were earned in agriculture and animal husbandry. Also 1300 masters degrees and 362 doctor's degrees were earned in these fields in a single year in 1951. In both farming itself and the systems and organizations which support agriculture, standards of training and specialization are ever on the increase. Rural sociologists are continually exploring the consequence of these developments.[34]

SELECTED BIBLIOGRAPHY

C. J. Galpin, *The Social Anatomy of an Agricultural Community* (Madison: Wisconsin Agr. Expt. Sta. Bull. 34, 1915). One of the earliest studies of a rural community made by one of the pioneers in rural sociology.

J. H. Kolb and E. deS. Brunner, *A Study of Rural Society* (Boston: Houghton-Mifflin, 1952). A textbook in rural sociology that stresses rural social organization, recent developments, and trends.

Paul H. Landis, *Rural Life in Process* (New York: McGraw-Hill, 1948). A textbook devoted to analysis of the structure and dynamics of rural life.

Charles P. Loomis and J. Allan Beegle, *Rural Social Systems* (New York: Prentice-Hall, 1950). An advanced text utilizing a theoretical framework in the analysis of social system components of rural society.

Charles P. Loomis and J. Allan Beegle, *Rural Sociology: The Strategy of Change* (New York: Prentice-Hall, 1957). A more elementary text stressing the processes of guided change in rural societies.

Charles P. Loomis and J. Allan Beegle, Editors, *Rural Social Systems and Adult Education* (East Lansing: Michigan State University Press, 1953). A research study of the major rural systems with respect to activities in the field of adult education.

Lowry Nelson, *Rural Sociology* (New York: American Book Co., 1948). This text emphasizes rural social institutions and various forms of social interaction.

Rural Life Studies, Culture of a Contemporary Community (Washington: United States Department of Agriculture). A series of six research monographs on selected rural communities of the United States.

T. Lynn Smith, *The Sociology of Rural Life* (New York: Harper, 1953). A text emphasizing demographic composition, settlement patterns, and systems of land division of rural society.

P. A. Sorokin, C. C. Zimmerman, and C. J. Galpin, *A Systematic Source Book in Rural Sociology* (Minneapolis: University of Minnesota Press, 1930. Three volumes). An historical source book containing materials from many periods and cultures.

P. A. Sorokin and C. C. Zimmerman, *Principles of Rural-Urban Sociology* (New York: Henry Holt, 1929). An early volume stressing rural-urban comparisons.

Carl C. Taylor and others, *Rural Life in the United States* (New York: Alfred A. Knopf, 1949). A text written by numerous experts and containing an emphasis upon the major types of farming areas in the United States.

Nathan Whetten, *Rural Mexico* (University of Chicago Press, 1948).

J. Allan Beegle (born September 13, 1918 near Bedford, Pennsylvania), attended the local high school and took his undergraduate degree at the Pennsylvania State University in 1939. His Masters degree in rural sociology is from Iowa State College and his Ph.D. degree in rural sociology and demography is from Louisiana State University (1946); now Professor of Sociology and Anthropology at Michigan State University. Among his publications are three books, published in collaboration with Dr. C. P. Loomis: *Rural Social Systems* (1950); *Rural Social Systems and Adult Education* (1953); and *Rural Sociology: The Strategy of Change* (1957); is also author of numerous journal articles and Experiment Station Bulletins in rural sociology and population.

(For *curriculum vitae* of Charles P. Loomis, see pp. 579-80.)

NOTES

1. Cf. Paul Honigsheim, "Max Weber as Rural Sociologist," *Rural Sociology*, XI (1946), 207-218.

2. P. A. Sorokin, C. C. Zimmerman and C. J. Galpin, *A Systematic Source Book in Rural Sociology*, Vol. 1, (Minneapolis: University of Minnesota Press, 1930), 54.

3. This portion of the chapter is based upon C. P. Loomis and J. A. Beegle, *Rural Sociology: The Strategy of Change* (New York: Prentice-Hall, 1957). Due to lack of space, we have omitted an analysis of processes in programs of directed change.

4. James West, *Plainville, USA* (New York: Columbia University Press, 1945).

5. Cf. Carle C. Zimmerman and Merle E. Frampton, *Family and Society* (New York: D. Van Nostrand Co., 1936).

6. Cf. Ralph Linton, *The Study of Man* (New York: D. Appleton-Century, 1936).

7. T. Lynn Smith, *The Sociology of Rural Life* (New York: Harper, 1953), 412-413. Smith lists the following functions: (1) the reproduction of the species; (2) the sustenance, care, and rearing of the offspring, especially during infancy and the years of complete dependency; (3) the education and training of the young; (4) the induction of the new members of the race into the larger society, particularly in helping to establish their status in society's various groupings; (5) recreation; (6) protection of members from enemies and dangers, including the shielding of members from psychological isolation and (7) the care of aged and other incapacitated members and relatives. Cf. Sorokin, Zimmerman, and Galpin, Vol. II, Chapter 4, *op. cit.*

8. See for example, Carl C. Taylor, *Rural Life in Argentina* (Baton Rouge: Louisiana State University Press, 1948); Nathan L. Whetten, *Rural Mexico* (University of Chicago Press, 1948); T. Lynn Smith, *Brazil: People and Institutions* (Baton Rouge: Louisiana State University Press, 1946); Lowry Nelson, *Rural Cuba* (Minneapolis: University of Minnesota Press, 1950); and Olen Leonard, *Bolivia: Land, People, and Institutions* (Washington: Scarecrow Press, 1952).

9. *Rural Life Studies* 1-6, (Washington: United States Department of Agriculture, Bureau of Agriculture Economics). These reports are studies of six selected communities in the U. S.

10. Olen Leonard and C. P. Loomis, *Culture of A Contemporary Rural Community, El Cerrito, New Mexico* (Washington: United States Department of Agr., Bur. of Agr. Econ., 1941), 19.

11. See items in bibliography on *Sociological Research on the Diffusion and Adoption of New Farm Practices* (Lexington: Kentucky Agricultural Experiment Station, 1952); also C. P. Loomis and J. A. Beegle, *Rural Social Systems* (New York: Prentice-Hall, 1950), Chapter 5. See also Herbert Menzel and Elihu Katz, "Social Relations and Innovation in the Medical Profession: The Epidemiology of a New Drug," *Public Opinion Quarterly*, XIX, (Winter, 1955-56), and Loomis and Beegle *op. cit.* Ch. 4.

12. See especially A. Demangeon "La Geographie de l'habitat rural," *Annales de géographie*, XXXVI, (1927); A. Meitzen, *Siedlung und Agrarwesen der Westgermanen und Ostgermanen, der Kelten, Römer, Finnen und Slaven,* (Berlin: Hertz, 1895); and Frederic Seebohm, *The English Village Community* (New York: Longmans, Green, 1926).

13. *Ibid.*

14. Smith, *op. cit.*, Chapter 10, and Loomis and Beegle, *Rural Social Systems, op. cit.*, Chapter 7.

15. For more complete discussions of methods of delineation, see Loomis and Beegle, *Rural Social Systems, op. cit.*, Chapter 6; Galpin, *op. cit.*; Irwin T. Sanders and Douglas Ensminger "Alabama Rural Communities, A Study of Chilton County," (Bulletin Published Quarterly by Alabama College, XXXIII, 1940); J. F. Thaden,

"The Lansing Region and Its Tributary Town-Country Communities," (East Lansing: Mich. Agr. Ext. Ser. Bulletin 302, 1940).

16. See A. R. Magnus, *Rural Regions of the United States* (Washington: Government Printing Office, 1940). Also C. E. Lively and R. B. Almack, *A Method of Determining Rural Social Sub-Areas with Application to Ohio* (Wooster: Ohio AES Bulletin, 1938).

17. See F. F. Elliott, *Types of Farming in the United States* (Washington: Government Printing Office, 1933); Carl C. Taylor, et al., *Rural Life in the United States* (New York: Alfred Knopf, 1949, Part IV).

18. P. G. Beck and M. C. Forster, *Six Rural Problem Areas* (Washington: Federal Emergency Relief Administration, 1935) and *Development of Agriculture's Human Resources: A Report on Problems of Low Income Farmers* (Washington: United States Department of Agriculture, 1955).

19. See especially the work of Smith, *op. cit.*, Chapter 11.

20. Smith, *op. cit.*, 284.

21. *op. cit.*, 559.

22. See especially, Sir Paul Vinogradoff, *The Growth of the Manor* (London: George Allen and Unwin, 1904); Frederic Seebohm, *The English Village Community* (London: Longmans, Green, 1905); Meitzen, *op. cit.*; M. Markovich, *Die Serbische Hauskommunion* (Leipzig: Duncher and Humblot 1903); B. Brutzkuss, *Agrarentiwickelung und Agrar-revolution in Russland* (Berlin: Sack, 1925).

23. See Joseph Ackerman and Marshall Harris, *Family Farm Policy* (University of Chicago Press, 1946).

24. Charles P. Loomis, et al., *Turrialba: Social Systems and the Introduction of Change* (Glencoe: The Free Press, 1953).

25. Personal notes of J. A. Beegle made during the year 1952-53.

26. See the treatment of these systems in *Systematic Source Book in Rural Sociology, op. cit.*; and in the following textbooks in rural sociology; Loomis and Beegle, *Rural Social Systems op. cit.*, Chapters 12-19; Smith, *op. cit.*, 18-20; J. H. Kolb and E. Des. Brunner, *A Study of Rural Society* (Boston: Houghton-Mifflin, 1946), Chapters 18-21 and 25; Paul H. Landis, *Rural Life in Process* (New York: McGraw-Hill, 1948), Chapters 22-25 and Lowry Nelson, *Rural Sociology* (New York: American Book Company, 1948), Chapters 17-23.

27. Carl C. Taylor, *The Farmers' Movement 1620-1920* (New York: The American Book Company, 1953).

28. See Carl C. Taylor and Wayne C. Rohrer, "General Farmers' Organizations and Cooperatives," and Wayne C. Rohrer and Carl C. Taylor, "Adult Educational Programs or Activities of the General Farmers' Organizations and Cooperatives," in Charles P. Loomis, editor, *Rural Social Systems and Adult Education* (East Lansing: Michigan State University Press, 1953).

29. Documentation for this development is provided in Loomis and Beegle, *Rural Sociology: The Strategy of Change, op. cit.*, Chapter 2.

30. Documented in J. Allan Beegle, "Mass Media of Communication," in *Rural Social Systems and Adult Education, op cit.*, Chapter 13.

31. Samuel A. Stouffer, *Communism, Conformity, and Civil Liberties: A Cross-Section of the Nation Speaks Its Mind* (Garden City, New York: Doubleday and Company, 1955).

32. "The Rural-Urban Fringe—A Special Feature," *Rural Sociology*, XVIII, (June 1953).

33. J. Allan Beegle and Widick Schroeder, "Suicide: An Instance of High Rural Rates," *Rural Sociology*, XVIII (March 1953), 45-52.

34. For documentation of these trends see T. Wilson Longmore and Frank C. Nall, Special Agencies Within the Department of Agriculture, in *Rural Social Systems and Adult Education, op cit.,* Chapter 7, and Loomis and Beegle, *Rural Sociology: The Strategy of Change, op. cit.,* Chapter 14.

EDUCATIONAL SOCIOLOGY

Philip M. Smith
Central Michigan College

The importance of educational sociology in the United States has been enhanced by at least three significant factors. (1) Probably in no other country in the world has there been greater interest in making free public education available to the masses. (2) Americans in general have a profound faith in the value of education as the principal means of building a democratic social order. (3) In no other country has greater emphasis been placed upon raising the educational level of the people on a comprehensive scale to meet the expanding requirements stemming from rapid technological progress.

Current definitions of educational sociology seem in complete agreement in at least one respect: the school is the focal point around which most of the child's significant learning experiences revolve. Since the school is the chief formal educational agency in the lives of citizens of a democracy, the school is expected to assume a position of leadership in regard to training our youth for effective living in a changing social order.

The historical roots of educational sociology can be found in the writings of European educational philosophers of the seventeenth, eighteenth, and nineteenth centuries. These writers were concerned with questions of *what ought to be* in relation to education in order to bring about socially desirable ends in a peaceful and efficient manner. Educational sociologists have been indebted to such men as Comte, Spencer, Tarde, and Durkheim for certain of their concepts and principles.

In the United States, Ward, Small, Ross, Giddings, Cooley, and Ellwood, and Znaniecki among others, made distinctive contributions to education from the standpoint of scientific sociological analysis. Perhaps no treatise on education by an American sociologist was more influential in shaping the trend of social thinking than Lester F.

383

Ward's "Education as the Proximate Means of Progress," which was included in his *Dynamic Sociology*. But it was the publication of John Dewey's *School and Society* in 1899 that created widespread interest in the role of the school as a social institution and helped to lay the foundaton for the development of educational sociology as a separate discipline.

Pioneer studies of various social aspects of education were those of Dutton (1907), Scott (1908), O'Shea (1909), King (1912), Bett (1912), Kirkpatrick (1916), Smith (1917), Robbins (1918), Chancellor (1919), Clow (1920), Snedden (1922), Peters (1924), Groves (1925), Good (1926), Finney (1928), Payne (1928), Smith (1928), Kinneman (1932), Waller (1932), Kulp (1932), Tuttle (1934), and Beard (1937). Some of the foregoing books dealt to a much greater extent with social education and the philosophy of education than with educational sociology. The first textbook to include the term *educational sociology* in its title was Walter R. Smith's *Introduction to Educational Sociology*, published in 1917. Interest in the social functions of education increased at an accelerated pace during the period between the two world wars especially, and educational sociology developed as a separate field of study in response to demonstrated needs.[1]

DIFFERENTIAL INTERPRETATIONS OF EDUCATIONAL SOCIOLOGY

No clearly defined American "schools" of educational sociology exist in the true sense because the views of leading exponents in this field involve so much overlapping. Nevertheless, the writings of certain authors reveal distinctive emphases with respect to their interpretations of the nature, objectives, and methods of educational sociology and these emphases are likewise carried over into important areas of research.

Probably the largest single group of educational sociologists consists of educators interested in placing greater emphasis upon social values and sociological orientation in education. They tend to regard educational sociology as a branch of education which can help them to determine desirable goals and methods in relation to the educative process in a dynamic society. As successors to the social philosophers of a former generation, they do not confine their activities to armchair theorizing but engage in empirical research on occasion to achieve their objectives. A second group of educational sociologists might well be referred to as the "applied school." Certainly, this is the largest single grouping of educators and sociologists combined that is devoted to the application of sociological principles to the problems of education. According to this particular view, educational sociology as a branch of general sociology is an applied social science in the same sense that educational psychology is a branch of general psychology. A third group, sometimes known as the "functional school," stresses the importance of sociological research as the chief basis for any educational program designed to meet the social needs of children. Thus, the exponents of the functional school are primarily sociologists rather than educators, although in their activities they combine the functions of both groups.

The functional school, centered largely at New York University, was an outgrowth of the teachings of Professor E. George Payne, whom Francis J. Brown has termed "the father of educational sociology." Under the inspiring leadership of Professor Payne, this group has not confined its researches to the school but it has constantly sought to broaden the scope of its participation in research and experimentation related to a variety of community educational agencies. It has conceived of education in terms of its broader implications, so that the media of mass communication, for example, are matters of recurrent interest to investigators. The functional group does not hesitate to capitalize upon research findings in cultural anthropology, social psychology, and other fields, and it has made outstanding contributions to interracial, intercultural, and international understanding. It was Professor Payne who established the first separate department of educational sociology in the School of Education of New York University. He likewise started the *Journal of Educational Sociology* in 1927 and was largely instrumental in organizing the National Society for the Study of Educational Sociology in 1923.

A fourth group might be designated as "the sociology of education" school of educational sociology. It is composed almost exclusively of sociologists who conceive of educational sociology as a branch of general sociology whose chief concern is with sociological analyses of educational institutions. From their analyses of sociological data derived from educational agencies, adherents of this particular school aim to develop concepts and formulate hypotheses which will contribute to sociological knowledge. The "sociology of education"

approach is concerned only incidentally with the application of sociological principles to educational problems. According to this view, it is
the educational establishment in our society which can prove to be
a fruitful source of information of lasting value to sociologists in their
efforts to gain a deeper understanding of social organization, social
structure, and social processes.

THE SCOPE OF MODERN EDUCATIONAL SOCIOLOGY

One of the most frequent criticisms of educational sociology pertains to the broad subject matter areas which it today includes within its scope. Some critics contend that the boundaries of educational
sociology cannot be determined because many of the topics with which
it is concerned belong in large measure to other fields of study, such
as social psychology, for example. But this criticism loses much of its
strength when it is realized that the trend in educational sociology is
toward greater integration of all data which have a bearing upon
educational problems in an atomic age. The very fact that educational
sociology in the United States has constantly extended its horizon is
an evidence of its adaptability to changing social conditions.

The present author is of the opinion that no better index of the
scope of educational sociology during the period 1946-56 can be found
than that afforded by a content analysis of articles appearing in the
Journal of Educational Sociology during this period. Since such a procedure would be time-consuming, and is likewise precluded by space
limitations of this article, a listing of some of the topics discussed in
special issues of the journal will present a fair picture of the wide
range of interests involved. For detailed information concerning the
mode of presentation of the data, the research methods used, and the
basic conclusions, the reader is referred to the original articles cited.
To conserve space, however, only the titles of the symposia included
in special issues, together with the names of issue editors, are listed
below:

Twenty-five Years of Educating Educators (E. George Payne; Oc-
tober, 1948); *Palestine* (Abraham I. Katsh; November, 1948); *Nu-
clear Energy* (Lillian Wald Kay; January, 1949); *Three Schools
Project, Bronx* (Mira Talbot; November, 1951); *Education-Industry
Cooperation in Higher Education* (Alonzo F. Myers; January, 1952);
Japanese Education Since the War (Yuzuru Okada; September;

1952); *Workshops in Human Relations* (Harold Schiff; March, 1953); *Aid in Indigenous Cultures* (T. L. Green; April, 1953); *Social Climate as a Factor in Education* (Dan W. Dodson; November. 1953) ; *Human Relations; Community Centered Professional Training* (Rhetta M. Arter; February, 1954); *Power and Social Status* (Louis Raths; November, 1954); *Education of Puerto Rican Children in New York City* (Joseph Monserrat; December, 1954); *Some Aspects of Education for Youth in India* (Theodore Rice and Binna Ray; January, 1955); *Athletics and Education* (Charles A. Bucher; February, 1955) ; *Teacher and Administrator Roles in the Educative Process* (Wilbur B. Brookover; September 1955); *Articulation Between High School and College* (Alonzo F. Myers; January, 1956); *Management Development; A Phenomenon in Adult Education* (John H. Herder; September, 1956); *Youth as Citizens: A Study of Adolescent Self-Direction and Social Responsibility* (Franklin K. Patterson; October, 1956) .

The following list of articles appearing in the *Journal of Educational Sociology,* which were selected at random, represents a fair cross-section of topics of current interest to educational sociologists: "A Need for Change in the Secondary-School Curriculum" (Howard B. Silsbee, December, 1948); "The Public School and Religion" (Rudolph M. Binder, January, 1950); "Education and Stratification" (Richard Stephenson, September, 1951); "The Sociology of the 'Born' Teacher" (Jean D. Grambe, May, 1952) ; "Status, Power, and Educational Freedom" (Israel Kugler, May, 1952); "The Social Drama Program: A Technique of Teaching Sociology" (Arthur Katona, October, 1952); "The Place of Local History in Modern Education" (Maurice P. Moffat and Stephen G. Rich, October, 1952); "Social Class: Conceptual and Operational Significance for Education" (Theodore I. Lenn, October, 1952) ; "New Jersey Leads in the Struggle for Educational Integration" (Marian Thompson Wright, May, 1953); "Conflict Episode Analysis—A Tool for Education in Social Technology" (H. Harry Giles, May, 1953); "A Formula for the Process of Socialization" (T. R. Schaffler; October, 1953); "The Teacher in the Authority System of the Public School" (Howard S. Becker; November, 1953) ; "Group Dynamics in Education" (Lloyd and Elaine Cook; May, 1954); "Democratic Leadership and Followership in the School Program" (Theodore Bienenstock; May, 1954); "Pupil-Teacher Rapport and the Teacher's Awareness of Status Structures Within the Group" (Isadore Bogen; November, 1954); "Social Class and Education" (Louis Raths;

November, 1954) ; "Effective Workshops in Human Relations" (Richard Franklin; May, 1955); "The Structure of Roles and Role Conflict in the Teaching Situation" (J. W. Getzels and E. G. Guba, September, 1955); "The Advantages and Disadvantages of Teaching as Judged by Parents of Differing Socio-Economic Status" (William F. Anderson, Jr.; November, 1955); "Leisure Pursuits by Socio-Economic Strata" (Lawrence G. Thomas; May 1956); "Relationship Between Ability, Socio-Economic Status and Choice of Secondary School" (Vernon C. Pohlmann; May, 1956).

It should be clear from the foregoing that the scope of studies in educational sociology is not limited to school situations and that the patterns of such studies are quite diversified. Certainly, the school does not operate in a social vacuum, for it is part of the community and the society that gave it birth. Hence, educational sociology has a legitimate interest in all aspects of school and community relationships.

RECENT DEVELOPMENTS IN EDUCATIONAL SOCIOLOGY

In some respects it can be said that educational sociology in the United States has followed a pattern of development since World War II which closely parallels that of general sociology. For example, there has been a growing interest among sociologists in studies of social class, social status, social role, social stratification, social mobility, social attitudes, community and institutional power structures, public opinion and propaganda, intergroup relations, the family, and group dynamics. This interest has been reflected in published articles in the field of educational sociology, as might be expected. Again, a trend toward a closer alignment of general sociology with other sciences has been much in evidence during the past few years. Interdisciplinary cooperation in large-scale research projects at various leading universities has shown promising results, and educational sociologists are today capitalizing upon the research findings of social scientists in allied fields.

Possibly the most striking development of the past ten years has been the movement in the direction of a true "sociology of education" designed to replace the older and more utilitarian type of sociology applied to educational problems. Of much significance, moreover, has been the strong emphasis on operational research as a substitute for older research methods which placed too much dependence upon subjective factors. Quantitative analysis has increased in popularity especially among many of the younger researchers in the field who hope to find their research pattern in the physical sciences.

In a timely editorial, "Educational Sociology Through Twenty-Five Years," Professor Dan W. Dodson, of New York University, has summarized some of the changes which have resulted from the impact of sociology upon education in this country. The quotations given below describe these changes briefly.[2]

> "(1) The changes of emphases from 'teach-learn' to a concept of 'growth and development.' From the beginning of the sociological impact upon education, educators who were sociologically oriented have kept hammering away at the need to take into account the total social milieu in which and through which personality is developed. . . .
> (2) The second great impact has perhaps been the discovery and interpretation of the meaning and function of culture. . . .
> (3) The third great impact of sociology in the interim has been an understanding of the impact of social change. . . .
> (4) The fourth dimension of the impact of sociology has undoubtedly been that of the understanding of group and the group process in relation to education. . . .
> (5) The dynamic of social class in the growth and development of school children. . . .
> (6) Explosion of the myth of racial superiority. . . .
> (7) The last item which will be listed as a part of this impact upon education is that of community. . . .

Looking ahead over the next twenty-five year period, Dodson made these observations:

> "Perhaps there is the necessity for further development of an integrative approach to the disciplines as they relate to education. . . . The second trend will probably be that the leadership of schools and agencies will become more definitely directed through the use of scientific data obtained from local surveys and research. . . . In these next twenty-five years, fraught as they undoubtedly will be with an increase of communication; increased aspirations of people who are not now fully sharing in the fuller life which modern technology has made possible, the school. . . . will find itself at the swirling vortex of social change with the responsibility to give direction to the social process. Hence, educational leadership in this larger frame of

reference will find itself increasingly dependent upon the types of competencies which sociological insight provides."

In his review of developments in the "sociology of education" during the period 1945-55, Professor Neal Gross has identified the following: (1) efforts to distinguish between "sociological" problems and practical problems of education which draw upon sociological data for their solution; (2) a growing appreciation of the fact that school systems and other educational agencies offer rich opportunities for sociological analyses of a scientific nature which will be based upon research findings rather than mere speculation; and (3) critical appraisals of the quality of research in this area of study, with special reference to their theoretical and methodological adequacy. Gross observed, however, that a number of outstanding research contributions had been made during the period surveyed and that these studies suggested further possibilities for fruitful sociological analyses of educational agencies and processes in the future.[3]

RESEARCH TRENDS DURING RECENT YEARS

In 1952 Richard Conrad summarized research trends in the sociology of education for the period 1940-50.[4] Articles published in three leading journals formed the basis of his analysis. Of a total of 2,245 articles appearing in the *Journal of Educational Sociology, Journal of Educational Research,* and *American Sociological Review* combined during the period studied, 118, or 5.3 per cent, were devoted to research in the sociology of education. Averages for the three journals were 6.4 per cent, 6.8 per cent, and 2.3 per cent, respectively. Peak years for the *Journal of Educational Sociology* in this connection were 1944 (12.8 per cent), 1950 (11.9 per cent), and 1949 (10.4 per cent). For the *Journal of Educational Research* the peak ratios were in 1948 (10.5 per cent), 1950 (10 per cent), and 1941 (9 per cent). The *American Sociological Review* reached its top figure (9.3 per cent) in 1942, while in 1948 and 1949 no researches in the sociology of education were reported.

Conrad classified the various articles pertaining to research in the sociology of education in terms of four "areas" previously suggested by Brookover. These areas and the percentage of articles included in each were listed as follows: (1) "relations of the school system to other aspects of society," 32 per cent; (2) "human relations within the school," 7 per cent; (3) "relations between school and society," 8 per cent; and (4) "the impact of the school on the behavior and personality of its participants," 53 per cent.

According to Conrad's findings, the most popular sources of research data were the opinion questionnaire (44 per ccent). The remainder of the researches (19 per cent) were distributed among four other methods, including interviews and observation. The most extensive use of the opinion questionnaire was reported by the *American Sociological Review* (75 per cent), while the *Journal of Educational Sociology* made use of records most extensively (31 per cent) as compared to the other journals.

A conspicuous weakness of current research in the sociology of education lies in the failure of investigators to develop theoretical concepts and to test significant hypotheses. Conrad noted that such concepts were present in only 14 per cent of the researches reported by the three journals as a group, while only 15 per cent of the studies involved the testing of various hypotheses. The smallest percentage of concepts (4 per cent) was found in articles included in the *Journal of Educational Research* and the smallest percentage of hypotheses (6 per cent) was found in articles in the *American Sociological Review.*

An interesting compilation in this connection is the annual census of research projects published by the American Sociological Society. In comparison with most other fields of study, the proportion of researches devoted to educational sociology is small. Typical percentages for selected years are as follows: 1945, 4.9 per cent; 1946, 5.4 per cent; 1947, 4.9 per cent; 1948, 4.4 per cent; 1949, 3.5 per cent. The number of projects listed under the heading of Educational Sociology during the period 1945-49 accounted for 4.5 per cent of the total number reported.

A better long-range picture of the status of research in educational sociology is perhaps afforded by the titles of Ph.D. dissertations reported by the *American Journal of Sociology.* The present writer checked the topics covered by persons who received the doctoral degree during the period 1944-55. Of a total of 1,122 doctoral dissertations completed, 84, or 7.5 per cent, were devoted to topics which ordinarily lie within the scope of educational sociology. What may be of some significance is the fact that while 4.0 per cent of the thesis subjects for the period 1945-49 were identified with educational sociology, during the period 1950-55 the proportion rose to 8.7 per cent. The problem of determining how certain projects are to be classified, of course, presents many difficulties. With respect to topics pertaining to educational sociology much cross-referencing usually has to be done.

The nature and scope of advanced studies in the field of educational sociology are well illustrated by the titles of doctoral dissertations completed in 1953, a typical year, and which are given below. *Stereotypes of Selected White College Students concerning Negroes* (Walter Cobb, Southern California); *The Role of the Institute in the Family-Life Education Movement* (Edwin R. Hartz, Duke); *An Analysis of the Social Distance Reactions of Students from the Three Major American Mennonite Groups* (Lee R. Just, Southern California); *The Relationship of Articulatory Disorders to Marital Adjustment and Parental Permissiveness in a Selected School District of Southern California* (William Klausner, Southern California); *Formal-Informal Leadership Relations in a New England High School* (Russell Langworthy, Yale); *Social Stratification and the Educative Process: An Experimental Study in Pre-service Teacher Education* (Theodore I. Lenn, New York University); *Selection of Academic Careers* (Margaret Hart Benson Matson, Pennsylvania State University); *Attitudes of High School Seniors in a Number of Selected Communities toward Marriage, Sex, and Parenthood as Correlated with Standard of Living and Subsequent Enrollment or Nonenrollment in College* (George Raglund, Iowa); *An Empirical Test of the Efficiency of Selected Methods of Forecasting University Enrollments* (Fred J. Shanley, University of Washington); *Involvement as a Basis for Stress Analysis: A Study of High School Teachers* (Chandler Washburne, Michigan State College); *Attitudes and Responses of Southern State College Students as Related to Their Residence in Urban Communities and to Their Socioeconomic Status* (Norman F. Washburne, Washington University, St. Louis).

Included in the foregoing are studies of attitudes, social adjustment, social stratification, group dynamics, school and community, and methodology. With regard to social processes there is doubtless considerable overlapping.

Judging from the research topics selected and from the way these topics are developed, it is clear that the great majority of persons obtaining advanced degrees in educational sociology are in close contact with the school situation. Doubtlessly, they are interested primarily in professional advancement in the field of education, and they usually find their research problems, their research data, and their facilities for experimentation near at hand. As a rule, professional educators are encouraged to study problems with which they are familiar in relation to the school setting and which also seem significant in terms of their larger sociological and educational implications.

Analysis of a sample of 100 titles of doctoral dissertations in educational sociology, by the present writer, disclosed the following percentage distribution in relation to specific areas of study: (1) student and teacher adjustment, 21 per cent; (2) measurement of attitudes, 16 per cent; (3) school and community, 15 per cent; (4) social stratification, status, and role, 14 per cent; (5) school organization, curriculum, and methods of teaching, 14 per cent; (6) intergroup relations, 12 per cent; (7) leadership and group dynamics, 8 per cent. In many instances the categories listed above represented research emphases rather than clear-cut subdivisions of educational sociology. For example, the study of attitudes, the school and community, and social stratification are often essential to the understanding of intergroup relations. They are all parts of the total picture.

Since the majority of doctoral dissertations in educational sociology are produced by students specializing in education rather than in sociology, the annual listings of thesis topics in the *American Journal of Sociology* serve only as a partial index of research interest in the field. Yet this compilation does reveal something of the nature of the emphasis placed upon educational sociology by departments of sociology in graduate schools of leading universities. In this connection, the distribution of doctoral dissertations on topics readily identified with educational sociology, according to the institution granting the degree during the period 1944-55, is perhaps more interesting than significant. These figures are as follows: New York University, 8; Southern California, 7; Chicago, 6; Columbia, 5; Wisconsin, 5; Washington (St. Louis), 4; Ohio State, 4; Michigan State, 4; Yale, 3; Pittsburgh, 3; Catholic, 3. The foregoing include only those institutions reporting more than two dissertations each in this area of study.

EDUCATIONAL SOCIOLOGY AND TEACHER TRAINING

It is a matter of historical record that courses in educational sociology were developed primarily to meet the practical needs of classroom teachers and school administrators. So great is the importance of the school in American society today that the value of such courses can hardly be overestimated, despite their acknowledged shortcomings in many instances. The school, as an enormous social enterprise, supplies the facilities and offers many opportunities for the development of educational philosophies and for the testing of sociological hypotheses. Yet most of the sociological research in this particular field is carried on with the aim of increasing the effectiveness of the school as the chief educational agency in a changing society, not merely to add to scientific knowledge.

Although "educational sociology" is not necessarily the same as "sociology for teachers," general sociology that is keyed to the needs of future teachers emphasizes both the social nature of the learning process and the importance of the school as a social institution. *In effect, therefore, most of the general sociology taught to prospective teachers becomes educational sociology when once it is applied to school situations.* From their study of the views of a cumulative sample of Michigan public school teachers over a period of years, Doby and Smith found evidence to support this contention. Analysis of the statements of several hundred teachers explaining how courses in sociology had helped them in their work showed that their reports could all be classified under one or more of the following headings: (1) Knowledge of Social Background Phenomena; (2) Understanding of Children's Attitudes and Behavior; (3) Social Adjustment of the Teacher; (4) Understanding of Social Problems; (5) Training for Citizenship in a Democracy.

When given an opportunity to enumerate specific areas of sociological study which had helped them, ranked according to order of preference, the teachers did not hesitate to select "practical" topics. Based upon frequency of mention, "Problems of the School and Community ranked first in order of importance. . . . Juvenile Delinquency ranked second. . . . Problems of Intergroup Relations (or Minority Group Problems) was third. . . . Problems of the Family (or Family Life Education) was fourth. . . . and Propaganda Analysis (or Public Opinion and Propaganda) ranked fifth. . . . Almost without exception, those replying tended to appraise general sociology courses, which should be indispensable for an understanding of social processes and social institutions, in terms of their value for helping with specific 'problem' areas of study."[5]

Sociology in the Teachers Colleges. Although the majority of persons who enter the teaching profession obtain their basic training in liberal arts colleges, it is the schools of education affiliated with large universities and the state teachers colleges which generally set the educational pattern. Certainly there is conclusive evidence that graduates of teachers colleges exert an influence upon teaching methods and curricula in the public schools which is out of all proportion to their numbers. Hence, the course offerings of these institutions in sociology have more than ordinary significance from the standpoint of future teachers and of the public schools themselves.

What sociology courses are most frequently offered in our teachers colleges? What sociology courses are most often required on teaching curricula? Is there any evidence that sociology is growing in popularity as an elective subject in college and that it is being introduced into an increasing number of high schools? These are questions which are not difficult to answer in the light of available data.

To determine the nature and distribution of course offerings in sociology, Landis examined the catalogs of 162 teachers colleges for the period 1944-45.[6] As might be expected, the introductory course (Principles of Sociology) was the one most often taught, since it has no prerequisites and is itself a foundation for the advanced courses. The 162 institutions reported a total of 169 introductory courses. Next in order of frequency was "Social Problems" (total of 95 courses), followed by "Marriage and the Family" (83 courses), and "Rural Sociology" (82 courses). A total of 52 "Criminology" courses was listed. Landis observed that the average number of sociology courses offered per school ranged from 9.8 in the Southwest to 1.9 in the Middle Atlantic and New England region. The second highest average, 8.6, was found in the Midwest, while the average for all regions was 6.3. A total of 113 different course titles was recorded, a figure which would have been larger if no effort had been made to place courses with similar content under the same heading. Landis also noted that as a result of growing emphasis upon the social studies in high schools there will be demands upon the teachers colleges for more offerings in sociology. As one of his more significant conclusions, he mentioned that "if sociologists feel that they should have a part in shaping the social thinking of the next generation there is no greater field of opportunity open than that presented by the teachers colleges."[7]

In 1953 Smith conducted a questionnaire survey of a sample of 100 teachers colleges to discover whether sociology courses were playing an expanding role in the training of teachers. The great majority of respondents (74 per cent) were optimistic about the future prospects of sociology in their own institutions. Smith noted that education courses in many instances are developing sociological emphases of their own, that "the extent to which education courses use the findings of sociological researches is both significant and impressive," and that "in practice, the line of demarcation between 'education' and 'sociology' seems at times to become almost completely obliterated. . . ."[8]

Among the more specific findings were the following: (1) The courses most frequently offered, in rank order, were Principles of Sociology (or its equivalent), Social Problems, and Marriage and the Family. Such courses as Juvenile Delinquency, Race and Culture, and School and Community have been growing in popularity. (2) In about three-fourths of the colleges major emphasis is placed upon interdisciplinary social science rather than on sociology, especially at the freshman level. (3) In spite of the growing interest in sociology courses on an elective basis, on most campuses not more than from 3 to 6 semester hours credit are required on teaching curricula. Students preparing to become high school teachers are usually advised to focus their attention on history rather than on sociology in view of its greater practical value as a "teaching minor." (4) About half of the colleges stated that their chief aim in sociology courses was "preparation for effective living through a better understanding of human relations in a complex society," in contrast to only one-fourth of them which regarded "preparation of students for greater usefulness when they enter the teaching profession" as of equal importance as an objective. (5) Less than one-third of the colleges offer courses in "Educational Sociology" as such. Yet there is "a growing tendency for 'education' teachers to use sociological materials to meet specific needs in this area of study. . . . while much educational sociology is taught by sociologists in courses having a variety of titles."[9]

At this point it might be well to mention an article by Zeleny pertaining to teacher education, which was published in 1947. Zeleny emphasized the role of public school teachers in "developing new understandings of social relations among the youth of the world" in an age of technology, and he suggested that sociology occupies a strategic position in this respect. But he regarded some areas of study as more important than others for the attainment of desired objectives:

> In the opinion of the writer, there are four areas of socio-
> logical study necessary for the twentieth-century training of
> teachers, namely *principles of sociology* (preferably called social
> relations), *the community, anthropology,* and *social philosophy.*
> A teacher who masters these areas of knowledge should obtain
> not only a deep insight into the dynamic nature of all human
> societies, and a detailed understanding of social relations, cul-
> ture, and social institutions in the local community where youths
> live, grow, and finally function as adults, but also an under-
> standing of particular human relations in many primitive and
> modern cultures of the world with a perspective of the total
> meaning of world institutions and a concept of ideal social
> relationships and social organization in the world of today and
> tomorrow.[10]

The relationship between "education" and "sociology" courses in
certain institutions may need to be more clearly defined if best results
are to be attained; however, as is noted below:

> In not a few instances is there evidence that sociologists with
> traditional training at the graduate level, who have served in
> other types of institutions, seem to resent what they consider
> the intrusion of "educators" into their field. But such a dispute
> in a teachers college should, of course, prove pointless, since a
> greater degree of correlation of content seems highly desirable.
> . . . Some sociologists suggest that in certain institutions the
> educational courses with sociological content tend to become a
> mixture of disconnected topics which lack an integrating con-
> ceptual framework. . . . There is always the danger, moreover,
> of so diluting the content and quality of traditional sociology
> courses, in order to adapt them to the requirements of teaching
> curricula, that they may become of limited value to the student
> planning to do graduate work in this field. But, by and large, the
> great majority of respondents were of the opinion that sociology
> courses are being adapted to the needs of future teachers with-
> out any sacrifice of standards.[11]

TRENDS IN THE TEACHING OF EDUCATIONAL SOCIOLOGY

Educational sociology in American colleges is taught both by professors of education and of sociology, depending upon the curricular
emphasis of the particular institution involved. To some sociology
departments it seems a sort of "orphan child" whom few may really
want but whose value cannot be denied. Courses offered by depart-

ments of education often include "educational sociology" under various headings, and there is no doubt as to the popularity of their content with students.

Yet "educational sociology" as a course title is not widely used in college catalogs today, and there are at least two plausible explanations for this situation. In the first place, the term *educational sociology* bears a connotation of specialization which may seem distasteful to general education students who might otherwise be interested in enrolling for such a course—and enrollments are important. In the second place, once such a course is taken it cannot be repeated. But students can enroll in several courses covering substantially the same area of study so long as the titles and the course emphases are different, and enrollments can thus be correspondingly increased. For example, "School and Community," "Social Aspects of Education," "The Sociology of Teaching," "Sociological Foundations of Education," "School and Society," and "Social Backgrounds of Education" are course titles which may not necessarily mean the same as "Educational Sociology" because of their generally broader scope and varying emphases.

Of interest in the foregoing connection is a report by Meltzer and Manis pertaining to the proportion of sociology departments in American colleges which offer courses in Educational Sociology. Only 18, or 18 per cent, of their sample of 100 colleges listed such a course, while only one department offered as many as three or more courses in Educational Sociology.[12]

But in those institutions where educational sociology is taught (or where "sociology" is applied to the problems of education), Zeleny thinks that there is a definite responsibility for educational sociologists to help in curriculum building and with methods of teaching and learning in the schools.[13] He thus conceives of educational sociology as a *practical technology*, in marked contrast to the views of Brookover and others who prefer to think in terms of a *sociology of education* which aims to develop concepts and to test hypotheses in a sociological analysis of education.

Course Offerings in Educational Sociology. Surveys of institutions offering courses in educational sociology have revealed a fairly wide range of course titles and a lack of uniformity in subject matter areas covered. Lee found that the number of institutions with such courses had increased from 40 in 1910 to 194 in 1926 but that less than half of the teacher training institutions required educational sociology for professional preparation.[14] His questionnaire was sent out under the auspices of the National Society for the Study of Educational Sociology. Probably the most extensive study in this field during recent years was that of George S. Herrington, "Educational Sociology as a Factor in the Training of Teachers." This was an unpublished Doctor of Education dissertation, School and Education, Stanford University, 1947. The findings were summarized by Herrington in his "The Status of Educational Sociology Today," which appeared in the *Journal of Educational Sociology*, 21 (November, 1947). He obtained his data from a total of 239 teacher-training institutions which were distributed throughout the country.

Herrington, in a later paper, reported on his analysis of 49 "required and partially required courses in educational sociology in terms of requirements and prerequisites, aims, topics, activities, texts, instructors' training, and proposals for changes. . . ."[15] These 49 courses were reported by a total of 45 institutions. For teaching credentials, 15 courses in all were required, while a total of 29 courses were "optional as part of general requirement for teaching credential candidates." For this latter group, 5 courses in "Educational Sociology" were required and 19 such courses were optional. "School and Society" was required in three instances and it was optional in two instances for this same group. For the master's degree, 3 courses in Educational Sociology were required and 10 such courses were optional. Other typical course titles were "Community Action and the School," "Social Orientation of Children," "Social Education," and "The Teacher and Community Problems." Of 36 institutions reporting, 23 had no prerequisites for courses in educational sociology. Topics most often covered by these courses were "The community and the school" (30), "Pressure groups, public opinion, propaganda, and education" (17), "Education and the family" (15), "Intercultural education" (14), and "Democracy and education" (12).

The aims of educational sociology courses mentioned with greatest frequency were: "To understand the role of the school as an instrument of social progress" (13), "To understand the democratic ideology" (13), "To understand social problems" (11), "To understand relations of school and community" (10), "To use techniques of research and critical thinking" (9), "To understand relations of education and society" (8), "To understand the teacher's role in the community" (8), "To socialize the curriculum" (7), "To understand the social functions of the school" (7). Herrington noted that "almost

all of the classified objectives stress understandings and knowledge"
and that "only a few of them relate to attitudes, skills, and abilities."

With respect to the preparation of college and university teachers
of educational sociology, Herrington found that of 46 instructors'
highest degrees reported 35 were doctor's degrees, 9 were master's
degrees, and only 2 had no more than a bachelor's degree. This
finding was in marked contrast with that of Lee whose 1926
survey showed that only 62 of 161 instructors reporting had received
the doctor's degree and that only 75 of them had the master's degree.
Thus the proportion of those holding the doctor's degree in 1947
(76 per cent) was twice as high as in 1926 (38 per cent), indicating
that steady progress relative to the raising of academic standards had
been made during the intervening years. It is noteworthy that, as
in 1926, teachers of educational sociology in 1947 had "a greater
amount of training in education than in sociology or educational
sociology."

CONTRIBUTIONS OF EDUCATIONAL RESEARCH

Although the broad field of educational research in general is more
closely related to educational psychology than to educational sociology, it must be credited with valuable contributions to the latter.
The following list of articles, which appeared in more recent issues
of the *Journal of Educational Research*, should illustrate this point:

"A Comparison of Teachers' and Administrators' Opinions on Personnel Administration Practices" (Eugene W. Bowman, November,
1955) ; "A Study of the Student Drop-Out Problem at Indiana University" (Charles L. Koelsche, January, 1956); "Social Characteristics
of High School Seniors in Urban Negro High Schools in Two States"
(Benjamin F. Smith, March, 1956); "The Social-Economic Background
of Negro Youth in California" (Russell Morris, April, 1956); "Social
Relationships and the Elementary Curriculum" (Thomas D. Horn,
September, 1956) ; "School Children's Problems as Related to Parental
Factors" (Jack Rouman, October, 1956); "Effect of Cohesion and
Intelligence in the Problem Solving Efficiency of Small Face to Face
Groups in Cooperative and Competitive Situations" (Beeman N.
Phillips, October, 1956); "An Analysis of Factors Related to With-
drawal from High School Prior to Graduation" (Edward S. Cook, Jr.,
November, 1956); "A Study of the Sociometric Hierarchy of Elemen-

tary Education Majors" (Curtis L. Drawhorn, December, 1956) ; "Does Teaching Change Students' Attitudes?" (Joseph C. Lagey, December, 1956).

An excellent picture of developments is presented in the June, 1956, issue of the *Review of Educational Research,* official publication of the American Educational Research Association, which is a department of the NEA. This issue was entitled, *Twenty-five Years of Educational Research,* and Helen M. Walker was the author of Chapter VII, "Method of Research." Observing that seven entire issues of the *Review* (in 1934, 1939, 1942, 1945, 1948, 1951, and 1954) had been devoted to methodology, she noted a definite trend toward raising the level of educational research by the use of methods which had proved their value in related fields. Referring to developments since World War II, she stated:

> The fourth issue on methods of research and appraisal in education, December 1945, introduced one new topic, research design, which was retained in the issues of 1948, 1951, and 1954. It also continued to treat recent developments in statistical theory and computational technics. The December 1951 issue contained chapters acknowledging the continued importance . . . of library and documentary research, of trend and survey studies, of observational procedures, and of tests as research instruments. However, 60 per cent of its page space and 60 per cent of the references quoted were devoted to "Applications of Experimental Design and Analysis," "Recent Developments in Statistical Theory," "Computational Technics," and "Factor Analysis in Educational Research." Three years later, in December 1954, the entire issue was devoted to "Statistical Methodology in Educational Research. . . . In December 1945, 28 pages were allotted to statistics; in 1948, 43 pages; in 1951, 82 pages. In December 1954, the entire issue of 132 pages was entitled "Statistical Methodology in Educational Research." (pp. 325-326, f.)

Of more direct interest from the standpoint of educational sociology is Chapter VI, "The Historical, Philosophical, and Social Framework of Education," by William O. Stanley and B. Othanel Smith. Under the sub-headings, "The Social Function and Framework of Education" and "Sociological Studies of Education," these authors review some of the outstanding investigations in those areas which are concerned with social aspects of educational systems. Among the more significant books cited are the following: August B. Hollingshead, *Elmtown's Youth* (1949) ; Theodore Brameld, *Patterns of Educational*

Philosophy (1950); Margaret Mead, *The School in American Culture* (1951); Vivian T. Thayer, *The Attack upon the American Secular School* (1951); Harold Rugg, *The Teacher of Teachers* (1952) ; John Dewey, *Society, Educational Freedom in an Age of Anxiety* (1953); William O. Stanley, *Education and Social Integration* (1953); Margaret Fischer, *Leadership and Intelligence* (1954) ; Robin M. Williams and Margaret W. Ryan, *Schools in Transition* (1954); Melvin C. Baker, *Foundations of John Dewey's Educational Theory* (1955).

J. Cayce Morrison was Chairman, Committee on Twenty-Five Years of Educational Research, Chester W. Harris planned the special issue of June, 1956, while Tom A. Lamke is editor of the journal.

TRENDS

Interestingly enough, during the period extending from 1951 through 1956, a total of 183 projects in Educational Sociology were reported in the Census of Research taken by the American Sociological Society. The proportion of all research projects which were devoted to this field amounted to 4.5 percent during this period. While the peak ratios, 7.7 percent and 6.7 percent, were attained in 1955 and 1956, respectively, figures for these two years are not strictly comparable with those of preceding years because they included projects which were either primarily or secondarily in Educational Sociology.

Although it is difficult in some respects to differentiate between general sociology, and between social education and educational sociology, perhaps the important thing to remember is that the new sociological approach to education transcends subject matter boundary lines in making its distinctive contribution. On the other hand, the difficulties involved in defining educational sociology and in determining its proper sphere of activity have been a handicap to sociologists who would like to develop a true sociology of education which will be a theoretical science rather than an educational technology. There is abundant evidence, however, that educational sociology occupies a unique position among the social sciences and that it meets a definite need in the field of education. By bringing together both educators and sociologists in an effective working relationship, and by relying to a greater extent upon modern scientific research methods in the future, educational sociology should continue to play a leading role in American education.

SELECTED BIBLIOGRAPHY

Frederick E. Bolton, and John E. Corbally, *Educational Sociology* (New York: American Book Co., 1941). Exemplifies the "educational" rather than the "sociological" approach; its treatment of the school and allied educational agencies is designed to emphasize the importance of education for democratic living.

Wilbur B. Brookover, *A Sociology of Education* (New York: American Book Co., 1955). Aims to define the term "sociology of education" and to analyze various aspects of school systems in relation to sociological concepts and from a socialpsychological viewpoint. (The latter section of the book, "The School in the Community," was written by Orden C. Smucker and J. F. Thaden.)

Francis J. Brown, *Educational Sociology* (New York: Prentice-Hall, Inc., 1947). The keynote is "social interaction," and emphasis is placed upon the social nature of education; the school is regarded as a central agency in social interaction which is closely related to other agencies of interaction. The author conceives of educational sociology as the application of sociology to educational problems in general.

Lloyd A. Cook, and Elaine Cook, *A Sociological Approach to Education* (New York: McGraw-Hill Book Co., 1950). Originally this was to be a revision of Cook's *Community Backgrounds of Education* (1938), but it developed into a new and larger book; the emphasis is more "sociological' 'than "educational," and considerable attention is devoted to the relationships among school personnel as a reflection both of the school culture and the larger community of which the school is a part.

Neal Gross, "Sociology in Education," in Hans L. Zetterberg (editor), *Sociology in the United States of America: A Trend Report* (Paris: UNESCO, 1956), 62-67. A review of developments in the sociology of education during the period 1945-55; much useful information is contained in this short chapter and current trends are clearly depicted.

Clyde B. Moore, and William E. Cole, *Sociology in Educational Practice* (Boston: Houghton Mifflin Co., 1952). Draws freely from sociological materials in its treatment of the educational process. At the same time, it indicates the strategic role of education in social change and social progress.

Edward G. Olsen, *School and Community*, rev. ed. (New York: Prentice-Hall, Inc., 1954). The major emphasis is upon the social orientation which the community can give the school and upon the contribution which the school can make to the community through participation in community activities.

Florence Greenhoe Robbins, *Educational Sociology* (New York: Henry Holt and Co., 1953). The major portion of this book is devoted to a discussion of the process of socialization as it relates to the cultural orientation of the child. The author draws freely from a wide variety of sources for appropriate illustrative materials.

Joseph S. Roucek, and associates, *Sociological Foundations of Education* (New York: Thomas Y. Crowell Company, 1942). This textbook was the joint product of a number of collaborators who wrote selected chapters; it presents a well-balanced sociological interpretation of education in a broad sense, with the school being regarded as only one of several basic educational agencies. Strong emphasis is placed upon education as a means of social control. A helpful discussion of trends in educational sociology adds to the value of the book. Roucek's *The Development of Educational Sociology* (Bridgeport, Conn.: The Author, 1956, mimeographed) is the extension of his original article, "Some Contributions of Sociology to Education," Chapter 22, 793-832, in Harry Elmer Barnes, Howard Becker & Frances Bennett Becker, Eds., *Contemporary Social Theory* (New York: D. Appleton-Century, 1940); it is a systematic survey of the theoretical developments of the predecessors and present proponents of Educational Sociology.

Walter R. Smith, *Principles of Educational Sociology* (Boston: Houghton Mifflin, 1928). One of the earlier treatises in the field, this book exemplifies the view that Educational Sociology consists of the amplification of sociology to educational problems.

William O. Stanley; B. Othanel Smith; Kenneth D. Benne; & Archibald W. Anderson, *Social Foundations of Education* (New York: Dryden Press, 1955). A book of readings which includes some excellent source material.

Willard Waller, *The Sociology of Teaching* (New York: John Wiley, 1932). A pioneer effort to make a sociological analysis of the culture of the school; as such, the book has much to offer to teachers especially who wish to gain a better understanding of teacher roles and of teacher-student interaction.

Philip M. Smith, B.S. (Temple University), Th.B. (Princeton University), M.Ed. (Pittsburgh University), and Ph.D. (Pittsburgh University), has been Professor of Sociology (1947–) in Central Michigan College (Mt. Pleasant, Mich.). Author of many articles in the field of sociology and education, of chapters in books, and joint author (with Bernard N. Meltzer & Harry R. Doby) of the forthcoming *Readings in Educational Sociology* (to be published by T. Y. Crowell).

NOTES

1. For what is perhaps the best condensed treatment of this topic that is available, see Joseph S. Roucek's chapter on educational sociology in Harry Elmer Barnes, Howard Becker, and Frances B. Becker, *Contemporary Social Theory* (New York: D. Appleton-Century Co., 1940), 793-828.

2. Dan W. Dodson, "Educational Sociology Through Twenty-five Years," *Journal of Educational Sociology,* XXVI (September, 1952) , 2-6.

3. Neal Gross, "Sociology of Education," in Hans L. Zetterberg (editor) , *Sociology in the United States of America: A Trend Report* (Paris: UNESCO, 1956), 52-67.

Regarding the matter of definitions of educational sociology, Professor Dan W. Dodson makes an interesting comment: "I have always thought 'Sociology of the Educative Process' would be a better term than 'Educational Sociology.' We have concerned ourselves with the sociological facets of those processes by which and through which people acquire and organize their experiences, i.e., the growth and development idea." (From a letter dated November 20, 1956.)

4. Richard Conrad, "A Systematic Analysis of Current Researches in the Sociology of Education," *American Sociological Review,* XVII (June, 1952) , 350-355.

5. Harry R. Doby and Philip M. Smith, "Sociology Study as an Aid to Teachers," *Journal of Educational Sociology,* XXVII (October, 1953) , 59.

6. Judson T. Landis, "The Sociology Curriculum and Teacher Training," *American Sociological Review,* XII (February, 1947) , 113-116.

7. *Ibid.,* p. 116.

8. Philip M. Smith, "Sociology in the Teachers Colleges," *Journal of Educational Sociology,* XXIX (February, 1956) , 265-267. This article is based largely upon a paper which the author prepared for the Forty-eighth Annual Meeting of the American Sociological Society held at Berkeley, Cal., in 1953.

9. *Ibid.,* p. 267.

10. Leslie D. Zeleny, "The Place of Sociology in Teacher Education," *Sociology and Social Research,* XXXI (May-June, 1947) , 383. (This was a paper presented at the meeting of the American Sociological Society held in Chicago in December, **1946.)**

See also Zeleny's "New Directions in Educational Sociology and the Teaching of Sociology," *American Sociological Review,* 13 (June, 1948) , 336-341.

11. Philip M. Smith, *op. cit.,* p. 266.

12. Bernard N. Meltzer and Jerome G. Manis, "The Teaching of Sociology," in *The Teaching of the Social Sciences in the United States* (Paris: UNESCO, March, 1954) , p. 94.

13. Leslie D. Zeleny, *op. cit.,* pp. 337-339.

14. Harvey Lee, *The Status of Educational Sociology in Normal Schools, Teachers' Colleges, and Universities,* (New York: New York University Press Book Store, 1927) .

15. **George S. Herrington,** "An Analysis of Courses in Educational Sociology with Proposed Changes," *Journal of Educational Sociology,* XXII (December, 1948) , 259-275. Note: numbers in parentheses below refer to frequency of mention

SOCIAL PSYCHIATRY

Jiri Nehnevajsa
Columbia University

"The impact of social and cultural environment upon the development of personalities is the central problem of social psychiatry," says Marvin K. Opler in the opening sentence of his outstanding integrative volume.[1] More specifically, it is the concern with the mentally ill and the deviant which lies in the focus of the field. The classical argument pertaining to the relation of the individual to the society yielding psychologistic and sociologistic theories of behavior has been largely discarded.[2] Monofactorial approaches have given way to more complex modes of interpretation. The very meaning of causality has been redefined in the course of the past fifty years. While we think this not unrelated to the growth of nuclear physics, and of symbolic logic (especially through general semantics), perhaps the crossfertilization of researchers from various fields accounts for this even more: physicians, anthropologists, sociologists, and psychologists have gradually been evolving a framework basically common to them all—to the benefit of all. The individual functions in an environment, and by his behavior, he alters the environment. The environment is operative with respect to the individual by channelling—broadly or narrowly so—his conduct. Nor is it the environment as some metaconstruct; it is the human context and the setting of man-made cultural elements which socializes the person into a personality.

This socialization process implies that norms are formulated, or traditional norms passed on; thus the very concept of "illness," mental or otherwise, is comprehensible only through the societal system of norms. Aberrations and deviant behavior, organization and disorganization, progress and regressions, are all determined normatively. Disagreements may result over the boundaries: where to draw the "line" between health and disease is precisely one such problem. But there exists, today, no disagreement as to the underlying relation of social norms to all that man do, think, dream, and anticipate. In as much

as the norm systems differ—from time to time, and place to place—
there is little wonder that cultural relativism on one hand, and operationalism on the other hand, have been the most salient currents in
behavioral sciences.

Symbols—or rather, the communication of symbols and by symbols—
are the basic tissue in all this: individuals, and the groups they form,
depend thoroughly on symbolic interactions. "Reality" is grasped by
the means of cues which acquire their meaning from what they stand
for, or symbolize. Whether we go then asserting that sanity, no matter
how normatively defined, is a function of adequate communication
processes,[3] or whether communication is seen as the proper "matrix"
of human life, seems less important than the ramifications of either
thought:[4] communication presupposes interacting individuals, and not
individuals alone as independent entities. It has as its prerequisite the
sharing of some basic symbols which may have very concrete, and
specialized, meanings for varying individuals, but whose core must be
understood, by, at least, two persons. In this sense, interpersonal
situations, group settings, become the focal point of attention. Yet,
since individuals enter such human situations not totally but merely
in terms of systems of acts seen appropriate (by them) under the
conditions, such systems of acts, or *social roles* are the units of analysis.

BASIC MODELS IN PSYCHIATRY

The very term "social psychiatry" implies a modification of "psychiatry," a departure from former notions: universalistic models,
bio-gentic and psychologistic in character (emphasizing either the
organism, or that aspect of the organism labelled the "psyche") are
supplemented by the inclusion of the sociological and anthropological
dimensions of conduct. Cultural relativism has the effect not of dis-
posing of universalistic concepts, or need for them, but of refining
them. It asserts, at least with respect to our immediate aims in this
paper, that the interpretation of conduct is meaningful contextually.
That is, that the norms governing behavior vary culturally, and that
this variability must be referred to both temporal and spatial loci.

The sociological axis of social psychiatry does pertain to universal
traits of social systems. Among these are such considerations as the
following: in all systems, and at all times, communication processes
can be so called only when some standardization occurs, when at

least crude relations between cues and symbols are understood. Such standardization, furthermore, amounts to establishing elementary "rules of the game," mechanisms of social control. Thus norms, too, are ever present. In all societies, so far as we can determine, systems of obligations emerge consisting of clusters of acts appropriate for specific occasions: the idea of social roles is then also universal. And finally, we think it only accurate to add that such clusters of acts are comprehended as means to *ends,* and that men everywhere and at all times have goals with respect to which they orient their actions.

The underlying functionalist model—stemming from the works of anthropologists, sociologists, and psychologists (social psychologists) alike—may well provide the basic frame of reference of analysis. Concrete-cultural settings clearly lead toward refinement: social systems vary as to the manner in which goals are set, and what kinds of goals they are; they vary as to the number of social roles in which individuals function, and in the number of social roles available throughout the system; they vary as to the definiteness with which the roles are delineated; they differ as to the extent to which the roles (qua means) are appropriate for the achievement of the desired goals. And so on.

We are far from saying that the socio-cultural model has been sufficiently developed. But it is such an incipient model that gives rise to social psychiatry. The individual psychopathology is thus placed into a societal context. Jung anticipates such thinking by his notion of "collective unconscious." Adler is preoccupied with the normatively organized *Lebensstil* of individuals whose behavior he sees clearly, and consistently, goal-oriented. J. L. Moreno insists upon differentiating between the aims for which men sociate, and interact, and employs an elementary theory of social roles in his psychodramatic and sociodramatic procedures. Kurt Lewin formulates his theory of tension systems. Here, the tension system pertains to some specifiable region of the individual (or group)—that is to some specific clusters of acts —and the idea of "tension" means no more than that the referent entity (individual, group) perceives of some need, end, goal.

EPIDEMOLOGY, ETIOLOGY, AND THERAPY

Although it may be clear that fruitful analysis takes into account not only the organism, or the single individual, but an *interpersonal situation occurring in a particular socio-cultural setting,* it is not equally easy to translate such a concept into the language of social research.

Psychiatry has been particularly suited to the investigation of etiological problems. And it has employed psychodynamic concepts in the process. But by far most psychiatrists have limited themselves to the study of but a few cases certainly not taking benefit from the advancement of sampling theory, and survey techniques.

On the other hand, social surveys lend themselves easily to simple epidemological inquiries. As a result, many have been structural in undertone: reports on the incidence of illness in various classes, ethnic groups, sex, and age groups. But such studies have been of little relevance to psychiatry[5] even were it not for additional methodological difficulties.[6]

Unless the etiology of illness in particular social subsystems becomes known, the epidemological findings have, indeed, little meaning in themselves. Incidence rate (epidemology) of an illness obviously depends on *how and why* the illness occurs (etiology) in given structures. The attitudes men have toward mental illness, for instance, and how these attitudes influence detection, and even treatment and cure, remain relatively unknown.

A consistent application of socio-cultural variables increases also the comparability of results of cross-cultural studies. For instance, the occupational distribution varies society by society in numerous ways: among these, in the number of available social roles, in the number of social roles any given individual will encounter, or perform in, in the manner in which these social roles are defined (as including more or less expectations), and so on. The stresses may be locatable in distinctly different segments of the respective social system, and thus affect different groups.

The personality equation makes it further possible to distinguish, *within* social subsystems how some individuals, say some unskilled workers, manifest psychotic or neurotic symptoms and others, belonging to the same statistical groupings, do not. This depends on the extent to which the social norms are internalized in an individual, and which ones are, an issue ultimately reducible to the interpersonal setting of individuals. An "unskilled worker" who is aspiring at making some money to enter a University (who is thus psychologically mobile) cannot be expected to manifest the behavioral responses of unskilled workers whose career expectations relate to their occupational group. The idea of level of aspiration of the Lewinian field theorists applies with a forceful meaning, here as an aggravating, there as an alleviating condition. To illustrate the cross-cultural differential on the same example: if expectations of stability are associated with an otherwise "insecure" social role, insecurity will not result. The classical Hindu pattern would exemplify this. The individual aspires at upward social mobility in the next life, and he achieves it by appropriate performance of any given task in the present life.

A METHODOLOGICAL NOTE

There is agreement generally, that the needed investigations have to incorporate medical, psychological, sociological, and anthropological dimensions to be truly meaningful.[7] The psychiatrists have accumulated rather inconclusive, though both salient and interesting, case study accounts. Even when the socio-cultural context is recognized, the sociologists have provided quite a bit of epidemological data of structural character. But such findings too, are questionable from the viewpoint of interpretation of psycho- and socio-pathological processes. The anthropologists have come forth with data on careful case studies in different cultures. But integration of these three types of results is wanting as much as is the development of a theoretical model which would address itself to etiological problems and, ipso facto, help generate epidemological hypotheses.

At the same time a gap of unknown magnitude exists between the actual incidence of illness, and the occurrence ascertainable by survey tools employed up to date. Admission rates to hospitals do not tell the whole story; and, for all we know, the story they tell may be greatly distorted. Such data obscure the fact of differential attitudes toward illness, toward detection, toward treatment, and they reflect incidence but also neglect successes and failures in treatment. In many cultures, epidemological data is deflated by the relative absence of proper medical facilities—both for detection, and for treatment. We can hardly accept, as valid, the finding that military discharges for psychoneurotic disorders were perhaps, twenty times as frequent in the United States Army than they were in the Nazi Army during the last world war. For, indeed, in the former setting discharges of vulnerable soldiers were favored, whereas the Nazis were as reluctant to grant discharges as they were anxious to uncover "malingerers."

If the problem of delineating the population frames for epidemological studies were solved (by conducting field studies on community, regional levels, and laboratory experiments matching ill and healthy individuals, and so on), the psychiatrist would decidedly benefit from the accumulation of such knowledge on the distribution of disease. This especially were the symptomatic distribution taken into account systematically. Nonetheless, more progress can be expected when such researches test hypotheses derived from one, or several, overall models.

On the other hand, the psychiatrists need to reconsider, as they have been doing, their own nomenclature. Such reconsiderations must be grounded, to be fruitful, in socio-cultural theories. A broad label, such as "schizophrenia," is too undifferentiated to be meaningful. The course of any of the schizophrenias is likely affected by personality patterning, and crucial in this patterning are interpersonal relations occurring in a normatively defined social and cultural setting.

DYNAMIC CONCEPTS IN SOCIAL PSYCHIATRY

It is certainly correct to say that the designations of normalcy, and thus of deviancy, are socio-cultural. But the concept of adjustment to society does not need to coincide with the concept of "mental health." Kardiner, among others, has reported severe neurotic symptoms in individuals perceived, in their community, as normal.[8] Individuals may be caught in severe dilemmas and conflicts, yet, they may perform —at least, for a time—adequately in their overt social roles. Adjustment by "conformity" has not been seen as a stamp of health by Horney,[9] or Fromm,[10] or Riesman.[11] In his latest volume, Erich Fromm[12] not only discusses the possibility of an ailing society (where predominant norms are conducive precisely to psychoneurosis) but again emphasized that emotional problems will ensue when an individual performs satisfactorily—yet against his own desires (and thus gives up his individuality). Our society, says Fromm, is so organized as to enhance guilt feelings whether the individual remains faithful to his Self, or whether he conforms to society. Like Horney, he has seen in competitiveness—and the values it implies—the main source of the problem.[13] Ruth Benedict[14] sees the persecutors of "witches" as more disturbed than the "witches" (although the social norms were those of the persecutors). Parsons goes a long way to analyze Nazism (and its popular support) along these lines. The "normative order" of a society provides a useful framework for the analysis of mental illness if it is comprehended, itself, as a dynamic concept, and not a structural one. The norms are not entities: they emerge and reemerge through interacting of people, and are altered, in part, and reaffirmed, in part, when the obligation systems are activated by real acting people. Whenever the normative system is rigidified (generally by superimposition of some fundamentalist orientation), it becomes really fruitful to speak of "sick societies" and healthy individuals within them, rather than of "sick individuals" within healthy societies.

Similarly, structural meaning was attached usually to the idea of anomie. It came to mean poverty, population density, or some fixed process of social disorganization—for instance, a "cultural lag" stemming from the discrepancy between the rate of development of "material" and "non-material" aspects of culture. In its modern sense, anomie has become a sociodynamic notion (Robert K. Merton, David Riesman, C. Wright Mills). Industrialization, though it may be crudely indicated—for instance—by the ratio of workers in industrial occupations to the total labor force—refers to the formation of patricular interpersonal patterns (based, say, on segmental relations among individuals, on increased depersonalization of contact, and such), and to particular means-ends schemas emerging from interaction of men in the industrial setting.

In a sense, the existentialists Heidegger, Sartre, Marcel, and others, with their concepts of "anxiety," "freedom" to which men are doomed, "involvement," and "responsibility," draw merely the gloomy conclusions from premises which, to a large extent, underlie the conceptualizations of alienation and anomie in Horney, Fromm, Merton, Mead, Benedict, de Mann, and Weil.

The Lewinian theories of positive and negative valances associated with specific goal regions (in individuals, as well as groups) have been particularly salient in generating research on conflicts between two, or more, regions of positive valance, two or more regions of negative valence, and positive *and* negative loadings corresponding to a given region.[15] J. L. Moreno[16] has been concerned with the discrepancy between the desired obligation systems and the normatively prescribed ones, something both Horney and Fromm have dealt with in discussing the relation between social adjustment and personal stability.

To emphasize dynamic aspects of human conduct is not a mere fashion of the day; it stems from recognition of their importance. Opler has pointed out that the structural label "Catholics," for instance, obscures the fact that Irish, Polish, Swiss, and Czech Catholics differ greatly (for in each case, "Catholicism" enters in a different social complex of values). Among the Irish, furthermore, there may be variability with respect to "socio-economic status." And within each socioeconomic status group, variability may be reduced to psychological locomotions; some individuals believe their status to be higher than it is by some objective measure; others believe themselves socially mobile; still others identify with a different socio-economic group than the one to which they belong by an objectified classification.

GROWTH OF MODERN SOCIAL PSYCHIATRY

The psychiatric nomenclature still remains under the influence of Kraepelin. At least initially, the classifications presume rather fixed processes of illness with strong organismic leanings. It is not without interest to note that it was Adolf Meyer who popularized the nomenclature in psychiatric circles: the same scholar who stands among the forerunners of a social psychiatry firmly grounded in socio-cultural considerations. Meyer's involvement in neuropathological inquiries gives way to social psychiatry.[17] While Freudian theories come to dominate the American psychiatric scene, introduced, among others, by Brill and White, some elementary knowledge on symptomatic variability by culture is already available. In fact, Kraepelin's "unintended influences" (as Opler puts it)[18] on Meyer lead him to observe the relative rarity of melancholias on Java, and the relative frequency of symptoms of dementia praecox (of Kraepelinian definition). Others observe cultural variability. Bleuler notices different behavior in English, Irish, and Bavarian patients, Van Loon (1928) speaks of particular disorders in those Malayan women who associated with Europeans, Ziehen notices differences in incidence in Holland and Thuringia, Germany, Dhunjibhoy draws the attention of psychiatrists to regional differences in India (1930).

Psychiatry is increasingly influenced by anthropology of functionalist orientation. Anthropology, in turn, is enriched gradually by inclusion of psychiatric categories in cultural studies.[19] The mutual effects foreshadow the gradual blending of concepts. At the same time, cultural anthropologists come to warn psychiatry against oversimplifying the concept of "normalcy" by applying Western standards and definitions.

Most sociologists of the 30's—following, in fact, Spencerian and Durkheimean views (and those of Tönnies)—relate mental disorders to the concept of social disorganization.[20] They agree that the accelerated tempo of modern civilization accounts not only for the increasing rate of mental disorder, but also provides adequate etiological explanations—a point, by the way, agreed to by Freud.[21] Others argue that there has been no increase in the frequency of disorders.[22] And still other writers attribute the manifest increases in psychopathology to increasing facilities for treatment.[23]

When cultural complexity is considered along structural lines, and identified with poverty, or population density, the relation between actual disorder and heterogenity of culture can be subject to serious doubts. But the same relation is found when dynamic concepts are employed. W. Lloyd Warner, for instance, notices a tendency toward disorders among Negroes aspiring at crossing the color line.[24] Faris and Dunham in their classical report emphasize that successful interactions over a period of time (interpersonal relations, as well as relations of individuals with respect to social organizations) lead to the development of normalcy and mental health.[25] Gerard and Huston speak of a drift of individuals into specific areas,[26] Morris S. Schwartz points out that schizophrenics are downward mobile in the occupational system prior to hospitalization.[27] In his overview of the African scene, Carothers has noted not only that the incidence rates in Africa are consistently lower than those in Western Europe and in America, but also that this holds only for areas unacculturated to Western standards.[28] Shelley and Watson concluded that radically different behavior of African whites to the natives seems to account, to a large extent, for the value conflict in the native, and subsequent psychopathological developments.

Similarly, Malzberg finds consistently higher rates of disorders among (especially urban) American Negroes, and comes to speak of the dynamics of low socioeconomic status in relation to the incidence rates.[29] Social factors, and chiefly value orientation and mutual obligation systems, are called for to explain the findings.

By and large, it seems to be fruitful to say that even structural findings in social psychiatry lend themselves, at least tentatively, to dynamic reinterpretations. In this sense, the results of Faris and Dunham appear consistent with hypotheses stemming from contemporary functionalist theories. The New Haven researches locating schizophrenias with much greater frequency in lower than in upper strata of society, can be similarly translated into the language of social dynamics.[30]

This means that understanding of family attitudes, of individual expectations in the context of ethnicity and the stratification hierarchies may help to elaborate the findings rather than defy them. Thus although various students find rural rates higher than urban rates, for instance Lemert in his five year study in Michigan, such results need not be incompatible with the "cultural heterogeneity" hypotheses when it takes into account the relevant value orientations, the types and intensities of interpersonal contacts, the manner in which social roles are designated and defined.

The weakness of such reinterpretations is obvious: etiological statements are made, so to speak, ex post facto, and on the basis of epidemological findings. What we mean is that additional careful studies which test etiological hypotheses may actually be compatible with the results of former ecological researches: this, in fact, we hypothesize to be the case.[31] Clausen and Kohn have noted, quite meaningfully, that modern ecological research leads to the discovery of not only structural subcommunities, but also of subcultures.[32]

CONCLUSIONS

We have, indeed, merely scratched the surface of some of the problems of contemporary social psychiatry. We have done even less in attempting to convey to the reader the richness of materials now available—theoretical and empirical. But, at least, on one point there seems to be rather complete agreement. Human behavior appears, to by far the most modern analysts—psychiatrists, sociologists, anthropologists, psychologists—goal oriented. Whether numerous goal regions are hypothesized (Lewin), or several are selected as basic (W. I. Thomas, Harry S. Sullivan), individuals acting to achieve goals are functionally interdependent. They live in a human context, and the groups they form are purposive (J. L. Moreno, H. S. Sullivan, K. Lewin). The social subsystems, in turn, operate in a larger context of the social system displaying both cultural continuities and discontinuities. That which is normal is culturally defined, although such definitions do not need to correspond to the physician's conception of mental health. Thus deviant behavior is also culturally delineated.

Disequilibria in the means—ends "ideal types" schema, that is anomic processes, render all individuals vulnerable, and at the same time, creative. The particular emphasis on certain values, the degree of general social differentiation and the norms channeling interaction, all account (on the theoretical level) for the cross-cultural differences in gross occurrences of psycho- and socio-pathological behavior, Within a given culture, subcultures are integrated with one another to a greater or lesser degree, dependent again on the extent to which they are in contradiction with the goals. Consequently, different subcultures within a cultural system are likely to be more or less vulnerable.

Individuals, too, need not be "perfectly" in the subcultures (these may be ethnic groupings, "racial" groups, socioeconomic strata, occupational groups—which of these would seem to be related to the paramount social values): their goals may be compatible with the subsystem goals only to a degree. And finally, the individual personality is an organization of actions-towards-ends, more or less integrated.

Etiological and epidemological considerations become two aspects of the same coin. Regardless of where the emphasis is placed, the interpretation of psychopathological behavior must cut across all these dimensions: personality organization, subsystem integration (interpersonal behavior), system integration (organization of subsystems within a society), and cultural integration. The tissue which binds all these referent "entities" is the tissue of communications. The stress on this by Ruesch and Bateson[33] is doubtlesly not misplaced especially when the contributions of general semanticists are considered, too. While the cultural values are, themselves, symbols, it is such values which specify the preferred directions, and contents of communication.

Social psychiatry is thus a study of communication wherein cultural variables determine the crude directionalities and content, social variables pertain to differential exposures of subgroups, and the personality variables underscore the particular communications fabric about an individual, or within him. All these dimensions deserve careful attention. Due to the interdependence of the systems, all the dimensions must be considered *simultaneously*.

This can be done when it is realized, both on the theoretical and on the practical research levels, that social psychiatry is truly cross-departmental. Volumes such as those of Mullahy (1949)[34] Ruesch and Bateson (1951), Weinberg (1952), and especially Opler (1956) go a long way in this desirable direction.

SELECTED BIBLIOGRAPHY

J. C. Carothers, *The African Mind in Health and Disease* (United Nations: World Health Organization, Monography No. 17, 1953).

Excellent summary of African materials with reference to more than 200 studies, including data on various parts of the Continent.

Raymond J. Corsini and Lloyd J. Putzey, "Bibliography," *Group Psychotherapy*, IX, 3 (November, 1956), 178-249. This is the best contemporary bibliography on group therapy covering the period 1906-1955; the materials are indexed both by the author and by the theme.

Sigmund Freud, *Civilization and Its Discontents* (London: The Hogarth Press, 1930). Classical analysis of the relation of culture to the superego.

Erich Fromm, *The Sane Society* (New York: Rinehart & Co., 1956). Systematization of Fromm's theories, formerly expressed in volumes such as *Escape from Freedom, Man for Himself*, with particular emphasis on psychopathological and sociopathological conditions in relation to dominant American values.

Frieda Fromm-Reichmann and J. L. Moreno, editors, *Progress in Psychotherapy: 1956* (New York: Grune & Stratton, 1956). An outstanding volume with contributions by psychiatrists from various schools of thought. Here, problems of contemporary psychiatry and social psychiatry are carefully discussed by proponents of various views. Under editorship of J. L. Moreno and Jules Masserman, the publishers are preparing the 1957 volume. *Progress in Psychotherapy* is to be appearing annually.

J. K. Hall, G. Zilboorg and H. A. Bunker, *One Hundred Years of American Psychiatry* (New York: Columbia University Press, 1944). A collection of papers on the growth of contemporary psychiatry.

Karen Horney, *The Neurotic Personality of Our Time* (New York: W. W. Norton & Co., 1937). The author analyzes the formation of neurotic responses in the context of prevailing social values in America in our time.

J. L. Moreno, *Who Shall Survive?* (Beacon, N. Y.: Beacon House, 2nd edition, 1953). Subtitled "Foundations of Sociometry, Group Psychotherapy and Sociodrama," the volume expresses Moreno's theories underlying the uses of psychodrama and group therapy in psychiatry. This is a statement of interpersonal models in social psychiatry.

Patrick Mullahy, editor, *A Study of Interpersonal Relations* (New York: The Hermitage Press, 1949). Coauthored by sociologists, anthropologists, psychologists, and psychiatrists, the volume is dedicated to H. S. Sullivan. Parsons, Sapir, Laswell, Clara Thompson, Fromm-Reichmann, Ruth Benedict are among the authors whose provocative contributions on the sociocultural dimension of psychiatry appear here.

Ruth L. Munroe, *Schools of Psychoanalytic Thought* (New York: The Dryden Press, 1955). The best up to date overview of psychoanalytic thinking. The theories of Freud and the Freudians, Adler, Jung, Horney, Sullivan, Fromm, and Rank are presented not only with great lucidity, but also integrated along topical lines, and critically (but always sympathetically and with profound objectivity) evaluated.

Marvin K. Opler, *Culture, Psychiatry and Human Values* (Springfield, Ill.: C. C. Thomas, 1956). Unmatched for exposition and thoroughness, this book surveys social psychiatry in the midcentury. While rich in detail, sight is never lost of the major substantive and methodological issues.

Jurgen Ruesch and Gregory Bateson, *Communication, the Social Matrix of Psychiatry* (New York: W. W. Norton & Co., 1951). Problems of social psychiatry, with particular reference to the American scene, are analyzed in a consistent frame of reference of communication theory. This is, perhaps, one of the most interesting theoretical models hitherto explored.

Harry S. Sullivan, *The Interpersonal Theory of Psychiatry* (New York: W. W. Norton & Co., 1953). Basic statement of Sullivan's psychiatric interpersonalism.

S. Kirson Weinberg, *Society and Personality Disorders* (New York: Prentice-Hall Co., 1952). Quite likely the best textbook for students of the behavioral sciences interested in social psychiatry. The author deals with topics of theoretical interest, with results of empirical research pertaining to anxieties, dissociations, schizophrenias, manic depression, psychopathic behavior, as well as with some of the main therapeutic procedures.

Jiri Nehnevajsa was born in Czechoslovakia; now Assistant Professor of Sociology, Columbia University, (1950——). Was educated at the University of Masaryk (Brno, Czechoslovakia), Université de Lausanne (Switzerland, and Universität von Zurich (Switzerland). Joined the research staff of Conservation of Human Resources Project (Columbia University) in 1951; Instructor on Sociology, University of Colorado (1951-1952); Assistant Professor (1953). As a research Training Fellow of the Social Science Research Council, he visited the University of Washington and Harvard University (1953-1954). An Associate Editor of the *International Journal of Sociometry* and of *Group Psychotherapy*. His articles have appeared in *Sociology and Social Research, Sociometry Kolner Zeitschrift für Soziolgie, Group Psychotherapy, International Journal of Sociometry, Die Heilkunst*. Coauthored, with Stuart C. Dodd and Edith Dyer Rainboth, *Revere Studies on Interaction* (1954, mimeographed report for the U. S. Air Force, to be published in 1957); contributed to *Sociometry and the Science of Man,* J. L. Moreno, editor (Beacon House, 1956), and with Stuart C. Dodd (in collaboration with others) he prepared the volume *Techniques for World Polls* (UNESCO project, completed 1956); is the author of *Soziometrische Analyzevon sozialen Beziehungen* (being published by F. Enke Verlagsbuchhandlung, Stuttgart, Germany), and *Social Stratification* (to be published by Harper); has also contributed some 90 brief articles to the *Soziologen-Lexikon,* edited by Wilhelm Bernsdorf (Ferdinand Enke Verlagsbuchhandlung, Stuttgart, Germany, 1956).

NOTES

1. Marvin K. Opler, *Culture, Psychiatry and Human Values* (Springfield, Ill.: C. C. Thomas, 1956).

2. We find the overview by Pitirim A. Sorokin, *Contemporary Sociological Theories* (New York: Harper, 1928) still unmatched when it comes to this kind of material.

3. A. Korzybski, *Science and Sanity* (New York: The Science Press, 1941).

4. Jurgen Ruesch—Gregory Bateson, *Communication, the Social Matrix of Psychiatry* (New York; W. W. Norton, 1951).

5. Marvin K. Opler, *op. cit.*, this writer strongly agrees with Opler on this point.

6. Some of these difficulties to be mentioned later.

7. Marvin K. Opler, *op. cit.;* also cf. S. Kirson Weinberg, *Society and Personality Disorders* (New York: Prentice-Hall, 1952).

8. Abram Kardiner et al., *Psychological Frontiers of Society* (New York: Columbia University Press, 1945).

9. Karen Horney, *The Neurotic Personality of Our Time* (New York, W. W. Norton Co., 1937).

10. Erich Fromm, *Escape from Freedom* (New York, N. Y.: Farrar & Rinehart, 1941).

11. David Riesman, *The Lonely Crowd* (New Haven: Yale University Press, 1950).

12. Erich Fromm, *The Sane Society* (New York: Rinehart Co., 1956).

13. Cf. Arnold W. Green, "The Middle Class Child and Neurosis," *American Sociological Review*, XI, 1 (1946), 31-41.

14. Ruth Benedict, *Patterns of Culture* (Boston: Houghton Mifflin, 1934).

15. Kurt Lewin, *Resolving Social Conflict* (New York: Harper, Bros., 1948); also, *Field Theory in Social Science* (New York: Harper, 1951).

16. J. L. Moreno, *Who Shall Survive?* (Boston: Beacon House, expanded edition, 1953).

17. Karl Menninger, "The Contribution of Psychoanalysis to American Psychiatry," *Bulletin of the Menninger Clinic*, XVIII (1954), 85-96.

18. Marvin K. Opler, *op. cit.*, p. 69.

19. Clyde Kluckhohn, "The Influence of Psychiatry on Anthropology in America during the Past One Hundred Years", in *One Hundred Years of American Psychiatry*, edited by J. K. Hall, G. Zilboorg, and H. A. Bunker (New York: Columbia University Press, 1944); cf. also Edward Sapir, "The Contribution of Psychiatry to an Understanding of Behavior in Society", *American Journal of Sociology*, XLII (1937), 826-870; George Devereux, "Psychiatry and Anthropology", *Bulletin of the Menninger Clinic*, XVI (1952), 167-177.

20. Mabel A. Elliott and Francis E. Merill, *Social Disorganization* (New York: Harper, 1941).

21. Sigmund Freud, *Civilization and Its Discontents* (London: The Hogarth Press, 1930).

22. Ernest Beaglehold, "Cultural Complexity and Psychological Problems," *Psychiatry*, III (August, 1940), 330-332.

23. Henry B. Elkind and Maurice Taylor, "The Alleged Increase in the Incidence of the Major Psychoses," *The American Journal of Psychiatry*, XCIII (1936), 817-825.

24. W. Lloyd Warner, "The Society, the Individual, and His Mental Disorders," *American Journal of Psychiatry*, XCIV (1937), 275-284.

25. Robert E. Lee Faris and D. W. Dunham, *Mental Disorders in Urban Areas* (University of Chicago Press, 1939).

26. D. L. Gerard and L. Huston, "Family Setting and the Social Ecology of Schizophrenia," *American Journal of Psychiatry*, CXI (1954), 422-425.

27. Morris S. Schwartz, *The Economic and Spatial Mobility of Paranoid Schizophrenics and Manic Depressives*, unpublished M.A. thesis, (University of Chicago, 1946).

28. J. C. Carothers, *The African Mind in Health and Disease* (New York: World Health Organization Monograph #17, 1953).

29. Benjamin Malzberg, "Rates of Mental Disease among Certain Population Groups in New York State," *Journal of the American Statistical Association*, XXXI (1936), 545-548.

Cf. by the same author, *Social and Biological Aspects of Mental Disease* (Utica, N. Y.: State Hospitals Press, 1940).

30. August B. Hollingshead—F. C. Redlich, "Social Stratification and Psychiatric Disorders," *American Sociological Review*, XVIII (April, 1953), 163-170.

31. Robert E. Lee Faris in *Social Disorganization* (New York, The Ronald Press, 2nd Edition, 1955) deals with the various criticisms of the Chicago results along such reinterpretative dynamic lines.

32. John A. Clausen and M. L. Kohn, *The Use of Ecological Method in Social Psychiatry* (Washington, D. C.: United States Public Health Service, National Institute of Mental Health, 1954).

33. Jurgen Ruesch and Gregory Bateson, *op. cit.*

34. Patrick Mullahy, editor, *A Study of Interpersonal Relations* (New York: The Hermitage Press, 1949).

SOCIOMETRY

Jiri Nehnevajsa
Columbia University

During World War II, Florian Znaniecki expressed rather succinctly the special kind of contribution sociometry has been making:[1] it made possible the measurement of phenomena which were of considerable interest to social philosophers, sociologists, and psychologists for, literally, millennia. These were, broadly speaking, the phenomena of interaction, of interpersonal relationships. On one hand, the relations among men, and of men to non-persons—that is to objects, animals, symbols—are normatively patterned. Systems of obligations define the forms, and directions, in interactance. A social system is thus delineated in terms of its *axio-normative order*: nor is it necessary to postulate some essentialist reality of the arrangement. The societal orderings can readily be assumed to be analytical constructs, or indeed, ideal types of the language of Max Weber. While the terminologies might differ, contemporary writers would largely concur that the social fabric has as its basic referents the personality, social, and cultural systems.[2] On the other hand, men relate affectively—their preferences are explicitly, and implicitly expressed: while grounded in experience, such preferences are, on the whole, concrete-situational. In theory, G. H. Mead makes this an important aspect of his philosophy of the present. J. L. Moreno, the founder of modern sociometry, speaks of the moment. Kurt Lewin, whose work generates group dynamics, thinks of the life span at one time as predictive of behavior at another, immediately subsequent, occasion.[3] Explicit preferential behavior may manifest itself in, for instance, frequency of contact, or withdrawal from it; in contact intensity; in scope, that is, whether it subsumes many, or but a few, activities of the referent actors.[4] On the implicit level, affective sociation takes the form of desires, wishes, psychological locomotions regarding other actors.

Sympathy becomes one of the basic notions with regard to these affective relatings: in its universalistic meaning, it enters the thoughts of numerous writers, from Aristotle's idea of man as a social animal, to the "gregariousness" of Giddings, or cooperativeness of a Kropotkin. In a more specific sense, the modern analyst might wish to draw on, at least, the *Smithian* theory of moral sentiments (in a volume so entitled), but above all, on Max Scheler. The significant contributions of C. H. Cooley are thoroughly unununderstandable without taking into account the concept of empathy, and the interactionist sociology of Leopold von Wiese (with its associative and dissociative processes) is firmly rooted in this tradition. Nor is it too difficult to see that the broadening of the Freudian "libido" by Adler leads to his sympathy-anchored "Gemeinschaftsgefuhl."

J. L. Moreno[5]—ignoring other aspects of his work—has rendered the interpersonal preferential behavior measurable: his interaction tests, in which sociation is plotted against time, are designed, although crudely at that time, to assess explicit behavior. His sociometric tests in which the referent subjects verbalize their preferences are geared to measure implicit preferences. His first locograms are conceived in fundamentally the same frame of reference as the life space diagrams of Lewin and Lewinians.

SMALL GROUP SOCIOLOGY

The affective interrelations produce very specific configurations. They are operative within the axio-normative system in functional interdependence. But it appears possible to isolate them, for the purposes of inquiry, from the normative structures. The tissue of these configurations consists then of explicit and implicit cathectic orientations.

Although such relationships interlink, somehow, all humanity, the sharpening of focus upon the personality, and social system tends to limit the volume[6] of the interactance. The two premises, one regarding preferential behavior, and the other its concrete-situational aspects, direct the analyst to center his attention upon relatively small groups. Microsociology, to borrow a term of Georges Gurvitch, emerges. And its growth is punctuated by the theoretical considerations of a Tönnies (on the Gemeinschaft-level), a Durkheim (organic solidarity), but especially Georg Simmel and C. H. Cooley.

The small groups become referents for research as soon as the theoretical concepts are translated into the language of the empiricist. On one hand, microsociological phenomena have been studied in their own right. The individual functions as a *socius* in predominantly small groupings. Indeed, he relates to the larger social system generally through the mediating context of small groups,[7] or else, through symbols (nationality, flag, national anthem, "ideology") whose meaning, in turn, he learns again in a microsociological configuration. Only recently has it been realized that, possibly, small groups may be studied as "miniature societies," and that large scale social phenomena may be regarded manageable for the researcher.[8] But on this matter, we may have different feelings. It may be argued, indeed, that microsociological phenomena cannot be understood by merely, in a way, enlarging the photographs one gets in small groups. Yet, it appears extremely fruitful to speculate whether this can be done, at least, as a basic approximation.

A METHODOLOGICAL DISTINCTION

We started out by saying that inferences about preferential behavior may be made on the basis of explicit and implicit behavior. Although the two processes are but two dimensions of the same configuration, the differentiation underlies the major methodological tracks in microsociology.

In as much as explicit behavior is operationally defined by actual contacts, and actual forms of sociation, it can be observed directly. Let now two points be made: no matter how observations are made, they will tend to restrict the analyst to the investigation of truly small groupings. It is thoroughly impossible (in practice, not in theory) to observe interactions among many individuals.[9] Secondly, observing presupposes that some units of observation be selected and reliably and validly defined. In the writings of Leopold von Wiese, "associative" and "dissociative" behavior may be selected to establish general directionality. While many schemas are imaginable, that of Robert F. Bales has gained scientific respectability.[10] The interaction analysis becomes formalized as content analysis of behavior, wherein standardization of the content units increases the utility of the instrument. Yet, invariably, the researcher is limited to the laboratory setting, or quasi-laboratory setting, in which only three, four, five, and generally very few, subjects can be studied. In-the-field observations are rarer: they occur in connection with research in infant, and child behavior —for instance in the valuable work of Mary L. Northway and her associates at the University of Toronto. Other analysts have utilized participant observers in factory, college, school, community settings —but they do not tend to rely solely on the observers for data. The participation observers generally add saliency to data obtained by other means (various forms of interview).

Data on implicit preferential behavior does not require a small group: a sociometric schedule can be administered to any number of people, and the usefulness of the questionnaire depends solely on its construction. The subjects report their preferences: their positive, negative, and indifference relations. Intensity measures can easily be built into the schedule. The scope of affective configurations depends only on the selection of criterion-purposes.

Finally, individuals also perceive others in relation to themselves, in relation to one another. The *perceptual dimension* of the test is added, systematically introduced in the field by Renato Tagiuri of Harvard.[11] Roughly speaking, investigations of overt behavior ally themselves with Lewinian topology: that is, they employ the field theory as their frame of reference. We speak usually of group dynamics in this connection. Sociometry, in its narrower sense, is the frame of reference for the study of implied preferential behavior, both projective and perceived.[12]

SCOPE OF PROBLEMS

We may now go about our business of stating the kinds of problems the small groups analysts are concerned with. One immediate distinction can be recognized: in a given social system, individuals are both normatively *and* affectively (say, sociometrically) related. Thus we may wish to study the sociometric configurations within given normative structures, and also in their relation to the systems of obligations. Secondly, we may be analyzing sociometric configurations —and observing how they relate to normative systems. Here, the points of departure differ: in the former case, a social subsystem is delineated as a closed system. In the latter case, sociometric patterns (which may cut across several normative patterns) are used as a closed system.

Next, let us consider another issue. The researcher may conduct his investigation with focus upon personality systems: he compares individuals with one another (whether they come from the same system or different ones: the difference is one of choosing appropriate index numbers). Also, he may be studying the very organization of personality, that is, the relations of formal and sociometric relations in a given individual, or the interrelations of different sociometric configurations (different as to the criterion, or purpose, or goal for sociation). Secondly, the analyst may be conducting his inquiry with emphasis upon the syntality system, that is with respect to specific group characteristics. Such group characteristics are social cohesion, social integration, cleavage, group climate, size, spatial relations of the subjects, form of leadership, group goals, and so on.

The research questions reduce to two very general ones (and even these are but the two sides of the same coin): (1) What variable(s) predict the affective relationships? And, (2) What variable(s) are the affective relationships predictive of? To rephrase this: we test for homogeneity-heterogeneity of relationships by making some other variable(s) the independent one(s). And similarly, we study individuals of homogeneous relations with respect to other variable(s). Do sociometric friends share the same vote intention? Do they have homogeneous values? Or, what kinds of configurations are associated with homogeneity of vote intention, or values? We shall now be even more concrete without losing sight of our main purpose of depicting overall problems. A typology of the relevant variables would reveal that the researcher studies (a) interaction phenomena in their interrelations (that is, relation of the configurations with respect to one purpose to those under other purpose(s)),(b) interaction phenomena in relation to personality traits (sex, age, I.Q., and so on), (c) in relation to attitudes and values (whether these are existing attitudes and values, or induced ones for the purposes of the investigation), and (d) in relation to socio-cultural traits (such as socio-economic status, income, residence, race, role obligations). Finally, the interactance patterns and processes are studied in relation to (e) behavior (such as communicating, electing of leaders).[13]

The last topic is of particular importance: How do individuals in particular groups solve problems? (personality system emphasis) How do groups of different kinds solve problems? (syntality emphasis) How do individuals arrive at decisions? (personality) How do groups arrive at decisions? (syntality) How do individuals produce? (personality) And groups (syntality)? How does news, rumor, propaganda, spread? (syntality) What roles do individuals play in the communications network? (personality) Answers to such problems, even crude ones, not only advance knowledge for its own beautiful sake. They also contribute to increased understanding of practical problems human groups encounter. It does make a lot of immediate practical difference to know whether democratic group atmospheres are more conducive to productivity than either autocratic or anarchistic climates.[14] It makes a lot of difference to know what variables, other than the normative ones (including pay!), maximize performance of individuals or of groups (Van Zelst, James Chabot, Paul Maucorps and others), and how the affective configurations influence efficiency and morale (Goodacre, Wherry and Fryer, Chesler, Van Steenberg and Brueckel, Hollander, Torrance and others). It is only natural that the microsociologists find their results of great usefulness to suppliers in various fields of human endeavor: in the industry, in the Armed Forces, in hospitals, in prisons, in schools—last but not least.[15] Both Moreno and Lewin have emphasized the connections between research and the problems men face. Moreno went as far as we to say that research without diagnostic-therapeutic aims (leading toward alleviating of some undesirable conditions) can only yield invalid results: the subjects have to be motivated to respond accurately by their belief that the problem in question matters to them, and that its soluion is desired.[16] Although Lewin never went this far, and his formulations presupposed that knowledge be gathered irrespective of the ends to which it may be used, he, like Moreno, was inclined to be greatly absorbed in the practical problems of our time.[17] The manner in which men set their goals, how they go about achieving them, what dilemmas they encounter in the process—these are truly issues at the roots of Lewinian theories. With Morton Deutsch,[18] we may speak of *action research*—a product as much of theoretical considerations as of the turbulences of our century which, like always, direct the scientist (by shaping his values as to what is important).

It is easy to see how *sympathy*—raising a host of serious empirical problems—can, at the same time, become a value in itself. This is, once again, especially understandable against the background of the turmoils of our age. Associated with the growth of role theory—especially since the rather crucial contribution of Ralph Linton—we can readily comprehend the emergence of group therapy, sociodrama, and role-playing[19] are designed to increase empathy in individuals by letting them behave in roles of others. There is a sense in which this amounts to an attempt to bring the normative and the affective societal fabrics into greater agreement.

SOME ANALYTICAL TOOLS

In addition to customary statistical instruments, and in addition to the possibilities of content analysis of interaction,[20] some specific analytical tools have been developed. The description of the configurations generally begins with some form of a sociogram (Moreno, early 1920's). Interaction diagrams do the job for recording the interaction patterns over time (Moreno, 1923). More systematic are Northway's target diagrams (1940) describing the relationships with respect to the frequencies of received preference selections. F. Stuart Chapin (1952) has proposed a three-dimensional model making the inclusion of some additional variable (such as socioeconomic status) possible.

In Lewinian theories, the geometrical diagrams of the life space play this role; but included are, by definition, also normative relations. These psychological space schemas are easily related to the contemporary sociological theories of Talcott Parsons and Robert K. Merton —cognitive, cathectic, as well as evaluational orientations can be simultaneously graphed.

The graphic presentation methods, lately further elaborated by Massarik, Tannenbaum, Wechsler and Kahane (1953) to incorporate normative, actual, perceived and the projected affects, have given way to the use of matrices. This tabulation, onto rows and columns, is both more precise and more parsimonious, something Stuart C. Dodd was among the first ones to strongly underscore (1940).

Numerous index numbers have been suggested. Some depict the standing of individuals, others refer to groups, or to subgroups: thus we have indexes of sociometric status, of choice-rejection status, of group attractiveness, of ingroup preference, of cohesion, interaction level, and so on.[21] While innumerable index numbers are possible, the better known ones are associated with the names of J. L. Moreno, H. H. Jennings, George A. Lundberg, Joan H. Criswell.

The use of sociomatrices for the presentation of data is of still another importance; in as much as the sociomatrix is a matrix, some operations developed by the mathematicians into a whole field (matrix algebra) have become applicable. This holds especially about multiplication of matrices to discover contingent relationships (such configurations which depend on some intervening individual[s]), and to delineate factions and cliques. In the early 1950's, Duncan Luce, Albert Perry, Leo Katz, and Leon Festinger are among the pioneers in this regard.

Probabilistic analysis starts with simple chance models. Empirically observed interactions are analyzed in terms of deviations from chance, wherein independence of the affects is assumed. The method was elaborated by Moreno and Jennings (1938), and placed into a center of attention, and controversey, by Bronfenbrenner (1941, 1942, 1943). In these early attempts, the distribution of choices was defined, and expectations of various choice patterns solved. Leo Katz (1952) reported the solution of the distribution of isolated individuals (the probability that there will be k-isolates in a group of size N), and work has been progressing on more complicated chain relations under Katz's direction at Michigan State University (a 1952 memorandum gives some of the solutions). Intergroup configurations have been studied, among others, by Criswell (1943, 1945), Edwards (1948), and this author (1955).

Moreover, these chance models may be often quite inappropriate. Leo Katz has been insistent on the fact that independence of the expressions of preference cannot be assumed (say, especially for mutual relations). Furthermore, the field is in need of models which stem from formalizations of the actual behavioral processes rather than of typical random models.

SOME SUBSTANTIVE ISSUE

It is clearly beyond the scope of the present discussion to attempt to give justice to the hundreds, if not thousands, of studies which have been conducted in the past twenty years or so. If we were to state one major trend, we would have to say that the growth of microsociological research is marked by both increasing quantity of studies and by increasing refinement of the designs. If we were to speak of the *locus* of research, we would come to the inescapable conclusion that the increase in laboratory experiments has been rather spectacular, and that the sophistication which goes into such investigations foreshadows the 'coming of age' of the behavioral science. Furthermore, we would bear witness to the fact that microsociology—more, perhaps, than any other field in sociology—has helped to bridge the gap between sociology and psychology: and that, related to the frame of reference of the cultural anthropologist, a *behavioral* science is growing. Nor can we miss to see that, in spite of all the limitations, modern functionalism of the Parsonian and Mertonian sociology has played this crucial unifying role, a framework into which other theoretical schemas fruitfully collapse. Rigorously speaking, we know little about the formation of the sociometric and interaction configurations. From studies of Moreno, Northway, Bonney, and others, we know that, with age, the configurations about an individual increase in complexity; and that age, sex, and race cleavages—leading to the growth of relatively homogeneous structures—emerge successively. Although several sociometric studies have been carried out over a prolonged period of time, such as the well-known research of Jennings[22], the investigators have not taken benefit from the development of panel techniques of analysis. This is rather evident from the systematic overview of 'reliability' of the data by Mouton, Blake and Fruchter (1955): changes in the configurations over time are treated as problems in reliabilty, whereas panel analysis would lead to their being handled as problems of turnover, that is, of actual change in the relationships.

When interacts, or selections in a sociometric test, are used as a measure of status of individuals, we find consistently that but a few individuals are in such leadership positions, and few others are in isolated positions. Thus groups are stratified with respect to the test criteria.

Testing for the relations among varying purposes of sociation, the investigators generally agree that individuals interact, and wish to associate, with about the same individuals under different conditions. Researches by Bronfenbrenner (1943), Bonney (1944–), Grossman and Wrighter (1948) point in this direction. Bonney's research among school children (in Denton, Texas) also indicates the manner in which intelligence is related to popularity. Like Wardlow and Greene (1952), Bonney concludes that the more popular subjects are also the more intelligent ones, a result confirmed, among others, by Howell (1942), Thorpe (1954). Furthermore, individuals in mutual friendship relations are reported homogeneous with respect to intelligence.

Kidd (1951) and Potashin (1946) as well as Bonney have found that isolated or rejected individuals have a lower achievement in school. Wherry and Fryer (1949) reported that ratings by friends were predictive of success in an Officer's Candidate School, and thus of performance.

Strong homogeneity with respect to race has been similarly discovered. In the study of Radke, Sutherland and Rosenberg (wherein the authors used the Protective Picture Test) in Pittsburgh, Pa., the Negro respondents preferred their 'own groups' less than did the white respondents, but both groups showed marked self-preference. Seaman conducted (1946) an interesting investigation disclosing that preferential stratification is operative also within the Negro groups, and that it roughly relates to the particular skin shade.

Both physical and mental health have been found associated with popularity, and, on the other extreme, with rejection and isolation. Northway and Widgor (1947) used the Rorshach Pattern test to assess mental health, Kuhlen and Bretch (1947) employed the Mooney Problem Check List. Among 692 pupils (9th grade), they found that less accepted children had consistently more problems. Thorpe obtained a small, but statistically significant, negative correlation between neuroticism and sociometric status. Urdan and Lindzey (1954) confirmed the work of Maucorps (1949), among French staff officers, and Richmond (1950): homogeneity with respect to general personality traits seems associated with the patterning of affective relationships.

Maisonneuve (1954) in France, and Muldoon (1955) in the United States have agreed that similarity in value profiles correlated with mutual affective relations. The perception of the appropriate membership role and sociometric popularity was studied by Bates (1952): individuals who have expressed themselves strongly in favor of general group norms were high in sociometric status. Maas (1949) reported that subjects prefer those individuals whose values will not be in conflict with theirs.

There is also agreement on the relationship between socioeconomic, and social, status and effective popularity. Bonney reported homogeneity of socioeconomic backgrounds in friends (his status ratings were based on the Minnesota Home Status Index of Leahy). Stogdill (1949), confirmed this in the military setting. Loomis and Powell (1949) reported that community leaders were selected from among the individuals belonging to the highest socioeconomic class. Lundberg and Steele (1937-38), in their Vermont village classic, found that individuals tend to express preferences for others who are in higher status group, a finding coming also from Loomis, and Proctor (1950).

Spatial proximity, too, relates to interaction. Dozens of researches have concurred in this finding, whether we think of the work of Loomis in a Spanish American village (1938), or of Seagoe's research

(1933), or of the investigation among office workers by Gullahorn (1952) or the French bording school study of Maisonneuve (1952). Impressive are findings of Dodd and associates (1954) who found a harmonic curve predictive of the spreading of messages over spatial distances, in a near-experimental setting in the field.

Numerous are studies of communications in groups; many are laboratory experiments. Potashin found that friendship dyads communicated more than paired non-friends. Lewin and Lippitt (1938) observed that, under democratic group conditions, there was less over-all interaction, and about thirty times less the volume of hostiity than under autocratic group climates. Researches of Northway and her associates lead to the conclusion that sociometrically preferred individuals were the ones who talked more, and evidenced more initiative. Bock found a correlation of .85 between communications sent out by an individual and his sociometric standing. Back (1951) reported that when the attractiveness of a group increases, the amount of influence exerted increases also, and it is directed pre-dominantly at the deviant individuals (Festinger and Thibault, 1951, Schachter, 1951).

In a careful research, Borgatta and Cottrell (1956) have aimed at a preliminary typology of groups. Their factor analytic design led to the disclosure of several factors: (a) tension-neutral activity (relating to groups under stress but responding with emotional neutrality), (b) involvement activity (the cluster included "giving opinion-actual behavior," "giving opinion-role-playing,") showing antagonism (role-playing), showing solidarity (role-playing), (c) group indentification, (d) leader structure, (e) discussional involvement, (f) task interest, and (g) maturity. Although the authors label their findings preliminary, they are extremely impressive precisely because it became possible to locate such well defined factorial structures.

From military settings come reports on efficiency and cohesiveness of groups. In groups of Army scouts in twelve tactical situations, Goodacre found significant correlations between effectiveness in the field (rated by observers) and group cohesion (defined by preferential behavior). We have already mentioned that Wherry and Fryer discovered that buddy ratings were good predictors of effectiveness of the candidates (in an OCS)—inferior only to one military aptitude test. The retention of candidates in the school correlated significantly with their sociometric popularity. Chesler, Van Steenberg and Brueckel (1955) designed an elaborate study to assess individual replacement in contrast with team replacement. Actual observations were made under combat conditions in the Korean theatre. The sociometrically selected teams proved superior to soldiers replaced individually.

Hollander (1954) found high relationships between rated officer's qualities and popularity in a Naval Preflight School. French discovered (1951) that isolated Naval recruits frequented the sick bay more often than individuals accepted by their colleagues. The isolated subjects had also more disciplinary offenses. Following a classical study by Zeleny (1947) among air-crews, quite a few studies have been done in the Air Force. Rohy (1952) reports that liking, that is group cohesion, was associated with superior performance of the whole crew, results confirmed by Fiedler (1954). Levi, Torrance and Pletts (1954) conclude that post-survival training popularity of the commanding officer of the crew was an outstanding indicator of the effectiveness of the crew. Hemphill and Sechrest (1952) investigated ninety-four B-29 aircrews in training, and again, in Korea. Sociometric relations among the crew members were related to bombing accuracy.

We could go on in this fashion. But the meaning of all this may now be somewhat clear: the configurations stemming from explicit or implied preferences of individuals are not only another interesting dimension of sociological and social psychological research. They truly matter, and they effect the behavior of the members considerably. In this sense, the configurations make the achievement of goals easier, or they present a formidable barrier to achievement.

CONCLUSIONS

Microsociological studies have been generally characterized by insufficient coordination of the efforts. This is understandable due to fascination of many researchers with the very problem raised, and the desire to contribute to the solutions. It is, in a way, the first stage of any scientific endeavor: numerous rather uncoordinated researches and experiments are conducted to supply the ingredients for the systematization which (we hope) follows.

While we feel that many of the elements for such a systematization are already available, some are definitely not. We know very little about the preferential configurations in other cultures, something which Margaret Mead emphasized early in sociometry's development (1943). Except for the French researches, the tradition of micro-sociology is yet to be established in other countries, and under variable cultural conditions.[23] Which theoretical framework will prove itself most fruitful in subsuming the various research results remains to be seen. Presently, we have, at least, four such frameworks of potential utility: those of Kurt Lewin and Talcott Parsons (the two being reconcilable with relative facility), and those of J. L. Moreno and Stuart C. Dodd.

All this attests to a more general trend in contemporary American sociology: the empiricist is increasingly more concerned with theory. But this is as it should be. For the contemporary return to theory in the United States (and we possibly overestimate the degree to which this has been happening) is really no return but a progression. The empiricist pauses, for a while, to see how far he has gone and where he is going. The theories that are in want and in vogue are the ones which are firmly grounded in research, and which are conducive to more and better research: thus we are not asserting a tendency toward the renewal of armchair speculations. In fact, the 'back-to-theory' trend is characterized by the emphasis on the need for formalization of theory in the language of the logician and the mathematician. Such theorizing does not include metapsychological and metasociological notions. These are, indeed, not needed and they are wanted even less.

SELECTED BIBLIOGRAPHY

Robert F. Bales, *Interaction Process Analysis* (Cambridge, Mass.: Addison-Wesley Press, 1950). A systematic overview of the methodology for observing, and analyzing, the direction of content of interaction in small groups.

D. Cartwright and A. F. Zander, editors, *Group Dynamics: Research and Theory* (Evanston, Ill.: Row, Peterson Co., 1953) .This is an excellent book of readings including forty-one essays concerned with theoretical problems in the field, as well as with selected empirical researches on group cohesion, integration, communication.

Paul Hare, Edgar F. Borgatta and Robert F. Bales, *Small Groups* (New York: Alfred A. Knopf, 1955). Another volume of pertinent readings. Included are a few pages on early theories by Durkheim, Simmel, Cooley and Mead, as well as reports on some early research investigations. The remaining sections of the volume deal with the individual as referent, and group as a referent. The volume has a good annotated bibliography.

George Homans, *The Human Group* (New York: Harcourt, Brace, 1950). The author presents a systematization of some researches in interaction. The book is written with particular lucidity and warmth.

Kurt Lewin, *Field Theory in Social Science* (New York: Harper, 1951). In this collection of papers, field theory is explained as a method of analysis. The topological approach is then applied to several selected problems—learning, group dynamics, regression, and so on.

J. L. Moreno, *Who Shall Survive?* (Beacon House, 2nd edition, 1953). This is an enlarged edition of the 1934 publication. The author deals with his theories of evolution of groups, sociometry of the community, and other topics. Bibliography is very adequate.

J. L. Moreno, editor, *Sociometry and the Science of Man* (Beacon N. Y.: Beacon House, 1956). The book is a collection of papers on sociometry. It includes theoretical discussions, research reports, as well as contributions to methodology. Almost all articles included here were written explicitly for the voume.

Jane Mouton, Robert R. Blake and Benjamin Fruchter, "The Reliability of Sociometric Measures," *Sociometry*, XVIII, 1(February, 1955), 7-48. A survey of some fifty researches with emphasis upon consistency of sociometric data under test-retest conditions, and with respect to different methods of gathering data.

Jane Mouton, Robert R. Blake and Benjamin Fruchter, "The Validity of Sociometric Responses," *Sociometry*, XVIII, 3 (August, 1955), 171-200. The authors review studies focussing their attention upon validation of sociometric tests. Numerous crosstabulations of the researches make this a very valuable survey.

Fred L. Strodtbeck and A. P. Hare, "Bibliography of Small Group Research," *Sociometry*, XVII, 2(May, 1955), 107-178. This is about the most comprehensive bibliographic listing of relevant materials covering the period 1900-1953. Over 1000 titles are included. The ones judged most important by the compilers are marked for the convenience of the reader.

The student of small groups will find three journals of particular relevance: *Sociometry* (1937-), a journal founded by J. L. Moreno, and currently published by the American Sociological Society under the editorship of Leonard S. Cottrell Jr.; *Human Relations* (1947-), a publication of the Tavistock Institute of Human Relations in London and the Research Center for Group Dynamics at the University of Michigan; and *International Journal of Sociometry* (1956-), a journal published by J. L. Moreno with contributions in several major languages.

(For the author's *curriculum vitae*, see the previous chapter.)

NOTES

1. Florian Znaniecki, "Sociometry and Sociology," *Sociometry* VI, 3 (1943), 225-233.

2. Talcott Parsons—Edward Shils, editors, *Toward a General Theory of Action* (Cambridge, Mass.: Harvard University Press, 1952).

3. It appears worthwhile to be reminded of several models of opinion change developed by T. W. Anderson wherein (and the author wonders about the substantive meaning of this) opinions held at some time, t, become probabilistically independent of opinions held at some previous time, t-n. Cf. Paul F. Lazarsfeld, editor, *Mathematical Thinking in the Social Sciences* (Glencoe, Ill.: The Free Press, 1954).

4. Two volumes are of particular relevance in this connection: William F. Whyte, *Street Corner Society* (University of Chicago Press, 1943), and George Homans, *The Human Group* (New York: Harcourt Brace, 1950).

5. Especially in his early writings; J. L. Moreno, *Das Stegreif-theater* (Potsdam, Germany: G. Kiepenheuer Verlag, 1925); also *Who Shall Survive?* (Washington, D.C.: Nervous and Mental Disease Publishing Co., 1934).

6. Volume is here used as a class concept; it has as its constituent elements (a) the number of interacts, (b) their intensity with regard to (c) different aims of association, and (d) of specific directionality along the continuum of positive-to-negative.

7. The term "socius" stands for the individual and his relations to others. It is pertinent to mention that Stuart C. Dodd in his *Dimensions of Society* (New York: Macmillan, 1948) makes the concept of "socius" basic to social psychology and to sociology.

8. Cf., among others, Guy E. Swanson, "A Preliminary Laboratory Study of the Acting Crowd," *American Sociological Review*, XVIII (1953), 522-533, "Some Problems of Laboratory Experiments with Small Populations," *American Sociological Review*, XVI (1951), 349-368.

9. Were it not for the expense we could, of course, use motion picture cameras to record behavior. The size of the group would determine the required number of cameras.

10. Robert F. Bales, *Interaction Process Analysis* (Cambridge, Mass.: Addison-Wesley Press, 1950).

11. Renato Tagiuri, "Relational Analysis: An Extension of Sociometric Method with Emphasis upon Social Perception," *Sociometry*, XV, 1-2 (1952), 91-104.

12. Ake Bjerstedt of the University of Lund (Sweden) has recently made a substantial contribution toward delimiting the scope of sociometry. His results show that sociometry is, perhaps, best defined in terms of inquiries into all "preferential behavior." In this sense, we would use the term sociometry both for group dynamics and sociometry in its narrower meaning. We are, however, using microsociology as the generic concept, and group dynamics and sociometry as particular (methodologically distinct) branches thereof. Cf. Ake Bjerstedt, *Interpretations of Soiometric Choice Status* (Lund, Sweden: C. W. K. Gleerup, 1956).

13. Jiri Nehnevajsa, "Decades of Growth," in *Sociometry and the Science of Man*, edited by J. L. Moreno (Beacon, N. Y.: Beacon House, 1956), 48-95 also: "Soziometrische Analyse von Gruppen," *Kölner Zeitschrift für Soziologie*, VII, I (1955), 119-157, and VII, 2 (1955), 280-302.

14. Kurt Lewin–Ronald Lippitt, "An Experimental Approach to the Study of Autocracy and Democracy," *Sociometry*, I, 3-4 (1937-1938), 292-300.

15. As a result of this realization quite a body of research has been supported by various organizations. It has been especially gratifying to the behaviorial scientists to find consistent support—in addition to the generous help of foundations—in the United States Navy (Office of Naval Research), and other governmental organizations.

16. The very title of J. L. Moreno's first major book published in the United States is indicative of this profound concern: *Who Shall Survive?*

17. Kurt Lewin, *Resolving Social Conflict* (New York: Harper, 1948).

18. Morton Deutsch, "Field Theory in Social Psychology," in *Handbook of Social Psychology*, edited by Gardner Lindzey (Cambridge, Mass.: Addison-Wesley Press, 1954), I, 181-222.

19. There is truly no difference, that this writer could detect, between role-playing and sociodrama.

20. Bernard Berelson, *Content Analysis* (Glencoe, Ill.: The Free Press, 1952).

21. The reader should consult, among others, Charles P. Loomis–Charles H. Proctor, "Sociometry," in *Research Methods in Social Relations*, edited by Jahoda, Deutsch, and Cook (New York: The Dryden Press, 1951). The reader familiar with German will find an overview in Jiri Nehnevajsa's paper referred to in (13) above.

22. Reported in Helen H. Jennings, *Leadership and Isolation* (New York: Longmans, Green, 1943).

23. This is strictly not the case. For, indeed, sociometric research has been done in several cultures, in Sweden, France, Costa Rica, Germany, Peru, Mexico. But the Studies are too few yet, and far between. Above all, they do not appear to be *systematically* related to attempts at exploring variable cultural settings.

THE SOCIOLOGY OF
SYMBOLS, LANGUAGE AND SEMANTICS

Clifton R. Jones
Morgan State College

THE NATURE OF LANGUAGE

Language is perhaps the most important single cultural trait which man has invented during the course of his existence as a human being. More than any other trait language distinguishes man from lower animal forms; for language is a distinctly human trait.

Language may be defined as a system of significant symbols through the use of which men are able to communicate with each other. It is, according to Sapir, ". . . an essentially perfect means of expression of communication among every known people. Of all aspects of culture it is a fair guess that language was the first to receive a highly developed form and that its essential perfection is a prerequisite to the development of culture as a whole."[1]

Language is symbolic behavior. It is symbolic in the sense that it stands for, or refers to, physical objects, persons, situations, or ideas, sentiments and other feeling states. Psychologically, it has a profound significance for the development of human personality; sociologically, it is the *sine qua non* of social organization and cultural development.

In view of the importance of language, the fact that it is so essential to the existence of human society, it is not surprising that it has been the object of so much critical study and analysis, as well as a great deal of uncritical speculation. In no less than seven specialized fields of study—linguistics, philology, semantics, anthropology, psychology and sociology—language as a form of human behavior has been a fertile field of study and research.

EARLIER STUDIES OF LANGUAGE

Earlier studies of language, especially in the social sciences, were concerned, to a very large extent, with its origin. The studies of

437

Wundt, Herder, and Noire are significant, largely, for their attempts to explain how language came into existence. The theory of each, (a) that language developed from gesture, the attempt of men to communicate through gesticulation (Wundt),[2] (b) that language had its origins in man's attempt to imitate the sounds of nature (Herder),[3] (c) that language had its origin in sense impressions (Noire),[4] though seemingly logical, proved to be fallacious as single explanations upon empirical study. It is now generally recognized that the origin of language is a mystery which defies solution. Research in that direction holds little promise and has largely been abandoned.

During the twenties and early thirties of the present century considerable attention was given to the study of the process by which the child acquires language: the development of the child's vocabulary, development in the child's use of sentences, and the formation of concepts by the child. In this area the works of de Laguna,[5] Piaget,[6] Smith,[7] McCarthy,[8] Rugg, Kreuger and Sondergaard[9] are significant. Their studies have provided us with a great deal more insight into the early development of personality and the role which language plays in that development.

Since the thirties the run of attention has been in the field of semantics. This field has attracted wide attention, and scholars in both the social sciences and the natural sciences have made significant contributions to this important aspect of language.

SEMANTICS

In the brief pages which follow it is impossible to describe in detail the major lines of development in semantics which have taken place during the past quarter of a century.

Many lines of inquiry have been pursued in the field of semantics recently, including significs, pragmatism, linguistics, general semantics, cybernetics, group dynamics, and psycho-therapy each of which merits critical examination. Here we can state only in a general way the central thesis of the various schools of thought and call attention to the scholars most responsible for their development. The reader's attention is called to the bibliography at the end of the chapter from which a more detailed analysis and description may be obtained.

Semantics may be defined as the science of meaning. Interest in this field is by no means new. The study of the laws and conditions under which signs and symbols, including words, may be said to be meaningful, and the study of the relationships between words and things, between language, thought and behavior, probably had its origin in Aristotelian logic.

Aristotelian logic was based on three principles: (1) the principle (or law) of identity; the object *is* what the word says it is; (2) the principle (or law) of all-ness; a thing is either A or *not*-A; and (3) the principle (or law) of non-self-reflexiveness; a thing cannot be both A and *not*-A. This system of logic influenced the study of semantics from 350 B. C. to the nineteenth century with little or no innovation.

Modern Semantics appears to have had its origin in the work of Lady Viola Welby. Lady Welby was critical of traditional Aristotelian logic because it was too rigid and inflexible, and when applied to modern educational methods it results in what she called a "senseless formalism" in which the study of meanings was a purely verbal discipline showing little relationship to reality. In place of the rigid formalism of Aristotelian logic she suggested "significs." Lady Welby defined significs as the science of significance provided sufficient recognition is given to its practical aspect as a method of mind.[10] Significs was intended to be not merely a reform of obsolete and inadequate linguistic practices; rather, it was to constitute a training to create an entirely new and more realistic attitude toward experience, upon which all language is based. Her most significant work, *What is Meaning?*, though published in 1903, still exerts considerable influence in the field of semantics, especially in psycho-linguistic studies.

Lady Welby's approach to the study of linguistic forms and meaning led others to examine more critically the Aristotelian system which had been so influential in the past. Whitehead and Russell, who were largely interested in the study of the foundations of mathematics, noted that formalism and inflexibility of Aristotelian logic resulted in certain ambiguities in language which made the solution of certain problems in mathematics impossible. This led Russell to formulate his theory of types, the principal point of which was that,

> ". . . ambiguities of language conceal certain "illegitimate totalities," which, undetected, lead to "vicious circle fallacies." For example, need a statment about all statements apply to itself? the following statement illustrates this type of proposition: (All statements in these parentheses are false). If we suppose the statement true, we must conclude that it is false; if we suppose it false, we must conclude that it is true. The "all" in such

propositions is the "illegitimate totality." The "all" must be limited so that a statement about the totality must itself fall outside the totality."[11]

This line of reasoning, credited to Whitehead and Russell, not only supported the significs of Lady Welby, but it influenced in no small degree the thinking of the "logical positivist" school of semantics, frequently referred to as the "Vienna Circle." The most significant contribution of this school was the sharp distinction which it made with regard to the functions of language. Ludwig Wittgenstein, one of its leaders, held that most philosophical propositions arose from a lack of understanding of the logic of language, and the traditional problems of philosophy were senseless. The logical positivists pointed out certain kinds of statements which were impossible to verify and, therefore, fruitless to discuss, and classified another large group of utterances which turn out on analysis to be statements not at all about reality, but about language.

Since 1935 the logical syntax of Rudolf Carnap has gained a considerable following. Carnap distinguishes sharply between semantics and syntax, that is, between semantical systems as interpreted language systems and purely formal, uninterpreted calculi. He further emphasizes the distinction between factual truth, dependent upon the contingency of facts, and logical truth, independent of facts and dependent merely on meaning as determined by semantical rules. This distinction he believed necessary for the logical analysis of science.[12] Carnap admits that he was influenced considerably by Tarski although their conceptions of semantics diverge at certain points. However, Carnap's point of view and that of others of the "Polish School of Semantics"—Lesniewski, Kotarbinski, and Chwistek—were not far apart. The influence of Carnap led to the founding, in 1938, of the publication, the *International Encyclopedia of Unified Science.* Associated with Carnap in the founding of this publication were Otto Neurath, Neils Bohr, Bertrand Russell, John Dewey and Charles Morris. Their purpose was to develop an adequate theory of signs which would provide the basis for the ultimate unification of knowledge. A major attempt by Charles Morris to state a theory of signs was an outgrowth of the ideas which stemmed from this group.[13]

Equally critical of the traditional study of semantics were the pragmatists, whose central thesis was that the meaning of any word or symbol lies exclusively in its practical effect on human behavior,

rather than in any transcendental realm of ideas, and the operationalists, who insisted that a statement can have meaning only if it can
be translated into physical operations to ascertain its truth or falsity.
In the former instance the works of Charles S. Pierce, George Herbert
Mead, and the earlier works of John Dewey stand out. P. W. Bridgman, the physicist, was one of the influential leaders who developed
the school of thought known as operationalism.

In their earlier studies of nonliterate groups anthropologists, when
concerned with language at all, except as a functional means of investigating the culture under study, devoted most of their time to
the study of the structure of language (morphology, or linguistic form),
phonology (the sounds of language), and syntax (rules for combining
words into sentences). More recently anthropologists have shown a
great deal more interest in the meaning of words and symbols as they
appear in context among the people who are using them. Since Malinowski interest in this aspect of language has increased, and has been
given a great deal of attention in the works of such scholars as Edward
Sapir, Clyde Kluckhohn, Dorothy Lee and Benjamin Lee Whorf. The
point which these writers emphasize so strongly is that language is
not merely a convenient vehicle through which thoughts are expressed;
but of equal, if not greater, importance, it actually determines the
character of reality which one sees. Whorf, an outstanding authority
on the Hopi, clearly points out that people think, feel and respond to
phenomena according to the meaning of the phenomena in their
culture. Furthermore, the mere fact that some phenomenon has universal existence is no reason to assume that the meaning of the phenomenon is also universal. The concepts of time, space and distance,
for example, have quite different meaning for us than what they have
for the Hopi. Hence the Hopi neither think nor converse about them
as we do:

> Such terms as summer, winter, September, morning, noon, sun-
> set, are with us nouns, and have little formal linguistic difference
> from other nouns. They can be subjects or objects and we say
> "at" sunset or "in" winter just as we say at a corner or in an
> orchard. They are pluralized and numerated like nouns of physi-
> cal objects. . . . Our thoughts about referrents of such words,
> hence, become objectified. . . .
> In Hopi, however, all phase terms, like summer, morning, etc.,
> are not nouns but a kind of adverb, . . . They are a formal part
> of speech by themselves, distinct from nouns, verbs, and even
> other Hopi "adverbs." Such a word is not a case or a locative

pattern like *"des abends"* or "in the morning." It contains no morpheme like one of "in the house" or "at the tree." It means "when it is morning" or "while morning-phase is occurring." These "temporals" are not used as subjects or objects, or at all like nouns. One does not say "it's a hot summer" or "summer is hot"; summer is *not* hot, summer is only *when* conditions are hot; *when* heat occurs. One does not say *"this* summer" but "summer *now"* or a region, an extent, a quantity, of the subjective-duration-feeling. Nothing is suggested about time except the perpetual "getting later" of it. And there is no basis here for a formless item answering to our "time."[14]

Similar observations have been made by Dorothy Lee in her studies of the Trobriand Islanders. She notes that in European languages there is a tendency to relate events to each other by means of imaginary lines—a *line* of trees, the *thread* of discussion, the sales *curve,* the *branches* of learning. The Trobriand Islanders have no such lineal perceptions in their language; they see in clusters or aggregates.

This newer approach to the study of semantics, the critical analysis to which traditional Aristotelian logic was subjected by pragmatists, logical positivists, empiricists, operationalists, and other schools of thought, revolutionized thinking in the field of semantics. No school of thought, however, was more revolutionary than "general semantics." And no figure was more controversial than the founder of the idea, Alfred Korzybski.

GENERAL SEMANTICS

General semantics is a new educational discipline whose function, according to its author, Korzybski, is to train people in proper evaluation. All day long, the author stated, human beings are required to evaluate—react to, think and feel about—events, words, and symbols in their environment. The evaluative habits which men rely upon are based upon the traditional Aristotelian system whose rigid inflexibility leads only to confusion, distortion, and frustration, because the system itself, and the evaluative habits which rely upon it, are inconsistent with reality. Korzybski suggested that the natural sciences and technology had, to some degree, rid themselves of the restraints of Aristotelianism, but in other areas of human activity, in ethics and politics, men were bound by them. As long as this condition exists there will continue to be a wide gap in progress in the two fields. Aristotelian exaluative habits are "intensional." They insist upon rigid definition applicable to all situations, and regard only incidentally relationships. General semantics, as a method of evaluation is extensional, and takes into consideration all possible relationships of the object under discussion to all the factors affecting it in the situation to which the discussion has reference. Such an approach, Korzybski holds, will free men's minds from dogmatism, and develop an awareness of the relativity of phenomena,—time, space, distance, and the relationships between human beings.

Since Korzybski objected so strongly to Aristotelian logic and the principles upon which it was based (see page 439), he constructed what he called a non-Aristotelian system which also rested on three basic assumptions in contradistinction to Aristotelianism. These are as follows: (1) the principle of non-identity: a map *is not* the territory (words *are not* the things they represent); (2) the principle of non-allness: a map *does not* represent all of a territory (words *cannot* say all about anything); (3) the principle of self-reflexiveness: a map is *self-reflexive* in the sense that an ideal map would have to include a map of the map, which, in turn, would have to include a map of the map, of the map, etc. The *etc.,* says Korzybski, represents the incompleteness of the knowledge we have about anything and initiates caution and preciseness as nearly as possible, rather than dogmatism and conclusiveness.

The essential ideas of Korzybski are set forth in his volume, *Science and Sanity.*[15] This volume was first published in 1933, and has since gone through two other editions, in 1941 and 1948. In neither of the later editions, however, were his essential ideas modified to any great extent.

There can be little doubt that Korzybski's influence has been strong. Through his influence the Institute for General Semantics, which is a center for training in non-Aristotelian methods, was incorporated in Chicago in 1938. It moved to its present headquarters in Lakeville, Connecticut in 1946. In 1942 the Institute began the publication of an official journal, *ETC: A Review of General Semantics*. His methods have had wide and increasing application in the field of psychotherapy where psychiatrists and clinical psychologists recognize that many of the problems of personality maladjustment stem from the patient's inability to establish an adequate relationship between the symbolic and reality. It appears, too, that Lewin's ideas of group dynamics were influenced by the general semantics of Korzybski. He had many followers, of whom Samuel A. Hayakawa may be said to be most representative. The latter's *Language in Thought and Action* contains exactly the thoughts and ideas of Korzybski's non-Aristotelian system. In much the same manner, though written in a more popular style, the works of Stuart Chase[16] show this influence.

In spite of the influence which general semantics has had during the past quarter of a century, an evaluation of Korzybski, the founder of the idea, is difficult. While he is regarded as an apostle of enlightenment by some, others considered him a dilettante, even a fraud; he is accused of having developed a cult rather than having established an empirical science as he claimed to have done. One of the most favorable criticisms of Korzybski is that of Anatol Rapoport who evaluates Korzybski's contributions as follows:

> "If Korzybski cannot be said to have established an empirical science, what then has he done? He has pointed a way toward the establishment of such a science. He was a precursor of an intellectual revolution which is just beginning and which promises to match that of the Renaissance. If Korzybski is seen in this role, then the question of his originality or erudition is not important. He might have had something of the dilettante in him. He might have pretended to have more specialized knowledge than he actually had. Great portions of his outlook might be found in the works of more modest and meticulous workers. That is not important. He was a man of vision and an apostle. Such men are all too rare in our age of specialization."[17]

Regardless of whether we agree with Rapoport or not, it can be said with a great deal of truth that general semantics has been the most influential movement in this aspect of language during the twentieth century.

THE SOCIOLOGY OF ART

Historians, traditionally, in recording the history of a nation or race, or era in the evolution of civilization, have given a great deal of attention to the development of the art of the group under study. Quite often art is cited as evidence of the level of culture achieved by the group. Anthropologists describe in minute detail the art of the non-literate groups which they study, carefully noting art forms, the materials with which the artist works, and, more importantly, the place of art in the life of the group. Archaeologists have made much of the discoveries of art in the uncovered ruins of ancient civilizations. From their discoveries they have reconstructed the past and, hence, have made more intelligible the kind of social life the people must have led. Philosophers, both ancient and modern, have not only suggested theories with regard to the origin of art, but have proposed explanations of the functions of art in the life of a people. In contrast to the attention which these scholars have given to art, sociologists have been slow in recognizing the significance of art as a social phenomenon. At an earlier period Taine, Spencer, Grosse, Guyau and Wundt were not so hesitant as modern sociologists in giving sociological treatment to fine art. Since their day, however, there is a considerable gap in our knowledge. Both Bellamy[18] and Mukurjee,[19] among others, have noted the dearth of sociological data in this important field.

More recently the sociologist's interest in art has been revived, and at least a sociological frame of reference for its proper study has been suggested. Mukurjee, who appears to have been most active in this field, defines the area of the sociology of art as follows:

> "The sociology of art is, . . . , an objective study of art work as (a) an expression of the man's personal striving and fulfillment in the ideal plane and his unique sense of values that orient, articulate or explain the social values of an epoch or culture; (b) a vehicle of communication of prevailing social values moulding the values and destiny of the individual; and (c) a record and celebration of a culture or age, an unerring clue to the life and aims of a civilization as judged by the larger conscience of humanity. It is less directly concerned, however, with dates, titles, names and biographies or with the sensuous values of works of art as individual, independent objects, which it would leave to art history. It confines itself to the social conditions of origin and operation of art work, to the background of regional, economic and social factors and forces that determine the forms of art and largely condition its motifs and themes, and also its aspirations, frustrations, and fulfillments."[20]

Within this frame of reference Mukurjee further suggests that a sociology of art can be achieved by an analysis of (1) the social and ideological background of the artist; (2) the individual artist's original or novel achievement and the art tradition; (3) the form, motif and theme of art in relation to the precise social historical setting; and (4) the acceptance or unpopularity of the art object.[21]

The author applies his method of analysis in a rather critical discussion of art, focusing attention primarily on the art of Asia and Europe. His major points of emphasis are as follows: (a) art is the medium *par excellence* of expression of the unique moods, sentiments, frustrations and fulfillments of the individual; (b) art, in whatever form it may take—painting, sculpture, architecture—expresses and symbolizes the wide range of values of society as no other form of communication can; (c) while art is an individual achievement, art for art's sake, the mere satisfaction of the individual artist's impulses irrespective of the demands of society, rests on a false basis. The artist always produces for an audience, an audience which may already exist or one that he wishes to create. (d) Historically, it has been periods of great social upheaval which have given birth to great art. He cites as evidence the development of Buddhist art in India which followed the ravages of the armies of Chandra Gupta Maurya which led to India's first unification, the bloody struggles and invasion of China in the fifth century A. D. which gave rise to art in the Wei tradition, and Italian art of the Renaissance which was nurtured among civil tumults, internecine quarrels, and the debauches of Italian cities.

Following rather closely the pattern set by Mukurjee, Gotshalk makes what may be described as a sociological analysis of art in his book, *Art and the Social Order.*[22] The central points in Gotshalk's analysis are as follows: (a) Art, in whatever form it appears, is expressive of the times and the spirit of the society in which it is produced. (b) Art is a process. It is the product of interaction between the artist and the society in which he lives. The artist, says Gotshalk, is not more percipient than the rest of the people; he is merely able to concentrate his percipient powers and thus produce the forms and expressions in art objects, which in turn become the overt symbols of the values, the wishes and frustrations of society. (c) Art has both aesthetic and non-aesthetic functions. Aesthetically, "a work of art can bring out excellently the qualities of all other dimensions as termini of intrinsic perceptions."[23] Art is also a spiritual asset. As a spiritual good, fine art has considerable magnitude actually and potentially.

> "It is a spiritual asset, yielding to the members of society a large variety of immediate goods which in themselves have a justification that is positive and decisive. It is also a civilizing force, capable of exerting a social influence along two different lines. It can make innumerable contributions to an enlightened social

life, . . . , and it can make at least three major broad contributions—developing the capacities, the value range, and personality
of the individual; fostering a sense of human dignity; and providing a vision of human purpose in ideal embodiment that can
serve as a guide for both personal and group life." [24]

The non-aesthetic functions of art are both individual and group.
For the individual, art provides satisfaction for the will or drive for
mastery and achievement for the artist. His art object may be the
means of making money, or winning fame and prestige and social
power. It may serve a similar purpose for those who obtain the objects
of art. For the group, art has manifold non-aesthetic functions:

> "A building may shelter an industry, an educational institution,
> a congregation, or a family. A sculptured figure may serve as a
> religious icon or as a memorial to the fallen soldiers of a nation.
> Poetry, music, the dance may bolster the morale of a group or
> play a vital part in a festive occasion. Painting may record the
> deeds of a celebrated citizen, a king, or a prizefighter." [25]

Art also satisfies certain "physical" group needs, such as shelter and
transportation, and certain "mental" needs, in the communication
of feelings and experiences. It also functions to weld the individuals
of a group into a purposively active, unified society. Art is also instrumental. It can be a great social force, convincing society of the validity
of a certain social direction or redirection—political, religious, economic, and the like—or it may indirectly imply the universality of
social values for all times rather than for a specific period. In the
latter sense art serves an aesthetic function and, hence, lives longer.

Mukurjee has served an important function in formulating a frame
of reference and suggesting a method of analysis for the sociological
study of art. Both Mukurjee and Gotshalk have taken important steps
in sociological analysis of art. In all probability future sociological
studies will follow their lead until more precise methods have been
suggested.

THE SOCIOLOGY OF LITERATURE

The observations made regarding the fragmentary sociological data
with regard to art may also be applied to literature, but perhaps to a
lesser extent. In its broadest sense, all written communication in a
literate society constitutes its literature. One may also include the

myths, legends, proverbs and other stories of the group. In this broader
sense there is no lack of study and analysis of the content of communication and its effect on human behavior. Students of public
opinion and propaganda have been preoccupied with such analyses
for some time. In the more limited sense as the term is used here to
include poetry, novels, and drama, sociological analysis and description
have been lacking.

On the other hand, sociologists have not been unaware of the
function of literature as an agency of social control. Every great social
movement has been marked by the emergence of a great body of
literature which dramatically described the conditions of the times,
and the hopes and fears of the oppressed. Along with historians,
sociologists point out the influence of the writings of Voltaire on the
French Revolution, of Harriet Beecher Stowe's *Uncle Tom's Cabin*
on the question of Negro slavery, of Upton Sinclair's *The Jungle*
on the stockyard scandals at the turn of the century, of John Stein-
beck's *Grapes of Wrath* on thought and action regarding the "Oakies"
of the late thirties, and many others of similar vein.

The most important sociological treatise on literature within the
recent past is Duncan's, *Language and Literature in Society*.[26] In much
the same manner as Mukurjee and Gotshalk have analyzed art Duncan
treats literature, suggesting in the latter part of his book a frame of
reference within which a sociological analysis of literature may be
made. Duncan regards literature as great art, in which the author
describes dramatically and emotionally both the world of reality and
the world of make-believe, consciously manipulating symbols—words
—directed toward a desired end. Literature is also great magical art.
Through prayers, incantations, liturgy and the like the supernatural
is implored or persuaded to do the bidding of the group; the group
is, in turn, controlled by such prayers and incantations as it utters
and engages in the appropriate action with reference to the supernatural power. In another sense the magical art of literature is observed in the persuasive power of the politician or the authoritarian
ruler as his words move the group to action. Literature is also make-
believe. The author constructs a world of fantasy which embodies the
hopes and fears of the group. The world of make-believe provides a
convenient means of escape from the world of reality. It also functions
as a means through which the inhibitions of the members of society
can be released in a socially approved manner. Literature is also a
social institution. The literary craftsman follows standardized forms,

rules of grammar, cliches, plots and situations. The roles of the characters are the roles of society, ideally or realistically portrayed. Finally, Duncan suggests a sociological frame of reference for the study of literature which would include an analysis of the persuasive function of symbols, and the relation of symbols to authority. In all probability future studies of the sociology of literature will follow the pattern suggested by Duncan.

SUMMARY

The importance of language has long been recognized and it has been the object of study by scholars in many specialized fields. Earlier studies of language focused attention on its origin. In the twenties and early thirties a great deal of attention was given to the process by which the child acquires language and the function of language in the development of his personality. From the thirties on semantics has been the focus of attention. For centuries studies in semantics were influenced by Aristotelian logic. With the publication of Lady Welby's *What is Meaning*, in which she developed her concept, "significs," there came a break with traditional Aristotelianism and formalism of the past. Since then there has been a long stream of scholars, including Whitehead, Russell, Tarski, Carnap, among others, representing various schools of thought—logical empiricism, logical positivism, operationalism and others—which revolutionized thinking in the field of semantics. One of the most controversial figures of the times was Alfred Korzybski. His non-Aristotelian system, set forth in what he called "General Semantics," aroused considerable comment and criticism. However, it has been perhaps the most important single influence in the field of semantics in the twentieth century.

In the fields of literature and art there has not been a great deal of activity. The works of Mukurjee and Gotshalk in art, and of Duncan in literature have set a pattern which holds considerable promise for future studies in these fields.

BIBLIOGRAPHY

Rudolf Carnap, *Introduction to Semantics* (Cambridge: Harvard University Press, 1948). A somewhat technical discussion of the author's thesis of logical syntax.

Ernest Cassirer, *Language and Myth*, translated by S. K. Langer (New York: Harper, 1946). The ideas of the late Professor Cassirer on the relation of language and thought, and the development of ideas, are set forth.

Stuart Chase, *Guides to Straight Thinking* (New York: Harper, 1956). A discusion of forty-three common fallacies in thinking and speaking; easy to read; the influence of Korzybski is unmistakable.

Hugh Dalziel Duncan, *Language and Literature in Society* (University of Chicago Press, 1954). A scholarly analysis of the sociology of literature; contains a representative and fairly comprehensive bibliography on the sociology of literature and art.

D. W. Gotshalk, *Art and the Social Order* (University of Chicago Press, 1947). An excellent sociological treatment of art, its functions, and place in society.

Samuel I. Hayakawa, *Language in Thought and Action* (New York: Harcourt, Brace, 1949). A discussion of language and meaning from the point of view of general semantics.

Samuel I. Hayakawa, Ed., *Language, Meaning and Maturity* (New York: Harper, 1954). A selection of articles of general semantics appearing in *ETC*, 1943-53; contributions made by anthropologists, linguists, philosophers, psychologists, and other specialists.

Harry Hoijer, Ed., *Language in Culture* (University of Chicago Press, 1954). A collection of papers and discussions by anthropologists, linguists, philosophers, and psychologists on language and its relation to thought.

Wendell Johnson, *People in Quandaries: The Semantics of Personal Adjustment* (New York: Harper, 1946). An excellent discussion by an eminent psychologist and speech specialist of the speech difficulties of people and the relationship of these difficulties to personality organization and disorganization.

Alfred Korzybski, *Science and Sanity* (Lakeville, Connecticut: The International Non-Aristotelian Library Publishing Company, 1948). The author sets forth his non-Aristotelian principles upon which general semantics is based.

Jakob S. Kasanin, *Language and Thought in Schizophrenia* (Berkeley: University of California Press, 1944). A series of papers organized around the central topic of schizophrenic language and thought.

Suzanne K. Langer, *Philosophy in a New Key* (New York: Penguin Books, 1948). A rather interesting discussion of symbolism in art, religion, myth and human behavior generally.

Radhakmal Mukurjee, *The Social Function of Art* (Bombay: Hind Kitabs, Limited, 1951). An excellent sociological analysis of art, in which the author suggests a method for its proper study.

George Herbert Mead, *Mind, Self and Society* (University of Chicago Press, 1934). A classic on the shared nature of symbols and the meaning of gestures.

Charles W. Morris, *Signs, Language and Behavior* (New York: Prentice-Hall, 1946). The author is concerned with the development of an adequate technical vocabulary for the discussion and analysis of sign behavior.

Benjamin Lee Whorf, "Science and Linguistics," in Newcomb and Hartley, *Readings in Social Psychology* (New York: Henry Holt, 1947), 210-218. A scholarly discussion on the conditioning of reasoning by language structure.

Clifton R. Jones, Professor of Sociology, Morgan State College (Baltimore, Maryland); B.A., Virginia Union University (1935); M.A., State University of Iowa (1939); Ph.D., State University of Iowa (1943); G.E.B. Research Fellow, Fisk University (1940-1941); Research Associate and Instructor in Sociology, Fisk University (1943); Professor of Sociology, Florida A & M University (1945-1946); Professor of Sociology, Morgan State College (1946–). Rosenwald Fellow, State University of Iowa (1941-1943); member: Pi Gamma Mu. Has published numerous studies in such periodicals as *Journal of Negro Education, Social Forces, Journal of Higher Education Among Negroes,* etc.; author of "The Negro Press," Chapter 14, pp. 401-415, in Francis J. Brown & Joseph S. Roucek, *One America* (1952).

NOTES

1. Edward Sapir, "Language," *Encyclopedia of the Social Sciences,* IV, 155.

2. Wilhelm Wundt, *Elements of Folk Psychology, translated* by E. S. Schaub (London: Allen and Unwin, 1928), Chapter 1.

3. J. G. Herder, *Abhandlung Über den Ursprung der Sprache,* in *Herder's Sammtliche Werke* (Berlin: Weidmannsche Buchhandlung, 1877-1913), V.

4. L. Noire, *The Origin and Philosophy of Language* (Chicago: Open Ct., 1917), 73-74.

5. Grace de Laguna, *Speech: Its Function and Development* (New Haven: Yale University Press, 1927).

6. M. W. Smith, *An Investigation of the Development of the Sentence and the Extent of Vocabulary in Young Children* (Iowa City: University of Iowa Studies in Child Welfare, 1930), No. 5.

7. Jean Piaget, *The Language and Thought of the Child* (New York: Harcourt, Brace, 1926).

8. Dorothy McCarthy, *The Language Development of the Pre-School Child* (Minneapolis: University of Minnesota Institute of Child Welfare Monograph, 1930), No. 4.

9. Rugg, Krueger and Sondergaard, "A Study of Language in Kindergarten Children," *Journal of Educational Psychology,* XX (1929), 1-18.

10. Charles K. Ogden and Ivor A. Richards, *The Meaning of Meaning* (New York: Harcourt, Brace, 1946), Chapter 1.

11. Samuel A. Hayakawa, *Language, Meaning and Maturity* (New York: Harper, 1954) , 20-21. Quoted by permission of the publisher.

12. Rudolf Carnap, *Introduction to Semantics* (Cambridge: Harvard University Press) , 1948, I, iv-ix.

13. Charles Morris, *Signs, Language and Behavior* (New York: Prentice-Hall, 1946).

14. Benjamin Lee Whorf, "The Relation of Habitual Thought and Behavior to Language," in S. A. Hayakawa, Ed., *op. cit.*, 225-226. Quoted by permission of the publisher.

15. Alfred Korzybski, *Science and Sanity* (Lakeville, Conn.: The International Non-Aristotelian Library Publishing Company, 1948) .

16. Stuart Chase, *Guides to Straight Thinking* (New York: Harper, 1956)

17. Anatol Rapoport, "What is Semantics?" in S. A. Hayakawa (Ed.) , *Language, Meaning and Maturity* (New York: Harper, 1954), 17. Quoted by permission of the publisher.

18. Joseph S. Roucek, Ed., *Social Control* (New York: D. Van Nostrand and Company, 1947) , 240.

19. Radhakmal Mukurjee, *The Social Function of Art* (Bombay: Hind Kitabs, Limited, 1951) , ix.

20. Radhakmal Mukurjee, *op. cit.*, 30-31.

21. *Ibid.*, 37.

22. D. W. Gotshalk, *Art and the Social Order* (University of Chicago Press, 1947).

23. D. W. Gotshalk, *op. cit.*, 163.

24. *Ibid.*, 217.

25. *Ibid.*, 158.

26. Hugh Dalziel Duncan, *Language and Literature in Society* (University of Chicago Press, 1953).

ANTHROPOLOGY AND SOCIOLOGY

Fred W. Voget
University of Arkansas

All sciences can be delimited by the kinds of problems investigated, by the assumptions and techniques that guide solutions, and by the objective reality in which the problems are seated. These separate yet interrelated aspects also serve as axes whereby the different sciences may become interrelated, if not united. Any science, too, has a history, in which problems, theory and methodology, and content may reveal shifts of both a qualitative and quantitative nature.

To understand recent trends in anthropology and its relations to sociology a short resume of the history and connections of these two sciences is in order.

ANTHROPOLOGY AND SOCIOLOGY IN HISTORIC PERSPECTIVE

Both anthropology and sociology emerged as sciences in the first half of the 19th century, and both were nourished on the philosophic and political thought of the 18th century, which had programmed a naturalistic view of man in relation to an ordered universe. Admittedly man in society was unordered yet, but with the use of applied reason man could progress without limit. This naturalistic, reasoning, and progressive view, when united with the developing experimental outlook of the biological sciences furnished the mortar for "scientific" anthropology and sociology at their beginnings.

Actually throughout the 19th century anthropology and sociology were hardly distinguishable, with the possible exception of some content. Both sciences were heavily oriented toward an historic development of man in society and culture. And both tied man to nature by showing that man's social relationships and customs, though of a different order of reality than the inorganic and the organic, still responded to principles of organization and process operating generally in nature. This naturalistic and evolutionary view is well-illustrated by Herbert Spencer, who, after reviewing the evolution of the inorganic and the organic, went on to show that the superorganic (society and custom) also moved from a simple yet discrete homogeneity to a complex yet "coherent heterogeneity."[1] Although a "sociologist," Spencer's tracing of the simple origins of man's economic, social, political, and religious organization and custom to more complex stages was no different at base than the efforts of "anthropologists" like Bochhofen, Morgan, and Tylor.[2]

Nineteenth century naturalistic humanism, with its comparative method and evolutionary stages, has provided a common floor for the programming of problems in both anthropology and sociology. And while differences that were to distinguish these two sciences gradually accumulated, scientific humanism nevertheless continued a predominant influence well into the 20th century.[3] At this time both anthropology and sociology made a significant turn by repudiating interpretations based on a universal human psyche in progressive evolution.

When Durkheim (1895) enunciated his dictum that "social facts" alone can interpret other social facts he not only denied psychogenic interpretations but also implied the uniqueness of each social and cultural system, although in practice he sought a type from which he could generalize all situations.[4] In his *Elementary Forms of the Religious Life* (1912), Durkheim illustrated and analyzed how the collective ideas and symbols to which men related themselves in action, feeling, and object originated not out of a common human psyche but out of social interaction.[5] Henceforth, sociologists, especially in the United States, were to turn their backs on the historic and humanistic approaches and to converge on a scientific sociology that found reality in social interaction and science in the mustering and manipulation of data in mass—impersonal yet mathematically precise.

In anthropology the repudiation of psycho-cultural evolution first took shape in an emphasis on the historic process of diffusion, which denied evolutionistic stages since interruptions to the sequence might arise through the spread of inventions and ideas. Secondly, anthropologists like Boas[6] began to assert the uniqueness of each social and cultural system (and situation) and to insist on first reaching into the historic past of a system and into its relations with other systems before admitting independent origin or common psychic responses. Thus, Boas' contribution in anthropology was much like that of Durkheim in sociology, only now the dictum might be phrased, "a culture fact is to be interpreted by a culture fact,—first."

However, scientific anthropology, unlike scientific sociology, remained committed to an historic approach. This followed naturally from a total view of man as a developing species and as a culture-builder. History is an important accent for any definition of culture, which Kluckhohn and Kelly describe as an "historically created design for living" transmitted by one generation to a succeeding generation.[7]

The link with history and the assumption that any culture possesses an integration that makes it greater than the sum of its parts led anthropologists to maintain a more humanistic approach to their subject, man in culture, than is the case for sociologists, despite the fact that neither are committed to description and analysis at the personal level. This holistic and humanistic trend has moved anthropologists to project their problems on a grand scale while sociologists have sought the exercise of scientific control by narrowing considerably the limits of their problems. Moreover, since the data that anthropologists required lay unrecorded, they found themselves of necessity engaged in a gigantic program of salvage in which single anthropologists entered the field and attempted the description of a unique culture. Guided at first by a growing list of descriptive categories to be covered, they moved gradually in the direction of descriptive or "depictive" integration and came to grips with the problems of function and of ethos in culture. To a large extent the very necessities of field operations turned anthropologists away from the use of numbers to convey validity to their results.

The emergence of the concept of function in anthropology in the twenties emphasized anew the integrative nature of cultural systems, but in this instance viewed it largely as a product of a kind of social physiology. Functionalism emphasized process in contradistinction to "static" description, whether historic or categoric. Malinowski[8] concentrated on processes essential to the maintenance of the culture-organism, for social structure and process in his view rested firmly upon the basic organic requirements of the human body. Culture patterns and social processes then grew out of and fulfilled basic human needs, as metabolism, reproduction safety, growth, health, etc. Other functionalistic exponents, as Radcliffe-Brown, developed an "institutional" approach in which function is tied to the maintenance of social structures, defined as "set(s) of relations amongst unit entities" (individuals).[9] Culture patterns in this case spring out of social interaction (as Durkheim asserted) and are functional insofar as they maintain the continuity of interaction essential to the social structure. This Durkheimian interactionist tradition has shaped contemporary British Anthropology and aligns it more with a sociological than with the usual cultural approach of anthropology.[10]

Functionalism, as noted above, is one approach to the problem of integration in culture. In the hands of Ruth Benedict cultural integration became a style of life based on an historic selection from a total range or "arc of culture."[11] Cultures now were delineated in terms of sociopsychological configurations in which Dionysian stylists exhibited tendencies to transcend routine human experience, whereas cautious Apollonian stylists tread a more sober and moderate path through life.

This fresh emphasis upon the psychological underpinning of culture patterns converged in the first instance on the problem of a culture-induced personality and in the second instance on the problem of values and motivation. For the first time a sober and intensive exploration of the psychological dimensions and variations of culture patterns began. Heretofore most anthropologists had treated human nature and how the individual actually learns and supports his culture patterns as "given." They had rested content with a learning theory that emphasized conditioning, since men in tribal societies gave every evidence of being habit-bound and in no hurry to separate themselves from tradition.

Yet learning theory could throw no light on the stimulus configurations that gave rise to patterned behaviors like totemism, social avoidances and licenses, shamanism, ritualized cannibalism, captive torture, homosexuality, and the like. Some of the dynamics of human personality must be sought elsewhere. Here anthropologists found the Freudian leads far more insightful than the rationalistic approach of the 19th century or the modified rationalism of stimulus-response psychology.[12] Of course this Freudian approach implied a reappraisal of human nature and the basic axes of response. Man now was essentially irrational, moved by sudden, yet persistent, non-cognitive impulses rooted in frustration, repression, guilt, anxiety, aggression, and insecurity. This new approach also implied that the dynamics of human motivation must be searched in the individual's reaction to the learning context rather than what he apparently learned in the socio-cultural context.

While accepting the psychological processes of Freudians, including the view that personality largely is structured during early childhood, grosser features based on a universal instinctual ontogeny generally were rejected. Moreover, concern with the group necessarily directed research toward modalities rather than to individual idiosyncrasies. And since these modal personalities could be delimited best through test materials devoid of cultural verbalisms and content specific to Western culture, special projective tests like the Rorschach and modified Thematic Apperception Tests found considerable favor.[13] "Personality in culture" monographs always included a description and analysis of the culture but first treatments proved to be highly selective and interpretive since the context for personality development alone defined the range of significant observation and description.[14] Owing to the assumption that man basically is non-cognitive and unable or unwilling to verbalize his motives in conflict with ideal patterns, there was a tendency to interpret the informant's behavior as covert or to use the projective test as the final arbiter of reliability. Since projective tests and interpretations were standardized on European populations, their cross-cultural validity early came to be questioned. While admitting that the validity of projective tests in the cross-cultural dimension has yet to be proved, anthropologists have found them to be a useful supplement to traditional techniques and are convinced that the tests reflect substantial agreement with the observations and independent interpretations of ethnographers.[15]

CONVERGENCE IN ANTHROPOLOGY AND SOCIOLOGY

The late twenties and thirties not only witnessed significant turns in both anthropology and sociology but considerable convergence in the development of similar problems,—e.g., personality development, structural-functional processes, the relation of attitudes and values to actual human behavior, and the application of social science to the persistent and demanding problems of man in society and culture. But in treating these common problems, each science tended to maintain its distinctive methodological character. This can be seen in the study of personality, where anthropologists explored Neo-Freudian psychodynamics while sociologists picked up the strands of Cooley's (1902) social role theory, freshly reinterpreted by Mead (1934).[16]

Nevertheless, some methodological convergence can be found. Theories and methods drawn from European sociologists, culture historians, and psychologists (notably Gestalt) conveyed a fresh holistic and interpretive strain that influenced American sociologists and anthropologists alike. The sociologically-trained Lynds[17] applied a combined sociological and anthropological approach to the study of an American industrial community, while Redfield,[18] an anthropologist, began the study of "folk" communities, comparing and contrasting their structural and functional qualities with those of urban communities.

Although community studies at first were conducted with the idea of depicting structures and processes within a timeless social and cultural system, it became evident that certain processes were changing. Moreover the changes were introducing functional disturbances that must be considered disorganizing to both the social and to the personality systems. Of course, social and cultural disorganization were strangers neither to sociologists, whose ecological studies of urban areas had produced apparent correlations between the socio-economic conditions of the slums and a higher incidence of delinquency and mental disease,—nor to anthropologists, who had become aware of the serious dislocation of the cultural systems that they sought to describe. Nevertheless, in anthropology theoretical interest in recording, even in reconstruction, the unique untouched system initially pushed the problems of change and of disorganization into the background. The advent of functionalism did not change this situation materially. Since functionalism by very definition focussed on the physiology of structures, it tended to be non-historical, and even to deny the legitimacy of interest in historic developments. For functionalism was "scientific," directed to the production of social laws, whereas history was developmental and concerned with unique and non-recurrent events, hence, non-scientific.[19] Functionalists thus aligned themselves squarely with the sociological approach.

However, the historic orientation in anthropology was too firmly embedded in some of its basic parts and problems (pre-history, human paleontology, and the distribution in time and space of races, languages, culture traits and complexes) to allow the amputation extreme functionalists called for.[20] The spread of industrialism into the remotest areas of the world also complicated structural-processual interpretations in present time alone and made use of a limited history imperative. Emphasis on process thus turned equally in the direction of on-going change, especially where persistent and intensified contact had altered but not destroyed the indigenous culture-system, as in Africa and Oceania, where the foremost exponents of functionalism operated.

However, new investigative areas like acculturation and applied anthropology might still be lying dormant but for the comprehensive disruption of the industrial societies of the West and their dependencies owing to the World Wars and the Great Depression. The stern need to control conflict and to restore the equilibrium of the socioeconomic system generated by depression and war paved the way for more realistic studies of human relations in the work world and for efforts at social planning with the help of social scientists. As culturally distinct minority groups grew restless and made demands for a better social and economic life and for political autonomy, Western governments turned to anthropologists for data and for advice that would implement their plans for westernization, or reorganizations that would give the subordinate groups more control over their future.[21] Governmental needs during the war also diverted research to the administration of conquered areas, enemy aliens, and the "national psychology" of the enemy.[22]

The continuing high-level crisis in the western world over the past twenty-five years thus has jogged anthropologists and sociologists alike into a kind of social practicality. For those who grew up with the scientific ideal at the start of the 20th century, this linking of social science with the life of the community in a planning capacity was particularly uncongenial because of its apparent subversion of "pure science." Actually the contrary prevailed, for attention to application not only broadened perspective by introducing new problems, but forced methodological changes also. Anthropologists, in tackling human relations in industry and in implementing administrative programmes for minority groups became more aware of the importance of social interaction and social structure whereas sociologists who investigated the industrial transformation of tribal societies were sensitized to the significance of cultural differences for social action.[23] By and large, however, the mutual influence which these two sciences have exerted upon each other never has extended to basic methodology.[24]

RECENT TRENDS IN ANTHROPOLOGY: 1947-57

Recent trends in anthropology largely continue or represent adjustments of the basic ethnopsychological, historical, structural-functional, and applied emphases that emerged during the ferment of the thirties. From the literature it is evident that anthropologists feel that they

again have completed an exploratory phase and that another significant turn in their science is at hand. This is demonstrated by concerted
efforts now being made to systematize the theory and method of the
anthropological "frontier" and to disseminate it throughout the scientific community. There is a call for more precise definitions of problems and for the use of techniques that will yield a more consistent
and a wider range of control for generalization.

Of necessity the summary of contemporary trends that follows must
be selective and incomplete. A number of major problems and fields
have been utilized in organizing the discussion: culture processes and
sequences, cultural integration, society and personality, linguistics,
applied anthropology, and theory and method.

CULTURE PROCESSES AND SEQUENCES

In some measure the scientific, functionalist, and psychological permutations in anthropology after 1930 produced an anti-historical and
non-comparative bias since the study of interrelationships was considered sufficient, or it was argued that the relevance of any cultural
datum must be sought in context. Gradually, however, a new historicism devoted to sequential developments derivable from controlled
comparisons of structures and processes arose in response to the challenging discoveries of archeologists. European prehistorians, as the
ancient civilizations of the Near East unfolded before pick and spade,
were in an advantageous position to compare and to advance structural sequences and processes in the development of complex civilizations.

At first efforts were devoted to the immediate effects of major
inventions (cultivation, metallurgy, writing) upon culture growth and
the transformations that followed in the wake of their spread. By 1936
Childe was arguing that prehistory was a "continuation of natural
history" and that "progress in culture," marked by a differentiation
and advance in control over environment was analogous to organic
evolution.[25] Advance in human history could be described, and more,
each major advance was signalized by "an economic revolution of
the same kind and having the same effect as the 'Industrial Revolution'
of the eighteenth century."[26] Culture advanced in mutative surges that
followed a signal change from food-gathering to food-producing econ-
omies, and this in turn prepared the way for a succeeding "urban

revolution" based on a "specialized manufacture and external trade" economy.[27]

The high civilizations of the New World have produced socio-economic sequences remarkably similar to those described for the Near East and Europe. In both Middle America and the Andes a food-gathering, formative (horticultural), efflorescent, and militaristic order can now be described, with urban settlements appearing in the efflorescent or classic phase but reaching their peak during the militaristic.[28] Yet it is not clear that the urban trends followed an independent and parallel development in each area since "original historical unity and later indirect diffusion" may have combined to produce these synchronous resemblances.[29]

When archeologists in the New World defined the essential unity of Middle and Andean America (referred to as Nuclear America, Kroeber, 1948; Bennett, 1951),[30] they advanced to a cultural universe of interaction comparable to that of the Ancient East, with a promise of significant generalizations. In 1949 Steward went on to compare structural regularities in the Near East, China, and the New World, and, finding them to be remarkably similar, he concluded that "wide diffusion of particulars within . . . and even between hemispheres . . . does not mean that diffusion must be accepted as the principal explanation of cultural development."[31] In 1955 Willey and Phillips compared areal and multi-areal regularities in the New World by means of a developmental classification that included six stages: "(1) Early Lithic, (2) Archaic, (3) Preformative, (4) Formative, (5) Classic, and (6) Postclassic."[32]

The grand rhythms and surges in cultural evolution now opening before prehistorians have not been too evident to ethnologists, although a number on both sides of the Atlantic have insisted that developmental regularities are a proper focus for cultural studies. In the United States, Leslie White has described three levels of reality —scientific (functional), historic, and evolutionistic—each with a special methodology.[30] After pointing out that all sciences "have traveled these three roads" White asserts that anthropology likewise must complete its conception of reality with a legitimate interest in depicting the "evolution of culture as a whole."[34] The key to cultural evolution employed by White is economic. As a people increase their ratio of energy to the individual and distribute it efficiently culture advances and grows more complex, socially, politically, and ideologically.[35] Admitting that a "social system may so condition the operation of a technological system as to impose a limit upon the extent to which it can expand and develop," White comes to deny the inevitability of evolution and progress, contending that "only by tapping some new source of energy and by harnessing it in sufficient magnitude to burst asunder the social system" can culture in this instance move ahead.[36]

Kroeber, by way of contrast, sought culture rhythms and the key to grand cultural processes in the documented creativity of geniuses, who have a way of "clustering" when patterns expressive of "high cultural values" are produced. While finding good evidence for a pulsative type of creativity and *value pattern* growth and decline, Kroeber[37] detected no inevitable systemic "culture-beat" like that of Toynbee[38] nor rhythmic alternation of "super-systems" as enunciated by Sorokin.[39]

In Redfield the approach to systematic changes again is through an economic door, but the significant effects are sought in the "moral order" rather than in the technological, social, and political contexts.[40] Beginning with the isolated but homogeneous "folk society," Redfield traces world culture history to a "peasant" and finally to an "urban" stage. The trend throughout is from a collectively-implemented moral order to a personally-implemented type—from social and cultural homogeneity to heterogeneity. Implicit in the approach is the idea that growth of alternatives in the cultural system has left urban man with a segmented, if not fragmented, social life and personality, and that he is more or less adrift since he has no strong group ties. In contrasting the moral tenor and primary group solidarity of the folk society with the isolating and segmentalizing quality of secondary interpersonal relations at the urban level, Redfield demonstrates his basic sociological orientation.

Anthropologists long have considered the study of social organization particularly advantageous for the discovery of regularities that may be defined as "laws." When citing "scientific laws" discovered by anthropologists, Lowie[41] turned immediately to the field of social organization as have functionalists and cross-cultural comparativists. In his *Social Structure*, Murdock eloquently affirms that "the elements of social organization, in their permutations and combinations, conform to natural laws of their own with an exactitude scarcely less striking than that which characterizes the permutations and combinations of atoms in chemistry and of genes in biology."[42]

This statement by Murdock followed his comparison of 250 tribal societies according to types of families, kin and local groups, and kinship and demonstration of functional relationships with the aid of statistical correlations. Besides testing statistically certain theories on the regulation of sex, the presence of incest taboos and extensions, he also developed seven "social laws" of sexual selection based on negative and positive gradients. His most enterprising contribution, however, was a technique for reconstructing the "evolution of social organization by recognizing 'survivals' from previous forms of organization" and utilizing them analytically to "yield reliable indications of historically antecedent types of social structure."[43] Under such a systematic procedure little could be offered about processes, but in Murdock's view altered economic conditions induced shifts in residence that affected family and clan organization, which in turn brought changes in kinship terminology and transitional social systems.[44] Although there is much in Murdock's method to warrant caution, there can be little doubt that he has advanced the study of social organization considerably.[45]

British and French functionalists have contributed some outstanding ethnographies and regional surveys (notably in Africa) of social, political, legal, and religious organization besides socioeconomic studies of labor mobility, urban slums, and mine locations.[46] Most studies are interlarded with propositions that relate certain qualities of the social structure to sociopsychological "syndromes."[47] Following the leads of Radcliffe-Brown[48] and Mauss[49] there also is a tendency to discover a basic or focal complex of social and psychological interrelations that will acount for a complex of sentiments that underwrites the total order. For Radcliffe-Brown the focal arena for these supporting sentiments was ritual, with which Nadel and Wilson are in agreement, following their studies of Nupe and Nyakyusa religion.[50]

Studies of cultural change resulting from contact also are producing some striking reorientations in views about the interrelations of the individual, society, and culture. Anthropologists have long maintained that peoples undergoing acculturation used their culture base as a measure for the selective rejection or adoption of novel traits and complexes, but the actual processes involved in perceiving, interpreting, and selecting received scant attention. Habituation was a sufficient explanation. But when personality-in-culture studies of Pueblo and Plains societies were made, it became evident that the seeming incapacity to adjust and adapt included modal configurations based on immobolizing anxieties and compulsive hostile withdrawal.[51] Projective test protocols and case studies also have posed the challenge of variation in individual response within the shared cultural milieu[52] (Vogt, 1951; Kaplan, 1954). New theoretical interest in the individual and categories of individuals in relation to variation has sundered the presumed social and cultural homogeneity of tribal communities undergoing acculturation, and promoted psychological studies of socio-cultural categories arranged along the acculturative continuum.[53] While there is a growing realization that the acculturative context may produce a "normless" and conflictive type of individual who fosters innovations out of personal impulse rather than by a cultural measure, anthropological interest and explanation do not lead to the conception of the innovator as a "marginal man."[54] Generally the focal problems of change are considered to lie in the processes of choice and what follows upon choice. Hence the importance of the desirable (values) in persuading people to choose one alternative over another, which has served as a guide for comprehensive research among the Navaho and adjoining Anglo, Mormon, Texan, and Mexican communities (See publications of the values study, Papers of the Peabody Museum, Harvard University).

The study of value choices in situations of contradiction and outright conflict is one way of testing the pervasive qualities of culture-percepts. Barnett following Linton[55] has analyzed culture-percepts in terms of a form-meaning-function-principle nexus and extended his analysis in depth by means of psychological theories of perception, principally Gestalt,—since "Acceptance [or rejection], like perception and conception, is by configurated wholes."[56] Throughout studies in acculturative processes a considerable strain toward an experimental approach within a limited universe can be detected, as in the testing of the responses of different peoples in comparable historic situations or in situations where a single variable has been altered.[57]

CULTURAL INTEGRATION AND PERSONALITY

Two basic assumptions stand behind the holistic approach to the study of culture. In the first instance, the parts of any culture are assumed to be interrelated functionally or "organically" so that a shift in one activity will carry important effects to another activity. In the second place it is asserted that fundamental principles drive the parts into a state of wholeness or integration that is beyond any simple addition of parts. Studies in functionalism largely account for the structure-maintenance process, whereas studies in ethos account for the configurational processes. In matters of ethos it is inevitable, perhaps, that values, goals, attitudes and world views come to be considered.[58]

Early studies in cultural ethos, like those of Benedict[59] and Mead[60] made use of polar entities to contrast different psychological configurations expressed in a "style of life" or in interpersonal orientations. Bipolarity is also fundamental to Redfield's folk-urban constructs, although he later interpolated the "peasant society" in his continuum. Behind the different type-societies Redfield ultimately discovered a basis for unity in the ethical principles that oriented individuals to the world and to their fellows. In 1945 Opler[61] introduced the concept of a cultural "theme," which he defined as a "postulate" or basic assumption that a people made about nature, man's relation to it, and man's relation to man, and by which they guided their decisions and actions. In his view cultural integration was an effect of the adjustment of inconsistent, variant, and contradictory themes.

As themes are basic orientations expressed or symbolized in specific situations or classes of situations, the approach is of the same order as the empirically-geared value studies carried out by Kluckhohn and associates to uncover the nature of cultural and personal unity and variation.[62] In a theoretical statement, "Dominant and Variant Value Orientations," Florence Kluckhohn aims "to show that different societies make different selections among possible [i.e., limited] solutions of common human problems."[63] And, although "one of the alternative principles" is raised to a "dominant position," she insists that "variant values," expressed in individual and group actions, are *"not only permitted but actually required"*[64] to maintain the system. The universals of cultural systems are derived from five common human problem areas, each of which allows for three basic solutions, besides limited variations, as shown in the table reproduced below:

Studies devoted to ethos configurations readily transpose into ethos-personality processes and *vice versa* since both imply a structured set of internal relationships. Analyses of cultures in their configurational aspects at the present time owe as much to the continued pursuit of personality-in-culture processes as to a specific commitment to cultural analysis *per se*. This is well-demonstrated by the "national character" and cultural studies "at a distance" carried out by Mead and associates.[66] The theoretical emphasis here is on a multi-dimensional thematic approach to cultural analysis and the effects which these themes exert in the socialization of the child.[67] In using a thematic approach Mead apparently has made an about-face in her personality and culture studies. In place of relying on early childhood syndromes to explain how the core patterns are supported (if they do not originate here), she now traces the effects of cultural orientations, as implemented in the child-training program, on personality development.

Human Problems and Type Solutions

Innate Predis- positions:	Evil (mutable or immutable)	Neither good nor bad (mu- table or im- mutable)	Good (mutable or immutable)
Man's Relation to Nature:	Man subju- gated to nature	Man in nature	Man over nature
Time Dimen- sion:	Past	Present	Future
Valued Person- ality Type:	Being	Being-in Becoming	Doing
Modality of Relationship:	Lineal	Collateral	Individual- istic[65]

This shift in ground by Mead is symptomatic of a general reevaluation of the contribution which the psychoanalytic approach can make to the study of personality-in-culture. It is now becoming evident that human personality may or may not be fixated by early childhood according to circumstances, thus allowing more significance to post-childhood role-playing. A reexamination of neo-Freudian theories of cultural integration also is in order. Kardiner[68] for example, argued that childhood frustrations and repressions precipitated unconscious "psychological constellations," which, when shared in a particular society, could be viewed as the "basic personality" of the group. The basic personality constituted the groundwork for the integration of culture, since core constellations, largely the result of frustration and repression, are expressed as unconscious projections in "secondary institutions."

Functionalist enunciation of the primal significance of maintenance processes deriving either from the biological needs of man[69] or from the requirements of the social order[70] leads them to declare a number of propositions to account for the integration of a specific sociocultural system. Maintenance processes also limit functionalists in their use of a values approach to integration since value tends to be swallowed up by function. As Bidney writes of Malinowski and Radcliffe-Brown, the "ultimate absolute value . . . is the survival value of the society, all other cultural values being subservient as a means or instruments to this end."[71] Thus, functionalist studies of institutionalized patterns —kinship, law, religion, political organization—eventuate in judgments as to interrelationships and significance for the maintenance of the social system in question, but there is no serious commitment to value-orientations and ethos as found among American anthropologists.[72]

Herskovits[73] has suggested that a cultural system may be analyzed meaningfully by way of its "focus," a manifest area of activity that demonstrates greater creativity and variation when compared with other activities. In like manner Voget[74] suggested that a culture may be integrated structurally and functionally by a primary institutionalized pattern which defines the basic role for individuals in the society and programs their socialization accordingly.

Redfield's continued pursuit of the "world view" and "moral order" as keys to cultural integration and change along the folk-peasant-urban continuum has enervated in a series of "Comparative Studies of Cultures and Civilizations."[75] These researches, when teamed with community studies (functionalist and cultural) and thematic analyses of cultures in the "national character" program, represent a considerable contribution of anthropologists to the understanding of complex civilizations.[76]

LINGUISTICS

There are two major areas where linguists touch upon issues of immediate interest to anthropologists generally. The first is broadly historic, and includes classifications and comparisons that may establish a connection between peoples at some point in time even though at present they may be spatially separated and culturally distinct. Recently Swadesh[77] has produced a technique for computing the time involved in linguistic differentiation. By using approximately 200 "conservative" type-words he discovered that in 1,000 years the retention was about 81% in the languages he investigated. Applying his formula to other languages he has been able in some instances to correlate his glottochronology with archeological estimates.[78]

The second problem-area of general significance focusses on the influence which linguistic categories may hold for the perception and interpretation of human experience. This issue was opened up recently by Benjamin Whorf who hypothesized that "each language is not merely a reproducing instrument for voicing ideas but rather is itself the shaper of ideas, the program and guide for the individual's mental activity . . ."[79] For Whorf linguistics could not remain a mere description and comparison of forms. Language in action is a psycho-cultural process. Studied analysis and comparison might begin profitably with an elucidation of basic categories for classifying and interpreting the world of nature and man's relation to it, since his analysis of Hopi had revealed considerable differences between the concepts of time, space, and matter of this Southwestern people and of Europeans.

This "Whorfian hypothesis," following earlier leads by Sapir (1929)[80] places language right where it should be—within the culture system—and gives to it the determinative influence usually attributed to culture patterns when accounting for uniformities in human behavior in a particular society. It obviously promises new leads in comprehending the psychological dimensions that separate one people from another. In the extreme, of course, linguistic determination denies a natural or "physiognomic" perception common to mankind at the biogenic level and calls into question the fondness of child psychologists like Piaget and Dennis that children generally may view the world in "realistic," "animistic," and "artificial" terms.[81] An extremist view, however, does not seem to have been the intent of Whorf nor of other linguists equally interested in exploring the relationship between linguistic patterns and other non-linguistic behaviors and in ultimately comprehending the metaphysics of a people and its bearing on cultural integration and change.[82]

APPLIED ANTHROPOLOGY

The application of anthropological methods to the solution of human problems, especially among peoples subject to westernization at the direction of European nations would appear a natural and inevitable outgrowth of research into the cultures of the peoples controlled. Such a development, however, must follow agreement on the part of anthropologists and administrators alike that cooperation is mutually beneficial. Administrative application of social science to "social engineering" largely turns on the climate of opinion that prevails and the press of necessity. In their turn anthropologists have been chary of diluting their science by limiting it to practical issues. It is also realized that if the social scientist starts from a given political position, he is certain to enter into complications of conscience and of morality.[83] For these reasons anthropologists have defined their role in any governmental program for economic and social change as that of advisor and fact-gatherers, and, in answer to imperious demands of administrators for data relevant to the timing of problems and the programming of solutions, they have insisted on the benefits that follow from unfettered investigations.[84]

Despite the "conflict of interest" between applied and pure research and the fluctuations of administrative necessity, anthropologists have been able to produce some significant research under government auspices. Under John Collier, Commissioner of Indian Affairs, anthropologists teamed with specialists in a number of disciplines, including public administration, ecology, pedagogy and psychiatry, to produce social, cultural and personality data designed to bring the government into cooperative partnership with the Indians in the working out of their problems in place of a director. What became most apparent to those engaged in personality research among the five Indian societies in the United States was the ultimate "significance of culture structure" without which men in society cannot function.[85] And out of close cooperation with practical administrators the anthropologist has been able to broaden his conception of the dynamics of westernization to include the "views and behavior of Europeans as actors in the situation as well as those of the Africans."[86]

Throughout acculturative studies agreement on a unitary structural functional approach to problems of change among colonial peoples and the use of scientific teams for their solutions is now common. However, differences of opinion exist concerning the significant features of the multi-dimensional reality. In British Africa, "basic ethnographic field investigation and fundamental studies of social structure were [considered] indispensable to provide the anthropological knowledge required for tackling the manifold prac-

tical problems involved in the development plans formulated by the colonial government . . ."[87]; and less consideration was given to the historic aspects of change than is the case for Americanists. By and large
the specific-problem orientation of British authropologists in Africa
has resulted in contemporary-minded, practical, and sociological types
of studies. Problems in method focus on the quantifying of data, the
use of censuses, schedules and questionnaires, and a minimal definition
of a "zero point" from which change may start. In contrast the problems engaged by Americanists face broader historic cultural issues,
value-orientations, and personality. Beals has even suggested that "the
development of theory and method is perhaps a particular responsibility of scholars in the United States" since they are not so subject
to "pressure . . . for applied studies."[88]

Theoretical and practical issues also merge in efforts to bring
modern sanitation procedures and a conception of physical and mental hygiene to non-westernized peoples under United Nations and
government auspices. Ackerknecht convinced that a "large comparative study of primitive medicine would be of great value for medical
history and medicine as a whole" has launched a series of comparative
studies to discover the role of medicine in the total life of a people.[89]
Specific investigations like those of Hsu and Foster[90] include descriptions of local medical belief and practice and analyses geared to the
easing of doctor-patient relations and to the implementing of scientific
medicine within native communities. The majority of anthropologists
participating in medical research on the social structure of hospitals,
interpersonal relations in the therapeutic context, and the professional roles of doctors and nurses have united psychiatric and cultural
theory in defining the scope of the problems and method. When
discussing the mental health implications of technical change in a
manual prepared under the auspices of UNESCO, Mead emphasized
the necessity for turning to "the disciplines of psychiatry and clinical
psychology" for the appropriate "frame of reference."[91]

Since the United Nations is weighted with the task of mediating
between non-industrialized peoples and the industrialized West, the
anthropologist as a specialist in a particular area has been utilized
as a research worker and advisor for U.N. programs. In Métraux's
view, however, the role of the anthropologist is far more comprehensive than this advisoral and research function. For the "extremely
delicate" task allotted to anthropology by the United Nations is that

of "guiding the transition from one form of culture to another . . . to avert the disastrous consequences that many countries of the world have suffered from such changes in the past." [92] It is doubtful, however, whether much guidance will take place before damage has been done. And in the meantime Tax is conducting an "experiment" in "action anthropology" in a situation of damage designed to awaken a new perception of the social and cultural context by both the minority people and their disinterested neighbors. [93] Sympathetic participant-observers are introduced into both groups to discuss important issues and to educate people to think through the prejudices and fears that maintain conflict and misunderstanding. Action and interaction are basic to the program since through these processes, it is hypothecated, new self-conceptions will arise to facilitate personal and group adaptation.

A multi-dimensional orientation also constitutes the anthropological leaven for human relations studies in industry, an approach first introduced by Elton Mayo, a psychiatrist influenced by the functionalists, Radcliffe-Brown and Malinowski. The new turn in industrial relations research also witnessed the introduction of the participant-observer method traditionally associated with anthropology, together with a new accent on "social groups as determinants of human behavior." [94] Although the anthropologically-trained E. D. Chapple[95] teamed with C. S. Coon to write an "interactionist" text without mentioning the concept of culture, his continued efforts in industrial relations rest on the assumption that "attitudes and emotional reactions as well as productivity are functions of the interactional situation and *this interactional situation represents the interplay of personality and cultural process and technique.*"[96] For this reason he insists that the answer to human relations problems for the most part must involve the alteration of systemic social interaction by changing the culture processes in place of transferring personalities to fit the situation or by taking oneself into a new self-conception and social role through group-dynamics procedures. Expansion of other specialists in the industrial relations field has led to the introduction of new methodologies and emphases, especially upon the quantifiction of data. This has meant a diminution in traditional anthropological studies, but tacit stress on a broad sociocultural context for investigation and analysis remains.

PHYSICAL ANTHROPOLOGY

The fundamental problems engaged by physical anthropologists turn on human origins and evolution. The complexities that flow from this broad issue are as limitless as man himself, involving not only the biology of man, but the interplay of biology and culture, the distribution of populations and their ecological relations, and the effects of comprehensive processes such as natural selection.

In the panorama of history it is possible to view the development of the sciences in perspective. First problems must come first, and in the beginning reporting and classification and the refinement of techniques appropriate to these ends predominate. Physical anthropology proves to be no exception to the above rule for sciences, since its basic technique, anthropometry, was developed at the start to provide a basis for classifications of man. Today physical anthropology is undergoing considerable revision in its purpose and methodology. The seed bed for this transformation is the "new genetics" focussed on the dynamics of structure and function, and the processes whereby these are changed.[97]

At base the new view is broadly ecological, emphasizing the interdependence of the organism and the total local environment. As applied to man the adaptive processes include the operation of specific environmental conditions, such as high altitude for enlargement of the thorax and greater hemoglobin count,[98] the effects of diet on body size,[99] climate and human physique,[100] mutations and genetic drift, and the selective effects of culturally defined mating patterns for genetic segregation and gene frequency.[101]

Problems and dynamic processes such as these were unheard of in anthropometry since primary concern was for observable, measurable, and unchanging characteristics that would have precise and final diagnostic value in the classification of types. A genetic connection always was implicit in such studies, since the non-adaptive morphological features and indices were presumed to be hereditary. However, in the finally analysis a "statistical type"—a Negroid, Mongoloid, or Caucasoid type of nose for example—would be defined for geographic populations and then substituted for the unknown genetic reality. Then, wherever or whenever a "Negroid type" of nose was found in a population exhibiting the hair-type of the Caucasoid, it was immediately concluded that Negroid and Caucasoid intermixture had occurred.

This view left no room for either genetic mutation, natural selection, or adaptation, but attributed intermediate forms to mixture from contact between two "pure" races. As knowledge of genetic processes has grown, and as empirical testing of the non-adaptive qualitiy of the morphological and metrical features used in race comparison has produced contrary results, the shortcomings of the limited theory and method of anthropometry, and the necessity for a reorientation, have become all too evident.

It does not seem, however, that the genetic approach will result immediately in any serious revisions of the major races or stocks first defined by the techniques of anthropometry.[102] For some time to come it is quite probable that a number of "genetic" racial classifications will stand in mutual contradiction, since the locating and plotting of genetic constellations or assemblages in space, from which racial distinctions can be made, is hardly under way. Garn and Coon contend that "what seems to be a disagreement of considerable magnitude [in the definition of human races] narrows down to a lack of agreement on just what taxonomic unit is properly designated as a race in man."[103] They propose that the broad geographic populations that conform to the old stocks (Caucasoid, Negroid, Mongoloid) be called "geographic races" and that the local populations that constitute a breeding unit be referred to as "local races." Continuing they observe that

"Counting up the number of geographical races is comparatively simple because there are a limited number of continents and islandic chains, and different human groups have radiated through and exploited each of them. A count of local and microgeographical races, however, is a more difficult procedure. Not only are we currently unable to enter into a very large section of the world, where many populations remain unstudied, but we have been remiss in investigating race-populations within our own national borders. These observations, plus the foregoing, should make it clear that in regard to the number of local and micro-geographical races of man, the count is thirty *plus*. And the "plus" represents an indeterminate number at least as large as the thirty."[104]

If, as Boyd[105] suggests, "a human race [is] a population which differs significantly from other human populations in regard to the frequency of one or more of the genes it possesses," then the local populations, which form "breeding units," appear to be the logical place to start the plotting of gene frequencies. Here too would be the place to tackle the problem of race classification, especially since breeding populations are more variable and perhaps more subject to evolutionary change under natural selection. Natural selection need not to be considered as a crude "struggle for existence" but simply as effective reproduction which preserves the genotype.[106]

More challenging than any classification effort, however, are the empirical studies that relate biogenic structures to the environments in which populations live and reproduce. Fleure's[107] (1945) plotting of skin pigmentation and ultraviolet radiation offers more than suggestive evidence for a direct connection between these two variables. The application of Bergman's and Allen's rules may reveal common evolutionary tendencies under natural selection that account for a greater body mass and shorter extremities in polar areas in contrast to lesser size and longer extremities in the warm and arid ranges.[108] Were these trends to be confirmed for man, and the genetic and selective processes stand revealed, a considerable contribution to the study of constitutional types[109] and to the range of human plasticity[110] would follow.

Of all the processes effecting human evolution (mutation, isolation, migration, selective mating, genetic drift, population size) natural selection proves to be the most controversial.[111] While some have assumed that civilized man is beyond natural selection and in future will degenerate both physically and intellectually, Dobzansky and Allen[112] counter that natural selection is still operative within the cultural context. Culture indeed has shifted the area of selection from the species to the individual and the family, and this shift in ground has introduced a selection for mental health and other psychosocial attributes. They feel that man soon will possess the knowledge to direct his own evolution, but in every instance the selective factor will be at work, depending upon the biogenic and psychosocial characteristics considered desirable. Perhaps, too, as Boyd has predicted, future miscegenation will so alter the genotypic and phenotypic structures that "races . . . will largely cease to exist. . .", and further, that current population proportions, which show a preponderance of the Asiatic and African groups, will favor the genetic emergence of a brachycephalic type, "perhaps about as tall as present-day inhabitants of Southern Europe, with dark brown eyes, a brown skin, and straight (or perhaps slightly wavy) hair."[113]

THEORY AND METHOD

This summary of recent trends in Anthropology can be brought to a close with some remarks on theory and method.

The basic orientation of anthropologists still centers in the concept of culture even though some in particular research and interdisciplinary projects have found the concept and its corollaries to be too general for their purposes.[114] Differences of this kind strike at the very heart of the "reality" which the theory and method of a particular discipline programmes for solution. It falsely distinguishes "positivists" who presume to "scientify" the discipline through controlled experiments of a limited nature from "humanists" who emphasize a dynamic configurational reality requiring "insight, empathy, intuition, and an element of art" for its comprehension.[115]

For anthropologists, by and large, the reality of culture is projected in terms of a dynamic unity, interrelated and structured by processes fulfilling maintenance and other special requirements for the group (and by implication for the individual), subject to change with a generalizing of effects along related structural-functional axes. This holistic approach makes for an extended comprehension that favors variations in problem-definitions and the appropriate methodology to be followed. There is little tendency for a special theory and method to establish itself as a dominant "school" since the fields of anthropology comprehend problems (and methods) as immediately diverse as human evolution, the development of culture, the forms and functions of language, and the effects of the sociocultural milieu on personality formation. The very diversity of anthropology determines its essential strength, uniting individuals "of broad interest in the nature and origin of man and his works." [116] Yet the immediate basis for this unity is the sociocultural milieu in which every man operates from his birth to death.[117] Even in the evolution of man it must now be admitted that the prevalence of genotypes in a population owes as much, if not more to sociocultural selection as to natural selection and genetic processes, for it is "the attitudes and role of the individual in his society" that defines who will mate with whom and thus determine the future distribution and frequencies of genes in the population.[118]

Any projected system of reality, such as the multi-dimensional yet culturally integrated view held in anthropology, immediately raises the issue of the type and extent of control to be exercised if valid generalizations are to follow. Comparison long has served anthropologists to contrast as well as to demonstrate similarities quantitatively within single cultures, among historically related peoples of a culture area, and among societies distributed around the globe. While the "development of field studies . . . led to a relative neglect of studies making use of the comparative method," as Radcliffe-Brown[119] states, there never has been an "abandonment" of comparison *per se* as some have suggested.[120] Rather there have been periodic shifts in theoretical emphasis and on the magnitude of comparisons. Under Boas, Americanists rejected the universalistic comparisons of their continental colleagues and turned to single and regional studies, whereas today continental anthropologists are urging intensive single and regional comparisons, and are seeking to restrain Americanists in their enthusiastic pursuit of statistical correlations based on global comparisons![121] There can be, of course, "no single method of comparison", statistical, regional, or global, as Singer writes (or in any science for that matter), for "method is largely determined by problem, and . . . a method appropriate for the comparison of kinship systems is not necessarily most appropriate for other types of cross-cultural comparisons." [122]

However, before comparison can be undertaken a precise and proper classification of the units must be made to insure that they are commensurable. Invariably those who have engaged in world-wide comparison have been forced to equate units that represent "ideal types" rather than empirically derived categories.[123] There can be little doubt, nonetheless, that cross-cultural comparisons now being carried out under the auspices of the Human Relations Area Files are producing some very original and challenging propositions.

Thus the very requirements of an adequate sample and a precise definition of the units compared are conspiring to drive anthropologists to quantify their data.[124] Applied programs also result in the compilation of statistical data, ranging from the usual census to household budgets, hours given to work according to season, and labor mobility.

To quantify where number extends control and allows a more exact statement of relationships is all well to the good, since control is the very stuff of science, however it be attained. Yet there are some problems that do not necessitate or may not allow quantification. This is the point made by Margaret Mead in defense of the use of "type" as a substitute for number in the thematic studies of cultures carried out under the Columbia University Research in Contemporary Cultures program.[125] Functionalists also are inclined to make use of empirically-derived types as a substitute for number when making comparisons for purposes of generalization.[126]

Actually the qualitative differences in their problems do not require that anthropologists select one method to the exclusion of all others. The study of man cannot become scientific simply by an espousal of statistical techniques, as some insist while ignoring the vital problem of control in the collection of data.

In other cases, as in a description of the usual, preferred, or prescribed patterns with observations on the variations permitted, quantification, though desirable, hardly seems necessary. In like manner there are no necessary numerical requirements when analysis of culture systems unveils contrastive orientations toward life and the enunciation of different values and ends, as pursued in ethos studies. But when inferences relate ethos to a specific and systematic organization of motivation, affect, and action in specific individuals and groups, the relationship must remain hypothetical until verified empirically with number,—and this despite the fact that there is good reason to assume that a majority are committed to the support of the cultural system, and hence, as personalities share the motivations, affects, and activities considered desirable.[127]

However, number need not be restricted to unit-individuals collected by schedules, interviews, and tests. Number can be attained within a single culture by a list of culture patterns that duplicate congruences defined in the ethos configuration, or in a situation of change by a popular selection of novel culture traits or patterns that are in essential agreement with the configuration hypothecated.

Better control over the collection, range, and interpretation of cultural data can be achieved by fielding "ethnographic teams" composed of workers specially trained in several disciplines. When team research is continued over a period of time, as for the Navaho under Kluckhohn, the promise of controlled observation and the recording of significant and numerically adequate data is greatly enhanced, and permits "controlled comparisons"[128] of a high order.

Despite some weaknesses, descriptive and analytic studies based on "presumptive" modes or averages do have a place as have the inferences that flow from them, since they serve to define probable relations and assist in the programming of systematic research. There can be little doubt, however, that in future anthropologists, while continuing to document the range and diversity of human behavior, gradually will join their "sociological brethren" in a "closer and more careful look at individual small societies." [129] It is also a certainty that they will do so without surrendering entirely their basic interests in cross-cultural comparisons, "a broad coverage of subject matter, a variety of methods and approaches, a wide range of objectives, and a healthy eclecticism . . ." [130], for these too are requirements for a science of social man.

SELECTED BIBLIOGRAPHY

Homer G. Barnett, *Innovation: The Basis for Cultural Change* (New York: McGraw-Hill, 1953). A sociopsychological approach to the study of cultural change.

David Bidney, *Theoretical Anthropology* (New York: Columbia University Press, 1953). A series of essays concerned with the concept interpretation.

J. G. D. Clarke, *Prehistoric Europe: The Economic Basis* (New York: Philosophical Library, 1952). An ecological treatment of the development of culture in prehistoric Europe.

Fred Eggan, *Social Organization of the Western Pueblos* (University of Chicago Press, 1950). A study in "controlled comparisons and interpretation."

A. L. Kroeber, Ed., *Anthropology Today: An Encyclopedic Inventory* (University of Chicago Press, 1953). An indispensable summary of current developments in Anthropology; *Configurations of Culture Growth* (Berkeley: University of California Press, 1944). A study of culture rhythms by way of "value-patterns" and the clustering of geniuses.

Claude Levi-Strauss, *Les Structures élémentaires de la parenté* (Paris: Presses universitaties de France, 1949). An original analysis and comparative treatment of social structures, in which the principles by which groups are related through marriage and the maintenance of relationships through reciprocities supply the keys to social morphology.

Oscar Lewis, *Life in a Mexican Village: Tepoztlán Restudied* (Urbana: University of Illinois Press, 1951). An example of the range and intent of the contemporary anthropological field research.

Ralph Linden, *The Tree of Culture* (New York: Knopf, 1955). A cultural history of man.

Margaret Mead & Martha Wolfenstein, *Childhood in Contemporary Cultures* (University of Chicago Press, 1955). An anthology demonstrating the cultural-thematic approach to the study of the child in society.

George P. Murdock, *Social Structure* (New York: The MacMillan Co., 1949). A effort to combine sociological, psychological, anthropological, and historical approaches in the study of social organization and to establish it upon a sound scientific basis by way of statistical techniques.

S. F. Nadel, *The Foundations of Social Anthropology* (Glencoe, Ill.: Free Press, 1951). A critical analysis of method in Anthropology.

A. R. Radcliffe-Brown, *Structure and Function in Primitive Society: Essays and Addresses* (Glencoe, Ill.: The Free Press, 1952). Analytical papers presenting a "functionalist" approach to kinship, law, and religion.

Robert Redfield, *The Primitive World and Its Transformations* (Ithaca: Cornell University Press, 1953). A grand description of trends in world culture development.

J. W. M. Whiting and Irvin Child, *Child Training and Personality: A Cross-Cultural Study* (New Haven: Yale University Press, 1953). A combination of psychoanalytic and learning theories to elucidate relationships between socialization, projected anxieties, and explanations of disease.

Fred Voget, Professor of Anthropology, University of Arkansas, received his B.A. degree from the University of Oregon (1936), and his Ph.D. from Yale University (1948); did field work among Crow Indians (1939, 1940, 1946), and Iroquois at Caughnawaga, Quebec (1949, 1950); was a member of the Committee on Indian Research, Canadian Social Science Research Council (1951-1952), and is currently engaged in the study of Pan-Indianism as an emergent phase in the acculturation of American Indians (supported by a grant-in-aid from the Wenner-Gren Foundation for Anthropological Research, 1956). Served also on the staff of the University of Nebraska (1947-1948), McGill University (1948-1952); his contributions have appeared in such periodicals as the *American Anthropologist, Social Forces, The American Journal of Sociology,* etc.

NOTES

1. Herbert Spencer, *First Principles* (New York: Appleton, 1920); *Principles of Sociology* (London: Williams and Norgate, Ltd., 1893).

2. J. J. Bachhofen, *Das Mutterrecht* (Stuttgart, 1861); Lewis H. Morgan, *Ancient Society* (New York, 1877); E. B. Tylor, *Primitive Culture,* 2 vols. (Boston, 1874).

3. For example, Robert Briffault, *The Mothers,* 3 vols. (New York: MacMillan, 1927), W. G. Sumner & A. G. Keller, *The Science of Society,* 4 vols. (New Haven: Yale University Press, 1927).

4. Emile Durkheim, *The Rules of Sociological Method* (edited by George E. G. Catlin) (University of Chicago Press, 1938).

5. Emile Durkheim, *Elementary Forms of the Religious Life* (trans. J. W. Swain), (New York: MacMillan, 1926).

6. Franz Boas, "The Limitations of the Comparative Method of Anthropology," in: F. Boas, *Race, Language, and Culture* (New York: MacMillan, 1940), 270-280.

7. Clyde Kluckhohn and William H. Kelly, "The Concept of Culture," in: Ralph Linton, Ed., *The Science of Man in the World Crisis*, '98 (New York: Columbia University Press, 1945), 78-108.

8. B. Malinowski, *A Scientific Theory of Culture and Other Essays* (Chapel Hill: University of North Carolina Press, 1944).

9. A. R. Radcliffe-Brown, "On the Concept of Function in Social Science," *American Anthropologist*, XXXVII (1935), 394-402.

10. The Functionalist-interactionist posture of contemporary British Anthropology made it the logical successor to the humanistic and evolutionistic sociology of the 19th century. The relation of sociology to anthropology in France is very nearly the same. See G. P. Murdock, "British Social Anthropology," *American Anthropologist*, LIII (1951), 465-573, & Raymond Firth, "Contemporary British Social Anthropology," *Ibid.*, 474-489.

11. Ruth Benedict, *Patterns of Culture* (Boston: Houghton-Mifflin, 1934).

12. Clyde Kluckhohn, "The Influence of Psychiatry on Anthropology in America During the Past One Hundred Years," in: J. K. Hall, G. Zilboorg and H. A. Bunker, Eds., *One Hundred Years of American Psychiatry* (New York: Columbia University Press, 1944).

13. Cora DuBois, *The People of Alor* (Minneapolis: University of Minnesota Press, 1944); Thomas Gladwin and Seymour Sarason, "Truk: Man in Paradise", *Viking Fund Publications in Anthropology*, No. 20. (New York: Wenner-Gren Foundation for Anthropological Research, Incorporated, 1953); A. I. Hallowell, "The Rorschach Method as an Aid in the Study of Personalities in Primitive Societies," *Character and Personality*, IX (1941), 235-245.

14. Margaret Mead, *Coming of Age in Samoa* (New York: William Morrow, 1928); G. Gorer, *The American People* (New York: W. W. Norton and Co., 1948); Abram Kardiner, *The Individual and His Society* (New York: Columbia University Press, 1939).

15. Jules Henry and Melford Spiro, "Psychological Techniques: Projective Tests in Field Work," in: A. L. Kroeber, Ed., *Anthropology Today* (University of Chicago Press, 1953, 417-429); Ivan N. Mensch and Jules Henry, "Direct Observation and Psychological Tests in Anthropological Field Work," *American Anthropologist*, LV (1953), 461-480.

16. C. H. Cooley, *Human Nature and the Social Order* (New York: Charles Scribner's, 1902); George H. Mead, *Mind, Self, and Society* (University of Chicago Press, 1934).

17. Robert and Helen Lynd, *Middletown* (New York: Harcourt, Brace, 1929); *Middletown in Transition* (*Ibid.*, 1937).

18. Robert Redfield, *Tepoztlan, a Mexican Village* (University of Chicago Press, 1930); & *The Folk Culture of Yucatan* (University of Chicago Press, 1941).

19. A. R. Radcliffe-Brown, "The Methods of Ethnology and Social Anthropology," *South African Journal of Science*, XX (1923), 124-147; see also: "The Social Organization of Australian Tribes," *Oceania Monographs*, No. 1 (Melbourne, 1931).

20. A. A. Lesser, "Functionalism in Social Science," *American Anthropologist,* XXXVII (1935), 386-393.

21. Daryll Forde, "Applied Anthropology in Government: British Africa," in: A. L. Kroeber, Ed., *Anthropology Today* (University of Chicago Press, 1953), 841-865; Laura Thompson, *Personality and Government* (Mexico: Inter-American Institute, 1951).

22. Ruth Benedict, *The Chrysanthemum and the Sword* (Boston: Houghton-Mifflin, 1946); Alexander Leighton, *The Governing of Men* (Princeton University Press, 1945).

23. Ralph Beals, "Urbanism, Urbanization, and Acculturation," *American Anthropologist,* LIII (1951), 1-10.

24. J. W. Bennett and K. H. Wolff, "Toward Communication Between Sociology and Anthropology," in: W. L. Thomas, Jr., Ed., (see footnote 29).

25. V. Gordon Childe, *Man Makes Himself* (New York: Pelican Books, 1952), 20.

26. *Ibid.,* 35.

27. *Ibid.,* 116.

28. Wendell C. Bennett and Junius C. Bird, "Andean Culture History." *American Museum of Natural History Handbook Series,* No. 15 (New York, 1949); Pedro Armillas, "A Sequence of Cultural Development in Meso-America," in: W. C. Bennett, Ed., *A Reappraisal of Peruvian Archaeology,* Memoirs of the Society for American Archaeology, 13, No. 4 (Menasha: George Banta Publishing Company, 1948), 105-111; W. D. Strong, "Cultural Epochs and Refuse Heap Stratigraphy in Peruvian Archaeology," *Ibid.,* 95-102.

29. W. D. Strong, "Cultural Resemblances in Nuclear America: Parallelism of Diffusion?" in: Sol Tax, Ed., *The Civilizations of Ancient America,* Selected Papers of the 29th International Congress of Americanists, 278 (University of Chicago Press, 1951), 271-279; Gordon Willey, "Archaeological Theories and Interpretation: New World," in: W. L. Thomas, Jr., Ed., *Yearbook of Anthropology—1955* (New York: Wenner-Gren Foundation for Anthropological Research, Inc., 1953), 361-385, and "The Prehistoric Civilizations of Nuclear America," *American Anthropologist,* LVII (1955), 571-593.

30. A. L. Kroeber, *Anthropology* (New York: Harcourt Brace, 1948); Wendell C. Bennett, "Introduction," in: Sol Tax, Ed., *The Civilizations of Ancient America,* Selected Papers of the 29th International Congress of Americanists. (University of Chicago Press, 1951), 1-16.

31. Julian Steward, "Cultural Causality and Law: A Trial Formulation of the Development of Early Civilization," *American Anthropologist,* LI (1949), 1-27.

32. Gordon Willey and Philip Phillips, "Method and Theory in American Archaeology II: Historical-Developmental Interpretation," *American Anthropologist,* LVII (1955), 723-819; also, Philip Phillips and Gordon Willey, "Method and Theory in American Archaeology: An Operational Basis for Culture-Historical Integration," *Ibid.,* LV (1953), 615-633.

33. Leslie White, "History, Evolutionism and Functionalism," *South-Western Journal of Anthropology,* I (1945), 221-248.

34. *Ibid.,* 245, 243. Cf. Julian Huxley, "Evolution, Cultural and Biological," in: W. L. Thomas, Jr., Ed., *op. cit.,* 3-25.

35. Leslie White, "Energy and Evolution," *American Anthropologist,* XLV (1943), 335-356. Cf. George A. Bartholomew, Jr. & Joseph B. Birdsell, "Ecology and the Protohominids," *Ibid.,* LV (1953), 481-498.

36. White, *op. cit.*, 338, 348.

37. A. L. Kroeber, *Configurations of Culture Growth* (Berkeley: University of California Press, 1944); also, "Is Western Civilization Disintegrating or Reconstituting?", *Proceedings of the American Philosophical Society*, XCV (1951), 100-104.

38. Arnold Toynbee, *A Study of History*, Abridgement of vols. 1-6 by D. C. Somervell (New York: Oxford University Press, 1947).

39. Pitirim Sorokin, *Social and Cultural Dynamics*, 4 vols. (New York: American Book Company, 1937-41).

40. Robert Redfield, *The Primitive World and Its Transformations* (Ithaca: Syracuse University Press, 1953).

41. Robert Lowie, "Cultural Anthropology: A Science," *American Journal of Sociology*, XLII (1936), 301-320.

42. George P. Murdock, *Social Structure* (New York: The MacMillan Co., 1949), 183.

43. *Ibid.*, 323.

44. Cf. Alexander Spoehr, "Changing Kinship Systems." *Anthropological Series, Field Museum of Natural History*, XXXIII (1947), 153-235.

45. See: Morris Opler, "Review of *Social Structure* by G. P. Murdock," *American Anthropologist*, LII (1950), 77-80; Claude Levi-Strauss, "Social Structure," in: A. L. Kroeber, Ed., *op. cit.*, 524-553.

46. W. V. Brelsford and W. Allan, *Copperbelt Markets: A Social and Economic Study* (Lusaka, Northern Rhodesia: Government Printer, 1947); K. A. Busia, *Report on a Social Survey of Sekondi-Takoradi* (London: Crown Agents, 1950); Meyer Fortes and E. E. Evans-Pritchard, *African Political Systems* (London: Oxford University Press, 1950); Max Gluckman, *The Judicial Processes Among the Barotse* (Glencoe, Ill.: Free Press, 1955); A. R. Radcliffe-Brown and Daryll Forde, Eds., *African Systems of Kinship and Marriage* (London Oxford University Press); Audrey I. Richards, Ed., *Economic Development and Tribal Change; A Study of Immigrant Labour in Buganda* (London; Heffer and Sons, 1954); I. Schapera, Ed., *The Bantu-Speaking Tribes of South Africa: An Ethnographic Survey* (New York: The Humanities Press, 1950); Georges Balandier, *Sociologie Actuelle de l'Afrique Noire: Dynamique les Changements Sociaux en Afrique Centrale*, Bibliotèque de Sociologie contemporaine (Paris: Presses Universitaires de France, 1955); P. Mercier (with collaboration of G. Balandier), "Particularisme et Evolution. Les Pécheurs Lébou," *Études Senegalaises*, No. 3 (Senegal: Saint-Louis de Senegal Centre Institut Français d'Afrique Noire, 1952); P. Métais, "Démographie de Néo-Caledonians," *Journal de la Société des Océanistes*, IX (1954), 99-128; J. Pauvert (with collaboration of G. Balandier), "Les Villages gabonáis," *Memoire de l'Institut d'Études Centrafricaines*, No. 5 (Brazzaville, 1952).

47. S. F. Nadel, *The Nuba* (New York: Oxford University Press, 1947); "Witchcraft in Four African Societies: An Essay in Comparison," *American Anthropologist*, LIV (1952), 18-29.

48. A. R. Radcliffe-Brown, *Structure and Function in Primitive Society* (London: Cohen and West, 1952).

49. Marcel Mauss, (with assistance of Henri Beuchat), "Essai sur les variations saissoniéres des sociétés eskimos. Étude de morphologie sociale", *L'Année sociologique*, neuviéme année (1904-1905), 39-132.

50. S. F. Nadel, "Two Nuba Religions: An Essay in Comparison," *American Anthropologist*, LVII (1955), 661-679; Monica Wilson, "Nyakyusa Ritual and Symbolism," *Ibid.*, LVI (1954), 228-241.

51. Gordon MacGregor, *Warriors Without Weapons* (University of Chicago Press) ; Robert Rapoport, "Changing Navaho Religious Values, A study of Christian Missions to the Rimrock Navahos," *Papers of the Peabody Museum of American Archaeology and Ethnology, Harvard University,* 41, No. 2 Reports of the Rimrock Values Series, No. 2 (Cambridge: Crimson Printing Company, 194); Laura Thompson and Alice Joseph, *The Hopi Way* (University of Chicago Press, 1944).

52. Evon Z. Vogt, "Navaho Veterans: A Study of Changing Values." *Papers of the Peabody Museum of American Archaeology and Ethnology, Harvard University,* 41, No. 1 Reports of the Rimrock Project Values Series, No. 1. (Cambridge: Crimson Printing Company, 1951) ; Bert Kaplan, "A Study of Rorschach Responses in Four Cultures." *Ibid.,* LXII No. 2; Reports of the Ramah Project No. 6.

53. George Spindler, "Sociocultural and Psychological Processes in Menomini Acculturation." *University of California Publications in Culture and Society,* 5 (Berkeley: University of California Press, 1955) ; Fred Voget, "The American Indian in Transition: Reformation and Accommodation," *American Anthropologist,* LVIII (1956), 249-263.

54. Homer Barnett, "Personal Conflicts and Cultural Change," *Social Forces,* XX (1941), 146-147; Laura Thompson and Alice Joseph, "White Pressures on Indian Personality and Culture," *American Journal of Sociology,* LIII (1947), 17-22; Richard Thurnwald, *Black and White in East Africa* (London: G. Routledge & Sons, 1935).

55. Homer Barnett, "Culture Processes," *American Anthropologist,* XLII (1940) 21-48; Ralph Linton, *The Study of Man* (New York: Appleton-Century, 1936) & Linton, Ed., *Acculturation in Seven American Indian Tribes* (New York: Appleton-Century, 1940).

56. Homer Barnett, *Innovation* (New York: McGraw-Hill), 338.

57. A. I. Hallowell, *Culture and Experience* (Philadelphia: University of Pennsylvania Press, 1955), 345-357; Edward P. Dozier, "Spanish Catholic Influence on Tewa Pueblo Religion," *Paper Read at the Fifty-Fifth Annual Meeting of the American Anthropological Association at Santa Monica,* (1956) ; Edward H. Spicer, "The Yaqui Adaptation of Christianity," *Ibid.;* George Spindler and Walter Goldschmidt, "Experimental Design in the Study of Culture Change," *Southwestern Journal of Anthropology,* VIII (1952), 68-83.

58. Walter Goldschmidt, "Ethics and the Structure of Society: An Ethnological Contribution to the Sociology of Knowledge," *American Anthropologist,* LIII (1951), 506-524; Clyde Kluckhohn, "A Comparative Study of Values in Five Cultures," in: E. Z. Vogt, *op. cit.,* vii-ix, & C. Kluckhohn, "Values and Value-Orientations in the Theory of Action: An Exploration in Definition and Classification," in T. Parsons and E. Shils, Eds., *Toward a General Theory of Action* (Cambridge: Harvard University Press, 1951), 388-434; Robert Redfield, "Relations of Anthropology to the Social Sciences and to the Humanities," in: A. L. Kroeber, Ed., *op. cit.,* 728-738.

59. Ruth Benedict, *op. cit.* (1934).

60. Margaret Mead, *Cooperation and Competition among Primitive Peoples* (New York: McGraw-Hill, 1937).

61. Morris Opler, "Themes as Dynamic Forces in Culture," *American Journal of Sociology,* LI (1945), 198-206.

62. Ethel M. Albert, "The Classification of Values," *American Anthropologist* LVIII (1956), 221-248; Clyde Kluckhohn, "The Philosophy of the Navaho Indians," in:F.S.C. Northrop, Ed., *Ideological Differences and the Moral Order* (New Haven; Yale University Press, 1949), 356-384; Robert Rapoport, *op. cit.;* E. Z. Vogt, *op. cit.*

63. Florence Kluckhohn, "Dominant and Variant Value Orientations," in: C. Kluckhohn, H. Murray, and D. Schneider, Eds., *Personality in Nature, Society and Culture* (New York: Knopf, 1953), 342-357.

64. *Ibid.*, 352.

65. *Ibid.*, 346.

66. Mark Zborowski & Elizabeth Herzog, *Life is with People: The Jewish Little Town of Eastern Europe* (New York: International Universities Press, Incorporated, 1952).

67. Margaret Mead and Martha Wolfenstein, Eds., *Childhood in Contemporary Cultures* (University of Chicago Press, 1955).

68. Abram Kardiner, *The Individual and His Society* (New York: Columbia University Press, 1939), *The Psychological Frontiers of Society*, (*Ibid.*, 1945).

69. B. Malinowski, *op. cit.*

70. A. R. Radcliffe-Brown (1952).

71. David Bidney, "The Concept of Value in Modern Anthropology," in: A. D. Kroeber, Ed., *op. cit.*, 682-699.

72. For a functionalist's discussion of values, see Monica Wilson, *Good Company: A Study of Nyakyusa Age-Villages* (London: Oxford University Press, 1951), 66-90.

73. Melville J. Herskovits, *Man and His Works* (New York; Knopf, 1948), 542-560.

74. Fred Voget, "The Folk Society—An Anthropological Application," *Social Forces,* XXXIII (1954), 105-113.

75. McKim Marriott, Ed., "Village India: Studies in the Little Community," Comparative Studies of Cultures and Civilizations No. 6 (Robert Redfield and Milton Singer, eds.), *American Anthropological Association Memoir 83* (University of Chicago Press, 1955); G. E. Von Grunebaum, "Islam: Essays in the Nature and Growth of a Cultural Tradition." *Ibid.*, No. 4, *Memoir 81* (Menasha: George Banta Publishing Company, 1955); Arthur Wright, Ed., "Studies in Chinese Thought," *Ibid.*, No. 1, *Memoir 75* (Menasha: George Banta Publishing Company, 1953).

76. Margaret Lantis, Ed., "The U.S.A. as Anthropologists See It," *American Anthropologist,* LVII (1955), 1113-1295; David Mandelbaum, "The Study of Complex Civilizations," in: W. L. Thomas, Jr., Ed., *op. cit.*, 203-226.

77. Morris Swadesh, "Lexico-Statistic Dating of Prehistoric Ethnic Contacts," *Proceedings of the American Philosophical Society,* XCVI (1952), 453-463.

78. Morris Swadesh and others, "Time Depths of American Linguistic Groupings," *American Anthropologist,* LVI (1954), 361-377.

79. Benjamin Whorf, *Collected Papers on Metalinguistics.* (Washington: Department of State, Foreign Service Institute, 1952), 5.

80. Edward Sapir, "The Status of Linguistics as a Science," in: David Mandelbaum, Ed., *Selected Writings of Edward Sapir in Language Culture and Personality* (Berkeley: University of California Press, 1949), 160-166.

81. Franklin Fearing, "An Examination of the Conceptions of Benjamin Whorf in the Light of Theories of Perception and Cognition," in: Harry Hoijer, Ed., "Language in Culture"; Comparative Studies of Cultures and Civilizations (Robert Redfield and Milton Singer, editors), *American Anthropological Association Memoir 79* (Menasha: George Banta Publishing Company, 1954), 47-81.

82. Harry Hoijer, "Cultural Implications of Some Navaho Linguistic Categories," *Language,* XXVII (1951), 111-120; "The Relation of Language to Culture," in: A. L. Kroeber, Ed., *op. cit.*, 554-573; "The Sapir-Whorf Hypothesis," in: Harry

Hoijer, Ed., *op. cit.*, 92-105; D. Demetracopoulou Lee, "Conceptual Implications of an Indian Language," *Philosophy of Science*, V (1938), 89-102; "Linguistic Reflection of Wintu Thought," *International Journal of American Linguistics*, X (1944), 181-187; Gladys Reichard, "Language and Culture Patterns," *American Anthropologist*, LII (1950), 194-204; E. H. Lenneberg and J. M. Roberts, "The Language of Experience: A Study in Methodology," *Indiana University Publications in Anthropology and Linguistics, Memoir, 13 of the International Journal of American Linguistics,* XXII (1956), 1-33.

83. G. Jan Held, "Applied Anthropology in Government: The Netherlands," in: A. L. Kroeber, Ed., *op. cit.*, 866-879; Godfrey Wilson, "Anthropology as a Public Service," *Africa,* XIII (1940), 43-61.

84. Daryll Forde, "Applied Anthropology in Government: British Africa," in: A. L. Kroeber, Ed., *op. cit.*, 841-865; Edward Kennard and Gordon MacGregor, "Applied Anthropology in Government: United States," *Ibid.*, 832-840; Alfred Métraux, "Applied Anthropology in Government: United Nations." *Ibid.*, 880-894; L. P. Mair, "Review of Lord Hailey's *Native Administration in the British Territories of Africa,*" *Africa,* XXI (1951), 336-339.

85. Laura Thompson, *Culture In Crisis: A Study of the Hopi Indians* (New York: Harper, 1950), 15; also, *op. cit.*

86. Forde, *op. cit.*, 849.

87. *Ibid.*, 853.

88. Ralph Beals, "Acculturation," in: A. L. Kroeber, Ed., *op. cit.*, (634), 261-641. For a contrary view, see: Elizabeth Colson, "The Intensive Study of Small Sample Communities," in: Robert F. Spencer, Ed., *Method and Perspective in Anthropology* (Papers in Honor of Wilson D. Wallis) (Minneapolis: University of Minnesota Press, 1954), 43-59.

89. Edwin H. Ackerknecht, "Primitive Medicine and Culture Patterns," *Bulletin of the History of Medicine*, XII (1942), 545-574; also, "Natural Diseases and Rational Treatment in Primitive Medicine," *Ibid.*, XIX (1946), 467-497.

90. Francis L. K. Hsu, *Religion, Science and Human Crisis: A Study on China in Transition and its Implications for the West* (London: Routledge and Kegan Paul, 1952); George M. Foster, Ed., "A Cross-Cultural Anthropological Analysis of a Technical Aid Program" (Washington: Smithsonian Institution, 1951, mimeographed), cited by William Caudill, "Applied Anthropology in Medicine," in: A. L. Kroeber, Ed., *op. cit.*, 771-806.

91. Margaret Mead, Ed., *Cultural Patterns and Technical Change,* A Manual Prepared by the World Federation for Mental Health (New York: The New American Library, Mentor, 1955), 269.

92. Metraux, *op. cit.*, 883.

93. Sol Tax, Ed., "Symposium: The Fox Indian Project, A Program of Action Anthropology," *Central States Anthropological Society*, Mimeographed (1955).

94. F. L. W. Richardson, Jr., "Anthropology and Human Relations in Business and Industry," in: W. L. Thomas, Jr., Ed., *op. cit.*, 397-420.

95. E. D. Chapple and C. S. Coon, *Principles of Anthropology* (New York: Henry Holt and Company, 1942)

96. E. D. Chapple, "Applied Anthropology in Industry," in: A. L. Kroeber, Ed., *op. cit.* (italics supplied), 819-831.

97. W. C. Boyd, *Genetics and the Races of Man* (Boston: Little, Brown 1950); Theodosius Dobzhansky, *Genetics and the Origin of Species* (New York: Columbia University Press, 1951, 3d edition); G. G. Simpson, *The Meaning of Evolution* (New

Haven: Yale University Press, 1949) ; T. D. Stewart, "Three in One: Physical Anthropology, Genetics, Statistics," *Journal of Heredity*, XLII (1951) , 255-56, 260;
S. L. Washburn, "The Strategy of Physical Anthropology," in: A. L. Kroeber, Ed.
op. cit., 714-727.

98. Carlos Monge, "Physiological Anthropology of the Dwellers in America's
High Plateaus," in: Sol Tax, Ed., *Indian Tribes of Aboriginal America* (Selected
Papers of the 29th International Congress of Americanists) (University of Chicago
Press, 1952) in: A. L. Kroeber, Ed., *op. cit.*, 127-144.

99. N. B. Talbot, "Nutrition and Pediatrics," *Nutrition Review*, IV (1946),
289-291.

100. M. T. Newman, "The Application of Ecological Rules to the Racial Anthropology of the Aboriginal New World," *American Anthropologist*, LV (1953)
311-327.

101. Frederick B. Thieme, "The Population as a Unit of Study," *American
Anthropologist*, LIV (1952) , 504-509.

102. Cf. W. C. Boyd, *op. cit.;* C. S. Coon, S. M. Garn, & J. B. Birdsell, *Races
. . . A Study of the Problems of Race Formation in Man* (Springfield, Ill.: Charles
C. Thomas, Publisher, 1950) ; Earnest A. Hooton, *Up From the Ape* (New York:
The MacMillan Co., 1946, rev. edition).

103. S. M. Garn and C. S. Coon, "On the Number of Races of Mankind,"
American Anthropologist, LVII (1955) , 996-1001.

104. *Ibid.*, 1000.

105. W. C. Boyd, *op. cit.*, 207.

106. Theodosius Dobzhansky and Gordon Allen, "Does Natural Selection Continue
to Operate in Modern Mankind?", *American Anthropologist*, LVIII (1956) , 591-604.

107. H. G. Fleure, "The Distribution of Types of Skin Color," *Geographical
Review*, XXXV (1945) , 580-595.

108. M. T. Newman, *op. cit.*

109. W. H. Sheldon, S. S. Stevens, and W. B. Tucker, *The Varieties of Human
Physique* (New York: Harper, 1940).

110. Bernice A. Kaplan, "Environment and Human Plasticity," *American Anthropologist*, LVI (1954) , 780-800.

111. G. S. Carter, "The Theory of Evolution and the Evolution of Man," in:
A. L. Kroeber, Ed., *op. cit.*, 327-342; also, G. G. Simpson, *op. cit.*

112. T. Dobzhansky and G. Allen, *op. cit.*; cf. Julian Huxley, *Evolution in Action*
(London: Harper, 1953) .

113. W. C. Boyd, *op. cit.*, 364-366.

114. J. W. Bennett, "Interdisciplinary Research and the Concept of Culture,"
American Anthropologist, LVI (1954) , 169-179; G. Gordon Brown, "Culture, Society,
and Personality: A Restatement," *American Journal of Psychiatry*, CVIII (1951),
173-175; C. W. M. Hart, "The Sons of Turimpi," *American Anthropologist*, LVI
(1954) , 242-261. For a compilation and comparison of variant definitions of culture,
see: A. L. Kroeber & Clyde Kluckhohn, "Culture: A Critical Review of Concepts
and Definitions," *Papers of the Peabody Museum of American Archaeology and
Ethnology*, Harvard University; XLVII, No. 1 (Cambridge: Crimson Printing Company, 1952) .

115. Oscar Lewis, "Comparisons in Cultural Anthropology," in: W. L. Thomas,
Jr., Ed., *op. cit.*, 259-292.

116. Sol Tax, "The Integration of Anthropology," in: W. L. Thomas, Jr., Ed.,
op. cit., 313-328.

117. This emphasis on the integrative quality of culture in anthropology does not deny the total bio-sociocultural and environmental universe of man. The debate over whether anthropologists should study man with relation to both the biogenic and/or cultural facies, to which Redfield (1953) refers, is quite superfluous. The nature of the interacting universe requires it.

118. Frederick Thieme, *op. cit.*, 507.

119. A. R. Radcliffe-Brown, "The Comparative Method in Anthropology," *Journal of the Royal Anthropological Institute, Great Britain and Ireland*, LXXXI (1951) 15-22.

120. Erwin H. Ackerknecht, "On the Comparative Method in Anthropology," in: Robert F. Spencer, Ed., *op. cit.*, 117-125.

121. I. Schapera, "Comparative Method in Anthropology," *American Anthropologist*, LV (1953) , 353-361.

122. Milton Singer, "Summary of Comments and Discussion (of I. Schapera, *Some Comments on Comparative Method in Social Anthropology*) ," *American Anthropologist*, LV (1953) , 363-366; cf. Ackerknecht, *op. cit.*

123. Elizabeth Colson, *op. cit.;* Claude Levi-Strauss, *op. cit.;* Clyde Kluckhohn, "Universal Categories of Culture," in: A. L. Kroeber, Ed., *op. cit.*, 507-523; G. P. Murdock, "Feasibility and Implementation of Comparative Community Research," *American Sociological Review*, XV (1950), 713-720; also, "Sociology and Anthropology," in: John Gillin, Ed., *For a Science of Social Man* (New York: MacMillan, 1954) , 14-32; G. P. Murdock and John W. M. Whiting, "Cultural Determination of Parental Attitudes; The Relationship between the Social Structure, Particularly Family Structure and Parental Behavior," in: M. J. E. Senn, Ed., *Problems of Infancy and Childhood* (Transactions of the Fourth Conference, March 6-7, 1950) (New York: Josiah Macy, Jr. Foundation, 1951) , 13-34.

124. Harold Driver, "Statistics in Anthropology," *American Anthropologist*, LV (1953), 42-59.

125. Margaret Mead, "National Character," in: A. L. Kroeber, Ed., *op. cit.*, 642-667; also, Margaret Mead & Rhoda Metraux, *The Study of Culture at a Distance* (University of Chicago Press, 1953) .

126. Claude Levi-Strauss, *op. cit.*, 531.

127. For Rorschach variation, see: Bert Kaplan, *op. cit.*

128. Fred Eggan, "Social Anthropology and the Method of Controlled Comparison," *American Anthropologist*, LVI (1954) , 743-763.

129. Oscar Lewis (1955) , 277.

130. *Ibid.*, 279.

III.

SOME APPLICATIONS OF SOCIOLOGY

THE SOCIOLOGY OF BUREAUCRACY AND PROFESSIONS

Robert C. Stone
Tulane University

HISTORY OF CONCEPTS

The history of the two terms bureaucracy and profession is curious in that they have developed quite separately, yet at the same time the notion of bureaucracy contains the notion of professionalism. By and large, the concept of profession has been studied from a social-psychological framework whereas the term bureaucracy has been employed to describe social structure.

Interest in the study of the professions appears to have been somewhat sporadic until the last fifteen years. The index of the *American Journal of Sociology* for the years 1895-1935 lists only one article under the heading of professions. An equal lack of interest appears with reference to the study of occupations. Impetus for the study of professions was given by investigation of social types in the city. These social types were frequently also occupational types and drew attention to professions as aspects of the occupational world. An emphasis upon social process also lead to the study of occupations in terms of professionalization. Today, the interest in professions is more or less divorced from interest in urbanism, but the notion of process is still utilized.

The emphasis in this field has centered upon social psychological elements in professionalization, the self conceptions, conflicts and stresses emerging from changing status and from the development of a specialized group of persons wielding highly developed occupational skills. The notion of *process*—ceaseless change and adaptation has been basic to the development of the field. Consequently, an interest in professions as a structural feature of modern occupational systems was not stressed.

491

One qualification to the emphasis upon social process was the use of the concept of natural history. Studies made by sociologists trained at the University of Chicago utilized this idea widely. Natural history refers to a sequence of changes or set of stages that pertains to a class of things. This is in contrast to history *per se* with its emphasis upon the unique. If the term natural history is applied to professions, then we may expect that any group undergoing professionalization will follow a sequence of changes. This ignores, of course, the particular and unique aspect of each professional group.

Much more recently, study in the professions has utilized a functional approach, and the emphasis has tended to shift then to matters of social structure with resultant lack of interest in the concept of social process. Parsons' analysis of the professions as a structural aspect of modern occupational life is the foremost example of this type of study.

Over and above the interests of sociologists there has been a lively and continuing interest by members of professional groups in their own occupations, and a quite considerable body of writing about particular occupations can be found in any good library. This volume of material has several functions, as it is on the one hand data for the social scientist, and on the other social interpretation and theory. Most of the theorizing about professions by members of a particular occupation has not been utilized by professional sociologists.

The development of the concept bureaucracy has a much different history. Despite usage of the term in other fields in the 19th century, the term as used in sociology is clearly linked to the work of Max Weber, the famous German sociologist. The concept is a key term in Weber's sociology and its meaning has been taken over wholesale by American sociologists. There have been a number of books recently published on this subject and every one of them starts with a discussion of Weber's usage of the term as the basic reference. This is even true of recent books on Public Administration in the field of Political Science.

Despite such clarity in historical sources there is also a popular conception of bureaucracy that seems inextricably mixed with the social science meaning that Weber developed. The public meaning of bureaucracy—government bureaus with emphasis upon rigid procedures and red tape—is mixed with the social science meaning regardless of efforts to separate them. There is more involved here however than a simple confusion of words, because the theoretical articles written by social scientists deal with the issues of rigidity and red tape as dysfunctions of bureaucratic structure. Consequently, we conclude that the total subject matter of bureaucracy legitimately includes not only the meaning intended by Weber, but also the older meaning which is the public and popular one.

It is clear from Weber's writing and from usage by other social scientists that bureaucracy refers to matters of social structure. Bureaucratic organization is the form that persists and that gives stability to organizations. Consequently, the notion of bureaucracy has not been studied from the viewpoint of social process. This is not to say that such could not be the case but only to point out that the development of the concept has been to describe matters of social structure.

Given these differences in history and development there is considerable difficulty in treating these concepts jointly, but despite the fact of being strange bedfellows, there are good reasons why they should be treated together in a chapter on trends in sociology. First, there is the important empirical fact that these two organizational aspects of the division of labor are becoming more and more important in American society. Secondly, the common and differential values that they express are of central importance in understanding the overall configuration of American society and of modern societies in general.

Thirdly, recent studies point to the actual inter-connection between the two organizational modes. As each of these modes becomes more widely diffused in the world of work, they can be found operating jointly within the same organization or social structure. The professional organization of doctors is incorporated within the modern hospital directly within the context of bureaucratic organization. Engineers, lawyers and scientists work within government and business bureaucracies. More and more professionals are employed by the federal government. It appears that these two modes constitute conflicting patterns of organization on many counts. Yet from a functional viewpoint, organizations can contain conflicts and continue as going concerns. The combination of these two organizational patterns results in a wide variety of structural patterns and social roles. Descriptions of organizations that are both bureaucratic and professional in their organization and operation are quite recent and a few in number.

Our procedure will be to discuss trends in the study of professions, in the study of bureaucracy, and last the research that deals with both of these concepts.

The term professions usually refers to a group of persons wielding a specialized set of occupational skills. This group is bound by a code of conduct called professional ethics, some control is exerted over membership in the occupation, long and extended training is characteristic and usually involves more than apprenticeship learning. The underlying note in professionalism is the rendering of a service either to a public or to clients. Characteristically professionals do not believe that outsiders can judge the quality of the work they perform. As Everett Hughes states it: "The people in a profession make their living by giving an esoteric service." [1]

Doctors are one of the professional groups that has interested sociologists. Oswald Hall[2] has shown how the stages of a medical career develop, and the informal social controls that are maintained by members of the profession. The doctor who wishes to succeed must accept these informal controls if he is to follow the accepted career pattern. The power of doctors in controlling the structure and functioning of hospitals has also been studied. Specialization of skills within the profession brings in its train rivalry and conflict focusing on matters of prestige and authority.

Nurses have been studied particularly with reference to their changing status and to developing professionalization. The tensions and problems that emerge with status changes have been described in a number of studies. The competition and conflicts between doctors and nurses have also been noted. Role relationships between two professional groups placed in a superior and inferior status position reveal clearly some of the basic attributes of professionalization, particularly when the statuses of the two groups are in process of change.

Lawyers have been the subject of several studies. The relationship of this group to the business world and the dual role of professional and business man has been described. Social ranking and prestige of the criminal, labor, and corporation lawyer has been described in detail.

The real estate man has also been described in terms of the competing pull of professional values and business considerations. The same conflicts show up in studies devoted to role conflicts among pharmacists.

Engineers have been described in terms of conflicts arising from their position as technical employees versus the role of manager and executive. In a recent article on *The Changing Status of the Engineer*[3] William Evan emphasizes increased length of training, higher prestige, and licensing as factors legitimizing the engineer's status as that of a professional. However, his employee status, and the bifurcation of career between technical and managerial lines leads to a continuation of confusion and doubts about professional and business roles.

A considerable number of papers have been written on military organization and some of these deal with problems of profession and career. The military journals themselves carry articles dealing with this subject. Matters of prestige and status are usually of central concern. Changes in type of career preparation and career pattern as well are also given consideration in these discussions. Role conflicts developing from additional officer duties not directly related to command have been studied in some detail.

Teachers and the teaching profession have also been scrutinized by sociologists. Logan Wilson's *The Academic Man*[4] throws light on the key importance of prestige as an element in professional organization and functioning. Studies of teachers also document the importance of the concept of career to professional status.

This very brief survey leaves out several occupational groups that have been studied and makes reference to only a handful of studies. However, there are a number of central issues or tendencies that are revealed from any survey of the sociological study of the professions.

Hughes[5] has posed several points which he says are universal problems for every occupational or professional group. The first characteristic is the potential conflict of interest between the professional and his client. The means of controlling this conflict may vary widely, and the results of such control also are variable. The underlying stresses and strains in patient-professional relations serves then as a focal point for the analysis of social process. A second universal feature is the social control by members of a professional group exerted against the inroads by outsiders. Licensing, informal controls, ideologies, etc., all can be analyzed as means of dealing with this fundamental problem. A third issue that is ever present is that of defining the amount and kind of work that is done.

Other central issues also emerge from the study of professions. Almost every study of an occupational group, and particularly of professions, deals with prestige. The range of possible subjects investigated under this rubric is large and includes matters of ideologies, cooperation and conflict between professional groups, internal rivalries of a given profession, and vertical mobility. In fact, the importance of prestige in determining the outlook and motives of professionals is so strong, that it may underlie some of the objections of sociologists to the current industrial emphasis upon group goals in contrast to the 19th century emphasis upon individualism and success. If success in the prestige realm is the ethos of professional life, it is small wonder that many professionals look upon the ideology of group participation and solidarity as indicative of a weakening of moral fiber. Some professionals even look upon their occupational groups as the last bastions for the defense of individualism.

Some interest has been displayed in studying the role of professionals in business, governmental, and medical institutions such as the hospital. The interest has focused upon the conflicts and difficulties in integrating professionals into an organization which itself can not be described as professional in character. We shall deal with these studies in the last section of the chapter.

Perhaps the most important analysis of motivation and professionalization, other than descriptions of the obvious facts concerning motives and prestige, is found in Talcott Parsons' essay on the professions.[6] Parsons argues that it is not individual motives of acquisitiveness that differentiate business from some corresponding individual service motives held by professionals. The difference between business and professions is to be found in the institutionalization of values. While the pecuniary orientation of the businessman and the service orientation of the professional appear on the surface as widely divergent motives, a functional approach indicates that they may stem from underying similarities in values. Prestige for the professional becomes much the same as profit for the businessman. Parsons extends his analysis of underlying similarities between business and professions and indicates that both modes of "work" are patterned in terms of functional specificity and affective neutrality.

One approach to the subject of professionalization that has been of interest to the businessman but not to sociologists is the notion of professionalization of business. Such interest is indicated by the continued publications of books on the subject. In a much more fundamental way, Émile Durkheim[7] has dealt with this subject, and was driven to the conclusion that the dysfunctions of the modern economic world could only be corrected through the development of "occupational societies" or "corporations." His descriptions of the functions of such institutions implies a professionalization of the business world. Durkheim argued that because economic affairs are of paramount importance in the modern world, they must be subject to some moral control over and above the ideology of economic individualism. The occupational group seemed to him the logical unit for the implementation of needed social control. This theoretical approach to professionalization has not been utilized by American sociologists. It obviously raises fundamental questions about the distribution of economic power in modern society.

In general, the study of the professions has centered upon social psychological matters of role and self conception. In analyzing client-professional relations, changing prestige and occupational status, and occupational conflicts the reference has usually been to the individual in his occupational role. The major modification to this approach has been through use of the concept of natural history. With the exception of Parsons' essays there has been little attempt to view the professions as elements of a larger social pattern—the occupational structure of the United States.

Perhaps one other exception to the social psychological trend is found in the field of Political Science. For some time professionalization along with civil service were considered to be twin solutions to the dysfunctions of government organization. However, an opposing view has also developed, namely that professionalization is not an adequate guarantee that a given occupational group will fulfill its responsibilities to the body politic. To quote one author's summary of this viewpoint: "It is generally agreed that the professional sanction does not of itself provide an adequate guarantee of responsibility in our society. Some students have even emphasized the special dangers of any heavy reliance on professional standards."[8] This viewpoint is also expressed in the criticisms that have been leveled at the medical profession in recent years.

BUREAUCRACY

One of the trends that has been noted by sociologists as well as by others is the spread and diffusion of the bureaucratic mode of organization in modern life. This trend validates Weber's conclusion that the movement of history is away from traditional modes of organization and toward increasing rationality as manifested in the spread of bureaucracy. At the same time, there is a literature of protest about this movement, just as there has been a literature of protest about increasing industrialization. Some sociologists see the dysfunctions of bureaucracy as a growing threat to the social order.

In simplest form, we may take increased size of organizations, proliferation of authority levels, development of systematic organization rules, standardization of tasks, emphasis upon impersonal obligations, and separation of personal from official affairs as evidence of increasing bureaucratization. We hardly need comment upon the growing influence of government and the growth of government bureaus as evidence of such a trend. But over and above growth of government other studies indicate the growth of bureaucracy in business, education, unions and even in the field of philanthropy.

C. Wright Mills[9] and Robert Dubin[10] have described the growth of bureaucratic forms as a functional necessity in the development of the giant modern trade unions. Emphasis upon rules, permanent officials, and a complex hierarchy of administration contrast with older personalistic methods of organizing trade union affairs. The growth of bureaucracy in business has been studied by many persons. The process of decentralization of decision making without loss of bureaucratic form has been described by Peter Drucker in his volume *The Concept of the Corporation.*[11]

Almost no realm of modern life seems to escape the need for bureaucratic administration. It has been suggested that the various Catholic orders have changed from a gemeinschaft towards gesellschaft structure with attendant bureaucratic administration. Weber himself pointed to the bureaucratization of research, and his trend has been described in recent studies of the impact of giant foundations on the academic world.

An older interest in bureaucratic centralization and its affects upon local community action has been carried forward by studies such as Selznick's *TVA and the Grass Roots.*[12] Not only in the TVA but also in the Soil Conservation Service attempts have been made to link bureaucratic administration with local participation and community involvement.

J. Donald Kingsley[13] in his study of the British Civil Service attacks the same problem of bureaucracy and power in a democracy. Herring[14] has summarized this problem in his analysis of politics as a method for dealing with power distribution and bureaucratic administration as a method for achieving efficiency. Government in modern society involves both of these logically opposed goals, and the functional problem is how to combine efficiency and politics within the same political system. Herring offers no answers but shows clearly the false character of many older arguments bearing on the problem.

Public Administration has traditionally been the prerogative of Political Scientists but there has been a significant and vital broadening of the field to include all types of administration whether governmental or not. Sociologists as well as political scientists have contributed to the recent studies on administration. One of the developments centers around the study of decision making. Herbert Simon's *Administrative Behavior*[15] presents a systematic approach to the study of decision making within bureaucracy. Harold Stein's casebook[16] on decision making in governmental administration utilizes the concept of process. Case studies of top level decision throw a great deal of light upon the dynamics of bureaucratic administration.

Another interest has been in the study of communication. An old maxim has it that the only way to run a large organization is to treat it like a small organization. The implications of this somewhat mysterious adage are being investigated through the studies dealing with communication in large complex organizations. Distortions, bias, and roadblocks in communication arising in the context of bureaucracy are problems that continue to hold the attention of researchers.

Alvin Gouldner's[17] study of leadership succession in a bureaucracy highlights problems of communication and consensus. Gouldner suggests a set of types; mock bureaucracy, punishment-centered bureaucracy, and representative bureaucracy. Each of these types has direct effects upon communications within the system. According to the argument, representative bureaucracy tends to maximize communication between sub and superordinate.

Selznick utilizing a functional approach, suggests the key importance of self-maintenance elements in determining the dynamics of bureaucratic administration.[18] This view has roots in political theory where the notion of vested interests and iron law of oligarchy have been advanced as theories about power arrangements. Selznick modifies these concepts and applies them to bureaucratic patterns of organization.

Another approach is suggested by Eric Josephson in his article on "Irrational Leadership in Formal Organization." [19] This emphasis upon irrational elements enlarges upon the ideas suggested by Weber's concept of "charisma."

Interest in informal organization is another trend that has extended to studies of bureaucracy. Relationships between these two modes have been explored in a series of case studies of military bureaucracy. Again, Alvin Gouldner's[20] study of business bureaucracy emphasizes the key importance of informal organization in a situation (mining) where danger is an important element. In general, the study of informal organization emphasizes the mediating effects of this mode upon the rigidity of formal organization. Such studies do not merit the conclusion, however, that informal organization necessarily destroys the bureaucratic features of an organization.

Finally, there is a continuing interest in 'bureaucracy and personality.' If there can be said to be a social psychology of bureaucrcy, it is to be found in this area of study. Merton's[21] classic article lays out in theoretical terms expected relationships between bureaucratic structure and personality organization. Tendencies toward slavish rule following and toward depersonalization of relationships are seen as the subjective side of structural aspects of the system.

Another set of conditions is suggested by studies of corporation executives. In this formulation it is held that the corporation "captures" the family system, and enmeshes not only husband but wife and children in its ethos. Emphasis upon adjustment, getting along, and solidarity with the company lead, then, to a synthetic kind of of welding together of family and occupational life. The obvious implication of this approach is to suggest that such integration of bureaucratic and family life destroys primary group values.

Still another permutation of bureaucracy and personality is found in the description of Soviet factory life given by Alexander Vucinich.[22] The ideology of Soviet society stresses not the integration of primary group and job, but rather the total divorcing of the two. Any loyalty that intercedes between the state—with its goals of ever-increasing productivity—and the efforts of individual workers is to be ruthlessly weeded out. Consequently, one would assume that the sharpest possible separation is maintained between family life and its demands and the world of work.

Continuing the trend for further investigation of this subject, Gouldner raises a number of questions in his article in the *Reader in Bureaucracy*[23] about the relationship between impersonality and bureaucratic structure, and questions some of the accepted theories. In a recent volume, Francis and Stone have made a study of personal obligations that developed among members of a bureaucratic organization. Parsons has pointed to the ideology of American society with its emphasis upon separation of job and family worlds. Empirically, it would seem that wide variation from this norm can and does occur.

The best summary volume dealing with trends in research on bureaucracy is found in the *Reader in Bureaucracy*. The most important trend in the research is the emphasis upon dysfunctions. Interest has continued to center on the curse of bigness. Studies dealing with communication, informal organization, levels of authority, and efficiency almost always have reference to malfunctions of the system. One aspect of dysfunction that comes to the fore is the emphasis upon government bureaucracy and democratic control. Lipset's[24] investigations of the political biases of bureaucrats with resultant effects upon policy implementation illustrates this interest. Dysfunctions due to the rigidity of bureaucratic structures also continue to hold the interest of researchers.

In one sense the problem of democratic social control over government bureaucracy is like the problem of civil liberties. The motto of the American Civil Liberties Union, "The price of liberty is eternal vigilance," is essentially a statement of process. According to this view there is no structural solution to the matter of civil liberties, because the same problem is being endlessly repeated, the process is one of endless solution. To date, the research on bureaucratic dysfunctions indicates much the same thing. There appear to be no structural solutions to the dysfunctions of bureaucracy, only an endless resolving of problems as they continue to arise. The process interpretation is much like Hughes' interpretation of relationships between clients and professionals. The relationship is an endless problem solving of latent conflict. Selznick describes the dysfunctions of bureaucracy in much this manner, as tendencies that always lurk beneath the surface. He says: "These tendencies are, however, analytical: They represent abstractions from concrete organizational patterns. To state these tendencies is to *set* a problem, for although they ascribe to organizations in general an initial presumption of bureaucratic consequence, it always remains to be determined to what degree the bureaucratic tendencies become dominant." [25]

Another major trend in studies of bureaucracy is toward more adequate description of particular cases. As case studies are developed, a more adequate understanding is gained of the variability in this shadowy but most important social pattern.

RESEARCH ON THE RELATIONSHIP BETWEEN BUREAUCRACY AND PROFESSIONS

Max Weber's concept of bureaucracy included professionals as a necessary element of such a system. Subsequent usage of the term has not, however, been consistent in this respect. Both factory systems and government organizations have been labeled bureaucracies and certainly the professional status of personnel in these two types of organization is vastly different.

Parsons has pointed to the analytical confusion that is involved here and indicates that Weber did not foresee the role of professional organization in modern occupations as distinct from the bureaucratic mode of organization.

A number of recent studies consider these two modes, the professional and the bureaucratic, as antithetical but co-existent within the same organization. Studies of hospital organization indicate that both of these modes operate within the hospital framework. Leonard Reissman's [26] study of a government office indicates that professional and bureaucratic orientations operative within the same system function to produce several social types: 1. the functional bureaucrat oriented to a professional group, 2. the specialist bureaucrat oriented both to professional and bureaucratic structures, 3. the service bureaucrat oriented to clients and to the bureaucratic structure, 4. and the job bureaucrat whose motives lead him toward conformity to bureaucratic rules.

Peter Blau's [27] study of two government offices indicates this same complexity in the inter-meshing of bureaucratic and professional modes. The study by Francis and Stone [28] focuses upon the ideological and role conflicts emerging from the dialectic operation of the two opposed patterns of organization.

Bureaucratic and professional modes are conflicting on many counts. The former centers on coordination of diverse groups for the purpose of efficiency in achieving clear cut organizational goals. The latter centers on a group wielding similar occupational skills for purposes of service to clients or a public. The skills of the individual and individual responsibility lie at the heart of professional ideologies, by contrast with the bureaucratic emphasis upon rationalization of skills, and distribution of authority throughout a highly coordinated system.

Now these two modes may combine in a large number of different ways. For example, the Soil Conservation Service of the Department of Agriculture employs persons in its field offices who, by and large, define themselves as professionals. Examination of the relations of one field office to another and to the regional headquarters indicates bureaucratic modes of organization and corresponding rationality. Investigation of the job activities of individual members within a given field office, and of their relationships to each other, reveals professional modes of conduct as the dominant theme. This structure may be contrasted with factory organization where the people at the bottom of the authority and status hierarchy are in no sense professional, but the persons in staff positions, such as accountants, engineers, etc., are professionals. The coordination of all the various skill groups is maintained by bureaucratic administration. Many other possibilities are suggested by the recent studies focusing on the joint operation of bureaucratic and professional principles.

One label that is beginning to appear with greater frequency in this field is the phrase "sociology of work," and it is frequently substituted for industrial sociology or the term "sociology of economic institutions." Bureaucratic and professional patterns fall quite conveniently together under this heading. However, with the possible exception of certain recent essays by European scholars, *work* has not been treated as a theoretical concept in the field of sociology. The recent studies on bureaucracy and professions as related but conflicting organizational modes, and the tendency to class these terms as aspects of work organization indicate a movement toward more interest in a general theoretical approach to this subject.

One suggested approach combining and enlarging the concepts of profession and bureaucracy has been made by Edward Gross.[29] Starting from the observation that work may be approached either from the viewpoint of occupations or from the viewpoint of an institutional unit such as company, bureau, etc., Gross points out that occupations may be conceived of as varying from the status of "job" to that of "profession." Organizations may be thought of as varying from symbiosis to consensus. It is obvious that these two axes of analysis are not unrelated. As the tendency for an occupation to become a profession increases, so emphasis upon consensus in organization increases and vice versa.

This theoretical formulation is indicative of the trend toward development of generalized schemes that will encourage description of the various combinations of bureaucratic and professional organization. Such theoretical schemes should function to bridge the gap created by the historical emphasis upon process in the study of professions and the emphasis upon structure in the study of bureaucracy.

SELECTED BIBLIOGRAPHY

Peter Blau, *The Dynamics of Bureaucracy* (University of Chicago Press, 1955). A report on research leading to the conclusion that professional values can and do operate within the bureaucratic concept; stresses the possibility of wide variation within the over-all pattern of bureaucratic administration; the study centers on application of functional theory.

A. M. Carr-Saunders & P. A. Wilson, *The Professions* (Oxford: The Claredon Press, 1933). An earlier study, devoted to the development of the professions in England.

Alvin Gouldner, *Patterns of Industrial Bureaucracy* (Glencoe, Ill.: The Free Press, 1954). Emphasizes the alternative forms of organization that develop within the bureaucratic mode; presents a typology of bureaucratic type and a general functional analysis of bureaucratic forms.

Edward Gross, "Some Suggestions for the Legitimation of Industrial Studies in Sociology," *Social Forces,* XXXIII (March, 1955), 233-239. One of the few articles attempting a theoretical linkage between the concept of occupations and bureaucracy.

Oswald Hall, "The Stages of a Medical Career," *The American Journal of Sociology,* LIII (March, 1948), 327-336. One of the best studies of social control and career within a professional group; the key elements in professionalism are highlighted.

Everett Hughes, "Institutional Office and the Person," *The American Journal of Sociology,* XLIII (November, 1937), 409-413. Analyzes the relationship between status positions viewed as objective aspects of structure and career viewed subjectively in terms of self-conceptions.; "The Sociological Study of Work: An Editorial Foreword," *Ibid.,* LVII (March, 1952), 423-426. The most general current statement about work as a subject for sociological inquiry; develops the approach to occupations and professions in terms of processes.

Robert K. Merton, "Bureaucratic Structure and Personality," *Social Forces*, XVIII (May, 1940), 560-568. Argues that bureaucratic structure gives rise to tendencies toward compulsive rule following and toward impersonality; discusses hypotheses about the source for such characteristics. Merton & *al., Reader in Bureaucracy* (Glencoe, Ill.: The Free Press, 1952). Some of the most recent thought on the subject of bureaucracy is contained in the essays contained here; problems of power, impersonality, and democratic control are among the topics treated.

Talcott Parsons, "The Professions and Social Structure," *Social Forces*, XVII (May, 1939), 457-467. An important essay analyzing the professions as an aspect of modern occupational structure; points to underlying similarities between professions and other occupations.

Max Weber, *The Theory of Economic and Social Organization* (trans. by A. M. Henderson & Talcott Parsons, New York: Oxford University Press, 1947); *From Max Weber: Essays in Sociology*, H. H. Gerth & C. Wright Mills, Eds. (New York: Oxford University Press, 1946). Several key passages from Weber's theories can be found here; the editors also provide a valuable commentary on Weber's theory.

Logan Wilson, *The Academic Man. A Study in the Sociology of a Profession* (New York: Oxford University Press, 1942). Lays bare the key importance of career and prestige striving in professional organization.

Robert C. Stone, A.B., University of California (1940), M.A. University of Chicago (1946), Ph.D., University of Chicago (1949). Research Associate (Instructor), Committee on Human Development, University of Chicago (1947-1948); Assistant Professor of Sociology, Stanford University (1948-1951); Assistant Professor of Sociology, & Staff Associate, Urban Life Research Institute, Tulane University (1951–). Co-author of *Service and Procedure in Bureaucracy* (with Roy G. Francis), a study of bureaucratic and professional aspects of work organization in a government agency.

NOTES

1. Everett Hughes, "Psychology: Science and/or Professions," *The American Psychologist*, VII, 8 (August, 1952), 441.

2. Oswald Hall, "The Stages of a Medical Career," *American Journal of Sociology*, LIII (March, 1948), 327-336.

3. William Evan, "The Changing Status of the Engineer," *Age of Science*, II (December, 1956), 57-60.

4. Logan Wilson, *The Academic Man* (New York: Oxford University Press, 1942).

5. E. C. Hughes, "The Sociological Study of Work: An Editorial Foreword," *The American Journal of Sociology*, LVII (March, 1952), 423-426.

6. Talcott Parsons, "The Professions and Social Structure," *Social Forces,* XVII (May, 1939), 457-467.

7. Emile Durkheim, *The Division of Labor in Society* (Glenkoe, Ill.: The Free Press, 1937); *Le Socialisme,* M. Mauss, Ed. (Paris: F. Alcan, 1928).

8. Arthur A. Maas and Laurence I. Radway, "Gauging Administrative Responsibility" in *Ideas and Issues in Public Administration,* Dwight Waldo, Ed., (New York: McGraw-Hill Book Company) 1953, 452.

9. C. Wright Mills, *The New Men of Power* (New York: Harcourt, Brace, 1948).

10. Robert Dubin, "Imperatives Affecting Industrial Relations Decisions," in *Human Relations in Administration* (New York: Prentice-Hall, 1951).

11. Peter Drucker, *The Concept of the Corporation* (New York: The John Day, 1946).

12. A. Selznick, *TVA and the Grass Roots* (Berkeley: University of California Press, 1949).

13. J. D. Kingsley, *Representative Bureaucracy* (Yellow Springs, Ohio: The Antioch Press, 1944).

14. E. P. Herring, "Logamachy and Administration," *Journal of Social Philosophy,* II (January, 1937), 95-117.

15. Herbert Simon, *Administrative Behavior* (New York: The MacMillan Co., 1947).

16. Harold Stein, *Public Administration and Policy Development* (New York: Harcourt, Brace, 1952).

17. Alvin Gouldner, *Patterns of Industrial Bureaucracy* (Glencoe, Ill.: The Free Press, 1954).

18. P. Selznick, "An Approach to a Theory of Bureaucracy," *American Sociological Review,* VIII (February, 1953), 47-59.

19. Erich Josephson, "Irrational Leadership in Formal Organization," *Social Forces,* XXXI (December, 1952), 109-117.

20. Alvin Gouldner, *op. cit.*

21. R. K. Merton, "Bureaucratic Structure and Personality," *Social Forces,* XVIII (May, 1940), 560-568.

22. Alexander Vucinich, *Soviet Economic Institutions* (Stanford University Press, 1952).

23. Robert K. Merton, Ed., *Reader in Bureaucracy* (Glencoe, Ill.: The Free Press, 1952).

24. *Ibid.*

25. Selznick, *op. cit.,* 47.

26. Leonald Reissman, "A Study of Role Conceptions in Bureaucracy," *Social Forces,* XXVII (March, 1949), 305-310.

27. Peter Blau, *Dynamics of Bureaucracy* (University of Chicago Press, 1955).

28. Francis & Stone, *Service and Procedure in Bureaucracy* (Minneapolis: University of Minnesota Press, 1956).

29. Edward Gross, "Some Suggestions for the Legitimization of Industrial Studies in Sociology," *Social Forces,* XXXIII (Marcn, 1955), 233-239.

THE SOCIOLOGY OF ECONOMIC ORGANIZATION

S. Earl Grigsby
and
Leonard L. Linden
University of Florida

What are some of the specific areas of the economic organization which have received the attention of the sociologists? A review of the voluminous, but unfortunately not always significant, literature in the field of socio-economic thought gives ample evidence that this area has been, and still is, the recipient of urgent and concentrated, though not always organized attention. This chapter does not attempt to review the literature but focuses its attention upon: (1) the organizational structure, concepts and values in the economic organization and (2) the "human social factors" and their influence on the economic organization.

In the analysis of a particular segment of socal activity it is frequently necessary to acknowledge either that this activity is governed by certain regularities of social action which are known (if not understood) or that the particular activity is in itself the determinant of all other social action. The rejection of economic determinism is a valid one which has widespread acceptance today and this necessitates the former proposition that we have sufficient sociological knowledge to analyze economic activity. This unfortunately is not true. A third alternative would be description in terms of perceptions. However, describing complex interaction without understanding its major component parts leads to endless description and becomes almost a cosmological explanation of human action.

It is for this reason that the present efforts to present a unified approach in the "social sciences" encounters its criticism. Attempts to do this at this time indicate that the very complexity of the subject has defied attempts to analyze the factors in depth. These attempts are usually analogous to those of biology when it analyzes physiological processes in terms of chemistry and physics. This can be done in biological science because there is now sufficient understanding of the relationships between these areas. The social sciences, perhaps in imitation of the physical and biological sciences, are attempting to accomplish this unified approach without first deciding upon the actual area(s) that are being discussed and "unified" and without a complete scientific understanding of the factors involved.

ECONOMIC ORGANIZATION

Economic organization and activity exists in our (Western) society because it is sanctioned by and is consistent with the societal value systems and norms. Man's efforts to satisfy his many wants through the use of the scarce resources of nature have risen to a primary goal through an inter-relationship of many factors.[1]

The emergence and rise of economic activity through and from these factors has constantly redefined and reshaped the societal norms and organizational structure of Western society. It is this reciprocal action between economic activity, societal norms and organizational structure and the group setting within which these reciprocal relations are manifested that are of primary interest to the sociologist. The sociologist is no longer content with the "residues" of social problems caused by supposed failures of the economic order to function according to its ideal pattern. The science of economics, one of the oldest social sciences, has defined its interests and itself as being "the science which deals with man's efforts to satisfy his wants through the use of the scarce resources of nature."[2] This definition may be interpreted rather narrowly as is done by the classical economic school so that it becomes an abstract science concerned with "ideal" types; or, in contrast, the encyclopedic (institutional) economists have interpreted this definition with the greatest latitude so that their investigations and analyses consider any area, which may give rise to economic consequences, as being within their scope.

In both definitions the concept of *homo-economicus* is present implicitly, even if not explicitly, for there is always the assumption that economic interests will prevail whenever there is a choice between a conflict of interests. However, there is no absolute *a priori* reason for supposing that economic interests will always prevail unless economic primacy is consistent with the total normative and value systems of the societal group.[3] It is now almost universally accepted that the economic side of social man is oriented toward the ends defined by his particular society and that motivation is primarily social in its origin.[4]

THE ECONOMIC SYSTEM: ITS CONCEPTS AND VALUES

Property. The economic value system has its basis in the concept of property. All economic motivation as we recognize it today is based upon this concept. The possession of exclusive right (as defined by the norms of the group) to an object or activity implies that possession is considered desirable by the other members of the group and that a comparative scarcity exists between its presence and the wants or needs of the group. The factor of scarcity establishes the right of possession.

Competition. Implicit and often explicit in the science of economics is the factor of free and open competition within an unrestricted market place where supply and demand can operate so that the economic motivations of man can be evidenced. In contrast to this ideal situation, society has always placed restrictions of some type upon economic activity even though they may be at a minimum as during the period of mercantilism when almost any economic activity was permitted, if it was consistent with the rise and improvement of the wealth of the state; or approaching the maximum as in the various socialist states where economic activities have been narrowly restricted so as to be consistent with the expressed value that wealth belongs to the total society or collectivity of individuals.

Wealth. In addition to the concepts of property and competition, economic activity is dependent upon the acquisition of wealth by the individual or group.[5] The intensity of the acquisition or accumulation is dictated by two factors: (1) the degrees of sanctification given to it and (2) the desirability that the society places on measuring wealth in terms of property. Sociological interest does not lie *solely* in the recognition of this socially determined goal as this would almost place the sociologist in identical position with the economist who accepts it as *a priori*. The sociologist is also concerned with the means which the group has accepted for achieving this goal as is evidenced in the normative behavior and the value systems of the group.

Without reference to economic activities as they may have existed during the feudal period or previous to it in European society, we would like to consider briefly the social values placed upon wealth.

After the feudal period and during the early rise of capitalism the right to the acquisition of wealth was limited, to a large extent, to the bourgeois who had overthrown the feudal system. Changes in religious dogma had permitted the acquisition and accumulation of wealth to become a desirable societal end. One historian has succinctly stated this transition as ". . . from spiritual being, who, in order to survive, must devote a reasonable attention to economic interests, man seems sometimes to have become an economic animal, who will be prudent, nevertheless, if he takes due precautions to assure his spiritual well being." [6]

The increasing emphasis upon wealth led to its being considered as the major criterion of status which relegated to those who did not possess property a social position only slightly higher than that of a draft animal. This emphasis plus the recognition of potential tendencies toward rebellion of those not having economic wealth was, seemingly, always present in the minds of the framers of the Constitution of the United States for ". . . they were anxious above everything else to safeguard the rights of private property against any leveling tendencies on the part of the propertyless mass." [7]

Economic Equality. The concept of equality was not stated originally in economic terms. Rather there was an increasing desire by some members of the social order to recognize the social equality of all humans as differentiated, if possible, from economic equality. The difficulty in separating these two factors in an economic-oriented society has led to the desire for economic equality. The efforts of both the Fabian and "scientific" socialists were very instrumental in spreading the doctrine of social and economic equality. This was not, and still is not, an entirely peaceful evolutionary process as testified by the history of the growth of labor unionism. Even today differences in historical backgrounds have produced division in thought between countries as well as within countries regarding the necessity of economic equality of man. For example in France the ". . . elite is divided, both because the various groups disagree about the present distribution of the national income and because the leaders believe in different Gods and their visions of the future are incompatible."[8]

The question of economic equality in the Western world has shifted slightly from implying social equality to that of ability to enjoy an increasing supply of the goods and services produced. This change has been aided, though sometimes reluctantly, by the gradual realization of the owners of the productive agents that consumption is an extremely vital factor influencing production, and that production must be of necessity limited by the demands of the consuming market. This change has given rise to a conflict between the businessman as an individual interested in the maximization of his "wealth" (as defined by one social group) and the businessman as a producer of goods and services which must be consumed regularly by the market, in order that he continue production with some assurance of stability. In attempting to maximize his own wealth, the businessman, in the long run, may very well be minimizing the potential demand for his goods and services, since demand is not desire only, but desire coupled with the ability to acquire goods and services.

This change in value orientation has been reflected in the increasing attention being paid to macro-economics which is concerned with levels of national income, propensities to save and consume, and levels and standards of living.[9] Micro-economics with its abstract of the ideal competitive order and its concern with the individual factors of production and the functioning of the "laws" of supply and demand in the market place, has been relegated to a much less important position in economic thought and investigation.[10] At least in some measure this illustrates the interrelationship between the value system of the society and the change in economic activities and thought within the group.

Specialization. Specialization and division of labor are inherent in the activities of man; even preliterate societies exhibit some degree of specialization. Technological advances and increasing emphasis upon economic activity have placed demands upon human action which could be met only through increased specialization. The individual today would find it impossible to engage actively in all phases of the productiton of goods and services which he demands. Technological efficiency has also placed a space-time limitation upon production.

Specialization in "modern" society has created new elements and questions regarding the organization of social groups and their relationship to each other. No longer can the individual or even the family be considered as even remotely capable of sustaining itself, rather it has become just one of the units in the interrelationships between persons and groups. From the analytical standpoint, this has brought about an increased complexity in modern societal life. It would be incorrect to assume that this complexity of relationships has brought about specialization as some have done. The apparent complexness is due to the fact that the social science analyst must now describe a multitude of interrelationships between various social units or groups. The complexity has increased only from the standpoint of the analytical observer; the inter-acting individuals and groups have devised means of simplifying these multitudinous relationships to comparatively understandable forms.

Bureaucracy. Bureaucracy is the logical outgrowth of increased specialization. Specialization and its accompanying complex relations inevitably evolve some types of "chain of command" or "chain of action." A bureaucracy, while exceedingly complex in its total structure, is readily understandable to its individual members in that they are directly concerned with only a fragment of the total structure: their immediate associates, those immediately above and those immediately below. Their activities and responsibilities are clearly defined and are usually arranged so that they may perform them with comparative maximum efficiency, which in itself necessitates a high degree of specialization. The rigidity of the structure encourages and necessitates an impersonal attitude. The definition of limitations for each activity tends to channel them according to the prescribed forms and discourages individual action, initiative, or responsibility.

Unfortunately, the "human factor" tends to offset the advantages in efficiency gained by bureaucracy; narrowness of perspective may be considered as its latent dysfunction.[11] The individuals have simplified for themselves, and have had simplified for them, their particular role in the activities of the organization. Thus the individuals, thinking in these simplified terms, regard the end of their individual activities as being the primary end-goal of the total action. This consequently distorts within themselves their relative importance in the entire organization. This distortion may be an under-evaluation of their importance and the attention paid to them.[12] Or it may be an over-evaluation, resulting in methodology assuming primary importance rather than the original goal of the organization.[13] In either case, a bureaucracy usually finds that it has built into itself a resistance to change in its methods, and attempts to change methods by the leaders or management frequently results in internal dissatisfaction and conflict.[14]

Interdependency and Conformity. Increased specialization has resulted in the necessity of increased cooperation among individuals. No longer is the individual able to produce the necessities of life as dictated by the "aspired to" standards of living, nor is he even capable of raising his children solely within the family if they are to have the minimum standards of health and education. This dependency upon others for his very existence has produced noticeable changes in his socio-psychological viewpoint.[15] This increased interdependency of individuals has necessitated a basic psychological change. The pioneer spirit, individualism, and independence cannot readily survive where the individual owes his very existence and the existence of his family to the cooperation of other individuals with whom he is necessarily in contact. He must avoid offense for this would jeopardize his very existence, and consequently conformity to group norms has become a virtue if not a vital element of existence.[16]

The Role of Economic Power and Influence. The "power relationship" implies that individuals or groups are subordinated to others in the fulfillment of their actions; this in turn implies the existence of inequality in the distribution of power. While the power relationships frequently imply an economic basis, it should not be forgotten that "power" may owe its existence to many factors.

A power relationship is inherent in economics by definition. The control of "scarce" materials or resources implies their desirability, and control over these scarce materials in turn lead to a dominant-subordinant relationship between those controlling and those seeking to use the materials. The current emphasis upon power relationships was not as dominant in our society until the economic organization assumed its present form which places economic considerations in a primary category. Increasing dependence upon others for gaining the basic necessities of life has heightened interest and awareness in this type of relationship. The very impersonal nature of meeting these needs has also contributed to this interest. In our society where the majority of men are dependent upon wages and salaries for their sustenance, the earning of this share of the money economy and the determination of its size has been and is a source of conflict. The owners of productive facilities, by virtue of ownership, have the power of decision over who shall earn and to some extent who shall share in the rewards of the enterprise. The societal indoctrination of the individual to maximize his share of the income precludes equal distribution of it, should he possess the power to prevent it.

The norms of an economic-oriented society, and particularly the norms of the group possessing economic power, make as synonymous as possible the relationship between economic power and social power. The limited authority that economic power actually gives to the individual or group is transcended beyond mere economic power and bestows upon them the role of the leaders of action and thought. If the holders of economic power were specifically limited to leadership in just the economic area, it is quite possible that the holders of non-economic power would develop more actions and thoughts which would be dysfunctional to the ends of the economic leaders. An extremely economic-oriented society makes non-economic and economic powers identical by fostering economic power as a universal goal within the social group. This aspiration to the universal goal reinforces its desirability until it becomes primary, with non-economic power being measured in terms of economic power. Then the holder of economic power (businessmen, entrepreneur, financier) through societal ascription assumes the role of the "prophet" or leader in the social group.[17]

This societal bred *"universal"* aspiration for economic power may produce a severe reaction depending upon the frequency with which the aspiration can be achieved. Aspiration to a goal without the possibility of successful fulfillment will not endure long in a social group where comparatively easy communication of thought is possible.[18]

A correlate of power is influence. Influence in itself assumes the form of power even if it is not consciously purposeful. The connotation of influence is a continuum. It may range from the unconscious "influence" of the socio-cultural backgrounds, which shape group thoughts and action, to a direct attempt to initiate thought and action by its use. In the latter case influence varies directly with power, and in this instance influence is the vehicle of a power relationship.

So obvious is the role of influence in the consumption phase of our economic organization that we often lose sight of the enormous effects of advertising upon our culture. Our standards of living for the most part are based directly upon the assimilation of advertising. Its direct influences upon the individual's desires and wishes necessitate a constant increase in the material standards of living, and this enables the productive facilities of the economic organization to be more fully utilized and expanded. This culturally bred demand has the "latent function" of producing an additional multitude of desires for the means to acquire an increasing standard of living. It is within such an area as this that relationships and other factors may best be observed in producing "social change."

The increasing awareness of the role of technology in raising our material standards of living has created in Western man a "future-oriented" type of society in contrast to the "tradition-oriented" Asiatic societies. The expectations placed upon our technology have been expanded to include science, and in many cases the two are considered identical. The comparative ease with which technology has solved some of the most burdensome physical problems of man has led to the expectation that science, *per se*, can solve all of the "problems" of mankind. The social scientist may well ponder the connotations and implications of these attitudes.

The more subtle aspects of influence in the life of man are a fertile field of investigation which sociology can rightly claim as its own domain. The role of influence within the relationships of the family, associations, and other socal groupings is perhaps one of the main "keys," to an understanding of social processes, and this could be no less important in understanding economic organization, where the many conflicting views, values, and attitudes demand a more basic understanding of the roles of power and influence.[19]

Population Factors. The influence of population upon economic organization is again becoming an area of intensive and fruitful study. After the eclipse into which it was thrown by the followers of Malthus, who attempted to explain and interpret all social change in terms of this unilateral theory, there is now a recognition that population, its size, composition, and change are in some respects specifically sociological elements that are economically relevant.[20]

There is little doubt that population is an important factor in the determination of economic organization and change. One needs only to witness the concern of the governmental agencies in the United States with the increasing size of the population, which has made it necessary for the economic organization to constantly expand in order to maintain its same relative position with respect to employment. The reciprocal relationship existing between the characteristics of the population and the cultural values of the group presents an extremely complex problem which sociological analysis is now meeting with some success.[21]

Density of population alone is not the exclusive criterion in the determination of the development of economic organization, but within a particular situation it may have great influence. Modern industrial organization demands great numbers of workers in its productive enterprises, and therefore is a factor leading to urbanization. At the same time the size of population controls the labor available and determines the market for the goods that are produced in that area.

A densely populated area need not necessarily be conducive to the formation of a complex industrial economy. China and India are examples of this, and the difficulties that many of the Latin American nations are now having in establishing industrial organization also illustrate this phenomenon. In order to have a complex industrial economy, there must first be a source of "capital" with which to build the productive facilities necessary for industrial development; and at the same time there must be an "optimum" population to aid in this.[22]

The composition of the population cannot be neglected in analyzing economic organization. A high birth rate with a correspondingly high mortality rate results in an unfavorable ratio of producers to dependents which is likely to act as a depressant upon the accumulation of "capital" necessary for industrial expansion. The opposite situation of a low birth rate and a correspondingly low mortality rate may at first give rise to a highly favorable (from a productive standpoint) ratio of producers to dependents, which may later increase the number of dependents due to the aging of the population. The value system of the society determines to a great extent the degree of dependency of the older population. The dilemma of whether a person should cease his productive life and become a dependent at age sixty-five is one that possibly can only occur in a wealthy, highly industrialized economy. This is an important problem which is now starting to receive attention in the area of gerontological studies.

CONCLUSION

Demographic study of a population may be considered as one of the major connections between sociology and the science of economics. An understanding of population forces (still to be achieved) may provide economics with the situational patterns within which it can achieve greater predictiveness.

The businessman, as well as the sociologist, is concerned with demography since the population furnishes his market. Increasing attention is being paid to population analysis by industry in determining sources of labor and the extent of the market. This concern has been made obvious in the United States by the placing of the Bureau of Census under the Department of Commerce.

The present role of sociology in its application to economic organization is that of analyzing the societal factors contained within it and attempting to reduce conflict, which is socially determined, between economic organization and society. In doing this the sociologist is dependent upon the present state of sociological knowledge available to him. Clarity of definition and conceptualization is vital to those who are attempting to apply scientific knowledge. It is within this area that further intensive effort must be made by the sociologist so that his analyses may be more valid and useful.[23]

SELECTED BIBLIOGRAPHY

Reinhard Bendix & Seymour Martin Lipset, Eds., *Class, Status and Power: A Reader in Social Stratification* (Glencoe, Ill.: The Free Press, 1953). Presents readings from most theories of social stratification with emphasis on economic factors.

Ralph H. Boldgett, *Our Expanding Economy* (New York: Rinehart and Company, 1955). Economics text presenting both macro- and micro-economics.

Elihu Katz & Paul F. Lazarsfeld, *Personal Influence* (Glencoe, Ill.: The Free Press, 1955). Theory and a new research design in the study of influence.

Elton Mayo, *The Human Problems of an Industrial Organization* (New York: Macmillan Company, 1933). Early study of the psychology and sociology of industrial organization; *The Social Problems of an Industrial Civilization* (Boston: Graduate School of Business Administration, Harvard University, 1945). Dicusses problems caused by industrial and economic organization.

Robert K. Merton & others, Eds., *Reader in Bureaucracy* (Glencoe, Ill.: The Free Press, 1952). Readings on administrative and industrial bureaucracies.

Robert K. Merton, *Social Theory and Social Structure* (Glencoe, Ill.: The Free Press, 1949). Chapters on functional analysis and bureaucracy.

Wilbert E. Moore, *Economy and Society* (New York: Doubleday, 1955). Short survey of the relationships between economics, the economy, society, and sociology.

Marbury B. Ogle Jr., Louis Schneider & Jay W. Wiley, *Power, Order and the Economy* (New York: Harper, 1954). A "unified" approach to the social sciences.

F. J. Roethlisberger & Wm. J. Dickinson, *Management and the Worker: Organization in an Industrial Plant* (Boston, Harvard Business School, Business Research Studies, No. 9, 1934). Classic study in industrial sociology.

T. Lynn Smith, *Brazil: People and Institutions* (Baton Rouge: Louisiana State University Press, 1954). Discusses the social factors influencing economic organization in Brazil.

Joseph J. Spengler & Otis Dudley Duncan, Eds., *Population Theory and Policy: Selected Readings* (Glencoe, Ill.: The Free Press, 1956). Many readings on the interrelationship between population and economic organization.

Leonard D. White, *The State of the Social Sciences* (University of Chicago Press, 1956). Papers presented at the 25th Anniversary of the Social Science Research Building, The University of Chicago, contains several good ones on economics and the economy.

Shaw E. Grigsby, a native of Winnfield (La.), was educated at Louisiana State University (B.S., 1935; M.A., 1937) and Cornell University (Ph.D., 1942); formerly director of the Institute of Social Science Research, Darmstadt, Germany, (Office of the High Commissioner for Germany) and Professor in the Institut fuer Socialwissenschaftliche Forschung, he has been associated since 1953 with the University of Florida, where he is presently Assistant Professor in the Department of Sociology and Anthropology.

Leonard L. Linden graduated (B.A.) from the University of Florida where he is currently engaged in graduate study; his main interests are in sociological theory and research in class, status, and stratification.

NOTES

1. See Max Weber, *Wirtschaft und Gesellschaft* (Tuebingen: J. C. B. Mohr, 1925). The author presented an extremely cogent, though not entirely conclusive, analysis of the historical development of Western economic organization; see also Talcott Parsons, *The Structure of Social Action* (Glencoe, Ill.: The Free Press, 1949), where Weber's analysis is discussed, analyzed and synthesized.

2. See Ralph H. Blodgett, *Our Expanding Economy* (New York: Rinehart and Company, 1955), 7.

3. See Wilbert E. Moore, "Sociology of Economic Organization," in Georges

Gurvitch and Wilbert E. Moore, editors, *Twentieth Century Sociology* (New York: Philosophical Library, 1945), 458.

4. *Ibid.*, 449.

5. "Wealth" is used here to mean the factors that give status to the owner (s). It may be material or non-material; it may have an economic basis in that it is accumulated property.

6. See R. H. Tawney, *Religion and the Rise of Capitalism* (New York: The New American Library, 1947), 228. The author presents a slightly different analysis of the historical basis of capitalism than Max Weber.

7. See Charles A. Beard, *The Economic Basis of Politics and Related Writings* (New York: Vintage Books, 1957), 141.

8. See Raymond Aron, "Social Structure and the Ruling Class" in Reinhard Bendix and Seymour M. Lipset, editors, *Class, Status and Power: A Reader in Social Stratification* (Glencoe, Ill.: The Free Press, 1953), 577.

9. See Ralph H. Blodgett, *op. cit.*, 14.

10. *Ibid.*, 14.

11. See Robert K. Merton, *Social Theory and Social Structure* (Glencoe, Ill.: The Free Press, 1949), 21-81. Discussed here is the theory of the "functional" approach which is proving of value in sociological analysis.

12. See F. J. Roethlisberger and Wm. J. Dickinson, *Management and the Worker: Organization in an Industrial Plant* (Boston, Harvard Business School, Business Research Studies, No. 9, 1934) ; see also Elton Mayo, *The Human Problems of an Industrial Civilization* (New York: The Macmillan Company, 1933), Elton Mayo, *The Social Problems of an Industrial Civilization* (Boston: Graduate School of Business Administration, Harvard University, 1945).

13. Robert K. Merton, *op. cit.*, 151-160.

14. Studies of individual psychological and social action in industry are plentiful and are useful to management (in many cases) in understanding these problems as they occur. Unfortunately most of these studies were not designed and cannot be utilized for generalization on a higher order. Therefore "applied social science" must treat, for the most part every case as a unique development.

15. See Max Weber, *The Protestant Ethic and the Spirit of Capitalism,* tr. by Talcott Parsons (London: G. Allen and Unwin, 1930), & Talcott Parsons, *op. cit.*

16. Riesman's recent study gives a penetrating insight into the role of the individual in a highly specialized industrial societal grouping. Further studies along these lines will be of great interest since they seem to provide the basis for generalizations and hypotheses upon which a predictive science can be built. See David Riesman, Nathan Glazer and Reuel Denney, *The Lonely Crowd* (New York: Doubleday and Company, 1954).

17. See Max Weber, *Wirtschaft und Gesellschaft, op. cit.*, and Talcott Parsons, *op. cit.*, p. 567.

18. See Robert K. Merton, *op. cit.*, pp. 125-149.

19. See Elihu Katz and Paul F. Lazarsfeld, *Personal Influence* (Glencoe, Ill.: The Free Press, 1955). The authors analyze the role of influence in societal behavior using an empirical approach.

20. See Wilbert E. Moore, *Economy and Society* (New York: Doubleday, 1955).

21. See Joseph J. Spengler and Otis Dudley Duncan, Eds., *Population Theory and Policy: Selected Readings* (Glencoe, Ill.: The Free Press, 1956). This volume investigates ". . . the implications of demographic phenomena for social structure and for socio-economic change and welfare . . ."

22. T. Lynn Smith, *Brazil: People and Institutions* (Baton Rouge: Louisiana State University Press, 1954), analyzes and discusses many of the population and cultural factors in the development of economic organization in Brazil. Most of this is applicable to other countries faced with similar problems.

23. See *International Encyclopedia of Unified Science* (Chicago: The University of Chicago Press, 1952), Carl G. Hempel, "Fundamentals of Concept Formation in Empirical Science," Volume II, Number 7.

SOCIAL STRATIFICATION

Gerhard E. Lenski
University of Michigan

Few fields of sociological inquiry have attracted more attention since the end of World War II than the study of social stratification. A series of recent bibliographies attest to the tremendous volume of activity in many corners of the world.[1] As a perusal of these bibliographies, or the literature cited in them, quickly indicates, the work in the field has been extremely scattered in character and reflects a wide range of interests and concerns.

Despite the heterogeneous character of recent work in the field, it seems possible to detect certain significant trends which differentiate the work of the post-World War II era from the preceding period. These trends are especially evident when one limits the comparison to work done by American scholars.

INCREASED CONCERN WITH STRATIFICATION IN THE TOTAL SOCIETY

One of the most obvious and also one of the more important trends of the last decade has been the shift from the local community to the total society as the basic object of analysis in stratification research. During the period from the end of World War I to the end of World War II a majority of the more important and more influential studies of stratification were concerned with one or more aspects of the system of stratification in some local community. This was true of the early work of the Lynds; it was equally true of the later work of Warner and his various students, and also of the work of Jones, the Useems, Dollard, Powdermaker, West, Davidson and Anderson, and others.[2]

This characteristic of stratification research was undoubtedly a reflection of the methodological difficulties of the time. Significant data on stratification in the total society were difficult to obtain, or

521

in many cases, simply were not available. As a result, those interested in problems of stratification were obliged to concentrate upon social units which were more amenable to study by available methods, and the relatively small community was the obvious unit. Furthermore, the fact that many of those concerned with the phenomenon of stratification in this period were persons with either training in, or an orientation to, anthropology further stimulated this tendency. Anthropology, by virtue of its strong emphasis on the methodology of participant observation, seems to have predisposed many of these scholars to concentrate upon local communities rather than the total society as their unit of analysis.

There were, of course, always some whose concern was with stratification in the total society. Names such as Sorokin, Taussig and Joslyn, Parsons, K. Davis, Davis and Moore, and Sibley remind one that this concern was not absent in this earlier period.[3] However, these writers seem to have been much less influential at the time, perhaps because their work was so seldom productive of significant research.

In the decade since the end of World War II there seems to have been a progressive decline in the degree of attention devoted to local systems of stratification, and a corresponding increase in the degree of attention devoted to stratification in the larger society. Hollingshead's study of Elmtown, and Kaufman's study of an upstate New York community are among the few postwar studies of local systems of stratification that have attracted attention, and it is significant to note that both of these studies are based on data gathered prior to World War II.[4]

As one reviews the postwar literature in the field of stratification, one cannot help but be impressed by the degree to which the concern of scholars has shifted to stratification phenomena in the total society. Centers' work on class consciousness is clearly of this character; so, too, is the writing of Mills, Hatt, North and Hatt, Lipset and Bendix, Rogoff, and others who have influenced postwar thought.[5] In some cases, the data on which their analyses have been based have been gathered in a single, local community, but they have been data which have more than local significance, and this more general significance has been stated explicitly. It is perhaps noteworthy, that certain prominent students of stratification whose earlier work was concerned with local systems of stratification, have, in their more recent research, concerned themselves with problems which take them well beyond the bounds of any local system of stratification, as in Warner's recent work on the business elite.[6]

The causes of this trend are not too hard to find. In large measure the trend reflects the growing awareness of the limitations of purely local studies of stratification. Warner's recent study, with Abegglen, of the social origins of the business elite seems to be a tacit admission that his earlier assertion that "Jonesville is America" is not defensible. This recognition seems to have been stimulated to a considerable degree by the increasing assimilation of continental European viewpoints, especially those of Marx, Weber, Pareto, Schumpeter, and others, into the mainstream of American stratification theory. This trend has also been facilitated greatly by methodological developments since the mid-nineteen-thirties, which have made it possible to obtain data about American society as a whole far more easily than in earlier times.[7]

RENEWED CONCERN WITH VERTICAL MOBILITY

A second important development of the postwar period has been a renewed concern with the phenomenon of vertical mobility. In the decade immediately following World War I there were several important studies of vertical mobility, most notably those of Sorokin, and Taussig and Joslyn.[8] During the nineteen-thirties and the early nineteen-forties, however, interest in vertical mobility declined. Attention was directed much more to the problems of defining class structures. This shift in interest was undoubtedly related to the depression and its influence on sociological thought. Many sociologists in this period seem to have adopted the pessimistic view that opportunities for mobility in this country were declining and that an increasingly rigid class system was emerging. Under the circumstances, the study of vertical mobility seemed to be passé. One of the few important studies of vertical mobility to appear during this period was Davidson and Anderson's study of occupational mobility in San Jose, California.[9]

Since the end of World War II, American sociologists have once again become interested in the subject of vertical mobility, and this revival of interest has largely coincided with a rejection of the doctrine of the nineteen-thirties that the rate of mobility in American society is declining. Among those who have published papers arguing this view one may note Sjoberg, Petersen, and Lipset and Bendix.[10] A more skeptical position on this matter has been adopted by Chinoy and Hertzler who, in recent papers, have maintained that the evidence is inconclusive (Chinoy) or even points to a declining rate of mobility (Hertzler).

Despite the increasing interest in the subject of trends in the rate of mobility, as yet only a limited amount of systematic quantitative work has been done. Among the more significant studies in this area are the work of Rogoff, Warner and Abegglen, Keller, and Adams.[11] In most of these studies the evidence indicates that the rate of mobility in American society is at least as high today as it has been at any time in the last fifty to one hundred years, if not higher. Since all of these studies involve but a limited segment of the American population, their findings can hardly be regarded as conclusive, but neither can they be ignored.

It may be worth noting here that most of the discussions of this important subject suffer from the failure of the writers to differentiate the various types of mobility. Casual observation suggests to this writer that it is very possible that counter-trends in the rate of vertical mobility may have developed in the last half century or more. The evidence presented by Rogoff and the others cited above, together with a vast body of scattered data of a less systematic nature, suggest that the rate of *inter*-generational occupational mobility may, in fact, have increased in American society, thanks in large measure to the increasing socialization of education. On the other hand, there is a considerable body of evidence which is equally impressive which suggests that the rate of *intra*-generational occupational mobility has declined. There seems good reason for asserting that an ever-increasing percentage of Americans are employed in large-scale organizations which possess something very much like a caste system which renders promotion from the bottom of the system to the top virtually impossible. It may well be that the explanation for the contradictory views which American sociologists have held on the question of the trend in the rate of vertical mobility in their own society may arise in large measure from the fact that some have conceived of vertical mobility primarily in *intra*-generational terms while others have thought primarily in *inter*-generational terms.

Another significant postwar development in the study of vertical mobility is the beginning of comparative studies in which total societies are the units of analysis. The paper by Lipset and Rogoff on comparative rates of mobility in the United States, France, and Germany is one example. Rogoff's paper on class consciousness and mobility in France and the United States is another.[12] As in the case of most new ventures, these papers raise almost more questions than they answer, but in any case they represent an important new development. This venture is one which has been dependent, of course, upon the postwar growth and expansion of sociological research abroad.

Finally, it may be well to note that this increased concern with vertical mobility has led to some interesting work on the social psychological correlates of vertical mobility. These will be discussed later in this chapter where the work on the social psychological correlates, not only of mobility, but also of status positions, will be reviewed more fully.

GROWING AWARENESS OF SYSTEM CHANGE

During the last decade American students of stratification have become increasingly concerned not only with problems pertaining to the circulation of individuals within established systems of stratification, but also they have come to be concerned with fundamental changes in the systems themselves. This concern is not entirely a new one among American sociologists, but it is surely one which has achieved a far greater degree of prominence in recent years than in the past.

There was a time not too long ago when most American students of stratification seemed to regard the prevailing system of stratification in their own and other industrialized societies as a relatively stable and fixed system which would not change greatly unless, perhaps, it were destroyed by violent revolutionary forces. More recently, however, it has become increasingly apparent that fundamental changes of major importance can and do occur in the systems of stratification in industrialized societies without the assistance of revolutionary violence.

In American society there have been four types of changes of this sort which have attracted increasing attention.[13] First, there have been changes in the relative positions of Negroes and whites. Second, there have been somewhat comparable changes in the relative positions of blue collar workers and white collar workers. Third, there have been important shifts in the distribution of workers among the several occupational categories. And finally, there have been important changes in the distribution of incomes in American society.

Individually, some of these shifts have been recognized for a considerable period of time. Thus, for example, some time before World War II, Warner developed his now familiar diagram to portray graphically the changing nature of the relative social status of the racial groups in the United States. Others were aware of the changing distribution of workers among the several occupational categories. Until recently, however, each of these changes seems to have been viewed as the exception to the rule in what was conceived of as a basically stable and unchanging system of stratification. Perhaps this was due to the degree to which the thinking of American sociologists was guided by a static structural-functional model of society, as Kaufman, Duncan, Gross, and Sewell suggested in a recent paper.[14]

Since the end of World War II a growing body of empirical data has forced a recognition of the changing nature of the American system of stratification on students in the field. The Bureau of the Census has been the most important single source of such data. However, the work of the Census has been supplemented in a significant way by the work of Kuznets, Goldsmith, and H. Miller on changing income structure, by the work of Burns on changes in the relative positions of blue collar and white collar workers, and by a vast number of students of race relations on changes in the relative positions of Negroes and whites in the American system of stratification.[15]

As evidence of basic structural changes accumulates, it has become increasingly evident that one can no longer conceive of the systems of stratification in industrialized societies as fixed and stable entities persisting without change from one generation to the next. Instead, those who concern themselves with problems covering a span of time find it increasingly necessary to take explicit recognition of the dynamic and constantly changing character of the system. Thus far, Mills has been the most prominent among those who have attempted to analyze such change, but his analysis has received, at best, only a mixed reception.[16] Among other discussions of this general subject, Mayer's recent paper on recent changes in the class structure of the United States is noteworthy, though far less ambitious in scope than the work of Mills.[17]

CHANGING VIEWS OF THE CLASS CONCEPT

In the whole literature on social stratification there is no single concept which has been employed more often than the concept class.

Although the uses of this term have been extremely varied, there is a common denominator which runs through most of them. This is the notion, either implicit or explicit, that the term refers to some kind of visible, self-evident, self-conscious set of collectivities into which the populations of communities and societies are divided.

This was surely the view of class which the community studies of the nineteen-thirties and early nineteen-forties promoted. It was also the view of the great majority of those who derived their inspiration from Marxist theory during this period. Thus, although they could not always agree as to the exact nature of classes, there was little doubt that such entities existed as fundamental units within communities and societies. Sometimes the existence of such units was reported as a finding of research, as in the Yankee City study or in Jones' study of Akron; more often their existence was simply assumed in advance by the investigators, as in the Lynds' work in Middletown.

As is so often the case in the development of a scientific discipline, that which is taken for granted by one generation of students often becomes the problem for research for the next generation. This has surely been the case with respect to the class concept. Since the end of World War II, an ever growing number of sociologists have re-examined the concept class and have concluded that the earlier uses were either naive or unrealistic. In a series of papers, directed often at the Warner school, writers such as Pfautz and Duncan, Sorokin, and others have raised a series of critical questions about the traditional use of the term class, questioning among other things whether the classes which have been described in American community studies actually have had the obvious, objective character ascribed to them.[18] Empirical studies of this matter by Kaufman, Duncan and Artis, and this writer indicated that although the residents of the three communities they studied were clearly aware of status distinctions, they did *not* perceive their communities to be structured in terms of any clearly defined or commonly recognized system of classes.[19] As a consequence, the current trend among American sociologists seems to be increasingly one which views classes as social categories which enjoy, at best, only a limited recognition by the rank and file of Americans.

This trend has been further reinforced by recent studies of class consciousness. This term, having its roots in Marxian thought, has been used primarily with reference to awareness by the individual of his membership in an economically defined collectivity. In most of the early studies of class consciousness in this country, it was taken for granted by those conducting the research that every normal, adult American was conscious of class, and that the important problem was that of discovering how many persons thought of themselves as members of this or that class, especially the middle and working class.[20] Thus, in these early studies, respondents were usually confronted with a predetermined set of alternatives which made no allowance for the possibility that the individual might have no consciousness of class as the investigators assumed.

Since the end of World War II several students have relegated the assumption of universal class consciousness to the level of an hypothesis to be tested. The studies of Sargent, Gross, and Manis and Meltzer are especially noteworthy in this connection.[21] Each of these writers found that when they approached the problem in this way, substantial numbers of Americans showed little or no consciousness of class. Thus, these findings have further accelerated the trend away from the older view of class.[22]

The newer view of class which seems to be emerging does not, of course, deny the existence of social stratification in either communities or societies. It only denies that systems of stratification are necessarily structured in terms of series of well-defined, discrete, self-evident, and self-conscious collectivities as so many have assumed until so recently. In this conncetion contemporary analysis seems to be moving in the direction of the view stated by Weber a generation ago when he argued that classes are not communities, but are merely possible bases for communal action. Also, this "newer" view of class hearkens back to Marx's distinction between classes as categories of people merely sharing a common position in society and classes as organized, self-conscious groups.

GROWING RECOGNITION OF MULTI-DIMENSIONAL CHARACTER OF SOCIAL STRATIFICATION

Until relatively recent times most social philosophers and social scientists have discussed the vertical structures of human groups in terms of some single hierarchy in which each member occupies a single position. Different exponents of this traditional scheme have not always agreed as to the nature or the characteristics of this hierarchical structure, but nevertheless, all shared the common conception of a unidimensional structure.

Early in the present century this view of stratification came to be questioned in Germany by Weber, and in this country by Cooley. For the most part, however, their views aroused little enthusiasm, at least among American sociologists. Almost the only American sociologist who incorporated this view into his research prior to the end of World War II was Homans, in his study of English villagers of the thirteenth century, which as might be expected from the subject, had little impact at the time on most American students of stratification.[23]

Since the end of World War II discussions of stratification couched in multi-dimensional terms have become increasingly common in American sociology. To a considerable degree this development reflects the postwar translation into English of Weber's work on classes and status groups. Much that has been written in this vein represents little more than an amplification and application of the Weberian scheme of analysis, as in the case of much of Mayer's work.[24] In other cases, however, perhaps most notably Sorokin, a more radical view is taken in which the possibility of far more than two dimensions is entertained.[25]

Thus far most of the research based on this multi-dimensional view has concerned itself simply with charting the interrelationships among various stratification variables. Perhaps the best known of these studies is Centers' study which examines the interrelationships between class self-identification on the one hand and various objective stratification variables on the other.[26] Warner, Meeker, and Eells examined interrelationships between community reputation on the one hand and various objective stratification variables on the other.[27] Other studies reporting on interrelationships among stratification variables of one sort or another are those of Hochbaum and others, Kahl and Davis, Gross, Duncan and Artis, and Turner.[28] Unfortunately, few of these studies attempted to go beyond establishing correlations, in order to discover in a systematic way the causes of the relationships observed.

Also, very little has been done, as yet, to determine the significance of variations in the degree of consistency among the several dimensions of a system of stratification. Thus far, limited studies of air force bomber crews by Adams and of the community of Detroit by Landecker and this writer suggest that this is a fruitful area of inquiry and that variations of this nature may be associated with significant differences in the behavior both of individuals and of the social organizations to which they belong.[29]

SHIFT IN EMPHASIS FROM PRESTIGE TO POWER

Somewhat related to the previous development is another change in the way in which stratification phenomena themselves are conceptualized. During the period in which stratification research was dominated by studies of relatively small communities, there was a pronounced tendency among American sociologists to think of the field of stratification analysis as being chiefly concerned with the study of the prestige structures of local communities. This view of the field was especially promoted by the work of the Warner school.

There always were a substantial number of critics who argued that local community prestige structures were not the central concern of stratification analysis, but during the early forties especially, their voices were drowned out by the veritable flood of community studies produced by the Warner school. Since the end of World War II, however, Warner's influence has waned, and with the waning of his influence the concern with local prestige structures in particular, and with prestige in general, has tended to decline somewhat. More and more American sociologists phrase their problems in terms of inequalities in power, especially in economic power. Even Warner's most recent work is phrased in these terms.[30]

That such a shift should have occurred seems to have been almost inevitable, if progress were to be made in the field. Systems of inequality in economic power are undoubtedly in some sense of the term a more basic aspect of society than systems of inequality in prestige. Moreover, so long as the central variable in the field is one which can be measured operationally only by asking people for their opinions of others, certain types of important research such as studies of mobility, of system change, and of very large social units such as the modern metropolitan community or the urban society are almost impossible.

However, while there is much that is sound in this newer trend, it may be that an undue emphasis is coming to be placed on economic power to the neglect of other forms of power. In American society it seems abundantly clear that one's position in the occupational hierarchy is not the only significant determinant of his access to the rewards which American society generates and distributes. In particular, it would seem that the power of individuals to obtain these rewards is influenced by their ethnic-racial (or perhaps religious-racial) status, their educational status, their age status, and their sex status, and that one's position in the occupational hierarchy is, at best, only imperfectly related to his position in the other hierarchies. Yet far too often studies of social stratification ignore these other dimensions of the phenomenon. If the trend to phrase questions pertaining to stratification in terms of power becomes a trend to phrase questions solely in terms of *economic* power, the gains which will accrue will very largely be offset by corresponding losses both in theoretical insight and in predictive value.

RENEWED CONCERN WITH ELITE STUDIES

Although the study of the social origins of elite groups is one of the older areas of empirical study, in the postwar years, this type of study, in more sophisticated form, has enjoyed a new vogue. The sources of this newer interest in elite groups are diffuse, though several prewar sources seem deserving of note. The most important of these would seem to be the work of Harold Lasswell.[31] His influence, however, has been supplemented by the influence of other prewar scholars such as Mosca, Pareto, Mannheim, Taussig and Joslyn, and also F. Lundberg.[32]

Prior to World War II the empirical work in this field was mainly confined to studies of the social origins of business and professional men. Little attention was devoted to the social origins of other elite groups, such as those found in political, military, religious, or labor organizations. Also, little concern was felt with problems relating to the functional significance of these elites for the larger society of which they were a part, except in so far as their recruitment was relatively broad or restricted.

Since the war, however, a considerable volume of research has appeared dealing with an ever widening range of problems. Representative of the newer range of interest is Mill's work on the labor elite, Bendix on the civil service elite, Janowitz, and de Sola Pool on military elites, and Warner and Abegglen, and Keller on the business elite.[33] In a number of these newer studies of elite groups one sees the beginnings of a rewarding interaction between theory and research which was so generally lacking in the earlier work in this area. In particular, one sees the emergence of a more explicit formulation of the study of élites in functional terms.

OTHER TRENDS

In view of the limitations of space, it is possible to note here only briefly several additional trends which have been indicated in passing in previous discussions, but which deserve explicit attention. In the first place, as indicated at several points, in the last ten years, American discussions of stratification seem to have been more greatly influenced by older European theorists than in the periods of the thirties and early forties. In particular, Marx and Weber seem to have become more influential. To a lesser extent one might note the influence of Mosca, Pareto, and Schumpeter.

Second, one should also note the expanding horizons of stratification research. More and more American students of stratification are venturing abroad and studying stratification in other societies. Especially noteworthy in this respect is the work of Ryan, Tumin, Gist, and of course Inkeles and his associates at the Russian Research Center.[34] Not only has there developed an increased concern with stratification in other societies, but also a similar development has occurred with respect to stratification at earlier periods in American society or in western societies. Illustrative of this trend is the work on system change cited earlier.

Third it seems worth noting that in the postwar years, the study of stratification has become somewhat less of an isolated specialized field of study than it once was, and more and more bridges have been built between the study of stratification phenomena and the study of other sociological and social psychological phenomena. Such a development was, it must be recognized, a prerequisite to continued growth and progress in the field.

Finally, there has been a continuing study of the social and social psychological correlates of stratification variables. Among the more important of these is the work of Hollingshead and his associates and the work of Swanson and Miller in the study of mental illness, the work of Bettelheim and Janowitz in the study of prejudice, the work of Lazarsfeld and his associates in the study of political behavior, and the work of A. Davis and his associates, Sears and his associates, and Swanson and Miller, in the study of child-rearing.[35] It should be noted, however, that these studies have generally contributed far more to the sociological understanding of the related fields such as mental illness and prejudice than to the understanding of stratification itself. This was, of course, in keeping with the intentions of the investigators themselves.

EVALUATION

During the last ten years the fund of accumulated knowledge in the field of social stratification has been greatly increased by the work of innumerable sociologists and other social scientists in related fields as indicated in the foregoing. Unfortunately, however, it cannot be said that this fund of knowledge is much better integrated today than it was immediately after the end of World War II. In their zeal for opening new frontiers, students in the field have largely ignored the pressing problem of establishing order within the older, more familiar, and better charted regions. This is the task which everyone leaves to someone else.

It would seem to be a hopeful sign, however, that in the last decade there has been a growing awareness of this problem. This is reflected in the renewed interest in European theorists such as Marx and Weber, and in the growing number of thoughtful critiques of the present state of knowledge in the field. Perhaps the most discouraging feature of the few recent attempts, thus far, to formulate an integrative theory is their rather slavish adherence to the older formulas and their apparent reluctance to stray too far from the fold of theoretical orthodoxy. Parsons' recently revised essay on stratification is a notable exception to this general tendency, but this writer is not yet convinced of the scientific promise of the general theoretical scheme on which this essay is based.[36]

It would seem, however, that Parsons is on sound ground when he argues that stratification theory must be related to a general social system, or social organizational, theory. Stratification is essentially a social organizational process, and therefore it seems probable that the development of stratification theory is, in some measure, contingent upon the prior development of social organizational theory. If this is true, it seems unlikely that a fully satisfactory theory of stratification can be hoped for in the next generation, since there is currently so little work of promise in the more general field. This does not mean, however, that substantial advance cannot be made in clearing up the current conceptual chaos in the field. On the contrary, such a development seems likely if for no other reason than that effective communication among students in the field increasingly demands it.[37]

SELECTED BIBLIOGRAPHY

B. Barber, *Social Stratification* (New York: Harcourt, Brace, 1956). Stimulating attempt to synthesize recent work in stratification and relate it to general sociological theory.

R. Bendix and S. Lipset (eds.), *Class, Status, and Power* (Glencoe: Free Press, 1953). A collection of reprinted materials in the field together with several original contributions.

R. Centers, *The Psychology of Social Classes* (Princeton: Princeton Press, 1949). Important early postwar study of class consciousness.

A. Hollingshead, *Elmtown's Youth* (New York: Wiley, 1949). Best of the community studies of stratification; concerned with impact of class system on youth of the community.

S. Lipset and R. Bendix, "Social Status and Social Structure," *British Journal of Sociology*, II (June and October, 1951), 150-168 and 230-257. Stimulating critique of recent work in stratification.

J. Manis and B. Meltzer, "Attitudes of Textile Workers to Class Structure," *American Journal of Sociology*, LX (July, 1954), 30-35. One of the most significant studies of class consciousness thus far; indicates limited consciousness of class even among workers who might be expected to be most highly class conscious.

K. Mayer, "Recent Changes in the Class Structure of the United States," *Transactions of the Third World Congress of Sociology*, 66-80. Summary of major changes in American class system in recent decades.

H. Miller, *Income of the American People* (New York: Wiley, 19). Intensive analysis of census data on income distribution in the United States.

C. W. Mills, *New Men of Power* (New York: Harcourt, Brace, 1948). One of the more stimulating studies of elites; in this case the elites involved are labor leaders; *White Collar* (New York: Oxford Press, 1951). One of the few attempts to deal with a major change in the societal system of stratification; stimulating though sometimes questionable scholarship.

C. North and P. Hatt, "Jobs and Occupations," *Opinion News* (September 1, 1947) 3-13. A national survey of the prestige of several score occupations.

N. Rogoff, *Recent Trends in Occupational Mobilty* (Glencoe: Free Press, 1953). Excellent analysis of trends in   Inter-generational ocpational mobility in one large American city.

B. Ryan, *Caste in Modern Ceylon* (New Brunswick: Rutgers Press 1953). Probably the best study of stratification in another society by an American scholar.

G. Sjoberg, "Are Social Classes in America Becoming More Rigid?" *American Sociological Review,* XVI (December, 1951), 775-783. One of the first and most effective challenges to the older view that the American system of stratification was becoming more rigid.

W. L. Warner and J. Abegglen, *Occupational Mobility in American Business and Industry* (Minneapolis: University of Minnesota Press). Follow-up of earlier study by Taussig and Joslyn of recruitment of American business elite.

Gerhard E. Lenski, Assistant Professor of Sociology, University of Michigan, was born in Washington, D.C. (1924); A.B., Yale (1947); Ph. D. (Yale, 1950); Instructor in Sociology, University of Michigan (1950-54), Assistant Professor, (1954-   ). Author of papers on stratification and sociology of religion and co-author with Ronald Freedman, Amos H. Hawley, Werner S. Landecker, and Horace M. Miner of *Principles of Sociology* (rvd. ed., 1956).

NOTES

1. Among the more important bibliographies of recent work in this area one should note Harold F. Pfautz, "The Current Literature on Social Stratification: A Critique and Bibliography," *The American Journal of Sociology,* LVIII (January, 1953), 391-418; D. G. MacRae, "Social Stratification: A Trend Report and Bibliography," *Current Sociology,* II, no. 1 (1953-1954), 74 pp.; Louis Wirth, "Social Stratification and Social Mobility in the United States," *ibid.,* II, no. 4 (1953-1954), 279-305; Gunnar Boalt and Carl-Gunnar Janson, "A Selected Bibliography of the Literature on Social Stratification and Social Mobility in Sweden," *ibid.,* 306-328; Tsutomu Himeoka, Kizaemon Ariga, and Kunio Odaka, "A Select Bibliography on Social Stratification and Social Mobility in Japan Since 1800," *ibid.,* 329-362; H. D. Lasswell, D. Lerner, and C. E. Rothwell, *The Comparative Study of Elites: An Introduction and Bibliography,* Hoover Institute Studies, Series B: Elites, No. 1 (Palo Alto: Stanford University Press, 1952); B. Barber, *Social Stratification* (New York: Harcourt, Brace, 1957), 503-527.

2. R. S. Lynd and H. M. Lynd, *Middletown* (New York: Harcourt, Brace, 1929); Lynd and Lynd, *Middletown in Transition* (New York: Harcourt, Brace, 1937); W. L. Warner *et al, Yankee City Series* (New Haven: Yale University Press), 6 vol.; A. Davis, B. B. Gardner and M. R. Gardner, *Deep South* (Chicago: University of Chicago Press, 1941); St. C. Drake and H. Cayton, *Black Metropolis* (New York: Harcourt, Brace, 1945); A. W. Jones, *Life, Liberty, and Property* (Philadelphia: Lippincott, 1941); J. Useem *et al,* "Stratification in a Prarie Town," *American Sociological Review,* VII (June, 1942), 331-342; J. Dollard, *Caste and Class in a Southern Town* (New Haven: Yale Institute of Human Relations, 1937); J. West, *Plainville, U.S.A.* (New York: Columbia University Press, 1945); P. E. Davidson and H. D. Anderson, *Occupational Mobility in an American Community* (Palo Alto: Stanford University Press, 1937).

3. P. A. Sorokin, *Social Mobility* (New York: Harpers, 1927); F. W. Taussig and C. S. Joslyn, *American Business Leaders* (New York: Macmillan, 1949); T. Parsons,

"An Analytical Approach to the Theory of Stratification," *American Journal of Sociology*, VL (May, 1940), 841-862; K. Davis, "A Conceptual Analysis of Stratification," *American Sociological Review*, VII (June, 1942), 309-321; K. Davis and W. Moore, "Some Principles of Stratification," *ibid.*, X (April, 1945), 242-249; E. Sibley, "Some Demographic Clues to Stratification," *ibid.*, VII (June, 1942), 322-330.

4. A. B. Hollingshead, *Elmtown's Youth* (New York: Wiley, 1949); H. Kaufman, *Prestige Classes in a New York Rural Community* (Ithaca: Cornell University Experiment Station Memoir No. 260, 1949).

5. R. Centers, *The Psychology of Social Classes* (Princeton: Princeton University Press, 1949); C. W. Mills, *The New Men of Power* (New York: Harcourt, Brace, 1948), and *White Collar* (New York: Oxford University Press, 1951); P. K. Hatt, "Stratification in the Mass Society," *American Sociological Review*, XV (April, 1950), 216-222; C. C. North and P. K. Hatt, "Jobs and Occupations: A Popular Evaluation," *Opinion News*, IX (September, 1947), 3-13; S. M. Lipset and R. Bendix, "Social Status and Social Structure," *British Journal of Sociology*, II (June and October, 1951), 150-168 and 230-257; N. Rogoff, *Recent Trends in Occupational Mobility* (Glencoe: Free Press, 1953).

6. W. L. Warner and J. C. Abegglen, *Occupational Mobility* (Minneapolis: University of Minnesota Press, 1956).

7. These developments have been of various sorts. The most important development in this period has probably been the development of techniques for sampling the American population. Another development of importance has been the improved collection of data by the Census Bureau, which since 1940 has begun to provide an ever-expanding body of data relevant to stratification analysis. Finally, one should also note the greater availability of research money which has made more ambitious projects feasible for the first time.

8. Sorokin, *op. cit.*; Taussig and Joslyn, *op. cit.*

9. Davidson and Anderson, *op. cit.*

10. G. Sjoberg, "Are Social Classes in America Becoming More Rigid?" *American Sociological Review*, XVI (December, 1951), 775-783; W. Petersen, "Is America Still the Land of Opportunity?" *Commentary*, XVI (November, 1953), 477-486; S. M. Lipset and R. Bendix, "Ideological Equilitarianism and Social Mobility in the United States," *Transactions of the Second World Congress of Sociology*, II, 34-54.

11. Rogoff, *op. cit.*; Warner and Abegglen, *op. cit.*; S. Keller, *The Social Origins and Career Lines of Three Generations of American Business Leaders* (unpublished doctoral dissertation, Columbia University, 1953); S. Adams, "Trends in the Occupational Origins of Physicians," *American Sociological Review*, XVIII (August, 1953, 404-409), Adams, XIX (October, 1954), 514-548; "Trends in the Occupational Origins of Business Leaders."

12. S. M. Lipset and N. Rogoff, "Class and Opportunity in Europe and the United States," *Commentary*, XIX (1955), 562-568; N. Rogoff, "Social Stratification in France and the United States," *American Journal of Sociology*, LVIII (January, 1953), 347-357.

13. In addition, that is, to possible changes in the rate of mobility which was discussed in the previous section, and concerning which evidence is still inconclusive.

14. H. F. Kaufman, O. D. Duncan, N. Gross, and W. Sewell, "Problems of Theory and Method in the Study of Social Stratification in Rural Society," *Rural Sociology*, XVIII (March, 1953), 12-24.

15. S. Kuznets, *Shares of Upper Income Groups in Income and Savings* (New

York: National Bureau of Economic Research) ; S. Goldsmith *et al*, "Size Distribution of Incomes Since the Mid-Thirties," *Review of Economics and Statistics,* 36 (February, 1954) , 1-32; H. Miller, *Income of the American People* (New York: Wiley, 1955) ; A. Jaffe and R. Carleton, *Occupational Mobility in the United States*: 1930-1960 (New York: King's Crown Press, 1954) ; R. Burns, "The Comparative Economic Position of Manual and White Collar Employees," *Journal of Business,* 27 (1954) , 257-267.

16. See, for example, Mills, *White Collar, op. cit.*

17. K. Mayer, "Recent Changes in the Class Structure of the United States," *Transactions of the Third World Congress of Sociology,* 66-80.

18. H. Pfautz and O. D. Duncan, "A Critical Evaluation of Warner's Work in Social Stratification," *American Sociological Review,* XV (April, 1950) , 205-215; P. Sorokin, *Society, Culture, and Personality* (New York: Harpers, 1947) .

19. H. F. Kaufman, *Defining Prestige in a Rural Community,* Sociometry Monographs, No. 10 (New York: Beacon House) ; O. D. Duncan and J. Artis, *Social Stratification in a Pennsylvania Rural Community,* Pennsylvania State College Agricultural Experiment Station Bulletin 543 (1951) ; G. Lenski, "American Social Classes: Statistical Strata or Social Groups?" *American Journal of Sociology,* LVIII (September, 1952) , 139-144.

20. The early study by *Fortune Magazine* in 1940 was an important exception.

21. S. Sargent, "Class and Class Consciousness in a California Town," *Social Problems,* I (June, 1953) , 22-27; N. Gross, "Social Class Identifications in an Urban Community," *American Sociological Review,* XVIII (August, 1953) , 398-404; J. Manis and B. Meltzer, "Attitudes of Textile Workers to Class Structure," *American Journal of Sociology,* LX (July, 1954) , 30-35.

22. For an interesting discussion of factors reducing consciousness of class see M. Rosenberg, "Perceptual Obstacles to Class Consciousness," *Social Forces,* XXXII (October, 1953) , 22-27.

23. G. C. Homans, *English Villagers of the Thirteenth Century* (Cambridge: Harvard Press, 1941) .

24. K. Mayer, *Class and Society* (Garden City: Doubleday) and "The Theory of Social Classes," *Harvard Educational Review,* XXIII (Summer, 1953) , 149-167.

25. *Society, Culture, and Personality, op. cit.*

26. R. Centers, *The Psychology of Social Classes, op. cit.*

27. W. L. Warner, M. Meeker, and K. Eells, *Social Class in America* (Chicago: Science Research Associates, 1949) .

28. G. Hochbaum *et al,* "Socioeconomic Variables in a Large City," *American Journal of Sociology,* LXI (July, 1955) , 31-38; J. Kahl and J. Davis, "A Comparison of Indexes of Socio-Economic Status," *American Sociological Review,* XX (June, 1955) , 317-325; N. Gross, *op. cit.;* O. D. Duncan and J. Artis, *op. cit.;* R. Turner, "Occupational Patterns of Inequality," *American Journal of Sociology,* LIX (March, 1954) , 437-447.

29. S. Adams, "Status Congruency as a Variable in Small Group Performance," *Social Forces,* XXXII (October, 1953) 16-22; G. Lenski, "Status Crystallization: A Non-Vertical Dimension of Social Status," *American Sociological Review,* XIX (August, 1954) , 405-413; Lenski, "Social Participation and Status Crystallization," *op. cit.,* XXI (August, 1956) , 458-464.

30. Warner and Abegglen, *op. cit.*

31. H. Lasswell, *Politics: Who Gets What, When, How* (New York: McGraw-Hill, 1936) .

32. G. Mosca, *The Ruling Class* (New York: McGraw-Hill, 1939); V. Pareto, *The Mind and Society* (New York: Harcourt, Brace, 1935); K. Mannheim, *Man and Society in an Age of Reconstruction* (New York: Harcourt, Brace, 1950); Taussig and Joslyn, *op. cit.;* F. Lundberg, *America's 60 Families* (New York: The Citadel Press, 1937).

33. C. W. Mills, *New Men of Power, op. cit.;* R. Bendix, *Higher Civil Servants in American Society,* University of Colorado Studies, Series in Sociology, I, 1949; M. Janowitz, *Working Paper on the Professional Soldier and Political Power,* mimeographed paper, Bureau of Government Institute of Public Administration, University of Michigan, July, 1953; I. de Sola Pool, *Satellite Generals,* Hoover Institute Studies, V, Series B (Palo Alto: Stanford University Press); Warner and Abegglen, *op. cit.;* Keller, *op. cit.*

34. B. Ryan, *Caste in Modern Ceylon* (New Brunswick: Rutgers Press, 1953); M. Tumin, *Caste in a Peasant Society* (Princeton: Princeton Press, 1952); N. Gist, "Caste Differentials in South India," *American Sociological Review,* XIX (April, 1954), 126-137; A. Inkeles, "Social Stratification and Mobility in the Soviet Union," *op. cit.,* XV (August, 1950), 465-480; R. Feldmesser, "The Persistence of Status Advantages in Soviet Russia," *American Journal of Sociology,* LIX (July, 1953), 19-27.

35. A. B. Hollingshead and F. Redlich, "Social Stratification and Psychiatric Disorders," *American Sociological Review,* XVIII (April, 1953), 163-169; Hollingshead and Redlich, "Social Stratification and Schizophrenia," *op. cit.,* XIX (June, 1954), 302-206; Hollingshead *et al,* "Social Mobility and Mental Illness," *op. cit.,* XIX (October, 1954), 577-584; G. E. Swanson and D. Miller, *Conflict and Defense in the Child* (New York: Holt, forthcoming); B. Bettelheim and M. Janowitz, *The Dynamics of Prejudice* (New York: Harpers, 1950); B. Berelson, P. Lazarsfeld, and W. McPhee, *Voting* (Chicago: University of Chicago Press, 1954); P. Lazarsfeld, B. Berelson, and H. Gaudet, *The People's Choice* (New York: Columbia Press, 1948); A. Davis and R. Havighurst, "Social Class and Color Differences in Child Rearing," *American Sociological Review,* XI (December, 1946), 698-710; M. Ericson, "Child-Rearing and Social Status," *American Journal of Sociology,* LII (1946-1947), 190-192; R. Sears *et al, Patterns of Child-Rearing* (in press); G. E. Swanson and D. Miller, *The Changing American Parent* (New York: Wiley, 1957).

36. T. Parsons, "A Revised Analytical Approach to the Theory of Social Stratification," in R. Bendix and S. Lipset, (eds.), *Class, Status, and Power* (Glencoe: Free Press, 1953).

37. As this manuscript was going to the editor, the writer received a new text in stratification which may contribute to this end. It is B. Barber, *Social Stratification* (New York: Harcourt, Brace, 1956).

THE SOCIOLOGY OF RELIGION

Chester L. Hunt
Western Michigan College

The development of the sociology of religion in the early part of the twentieth century might be referred to as the incubation in the American environment of ideas contributed by European scholars. In this procedure the borrowed concepts were not, of course, taken over without change but were modified to suit the climate of opinion among American sociologists. Typical of this process was the influence of August Comte's hierarchy of intellectual disciplines. The Comtean classification began with the theological and moved to the philosophical and then the positive or scientific. This approach clearly stated that the theological was a primitive approach soon to be outmoded in a progressive society. Theological thinking was considered completely without value and religion itself would survive only in the form of liturgy used in the service of a "religion of humanity," which would be based on science rather than revelation.

When sociology developed vigor in the United States the Comtean analysis was utilized by two different groups of American sociologists. One group was affected by a stream of thought which regarded religion as an impediment to the development of a rational society. For this group religion was viewed chiefly as a type of cultural lag in which institutions outmoded by scientific advance survived for a period of time in the sentiments of the people. Others, of whom C. A. Ellwood[1] was the most striking example, were fascinated by the possibility of a "Social Gospel" and looked at sociology as the source of guidance for the moral norms and institutional practices of a socially relevant religion. In this respect it is worthy of note that many of the early sociologists had been recruited from the ranks of the Protestant clergy. They tended to use sociological activity as a method of working out the frustrations which affected the socially conscious pastor. This is probably less true today since the shift away from a normative viewpoint in sociology, along with the rise of Social Work as a separate discipline, has made Sociology less attractive to this type of personality. The change is not yet complete and there are still sociologists who look to their discipline as a basis for religious reform along with another group whose aversion to everything connected with the church makes it difficult for them to take the sociology of religion seriously.

TRANSITION TO FUNCTIONALISM

The attack on the concept of religion as merely a mechanism by which pre-scientific man uses the supernatural as a substitute for scientific technology came from the field of anthropology. Malinowski[2] found that primitive man was impelled by the forces of culture to seek answers to the unknown which could not be granted to him by any conceivable advance in human knowledge. Religion thus had a functional value in enabling man to meet the inevitable hazards of life and religious ritual undergirded the moral beliefs and social cohesion essential to community life. Pareto's[3] insistence upon the survival of sentiments as a non-rational influence affecting human conduct also made it more difficult to consider religion either as a phenomenon peculiar to the pre-scientific stage of culture or as an institution which could easily be moulded to the needs of any current ideological framework. Durkheim's[4] emphasis on the role of sacred objects as symbolizing the values of the group added another concept to what has come to be known as the functionalist position.

Largely through the writings of Max Weber the topic of the relationship of religion to modern capitalism came to exemplify the relationship between attitudes toward the supernatural and adjustment in the mundane world. Weber reasoned that the attitudes of the Calvinist, although reached without regard to secular objectives, were such as to facilitate the acceptance of norms of conduct congenial to success in business enterprise. This was cited as an explanation of the data which indicated that business enterprise along with scientific advance and political democracy, seemed to flourish best in Calvinist groups. It is a thesis which has provoked both discussion and research, and while it has occasionally been challenged, the main aspects of the idea have gained rather general acceptance.

While the writings of the men who contributed to the functional analysis of religion made a direct impact upon American sociology, this was strengthened by the work of Talcott Parsons, who has trans-lated writings of Max Weber and whose approach to social systems represents an effort to systematize the ideas of the structure-function approach. Parsons has enabled sociologists to shift rather completely from the Comtean emphasis on religion as a passing phenomenon linked to pre-scientific culture to a study of the manner in which religion institutions although shaped, at least in part, by features without any utilitarian basis nevertheless enter into interaction with society. Perhaps typical of Parsons' approach is his analysis of the apparent discrepancy between the Calvinist and the Catholic success in economic development.[5] In this analysis the non-empirical goals of Calvinism give rise to direct empirical goals symbolized in the King-dom of God on Earth. Catholicism, on the other hand, is organized toward non-empirical goals with no empirical implications. This leads to a concern with stabilization through traditionalism and authority rather than continuing development.

IMPACT OF OTHER EMPIRICAL INTERESTS

Parsons' concept of structure and function furnishes a theoretical framework which would be expected to stimulate a variety of empiri-cal studies with reference to the interaction of religious and secular phenomena. In point of fact, however, theoretical frameworks have had less influence on the work of American sociologists than the transfer to the study of religious institutions of the concepts which have been developed in general sociology. This statement finds a rather interesting expression in a review by Faris of the book *Types of Religious Experience* by Jaochim Wach. This book is an encyclo-pedic type of treatment with an elaborate discussion of religious forms, leadership and ritual in many types of societies. In his review Faris dismisses the volume with the comment that "American soci-ologists will find only marginal contact with the issues which are of central concern to them."[6]

To indicate the issues of principal concern to American sociologists one would simply list many of the major fields of concern and speak of their application to the study of religious phenomena. These would include the detailed study of both rural and urban institutions, the analysis of social differentiation and stratification, the study of status and role, research on the effect of religion in reinforcing ethnic distinctions, the classification of religious authority and leadership and the measurement of attitudes which are assumed to be affected by religious groups. Somewhat independent of the interests already named is an interest in typology represented in the classification of religious groups according to their relation to the total society. Another interest which may not fit into the previous list is the study of the formation and development of the small "sect type" religious groups which have a special fascination for American sociologists and have attracted more academic attention than the major religious organizations.

RURAL RESEARCH

There is more empirical data about the functioning of religious institutions in the rural field than in any other phase of the sociology of religion. In part this attention is due to the impact of the problems which social change has brought to the churches of the traditionally religious countryside. Migration to the cities has decreased the constituency of the rural church while the influence of the automobile and mass communication has brought the spread of secularization. In some areas these changes are accompanied by a shift from small family size, owner operated farms to a large scale corporation type of agriculture in which the tenant or the wage laborer has replaced the independent farmer. All this has taken its toll of the rural church so that rather than being the nation's chief source of religious vitality it is often a feeble unit kept alive by subsidies raised in urban areas. Faced with these problems, church authorities have sought for a change of strategy which might enable the rural church to function more effectively in this new environment. Under this stimulus a number of men were employed by theological seminaries and church boards who might be labeled "applied rural religious sociologists." Their work has been supplemented by rural sociologists in the land grant agricultural colleges who have usually enjoyed larger research funds than their colleagues in other institutions.

Most of these studies have been concerned with the factors which appear to affect participation in religious institutions.[7] These studies have confirmed the belief in differential age and sex roles since women are more involved in church activities than men although the leadership in churches, both lay and clerical, is mainly male. Similarly the rural churches were more successful in attracting the group over forty-five than those in the younger age group. Other findings support the hypothesis that lack of participation is related to *anomie* while involvement in church activities is highly correlated with integration in the community. Thus factors such as distance from the church building, length of time in the community and participation in other organizations all correlate positively with church attendance. Traits which might enhance status in the community such as income, education and farm ownership tend to encourage religious participation. Ethnic minorities are usually non-participants except in churches specifically related to their group. Although in general the higher status rural residents are more apt to be religious participants, this tendency is not so pronounced in regions where a stable peasant type of agriculture has persisted such as New Mexico and a few portions of the deep South. Denominational membership seems to be one method of social stratification and differentiation and the different churches have a differential attraction for the different social classes. Similarly denominational affiliation is related to total community participation with Catholics and members of the "sect type" churches showing less participation than members of other churches.

In general these studies of religious institutions in relation to the community serve to verify the hypothesis that religious institutions can only be understood by gaining an insight into their relation to the total community life. This does not imply that the church is simply the reflex of secular society but it does mean that a viable religious institution is one which occupies a meaningful place in the social structure.

URBAN RESEARCH

Somewhat similar to this aspect of rural sociology is the utilization of urban sociologists in solving the problems of the city churches. Here the influence of the University of Chicago and its emphasis on ecological research may be noted. In the rapidly growing and expanding cities a given church was apt to be robbed of its normal constituency by a population shift. Thus sagacious churchmanship demanded an understanding of the dynamics of changing land use. Even as other scholars went in for market analysis, so the religious sociologist made city surveys and drew maps and charts indicating the present location of members and churches and probable future trends. There still remained the question as to whether a church of a given denomination could shift its program to a different population group and attempts were made to analyze the folkways of various groups and the methods the church might use to reach their attention. Problems of this type along with a good deal of statistical inquiry stimulated the development of the Institute for Social and Religious Research, which became a depression victim in the mid thirties. Currently research in this field is carried on by teachers in seminaries and research staffs of church federations with an occasional contribution by a sociologist not connected with religious institutions.

Closely related to this interest in the urban community is the recent research of Roman Catholic sociologists in the social structure of the parish. In its most common form this is simply an effort to discern the extent to which Catholic institutions are involving their nominal constituency in religious activities. A great deal of research in Europe, particularly in France and the Netherlands, has been devoted to such topics as attendance at Mass, performance of minimum obligations, recruitment for the priesthood and other questions relating to the operational efficiency of particular Catholic parishes. In the United States, Nuesse and Harte have given a presentation of the technique and rationale of this type of research in their book, *Sociology of the Parish*.[8]

An attempt to consider the parish from the standpoint of a social institution has been made by Father Fichter.[9] He finds the principal issues of Parish Sociology to be: the impact of urban change on Catholic parishioners, the church as a power structure in relation to the larger society, the effect of free religious choice on social integration, the motivation of religious behavior and the relationship of parish structure to the functioning of the parish. This statement of issues is still concerned mainly with the operational problems of Catholic institutions but they are stated in a manner which enables them to be studied in the framework of general sociological theory and research. His tentative conclusions are that the empirical evidence shows Catholics to be more firmly united on the secular values they hold in common with non-Catholics than on viewpoints which are uniquely Catholic. He finds no convincing evidence that urbanization leads to secularization and observes that, although some types of religious observances have declined in recent years, others have attracted increased participation. His most interesting thesis is that the territorial parish which, with the decline of parishes based on ethnic grouping, is dominant in American Catholicism is inconsistent with the trends of American life. He feels that urban society is moving away from any type of ascribed groupings and towards association based on voluntary choice. In view of this trend it is possible that small chapels with an intimate priest-parishioner relationship, extra-parochial interest groups and loosely structured mass movements might be more effective than the territorial parish in sustaining a viable structure of Catholicism. Research has not yet progressed to the point where this hypothesis can be tested but it points out the direction of important inquiry both for the sociology of religion and for the general analysis of urban associational patterns.

Fichter's work illustrates the manner in which social research which begins as a narrowly conceived adjunct to institutional management may broaden in conceptual depth to a point where it develops important theoretical insights. Along with an interest in the functioning of the parish is a concern for the social role of the clergyman. This has been stimulated by the study of occupations in the rapidly developing field of Industrial Sociology. Recent studies have analyzed the social origins of clergymen, the mobility processes in clerical careers and the comparative incidence of insanity among different Catholic orders. Currently a good deal of attention is being given to "job analysis" in which the day by day routine is examined to delineate the various roles which the clergyman is required to play.[10]

Comparatively little sociological attention has been given to what might be termed "subsidiary religious institutions" such as schools and welfare organizations. Critics of the parochial schools have charged that they lead to a fragmented society and group misunderstanding, while the advocates of parochial schools defend them as the best means of instilling a religious philosophy of life and of maintaining loyalty to the church. Such empirical research as has been done is inadequate to test any of these hypotheses but does suggest that parochial schools tend to attract a predominantly lower class constituency which develops a higher degree of ethnocentrism than students in a public system. Some observations on the comparison of societies with a church monopoly of educational institutions with those in which the church has to compete with secular agencies indicate that there may be a divergence between the manifest and the latent effects of these systems which is contrary to the popular conception. Thus American Catholics who have no public protection against hostile propaganda and have at least half of their children educated in public schools are known for their religious activity while Spanish Catholicism has a maximum of state protection accompanied by empty churches and a long history of anti-clericalism. Similarly in Germany the existence of a publicly supported educational system operating under religious auspices did not succeed in developing either institutional loyalty or a general respect for the Christian view of life. Obviously other factors are involved in these situations besides the religious control of the educational system, but such examples do support the hypothesis that religious loyalty is not necessarily stimulated by church operation of related social institutions.

RELIGIOUS CONFLICT

Statistics on religious affiliation in the United States indicate that about sixty per cent of Americans are church members and that of these a little over a third are Catholic. Since the non-church members seldom identify themselves with a cultural catholicism this means that Catholics, although comprising the largest single church, are definitely a minority of the total population. Relations between Catholics and the rest of the populace have varied from the riots and discrimination of the mid-nineteenth century to the current uneasy tolerance which accepts the existence of American Catholicism but rejects any attempt to impose Catholic patterns on a culture in which Protestantism has been the strongest single religious influence. This situation has led sociologists to analyze religious conflict in a manner similar to that used in the discussion of race relationships. A recent evidence of this is the work of John Kane on Catholic-Protestant tensions.[11] Kane's major thesis is that, while religious tensions reflect other tensions in the society, they are due fundamentally to a disagreement on the nature of assimilation. Supposedly Protestants are committed to a melting pot viewpoint in which minorities take on the folkways and support the institutions of the majority, while Catholics prefer a position of cultural pluralism in which their unique social institutions, such as parochial schools, will not only be tolerated but will receive open support by the total society.

Another hypothesis is that Catholic-Protestant tensions are the result of social status differentials. Catholics representing a late stream of immigration are disproportionately lower class and manifest the defensiveness and withdrawal tendencies associated with such status. Protestants are characterized as a higher status group fearing the growing power of late arrivals on the scene. In promulgating this view Kane describes the social status of Catholics in a manner which indirectly supports Weber's position that Catholicism tends to retard adjustment to the norms of a commercial society.

ETHNIC-RELIGIOUS DEMARCATION

Considerable sociological attention has been focused on the topic of ethnic-religious differentiation. On the Canadian scene a good example of this work is Hughes' treatment of French Canada,[12] a situation in which English Catholics form a marginal group in relation to cultural complexes based on French Catholicism and English Protestantism. In the United States the association of religion with nationality meant that each group of immigrants tended to develop distinctive religious institutions. With Scandanavian and German Lutherans this resulted in separate denominations while the various European Catholic groups were represented in nationality parishes and the American Negro worshipped in segregated Baptist and Methodist churches. Similarly lower class elements tended to break away from the traditional churches and to flock to churches whose religious expression and social milieu was more congenial to their tastes. This dual development of religious differentiation is the theme of Richard Niebuhr's *Social Sources of American Denominationalism*[13] as well as numerous other works.

The progress of assimilation together with the shutting off of mass migration has led to a diminution of the linguistic and economic basis of differentiation while the mobility of Americans within the country has prevented the rise of a regionalism as strong as that in European areas. These developments have led to the gradual abandonment of the national parish in Catholicism and to the elimination of foreign language services in Protestant churches. On the other hand, in a nation in which the simple badge of American nationality is not enough to establish the feeling of identity and belonging, religious differences now serve as lines of social demarcation. Paradoxically, this thesis is consistent with the idea that the processes of diffusion have developed an "American" religion which is found in all religious groups. In Catholicism, Judaism and Protestantism one finds an emphasis on lay participation, religious "activism," some remnants of puritanism together with a confidence in progress (except for a few theologians). Clergymen such as Bishop Sheen, Norman Vincent Peale and the late Rabbi Liebman, who regard religion as a means of personality adjustment, operate with equal effectiveness in their respective churches. Thus middle class Catholics, Protestants and Jews find in their religious affiliation an acceptable group label which combines a means of identification with an affirmation of their common Americanism. Some inconsistencies have to be recognized in the picture such as the survival of an uncertain degree of anti-semitism, the identification of Negroes as members of a minority race rather than as adherents of a majority religious group, and the clash between middle class norms and the official Catholic opposition to birth control. These reservations, however, are not sufficient to destroy the validity of the idea and it is certainly possible to visualize a situation in which ethnic and class stratification has become blurred while an "Americanized" Catholicism, Judaism and Protestantism provide the significant sub-group boundary lines within the society.

The thesis has been brilliantly developed by Herberg in *Protestant, Catholic, Jew*,[14] but there is still some doubt as to whether the foundation of empirical data is adequate to support the theoretical superstructure. The central concept here is that while in 1900 the churches adapted to the folkways of the foreign born that fifty years later they are dominated by the third generation. Each generation is assumed to have a different attitude toward its ethnic origin. The first generation seeks to reestablish on American soil the institutions of the old country; the second generation, avid for assimilation, seeks to avoid everything "foreign"; while the third generation, confident of its "Americanism," looks for ancestral roots. The third generation seeks a distinctive heritage which is still compatible with Americanism and finds this in a return to the distinctive religious loyalties partially abandoned by the second generation.

Evidence to support this idea comes from the study of mixed marriages, a natural topic of religious sociology since sociologists have largely preempted the study of the family while religious functionaries are concerned about the impact of such marriages on religious loyalties. In one of the most famous such studies Ruby Jo Kennedy reported on intermarriage in New Haven, Connecticut, in an article entitled "Single or Triple Melting Pot?"[15] This study found that while there was increasing intermarriage between ethnic lines, religious barriers still tended to hold. Thus German and Polish Jews might intermarry but not Jews and gentiles. Intermarriage took place between ethnic stocks within the three major religious divisions but not across religious lines. This evidence substantiates the belief that although ethnic social distance may be decreasing, religious affiliation provides a more durable type of social demarcation.

Other studies, however, indicate that the New Haven pattern may not be typical of the nation as a whole. These studies show that, while intermarriage between Jew and Gentile in the United States is infrequent, the rate between Catholic and Protestant is rather high. They also indicate that when a Catholic Parish changes from a unitary to a plural ethnic composition the rate of intermarraige with non-Catholics tends to increase. In a few areas the rate of Catholic marriage to Protestants and Jews is actually higher than the marriage rate within the fold. The rate of interfaith marriage varies with the relative size of different groups, ethnic composition and the social status of the individuals comprising the membership of the three major faiths. In general people tend to marry out of the faith when they are in a minority in a community but are not sharply separated from other faiths by class level or ethnic background. Intermarriage is reduced in groups which form a large proportion of the local population and religious endogamy is further facilitated when religious affiliation is correlated with a particular class level or ethnic origin.

Further doubt on the concept that third generation religious ties are firmer than in preceding generations is provided by a few studies of Catholic parishes which reveal that the amount of "leakage" (loss of Catholics to other religious groups) and of inactivity seems to be just as great now as in the twenties or thirties. The hypothesis that in a modern nation of diverse ethnic origins religious differences will be the principal lines of social division is still to be proved. It is, however, an interesting challenge to the thinking of a previous era which assumed that secularization was steadily reducing the importance of all types of religious institutions. The concept is so challenging that surely some research group will eventually make a thorough study of the variations in generational behavior within religious groups. In the meantime we have the presentation of an interesting hypothesis whose testing is delayed by the scattered, fragmented nature of research in religious sociology carried on as a part time avocation by individual scholars.

Apart from the thesis treated above, the reciprocal effect of interfaith marriage on religious and family life has been the object of occasional research. While there is some variation in the research results, the majority of the reports would indicate a confirmation of Parsons' theory of the "imperatives of compatibility in a social system."[16] Thus the wife, as the parent who has the most contact with the children in the family system (primary group relationship), tends to determine the course of the children in the religious system, a secondary type of relationship. Again, since church and family ties operate in some degree of opposition one would expect adherence to both institutions to be weakened. This is borne out by indications that both divorce and religious inactivity is higher in mixed marriages than in those within the same faith. Evidently in some marriages differing religious loyalties lead to a weakening of marital ties while in others the solidarity of the family is secured by minimizing the claims of the religious institution. All of the studies indicate the ineffectiveness of the promise often made by the non-Catholic partner to rear the children in the Catholic faith, which could be cited as another evidence of the limited power of formal contractual ties as opposed to other types of social cohesion.

RELIGIOUS ATTITUDES

Much as the development of family research among sociologists led them to consider the religiously divided family, so the development of attitude testing among the social psychologists prompted many studies of religious attitudes. A very high proportion of such studies consisted of classes of the professor-researcher and often the results indicated only the type of verbal responses apt to be given by certain types of college students in a classroom situation. Perhaps the most interesting results to come from such studies are the frequent correlation of religious conformity with ethnocentrism and intergroup prejudice and the indication that verbal responses did not necessarily indicate overt behavior. Although most studies of this type could be criticized because they failed to differentiate between a nominal and a faithful member of a religious group, yet some valuable evidence did emerge. Hartshorne,[17] for example, challenged many of the usual notions of the effect of religion on behavior when he found that there was no relation between knowledge of moral rules or religious precepts and behavior.

SOCIAL CLASS

Students of social class have found intriguing material in the study of stratification manifested by religious institutions. Not only does the diversity of religious groupings allow churches to have a differential class representation, but even when found within the same church, variation in social class affects the participation of members. Thus we have Congregationalists, Presbyterians and Episcopalians, the traditional churches of the early Americans, attracting a disproportionate amount of upper class membership. At the other extreme, the Pentacostal storefront churches are the refuge of the disinherited and afford them religious institutions free from control of other groups. Not only do churches have a differential class attraction, but a given church will show the effects over a period of time of a change of class status within its membership. A hundred years ago the Methodists were a church of the frontier proletariat. The passage of time and the practice of thrift, hard work and sober living have encouraged upward mobility in Methodist ranks, and today that church is predominantly a middle class institution. As such the "shouting Methodists" have given way to an orderly group of respectable citizens who worship sedately in neo Gothic structures which are usually located in the better residential neighborhoods.

This type of phenomenon has been taken by David Riesman[18] to support his notion of an "other directed" society. He finds that even in relationship to religious behavior, internalized goals have been replaced by a desire to conform to the popular norms of behavior. Thus both the village atheist and the bitter sectarian no longer have a place in the picture. Everyone should belong to some church so to the extent that the citizen is involved in the new society he too will affiliate with a religious institution. This, however, is not selected on the basis of dogmatic belief so much as on a combination of ancestral influence and the extent to which a given congregation helps him to be integrated in the community at the desired social level. Clergymen cease to be vigorous proponents of dogmatic views and become either amateur psychologists utilizing a religious frame of reference or skilled public relations men who offer their congregations an acceptable blend of viewpoints adapted to the social milieu of their parishioners.

The Reisman hypothesis is another brilliant analysis even more difficult to test through empirical research than the triple melting pot theory. While many instances of religious behavior support the notion of religion as a vehicle of social adjustment, some contrary evidence can also be cited. Thus the fastest growing churches in the United States include the highly dogmatic Missouri Synod Lutherans and Southern Baptists. On the other hand, their success could be interpreted in terms of the rising status of their members who are making the ascent from lower to middle class status with a consequent increase in the prestige and effectiveness of their religious institutions.

TYPOLOGY OF RELIGIOUS INSTITUTIONS

The influence of class status is also linked to another perennial question of religious sociology: that of the adjustment of religious institutions to the secular power structure. This question led to the formulation by Troeltsch[19] of the religious typology of sect, denomination and ecclesia indicating different types of adjustment by the church to secular power. The sect, often drawing a large part of its membership from the lower classes, adheres to a radical literal interpretation of the gospel which rejects the secular patterns in favor of pacifism, equalitarianism and other patterns antithetical to an organized power structure. The ecclesia is coterminous in membership with the total society, and while it may maintain a degree of tension between religious and secular norms, it usually accepts and supports the secular power structure. The denomination is a group larger than the sect but not coterminous with the total society which has made a considerable adjustment to the norms of the greater society. This classification has been elaborated and modified by a number of European and American sociologists and is still a favorite theme of systematic analysis. One of the most pertinent contributions is that of H. Richard Niebuhr[20] who offers a dichotomy of "Culture Christians" and "anti-Culture Christians" on the theory that religious groups eventually come either to accept the world while still seeking to modify secular viewpoints with the gospel ethic or seek to maintain the purity of religious idealism by avoiding responsibility for the culture in which they live.

American society is so religiously fragmented that there can be nothing approximating an ecclesia, and sociologists have given far more attention to the peculiar patterns of the sect than to the adjustment of the denomination to the greater society. The sect was usually a small group living in either social or geographic isolation and offered a fascinating possibility for research at the doctoral thesis level. The denomination is dispersed, its members are an integral part of the total society and sociological inquiry was apt to run onto resistance by powerful vested interests. Under these circumstances it is perhaps not surprising that sociological research gravitated in the manner it has.

Such research emphasizes the mechanisms by which the sect keeps itself unspotted from the world and the resulting personality types which appear among members of the group. It has often been assumed that life in the sect provided a refuge from the strains of modern life and resulted in better integrated individuals less subject to mental disease. Some light on this idea was shed by a recent study of the Hutterites conducted by a team of psychiatrists and sociologists.[21] Their studies indicated that even the society of such a sect contained perils to personality integration, since the prevalence of mental difficulty was found to be about the same as in adjacent areas although there was a variation in the incidence of particular types of mental illness.

Since religious organizations have the longest recorded history of any human institutions, are found in all parts of the world and embrace the majority of mankind, it is inevitable that sociologists should look to them for data on the operation of social processes. Since the functionaries of religious institutions usually become aware that they work in a social context, there has been a union of interest between clerics seeking to gain data helpful to the operations of the church and sociologists seeking to validate hypotheses concerning social organization. The development of sociology of religion requires such cooperation, since it must combine a knowledge of the techniques and theories of sociology with an acquaintance with the ideology, structure and functioning of religious groups. This cooperation has been impeded by various factors. The clerics seldom understand sociology, often resent description of religious institutions on an objective basis and are afraid that this approach will reduce religion to a purely social phenomenon. Sociologists in the past were inclined either to view social analysis of religious relationships simply as a measurement of the secularization of society or to have a naive optimism that religion could give emotional weight to norms established by social science. Current social scientists are both more respectful of the role of religious institutions and more thorough in the effort to safeguard research from the bias imposed by the value judgments of the researcher. Further, they have abandoned theories dealing with the ultimate nature of religion in favor of the hypotheses of the "middle range" which have less cosmic significance but are more susceptible to empirical inquiry. The *Zeitgeist* is compatible with a scientific interest in the social aspects of religion, and if funds are made available for systematic research, the results should give us more understanding of the nature of both religion and society.

SELECTED BIBLIOGRAPHY

Emile Durkheim, *The Elementary Forms of the Religious Life,* Trans. by J. Swain (Glencoe, Illinois: The Free Press, 1947). Classic treatment of the role of religion in social solidarity.

Joseph W. Eaton in collaboration with Robert J. Weil, *Culture and Mental Disorders: A Comparative Study of the Hutterites and Other Populations* (Glencoe, Illinois: The Free Press, 1955). Inter-disciplinary study of social organization and mental health in a sect type religious group.

Joseph Fichter, *Social Relations in the Urban Parish* (Chicago: University of Chicago Press, 1954). An attempt to apply sociological analysis to an urban Catholic parish.

William J. Goode, *Religion Among the Primitives* (Glencoe, Illinois: The Free Press, 1948). Treatment of primitive religion from a functionalist viewpoint.

Will Herberg, *Protestant, Catholic, Jew* (Garden City, N. Y.: Doubleday, 1955). A popular, yet scholarly, presentation of the thesis that religious demarcation has replaced ethnic background as the major source of group identification and social cleavage in American life.

John J. Kane, *Catholic-Protestant Conflicts in America* (Chicago: Henry Regnery Co., 1955). A Catholic view of religious tensions in which the recognition of cultural pluralism is urged as the best means of amelioration. Contains excellent analysis of the social structure of American Catholic society.

Murray H. Leiffer, *The Effective City Church* (New York: Abingden-Cokesbury, 1949). An attempt to formulate a strategy for urban Protestantism based upon sociological analysis.

Frank S. Loescher, *The Protestant Church and the Negro* (Philadelphia: University of Pennsylvania Press, 1948). A thorough treatment of the role of religious institutions in the Negro community.

Robert K. Merton, *Social Theory and Social Structure* (Glencoe, Illinois: The Free Press, 1949). Collection of essays which includes a lengthy exposition of the functionalist approach.

H. Richard Niebuhr, *The Social Sources of Denominationalism* (New York: Henry Holt & Co., 1929). An analysis of the ethnic, regional and economic factors which have affected the development of denominations in the United States.

Liston Pope, *Millhands and Preachers* (New Haven: Yale University

Press, 1942). A case study of religious stratification in a southern mill town in the United States.

Ernst Troeltsch, *The Social Teachings of the Christian Churches* 2 vols. trans. by Olive Wyon, (New York: Macmillan Co., 1931). Discussion of the reaction of different churches to the rise of capitalism and to political democracy largely in terms of the "sect"–"church" typology.

Joachim Wach, *Sociology of Religion* (Chicago: University of Chicago Press, 1944). An encyclopedic treatment of the social basis of religious phenomena.

Max Weber, *The Protestant Ethic and the Spirit of Capitalism*, Trans. by Talcott Parsons, (London: George Allen and Unwin, 1930). Basic presentation of the theme that one of the indirect results of Calvinism was a stimulation of attitudes favorable to business enterprise among its adherents.

Milton Yinger, *Religion and the Struggle for Power* (Durham N.C.: Duke University Press, 1946). A treatment of the "sect"–"church" typology in reference to response of religion to economic institutions and to military conflict.

Chester L. Hunt, Associate Professor of Sociology at Western Michigan University; received his Ph.D. at the University of Nebraska and his Master's Degree at Washington University in St. Louis; Professor of Sociology and Research Associate at the University of the Philippines (1952-1954). He is principal author of *Sociology in the Philippine Setting*. Among his publications with relevance to the sociology of religion are: "Religion in the Sociology Texts," *Midwest Sociologist* XVII, 2, 26-29; "Moslem and Christian in the Philippines," *Pacific Affairs* XXVIII, 4, 331-350; "Religion and the Businessman," *Diliman Review* I, 4, 302-312; "An Arrested Reformation," *Christian Century*, LXXIII, 4, 108-111; "Kremlin, Vatican and White House," *Antioch Review*, IX, 4, 549-553; "Religious Instruction Versus Secularization: The German Experience," *Journal of Educational Sociology*, XXII 6, 304-310; "Life Cycle of Dictatorships as Seen in Treatment of German Religious Institutions," *Social Forces*, XXVII, 5, 365-369; "Religious Ideology as a Means of Social Control," *Sociology and Social Research*, XXIII, 1, 180-187; "The German Protestant Church and the Third Reich: A Study in Institutional Conflict," *Social Science*, XXV, 2, 111-118.

NOTES

1. Charles Abram Ellwood, *The Reconstruction of Religion* (New York: Macmillan, 1925).

2. Bronislaw Malinowski, *The Dynamics of Cultural Change* (New Haven: Yale University Press, 1945).

3. Vilfredo Pareto, *The Mind and Society* (London: Jonathan Cape, 1935).

4. Emile Durkheim, *The Elementary Forms of the Religious Life* (Glencoe, Illinois: The Free Press, 1947).

5. Talcott Parsons, *The Social System* (Glencoe, Illinois: The Free Press, 1951), 190-191.

6. Ellsworth Faris, "Review of Jaochim Wach, Types of Religious Experience," *American Sociological Review*, XVII, No. 2 (April, 1952), 253-254.

7. John A. Hostetler and William G. Mather, *Participation in the Rural Church* (Pennsylvania State College; October, 1952), Paper #1762.

8. Thomas J. Harte and C. J. Nuesse, *The Sociology of the Parish* (Milwaukee: Bruce, 1954).

9. Joseph H. Fichter, S.J., "Major Issues of Parish Sociology," *American Ecclesiastical Review*, CXXVII (May, 1953).   •

10. E.g., Jean M. Jammes, "The Social Role of the Priest," *American Catholic Sociological Review*, XV, No. 2 (June, 1955), 94-104. Myles W. Rodenhaver and Luke M. Smith, "Migration and Occupational Structure: The Clergy," *Social Forces*, XXIX (1951), 416-421. Don Thomas Verner Moore, "Insanity in Priests and Religious," *American Ecclesiastical Review*, XCV (1936), 485-498.

11. John J. Kane, *Catholic-Protestant Conflicts in America* (Chicago: Henry Regnery Co., 1955).

12. Everett C. Hughes, *French Canada in Transition* (Chicago: University of Chicago Press, 1943).

13. Helmut Richard Niebuhr, *The Social Sources of American Denominationalism* (New York: Henry Holt, 1929).

14. Will Herberg, *Protestant, Catholic, Jew* (Garden City, N. Y.: Doubleday, 1955).

15. Ruby Jo Reeves Kennedy, "Single or Triple Melting Pot?", *American Journal of Sociology*, XLIX, No. 4 (January, 1944).

16. Parsons, *op. cit.*, 177-182.

17. Hugh Hartshorne and M. A. May, *Studies in Deceit* (New York: The Macmillan Co., 1929).

18. David Riesmann, "Some Informal Notes on American Churches," *Confluence*, IV (1955), 127-159.

19. Ernst Troeltsch, *The Social Teachings of the Christian Churches*, Trans. by Olive Wyon (New York: The Macmillan Co., 1931).

20. H. Richard Niebuhr, *Christ and Culture* (New York; Harpers, 1951).

21. Joseph W. Eaton in collaboration with Robert J. Weil, *Culture and Mental Disorders: A Comparative Study of the Hutterites and Other Populations* (Glencoe, Illinois: Free Press, 1955).

THE TYPOLOGICAL TRADITION

John C. McKinney
Duke University
and
Charles P. Loomis
Michigan State University

One of the persistent aspects of sociological enterprise is the very old tradition of typing social entities antithetically. As Sorokin pointed out, the tradition may be traced back to the philosophical speculation of the Classical Greeks and to the epoch of Confucius.[1] Despite the age of the tradition it still has a marked vitality, and appears to be one of the fundamental approaches to sociological phenomena. Such familiar conceptualizations as Maine's status society and contract society; Spencer's militant and industrial forms; Ratzenhofer's conquest state and culture state; Wundt's natural and cultural polarity; Tönnies' *Gemeinschaft* and *Gesellschaft* forms; Durkheim's mechanical and organic solidarity; Cooley's primary and secondary (implicit) groups; MacIver's communal and associational relations; Zimmerman's localistic and cosmopolitan communities; Odum's folk-state pair; Redfield's folk-urban continuum; Sorokin's familistic vs. contractual relations; Becker's sacred and secular societies; as well as such non-personalized but common dichotomies as primitive-civilized; literate-non-literate; and, rural vs. urban are examples of this tradition.

Obviously these varied polarizations are not interchangeable and do not abstract the "same things" out of the social world, but they do have something in common. Not only do they frequently represent similar "content," but perhaps more important, they in common exemplify the view that it is necessary to distinguish fundamentally different types of social organization in order to establish a range within which transitional or intermediate forms can be comprehended. The polar extremes in point are clearly ideal or constructed types despite the fact that some of the aforementioned theorists tended to treat their types as ontological entities rather than as conceptual devices.[2] The polar type formulations, implicitly at first, but in recent years with increasing explicitness have firmly established the point that the *continuum* is a vital notion in the comparative analysis of social phenomena. The types establish the "outer limits" or standards by means of which the processes of change or intermediate structural forms can be comprehended from the perspective of the continuum. It is in this sense that "general" types such as those we have mentioned continue to play an important role in sociological analysis. A brief examination of the historical significance of some of the type constructs would therefore seem to be pertinent. In addition a demonstration of the current applicability of one of the typologies will be undertaken to illustrate the continuing utility of the approach.

TÖNNIES: GEMEINSCHAFT AND GESELLSCHAFT

Tönnies conceived of all social relations as products of human will. He states:

> The concept of human will . . . implies a twofold meaning. Since all mental action involves thinking, I distinguish between the will which includes the thinking and the thinking which encompasses the will. Each represents an inherent whole which unites in itself a multiplicity of feelings, instincts, and desires. This unity should in the first case be understood as a real or natural one; in the second case as a conceptual or artificial one. The will of the human being in the first form I will call natural will (Wesenwille); in the second form rational will (Kurwille).[3]

The three simple forms of natural will are: (a) linking, (b) habit, and (c) memory. In contrast the three simple forms of rational will are: (a) deliberation, (b) discrimination, and (c) conception. Emanating out of these 2 different wills are the 2 fundamentally different forms of human bond. Tönnies calls all associations in which natural will predominates *Gemeinschaft,* and he views all those which are formed and conditioned by rational will *Gesellschaft.*

A *Gemeinschaft*-like entity may be distinguished by virtue of its possession of the following attributes: unity, a division of labor based upon mutual aid and helpfulness; an equilibrium of individual wills in mutual interdependence; authority based upon age, wisdom, and benevolent force; common habitat; common action directed toward common goals understood as given; kinship; friendship; reciprocal and binding sentiment; diffuse or blanket obligations, common language, custom, and belief; mutual possession and enjoyment; sacred tradition; and the spirit of brohterhood. In sum, *Gemeinschaft* is a relationship of concord based upon bonds of: (a) blood (kinship), (b) place (neighborhood), or (c) mind (friendship).

In contrast a *Gesellschaft* may be distinguished in terms of the following characteristics: separation rather than unification, individualism; action in terms of self-interest; conventions or positive and specific definitions and regulations; delimited spheres of contact; money and credit relationships, dominance by merchants, capitalists, and a power elite; obligations limited and the feelings and strivings of others disregarded on the level of sentiment; and lack of mutual familiar relations. In sum, the *Gesellschaft*-like entity based upon rational will consists in contractual and functionally specific relationships consciously established for the attainment of planned objectives. The *Gesellschaft* is articulated through (a) convention, (b) legislation, and (c) public opinion, and exists in city, national, and cosmopolitan life.

Tönnies utilized the concepts of *Gemeinschaft* and *Gesellschaft* first of all as "normal types," or what Weber later called "ideal types" in the analysis of social structure. In addition, however, he utilized them to analyze the data of history and discovered them to be transhistorical sociological categories. Tönnies found the main evolutionary path of history to be the transition from *Gemeinschaft* to *Gesellschaft* and in so doing indicated that they may coexist and be intertwined in various empirical structures in different degrees at different times. In viewing *Gemeinschaft* and *Gesellschaft* as trans-historical and historical simultaneously, Tönnies helped to free sociology from its entanglement with the historical viewpoint so common in Germany. Moreover, although his concepts are psychologically relevant and psychologically based he helped begin a tradition of thinking which may eventually articulate the relationship between the social system and the personality system without psychologizing the former.[4] In brief, Tönnies not only aided significantly in the establishment of a *de facto* field of sociology, but also contributed sociological conceptual forms that are still useful.

DURKHEIM: MECHANICAL AND ORGANIC SOLIDARITY

Describing not merely the range of human existence, but what to him appeared as an irreversible historical trend, Durkheim in his study of the division of labor polarized society into two types.[5] The first type is the *mechanically solidary society* wherein beliefs and conduct are alike. People are homogeneous mentally and morally, hence communities are uniform and non-atomized. It is in this type of society that a totality of beliefs and sentiments common to all men exists, and which Durkheim called the *conscience collective*. This conscience is characterized by the attributes of *exteriority* and *constraint*. Exeriority refers to the fact that the conscience as totality is never a product of the members of society at any one point in time; constraint has reference to the significant point that the membership of a mechanically solidary society cannot morally refute its collective conscience. Offense against the collective conscience is moral offense and is punishable by repressive law.

Durkheim's second polar type, defining the direction of historical development, is the *organically solidary society* wherein society is held together by the interdependence of its parts. The division of labor is a result of the struggle for existence, and the specialization of labor stimulated individualism and differentiation. People in the society are heterogeneous; their mental and moral similarities have disappeared. Volume, and material and moral density of people are the necessary conditions for the division as they make it possible for more individuals to make sufficient contact to be able to act and react upon one another. This in turn makes possible the contact and interconnection of formerly separate collectivities and breaks down the insulation between them, with resultant diversification. The primary consequence of this whole process is the weakening of the *conscience collective*. Crime ceases to be an offense against common moral sentiments and becomes an offense against personal "rights." Spontaneous relations between individuals are replaced by contractual associations. Offensive acts then lose their sacrilegious character and "repressive" law is replaced by "restitutive" law.

Durkheim's investigation of suicide[6] brought about a fundamental change in his conception of the *conscience collective* as put forth in *The Division of Labor*. The emphasis on the strong predominance of the *conscience* in the mechanically solidary society and the weakening of the *conscience* in the organically solidary society was supplanted by a recognition of the existence of the *conscience collective* in the differentiated, heterogeneous, organically solidary society as the basis of either egoistic or altruistic order. A more specific definition of its absence was arrived at— the *anomic* society, wherein the collective beliefs and sentiments no longer effectively regulate social action and society persists only on the basis of a shifting and precarious consensus. The change from mechanical solidarity to organic solidarity does not result in an automatic loss of *conscience collective,* but an alteration in its forms. The "non-contractual basis of contract" is a moral, and hence collective foundation for individualistic and secular association. Durkheim's recognition of this, based upon the research use of his types, has given an undeniable impetus to the specialized sociological study of law, religion, and knowledge due to the now obvious relation of these phenomena to social structure.

COOLEY: THE PRIMARY GROUP

Cooley, an American contemporary of Durkheim's, maintained that neither the individual nor the group has primacy in social action. Contrary to Durkheim, who gave the group primacy over its individual members, and contrary to Spencer who asserted that the individual is basic and the group only the sum total of its members, Cooley perceived the importance of interactive process, of mutual influence between group and individual. For him the most important groups in the formation of individual human nature and the development of norms and ends are what he called *primary groups.*[7]

> Type examples of the primary group are the family, or household group, the old-fashioned neighborhood, and the spontaneous play-group of children. In such groups all children everywhere participate, and the intimate association there realized works upon them everywhere in much the same way. It tends to develop sympathetic insight into the moods and states of mind of other people and this in turn underlies the development of both the flexible type of behavior and the common attitudes and sentiments which we have mentioned. . . .
> The chief characteristics of a primary group are:
> 1) Face-to-face association.
> 2) The unspecialized character of that association.
> 3) Relative permanence.
> 4) The small number of persons involved.
> 5) The relative intimacy among the participants.

Such groups are primary in several senses, but chiefly in that they are fundamental in forming the social nature and ideals of the individual. The result of intimate association, psychologically, is a certain fusion of individualities in a common whole, so that one's very self, for many purposes at least, is the common life and purpose of the group. Perhaps the simplest way of describing this wholeness is by saying that it is a "we"; it involves the sort of sympathy and mutual identification for which "we" is the natural expression. One lives in the feeling of the whole and finds the chief aims of his will in that feeling.[8]

Cooley's combination of organic theory and psychological orientation which led him to the invention of the concept, "looking-glass" self, and to say that "self and society are twin born,"[9] resulted in the conceptualization of the primary group, apparently independently of the other theorists we discuss. He did not use the term "secondary group," permitting the implicit type under which groups with characteristics opposite to the primary groups to go unnamed. Since the time of Cooley, the primary group, in one form or another, has been a focal point of attention in American sociology. From the mid-thirties on a tremendous amount of research pertaining to this form of social structure has been conducted.[10]

REDFIELD: THE FOLK-URBAN CONTINUUM

The folk-urban typology of Redfield has been the best known and most controversial typological formulation in cultural anthropology for the past twenty-five years. It has often been criticized, particularly by idiographically-minded field workers, but it nevertheless has been the stimulant for a great amount of research.[11]

Redfield has formulated an ideal-type version of folk society by linking together a set of attributes. In the absence of explicit delineation the "urban" type is simply composed of the opposite attributes, and hence becomes the polar antithesis.

To Redfield, the folk society is a small collectivity containing no more people within it than can know each other well. It is an isolated, non-literate, homogeneous grouping with a strong sense of solidarity. Technology is simple, and aside from the division of function between the sexes there is little other division of labor, hence the group is economically independent of other groups. The ways in which problems are met by the society are conventionalized by long intercommunication within the group, and these ways have become interrelated with one another to constitute a coherent and self-consistent system: a culture. Behavior is spontaneous, traditional, personal, and there is no motivation toward reflection, criticism, or experimentation. Kinship, its relations and institutions, is central to all experience, and the family is the unit of action. The value of traditional acts and objects is not to be questioned; hence they are sacred. The sacredness of objects is apparent in the ways in which objects are hedged in with restraints and taboos that keep them from being commonplace. All activities, even those of economic production, are ends in themselves. The more remote ends of living are taken as given; hence the folk society exists not so much on the basis of exchange of useful functions as in common understandings as to what is to be done.

Redfield contends that understanding of society in general and of our own modern urbanized society in particular can be gained through consideration of the societies least like our own—folk societies. His scheme defines an ideal type, the *folk society,* which is the polar opposite of urban society. The type is a construct and no known society precisely corresponds to it. It is "created only because through it we may hope to understand reality. Its function is to suggest aspects of real societies which deserve study, and especially to suggest hypotheses as to what, under certain defined conditions, may be generally true about society."[12] The fact that the typology has served this function to a significant degree is evidenced by the gratifying amount of research done in terms of it since the initial tentative type formulation in 1930 in the study of Tepoztlan.[13]

Redfield explicitly indicates his indebtedness to Maine, Durkheim and Tönnies and points out that his folk society type results from a restatement of the conceptions of these three men in the light coming from consideration of real primitive societies.[14] It is less generalized and abstract than any of the sets of concepts formulated by Maine, Durkheim, and Tönnies, but it contains essentially the same attributes. As a consequence Redfield has succeeded in transforming the central considerations of these concepts to a cross-cultural basis and facilitated the comparative study of societies.

BECKER: SACRED AND SECULAR SOCIETIES

The sacred-secular antithesis has been utilized by many people, but it finds its most elaborate construction in the work of Howard

Becker.[15] Becker makes it very explicit that sacred and secular societies are constructed types. He has meticulously and skillfully preserved their conceptual character and in so doing has contributed significantly to the methodology of typing.

The *sacred society* is isolated vicinally, socially, and mentally. This isolation leads to fixation of habit and neophobia, relations of avoidance, and traditional in-group—out-group attitudes. The concrete is emphasized at the expense of abstraction; social contacts are primary; and tradition and ritual play a large part in the life of the individual. There is the dominance of sacredness even in the economic sphere which works toward the maintenance of self-sufficiency, and against any development of the pecuniary attitude. The division of labor is simple. Kinship ties are strong and are manifest in "great family" relationships. All forms of activity are under sacred sanctions, and hence violent social control is at a minimum. The forces of gossip and tradition are powerful tools of control. Non-rational behavior is predominant, with an important element of supernaturalism present. Rationalism, particularly in the form of science, is largely absent. The value system is impermeable.

The *secular society* lies at the opposite pole of the continuum and is vicinally, socially, and mentally accessible. Habit fixation is rendered difficult by the accessibility of the social structure. There is an absence of social barriers. Social circulation is unimpeded. Ends are evaluated in terms of "happiness," and means according to the norm of efficiency. Tradition and ritual are minimal. Rationality is dominant, and science is pervasive and powerful. The kinship group is manifest in the conjugal family form. Innovation is frequent; change is sought after and idealized as progress. Informal sanctions are weak and formal law prevails. Offense against the law invokes little social disapproval. Legal contracts are the rule. Individuation is prominent in society and the value system is permeable.

These two constructed types cannot be found except in empirical approximations to the major sub-types derived by Becker. The *folk-sacred* society is best exemplified by the old-fashioned and primitive groups in the world. The *prescribed-sacred* finds its closest approximation in the Geneva theocracy of Calvin, the Jesuit state of Paraguay, Fascist Italy, Nazi Germany, and Soviet Russia. The *principled-secular* is an equilibrating society wherein the extreme aspects of the sacred are lost, and yet a principle derived from the sacred value system puts a check on rampant change and reduces the potential of mental accessibility. The *normless-secular* is the anomic form of the secular society. Instances are most frequently found in centers of culture contact wherein the devices of communication generate social accessibility.

The primary value of the Becker polarity lies in its use in getting at the sacred or secular aspects of a group relationship conceived of as *system,* and in exposing the process of secularization or sacrilization that might be taking place. In contrast to the preceding typologies there is no notion of irreversible process in the sacred-secular schema. Although the main historical trend has been toward secularization it is equally permissible to speak of specific cases of sacrilization, as for instance in the Nazi movement.[16] Also in contrast to earlier typologists, Becker has recognized the fundamental limitations of the general types: That is, that their construction on a very general level makes them "sponge" types, and hence precludes their use for many specific research purposes. As a consequence Becker has derived a large number of sub-types incorporating particular combinations of attributes for which empirical approximations can readily be found in quite specific research contexts.[17] Due to the fact that the sub-types are derivations, theoretic articulation is retained and hence the comparative study of concrete groupings is facilitated. The sacred-secular polarity has been constructed along comprehensive lines, and yet remains versatile and flexible.

SOROKIN: FAMILISTIC, CONTRACTUAL AND COMPULSORY RELATIONS

As Sorokin states in the foreword to the English edition of *Gemeinschaft and Gesellschaft,* these types are reiterated up to and presumably in his own thinking. Sorokin's *familistic* and *contractual* relationships correspond respectively to *Gemeinschaft* and *Gesellschaft* and have been used as pairs to accompany these concepts, i.e., *familistic Gemeinschaft* and *contractual Gesellschaft.*[18] Sorokin has himself stated that his third type, *compulsory* relations, represents conceptualization on a different level. Either *familistic* relationships or *contractual* voluntary relationships may be more or less the opposite to compulsory relations. We shall here treat only the *familistic* and *contractual* relationships. For Sorokin *familistic* relationships are permeated by mutual love, sacrifice and devotion. They are most frequently found among members of a devoted family and among real friends. Familistic relations represent a fusion of the ego into "we." Both joys and sorrows are shared in common and those involved need one another. Norms of such relations require that the participation be all-embracing, all-forgiving, all-bestowing and unlimited.

The *contractual* relationship is limited and specified, covering only one narrow sector of the lives of the parties involved. Typical contractual relationships are those of employer and employee, buyer and seller, plumber and householder. The rights and duties of each party are specified by contract. The unity of such groups is rooted in the sober calculation of advantage. It is self-centered and utilitarian. Typically one member of the relationship tries to get as much from the other as possible with the smallest possible contribution. They may remain strangers to each other, one party little interested in the well-being, activities and philosophy of the other. There is no fusion to produce a homogeneous "we." Such relations are usually of limited duration, voluntary and stand in contrast to those which are compulsory. Relationships may develop from familistic to contractual or vice versa.[19]

WEBER: TYPES OF ACTION ORIENTATION

Although not following properly in the tradition of dichotomously typing society, the types of action constructed by Weber are directly relevant to the Tönnies formulation, the Parsons formulation which is to follow, and the present context in general. All the relationships discussed here, indeed all relations, are based upon a continuity of social action.[20] Weber starts by typing the action context, and then constructs his varied relationships types on the basis of the underlying typical lines of action. Action is typed:

> . . . in terms of rational orientation to a system of discrete indi vidual ends (*zweckrational*), that is, through expectations as to the behavior of some objects in the external situation and of other human individuals, making use of these expectations as 'condition' or 'means' for the successful attainment of the actor's own rationally chosen ends; (2) in terms of rational orientation to an absolute value (*wertrational*); involving a conscious belief in the absolute value of some ethical, aesthetic, religious, or other form of behavior, entirely for its own sake and independently of any prospects of external success; (3) in terms of affectual

orientation (*affektuell*), especially emotional, determined by the specific affects and states of feeling of the actor; (4) as traditionally oriented (*traditionell*) through the habituation of long practice.[21]

It may be seen that *zweckrational* is essentially expedient rationality and denotes a system of action involving an actor's motives, conditions, means, and ends wherein the actor weighs the possible alternative ends and means available to him in terms of his purposes and selects the course of action most expedient to him. A system of discrete ends exist for the actor, and an orientation toward them involves such considerations as "efficiency," "counting the cost," "undesirable consequences," "amount of return," and "figuring the results" which condition the otherwise unrestrained adaptation of means to the achievement of ends. This form of rationality plays a dominant role in Weber's overall sociological analysis.

Wertrational orientation is differentiated from expedient rationality by Weber through the inclusion of an "absolute value" which eliminates the possibility of the actor's selection from alternative ends, and ultimately, therefore, bars the possible selection of certain means. This is a sanctioned form of rationality wherein the actual adaptation of means toward the achievement of the absolute, or ultimate end (value), may comply with the criteria of expedience but cannot in itself be *zweckrational* in view of the lack of a discrete system of ends and the possibility of weighing them in terms of available means and prevailing conditions. The sole important consideration of the actor is the realization of the value.

Affectual action is actually treated by Weber as a form of nonrationality (possibly even irrationality) wherein means and ends become fused, and therefore insusceptible of delineation in behavior. This form of action is dominated by emotional states of feeling of the actor and involves an impulsive or uncontrolled reaction to some exceptional stimulus. It occurs as a release from tension, and therefore the later phases of an affectual act may become increasingly "rational."

Traditional action is also treated by Weber as a deviation from rational orientation in that the means involved become ends in themselves or hold the same rank as ends. This type of action is an almost automatic reaction to habitual stimuli which guide behavior in repeatedly followed and prevailing courses. Typically this means a conformity with the accepted and prevalent ways of behavior, with little evaluation or consideration of their expedience.

These four ideal-typical modes of social action were formulated by Weber for purposes of comparison with actual occurrences of behavior. Such behavior of course shades across the types in various degrees of approximation. It is important to note, however, that in Weber's actual analysis of empirical occurrences there is a marked tendency on his part to utilize the *zweckrational* orientation as the basis for "understanding" and "interpreting" behavior, thereby reducing the other forms to the status of residual categories. In effect, this produces an implicit rational-nonrational dichotomy underlying the action types, which in turn results in the conceptualization of relationships in these terms. Weber's *Vergemeinschaftung* and *Vergesellschaftung* are directly modeled upon Tönnies' formulations, although Weber does introduce a third category of *Kampf* (conflict) that is not provided for in Tönnies' system. *Zweckrational* may be compared with Tönnies' *Kurwille* and the resulting *Gesellschaft,* whereas *wertrational, affectual,* and *traditional* behavior may be identified with Tönnies' *Wesenwille* and the resulting *Gemeinschaft.*[22] It is easy to see then how Weber reached his conclusion that the main trend of history was that of increased rationalization. This compares directly with Tönnies' conclusions regarding the trend toward *Gesellschaft,* and also with the related conclusions of Sorokin, Becker, Durkheim, and Redfield.

PARSONS: THE PATTERN VARIABLES OF ACTION ORIENTATION

The pattern variables of action orientation (or of value orientation or role definition, as they are variously called) constitute the most persistent link between personal, cultural, and social systems in Parsons, theory of social action.[23] As a consequence they are of central importance in articulating the scheme. It is apparent that the pattern variables were born as a negative reaction to what Parsons conceived of as the inadequacies of Weber's types of action and Tönnies' polar types. Parsons ends his classic discussion of *Gemeinschaft* and *Gesellschaft* with the following comment:

> . . . this discussion of *Gemeinschaft* and *Gesellschaft* should not be taken to mean that these concepts are unreservedly acceptable as the basis for a general classification of social relationships

or, indeed, that it is possible to start from any dichotomy of only two types. The basic types cannot be reduced to two, or even to the three that Weber used. To attempt to develop such a scheme of classification would be definitely outside the scope of the present study. Such an attempt would, however, have to make critical examination of the schemes of Tönnies, Weber and some others one of its main tasks.

However, the aspects of Tönnies' classification with which this discussion has been concerned do involve distinctions of basic importance for any such scheme and would hence have to be built into the wider scheme, which would probably involve considerable alteration in their form of statement.[24]

At base the attitude of Parsons indicated a recognition of the fact that general "sponge" types had inherent limitations with respect to the handling of many specific problems. Weber manifested some recognition of this; Becker has been acutely aware of it; and the present writers among others in recent years have been directly concerned with the problem. Whereas Becker approached the problem by deriving a series of sub-types for empirical purposes, Parsons, in line with his propensity for systematic theory, chose the approach of deriving the components of action orientation directly from the structure of social action.

In starting his analysis with an actor in a situation Parsons contends that any actor must make five separate choices before the action will have a determinate meaning for him. Meaning does not automatically emerge in a situation, but rather, is based upon the actor's selections from the five sets of alternatives posed for him in any situation. These dichotomies are termed the pattern variables of action orientation, and the problems of choice between them are termed the dilemmas of action.

Affectivity vs *affective* neutrality is the gratification-discipline dilemma and involves the problem of accepting an opportunity for gratification without regard for its consequences. It is a matter really of whether evaluation will take place or not in a given situation.

Particularism vs *universalism* is the dilemma of choice between types of value standards, and involves evaluating an object of action in terms of its relations to the actor and his specific object relationship situation, or in terms of its relations to a generalized frame of reference. This dilemma is one concerning primacy of cathectic or cognitive standards.

Ascription vs *achievement* is the dilemma of choice between "modalities" of the social object, and involves the actor's seeing the social object as a composite of ascribed qualities, or conversely, as a composite of performances. This dilemma concerns the conception of objects as "attribute" or "action" complexes.

Diffuseness vs *specificity* is the dilemma of the definition of the scope of interest in the object, and involves the concession to a social object of an undefined set of rights to be delimited only by conflicting demands, as over and against the concession to a social object of a clearly specified and limited set of rights. This dilemma concerns the scope of significance of the object in action.

Collective orientation vs *self orientation* is the collective interest vs private interest dilemma and involves the problem of considering an act with respect to its significance for a collectivity or a moral code, or with respect to its personal significance. This dilemma concerns the primacy of moral standards in a procedure of evaluation.[25]

Parsons contends that these pattern-variables are the single most important thread of continuity in the action frame of reference and that they enter in at four different levels. On the concrete level of empirical action they exist as five discrete choices an actor must explictly make before he can act. They enter on the collectivity level as role definitions wherein actions of role-incumbents tend to be specified in terms of one side or another of a dilemma. The variables also enter on the cultural level as aspects of value standards. In that value-standards are rules governing action and insofar as an actor is committed to a standard he will habitually choose the horn of the dilemma specified by adherence to that standard. As a consequence the variables also enter at the personality level.

In view of their history, derivation, and content, it seems justifiable to conclude that the pattern-variables represent a further and more elaborate specification of the aspects of society dealt with by *Gemeinschaft* and *Gesellschaft*.[26] In our judgment, then, it is legitimate to speak of them as theoretical components of the more general types. On the basis of our analysis we feel that it is possible to take Parsons' first four variables, add Sorokin's familistic-contractual dichotomy, and Weber's rational-traditional pair and conceive of them as sub-types of *Gemeinschaft* and *Gesellschaft* or sacred-secular. In so doing it is our judgment that all of the major implications and content of these two typologies are covered, and in addition the advantage of having more specific categories to work with is gained. The fit with the Durkheim, Cooley, and Redfield typologies is not as good because of the differences in construction and levels of abstraction, but nevertheless it seems obvious that there are basic similarities between all of the typologies treated here; hence the things that can be empirically said about *Gemeinschaft* and *Gesellschaft* or sacred and secular at least have implications for the other typologies. We shall attempt an operational demonstration of our type usage.

APPLICATION OF TYPES USED BY PARSONS, SOROKIN, WEBER AND BECKER IN RELATION TO TÖNNIES' GEMEINSCHAFT AND GESELLSCHAFT

In a recent article the present authors attempted to describe what they considered to be essential differences in the systemic attributes of communities of family farms and large estates through a tentative demonstrational analysis of two communties in Costa Rica.[27] Both the concrete and abstract or typological attributes were presented, but we shall here concern ourselves primarily with the application of Tönnies' concepts *Gemeinschaft* and *Gesellschaft* and pertinent concepts as used by other theorists. The two communities to be described are Atirro, a hacienda community with 65 families, and San Juan Sur, a near-by community of family farms including 75 families. Both these communities are located in the Turrialba Canton of Costa Rica 6 miles and 3 miles respectively from the town, Turrialba, in which 6,500 people live. They are, we believe, typical communities of rural Latin America. If they are typical, the differences are all the more significant in view of the ideological struggles going on in the world today concerning the relative merits of various forms of land tenure and settlement form.

A. The Procedure. In an attempt to avoid some of the shortcomings of previous typological descriptions of communities, we have introduced the following innovations: First, what we believe to be the important subtypes of the major general types have been introduced as continua. Second, in the analysis we use subtypes in the form of variable polar components of more general types. These subtypes, although varied and to a certain unavoidable degree overlapping, represent similar levels of abstraction. Third, we have used the concept of the "social system" and consequently are able to treat these subtypes as systemic attributes. This establishes the theoretical possibility of finding similar attributes in apparently different empirical groups. Fourth, we apply the types to only one social system or reference group at a time. We do not attempt to apply the types to many reference groups, such as the family, church groups, occupational groups, political systems, etc., simultaneously. The level of abstraction is thereby held constant. It should also be noted that our types are applied to *social* systems, not cultural systems or personality systems. Fifth, we apply the types to specific and comparable status-roles in specific social systems. Sixth, to standardize the typing of the relationships, a specific category of action is supplied.

In order to make our hypothetical treatment of these systems pertinent to intercultural accessibility or to resistance to change, we are considering changes which require community action, not "normal" or gradual infiltration of ideas or techniques. On the contrary, we are referring to instigated change involving the articulation of the entire community in a common course of action, such as proposals to introduce organized sanitation to prevent spread of communicable diseases, or quarantine regulations of sick persons with such diseases, or to set up community-wide co-operatives, schools, and the like.

B. The Social Relationships to be Compared. In order to arrange for typing of communal action, we chose a status-*role* in each community which articulated the power structure of the whole social system. The status-*role* of the administrator was chosen as the subject, and the status-*role* of an immediate subordinate, the supervisor, was chosen as object on the large estate, Atirro. The administrator initiates action continuously to the supervisor, who is in daily contact with most families in the hacienda community.

Since the power structure of San Juan Sur is articulated only during fiestas and times of crisis and since there are no formally elected or appointed governmental administrative officials, obviously there are no status-*roles* exactly comparable to those of the administrator and supervisor at Atirro. The local informal leader of the community, the *gamonal,* most frequently initiates action in the community as a whole. In our typology the gamonal is considered as subject, and a fellow community member whom he chose to help him is considered as object.

C. The Specific Category of Action. Several social scientists who are Latin-American specialists were asked to function as "judges" in the typing of the two communities under consideration. Each is intimately acquainted with Atirro and San Juan Sur. The instructions that they followed, as well as one example of the continua offered them, are seen in Figure 1; continua which we believe may be communicated across cultures.

D. Subtypes or Component Continua of the General Types. On hypothetical grounds we have accepted the *Gemeinschaft* and *Gesellschaft* types as the most general forms relevant to our problem. Figure 2 provides the subtypes or component continua which we believe are the chief constituents of these general types. In typing the relationships an attempt was made to communicate the meaning of the continua through characteristics of their poles.

The judges' reactions are portrayed schematically in Figure 2. Different "profiles" emerged for the two communities. These are marked F and H. The two systems tended to scale out toward opposite poles of the typology, sharp and significant differences being thereby established.[28]

CONCLUSIONS

Insofar as a specific manifestation of the employment of power in San Juan Sur tended toward the affectivity, particularistic, ascription, diffuseness, traditional, and familistic poles, it becomes subject to the hypotheses and statements made about *Gemeinschaft* or sacred communities. On somewhat more tenuous grounds, and with the proper interpretive care, it also becomes subject to many of the hypotheses and statements typically related to the primary group, and mechanical and folk societies.

In contrast, Atirro under comparable conditions tended toward the opposite poles of affective neutrality, universalism, achievement, specificity, rationality, and contractuality and hence becomes subject to hypotheses, and statements made about *Gesellschaft* or secular communities. Again the specific social system being considered with the proper interpretive care and recognition of limitations of transfer, it also becomes subject to treatment in terms of secondary, organic, and urban theory.

It is now a commonplace in the sociology of knowledge that different types of knowledge, as well as the techniques and motivations for extending knowledge are bound up with particular forms of groups.

Gemeinschaft types of society have a traditionally defined fund of knowledge handed down as conclusive and final; they are not concerned with discovering new ideas or extending their spheres of knowledge. Any effort to test the traditional knowledge, insofar as it implies doubt, is ruled out on moral grounds. In such a group, the prevailing methods are ontological and dogmatic; its mode of thought is that of conceptual realism. In contrast, *Gesellschaft* types of organization institutionalize techniques for the attainment and codification of knowledge. In such a group the methods are primarily epistemological and critical; the mode of thought nominalistic.

If the communities of Atirro and San Juan Sur are actually representative of other large-estate and family farm communities in Latin America, then we have solid grounds for saying that the large-estate community possesses a different order of accessibility, socially and culturally, than the family-farm community. Moreover, we are justified in saying that the instigation of any change will necessarily have to follow different procedures, adapted to the two distinctly different social structures.

The specific and very limited problem we have dealt with here with respect to these communities is part of a much larger problematic area, that of *social change*. If sociology is to play a key role in contemporary research, then the major inquiries must be made in a world where the patterns of the past are under increased pressure from a dynamic future. The frames of reference utilized in the past to analyze social change appear to be either over-simplified; too much identified with Western ideologies; or overly impressed with an inevitable one-way direction of progress. From out of this heritage it seems possible, however, to salvage a fundamental starting point—the idea of the societal continuum. The dynamics of a societal continuum so formulated as to comprehend the concept of constant polarity and transitional society in which empirical regularities, constant societal denominators, and universal norms can be recognized cannot be sterile. Tönnies' analysis of *Gemeinschaft* and *Gesellschaft* and the related work of other theorists attacking similar problems is still relevant, and continues to pose pertinent problems for contemporary sociologists. Our analysis of San Juan Sur and Atirro represents an attempt to demonstrate the utility of general typologies, for even relatively specific research problems, when implemented with suitable conceptual tools.

FIGURE 1

THE SCHEDULE: AN ILLUSTRATION*

INSTRUCTIONS: Assume that in both the community of family-sized farms (San Juan Sur) and the large estate community (Atirro) two leaders are organizing a reception for the national president who has just informed the leader in the subject role that he will arrive on the next day. The status-*roles* which structure the interaction which is to be placed on the continua are the following: Hacienda community—Subject is the administrator and object the next subordinate, e.g., the supervisor; Community of family-sized farms—Subject is the most powerful informal leader, the *gamonal*, and the object whoever helps him most in the execution of the act. In both cases the initiator of the action is the subject, administrator in the hacienda community and *gamonal* in the community of family-sized farms.

Place an H on each continuum below for the above described action between the specified roles for the event and situation as indicated, for the Hacienda Community. Place an F on each continuum to indicate how the interaction event and situation for the *roles* specified would compare in the community of family-sized farms.

NORMS OF ORIENTATION OF THE SUBJECT TO OBJECT

AFFECTIVITY						AFFECTIVE NEUTRALITY				
5	4	3	2	1	0	1	2	3	4	5

Note: Position No. 5 as the polar type represents action determined completely by emotions—love, hate, fear and other emotions. Examples of interaction which would fall toward this pole are the following: Mother as subject loving her child, Damon as subject pleading to die for his friend Pythias.

Position No. 5 as a polar type represents action completely devoid of feeling. Examples of hypothetical interaction which would fall close to this pole are the following: A robot commanding another actor: the hired gunman "cold-bloodedly" shooting his victim, a telephone operator giving the object the time of day at the response to a dial signal, etc.

*Other component sub-types were similarly polarized and illustrated. The complete schedule can be seen in Charles P. Loomis and John C. McKinney, *op. cit.* pp. 410-411.

FIGURE 2

PROFILES TYPING THE NORMS OF ORIENTATION OF SUBJECT TO OBJECT IN AN ACTION CONTEXT

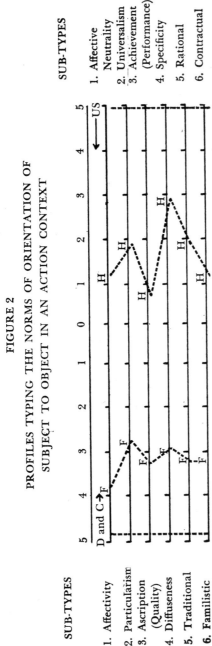

F designates the profile of the relationship of informal community leader and an assistant in a community of family-sized farms.

H designates the profile of the relationship of the manager to an immediate subordinate, the supervisor, in the large estate community.

D and C designate the hypothetical polar profile of the relationships of president and cabinet subordinate in the Dominican Republic and the Republic of Cuba. On analysis of empirical action the profile will move to the right.

US designates the hypothetical profile of the relationship of the president and a cabinet subordinate in the United States. On analysis of empirical action its position to the left may be determined.

SELECTED BIBLIOGRAPHY

Howard Becker, *Through Values to Social Interpretation* (Durham, N.C.: Duke University Press, 1950). An essential introduction to typological procedure, both methodologically and substantively.

Howard Becker, and Harry E. Barnes, *Social Thought from Lore to Science* (Washington D.C.: Harren Press, 1952). The most comprehensive history of social thought extant, and as such has reference to many historically important typologies.

Charles H. Cooley, *Social Organization* (New York: Scribners, 1909). Contains the classic development of the "primary group" and relates it to the wider society.

Émile Durkheim, *The Division of Labor in Society,* translated from the first French edition, 1893, by George Simpson (Glencoe, Illinois: The Free Press, 1949). The first work of a man who dominated French social thought for a quarter of a century. Utilizes the "mechanical" and "organic" societal types as well as the "repressive" and "restitutive" law types in a functional analysis.

Émile Durkheim, *Suicide,* translated from the 1930 French edition (first edition 1897) by John A. Spaulding and George Simpson (Glencoe, Illinois: The Free Press, 1951). A classic typological study that still serves as a model in research design with respect to the articulation of theory and empirical inquiry.

Charles P. Loomis and J. Allen Beegle, *Rural Social Systems* (New York: Prentice Hall, 1950). A book manifesting a convergence of the thought of Tönnies, Sorokin, and Parsons in particular and one that uses the Gemeinschaft-Gesellschaft typology as a basic referent.

John C. McKinney, "Constructive Typology and Social Research" in John T. Doby *et al.* (eds.), *An Introduction to Social Research* (Harrisburg, Pa.: Stackpole Co., 1954), 139-198. An extensive treatment of the methodology and procedure of typing. Assesses the relation of typology to other methodological devices.

Talcott Parsons, *The Social System* (Glencoe, Ill: The Free Press, 1951). Contains in systematic and generalized form the main outlines of a conceptual scheme for the analysis of the structure and processes of social systems. Abounds in types.

Talcott Parsons, *The Structure of Social Action* (Glencoe, Ill.: The Free Press, 1949). An analysis in relation to a group of authors of the nature and implications of the action frame of reference. See especially the section on Max Weber's "ideal" type and Tönnies' *Gemeinschaft* and *Gesellschaft*.

Robert Redfield, *The Folk Culture of Yucatan* (Chicago: University of Chicago Press, 1941). A comparative study of a city, town, village, and tribe within the framework of the Folk-urban typology.

Pitirim A. Sorokin, *Social and Cultural Dynamics*, 4 vols. (New York: American Book Co., 1937-41). The master work of the erudite and prolific Sorokin. Contains a wide range of types; see especially the "idealistic-ideational-sensate" triad.

Ferdinand Tönnies, *Community and Society: Gemeinschaft und Gesellschaft* translated and introduced by Charles P. Loomis (East Lansing: Michigan State University Press, 1957). The original and classic exposition of *Gemeinschaft* and *Gesellschaft* supplemented by introductory comments of Sorokin, Heberle, McKinney and Loomis.

Max Weber, *The Methodology of the Social Sciences* translated and edited by Edward A. Shils and Henry A. Finch (Glencoe, Ill.: The Free Press, 1949). Contains the best translation extant of Weber's treatment of the "ideal type."

Max Weber, *The Theory of Social and Economic Organization*, translated by A. M. Henderson and Talcott Parsons (New York: Oxford University Press, 1947). An essential introduction to the use of types in a systematic fashion. See especially "The Fundamental Concepts of Sociology," pp. 87-157.

John C. McKinney, Professor of Sociology and Chairman of the Department of Sociology and Anthropology, Duke University; his primary areas of interest lie in sociological theory, the sociology of knowledge, and the sociology of complex organization; co-author with J. T. Doby et al. of *An Introduction to Social Research* (Harrisburg, Pennsylvania: Stackpole Press, 1954). Among the symposia chapters and journal articles he has published, the following would be representative works: "The Role of Constructive Typology in Scientific Sociological Analysis," *Social Forces*, XXVIII (March, 1950); "Methodological Convergence of Mead, Lundberg, and Parsons," *American Journal of Sociology*, LIX (May, 1954); "The Development of Methodology, Procedures, and Techniques in American Sociology Since World War I" in Howard Becker and Alvin Boskoff (eds.) *Modern Sociological Theory in Continuity and Change* (New York, Dryden Press, 1957); and "The Contribution of George H. Mead to the Sociology of Knowledge," *Social Forces*, XXXIV (December, 1955).

Charles P. Loomis, Head of the Department of Sociology and Anthropology, Director of the Social Research Service and Area Research
Center, Michigan State University. Prior to this, head of the Division
of Extension and Training in the Office of Foreign Agricultural Relations of the United States Department of Agriculture. His works
include *Community and Society, Gemeinschaft und Gesellschaft,* a
translation and introduction to Ferdinand Tönnies (East Lansing:
The Michigan State University Press, 1957). Other works of which he
is senior author are the following: *Rural Sociology-The Strategy of
Change, Turrialba—Social Systems and the Introduction of Change,
Rural Social Systems,* and *Rural Social Systems and Adult Education.*

NOTES

1. Pitirim A. Sorokin in the "Preface" to Ferdinand Tönnies, *Community and
Society: Gemeinschaft und Gesellschaft* translated and introduced by Charles P
Loomis (East Lansing: Michigan State University Press, 1957).

2. For an extensive treatment of the methodology of typing see John C.
McKinney, "Constructive Typology and Social Research" in John T. Doby *et al.*
(eds.), *An Introduction to Social Research* (Harrisburg: Stackpole Co., 1954),
139-198.

3. Ferdinand Tönnies, *Fundamental Concepts of Sociology (Gemeinschaft und
Gesellschaft),* translated and introduced by Charles P. Loomis (New York American
Book Co., 1940), 119.

4. As Hans Freyer says: "His system was no geometry of social forms and also
no psychology of social situations. Rather it is composed of true structural concepts
with which the social structures of man may be ordered." See Hans Freyer, *Sociologie als Wirklichkeitswissenschaft* (Leipsig and Berlin: B. G. Teubner, 1930),
p. 188.

5. Émile Durkheim, *The Division of Labor in Society* translated from the first
French edition, 1893, by George Simpson (Glencoe: The Free Press).

6. Emile Durkheim *Suicide,* translated from the 1930 French edition (first edition 1897) by John A. Spaulding and George Simpson (Glencoe: The Free Press, 1951).

7. Charles H. Cooley, *Social Organization* (New York: Scribners, 1909), 23-31

8. Charles H. Cooley, *Social Organization op. cit.,* 5.

9. Charles H. Cooley, Robert C. Angell, and Lowell J. Carr, *Introductory Sociology* (New York: 1933), 55-56.

10. For a brief and yet comprehensive statement on the study of the primary group with particular attention to the contributions of Mayo, Lewin, and Moreno, see Edward A. Shils, "The Study of the Primary Group," in Daniel Lerner and Harold D. Lasswell, *The Policy Sciences* (Stanford University Press, 1951), 44-69.

11. To cite just some of the examples of the use of the continuum see Horace Miner, *St. Denis: A French-Canadian Parish* (Chicago: University of Chicago Press, 1939); Herbert Passin and John W. Bennett, "Changing Agricultural Magic in Southern Illinois: A Systematic analysis of Folk-Urban Transitions," *Social Forces,* XXII (October, 1943), 98-106; Edward Spicer, *Pasqua: A Yaqui Village in Arizona* (Chicago: University of Chicago Press, 1940). Some of the more significant criticisms are contained in the following: Neal Gross, "Cultural Variables in Rural Communities," *American Journal of Sociology,* LIII (March, 1948), 344-350; Oscar Lewis, *Tepoztlan Revisited* (Urbana: University of Illinois Press, 1951); Julian Steward, *Area Research: Concepts and Methods* (New York: Social Science Research Council, 1950); Gideon Sjoberg, "The Preindustrial City," *American Journal of Sociology,* LX (March 1955) 438-445; and Howard Becker, "Sacred and Secular Societies: Considered with Reference to Folk-State and Similar Classifications," *Social Forces,* XXVIII (May, 1950), 361-376.

12. Robert Redfield, "The Folk Society," *American Journal of Sociology,* LII (January, 1947), 295.

13. Robert Redfield, *Tepoztlan, A Mexican Village* (Chicago: University of Chicago Press, 1930).

14. Robert Redfield, "Rural Sociology and the Folk Society," *Rural Sociology,* VII (March, 1943), 68-71.

15. See in particular: Howard Becker, *Through Values to Social Interpretation* (Durham: Duke University Press, 1950), 248-280; "1951 Commentary on Value-System Terminology" in Howard S. Becker and Harry E. Barnes, *Social Thought from Lore to Science,* second edition (Washington, D. C.: Harren Press, 1952), i-xxii; and "Current Sacred-Secular Theory and Its Development" in Howard Becker and Alvin Boskoff (eds.), *Modern Sociological Theory in Continuity and Change* (New York: Dryden Press, 1957).

16. Becker describes a sacrilization process in *German Youth: Bond or Free* (New York: Grove Press, 1946).

17. See Howard Becker, *Through Values to Social Interpretation, op. cit.,* 264 and 276 for schematic presentation of the sub-types.

18. Charles P. Loomis and J. Allan Beegle, *Rural Social Systems* (New York: Prentice Hall, 1950).

19. Pitirim A. Sorokin, *Social and Cultural Dynamics* (New York: American Book Co.) Vol. 3, 40. See also *Society, Culture, and Personality* (New York: Harper, 1947), 93-118.

20. We define as "action" any concrete system maintained by a sequence of what Parsons calls "unit acts." "In a unit act there are identifiable as minimum characteristics the following: (1) an end, (2) a situation, analyzable in turn into (a)

means and (b) conditions, and (3) at least one selective standard in terms of which the end is related to the situation." *The Structure of Social Action,* second edition (Glencoe: The Free Press, 1949), 77.

21. Max Weber, *The Theory of Social and Economic Organization,* translated by A. M. Henderson and Talcott Parsons (New York: Oxford University Press 1947), 115.

22. Four years before his death Tönnies discussed his own typology in relation to these ideal types of Max Weber. His analysis concurs with the view presented here. See Ferdinand Tönnies, *Einfuehrung in die Sociologie* (Stuttgart: Ferdinand Enke, 1931), 6 and 8.

23. Talcott Parsons and Edward A. Shils (eds.) *Toward a General Theory of Action* (Cambridge: Harvard University Press, 1951), 76-91.

24. Talcott Parsons, *The Structure of Social Action, op. cit.,* 694.

25. For an extensive development of the pattern-variables and their relation to social structure see Talcott Parsons, *The Social System* (Glencoe: The Free Press, 1951), esp. Chs. 2 and 3.

26. Parsons has stated that he had been dissatisfied with the concepts *Gemeinschaft* and *Gesellschaft* in handling the professions, especially the doctor-patient relationship. However, four out of his five variables place this on the same side; namely, the *Gesellschaft* side. Only on the collectivity orientation vs self orientation does it fall on the *Gemeinschaft* side. It is interesting to note, however, that the collectivity orientation in this relationship rests on an institutional rather than a motivational base. The collectivity orientation of the physician has become built into a set of institutionalized expectations, and hence it is to a physician's self-interest to act contrary to his own self-interest in an immediate situation (collectivity orientation) —but *not in the "long run."* The long run orientation is self rather than collectivity, and hence in this sense all the variables fall on the *Gesellschaft* side. See Talcott Parsons, *The Social System,* op. cit., 473.

27. Charles P. Loomis and John C. McKinney, "Systemic Differences Between Latin American Communities of Family Farms and Large Estates," *American Journal of Sociology,* LXI (March, 1956), 404-412.

28. The D and C profile on the *Gemeinschaft* side in Figure 2 and the U.S. profile on the *Gesellschaft* side in the same figure represent typological descriptions of relations within national governments. The governments of the Dominican Republic and of Cuba are filled with many relatives of the respective presidents. In the Dominican Republic for instance, the son of President Trujillo was a colonel in the army by the age of three, and a brigadier general by the age of ten. Moreover, with the impending retirement of Trujillo after a quarter century in office, the president is throwing the weight of his influence behind the candidacy of his brother for the post. This state of affairs does not exist in the United States. As a matter of fact, norms of bureaucratic action of all kinds in the United States quite generally forbid relatives working in the same section or even organization. For example, once when "unofficial advisor" Milton Eisenhower left a meeting at the White House early, the President of the U.S. turned to his associates and said: "Gentlemen, the man who just left the room would most certainly be a member of my Cabinet except for one, just one, disqualifying factor. He happens to be my brother." *Time,* LXVII (June 18, 1956), 74. In typing the action of the three national governments of the United States, Dominican Republic, and the Republic of Cuba, we have followed the same procedures used in typing the farm and

estate communities. The status-*role* of the president was chosen as the subject, and the role of an immediate subordinate in the cabinet as object; in each case this was the cabinet official having the most power in the military situation involved. The specific category of action is that of preparation resulting from an actual or rumored threat of invasion. The profiles are hypothetical but suggestive.

Figure 1 and Figure 2 are taken from pages 26 and 27 of the book, Ferdinand Tönnies, *Community and Society—Gemeinschaft und Gesellschaft*, East Lansing, Michigan State University Press, 1957.

SOCIOLOGY AND SOCIAL WORK

Philip M. Smith
Central Michigan College

Sociology continues to be more closely related functionally to the field of social work than do any of the other social sciences. But this relationship is not as clearly defined as formerly because social work now draws upon several different fields for the knowledge which today is considered essential to professional training. The growth in popularity of the interdisciplinary approach to the study of the social sciences, moreover, has tended to place various subject matter areas in their proper perspective in relation to an integrated basis for preprofessional education. Much of the compartmentalization that once characterized undergraduate preparation for social work has been superseded by an new emphasis upon the contributions which a number of disciplines make in common. Sociology, of course, plays a leading role in this integrating process, partly because it was first on the scene historically and partly because of the nature of its subject matter.

Among the factors responsible for the close relationship between sociology and social work are the following: (1) their joint historical origins which involved a mutual interest in social problems and social reform; (2) overlapping of leadership and of functions in their attempts to find solutions to social problems during the late nineteenth century; (3) recognition of the need for special academic training for persons who wished to become social workers, after the turn of the century; (4) the contributions of sociology to social work in terms of social surveys of problem areas, case studies, and community analyses; (5) the formulation of useful hypotheses pertaining to social groups, institutions, and processes; (6) the training of students in such a way that they will have a good understanding of the structure and functioning of our society. As specialists in research methodology, some sociologists made contributions of inestimable value to administrators of social agencies who desired scientific appraisals of the effectiveness of their welfare programs. In fact, for more than half a century sociologists and social workers have cooperated closely in a wide variety of activities designed for community betterment.

Familiarity with the historical background is essential to a full understanding of the relationship of sociology to social work in the United States. Developments in both fields were the products of social forces that have profoundly influenced our way of life. Many who became "social workers" after the turn of the century did so because of a serious interest in social problems which stemmed from the Industrial Revolution. Among the outstanding pioneer social workers were persons primarily concerned with social reforms. Hordes of immigrants from Europe who settled in our largest cities intensified such social problems as poverty and unemployment, housing, vice and crime, and public health. Associated with a small devoted group of social workers in their efforts to improve the lot of the underprivileged were clergymen, college professors, philanthropists, humanitarians, and public-spirited citizens in general. But the early approach to social work was marked more by zeal than by knowledge, however commendable its motivations may have been. In view of the prevailing *laissez-faire* social philosophy of the times, moreover, it is not surprising that reform movements usually encountered strong resistance.

During the latter part of the nineteenth century a new and more scientific approach to social welfare problems was exemplified by the Charity Organization Society movement. The idea was conceived in England and took tangible form in London in 1869. The movement soon spread to America, and the first COS was established in Buffalo, New York, in 1877. Because one of the cardinal principles of the new movement was elimination of wasteful duplication in the administration of funds by private charities, the advantages of the plan soon gained wide recognition, and similar societies, under various names, were organized in many other cities. An important step in the direction of better cooperation between charitable and correctional agencies had previously been taken in 1873, when the National Conference of Charities and Correction was organized. It was first known as the Conference of Boards of Public Charities, and it later became the National Conference of Social Work. Social scientists, including sociologists, played an important part in Conference programs and activities, just as they have done in relation to the COS movement and its successors, the modern federations and councils of social agencies.

What is perhaps most significant about the relation of sociology to social work is the latter's dependence upon the former for helping to determine the direction of its development. In fact, such leading pioneers in social group work as Jane Addams and Ellen Gates Starr, at Hull House, were much concerned with finding solutions to urban social problems, while such a distinguished exponent of social case-work as Mary Richmond typified the "sociological" stage in the evo-lution of social work. To obtain the facts about the social conditions under which many of the proper people lived, it was necessary to enlist the aid of social scientists and graduate students from the universities. A similar procedure was followed with reference to the problem of matching resources and needs as well as in the planning of agency programs. With the passing of time, and as sociology became a well established discipline, it became customary for social agencies to look to the sociology departments of the colleges for advice and practical assistance. On the other hand, graduate students in sociology profited by the opportunities which social agencies afforded them to participate in social surveys and to observe social workers as they discharged their duties.

RELIGIOUS ORIENTATION OF EARLY SOCIOLOGISTS

It is noteworthy that while modern social work is largely an out-growth of efforts by religious leaders to help the needy in a system-atic way, at the same time many men who became sociology teachers were also motivated by a strong desire to improve society on the basis of the Judeo-Christian ethics. In both instances, humanitarian considerations were factors of importance in attracting competent personnel and in shaping the trend of development. So interested were the economists, John R. Commons and Richard T. Ely, in the relation of Christianity to social problems that at one time—as soci-ologists—they had advocated the founding of an American Institute of Christian Sociology.

The close relationship historically between sociology and social work in this country was undoubtedly facilitated by the presence on the sociology staffs of leading universities of men trained for the ministry or whose fathers were clergymen. Chiefly because of their early conditioning, with its emphasis on human values, certain of these men became much concerned about various social injustices which followed in the wake of the Industrial Revolution. It was only

natural, therefore, for them to view the activities of social reformers
in the light of the societal goals which their own religious training
had suggested would be desirable. In like manner, many of them
regarded organized social work as a more scientific means of helping
the underprivileged than was true of the methods employed by over-
zealous individuals of the reformist type. In each instance, the religiously oriented sociologist tended to think that sociology had much
to contribute to social action and to social work programs, especially
since the values involved were primarily human values.

Among the distinguished sociologists of an earlier day whose fathers
served churches as pastors were Franklin Giddings and Albion Small.
A fairly long list of sociologists with ministerial training would include such notables as Ellsworth Faris, John M. Gillette, John M.
Gillin, Edward Carey Hayes, Jesse Steiner, and Ulysses Weatherly,
in addition to William Graham Sumner.

EARLY SOCIOLOGICAL ORIENTATION OF SOCIAL WORK

In view of the fact that "social work" was at one time regarded
as "applied sociology," it is understandable how laymen tended to
confuse social workers with sociologists. Even at the present time
newspaper accounts of social work conventions occasionally include
references to them as meetings of "sociologists." There are borderline
professional classifications, of course, which involve a certain amount
of overlapping, as in prison work, but sociology and social work are
separate and distinct as fields of professional activity.

The factor of greatest significance in this connection was the historical origin of courses in social work at the undergraduate level and
the inauguration of professional social work training at the graduate
level. The first training course was offered by the New York Charity
Organization Society during the summer of 1898. A later training
program for social workers developed into the New School of Philanthropy, which became the New School of Social Work, affiliated with
Columbia University. In 1908 the Chicago School of Civics and Philanthropy was started, and it later became the School of Social Service
Administration of the University of Chicago. In both instances, social
scientists, including sociologists, played an important role in the
initiation of social work education.

Almost without exception, courses in social work for undergraduates are offered in departments of sociology or social sciences. Graduate schools of social work generally assume that the easiest way to contact students interested in social work as a profession is to get in touch with the heads of sociology departments in the undergraduate colleges, assuming that the instructor who teaches a beginning course in social work will likewise be a member of the sociology staff. To verify this assumption, the present writer checked the catalogues of a sample of 50 liberal arts colleges in 1956 and found that all courses offered in social work were listed under the heading of "sociology" or "social science" with such courses in departments of "sociology and social work," while two of the largest of them maintained small departments of social work and provided undergraduate field work under the supervision of a professionally trained caseworker.

The sociological orientation of social work is best exemplified by listing the names of some of the American sociologists who were largely instrumental in establishing schools of social work and in promoting social welfare programs. One of the outstanding leaders in this respect was Professor Charles R. Henderson, of the University of Chicago sociology department, whose pioneer work led to the establishment of the School of Social Service Administration at that university. Another example was Professor F. Stuart Chapin who headed the social work training program at the University of Minnesota, following similar experience at Smith College. Both Professor Emory S. Bogardus, who became head of the graduate school of social work at the University of Southern California, and Professor Eduard C. Lindeman, who was in charge of the program at the New York School of Social Work, gained wide recognition in sociological circles. The same was true of Professor Howard W. Odum, who served as head of the School of Public Welfare at the University of North Carolina. Professor Jesse Steiner, of the University of Washington, had considerable experience in social welfare administration, while Professor Stuart A. Queen, of Washington University (St. Louis), was perhaps linked more closely with professional social work than was true of the great majority of his colleagues in the field of sociology. The list of well-known sociologists who were oriented toward social work would also include such men as Blackmar, J. E. Cutler, Dawson, Ellwood, Eubank, Gillin, Hayes, M. J. Karpf, Sutherland, Weatherly, and A. E. Wood. In fact, sociologists have probably contributed more to education for social work than have members of any other social science group.

SOCIOLOGY AND SOCIAL WORK EDUCATION

Although graduate schools of social work continue to stress the importance of a broad foundation in the social sciences as a basis for professional training, sociology is the subject matter area which seems to meet the needs of the largest group of preprofessional students most effectively. One reason for this is that sociology majors, in particular, tend to cultivate an interest in social work as a profession through their study of social problems. Another factor contributing to students' decisions to become social workers stems from contacts with social agencies which they often make as sociology students and which afford them opportunities for observing social workers in action.

OCCUPATIONAL INTERESTS OF SOCIOLOGY MAJORS

In order to determine the relationship between the student's preference for sociology as a major field of study and his occupational interests, Chester Alexander compiled data covering a sample of 4,614 sociology majors enrolled in 124 colleges during 1947-48.[1] Analysis of the data yielded results which were especially significant from the standpoint of undergraduate preparation for social work. For example, Alexander found that the largest single group of women students majoring in sociology, who expressed an occupational preference (32 per cent), desired to become social workers. The second largest group (20 per cent) had failed to make a definite decision regarding an occupation, while the third largest group (14 per cent) planned to become teachers.

Occupational preferences of men students who were majoring in sociology differed significantly, percentagewise, from those designated by the women. Thus, the largest single group of men (24 per cent) intended to enter the teaching profession, while the second largest group (21 per cent) planned to become social workers. The third largest group of men majoring in sociology (11 per cent) expressed a preference for religious work, including the ministry and religious education.[2]

In addition to the data pertaining to undergraduate majors in sociology, Alexander obtained information from 1,377 graduates regarding the nature of their employment. A drift toward social work on the part of women graduates who had not previously planned

to enter the field was clearly in evidence. In contrast to 32 per cent
of women sociology majors who preferred social work as a career, a
total of 50 per cent of women college graduates in the sample actually
had entered this profession, while 26 per cent of the male graduates
became social workers as compared to 21 per cent who had expressed
a preference for social work while still in college.[3]

It is noteworthy that although the largest single group of undergraduates interrogated (23 per cent) were of the opinion that courses
in the area of The Family had proved most helpful to them the
second largest group (14 per cent) thought that they had derived the
greatest benefit from courses in Social Work.[4]

EFFORTS TO MEET THE NEED FOR TRAINED SOCIAL WORKERS

The passage of the Social Security Act in 1935 created such a
demand for caseworkers (or case visitors), especially under the Public
Assistance programs, that persons with no graduate training had to
be drafted into service. Thus, the sociology departments of the colleges
attempted to meet the need by offering regular courses in social work
at the undergraduate level, in addition to off-campus extension classes
for the benefit of public assistance workers who were still earning
credits for their baccalaureate degrees.

The formation of the National Association of Schools of Social
Administration in 1942 was largely the result of a realistic approach
to the problem of recruitment of personnel for social work. Beginning
in 1919, the American Association of Schools of Social Work became
the official accrediting agency for social work education in the United
States and Canada, and it continued to function in that capacity until
1952. Approved training programs in the field of social work were
those offered by graduate schools on a professional basis. Two years
of graduate training were required for the completion of programs
leading to the master's degree in social work, and field work in a
social agency under professional supervision became a standard requirement. Because of the high academic standards involved, as well
as the time and expense which the program entailed, there were not
enough applicants for graduate training to meet the need for social
workers. The National Association of Schools of Social Administration
provided for social work education at the undergraduate level which

would receive both academic and professional recognition and which would attract more college students to the field. On some campuses, undergraduate and graduate training were combined, or closely integrated, to save time.

In 1946 the National Council on Social Work Education was formed for the purpose of making a thorough study of the problem of accreditation especially. As a sequel to the report of the Council, issued in 1951, the American Association of Schools of Social Work, the National Association of Schools of Social Administration, and the National Council on Social Work Education joined forces in 1952 to form the new Council on Social Work Education. In this new organization every effort was made to coordinate undergraduate and graduate training for social work, so as to provide professional education of high quality. It was realized, of course, that graduate training for all social workers was the ideal to be attained in the long run. From the standpoint of immediate needs, however, the role of sociology departments in offering courses in social work at the undergraduate level was recognized as a contribution of major importance because numerous positions in the field had to be filled as soon as possible, and partly trained workers were thought to be better than those with no special training at all.

By 1956 the Council on Social Work Education included in its membership 59 graduate schools of social work, the National Association of Social Workers, some 36 national employing agencies, and numerous local agencies and individuals. It might be well to note at this point that the American Association of Social Workers, which began in 1921 as the successor to the National Social Workers Exchange, became the National Association of Social Workers in 1955. The Association seeks to maintain high educational and professional standards for social workers, largely through its requirements for membership.

Beginning in 1944, the American Association of Schools of Social Work adopted a curriculum, known as the "basic eight," which was designed to provide future social workers with a well-rounded professional education. Included in the "basic eight" were these subject-matter areas: community organization, medical information, psychiatric information, public welfare, social administration, social casework, social group work, and social research.

In 1952 the AASSW re-examined its curriculum policy and concluded that all member schools should provide an integrated two-year professional program at the graduate level and that schools with only a one-year program could no longer be eligible for membership. This statement of policy was accepted by the Commission on Accreditation of the Council on Social Work Education. Three distinct areas of study were included in the new program: (1) the social services, (2) human growth and behavior, and (3) the practice of social work.

Despite the steady progress in education for social work that was so noticeable after World War II, there were several issues which called for further clarification. The lack of adequate data of a factual nature handicapped persons responsible for programs of professional education who desired to organize their curricula in terms of the realities of the situation rather than on a basis of mere speculation. One of the important questions to be considered was the relation of pre-professional education to professional education for social work. Then, too, there were recurrent problems related to accreditation, curricula, and recruitment of social workers.

In response to numerous requests, the National Council on Social Work Education had made a comprehensive study of professional preparation for social work, aided by a grant from the Carnegie Foundation, but its findings left many questions unanswered. The report, *Social Work Education in the United States,* was written by Ernest V. Hollis and Alice L. Taylor and was published in 1951. The thorough investigation which preceded the writing of the report created a great deal of interest in educational and professional circles throughout the nation, and the report itself pointed up the need for a careful study of the social work curriculum. As the logical group to carry out such an assignment, the Council on Social Work Education initiated a three-year study late in 1955.

SOCIAL RESEARCH AND SOCIAL WORK

Social work research has been growing in importance, especially during the past decade, and it continues to draw heavily upon sociology for its methods, personnel, and much of its material. Sociology, in particular, has made contributions to research in the field of social work which have proved of great value. Among the reasons why such research is today deemed essential are the following: (1) the need for social agencies to plan programs of expansion, or to modify existing programs, on the basis of changing community requirements; (2) the desirability of evaluating the effectiveness of agency programs in order to make such revisions as will result in greater over-all efficiency (3) the importance of discovering the relationship of an agency's program to those of other agencies in the community, and the need for measuring these relationships with some degree of objectivity; (4) growing recognition of the value of studies of people's attitudes toward welfare programs which are not tax-supported, especially in relation to fund-raising campaigns; (5) the need to determine what social policies and what social action programs will contribute most effectively to the solution of problems of great concern to social workers and their clients; (6) the need for developing a research methodology in the field of social work which will be an outgrowth of repeated tests under actual working conditions and which will help the investigator to make substantial contributions to knowledge. Since social work is an art rather than a science, it is to be expected that research in this field will have utilitarian emphases. Social workers are concerned with scientific abstractions only as they have a bearing upon the practical problems with which they are confronted, since they have dedicated their lives to "the art of helping people in trouble."

In this connection, Ernest Greenwood and Fred Massarik have observed that individuals "trained in social research are increasingly being called upon by social workers to gather accurate data which will assist the latter in the solution of their professional problems."[5] They also noted that "the scientific approach and technical skills which the social researcher brings to a social work problem are essentially the same as those he employs when he works with a problem laden solely with theoretical implications."[6] As an example of how social research can be of practical value to social agencies, Greenwood and Massarik explained how they gathered and interpreted data pertaining to a problem of concern to administrative officials of the Jewish Centers Association of Los Angeles and conducted research which required the formulation and verification of a reasonable hypothesis.

As already noted, it is customary for specialists in social research to draw upon the social sciences for helpful information when they investigate problems in the field of social work. But not often is the latter regarded as of special value in helping the researcher with his studies of the social sciences. The truth is that the various areas of study are interdependent in that each contributes to a better understanding of the others. Olive M. Stone contends that social casework "can contribute to the social sciences in at least three significant ways: (1) in the use by social scientists of methods and techniques common to social science research and social casework; (2) in the use by social scientists of analyzed and unanalyzed casework data; (3) in the review or analysis by social scientists of their own data as tested through casework practice."[7] She thus indicates some of the possibilities for scientific research that might result from a closer relationship between theory and practice in this important area of study.

THE PSYCHOLOGICAL VERSUS THE SOCIOLOGICAL EMPHASIS

Perhaps the most significant development in social casework since 1945 is the strong trend in the direction of greater emphasis upon the psychological approach, with special reference to the contributions of the psychoanalytical school. The impact of World War II upon the thinking of social workers was a particularly important factor in accentuating psychologically-oriented treatment programs. For example, the study of neuropsychiatric conditions among hospitalized veterans indicated that the nature of an individual's attitude toward his handicap, whether physical, mental, or social, could be a decisive factor in relation to his ultimate rehabilitation. In addition, a great deal was learned concerning psychosomatic conditions, so that the contributions of psychology (and psychiatry) to the understanding of their clients became increasingly appreciated by social caseworkers. So powerful is the psychiatric influence upon social casework today that a worker who is unfamiliar with the most commonly used technical terms may be at a distinct disadvantage. Fortunately, the profession of social work has taken the stand that one does not need to be a psychiatrist, a clinical psychologist, or a psychiatric social worker to help people who are mentally ill, although the treatment team of a psychiatric clinic consists of the foregoing. The psychological influence is especially strong in family casework, as well as in some types of child welfare work, and it also assumes a position of much importance in correctional work.

In view of the popularity of the psychological approach to social casework, it was to be expected that a reaction would set in. Some sociologists, and social workers trained in the "sociological school," have raised serious questions as to the over-all effectiveness of the individualistic, "personal adjustment" approach which characterizes much of the psychological orientation of modern casework. They suggest, for example, that trying to adjust to slum housing, poverty, and racial discrimination, in the long run, helps neither the individual nor society, and that failure to recognize the impact of powerful social forces upon the individual in our complex society may actually magnify the task confronting social workers.

There are those in the profession who contend that social work in the United States has lost its vision, that it has no truly constructive philosophy to determine its goals, and that social workers themselves are apathetic toward social action and social reform. Doubtless there is much truth in this contention. Yet there are many signs that organized social work, conducted on a more "scientific" plane than ever before, is helping to cure some of our social ills, although progress is being achieved without extensive social reforms of the type which were effected during the New Deal era.

During the past ten years especially there has been a phenomenal growth of interest in community organization—in city planning, in coordinating councils, in united fund drives, in improvement of living conditions at the local level. This activity has led to a revival of interest in "sociological" factors on the part of social workers. Such significant problems as juvenile delinquency, adult crime, slum clearance, public housing, desegregated schools, the promotion of interracial understanding, and elimination of racial and religious bigotry have led to a number of research studies which capitalized upon an integrated sociological-psychological approach and from which social workers have derived considerable benefit.

THE TREND TOWARD COOPERATIVE COMMUNITY STUDIES

One of the significant developments since World War II has been the growth in popularity of studies of community social services which have exemplified the "team" approach. Representatives of various social agencies, educational institutions, churches, women's groups, and service clubs, for example, have pooled their resources as they cooperated with specialists in social research and community organization engaged in conducting surveys of community needs and resources, usually in connection with some aspect of social service. Although space limitations prohibit a listing of the most significant studies of this type, a few of them are mentioned below for illustrative purposes:

(1) Bradley Buell and Associates, *Community Planning for Human Services* (New York: Columbia University Press, 1952); (2) Edwin Powers and Helen Witmer, *An Experiment in the Prevention of Delinquency: The Cambridge-Somerville Youth Study* (New York: Columbia University Press, 1951); (3) Gordon W. Blackwell and Raymond F. Gould, *Future Citizens All* (Chicago American Public Welfare Association, 1952); (4) *Reaching the Unreached* (New York: New York City Youth Board, 1952); (5) Sherwood Norman, *The Detention of Children in Michigan: A Study Requested by the Michigan Probate Judges Association* (New York: National Probation and Parole Association, 1952).

Although it is usually deemed best to place an "outside expert" in charge of a community survey, or a study of some aspect of community life, every effort is made to enlist the cooperation of as many volunteers as possible in order to obtain the wholehearted support of the local citizenry. Sociologists from colleges and universities, or specialists in community organization from graduate schools of social work, are often among the first to be invited to conduct surveys for the reason that they generally have had the requisite training and experience to do a good job.

SOCIOLOGY, SOCIAL WORK, AND THE CORRECTIONAL SERVICES

Since courses in Juvenile Delinquency and Criminology are almost always taught by members of the sociology department on the average college campus, sociology continues to play a strategic role in helping to train young men for probation and parole work. A minimum of one year of advanced study, preferably in a graduate school of social work, is required of applicants for the better-class correctional positions, but only a small proportion of those interested in this type of work seem willing to spend an extra year in school before they apply for their first job. As a result, the bulk of the positions are filled by persons without graduate training. An encouraging development during the past ten years was the growth in popularity of in-service training programs for correctional personnel, under an arrangement which enables college graduates to obtain certain types of positions while studying for advanced degrees.

Many social workers still raise serious questions as to whether social casework, in the true sense, can be carried on in the authoritarian atmosphere of the prison setting, and some are likewise skeptical concerning casework procedures used in relation to probation and parole. But, in general, the past ten years have been a period of progress in this connection. Both casework and group work have become an important aspect of programs of rehabilitation in the correctional services. Until salary scales become more attractive, and until prison personnel are fully protected from political interference with their professional activities, the great majority of positions will continue to be filled by applicants with little or no graduate training. Thus, the responsibility of teachers of sociology for the recruiting of correctional personnel at the undergraduate level has become increasingly apparent. It is perhaps unfortunate that the correctional services have not succeeded in attaining equal status from a professional standpoint with those areas of social service which have higher academic requirements for their practitioners.

UNDERGRADUATE FIELD WORK

A significant development since World War II has been the growing popularity of field courses in social work at the undergraduate level. It should be noted, however, that the great majority of such courses are offered by sociology departments, and they are usually listed under the heading of "sociology" rather than "social work." In some institutions the "field laboratory" approach is used, particularly in large cities where the social agencies of the community can supply the facilities for observation and practice which are required. Students, as a rule, work under supervision in order to be of some use to the agency while they learn how it serves its constituency. Those who have completed at least two years of college, and who have been carefully screened, can do a creditable job as student assistants in settlement houses, boys' clubs, Y.M.C.A.'s, city recreation departments, Boy Scout activities, C.Y.O.'s, and church groups—to name only a few of the many possibilities.

Some of the larger colleges located in the urban areas, and which have social work departments, offer regular field training in social agencies under the direction of a staff member who holds a master's degree in social work. This type of program is designed to enable the student who does not plan to attend a school of social work to fill a responsible position immediately upon his graduation from college. One of its best features is the opportunity thus afforded the student-trainee to decide whether he actually wants to become a social worker. After a suitable try-out experience, some students change their minds and decide that they are not fitted for social work, temperamentally and otherwise. Those who continue on the job after graduation find their undergraduate experience of considerable value.

Central Michigan College Program. As an illustration of what the sociology departments of many of the schools are doing, the experience of Central Michigan College may be fairly typical, with one exception: the field courses are offered only during the summer months when students can concentrate upon what they are doing without being distracted by campus social life. So far as practicable, student-trainees are encouraged to live in or near the institution or agency which makes use of their services. They usually receive free room and board and a small amount of compensation. Such an arrangement is usually made to prevent their being exploited.

Among the institutions and agencies which have accepted Central Michigan College students for summer training are the following:

Boys Republic, Starr Commonwealth for Boys, Traverse City State Hospital, Detroit Recreation Department, Camp Oakland, Boys Ranch, Wexford County Bureau of Social Aid, Saginaw County Juvenile Court, Oakland County Children's Home, Children's Village, Michigan State Reformatory, State Prison of Southern Michigan, Muskegon County Juvenile Court, Oakland County Juvenile Court, The Haven, The Institute of Living (Hartford, Conn.). In addition, camp counselors and group work leaders, under competent supervision, in several of the summer camps for which Michigan is noted.

ATTITUDES OF GRADUATE SCHOOLS TOWARD UNDERGRADUATE FIELD WORK

As might be expected, graduate schools of social work do not recommend that students try to do bona fide work while they are still undergraduates. There are several reasons why this is so, among which are the following: (1) They need to spend most of their time obtaining a broad liberal arts education, including a good understanding of the social sciences. (2) They are usually too immature, in terms of academic background and life experience, to obtain the most benefit from such training. (3) The amount of field work ordinarily available to undergraduates is so limited as to be of little practical value. (4) The student generally lacks sufficient preparation in social work to profit significantly from his field experience. (5) He is apt to form bad work habits which can be corrected later only with considerable difficulty. (6) He often lacks supervision of the quality and type which are essential if he is to derive any substantial benefit from the program. (7) Such an experience may result in the student overemphasizing the practical aspects of social work, thus causing him to underestimate the importance of the thorough academic training which is today considered so essential. (8) Only graduate field work is recognized professionally.

The preceding statements were derived from the results of a questionnaire survey made by the present author in 1948. Of a total of 32 directors of graduate schools of social work, only 7 expressed their approval of undergraduate field work, while 4 gave their qualified approval. Among the reasons advanced for endorsing the undergraduate program were the following: (1) It gives the student an opportunity to combine theory and practice. (2) It helps him to find the type of work in which he is most interested. (3) It aids him in discovering the kind of work for which he is best adapted. (4) It is useful as a partial basis for predicting future success or failure.

TRENDS

In contrast to the close relationship between sociology and social work during the early part of the century, the period since World War II has been marked by social work becoming a field of knowledge in its own right, with its dependence upon sociology reduced to a minimum. The trend in social work is toward ever higher academic standards, and 12 graduate schools of social work in the United States now offer programs leading to the doctoral degree.

The impact of the "psychological school" upon theory and practice in social work in recent years has tended to result in overemphasis on individual factors at the expense of what some consider to be factors of greater importance because of their social-environmental nature. There are signs that certain of the views of the older "sociological school" are being revived and that a combined psychological-sociological approach to social casework has much to offer.

Social work is now capitalizing upon the research findings of allied disciplines and is using tested research methods to improve welfare programs. One of the most promising developments during the past decade has been the growth in popularity of "team" research and of the community organization approach to the solution of welfare problems.

Graduate schools of social work still expect undergraduate departments of sociology to furnish a substantial proportion of all students expecting to take advanced study in the field. Social agencies likewise continue to recruit personnel in significant numbers from among graduating students who are Sociology majors.

Field courses on the undergraduate level are now offered in many colleges both to supplement campus courses in sociology and to help students to decide whether they would like to become social workers.

SELECTED BIBLIOGRAPHY

Helen I. Clarke, *Social Legislation* (New York: Appleton-Century-Crofts, Inc., 1957). An extensive revision of an authoritative text, new materials on marriage, divorce, juvenile delinquency, and social security have been added.

Nathan E. Cohen, "Social Work as a Profession," in *Social Work Year Book 1957* (New York: National Association of Social Workers, 1957), 553-562. An excellent article on professional developments in the field of social work, beginning with the early organizations.

M. C. Elmer, *Contemporary Social Thought: Contributors and Trends* (Pittsburgh, Pa.: University of Pittsburgh Press, 1956), Chapter IX, "Social Work and Social Reform," 137-155. Includes a descriptive analysis of salient trends, using the historical approach to advantage.

Arthur E. Fink, *The Field of Social Work* (New York: Henry Holt, 1955). This widely used text contains all the essential information needed for teaching the introductory course.

Walter E. Friedlander, *Introduction to Social Welfare* (New York: Prentice-Hall, 1955). Both comprehensive in its coverage and thorough in its treatment of the major aspects of social welfare services.

Ernest V. Hollis and Alice L. Taylor, *Social Work Education in the United States* (New York: Columbia University Press, 1951). The most complete and authoritative study of its kind which is available.

Cora Kasius, Ed., *New Directions in Social Work* (New York: Harper, 1954). Presents a variety of views of interest to social workers in a thorough manner.

Katherine A. Kendall, "Education for Social Work," in *Social Work Year Book 1957*, Russel H. Kurtz, editor (New York: National Association of Social Workers, 1957), 217-232. Clearly traces the significant developments from the early years to the present.

Philip Klein and Ida C. Merriman, *The Contribution of Research to Social Work* (New York: American Association of Social Workers, 1948). A short but especially timely treatment of a topic of growing interest to social welfare administrators and practitioners.

Mary E. MacDonald, "Research in Social Work," in *Social Work Year Book 1957*, Russell H. Kurtz, editor (New York: National Association of Social Workers, 1957), 489-500.

Otto Pollack, *Integrating Sociological and Psychological Concepts* (New York: Russell Sage Foundation, 1956). A significant study, representing an approach which may prove to be most fruitful from the standpoint of the practice of social work in future years.

Marion K. Sanders, "Social Work: A Profession Chasing Its Tail," *Harper's* CCXIV, 1282 (March, 1957), 56-67. A penetrating description of the inability of the social workers to define their field and their tendency to get lost in semantics.

(For the *curriculum vitae* of the author, see p. 404.)

NOTES

1. Chester Alexander, "Occupational Interests of Sociology Majors," *American Sociological Review*, XIII (December, 1948), 758-763.

2. *Ibid.*, 761.

3. *Ibid.*, 761.

4. *Ibid.*, 760.

5. Ernest Greenwood and Fred Massarik, "Some Methodological Problems in Social Work Research," *American Sociological Review*, XV (August, 1950), 546.

6. *Ibid.*

7. Olive M. Stone, "What Can Social Case Work Contribute to the Social Sciences?," *American Sociological Review*, XV (February, 1950), 68.

THE USE OF STATISTICS
IN SOCIAL SCIENCE RESEARCH

Roy G. Francis
University of Minnesota

If the changes which occurred during the last thirty years continue in direction and speed, the use of mathematics is likely to change the contours of several social science fields. This statement, however, is not cast as a hypothesis; it is merely a conditional observation. The likelihood of continuous change, in either direction or speed, is contingent upon a large number of factors and conditions which are not contained in the notion of the mathematization of any science.

All science proceeds in a social situation. And as the social situation —its rewards, its status systems, it motivations, its actors—changes, so will the science that is generated in the situation of interest. A discussion, then, of the changing use of statistics in social science is a proper task of the sociologist.

In order for one to speak intelligently of change, certain preconditions must be met. First, the social unit in question must be *generically* unchanged. For example, it would be improper to describe the difference between American Indian culture and contemporary American culture as change unless one used as the unit of inquiry "human behavior on the North American Continent."

Secondly, although the social unit is generically unchanged, some difference must be observed where the social space is known to be continuous. Now mere difference is insufficient for the argument of change. Implicit in the requisite of social spatial continuity is the notion of the passage of time. This we can elevate to a third condition, perhaps. That is, that a real difference be observed between at least two units of the same generic thing and that these units be connected through time. To observe the difference between two instances of "family patterns" does not imply change. Even the comparison of a family pattern of 1400 and 1950 does not imply change by itself. After all, one could compare the pigmy family pattern of 1400 with the Hopi family pattern of 1950—and this certainly does not imply change. Notice that, in this case, the social unit (the family pattern) is a generic concept and as a concept an absence of change is noted. Observe, moreover, that differences in the empirical instance are noted. Observe that a temporal difference exists. What is lacking is the continuity of the social space.

The notion of "Time" in a discussion of change requires some careful consideration. First, consider the dangerous practice of many demographers of using calendar years as a measure of time. The attempts to extrapolate birth rates through time were all based on the assumption that historical time is a unidimensional thing. Nothing could be further from the truth. Teggart[1] has ably argued that historical time contains at least three basic social processes. Basically, there is a pattern of persistence—the implication behind "tradition" is that of fixity and no change. Next there is the process of relatively slow change: and, finally, a process of rapid or eventful change. The distinction between the latter two is at least operationally real: rapid or eventful change can be located in time and space. Even though the event may be an eruption culminating a longer period of slow change, the two are observably different. Teggart merely elevated an observed difference to the status of an analytical difference.

When one correlates historical time with any dependent variable—as one necessarily does in "time series analysis"—one is correlating at least three processes against the problematic data. Note that in time series analysis, a fundamental assumption of some persisting feature is made. Note, too, that "cyclic" and "seasonal" variation are distinguished from the "secular trend." Time series analysis is not as simple as it might first seem. But it does ordinarily involve an assumption which is not necessary, from the propositions suggested by Teggart. As ordinarily used in research time series analysis requires a notion of functional continuity: a line is fitted over the entire series. The idea of eventful change permits the possibility of fitting one kind of line (say a straight line) up to year X, after which another kind of line (say a second degree parabola) can be better fitted. There is nothing fundamentally inconsistent, then, between Time Series analysis as an argument, and Teggart's methodological requirements for studying change. All that is needed is an explicit decision regarding the proposition offered by Liebnitz: "Nature never takes leaps."[2] A priori commitment to this proposition determines, to a large extent what answer one will accept when studying change. Although it might be an empirically correct statement, failure to accept the doctrine by Liebnitz does not *require* one to observe gaps in "nature." Neither, then, does it force one to live in a world of buzzing confusion. It does, however, require a rather careful statement regarding how one distinguishes between a "leap" or discontinuity in nature and in paucity of data. In the case of categorical material, not much can be said. But in the matter of mathematical argument, well known traditional tests can be applied: by using the F test, the question "does an alteration of the functional argument at any point reduce variance significantly, or is the reduction within the realm of change explanations?" can be answered.

A second difficulty with the naive use of historical time is the failure to note that certain processes take time without denoting social change. Thus, it take time for a graduate student to learn how to think mathematically; but this passage of time does not imply *social* change. Again, it takes time for marital partners to adjust: but this time does not imply *social* change. These are cases of activity going on in a social matrix. Alas, however, this process time occurs precisely when historical time containing change does occur. Consider the graduate student who is learning mathematical thinking in the social sciences: while he is learning what has been used before and is used today, some changes are being made in the subject matter itself. Care must be taken not to confuse the two kinds of time which are analytically distinct. For the most part, we are here concerned with historical, not process, time.

A third difficulty flows from starting at a given time and looking back. Teggart[3] asserted that this forced history into a narrative which predetermined the outcome of the inquiry. Consider an example not offered by Teggart: an old man dies. Apparently we can look back on his life and discern several basic "stages" through which he passed. We note infancy, childhood, adolescence, young manhood, middle age, and old age. These seem natural and necessary; similar stages are seen in "biology." But these "stages" are all *after the fact.*

Begin, not with death, but with birth: what *necessary* stages are seen now? None can be seen, for there are no necessary stages. Death is as much a natural process as is life; is the consequence of natural causes as much as is the continuation of life. If one alters conditions, one alters the consequence. There are no "stages," but "states." In certain spheres of activity, one cannot enter state X_7 without having been in state X_6, nor can an object in state X_7 return to state X_6—as in biological maturation. In other spheres, being in state X_7 does not imply ever having been in X_6; or, if one were in X_7, having passed through X_6 deny the possibility of returning to an earlier state. Consider an example from race relations: if X_7 is "Accommodation" and X_6 is "War," having achieved accommodation after having been at war does not preclude the possibility of returning to a state of war.

We here will attempt to describe five major "states" regarding the use of mathematics in the social sciences. Historically, the first one to be described dominated the field some years ago; it still persists, though with less force than before. The second one to be described was the next to dominate the field. If it has given way to the third, the relinquishment of the throne has been recent. Indeed, the "fourth" state may have so quickly succeeded the third that few noted the existence of the third. The fifth state to be noted shows some signs of dominating the future—or of passing from the scene. We are not, therefore, committing ourselves to a revolutionary argument. It happens that we prefer the fifth "state," and would like to see the day when the social sciences are characterized by it. This preference, however, does not permit the inference that this will be so. In the sociology of knowledge, it will be clear that the fifth state could not have preceded the others. But the existence of any dominating state does not preclude a return to an earlier state of affairs.

THE FIVE "STATES" OF UTILIZING MATHEMATICS IN SOCIAL SCIENCES

Briefly, the five major states are: (a) Descriptive statistics; (b) Analytic statistics; (c) Formal statistics; (d) Non-parametric statistics; and (e) Substantively parametric statistics. We will describe each in turn.

DESCRIPTIVE STATISTICS

Helen Walker has interestingly accounted for the early history of statistics in the social sciences.[4] The word itself derives from "State" (or "Stadt" in the German) and suggests its origins were in the domain of the social sciences. For a long time, it was basically an enumerative activity, the census being an example of simple enumeration. But this type of statistical work is not without faults: it is almost completely dependent upon the intellectual climate of the times. Thus, the 17th century statistician would gravely note the increasing number of deaths due to "rising of the lights"; and the contemporary demographer of Mexico finds it convenient to classify people according to whether they do or do not wear shoes.

Historically, the interest in probability theory comes from the interest of early western man in gambling. We will only note that aspect in passing. Suffice it here to say that the day-by-day observations of inveterate gamblers were sufficiently accurate to note a difference between outcome and the common sense theory of chance. Sufficiently, that is, to prompt the gamblers to take their problems to mathematicians who noted fundamental errors in assumptions by the common sense idea of chance. What is important here is not the development of theory but the actual use of statistics. As long as everyone who uses the data are agreed upon the propriety of the categories used, simple enumeration generates no trouble. But when a radical change in use occurrs—as in the famous studies by the Webbs[5] in studying poverty in England—then certain problems emerge. When there is disagreement as to the correctness of the classifications employed, the problem becomes explicit.

Historically, when the social sciences began the survey taking business, researchers were unable to employ ready made categories. It was necessary to develop a model for defining categories. Such a model was the "natural sciences"—and particularly, the biological sciences. Here the "theory of classification" apparently was well developed. Certain rules were adopted: To have only one system of classification. To allow each object to fall into one and only one category. To make sure that all objects in the study would be put into its proper category —even if it were only a residual category called "all other."

This system has not been completely followed. For example, today we find some difficulty in working out a system for classifying occupations: the category "farmer" almost always includes "residence," and it is easy to work out a system with more than one basis of classification. The difficulty lay in a philosophical orientation: the original point of view was to describe nature as she was. The original notion of categories was taxonomic. The analytic notion is of recent origin.

Enumerative statistics tended to beg these questions. Those who felt a bit uncomfortable with this kind of statistical argument called survey research "toilet counting" and "pebble picking." To a large extent the name calling was quite accurate. But this was a case in which accuracy did not improve the activity. All that it did was to prevent the critics from seeing the crux of the problem. Intuitively they felt themselves to be correct; but they could not even manipulate the right vocabulary to express their criticism. All that was generated was polemics and harangue. Reputations were established, that is true. But this could have been accomplished by other means.

Those using enumerative statistics sometimes took time out to reply to their critics. Mostly, however, they were busy with problems of their own. For the use of the survey turned out to be another Pandora's Box.

When making comparisons, it turned out that *frequencies* could be misleading. Suppose that for a given year, two cities both had 10 murders committed. But suppose that one had a population of 273 and the other a population 273,000: clearly the observation of "10 murders during the year" would have different implications. So the size of the survey became important, if comparisons were to be meaningful.

At any rate, in the course of arguing the relative merits of the various "measures of central tendency," it became apparent that a single number could not properly summarize a complete distribution. Some notion of the variation had to be developed. One early idea was the range: the difference between the largest and smallest value in the distribution. It is only recently that the distribution of the range has been known.[6] Without this knowledge, judgments about the range were difficult to make. So other measures of "dispersion" were proposed.

One simple-minded idea was to subtract each object's measurement from the mean, then sum these and get the average deviation. Unfortunately, this sum always turned out to be zero. So the old dodge of "signs disregarded" was employed. Although seldom used today, the average deviation, the sum of the differences about the mean disregarding the algebraic sign and divided by the number of objects measured, gives a fairly simple description of how much each member deviates from the basic summary measure. It, too, gave away to another measure.

Hence a need for a summary statement of a lot of data was felt. All sorts of *averages* were developed. The median, that value which found half of the survey being larger and half smaller, was preferred by some. Others thought that the mode—the value which had the largest number of members—was a better average. If the distribution (to use modern vocabulary) was rectangular, a good case could be made for the median; if the mode clearly dominated the distribution, it undoubtedly said something important. These "measures of central tendency" are still employed, particularly in surveys rather than researches to test hypotheses.

They gave way to the "arithmetic" mean: the sum of all quantities divided by the number of objects measured. This measure was more dependent upon extremes than other measures, but it turned out to have certain mathematical qualities—like being normally distributed regardless of the distribution of the basic data—that has resulted in its being the most widely used summary statement of a single distribution. Less known and less used, apparently because too few social science distributions require the assumptions as a model, are the geometric and the harmonic means. Even so, most students are dutifully required to know something about these measures.

The sum of the deviations around the mean was zero because the "plusses and the minusses cancelled" to use a schoolboy's somewhat incorrect accounting. Not only does "disregarding the algebraic sign" prevent this, but squaring the difference also allows the sum to be other than zero. From classical physics, a theory of mathematical moments had been developed. Squaring these deviations was precisely the operation involved in obtaining the so-called second moment. A mathematical argument of developing moments about the mean was easily developed and rapidly accepted. For, as history was to show, the measure of dispersion around the mean also had an interesting statistical distribution. It was an enormously happy moment.

But the users were not any more gifted with foresight than were the critics. The happy discovery that the "normal distribution" was completely described by two and only two numbers cheered research. These numbers were the mean and the standard deviation, as the square root of the second moment about the mean came to be called. Now, the knowledge that these two numbers told all one needed to know about the distribution generated a feeling that a lot of things were normally distributed—height, weight, intelligence, and almost everything else. As if to demonstrate their lack of analytic understanding, the users of "quantification" developed a thing called the "probable error"; this was an adjustment of the standard deviation (soon called "standard error") by a multiplicative constant, which gave an interval which contained 50% of all cases, with the mean in the middle. One seldom encounters the probable error, today.

Indeed, one finds a waning of the demand of getting normal curves. At least, among those who are serious about the use of statistics in modern research, there is a decline in desiring to find a normal curve. Its only advantage today lies in the ease of analysis. But when most quantifiers were busily searching for, adjusting data and obtaining normal curves, the critics were humbled. By this time, the quantifier began to speak a queer language:

$$Y = \overline{\sigma\sqrt{2\pi}} \ e-\frac{1}{2} \ \left(\frac{x-u}{\sigma} \right)^2$$

and of the truth of this there could be no doubt. But many were curious as to why the insistence upon normal curves. This became especially important during the state typified by "analysis."

ANALYTIC STATISTICS

The quantifiers began to feel their oats, as it were. Statistical analysis was the way in which one did research. After all, had not Fisher himself said that statistics constituted "Inductive logic?"[7] By this time, statisticians began to concern themselves with more than one kind of problem: not only the survey description of a single dimension, but the joint distribution of two or more variables. This was accomplished by two devices: chi-square and the straight line. The straight line began to be as popular as the normal curve. And correlation analysis began to be the basic task of modern research.

Correlation analysis had a curious beginning. Initially, the mathematics involved deviations around a "fitted line" clearly analogous to deviations around the mean. Indeed, teachers often point out the similarity to beginning students. The logical argument was to get that line which will insure the sum of deviations being a minimum (i.e., equalling zero). The extent to which this kind of a line reduced variance is the basic idea to correlation; as a matter of fact, this reduction is measured in percentage terms. Mathematically, this notion of developing an analytic argument became known as "the method of moments," and has been contrasted to the "maximum likelihood" argument. The argument is not yet resolved, except for those who adhere to either side.

The "straight line" analysis became popular. Now, the fundamental idea behind "analysis" is that the form of the argument is assumed to be true; the contents of the variable are without question. All that is "unknown" is the existence degree, and direction of the relationship. Data could be analyzed statistically.

We should recur to the development of probability theory. Beginning about the time that von Mises[8] began to challenge the traditional definition of probability, an operational (sometimes called sampling) approach to probability emerged. The importance is in the ability to integrate mathematically a host of previously discrete arguments. Not only did the method of moments show itself to be based upon probability logic, but a host of other distributions than the binomial were shown to be related. A number of distributional families were shown to exist. A general probability theory was developing. The modern developments have since shown that these were really humble beginnings, merely special instances of an even more general theory.

Actually, this argument was not immediately felt by those doing research. Instead, concern over sampling became paramount. The "least squares solution" to the correlation problem could be applied to a finite population; no knowledge of the distribution of the measure of correlation was really needed. When one considered comparing surveys, then all differences appear to be real ones. But trouble begins when one realizes that instead of having an entire population, one merely has a part of it. The question is, "what part of the population which I am interested in do I actually have?" If the answer is, "a randomly selected part," then inferences regarding the parent population became possible.

While the "analyst" contented himself to the feeling that he was inductively testing hypotheses, he became aware that he must have some alternative explanation than the one entertained. In time, this became known as the "null" hypothesis—the indifferent hypothesis of no difference.

One major aspect of analysis became known as "chi-square analysis." Chi-square is an argument which is based upon *frequencies,* or the number of instances of various possibilities. A comparison is made between some system of expected frequencies with "actual" or "observed" frequencies. By and large, the "expected frequencies" are usually ad hocly determined from probability inferences of the marginal totals of the observed frequencies. That this often implies the marginal values as sampling estimations of a parametric value is generally ignored; chi-square is treated as being non-parametric.[9]

Now, any cook-book treatment of statistics will indoctrinate the student, who later becomes a professional researcher, to think that all one needs to do is to test the idea that "there is no association between the variables" being considered. This is called the "null hypothesis"; and, as a matter of fact, really says that the researcher is without any hypothesis—although this is not the strict semantic interpretation of the phrase. At any rate, a generation of social scientists went busily about testing a set of null hypotheses; research designs were replete with hypothetical assertions: "there is no relationship between. . . ." This required a tremendous faith in the power of statistics to generate truths. This was Baconian science epitomized. Here was a technique which was truly independent of the user. Even an idiot could conduct research. Sometimes it seemed as if one had.

The point regarding "analysis" must be considered carefully. Analysis must assume that *something* is true: the something in this case was the appropriateness of the statistical argument. It was explicitly assumed that, since statistics formed a basis for "inductive logic," statistical analysis was the true way which would permit a leap from particular cases to a general statement.

The error is two-fold. First, as a matter of logic, an error existed in the failure to see that any formula is a system of deduction. Francis and Golightly[10] have shown and illustrated the argument elsewhere utilizing chi-square as a vehicle of discussion. The other error is no less serious. It is a failure to distinguish between a summary statement and a generalization. Grammatically, the two statements seem to involve the same form. But the two are different in respect to the inferences which are warranted from either. The summary statement merely asserts what is known from the data at hand: a mean, a chi-square value for a given set of data, the value given to the constant terms of a straight line equation, all these are at least summary statements. To argue as though they represent generalizations is to commit the fallacy of "hasty generalization"—of leaping to conclusions.

Although the distinction is significant, few analysts appreciate the difference. Such argument is dismissed as "philosophizing," or, what is worse, as being "theoretical." Yet the other states which will be considered are predicated upon the assumption that the distinction is real and theoretically important.

FORMAL RESEARCH STATISTICS

There was little time wasted between the "analytic" state and the "formal" state as far as basic operations were concerned. But in terms of orientation, there is still a considerable difference. Many statistical researches are written as though they were research in character when they actually are analytic in spirit. The difference lies in what one means by "induction." As we saw, the "analyst" thought an equation forced a generalization to leap from discrete facts. The formal researcher knew otherwise. He states his hypotheses and the statistical design for testing his hypotheses *before* the test.

In an attempt to be rigorous in testing hypotheses instead of ad hoc analysis, a change of spirit was manifest in the social sciences. This will become doubly important in the final "state" to be considered. It begins with considering alternative explanations. There are, from the vantage of statistics, at least two explanations for any observation of a repetitive event: either chance or something else. It will usually turn out that "something else" is really a set of alternatives and that, finally, in sub-categories of the "correct" alternative a chance factor remains (i.e., that error is never reduced to zero).

In attaching his faith to the "null hypothesis," the run of the mill researcher was showing a lack of understanding of the major statistical theorists. Like any innovator—like Pavlov with his animal experimentation in psychology, and Freud in psychoanalysis—important statisticians like Pearson, von Mises, "Student," Schnedecor, and the other leaders had a following who imitated but did not ken the thrust of statistical logic. The argument of the critical ratio, for example, was a standard piece of equipment of the analyst. Sampling was seen as simply another way to test the null hypothesis.

But when careful thought was given to over-all design; to wondering where hypotheses came from; to recognizing that a considerable body of empirical findings was established; the logic of such things as the critical ratio began to attract attention. Mathematically, an enormous change occurs in noting the difference between "point estimation" and "interval estimation." The former was of special interest in surveys, where measurement is the proper task; the latter is more important in testing substantive hypotheses.

Possibly the greatest single step in clarifying the distinctions came with noting the existence of two possible errors.[11] Now, western man had long known there were the two kinds of sins—the sin of omission and the sin of commission. It took some time and doing for quantifiers to recognize the same thing. These became known as "Alpha error" (or "error of the first kind"; or "Type II error"). This is semantically sad: the word "error" is used to mean something else

in statistical literature (standard error). But this is no cause for dis-
comfort.

The alpha error is the rejection of a true hypothesis; the beta error
is the acceptance of a false hypothesis. Stated this way, the issue is
simple enough. But this becomes somewhat difficult to follow when
the statistical hypothesis is the "null" one, and the scientific hypothesis is at least contrary (but not necessarily contradictory) to the
null one. Hence, rejecting a true (null) hypothesis *seems* to be the
same as accepting a false (substantive) hypothesis. It is no surprise
that many students get the two confused. The issue gets complicated
when one introduces the problem of measuring the probability of
committing either of two errors. Suffice it to say here, if one truly
believes chance as the explanation, then he is required to minimize
the likelihood of the "beta" error. Etc.

This distinction is important because it requires a way of thinking
which virtually destroys the analytic use of statistics. Theoretical
issues arise which must be decided prior to the actual research. Consider the "alpha error"; traditionally, in sociology we have accepted
the "five per cent level of significance." In psychology, we have accepted the "one per cent level." Why either level? In the industrial
world, the level of significance is often decided in terms of the cost
involved the higher the cost, the smaller the probability of the alpha
error is accepted. Something similar seems to be true in science
(except that the cost is more difficult to measure). But certainly, a
hypothesis the truth of which would upset the basis of a science
ought to require a more costly entrance ticket than a hypothesis the
truth or falsity of which has little theoretical significance.

The mathematical operations of analytic and formal statistics are
precisely the same. Usually, the thought processes alone differ. Or if
not, then the acceptance of intellectual honesty seems to suffer.

Most modern statistical texts distinguish between descriptive and
inferential statistics. I wish I could happily report that most social
scientists are properly using inferential statistics. More and more of
them are doing that, but a very simple-minded operationalism still
persists. And "simple minded operationalism" is simply another way
to describe statistical analysis.

One way of stating the difference is this: formal statistical inference
requires the use of a priori hypotheses; analytic statistics involves the
use of the ad hoc hypothesis. There is really nothing wrong with

the ad hoc hypothesis—if it is properly labeled and the user does not think he has *tested* any empirical statement.

As the mathematical theory underlying statistics in the social sciences became more and more complex, requirements for statistical inference become more and more rigid. It is true, the analytical use of statistics might pretend that these requirements are not serious. But as a system of logic designed to permit the researcher to arrive at necessary inferences, the requirements for inference must be met.

An example of the increasing complexity of modern statistical work is found in the work called "the analysis of variance."[12] The name of this activity seems to suggest belonging to that state called "analysis." Many researchers have used anova in an analytic way. But if one seriously means to draw generalizations from the "analysis of variance," as distinct from using this as a summary statement of an ad hoc solution to a set of historical data, then anova must be regarded as a set of inferential rules. To use anova as a set of rules, the mathematical assumptions must at least square with the operations performed.

The price of rigor comes high. Sloppy research does not warrant rigorous inferences. It is not a matter of having a good statistical argument. It is a matter of having research operations correspond to theoretical assumptions. It is a matter of having substantive hypotheses prior to the acquisition of data. It is the difference between analysis and inference, when the latter is something more than a classroom game.

The primary distinction between analytical statistics and formal statistics lies, as we said, not in the operations performed but in the spirit of inquiry. Analytical statistics is used to denote that "research activity" best characterized by a concern for technique; formal statistics is more concerned with the theoretical problem. The *logical character of the statistical argument dominates the attitude towards statistics in the state called "formal statistics."*

Clearly, there are still those whose orientation to research begins with a technique. Problems are selected because they fit (or very nearly do) some technique. A kind of fadism does pervade the analysts;[13] status is achieved by a demonstration of ability to use a modern technical device. Methodological problems sometimes are viewed as technical ones. Theoretical issues are ignored, if considered at all. A contemporary example of this sort of orientation is found in a paper offering a short-cut way to create indices.[14] This is done by transforming raw data into ranks. Then the ranked data are put into an arbitrary distribution that is "almost normal"; at least the mean and the variance is constant for any distribution. Correlation then depends only upon cross products. The fact that a skewed distribution is forced into a "normal" curve is highly regarded as a clever way to reduce computational time. What happens to one's problems is of no concern: one begins with a concern for technique, not with solving theoretical problems. "Analysis" has not entirely disappeared; it persists and will find acceptance by many yet to come.

NON-PARAMETRIC STATISTICS

The thrust of modern sampling lies in mathematical statements describing the theoretical distribution of those numbers used in making summary statements—as a mean summarizes a set of data; as does a variance; as does the slope of a line, as does every statistic used descriptively. These numbers (for any set of data, they are "constant," but for all possible sets, can "vary") are called "parameters" if they have a distribution—if, themselves, they have an expected value and measurable variation when one deduces simply from the theory of probability.

It is the estimation of parameters that requires the most stringent set of assumptions. Sometimes the researcher thinks in terms of either analysis or inference, but finds that he cannot meet the assumptions of a parametric statistic as in the analysis of variance. What is he then to do? Quit and go home? Pretend that the assumptions really are not important? Or develop an argument which is independent of any theoretical distribution?

The latter generates the "non-parametric" statistic. We have already encountered chi-square. Although this often involves some theoretically defined estimation of probability, the distribution of chi-square is independent of the source of definition of theoretical probability. Chi-square is a function of the number of "degrees of freedom" involved in its computation; roughly, it depends not upon the size of the sample, but more upon the number of categories used on the analysis.

A host of non-parametric statistics exist today. Most of these are based upon a simple transformation of data: the ranking operation. Sometimes the data come to the scientist in the form of ranks.

Spearman's rank order correlation is, perhaps, the most widely known statistic of this sort.[15] Friedman's chi-square of ranks[16] is gaining in popularity and has been used in a variety of problem areas. The Mann-Whitney "U-test" and similar statistics, have been used with apparently good results in psychological research.

In a manner of speaking, many so-called "parametric" statistics have been used as though they were non-parametric in character. When the sociologist studies class differences and establishes this through a critical ratio of mean annual incomes, the *mean* is *statistically* a parameter. But from the point of sociology, it has no theoretical status. There is nothing other than a vague operational specification of the concept purportedly being measured by income. No one really believes that an average income of "$5,478.35" says anything interesting to sociology. The statistical parameter is not a theoretical one.

Consider the present status of variance in sociological research. Suppose that a person has "measured" attitudes towards negroes; and, further, intends to test the hypothesis that "there is no difference between lower class southern whites and college educated northern negroes." Aside from the ridiculous use of the word "hypothesis," which is not at all uncommon, this seems like a good statement to test. But do we not seriously attach a theoretical value to any reported mean attitude score. We do not have faith enough in the measuring device to elevate it to theoretical status. But we will use a critical ratio, and test the difference between means.

We ignore the other parameter, the variance.[17] It could well be true that one group (perhaps the college educated northern negro) has a higher consensus regarding Negro status than the other. This could be tested by the F ratio. But we are disinclined to do so: because we have, for the most part, failed to give statistical parameters any theoretical meaning. We use the most powerful statistics heuristically. Even when we have a priori hypotheses, when we use statistics inferentially, we are disinclined to attach any real importance to our statistical parameters.

The social sciences have, for the last two or three generations, thrown away at least half of their most important information.

Not all have been happy about this. Many have been struck with the way in which summary statements *look* like laws. Many have been impressed with the developments of inferential statistics; many have been unhappy about developing only ad hoc hypotheses, with analytic statistics. More and more are beginning to propose mathematical models for the social sciences. This will be the final state to be considered.

THE SUBSTANTIVELY PARAMETRIC STATISTIC: THE MODEL

The history of the model does not begin in the last few years. The mathematical model has had a rather long history, considering its recent acceptance by younger social scientists. Stuart Dodd, with his ill-fated "S-curve,"[18] was an early pioneer in the model-building business. Part of the failure of the S-curve to catch on might be due to the situation in which it was proposed. Mostly, however, its failure stems from lack of theoretical contact. It was developed whole-cloth. It had no history. It was an unwarranted intruder.

The "Simons-Homans" model[19] enjoyed some recent prestige. But this was not a model in any real sense. This was simply the employment of mathematical form for logical clarity. Nothing new was added; indeed, some original assumptions became strained, and a lack of operational contact with the real world must be noted. It is important, however, in that it excited a group of youngsters and showed that mathematical logic was not the sole property of the physical sciences.

An early attempt to make a workable model, with operational specification for testing ideas, was the Stouffer argument in respect to migration.[20] Both the theoretical and empirical criticisms are too well known here to require comment. But the idea of deducing the form of a mathematical line is a powerful one. It is too bad that insufficient attention was paid to bring this model in line with theory.[21]

There have been other attempts to depict mathematical models. One notable example is that of Wiener.[22] This "attempt" is almost completely devoid of sociological thought. It is almost completely sterile. For the most part, the same results could be achieved by taking a textbook in differential equations and giving social science sounding names to various variables. The gamesmanship spirit finds this a happy exercise. But the person who seriously seeks to solve problems of considerable importance in contemporary social science must find this hard to take. The critics of "mathematization" have a field day; this type of argumentation is scarcely defensible. The defenders of "mathematization" are even more disturbed: this has the *form* of their argument, but not the content. To them, this use of mathematics is not really different from what a charlatan would do.

All sorts of subtleties creep into the problems of employing a mathematical logic. Many attempts to seem erudite and precise have involved the use of the differential equation. Few of those who have made these attempts have realized that the differential is predicated upon the notion of causation—a mechanical notion—that existed in Newton's day. The idea is simple: let X increase ever so little and then mechanically and instantaneously a change occurs in Y. Not all of those who use differential equations like to employ notions of mechanical causation in respect to human behavior.

Other attempts to develop models have been more promising. The field of population contains more good examples than others. As long as these models have been demographic in character—as the Gompertz death curve—they have not been social science models in the strictest sense of the word. Sagi[23] has made a serious attempt to bring demographic model building in line with sociological theory.

This requires a formal statement of the model, as distinct from other research operations. The model differs from "curve fitting" in that the fitted curve is always ad hoc. The *form* of the line in the case of the model follows from the definitions which are stated, and the conditions which are admitted. If these primitive ideas have theoretical commitments, then the resulting inference has the status of a model. It then is tested, and data are "fitted to the model" to see how appropriate the model actually is. Science does not trust mere deduction in building models. Many previous efforts in demography have looked like models because the form of the curve follows from the assumptions: but unless these assumptions are grounded in an empirical science, the result is not, properly, a model.

Perhaps the attempt that most completely conforms to these specifications of a model is that of the Mosteller-Bush stochastic model for learning.[24] In that instance primitive terms are defined, and shown to fit into "theory." Mathematical deductions are made: a form of the curve is required. Then operational specifications are attempted (the argument is weakest at this point), and the model submitted to empirical test.

The model has a scientific "ring" to it. There is something missing in the ad hoc solution: it cannot be false. It merely summarizes a set of data. But modern science requires that hypothesis must be capable of being shown to be false. If it cannot be falsified, it is not subject to test. The fitted curve is "right"; *any* set of data can have the "best" straight line. The model, however, can be wrong. It can be tested and found wanting.

Most contemporary thinking has put the "model" in terms of quantification. Yet a fundamental assumption of the social sciences has long the desirability of "if A, then B" statements. While a considerable confusion has existed regarding this endeavor,[25] there is no reason why logical forms cannot be regarded as models. Indeed, a recent study on bureaucracy has shown the feasibility of using the logical form as a model in precisely the same sense as the mathematical model.[26] This model can be tested by the ordinary statistics of chi-square or critical ratio of proportions.

What the model requires is simple: both the content and the form of the argument must have theoretical relevance and a theoretical requirement. At this point the polemic of theory, research, and mathematics disappears. They are all seen as different aspects of a total activity.

A BRIEF SUMMARY

The basic states of statistical inquiry all co-exist at the present time. It is perhaps safe to say that "inferential statistics" shares the spotlight with analytical statistics. The thrust of modern thinking seems to be tending towards the creation of models, both mathematical and the more traditional categorical logic in form.

Historically, description was the initial type of activity, and dominated research for a long time. The objectors to it intuitively felt a sterility to this as "science," although they were without the proper vocabulary to argue correctly. Then as this new kind of operationalism began to develop a formal mathematical theory, substantive theorists were quite helpless, except to plea "no, no, a thousand times, no."

The new priesthood felt its power, though their strength was some time in coming. But as "empiricists," originally (apparently) in defense of their new-found activities, looked askance at "theorizing" and "philosophizing," research became a quest for normal distributions and straight lines. The weaker minds contented themselves with chi-square analyses.

There is a saying, "If you can't lick 'em, join 'em." Some social scientists, with a theoretical bent, looked closely at this new way of thinking. They looked hard at the changes in other sciences. And they noted the possibility of incorporating mathematical argument with substantive theory. They found that they did not have to subvert the problem for the technique. Ad hoc analysis need not dominate thinking; statistical inference could be used to test substantive hypotheses.

In fighting about the assumptions required for rigorous inference, attention was called to the distribution-free statistics, the so-called non-parametric tests. This called attention, or, rather, renewed interest in looking at research measures in terms of theory. Substantive research had not used the "parametric" statistical test with any real commitment to the existence of the "parameter." When one raised the question as to the "existence" of the parameter in theory, the use of statistical forms as models became apparent. And if one could use a mathematical form as a model, it became apparent that one could also use a more traditional form of logical argument as a model.

Whether the future sociologist of knowledge will be able to report the fifth state as ever characterizing social science remains to be seen. But the possibility is real. The probability is greater than zero. At the same time, an anti-intellectualist revolt could conceivably reduce social science inquiry to that curious state of affairs known as "descriptive statistics." Even the modern statistician finds his viscera tightening at the thought of toilet-counting.

SELECTED BIBLIOGRAPHY

Thomas C. McCormick, *Elementary Social Statistics* (New York: McGraw-Hill & Co., 1941). An outstanding book giving, in a form understandable by the average social science graduate student, an excellent presentation of basic statistical argument. Can be used as a summarization. A bit old in terms of modern terminology; but, for that reason, communicates well to social scientists.

Wilfred J. Dixon and Frank J. Massey, Jr., *Introduction to Statistical Analysis* (New York: McGraw Hill Book Corp., Inc. 1951). Rapidly accepted as a standard text, this took is more advanced, both in symbols and adherence to statistical argument, than the McCormick one. Hardly usable as a beginning book, since some sophistication in manipulation of symbols is required, whether the authors recognize this or not.

A. C. Rosander, *Elementary Principles of Statistics* (New York: D. Van Nostrand Co., Inc., 1952). A highly usable text beyond the real introductory level. Many excellent books are "elementary" in respect to statistics, but not from the point of view of students nursed on non-statistical theory of many social sciences. This is one such book. For the "second course," this is excellent. If the instructor loves his task, however, this can be used for the first book.

A. L. Edwards, *Statistical Analysis for Students of Psychology and Education* (New York: Rinehart and Co., 1946, revised 1955). An outstanding book, including (in a revision) a chapter on simple mathematics designed to alleviate fear and teach some fundamentals. This is clearly a book grown out of teaching social science majors and has tremendous value for that reason.

Quinn McNemar, *Psychological Statistics* (New York: John Wiley & Sons, 1949). This is the kind of text book that graduate students in the social sciences are willing to read. Often an excellent development of statistics fails in its ability to reach those who need it most. McNemar's book is exemplary in its ability to contact graduate students.

P. G. Hoel, *Introduction to Mathematical Statistics* (New York: John Wiley & Sons, 1947). An excellent, if elementary treatment of mathematical statistics. Develops the "method of moments" which, while not in current vogue, is easily grasped by most students. Requires relatively little mathematical sophistication.

Alexander M. Mood, *Introduction to the Theory of Statistics* (New York: McGraw-Hill Book Co., 1950). Those who desire more sophistication than Hoel's volume, and especially like to see an introduction to the "Maximum likelihood" argument will find this an outstanding contribution. No one seriously in the business of teaching statistics ought exclude this from his library.

G. Udney Yule and M. G. Kendall, *Introduction to the Theory of Statistics* (London: C. Griffin and Co., 1937). A classic. A must. No social science student can be considered adequately trained unless he understands the material covered by the first five chapters of this volume. A bit rigorous, but there is no harm in that.

J. V. Uspensky, *Introduction to Mathematical Probability* (New York: McGraw-Hill Book Co., 1937). A classic. Requires a sound conception of mathematical analysis, and is not recommended for the novice nor the dilettante. For serious students, it is difficult to imagine ignoring this volume.

W. E. Deming, *Some Theory of Sampling* (New York: John Wiley & Sons, 1950). A good summarization of the major sampling problems and their statistical solutions. Does not require too much preparation; can be understood by a well trained social scientist.

G. W. Snedecor, *Analysis of Variance* (Ames, Iowa: Iowa State College Press, 1934). Anyone seriously considering analysis of variance would be a fool to ignore this volume.

R. A. Fisher, *Statistical Methods for Research Workers* (Edinburgh: Oliver and Boyd, 8th Edition, 1941). Fisher has contributed so much to modern statistical thought that some contact with him is mandatory. Other books, perhaps, contain more solid contributions to statistical theory, but for most social sciences none can be more immediately useful.

Mordecai Ezekial, *Methods of Correlation Analysis* (New York: John Wiley & Sons, 2nd Edition, 1941). There are those who belittle correlation analysis, but for those who, recognizing the relation between correlation and anova, are not swayed by appeals to fads and traditions, this book is a near must. Like Deming's book on sampling, this book is devoted to correlation and makes an excellent complement to the former. Good cautions for multiple measure analysis are contained in a readable and convincing format.

Margaret J. Hagood and Daniel O. Price, *Statistics for Sociologists* (New York: Henry Holt and Co., 1952; Revised edition). For research workers and students who want to know, in detailed ways, precisely how one can proceed from data to the standard statistical equations employed in sociology, this book has become a must. Shorter than the previous edition (mainly due to the omission of the demographic materials), few sociology students are without this volume. Sooner or later, they get it. Insightful.

Richard von Mises, *Probability, Statistics and Truth* (New York: The Macmillan Co., 1939). While vehemently castigating "philosophers," von Mises proceeds to develop a positivist conception of probability. A major step in breaking the bonds of traditional definitions of probability. A challenge to those who dislike statistics; re-enforcing to those who do. Not that the latter will let the arguments of this book go unchallenged; they will, however, be happy about their task.

William Kneale, *Probability and Induction* (London: Oxford University Press, 1949). A modern philosophical approach to the problems von Mises asserted did not exist. He takes a non-positivist position, while trying to maintain the mathematical developments that flowed from the positivist definition of probability. Not all mathematical statisticians will be sleeping comfortably after reading this book. Nor will many who are already unhappy with statistics find comfort here. Take a dare: read this one.

Roy G. Francis, Associate Professor in the University of Minnesota, received his B.A. (Magna Cum Laude) from Linfield College, M.A. (with honors) from University of Oregon, and Ph.D. from University of Wisconsin (1950). Taught at University of Oregon, Wisconsin, and Tulane Universities. In addition to *An Introduction to Social Research* (with Doby and others) and *Service and Procedure in a Bureaucracy* (with Robert Stone), has published numerous articles in the field of logic, scientific procedure, prediction and other methodological problems.

NOTES

1. Frederick J. Teggart, *Theory and Processes of History* (Berkeley: The University of California Press, 1941), especially from 148 ff.

2. Cited by G. H. Hildebrand (ed.), *The Idea of Progress* (Berkeley: The University of California Press, 1949), 204.

3. Teggart, *op. cit.,* variously throughout the reprinting of "Processes of History."

4. Helen Walker, *Studies in the History of Statistical Method* (Baltimore: The Williams and Wilkins Co., 1929).

5. Beatrice and Sidney Webb published many relatively important works. Those that illustrate the sophistication of their survey techniques include: *Industrial Democracy* (New York: Longmans, Green & Co. 2d ed., 1908), esp. the preface; *History of Trade Unionism* (New York: Longmans, Green & Co., 1920); and their famous nine volume study, *English Local Government* (London: Longmans, Green & Co., 1906-1909).

6. For example, see R. F. Link, "On the ratio of two ranges," *Annals of Mathematical Statistics,* XXI (1950), 112.

7. R. A. Fisher, *The Design of Experiments* (London: Oliver & Boyd, 1937), 8-9.

8. Richard von Mises, *Probability, Statistics and Truth* (New York: The MacMillan Co., 1939).

9. For a general introduction chi-square, see almost any introductory text, e.g., Thomas C. McCormick, *Elementary Social Statistics* (New York: The McGraw-Hill & Co., 1941). For a sound introduction of non-parametric statistics, see F. Stuart Chapin, *Experimental Design in Sociological Research* (New York: Harpers & Bros., Revised edition, 1956).

10. Roy G. Francis and Cornelius Golightly, "On Scientific Inference," *The Midwest Sociologist,* XVII, No. 1, 1955, 27 ff.

11. A good treatment is found in Wilfred J. Dixon and Frank J. Massey, Jr., *Introduction of Statistical Analysis* (New York: McGraw-Hill Book Co., Inc., 1951), especially Chapter 14, "Probability of accepting a false hypothesis."

12. The basis of this was formulated by Fisher, in whose honor Snedecor named the "F-test" (or "F-ratio"). Hence, see G. W. Snedecor, *Analysis of Variance* (Ames, Iowa: Iowa State College Press, 1934).

13. Not necessarily in the mood of P. A. Sorokin, *Fads and Foibles, in Modern Sociology and Related Science* (Chicago: Henry Regnery Co., 1956).

14. Charles H. Coates and Alvin L. Bertrand, "A Simplified statistical methodology for deeloping multi-measure indices as research tools," *Rural Sociology,* XX, No. 2 (June, 1955), 132-141.

15. Thus, see McCormick, *op. cit.,* 191-192.

16. Milton Friedman, "Use of Ranks to Avoid the Assumption of Normality Implicit in the Analysis of Variance," *Journal of American Statistical Association,* XXXII, (1937), 685-701.

17. Demographers have assessed variance in the way suggested here. See the discussion of the Lexis ration in Henry L. Dietz, *Mathematical Statistics* (LaSalle, Illinois: The Open Court Publishing Co., 1927), 152-155.

18. Stuart C. Dodd, *Dimensions of Society* (New York: The MacMillan Co., 1941).

19. Herbert A. Simon, "A formal theory of interaction in social groups," *American Sociological Review,* XVII (1952), 202-211.

20. Samuel A. Stouffer, "Intervening opportunities: a theory relating mobility and distance," *American Sociological Review*, V, No. 6 (December, 1940), 846 ff.

21. Roy G. Francis and Don A. Martindale, "The scientific status of mathematical models and ideal types as illustrated in demographic research," *The Alpha Kappa Deltan*, XXV (1955), 16 ff.

22. Norbert Wiener, *Cybernetics* (New York: The Technology Press, John Wiley & Sons, 1948).

23. Philip C. Sagi, *Mathematical Models for the Analysis of Fertility Data* (Minneapolis: Unpublished Ph.D. thesis, University of Minnesota Library, 1956).

24. Robert R. Bush and Frederick Mosteller, *Stochastic Models of Learning* (New York: John Wiley & Sons, 1955).

25. For example, both George Lundberg and Howard Becker seem to agree that science seeks such statements.

26. An illustration can be found in Appendix IV in Roy G. Francis and Robert C. Stone, *Service and Procedure in Bureaucracy* (Minneapolis: University of Minnesota Press, 1956), 181-183.

PUBLIC OPINION AND PROPAGANDA

Joseph B. Ford

Los Angeles State College

A quarter of a century ago, Walter Lippmann wrote: "Since public opinion is supposed to be the prime mover in democracies, one might reasonably expect to find a vast literature. One does not find it." [1] Today, however, one does find a literature exceeding in quantity, though perhaps not in quality, all of Lippmann's fondest wishes. Sociologists have joined political scientists, psychologists, and a host of other academic and non-academic "communication specialists" in the production of general works and special studies of public opinion, propaganda and related topics.

The result has been, all but literally, a deafening echo of communication. Sifting sounds out of an echo is indeed a challenging task, but any survey of current trends in this field must face such a challenge.

2,558 titles were covered in a bibliography at the end of World War II, and since that time this mass-production has become even more massive. [2] Highlighting the trends, we focus only on the more prominent and paramount aspects.

The chief studies of public opinion may be divided into the theoretical and general treatments, usually including a coverage of propaganda as well, and the more specialized cross-sectional and dynamic inquiries. For propaganda, these may be divided more specifically in terms of the subject matter.

PUBLIC OPINION

Theoretic and General. As in many fields of social science, theoretical and general considerations of public opinion and propaganda are to be found largely in texts. Furthermore, the growing tendency to hit only the lowest-common-denominator in college texts is exemplified, quite pointedly, in texts on public opinion and propaganda.

Nonetheless, several recent texts seem worthy of note, both in themselves and in virture of their theoretic contributions. With the obvious exception of those fitting the anthological model,[3] the most outstanding recent texts are those of Albig, Bogardus, Doob, and Irion.

Albig's *Modern Public Opinion* is a revision of an earlier work.[4] Along with its competent general survey of the history and current developments in research goes the author's own considerate comment on the condition of theory and research, so apt as to be worthy of full quotation:

> "When I contemplate the materials with which I had to work fifteen years ago in constructing my *Public Opinion* of that day and then look at the contributions of the intervening years, I am amazed and encouraged by the energy and productivity of American scholarship, once attention is centered on an area of knowledge. There are the numerous bibliographies which have made unnecessary the fairly extended bibliographies of *Public Opinion*. During the past fifteen years several thousand articles dealing with public opinion, the mass media, and communication have been published. An industry devoted to polling, to the measurement of attitude, and market research, has expanded to a research activity expending not less than $100 million a year. Propaganda has been practiced and studied ad nauseam. The study of mass communication content and effects has been conducted with enormous gusto. And, latterly, we are supposed to have learned a great deal about the theory of communication from the contributions of physical scientists to information theory. During the past decade I have come across thousands of interesting fragments. And yet, when I review what I have learned of meaningful, theoretical significance about communications and about the theory of public opinion, I am not so encouraged. Gross generalization and theory have made little advance during these years. The bulk of research contributions are usually avoided generalizations, and skillful syntheses have been rare. The intellectual climate has been unfavorable to the emergence of logical theory, while the objectively accumulated data are far too fragmentary to provide the basis for much generalization or grand theory." [5]

Bogardus' briefer work[6] is noteworthy for a fuller assessment of the factors entering into the "making of public opinion," especially the somewhat slighted role of personal and primary associations.[7] He thus moves toward an integration of some classic insights of earlier American sociologists into the limited body of basic theory on public opinion. Irion, though a political scientist, does much the same in his own text.[8] Both of these works offer measured attention to the various institutional influences neglected by many sociologists and others hypnotized by concepts of "mass" behavior. Recently the theories—or better, the implied assumptions—of researchers on public opinion seem to have achieved more balance, and works such as these has played an appreciable role in achieving this balance, as have indeed critiques of the sociological conceptual arsenal by sociologists themselves.[9]

On the other hand, Doob's concepts are those of an eclectic psychologist. He starts with a stimulus-response notion of "social behavior," but uses this in a sophisticated and extended form so that he is able to embrace social organization and cultural background in studying and explaining the phenomena of public opinion and propaganda.[10] This leads him to a more or less catholic theory, exploiting a wide variety of psychological concepts. Distinguishing "latent" and "actual" public opinion, he views the actual form as "an attempt to diminish conflict, anxiety, and frustration." Rationalization, displacement through aggressive behavior, or a substitute compensatory activity may result, according to the circumstances.[11] Doob recognizes these and other "crude principles" as only efforts at stating the problem, and his work merits attention as one of the better efforts to order the chaos of data on the psychological side of the equation. The lacunae and ambiguities in his hypotheses exemplify the perils of attacking what Albig calls the basic "logical theory," but Doob at least faces the problem, which so many others evade with compensatory specialization on unrelated and irrelevant details.

Suggestive theoretic frameworks have been attempted in other general works. Powell seeks to develop an "anatomy of public opinion" in terms of power theory. He views public opinion and propaganda as "power phenomena." [12] This typifies a primarily political approach, as do such attempts as that of Ogle[13] to consider public opinion in its relationship to "ideological forces." These recent works continue a great tradition in political science and sociology, but like their forerunners in the writings of Machiavelli, Mosca, Michels, and even Mannheim, they too neglect other facets of the complex-phenomena.

Dubious Orientations. A dubious theoretic orientation is exemplified by a psychologist, George Miller of the Massachusetts Institute of Technology. Miller tends to reduce public opinion, propaganda, and other aspects of communication to their *sub-social* aspects. In his *Language and Communication*, Miller pays lip-service to the truism that "communication, if it is anything at all, is a *social* event," [14] but then proceeds to distribute his coverage as follows: two-hundred and forty-eight pages to what may more properly be called the psychological, phonetic and other *substrata* of communication, and then twenty-six pages to a final chapter entitled "The Social Approach." Whatever may be the role of the substrata, it is doubtful that any adequate theory of communication can be developed from all the conceivable information to be garnered now or later on them alone. The analysis of acoustics, physiology, and other sub-social aspects cannot alone explain this admittedly *social* phenomenon.

At the other end of the spectrum are the works which tend to minimize the role of public opinion and propaganda as minor events, possibly only "speech reactions," in the broad sweep of social and institutional change. Generally, upon close examination, even those works will be found to embrace the phenomena of public opinion in connection with lesser fluctuations in large cyclic movements (as in Pareto, Sorokin, *et al*).

Between these two extremes lie most orientations of the general and special theorists today. Empirical studies are being heaped one upon the other in an ever expanding but ill-assorted conglomerate, but an adequate theoretic frame-of-reference remains the paramount need.

Cross-sectional Studies. The overwhelming majority of empirical studies of public opinion have been *cross-sectional* in that they have tended to focus upon the analysis of *states of opinion* at given times, rather than the processes of formation, influence, and change.

Public Opinion Polls. The most obvious and numerous of these studies have been the so-called polls. These are now so universally known as to be part of popular folklore as well as an area of legitimate scientific concern. Unfortunately, much of the scientific as well as popular evaluation of their worth has been scaled to the relative success or failure of short-term predictions. These predictions have been hazarded by ebullient and often overconfident exponents, and have, in turn led to shallow and purely hypothetical explanations when the incorrect guess-work has to be supplemented with *ex post facto* patchwork.

Actually, polling methods are but one aspect of a wide assortment of methods of studying attitudes and opinions. Without embarking on a history of attitude-studies, we may note that over the past decades methodologies have been refined from the pioneer efforts of the 1920's (Bogardus, Thurstone, *et al*) to procedures and techniques adapted to gauge virtually a whole gamut of political, economic, and other social conditions and events.

Polling of public opinion has a long history. In the United States, "straw votes" are recorded as early as the first quarter of the 19th Century. Nationwide polls on presidential elections achieved prominence under the aegis of the *Literary Digest*. The Digest poll, though not the first or only one, enjoyed almost sole dominion of the field from 1916 to 1932 but collapsed utterly in 1936 when it predicted a landslide for Landon.

During the same decade, the modern "scientific" polls, utilizing standard statistical sampling procedures, came into vogue. These received a severe setback in 1948. All the major polls erred in predicting a victory by Dewey, but some consolation was found in that the percentage error of the Digest Poll or '36 (*circa* 20%) was reduced to a mere 5% in the case of the Gallup and Crossley polls of '48.[15] Though battered and bloody, the heads of the pollsters remained unbowed, and their work continued with somewhat shaken but not yet shattered popular and even scientific support.

Polling procedures are today applied on a large scale, not only to political matters, but to opinions and attitudes toward purchases, housing, and other aspects of "market research." Pollsters have inquired also into opinions on virtually every aspect of socal life, often utilizing the personnel organized initially for political inquiries. Some of these ventures have carried them outside the pale of public-opinion research as such, but have always retained at least some peripheral contact.

Current trends in polling include a constant refinement of techniques as well as their application to these manifold spheres. No summary could do justice to the technical developments, but those interested in these may refer to any of several excellent longer works.[16]

Broadly, despite the improvements, the true situation of public opinion polling even a decade later may perhaps be found in the statement of the Committee appointed by the Social Science Research Council to investigate the errors of the pollsters in the 1948 election. This committee indicated that "the pollsters over-reached the capabilities of the public opinion poll as a predicting device" and had been "led by false assumptions into believing their methods were much more accurate than in fact they are." [17]

This seems a reasonable position and recognizes the limited predictive value of the polls, while leaving unanswered the question of whether the attempts at specific prediction offer a real test of the true value of such procedures.

Like other research-techniques in social science today, these polling devices have operated on certain fundamentally *static* presuppositions and in connection with largely *structural* rather then dynamic theoretical assumptions. Thus, even the weak explanations of the pollsters in 1948 (i.e, that there had been a sweeping last-minute shift in opinion) recognized the ever-present dynamism of their object of study, and betrayed on the other hand the superficial level on which they are willing to admit this dynamism.

Once the refined and improved polling techniques are utilized fully in connection with dynamic hypotheses, one may expect a richer body of meaningful empirical data to emerge from them.

The Dynamics of Public Opinion. This contrast between cross-sectional and dynamic approaches to public opinion is suggested by Kimball Young, who notes that we may either view public opinion "cross-sectionally, that is, in terms of the convictions on public issues at a given point in time" or else "dynamically in terms of the interactional processes involved in the formation of a consensus or common opinion." [18]

But, the dynamics of public opinion should be considered far more broadly. Dynamic studies should embrace all the factors in the initial formation, the source, and the shifts in public opinion, as well as the role of public opinion itself in social change and control. But the few dynamic studies made to date embrace, at best, only a small portion of this vast and vital area of concern.

Herbert H. Hyman and Paul B. Sheatsley in "The Current Status of American Public Opinion" [19] recognize the *ephemeral* character of most of the polling data and seek to find beneath these "occasional data which reveal the underlying characteristics and nature of American public opinion." In this, they excel their colleagues by assorting and integrating these data into a "collective statistical partrait." Still their task is limited to what can be achieved with the data on hand. The limitations are exemplified in the very title of "status" as used to describe a type of phenomenon which, as even the most redoubtable pollsters attest, can shift beneath their feet during the week-end before election. On the other hand, if the authors are seeking to delineate, as they also say, "some of the basic beliefs and ideals of the people" as seen even in the "fluctuating votes"—then, this is not a matter of the "status of public opinion" as such, but of the deeper values in the folkways, mores, value-systems, or whatever we may label them.

Many general and special works treat the psychological and social processes in the formation and changing of opinion, the effect of censorship, authority, leadership, and the mass-media, and so on. Some of the studies of the effects of propaganda have also cast considerable "reflected glory" on the processes of public opinion (e.g. those of Merton, Lazarsfeld, and others discussed later). But, by and large, the dynamics of public opinion constitute a much neglected field, especially when contrasted with the immense production of studies of cross-sectional aspects.

The meaningful study of dynamics must accompany and make possible the further development of basic theory. For this, added historical and comparative studies are clearly in order. Some comparative value and conceptual clarification may also be found in anthropological materials, as already attempted by Mead. It is extremely doubtful if these cross-cultural comparisons can illuminate greatly the far more complex processes in civilized societies, but they may be of real assistance, as she states, "in helping to clarify, sharpen, limit and enlarge the instrumental concepts which are being used in the analysis of our own society." [20]

Narrative Accounts of Propaganda. The crowded years of World War II and the post-war period have witnessed a tremendous increase in the already ample descriptions of specific instances of propaganda and accounts of activities of leading propagandists (e.g. Goebbels). All of these writings, taken together, have contributed little to the understanding of propaganda, though some of the better ones do illustrate its potency, if further evidence were needed for that. All in all, the judgment made a generation ago by Doob still fits today:

> "The truly voluminous and sometimes inspiring literature on the subject of propaganda has confined itself largely to the method of narration. Either with gusto or with groans of despair, most authors have deposited choice illustrations of propaganda between the covers of their books. Unfortunately these writers have become too engrossed in their stories to explain the implications or to analyze the subtleties of the propaganda they have been describing." [21]

Psychological Techniques. Many psychologists have analyzed propaganda in terms of the techniques employed by the propagandist and the psychological processes presumed to be wrought in the audiences. Thus, Doob's own principles, as stated in his two main works, involve the analysis of the technical side of the propagandist's art in terms of key psychological concepts congenial to his own approach. Technique-analysis by other psychologists likewise has tended to reflect the varying orientations of the writers. Brilliant analyses have been made in psychoanalytic terms, in Gestalt terms, in behavioristic terms, and of course more frequently in the catholic terminology of Doob's later work. But these analyses have abounded in interesting details while offering few illuminating hypotheses.

Sociologists, on the whole, have paid less heed to the tactical employments. Yet two sociologists contributed the most widely known catalogue of techniques—that used by the pre-war Institute for Propaganda Analysis. In *The Fine Art of Propaganda*[21] Alfred McClung and Elizabeth Briant Lee set forth their famous list of key devices. These were seven in number: Name-Calling, Glittering Generality, Transfer, Testimonial, Plain Folks, Card-Stacking, and Bandwagon. In a later work, Alfred Lee revised this classification somewhat and notes at the same time the inadequacy of a purely technical analysis unless it is made in relationship to other "approaches."[23]

The truths of Lee's newer position is evidenced by the fact that those specializing solely in the analysis of techniques have contributed little more than the narrators. Technical and tactical analyses can be of great value, when linked to the study of broader features, but otherwise tend to offset this value by distracting from the main issues.

One source of confusion has been the effort to develop generalizations solely on the tactical level, when in practice propagandists vary their tactics in accord with varying strategies and objectives. Generalizations on propaganda-tactics are surely within the realm of possibility, but not if the tactics are conceived apart from the central features. The parts must be fitted into the picture.

PROPAGANDA

Effects of Propaganda. The effects of Propaganda have been investigated in two main ways: the case-study method and the experimental method.

Of course, all studies of propaganda have hypothesized—or assumed —some propositions regarding the results. Thus, the analysis of techniques is linked to the consideration of at least the resulting psychological processes. But studies of effects, as such, have either focussed on specific cases, on compiling and correlating cases, or on what have been regarded as crucial experiments.

Case-Studies of Effects. The most comprehensive case-studies have been those of large-scale propaganda, such as Nazi or Communist. There also have been many intensive inquiries into propaganda on a smaller scale, such as Kate Smith's bond-selling marathon.[24] Other studies have compiled data on the effects of specific media, such as radio, motion pictures, or reading;[25] and there have been a few efforts to make comparisons of the effects of various media.[26]

Unfortunately, there have been very few serious attempts to interrelate the case-studies to make a general theory of propaganda and its effects. Those at the text-book or popular levels have been breezy and occasionally informative, but have contributed little to our total knowledge of the subject.

Polling procedures have been used to test the effects of this or that sort of propaganda. Generally, however, the brief replies to polling questions reflect only superficial aspects. Exceptions would be such intensive studies of pressures, cross-pressures, and other factors in the decision-process, as those reported in a work like *The People's Choice.*[27] A few more investigations of this sort would contribute far more than any number of additional barrages of miscellaneous polling data.

Experiments in Attitude-Change. In recent decades sociologists and psychologists have conducted numerous experiments on the effects of propaganda. Unfortunately, most of these have been confined to specialized and frequently artificial situations, and students have been the principal "experimentees." While experimenters have sought to correct this obvious source of bias in the results, the variety of other experimental groups remains quite limited, and these have often been ones subject to authoritarian supervision (e.g., soldiers).

A few attempts have been made to study attitude-change in real rather than artificial contexts, thus approximating in a partially controlled situation the type of facts studied by Lazarsfeld and his collaborators in *The People's Choice.* One of the examples of this is Leon Festinger's *Changing Attitudes Through Social Contact.*[28] Here, a report is made on actual changes in attitudes and behavior taking place during a program designed to change attitudes. In this study, there was also an attempt to differentiate changes coming about through other factors.

Another type of effort to approximate a real-life situation is through the presentation of more than one type of propaganda on the same issue in an effort to sift out the effects of prestige, source-credibility, etc.[29] This aims to correct some of the grosser sources of bias in the usual experiments. However, it still treats attitude-change as an isolated process, rather than as one of a number of behavioral processes in an actual situation.

All this brings to the fore the question, always present in such considerations, of how and in what degree meaningful experiments may be conducted in social science. Whatever may be the future of such experimentation, the results to date have been quite limited. Collectively, however, these experiments do at least serve to demonstrate that propaganda does have effects, even when only trivial instances of such effects can be tested.

None the less, some of the experiments with propaganda are veritable models of experimentation in the social sciences—for example, those reported in Vol. III of the *Studies in Social Psychology in World War II.*[30]

The amazing thing about these experimental materials—despite the more than ample financing of the Research Branch, Information and Education Division, War Department, and the participation of first-rate sociologists, socal psychologists, and statisticians, all collected and reported under a grant of the Carnegie Corporation of New York—is the *utter triviality* of the results. With all these excellent auspices, generous budgetary allotments, and wartime governmental backing, Hovland and his co-experimenters, were able to reveal, for example, that a film, especially designed to show Hitler's intention to attack the U.S.A. after victory over Britain, increased an affirmative opinion on this point from 27% in the "control group" to 36% in the film group.[31] Lest it be thought that this instance represents a biased selection, let us take the summation of the "results of evaluative research" in the author's own words, bearing in mind the high competence and enormous financial and authoritative backing of these experimenters, who were taking advantage of an unprecedented wartime opportunity to experiment *en masse*:

> "The films had marked effect on the men's knowledge of factual material concerning the events leading up to the war.

The fact that the upper limit of effects was so large—as for example in the cases where the correct answer was learned and remembered *a week later*[32] by the majority of the men—indicates that highly effective presentation methods are possible with this type of film.

"The films also had some marked effects on opinions where they specifically covered the factors involved in a particular interpretation, that is, where the opinion test item was prepared on the basis of film-content analysis and anticipated opinion change from such analysis. Such opinion changes were, however, less frequent and, in general, less marked than changes in factual knowledge.

"The films had only a very few effects on opinion items of a more general nature that had been prepared independently of film-content, but which were considered the criteria for determining their orientation objectives.

"The films had no effects on items prepared for the purpose of measuring effects on the men's motivation to serve as soldiers, which was considered the ultimate objective of the orientation program."[33]

This must be viewed as undoubtedly among the *best* studies of this sort. Indeed, the very caution and restraint exercised in the conclusions attest to its quality. If this is the best of the sort, however, what hope does this sort of approach offer for the handling of truly significant data on mass communication? A book that could well serve as a textbook or model of this type of method offers less almost than one would exepct to know from "common sense"—less, that is, save the disconfirmation of some hypotheses (a contribution not entirely without value) and in the cumulation of further empirical evidence that, at least, some propagandic communications *do have effects*.

Content-Analysis. The analysis of communication-content has become a highly refined and systematic pursuit. A substantial literature has emerged. While much of this has to do with topics only indirectly related to propaganda, the content-analyses of propaganda have been numerous, illuminating, and often quite valuable.

Content-analysis may be either qualitative or quantitative, but usually the term is reserved for the "objective, systematic, and quantitative description of the manifest content of communication."[34] Such quantitative content-analysis has been applied to three main types of variables: the characteristics of the communicator (position in the social structure, intentions, interests, etc.); those of the communication itself (techniques, style, trends, etc.); and those of the audience (position in the social structure, personality-factors, reactions, etc.).[35] In all these cases, the focus is still upon the indications in the content itself, but the variety of outcomes and applications is manifest. Indeed, the manifold applications to propaganda alone defy summation here, and one must refer to such a compilation as that of Berleson, which is, even so, only an introduction to this interesting and promising zone of inquiry.

In passing, however, it may be worthy of note that content-analysis has passed the stiff tests for admission as evidence in court under the rules of Anglo-Saxon jurisprudence. In *Language of Politics*, Lasswell and his associates set out to show how studies made of the correspondence between the themes of Nazi propaganda and those of Pelley's *Gallilean* and the Transocean News Agency (two sources of pro-Nazi propaganda) were used as evidence in a trial during World War II for failure to register under the McMormack Act.[36] The tests applied were Laswell's "standards of detection," summarized by him as follows:

"In the *Bookniga* case most of these tests were utilized. The consistency (with Nazi aim) test was applied to the *Auhagen* and *Transocean* material. The paralleling of Nazi themes figured in the *Pelley* case, and the distortion test was used in the preparation of *Transocean* data." [37]

The key problem, however, has always been how to *validate* the results. Most practitioners stress that the analysis must be confined to the manifest content. It would seem that objective validation of the results calls for the correlation of such content-analysis with other research procedures.[38] This is certainly true in the sociological study of propaganda, where the manifest content must be studied in its social context and interpreted in the light of data from other sources.[39]

"The thousands of 'variable' studies of attitudes, for instance, have not contributed to our knowledge of an attitude; in a similar way the studies of 'social cohesion,' 'social integration,' 'authority,' or 'group morale' have done nothing, so far as I can detect, to augment generic knowledge of these categories." [40]

ASSESSMENT

Even so brief a reconnaissance calls for a concluding assessment of the situation. In this phase of social science, as elsewhere, one cannot help thinking of Goethe's:

> "Das Wenige verschwindet leicht dem Blicke,
> Der vorwärts sieht, wie Viel noch übrig bleibt."

The very quantity of the output in recent years highlights all the more vividly how much work remains to be done, because so little of quality is known amidst all this massive quantity. The little that is done seems as naught to what there is yet to do.

So many so-called *variables* have been dissected. There are so many tests of minor changes, as that from 26% to 37% *pro* or *con* an issue after a brief dose of film-propaganda. Yet how many studies do we have of the role of propaganda in major social change? How many studies cast any light upon the *larger* (or indeed even upon the *lesser*) aspects of social control? How many studies embrace a long enough time-span to make possible any but limited *static* insights? How many produce comparisons of data in historical perspectives that would enable us to do so much as hazard genuine generalizations?

Indeed, even with regard to the variables that have been highlighted, how much have we really learned about them? How much of this knowledge is even *susceptible* of generalization? How much of it is even sufficiently unambiguous to be capable of testing? How much fails of fundamental logical coherence, as well as empirical validity? Somewhat in these terms, Herbert Blumer has recently called attention to the plight of much sociological analysis:

1. *The Avowal Test.* Explicit identification with one side of a controversy.
2. *The Parallel Test.* The content of a given channel is compared with the content of a known propaganda channel. Content is classified according to themes.
3. *The Consistency Test.* The consistency of a stream of communication with the declared propaganda aims of a party to a controversy. The aims may be official declarations or propaganda instructions.
4. *The Presentation Test.* The balance of favorable and unfavorable treatment given to each symbol (and statement) in controversy.

5. *The Source Test.* Relatively heavy reliance upon one party to a controversy for material.

6. *The Concealed Source Test.* The use of one party to a controversy as a course, without disclosure.

7. *The Distinctiveness Test.* The use of vocabulary peculiar to one side of a controversy.

8. *The Distortion Test.* Persistent modification of statements on a common topic in a direction favorable to one side of a controversy. Statements may be omitted, added, or over- or under-emphasized (for example).

In the light of present trends, what does the future promise? Probably, for the present, much more of the same. More highly refined experiments, telling us little either new or important. Improved and more extensive content-analyses, increasing our already valuable store of data in this one vital sub-area, but limited in value because the area is at present an island of clarity in a sea of confusion. More and more polls on more and more subjects, extending our thin veneer of superficial knowledge of some of the outcomes of the processes of public opinion. Of all this, and more akin to it, we can be fairly confident.

But all this cannot add much of value to the present miscellany unless these studies are integrated into meaningful contexts of theory. Nor can this theory be meaningful if the hypotheses, whose tests shall contribute to it, and the frames-of-reference, in terms of which it shall develop, are not broad enough to embrace historic and comparative analyses. Knowledge of the ephemeral and the static must be supplemented with investigation of *dynamic realities over longer spans of social time.*

Above all, the development of meaningful hypotheses regarding important aspects of public opinion and propaganda, in their historical and contemporary settings, must take place in the light of the role of these in *social control* and *social change*—two old-fashioned branches of sociology too much slighted in recent years. Some of the insights of pioneer researchers in these realms may stand us in good stead as anchorage-points in the vast sea of confusion where the many pilots (and their "pilot-studies") seem to have led us. But that, as Kipling would have it, is another story.

SELECTED BIBLIOGRAPHY

William Albig, *Modern Public Opinion* (New York: McGraw-Hill, 1956). A well-known text; good on theoretical aspects.

Bernard Berelson, *Content Analysis* (Glencoe, Ill.: Free Press, 1952). A systematic approach.

Serge Chakhotin, *The Rape of the Masses* (London: Routledge, 1940). The title indicates its exciting but valuable approach.

Ladislas Farago, *German Psychological Warfare* (New York: G. P. Putnam's Sons, 1945). One of the best analyses of World War II propaganda.

Leon Festinger, *Changing Attitudes Through Social Contact* (Ann Arbor: University of Michigan Press, 1951). A provocative effort to apply a theoretical approach.

G. I. Hovland & A. A. Lumsdaime & F. D. Sheffield, *Experiments on Mass Communication* (Princeton University Press, 1949). Quite original in its approach.

Alex Inkeles, *Public Opinion in Soviet Russia* (Cambridge: Harvard University Press, 1952). Quite original.

F. C. Irion, *Public Opinion and Propaganda* (New York: Crowell, 1951). A systematic summary of the most pertinent literature.

E. Katz & P. F. Lazarsfeld, *Personal Influence* (Glencoe: Free Press, 1955). As other studies by the same authors, quite suggestive.

Paul Kecskemeti, *Meaning, Communication, and Value* (University of Chicago Press, 1952). Stresses the theoretical side.

Ernst Kris & Hans Speier, *German Radio Propaganda* (New York: Oxford University Press, 1944). Altough somewhat outdated, still a good analysis of the workings of war propaganda.

H. D. Lasswell & Nathan Leites & Associates, *Language of Politics: Studies on Quantitative Semantics* (New York: Stewart, 1949). A heavy theoretical going, but most important for its hypothesis.

Robert K. Merton, et al., *Mass Persuasion* (New York: Harper, 1946). Good on the application of propaganda to masses.

Mildred Parten, *Surveys, Polls, and Samples* (New York: Harper, 1950). Excellent in its critical approach.

H. H. Remmers, *Introduction to Opinion and Attitude Measurement* (New York: Harper, 1954). An Introduction to the application of statistics.

Joseph B. Ford, Associate Professor of Sociology, Los Angeles State College, received his B.A. with Highest Honors from the University of California, Los Angeles (1937) and his Ph.D. from the University of California at Berkeley (1951); in between he studied at the University of Munich on an exchange-scholarship as an undergraduate, and as a graduate at Harvard and University of Southern California (receiving Master's Degrees from both these latter institutions); also studied law at Southwestern University for one year. During World War II, served in the Navy, primarily as a Japanese Language Officer; after the war continued in government service for several years as a Vocational Counsellor with the Veterans Administration and as a Special Agent in the investigation of war-surplus frauds; also spent several years in business activities before returning to a full-time academic career. Is the author of numerous papers and articles in sociological and other journals and has written extensively on the topics of public opinion and propaganda (the subject-matter of his Master's and Doctoral dissertations); is co-author (with Professor Zimmerman of Harvard) of a work on Social Change (to be published). In 1955-56, did research on Italian towns and cities under a Fulbright Research Grant, having been during that period a Visiting Professor in the Institute of City Planning at the University of Rome.

NOTES

1. Walter Lippmann, *Public Opinion* (New York: Harcourt, Brace, 1922), 253.

2. B. L. Smith, H. D. Lasswell and R. D. Casey, *Propaganda Communication and Public Opinion* (Princeton University Press, 1946). See other figures cited in J. B. Ford, "Is There Mass Communication?," *Sociology and Social Research* XXXVII (1953), 244-250.

3. Two well-selected sets of readings are *Public Opinion and Propaganda,* edited by Daniel Katz et al. (New York: Dryden Press, 1954) and *Reader in Public Opinion and Propaganda* edited by Bernard Berelson and Morris Janowitz (Glencoe: The Free Press, 1950).

4. William Albig, *Modern Public Opinion* (New York: McGraw-Hll, 1956).

5. *Ibid,* v-vi.

6. Emory S. Bogardus, *The Making of Public Opinion* (New York: Association Press, 1951).

7. *Ibid,* Chapters III, VIII, IX, and *passim.*

8. F. C. Irion, *Public Opinion and Propaganda* (New York: Thomas Y. Crowell, 1951).

9. Some of the more important studies and critiques are cited in J. B. Ford, "The Primary Group in Mass Communications," *Sociology and Social Research,* XXXVIII: (1954) 152-8. Greater research-attention is well exemplified in E. Katz and P. F. Lazarsfeld, *Personal Influence* (Glencoe: The Free Press, 1955). Some of the proliferating studies on "small groups" have made peripheral contributions amid many oddities and artificialities.

10. Leonard W. Doob, *Public Opinion and Propaganda* (New York: Henry Holt, 1948); see especially Chapters II through IV.

11. Doob summarizes these and other "principles of public opinion" in *ibid.,* 87-9. The "principles" of propaganda have perhaps a more specific but equally eclectic cast. Cf. also his earlier *Propaganda: Its Psychology and Technique* (New York: Henry Holt, 1935).

12. Norman J. Powell, *Anatomy of Public Opinion* (New York: Prentice-Hall, 1951).

13. M. B. Ogle, Jr., *Public Opinion and Political Dynamics* (Boston: Houghton Mifflin, 1950).

14. George A. Miller, *Language and Communication* (New York: McGraw-Hill, 1951); quote is from Preface, v.

15. Actually, Gallup's own poll had missed the Democratic vote in 1936 by 6.9% —a fact that was forgotten in the clearly demonstrated superiority of even crude sampling techniques to the "shot-gun approach" of the Digest Poll.

16. Among these are: Mildred Parten, *Surveys, Polls, and Samples* (New York: Harper, 1950) H. H. Remmers, *Introduction to Opinion and Attitude Measurement* (New York: Harper, 1954); and a host of others.

17. Social Science Research Council Bulletin No. 60, *The Pre-Election Polls of 1948.*

18. These and other pointed and penetrating remarks on public opinion may be found in Kimball Young's "Comments on the Nature of 'Public' and 'Public Opinion,'" in the *International Journal of Opinion and Attitude Research,* II (1948), 385-92.

19. *In the National Council for Social Studies Yearbook,* I (1950), 11-34.

20. Margaret Mead, "Public Opinion Mechanisms Among Primitive Peoples," *Public Opinion Quarterly,* I (1937), 5-16. Some of the data in this exploratory excursus seem stretched to fit the last.

21. Doob, *op. cit.,* 6.

22. Alfred M. Lee and Elizabeth Briant Lee, *The Fine Art of Propaganda* (New York: Harcourt, Brace, 1939).

23. Alfred McClung Lee, *How to Understand Propaganda* (New York: Rinehart, 1952); see chapters 3-8.

24. For examples of case-studies of large-scale propaganda see Ernst Kris and Hans Speier, *German Radio Propaganda* (New York: Oxford University Press, 1944); E. A. Shils and Morris Janowitz, "Cohesion and Disintegration in the Wehrmacht in World War II," *Public Opinion Quarterly,* XII (1948), 280-315 or Alex Inkeles, *Public Opinion in Soviet Russia* (Cambridge: Harvard University Press, 1950). For a study of Kate Smith's marathon and its effects, see R. K. Merton et al., *Mass Persuasion* (New York: Harper, 1946). Most of these works consider content as well as effects, but none would be considered a content-analysis in the strict sense.

25. Again, as examples, see P. F. Lazarsfeld and F. N. Stanton (eds.), *Communications Research* (New York: Harper, 1949); J. T. Klapper, *The Effects of Mass Media* (New York: Columbia Bureau of Applied Research, 1949); Douglas Waples, et al., *What Reading Does to People* (University of Chicago Press, 1940). All of these consider other effects, as well as those of the propaganda-content.

26. Most studies make some comparisons, or assumptions regarding contrasting effects. Among the few which attack the problem more seriously are Angus Campbell and C. A. Metzner, "Books, Libraries, and Other Media of Communication," in *Public Use of the Library* (Ann Arbor: University of Michigan, Survey Research Center, 1950) P. F. Lazarsfeld and P. Kendall, *Radio Listening in America* (New York: Prentice-Hall, 1948); and Klapper in *op. cit. supra.* Some content-analyses are also relevant.

27. P. F. Lazarsfeld, B. Berelson and H. Gaudet, *The People's Choice* (New York: Columbia University Press, 1948).

28. Leon Festinger, *Changing Attitudes through Social Contact* (Ann Arbor: University of Michigan, Institute for Social Research, 1951).

29. See: C. I. Hovland and W. Weiss, "The Influence of Source Credibility on Communication Effectiveness," *Public Opinion Quarterly,* (1952), 635-50; S. E. Asch, "The Doctrine of Suggestion, Prestige, and Imitation in Social Psychology," *Psychological Review,* LV (1948), 250-56; also revelant is Asch's "Opinion and Social

Pressure" in *Scientific American,* CXCIII, No. 5 (Nov. 1955), 31-35, and H. B. Lewis's "The Operation of Prestige Suggestion," in *Journal of Social Psychology,* XIV (1943), 229-250; and some of the data in R. K. Merton's "Patterns of Influence," in *Communications Research,* cited *supra,* 180-219. The latter, like the work of Festinger, is more of an effort at a "natural experiment" than a designed experimental study of the usual variety. Thus both of these are, in a strict sense, more intensive case-studies.

30. C. I. Hovland, A. A. Lunsdaime, and F. D. Sheffield, *Experiments on Mass Communication* (Princeton Unniversity Press, 1949).

31. *Ibid.,* 38.

32. Underscoring added. If this represents the "upper limit" of the positive results of this research, one can only wish that somehow a small fraction of the ability, finance, and backing might someday be applied to materials better selected for significance and comparative applicability. Even in the hurly-burly of wartime, a comparative or historical study could hardly be less fruitful than this.

33. *Ibid.,* 254-5.

34. Bernard Berelson, *Content Analysis* (Glencoe: The Free Press, 1952), 18. This is the most comprehensive work to date on this topic.

35. I. L. Janis, "Meaning and the Study of Symbolic Behavior," *Psychiatry,* VI (1943), 423-39. A somewhat parallel and more detailed classification is given in Berelson, *op. cit.,* 26-9.

36. Harold D. Lasswell, Nathan Leites, and Associates, *Language of Politics: Studies in Quantitative Semantics* (New York: Geooge W. Stewart, 1949); see especially Chapter IX, "Propaganda Detection and the Courts."

37. *Ibid.,* 177-8.

38. One of the best exponents of content-analysis has made interesting suggestions for inferring validity through "productivity." See I. L. Janis, "The Problem of Validating Content Analysis," Chapter IV, in Lasswell et al, *op. cit.*

39. This theme is more fully developed in Chapter VIII, "Content Analysis," of J. B. Ford, *The Sociological Analysis of Propaganda Campaigns* (Ph.D. Dissertation, University of California, Berkeley, 1951).

40. Herbert Blumer, "Sociological Analysis and the Variable," *American Sociological Review,* XXI (1956), 684. By the same token, the researchers and theorists have not necessarily been even treating or thinking of the same "variables" when conducting their experiments on "attitudes," "opinion," etc. Perhaps they have been barred from success in generalizing by the very lack of a general (logical) fundament. This, too, would apply to other areas of sociology and social science.

ROLE THEORY AND SOCIODRAMA

Jacob L. Moreno
New York University
and
Leslie D. Zeleny
Colorado State College

Since the behavior of individuals is usually "reciprocal action" with a person or persons occupying one or more statuses, *a role may be defined as the human interactions coordinated with the norms of two or more statuses.*[1] To understand role theory one must begin with *culture* and *status*. Some define *culture* as an organization of behavior expectancies and *status* as a unit of these expectancies "de- manding" certain behavior of an individual functionary in a group.[2]

Our definition of a role is different from the one of Linton which considers the role "the sum total of culture patterns associated with a particular status."[3] But many have accepted this definition without realizing that Linton also said that one must recognize the "legitimate expectations of such persons with respect to the behavior toward them of persons in other statuses."[4] Mead, too, declared that, "The indivi- dual possesses a self only in relation to the selves of other members of his social group."[5] Consequently, we believe that any consideration of role must recognize that it is *a system of interpersonal relations in a group*[6] rather than the mere enacting of the expectations of one status.

Another important consideration in connection with role theory is that the human *self* develops through participation in systems of interpersonal relations or roles. "The tangible aspects of what is known as 'ego' (or self) are the roles in which he operates."[7] Accord- ingly, one can define the *self* as the role-taking ability of a person. "A new role—when it is in its infancy—*leans* upon an older role until the time comes when it is able to free itself and operate alone. . . . In the course of time, this new role may become the mother pattern for other new roles."[8] Consequently, the human personality may be conceived as an "action system" built into the human organism "out of the interplay of self and role."[9]

If role theory is even moderately related to the actual facts of social life, the implications for the growth of the role and the human personality are great. It means that more is involved in human learning than the manipulation of symbols. Rather, it implies that *cognition* must be accompanied by *action* in a role, real, vicarious or simulated. Role "perception" and skill in role "enactment" develop hand in hand.[10]

Real action in a role may be called role-taking or "'being' in a role in life itself within its relatively coercive and imperative contexts."[11] Thus, a married man must actually assume the status of a husband and carry into action the expectancies associated with that role. Obviously, the role of a husband can only be activated in relation to the role of a wife. It may be coordinate with the two statuses, but not precisely the same, for the role-taking ability of each of the two selves may not be fully equal to the expectancies of the situation. More than this, the expectancies at best are not sufficiently definitive to provide all the "answers"; consequently, for satisfying role-taking some degree of *spontaneity* or *creativity* is necessary to meet situations which have not been anticipated in the culture or by the two selves. Without spontaneity, a kind of "dead" living takes place based entirely on the "culture conserve" in the two interrelated statuses.[12]

An excellent analysis of the effect of role-taking upon the attitudes and actions of an individual participant has been made by Turner.[13] Participating in role behavior may (1) cause one to adopt the norms of behavior of the other, or (2) cause one to adjust one's behavior to act in a way to conform to the expectancies of the other. Either way of determining behavior has a profound influence upon the self; and the totality of influences has a bearing upon the self and the action pattern of the total personality of each individual involved in the role-playing process. Turner believes that "the fundamental source of social values appears to be the standpoint of the other,"[14] (or of the generalized other) and the norms of a reference group with which one compares himself.

One may go further than role-taking in the development of the self in real situations and *practice* or *play* roles for the purpose of learning more than a "normal" life experience might give by role taking only. When one "plays" a role involving two or more "individual" statuses in a particular group (psychodrama) one is learning "individual" adjustments; but when one "plays" a role involving "collective" representations of norms in two or more "reference groups" or cultures (sociodrama) one is learning understandings with respect to adjustments between or among the cultures of two or more groups. Both types of learning are of great importance; but the *second type* provides the opportunity for individuals to assume the role of representatives of other groups or cultures in practice and, consequently, to understand the attitudes of other groups that he may broaden his insights and/or deal with representatives of other groups and cultures more intelligently. Sociodrama, then, is a means for learning cultural understandings *in depth,* including appropriate actions. In the sociodrama one can play roles for the purpose of exploring, experimenting and developing new concepts of role systems.[15]

Sociodrama, therefore, may be used as a means for exploring relationships between groups by means of role playing. The situations may be those involving relationships, especially issues between local groups or peoples like between capital and labor or Negro and White in a local community or between Arab and Jew or Western Peoples and Russian Peoples in the World Community or even historical situations like the strife in Rome during the period of Augustus. Thus, with the sociodrama one may "bring the cultural order to view by dramatic methods." One may "explore and treat at one stroke, the conflicts which have arisen between two cultural orders, and at the same time by the same action . . . change the attitude of the members of one culture versus the members of the other." [16]

Sociodramatic role-playing is not too difficult to organize when representatives of different groups between which an issue is involved are in an audience or a classroom; but when the cultural backgrounds of an issue are not in the previous experience of an audience or a class, a great deal of preliminary study may be necessary before viewpoints can be properly represented.

It is difficult for young people studying "strange" roles to volunteer to reenact them before a large group; therefore, some form of "warming up" is necessary.[17] The recognition of the situation is a preliminary "warming-up" process; but a class may be divided into many small compatible groups, with the aid of sociometry when possible, to permit each group to re-create the problem in social relationships.[18] For example, each group in the class may reenact the relationships between representatives of various nations in an international dispute in the Middle East over the Suez Canal and other issues. One person or student in a small group may take the position of Israel, another the position of Egypt, another the position of the United States and another the position of the United Nations. This procedure gives *every one* in an audience or a class an opportunity to play a role, to "warm up" to a role, to express feelings spontaneously, to reverse roles, etc. Theoretically, role-playing in small groups can have a marked educational effect upon the development of the self and of the action pattern of the individual or his personality.

Although the interaction in small groups as just described may be considered role-playing, the more formal role-playing and sociodrama is carried on *before* and *with* an audience or class. Volunteer role-players may be obtained from small groups. After a short conference with respect to the "locale" of the interaction and upon the exact nature of the issue to be discussed and/or acted out, the volunteer role players may precipitate a spontaneous discussion or drama which, shortly will involve the whole audience or class.

As the sociodrama unfolds—as the nature of a reality is progressively revealed, the emotions of the audience or class may be deeply aroused; consequently, more and more members may take part in the role playing until nearly every member in the room is involved. Persons who may not have volunteered to play roles at first may wish to take part and even suggest new ways of role-playing which may represent possible solutions to the problem being portrayed.

Through continued role playing, role analysis and replaying for solutions participants themselves may apply or even build ethical standards which apply to the situation. In this way a practical application of ethics may be realized by the participants.

Role theory can be made an educational instrument of great significance when applied in the form of sociodrama. It can *demand knowledge, develop insight into social life* and *produce wisdom*. This result may be obtained with respect to social relationships and roles related to local, national and international issues of the present time or of the past. Thus, the sociodrama may be considered an application of role theory to education in the social sciences and in history.

Persons may play roles of *representative* persons with respect to world *issues*. They may *re-create* the controversy by *playing* the roles actually taken by the real participants. For example, students may play the controversy between West Germans and East Germans with respect to the unification of Germany. Also, role-playing may be

"reversed" so that the participants may "see" the dilemma from two
(or more) different positions or roles and, thus, understand the sentiments felt by the representative persons on both (or several) sides of
an issue. In this manner, those who participate in role-playing exercises
may learn to understand social reality, including the facts involved
and the feelings and aspirations of different groups or peoples as
well as possible solutions to social dilemmas.[19]

Thus conceived, the sociodrama can become an important aid in
helping students understand sentiments and aspirations associated
with great issues of modern times and of history. Some contemporary
international dilemmas which could be recreated sociodramatically
and studied are: the conflict between the Frenchmen and Arabs in
Algeria, the issues between the British and the Cypriotes in Cyprus,
the conflict between Nationalist China and Communist China, the
Arab-Israeli conflict in the Middle East, the West-East conflict, etc.
Today these and many other international issues have become great
dilemmas of our times partly because of the ineptitudes of the representatives of these peoples in their international relations. These
ineptitudes are legion today; they may even provoke the release of
explosive power sufficient to destroy the pattern of Western Civilization, including a significant portion of the people who are now
operating it. One cause of these profound ineptitudes is ignorance—
ignorance of the culture and sentiments of other peoples. Another
probable cause is the possession of distorted ideas with respect to
other peoples. If ignorance and distorted ideas are causes of many
of our miserable failures in international relations, then one approach
to the reduction of current ineptitudes in human relations with respect to peoples and relationships among peoples is to introduce
representatives of these peoples to experiences which promise to reduce ignorance and correct distortions.

The sociodrama, by stimulating actual intergroup relations, can
be used as an instrument for experiencing the views and feelings of
others, thus a basis for more intelligent thinking and acting is provided.

If contemporary world dilemmas can be replayed for analysis vital
problems faced by persons in historical times may be brought to life
too. Kaminsky,[20] for example, directed his students in the "bringing
to life" of the French Revolution and the relationships among nobility, clergy, bourgeoisie, and peasants at the time of the meeting of
the National Assembly on the fateful night of August 4, 1789.

This sociodrama required a careful analysis of such roles as the chairman of the committee to investigate disturbances, a representative of the clergy who deplored the loss of faith among the people, a noble who called for unity among his peers, and a spokesman for the common people (Third Estate) who demanded immediate reforms. The settings were the meeting hall, lobby, and courtyard of the National Assembly building. Student participation and interest was very good. Kaminsky reported that the sociodrama (adapted from a TV program, *You Are There*) contributed to an understanding of the conflicting interests of the different groups involved in the French Revolution as well as to the development of self-confidence and the ability to think in a difficult situaton.

Some issues of history which could be studied by means of role-playing are: the conflict betwen Socrates and the Athenian Senate, the French Revolution, the battle between King John and his nobles, etc.

The efficacy of the sociodrama is predicated upon the validity of the observation that meaning in the mind of an individual is developed when one takes a role in "real life." The converse of this may also be true; i.e., ignorance remains in the mind of an individual to the degree that he does not take or experience roles. One cannot have all experiences, but one can simulate the taking of a role as it is called, play a role. Thus, one who would understand the current Jewish-Arab conflict in the Middle East, for example, can play the role of the Jew in the conflict and then "reverse" his role and play the role of the Arab. When one thus "practices reality," one learns to understand the "reality" better. And, when one understands "reality" better he may be able to make a better adjustment to it because, "one becomes an object to himself." [21] If the role-playing experience requires one to play roles typical of those played in a group different from his own one creates his concept of the "generalized other" or in other words one comes to true consciousness of the interests and needs of the other group.

But, without specific techniques for putting the sociodrama into operation the potentialities of it remain latent. One cannot go before a group and say, "Now we are going to have a sociodrama," and expect it to work. If in the group there are representatives of people now in conflict, volunteers may be immediately available who will stage an excellent sociodrama. However, many issues not immediately experienced by the members of a class which one is teaching may be

considered important to understand—either from the point of view
of contemporary affairs or of history. To "sociodramatize" these issues
preparation is essential, for many people are either completely ignorant of the problem or have incomplete or biased information with
respect to it. A problem of the director or teacher, therefore, is to
present the important dilemma to be considered in a manner which
will arouse a genuine interest in the social problem to be studied. The
following practical steps are suggested for the conduct of a successful
sociodrama with a group who may have no primary or "natural"
knowledge or interest in the problem.

RECOGNITION OF A DILEMMA IN HUMAN RELATIONS

The easiest approach, as has been pointed out, is to ask the group
to introduce its *own* problem with respect to a social dilemma. There
is always more interest in a problem thus selected than in one selected
by a director or teacher. But the range of problems which is readily
recognized by a group of students or the information with respect
to the issues involved is very limited. Since a function of the director
is to educate youth or adults with respect to matters on which they
are ignorant or misinformed, great care must be taken in introducing
new issues. To accomplish this any one or any combinations of the
following may help: field trips, films, phonograph records, lectures,
readings, discussions, or other resource information. This preliminary
study must be carried on *until the problem situation becomes significant to a large number of the members of the class and until the
fundamental roles in the conflict are identified and understood and
the feelings associated with the roles are recognized.*

Identification of roles. When a problem situation becomes significant
in the minds of students they can identify the roles taken in the
conflict. These are the roles, which may be played to re-create the
conflict situation or other problem situation. In preparing to re-create
the Arab-Jewish conflict in the Middle East, for example, Gurion's
role may be played to represent the *Jewish* position, Nasser's role
can represent the *Arab* point of view, Anthony Eden may represent
the *British* viewpoint, Dulles, the *American* and Gromyko, the *Russian* angle. Of course, the students must do much more than mention
the names of these men. The main points of the position of each
may be outlined on the blackboard by the class and the teacher or
director. It may take considerable study to make clear the fundamental

position of each of the groups in the conflict; but these positions must be clearly delineated before adequate role-playing can take place.

Practice role playing in small groups. It may be of value to divide a large class into a number of small groups each equal in size to the number of roles to be played. This procedure has several purposes. Informal practice in small groups gives *every one* in the class an opportunity to play a role. It provides a period of "warming up" or breaking down reserve and of increasing feelings of *spontaneity.* Good sociodrama *cannot* be developed by writing out and memorizing roles. The give and take of the discussion must spontaneously arise out of a rich background of understanding which is a product of real or vicarious experience acquired by reading and observation. The small group discussion can be informal preparation for a better quality of role playing which may later be made before the group, especially when the problem involves considerable learning *before* the sociodrama proper can be introduced.

Selection of role players. At this point students may be invited to volunteer to play the roles involved in the issue before the class. Students who do not volunteer should never be forced into the socio-drama; some who may not at first volunteer will be anxious to take part later.

Role-playing. Before role playing begins it may be desirable for the "players" to confer for a short time to agree upon the setting for the action and upon the definition of the issue to be discussed and/or acted out. Also, players must examine their own biases and try to free themselves from them so that they may represent freely the role they are to play.

The role-playing itself should go along nicely because of interest which has been generated over the period of preparation, including the practice in small groups. In sociodrama participants should re-member, says Moreno, that individual participants are representing the position of *groups* rather than (as in psychodrama) the position of *persons.* True it is that interpersonal and intergroup relations cannot be completely separated; but a distinction should be made with respect to emphasis or orientation. Thus, if the sociodrama is to portray the reality of the great issues between the Arabs and the Jews in the Middle East, the personal uniqueness or problems of Gurion and of Nasser, as persons, are of negligible importance; but their views as representatives of the wishes and policies of two great groups of peoples are of great importance.

It may be noted at this point that the role-playing described here was *prepared for*. The reason for this is that youths in school have had limited experiences, making it possible for them to dramatize spontaneously only a very limited number of problems in intergroup relations outside of *local* intergroup problems. This article, however, deals with the sociodrama applied to the education of youth with respect to problems in international relations or historical issues both of which are remote from the experience of youth. Consequently, a background of knowledge must be acquired *before* roles can be understood or played.[22] This requirement, of course, is something of a departure from the important principle of *spontaneity* which has been fundamental to Moreno's success with the sociodrama. But he has emphasized that considerable spontaneity is possible even under the limitations imposed by this plan.[23]

Analysis. But a sociodrama exercise is not complete with the role-playing of a small group before the class. As the sociodrama unfolds, as the nature of the social reality is re-created by the role-playing the feelings of all in the room may be deeply aroused. Consequently, class members who may not have volunteered to represent positions at first may now feel urged to supply information, to suggest how the roles may be played better, and to indicate possible solutions to the dilemma which is being portrayed.[24]

The process of dramatization to this point can be of great interest to many in the class. New social insights are acquired with respect to intergroup conflict and a deep interest is aroused in a search for solutions.

Replaying of roles. The development of the sociodrama exercise so far may have shown to the group the need for an improved representation of positions. A new "cast" may re-create the situation in an "improved" manner.

The group may also suggest one or more possible solutions to the dilemma including ways of portraying these by means of the sociodrama.[25] For example the group may have portrayed the present impasse in Arab-Israeli relations by the following:

> Gurion: "The Jewish homeland must be expanded now before you Arabs get too strong."
> Nasser: "The Middle East is our Arab country. The Jew is a foreigner. You and your peoples must be stopped now before your population gets any larger."

Someone then may suggest that a conference of Arab and Jew with a representative of the people of the World, like Dag Hammerskjold. The probable views of Hammerskjold are then reviewed. Following this, a likely conference is enacted; and the problems involved in working out a "solution" are revealed.

Democratic development of ethical standards. Through the whole emerging sociodramatic process it is possible that many may under-stand that certain combinations of roles in international relations or world history produce serious dilemmas while other combinations may lessen them. The recognition of these differences may be called training in the *ethics* of democratic citizenship, including depend-ability, respect for the personalities of others and ability to cooperate ("axiodrama").

Informed and interested persons can re-create many of the great scenes and issues of our times and of history in the classroom by means of the sociodrama. This procedure can have great value not only for teaching the deeper meanings associated with these events but to place these great events before a "social microscope," where they can be analyzed for mistakes made and for successes achieved. In this way students may create their own version of the intergroup relations as they might have been and thus acquire *understanding* and *wisdom.* They might even achieve "solutions" to problems in human relations never before conceived. Consequently, role theory and its practical application in the form of the sociodrama may be expected to become of great significance in the future with respect to the education of peoples for living in the second half of the Twentieth Century.

TRENDS

It should be noted that the fundamental ideas of role-playing and sociodrama are being adapted in many areas of our society including business. According to Gordon[26] adaptations of role-playing are being used to iron out difficulties with respect to production and to improve production standards, to give salesmen opportunities to practice im-proving customer relationships, to increase selling effectiveness, to iron out difficulties between factory representatives and field office representatives, to improve foreman-worker relationships and to im-prove the executives understanding of the problems of other workers in the business. The point is that the problems in human relationships for these areas are simulated in business conferences. The role-playing makes the problem real and has been found to be a better instructional method than plain lectures.

(For this chapter the annotated footnotes represent a selected bibliography on the subject of role-playing and sociodrama.)

Leslie D. Zeleny (1898——), B.S., University of Minnesota (1922), M.A., Columbia University (1923), Ph.D., University of Minnesota (1931); post-doctorate study, The London School of Economics and Political Science. Five years of military service in World War I and II; Chairman, Division of the Social Studies and Professor of Sociology, Colorado State College (Greeley). Author of: *Practical Sociology* (New York: Prentice-Hall, 1937); *An Introduction to Educational Sociology* (Boston: D. C. Heath, 1934 with Ross L. Finney); *Problems of Our Times* (New York: McGraw-Hill Book Co., 1935, 1936, 1937, 3 vols., co-author D. S. Brainard); contributor to such books as: "A Sociological Curriculum," Chapter 14, in Joseph S. Roucek, Ed., *Sociological Foundations of Education* (New York: T. Y. Crowell, 1942); "The Leadership Process," Chapter 17, in Joseph S. Roucek, Ed., *Social Control* (Princeton, N. J.: D. Van Nostrand Co., 1956); "Intergroup Understanding in Colleges," Chapter 29, in *One America*, edited by Francis J. Brown & Joseph S. Roucek (New York: Prentice-Hall, 1952) etc. Onetime Associate Editor & Contributing Editor, *Journal of Educational Sociology*; Contributing Editor and Issue Editor, *Sociometry*.

Jacob L. Moreno (Bucharest, 1892——); University of Vienna (1910-1912); medical school, Vienna (1912-17); M.D. (1917); came to the United States (1927), naturalized (1935). Superintendent, Mitterndorf State Hospital, Vienna (1918); officer of health, Voslau (Austria, 1919-25). Originated "Living Newspapers" and the idea of psychodrama (1923); inventor and patenter of "radio film" for electro-magnetic recording of sound on discs for radio transmission and reception (1924); licensed physician (New York State, 1927); engaged in private psychiatric work, New York City (since 1928); began psychodramatic work with children, Plymouth Institute, Brooklyn, and introduced "spontaneity test" at mental hygiene clinic, Mt. Sinai Hospital (New York City, 1928); did psychodramatic work, Grosvenor Neighborhood House and Hunter College (1929); made sociometric studies, Sing Sing Prison (1931-32); responsible for the first Sociometric Conference in the United States, Philadelphia, 1932); Founder and Physician in charge, Beacon Hills Sanatorium (now Moreno Sanatorium (1936——); founded "therapeutic Theater," first Theater for Psychodrama (1936); founded *Sociometry, a Journal of Interpersonal Relations* (1937); Lecturer, New School of Social Research (1937-38); Columbia University, Teachers College (1939-40); assisted in Foundation of Theater for Psychodrama, St. Elizabeth Hospital (Washington, D.C.); Founder, Sociometric & Psychodramatic Institute (now Moreno Institute); Fellow A.M.A., American Psychological Association; American Sociometric Association (President, 1945). Among his numerous works, the latest: Sociometry, *Experimental Method and the Science of Society* (1951); *Who Shall Survive?* (rev. ed., 1953). *Sociometry and the Science of Man,* 1956.

NOTES

1. J. L. Moreno and F. B. Moreno, "Role Tests and Role Diagrams of Children," in *Psychodrama* (New York: Beacon House, 1946), 161-177. In this article Moreno states that "roles are not isolated; they tend to form clusters;" see also: *Who Shall Survive?* (Beacon, N. Y.: Beacon House, 1953), 326.

2. Theodore R. Sarbin, "Role Theory," in *Handbook of Social Psychology* edited by Gardner Lindzey (Cambridge, Mass.: Addison-Wesley Publ. Co.), states, 223-258, that "culture appears to be no more than actions of persons."

3. Ralph Linton, *The Cultural Background of Personality* (New York: D. Appleton-Century, 1945).

4. *Ibid.*

5. George H. Mead, *Mind, Self and Society,* ed. by Charles W. Morris (University of Chicago Press, 1934).

6. J. L. Moreno, "Psychodrama and the Psychopathology of Interpersonal Relations," in *Psychodrama, op. cit.,* 177-216. Moreno states that "a role is an interpersonal experience and needs two or more individuals to be actualized."

7. Moreno, "Psychodramatic Treatment of Marriage Problems," *Sociometry,* III (1940), 2-23.

8. Moreno, "Psychodramatic Treatment of Psychoses," *Sociometry,* III (1940), 115-122.

9. T. R. Sarbin, "Role Theory," *op. cit.*

10. Moreno, "Role Tests," *op. cit.*

11 Moreno, *Who Shall Survive?*

12. *Ibid.*

13. R. H. Turner, "Role-Taking, Role Standpoint, and Reference Group Behavior," *American Journal of Sociology,* XLI (January, 1956), 316-328.

14. *Ibid.*

15. L. D. Zeleny, "The Sociodrama as an Aid in Teaching International Relations and World History," *International Journal of Sociometry,* I (September, 1956), 29-32.

16. Moreno, "The Concept of Sociodrama," *Sociometry,* III (November, 1943), 434-449.

17. For procedures in producing a sociodrama, see: Moreno, *op. cit.,* Helen Jennings, "Sociodrama as an Educative Process," in *Fostering Mental Health in Our Schools* (1950 Yearbook, Association for Supervision and Curriculum Development, Washington, D. C.: NEA, 1950); Charles E. Hendry, Ronald Lippitt and

Alvin Zander, *Reality Practice as an Educational Method* (Beacon: Beacon House, 1947).

18. L. D. Zeleny, *How to Use Sociodrama* (Washington, D. C.: National Council for the Social Studies, 1955); this article introduces the use of small groups into the sociodramatic procedure.

19. A source for much of the material in this section is: Leslie D. Zeleny's *How to Use Sociodrama* (published as a pamphlet by the National Council for the Social Studies) and the same author as "The Sociodrama as an Aid in Teaching International Relations and World History," *International Sociometry*, I (1956), 29-32.

20. Albert Kaminsky, "'You are There' in the Social Studies Classroom," *High Points*, XXXVI (May, 1954), 36:43-48.

21. Moreno, *Sociodrama—A Method for the Analysis of Social Conflicts* (Beacon, N. Y.: Beacon House, 1944), Psychodrama monographs, No. 1.

22. R. B. Haas, "Sociodrama in Education," *Sociometry*, II (December-March, 1948), 240-249.

23. C. C. Bowman, "Role Playing and the Development of Insight," *Social Forces*, XXVIII (December, 1949), 195-199.

24. Leopold von Wiese, "Role Playing as a Method of Academic Education," *Group Psychotherapy*, V (April-July-November, 1952), 73-77, shows how the sociodrama can be used to teach the meaning of social reality in college classrooms.

25. Zeleny, "Sociodrama as a Means of Studying Controversial Issues," *Southern California Social Science Review* (October 18, 1948), shows the use of sociodrama in teaching the meaning of international issues.

26. Mitchell Gordon, "Role-Playing," *The Wall Street Journal*, CXLIX (March 15, 1957), 1.

MILITARY SOCIOLOGY

Paul Walter, Jr.
University of New Mexico

From the beginning of the development of sociology, as well as in the philosophical probings which preceded the efforts to develop a science of human relations, war and military phenomena have been of especial interest. This has been an interest which has been shared by other social scientists such as political scientists, economists, and, more recently, social psychologists. It is not surprising, therefore, that a great number of "determinisms" have arisen to account for military phenomena, and to explain their various aspects.

Within sociology itself, the early inquiries and contributions were centered in the phenomenon of war itself. The "sociology of conflict" at one time came near to occupying the center of the stage, to speak figuratively; and the running controversy between the conflict sociologists and the positivists, who sought rational solutions for war as for other "social problems," gave considerable stimulus to sociological thinking, whether or not it added much to scientific understanding. This early probing into the sociology of war was a search, primarily, for an adequate theory to account for international strife, revolutions, and mob violence. It largely drew its factual content from history and, to a lesser extent, from anthropology; but the thoroughness and objectivity with which it probed into historical fact varied greatly and was, at best, short of true scientific inquiry.

While there are still sociologists who are primarily interested in war as a social phenomenon, the later and present concentrations have been on the study of military organization as such. This has been especially true in the United States since the military establishment has become such an extensive and important aspect of the national group life, starting with the First World War, and greatly accelerated during and since the Second World War. The study of military structure has taken two directions, one emphasizing the external relations of military organization to other organized phases of

SOME APPLICATIONS OF SOCIOLOGY

a society, the other concentrating upon aspects of the internal relationships within the military. One important aspect of the latter has been the socio-psychological, which relates the military organization and its implied processes to the behavior and attitudes of persons involved in it.

The recent study of military organization has been largely in disregard of the larger problem of war, and thus has been less of a search for sweeping theory than an analysis of directly observable and measurable phenomena. Very largely, it has been applied sociology, starting with particular problems to be isolated and "solved," in the sense of increasing the efficiency of the military, without regard to the moral issues of warfare. This type of study has borrowed much from other fields such as industrial sociology, industrial psychology, and political sociology in which there now is a considerable accumulation of materials on power structure, bureaucratic organization, channeled communication, etc. It has also contributed great impetus to, and drawn heavily upon, the interdisciplinary study of the "small group," channeled communication, etc., an emphasis which has increased rapidly in recent years.

THE SOCIOLOGY OF WAR

To return to the sociology of war, at first glance it would seem, as has largely been the case, that any such inquiry must be based in historical knowledge, primarily. Modern war is an historical phenomenon which has been treated in great historical detail and thoroughly documented. But the problems of deducing a sociological theory of war from historical facts are enormous, and perhaps insoluble. Certainly, no sociological theory of war is self-evident in the welter of historical data. One way of stating the problem is that "you can prove anything by history." And conversely you can "disprove" any sweeping theory. From history Ludwig Gumplowicz could "prove" that conflict is the norm in human affairs; while from the same history Prince Kropotkin could "prove" that war is the exceptional and unusual, while human cooperation and mutual aid are the normal.[1] It must be said, and sociological writings appear to support the notion, that the sociological theory must exist, either explicitly or implicitly, *before* one can approach historical facts; and this because of the tremendous range and variety of facts that make up history. The history of war and militarism, *as history*, is noncommittal.

A few early sociologists who worked more with anthropological materials bearing upon simple primitive groups came closer to developing a tenable theory of war in human relations than did those who worked mainly with history. But a part of their advantage lay in the relative paucity of anthropological materials at the same time they wrote, and their theories become less convincing as more data accumulated and became available. Nevertheless, probably the best basis for a general sociological theory to account for war has been that propounded by William Graham Sumner at the turn of the century. He deduced that, inherent in the very nature of social organization, is the in-group and out-group (we-group and they-group) dichotomy. He presumed such a division to be universal and posited that the solidarity of any group was directly related to the threat of real or imagined enemy or out-groups; that, indeed, the very concept of belonging to a group depended upon some prior (and antagonistic) conception of other groups to which one did not belong. With progressive accumulations of data this theory has held up well.

Sumner's thinking did not differ widely from that of Gumplowicz whose writings Sumner had read. While Gumplowicz used considerable historical material, the basis of his reasoning lay largely in his concepts of the prehistorical backgrounds of modern societies. He raised the question of how small, loosely knit hoards developed through time into the modern highly complex nation-state. The steps, as he posited them, were chiefly associated with warfare. As the art of war developed, he held, two consistent by-products were evident. One was the conquest of one group by another, which became the basis for a larger and more complex group; the other, the development of alliances among the weak to protect themselves from stronger groups, the alliances also making for greater and more differentiated societies. Only in such terms, in Gumplowicz' thinking, could we account for the great nation states of this era.[2]

Other sociologists, in attempting to develop theories to account for war, have produced a variety of answers which are drawn less from sociological principles than from other fields. In the period when Darwin's theory of evolution was radically changing biology, it also had its impact upon the speculations of sociologists. In such cases there was a tendency to explain war as a quasi-biological mechanism necessary to eliminate the "unfit" in order that the "fittest" might survive. A later type of theory, resting upon biological assumptions, attempted to relate war to demographic facts, especially the different rates of population growth, and the resulting competition for land and food. And, it is not surprising that in the hey-day of the instinct theory in psychology, some sociologists thought that war could be explained in terms of innate individual pre-dispositions of one kind or another.

Inescapable in the long quest have been, of course, such facile types of explanation as those ascribing warfare to the evil genius of certain individuals, various economic determinisms, and political theories which stress one type of government as over others as being more, or less, conducive to military activity and international aggression.

One type of theory that would appear to follow from the doubtful validity of "simple" explanations has naturally arisen, as it has in criminology and other areas of sociological concern. This is the "multiple factor" type of theory which, in its logical extreme, is the notion that everything enters into the explanation of warfare. Usually, in its statement, this type of theory is somewhat delective of factors to be emphasized, but it is difficult to defend one selection as over other possible ones, and little has been added to understanding.

Suffice it here to say, in summary, that there is as yet no completely adequate, usable, or generally accepted sociological theory of war.

MILITARY STRUCTURE IN SOCIETY

A more recent and, in many ways, more promising type of study has been based upon the acceptance of military organization as an existent fact, being a part of the more inclusive social structure of the modern nation-state. The larger problems of the evolution of such a substructure, its necessity, or its desirability can then be avoided simply by noting that it is universal at present, and therefore may be assumed to have a functional significance which can be examined. Attention can then be focused on its relations to other sub-structures within a national society, and the current trends in such structures and relationships. The relationships as between military and other substructures may be those of dominance or subordination, or a combination of the two. They imply such processes as cooperation, competition, and, at times, conflict within the social structure, or varying combinations of these. A rapidly expanding military organization will present, often, acute problems which may be analyzed in such terms.[3]

The military sub-structure has its distinctive characteristics, among which is the rigid separation from other sub-structures. A person either belongs to it, or does not. Such sharp distinction is reenforced by obvious symbols such as uniforms and insignia of various kinds. There are formalities of induction and initiation into the military which are somewhat similar the world over; and there is a definite point at which persons are separated from the military upon expiration of their terms or for other reasons. The military establishment is usually spatially separate from the general community and access to it is somewhat restricted. While there are some departures from these characteristics (as when military personnel are permitted to wear civilian clothes), the departures are the exceptional.

The military has both latent and manifest functions which are relatively clear as to occasions and circumstances. In some periods it is relatively subordinated to the functions of other sub-systems while, in others, such as those of warfare, it tends to dominate and give direction to all other aspects of society. Always it is in a position of potential domination, and at times and places is thus a great political force. It is in these functions that we have the immediate basis for peaceful relations among nations, even when there is conflict of interests; and at the same time, the actual or potential irritants that are usually the precipitants of armed conflict.

As to trends, these are many and marked in recent times but, as might be expected, changes meet with strong opposition both within and outside the military organization. Certainly, in our own case as a nation, the military, in recent decades, has become a dominant factor in our whole economic structure, in our industrial development, in political organization and, generally, in all power relations within our society.[4] These shifting relations result largely from the existence and recognition of an international situation which is neither entirely peaceful, nor technically war. The term developed to describe the situation is "cold war," and a major adjustment of social structure has been necessary because of it.

Examples of far-reaching effects of military influence and requirements are the organizations and requirements centered in the development of atomic weapons and atomic-powered machines; and the greatly intensified concerns with secrecy in governmental and related activities considered sensitive because of their relations to possible future military activities. While in both cases the focus often lies outside the military establishment itself, the problems can only be fully understood in terms of military potentialities.

The transitions evident in our social structure with the expansion and increased importance of the military have been reflected within the military as well as in the impact of the military on other sub-structures. Increasingly the military has become involved with and dependent upon scientific, technological, and industrial structures lying outside of direct military control. This has been because warfare has become, to a very great extent, a technological and scientific procedure. The military, to a greater extent than ever before, has come into competition with other aspects of society for highly trained specialists in its multi-directional activities.

Suggested in the foregoing incomplete summary of the various aspects of the military as a sub-structure in the larger society are numerous problems which have been the centers of voluminous research. Much of this research has been instigated and carried out by the military organization itself, through its various branches. One of the newer characteristics of military organization is that it maintains within its sub-system large divisions devoted to research and in part, at least, behavioral and sociological research.

Studies can be and are made in a wide variety of frames of reference. There are comparative studies of the societal position of the military in various nation-states, where the focus is upon the relation of the military to other structured aspects of the total society.[5] Other studies have probed into relations of the military establishments to "host" communities, at the local level, where the military is both apart from, yet largely dependent upon, the community. Some studies have centered upon relations between the military and family organization, in cases in which the breadwinner owes his chief allegiance and obedience to the military, often causing unusual strains upon family ties. Within the range of such historically limited research, much objectivity is possible, as are the development and adaptation of techniques for careful observation and measurement, so necessary to scientific progress.

In the sociological focus indicated, wider issues can be subordinated to fact finding to a great extent, simply by overlooking them as issues. In this way research is largely applied sociology based upon the facile assumption that desirable ends are obvious. The applied aspect can be simply stated: given desirable ends (increased efficiency, suppression of prostitution in a "host" community, stability of service men's family relations) what are the most effective means for achieving these ends by deliberate manipulation of sociological elements?

INTERNAL STRUCTURES AND PROCESSES

Military organization is distinctive, has clear boundaries, and can be studied as a unit within the total social system. It is also highly differentiated internally. There are the various services, such as, in this country, the Army, the Navy, and the Air Force, each with its own somewhat unique structure, although all conform to a general pattern which is recognizably military. Each has its somewhat unique functions, trends, and problems, and there are, of course, rivalries among them. Often the rise in importance of one branch becomes a threat to others, and, in some cases, may mean a reduction in the prestige and support of others.

Most of the work of those engaged in the study of the military in recent years, and increasingly, has gone into research in problem areas which are mainly internal to the armed services. There is, however a considerable overlap of such studies with those of external relations. In this concentration on internal organization and processes it is even more characteristic that problems are isolated from larger issues such as were dealt with in the earlier sociology of war. This tends to simplify problems of approach and techniques: and, in turn, to reduce the general significance of findings.

Internally, military social structure may be considered in terms of horizontal relationships, since armed forces are aggregates of functional units. Armies, divisions, fleets, wings, squadrons, and lesser component units have functions identical with those of the same class within each of the services, and may be compared as to performance and other variable characteristics. Experiments may be conducted in which particular controlled units are varied in one or more particulars and results then measured on scales of relative efficiency. Throughout the military organizations there are divisions between and among the strictly military and various supporting and auxiliary arms; and within the military as between staff and line functions, just as are found in industrial organizations.

In greatly expanded organizations which, while they are expanding, are also changing from strictly traditional military to increasingly technological operations, there arise confusions and strains among all these various horizontal groupings, and here lies a great area for sociological research. The strictly military organization of an air squadron, for example, may have a mission to perform; but unless the more technological operational branch has planes ready to fly, it cannot function. And in such situations a multitude of problems arise, some of them falling within the area of the human relations which are involved.

The overall problems are, chiefly, those of coordination of command units. But general coordination involves a multitude of difficulties such as those of clear and prompt communication as between the arms of the various services, and within each arm. There are problems of priority of given functions and tasks as over others, which may be seen differently in different branches of the service. There are also problems of procedural routines which may be more rigid in some services than in others, or as among various branches of the same service. There are also the very human problems of jealousies and competition which may stand in the way of effective cooperation.

These problems are not unique to the military, but they have special importance and meaning there. Certainly, a great deal of time and effort has been expended by research workers in defining and studying them, and in experimental efforts to find solutions. Neither the problems nor the study of them exist in isolation from similar problems and studies in the industrial and political realm; but always, in the military setting, they have special aspects which arise from the organizational and functional settings within which they occur.

As critical as the horizontal relationships are within military organization, they are probably secondary to those of vertical differentiation. Highly characteristic of military sub-systems, and more so than of other structural aspects of a democratic society, is strong emphasis upon vertical position, or rank. Starting with the General Staff and the top command of each of the services, there are successive levels of command and authority down to the least unit of operation. Decisions of those at the top rank must be transmitted, somehow, to those at the lowest levels, in most cases, if they are to be actuated. Thus the chain of command and vertical communication are critical, and problems arising within them are of acute and immediate importance. Most usually, the commands from the top must be amplified and interpreted at various levels as they move downward toward those who will ultimately perform the indicated tasks at the proper place and time. A brief, terse command from a general may have to become a mass of detailed directives at various levels before it can become operative.

In the armed services of a democracy the problem is intensified. Implicit in such services, which recruit from a permissive democratic society, is the notion that the system of communication operates *both* upward and downward. This imperative, made operational on a large scale, can complicate problems of the efficiency and effectiveness of communication.

Also implicit in the armed forces of a democracy are peculiar problems of discipline. In the strong traditions of the armed services, discipline is rigid and stern, but in practice in our own services there is the ever-present tendency to relax requirements in order to give recognition to the "rights" of those in the lower echelons somewhat resembling the rights of citizens, as, indeed, they are.

The vertical ranks in the military are sharply demarcated and the divisions are reenforced by many outward symbols, such as the differences in the uniforms for the different ranks, and the insignia; in quarters, mess halls, and clubs on military posts; and in deferential behavior of those of lower ranks when in the presence of superiors. Such deferential behavior is especially marked when military personnel are in public view.

A complicating factor in both the horizontal and vertical division of persons in the armed forces is the development of unofficial counterparts of the official requirements as, again, happens in industrial organizations; and all routine functions tend to develop unofficial rivals. This is especially true in the area of communications where, side by side with official channels, there will develop unofficial channels which may often be more rapid, if less accurate, in transmitting messages from the command downward, or from lower echelons to those above, or laterally among branches of each of the services. Quite often such contacts at lower echelons may be more effective in "getting the job done" than are the official channels, as every person in the armed services learns sooner or later. But unofficial channels of communication can work both ways. Not only can they be short cuts leading to more efficient and effective operation, but they can also serve to slow up or sabotage plans and procedures developed at higher levels. In similar ways, unofficial relationships tend, inevitably, to develop within the armed services, and often come to supercede their counterparts as described in the official regulations and traditions.

The critical problem areas change as rapidly as do the modes of warfare and of anticipated warfare. The techniques used in research vary, and include, principally, those developed and used outside of military research, ranging through various types of interviews, extensive use of questionnaires and schedules, direct and participant observation, and artificially set up and largely controlled experiments with groups of various size. Possible theoretical significance of the findings is most usually subordinated to more immediate and practical considerations, and relatively few of the studies have been published outside of military channels.[6] This is largely because, even though outside publication is usually encouraged, the volume of research far exceeds the capacity of facilities for editing and dispatch. But the military is one of the most active sections in sociology and related sciences at the present time, reckoning in terms of the numbers engaged and the man-hours of research involved.

SMALL GROUP RESEARCH

Bridging the gap between the study of internal structure of the military branches and the social psychology of those in the armed forces is the study of "small" groups, ranging from two persons to a dozen or even more, an area of concentration which is rapidly expanding as a specialty in sociology and social psychology. While usually treated as a somewhat unique field of concentration, the focus on the small group had earlier beginnings in the work of Cooley and Simmel decades ago.[7] The work of S. A. Stouffer and his numerous associates during the Second World War[8] definitely paved the way back to the approaches of these earlier thinkers. Following what was then current thinking in seeking explanations of attitudes in mass phenomena, these researchers were forced, by the nature of their findings among American soldiers, to give greater and greater emphasis to small groups of men within the armed services in order to understand their thoughts and feelings under stress conditions. Much of their work falls most properly under Social Psychology, which will be treated below, but it also requires mention, in passing, here.

Throughout the military, most frequently small groups are characteristic at the functioning level. In fact, the closer one comes to the all-important operations of military forces in battle, the more one is impressed that it is small groups of a handful of men in the final analysis who must meet the critical tests.

There are many advantages for research in the focus on small groups. Such groups can easily be assembled, subjected to artificial controls, submitted to various careful tests and observations, and the results carefully tabulated for statistical analysis. Because larger groups are unstable, in the military as elsewhere, and it takes longer to make any kind of study of them, they are constantly baffling research workers who concentrate upon them. Not only are small groups easy to assemble, but experimental projects with them take relatively little time. There can be many replications of a given problem in a variety of settings with only given conditions controlled, and thus the possibilities for cumulative research findings are enormous.

Key concepts, which lie at the very heart of sociological theory, and which dominate in small group study, are those of status and role. Each of these terms has meaning in, and application to, all sizes of groupings, but they become poignantly significant, controllable, and measurable in studies of the small group. That status which counts most, whether for the juvenile delinquent or the military hero, is the one within his immediate reference group, usually a group of three, four, or a few more of his closest associates. And while the individual, whether in the armed forces or elsewhere, enacts numerous roles, and these, in composite, make up his "personality," those roles with the most immediate application for a limited number of immediate associates are the keys to his attitudes and behavior.

MILITARY SOCIAL PSYCHOLOGY

Military organizations are, in the last analysis, made up of men and women who have personality traits and characteristics, hopes and aspirations, doubts and fears, and other subjective qualities which are largely determinant of the ways in which they will behave in the monotony of daily routine, or in the rare crisis of mortal combat. As people, the military may perform well or poorly in either type of situation, and the keys to such differentials in behavior lie largely in the realm of social psychology. The situations of military personnel differ from those of other persons in their larger societies in that they presumably are trained deliberately to face deadly danger, to inflict death cold-bloodedly on other human beings at the stimulus of a verbal command, and to behave otherwise in what, from other viewpoints, are peculiar ways. It is men and women who are submitted to disciplinary codes, who give and receive commands, who, in a word, make up the armed forces. Their situations and experiences are in many ways unique, as has been suggested in what has been said about military structure and processes. Their life conditions are "unnatural" in the sense that they are often separated from such normal settings as are provided by proximity of family and home, and the usual satisfactions and curbs of non-military life.

The military is made up, for the most part, of a highly selected age group, those just entering upon maturity, in their late teens and early twenties. Gradations in age are, to a large extent, paralleled by gradations in military rank, but in newer and rapidly expanding services, younger men often are in command over those of greater age, maturity and longer backgrounds of military service. The "old man" (colonel, general, etc.) may, in such cases, turn out to be a youngster by comparison with many of his subordinates.

All of these, and many other facets of military life, must be somehow assimilated by persons engaged in it. The experiences of induction, indoctrination and rigid training can have many effects on the life philosophies, the goals and satisfactions or feelings of deprivation of those who undergo them. In some cases military experience may be neatly rationalized; in others, it can lead to almost disastrous confusions, puzzlement and painful disillusionment.[9] In most cases, of course, the experiences and results lie somewhere between such extremes. As those versed in social psychology know, the nature of the experiences of those in the military, as well as their impacts and eventual results, are not uniquely determined by individuals psychically isolated, but to a large extent are mediated by influences of the immediate group surroundings. Older men in the services translate their mysteries to the newer recruits; the men talk over among themselves in informal groupings the impacts of their experiences and their interpretations of them. They are influenced by, and influence, their immediate group environments.

In the current studies of the socio-psychological aspects of military organization and life, the turning point has largely been, as in the case of the small group focus, the voluminous studies of Stouffer and his associates, previously noted. But, again, the background is older and the work of these scientists is more a revival of earlier socio-psychological theory and findings than a new discovery.

Those in the military do not respond uniformly to the situational stimuli which impinge upon them. Most serve out their terms in the service, then some re-enlist, others do not. A few "go over the hill," usually to be arrested and punished for their defections. For some, the military atmosphere becomes a comfortable setting for living out their lives or their active years. For others, it is something to escape as quickly and completely as possible. Some react by becoming highly efficient service men; others are indifferent in attitude and performance, while still others become habitual "gold-brickers." Some find their ways repeatedly to the guard house, others become models of decorum and behavior. Some are exceedingly careful of the expensive equipment which the man of arms must now have; others are reckless out of seemingly sheer exuberance; and others are careless out of indifference or sheer lack of basic abilities. All of these variables are problems of importance to the military establishment, and their understanding and control is the center of much of the behavior research, most usually psychological in nature, but often, as well, of socio-psychological import.

The range of behavioral and attitudinal variables among those in the services comes to its critical peak of importance during war, and then especially among those who are in direct contact with the enemy. There is no other test of personality factors quite equal, probably, to that of entering battle to kill and, perhaps, be killed. Some men behave bravely and effectively under such extreme stress and others do not. Much may depend upon those in command responsibilities being able to discover in advance to action the clues to such differences, usually covered inexactly by such terms as "cowardice" and "courage." As Stouffer and his associates have shown, and as battle veterans freely testify, nearly all are afraid in battle, yet many perform beyond the call of duty.

Problems of morale are of obvious importance for organizations geared to the dangers and hardships of war or, even, of military training. They gain in peacetime importance for the military as the training and equipment of each man becomes more expensive in terms of money and time to produce them. Morale also has an obvious relationship to the problems of recruitment and retention of military personnel within the military organization in times of full employment when most of those of military age may choose more or less freely among competing occupations.

The social psychological studies have had more of an impact upon prevailing theories than have other types of study previously described. This has been, perhaps, because findings have been somewhat more surprising, and have tended to challenge many current notions regarding morale and related phenomena. And, perhaps, the findings have more obvious relevance for problems lying outside the military setting.

In general, the findings have tended to refute many of the assumptions which have long supported mass psychology as a system of theory. In this, they have tended to minimize the forces emanating from large groups and distant sources; in a word, the effectiveness of mass communication. And they have reemphasized the effectiveness of immediate and primary or quasi-primary group relationships.

A special field of growing importance with the changes in methods and equipment in warfare has been what has been called "survival" research.[10] It envisions groups of men, such as crews of war planes, stranded behind enemy lines, and attempts to find the best and most efficient methods of again getting back to their own forces intact. The urgency behind such research, again, lies partly in the greatly increased investment of time and money which goes into the preparation of each man for combat, and therefore, the increased importance of keeping as many operative during wartime as possible. Such survival research ranges over a wide area, from means and methods of remaining alive on scanty rations of water and food to tricks for the deception of the enemy. But the main focus is again on socio-psychological aspects of such situations. Who shall be the group leader, under "survival" conditions? Shall the men stay closely together or separate? How may morale of the weaker men be bolstered and maintained under the most extreme hardships? These and many other questions appear to need dependable answers.

Closely related to survival research is the problem area related to the new prominence of "Brain washing" as a wartime technique. How may men captured by an enemy anticipate and resist their highly developed skills in enforced conversion to enemy loyalties and points of view? Here, again, the answer must lie in the field of psychology, but also it has import for social psychology and sociology.

One emerging problem area, again largely socio-psychological in nature, has to do with the rapidly increasing mechanization of warfare in which many purely human aspects of military life must be subordinated to the relatively inflexible requirements of technological equipment. A dramatic type of case is that of the atomic-powered submarine, in which a crew of men may remain isolated from outside contacts and relatively idle over long periods of time running, perhaps, to months. Under such conditions, what behavioral problems will arise, and what precautions may be taken to meet them? Similar problems will arise in connection with air crews who may be aloft for days at a time without any but the most meager outside contacts. Such problems, and others suggested before, are stated in question form, since in most cases, answers remain to be found which may be considered final or definitive.

CURRENT CHARACTERISTICS AND TRENDS

Presently military sociology is chiefly research, and is relatively little concerned with or productive of theory. What theoretical concern there is is largely "operational," limited in its pertinence to the immediate and limited problems at hand. Method aims increasingly at precision with considerable reliance on sophisticated mathematical manipulations. The research is very largely team research and quite usually, although not invariably, the sociologists on the teams have roles subordinate to those of psychologists or other scientists. In fact, the terms "behavioral science," "human component," and "human factor" are increasingly used to describe the focus and type of work undertaken, rather that of the terminology derived from the more traditional academic division of labor among the various sciences.

The volume and variety of research in these areas is enormous and tends, through time, to grow; but the growth is not steadily maintained or consistent since it is usually linked to annual budgets and to the growth or contraction of various arms and branches of the military establishment. Very little of the research extends over periods longer than a few weeks to a few months and this is for two reasons: one, again, is the limitation imposed by annual budgets; and the other lies in the relative instability of the groups upon whom the research is being conducted, both as to membership and as to fixity of location and assignment.

Another limiting condition is that the research is carried on, for the most part, by scientists drawn from civilian life. Often they do

not recognize that in the armed services as in other areas of group
life, there are "sensitive" zones where there is great resistance to
scientific probing, on the part of those in authority. Also, there are
inherent communication difficulties, both in the conduct of the research, and in the transmission of findings to military personnel. A
finding, couched in terms meaningful and clear to sociologists and
social psychologists, often "just doesn't make sense" to listeners or
readers who have their own peculiar and restricted modes of communication. In connection with the latter difficulty, where behavioral
science research is now inaugurated in the setting of the armed services, it is increasingly the practice to spend a large part of the time
and effort in attempting to anticipate and surmount just such communication barriers.

While sums of money and the time of sociologists and other behavioral scientists now go into military research which far exceed the
wildest dreams of a few decades ago, the cumulative results, from the
point of view of the sciences, is relatively small. Reasons for this are
several, including some which have been suggested above. Certainly,
the close adherence to "operational" research into restricted problem
areas account for a part of the paucity of general results for sociology.
A practical answer to an existent problem in a situationally limited
set of circumstances does not, of itself, add to the sum of understanding in a science, even though the approach may be sociological or
socio-psychological.

Yet many of the findings arising from the widespread military
research might be highly suggestive were there ready and easy communication of the findings and methods used. Such easy communication does not exist, and the greatest part of military research in the
behavioral fields does not gain general currency. There is no effective
program for regular and continuous publication of research carried
on in military settings, nor are there adequate avenues for communicating such research from one major branch of the services to another,
or even from one installation within a branch to other installations.

Trends, however, give promise of future improvements in this
regard, which may help to solve many of the limiting problems of
military research. In recent years, national and regional organizations
of professional sociologists have included in their programs sections
on military sociology, which helps to give currency to their work and
findings.

SELECTED BIBLIOGRAHY

L. L. Bernard, *War and Its Causes* (New York: Henry Holt, 1944). A systematic institutional analysis with suggested remedies, but without much optimism.

Maurice R. Davie, *The Evolution of War* (New Haven: Yale University Press, 1929). In effect, a search for a solution to the problem of war through a better understanding of underlying causes.

Arthur A. Ekirch, *The Civilian and the Military* (New York: Oxford University Press, 1956). An historical treatment, strongly antimilitaristic in tone.

Floyd N. House, *The Development of Sociology* (New York: McGraw-Hill Book Company, 1937); chapter XIV, "Social Darwinism"; Chapter XXIII, "William Graham Sumner." Condensed summary statements of early theoretical contributions to the understanding of underlying causes of war.

Frederick C. Irion, *Public Opinion and Propaganda* (New York: Thomas Y. Crowell, 1950); chapter XX, "War and Peace." An abbreviated coverage of some of the more recent literature of pertinence to the understanding of war.

M. A. May, *A Social Psychology of War and Peace* (New Haven: Yale University Press, 1943). An analysis of the social conditioning processes which make war accepted practice.

Ithiel de Sola Pool, *Satellite Generals: A Study of Military Elites in the Soviet Sphere* (Stanford University Press, 1955). A study of the deliberate manipulation of military command to gain and retain political ascendency.

P. A. Sorokin, *Contemporary Sociological Theories* (New York: Harper and Brothers, 1928); chapter VI, "Sociological Interpretation of the Struggle for Existence and the Sociology of War." A comprehensive, but highly condensed, study of the literature.

Samuel A. Stouffer and Associates, *Studies in Social Psychology in World War II* (Princeton University Press, 1949). A recent classic, describing numerous studies conducted, in many cases, by cross-disciplinary teams.

E. C. Tolman, *Drives Toward War* (New York: Appleton-Century Company, 1942). An analysis in terms of dominant psychological types characteristic, presumably, of different eras.

Alfred Vagts, *A History of Militarism* (New York: W. W. Norton, 1937). Somewhat dated, but thought-provoking and informative.

Willard Waller, *War and the Family* (New York: Dryden Press, 1940). How family life and ideals are affected by the disruptions of war; *War in the Twentieth Century* (New York: Random House, 1940). A study of the varied direct and indirect effects of modern war on all types of individuals.

G. B. Watson, *Civilian Morale* (Boston: Houghton Mifflin, 1942).

A definitive analysis of factors involved and an assessment of their operation.

Quincy Wright, *A Study of War* (University of Chicago Press, 1942). The approaches of the various social sciences to the understanding of war—law, political science, sociology, social psychology, anthropology, and history.

Paul Alfred Francis Walter, Jr. (1901—) received his Ph. D. from Stanford University (1937); newspaper reporter (1921-1929), Instructor in Journalism, University of New Mexico (1930-1937), Assistant Professor of Sociology (1946), and today Professor and Chairman of the Department of Sociology. Author of such volumes as *Social Sciences* (1949) and *Race and Culture Relations* (1952), and co-author of *An American Philosophy of Education* (1942), *The Sociological Foundations of Education* (1942), *Social Control* (1947, 1956), etc.

NOTES

1. There are numerous histories of social thought which give brief statements of these theories. See "Selected Bibliography" at end of the chapter.

2. See W. G. Sumner, *War and Other Essays* (New Haven: Yale University Press, 1911); and Ludwig Gumplowicz, *Der Rassenkampf* (Innsbruck, 1883).

3. Examples of the variety of approaches to such problems in two distinct settings may be found in issues of *The Annals of the American Academy of Political and Social Science;* see CCXLI (September, 1945), "Universal Military Training and National Security"; & CCXLV (May, 1946), "The Netherlands During German Occupation."

4. The large proportion of the Federal budget absorbed by the military is but one index of this trend.

5. For the setting of such investigations, see Harold W. Stoke, "The New Nationalism," in T. C. McCormick (Ed.) *Problems of the Postwar World,* (New York: McGraw-Hill, 1945).

6. A check of three recent issues of *Sociological Abstracts* indicated that slightly more than three per cent of the items included could be classed as military sociology. A smaller percentage emanated from the armed forces themselves.

7. See histories of social thought cited in "Selected Bibliography" at end of chapter.

8. See "Selected Bibliography."

10. E. Paul Torrance, *Psychological Aspects of Survival: A Survey of the Literature,* (Washington, D. C.: Human Factors Operations Research Laboratories, Bolling Air Force Base, 1953).

9. A. M. Rose, "Neuropsychiatric Breakdown in the Army," *American Sociological Review,* XXI, No. 4, (August, 1956).

SOCIOLOGICAL ASPECTS
OF PSYCHOLOGICAL WARFARE

Robert C. Sorensen
Munich (Germany)

PSYCHOLOGICAL WARFARE AND THE SOCIOLOGIST

Psychological warfare has witnessed a modern revival among nations anxious to influence the minds and behavior of people in other lands. Waged by information, propaganda, diplomacy, boycott, and various forms of technical assistance, psychological warfare for political ends plays a vital role in the lives of millions of people today. To participation in psychological warfare can often be attributed major tenets of a government's domestic and foreign policy, the relationship between a government and its people, and the ideologies to which people adhere.

The study and practice of psychological warfare involves many fields of Sociology. Political Sociology has a very important role to play. The political behavior of the participating countries must be accurately diagnosed, both to understand the role of given objectives in the formulation of *techniques* of warfare and to study their effects on relationships between government and people in the target system. The acts of individuals and power alignments both in and out of government, whether planned or spontaneous, may indicate behavior which might escape the notice of an unsophisticated observer.

In addition, the student of psychological warfare must have an appreciation of the circumstances under which the objectives of psychological warfare are framed. The art of decision making and the relationship between impact and purpose require careful study if one is to understand the process of psychological warfare.

Interwoven throughout these considerations is the relationship between the warfare agency and the target system. Thus the area of social psychology assumes a role of major importance. The maintenance of this relationship is governed by basic considerations with respect to public opinion and collective behavior. These same conditions in fact govern the limits within which psychological warfare can be effectively conducted. So-called "rules" do not provide a basis for judging either the process or effectiveness of psychological warfare.

It is in formulating models of effectiveness (or lack of it) and assessing the relevant data thereto, that sociological method makes its greatest contribution to the study and practice of psychological warfare. The task of assessing effectiveness has grown in stature during the last decade. Psychological warfare agencies have gradually come to realize that the measure of their effectiveness does not rest alone with technical facilities, manpower resources, and intellectual adeptness. The effectiveness of the application and results of psychological warfare techniques requires analysis in light of the social structure of the target system, public sentiment and personal prejudices therein, and resulting behavior. These have long been areas of inquiry for the social scientist, particularly the sociologist.

Psychological warfare as described herein is practiced to varying degrees by nations of many political persuasions. This is not a discussion of psychological warfare in terms of any single country's point of view or techniques. This chapter is confined to a general inquiry into the theory and practice of psychological warfare from a sociological perspective, with specific examples from various countries often lacking due to space limitations.

THE NATURE OF PSYCHOLOGICAL WARFARE

"Warfare" of Psychological Warfare. War constitutes organized fighting between men. *Warfare* is the rational application of violence through devices of influence calculated both to provoke this organized fighting and to affect its outcome. Warfare embodies technique, and techniques chosen to wage war differ in method and consequence according to the potentialities, objectives, and expectations of the parties at war with each other.

In this discussion, we speak of *war* between nations. War requires a systematic undertaking (warfare) by the government of one nation to compel certain prescribed behavior on the part of the government and people of another nation. This undertaking (for offensive or defensive reasons) exerts *influence by force of arms* or *influence by persuasion* in order, consistent with political objectives, to undermine the power and prestige of the opposing government, minimize the control it exercises over its peoples, subvert people's loyalties to their government, and undermine their adherence to certain ideologies and goals considered crucial by the warmaker.[2]

The key difference between psychological warfare and the more orthodox forms of military warfare is that psychological warfare exerts influence *mainly* by persuasion rather than by force of arms.

Each is capable of doing violence to people's lives, the former to men's minds, institutions and welfare; the latter to people's physical survival. In this respect, each complements the other.

It is equally evident that all war, no matter what its mode of implementation, has psychological effects as well as physical ones. There is no substitute in armaments for the morale of people however their mode of warfare.

The "Psychological" of Psychological Warfare. Harold D. Lasswell once observed: "The study of politics is the study of influence and the influential." From this perspective, politics has proven to be the purposeful, organized shaping and sharing of values in human society. The place of violence in politics as a means of elite attack and defense has been impressive. All warfare, as discussed herein, is for political purposes.

Psychological warfare is an undertaking by any given power to compel a nation by persuasion in the direction of pre-determined political objectives whose accomplishment has met with resistance. Its consequences involve the forced redistribution of power and values in the target system in accordance with the desires of the victor.

Thus it is the *type of influence* for which each *mainly* strives which distinguishes psychological warfare from other types of warfare. In warfare which is waged by armaments, the object is that the enemy *perish* if necessary. In psychological warfare where ideas are the primary weapon, the object is that appropriate elements of the target system be *persuaded* to behave in accordance with the goal of the opponent.

The term "political warfare" is sometimes confused with psychological warfare. Some observers consider the two types of warfare synonymous. In reality they are not. All warfare is "political warfare" in terms of end purposes. Psychological warfare has political goals for whose achievement its particular devices are utilized in conjunction with those of armed warfare. By this definition, it is acceptable to speak of "psychological warfare waged for political or military ends."

Propaganda is a leading element in psychological warfare. The increased belief in the role of irrationality in human affairs has led to a more widespread use of propaganda in psychological warfare than ever before. Moreover, "since war creates an atmosphere of tension and excitement peculiarly prejudicial to independent judgment and also provides warrant for censorship of both fact and opinion, it is not surprising that it has been the ideal breeding-ground of propaganda."[3]

Objectives of Psychological Warfare. A nation waging psychological warfare is ultimately concerned with its own best interests and those of its allies. In this sense, a nation's best interests will sometimes include concern for the integrity and/or welfare of other countries even though such concern brings no promise of material benefit. Needless to say, psychological warfare is also waged as a defense against psychological warfare efforts of other nations.

Important objectives for which psychological warfare is waged by a nation of any political complexion have been one or more of the following: (1) Protection of the integrity of a nation's own ideologies and infiltrating the prevalent ideologies of another nation. (2) Defense (and counter-offensive) against psychological warfare efforts of another nation. (3) Insuring the existence of a government and people who are friendly to a nation's people and/or specific aims (trade, alliances, etc.). (4) Persuading people to favor an acceptable ideology and to reject another. (5) Maintenance of opposition to a government for purposes of weakening its ability to function and with a view to its eventual subversion or overthrow. (6) Persuasion of a nation or segment thereof to surrender its objectives (e.g., surrender to military conquest, acceptance of military occupation, agreement to important political or economic concessions, trade domination in a particular area). (7) Securing a government's willingness to receive or provide assistance in place of another nation whose strength and prestige is thereby reduced.

Emergence of Psychological Warfare as a Substitute for Traditional Warfare. Psychological warfare, particularly its propaganda aspects, is not new to relationships between groups and nations. Linebarger, Scott and others have pointed out many instances of psychological warfare which date back to ancient times.

But ancient wars permitted only limited displays of psychological warfare. Throughout most of history nations fought to decimate ene-mies and whole peoples were wiped out. Later the scope of the objec-tives of wars and the conditions under which they were fought changed. Wars were fought less often between civilizations and more among nations or societies devoted to their own political and geographic aggrandizement. But in recent years, nuclear weapons and mass com-munications being what they are, wars can involve civilization as a whole. At the same time, all kinds of local forays and probings con-tinue, sometimes involving many nations but now euphemistically called "local wars."

Many conditions have emerged which account for psychological warfare activity both for its own sake and as a "substitute" for armed warfare. Because these conditions cast considerable light on the nature of psychological warfare, they are briefly set forth here: (1) War between nations no longer constitutes organized fighting between small, compact, disciplined groups. Such groups are still the spearhead of armed warfare, but the balance is often tipped by the millions of people involved who have demonstrated a growing independence of established concepts of loyalty. Yet, "increasing numbers of people have displayed a disposition to give support to their government or to withhold it in accordance with their personal attitude to some great over-all political issue . . . rather than adhere to the principle of unqualified loyalty to *their government*."[4] On occasions when people may surrender without physically fighting, if people have vulnerabilities in their ideals and motive power to which violence may be done by persuasion, then force of arms is clearly not the only choice of warfare against them.

The greater psychological independence of large masses of people whose loyalty can place the outcome of war in balance is a factor which has undoubtedly contributed much to the current prevalence of psychological warfare.[5]

In view of the cost of modern war, consideration is inevitably given by any rational power to the ratio of cost and effectiveness in the choice of warfare. The vulnerabilities of the target are assessed and the weapon chosen that will accomplish a government's goal most effectively with the least deprivation to its resources. Thus, for ex-ample, if a government can win by diplomacy or subversion what it would have to take by sacrificing an army, it will ordinarily under-take the former unless it is employing the mobilization of manpower and material resources to satisfy the requirements of domestic policy.

(2) Except for that society in which war is an end in itself, care must be taken that the fabric of any victory or stalemate is not ravaged by the consequences of the physical violence which obtains in *armed* warfare. Where it can be avoided,[6] it deserves to be more than ever before. Through martyrdom and myth, those who perish as a consequence of physical violence have a way of rising from the dead to inspire their fellows to further conflict or grudging accommodation which can prolong the very conditions which a war was fought to eliminate.[7]

(3) Victory over an idea, unless every instance of its communication and influence is eliminated, cannot be eliminated through sheer physical suppression. Thus, for example, the world which has been the target of Soviet Union efforts to explode pockets of nationalism and inspire class warfare cannot meet the challenge by force alone.

Robert Holt lends support to this thesis when privately discussing the strengths of communism that are not amenable to armed warfare: "Ideologies compete not only on the grounds of what they promise but also on the *prospects* of achievement. . . . Their philosophy is not only a philosophy of ends; it also provides a 'Weltanschauung.' The communists have captured the Muse of history and employed her to their ends. . . . Every event, every trend can be fitted into their vast pattern. Everything is leading toward eventual victory. To the less empirically oriented peoples of the world, this can have tremendous appeal."

Every sign points to the conclusion that communism would exist under given circumstances in spite of (if not sometimes partly because of) armed efforts to destroy its adherents or those who fight at the command of the "dictatorship of the proletariat." As a technique of warfare, force of arms fails to establish adequate contact with an ideological target. Each is on a different level of abstraction; neither can wholly collide with tne other.

(4) The potential consequences of nuclear warfare have convinced political leaders that it is to be avoided at almost all possible costs, according to available opinion surveys and the statements of leaders themselves. This reaction has resulted in two types of departure from war as it was once fought: (1) "Rules" of war (not to be confused with rules of ethical warfare) have been established in various combat theaters about weapons utilization and the territories in which war is fought. (2) Psychological warfare as a "substitute" form of warfare is sought after in the hope of accomplishing telling blows against

the enemy without the risk of a contest in "mass retaliation" with death-dealing weapons.

(5) The availability of psychological warfare techniques has enabled governments to contemplate goals which otherwise might have been impossible. Two hundred years ago, for example, it would have been impossible for one nation to employ radio broadcasts and leaflets to persuade the peoples of another nation thousands of miles away to work for the day of eventual freedom from enslavement.[8] The refinement of intelligence devices, another consequence of the new era of mass communication and technology, has also made it possible to *hold out goals of war* which fifty years ago would not *have been imagined* possible.

(6) One emerging function of psychological warfare has in fact been victory through deterrence. In regard to this variation of warfare which some have called *peacefare,* James Forrestal often asserted: "The surest way to avoid war is to make it clear to any possible group of enemies that the risks of engaging us are too great to make it worth while." This philosophy has since been maintained through the concept of the "atomic stalemate" via well publicized nuclear bomb experiments, the threatened unleashing of other powers by publicly subsidizing them for that purpose, the mutual defense treaty, and the unilateral assurance to a country that to protect mutual interests it will be militarily defended if it is invaded by a power considered unfriendly to the protector.

In outline form we have discussed the nature of psychological warfare and the situations from which it emerges. Warfare is not only a function of politics but also is an outgrowth of national conflicts and personal insecurities in the world community; this becomes increasingly clear in the two following sections dealing with the process of psychological warfare and the conditions for its conduct.

THE PROCESS OF PSYCHOLOGICAL WARFARE

Parties to Psychological Warfare. Psychological warfare is initiated and regulated by governments which operate either directly through their own agencies (e.g., foreign service, information centers, broadcasting stations) or through the controls exercised over the activities of business firms (e.g., export-import regulations). An exception is the occasional private agency in democratic countries for which funds are provided by private subscription but whose policies are ordinarily consistent with those of its country's government. The nature of government departments directly concerned with psychological warfare policy-making and implementation depend upon the nature of the government and the sophistication of its techniques.[9]

The Substance of Psychological Warfare. As previously mentioned, the nature of the policy objectives and the target, the time and cost permitted, and other intervening variables (including domestic considerations) determine selection of the means by which *influence,* the *sine qua non* of psychological warfare, is communicated *to the target.* The means of psychological warfare are its weapons, *words* and *deeds* are its ammunition, with the added consideration that words and circumstances under which they are conveyed often are viewed as deeds *per se* in the target system. Words and deeds, both offensive and counter-offensive, convey various degrees of influence—propaganda, inspiration, intimidation, example, assurance, fulfillment, and deprivation.

Unfortunately, the opportunity does not exist to describe in detail the functions of some psychological warfare weapons outlined below. The way in which each one of these weapons is utilized would require a book in itself.

Weapons of Psychological Warfare. Means by which influence is (verbally) communicated are mainly the following: (1) The radio broadcast (external, internal, internal "black"); (2) the leaflet (conveyed by balloon, projectile, airplane drop or mail); (3) Protesting to another government (conveyed and publicized in a variety of ways); (4) Debate in an international body (e.g., UN); (5) Diplomatic activity (overt and covert); (6) Announcements by government officials (press conferences, debates in government forums, publicized speeches, "trial balloons" and "planted" material in domestic media); (7) Television and films; (8) Information centers.

Deeds as means of communicating influence are mainly the following: (1) A show of military power, political unity at home, etc.; (2) Provision of economic, political, or medical assistance (to target countries but also to other countries as a means of penalizing the target country); (3) Discrimination in provision of trade (including boycott) and assistance; (4) Formation or breakoff of diplomatic representation, alliances, etc., for a variety of purposes; (5) Sponsorship of cultural exchanges, trade fairs, professional associations, youth festivals, etc; (6) Movements for defection and redefection (physical) through organizations, changes in the law regarding returning emigres, etc.; (7) Exercise of censorship over outside media and border restrictions governing travel in or out of the country; and (8) Creation of "front groups" and political parties within the target country for propaganda and subversion purposes.

Psychological Warfare Weapon Capabilities. As an atomic warhead or a 30 mm howitzer artillery piece is utilized to accomplish certain purposes, so do the weapons of psychological warfare have certain capabilities of individual and group influence. The following are typical examples: (1) Provision of prohibited information and culture in competition to normally available and/or accepted media; (2) Deliberate provocation of rumor; (3) Promise of higher standards of living under certain circumstances; (4) Encouragement of feelings of gross insecurity about the future; (5) Provision of inspiration whch is an essential ingredient in maintaining a challenge to the government; (6) Successful persuasion that items such as food, clothing, etc., are in short supply because normal trade relationships are impossible under present circumstances.

CONDITIONS FOR THE CONDUCT OF
PSYCHOLOGICAL WARFARE

The objectives of psychological warfare, its techniques of implementation, its communication devices, its impact on the target, and the extent to which psychological warfare succeeds in implementing its objectives can be evaluated by the sociologist from the standpoint of the relationship between the agency waging psychological warfare and its target system.

The significance of the relationship between a psychological warfare agency and target system lies in the "feedback" of the latter upon the purposes and methods of the former. What the target population has done or is capable of doing under given conditions is an important factor in both the provocation of psychological warfare efforts and the resolution of their outcome.

In this connection, it is pertinent to note that the relationship between two warring states is seldom completely severed. More often the opposite occurs, in that each country loses something of its ethnocentricity with respect to the daily affairs and the culture of the other. Strengths and weaknesses are carefully scrutinized, albeit usually from a distance. This exigency of war has, as in many other aspects of the social sciences, provoked experimental scientific investigation and refinements in research methodology which might otherwise have never been made.[10]

Four important conditions require persistent consideration in psychological warfare operations: (1) *Attention and awareness* must be secured from crucial elements of the target system. (2) *Credence* with respect to psychological warfare efforts must also be sought from crucial elements of the target system. (3) Modification sought in target attitudes and behavior must take the *existing predispositions* of the target people into consideration. (4) Prescribed behavior must be restricted to possibilities permitted by *environmental factors.*[11]

But at the outset, this caveat must be added: Just as policy makers cannot pretend that a particular event has never occurred, neither can it be assumed that psychological warfare efforts are the sole determinant of what happens in the target country. People are also affected by extraneous political, military, and economic events over which psychological warfare exercises no control. At the same time, of course, a psychological warfare effort can seize upon such occasions and endeavor to exploit them for its own purposes.

Target System Attention and Awareness. In establishing contact with the target system, the psychological warfare operator is immediately challenged by the necessity to secure attention and awareness from significant elements therein. Contact is not established without notice of the warfare effort and/or without awareness of the consequences which members of the target system should feel persuaded *may* befall them. Thus, for example, people are not going to seek freedom from a regime imposed by another country if they are not aware of the issue of self-determination. Or, if people have such an antagonism against their government, they will still not think and act in line with the policy objectives of psychological warfare if their expectations for possible change have not been aroused.

As one observer put it: "Human beings can only sample the sensory world." So much is available that the average person can only select and assimilate a tiny fraction of his symbolic environment.[12] This point has been supported by Hoffer who has described the sheer comfort of forgetting and Zipf whose "principle of least effort" postulates, in this case, that the exertion of effort is minimized in accordance with people's needs and expectations. The instances are relatively few in which ideas newly clamoring for attention do not have to "push out" ideas normally occupying the attention and testing the awareness of people.

Exposure to armed warfare usually provokes imagery of one's self as an enemy target of destruction. There are many typical instances of behavior among those who want to avoid any posture by which their chances for physical survival may be compromised; people will change their jobs, move from their homes, forsake their friends, and suffer almost any privation in order to secure some degree of self-protection.

This is seldom the case within the psychological warfare target system. People do not conceive themselves in the same role as those who contemplate the armed enemy. Depending upon the circumstances, peoples must sometimes be aroused to protect themselves from exposure to influence. Some do not view the psychological warmaker as an enemy.

Why are people so unconcerned about being the targets of propaganda or diplomatic activity, for example?

(1) In some cases, psychological warfare efforts are focused against an elite group (e.g., government officials) so that relatively few people are aware of negotiations which in turn will affect them. In many cases, the government will do its best to "protect" its population from awareness of events such as these. (2) No feeling of crisis exists for people in many cases. People define a crisis on the basis of personal experience and needs which, as mentioned elsewhere in this chapter, have little basis in objective reality. Thus an impending economic depression which would engulf one's entire country might be overshadowed for some people by the robbery of a savings bank in a neighboring village. (3) Where people's predispositions (see below) sometimes permit little or no modification in expectations for which a given psychological warfare effort is striving, such people may be closed off to these specific efforts at influence.

Persons who fit this category in the extreme will survive even if deliberately "sighted" and struck by all of the "firepower" of a psychological warfare weapon because (a) they are as of that moment incapable of being persuaded from their present course; and/or (b) they will not be aware that any effort was made to influence them.

The question might be asked: Is not the social psychological warrior more interested in influencing people without their realizing it? The answer is yes *and* no. Although it can easily be understood why the social psychological warrior would like his target to be affected unknowingly, the following also deserves consideration: (1) Awareness often signifies conscious concern directed in channels which arouse the concern of others (e.g., the dissemination of rumors). Moreover, measurement of effectiveness (where contacts with the target system are possible) is easier with respect to reactions deriving from awareness rather than unconscious feelings. (2) Where some degree of acceptance is won on the part of persons in the target system, any conscious support for the psychological warmakers' objectives will undoubtedly encourage them to resist defensive efforts at least partially, and to alert others to side with them. (3) In some cases, people will more persistently and intensively search for alternatives of action in behalf of psychological warfare objectives if they have given conscious attention to the psychological warfare effort.

The quality of awareness within the target system is gained for psychological warfare efforts by utilizing the following techniques:

(1) Simplicity, starkness and repetition; (2) Exploitation of the support and opposition given by already existing friends and enemies of the psychological warfare cause who constitute "special interest" groups already working within the target system; (3) Availability and accessibility of contents of psychological warfare communication; and (4) the extent to which the effort as an incident is differentiated from the ordinary events of people's lives.

The first three techniques involve well known findings with respect to human behavior which are frequently described in many text books. The last deserves brief mention in terms of these findings: (1) Words or deeds of opposing forces sometimes tend to negate each other when they are very similar to each other in technique of influence. If one adversary utilizes propaganda, the other might be wise to employ information or a show of strength so that the target audience will not lose interest and say in effect: "A plague on both your houses." "You are both dull, evil intentioned," etc. (2) People who are accustomed to crises are not always impressed by the announcement that another one is impending. Until the "enemy" successfully interprets this crisis to foreshadow certain very definite consequences for themselves they will not view it as a departure from the normal expectations. (3) Many members of the target population are engulfed to varying degrees in the routines of their lives. They are inevitably wedded to their families, jobs, homes, personal obligations, and other social imperatives. An effort which does not loosen a person's preoccupation with his daily regimen, or which is very quickly assimilated into a person's routine perceptions may be dissolved and lost forever as an irritant in his field of awareness. (4) This principle applies to physical and sense characteristics as well. Radio broadcasts must be transmitted on sufficient frequencies and with the necessary power to withstand the efforts of jammers; they must also emphasize language and tone which is least susceptible to the noise caused by jamming. Words which provoke basic sentiments will usually attract more attention than words which do not. Leaflets of particular colors, dimensions, and art also attract more attention than others.

Credence and Psychological Warfare Communications Efforts. Credence is a necessary prerequisite of influence. If an effort at persuasion is not believable, it is doomed to minimum impact.

Unfortunately, there has been little relatively empirical research done in the area of political warfare credibility. Sociological studies of credibility in the orientation of soldiers and in advertising campaigns have only limited application for the target systems of psychological warfare. The Audience Analysis Section of Radio Free Europe has conducted studies in the theory and practice of credibility which will be available at the time this chapter is published.

The following hypotheses regarding credibility do emerge from preliminary evidence regarding the effects of psychological warfare broadcasts and leaflets: (1) A high correlation exists between the objectivity rating assigned to communications content by the target "audience" and its tendencies to believe what it sees or hears. (2) An effort-at-influence which is *relevant* to people's hopes and fears has greater opportunity to be believed than one which lacks relevance. This appears to be the case even if the effort at persuasion is not considered objective by the target audience.

No matter how objective an effort at influence may be or pretends to be, the decision of what is "propaganda" lies almost completely with the state of mind of the target peoples rather than with the initiative of the social psychological warrior. In broadcasting, for example, the psychological warfare radio station is confronted with the problem of presenting information in which listeners who look for propaganda will not find it. Even news which meets all of the requirements of objective truth may deserve to be rejected for broadcast purposes if it is likely to be disbelieved or seriously challenged by the listener.

Circumstances often encourage people to be propaganda conscious. When the psychological point of satiety is reached by the propaganda efforts of one government, persuasive efforts of another government which for any reason seem "propagandistic" will sometimes be summarily rejected without regard for other considerations. With others in these circumstances, efforts at influence are sometimes suspected of concealing "selfish aims" or "bad news" or "real truth."

This is recognized by those assigned to defend the target system against influence fostered by psychological warfare efforts. A counteroffensive ensues wherein accessible and officially sanctioned media assume the greatest pretense of objectivity possible under existing conditions. In addition, every effort is made to detect factual flaws in "enemy propaganda" so that people can see with their own eyes that they are not being told the truth.

In this context, the *effect of objectivity* should be contrasted with *inherent objectivity* (i.e., objectivity for objectivity's sake). Both qualities can have the same effect on the target population, but each springs from different motives and is designed in a different way. The psychological warfare effort which reflects the integrity of its sponsor and its hopes for the well being of the target population strives for inherent objectivity. The propagandist who is oblivious to these considerations will prefer effect of objectivity. However, expediency will from time to time favor one quality over the other regardless of regular practice.[13]

Thus, the *effect of objectivity* is a vital characteristic of any psychological warfare effort. The extent to which this is achieved depends on the accuracy with which predispositions and events in the target system are appraised by the social psychological warrior.

As for the second hypothesis, individuals can be provoked into giving credence to an idea in which they do not believe if it has a strong bearing upon their hopes and fears. It is not a rational credence but a kind of tentative acceptance which provisionally exploits their sentiments. A threat of atomic war may, for example, inject feelings of dread, rumors of the "possibility" of war, and dissatisfaction with what one's government is doing to prevent war; this in spite of the fact that people may believe that the threat is a "bluff," lacks any basis in military strength of the country making the threat, etc. Allport and Postman, as well as other students of the subject of rumor, have demonstrated that rumors received under these circumstances are particularly capable of assimilation.

Predispositions of The Target and Psychological Warfare Objectives. Any efforts at influence on the part of psychological warfare must recognize the predispositions of the target peoples. By predis-positions is meant the effects of personal experience and prejudices on perception.

People tend to perceive so as to resist any challenge to their experi-ence with people and events. The world, as Lippmann has described it, is structured by the individual in terms of what "on the scale of time are but a few moments of insight and happiness"; both his ego and peace of mind hold a strong stake in what for him is both a meaning-ful and functional structure of experience.

Psychological warfare must be concerned with the nature of the prejudices operating when the effort at influence is "received." If people in a given target system are very rational along a particular line, possess unlimited loyalty toward their government, exercise complete self-confidence in their particular ideology—to cite possible examples—the potential effectiveness of certain psychological warfare weapons is limited accordingly. Frames of reference such as these may afford a defense as effective as physical protection from the effects of armaments, and they can be exploited in counter offensive tactics.

Thus, as is the case with credence, facts, no matter how true they are or how sincere their sponsorship, rank second to the language by which they are transmitted. These symbols must be in accord with what is *possible* as defined by people's predispositions described above and by people's environment as described below. The challenge to the social psychological warrior lies in the fact that information and ideas both lack a logic of their own which would enable the "receiver" to perceive them as they were intended.

A further complication which is less frequently understood is that words themselves stand for slices of reality apart from any actual ex-perience they may symbolize, and about which people are by no means always cognizant. In this connection, Katz has observed: "Viewed realistically, language as a living process has other functions than accurate communication. It did not arise . . . solely in the interests of precise interchange of information. Language as it exists is not the product of scientists trying to perfect an exact set of symbols; it is the product of an arena of everyday life, in which people are con-cerned with manipulating and controlling their fellows and with expressing their emotional and psychological wants."[14]

If language is intended to propagate special meaning in the interests of a particular propaganda effort, it is equally true that past language habits of people in the target system will constitute a potential barrier

to the effective accomplishment of influence. And when the language
of psychological warfare conflicts with the target system's language
structure, a "built-in" dilemma emerges with respect to people's predispositions which may be grounded in an entirely different universe
of discourse.

Environment and the Ability to Respond. If people's expectations
are successfully modified under pressure of psychological warfare activity, their resulting behavior is nevertheless limited by the conditions of their environment. Thus, for example, while people may
be encouraged to reformulate their attitudes toward their government,
they may find it totally impossible to speak out against their regime
in union meetings and on public street corners. In another kind of
stiuation, a government—whose top officials have become convinced
by virtue of psychological warfare efforts that they must make concessions to a particular country—may nevertheless be strongly restricted
by the attitude of its own people or of a neighboring government.
Thus, psychological warfare must limit itself to achieving changes of
attitude and behavior within a realistic range of possibilities.

When people believe that action consistent with the objectives of
psychological warfare against them is limited by their environment,
effectiveness cannot be achieved until they are persuaded that the
limitations are not as great as they may seem. With few exceptions,
no social psychological warrior will deliberately invite resistance which
might provoke consequences (e.g., military intervention by another
nation) that would undermine the eventual psychological warfare
objective.

THE ASSESSMENT OF PSYCHOLOGICAL WARFARE
EFFECTIVENESS

Definition of Effectiveness. Effectiveness can be considered in terms
of the manner in which an entire psychological warfare operation
is conducted and in terms of the extent to which behavioral outcomes
indicate an achievement of objectives. The former inquires into the
extent to which the four above-mentioned conditions are fulfilled by
each step of a given psychological warfare effort and the reliability of
the information and intelligence employed in their application. No
further attention need be given this point, beyond reference to sources
and methods of obtaining this information below. The second ap-

proach to effectiveness, determining the extent to which the objectives of a given psychological warfare effort are being fulfilled, will be discussed at the close of this section.

Sources of Information About Effectiveness. Four basic sources of information about the target system are available from which indices of effectiveness may be formulated and tested: (1) individual and public opinion; (2) individual and group behavior; (3) contents of press and radio; and (4) actions within and on the part of the target government.

The six basic methods for obtaining this information are: (1) The personal interview and questionnaire; (2) Content analysis of mass media (3) Letters to the psychological warfare agency; (4) Participant-observation in private and government meetings, government parliamentary and policy-making meetings, etc.; (5) Access to private letters, diaries, etc. as well as to official documents; (6) Monitoring of target system communications; and (7) Reports from eye witnesses.

These information sources and methods are well known to the social scientist and need not be detailed here. The manner in which they can be most reliably employed is a function of the circumstances under which psychological warfare intelligence is being gathered. The reliability of the information obtained depends upon the adequacy and representatives of available sources, the extent to which first hand contact with various elements of the target system is possible, the degree to which intervening variables are subject to identification and isolation, and the rigor of the methods of inquiry.[15]

Main Areas of Inquiry Regarding Effectiveness. The proving grounds for effectiveness and the basis for a theory of effectiveness lie in the four conditions explained in the previous section. The student of effectiveness must also have an appreciation of the objectives of the particular psychological warfare effort under consideration. Impact without regard for success or failure in accomplishment of purpose offers little and often misleading evidence about the results of psychological warfare.

The specific points to be considered in appraising the significance of behavioral outcomes depend on the type of psychological warfare effort made to accomplish given objectives. Lawrence Schlesinger in a private paper has discussed psychological warfare in terms of particular and distinct models which deserve mention in this overall survey of psychological warfare. The first and most familiar model is concerned with the relationship between the target system and its environment. The second focuses on the commitment and participation of members in the target system's organization and goals. The third views the target as a communication and control system.

Actually no inquiry into effectiveness can assume the existence of any single model. One value of constructing models such as the above is to better calculate the implications for effectiveness of psychological warfare objectives. More important is their use for determining the limitations imposed upon objectives and techniques of psychological warfare by the nature of the target system.

Government Response. The person investigating effectiveness with respect to target government response inquires into the *meaning* of any verbal references to the psychological warfare effort and the meaning of any changes in attitude and behavior by the target government. These questions concern the significance of the government's conduct in terms of compliance with the psychological warfare objectives or awareness that all or significant portions of the community have been influenced in the direction of these objectives.

Summarized, the major points of inquiry are as follows: (1) Possible meanings of target government references to enemy psychological warfare efforts (PW): (a) Target government sensitivity to particular types of PW; (b) Genuine concern regarding impact of PW on its relationship with the population within the target system; (c) Attachment of blame to PW for failures which in fact are due to inefficiency and/or lack of popular support totally independent of PW; (d) Linkage of already discredited ideas, events, or personalities to discredit PW through "guilt by verbal association" techniques; (e) Use of PW as a vehicle to discredit ideas, events, or personalities through "guilt by verbal association" techniques; (f) Unconcern for some aspects of PW and more concern for others; (g) Occasion for guidance to local agit-prop elements; (h) Occasion for intimidation; (i) Occasion for rallying support of particular group; (j) Effort to discredit PW in minds of other nations; (k) Exploitation of error or vulnerability on the part of PW; and (l) Reflection of power struggle with government ranks which is attributable to PW efforts.

Two observations should be made about target government references to antagonistic psychological warfare efforts. Differences in subject matter and intent often exist between those references appearing in the radio and press and those which are made in interpersonal communications which are usually not available to the analyst. A point which may appear ridiculous in print but be far more persuasive in the form of a rumor may therefore deliberately be disseminated in the latter form. An idea which is crowded out of limited newspaper space may be pursued at greater length during a meeting of intellectuals or a labor union rally. Moreover, efforts at intimidation and admissions of impact are more likely to occur in personal conversations than in the public print.

Second, effectiveness of a psychological warfare effort is by no means always reflected by the frequency with which it is mentioned by the target government. As the above list indicates, references to PW are not always acknowledgements of effectiveness. They indicate an awareness of PW existence to be sure, but they sometimes signify domestic (even personal) considerations or successful counter PW efforts. In addition, those aspects of PW which are never or very infrequently discussed by government propagandists may be forbidden as objects of discussion for reasons which are significant to a study of effectiveness. Finally, many governments believe that it does not pay to advertise the hostile efforts of another nation or to concede that they have any concern whatsoever for their outcome.

Needless to say, these references must be appraised in terms of known audience reaction, the known vulnerabilities of the target system, and the counter weapons at the command of the target government.

(2) The following activities on the part of the target government need *to be* continuously appraised in order to determine whether any departures from the *status quo* have occurred which are meaningful in resolving the question of effectiveness: (a) Provision of information and propaganda for internal consumption; (b) Internal policies regarding standard of living, working conditions, representative government, etc.; (c) Stability or shifts in personnel of officialdom; (d) Tactics of diplomacy and negotiations (particularly with government waging PW); (e) Types of behavior defined as anti-government; (f) Degree of toleration with respect to freedom of speech, press, religion, and the arts; (g) Status of individuals formerly very much accepted, censured, or repudiated; (h) Status of censorship efforts, jamming of radio broadcasts, boundary restrictions, trade restrictions; and (i) Policies with respect to other countries.

Audience Reaction. The following points are typical of those to be studied in determining the effects of a given psychological warfare effort on the population of a target system: (a) Extent to which people seek exposure to PW efforts at influence (e.g., purchase and conversion of radio sets, participation in rumor and group discussion, visits to foreign legations); (b) Popularity or lack of popularity of devices communicating influence; (c) Target audience imagery of PW agency and factors affecting it; (d) Extent to which people identify themselves and their problems with psychological warfare goals; (e) People's current reactions to their government (respect, loyalty, submission, willingness to endure deprivation, belief in "lasting power" of regime, etc.); (f) Extent to which people credit particular happenings to PW effort; (g) Extent to which popular interest is sustained in PW; (h) "Communicability" of influence, i.e., extent to which people pass on to others what they have or think they have perceived (heard, seen, felt, thought) as a result of PW effort; (i) Extent to which reaction is voluntarily expressed through letters, visits, protests to own government, indignation about own government or PW, resistance to government countermeasures calculated to bar exposure to and/or discourage people from influence by PW objectives; and (j) Extent to which people's actions do or do not coincide with actions predicted after any given PW efforts.

The ultimate measure of effectiveness is the extent to which the target population is influenced to think and act in accordance with the prescribed objectives of a given psychological warfare effort.

CONCLUDING NOTE

Without attempting to summarize what is an altogether too brief survey of this field, some points are particularly clear with respect to the sociological implications of psychological warfare: (1) Psychological warfare more frequently characterizes conflict between nations than ever before. In some cases it has *substituted* for armed warfare; more frequently it has been utilized to achieve political goals which are possible because of developments in the technology and techniques of mass communications. (2) Although warfare (influence) by force of persuasion rather than force of arms has come to be known as psychological warfare, its sociological implications are many. This has been tacitly recognized by the increasing participation of sociologists in both the conduct and the study of psychological warfare techniques. (3) Psychological warfare does not manufacture opinions. But it does endeavor to engineer consent within the target system by seeking to influence people's attitudes and behavior in the direction of prescribed objectives.

(4) Psychological warfare is best understood in terms of the relationship between a psychological warfare agency and its audience. This situational relationship in effect posits certain conditions which need to be met if psychological warfare techniques are going to achieve maximum potential effectiveness. *Rules* of *how* to conduct psychological warfare without regard for these conditions are of small avail. (5) Although both the techniques and purposes of psychological warfare clearly distinguish it from other forms of warfare, psychological warfare is never independent of other events. All warfare has political goals, psychological warfare included, and events over which the psychological warmaker has no control may substantially alter the circumstances under which influence is being exerted.

SELECTED BIBLIOGRAPHY

Edward W. Barrett, *Truth is Our Weapon* (New York: Funk & Wagnalls, 1953).

R. M. Collier, "The Effect of Propaganda upon Attitude Following a Critical Examination of the Propaganda Itself," *Journal of Social Psychology,* XX (1944), 3-17.

E. Cooper and Marie Jahoda, "The Evasion of Propaganda: How Prejudiced People Respond to Anti-Prejudice Propaganda," *Journal of Psychology,* XXIII (1947), 15-25.

F. Bowen Evans, *Worldwide Communist Propaganda Activities* (New York: The Macmillan Co., 1955).

Eric Hoffer, *The True Believer* (London: Secker & Warburg, 1952).

Carl I. Hovland, Irving L. Janis and Harold H. Kelley, *Communication and Persuasion* (New Haven: Yale University Press, 1953).

Alex Inkeles, *Public Opinion in Soviet Russia: A Study in Mass Persuasion* (Cambridge: Harvard University Press, 1950).

Elihu Katz and Paul F. Lazarsfeld, *Personal Influence* (Glencoe: The Free Press, 1955).

Evron M. Kirkpatrick, *Target, The World* (New York: The MacMillan Co., 1956).

Harold D. Lasswell, *The Analysis of Political Behavior* (London: Routledge & Kegan Paul, 1948).

Harold D. Lasswell, *Politics: Who Gets What, When, How* (Glencoe: The Free Press, 1951).

Daniel Lerner, *Propaganda in War and Crisis: Materials for American Policy* (New York: George W. Stewart, 1951).

Daniel Lerner, *Sykewar: Psychological Warfare Against Germany, D-Day to VE Day* (New York George W. Stewart Publisher, Inc., 1949).

Paul M. A. Linebarger, *Psychological Warfare* (Washington, D.C.: Infantry Journal Press, 1948).

Walter Lippmann, *Public Opinion* (New York: Harcourt, Brace and Company, 1922).

Wilbur Schramm, Daniel Katz, Willmoore Kendall, Theodore Vallance, *The Nature of Psychological Warfare* (Chevy Chase: Operations Research Office, 1953).

Wilbur Schramm, Ed., *The Process and Effects of Mass Communication* (Urbana: University of Illinois Press, 1955).

John Scott, *Political Warfare* (New York: The John Day Co., 1955).

Philip Selznick, *The Organizational Weapon: A Study of Bolshevik Strategy and Tactics* (New York: McGraw-Hill, 1952).

Chitra M. Smith, Berton Winograd, and Alice R. Jwaideh, *International Communication and Political Warfare: An Annotated Bibliography* (Santa Monica: The Rand Corporation, 1952).

Bruce Lannes Smith, Harold D. Lasswell, and Ralph D. Casey, *Propaganda, Communication, and Public Opinion: A Comprehensive Reference Guide* (Princeton: Princeton Univ. Press, 1946).

Hans Speier, "Psychological Warfare Reconsidered," in Daniel Lerner and Harold D. Lasswell (eds.), *The Policy Sciences* (Stanford: Stanford University Press, 1951).

Oren Stephens, "Facts to a Candid World" (Stanford University Press, 1955.)

Dr. Robert C. Sorensen is Chief of the Audience Analysis Section of Radio Free Europe in Munich, whose purpose is to study listener and communist regime response to Western radio broadcasts, the attitudes of people in the target countries, and other factors bearing upon the relationship between Western broadcasters and their audiences. Before coming with Radio Free Europe, he was associated with Operations Research Office of the Johns Hopkins University (Washington, D.C.). In the five years preceding, he was Assistant Professor of Law at the University of Nebraska College of Law, and Lecturer in Sociology for one summer at Northwestern University. He has conducted several studies in the fields of opinion research and in the impact of social research findings on legal policy problems. His articles have appeared in several periodicals including *The Journal of Marketing, Social Forces, Journal of Criminal Law, Criminology and Political Science, New York University Law Review,* and *Journalism Quarterly.*

NOTES

1. Defining psychological warfare is necessarily an arbitrary undertaking, because it has been so seldom formally defined. That differences of opinion exist regarding the nature of psychological warfare is seen from the discussion along different

lines by Hans Speier who also asserts the lack of a more basic agreement on the nature of war itself.

2. Thus it should be clear that wars fought for these ends, even if the techniques of warfare utilized are wholly those of persuasion by "psychological means," cannot be compared to advertising and propaganda campaigns on the home front.

3. "Propaganda," *Chambers Encyclopedia* (London: George Newnes, Ltd., 1950), II.

4. Oleg Anisimov, "A New Policy For American Psychological Warfare," *The Russian Review* (July, 1955).

5. This is not to say, however, that psychological warfare has either replaced what otherwise would inevitably have been the more conventional military warfare or that psychological warfare has introduced warfare into situations where otherwise warfare would be non-existent. This question is beyond the purview of this chapter.

6. At the same time, the only military defense against nuclear attack is massive retaliation in kind.

7. An ancient Chinese military classic warned of the limits of physical violence in 500 B.C.: "Now, of the fighting races below heaven; those who gained five victories have been worn out; those who have won four victories have been impoverished; three victories have given dominion; two victories have founded a kingdom; and upon one victory an empire has been established. For those who have gained power on earth by many victories are few; and those who have lost it, many."

8. This type of goal, among others, provoked John Scott to categorize political warfare as either constructive or destructive. Constructive political warfare, says Scott, is "aimed at making friends and allies by organized persuasion".

9. Needless to say, although a country's population is often a target of political warfare techniques, the masses seldom initiate them. Some governments, particularly totalitarian ones, make particular efforts to organize a continuous civil defense program among their populations with respect to psychological warfare.

10. See, e.g., Margaret Mead and Rhoda Metraux, (eds.), *The Study of Culture at a Distance* (University of Chicago Press, 1953), for an excellent manual based on the researches of other countries from the outside inaugurated by the late Dr. Ruth Benedict.

11. Daniel Lerner has posited similar conditions (see *Sykewar*) for psychological warfare from which the titles though not the subject matter were taken in considerable part.

12. Wilbur Schramm, Daniel Katz, Willmoore Kendall, Theodore Vallance, *The Nature of Psychological Warfare* (Chevy Chase, Maryland: Operations Research Office, The Johns Hopkins University, 1953), 35.

13. Thus, for example, a given piece of news or information may in fact seem destined to have an undesired non-objective effect (not believed even though true).

14. Daniel Katz, "Psychological Barriers to Communication," in Wilbur Schramm, Ed., *Mass Communication* (Urbana: University of Illinois Press, 1949).

15. For a discussion of psychological warfare effectiveness study, see (1) Daniel Lerner, *Sykewar* (New York: George W. Stewart), Chapter 11; (2) Selected studies of effectiveness by Radio Free Europe, Munich; Intelligence and Research Division of United States Information Service; and Operations Research Office of the Johns Hopkins University; (3) Richard Sheldon and John Dutowski, "Are Refugee Interviews Projectable?", *Public Opinion Quarterly* (Winter, 1952); (4) Robert C. Sorensen, "Radio Free Europe and Its Audience Publics", *Midwest Sociologist,* XVII (Spring, 1956).

IV.

TRENDS ABROAD

GREAT BRITAIN

Donald MacRae
London School of Economics

There was sociology before Comte invented the word. In Britain where tradition is strong and where it is customary to pretend that something done yesterday for the first time has been done ever since that period "whereof the memory of man runneth not," it is necessary to keep the fact in mind. An account of sociology in modern Britain must reach far back—not just to the end of the second German war, nor even to the first academic recognition of the subject in 1907, but further still to the eighteenth century where two of the dominant traits of British sociology were established to influence most of what is done today. Some, indeed, would go back further to the political arithmeticians of the late seventeenth century with their demographic interests, their concern to number and define the social groups of English society. The interests of these men were practical—administrative and meliorative—and they were not professional academics but men of affairs with strong social concerns. This pattern of interest and concern is one of the main themes of British sociology, and today, as two hundred and fifty years ago, many of those who continue it are not professionals—though it would be hard and untrue to describe their work in any way amateur.

The second theme has been the making of institutional and comparative studies. What is sometimes called the prehistory of our subject has no larger mass of material still usable than the books of the eighteenth century Scottish investigators of society. Hutchison's *De naturali hominum socialitate* was an inaugural lecture at Glasgow in 1730. Twenty years later and more came the flood. As everyone knows Adam Smith's *Theory of Moral Sentiments* (1759) and *Wealth of Nations* (1776) are based, like Hume's *The Natural History of Religion* (1757) on wide comparative studies of the appropriate insti-

699

tutions. Specifically on the nature and growth of social institutions
in general were Adam Ferguson's *An Essay on the History of Civil
Society* (1776), John Millar's *Distinction of Ranks in Society* (1771),
and a host of lesser works by Kames, Monboddo, Stewart and others.
This tradition continued in Scotland into the early nineteenth century, and was continued by English writers from that time to the
present. The reasons for its ultimate failure in Scotland would provide material for a pretty essay in the sociology of knowledge—it
would, alas, be irrelevant.

The history of the other tradition is more continuous. In the
1790's appeared the first (or "old") *Statistical Account of Scotland*
under the direction of the agriculturalist, administrator and politician, Sir John Sinclair. The title may mislead, for here, "by Statistical is meant . . . an inquiry into the state of a county for the
purpose of ascertaining . . . the quantum of happiness enjoyed by
its inhabitants and the means of its future improvement." Its twenty-
one volumes are based on the replies from the ministers of religion
in each parish to a questionnaire of one hundred and sixty items—
not all of them sociological. A committee supervised the second
Statistical Account on the same basis in the 1840's. *The Third Statistical Account of Scotland* on a more scientific but less uniform plan
under the supervision of the four Scottish universities began with
Ayrshire (Edinburgh, Oliver and Boyd, 1951). So far four volumes
have appeared. When it is completed we will thus have a unique
record of the total social composition and social structure of a single
society over a period of some one hundred and seventy years. Clearly
such work is sociological, but professional sociologists will have had
little enough—too little—to do with any of it.

In England Sir Frederick Eden, influenced by Kames and Smith,
produced his three volume *The State of the Poor* in 1797 and his
Estimate of the Number of Inhabitants in 1800. He adapted his
questionnaire from Sinclair's, made use of the clergy as informants,
and employed a research assistant on his field work. His *Estimate*,
which anticipated the first British census of 1801, is the earliest attempt known to me to use rudimentary sampling methods to cut
down the time, tedium, and expense of social research.

Given this background it will readily be seen why sociology in
Britain cannot be treated separately from the practice and study
of social administration and social work. It will also have begun to
appear why this is also true of social anthropology which in these

islands and the Commonwealth and British Colonial Empire forms
an integral part of sociology. A fuller development of this point will
be found later in this paper.

It would be inappropriate to pursue the story of British sociology
in the last century on even the summary scale which has so far
been used. Certain landmarks, however, can and should be quoted.
Industrialism as a social system developed first in Britain. The positive and meliorative social philosophy of utilitarianism—influential,
let us say, from Bentham's first published work in 1776 to the death
of J. S. Mill in 1873—interacted with the social, administrative, and
political problems of the new society to maintain a lively stream of
social investigation into particular problems at every level from that
of private and local research to government commissions. On the
whole the universities—even that product of the 1820's, the University of London—stood aloof from these developments. The education
of the gentleman and the dedication of the scholar remained unsullied
by the filth of Dickens' London or the grime of the industrial urbanism described in Engels' *The Condition of Working-Class in England*
(Leipzig, 1845) or Disraeli's *Sybil* (1845)...

It is however in the 1830's that the Royal Statistical Society was
founded. It was followed by a remarkable, if less enduring body, The
National Association for the Promotion of Social Science. Neither
academic purism nor a vulgarized *laisser faire* could prevent practical
benevolence and administrative need from satisfying their appetite
for precise social data.

The National Association had an interesting and largely unwritten
story. It flourished from 1856 to 1886; it was important enough to be
attacked by powerful interests and to rebuff their attacks; its annual
conferences were public and important events for the cities that
housed them; yet it perished in obscurity and what is most remembered about its guiding spirit, G. W. Hastings, is that from being
a prison reformer he became an embezzler and a convict. Part of its
legacy is that in English usage "social science" is often a synonym
for social welfare work and, sometimes, for the study of social
administration.

The *Transactions* of the Association are of great interest not just
as a record of Victorian social life and attitudes, but as embodying
research—as we would now call it—of diverse kinds and values. The
tradition of practically oriented social empiricism remained unbroken.
In a sense the Association failed because of its success: smaller, spe-

cialized bodies were established in particular fields, legislation and charitable action reduced something of the urgency which had inspired its endeavors, and such bodies as the Charity Organization Society founded in 1869 on the ungenerous principles developed earlier by a Glasgow clergyman and economist, Thomas Chalmers (1780-1847), narrowed the concept of "social science" to more limited purposes and more confined interests.

During this period comparative studies flourished. Their success in geology, the biological sciences, philology, and prehistoric archaeology combined with the mass of new and exciting data brought before the educated public by the expansion of British power in Asia, Africa, and Oceania to produce both numerous schemes of social evolution and genetic studies of particular institutions. Despite the examples provided of the careful use of the comparative method in other subjects this work was often slipshod, and most of it compares unfavorably with what had been achieved in the eighteenth century. The writings of Maine, whose *Ancient Law* appeared three years after the *Origin of Species*, provide a rare exception in a period more ambitious than effective. Yet out of these interests evolved modern British social anthropology with its sociological and administrative bias.

J. S. Mill's *Auguste Comte and Positivism* appeared in 1865. In 1843 the sixth book of his *Logic*, concerned with the methodology of the social sciences, had proposed a discipline of "ethology," not unlike what I now take it to be understood by the term "behavioral sciences" in the United States. Otherwise the period is barren of serious theoretical interest. The influence of Comte remained rather ethical and religious than sociological. It was, however, in these years that Herbert Spencer was shaping his system. It is not Spencer's finished system, however, that is at work in modern British sociology—whatever textbooks of the history of sociology may say to the contrary. His influence, often unrecognized but profound and pervasive, is to be found elsewhere.

No-one today reads Spencer: his style is repellent, his illustrative material always copious but sometimes ludicrous, his evolutionism dated and his metaphysics unacceptable. If he gained—as J. S. Mill certainly did—from an education and a career outside the walls of the university, he suffered in a way that Mill did not from a consequent lack of discipline and criticism. Yet in Britain and to a large extent in the United States and France the vocabulary and concepts of sociology are predominantly Spencerian even if his ideas are rejected or forgotten. When we define institutions, use such words as "structure" and "function," attempt the analysis of social control or of social roles we are indebted to Spencer. *The Principles of Sociology* (1876-96) are far less important than the heroic taxonomic effort of the *Descriptive Sociology* (classified and arranged by Spencer, 1874-1933) wherein an attempt is made to classify societies in terms of their social structures and to depict these structures as changing processes. For many reasons the attempt failed, and was bound to fail, but the lessons of that failure are at least as valuable as certain fruitful and widely praised theories and first approximations in the history of the natural sciences. Nor is this influence for good exhausted.[1]

British Sociology After Spencer.[2] Meanwhile the academic situation had begun to change. Oxford was not to recognize sociology until 1949, but in 1884 began the association of E. B. Tylor with the university from which his family's religious affiliations had barred him as youth. Cambridge followed Oxford's lead in 1900, and in 1908 London followed suit, and the phrase "Social Anthropology" was used academically for the first time in the new University of Liverpool. Tylor's influence was not merely one of books and such famous papers as *On a Method of Investigating the Development of Institutions* (1889). Classical scholars such as Cornford, Jane Harrison and Gilbert Murray found in anthropology a clue to the interpretation of their own problems. James Frazer, unjustly neglected today, deserted the classics for anthropology, and gave the subject a public respect it has never lost.

Thus by the end of the century there was in Britain an established tradition of social investigation, of social work, and of the comparative study of the institutions of both primitive and advanced societies. In 1895 the London School of Economics and Political Science was founded by Sidney and Beatrice Webb for the pursuit of all the social sciences. Modern British field work in anthropology dates from A. C. Haddon's expedition to the Torres Straits in 1898. The most important of English social surveys—Booth's *Life and Labour of the People of London*—took its definite form in seventeen volumes in 1902. In 1906 Sir Arthur Bowley suggested how such work might be achieved with less labor by the scientific use of sampling. In 1903 began a series of *Sociological Papers*. The whole period of the 1890's and the Edwardian era were marked by a new growth of demography and great advances in the theory of statistics. The situation for sociology appeared promising as never before.

At first it might have seemed as if the promise were to be rapidly fulfilled. In the University of London and at the London School of Economics L. T. Hobhouse became the first Professor of Sociology in these islands (1907); with him, in a personal chair, was Edward Westermarck.[3] Both were already widely known for their comparative studies and philosophical interests. Both continued to add to their repute in both fields, and in 1915, a new name, that of Morris Ginsberg, joined those of Hobhouse and G. C. Wheeler on the title page of *The Material Culture and Social Institutions of the Simpler Peoples*. That name has remained before the public ever since—as colleague and successor to Hobhouse and the central figure for praise or blame in British sociology.

THE PERIOD AFTER WORLD WAR I

Two things chiefly prevented the full expectation of the period 1907-1945 from being realized. The 1914-18 war removed by death nearly a generation of young men, and service in the trenches weakened and brought to premature graves many of the survivors. (In this respect the consequence of the 1939-45 war have been less severe.) The 1920's and '30's were years of stagnation, poverty and unemployment and academic penury. Secondly the extra-academic impulse, so often rich and rewarding, turned sour in the '20's. *The Sociological Review* despite some excellent articles touched a nadir of quality and sentiment in these years. It improved greatly after 1930 under the influence of Ginsberg and others, and an Institute of Sociology formed in that year did some useful work, notably in its excellent conference reports on such topics as *Class Conflict and Social Stratification* (ed. T. H. Marshall, 1938). Unfortunately both the *Review* and the Institute suffered greatly from the second German War, and though the new University College of North Staffordshire saved the former the latter has disappeared.

During these years the number of social surveys increased, social work training became widely established in the universities, and both the teaching and the researches of Radcliffe Brown and Malinowski, and the administrative success of Rattray in Ashanti, consolidated the position of social anthropology. Ginsberg's *Sociology* (Oxford

University Press, 1934) gave a scholarly summary of the position of sociology at that date and at the same time possessed an originality not always fully appreciated. Significantly, given its date, it devoted much space to the examination and refutation of racial theories. Refugee scholars from Nazi Germany were already introducing a new element into British sociology.

It was not that the work of continental sociology was unfamiliar, but that its spirit had little affected British thought. One exception to this is undoubtedly Durkheim, but he was less alien to the tradition I have tried to delineate than might at first sight appear. Indeed I believe that a most fruitful historical enquiry would be one into the English influence on Durkheim and his successors. When such a work has been achieved I believe that the influence of Spencer will be found to have been far more powerful than has hitherto been conceived. Nor was Weber neglected—Tawney and Ginsberg in different ways saw to that. But Nazism produced a new urgency, and German sociology in the person of Karl Mannheim seemed to hold a new, an almost messianic hope that spread for beyond the walls of the London School of Economics and the Institute of Education where he later went. Perhaps sociology both existed as a developed discipline and could help solve the political and social problems of the time? The thought was a heady one.

Unfortunately Mannheim's best work was done ere he left the continent and if he intoxicated such unlikely people as the Archbishop of Canterbury, he was also intoxicated by them. Certainly something was done to cure British insularity, but solid achievement was rather to seek. Yet 1945 saw a new situation, a new optimism about the utility and even the necessity of an expansion of sociology in the universities and about its possible influence on intellectual and administrative life.

During the 1939-45 war the London School of Economics had been evacuated to Cambridge. It returned to London to find its building unique amongst those of the colleges and schools of the university in having escaped bomb damage. Two of its departments can be regarded as specifically concerned with sociology—Ginsberg's Department of Sociology engaged in undergraduate and postgraduate teaching and research, and the Social Science Department (social administration and social work) then led by T. H. Marshall and now by Richard Titmuss. Also at the School was the Population Investigation Committee directed by D. V. Glass.

In addition to these bodies there was Mass Observation with its ideology of "every man his own anthropologist," which had been founded in 1937. Its reports, always stimulating but unsystematic, became of less and less frequency and importance during the postwar years. In 1941 a Government Social Survey—today directed by Louis Moss—had been instituted the better to guide policy and administration by the provision of social data on public need and demand. Its work has been of constant value not merely for its official purposes but also as providing social data to other researchers and as a laboratory of the techniques of social investigation.

THE PERIOD AFTER WORLD WAR II

In 1946 a committee under the Duke of Devonshire recommended a special course of social training for recruits to the Colonial Service. The Colonial Office had long been interested in social research, and in 1944 had set up a Colonial Social Science Research Council under Sir Alexander Carr-Saunders, then, Director of The London School of Economics, with members from the universities of Cambridge, Edinburgh, London and Oxford. The primary impact of all this was, of course on social anthropology. This subject, however, it might be remembered had been defined in Britain by Radcliffe Brown as "comparative sociology," and if the subject had tended in the inter-war years to move away from sociology, it would I think be fair to say that the last ten years have seen an ever increasing rapprochement of the two. The problems of colonial territories have, at any rate, become increasingly those of urbanism and industrialism, and research in them more strictly sociological. (This is not the place to write of social research in the new colonial universities—which is extensive— or of their one major teaching department of sociology in Ghana.)

In 1946, another government committee, this time under the direction of the economic historian Sir John Clapham, was appointed to "consider whether there was need for additional provision for research into social and economic questions." In 1947 the Universities Grant Committee (itself appointed by the Treasury) established an advisory sub-committee on the social sciences. Both agreed that available resources were inadequate, and by 1951-52 some £400,000 were available in addition to grants made by independent trusts and foundations.

The period from the beginnings of the Churchill government in 1940 to the fall of the Attlee administration in 1951 was one of great social optimism—the planning and establishment of new social services, the reform of old. In this atmosphere new teaching and research departments came into being, and existing ones were reformed and expanded. Student demand increased enormously and, at the time of writing, shows no abatement. Glasgow and Edinburgh developed primarily in the field of research, while Birmingham, Leeds, Liverpool, Exeter, Nottingham and Leicester expanded the teaching of sociology. In January 1949 the present writer became the first sociologist engaged as such in Oxford—an isolated, not very important, but symptomatic fact. Even Cambridge unexpectedly, briefly, and experimentally brought over visiting professors of sociology from the United States.

In 1946 the social anthropologists founded a professional association. In 1951 the sociologists followed suit with a less exclusive body, the British Sociological Association which has today about five hundred members. A year earlier the *British Journal of Sociology* made its first appearance—its present editorial board of four sociologists, a social administrator and a social anthropologist itself illustrates something of the thesis of this paper about the nature of British sociology. Shortly afterwards the veteran *Sociological Review* was drastically reformed and improved. From 1944 onwards an International Library of Sociology had been produced by a leading London publishing house. A new, differently conceived series of sociological books began in 1956, and at the time of writing a third is planned.

TRENDS IN DEVELOPMENT

Let us now try to delineate the main lines of progress in these post-war years. Demography received an impetus from official concern about the falling birth-rate and the appearance of the possibility of an absolute decline in population which first seriously attracted attention in the 1930's. A Royal Commission was established and commanded resources quite new in character. Its Report (Cmd. 7695) has proved of less importance than the body of technical papers which it has published and new information contained in its sample family census. For sociologists who are not themselves demographers particular interest attaches to D. V. Glass and E. Grebenik's *The Trend* and *Pattern of Fertility in Great Britain: a Report on the Family Census of* 1946 (London, 1954). The motivation of reproductory patterns—social and individual—remain despite this work, little understood.[4]

Demographic research still reveals medical, social and perhaps psychological differentia between the classes—differentia which have direct bearing on the trends, quantity and quality of the population. Their study fills much of the space of Britain's leading demographic journal, *Population Studies.* Their consequences in a society dedicated to the making of public provision for individual need and against individual disaster—i.e in a self-conscious welfare state—are part of the subject matter of what is often called in Britain either 'social science' or 'social work.' In nearly every British university there is a department dedicated to these disciplines, and as the emphasis of these departments changes from a total concentration on case work to a greater admission of the place of social administration, so do they become more sociological. In the past their students were highly class selected from the daughters of the upper middle classes, and they engaged in instruction at what was often a lower level (and was always for a briefer period) than the usual courses for first degrees. Today their work is increasingly with undergraduates reading sociology, with postgraduates, and with research. The old class bias is much reduced, and the area now attracts men as well as women. This trend is particularly marked in large departments, such as those at Liverpool or London. No good book has yet been written on the principles of social administration, but there has been and is a mass of useful research, and at least one admirable synthetic study. R. Titmuss, *Problems of Social Policy* (H.M.S.O., London, 1950).

One conspicuous study in this area, criminology, has benefitted more from general sociology than it has contributed. This discipline is particularly well established in Bristol, Cambridge, Oxford and London. No other branch of British sociology has gained so much from refugee scholars—in particular K. Mannheim. (A post-war journal, *The British Journal of Delinquency* published by the independent Institute for the Scientific Treatment of Delinquency might be mentioned here for its consistent quality).

The sociologies of special topics such as religion have been but little pursued. The only work that readily springs to mind is J. Highet's *The Churches in Scotland,* though one looks forward with eagerness to the publication of B. R. Wilson's study of three sects in

a midland city of England as a pioneer study of the sociology of contemporary religious behavior in Britain.

The sociology of politics has taken two forms: the sociologising of
political science—to which we can pay but little attention—and the
study of the political process directly by sociologists. British political
scientists have been so afraid of the name of sociology that some of
them have even invented the pompous term "psephology" to
avoid using the phrase "electoral sociology." (Others among them
have been less bigoted—for example S. E. Finer of North Staffordshire.) These "psephological" studies have taken over some, but not
enough, of the techniques of the social surveyors, and have also
learned something from the pollsters. Five of them are of particular
importance—the accounts of the general elections of 1945, 1950, and
1951, and two detailed studies of Bristol and Glasgow respectively.
Two directly sociological electoral studies have been J. Bonham, *The
Middle Class Vote* (London: Faber and Faber, 1954) and a detailed
analysis of the London borough of Greenwich: M. Benney, A. P. Gray,
and R. H. Pear, *How People Vote* (London: Routledge, 1956); the
latter stemming directly from the interest of London School of Economics sociologists in social stratification and mobility. In 1955 a Canadian sociologist at the London School of Economics, R. T. McKenzie,
produced what is by far the most important study of parties at the
national level as working institutions in *British Political Parties* (London: Heinemann, 1955).

Probably the most thoroughly cultivated of special sociologies has
been the sociology of education—both for its own sake and for the
light which it throws on social stratification and mobility in Britain.
Education in England—not in Scotland or Wales—is completely class
dominated. Until the rise of the Labor Party our political elites were
overwhelmingly recruited from a small number of schools, and at the
time of writing (March, 1957) a conservative journal, *The Spectator,*
was engaged in criticising a Conservative Party administration as being
"government by old Etonians."[5] To understand the social composition of English society and to make any sense of social and political
change it is thus centrally necessary to understand the structure and
functioning of English education in its social setting.

It is this impetus that has produced such books as those by Banks,
Floud, Halsey and Martin;[6] it also underlies such a study of professionalization as Tropp's contribution,[7] where the changing prestige
of the teachers in the public elementary schools which deal with the

mass of the population is an index of social conflict and social change. The careful study of the institutionalization of science and technology in Cardwell[8] illustrates class resistance of a most interesting kind to changes in the content of education. It is not surprising therefore that five out of thirteen chapters of D. V. Glass (Ed.), *Social Mobility in Britain* (London: Routledge, 1954) should be concerned with education.

This latter study, based on a careful occupational ranking, new statistical techniques, research in time and in depth in selected localities, is perhaps the most important document of its kind yet to appear in any country. I tried to place this work in its international context and to summarize its conclusions:[9]

> "Although the generation of adults born in the 1920's is likely to be still highly mobile, and no generalization made about it is as yet certain, we can say that there had been no significant change in mobility over the previous three generations. This conclusion contradicts the common picture of mobility constantly increased by public educational provision and the welfare state; but, for all that, it confirms too much other work, is consistent with too many other facts, and is too carefully established for there to be much doubt that it is correct. Secondly, the decisive factor in assigning individuals to one or another of the seven classes into which the population is divided, is the educational divide: does one, in England, have access to grammar or public school education, then one's path is smooth; if not, not. This is hardly surprising, for it is clear to all that for over a century the English have institutionalized their class structure through their educational system, but the degree to which this remains operatively true is surprising and overwhelming. Thirdly, despite this long immobility based on a partial system of schooling, British society as compared with most others is relatively fluid. That there is more social mobility in Britain than in France (and more in France than in Italy) is not a very striking discovery, but that there is, and has been as much social mobility in our country as in the United States is surely astonishing. Yet American investigators have confirmed this fact.
>
> This situation of a fairly high but apparently constant rate of social mobility has been accompanied by a reasonably static distribution of money income before taxation, and by a more significant—and far greater—inequity in the distribution of capital in private hands. It does not mean, however, that the 'social distance' between classes has remained constant, and I believe indeed that this distance both has decreased and is lessening. The

general rise of the national income and the tendency of modern industry to satisfy mass rather than luxury demand have united to produce this result. Poverty is no longer so extreme, or the consuming habits of the classes so different as even a generation ago and, in addition, fifteen years of full employment have made a real difference to the attitudes of every class. The old contempts, deferences, hatreds, and condescensions have lessened or gone underground. What is more, the new respect for the working class movement has tended to create if not a class, at least a stratum of trade union and Labour Party office-holders, etc. which has to be accepted and reluctantly recognized if only because it is feared."

Since Glass' volume appeared, research in this area had gone forward in London, Liverpool and elsewhere. An unusually clear and full summary will be found in Simey.[10] The Liverpool investigations by Scott, Banks, and others make particularly clear how stratification differences operate within the working class, in industrial units, and affect labor relations. In every country the study of industrial sociology must involve the study of status differences: in Britain where these differences are unusually complex and deep rooted one may feel that industrial sociologists have neglected both a challenge and an opportunity. Certainly their researches have so far been marked by a concentration on either formal structure,[11] or on the pursuit of themes suggested by American example rather than by the peculiar character of industrialism in this, the oldest and most thoroughly industrialized —though not most highly developed—industrial society in the world. Happily this state of affairs is changing. The post-war years have seen a number of social surveys continuing an already well-established tradition. These have ranged from enormous and scientifically unsatisfactory studies on a national scale (such as Rowntree and Lavers,[12] or G. Gorer)[13] to detailed urban surveys like R. Glass on Middlesbrough[14] and the beginning of an English rural sociology with such books as W. R. Williams' *Sociology of an English Village* (London: Routledge, 1956). However various their merits these surveys have all contained data of interest, but none has, I think, done much to alter English techniques, change English picture of English life[15] or deflect a course of worthwhile laboratory for the student of society.[16]

The first point has been well discussed by L. Silberman,[17] and though the situation has altered since he wrote, and altered for the better, yet is remains true that while sociologists can readily find employment yet the discipline is still regarded with suspicion and only a few of its most distinguished practitioners awarded a public esteem. It is a remarkable fact that neither the recent Royal Commission on Divorce nor that on Capital Punishment contained a sociologist nor made use of any weight of sociologically derived evidence. I think the same is true of the Duke of Edinburgh's Study Conference (Oxford, 1956) on the human problems of industrial communities, but so many people were involved in this that I might well be mistaken. Certainly any such participation was merely peripheral. Part of the blame for this lies with the sociologists themselves, but the primary factors are deeply imbedded in English social structure and English educational practice. Happily time and circumstances are eroding these influences and hope is not unreasonable.

The situation with regard to social theory is open, I believe, to more dramatic transformation. The doyen of our sociology, Morris Ginsberg, has never been the preacher of a doctrine more constricting than one of tolerance and scholarship. He has made his own contribution by exposition, selection and elucidation rather than directly. Consequently his contribution has had its originality underestimated. His very lucidity has disguised the difficulty and importance of what he has had to say. His constant—and I believe correct—attempt to keep sociology in harness with social philosophy has not always been popular. Yet most of us are, directly and indirectly, his pupils. The two volumes of his collected essays and his pre-war *Sociology*[18] provide foundations for a solid and realistic social theorizing of which any country might well be proud. Something of the same sort could be said of the more slender work of W. J. Sprott.[19] T. H. Marshall[20] showed a unique sensitivity to the issues of theoretical sociology, social administration and the problems of policy. An archaeologist like V. G. Childe[21] and an anthropologist like I. Schapera[22] have shown the continuing value of the comparative method and in so doing have cast real light on the content and procedure of sociological theory.

It is therefore possible to be sanguine. Sociology is becoming an established reality in teaching, research and among the professions. The traditions with the description of which I began are still vital. There are new forces at work to match new conditions. Status will come. As in no other country sociology and social anthropology can draw strength from each other. Most important of all, there is a new generation of sociologists, younger than the present writer, larger than ever before, and already rich in achievement as well as promise.

SELECTED BIBLIOGRAPHY

M. Abrams, *Social Surveys and Social Action* (London: Heinemann, 1951).

J. A. Banks, *Prosperity and Parenthood* (London: Routledge & Kegan Paul, 1954).

Harry Elmer Barnes, Ed., *An Introduction to the History of Sociology* (University of Chicago Press, 1948), has valuable studies of the following English sociologists: Barnes, "Herbert Spencer and the Evolutionary Defense of Individualism," Chapter IV, 110-137; Barnes, "The Suprarational Social Philosophy of Benjamin Kidd," Chapter XXXI, 606-613; Barnes, "Leonard Trelawney Hobhouse: Evolutionary Philosophy in the Service of Democracy and Social Reform," Chapter XXXII, 614-653; C. Wright Mills, "Edward Alexander Westermarck and the Application of Ethnographic Methods to Marriage and Morals," Chapter XXXIII, 654-667; Huntington Cairns, "Robert Briffault and the Rehabilitation of the Matriarchal Theory," Chapter XXXIV, 668-676; Lewis Mumford, "Patrick Geddes, Victor Branford, and Applied Sociology in England: The Social Survey, Regionalism, and Urban Planning," Chapter XXXV, 677-697; Barnes, "Graham Wallas and the Sociopsychological Basis of Politics and Social Reconstruction," Chapter XXXVI, 696-716; Barnes, "Arnold Joseph Toynbee: Orosius and Augustine in Modern Dress," Chapter XXXVII, 717-738.

Howard Becker & Harry Elmer Barnes, *Social Thought from Lore to Science* (Washington, D. C.: Harren Press, 1952), II, "British Sociology," 793-814, a valuable synthesis, with numerous bibliographical references.

H. C. Brearley, "Contemporary English Sociology," *Sociology and Social Research,* XXIV, 6 (July-August, 1940), 503-510.

J. E. Floud, A. H. Halsey & F. M. Martin, *Social Class and Educational Opportunity* (London: Heinemann, 1956).

Morris Ginsberg, *Sociology* (London: Oxford University Press, 1934); *Essays in Sociology and Social Philosophy* (London: Heinemann, 1956): I: *On the Diversity of Morals*; II: *Reason and Unreason in Society*. Studies by a leading English sociologist.

D. V. Glass, Ed., *Social Mobility in Britain* (London: Routledge, 1954).

A. E. Heath, Ed., *Scientific Thought in the Twentieth Century* (London: Watts, 1951); chapters on "Psychology" by Sir Cyril Burt, "Social Anthropology" by Meyer Fortes, & "Sociology" by Donald G. MacRae.

John Madge, *The Tools of Social Science* (London: Longmans, 1953).

T. H. Marshall, *Citizenship and Social Class* (Cambridge University Press, 1950).

J. Rumney, "British Political Thought," Chapter XX, 424-443, in Joseph S. Roucek, Ed., *Twentieth Century Political Thought* (New

York: Philosophical Library, 1946). A survey of works in the field
of "Political Sociology."

L. Silberman, *Analysis of Society* (London: Hodge, 1951); see especially Chapter III, "The Education of the Governing Classes."

W. J. H. Sprott, *Sociology* (London: Hutchinson, 1949); *Science
and Social Action* (London: Watts, 1954); "Sociology in Britain: Preoccupations," Chapter 21 in Howard Becker & Alvin Boskoff, Eds.,
Modern Sociological Theory (New York: The Dryden Press, 1957).

R. M. Titmuss, *Problems of Social Policy* (London: H.M.S.O., 1950).

Donald G. MacRae was educated at the Universities of Glasgow and
Oxford, where he studied under Radcliffe-Brown; worked at the Oxford Institute of Statistics; joined the Sociology Department, London
School of Economics (1945). In 1949 returned to Oxford as University
Lecturer in Sociology. Is now Reader in Sociology in the University
of London; has been Review Editor of the *British Journal of Sociology*
since its foundation and is now Managing Editor; also edits Heinemann books on Sociology. He published some 40 articles and pamphlets on sociological and philosophical topics, and is particularly
interested in the history and theory of sociology and the development
of comparative studies.

NOTES

1. As I write I have before me Reuben Levy's *The Social Structure of Islam*
(Cambridge University Press, 1957), the latest fruit of the activity of Spencer and
his trustees. For more details on this period of British sociology, see: Howard
Becker & Harry Elmer Barnes, *Social Thought from Lore to Science* (Washington,
D. C.: Harren Press, 1952), II. Chapter XXI, "British Sociology," 793-815, and
especially "The Development of British Social Science Before 1859," 797-799, and
"The Place of Spencer in British Social Science," 799-800.

2. Becker & Barnes, *op. cit.*, "Sociologically Relevant Phases of British Social Science After 1850," 800-809; Harry Elmer Barnes, Ed., *An Introduction to the History
of Sociology* (University of Chicago Press, 1948), Part V, "English Sociologists Since
Herbert Spencer," 603-738.

3. For details on their contributions, see: Harry Elmer Barnes, "Leonard Trelawney Hobhouse: Evolutionary Philosophy in the Service of Democracy & Social
Reform," Chapter XXXII, 614-653, & C. Wright Mills, "Edward Alexander Westermarck and the Application of Ethnographic Methods to Marriage and Morals,"
Chapter XXXIII, 654-667, in Barnes, *An Introduction to the History of Sociology*,
and the bibliographical references at the end of each chapter.

4. An interesting attempt, making novel use of historical data, to throw light on
these matters is J. Banks, *Prosperity and Parenthood* (London: Routledge, 1955).

5. Cf. H. J. Laski, "The Personnel of the British Cabinet, 1801-1924," *American
Political Science Review*, XXII (1928), and W. L. Guttsman, "The Changing Social
Structure of the British Political Elite," *British Journal of Sociology*, II (1951).

6. O. Banks, *Parity and Prestige in English Secondary Education* (London: Rout-ledge, 1955); J. Floud, A. H. Halsey, & F. M. Martin, *Social Class and Educational opportunity* (London: Heinemann, 1956). A. K. C. Ottaway, *Education and Society*: *An Introduction to the Sociology of Education* (London:Routledge & Kegan Paul, 1953), is an introduction to the Sociology of Education from an English point of view; especially valuable are the chapters devoted to the social determinants of education in England in the second half of the 20th century.

7. A. Tropp, *The School Teachers* (London: Heinemann, 1957).

8. D. Cardwell, *The Organisation of Science in England* (London: Heinemann, 1957).

9. Donald G. MacRae, "Social Stratification," *Current Sociology*, II, 1953-1954; "Social Mobility and Social Leadership," *Highway*, XLVI (1955).

10. T. S. Simey, "Class Conflict and Social Mobility," *Journal of the Royal Society of Arts*, CIV (1956).

11. H. Clegg & A. Flanders, Eds., *The System of Industrial Relations in Great Britain* (Oxford: Blackwell, 1955).

12. Rowntree & Lavers, *English Life and Leisure* (London: Longmans, 1951).

13. G. Gorer, *Exploring English Character* (London: Chatto, 1955).

14. R. Glass, *Social Background of a Plan* (London: Routledge, 1950).

15. There are very few real problems of race relations in Britain. Of the most important of these, the relation of the indigenous population to Irish immigrants, there is as yet no adequate survey. Anthropologists and sociologists from Edinburgh such as K. Little, A. Richmond and M. Banton have produced a number of studies of the position of West African and West Indian immigrants in various parts of the country. Their work has, I think, been vitiated by a failure to assess properly the comparable circumstances of native unskilled laborers. An anthropologist, M. Freedman, has produced with some collaborators in *The Jewish Community* (London: Mitchell, 1955), an uneven but excellent study of a more important minority.

16. The author has tried to comment on the latter point in "Sociology in Transitional Societies," *Universitas*, II (1956); two things perhaps are lacking: a satisfactory status for sociology and a higher development of social therapy

17. L. Silberman, *The Education of the Governing Classes, Analysis of Society* (London: Hodge, 1951).

18. Morris Ginsberg, *Sociology of Social Philosophy* (London: Oxford University Press, 1934).

19. W. J. Sprott, *Sociology* (London: Hutchinson, 1949).

20. T. H. Marshall, *Citizenship and Social Class* (Cambridge University Press, 1950).

21. V. G. Childe, *Social Evolution* (London: Watts, 1951).

22. I. Schapera, *Government and Politics in Tribal Societies* (London: Watts, 1956).

FRANCE

A. Cuvillier

French Institute of Sociology

THE DURKHEIM TRADITION

French sociology was for long dominated by the influence of the Durkheim school of thought. Between the wars, this influence had already weakened, in great part to the decimation in the first World War of the cohort of young research workers who had formed a group around Émile Durkheim. The second War, too, deprived the school of one of its more eminent representatives, Maurice Halbwachs, who died in a German camp after deportation.

It would seem, however, that there has been a revival of interest, especially since 1945, for the thought of the man who was the undisputed head of the French sociological school. This movement has been perhaps more marked abroad than in France itself.[1] At all events, *L'Année Sociologique*, resuscitated in 1949, appears regularly once more, though, it must be admitted, not always presenting the same unity of inspiration as animated it formerly. Two important works of the master have been published for the first time: his *Leçons de Sociologie*[2] on morals and law, in 1950, and his lectures on *Pragmatism*[3] in 1955. These two works has enabled us to form a more adequate idea of his thought.

Durkheim had been accused of being misled by a "false problem": the opposition of the individual and society,[4] and of ending in the "anemia of the Ego."[5] However, the first work states as a law "the more he advances in history," the more does the individual personality detach itself from "the social mass," and the second, justifying "intellectual individualism," goes as far as to declare that "truth is expressed only by individuals."—Another criticism was that Durkheim had brought social values down to the level of the *institutional* and thus failed to recognize the importance of all the dynamic and "effer-

vescent" elements in social life.[6] Yet in this very lecture on Pragmatism, he asserts that, while fulfilling functions which are constants,
institutions are perpetually evolving and that society is a milieu in
which we endlessly witness "the birth of new forces" and syntheses
"rich in unlimited possibilities."—The really new element in the
thought of Durkheim, brought to us by this last lecture, is just this
concern, as he himself says, to "link thought to existence and to life."
It reveals to us, indeed, a Durkheim intent on rooting value judgments—whether they concern thought or action—*in existence actually
lived,* that is to say in the social life of men, and, at the same time,
to rationalize this lived experience, to think it out scientifically.

It should be added that the disciples of Durkheim often developed
his ideas along lines at variance with the rather systematic dogmatism
of the master. This was the case with the interpretations of C. Bouglé
and Fr. Simiand, also of M. Halbwachs and M. Mauss. In 1949 was
published a study in social psychology by M. Halbwachs called
Mémoire et Société,[7] which completes his *Cadres sociaux de la
mémoire* of 1925, and, in 1955, an *Esquisse d'une Psychologie des
Classes sociales.*[8] The lectures delivered by Marcel Mauss at the
"Institut d'Ethnologie" have been collected in a *Manuel d'Ethnographie*[9] which begins with some important methodological remarks,
and several of his articles have been grouped under the title of
Sociologie et Anthropologie.[10] This latter work is prefaced by an
interesting introduction by Cl. Lévy-Strauss, drawing the reader's
attention to the change brought about in the viewpoint of French
sociological thought from Durkheim to Mauss: what for the former
was still an archaic or semi-archaic *stage* in the evolution of the
human mind, becomes for the latter a social *species* or *type,* and, in
fact, a "universal and permanent form of thought"[11]: in other words,
we have passed from the viewpoint of *genesis* to that of the *structure.*
It is interesting to note the same transformation of viewpoint in
another author, one who, without actually being of the Durkheim
school, nevertheless had many affinities with it: Lucien Lévy-Bruhl.
The "primitive mentality," characterized by "participation" and in
which he seemed, in his early works, to see a stage in the history
of human thought, appeared to him later—witness his *Carnets*[12] published in 1949—as a feature "essential to the structure of the human
mind," which is more frequent in those societies called "primitives,"
only because it is "repressed" in ours, while continuing nevertheless
to exist.

THE NEW TRENDS

Durkheim's mistake, drawing his inspiration as he did from Auguste Comte, was to link too closely sociology and philosophy, claiming to deduce from the science of social facts an ethics, a theory of knowledge and, in fact, a whole system,—that is known as *sociologism*. On the other hand he had had the double merit, firstly of presenting sociology as an *objective* science, asserting that "sociology is a science of the same type as the other sciences," [13] and secondly of never divorcing theory from empirical research, a position fairly summarized by the formula of François Simiand: "No facts without ideas; no ideas without facts."—Now, as we have attempted to show in our small book *Où va la Sociologie française?*,[14] there has arisen in France, since the last war, a double tendency—in our opinion, a most regrettable one— to discredit firstly the efforts of the human sciences, and especially sociology, towards *objectivity*, and secondly to treat *separately* abstract systematization and concrete research: whence, paradoxically, comes a return to theoretical dogmatism and "social philosophy" under the pretense of sociology, and on the other hand a fragmentation of research into a multiplicity of separate inquiries, surveys or monographs, often interesting, it is true, but lacking at times in guiding principles or ideas.

THE CRISIS OF OBJECTIVITY

We may consider as representative of the first tendency—the renunciation of objectivity—the book of Jules Monnerot: *Les faits sociaux ne sont pas des choses*,[15] the mere title of which is eloquent. The author, who takes his inspiration from the philosophy of Dilthey and Jaspers and from the German distinction between *Naturwissenschaften* and *Geisteswissenschaften*, especially criticizes Durkheim, who recommended to "treat social facts as things," which, in his opinion, was tantamount to "refusing psychology" and "giving up all hope of understanding and turning one's back on living experience."

We have already seen the worth of the last point; and, as for the rule laid down by Durkheim, it is a complete misconception to see in it a repudiation of psychology. On the contrary, the merit of Durkheim had been to demonstrate, while defining social life by its "hyperspirituality," [16] that there exist psychic realities only to be understood by treating them objectively,—precisely because they are at the same time social realities,—and that it is naive to believe the latter *understood* simply because they are *lived*. The vague and equivocal character of the "sympathetic comprehension" recommended by J. Monnerot has long ago been denounced.[17] As said C. Lévi-Strauss[18] concerning the use of "personal documents," scientific study stands on another plane than that of subjective experience and, in this sense, we may "remain convinced that social facts must be studied as things."

THEORETICAL CONSTRUCTIONS

Among the theoretical constructions exercising the greatest influence in France at the moment, must be placed the sociology of Georges Gurvitch. This author was originally a philosopher. The writer of studies on *Otto von Gierke als Rechtsphilosoph*,[19] on *Fichte's System der konkreten Ethik*,[20] on *Les Tendences actuelles de la Philosophie allemande*,[21] etc., he shows himself, in the last work, very much influenced by Phenomenology and the theories of Max Scheler.

His sociological doctrine to which he seems to have come through the Philosophy of Law, has also been strongly influenced by the former, at least in its origin. In his *Essais de Sociologie* of 1939, he had presented "the phenomenological inversion or reduction (of Husserl), immanent decomposition, searching deep down for the superposed strata of social reality," as the fundamental sociological method. There we had, writes C. Lévi-Strauss,[22] "a clear-cut philosophical position." Later, in his *Vocation actuelle de la Sociologie*,[23] which is in fact, an augmented re-casting of the *Essais* of 1939, the author abjured this position and declared unambiguously that he refused the "patronage" of Phenomenology. Lastly, he sheltered himself behind a "dialectical hyper-empiricism," completed by a "super-relativism in its most extreme form." [24] However that may be, the primitive construction of social *types* has remained identical in its main lines[25]: "sociological pluralism," both vertical and horizontal, which denies the unity and continuity of the social aspect; "pluri-dimensionalism" which multiplies and intermingles the perspectives; "sociology in depth" which recognizes up to ten "strata" (*couches*), "flats" (*paliers*) or "levels" (*niveaux*) in social reality, from the "morphological surface" and the "organized superstructures" to the "free currents of collective psychism"; "differential sociology" which distinguishes, going from the *mass* to *communion* passing through *community*, according as the *pressure* is more or less strong and the *fusion* of the "Ego" into the "We," on the contrary, less or more intimate (here "micro-sociology" has a close affinity to the "sociometry" of J. Moreno);— secondly, types of *groupings* which may themselves be classified according to fifteen different criteria: content, scope, duration, rhythm, functions, etc.;—thirdly and lastly, types of *global societies*, which may be constructed (for even those types which are the most concrete ones, must be "constructed") according to a great variety of criteria: one may, however, distinguish four *archaic* structures, six *civilized* or *historical* structures and four types in conflict within our transitorial societies.[26]

It would seem necessary to add a few remarks. The first which the very brief summary we have just given would sufficiently suggest, concerns the complexity of this classification and those distinctions, the almost infinite multiplication of which, "added to the ambiguity and lack of precision of the definitions, runs the risk of reducing or annulling their usefulness as guides to concrete research."[27] The second is that "the network of these relations fails to reveal any historical form:"[28] the typology thus constructed contains indeed no element of a genetic explanation with a historical basis, however slight, to such an extent that the fear has been expressed that this typology, situated outside time, may result in an "anti-historicism" refusing all help from history.[29] Third and last difficulty: although the author vigorously denied having built up a *formalistic* sociology, it may be asked, given the absence in his works of any concrete data— geographical or economic[30] as well as historical,—if he is not falling into a formalism analogous to that of Simmel or L. von Wiese,[31]— all the more so as he does not hesitate to declare that the global societies are "macrocosms of particular groups" which are themselves "microcosms of forms of sociability."[32] Here it is that appears the danger of the "ideas without facts" mentioned by Fr. Simiand. We are not mistaken, for the "experience" of Gurvitch has nothing in common with the inductive experiment, based on facts, used by the experimental sciences: "All direct inductive observation," he writes,[33] "if only to serve as basis for verification, proves impossible or almost." *Hyper-empiricism* must be understood here to mean "lived" experience in the phenomenological sense. From this it may readily be understood that certain critics should have been able to reproach the author with either "a return to metaphysics, which, however, he denies,"[34] or "a philosophical position [this time] unconfessed" which, in reality, "founds a new sociologism."[35] In fact, as Durkheim had attempted to make sociology a basis for an Ethics and for a Theory of truth, G. Gurvitch in his latest book strives to provide a sociological answer for that essentially philosophical problem which is the problem of human liberty.

B) Another attempt at theoretical systematization which appears to us worthy of interest, is that of Claude Lévy-Strauss. In contrast to the previous writer, Lévy-Strauss is not a pure theorist. He is an ethnologist who has done concrete research and accomplished *field work*.[36] It is through his research into systems of kinship that he has been led to emphasize the notion of *social structure*. Ethnology, according to him, allows us to distinguish "what presents the attributes of the relative and the particular," regulated by social norms and thus belonging to *culture*, from what is constant and universal among all men and which is therefore the domain of *nature*.[37] Ethnology also has to deal with the *unconscious* character, as Fr. Boas had said concerning language, of certain expressions of social life, while history studies mainly its *conscious* expressions: "The unconscious activity of the mind consists in imposing forms on a content, and these forms are fundamentally the same for all minds, both ancient and modern, primitive and civilized."[38] One must therefore strive to reach the unconscious structure underlying each institution or custom, to obtain a single schema which, behind the chaos of cultural rules and patterns, remains present and active in different local and temporal contexts. Lévi-Strauss bewares, however, of repudiating history: "All is history," he writes,[39] and "even the analysis of synchronous structures implies constant reference to history": for, by showing institutions in process of transformation, history enables us to bring out the permanent structure and the unconscious relations of correlation and opposition which must also be present even in peoples which have never known the institution under consideration.

This does not mean that the term *social structure* applies to empirical reality. It means a pattern to be constructed according to this reality and which must satisfy the following three conditions. It must: 1) constitute a system, the elements of which are conjoint; 2) make possible a series of transformations resulting in one or several groups of patterns of the same type; 3) allow the sociologist to foresee how the pattern will react if one or more of its elements are modified.[40] The sociologist (or anthropologist) will be in position here to

be guided by "structural Linguistics," and the notion of *communication* will enable him to provide a mathematical expression for the
phenomena without, at the same time, depriving them of their qualitative character. For this, however, new systems of Mathematics are
necessary.[41] These new paths have already been open for Economics,
by the *Theory of Games* of von Neumann and Morgenstern, and, for
the interpretation of psychological tests and factorial analysis, by Louis
Guttman. The social sciences which, until now, like Psychology in its
first stages, had called upon Mathematics mainly to *measure* sizes
(population figures, economic resources, etc.), must now profit from
these new prospects and make use not only of the Calculation of the
probabilities but of Topology, Theory of Sets and Theory of Substitution Groups, etc. It may be possible, for instance, to put in equation form the rules of marriage in a given society and to treat these
equations according to rigorous methods, while leaving entirely aside
the nature of the phenomena under study,—in this case, marriage.

These views are in harmony with certain of the latest tendencies
in contemporary social sciences, for instance these expressed recently
by Daryll Forde, who wrote: "Anthropologists have, in growing
measure, recognized that the corresponding features between particular societies must not be looked for in concrete cultural forms, but
in their more abstract sociological properties."[42]—This opinion has
nevertheless given rise to criticisms, some of them very violent,[43] the
most valid of which seems to us to be that it may result, if taken to its
logical conclusion, in a mathematical formalism in which the specific
character of social phenomena would disappear. P. A. Sorokin[44] recently drew attention to the fact that even mathematical formulation
supposes certain assumptions, and gave a timely reminder of the reflexion of Auguste Comte that the precision of a formula—or the
elegance of a mathematical model—must not be confused with its
truth or certainty.

CONCRETE RESEARCH

Parallel to these theoretical constructions, French sociology since
1945 has made a remarkable effort in the domain of concrete research.
To the *Institut français de Sociologie* have been added new organisms
which are above all research organisms. The *Centre d'Etudes Sociologiques* (C.E.S.), founded in 1946 by the *Centre National de la Recherche scientifiqe* (C.N.R.S.), has organized "sociological weeks," the

first under the direction of G. Gurvitch on the theme *Industrialisation et Technocratie* (A. Colin, 1949), the second under the direction of G. Friedmann on the theme *Villes et Campagnes* (A. Colin, 1953), the third under the direction of Max Sorre on *Sociologie comparée de la famille contemporaine* (ed. C.N.R.S., 1955). The *Centre* has also supported very many studies of Social Psychology and Sociology: urban, industrial, educational, criminal, religious sociology, etc.[45] The same concrete orientation can be found in the research carried out by the *Institut d'Etudes démographiques* (I.N.E.D.), the *Fondation Nationale des Sciences politiques* (F.N.S.P.), the *Institut français de l'Opinion publique* (I.F.O.P.), the *Institut d'Ethnologie*, etc. Let us mention also that the *Ecole pratique des Hautes Etudes*, which already included a Department of *Sciences religieuses,* has created in 1947, with the name of Department of *Sciences économiques et sociales,* a "sixth section" which is, in reality, destined to promote all research concerning the human sciences.—Many other research organisms, private or local, are worthy of mention. Let us limit ourselves to naming the *Institut de Sociologie économique et de Psychologie des Peuples* which has its headquarters at Le Hâvre and which publishes the *Revue de Psychologie des Peuples* (dir.: A. Miroglio), and the group *Économie et Humanisme* of L'Arbresle near Lyon, which continues, while modernizing it, the tradition of surveys in the manner of Frédéric le Play. The leading figure of this last group, Father L. J. Lebret, has published a precious *Guide pratique de l'Enquête sociale* (3 vol.: see *Bibliography*).

Pursuing rather a different line of thought, the interest should be mentioned of the *Guide d'étude des comportements culturels* published by Marcel Maget, director of the *Laboratoire d'Ethnographie française* in the *Musée des Arts et Traditions populaires.*[46] As the author says, the hiatus is much less marked "between ethnographic and ethnographiable peoples" than in former times; and the work draws up a framework extremely rich as well as strongly structured, borne out also by numerous schemas concerning all the methods borrowed from ethnographical investigation, but applicable to the societies surrounding us.

On the field of *Demography,* mention must first be made of the publications of the I.N.E.D., either in its collection *Travaux et Documents* or in the review *Population,*[47] and especially of the two important volumes of the *Théorie générale de la population*[48] by its director Alfred Sauvy, the first more classical and economical, the second confronting the laws stated in the first with the moving phenomena of human reality, studying for instance the increase of the Elders,[49] the social factors for mortality and fecundity, etc. Working along rather different lines is the *Introduction à l'étude géographique de la population du monde* (P.U.F., 1951) by Pierre George, where the author links the teaching of demography with that of geography. It is the same with the suggestive book published by Max Sorre on *Les Migrations peuples* (Flammarion, 1955).

The study of *Urban Sociology* was inaugurated with the inquiry, in imitation of the studies on *Middletown,* concerning *Auxerre en 1950.*[50] The survey on *L'agglomération parisienne,*[51] taken up under the auspices of the C.E.S. and under the direction of P. Chombart de Lauwe, shows that the limits and divisions of the "social space" in a large city evolve not only according to *ecological* processes but also in accordance with the attitudes and ideas of the groups: "Collective ideas control spacial distributions as much as the contrary." The work written by Pierre George on *La Ville*[52] attains to a truly sociological typology: the author distinguishes the market towns of the rural economy, the trading towns of the pre-capitalistic era, the industrial towns of capitalistic economy, the "socialistic" towns of the USSR and of the countries of "popular democracies," etc. He reserves a chapter for colonial towns and, on this last point, his book finds a useful complement in the work of Georges Balandier on the *Black Brazzavilles,*[53] which reveals, in such a living way, the persistence of the patterns of traditional society within the framework of a completely new social context, dominated by economic factors.

Research into *Rural Sociology*, although often taking the form of monographs of villages, have sometimes resulted in analogous conclusions. Thus, for example, the study on *Les Paysans de Morette,*[54] in which Joseph Garavel notes that, "faced with modern technical civilization, the peasants remain strangely faithful to the traditional way of life" and states the whole "peasant problem" in these words: "Two ways of life, two civilizations, perhaps, exist side by side." More closely resembling the monograph is the work by L. Bernot and R. Blancart, *Nouville, village français,*[55] in which the problem is above all relationship "between collective attitudes and the character of the individual." May one speak of comparative study for the work of Henri Mendras on *Novis*, a French parish in the Aveyron, and *Virgin*, a Mormon community in the United States?[56] Rather is it a parallel, though one which reveals, amid all the differences in milieu, a very general phenomenon: that of the growing mechanization and urbanization in our societies. These general problems have been studied in different articles by Henri Lefébvre[57] and in the works of Daniel Faucher,[58] as also in the above mentioned symposium on *Villes et Campagnes: civilisation urbaine et civilisation rurale en France.*

This leads us to the studies on *Industrial Sociology.* The writings of Georges Friedmann[59] in this domain must be given pride of place. As early as 1936, he was drawing attention to the coming of a second industrial revolution resulting from technical transformations and the development of the means of production. But he has been led to insist more and more on the *human* element in production and to express on this account certain doubts and fears which the progress of technique is unable to calm: his latest work shows the responsibility of the fractionizing, the "crumbling" of work into elementary mechanized gestures in the present crisis of the human being. With greater optimism, Jean Fourastié[60] has used the notion of "three sectors" distinguished by Colin Clark, but defining each of them by the physical productivity in work. In his opinion, if technical progress does not imply *ipso facto* social progress, it nevertheless tends towards it by raising the standard of living and freeing man from drudgery. In a similar field, we must point out the considerable work done by Paul Combe on *Niveau de vie et Progrès technique en France depuis 1860,*[61] inspired by the method of objective and quantitative observation of Fr. Simiand. We may also add the many inquiries or surveys led either by the F.N.S.P.,[62] by the I.N.E.D.[63] or again and especially by the C.E.S.[64] In a rather different vein, must be noted the curious essay by A. Vexliard, *Introduction à la Sociologie du vagabondage*[65] recalling to mind the American studies on the *hobos* and breaking new ground in France. Let us mention, in concluding, a practical step, the creation in 1952 of the *Institut des Sciences sociales du Travail*, which aims at studying all problems relating to the condition of the workers in the modern world.

In France at the moment there is a revival of interest in *the Family,* as is shown by the publication of the I.N.E.D. *Renouveau des idées sur la famille*[66] and by the international symposium, already mentioned, at the C.N.R.S. on the *Sociologie comparée de la famille contemporaine.* While showing the diversity of the types of family structures according to the social milieux as well as the transformation in time of family functions, these two studies reveal certain "elements of permanence" and the stable part played by the family as a "social cell." Another study by G. Duplessis on *Les Mariages en France*[67] demonstrates, contrary to the prejudice which connects essentially the marriage and the birth rates, "a phenomenon rarely noted until now: the growing generalization of marriage in the course of the last century correlated with diminishing fecundity." Finally, because they are almost the only one to have touched this field in France, we must underline the importance of the studies of Émile Sicard on the *Zadruga* and the family communities of the Southern Slavs.[68]

A branch receiving the greatest attention today is that of *Religious Sociology*. The initiator of research in this domain was Gabriel Le Bras, whose numerous studies have recently been conllected in the two volumes, so rich in substance, of his *Etudes de Sociologie religieuse*.[69] Centered at first on religious *practices*, mainly catholic, this vast inquiry has spread on the one hand to the other religions and on the other to the correlations of religious practice with manners, family life, political attitudes, socio-professional conditions, etc.[70] It is fair to recall, in this connection the work done by the whole team of his collaborators among whom are numbered Canon Boulard,[71] F. Isambert,[72] Professor G. H. L. Zeegers[73] of Nimegen, Canon Leclercq[74] of Louvain, etc. Among the local studies we will mention the *Aspects de la pratique religieuse à Paris* by Abbé Y. Daniel[75] and the interesting study by Mme. Jean Perrot of *Grenoble, essai de sociologie religieuse*.[76] Noteworthy is also the birth, under the patronage of the C.N.R.S., of the *Archives de Sociologie religieuse*, the first fascicule of which (June 1969) contains a precious bibliography which completes opportunely that contained in vol. V of the UNESCO publication *Current Sociology*. As we have said, the inquiry extends today beyond the limits of the catholic religion and even to non-christian religions.[77] At last let us name some more synthetic studies: the *Essai sur la religion bambara* by Germaine Dieterlen, *Le Sacrifice chez les Arabes* by Joseph Chelhod,[78] different studies by Roger Bastide[79] who had published in 1935 the most valuable *Éléments de Sociologie religieuse*.

Another branch which provides today a fairly rich literature is that of *Electoral Sociology*. André Siegfried who had inaugurated it as early as 1913 with his *Tableau politique de la France de l'Ouest*, has, in company with Fr. Goguel, Ch. Morazé, etc., led very many studies.[80] He himself demonstrated in his *Géographie politique de l'Ardèche*[81] the persistent action of historical causes, at least in old countries like France, on the present division of political opinions, the parts of the country formerly affected by the Reform, for example, behaving differently from regions with a Catholic tradition. Particular attention has been paid to the relationship of political opinions to religious beliefs[82] and also to other social realities; national factors, stratification of classes, etc.[83]

The studies by Ch. Morazé on *La France bourgeoise* and by M. Duverger on *Les Partis politiques*[84] lead us to researches on *Public Opinion*. Inaugurated by Jean Stoetzel, today director of the I.F.O.P., in his two works *Théorie des Opinions* and *L'étude expérimentale des opinions*[85] and inspired by American research in this field, such studies have given rise to various "sample surveys" published in a special review.[86]

Finally, where Psychology and Sociology melt, studies in *Social Psychology* are represented by three works of prime importance:[87] *Sociologie et Psychoanalyse* by Roger Bastide, a book in which the role of Psychoanalysis is rightly shown to be limited by the conditions imposed on the "instincts" by cultural norms;—*Attitudes collectives et relations humaines* by Roger Girod, where are analyzed and reconsidered the *social field* theories of Kurt Lewin and the results of inquiries such as *An American Dilemma* and *The American Soldier*; —and lastly, but not least, *La Personnalité de base* by Mikel Dufrenne, in which this notion is discussed as a "sociological concept" and the emphasis placed on the historical character of the "basic personality." The suggestive book of the late deceased ethnologicist Maurice Leenhardt, *Do Kamo*,[88] may be considered as a study on the personality in the Melanesian world.

CONCLUSION

The mere enumeration of these researches gives the impression of incontestable wealth of documentation. We may, however, be justified in wondering if from this accumulation of material there emerges any results of general significance. Thus it is in 1951 that one of these research workers, the author of remarkable studies on the sociology of the cinema, Edgar Morin,[89] questioned the results attained: "Will the remanipulation of diverse elements by the C.E.S. give a unity to this generation? Will a theory arise from its experiences?"[90] The problem undoubtedly exists. Let us say immediately that it would be very unfair, in our opinion, to give a biased negative answer. From these researches itself there often emerge certain general ideas.

One of the more incontestable,—one which we have already mentioned on several occasions,—is the necessity for Sociology to *maintain
its links with History*. To refer in this matter to the opinions quoted
above of Lévy-Strauss or Siegfried, is to understand that, the role
of Sociology is to build up a *typology*, and typology without a *historical* basis is arbitrary and valueless. If there is "no fully intelligible
history of law without sociology," G. Le Bras says also, there is in
other hand "no sociology independent of time."[91]—A second lesson
emerging from these researches is, as Aug. Comte said, that social facts
are *"profoundly interconnected."* Most of those are, as Marcel Mauss
phrased it, "total facts." It is therefore impossible to isolate permanently any one of them from their general context. Thus it is, as we
have seen, that the practice of religion itself had to be recognized as
forming part of a whole social entity.—Third lesson: *the necessity
of leading ideas*. No "facts without ideas." Any study of rural
sociology would be a mere monograph if it did not reveal the *general*
problem of the urbanization and mechanization of modern life. Such
a study of electoral sociology stands out from the others as being more
enlightening[92] because the author does not fear to announce from the
first his *working hypothesis*: "The ensemble of the determining factors
in the political opinions of the majority stems from the economic and
social condition of the citizens."

A comforting fact is that these general views are often to be met
with in the specialists of particular sciences, who, while fighting shy
of certain types of over-doctrinal sociology, sometimes come to introduce into their writings various specifically sociological points of view.
It will be sufficient to remember here the names of Marc Bloch and
Lucien Fébvre, the founders of the historical review *Annales*, of Henri
Berr, the author of *La Synthèse en histoire* (new ed., 1953) and the
director of the collection *L'Evolution de l'humanité*, and, among the
now living historians, of Georges Bourgin, Louis Gernet (the historian
of the juridical thought in ancient Greece), Fernand Braudel, etc.
Among the geographers, we will quote the names of Roger Dion, the
writer of the *Essai sur la formation du paysage rural français*, and
chiefly Max Sorre, the author of the four volumes *Les Fondements de
la Géographie humaine*[93] where he shows the geographical importance
of the human groups and emphasizes the many points of contact
("rencontres") between Geography and Sociology.—But the most symptomatic feature is the attention paid today to Sociology by two University Departments which in France come under the Faculties of

Law and which, perhaps for that reason, had remained until now somewhat distant. There is first of all *Law* itself. An advent of importance is the quite recent creation, at the Faculty of Law in Paris, of a chair of "Sociology of Law." A Romanist such as Henri Lévy-Bruhl, who is incontestably as much a sociologist as an eminent jurist, has established in his *Aspects sociologiques du Droit*[94] the competence of Sociology in this matter. On the other hand, *Economic Science* shows analogous tendencies. The sociological viewpoints prevail in the works of economists such as Jean Marchal and André Marchal: the latter asserts that "the sociological factors are not only the framework of economic activity," but its "very essence."[95]

There is, then, reason to hope that the danger of divorce which we mentioned earlier between theoretical systematization and empirical research may be averted. French Sociology is not reduced to a choice between one or the other, and we may trust that she will find once more the path drawn for her by the formula of Simiand quoted earlier.

SELECTED BIBLIOGRAPHY

L'Année Sociologique, third series (Paris: Presses Universitaires de France, 6 vol. publ. since 1949). Original studies, critical book reviews and summary of the sociological researches.

Harry Elmer Barnes & Howard S. Becker, *Social Thought from Lore to Science* (Washington, D.C.: Harren Press, 2nd ed., 1952), II Chap. XXII, "Sociology in the French Languages," I. "France & French Switzerland" 815-866. A valuable summary, mostly of secondary literature, from the environmentalist theories to Richard and other critics of Durkheim; now outdated, since the original edition appeared in 1938.

Armand Cuvillier, *Manuel de Sociologie* (Paris: Presses Universitaires de France, 1950; 3rd ed., 1956, 2 vol.); vol. I: *Objet et Méthodes, Morphologie sociale (Sociologie structurale)*; vol. II: *Physiologie sociale (Sociologie fonctionnelle).* According to B. K. Francis, in *The American Journal of Sociology* LVII (January, 1952), 417: "A very useful instrument de travail, far more readable and lucid than most American texts on the history of sociology." Extensive bibliographies; *Ou va la sociologie francaise?* (Paris: M. Rivière, Petite Bibliothèque Sociologique Internationale, 1953). A polemical survey of the contemporary trends in French sociology.

Émile Durkheim, *Leçons de Sociologie. Physique des Moeurs et du*

Droit (Paris: Presses Universitaires de France, Bibliothèque de Philosophie contemporaine, 1950). With a foreword by Hüseyin Nail Kubali and an introduction by Georges Davy. An exhaustive bibliography of Durkheim's works.

Émile Durkheim, *Pragmatisme et Sociologie, cours inédit pronouncé à la Sorbonne restitué d'après des notes d'étudiants* (Paris: Librairie Vrin, 1955). According to K. H. Wolff, in *The American Journal of Sociology*, LXII (July, 1956), 101: "An intrafamiliar, intracultural controversy which . . . deeply lights up the 'family' and culture we still participate in."

George Friedmann, *Le Travail en miettes (The Crumbled Labor)* (Paris: Gallimard, 1956). A masterly writing in industrial sociology; see the other works of this author in the text.

Gino Germani, "La Sociologia en Francía," *Ciencias Sociales* (Washington, D.C.: Union Panamericana), VI 31 (February 1955), 12-27. An up-to-date survey with a bibliography.

Georges Gurvitch, *La Vocation actuelle de la Sociologie; vers une sociologie différentielle* (Paris: Presses Universitaires de France, Bibliothèque de Sociologie contemporaine, 1950). An exciting but merely theoretical work by the co-editor of the *Twentieth Century Sociology* (New York: Philosophical Library, 1945); *Determinismes sociaux et Liberté humaine* (Paris: Presses Universitaires de France, Bibliothèque de Sociologie contemporaine, 1955). The problem of the human freedom sociologically discussed.

Maurice Halbwachs, *Esquisse d'une Psychologie des Classes sociales* (Paris: M. Rivière, Petite Bibliothèque Sociologique Internationale, 1955). English translation under preparation, London: W. Heinemann, and Glencoe, Ill.: Free Press, 1957; with a bibliography of Halbwachs' works.

Gabriel Le Bras, *Études de Sociologie religieuse* (Paris: Presses Universitaires de France, Bibliothèque de Sociologie contemporaine, 1955 and 1956, 2 vol.); vol. I: *Sociologie de la pratique religieuse dans les campagnes françaises*; vol. II: *De la morphologie à la typologie*. An important collection of the many writings of the author on Religious Sociology.

L. J. Lebret, *Guide pratique de l'Enquête sociale* (Paris: Presses Universitaires de France, 1952-1955, 3 vol.); vol. I: *Manuel de l'enquêteur;* vol. II: *L'enquête urbaine, l'analyse du quartier et de la ville.* A very useful guide-book for the social surveys.

Claude Lévi-Strauss, *Les Structures élémentaries de la parenté* (Paris: Presses Universitaires de France, Bibliothèque de Philosophie contemporaine, 1949). A basic book by the great ethnologist concerning the kinship and the relationships between nature and culture; "French Sociology," Chap. XVII, 503-537, in Georges Gurvitch and W. E. Moore, Eds., *Twentieth Century Sociology* (New York: Philosophical Library, 1945).

Talcott Parsons and Bernard Barber, "Sociology 1941-46," *The American Journal of Sociology*, LIII, 4 (January, 1948), 245-257.

Alfred Sauvy, *Théorie générale de la Population* (Paris: Presses Universitaires de France Bibliothèque de Sociologie contemporaine, 1952 and 1954, 2 vol); vol. I *Économie et Population*; vol. II: *Biologie sociale*. A fundamental work in demography.

Jean Stoetzel, *Théorie des Opinions* (Paris: Presses Universitaires de France, Bibliothèque de Philosophie contemporaine, 1943). The best French book on the theory of public opinion.

René Toulemont, *Sociologie et Pluralisme dialectique: Introduction à l'Oeuvre de Georges Gurvitch* (Paris: Beatrice-Nauwelaerts, 1955). An analysis of Georges Gurvitch's work tracing especially the abiding philosophical influences of Fichte, Husserl and Scheler.

Armand Joseph Cuvillier (1887——); entered the École Normale Supérieure in 1908. Served in World War I as a machine-gun officer; admitted as an "agrégé de l'Université" (1919) and taught philosophy in different lycées in the provinces and later in Paris. His *Manuel de Philosophie* (Paris: Armand Colin, 16th ed., 1950) has been used as a textbook and revised as *Précis de Philosophie* (Paris, A. Colin, 1956). His *Introduction à la Sociologie* (Paris: A. Colin, 5th ed., 1954) has been translated into many languages; has also published numerous studies on the history of social ideas of Proudhon, the Saint-Simonians, etc., *Manuel de Sociologie* (Paris: P.U.F., 3rd ed., 1956), and other works. Lectured on Sociology at the Sorbonne (1945-1953). A member of the French Institute of Sociology and of the Teaching and Training Committee of the International Association of Sociology; is the editor of the *Petite Bibliothèque Sociologique Internationale* of the Librarie Marcel Rivière, Paris.

NOTES

1. Cf. T. Parsons and B. Barber, "Sociology 1941-46," *The American Journal of Sociology*, LIII, 4 (January, 1948) , 253-254.

2. Émile Durkheim, *Leçons de Sociologie, Physique des Moeurs et du Droit* (Paris: Presses Universitaires de France, 1950) .

3. Émile Durkheim, *Pragmatisme et Sociologie, cours inédit prononcé à la Sorbonne et restitué d'après des notes d'étudiants* (Paris: Librarie Vrin, 1955).

4. G. Gurvitch, *La Vocation actuelle de la Sociologie* (Paris: Presses Universitaires de France, Bibliothèque de Sociologie contemporaine, 1950) , 26-27.

5. R. Le Senne, *Traité de Morale générale* (Paris: Presses Universitaires de France, 1942) , 362 & 513.

6. G. Gurvitch, *op. cit.*, 64, 82, etc.

7. *L'Année Sociologique* (3rd series, Paris: Presses Universitaires de France, 1949)

I, 3-89; this study was reproduced under the title *La Mémoire collective* in the "Bibliothèque de Sociologie contemporaine," dir. by G. Gurvitch (Paris: Presses Universitaires de France, 1950).

8. Maurice Halbwachs, *Ssquisse d'une Psychologie des Classes sociales* (Paris: M Rivière, Petite Bibliothèque Sociologique Internationale, 1955) (English trans. Glencoe, Ill.: Free Press, 1957).

9. Denise Paulme, *Manuel d'Ethnographie* (Paris: Payot, 1947).

10. (Paris: Presses Universitaires de France, Bibliothèque the Sociologie contemporaine, 1950).

11. Cf. Claude Lévi-Strauss, "French Sociology," in G. Gurvitch and W. E. Moore, Eds., *Twentieth Century Sociology* (New York: Philosophical Library, 1945), 525.

12. *Les Carnets de Lucien Lévy-Bruhl,* Foreword by Maurice Leenhardt (Paris: Universitaires de France, 1949).

13. Lévi-Strauss, *op. cit.,* 504.

14. Armand Cuvillier, *Où va la Sociologie française?* (Paris: Marcel Rivière, Petite Bibliothèque Sociologique Internationale, 1953).

15. Jules Monnerot, *Les Faits sociaux ne sont pas des choses* (Paris: Gallimard, 1946).

16. É. Durkheim, "Représentations individuelles et représentations collectives," *Revue de Métaphysique et de Morale* (Paris: A. Colin) VI, 3 (May, 1898), 273ff., reproduced in *Sociologie et Philosophie* (Paris: Presses Universitaires de France, 1951), 48.

17. Cf. among others, Th. Abel, "The operation called *Verstehen*," *The American Journal of Sociology,* LIV, 3 (November, 1948), 211ff.

18. *L'Année Sociologique,* third series (Paris: Presses Universitaires de France, 6 vol. published since 1949) (General secretary: Louis Gernet), vol. 1949-I, 331.

19. Georges Gurvitch, *Otto von Gierke als Rechtsphilosoph* (Tübingen: Mohr 1922).

20. Georges Gurvitch, *Fichte's System der konkreten Ethik* (Tübingen: Mohr 1924).

21. Georges Gurvitch, *Les Tendances actuelles de la Philosophie allemande* (Paris: Vrin, 1930).

22. Claude Lévi-Strauss, "French Sociology," XVII, 503-537, in Georges Gurvitch & Wilbert E. Moore, Eds., *Twentieth Century Sociology* (New York: Philosophical Library, 1945), 533.

23. Georges Gurvitch, *La Vocation actuelle de la Sociologie* (Paris: Presses Universitaires de France, Bibliothèque de Sociologie contemporaine, 1950).

24. Georges Gurvitch, "Hyper-Emperisme dialectique," *Cahiers internationaux de Sociologie,* XV (Paris: Ed. du Seuil, 1953), 3-33.

25. As may be realized by comparing the article "Essai d'une classification pluraliste des formes de la sociabilité," *Annales sociologiques,* series A, fasc. 3 (1938), 1-48 (or the *Essais de Sociologie* of 1939, 9-112) with *La Vocation actuelle* . . . of 1950, 99-235.

26. Georges Gurvitch, *Déterminismes sociaux et Liberté humaine* (Paris: Presses Universitaires de France, Bibliothèque de Sociologie contemporaine, 1955), 200-292.

27. Gino Germani, "La Sociologia en Francia," *Ciencias Sociales,* VI, 31 (February, 1955), 17.

28. E. Gomez Arboleya, "Sobre el porvenir de la Sociologia francesa," *Revista de Estudios politicos,* LXXV (May-June, 1954), 85.

29. F. Braudel, "La discontinuité du social," *Annales: économies, sociétés, civilisations*, VIII, 3 (July-August, 1953), 349 & 351.

30. F. Braudel, *op. cit.*, 360.

31. Cf. Armand Cuvillier, "La Noicón de *forma* en sociologia," *Revista Mexicana de Sociologia*, XVII, 2-3 (May-December, 1955), 277 ff.

32. Gurvitch, *La Vocation actuelle de la Sociologie, op. cit.*, 9.

33. *Ibid.*, 109.

34. L. von Wiese, "Gurvitch's Beruf der Soziologie," *Kölner Zeitschrift für Soziologie*, 4. Jahrgang, Heft 2/3 (1951-52), 369.

35. E. Gomez Arboleya, *op. cit.*, 85.

36. Cf. Lévi-Strauss, *La vie familiale et sociale des Indiens Nambikwara* (Paris: Société des Américanistes, 1948).

37. Claude Lévi-Strauss, *Les Structures élémentaires de la parenté* (Paris: Presses Universitaires de France, Bibliothèque de Philosophie contemporaine, 1949), 9.

38. Lévi-Strauss, "Historie et Ethnologie," *Revue de Métaphysique et de Morale* (Paris: A. Colin), LIV, 3-4 (July-October, 1949), 386.

39. *Ibid.*, 376.

40. Lévi-Strauss, "Social structure," a communication to the *Symposium of the Wenner-Gren Foundation on Anthropology* (New York, 9-20th June, 1952). We quote from the French translation published in the *Bulletin de Psychologie* (Paris), VI (May, 1953), 359.

41. Lévi-Strauss, "Les Mathématiques et l'homme," *International Social Sciences Bulletin*, VI, 4 (1954), 643 ff.; cf. *Structures élémentaires de la parenté*, Chap. XIV and conclusion.

42. D. Forde, "Anthropologie und Soziologie," *Kölner Zeitschrift für Soziologie*, 8. Jahrgang, Heft 2 (1956), 180.

43. Especially G. Gurvitch, "Le Concept de structure sociale," *Cahiers internationaux de Sociologie*, XIX (1955), 2ff.; this article, very harsh, had been published in Spanish in the *Revista Mexicana da Sociologia*, XVII, 2-3 (May-December, 1955) 299ff.

44. P. A. Sorokin, *Fads and Foibles in Modern Sociology and Related Sciences* (Chicago: H. Regnery, 1956), 134-135.

45. A list of these surveys will be found in *Cahiers internationaux de Sociologie*, VII (1949); in *L'Année Sociologique*, third series (1949-1950) 517-523, & (1951) 555-559; & in the bulletin *Recherches Sociologiques* published by the Centre.

46. Marcel Maget, Ed., *Civilisations du Sud* (Paris, 1953).

47. *Population*, quarterly review (Paris: Presses Universitaires de France, since 1946).

48. Alfred Sauvy, *Théorie générale de la Population* (Paris: Presses Universitaires de France, Bibliothèque de Sociologie contemporaine, 1952 & 1954), vol. I: *Économie et Population;* vol. II: *Biologie sociale.*

49. Cf. also on this problem Jean Daric, *Vieillisement de la Population et Prolongation de la vie active*, Institut d'Études demographiques, Travaux et Documents, #7 (Paris: Presses Universitaires de France, 1948).

50. Charles Bettelheim and Suzanne Frère, *Une ville française moyenne: Auxerre en 1950, étude de structure sociale et urbaine*, Cahiers de la Foundation Nationale des Sciences politiques, #17 (Paris: A Colin, 1950).

51. P. H. Chombart de Lauwe, Ed., *Paris et l'agglomération parisienne* (Paris:

Presses Universitaires de France, 1952), vol. I: *L'espace social dans une grande cité;* vol. II: *Méthodes de recherche pour l'étude d'une grand cité;* see also P. George, *Études sur la banlieue* (suburbs) *de Paris,* Cahiers de la Fondation Nationale des Sciences politiques, #12, and J. Gouhier, *Naissance d'une grand cité: Le Mans,* Cahiers de la Fondation Nationale des Sciences politiques, #48.

52. Pierre George, *La Ville, le fait urbain à travers le monde* (Paris: Presses Universitaires de France, 1952).

53. G. Balandier, *Sociologie des Brazzavilles noires,* Cahiers de la Fondation Nationale des Sciences politiques, #67 (1955); *Sociologie actuelle de l'Afrique noire* (Paris: Presses Universitaires de France, Bibliothèque de Sociologie contemporaine 1955).

54. Joseph Garavel, *Les Paysans de Morette,* Cahiers de la Fondation nationale des Sciences politiques, #2 (1948).

55. L. Bernot and R. Blancart, *Nouville, village français* (Paris: Institut d'Ethnologie, 1953).

56. H. Mendras, *Études de Sociologie rurale, Novis et Virgin,* Cahiers de la Fondation Nationale des Sciences politiques, #40 (1953).

57. Especially: Henri Lefébvre, "Problemes de Sociologie rurale," *Cahiers internationaux de Sociologie,* VI (1949), 78; "Perspectives de Sociologie rurale," *ibid.,* XIV (1953), 122ff.

58. Daniel Faucher, *Géographie agraire* (Paris: M.-Th. Genin, 1949), & *Le Paysan et la Machine,* in the collection *L'Homme et la Machine,* dir. by G. Friedmann (Paris: éditions de Minuit, 1952).

59. Georges Friedman, *La Crise du Progrès* (Paris: Gallimard, 1936); *Problèmes humains du Machinisme industriel* (Paris: Gallimard, 1950); *Le Travail en miettes* (*The Crumbled Labor*) (Paris: Gallimard, 1956).

60. Jean Fourastié, *Nouvelles formes de la civilisation économique* (Paris: 1947); *Le grand Espoir du XXᵉ siècle* (Presses Universitaires de France, 1949); *Machinisme et Bien-être* (éditions de Minuit, 1951).

61. Paul Combe, *Niveau de vie et Progrès technique en France depuis 1860* (Paris: Presses Universitaires de France, 1956).

62. Especially Pierre Naville, *La vie de travail,* Cahiers de la Fondation Nationale des Sciences politiques, #56 (1954), predominantly statistical study.

63. Among others: Alain Girard, *Développement économique et mobilité des travailleurs,* Travaux et Documents (1956), examines the problem of transferring manpower.

64. Among others: M. Verry, *Les Laminoirs ardennais* (Paris: Presses Universitaires de France, 1955); Alain Touraine, *L'évolution du travail ouvrier aux usines Renault,* Ed. Centre National de la Recherche scientifique (1956); Viviane Isambert-Jamati, *Travail féminin et Travail à domicile,* Ed. Centre National de la Recherche scientifique (1956).

65. A. Vexliard, *Introduction à la Sociologie du vagabondage* (M. Rivière, Petite Bibliothèque Sociologique Internationale, 1956).

66. Under the direction of Robert Prigent, *Travaux et Documents,* 1954. Cf. also P. Chombart de Lauwe, *La Vie quotidienne des familles ouvrières,* Ed. Centre National de la Recherche scientifique (1956).

67. Gérard Duplessis-Le Guélinel, *Les Mariages en France,* foreword by P. Gemaehling, Cahiers de la Fondation Nationale des Sciences politiques, #53 (1954).

68. Émile Sicard, *La Zadruga sud-slave dans l'évolution du groupe domestique*

(Paris: Éditions Ophrys, 1943) ; *La Zadruga dans la littérature serbe* (Paris: Éditions Ophrys, 1943) ; *Problèmes familiaux ches les Slaves du Sud* (Éd. Familiales de France, 1947) ; *Études de Sociologie et de Droit slaves* (Paris: Ophrys, 1950) .

69. Gabriel Le Bras, *Études de Sociologie religieuse* (Paris: Presses Universitaires de France, Bibliothèque de Sociologie contemporaine, 2 vol., 1955 & 1956) , vol. I: *Sociologie de la pratique religieuse dans les campagnes françaises;* vol II:*De la Morphologie à la Typologie.*

70. Cf. F. Isambert, "Développement et dépassement de l'étude de la pratique religieuse chez G. Le Bras," *Cahiers Internationaux de Sociologie,* XX (1956) , 149ff.

71. F. Boulard, *Premiers Itinéraires en Sociologie religieuse* (éd. Ouvrières, Économie et Humanisme, 1954). Canon Boulard had composed, as early as 1948, an interesting *Carte religieuse de la France rurale,* brought up to date in 1952 (see Le Bras, *op. cit.,* vol. I, 324) .

72. F. Isambert, "Classes sociales et pratique religieuse paroissiale," *Cahiers internationaux de Sociologie,* XIV (1953) , 141ff.

73. See his communication in the 3rd *Congress of the international Conference of Religious Sociology,* in the review *Lumen Vitae,* Brussels, VI, 1-2 (January-June, 1951) , 43ff., with a map enabling a comparison to be made between the confessional and the economic structure of the Netherlands.

74. See his Introduction, along with that of G. Le Bras, to *Sociologie religieuse et Sciences sociales* (The Acts of the 4th international Congress of religious sociology) (Paris: éd. Ouvrières, Économie et Humanisme, 1955) .

75. Abbé Y. Daniel, *Aspects de la pratique religieuse à Paris* (Paris: Éditions Ouvrières, 1952) .

76. Mme. Jean Perrot, *Grenoble, essai de sociologie religieuse* (Grenoble: Centre d'Étude des complexes sociaux, 1953) .

77. See Maurice Leenhardt, "Questionnaire en vue de l'établissement d'une carte religieuse de l'Afrique occidentale française," *Bulletin de l'Institut fr. d'Afrique noire,* XV, 2 (April, 1953) , 768. Cf also, on the prophetic movements in South Africa and the ba-kongo "messianism," G. Balandier, *Sociologie actuelle de l'Afrique noire, op. cit.,* 219ff. & 417ff.

78. Both works in "Bibliothèque de Sociologie contemporaine" (1951 & 1955) ; cf. also, by the late lamented Marcel Griaule, *Dieu d'eau* (éd. du Chêne, 1948) .

79. Among others: "Immigration et métamorphoses d'un dieu" (a Yoruba God to Brazil) , *Cahiers internationaux de Sociologie,* XX (1956) , 45ff.

80. *Colloque de Sociologie électorale* (éd. Domat-Montchrestien, 1948); Ch. Morazé, R. MacCallum, G. Le Bras, P. George, *Études de Sociologie électorale,* Cahiers de la Fondation Nationale des Sciences politiques, #1 (1946) ; François Goguel, *Géographie des élections fr. de 1870 à 1951,* Cahiers de la Fondation Nationale des Sciences politiques, #27 (1951) ; by the same, *Nouvelles Études de Sociologie électorale,* Cahiers de la Fondation Nationale des Sciences politiques, #60 (1954) .

81. André Siegfried, *Géographie politique de l'Ardèche,* Cahiers de la Fondation Nationale des Sciences politiques, #9 (1949) .

82. A. Latreille and A. Siegfried, *Les Forces religieuses et la vie politique,* Cahiers de la Fondation Nationale des Sciences politiques, #23 (1952) .

83. G. E. Lavau, *Partis politiques et réalités sociales,* Cahiers de la Fondation Nationale des Sciences politiques, #83 (1953) ; M. Duverger, *Partis politiques et Classes sociales,* Cahiers de la Fondation Nationale des Sciences politiques, #74 (1955) .

84. Both published by Libr. Armand Colin, 1946 & 1951.

85. Both in 'Bibliothèque de Philosophie contemporaine" (Paris: Presses Universitaires de France, 1943); Alfred Sauvy, *Le Pouvoir et l'Opinion* (Paris: Payot, 1949).

86. *Sondages de l'Opinion publique française,* dir. by Max Barioux.

87. These three works in the Bibliothèque de Sociologie contemporaine (Paris: Presses Universitaires de France, 1950; 1953; 1953).

88. Maurice Leenhardt, *Do Kamo, la personne et le mythe dans le monde mélanésien* (Paris: Gallimard, 1947).

89. Edgar Morin, *Le Cinéma ou l'Homme imaginaire, essai d'anthropologie sociologique* (Paris: éditions de Minuit, 1956).

90. *L'Année Sociologique,* 3rd series (1950), 559.

91. Le Bras, *Études de Sociologie religieuse,* II, 801.

92. Pierre George, in the above quoted *Études de Sociologie electorale, op. cit.* (1946), 67, on the suburban locality Bourg-la-Reine, near Paris.

93. Libr. Armand Colan, 1943-1955. Cf. by the same author *Recontres de la Géographie et de la Sociologie* (M. Rivière, Petite Bibliothèque Sociologique Internationale, 1957).

94. Petite Bibliothèque Sociologique Internationale (1955).

95. *Méthode scientifique et Science économique,* Libr. Médicis (Paris, 2 vol., 1952 & 1955), I, 33.

THE LOW COUNTRIES

I. Gadourek

Netherlands Institute of Preventive Medicine (Leiden)

In spite of its relative autonomy, sociology (like any other empirical science) does not operate in a vacuum. Any attempt at the interpretation of its scope and its development in a certain culture-area should be based on the description of the most relevant factors of the culture-pattern and of the social structure concerned. There are, however, two reasons why certain reserve must be imposed on such a description of social and cultural determinants of the science of sociology: (1) the limitation of space; (2) the rather poor state of research and of theorizing in this field of sociology of knowledge. The following remarks are, therefore, rather impressionistic than systematic, more informative than solely explicative.

First we have to note the question of unity of the area concerned. In political respect, both present sub-groups, Belgium and the Netherlands, were incorporated in a common state until 1830; then they split and founded independent realms. This political cleavage accentuated other cultural differences which existed between the two ethnic areas already before and were, probably, also manifested in differences of national character. In an article published during the war, J. P. Kruijt, a Dutch sociologist, brings this mentality differential in connection with another factor—religious denomination.[1] Though the question whether the mentality or the religion had been the primary causal factor is not yet settled, the fact remains that in the Netherlands, the Reformation, especially Calvinism, became a majority church, while it had hardly set foot in Belgium. The language barrier is another factor making for disunity; Dutch and French are quite different languages, and French is less known and spoken by the intellectuals in Holland than is German or English for instance. As most sociological publications in Belgium appear in French, a considerable barrier arises between the groups of Dutch and Belgian sociologists.

The language-differential, finally, goes hand in hand with the different cultural orientation in either country. While, in the Netherlands, the sciences of man traditionally were saturated by the stimuli from the neighboring Germany, Belgium has been more influenced by French contributions.

In addition to these factors directly affecting the solidarity between the two countries, there are some minor points of difference. The industrial revolution seems to have affected the life in Belgium to a larger extent in the nineteenth century, than it did in Holland where rational town-planning helped to mitigate the most awkward aspects of the growing population-agglomerations.

As the intensity and occurrence of sociological interest is said to correlate with the occurrence of social problems and upheavals, it is worth mentioning that both countries enjoyed decades of peaceful development. In contrast to the neighboring Germany, for longer than a century (1830-1940), Holland was not engaged in a war; more shocking was the experience of the Nazi-occupation in World War II which, without doubts, accounts (in addition to other factors) for the upsurge of public interest in sociology, after 1945. Belgium, in political respect, too, more tied with France than with Germany, received its blow in World War I. In contrast with the Netherlands, who lost her largest part of overseas territories as the result of the last war, Belgium succeeded to keep her uranium-rich Congo and could proceed to the restoration of its devastated economy immediately after 1945.

In spite of these minor differences the basic nature of social problems are similar in the two countries: (1) both of them are old colonial countries, still assuming the responsibility for the cultural, technical and political assistance to the colored peoples outside Europe; (2) both countries are split into two important cultural sub-groups. Holland has the Roman Catholic and the Protestant creeds coinciding with the ethnic differences between "the South" and "the North." Belgium struggles with the problems of bilingualism which are symptomatic for a deep-going split into two different ethnic groups, the Wallons and the Flemings. (3) Another common source of problems in the two areas is the high population density; they belong to the most overcrowded countries in the world (the density index for Holland being 330 inhabitants per square kilometer, that for Belgium about 290 inhabitants). Of the two, Holland is faced with more serious problems owing to a high net to reproduction rate (141 in 1954) and to the loss of overseas territories. Under the severe population pressure, the government advocates an active emigration policy; industrialization is seen as a way-out of the population-impasse in both countries, while the reclamation of new lands seems to be a specific Dutch solution to the problem. These three processes, migration, industrialization and reclamation of lands lead to a great number of adjustment-difficulties which form the subject-matter of sociological studies in the two countries. Other social problems are linked with the prevalent social taboos to the extent that they have escaped the attention of the Dutch and the Belgian sociologists. To take up these "suppressed," neglected themes, and to clarify them by means of systematic analysis and empirical research, is one of the future prospects of sociologists in this area. (Some of them will be specified in the closing section of this chapter.) Meanwhile, let us deal with the present state of sociological thinking and research by briefly tracing its recent developments.

GENERAL CHARACTERISTICS OF SOCIOLOGY IN THE AREA

As might be expected in the social and cultural situation (some features have been described above), sociology in the Low Countries remained for a long time closely tied with other disciplines. In the Netherlands, as Van Doorn describes in his recent survey of Dutch sociology,[2] it was linked for years with social geography. It is still an open question as how far this should be accounted for by the fact that the first Dutch sociologist of international fame, R. Steinmetz (the author, among others of Soziologie des Krieges, [The Sociology of War, 1929]), was appointed the chairman of the Department of Social Geography at the University of Amsterdam.[3]

The fact remains that until the dire experience of war in the forties, sociological research was mainly confined to the problems of town planning and of the reclamation of lands. Specific sociological themes, such as war (Steinmetz), the loss of religious denomination (J. P. Kruijt), acculturation (Van Heek) were rather exceptional and were taken up by individual scholars rather than by research-teams. In addition to orientation towards geography, the impact of criminology (W. A. Bonger) and of economics (F. van Heek) were also strong, in Holland.

In Belgium, at most universities, sociology used to be considered as one of the auxiliary subjects which were taught at the faculty of law. A rather exceptional position was taken by the Solvay Institute of Sociology which (founded as early as 1895 in Brussels), for years was the only sociological institute in the European continent.[4] How-

ever, even this institute concentrated for years on the interpretation
and elaboration of the sociological concepts and ideas of its founder,
the industrialist Ernest Solvay, as well as on the documentation of
the related sciences (such as economy, political science and law).
Thanks only to persons like G. De Greef and E. Waxweiler, significant
contribution was made to theoretical sociology in the country which
gave the world no less a pioneer of social science than Adolph Quetelet.

While the lack of emancipation of sociology can, probably, be traced
down to the peaceful development and the lack of vast social interest
in both countries, the general cultural orientation in these areas accounts, without doubt, for its philosophical foundation.

In Holland, for years, the German influence dominated the field of
sociological thinking. W. Sombart was esteemed as a progressive thinker
whose periodization of modern history was accepted and whose plans
for social reform were considered as a remedy for the crucial social
problems of the time, even accepted by those who could not subscribe
to more dogmatic doctrines of orthodox Marxism. More recently, the
works of Karl Mannheim exercised similar influence. Though critical
of the concrete economic and social theories of Marxism about
the disappearance of the middle-class, about the accumulation of capital and the pauperization of the working-class, the Dutch scholars
were more positive in their appraisal of the dialectical method. Probably owing to the impact of Hegelian philosophy in Holland, Hans
Freyer's dialectical *Soziologie als Wirklichkeitswissenschaft* (1930) was
an often used and an often quoted handbook of sociology. Dutch
sociologists thought to have found in it an answer to a question that
puzzled them ever since Dilthey, Spranger, and, especially Rickert,
started criticizing the use of the natural science method in the field
of social and cultural sciences. Is sociology only another "cultural
science" whose model should be patterned in analogy to linguistics,
logic, or aesthetics, or is it an empirical science? Even when deciding
for the latter, the majority of sociologists of the generation between
the wars still emphasized that sociology should by no means be reckoned to the natural science. They would quote A. Vierkandt to prove
that the operation called *"Verstehen"* (i.e., intuitional, sympathetic
understanding) should be applied in the study of social phenomena
and would mention Rickert in order to demonstrate that sociology
can never reach the generalization-level of natural science, shortly,
that it remains a "nomothetic" rather than an "ideographic" science.

We shall understand now why the notion of "ideal type," which takes both elements of "understanding" and of time-and-space-bound nature of the social phenomena into consideration, was the main conceptual tool which they borrowed from Max Weber, a highly esteemed thinker in the sociological circles in Holland. We shall also understand why "sociography," which unites these two aspects of sociological thinking, appealed to the research workers and teachers of sociology in Holland. Sceptical about the possibility of finding generally valid laws of social developments Dutch "sociographers" preferred to describe social life in *one* definite area, in *one* period of time, by pointing out how social structure changes from the emotionally satisfactory *Gemeinschaft* (i.e. community) to the businesslike, "uprooted" *Gesellschaft* (i.e. society) in our era of late-capitalistic development. The sober, unphilosophical outlook of the Dutchmen are probably responsible for the preference for this descriptive science over the systematization of philosophical axioms that underlie any system of sociology.

In Belgium, on the contrary, an orientation towards the French sociology could be noticed. While in Holland sociology is reckoned to the sciences of culture (*Geesteswetenschappen*), and the method of natural science is banned from its field, Belgian sociology continues the French positivistic tradition.

E. Solvay, one of the founders of social science in this country, was an advocate of a mechanistic school, reducing sociology to a kind of social physics and energetics. The syndicalist De Greef adhered to the organismic interpretation of society in which some concepts of A. Comte were merged with the biological views of H. Spencer, and E. Waxweiler, on the other hand, lays emphasis on the psychological basis of social phenomena, thus taking a similar position to De Greef's organistic system as G. Tarde did with regard to E. Durkheim, in France.

The Comtean conception of sociology as a tool for social policy and reform, though promising and rich in intention, appeared somewhat fruitless in its realization. In spite of vast documentation and encyclopedic work carried out by the Institute *Solvay* not many large sociological research-projects have been carried out between the wars. Even in the educational field, the training was of such a wide scope (law, economics, political science) that we hardly can speak of sociologists in the sense of specialized professional workers trained by the universities.

POST-WAR BREAK-THROUGH

World War II brought about a sudden and penetrating change in the situation of sociology in the Low Countries. Most universities were closed, the teaching of social science was either prohibited or censored by the Nazi-occupants, government-sponsored research was impossible, import of sociological literature from abroad, and the mutual contacts between social scientists were stopped.

In spite of all this, we witness a rapid growth of sociology in this area; within some seven years since the occupation, sociology received a chair almost at every university, a number of university professors were appointed, hundreds of students enrolled, new research-projects were successfully conducted by teams of sociologists, and the former narrow, one-sided orientation was abandoned. How was this change achieved?

In spite of the temporary stagnation, the war brought about new conditions for development of social science. To mention first was the mass-confrontation of the population with another, strange way of life which the Nazi-occupants tried to impose on the temporarily subdued nations. This led to the awakening of public interest in the science which might offer answers to the salient social problems which one was confronted with. Another factor was just the very disruption and disorganization of existing institutions which made a fresh start possible; re-opened universities were not only overcrowded with students but could be and also were re-organized. They were adapted to the actual public needs and interests.

The general cultural orientation also changed during the war. Germany being an aggressor and France an occupied country, neither of them could bind the attention and the sympathy of the people in the Low Countries. Instead, Dutchmen and Belgians alike, focussed their attention on the remaining part of the free world. The Anglo-Saxon countries became better appreciated and also better known than before the war.

Immediately after the end of hostilities, material help began to pour in, not only in the form of food, economic loans, and industrial equipment, but also in the form of recent books on sociology of travel grants, and scholarships. If one realizes, that in Germany and in Italy sociology was silent after the totalitarian regimes were established there, and that in most other European countries with longer sociological erudition the academic activities were stopped for about five

years, one will understand the impact that these imported periodicals
and books had on the European scholars and scientists. It was not
only the temporal lag of European science but the inherent quality
of the recent works on sociology in the U.S.A. that appealed to many
an European reader. The war, which formed an impediment for the
development of social science in Europe, seems to have helped the
American social scientists to concentrate on more relevant subjects
and to elaborate new quantitative methods (such as: the *Authoritarian
Personality, Content Analysis,* the scaling methods as developed in
the American Soldier, etc.).

Finally, in addition to the travel grants (e.g., the Fulbright program)
which made intensive contacts of the European social scientists with
their American colleagues possible, research grants became available.
Several international or foreign agencies, such as UNESCO, the Rockefeller Foundation, the Ford Foundation, the Disaster Committee of
the National Research Council, became interested in research in this
area. Later on, when material help in the form of Marshall Aid and
F.O.A. was forthcoming, the need was growing for evaluation research,
efficiency-research, and the study of human factors in industrial production process. If we add to these new stimuli the fact that several
scientists proceeded to carry out the research-plans of their own which
they conceived or partly elaborated during the war, and the fact that
the government and other national agencies realized the contribution
which sociology could make to the reconstruction effort, we shall
understand why several new projects were launched, after the war.
Whether due to the favorable influence of Anglo-Saxon science or to
the indigenous factor, the projects were undertaken by teams of
research-workers of which some were multi-disciplinary and a few were
international. The traditional isolation of scholars seemed broken
after the war.

MAIN FIELDS OF INTEREST AND PROGRESS

Theory and Frame of Reference of Sociology. The old traditions
have not yet been abandoned and the new trends have been less conspicuous in the field of sociology in the Netherlands. P. J. Bouman's
Sociologie, Begrippen en Problemen [*Sociology, Its Concepts and
Problems*] (Antwerpen: N. V. Standaard-Boekhandel, 1946) remains
one of the main systematic handbooks; the same applies to the smaller

book by J. Bierens de Haan, *Sociologie, Ontwikkeling en Methode*
[*Sociology, Development and Method*] (Den Haag: Servire, 1947) which
deals more with history than offering a systematic body of knowledge;
the works of R. van Dijk and J. Ponsioen would be classified by English or American sociologists as belonging rather to the field of social
philosophy than to sociology; the former builds up, in his *Mens en
Medemens* [*Man and Neighbor*] (Wageningen: Zomer & Keuning,
1953), a system of social thought which would be compatible with the
Fundamentalist Calvinist ethics and theology; the latter, in his *De
Menselijke Samenleving* [*Human Society*] (Bussum: Paul Brand, N. V.
1953) tries to offer an official Roman Catholic interpretation of society.
Bouman's handbook is based on his earlier *Maatschappijleer* [*Science
of Society*]; it describes sociology as an independent science which
should be freed from the impact of natural science, at present, and
should follow the line which was drawn by "the precursors of a me-
thodically autonomous sociology in the 18th and the 19th centuries:
Fichte, Novalis, Miller, Hegel, etc." (*Ibid.* p. 13). The 200 pages are
evenly divided between the subjects on general and on special sociology; another traditional division of social science into statics and
dynamics is on the other hand, abandoned, though not explicitly but
rather as a matter of fact. In the first part, important concepts referring to the social structure are described and exemplified. In the latter,
the main contributions to the sociology of law, to sociological criminology, to the sociology of economic life, to that of religious life, of
art, of knowledge and of culture in general are briefly reviewed and
discussed on the hand of ample sources.

In spite of the author's acquaintance with "the American Way of
Life" (See his *Volk in Beweging*), no attempt has been made to admit
the recent elements of American sociology into his sociological system;
the author's broad interest and philosophical orientation give grounds
for belief that a theoretical synthesis will be undertaken in the future.

While Bouman's *Sociologie* is mainly appreciated owing to its di-
dactic value, and as a textbook, F. L. Polak's thought provoking dissertation can be considered as a contribution to the discussion about
the philosophical assumptions underlying the framework of reference
of a social scientist.[5] Starting with the criticism of Max Weber's attempt to establish economics as a value-free science, Polak comes to
the conclusion that all science necessarily implies value-judgments and
that, in terms of an English summary of his book, "science has been,

is and will always be in a certain way and to a certain extent: value judgment and evaluating" (p. 293).

A rather extensive series of arguments about these challenging views took place between Polak and J. P. Kruitjt[6] who tried to show that Polak did not grant justice to Weber's discriminative thought and that his main argument in favor of valuative basis of all science is based on a paralogism. (Polak uses the term "value" with the implications of "ethical, religious or philosophical value" and then in the sense of "rational interpretation of facts" and places both, without distinction, into the same syllogism).

More recently, theoretical sociology in Holland was enriched by two sociological dissertations: Dr. J. Ponsioen's *Symboliek in de samenleving* [*Role of Symbols in Human Society*] (Utrecht: Bijleveld, 1952) and Dr. J. A. A. van Doorn's *Sociologie van de organisatie* [*The Sociology of the Organization*] (Leiden: S. H. Stenfert Kroese, 1956). Ponsioen here tries to break the barrier between the French and the Dutch sociologists by introducing the concepts of Gurvitch to the readers in the Netherlands. In contradiction to the broad definitions of Morris and Mead, Ponsioen defines the symbol as "a sensible sign which is considered by the interested subject as containing deeper meaning of the natural or human events, i.e., the world of values, ideas, or of hidden realities as, for instance, the psychical life or spiritual values; it makes the participation in these hidden realities possible without, however, losing its hidden nature" (109). After having limited symbolic thinking to the attempts of expressing the non-empiric realities (117), Ponsioen discusses the problems of social origin of symbols as well as the influence of elements of social structure on symbolic thinking. A short survey of the main forms of symbolic systems in the archaic, the theocratic, the familial, the Middle-Age Christian, the rationalistic, the technocratic, and the relativistic patterns of culture closes the book.

Van Doorn describes "organization" as an inherent part of the system of social control; he sees in it a process by means of which a group of persons consciously pursue their goal by cooperating with each other, by dividing their tasks and by seeking their means in a rational way. On the other hand, in a concrete example, the organization of the western army, he discusses the functional aspects (rather dysfunctional aspects) and the limits of organization (the possibility to become organized), the impact of the organization on human groups, and the relation between the organization and the ideology. Having confined his work to the study of the organization as a process, he refutes the concepts of "informal organization" of the "blue-print of organization" as being too narrow and meaningless.

With the exception of the above mentioned works, little contribution is made to the sociological theory in Holland. S. Hofstra, in two minor works ably clarifies the concepts of "function" and of "normalcy," by semantically distinguishing their various connotations which lead to confusion when used in an unsophisticated, undiscriminative way. J. P. Kruijt tries to arrive at a more critical attitude to the well-known dichotomy of "community-society" by Tönnies; A. Oldendorff clarifies the notion of "a stranger" in his recent inaugural address.

As far as methodology is concerned, no proper sociological handbook is available. Sj. Groenman's *Methoden der sociographie* [*The Methods of Sociography*] (Assen: Van Gorcum & Co., 1950), though describing sociography as a concrete counterpart to a more abstract sociology, is much more limited in scope than the books which appeared in this field abroad (e.g., by A. S. Rice, P. Young, G. Lundsberg, M. Parten, J. Madge). What is still lacking is, on the one hand, a fundamental treatment of the basic methodological problems in the way Max Weber, E. Durkheim, F. Kaufman did it abroad; on the other hand, a systematic description and evaluation of the new techniques of sociological research such as new forms of interview and data-gathering, sociometric analysis, scaling analysis, multiple factor analysis of qualitative data, content analysis, non-parametric statistics, etc.

In Belgium, a short textbook was written by J. Leclercq in 1948 (*Introduction à la sociologie,* Louvain: 1948); here sociology is defined "as a positive science of interhuman facts," "a science that studies human factors in their relation to collective life, in a positive way" (93). The positivist standpoint of the French sociological school is not yet clearly surpassed. In comparison with the book of Bouman, *Introduction à la sociologie* does not present the body of knowledge, which the social science has to offer, but rather introduces the reader into the problems around sociology. It contains chapters on the origin and history of sociology, on its various "schools," on its object, method, and subdivision, on its relation to philosophy, on "the nature of social phenomena" and on the true sociological spirit. Like Bouman, Leclercq mainly refers to foreign sources published before the war.

Remarkable contributions to the theoretical sociology were made by E. Dupréel and J. Haesaert, each of whom wrote a treatise on general sociology under the title of *Sociologie Générale* (Paris: Presse Universitaire Française, 1948; Brussels, 1956). Either of these works presents a contribution to systematic sociology and as such can be compared with the systems of Comte, Simmel, Vierkandt, Von Wiese, Cooley, Sumner, Sorokin, etc.

The earlier of the two, the system of E. Dupréel, is original not only in that it contains practically no references to the work of other sociologists, but also in its conception of the object of sociology and its sub-division.

Dupréel sees the basic element of social reality in "social relationship" (*le rapport social*). This is described as an external relation between any two individuals who mutually influence each other either by their activity or by their mere existence (5). Two friends, two rivals, husband and wife, salesman and his client—these are, according to Dupréel, examples of social relationships. They are classified into positive relationships, based on association and cooperation, and into negative relationships, based on antagonism and alienation; there are, in addition, complementary relationships—that do not exist separately but are mutually dependent. The group or the society at large are defined as collectivities of individuals who are united and distinguished from other individuals by positive, complementary relationships (20). After having found, in accordance with G. Tarde, the basic elements of society in psychological make-up of individuals, Dupréel discusses various forms of human instincts under a somewhat strange term of "paleo-sociology" (*paléo- et néosociologie*), while trying to find hereditary conditions for the adaptation of man to his environment.

In the next section, Dupréel describes various aspects of living in groups: their growth, their tendency to endure, their typical "mentality," structure, and their dissolution. After a short chapter on the relation of the group to the individual, the relationships between the groups are discussed from the dynamic standpoint, in terms of antagonisms, conflicts, and of assimilation and "social symbiosis." A special section is added to describe the social equilibrium and "disproportionate ascendency" (*la démesure*) resulting in social hierarchy and in the hierarchy of values. In accordance with the German dichotomy of "culture" and "civilization," Dupréel chooses the latter concept to close his book by discussing "the demographic variable" and the technic as the main feature of both civilization and progress. (The notions of pattern of culture and of cultural sociology are not included in his system.) Demographical population-growth and technical progress are the main factors of social change which is, however, not of a linear but rather of an S-form; after an initial rapid development of both (techniques and population-increase), a period of stagnation, at a very high level, will be reached (*le plafond de civilization*).

Without abiding for long on the formal problems of sociology as a science, Haesaert like Dupréel, starts his work by directing the attention of the reader to the subject-matter of sociology—the human community, the culture-group, that is built on mutual human relationships (those of individual to individual, of individual to group, the relationships between the groups, or those of the group to individual). In accordance with the ethnological school, Haesaert looks for "the origin" of the community and finds it in the yet undifferentiated tribal organization in which the elements of religion, public law, and of war can already be discerned. When the tribes engage in wars, dominate each other, a mixed association of "people" under the common sovereignty is formed. By getting conscious of their common backgrounds, "people" become a nation, which is dominated by the same spirit as the community.

After having thus defined his starting point by briefly describing the limits (as expressed by the notions of "hostility" and "frontier"), as well as the organization and the disruption of communal life, Haesaert proceeds to the treatment of the three "typical forms of sociability" (39), namely, social statics, dynamics, and mechanics. In social statics, the general nature of collective life is described in terms of various "sociotypes." "Sociotype" is defined as a totality of similar or collective activities and forms of behavior which result from the reciprocal relationships between the men (40). The author reviews the various attempts to classify the sociotypes in order to take up one of the most important tasks of his statics: the description of the psychological basis of the community. This is in agreement with the basic assumption of his work that the individual and his needs form the very essence of every society (7). Various collective manifestations of psychological functions are described: (1) collective reactions to the same or similar stimuli which are called "concordant formations;" (2) the more diffused, the less stabilized structures, "coordinated formations;" and, (3) mental manifestation which form consistent, autonomous structure, the so called "consolidation formations." To the latter, religious life is reckoned; the author takes much pains to describe the various forms of religious institutions and activities, in this connection, while art and science are only briefly mentioned.

In the rest of his statics, Haesaert gives a brief description of the social structure by introducing a new term for it, "synergy." Elements of disintegration of social system are discussed under the term of "disergy." For the rest, Haesaert treats the more conventional elements of social structure (group, mass, family, clan, social stratification, political and economic organization) as always strongly leaning on the findings of comparative ethnology.

The social dynamics are even more original in conception. It describes the forces which result in maintenance or disruption of human communities. Human effort, individual or collective, and the resistance to this effort, either social or biological, economic, and geographic—these are the main mechanisms of the societal life. Besides the driving forces of religion, science, art and of other "less consolidated" forms of human effort, and the resistance to these forces of individual mental structure, of population factors, of fatigue, sexuality, age, emigration, physical distance, elements of social structure—there is no mechanism of social change; there is neither progress nor regress nor continual social development. We cannot even speak about a periodicity of universal history, nor about the development of social institutions; they do not change according to some preconceived curve or social law. There is only one change—that of re-assumed equilibrium that the man reaches when adopting to his environment (381-382).

By having limited social dynamics to the process of overcoming the resistance to change, Haesaert finds it necessary to add another part to his book—the social mechanics. He understands by social mechanisms the habitual practice of using material tools ("instrumentalles techniques") or the habitual ways of functioning ("fonctionneles techniques"), such as language, publicity and transportation. The mobility (both social and spatial), the centralization, the social norms, and the competition area, are fully discussed under the heading of "instrumental techniques." A short chapter on "disergy" concludes the book by describing the usual social problems: epidemics, catastrophies, wars, unemployment, sickness, delinquency, prostitution, a-social, anti-social and non-social collectivities.

An analysis of the texture of Haesaert's general sociology would indicate that in spite of the work's originality, it is not difficult to trace the impact of the Belgian sociological tradition of Haesaert's thought. The conception of sociology as consisting of statics, dynamics, and mechanics reveals distant Comtean, positivist influence. His method of searching for the origin of social phenomena in distant cultural areas is Durkheimean in essence. As compared with the comparative ethnology, other social sciences related to sociology are given much less attention. The results of the modern socio-psychological research are somewhat neglected—in a system that tries to explain the social structure by tracing its elements back to the individual needs. While the Anglo-Saxon influence can still be enlarged in this field, in the future,[7] the stress which is laid on "community aspects" of social organization, though not yet consistently incorporated in the entire system, seems to form a basis for a synthesis of German and French sociological thinking. The author's vast erudition (French, German, English and Dutch) gives every hope that such a synthesis will be achieved in the future.

In summing up this section, we should stress that traditional elements of thinking are strong in the field of theoretical sociology in both countries. The field of methodology is still neglected, the gap between the theory and the research is still very wide. Symptoms of broader cultural orientation can, however, be noticed.

Human Ecology. The old tradition of the geographic orientation of the sociological research in Holland was continued after World War II. As early as 1943, the "Stichting voor Maatschappelijk Werk ten Plattelande" [The Foundation for Rural Welfare Work] assigned one of the institutes for social research (ISONEVO) with a vast project in rural sociology covering about twenty-five hundred communities. The first monograph appeared in 1947; it is still considered a model-report in this field.[8] Since then, other studies by De Vries Reilingh, W. Sleumer, and others, have been published; in addition to them, several dissertations in sociography, social or economic geography should be mentioned, as well as a number of reports published by several sociographers working in single communities. Though there are more than a dozen monographies about various places, there is a striking uniformity of approach. This is partly due to a convention, the Dutch sociographers agreed on a standard research-plan to which one had to adhere in order to obtain comparable data. As the sponsors of the research were either planologists, the authorities of the local, the provincial or the national governments, as the economic objectives were predominant and the persons to carry out the research were trained economists, geographers or social historians, the proper subject-matter of rural sociology, the description of the local social process and of the social structure, were restricted to about one third, or even less, of the work, while geographic description and the presentation of demographic and economic data filled the largest part of the reports. Now and then, social and cultural history takes the place of economic analysis.[9]

The studies have an essential aspect in common; they are based on secondary data (statistical tables, documents from archives) and on impressionistic, by exception participant, observation. The few generalizations which can be found in these reports usually refer to "the group-character" of the inhabitants. One understands hereby the dominant personality-traits in the population-group under study. It is especially in this field where the absence of modern diagnostics and modern, inductive statistical approach makes itself felt. Instead of using tests or batteries of scale-questions in representative samples of populations, most sociographers search for occasional remarks of strangers or for the characteristics of the local people as seen by the novel-writers. At best, they select one or two persons and try to assess their qualities and personality-type by the descriptive method of the Dutch sociologist G. Heymans that was designed some twenty-five years ago. In spite of these shortcomings, some of these reports contain a rich treasury of social data and, in so far as they are based on intuition and sympathetic understanding, give a good, workable picture of the local communities, satisfying the major needs of the planners of local building projects or enterprise, somewhat less the needs of social welfare planners.

Ecological studies are not confined only to the field of social statics. On the initiative of Dutch scientists, an international "Research Group for European Migration Problems" was established in the Hague. In 1952, a number of English written publications appeared.[10] Van der Brink, one of the authors, who traced the variations in natality to the single war-events in his earlier Dutch publications, arrives here to a well-founded population prognosis; he concludes that natality is to remain, in the future, the dominant factor of growth; as a slow decrease in mortality also is to be expected, emigration seems to be the only outlet and the population will even then increase. The age composition will change, too; in 30 years ahead the care of the aged will require an expenditure by the productive age-groups some 40 per cent higher than at present.

Beijer and Oudegeest discuss (on the basis of quantitative data of the Central Bureau of Statistics) the birth-rate differential and the industrialization as factors in overseas migration and analyze the composition of the group of emigrants according to their age, sex, occupation, and area of destination. Petersen carries the analysis a bit farther by taking the problems of motivation, selection, and assimilation of emigrants into consideration. Hofstee, finally, takes up a more general theme and tries to discard the older theory about the negative selection of average intelligence due to emigration. In his view, migration is merely a secondary, indirect factor; the occupation plays a primary role both in intelligence-differential and in migration.

While most of the above mentioned studies are based on secondary data, recently, a large project of the assimilation of the migratory mineworkers in the southern province of the Netherlands was launched, under the general supervision of a psychologist, F. J. Th. Rutten.

Meanwhile, a similar study of assimilation has already been completed in Belgium by a team of sociologists in Liége, under the general supervision of R. Clèmens. The final report which covers the results of years-long research[11] reveals a fine balance of both primary and secondary sources and a variety of techniques and ways of approach. After having shown the relevancy of the problem (the assimilation of about 140,000 Polish and Italian immigrants to Belgium), the authors survey the results of monographic studies of assimilation in various areas, the results of the interviews with key-persons (Trade-Union leaders, employers and supervisors, teachers, clergymen); they refer to their study of the vertical mobility among the migrants and, finally, to a study of the attitudes of the autochthonous population towards the immigrants, covering structured interviews with 262 persons. As compared with the previous studies, more attention is paid to the role that the marital status, cultural distance, in-group out-group relationship, and other specifically sociological variables play in the process of assimilation of migrants.

In summary, we may state that, with a few exceptions (that of the migration project of Liège), a large part of the ecological studies are still somewhat unwilling to pay attention to the various aspects of social structure and cultural pattern. They should use less subjective, more reliable techniques of collecting and evaluating the data from primary sources. Thanks to the efforts of skilled sociographers and sociologists working in this field, the situation favors future development; the public authorities became more research-minded; several research-institutes and sociological departments were founded, and a number of qualified research-workers are leaving the universities with more insight in the proper sociological problems, in methodology, in social psychology, and in inductive statistics than before the war. While the primary objective in the Netherlands is thus to specialize and intensify the work, in Belgium, the decentralization of research, that still remains a monopoly of the universities, should be expected.

Occupational Sociology. This branch of sociological thinking has witnessed a rapid development after the war. Strangely enough, the main impetus did not come from abroad. In Holland, it got a stimulus in the work of two researchers, F. van Heek and M. G. Ydo, who started the studies of occupational problems in the days of war.

In order to ascertain the factors that influence the satisfaction in work, Ydo interviewed 1642 employees in 26 plants in the Netherlands.[12] By means of structured, standardized interviews and the mechanical cross-tabulation of data, he was able to state that the physical factors (such as illumination, noise, ventilation, heating) are far less relevant than "the social factors within the plant" (such as identification with the firm, chances for promotion, satisfaction with wages, etc.). Out of the thirty-seven factors that Ydo examined, the family-judgment of a worker's job appeared to be the most important condition for his satisfaction with work; the identification with the firm, the nature of his relationships to his "boss," followed in the same order of importance. Women and older people turned out to enjoy more satisfaction, but the association with age is not, according to Ydo, of a linear form.

The work of Ydo got surprising publicity in the Netherlands. Several research-projects were carried out and a number of publications appeared since. The Department of Mental Health of the Netherlands Institute for Preventive Medicine, in the association with which Ydo published his study, undertook a series of industrial studies which were mainly concerned with the problems of "human relations." They were carried out by multi-disciplinary teams organized by the Head of the Department, J. Koekebakker.

Among others, an inventory was developed to study "the moral in industry" ("Hoe denkt U over Uw werk"—"What do You Think about your Work?") by means of standardized scales (over 10,000 employees from forty industrial plants have already been interviewed in the process of standardization). In another study a verification was attempted of Bavelas' hypotheses about influence of the group-structure upon the communication process—both in the field and in the laboratory experiments. In addition to the work that is done by social pedagogists and psychologists within the plant, regional surveys of attitudes by sociologists were held. In one of them, about 550 steel-workers were interviewed in their homes to assess their attitudes to technical changes in the plant; in another one, 660 workers in an agricultural province (Zeeland) were questioned about their attitudes to industrial work in order to ease the on-going industrialization process.

In the academic circles, a number of sociological dissertations on occupational sociology appeared. D. Horringa (*Mens en Groep in het Moderne Bedrijf* [*Man and Group in a Modern Enterprise*] Assen: Van Gorcum, 1951) reviews the recent literature in this field by dis-cussing the problems which are rooted in the individual, those stemming from the group relations, and those caused by the organi-zational structure of the enterprise. A. M. Kuylaars's *Werk en leven van de industriële loonarbeider als object van een sociale onder-nemingspolitiek* [*Life and Work of the industrial Wage Earners as the Object of the Social Policy of the Enterprise*] (Leiden: H. E. Sten-fert Kroese, 1951) directs the attention of the Dutch readers to the problem of monotony and de-personalization of work; task-enlargement is seen as one of the humane solutions to the problem. H. Haveman's *De ongeschoolde arbeider* [*The Unskilled Worker*] (Assen: Van Gorcum, 1952) describes the pattern of living of the low-class workers as substantially different from that of other classes; in order to explain this difference Haveman is the first to introduce the concept of sub-culture to the Dutch readers.

All of those dissertations are prevalently based on the extensive study of sociological literature and on personal experience or participant observation; mass-interviewing of representative or analytical samples was not referred to.

Another origin of occupational sociology in the Netherlands can be traced down to the pioneer work of F. van Heek who started his study of social stratification in Enschede (a textile center in the north-eastern parts of the country) early in the war time.[13]

After a critical review of the literature on this subject, Van Heek comes to define social stratification as based on occupational prestige.

He uses Thurstone's method of judges (46 persons of various occupations in Enschede). This scale was applied to hundreds of inhabitants and to their fathers' occupations. In this way, Van Heek was able to follow the occupational (and social) origin of the population in various classes that are found very rigid and "closed" in Enschede—quite in agreement with his working hypothesis.

Being convinced that one should study the social phenomena in their extreme manifestations, Van Heek charged his assistant, I. van Hulten, with the study of the occupational mobility at the Philips' concern in Eindhoven.[14] Van Hulten used a vast sample (3,284 persons) and somewhat more sophisticated techniques of evaluation (chi-square tests of cross-tabulated data) to analyze the factors that influence mobility; the region of origin, the social status of the wife, and the training were identified as the main variables while the number of siblings, age, seniority, religion, etc., were found to be of less importance.

Two other projects directly stimulated by Van Heek approach the stage of final evaluation: (1) a statistical survey of mobility on a national scale (by Van Tulder), and (2) a study of the social origin of the employers and of the industrial captains in the Netherlands.

Inspired by the work of Van Heek though independent in the organizational setting of his research, G. Kuiper studied occupational mobility in Zwolle.[15]

In trying to bridge the various trends of occupational sociology in the Netherlands, Van Heek started the study of human and industrial relations in the textile region of Twente that is now conducted under the supervision of Th. J. Yzerman.

In order to test some of his earlier insights[16] by empirical research, A. Oldendorff helped to organize multi-disciplinary teams in the southern Roman-Catholic provinces. Sponsored by the Dutch Productivity Center, two studies are undertaken by these teams: (1) a study of the recognition, prevention, and treatment of mental disturbances among the industrial empolyees; (2) a study of the differential selection and the training of foremen. Finally, mention should be made of the attempt to develop the theory of human relations from the standpoint of the Roman Catholic ethics and theology that was made by this combined group.[17]

Industry is not the only object of interest for Dutch occupational sociologists. E. J. Tobi and A. W. Luijckk[18] started to study the social origin of the shopkeepers and of independent tradesmen; though depending on Van Heek in the choice of their problem, they followed rather their own way of approach.

Since 1953, E. W. Hofstee has published a *Bulletin* of the Department of Sociology and Sociography at the Agricultural College in

Wageningen showing the results of empirical research of farmers' problems. They are based on quantitative analysis and touch even on such social psychological questions as the personality traits of progressive farmers, the problems of public instruction and enlightenment of farmers. In addition to these subjects, the class-organizations of farmers and the cooperative movement in the Netherlands were studied by the co-workers of Hofstee.

In Belgium, the dispersion of professional workers of certain categories (physicians, dentists, pharmacists) were studied by the sociological seminar of R. Clèmens in Liège (*Médecins, Dentistes et Pharmaciens dans la Province de Liège*, Liège, 1954); H. Mayer worked on the participation of workers and employees in workshop committees, while H. Janne gave us a good survey of the theory of technical development.[19]

In summary, we may state that the occupational sociology belongs to one of the promising fields of sociological research in the Netherlands. In Belgium, research is still scarce or, with a few exceptions that have been mentioned above, is not carried out by qualified sociological research-workers. The high level of theorizing and the lively practical interest still wait to be bridged by the organized, specialized social research.

Sociology of Culture: There are as yet few studies which take the configuration of cultural traits in the Netherlands or in Belgium as their object of investigation. D. C. van der Poel's *Inleiding tot de sociologie van Nederland* (i.e., Introduction to the Sociology of the Netherlands, the Hague, 1950), contains only a few impressionistic remarks on the subject. In our own study we tried to analyze the inter-relationship of the social structure, culture-pattern, and the attitudes and values of people in a local community with the help of a large representative sample of the adult population.[19a] The pattern of culture was interpreted in terms of causal relationships that have been ascertained by means of a statistical analysis (cross-tabulation of clusters of variables that had been identified on the multiple-factor matrix).

The studies of the single cultural traits and institutions (religion, science, etc.) are more frequent. J. P. Kruyt, noted for his earlier works on sociological factors in the loss of religious affiliation and of the personality characteristics of persons of various religious denominations, is directing research on the social and cultural consequences of living in a society split up into distinct religious sub-groups. W.

Banning is editing a handbook of pastoral sociology which would cover, in several volumes, the religiography of the entire country. The Sociological Institute of the Dutch Reformed Church conducted several surveys (the material circumstances of the preachers, the attitudes to the mission, etc.) which are published in the *Sociologisch Bulletin*, the organ of the Institute. In order to demonstrate the typical mentality of the Roman Catholics in the Netherlands, Van Heek examined the natality figures in the communities along the Dutch borders by matching local places that were alike in all relevant respect except one—the national structure. He found higher natality-figures in Dutch communities in the neighboring Belgian and German communities, and explains this fact by the mentality of an emancipated minority group that strives for ascendancy.[20]

The sociologists of Roman Catholic backgrounds produced a number of monographies in which the description of religious practices is intermingled with various kinds of data which had been collected by the usual sociographic method.

In Belgium, more homogeneous in religious respect than Holland religiography is still in the hands of clergy or other non-sociological writers. Troubled with a problem of their own—the bilingualism—Belgian sociologists publish more in the field of sociology of language than their Dutch colleagues. They apply the method of comparative linguistics rather than that of social surveys.

A critical contribution to the sociology of knowledge was made by J. Maquet, [21] who compared the epistemological premises of Sorokin and Mannheim and came to the conclusion that *Wissenssoziologie* is a positive, empirical science.

With the exception of two minor studies of public libraries in Maastricht and in Amsterdam,[22] the sociology of literature and that of art are still rather neglected. The sociological study of leisure activities has been enriched by a very thorough survey of radio listening habits that was conducted by the Central Bureau of Statistics.[23] A study of Television habits is now under way under the direction of T. B. ten Have (University of Amsterdam).

In summary, we can note again the differential in Belgium and in the Netherlands. While in such fields as the sociology of religions and the sociology of leisure activities a good start has been made towards the application of scientific research, in other areas (the sociology of art, of morals, of language, of political institutions) very little has been done.

FUTURE PROSPECTS

The preceding survey of the fields of interest of sociologists in the Low Countries should not be considered as exhaustive or complete. In addition to the personal bias (due to "the human equation") the question remains open what should and what should not be reckoned to sociology. For instance, good social research is being done by criminologists, in Holland; there also is a very promising development of the experimental research in "group-dynamics" initiated and supervised by social psychologists (Koekebakker, Duycker, Hutte, Mulder). This does not, however, imply that there are no fields which have been neglected by social scientists up to now. To uncover "the under-developed areas of research" will become one of the main future objectives of Dutch and Belgian sociologists.

They will, without doubt, profit from their favorable geographical position—at the crossway of three rich European cultures. To try to unite the elements of German, French, and American sociologies in one coherent, "organic" system is, without doubt, the primary objective of the social scientists in this region that is already by its geographic conditions destined to become a melting-pot of the main western national currents of thought. Even more now, than in the past, Holland probably will mediate between the English-speaking and the German-speaking sociologists, while Belgium will try to bridge the French and the German sociological schools. In terms of theoretical sociology the cultural synthesis will imply a sincere attempt to re-assess the positive aspects of empiricism and of logical positivism on the one hand, and of phenomenology and of "Verstehen" on the other hand, and try to merge both in one common frame of reference. Such a synthesis would bring the present sterile controversy between "natural" and "cultural" sciences to an end and would open new fields for research that remained "a taboo" for the "geisteswissenschaftliche" sociology. First to mention is the entire field of the sociology of culture. The concrete configuration of culture-traits in this area remained a subject of reflection and mediation of *beaux esprits* and evaded attacks of empirical research. As mentioned above, the sociologies of language, of art, of literature, and of morals, are lagging behind the occupational sociology in which, for obvious reasons, the application of research found wide acceptance.

Another neglected field is that of the family-sociology. In spite of the dominant role which the familial structure plays in the pattern of culture in this area, as yet no basic research on family was carried out. Intimate sphere of family-relations seems to have been another taboo banning empirical research, in the past. Closely related to it, perhaps its subdivision, is sociology of housing, which is much needed in the country with high population pressure.

Thorough research in these three fields is not difficult to stimulate; since, especially in Holland, the need for planning of housing, of social welfare, and of cultural development is generally recognized on both national and local levels.

It is remarkable that very little has been done by the sociologists in either country to meet the present need for planning on an international level. Systematic studies of cultural and social differences between the Benelux countries, should be mentioned in the first place. It seems to be the case with the small nations that they are much more willing to learn from their great cultural paradigms than from each other. Only after Holland will learn to appreciate the Belgian, more theoretical, orientation, and Belgium will take over the Dutch way of organizing and developing research, after they both will have assimilated the sociological stimuli coming from their great neighbors into their own systems of national sociologies, the wish of J. Haessaert, the President of the Belgian Inter-University Center for Sociology, will materialize: to bring an independent European contribution to world-sociology.

Though written from a standpoint of a sociologist working in the Netherlands, the present survey was meant as a modest step towards this, yet distant, goal.

SELECTED BIBLIOGRAPHY

P. J. Bouman, *Sociologie, Begrippen en Problemen* [*Sociology, Its Concepts and Problems*] (Antwerpen: N. V. Standaard-Boekhandel, 1946). A textbook dealing with problems of general as well as special sociology.

R. Clèmens, G. Vosse-Smal, P. Minon, *L'assimilation culturelle des immigrants en Belgique.* [*Cultural Assimilation of Immigrants to Belgium*] (Liège: H. Vaillant-Carmanne, S.A., 1953). A report of a series of field studies in the mining regions in Belgium, carried out by the Seminar of Sociology at the University of Liège.

J. A. A. van Doorn, "The Development of Sociology and Social Research in the Netherlands," *Mens en Maatschappij* [*Man and Society*]

(1956), xxxi. An important survey of the sociological institutions, education, and research organizatons in the Netherlands, since the beginning of the 19th century to the present; an extensive, classified and annotated bibliography, with English translations added.

E. Dupréel, *Sociologie générale* [*General Sociology*] (Paris: Presses Universitaire de France, 1948). Describes M. Dupréel's system of sociology; no reference is made to other sociological works in Belgium.

I. Gadourek, *A Dutch Community. Social and Cultural Structure and Process in a Bulb-Growing Region in the Netherlands*. (Leiden: H. E. Stenfert Kroese, 1956). Describes the Dutch pattern of living and tries to explain the associations of the main cultural and social variables.

Sj. Groenman, *Methoden der sociography* [*Methods of Sociography*] (Assen: Van Gorcum & Co.) A handbook of methodology used by the students of sociography and by several sociologists in applied, sociographic research.

J. Haesaert, *Sociologie générale* [*General Sociology*] (Brussels: Editions Erasme, 1956). Describes Haesaert's system of general sociology; countless references to ethnological studies and to the sociological thinking of European scholars.

F. van Heek, *Stijging en daling op de maatschappelijke ladder* [*Upward and Downward Social Mobility*] (Leyden: E. J. Brill, 1945). A general discussion of the social mobility problems and a report of the author's research in Enschede, a textile industry center in the northern part of the Netherlands.

D. Szabó, "Développement de l'enseignement et organisation de la recherche sociologique en Belgique" ["Development of Training and Organization of the Sociological Research in Belgium"] *Transactions of the Third World Congress of Sociology* (London: International Sociological Association, 1956), VII, 7-13. A concise survey of the recent trends of sociological training and activities in Belgium.

Ivan Gadourek, a graduate in Philosophy and English, the Masaryk University, Brno (Czechoslovakia); a member of the Sociological Seminar of Prof. Dr. A. I. Blaha and an active member of the Masaryk Sociological Society. Participated in the organization of the resistance movement against the communist regime; forced to go to exile, he settled in the Netherlands (July, 1948). Studied sociology at the University of Leyden, graduated with honor, and awarded the Doctor's degree in sociology (1953) for his thesis about the social control in sovietized Czechoslovakia. At present, the head of the Sociological sub-department of the Netherlands' Institute of Preventive Medicine (Leyden), conducting surveys of workers' attitudes and planning research in the fields of medical sociology, social pathology, and basic research in methodology. A member of the Dutch Sociological Society, of the American Academy of Political and Social Science; a co-founder and co-worker of the Czechoslovak Foreign Institute in Exile. Among his publications: *The Political Control of Czechoslovakia* (New York: Praeger, 1956): *A Dutch Community* (Leyden: Stenfert Kroese, 1956); *Kennissociologie* (The Hague: Servire, 1955); etc.

NOTES

1. J. P. Kruijt, "Mentaliteitsverschillen in ons volk in verband met godsdienstige verschillen" ("Personality Traits as Related to Religious Differential of Our People"), *Mens en Maatschappij* (*Man and Society*), XIX (1943), 1ff., 65ff.

2. See his compact and informative article in English, "The Development of Sociology and Social Research in the Netherlands," presented in the form of a special issue of the *Mens en Maatschappij* (*Man and Society*), XXXI, 4 (August, 1956), 189-264, to the Third Congress of Sociology in Amsterdam. In this issue, the general orientation, the organization of research and of training in the field of sociology are described. A classified list of bibliography is added.

3. De Vries Reilingh, the present Professor of Sociography in Amsterdam, calls Van Doorn's statement about the existential factors of Steinmetz' linkage with social geography "a bold insinuation;" see his article, "Heeft de Sociographie haar tijd gehad?" ("Did Sociography Survive Her Time?"), *Mens en Maatschappij* (*Man and Society*), XXXI (November, 1956), 363-372.

4. See a short but succinct survey of the sociology in Belgium by Denis Szabó (University of Louvain), "Développement de l'enseignement et organisation de la récherche sociologique en Belgique" ("Development of Training and Research in Belgium"), in Transactions of the *Third World Congress of Sociology* (London: International Sociological Association, 1956), VII, 7-13.

5. F. L. Polak, *Kennen en Keuren in de Sociale Wetenschappen* (*Knowledge and Judgment in Social Sciences*) (Leiden: H. S. Stenfert Kroese, 1948).

6. J. P. Kruijt, "De waarde-vri jheid bij Max Weber" ("Max Weber's Concept of Value-Free Judgments"), *Mens en Maaschappij* (*Man and Society*), XXVII, 6 (1952), 353-380, and the continuation of the discussion in *Ibid.*, XXVIII (1953), 129-152.

7. Dr. Haesaert, in an introductory article to a new Belgium *Tijdschrift voor Sociale Wetenschappen* (*Social Science Review*), I, 1 (1956), gives a succinct and critical survey of the recent developments in the fields of group-dynamics, soc.-ometry, and quantification of the sociological variables in the United States.

8. Sj. Groenman, *Staphorst* (Meppel: M. Stenfert en Zoon, 1947).

9. Cf. the earlier study by E. W. Hofstee, *Het Oldambt* (Groningen: Wolters, 1937); more recently, H. J. Prakke, *Deining in Drente* (*Agitation in Drenthe*) (Assen: Van Gorcum, 1955).

10. T. van der Brink, *Some Quantitative Aspects of Future Population Development in the Netherlands* (The Hague: Martinus Nijhoff, 1952); G. Beijer, J. J Oudegeest, *Some Aspects of Migration Problems in the Netherlands* (1952); W Peterson, *Some Factors Influencing Postwar Emigration from the Netherlands* (1952); E. W. Hofstee, *Some Remarks on Selective Migration* (1952).

11. R. Clemens, G. Vosse-Smal, P. Minon, *L'Assimilation culturelle des Immigrants en Belgique* (*Cultural Assimilation of Immigrants to Belgium*) (Liége: H. Vaillant-Carmanne, S.A., 1953).

12. M. G. Ydo, *Plezier in het werk* (*Pleasure in Work*) (Leiden: H. E. Stenfert Kroese, 1947).

13. F. van Heek, *Stijging en daling op de maatschappelijke ladder* (*Ascending and Descending the Social Ladder*) (Leiden: E. J. Brill, 1945).

14. I. E. van Hulten, *Stijging en daling in een modern grootbedrijf* (*Social Mobility in a Modern Big Industry*) (Leiden: H. E. Stenfert Kroese, 1954).

15. G. Kuiper, *Opklimmen en dalen in beroep en samenleving* (*Upward and Downward Occupational and Social Mobility*) (Assen: Van Gorcum, 1954).

16. A. Oldendorff, *Sociale en psychologische arbeidsproblemen in de zelfstandige onderneming* (*Social and Psychological Problems of Labor in Independent Enterprise*) (Antwerpen: A. J. G. Strengholt, 1950).

17. F. J. Th. Rutten, *Menselijke verhoudingen* (*Human Relations*) (Bussum: Brand, 1955).

18. E. J. Tobi & A. W. Luyck, *Herkomst en toekomst van de middenstander* (*The Social Origin and the Future of Middle Class*) (Amsterdam: A. J. G. Strengholt, 1950).

19. See *Revue de l'Institut de Sociologie*, XXIX (1951), 551-585, 587-605, & XXV (1952), 531-652.

19a. I. Gadourek, *A Dutch Community. Social and Cultural Structure and Process in a Bulb-Growing Region in the Netherlands* (Leiden: H. E. Stenfert Kroese, 1956).

20. F. van Heek, *Het geboorteniveau van de Nederlandse Katholieken* (*The Natality Level of the Roman Catholics in the Netherlands*) (Leiden: Stenfert Kroese, 1954).

21. J. Maquet, *La sociologie de la connaisance* (The Sociology of Knowledge) (Louvain: Nauwelaerts, 1949).

22. *Mens en Maatschappij* (Man and Society) XXIV (1949) & XXV (1950).

23. G. B. S., *Radio en Vrijetijdsbesteding* (*Radio and Leisure Activities*) (Utrecht: W. de Haan, 1954).

SCANDINAVIA

Gunnar Boalt
University of Stockholm
Gösta Carlsson
University of Lund
and
Mia Berner Öste
University of Stockholm

Even if it were true that the Nordic countries represent a relatively "underdeveloped area" as far as sociology is concerned (a debatable point), the following pages, being only a summary, obviously cannot adequately survey the accomplishments in this field. Nor do the authors claim infallible judgment in their selection of items mentioned; they are all writing from the Swedish scene, and although the Nordic countries can be regarded for many purposes as one cultural area, this circumstance will make the present report probably more accurate with respect to Swedish sociology and less accurate for the other countries.[1]

DENMARK[2]

Denmark got its first sociology chair at a comparatively early date, in 1937, at the University of Aarhus, but World War II broke up teaching as well as research in the field. Not until after the war was sociological research work resumed at the universities. Shortness of funds has been a persistent problem, large-scale projects are therefore few and largely dependent on the support of international organizations.

Reports from investigating bodies or committees, appointed by the state or local authorities, form a very important part of sociological literature in Denmark. In main such reports fall into either one of the following two areas: social problems and policy on the one hand, town planning on the other. The Social Science Adviser to the Ministry of Labor and Social Affairs directs research serving the social welfare work. In town planning the city of Copenhagen, quite naturally, takes a leading part through the City Engineer's Directorate, and the Regional Planning Committee of Greater Copenhagen.

Among academic sociologists Geiger was the most prominent until his death in 1952. He started his academic work in Germany, by specializing in the field of legal science, but switched over to sociological problems, was attached to the statistical departments of Munich and Berlin, and appointed Professor of Sociology at the Technical Institute at Brunswick in 1928. In 1933 he emigrated to Denmark, where he published a volume on sociological theory. The German invasion into Denmark made him a refugee again, this time in Sweden, where he stayed for the duration of the war. After his return to Denmark he carried through important research in the field of social stratification and social mobility, and took a part in the ISA efforts to coordinate research in this field in different countries.

Danish sociologists, like their colleagues in the other Nordic countries, have learned to utilize existing archives and records to supply them with data. Academic sociology has definitely changed from a philosophical to an empirical approach, utilizing sampling and other modern techniques. At the same time, government agencies have started to use identical methods in their research; thus the difference between sociological research within and outside the universities is diminishing.

To the field of sociological theory belong some of Geiger's later works, where he dealt with the sociology of law,[3] ethical systems and moral valuations,[4] and problems centered around the concept of ideology.[5]

As already noted, the rapid growth of the city of Copenhagen has created many problems, and made necessary research which partly falls into the area of community studies. A number of publications from different parts of the city administrations deal with problems like the territorial or ecological distribution of over-crowding, crime, and suicide; communications; land use; the journey to work; and so on. A general plan for Copenhagen was published in 1948. Although it is not to any great extent based on empirical research of a sociological nature, it is of great interest because it proposes a concentration of habitation to one single city-area, strongly held together.

Two individual studies, by Halberg[6] and Rasmussen[7] treat the relation between city plan and industry (Halberg); and the differences between districts in the inner part of Copenhagen, and its consequences for planning (Rasmussen). Geiger's interest in stratification and mobility research has already been mentioned. He followed several different lines of enquiry; a study of the social origin of famous people by means of a biographical work, or the background of students, and finally the total social mobility in a Danish city, Aarhus.[8] Geiger's mobility data have been re-analyzed by Svalastoga, who used prestige-classes.[9]

In the field of criminology and social problems a somewhat unusual and interesting problem has been investigated by Christiansen, who studied some 5000 males convicted of treason against the Danish state and people during the war.[10] Christiansen investigated their physical and mental state and their environment from childhood and on.

In this context should also be mentioned studies by Kjems[11] of maladjusted children, and by Teilman[12] of relief clientele. Teilman's study is part of a greater project aiming at the causes of need and destitution.

In the field of mass-media and audience research there is an investigation by Agersnap,[13] who drew a cross-national sample and inquired about listening habits by means of mail questionnaires. Some 5000 persons were asked, and the results have been used for evaluating the program policies of the Danish radio system.

Finally there is an enquiry by Goldschmidt[14] into the social role of judges and administrators of law. The data were collected by the author when he was active in Greenland, first in the preparations for making a new law for the territory, then as a judge.

FINLAND[15]

Both in terms of general cultural conditions and the status of sociological teaching and research, Finland differs somewhat from the rest of the Nordic countries. It is a bi-lingual community, with a Finnish-speaking majority and a Swedish-speaking minority. Although educated people within the country usually master both the native languages, this creates a problem of communication, especially between Finland and the other Nordic countries. The linguistic rift also seems to offer a number of very interesting research problems, although Finnish sociologists do not appear to have ventured into this domain to any great extent.

The academic situation has been characterized above all by the comparatively strong position of anthropology (and related fields like comparative religion and ethics). Here, of course, the influence exerted by Westermarck is the explanation. Accordingly, there was for a long time a tendency to define sociology in anthropological terms, or at least to cultivate fields close to the anthropological domains, like folklore, customs in the pre-industrial society (Wikman), or primitive religion (Karsten).

Separate sociology departments have been, however, created at different institutions of higher learning since the beginning of the 1940's. In Helsingfors Verkko has been teaching sociology since 1945.[16] As in the other Nordic countries, sociology developed rapidly after the second world war. In Finland, too, the impact of American sociology has made itself felt. Some of the younger sociologists, like Pipping and Sariola, have themselves studied and carried through research outside Finland. A lively exchange of ideas with other countries, and a readiness to try new methods of data-collecting and interpretation, is as characteristic of Finland as of the other Nordic countries.

The war, in which Finland took a more active part than any of the other countries in the North, and the aftermath of the war with its many problems of social policy, has made its mark on Finnish sociology. This, however, has not prevented the sociologists from taking up theoretical problems of great interest in their research. Thus Pipping used the military unit for a study of group processes and attitudes.[17] In his later work he has studied attitudes among German youth,[18] and community problems.[19]

Problems of marriage and divorce have been made the object of enquiries by Allardt[20] and Nieminen.[21] Allardt has also published a study of political attitudes and social stratification.[22]

Another investigation in the field of stratification is that by Sariola, who studied class and stratification in a Costa Rican town.[23] When Finland had to give up parts of the Eastern provinces to Soviet Russia, the population of these parts was evacuated and moved to other parts of Finland. This was a huge undertaking, to which there was no previous counterpart in Finland. Quite properly, the resettlement of the Karelian evacuees, and their later adjustment in the new locality, was made the target of a sociological study by Waris.[24]

In Finland, and incidentally in Sweden too, the problem of alcoholism and the control of the use and misuse of alcohol looms large in the public debate, and is counted one of the major social policy issues. In Finland the state monopoly organization for the manufacturing and retailing of alcoholic beverages has a special research department working on these problems. We also find several sociological studies in this field: by Kuusi[25] on the effects of different restrictive measures (on consumption involving experimental procedure); by Lanu[26] on the effects of probation or supervision methods for alcoholism; and finally by Sariola on drinking habits in the northern part of Finland.[27]

Industrial sociology and related problems has received its customary share of the research resources, and we note several dissertations in the field; by Koivisto[28] on working and employment conditions of stevedores and longshoremen; by Koli[29] on the attitudes and adjustment of manual workers in three industrial enterprises; by Siipi[30] on the adjustment and satisfaction in certain rural or semi-urban industrial communities; and by Rainio[31] on leadership qualities, involving a factor-analysis of leadership variables.

To this group of studies of social or industrial problems may also be referred an investigation by Littunen[32] of environmental factors of importance for success in academic studies.

NORWAY

During the second world war some Norwegian psychologists and philosophers joined forces with ethnologists and linguists in order to acquaint themselves with sociological theory and methods. The first, rather informal seminars offered at the University of Oslo dealt with the sociology of Durkheim, conducted by professor Sommerfelt.

After the war, a group of psychologists, economists and other social scientists gathered in loosely organized research teams that made attempts at developing the social sciences at the University of Oslo. A first result of the efforts that were made in this direction was the invitation of Dr. Paul F. Lazarsfeld as a visiting professor. Following this successful attempt, there has been an unbroken series of eminent American sociologists visiting Oslo, mainly on the Fulbright plan. These experts promoted various fields of sociological research, e.g. social stratification, social psychology, rural and industrial sociology.

The need for continuity and for institutional support to these different projects and research programmes eventually led to the foundation of two Norwegian sociological institutions, both in 1950. *The*

Institute of Sociology is attached to The University of Oslo. The other one, *The Institute for Social Research* was started on private grants though it is officially recognized by the Norwegian Ministry of Education and by the University of Oslo.

The most appropriate way of presenting current Norwegian sociology seems to be to give a brief account of the activities carried out at these two research centers.

The Institute of Sociology is a regular department of the University of Oslo and therefore has primarily educational and training functions. Dr. Sverre Holm, professor of sociology, and several assistants give courses and seminars in sociological theory, methodology, research techniques, etc. As a part of this educational program, a section for mathematics and statistics has been established at the Institute. This section also aims at developing the use of mathematical models in sociology.

The Institute of Sociology has at present two research projects under way. Both of them are community studies; one is being undertaken of Mo in Rana (in northern Norway), and the other at Stranda in Sunnmöre (on the West coast).

The Mo in Rana project includes a general analysis of social change as a function of industrialization. In 1946, the Norwegian government began the construction of iron works in Mo. Production started in 1954-55. One hopes to get an overall picture of the social change that has taken place and is still going on in this community. Several reports have been mimeographed at the Institute.

In the Stranda project the Institute is making a study of the increasing migration from rural areas to cities that has been going on in Norway for some time. The analysis is concerned mainly with young people's choice of occupation. At Stranda three major occupational areas are represented: fishing, agriculture, and industry. This particular community was picked in order to test the hypothesis that there will be less migration among young people in a rural community with an occupational structure of this kind. Thus both the Stranda and the Mo in Rana projects are concerned with aspects of social change. Mimeographed reports are available from the Institute.

In addition to these major projects some laboratory experiments on small groups have also been conducted at the Institute. A study of the relationship that develops between old members of a small group, and a newcomer, was undertaken 1955-56 under the guidance of Theodore M. Mills (report not yet published).

Research projects in connection with individual dissertations have been carried through in a variety of fields, like a study of refugee problems in Norway, educational sociology, etc. These dissertations and papers have all been mimeographed at the Institute. There are also some printed publications.[33]

In November 1956, The Institute of Social Research had twenty university-trained social scientists on its staff, and two American visiting scholars, as well as a number of clerical and statistical assistants. All these members are engaged in full-time research work.

Methodologically, the work of the Institute has been characterized by the predominance of the newer techniques of data gathering and analysis; the emphasis has been on sample interview inquiries, attitude and personality testing, group experiments and observation studies, as well as content analysis of available documentary material.

The different activities of the ISR may be classified along the following lines (disregarding the overlappings that necessarily occur in reesrach of this kind): (1) *Basic Processes of Behavior.* Among the theoretical studies may be noted analyses of concepts in learning theory, and of the foundation of psychology (Smedslund),[34] models and operational anchoring (R. Rommetveit);[35] and an interpretation of the concept of "Freedom of decision" (H. Ofstad).[36] Smedslund has undertaken experiments on multiple probability learning.[37] (2) *Personality.* A validation of Rosenzweig's picture frustration test and a study of personality and international attitudes has been undertaken by Christiansen. (3) *Communication.* Semantic analysis has been characteristic of the Norwegian philosophical school. Among other concepts, "type," "law" and "meaning" have been analyzed at the Institute. The "definiteness of meaning"[38] has been tested empirically and different interpretations of "free enterprise" and arguments concerning the treatment of ex-Nazis have been collected by means of interviews. (4) *Norms and Roles.* The problem of the objectivity of norms has been investigated by Ofstad. Rommetveit has studied norms and role-behavior in a combined theoretical and empirical study.[39] The OCSR's (The Organization for Comparative Research) group experiments on the effects of threat on group intolerance were carried out under the guidance of S. Schachter.[40] (5) *Sociology of Law.* Several studies of attitudes towards law, among others laws on price-control and rationing, and domestic labor, have been completed, as well as, other sociologically oriented criminological research mainly directed by W. Aubert.[41] (6) *Attitudes, ideologies, political behavior.* Attitudes towards democracy, freedom of expression and nationalism have been studied theoretically and empirically. We also find ecological and attitudinal research in connection with the elections. Another field study is S. Lysgaard's investigation of attitudes, stereotypes and adjustment problems of exchange students.[42] (7) *Occupational, organizational and industrial studies.* Here we note a big attitudinal study on representatives and representees in industry.[43] Organizational structure and group formation was studied, partly through participant observation (not yet published). Interviews have been used to find factors in occupational choice. In a combined experimental and interview study, factors determining reactions to change in an industrial organization were studied by J. P. R. French Jr., Israel and D. Aass (forthcoming).

In a larger country, such disparate research activities would normally be assigned to a series of separate institutions. In Norwegian setting, it has been found to be a great advantage to assemble in one institution representatives of so many different academic disciplines.

A number of long-term research programs have gradually taken shape and provided the basis for some degree of structural differentiation within the Insttitute. So far, two Divisions have been set up as separate units within the general framework of the Institute, one for Industrial and Organizational Studies, the other for International Studies.

The Institute plans to continue its efforts to promote comparative research, particularly in the Scandinavian countries. In the present phase, attempts are being made to launch a series of secondary analyses of survey materials from the different countries in Scandinavia: particular emphasis will be put upon relationships between social class, communication processes and political behavior.

SWEDEN

Sociology is emerging as an independent academic discipline, with its own chairs and departments at the Swedish universities, and with a growing number of students. This development has taken place mainly after the Second World War; since 1945 three of the four universities have got a sociology department, with a full or associate professor at the head, and a varying number of assistants at his side. It is to be expected that the fourth university, Gothenburg, will follow shortly. Sociology is represented in the State Social Science

Research Council, an important organization for distributing research grants, and is thus officially defined as one of the social sciences, like political science, economics, statistics, economic history, human geography, but unlike psychology.

Parallel with this development on the institutional level we find a complete acceptance of empirical and quantitative methods in sociological research. Sociology has divorced itself from social philosophy and lofty speculation about society in the abstract. Instead it has allied itself closely with the other social sciences and psychology.

Perhaps Swedish sociologists have moved closer to the psychologists, and psychological problems than in many other countries, and it is arguable that this may, in the long run, lead to a corresponding neglect of certain other problems which are left to the other social sciences. There is a keen interest in social psychology as a branch of sociology. Swedish sociologists seem to be more interested in small group oriented research, and less interested in the description of social institutions on the mass-society or even community level, or the impact of this institutional system on individuals in large segments of the population. It must be clearly understood, however, that this rule, like every similar generalization, is subject to many exceptions.

If we look at this from the "instrumental" point of view, such research seems much more suited for application within certain areas, notably in industry, education and some varieties of therapy, and less suited for many labor market and social policy problems. Of course, the tendency to concentrate on some types of research problems can be explained to a large extent by pointing to the fact that sociologists found certain areas unoccupied and therefore invaded these more quickly than others. No social science of older standing has concerned itself with group dynamics, or social psychological problems, nor did the psychologists some ten or twenty years ago. But in the domain of population, labor market, and social welfare and policy problems, economists and statisticians were strongly entrenched.

Whatever the explanation, it is certainly true that industrial sociology has flourished more than any other comparable area. To this has contributed the availability of research funds from industrial enterprises or organizations, harassed by the recruitment problems characteristic of a labor market with over-full employment. To this domain belong studies by Lundquist and Segerstedt, Westerlund, Dahlström and Boalt.[44]

In terms of methods and specific objectives there are many differences between these studies. Thus Segerstedt and Lundqvist have employed questionnaires to determine the satisfaction and adjustment to the work situation, as well as adjustment within the community. Westerlund's study, on the other hand, is an experimental one in the strict sense of the word. Two methods of supervision, one the traditional (functional), the other one based on the principle that there should be one leader for each group, no matter what kind of problem or phase of work, were contrasted.

In main, surveys (interview and questionnaire studies) rather than manipulative experiments form the basis of industrial studies; at least this is true of the rest of the studies here listed. Within this frame, however, there are diversities in terms of the dominant theoretical themes: formal versus informal group organization (Boalt), communication problems (Dahlström), or status and social class within the enterprise (Dahlström).

Although a very important one, industrial sociology is not by any means the only area into which sociologists have moved with a desire to apply modern research methods to current social conditions and problems. There is at least one major study of community problems, by Dahlström.[45] He has studied one of the sub-urban communities bordering the city of Stockholm. The likes and dislikes of the inhabitants with respect to the district as a whole, the individual houses and flats, or collective arrangements and facilities, are ascertained by means of interviews.

It is more doubtful whether Hanssen's *Österlen*[46] should be placed in this category or referred to the domain of social anthropology, or perhaps social history. Hanssen takes up for treatment the past rather than the present. Österlen is a part of eastern Scania in Sweden, and the author has investigated, by means of existing records and other source material, community structure and relations between different social groups in the seventeenth and eighteenth centuries.

By two other authors, also working within a department of sociology (Uppsala), the orientation towards social or cultural anthropology is still more pronounced in that they have picked primitive or preliterate cultures as their object of study.[47]

In the field of the sociology of the family there is at least one Swedish major study, by George Karlsson.[48] This study involves among other things a replication of American research (by Locke). The results support Locke's findings.

In the field of social class and stratification there is one enquiry primarily directed to the analysis of a particular "functionally" defined group, namely the white-collar workers in Swedish society.[49] The conclusion is reached that this group forms a social class. By means of questionnaire data the social origin and present situation of white collar workers is determined.

The keen interest in small-group processes, mentioned previously and mainfested by some of the works listed here, has resulted in one study, or rather a collection of three studies presented in one book, by Israel.[50] Some of the current theories and hypotheses in the field of group dynamics have been tested on experimentally created groups. A part of the experimental work was coordinated with parallel studies in several other countries.

For all these particular areas of research the central field of theory and general methodology should not be forgotten. The philosophical background of many sociologists, particularly those whose own basic training came before the advent of sociology as an independent academic discipline, has had as one of its consequences a keen interest in theoretical problems.

Zetterberg's[51] examination of the methods of sociology stresses the advantages of "verificational" studies. An interesting contribution to general theory is made in a series of studies published by Segerstedt.[52] He has taken up a theme classical in sociology since Durkheim's days, namely the problem of uniform and norm-conforming behavior, and the processes by means of which such conformity or uniformity is brought about, notably the process of communication, and the role played by language and symbols. This, obviously, is a kind of theory which can be applied both on the small-group and on the mass-society level.

There remain to be mentioned, still more briefly, a number of research projects going on when this is being written. They will only be identified by a short label and the place (department) where the work is being done.

In the field of stratification and social mobility a study is under way in Lund, which fits into the international program for research in this field sponsored by ISA. At least two different research projects within the general domain of social problems are carried through in Stockholm, one directed to the problem of the use and misuse of alcohol, the other one to the problem of crime. Two studies verging on the economic field have been started at Uppsala; one centering on consumer behavior, the other on labor market problems. We also find studies of political activity (Lund) and the role of spatial contiguity for development of attitudes (Lund).

SELECTED BIBLIOGRAPHY

G. Boalt and G. Carlsson, "Current Trends in Swedish Sociology," *Transactions of the Third World Congress of Sociology*, Vol. VII, 1956, 130-137.

G. Boalt and C-G. Janson, "A Selected Bibliography of the Literature on Social Stratification and Social Mobility in Sweden," *Current Sociology*, II (1954), 306-328.

K. Bruun, "Sociological Teaching in Finland," *Transactions of the Third World Congress of Sociology*, VII (1956).

K. Bruun, "Institutional Sociological Research in Finland 1950-55," *Ibid.*, 65-68.

Danish Sociological Society, "Recent Sociological Research in Denmark," *Transactions of the Second World Congress of Sociology*, I (1954), 6-10.

L. Gråby, *Sociologi* (in Swedish, *Sociology*) (Stockholm: Ehlin, 1954).

J. E. Owen, "Sociology in Finland," *American Sociological Review*, XIX, (1954) 62-68.

S. Rokkan, "Current Sociological Research: A Note on Trends towards International Comparability," *Transactions of the Third World Congress of Sociology*, VII (1956), 51-60.

S. Rokkan, "The Institute for Social Research, Oslo: A Brief Summary of Activities 1950-55," *Ibid.*, 112-120.

T. Segerstedt, "The Uppsala School of Sociology," *Acta Sociologica*, I, (1956), 85-119.

R. Sjödén, *Översikt över svensk sociologisk och socialpsykologisk forskning.* In Swedish, "A Survey of Sociological and Social Psychological Research in Sweden." Mimeographed, (Uppsala: Inst. for Soc., 1950).

E. Tegen, "Soziologische Forschung in Schweden seit 1935," *Kölner Zeitschrift für Soziologie*, I (1949).

J. Westergaard, "The Scope of Urban Social Studies in the Scandinavian Countries (Sweden, Norway and Denmark)," *Current Sociology*, IV (1955), 77-80.

Gunnar Boalt (1910——) studied botany, zoology and chemistry at the University of Stockholm; after graduation (1933) taught biology at the High School and College level; became interested in the social factors related to secondary education and turned to social philosophy, psychology and statistics; wrote a thesis on educational selection (1947). Assistant Professor of Sociology (1949) at the University of Stockholm; Professor (1954——); Dean of the Stockholm School of Social Work and

Public Administration (1954); Editor: *Stockholm Studies of Sociology*; Chairman, the Central Union for Social Work (1955). Has published textbooks in biology, social psychology, sociology, industrial sociology and group psychology and has done research in industrial sociology and social problems.

Gösta Carlsson (1919——), Ph. D., University of Stockholm (1949), visited the United States as a post-doctoral student (1949-1951); after a short period in a government research organization, attached to his *alma mater*, first as Acting Professor of Social Philosophy and then as a Reader in Sociology: head of the Department of Sociology, University of Lund (1956——). Has done research in the field of general methodology and the history of sociology, public opinion and attitudes, social and differential psychology, family, and social class. In addition to articles, has published: *Dimensions of Behavior* (Lund: Gleerup, 1949); *Socialpsykologisk metod* (Stockholm: Svenska Bokförlaget, 1949).

Mia Berner Öste (1923——) studied philosophy and psychology at the University of Oslo; Assistant Teacher of Logic, University of Oslo (1945-1946); graduate from the University of Uppsala (1950); diploma from the Child Guidance Clinic, Stockholm (1951); Phil. lic. degree in Sociology, University of Stockholm. Published a text in Social Psychology (with G. Boalt) and some mimeographed papers on Group Dynamics, Information and Communication Theory; articles on "Attitude and Role" in *Pedagogisk-Psykologisk uppslagbok (Psychological Encyclopedia)*. Since 1948 writing reviews in the educational, psychological and sociological fields for the periodical *Dagens Nyheter*.

NOTES

1. Three of the four countries described here have been recently covered by: G. Boalt & G. Carlsson, "Current Trends in Swedish Sociology," *Transactions of the Third World Congress of Sociology*, VII, 130-137; K. Bruun, "Sociological Teaching in Finland," and "Institutional Sociological Research in Finland," *Ibid.*, 23-24, 65-68; S. Rokkan, "The Institute for Social Research, Oslo: A Brief Survey Summary of Activities, 1950-55," *Ibid.*, 112-120. See also: J. E. Owen, "Sociology in Finland," *American Sociological Review*, XIX (1954), 62-68.

2. We are indebted to Mr. T. Agersnap for advice and criticism of this section.

3. Th. Geiger, *Vorstudien zu einer Soziologie des Rechts (Acta Jutlandica,* Århus, 1947).

4. Geiger, *Forstidens moral och Fremtidens* (Copenhagen: Reitzel, 1952); in Danish: "Past and Future Ethics."

5. Geiger, *Ideologie und Wahrheit* (Vienna, 1953).

6. H. Halberg, *Industri-byplan* (Copenhagen, Teknisk forlag, 1950); in Danish "Industry and City-Plan."

7. S. E. Rasmussen, *Köbenhavn 1950* (Copenhagen, Nyt Nordisk Forlag, 1950); in Danish.

8. This part of Geiger's research is briefly summarized in English in *Acta Sociologica*, I, (1955), 10-82.

9. K. Svalastoga, *Vertikal social mobilitet i en dansk by;* in Danish, "Vertical Social Mobility in a Danish City" in *Sociol. Meddelelser*, I (1953), 75-86.

10. K. O. Christiansen, *Landssvigerkriminaliteten i sociologisk belysning*, (Copenhagen: Gad, 1955); in Danish, "Sociological Aspects of Treason"; summary in English.

11. Ungdomskommissionen, *Den tilpasningsvansklige ungdom* (Copenhagen: Schultz, 1952); in Danish, report published by "Youth Problem Commission," on "Maladjusted Youth."

12. K. Teilman, *Sicialmedicinske undersögelser over legemlig sygdom og offentlig hjaelp* (Copenhagen: State Publ. Office, 1954); in Danish "Somatic Illness and Public Relief"; Summary in English.

13. T. Agersnap, "Radio Listening in Denmark," *Acta Sociologica*, I (1955), 120-148.

14. V. Goldschmidt, "The Greenland Criminal Code," *Acta Sociologica*, I (1955), 217-255.

15. Doctor K. Pipping has kindly furnished much of the information utilized in this section.

16. V. Verkko, *Homicides and Suicides in Finland and Their Dependence on National Character* (Copenhagen, Gad, 1951).

17. K. Pipping, *Kompaniet som samhälle* (Abo: University of Abo, 1947); in Swedish, "The Military Company as a Social Unit."

18. K. Pipping, R. Abshagen & A. E. Brauneck, *Gespräche mit der Deutschen Jugend* (Helsingfors: Societas Scientiarum Fennica, 1954).

19. K. Pipping, "Soziale Veränderungen in den Finischen Schären," *Kölner Zeitschrift für Soziologie*, Sonderheft I, 26-50.

20. E. Allardt, Miljobetingade differnser i skilsmasso frekoensen (Helsingfors. 1952); in Swedish, "Environmental Factors and Divorce."

21. A. Nieminen, *Taistelu sukupuolimoraalista* (Helsingfors, 1951).

22. Allardt, *Social structure och politisk aktivitet* (Helsingfors: Söderströms, 1956); in Swedish, "Social Structure and Political Activity."

23. S. Sariola, *Social Class and Social Mobility in a Costa Rican Town* (Turrialba: Inter-American Institute of Agricultural Sciences, 1954); *Drinking Patterns in Finnish Lapland* (Stockholm: Almqvist & Wiksell, 1956).

24. H. Waris, *Siirtoväen sopeuluminen* (Helsingfors: Otava, 1953); in Finnish, "Adjustment of Evacuees."

25. P. Kuusi, *Alkoholijuomien käyttö maaseudulla* (Helsingfors: University of Helsingfors, 1955); in Finnish, "Alcohol Sales Experiment in Rural Finland" (Stockholm: Almquist & Wiksell, 1957).

26. K. E. Lanu, *Poikheavan alkoholikäyttäytymisen kontrolli* (Helsingfors: University of Helsingfors, 1955); in Finnish, "Control of Deviating Drinking Behavior."

27. S. Sariola, *Lappi ja väkijuomat* (Helsingfors: Väjuomakysymksen tutkimussäätiö 34, 1954); in Finnish, "Alcohol and the Lapps."

28. M. Koivisto, *Sosiaaliset suhteet Turun satamassa* (Abo: University of Abo, 1956); in Finnish, "Social Conditions in the Port of Abo."

29. P. Koli, *Ennakkoluuloista teollisessa organisaatiossa* (Helsingfors: University of Helsingfors, 1955) ; in Finnish, "On Prejudice in an industrial organization."

30. J. Siipi, *Palkkatyöväen viihtyvyys* (Helsingfors: University of Helsingfors, 1954) ; in Finnish, "Satisfaction among Workers."

31. K. Rainio, *Leadership Qualities; A Theoretical Enquiry and an Experimental Study of Foremen* (Helsingfors: University of Helsingfors, 1955).

32. Y. Littunen, *Opintoympäristön vaikutus korkeakouluopiskelussa* (Abo: University of Abo, 1956) ; in Finnish, "Environmental Influences on access in Academic Studies."

33. E. Groenseth, *The production Committees in Norwegian Industry—An Attempt of Functional Analysis* (Oslo: Institute for Sociology, 1952) ; K. Herredsvela, *Sex Role Pattern and Political Level of Aspiration; A Study in Women's Attitudes towards Female Participation in Politics* (Oslo: Institute for Sociology, 1954) ; M. Peterson, *Slum Clearance and Rehousing* (Edinburgh: International Congress for Housing and Town Planning, 1954), and *Urban Fringe and Metropolitan Structure* (Wien: International Congress for Housing and Town Planning, 1956) ; D. Sievertsen, *Goal setting and Social Norms* (Oslo: Institute for Sociology, 1953, mimeographed) ; Oe. Oeyen & M. DeFleur, "The Spatial Diffusion of an Airborne Leaflet Message," *American Journal of Sociology*, 1953 (1953) 144-149.

34. J. Smedslund, *A Critical Evaluation of the Current Status of Learning Theory* (Nordisk Psykologi. Monografiserie, No. 2, 1952, 27 pp.) ; "The problem of What is Learned?" *Psychological Review*, LX, 3 (May, 1953), 157-158.

35. R. Rommetveit, "Model construction in psychology. A defense of surplus meanings of psychological concepts," *Acta psychol.*, XI, 2 (1955), 335-345.

36. H. Ofstad, *An Inquiry into the Freedom of Decision: An analytical approach to a classical problem.* Vols. I-IV (Oslo, ISR, 1953-55), 687 pp. mimeo.

37. J. Smedslund, *Multiple-probability learning. An Inquiry Into the Origins of Perception* (Oslo: Akademisk Forlag, 1955).

38. Gullvaag, *Criteria of Meaning and Analysis of Usage* (Amsterdam, 1956).

39. R. Rommetveit, *Social Norms and Roles* (Oslo: Akademisk Forlag, 1953).

40. S. Rokkan, "An Experiment in Cross-National Research Cooperation. The Organization for Comparative Social Research," *International Social Science Bulletin*, VII, 4 (1955), 645-652; S. Schachter, J. Nutting, C. de Monchaux, P. Maucorps, D. Osmer, H. Duijker, R. Rommetveit & J. Israel, "Cross-Cultural Experiments on Threat and Rejection," *Human Relations*, VII, 4 (1954), 403-439.

41. W. Aubert, *On the Social function of Punishment* (Oslo: Akademisk Forlag, 1954) ; in Norwegian; W. Aubert, T. Eckhoff og K. Sveri, *En Lov i soekelyset* (Oslo: Akademisk Forlag, 1952) ; in Norwegian, "A Law in the Search Light."

42. S. Lysgaard, *A Study of Intercultural Contact: Norwegian Fulbright Grantees Visiting the United States* (Oslo: Institute for Social Research, May 1954).

43. H. Gullvaag, et. al., *Attitudes and Perceptions of Representatives and Representees in Industry. A Study of Some Attitudinal Differences, as Related to Differing Group Memberships and Roles, of Workers in Norwegian industry* (Oslo: ISR, 1952-53), vol. I-III, mimeo.

44. T. Segerstedt and A. Lundquist, *Människan i industrisamhället*, vol. I and II (Stockholm: Studieförbundet Näringsliv och Samhälle, vol. I, 1952; vol. II, 1955) ; summary in English as separate publication, *Man in Industrialized Society* (Stockholm: Studieförbundet Näringsliv och Samhälle, 1956) ; G. Westerlund, *Behaviour in a Work Situation with Functional Supervision and with Group Leaders* (Stock-

holm: Nordisk Rotogravyr, 1952) ; E. Dahlström, *Tjänstemännen, näringslivet och samhället* (Stockholm: Studieförbundet Näringsliv och Samhälle, 1954) ; in Swedish: Engl. title: *Management, Unions and Society;* Dahlström, *Information pa arbetsplatsen* (Stockholm: Studieförbundet Näringsliv och Samhälle, 1956) ; in Swedish, *Internal Communication.* G. Boalt, *Arbetsgruppen* (Stockholm: Tiden, 1954) ; in Swedish, *The Work Group.*

45. E. Dahlström, *Trivsel i Söderort* (Stockholm: Monografier utgivna av Stockholms kommunalförvaltning, 1951) ; in Swedish, "A Community Study for Social Planning."

46. B. Hanssen, *Österlen* (Stockholm: LT, 1952) .

47. B. Lindskog, *African Leopard Men* (Uppsala: Almqvist & Wiksell, 1954) ; B. Danielsson, *Work and Life on Raroia* (Uppsala: Almqvist & Wiksell, 1955) .

48. Georg Karlsson, *Adaptability and Communication in Marriage* (Uppsala: Almqvist & Wiksell, 1951) .

49. F. Croner, *Tjänstemannakaren i det moderna samhället* (Uppsala: Almqvist & Wiksell, 1951) ; in Swedish, "White Collar Workers in Modern Society."

50. J. Israel, *Self-Evaluation and Rejection in Groups* (Stockholm: Almqvist & Wiksell, 1956) .

51. H. Zetterberg, *On Theory and Verification in Sociology* (Uppsala: Almqvist & Wiksell, 1954) .

52. T. Segerstedt, *Social Control as a Sociological Concept* (Uppsala: Almqvist & Wiksell, 1948) ; *Slutna och öppna arbetsgrupper* (Uppsala: Lundequistska bokhandeln, 1956) ; in Swedish, "Closed and Open Work Groups"; *Gruppen som kommunikationssystem* (Uppsala: Lundequistska bokhandeln, 1955) ; in Swedish, "The Group as a Communication System."

GERMANY

René König
University of Köln

The still somewhat awkward situation of sociology in Germany may be illustrated by the recent statement of one of the most outstanding German sociologists of the older generation, Alfred Weber (born in 1868), that the best introduction into German sociology has been written by the Frenchman Raymond Aron.[1] It is true, one can easily enumerate many important sociologists in Germany, in the middle of the nineteenth century (W. H. Riehl, L. von Stein, K. Marx), towards the end of the nineteenth and the beginning of the twentieth centuries (the "historical" school in economics corresponding in some way to American "institutionalism" in economics, furthermore F. Tönnies, G. Simmel, Max and Alfred Weber, E. Troeltsch and others), and finally during the twenties of our own age. Yet, the lack of public recognition of sociology in Germany remains a rather striking feature.

This fact, by the way, is emphasized in the most impressive manner by the practically nearly complete exodus of German sociologists in 1933, under the impact of National Socialism. Indeed, if sociology is a science dealing with man, and trying to protect human dignity, it simply had to strike sail under the assault of an inhuman ideology like that of National Socialism. Incidentally, this also holds true in front of Bolshevism, both systems being closely related to each other.

THE IMMEDIATE POST-WAR NEEDS

After World War II, German sociology came to life again. But nobody will be astonished that this revival developed slowly if only because teaching in sociology had come to a complete standstill for more than 12 years. There were a few survivors of the great German tradition in sociology like Alfred Weber and Leopold von Wiese (born in 1876) who, notwithstanding their old age, displayed an extra-

779

ordinary activity after 1945, and others like Alfred Vierkandt (1867-1953) and Richard Thurnwald (1869-1954) who limited themselves more or less to re-publication of older writings. But very few names were to be noticed among the younger generations. During these earlier years after the war, the most promising representatives of German sociology were still living abroad. Inside Germany the main activity consisted in fighting for the immediate needs of reorganizing scientific and academic teaching in the field of sociology, in re-establishing the German Sociological Association, and in publishing again a Journal of Sociology. In all these tasks the accomplishments of Leopold von Wiese were of a decisive importance. The German Sociological Association, revived in April 1946, held its first regular convention (the eighth in the total series) in September 1946, after a break of sixteen years (the seventh having taken place in Berlin, 1930). Leopold von Wiese acted as the new president of this Association as he also had been its last when it was dissolved in 1934. Early in 1947 the third edition of an old booklet of von Wiese came out and has been widely used ever since as an introduction into sociology (*Soziologie: Geschichte und Hauptprobleme*. Walter de Gruyter-Verlag: Berlin 1947, fifth edition 1955). Finally, the first issue of the *Koelner Zeitschrift für Soziologie* (the new series of the former *Koelner Vierteljahrshefte für Soziologie*, 1921-1934, XII volumes) came forth under his editorship in May 1948, again after an interval of fourteen years.[2]

Thus far for the external outlines of the movement of revival in German sociology immediately after 1945.[2a]

REFUGEES & OTHER INFLUENCES FROM ABROAD

When we take into consideration, however, that "sociology in Germany had never had an undisputed place in the scientific hierarchie," as Max Horkheimer (born in 1895) puts it in his Report for the Library of Congress, 1952,[3] we easily understand that a substantial renewal of sociology in Germany could not be carried through without a stimulation from outside. It seems self-evident that the natural connecting link between the few sociologists who remained inside Germany during Nazism, and the outside world, could be represented by the many refugee sociologists from Germany, both in Europe and overseas, especially in the United States. As a matter of fact, many of them started lecturing at German universities rather early, like Theodor

Geiger (from Denmark) and René König (from Switzerland) in 1947.
A few years later, some of them were appointed to the vacant chairs
of sociology in Germany: Herbert Sultan (1894-1952) from England
in Heidelberg (1947); Alexander Rüstow from Turkey in Heidelberg
(1949); R. König in Cologne (1949); Theodore W. Adorno from U.S.A.
in Frankfort (1950); M. Horkheimer from U.S.A. in Frankfort (1951);
Helmuth Plessner from Holland in Göttingen (1951); Siegfried Landshut from Israel in Hamburg (1951); Arnold Bergstraesser from U.S.A.
in Freiburg (1954). Apart from these names, however, many more
could be enumerated who never came back, either because they died
too early like Karl Mannheim in London (1947) or Th. Geiger (1952)
or because they chose to remain in their respective new home countries. In some cases their writings had to be translated into German
like e.g. Joachim Wach's (1898-1955) *Sociology of Religion* (by H.
Schoeck).

In trying to make an approximate account of all German refugee
sociologists in the world, and adding to them some of their Austrian
colleagues who joined them in exile from 1938, after Hitler's annexation of Austria, it is rather amazing indeed to see how important the
total figure is. This, sometimes, has created the illusion in Germany
of a general fertilization of world sociology by German ideas. However,
apart from the fact that these men had perhaps been pushed off owing
to the reason that they represented ideas which did not fit into the
German tradition, it has to be noticed that most of them went through
a far-reaching process of transformation. Thus, one could say that they
were not the same men any more after these years. They were still
perhaps sociologists of German origin but no more German sociologists.

Incidentally, we would like to mention that for most of the Austrian
colleagues, the situation in this regard was quite different insofar as
the Austrian traditions, both in social sciences and in methodology,
are completely incomparable   with the German conceptions in this
field. Therefore, the Austrian refugees and emigrants did not have to
undergo the same changes as the German refugees. On the contrary,
the continuity of their work has remained extraordinarily strong. This
is the case for Paul F. Lazarsfeld, Marie Jahoda, Hans Zeisel and
others from the same group. Since their first research report on *The
Unemployed of Marienthal*, from 1932, they have indeed contributed
in the most impressive way to the development of empirical research
in sociology. But this achievement was, for them, much easier to attain,
since the Austrian logic of science had always been very different from

German philosophical logics, in science in general, and in social sciences as well. Today, this is best attested by a man like K. Popper in London.

The most interesting case of transformation of a German sociologist is perhaps Theodor Geiger (1891-1952) who started, under the influence of A. Vierkandt, as a representative of phenomenology in sociology, which produced so much obscurity both in German philosophy and in sociology, and finished as one of the most outstanding advocates of empiricism in sociology.[4] It seems to us that this antithesis between phenomenology and empiricism, has, beyond the particularities of the special case, a symptomatic bearing on the general changes which have occurred during the period with most of the German refugee sociologists, both in Europe and in the United States. The same could be said of Karl Mannheim (1893-1947) even though his starting point may be somewhat different. Here the essential shift comes from Neo-Kantianism. But this attitude, too, is as far from research as phenomenology.

New stimuli besides those exerted by German refugee sociologists came also from several foreign experts who were active for a shorter or a longer period in Germany. Among these, we would like to draw special attention to Nels Anderson who directed the important Darmstadt project: the first community survey of its kind in Germany, and mainly conducted by younger sociologists under the guidance of American experts. Anderson started this work in 1948; between 1952 and 1954 the final report came out in print, eight volumes totaling about 1,500 pages. Since 1954 Anderson has been appointed director of the UNESCO-Institute of Social Sciences in Cologne. Another important influence of the same kind was represented by a second American scholar, Conrad M. Arensberg, who first (1950) had his main field of activities in Dortmund, in the middle of the most important industrial area of Germany. Later on he became involved in another community survey carried through by the UNESCO-Institute of Social Sciences in Cologne (1951/2). Unfortunately, he had to leave before the end of the study.[5] Other American colleagues had the opportunity either to do research work in Germany, or to teach, or both. It seems impossible to list all their names. A last source of influence, however more important for the younger generation than for the academic teacher, has been exerted by the *Salzburg Seminar on American Studies,* in Austria, which started working early in 1948 and gathered together many representative American sociologists with young people of the different European countries, among them many young Germans. As seen from today, these men certainly will shape the future of German sociology.[6] But before we go into conjectures regarding the future, we still have got to deal with contemporary German sociology.

A FEW WORDS ON NATIONAL SOCIALISM

It has been said above that many, perhaps nearly all, German sociologists had left Germany in 1933 owing to the fact that some of their central ideas did not fit into the German tradition of thought. We shall, now, have to consider the meaning of this statement which is rather ambiguous. First it can be understood that the special kind of German tradition which came to light in National Socialism was the reason for the withdrawal of so many German sociologists. This would lead us back to a source like Heinrich von Treitschke (1834-1896) who violently opposed sociology with a combined theory of nationalism and the omnipotence of the State. During the period of National Socialism many elements of Treitschke's thought came to life again, either in their original form, or in a modified form taking up other more recent themes.[7] Another source of anti-sociological arguments which also has its roots in the German past was the German version of the science of folklore. In Gunther Ipsen (born in 1899) this branch of National Socialist thinking found one of the most vigorous pamphleteers against sociology, whereas a man like Max Rumpf (born in 1878) was more or less of the contemplative romantic kind and limited himself to discover through literary documents the traces of the ancient folkways.[8] Even though both these points play an important role in German tradition, it still could be stated that they were of a minor importance given that the traditions they represented are themselves of secondary importance for German thought. Therefore, this is only one side of our problem, one which is more connected with the history and origins of National Socialism than with sociology.

THE PHILOSOPHICAL BACKGROUND: HEGEL

On the other side, we have to take into consideration a much more important adversary, one who extends his roots far away in the German past and is what could be called the core of German social thought. It is, of course, impossible to develop this rather complex argument at any length, but it also seems to us that, if one is really interested in analysing the special situation of sociology in Germany, he must consider the following series of arguments which try to give an account of the situation without surrendering oneself to the peculiarities of a transitory constellation. Moreover, this leads us to some important sociologists who are not so well known in the United States, even though their weighty influence on German sociology and its evolution in the twentieth century simply cannot be overrated.

As in other countries, German sociology and its forerunners have a philosophical background. In this particular case, the most important ancestor is G. W. F. Hegel (1770-1831) whose influence on German sociology is at least of a threefold kind: (1) The most formal influence is exerted by his dialectic method. This influence extends to and joins Hegel with Marx and Marx with the different kinds of Marxian (this does not necessarily mean Marxist) social thought down to M. Horkheimer and Th. W. Adorno. (2) A more particular influence is Hegel's conception of culture. This line joins Hegel with the more conservative wing of social thought in Germany, reaching from Wilhelm Dilthey (1833-1911) through (at least partly) G. Simmel to Hans Freyer (born in 1887) and Theodor Litt (born in 1880). Of minor importance, though exerting a great influence through his teaching is Eduard Spranger (born in 1882). (3) The most concrete influence, however, that radiated from Hegel to the following generations of sociologists was Hegel's own outline of a system of sociology developed in his *Philosophy of Law* (1816) and elsewhere. This is much more formative of German sociology than is commonly known. This theory of society has not only been literally taken over by L. von Stein and by Marx, but especially by F. Tönnies whose concept of "Gesellschaft" as contrasted to "Gemeinschaft" has by no means been deducted from a series of corresponding experiences but has rather been borrowed from Hegel's *Philosophy of Law* and other similar sources.[9] From Tönnies, further influences go to a man like Werner Sombart (1863-1941) who both with his important volumes on the origins and evolution of capitalism and his more systematic writings on economic and sociological theory has most of all contributed to the popularization of the Hegelian concept of society as "a mechanism of needs."[10] Finally, it should be mentioned that a man like Alfred von Martin (born in 1882) also represents the influence of Hegel both in his concept of culture and in his different writings on the origins of contemporary society, especially his *Sociology of the Renaissance*.[11]

DIALECTICS & PHILOSOPHICAL TOTALITARIANISM FROM RIGHT TO LEFT

(1) The influence of Hegel's dialectic method. It seems necessary to have this philosophical background in mind in order to understand certain fluctuations and shades in evaluation of the specific task of sociology in Germany, especially its thoroughly ambiguous position towards research. Even in cases where this philosophical approach comes to a kind of compromise with empiricism and research in social sciences, it still does not admit the productivity of research in co-operation with sociological theory but rather emphasizes the unique, all embracing nature of a so called "theory of society." This comes up under the most different forms. However, all of them have in common one important feature, i.e. they rest upon the category of "totality" as it is the case for Hegel and Marx. This involves of course, a depreciation, if not more, of R. K. Merton's "theories of the middle range" in favor of a wholistic interpretation of the totality of social being. One of the most extreme cases of this attitude is to be found in Othmar Spann (1878-1951) and his organistic universalism.[12] To him, any attempt to do empirical research conveys the attribute of "individualistic," the most severe condemnation in his vocabulary. Speculative systems of this kind could be entirely omitted from our survey if they did not deeply influence German social thought in general, even if they have been expelled, at least in this primitive form, from sociology as such a long time ago. Also some aspects of this conception still survive in many minor forms, especially of popular social thought in Germany, first of all in the frequent emphasis on the "wholeness" of social "bodies."

It must be kept in mind, however, that the same dichotomy between a theory of society and a sociological theory regularly comes to life with the Hegelian heritage, both in its right or in its left wing. One could even say that the existence of this dichotomy in any form is symptomatic of Hegelianism. Since, here, philosophical thought is contrasted as essentially "dialectic" in character with the merely causal analysis of natural science, one could also say that dialectics constitutes the crucial feature of the philosophical approach. For its part, totality actually embraces everything, the one and the other, the being and its contrary. This, in itself, proves that dialectics are nothing but metaphysics which one is free to accept or to reject; sentences of this kind can never be verified following the rules of ordinary logics and methods of science. Therefore it seems wise to keep away from this very controversial approach as long as it does not impose itself as the only way out of our difficulties. Here, I would like to say that before we have reached this point, we have certainly so many other questions to settle that it seems rather premature to start from the very beginning with this fundamental dichotomy between a theory of society and a sociological theory.

The right wing of this approach is best represented by Karl Dunkmann (1867-1932) and his group.[13] In some way, Theodore Litt could also be cited in this context, at least with regard to his rightist attitude, even though he is more critical than most of the others.[14] This is probably the consequence of the purely "formal" character of his conceptual analysis. With Litt, the dialectic approach has probably produced his most important concept the importance of which for a general sociological theory has not yet been recognized to its full extent. We have in mind his concept of "reciprocity of perspectives" used as a label for the mutual relationship, either in behavior or perception, of the members of a group. As far as I can see, the French sociologist Georges Gurvitch is perhaps the only one contemporary sociologist who has taken up this concept and developed it further. The left wing of the dialectic approach is best represented by Georg Lukács (born in 1885), perhaps the most important communist refugee from Germany to Soviet Russia. After 1945 he went back to his native town Budapest, from where he seems to have been exiled again during the revolution of Winter 1956. In this case, we do not encounter any difficulties of classification. Irrespective of any criticism, he is above all a philosopher, even though interested in the general relationship of products of thought on one side and socioeconomic evolution on the other. Consequently, research does not play any role in his thinking.[15] In comparison with Lukács, the situation is very much different with two other partisans of the Hegelian and Marxian left wing like Max Horkheimer and Theodor W. Adorno (born in 1903).[16] Again, the core of their theory of society is of a highly philosophical character and falls completely in line with the German tradition of dialectics. But beyond that Horkheimer has given a rather strong stimulation to sociological research in Germany with his older book on

Family and Authority which came out in France, a few years after he had emigrated from Germany with most of his collaborators (1936). When he came back after the war, he immediately reorganized his former *Institute of Social Research* in Frankfort which has carried through ever since rather interesting research projects. On his side, Adorno, too, has given a likewise generous effort to promote socio-logical research both through his *"Authoritarian Personality"* in the United States and with his present activity at the Frankfort Institute. However, it must be underlined that Adorno is not interested in research as a means of checking and furthering sociological theory. With regard to this last point, he proved to be a pure and primarily critical philosopher who admits research just as a means of disclosure of ideologies and with no meaning of its own. It might be illuminating to stress the fact, that both, Lukács and Adorno, did their best work in aesthetics, Lukács in his different writings on literature, Adorno in important essays on musicology.[17]

THE CONCEPT OF CULTURE

(2) The influence of Hegel's concept of culture. Even if it is true that our differentiation between the three kinds of Hegelian influence is not intended to separate single aspects from the total body of Hegel's philosophy, one can state that there is in Hegel a particular conception of culture which could be discussed without reference to dialectics. The different contents of culture like art, religion, law represent special forms of ideas, but they cannot be conceived independently from man and society. Even though art is perfect in itself and does not need either a real audience or a real existence, e.g. as an economic good, it still realizes itself through many social channels. Without them the work of art would be non-existent. However, they do not add anything to the understanding of art. This is what is sometimes called in German a Theory of the Objectivations of Ideas.

In his systematic sociology Georg Simmel (1858-1918) clearly distinguished between the different cultural contents and the social forms through which they become real entities. This was perhaps the most ingenuous conception of sociology in Germany. In any case, Simmel has considerably contributed to the differentiation of sociological concepts, and he has therefore justly been known the world over.[17a] Perhaps so much that another important German philosopher who has dealt a good deal with sociology, Wilhelm Dilthey (1833-1911), has been nearly forgotten outside of Germany.[18] Dilthey is at least partly responsible for the unfortunate differentiation between natural sciences and the cultural sciences ("Geisteswissenschaften") and for the theory of understanding ("Verstehen"). Even though Dilthey himself came to the conclusion that sociology was non-existent as a science, he contributed greatly to this very German conception of sociology as a "Geisteswissenschaft" different from the traditional kind of science with its causal explanation. His main point was what has been later called the identity of subject and object in social sciences. According to this view, the man who is observing social life is himself part of this social life and, therefore, has knowledge of the meaning of all social phenomena before scientific knowledge. This immediate knowledge is what Dilthey calls "Verstehen." In our contemporary language we would speak of commonsense knowledge. We all know how important it is but we also know how erroneous it can be. Paul F. Lazarsfeld gave the following formula for this danger: "Obviously there is something wrong with obviousness." But this is no argument for Dilthey nor for his followers who essentially try to distil sociological theory out of this immediate commonsense knowledge. The result is a continuous sociological subjectivism confounding the objective function of a given social event with the impression I get when meeting this datum. Now, given the fact that at the close of the nineteenth century most of the existing sociological systems were more or less of the naturalistic kind, Dilthey concluded that sociology did not exist.

This verdict did not last too long, especially after the general influence of Dilthey had made itself conspicuous in social sciences. It seems rather typical that Dilthey restricted himself to psychology, pedagogics and, like Adorno and Lukács, aesthetics. But his attempt to establish sociology as a *Geisteswissenschaft* was then implemented by Hans Freyer. His chief work is nothing but the actual performance of Dilthey's program. Simultaneously, he shifted with his interests in human action from psychology and pedagogics to politics and became rather influenced by National Socialism; he could even be designated as a forerunner of National Socialism in social sciences. He is also the only important German sociologist who was able, during the Nazi Regime, to go on teaching without any hindrance by the official party agencies; one of his books on Macchiavelli even appeared with the "imprimatur" of the National Socialist party! His interest in contemporary society proved perhaps to be of a more conformistic character than is good for science! Like many others of the right Hegelian wing, he has never done any real piece of research. It is symptomatic to see that he has withdrawn completely into history after the war. His interest into contemporary society has faded away with National Socialism. On the other hand, his influence must not be underrated. Freyer is a most brilliant writer, and many of his former students are teaching sociology at several important places.[19] The same holds for a man like Eduard Spranger who is mainly responsible for the popularization of Dilthey's ideas through pedagogics, the main difference being that Spranger has kept away from Nazism.[20] On the other hand, it could be stated that some of the most primitive prejudices against sociology and research in social sciences have been spread by Spranger, especially through many generations of high school teachers who prove to be, still today, particularly resistent to the lessons of social sciences. They close themselves up in a sometimes rather puerile and cheap idealism whose main function is to supply its partisans with a sentiment of superiority against all men who regularly deal with such dirty things as economic life, social organization and disorganization and the like. To them, sociologists still are the muckrakers of the late nineteenth century.

THE COMPETITIVE SOCIETY (GESELLSCHAFT)

(3) The influence of Hegel's theory of society. The last group of Hegelian sociologists has taken over literally his description of contemporary society as Hegel himself had borrowed it from Adam Smith. It is the same materialistic conception of economic life as we meet in Ricardo, Marx and many others. Perhaps the most important sociologist who gave a thoroughgoing anatomy of economic society as a competitive society, in Germany, was Lorenz von Stein (1815-1890). Three years the senior of Karl Marx (1818-1883), he came in contact with French sociology rather early and discovered the importance of class stratification in social life without, for that, becoming a communist. His political attitude was inclined towards a social monarchy. Being a brilliant writer, his influence on German sociology simply cannot be overrated even though Franz Oppenheimer (1864-1943) and Gottfried Salomon had to rediscover von Stein after the first World War.[21] On the other hand, one could say that his teaching had become so popular in German sociology that it was able to survive without the name of its author.

Probably his main importance is given by the fact that F.
Tönnies (1855-1936) borrowed from him and from Hegel his concept
of society as contrasted to *Gemeinschaft* which has been more or less
derived from romantic conceptions. Now, we do not want to take up
once more the arguments in favor or against this classical dichotomy
of *Gemeinschaft* and *Gesellschaft*. This has been done often enough.
We rather want to comment upon another problem which, in our
eyes, seems much more symptomatic than the question of validity of
this dichotomy. This dichotomy has so much been discussed ever
since its first appearance (1887), that people inseparably linked the
name of Tönnies with those concepts. With that it was completely forgotten that Tönnies has been one of the first empirical sociologists in
Germany: he was thoroughly convinced of the power of research in the
social sciences.[22] However, it will always remain one of the most
startling puzzles of German sociology that Tönnies himself did not use
his own key terms of sociology in research. On the contrary, he proved
to be a rather sober minded and clear-cut scholar who knew how
to make a reasonable use of the most different research techniques,
statistics included. In my eyes, this fact is a much more severe verdict
against the use of his categories *Gemeinschaft* and *Gesellschaft* than
the keenest conceptual argumentation. This aspect of Tönnies has
been carried on successfully by his son-in-law Rudolf Heberle (born
in 1896) who left Germany under the threat of National Socialism
and has been teaching ever since in the United States (at the Louisiana State University in Baton Rouge, La.). But it is interesting to
remark that this side of Tönnies has remained completely deficient in
his many followers.[23] Tönnies can be designated as the only German
sociologist influenced by Hegel who nevertheless has been open to the
necessities of research in sociology. The only reproach that could be
formulated against him would be the fact that his experimental attitude is sometimes rather crude insofar as he does not see the necessity
of linking together sociological theory with research. Therefore, the
results of his research remain rather often somewhat descriptive in
the sense of "sociography," and less useful than they would otherwise
be.

LUTHERANISM VS. CALVINISM IN GERMAN SOCIOLOGY

In terminating the survey of these different groups of Hegelian
sociologists in Germany, we would like to draw the attention to the

fact that independently from all these efforts to establish sociology as a science of its own, an obvious anti-sociological feeling pervades all these considerations. It seems that German scholars are more or less unwilling sociologists, because the dimension of social life has not so well been integrated in the cultural system, at least not in this important current of German thought. It might be important, in this context, to expand our inquiry to the general cultural background of social thought in Germany. This can easily be done following some central ideas of Hegel himself who speaks about the great German revolution in the past as performed by the *Lutheran* reformation. Now, it seems clear that Catholicism had achieved the integration of social life in its general system of cultural values. We do not raise the question here whether or not such a system could survive under new conditions of life, we just want to stress that Catholicism had overcome the challenge of social life during the Middle Ages and succeeded in elaborating a cultural system of its own. With Luther, however, the situation is different in a most decisive way. Luther does not acknowledge a reconciliation between norms and life in the social community, but rather in man's conscience exclusively. With that, the essential link in its system of thought simply cannot be represented by a social system of any kind but only by internalization in the soul, i.e. the personal system completely overshadows the social system whose formation is for his part left to the traditional State. For Hegel, too, reconciliation of the spirit with itself can only be realized through tracing itself back into the depth of the soul. The cultural values are those of the personality. This, of course, means a general depreciation of the dimension of social life. Therefore, all the German sociologists of this group, even though dealing with social life and accepting it to some extent as a dimension of life in general, always shrink back from the recognition of the social system as a system in the same sense as the personal system or the cultural system. To them, social life will always remain a dimension of life with a lower status. Or, to put it into a different and somewhat antiquated language which, however, unites Hegel and the Hegelians both with Marx and the Marxians down to Lukács and Adorno, social life is nothing but the "self-alienation" of the human personality. These social philosophers altogether also exhibit a remarkable tendency to misunderstand the problems of social adjustment as mere conformism.

This Lutheran approach has been considerably modified by the different branches of Reformation, especially by Calvinism which is certainly at least partly responsible for the emphatic value attributed to community life in Anglosaxon countries. In my mind, this particular point explains many fundamental differences in the respective attitudes of German social thinkers towards the dimension of social life in general, and the same attitudes in England and especially in the United States. This discussion has been raised by Max Weber (1864-1920) and by Ernst Troeltsch (1865-1923). Unfortunately, both these men died rather early and promising students of theirs left Germany, like Hans Baron (born in 1900) and Hans Gerth (born in 1903) who are now teaching in the United States, or like Alexander von Schelting (born in 1894) who is now teaching in Switzerland. Gerth has gained a special merit by translating some writings of Max Weber into English.[24] Therefore, one could say that this rather important problem, in Germany, has never been brought to fruition. On the contrary, it has remained in suspense, it might even be that it has been repressed in the strict sense of the term.

Whereas Troeltsch was mostly interested in the history of religious ideas[24a] and only incidentally concentrated on purely sociological terms like those of sect and church, Max Weber is perhaps the most sociological minded German sociologist. To him, the dimension of social life is not only one object beside many others but rather the main dimension of human achievement. In that sense, Weber is perhaps the most Anglosaxon German sociologist.[25] On the other side, it is to be regretted that there is nothing comparable in Germany to the influence of Weber on Talcott Parsons in the United States. On the contrary, it could easily be shown that the specific German tradition in sociology explicitly rejects the Weberian concept of sociology. This is done in two different ways: on one hand, Weber is misinterpreted as a partisan of the method of understanding in sociology even though he only conceived a rational understanding as an adequate method for sociology, and this is practically identical with causal explanation. On the other hand, both the leftist Hegelian group like for instance Th. W. Adorno, and the personalistic approach like that of Gerhard Mackenroth (1904-1955) or of Werner Ziegenfuss (born in 1904), explicitly reject the approach of Weber.[26] In this way, many German sociologists prove to be unable to live up to the greatest accomplishment in German sociology hitherto existing, the only one that has been justly known the world over.

SOME RECENT ACHIEVEMENTS

Rather different is the approach of Max Weber's brother Alfred Weber who, curiously enough, produced enormously after the war even though he was already 77 years old when the war ended. Alfred Weber, in contrast to his brother, most emphatically stresses the necessity of value judgments in sociology and completely falls back upon a kind of philosophical morphology of cultural systems.[27] He is, of course, a most ingenious writer, but his work belongs much more to cultural criticism and to philosophy of history than to social science in general and especially to sociology. It may, however, be noted that Alfred Weber like his brother Max Weber, before the first World War, made interesting contributions to research work in sociology as did also the *Verein für Sozialpolitik* (Association for Social Policy) which has been influenced by both of them. The same holds true, incidentally, for G. Mackenroth who being an economist and a statistician by training, knew how to deal with the problems of research.[28] His premature and regretted death brought all his plans to an end before they could expand and come to maturity. His last assistant, Karl Martin Bolte (born in 1920) seems to stress this side of Mackenroth's work. Also Gerhard Wurzbacher (born in 1912) who has been appointed to Mackenroth's chair at the University of Kiel (in 1956) has shown strong interest in sociological research during the last few years.[29] The only point that could be raised in connection with the University of Kiel where Tönnies taught during his whole career, and also in connection with the strange disparity between Mackenroth's theory of science and his actual accomplishments, is the question whether or not sociological theory and research will grow together into a single body of rational science.

For the time being, it still seems as if research on one side and understanding and interpreting ("deuten") on the other could not yet come to a sound compromise. Nobody perhaps has done so much for the stimulation of research in German sociology during the last few years as Helmuth Schelsky (born in 1912) who now has the chair of sociology at the University of Hamburg.[30] And still the question could be raised whether his description of the German post-war family is the result of a methodologically conducted research or just an interpretation based on commonsense knowledge. The same holds true in some way for his former student G. Wurzbacher. We would like to stress that experience in research methods is still rather weak in Germany; therefore, there are fewer inhibitions to making precipitate interpretations instead of a step by step analysis. In looking upon a recent publication of H. Schelsky's on the Kinsey-Report, one could even assume that value judgments in the proper meaning of the word are still overriding rational analysis. On the other side, it may be welcomed in general that the importance of research is stressed even though the performances might still be unsteady. It is to be noted, however, that this unsteadiness shows a remarkable tendency to disappear as soon as less controversial topics are chosen. Thus, industrial and rural sociology have made some important progress in Germany.[31]

The same can be stated for social psychology and its most outstanding representative in the German-speaking countries, Peter R. Hofstätter (born in 1913) who has developed a most interesting synthesis of recent American trends in social psychology with European traditions.

In this regard it has to be deeply regretted that Theodor Geiger died so early. Given that he knew perfectly well the German tradition in sociology and that he had broadened his views after his emigration to Denmark after 1933 and to Sweden after the Germans invaded Denmark, he would certainly have been able to make a substantial contribution to the basic problem of the relationship between theory and research in sociology. Since he had worked his way through from phenomenology to empiricism, his answer, no doubt, would have been at least very illuminating. Geiger's case is especially interesting as he has dealt with one and the same problem of stratification at two different times in his life, once when he still was completely under the impact of the German tradition in sociology (1932), and a second time (1951) after he had experienced many other influences abroad.[32] Geiger is probably the only German sociologist of the last generation who combined research experience with theoretical and even epistemological interests. He left an empty place when he died. It can be said that his teaching has not yet been accepted in Germany.

OUTLOOK ON THE YOUNGER GENERATION

Our survey of contemporary sociology in Germany would be incomplete if we did not say a word of the younger generation. Given the fact that teaching in sociology came to a nearly complete standstill from 1933 to 1945, there is today not only a considerable lack of personnel for the chairs of sociology (as a matter of fact, most of them are actually held by former refugees), but also the middle generation is missing, those who would be approximately 35 to 40 years old. This means that the future of German sociology rests upon young scholars who are today between 25 and 35 years old. This, too, is a completely new feature for the German social sciences.[33]

It can be said that most of these young scholars, if not all, have undergone a more or less decisive influence by American sociology. The difference between this generation and the representatives of the old German sociological school who still survive, is indeed enormous. This means that a deep change is to be expected within a few years, provided that the older generation succeeds in keeping the younger sociologists in the career of academic teaching. Since government agencies, private enterprises, and also marketing and public opinion research institutes offer interesting jobs to well trained young research workers, the temptation is rather great to exchange an insecure academic career for a well paying job. This issue is moreover suggested by the fact that most of the young scholars are not yet so thoroughly trained that they could be immediately appointed to a professorship. One has even to keep in mind that at least some of them have a rather one-sided training. They may have carried through a good piece of research but their theoretical background remains rather weak. This, in general, seems to be one of the most important handicaps of German sociology: it suffers from an abundance of philosophical speculation and in the same time of a remarkable deficiency of theoretical viewpoints. One cannot expect that the younger sociologists will overcome this difficulty by themselves. Therefore, it can be stated that a strong stimulation from outside is still necessary to German sociology in order to bring it back to the level it once had and to the level of sociology in the Anglosaxon world. This will surely create a lot of troubles and difficulties. In order to understand our reserve, one has to look at the reports of the different meetings of the German Sociological Association. At its last convention, in 1956, an appeal was made to go back to the problems and attitudes of the 'twenties. Therefore, we cannot agree wholeheartedly with the optimism of one of these younger scholars that the new conception of sociology could be expected to be victorious in a few years.[34] On the contrary, I am rather inclined to be prepared for a strong reactionary movement the forerunners of which are easily to be felt today already. On the other hand, I do not want to give too pessimistic a picture. But German sociology surely will not free itself from many old prejudices without a long period of interior adjustments, even of violent struggles and breakdowns.

SELECTED BIBLIOGRAPHY

Theodore F. Abel, *Systematic Sociology in Germany* (New York: Columbia University Press, 1929). Mainly dealing with methodological questions.

Harry Elmer Barnes and Howard Becker, *Social Thought from Love to Science* (2nd edition New York: D. C. Heath Co., 1952). Chapter XXIII gives a rather useful survey on sociology in Germany.

Wilhelm Bernsdorf and Friedrich Bülow, Editors, *Wörterbuch der Soziologie* (Stuttgart: Ferd. Enke-Verlag, 1955). A dictionary of sociological concepts, of very uneven value.

Carl Brinkmann, Editor, *Soziologie und Leben* (Tübingen: Rainer Wunderlich-Verlag, 1952). Collected essays by various authors.

Gottfried Eisermann, Editor, *Gegenwartsprobleme der Soziologie. Alfred Vierkandt zum 80. Geburtstag* (Potsdam: Athenaion, 1949). Collected essays by various authors in honor of Vierkandt's 80th birthday.

Don J. Hager, "German Sociology under Hitler, 1933 to 1941," *Social Forces* XXVIII (1949), 6-19. A survey of sociology during Nazi times.

René König, "Die deutsche Soziologie im Jahre 1955," *Kölner Zeitschrift für Soziologie and Sozialpsychologie* VIII/1 (1956), 1-11. A rather critical survey on some new sociological publications in Germany.

William C. Lehmann, "Some Observations of a Visiting Sociologist on Tendencies and Trends in Sociology in Germany Today," *Sociologus. A Journal for Empirical Sociology, Social Psychology and Ethnic Research*, N.S. VI/2 (1956), 115-126. A rather critical survey on recent trends in German sociology.

Heinz Maus, "*Universitas Litterarum. Handbuch der Wissenschaftskunde*" (Berlin: Walter de Gruyter-Verlag, 1955). A systematic survey on different fields of sociology, rather incomplete bibliography; "Geschichte der Soziologie," *Handbuch der Soziologie*. Edited by W. Ziegenfuss (Stuttgart: Ferd. Enke-Verlag, 1955) 1-120. General historical survey of sociology in different countries. Valuable bibliographical notes on recent German sociology.

Wilhelm E. Mühlmann, "Sociology in Germany: Shift in Alignment," *Modern Sociological Theory*, ed. by Howard Becker and Alvin Boskoff (New York: Dryden Press, 1957). Survey on pre-war and recent sociology in Germany stressing the continuities in post-war developments.

Albert Salomon, "German Sociology," *Twentieth Century Sociology,* ed. by Georges Gurvitch & Wilbur E. Moore (New York: Philosophical Library, 1945). Critical review of pre-war German sociology with important evaluations.

Edgar Salin, Ed., *Synopsis. Festgabe für Alfred Weber* (Heidelberg: L. Schneider-Verlag, 1948). Collected essays by various authors in honor of Weber's 80th birthday.

Karl Gustav Specht, Ed., *Soziologische Forschung in unserer Zeit.* Leopold von Wiese zum 75. Geburtstag gewidmet (Köln: Westdeutscher Verlag, 1951). Collected essays of various authors in honor of von Wiese's 75th birthday.

Hilde Tönnies, Editor, *Beiträge zur Gesellungs- und Völkerwissenschaft.* Richard Thurnwald zu seinem 80. Geburtstag gewidmet (Berlin: Gebr. Mann-Verlag, 1950). Collected essays by various authors in honor of Thurnwald's 80th birthday.

Leopold von Wiese, "The Place of Social Sciences in Germany," *American Journal of Sociology* LVII (July 1951), 1-6. General survey concerning the importance of social sciences in the German university teaching system; Editor, *Abhängigkeit und Selbständigkeit im sozialen Leben* (2 vols. Köln: Westdeutscher Verlag, 1951). Collected essays by various authors dealing with the problems of dependence and independence in social life; "Soziologie," *Handwörterbuch der Sozialwissenschaften,* edited by H. Jecht and R. Schaeder (Stuttgart-Tübingen-Göttingen: G. Fischer, J. C. B. Mohr, Vandenhoek and Ruprecht, 1955), 626-648. A general survey on contemporary sociology, bibliography rather outdated.

René König (1906——), Ph.D. (Berlin, 1930); persecuted by the Nazis, left Germany in 1937; appointed Assistant Professor of Sociology at the University of Zurich (Switzerland, 1938); after World War II, appointed successor to Leopold von Wiese's Chair of Sociology in the University of Cologne (1949). Took part in the Preparatory Committee for the establishment of the International Sociological Association (ISA); organized the first World Congress in Zurich (1950). Director of the Sociological Research Institute, University of Cologne; editor of the *Kölner Zeitschrift für Soziologie und Sozialpsychologie;* Vice-President, the German Sociological Association (1955); Visiting Professor, University of Michigan (spring, 1957), and summer school, University of California (summer, 1957). Main publications in the field of sociology: *Die naturalistische Aesthetik in Frankreich* (Leipzig: Universitätsverlag, 1931); *N. Macchiavelli* (Zurich: Eugen Rentsch-Verlag, 1940); *Materialien zur Soziologie der Familie* (Bern: Verlag Francke, 1946); *Soziologie heute* (Zurich: Regio Verlag, 1949); Editor: *Praktische Sozialforschung,* I: *Das Interview* (2nd revised ed., 1957); II: *Beobachtung und Experiment* (1956); III: *Testen und Messen* (Köln: Verlag für Politik und Wirtschaft, 1956-1958); *Zur Soziologie der Gemeinde* (special issue to the *Kölner Zeitschrift für Soziologie und Sozialpsychologie*, VII, 1956);*Die Mode in der menschlichen Gesellschaft* (Zurich: Verlagsgesellschaft Modebuch, 1958). Editor of *Beiträge zur Soziologie und Sozialphilosophie* (Bern, Zurich, Cologne: Francke Verlag, Regio Verlag, Verlag für Politik und Wirtschaft, 1946-1957, 7 vols., continued); some 60 articles in periodicals and handbooks in Switzerland, Germany, France, and England.

NOTES

1. See Alfred Weber, and others, *Einführung in die Soziologie* (Munich: R. Piper-Verlag, 1955), 17; Raymond Aron, *Deutsche Soziologie der Gegenwart* (Stuttgart: Alfred Kröner-Verlag, 1953).

2. In 1955, the editorship of this Journal has been taken over by René König who, once again, slightly changed its title into *Koelner Zeitschrift für Soziologie und Sozialpsychologie*. This alteration is, however, symptomatic of a general change in the direction of this only Journal in German language, specialized in sociology. The new editor is trying to open this Journal both to the younger generations of sociologists in Germany and to new and more realistic trends.

L. von Wiese's publications since the war have more or less shifted away from sociology properly speaking to ethics. This is demonstrated by two major publications: *Homo Sum. Gedanken zu einer zusammenfassenden Anthropologie* (Jena: G. Fischer-Verlag, 1940); *Ethik in der Schauweise der Wissenschaften vom Menschen* (Bern: A. Francke-Verlag, 1947). Of a more sociological character: *Gesellschaftliche Stände und Klassen* (Bern and Munich: A. Francke-Verlag, Leo Lehnen Verlag, 1950). Two other recent publications: *Spätlese* (Köln: Westdeutscher Verlag, 1954) and *Das soziale im Leben und im Denken* (Köln: Westdeutscher Verlag, 1956) are either reprints of older papers or summaries of older theories of his. In 1955, a reprint of his main work *System der allgemeinen Soziologie* (3rd ed. Munich: Verlag Duncker und Humblot, 1955) came out without any changes. Therefore, the American reader can still use Howard Becker's translation in order to get himself informed about this formalistic sociology. Lately, this approach has been developed in an original manner by the Count Max zu Solms (born in 1893), *Analytische Gesellungslehre* (Tübingen J. C. B. Mohr, 1956) where an attempt is made to open the analytic and formalistic sociology to social psychology. However, it is to be said that this publication like so many others in Germany more or less ignores the evolution of sociology in the rest of the world.

2a. It could be added to these few indications that another representative of the older generation of German sociologists, the Count Max zu Solms of the University of Marburg, started a series of books in 1946, *Civitas Gentium*, wherein he published either monographs on special topics, or classical texts (M. Weber, V. Pareto, Ad. Smith, Ibn Khaldun) which were mainly intended to serve for teaching purposes. In 1947, the *Dortmund Institute on Social Research* also started a series of books with the German translation of the *Introduction into Sociology* by a Dutch scholar P. J. Bouman, *Allgemeine Gesellschaftslehre* (New Edition, Stuttgart: A. Enke-Verlag, 1955). Some latecomers of the same kind and with the somewhat identical intention to be used for teaching purposes came from America, e.g. J. Rumney and J. Maier, *Sociology: The Science of Society* (German translation Nurnberg: Nest-Verlag, 1954). Another case of a similar kind is furnished by Helmut Schoeck, Professor at Fairmont State College in Fairmont, West Virginia

(*Soziologie. Geschichte ihrer Probleme:* Munich: Verlag Karl Alber 1952) who, combines many wisely chosen selections with comments into a rather useful instrument.

3. Max Horkheimer, *Survey of the Social Sciences in Western Germany. A Report on Recent Developments* (Washington, D. C.: Library of Congress. Reference Department. European Affairs Division, 1952). Horkheimer gives a very rich bibliography and a rather comprehensive survey of the different centers in Germany.

4. Vide the necrology by René König, "Theodor Geiger (1892-1952)," *Acta Sociologica. Scandinavian Review of Sociology,* I (1955), 3-9.

5. An informal report on the Darmstadt study is given by Nels Anderson, "Die Darmstadt-Studie, ein informeller Rückblick," *Koelner Zeitschrift für Soziologie und Sozialpsychologie,* Sonderheft 1: *Zur Soziologie der Gemeinde,* VIII (1956), 144-151; see also N. Anderson, "A Community Survey of Darmstadt," *International Sociological Association. Second World Congress of Sociology* 1953, Sect. III, 1. We give the complete list of the different volumes of the Darmstadt-Study. 1) Herbert Kötter, *Struktur und Funktion von Landgemeinden im Einflussbereich einer deutschen Mittelstadt;* 2) Karl-Guenther Grüneisen, *Landbevölkerung im Kraftfeld der Stadt;* 3) Gerhard Teiwes, *Der Nebenerwerbslandwirt und seine Familie;* 4) Gerhard Baumert, *Jugend der Nachkriegszeit;* 5) Gerhard Baumert, *Deutsche Familien nach dem Kriege;* 6/7) Irma Kuhr, *Schule und Jugend in einer ausgebombten Stadt;* Giselheid Koepnik, *Mädchen in einer Oberprima;* 8) Klaus A. Lindemann, *Behörde und Bürger;* 9) Anneliese Mausolff, *Gewerkschaft und Betriebsrat im Urteil der Arbeitnehmer* (Darmstadt: Eduard Roether-Verlag 1952/4). Conrad M. Arensberg was first mainly concerned with supervising a study on the coal miners in the Ruhr area. Vide Carl Jantke, *Bergmann und Zeche* (Tübingen: J. C. B. Mohr-Verlag, 1953). The UNESCO community study which had also been started under the supervision of Arensberg has been reported by Gerhard Wurzbacher, with Renate Pflaum-Mayntz, *Das Dorf im Spannungsfeld industrieller Entwicklung* (Stuttgart: Ferdinand Enke-Verlag, 1954).

6. See for further information to this point footnote No. 33.

7. One of the advocates of National Socialist sociology also quotes Paul Anton de Lagarde (1827-1891), a representative of romantic nationalism, as a forerunner of German sociology. Vide Karl Heinz Pfeffer, *Die Deutsche Schule der Soziologie* (Leipzig: Verlag Quelle und Meyer, 1939).

8. Vide Gunther Ipsen, *Programm einer Soziologie des deutschen Volkstums* (1933). Ipsen is today connected with the *Dortmund Institute of Social Research* where he does quite normal research work. See also Max Rumpf, *Das gemeine Volk,* Vol. I, *Deutsches Bauernleben* (Stuttgart: Verlag W. Kohlhammer, 1936); Vol. II, *Religiöse Volkskunde* (Stuttgart: Verlag W. Kohlhammer, 1933). It is interesting to remark the totally ideological character of this folkloristic approach. No research is being done, all the conclusions are drawn from secondary materials, literary sources, novels, etc. A couple of years earlier, M. Rumpf had published two volumes of a more theoretical kind dealing both with "sociology of the folk" and a theory of social life: *Deutsche Volkssoziologie im Rahmen einer sozialen Lebenslehre* (Nurnberg: Verlag der Hochschulbuchhandlung Krische u. Co., 1931); *Soziale Lebenslehre. Ihr System und ihr wissenschaftlicher Ort* (Nurnberg: Verlag der Hochschulbuchhandlung Krische u. Co., 1932).

9. Vide P. König, "Die Begriffe Gemeinschaft und Gesellschaft bei Ferdinand Tönnies," *Kölner Zeitschrift für Soziologie und Sozialpsychologie,* VII (1955), 348-420.

10. From his many writings, especially in the field of economic history, we only quote a few with a more specific sociological character. W. Sombart, *Soziologie: was*

sie ist und was sie sein sollte (Berlin: Akademie der Wissenschaften, 1936); *Die drei Nationalökonomien* (New edition Munich and Leipzig: Verlag Duncker und Humblot, 1950); *Vom Menschen* (New edition Berlin: Duncker und Humblot, 1956). The American reader will find a good introduction into the writings of Sombart by F. X. Sutton, "The Social and Economic Philosophy of W. Sombart: The Sociology of Capitalism," in: H. E. Barnes, *An Introduction to the History of Sociology* (Chicago: The University of Chicago Press, 1948). Curiously enough, all the purely sociological writings of Sombart are missing in the bibliography.

11. Here, too, we only quote the more sociological publications. A. von Martin, *Soziologie der Renaissance* (2nd ed. Frankfort: Verlag Knecht, 1949; English translation by W. L. Luetkens, 1st impression, London: Routledge and Kegan Paul Ltd., 1944); *Geist und Gesellschaft* (Frankfort: Verlag Knecht, 1948); *Ordnung und Freiheit* (Frankfort: Verlag Knecht, 1956). Besides that see also his interesting contributions to Anton Wittman, Ed., *Handbuch für Sozialkunde* (Berlin-Munich: Verlag Duncker & Humblot, 1952-56). Incidentally, although A. von Martin remained in Germany, he always behaved as an adversary of National Socialism as can easily be proved by his writings during the war.

12. Even though Spann's economic and social ideas have played a very important role in the period immediately preceding the rise of National Socialism, he seems to be more or less forgotten today. A recently published choice of his more philosophical writings remained rather unnoticed: Hans Riehl, Editor, *Othmar Spann. Das philosophische Gesamtwerk im Auszug* (Vienna: Wilh. Braumüller, 1950). The best introduction in his thinking: O. Spann, *Gesellschaftslehre* (3rd edition, Leipzig: Quelle und Meyer, 1928). Vide Karl Dunkmann, *Der Streit um O. Spann* Leipzig: Quelle und Meyer, 1928), where an attempt is made to settle down the sometimes rather agitated discussion pro or contra Spann. After the war Spann completely shifted to philosophy of religion (1947).

13. After several publications of a more philosophical character, he published a textbook of sociology. Vide Karl Dunkmann, with Gerhard Lehmann and Heinz Sauermann, *Lehrbuch der Soziologie und Sozialpsychologie* (Berlin: Junker und Dünnhaupt-Verlag, 1931). G. Lehmann became later on a follower of National Socialism and published a most ignominiously antisemitic *History of Contemporary Philosophy*. H. Sauermann (born in 1905) specialized more and more in economics, but still has strong sociological interests. During a couple of years this group published a very interesting Journal of its own: *Archiv für Angewandte Soziologie*, V volumes (Berlin: Junker und Dünnhaupt-Verlag, 1929-1933). It might be interesting to remark that Dunkmann has dealt with sociology of the professions and sociology of work rather early. See his: *Die Lehre vom Beruf* (Berlin: Trowitsch und Sohn, 1922); "Soziologie der Arbeit," *Handbuch der Arbeitswissenschaft*, ed. by F. Giese (Halle: Verlag Marhold, 1931).

14. See especially Th. Litt, *Individuum und Gemeinschaft* (3rd edition, Berlin: Verlag B. G. Teubner, 1926).

15. G. Lukàcs, *Geschichte und Klassenbewusstsein* (Berlin: Malik-Verlag, 1923). From his many other writings we only mention: *Der junge Hegel. Über die Beziehungen von Dialektik und Oekonomie* (Zurich-Vienna: Europa-Verlag, 1948).

16. Max Horkheimer, *Autorität und Familie* (Paris: Félix Alcan, 1935). He also acted as the editor of an interesting sociological Journal the *Zeitschrift für Sozialforschung* (1933-1939). We do not need to quote explicitly his American publications, we only would like to remark that they did not meet with great interest in Germany, although a profound knowledge of his series *Studies in Prejudice* could be very helpful as an antidote against certain tendencies in Germany to underestimate the impact of prejudices. After the war came out the very important

collection of philosophical essays by M. Horkheimer and Th. W. Adorno, *Dialektik der Aufklärung* (Amsterdam: Querido-Verlag, 1947). Here the question is raised for the meaning of science and the above mentioned dichotomy introduced. We also would like to mention Th. W. Adorno and Walter Dirks, Editors, *Soziologische Exkurse* (Frankfurter Beiträge zur Soziologie, vol. 4. Frankfort: Europäische Verlagsanstalt, 1956). In this volume like in other ones the problem of dialectics and its relationship to theory and research is developed. See also the article "Empirische Sozialforschung," *Handwörterbuch der Sozialwissenschaften* (ed. by H. Jecht and R. Schaeder. Stuttgart-Tübingen-Göttingen: Gustav Fischer, J. C. B. Mohr, Vandenhoek und Ruprecht, 1954). A special device for research was developed in the Frankfort Institute by Friedrich Pollock (born in 1894), *Gruppenexperiment* (Frankfurter Beiträge zur Soziologie, vol. 2. Frankfort: Europäische Verlagsanstalt, 1955).

During the war a German communist refugee to Switzerland, Leo Kofler (born in 1907) published an introduction into dialectical sociology under the assumed name Stanislaw Warynski, *Die Wissenschaft von der Gesellschaft* (Bern: Verlag A. Francke, 1944). After the war he went to Eastern Germany where he has been teaching a few years at the University of Halle. There he published under his real name: *Zur Geschichte der bürgerlichen Gesellschaft* (Halle: Verlag Niemeyer, 1948). Later on he went to Western Germany where he published: *Geschichte und Dialektik* (Hamburg: Verlag Kogge, 1956), and: "Die Gesellschaftsauffassung des historischen Materialismus," *Handbuch der Soziologie*, edited by W. Ziegenfuss (l.c.).

17. All these writings have insofar at least indirectly a sociological character as they are mainly concerned with the position of art in the contemporary and nineteenth century "Bourgeois"–society. G. Lukács, *Goethe und sein Zeit* (Bern: A. Francke-Verlag, 1947); *Thomas Mann* (Berlin: Aufbau-Verlag, 1953); *Probleme des Realismus* (Berlin: Aufbau-Verlag, 1955); *Beiträge zur Geschichte der Aesthetik* (Berlin: Aufbau-Verlag, 1956) and several other publications in the same field. Th. W. Adorno, *Minima Moralia. Reflexionen aus dem beschädigten Leben* (Berlin and Frankfort: Suhrkamp-Verlag, 1951); *Versuch über Wagner* (Berlin and Frankfort: Suhrkamp-Verlag, 1952); *Prismen* (Berlin and Frankfort: Suhrkamp-Verlag, 1955); *Dissonanzen* (Göttingen: Vandenhoek-Verlag, 1956). Our above statement that Adorno is not interested in research as such is fully corroborated by the interesting critical review by Herbert H. Hyman and Paul B. Sheatsley, "The Authoritarian Personality. A Methodological Critique," *Studies in the Scope and Method of the Authoritarian Personality, Continuities in Social Research II*, Edited by Richard Christie and Marie Jahoda (Glencoe, Ill.: Free Press, 1954), 50-122.

17a. Simmel has been widely known in the United States as may be proved by some interesting and valuable books dealing with his sociology, some of which have come out quite recently. Vide N. J. Spykman, *The Social Theory of Georg Simmel* (Chicago: The University of Chicago Press, 1925); also Kurt H. Wolf, *George Simmel, Translated, Edited and with an Introduction* (Glencoe, Ill.: Free Pres, 1950); still more recently G. Simmel, *The Web of Group Affiliation*, transl. by K. H. Wolff and R. Bendix with a foreword by E. C. Hughes (Glencoe, Ill.: The Free Press, 1955).

18. Recently a choice of readings out of Dilthey's writings has been translated into English. Vide H. A. Hodges, *Wilhelm Dilthey. An Introduction* (London: Routledge and Kegan Paul, 1944, 2nd printing 1940), especially Chapter Four, pp. 52-67; 139-141. From the same author *The Philosophy of Wilhelm Dilthey* (London: Routledge and Kegan Paul, 1952), 186-190. As an introduction into his thinking see also Alexander Goldenweiser, "The Relation of the Natural Sciences to the Social Sciences, I. Wilhelm Dilthey," *Contemporary Social Thought*, ed. by H. E. Barnes, H. Becker, and F. B. Becker (New York: D. Appleton-Century Co., 1940), 93-98.

19. His main work in sociology has been widely discussed in pre-Nazi Germany: Hans Freyer, *Soziologie als Wirklichkeitswissenschaft* (Leipzig and Berlin: Verlag B. G. Teubner, 1930). His theory of culture is developed in: *Theorie des objektiven Geistes* (3rd ed. Leipzig and Berlin, Verlag B. G. Teubner, 1934). He becomes a forerunner of National Socialism mainly under the influence of the German youth movement. Vide: *Antaeus* (Jena: Eugen Diederichs-Verlag, 1918); also: *Revolution von Rechts* (Eugen Diederichs-Verlag, 1931); "Die Gegenwartsaufgaben der deutschen Soziologie," *Zeitschrift für die gesamte Staatswissenschaft* 95 (1934), 116-144; "Das politische Problem der Philosophie," *Blätter für deutsche Philosophie*, IX, 4 (1936); *Pallas Athene. Ethik des politischen Volkes* (Jena: Eugen Diederichs-Verlag, 1935); *Macchiavelli* (Leipzig: Bibliographisches Institut, 1938); *Die politische Insel. Eine Geschichte der Utopie von Platon bis zur Gegenwart* (Leipzig: Bibliographisches Institut, 1937). After the war he did not come back to ordinary teaching. His main publications are: *Weltgeschichte Europas* (Wiesbaden, Dieterich-Verlag, 1948) and: *Theorie des gegenwärtigen Zeitalters* (Stuttgart: Deutsche Verlagsanstalt, 1956). Vide Ernst Mannheim, "The Sociological Theories of H. Freyer. Sociology as Nationalistic Program of Social Action," *An Introduction to the History of Sociology*, ed. by H. E. Barnes (Chicago: University of Chicago Press, 1948).

20. Others to be quoted in his context are e.g. Erich Rothacker (born in 1888), Alfred Müller-Armack (born in 1901), Edgar Salin (born in 1892), and others of secondary importance.

21. F. Oppenheimer, "L. von Stein und die deutsche Soziologie," *Neue Rundschau*, Berlin, 1920. L. von Stein, *Der Begriff der Gesellschaft*, edited by G. Salomon (Munich: Drei Masken Verlag, 1921).

22. This point has recently been stressed by E. H. Jacoby, "F. Tönnies Sociologist: A Centennial Tribute," *Kyklos. International Revue for Social Sciences*, VIII, 2 (1955). Vide also Rudolf Heberle, "The Sociological System of F. Tönnies," *The American Sociological Review* II (1937), reprinted in: 1. c. "Das soziologische System von F. Tönnies," *Schmoller's Jahrbuch* 75 (1955).

23. After the war, the question of the empirical use of the categories of *Gemeinschaft* and *Gesellschaft* has been critically discussed by G. Wurzbacher, "Beobachtungen zum Anwendungsbereich der Kategorien Gemeinschaft und Gesellschaft," *Kölner Zeitschrift für Soziologie und Sozialpsychologie*, VII, 3 (1955). *Eodem loco:* R. König, "Die Begriffe Gemeinschaft und Gesellschaft bei F. Tönnies."

24. Max Weber, *Essays in Sociology*, transl. & edited and with an introduction by H. H. Gerth & C. Wright Mills (New York: Oxford University Press, 1946); *Ancient Judaism*. Trans. and edit. by H. H. Gerth and Don Martindale (Glencoe, Ill.: Free Press, 1950); *The Religion of China: Confucianism and Taoism*. Transl. by H. H. Gerth (Glencoe, Ill.: Free Press, 1951); other translations: *General Economic History*, Transl. by Frank H. Knight (New York: Greenberg, 1927; new edition Glencoe, Ill.: Free Press, 1950); *The Protestant Ethics and the Spirit of Capitalism*, Transl. by Talcott Parsons with a Foreword by R. H. Tawney (New York: Scribner's Sons, 1930); *The Theory of Social and Economic Organization*, Transl. by A. M. Henderson and Talcott Parsons (New York: Oxford University Press, 1947); *On the Methodology of Social Sciences*, Transl. and edited by Edward Shils and Henry A. Finch (Glencoe, Ill.: Free Press, 1949); *On Law in Economy and Society*, Translated and Edited with Introduction and Annotations by Max Rheinstein and Edward Shils (Cambridge, Mass.: Harvard University Press, 1954).

24a. Two English translations are available illustrating his contribution to the evaluation of protestantism in Germany, vide Ernst Troeltsch, *Protestantism and Progress*, Transl. by W. Montgomery (London: Williams and Norgate, 1912); *The Social Teaching of the Christian Churches*, Transl. by Olive Wyon (New York:

The Macmillan Co., 1931, new ed. London: Allen and Unwin, 1950). Vide also J. Milton Yinger, "The Sociology of Religion of E. Troeltsch," *An Introduction to the History of Sociology*, ed. by H. E. Barnes, l. c.

25. This point has recently been stressed by René König, "Max Weber," in *Grosse Deutsche*, ed. by Theodor Heuss (Berlin: Propyläen Verlag, 1957). For other references see the rather comprehensive bibliography in: Max Weber, *Schriften zur theoretischen Soziologie*, edited by Count Max zu Solms (Civitas Gentium. Frankfort: Kurt Schauer Verlag, 1947).

26. For Adorno vide *Soziologische Exkurse* (l.c.), 106 ff. G. Mackenroth, *Sinn und Ausdruck in der sozialen Formenwelt* (Meisenheim/Glan: Westkultur-Verlag, 1952), 74 ff., especially 83/4. W. Ziegenfuss, "Wesen und Formen der Soziologie," *Handbuch der Soziologie*, edit. by W. Ziegenfuss (Stuttgart: Verlag Ferd. Enke, 1955), pp. 215 ff. A similar criticism of Weber has been put forward many years ago by another Marxist and dialectic sociologist, Siegfried Landshut, *Kritik der Soziologie* (Munich-Leipzig: Duncker und Humblot-Verlag, 1929). In this regard, Landshut is the leftist parallel to Freyer.

27. The most violent criticism of his brother Max Weber is to be found in Alfred Weber and others, *Einführung in die Soziologie* (l.c.), pp. 162 ff. From his older writings we only mention: *Kulturgeschichte als Kultursoziologie* (2nd ed., Munich: R. Piper-Verlag, 1950); *Abschied von der bisherigen Geschichte* (Hamburg: Claassen and Goverts, 1946; English translation London: K. Paul, Trench, Trubner, 1947); *Prinzipien der Geschichts- und Kultursoziologie* (Munich: R. Piper-Verlag, 1951); *Der dritte oder der vierte Mensch* (Munich: R. Piper-Verlag, 1953).

28. See his very interesting report: *Die Verflechtung der Sozialleistungen. Ergebnisse einer Stichprobe* (Berlin: Duncker-Humblot-Verlag, 1954). His main book on demography also exhibits a purely sociological attitude: *Bevölkerungslehre. Theorie, Soziologie und Statistik der Bevölkerung* (Berlin-Göttingen-Heidelberg: Springer-Verlag, 1953).

29. Vide G. Wurzbacher, *Leitbilder des gegenwärtigen deutschen Familienlebens* (2nd ed. Stuttgart: Ferd. Enke Verlag, 1954); with R. Pflaum, *Das Dorf im Spannungsfeld der industriellen Entwicklung* (Stuttgart: Ferd. Enke-Verlag, 1955); also his contributions to H. Schelsky, Editor, *Arbeitslosigkeit und Berufsnot der Jugend* (2 vols. Köln: Bund-Verlag, 1952).

30. H. Schelsky, "Die Aufgaben einer Familiensoziologie in Deutschland," *Kölner Zeitschrift für Soziologie* II (1950); "Die Flüchtlingsfamilie," *Kölner Zeitschrift für Soziologie* III (1951); "Die gegenwärtigen Problemlagen der Familiensoziologie," *Soziologische Forschung in unserer Zeit*, edit. by K. G. Specht (Köln: Westdeutscher Verlag, 1951); *Wandlungen der deutschen Familie in der Gegenwart* (3rd edition Stuttgart: Ferd. Enke-Verlag, 1955); *Soziologie der Sexualität* (Hamburg: Rowohlt-Verlag 1955). Schelsky also edited besides the two volumes mentioned in note 29 another collection of research reports on youth problems: *Arbeiterjugend gestern und heute* (Heidelberg: Quelle und Meyer, 1955). See also Arnold Gehlen and H. Schelsky, *Soziologie. Lehr- und Handbuch zur modernen Gesellschaftskunde* (Düsseldorf: Eugen Diederichs-Verlag, 1955).

31. For bibliographical references see Ralf Dehrendorf, *Industrie- und Betriebssoziologie* (Berlin: W. de Gruyter-Verlag, 1956). The rural sociology has been organized in an association of its own the *Forschungsgesellschaft für Agrarpolitik und Agrarsoziologie*. For bibliographical references see: Dissertationen aus Agrarökonomik und Agrarsoziologie (1945-1955), mimeographed (Bonn, 1956).

32. Th. Geiger, *Die soziale Schichtung des deutschen Volkes* (Stuttgart: Ferdinand Enke-Verlag, 1932); *Soziale Umschichtungen einer dänischen Mittelstadt* (2 vols. Kopenhagen: Munksgaard, 1951); of his older writings we would like to mention:

Die Masse und ihre Aktion (Stuttgart: Ferd. Enke-Verlag, 1926); after the war he published: *Vorstudien zu einer Soziologie des Rechts* (Kopenhagen: Munksgaard, 1947); *Die Klassengesellschaft im Schmelztiegel* (Köln: Verlag Kiepenheuer, 1949); *Ideology und Wahrheit* (Stuttgart and Vienna: Humboldt-Verlag, 1953).

33. We give a sample of promising younger German sociologists interested in empirical research, in alphabetic order. Gerhard Baumert (born 1923) vide note 5; furthermore "Some Observations on Current Tends in the German Family," *Transactions of the Third World Congress of Sociology* vol. IV (London: International Sociological Association, 1956); "Methoden und Resultate einer Untersuchung deutscher Nachkriegsfamilien," *Recherches sur la famille*, vol. I (Tübingen: J. C. B. Mohr, 1956); "Ehe," "Familie," *Die Religion in Geschichte und Gegenwart*, forthcoming. Karl Martin Bolte (born 1925, University of Kiel), "Bevölkerungsentwicklung und Bevölkerungspolitik," *Weltwirtschaftliches Archiv* 1954, 1; "Prestigestrukturen in der industriellen Gesellschaft," *Gewerkschaftliche Monatshefte* 1956, 2; "Strukturwandlungen der Gesellschaft als Hintergrund der Bestrebungen zur Sozialreform," *Zeitschrift für Sozialreform* 1955, 2; "Ein Beitrag zur Problematik der sozialen Mobilität," *Kölner Zeitschrift für Soziologie und Sozialpsychologie* VIII, 1 (1956); "Getrennte Versicherungsgesetze für Angstellte und Arbeiter," *Zeitschrift für Sozialreform* 1956, 8; with G. Mackenroth, "Bevölkerungspolitik," *Handwörterbuch der Sozialwissenschaften*, ed. by H. Jecht and R. Schaeder (Stuttgart-Tübingen-Göttingen: G. Fischer, J. C. B. Mohr, Vandenhoek und Ruprecht, forthcoming); "Bevölkerungspolitik," *Religion in Geschichte und Gegenwart* (Tübingen: J. C. B. Mohr, 1957); "Angestellte," *eodem loco*; *Berufsprestige und Berufsmobilität*, forthcoming 1958. Ralf Dahrendorf (born 1929, Akademie für Gemeinwirtschaft, Hamburg), *Marx in Perspektive. Die Idee des Gerechten im Denken von Karl Marx* (Hannover: J. H. W. Dietz Nachfolger, 1953); *Industrie- und Betriebssoziologie* (Berlin: De Gruyter Verlag, 1956); "Struktur und Funktion. Talcott Parsons und die Entwicklung der soziologischen Theorie," *Kölner Zeitschrift für Soziologie und Sozialpsychology* VII, 4 (1955); "Industrielle Fertigkeiten und soziale Schichtung," *eodem loco* VIII, 4 (1956); *Soziale Klassen und Klasenkonflikte in der industriellen Gesellschaft* (Stuttgart: Ferd. Enke-Verlag, 1957). Ludwig von Friedeburg (born 1924, Institute for Social Research, University of Frankfort), *Die Umfrage in der Intimsphäre* (Stuttgart: Ferd. Enke-Verlag, 1953); *Betriebsklima* (Frankfort: Europäische Verlagsanstalt, 1955). Friedrich Fürstenberg (born 1930, University of Tübingen), "Empirische Sozialforschung im Industriebetrieb," *Kölner Zeitschrift für Soziologie und Sozialpsychologie* VI, 3/4 (1954); *Money and Motivation*, ed. by W. F. Whyte (New York: Harper and Brothers, 1955); "Die soziale Funktion der Leistungsanreize (Incentives) im Industriebetrieb," *Kölner Zeitschrift für Soziologie und Sozialpsychologie* VII, 4 (1955); "Die soziologische Dimension wirtschaftstheoretischer Aussagen," *Zeitschrift für die gesamte Staatswissenschaft* 1956, 3; "Das Strukturproblem in der Soziologie," *Kölner Zeitschrift für Soziologie und Sozialpsychologie* VIII, 4 (1956). Peter Heintz (born 1920, University of Cologne), "Lauderdales Kritik an der klassischen Oekonomie," *Schweizerische Zeitschrift für Volkswirtschaft und Statistik* 86, 1 (1950); *Anarchismus und Gegenwart* (Zürich: Regio Verlag, 1951); "Neue Forschungsergebnisse der Soziologie der Gruppenführung," *Schweizerische Zeitschrift für Volkswirtschaft und Statistik* 90, 1 (1954); "Betrachtungen zur soziologischen Theorie der Revolte," *eodem loco* 90, 4 (1954); "Von den Ansätzen einer neuen Soziologie der Technik bei Thorstein Veblen," *Zeitschrift für die gesamte Staatswissenschaft* 110, 3 (1954); "Die Struktur der spanischen Persönlichkeit," *Kölner Zeitschrift für Soziologie und Sozialpsychologie* VII, 1 (1954); "Die Technik im sozio-kulturellen Wandel," *eodem loco* VII, 2 (1955); "Einige theoretische Ansätze zu einer Soziologie der kriminellen Angriffe

gegen die Person," *Monatsschrift für Kriminologie und Strafrechtsreform* 1956; *Die Autoritätsproblematik bei P. -J. Proudhon* (Köln: Verlag für Politik und Wirtschaft, 1957); *Die sozialen Vorurteile* (Köln: Verlag für Politik und Wirtschaft, 1957); "Zur Soziologie der Grosstadt," *Schweizerische Rundschau* 56. 1957; "Zur Problematik der autoritären Persönlichkeit," *Kölner Zeitschrift für Soziologie und Sozialpsychologie* IX, 1 (1957); with René König, *Soziologie der Jugendkriminalität* (Opladen: Westdeutscher Verlag, 1957); "Anarchismus," *Die Religion in Geschichte und Gegenwart*, forthcoming. Heintz Kluth (born 1921, University of Hamburg), "Die Gemeinschaftfähigkeit der arbeitslosen Jugendlichen," "Das Verhältnis der arbeitslosen Jugendlichen zum Staat und zur Politik," "Die methodologischen Erfahrungen bei der Fragebogenerhebung," *Arbeitslosigkeit und Berufsnot der Jugend*, ed. H. Schelsky (Köln: Bund-Verlag, 1952); "Arbeiterjugend: Begriff und Wirklichkeit," *Arbeiterjugend gestern und heute*, ed. H. Schelsky (Heidelberg: Quelle und Meyer, 1955); "Kräfte und Tendenzen im gesellschaftlichen Spannungsfeld der Gegenwart," *Gewerkschaftliche Monatshefte* VI (1956); *Sozialprestige und sozialer Status* (Stuttgart: Ferd. Enke-Verlag, 1957). Herbert Kötter (born 1916, Secretary, German Association for Rural Sociology), vide note 5; furthermore: "Agrarsoziologie," *Soziologie. Lehr- und Handbuch zur modernen Gesellschaftskunde*, ed. by A. Gehlen and H. Schelsky (3rd ed. Düsseldorf: Eugen Diederichs-Verlag, 1957); "Der Einfluss der sozialen und wirtschaftlichen Differenzierung der Landbevölkerung auf die Landbewirtschaftung," *Dorfuntersuchungen, Berichte über Landwirtschaft* 162 (Hamburg: Verlag Paul Parey, 1955); "Die Gemeinde in der ländlichen Soziologie," *Soziologie der Gemeinde*, ed. by R. König (Opladen: Westdeutscher Verlag, 1956). Renate Mayntz (born 1929, University of Berlin), with G. Wurzbacher, *Das Dorf in Spannungsfeld der Industrie* (Stuttgart: Ferd. Enke-Verlag, 1954); *Die moderne Familie* (Stuttgart: Ferd. Enke-Verlag 1955); "Lokale Parteigruppen," *Zeitschrift für Politik* II, 1 (1955); with Howard V. Perlmutter, "Einige Versuchsergebnisse zum Problem der Vorstellungsbildung und Interpretation von Kommunikationen," *Kölner Zeitschrift für Soziologie und Sozialpsychologie* VIII, 3 and 4 (1956); *Soziale Schichtung und sozialer Wandel in der Industriegemeinde* (Stuttgart: Ferd. Enke-Verlag, 1958); *Die soziale Organisation des Industriebetriebs* (Stuttgart: Ferd. Enke-Verlag, 1958). Heinrich Popitz (born 1925, University of Freiburg in Baden), *Der entfremdete Mensch* (Basel: Verlag für Recht und Gesellschaft, 1953); with H. P. Bahrdt, E. A. Jüres, H. Kesting, *Technik und Industriearbeit, Soziologische Untersuchungen in der Hüttenindustrie* (Tübingen: J. C. B. Mohr, 1957); with the same co-authors, *Das Gesellschaftsbild des Arbeiters, Soziologische Untersuchungen in der Hüttenindustrie* (Tübingen: J. C. B. Mohr, 1958). Kriphal Sodhi (born 1911, University of Berlin), *Urteilsbildung im sozialen Kraftfeld: Experimentelle Untersuchungen zur Grundlegung der Sozialpsychologie* (Göttingen: Hofgrefe-Verlag, 1953); with R. Bergius, *Nationale Vorurteile. Eine sozialpsychologische Untersuchung an 881 Personen* (Berlin: Duncker and Humblot, 1953); "Strömungen der Sozialpsychologie Mittel- und Westeuropas," *Bericht über den 19. Kongress der deutschen Gesellschaft für Psychologie*, ed. by A. Wellek (1953); "Der sozialpsychologische Aspekt in der forensischen Psychologie," *Psychologische Rundschau* VI (1955). Finally, we want to draw the attention to some interesting books, also more or less representative for recent trends in German sociology: Hans Joachim Lieber, *Wissen und Gesellschaft* (Tübingen: Max Niemeyer, 1952); Erich Reigrotzki, *Soziale Verflechtungen in der Bundesrepublik* (Tübingen: J. C. B. Mohr, 1956); Theo Pirker, Siegfried Braun, Burkart Lutz, Fro Hammelrath, *Arbeiter, Management, Mitbestimmung* (Düsseldorf: Ring-Verlag, 1955); Gottfried Eisermann, *Die Grundlagen des Historismus* (Stuttgart: Ferd. Enke-Verlag, 1956); Helmuth Plesner, editor, *Untersuch-*

ungen zur Lage der deutschen Hochschullehrer, vol. I: Nachwuchsfragen im Spiegel einer Erhebung 1953-55; vol. II: Alexander Busch, *Stellenplan und Lehrkörperstruktur der Universitäten und Hochschulen in der Bundesrepublik 1953/54;* vol. III: Christian von Ferber, *Die Entwicklung des Lehrkörpers der deutschen Universitäten und Hochschulen 1864-1954* (Göttingen: Vanderhoek and Ruprecht, 1956).

34. Ralf Dahrendorf, "Soziologie in Deutschland," *Annales Universitatis Saraviensis,* IV (1955), 98-106.

AUSTRIA

August M. Knoll
University of Vienna

SOCIOLOGY IN AUSTRIA 1918-1938

Austrian sociology achieved many important results by influencing various social and cultural sciences during the period of 1918-1938. The sociological influence was especially felt in the field of historiography. In economic history, Alphons Dopsch[1] demonstrated the cultural continuity between antiquity and the early Middle Ages. Hans Hirsch[2] laid the fundaments of the history of the ecclesiastic and profane constitution of the medieval empire. Otto Brunner[3] and Otto H. Stowasser[4] studied the feudal system and its specific form of domination. Social and legal history primarily in connection with the development of settlements and towns were developed by Max von Vancsa,[5] Karl Lechner[6] and Ernst Klebel.[7]

The leading man in political history was Heinrich von Srbik[8] with his works on "Wallenstein" and "Metternich." Oswald Redlich[9] studied the Austrian and Austro-Hungarian Monarchy for which Viktor Bibl[10] had only negative criticism. Many stimulating ideas in terms of the philosophy of history were offered by Richard von Kralik[11] and Hans Eibl.[12] A new school of anthropology, the "Cultural Regions-Theory," directed against a-historical evolutionism and psychologism, was created by Wilhelm Schmidt and Wilhelm Koppers.[13] This view of history also prevailed in Oswald Menghin's,[14] an archaeologist's study of the Iron Age.

The contribution to sociology that Austrian economics made is of great importance indeed. We have to mention Carl Grünberg,[15] a representative of the farmers' and peasants' interests in political life and the historian of the liberation of the rural population in the 19th century to the status of full civil rights. Also the right wing economists Josef Gruntzel,[16] Michael Hainisch,[17] Viktor Mataja,[18] Eugen Schwiedland[19] have to be thought of. Still more sociological

807

was the work of Friedrich von Wieser,[20] one of the founders of the Austrian "Marginal Utility School." He wrote a theory of social economics and demonstrated the "law of power." The neo-*laissez-faire* school was founded by Ludwig von Mises[21] in 1922 by his study on "Gemeinwirtschaft." Questions of "Ideas and Economics," industrialization and de-proletarization were treated by Ferdinand von Degenfeld-Schonburg.[22]

Adolph Menzel[23] first working in the tradition of a jurist and a political scientist turned to sociology. He wrote a "System of Sociology," a history of "Greek Sociology." His study on "Natural Law and Sociology" may be called a classic. He tried to demonstrate that sociology essentially is ethico-political speculation. Also modern sociology, as positivism has created it, is, according to Menzel, only a version of "natural law" covered up by the terminology of the natural sciences.

Hans Kelsen,[24] one of the founders of a new type of jurisprudence of the so called "Theory of Pure Law," greatly furthered the development of sociology. Special attention has to be given to his "Juridical and Sociological Conception of the State," his essay on "Gott und Staat" (God and the State), his criticism of Natural Law and Marxist theory of the state. Despite many doubts Kelsen took position for sociology being a science of its own, a special method in the realm of the criticism of ideologies. Together with Kelsen his school undertook studies in sociology; Fritz Sander[25] edited a "Theory of Society" and Erwin Voegelin[26] studied political and racial problems.

Also a philosopher concentrated on sociology: Wilhelm Jerusalem.[27] His introduction to philosophy was translated into 7 different langauges and read all over the world; it contains many sociological digressions. This may suffice for a brief survey of some bordering disciplines, the sociological aspects contained therein and their contribution to sociology. It should be mentioned here that the work of the Vienna born Sigmund Freud,[28] his philosophy of drives, the methods and perspectives of his psychoanalysis and the understanding of subconscious desires and tendencies offered by such method proved to be of the greatest importance to sociology far beyond the borders of Austria.

As far as sociology as a University discipline goes their representatives in Austria between 1918 and 1938 were the following: Othmar Spann[29] whose life-work may be characterized by the Aristotelian phrase that the whole precedes its parts. With the zeal and emotion of a missionary Spann tried to demonstrate the "divine" and "wholistic" harmony of all things and all men. Every being is part of a whole and this again element of another, higher form of unity. Spann's economics, politics and sociology are characterized by this wholistic approach; the same holds true for his "universalist" school. His disciples Jakob Baxa[30] and Johannes Sauter[31] wrote histories of the Austrian and of the South German schools of Romantic Social and Political Thought. Platonic Social Philosophy was interpreted by Spann's disciple Wilhelm Andrea,[32] Thomist Social Thought by Friedrich Schreyvogl[33] and Fichtean theory by Hans Riehl.[34] A methodological continuation of Spann was offered by Karl Faigl,[35] and Walter Heinrich[36] follows Spann in some basic ideas. During early phases of their research several Austrian scholars were influenced by Spann: Gustav Seidler-Schmid[37] in his criticism of classical economics, Viktor Gutmann,[38] Ferdinand von Westphalen[39] and Ernst Lagler[40] in their dealing with problems of industry and agriculture.

In 1907 a "Sociological Society" was founded in Vienna by Max Adler, Rudolf Eisler, Rudolf Goldscheid, Michael Hainisch, Ludo Hartmann, Bertold Hatschek, Wilhelm Jerusalem, Josef Redlich and Karl Renner. This society published a series of works in Sociology and Social Philosophy. Seven different studies appeared. Ernst Gruenwald,[41] known by his study on the Sociology of Knowledge may be considered as one of the disciples of this group of sociologists.

Marxist ideas were aptly presented and interpreted in Austria by Karl Kautsky,[42] a friend of Friedrich Engels. The studies by Otto Bauer[43] and Karl Renner[44] concerning social political and government problems demonstrate the sociological interest of these two authors. Max Adler,[45] a sociologist by profession and professor of this discipline at the University of Vienna developed a theory of his own. Starting from the philosophy of Kant in general and his theory of knowledge in particular he gave new impulses to socialist theory.

The sociology of Natural Law as developed by the Roman Catholic Church after 1918 was represented by Franz Martin Schindler[64] and Ignaz Seipel.[47] Their basic ideas were woven into a system by Johannes Messner.[48] By this type of sociology the latter attempted to adjust the christian social teaching to the realities of Capitalist society. In radical opposition to these attempts Anton Orel[49] and Ferdinand Frodl,[50] together with their friends, formed the so called "Viennese

Currents"[51] and attempted an anti-capitalist interpretation on the basis on Christian-socialist and cooperative movements and successes of the first postwar period.

This quarrel concerning the possible meanings of "natural law" in catholic circles (for the first time in the history of ideas this occurred in Austria) led to a negation of "natural law." This tendency was formulated by Ernst Karl Winter[52] who, influenced by Hans Kelsen, wrote a criticism of the social metaphysics of scholasticism and a Sociology of Plato's theory of ideas.

During the years from 1934-1938 much sociological knowledge was gained; it was, however, of a particular kind, namely publications interpreting the papal encyclical "Quadragesimo anno," the controversy concerning the "May-constitution" of 1934 and general writings on the social order created by the Dolfuss system giving special consideration to the different types of economic production and professional specialization. The pros and cons are reflected in my study "Why did the Austrian 'Ständestaat' (state structured according to its occupational strata) 1934-1938 break up?" In this article, published by the Swiss periodical "Civitas" historical source material is given.

As far as my own sociological studies before 1938 are concerned I have to mention: "The Problem of Interests in Scholasticism." [54] Therein I tried to show that in the medieval church beside the canon law regulation forbidding the taking of interests also a more permissive attitude in this matter existed. Also in this work I tried to correct the Calvinism-Capitalism-thesis of Max Weber. My tenets were the following: Max Weber had specially treated the genesis of the "Calvinist Spirit" in Protestantism as a result of the Calvinist mentality (opposed to the conservative Lutherans), but he had neglected the Jesuits' opposition against the conservative Dominicans (a parallel development of socio-economic history in the catholic culture of the post reformation period). In a supplementary study "Grace and Interests" [55] I demonstrated that the controversies between Dominicans and Jesuits centering around the theological alternative: "human freedom through grace"—"human commitment to God through grace" in many ways were reflexions of their controversies concerning interest problems and thereby a product of their socio-economic ties. Jesuits and Calvinists are rooted in early Capitalism just as Dominicans and Lutherans have their roots in the feudal system.

AUSTRIAN SOCIOLOGY BETWEEN 1945 AND
THE PRESENT TIME

The sciences contributing toward development of sociology yield the following picture for Austria during this period:

As early as 1946, there appeared in Vienna a sociologically minded self-criticism of philosophy by Alois Dempf[56]—a fruit of politically enforced silence; he linked the process of philosophical thought with twelve social types and made these the empirical base for comparative philosophy. We also find the sociology of knowledge together with a critique of value systems in numerous articles by Ernst Topitsch.[57] Rudolf Stemberger[58] wrote on Kant as a philosopher and sociologist. A philosophical contribution toward political problems of the present time was given by Felix Klezl-Norberg[59] in his treatise on ideas as foundations of political and economic life. The family problem was considered by Albert Mitterer[60] from the standpoint of natural philosophy. A corpus of social medicine in six volumes was written by Albert Niedermeyer.[61]

Also during this time most important contributions toward sociology came from the historical sciences. A history of historiography and of its methods relevant to sociology is the book of Heinrich von Srbik[62] which he wrote in his old age on the concepts of Mind and History since the 18th Century Humanistic thought. Thorough insights into the social structure of the Middle Ages are conveyed by Hans von Planitz's[63] work on the medieval city, Heinrich von Fichtenau's[64] book on the empire of Charlemagne and Otto Brunner's[65] Feudal Culture and the European Mind. A collection of material concerning the peculiar types of constitution of social units within the church which aims at completeness is being undertaken by Leo Santifaller.[66]

Ambiguously judged by experts but very stimulating and reaching far beyond Austria are the books by the Viennese historian and philosopher Friedrich Heer;[67] they belong to the history of ideas and to social history. In his two volumes on the origins of modern Europe he traced the connections between politically minded religiosity and the rise of Europe in the 12th century. A continuation of this Friedrich Heer gives in his works: The Tragedy of the Holy Roman Empire and European History of Ideas.

More recent social history comprising also the history of social movements and parties in Austria and the connected trends of "world views" are and were treated by Heinrich Benedikt,[68] Hugo Hantsch[69] and Karl Eder[70] and their students. Furthermore Albert Fuchs,[71] Leopold Lentner,[72] Johann Christoff Allmayer-Beck,[73] Rudolf Till,[74] Kurt Skalnik[75] are to be mentoned here. 1948 a series of historical, ethico-political publications was edited, celebrating the 100th anniversary of the Austrian Revolution of 1848: by Robert Endress,[76] Ernst Fischer,[77] Alexander Novotny.[78] My own study on the Sociology of the Austrian Revolution 1848[79] appeared in the volume presented by the Government of Lower Austria on occasion of the same anniversary. Important for the Austrian ecclesiastical and social history of the years 1938-1945 are Jakob Fried's[80] and Karl Rudolf's[81] studies on Roman Catholic resistance against National Socialism in Austria.

In Vienna the following works contributed toward the political and social history of philosophy: Alfred von Verdross'[82] *Main Theories of Classical Legal and political Philosophy,* Otto Weinberger's[83] *Economic Theories of the Old Testament,* Rudolf Stanka's[84] *The Political Philosophy of Classical Antiquity* and Gustav Wetter's[85] *Dialectic Materialism,* the latter being a history and critique of bolshevist philosophy. A very ingenious study on Dante as a political philosopher was written by Robert L. John.[86]

Viennese representatives of the sciences of man are: the natural philosopher Ullrich Schöndorfer,[87] with a study of the Philosophy of Man; the biologist Otto Storch[88] with a study of the special rank of man within the animated world, the anthropologist Wilhelm Koppers[89] with many studies of primitive man and his concept of the world, the psychologist Viktor E. Frankl[90] with publications on the "unconditional" and the "suffering" man, and the atomic physicist Hans Thirring[91] with a publication on the "wise" man. From a natural science point of view, Hubert Rohracher[92] is dealing with the main physiological aspects of gerontology.

A general impression of both the achievements and the irradiations of the Austrian economic sciences in connection with sociological problems is to be gotten from two publications edited by Alexander Mahr in 1949 and Ernst Lagler in 1952 presented in honor of the 70th birthday of the economic scientists Hans Mayer[93] and Ferdinand von Degenfald-Schönburg.[94] Richard Kerschagl,[95] Anton Tautscher[96] and Wilhelm Weber[97] contributed to the history of socio-economic sciences, Hans Bayer[98] and Theodore Bütz[99] to the sociology of economy.

The most important Austrian representative of sociology in the more technical sense of the word before 1938, Othmar Spann,[100] moved beyond it in his late years. In 1947, three years preceding his death he published his last work in Vienna. The same distance to sociology is to be found in the publication edited in honor of Spann's 70th birthday with mostly philosophical and methodological contributions of his former students and admirers. There are practically no disciples of Spann's ideas left now. His most gifted followers like Walter Heinrich[101] and Hans Riehl[102] withdrew. Heinrich mostly works in the field of economics and Riehl in the field of philosophy.

Overlooking the present situation of sociology in Austria we have to quote first two studies of a wide scope. Of these one adheres to the socialistic and natural scientistic trend, the other one to the ecclesiastical trend connected with Natural Law. The former's author is the late President of Austria Karl Renner, the latter's the moralist of Vienna University Johannes Messner.

Renner's work[103] was posthumously edited in Vienna in 1952 (Renner died in 1950) and bears the title: *Man and Society, A System of Sociology*. For him the utmost ideal of presentation is the empiricism and materialism of the 19th century according to which "body and soul are one thing, a thing like the vibrating string, being catgut and sound at the same time," according to which the personal "Ego" is but a "product of its society" and its reflexion. Also the social essence in itself is explained in a naturalistic sene, following completely the tradition of the sociology from Hobbes onward to Spencer, who primarily see the "other" as an enemy and who consider fight being the primary sociological condition. Furthermore society and economy are viewed not only from the standpoint of a "zoologist" but also from that of a Marxist. Admittedly it is no dogmatic but a critical marxism which arrives at applications. The fact of the Iron Curtain which marxism finally had to face induced Renner to make some radical cuts. He postulates an "empirical socialism" which is a "frame of mind" having learned from "the experiences of the last generation" and not willing to press everflowing life into prefabricated moulds.

Connected with Renner's way of thinking is Robert Endress,[104] historian and sociologist. He wrote a History of Europe in two volumes from the standpoint of historical materialism. In his work *State and Society* he drafted the evolution of mankind from prehistoric ages to the present time. Of a like extensive kind and belonging to the same trend are the studies of Ernst Glaser.[105] His book, *Man and Society*, offers a "short sociology and social psychology," an analysis of the basic forms of human interrelations, of social groups and classes. Especially his second book on family, work and leisure found wide attention; it depicts and exercises these "three milieus of man." The ideas of Karl Kautsky were preserved and augmented by his son Benedict Kautsky.[106] He published "Friedrich Engels' exchange of letters with Karl Kautsky." Working in the tradition of the latter (which is certainly socialist but anticommunist) he wrote the book: *American Workers Advancing.* He also published a great number of sociological studies in the monthly magazine for politics, economy and culture *Die Zukunft* (The Future), edited by him and Oskar Pollak.[107]

Johannes Messner[108] stands for the ecclesiastical trend connected with the theory of Natural Law. His main work which first appeared in 1949 in the United States, in St. Louis (Mo.) and only afterwards, 1950, in Vienna, bears the title "Naturrecht" (Natural Law) and draws on almost 1000 pages a "natural" system of norms from which a "naturally correct" social standard is being deducted as the outcome of his investigation. Messner calls it "social democracy" and treats this by means of social and economic ethics as relevant to the "social question" after having given an introduction of moral-sociological philosophy and of philosophy of law. Because of the extremely formal character of natural law Messner admits himself to have given "but a very basic scheme of order for any system and not a concrete system as such." The same results show also the studies concerning Natural Law by Josef Funk,[109] Albert Auer,[110] Walter Riener,[111] Johann Schasching[112] and others.

As "Natural Law" does not yield a "concrete system" Christian social politics in Austria try to find concrete ways with or without Natural Law. Indeed these are two basically different ways! It is either an adaptation to the socialist concept of facts or a standing in the tradition of Vogelsang.

"Socialistically" oriented is Josef Dobretsberger.[113] His creed is laid down in his book on Catholic Social Politics. Of a socialist but not "peoples' democratic" or protocommunistic conviction is August Zechmeister[114] in his pamphlet on church and socialism. The reforms he aims at are well explained and prepared in his thorough study on the freedom of individual conviction in the Catholic Church. This is the first publication of the series edited by him: Elements of a Theological Sociology.

More successful was the trend of social thinking in Austria standing in the tradition of the great Austrian sociologist and social reformer Carl Freiherr von Vogelsang (+ 1890).[115] His basic idea which today is being practically discussed in all modern states, in the United States as well as in Europe, was the one of a reunification of labor and capital—by cooperative societies and partnership, by profit sharing and employee stocks. The center for these endeavors in Austria is today the "Institute for Social Politics and Social Reforms" founded by Nationalrat Dr. Karl Kummer,[116] Prof. Dr. Anton Burghardt and myself. Its series of publications (up to now seven have appeared) document the new ways and goals. As an example of these Anton Burghardt's[117] work on the ethics and control of property should be mentioned.

Furthermore Austrian sociology is characterized by a number of investigations on the specific systems of objectivation of society.

Thus the sociology of religion was furthered as to its material by the *Handbook of the History of Religions,* edited by the Archbishop of Vienna Franz König.[118] Bernhard Häring[119] wrote a study: *Power and Agony of Religion* with special consideration of the formation of religious elites and masses, of the spirit of epochs and the evolution of society. Ingenious (like everything coming from his pen) is Ernst Karl Winter's[120] *Christianity and Civilization.* Winter is a sociologist and historian, a philosopher and politician at the same time, furthermore an enthusiastic Austrian, even as an emigrant to the U.S.A. since twenty years, and one of the few connoisseurs of philosophy of Thomas Aquinas and Kant. As a political thinker standing on the right and "thinking on the left wing" and having an extraordinary knowledge of the historical contacts between Church and State Winter shows the basic theological problems and their sociological bearings and vice versa.

Empirical sociology geared at the description of certain points of the ecclesiastical situation in Austria is being done by the "Institute for Social Investigations within the Church" under the direction of Linus Grond. Up to now 21 interesting publications are available, by Erich Bodzenta, Andreas Liebscher and others.[121]

Toward the "Sociology of the Arts" contributed Kurt Blaukopf:[122] "Sociology of Music" and Hans Georg Marek:[123] *The Actor in the Light of Sociology.* Concerning the sociology of knowledge Ernst Topitsch[124] should be mentioned once more. His book: *Structural Analysis of World Views* will be published in the near future. "Sociology of language" is being treated by Friedrich Kainz[125] in the four volumes of his Psychology of speech and language. Rudolph Blüh-dorn[126] is working in the sociology of International Relations.

A number of sociologists are treating as their topic the working classes, the industrial society and its strata. In this line is lying the book of Johann Mokre:[127] *Our Changing Society*, edited by a commission of UNESCO, and his book on *Work and the Worker*.[128] Ernst Lagler is a pioneer in Austria of "rural sociology." [129]

The Institute of Sociology at the University of Vienna, headed by August M. Knoll, and helped by American money, is working on the sociology of the family, the housing problems and the town and area planning.

SELECTED BIBLIOGRAPHY

Howard Becker & Harry Elmer Barnes, *Social Thought from Lore to Science* (Washington, D.C.: Harren Press, 1952), II, Chapter XXIII, "Germany and Austria," 879-931. A good synthesis of the whole development of sociology in the German-speaking countries.

Samson B. Knoll, "Austria," Chapter 23, 313-324, in Matthew A. Fitzsimons, Alfred G. Pundt & Charles E. Nowell, Eds., *The Development of Historiography* (Harrisburg, Pa.: The Stackpole Co., 1954). Especially valuable on the works in the field of historical sociology.

Ferdinand A. Westphalen, *Sociology and Economics in Austria* (Washington, D.C.: Library of Congress, 1953). A brief survey.

August M. Knoll, Head of the Department of Sociology, University of Vienna, is the author of numerous sociological studies (*The Basic Theories of Society. Ignaz Seipel, The Problem of Capitalism in Modern Sociology, etc.*); also heads the Institute of Sociology, University of Vienna, which is conducting research in the field of the sociology of the family and community ecology.

NOTES

1. Alphons Dopsch, *Wirtschaftliche und soziale Grundlagen der europäischen Kulturentwicklung* (*The Economic and Social Basis of European Cultural Development*) (Wien, 1923-4); *Die Wirtschaftsentwicklung der Karolingerzeit* (*The Economic Development of the Carolingean Period*) (Weimar, 1921-2); *Verfassungs-und Wirtschaftsgeschichte des Mittelalters* (*Constitutional and Economic History of the Middle Ages*) (Wien, 1928).

2. Hans Hirsch, *Die hohe Gerichtsbarkeit im deutschen Mittelater* (The Position of the Judge in the German Middle Ages) (Prag, 1922)

3. Otto Brunner, *Land und Herrschaft* (*Region and Power Structure*) (Wien 1939).

4. Otto H. Stowasser, *Land und Herzog* (*The Regional Unit and Its Duke*) (Berlin, 1925).

5. Max von Vancsa, *Geschichte Nieder- und Oberösterreichs* (*The History of Lower and Upper Austria*) (Wien, 1927).

6. Karl Lechner, *Ausgewählte Schriften,* herausg. von Kurt von Vancsa (*Selected Studies,* ed. by K. v. Vancsa) (Wien, 1947).

7. Ernst Klebel, *Gedanken über den Volksaufbau während des Mittelalters, Typen weltlicher Grundherren und Grundherrschaften* (*An Essay on the Social Structure of the Middle Ages, Types of Secular Feudal Lords and Their Possessions*) (Leipzig: Deutsches Archiv für Landes und Volksforschung, 1938).

8. Heinrich von Srbik, *Wallensteins Ende* (*The End of Wallenstein*) (Wien, 1920); *Metternich* (München, 1925).

9. Oswald Redlich, *Ausgewählte Schriften,* hsg. von O. H. Stowasser (*Selected Studies,* ed. by O. H. Stowasser) (Wien, 1928).

10. Viktor Bibl, *Der Zerfall Österreichs* (*The Disintegration of Austria*) (Wien, 1922-24).

11. Richard von Kralik, *Grundriss und Kern der Weltgeschichte* (*The Structure and Nucleus of World History*) (Wien, 1920).

12. Hans Bibl, *Vom Sinn der Gegenwart* (*On the Meaning of the Present Age*) (Wien, 1934).

13. Wilhelm Schmidt & Wilhelm Koppers, *Gesellschaft und Wirtschaft der Völker* (*Society and Economics of the Nations*) (Regensburg, 1924).

14. Oswald Menghin, *Weltgeschichte der Steinzeit* (*World History of the Stone Age*) (Wien, 1931).

15. Carl Grünberg, *Archiv für die Geschichte des Sozialismus* (Leipzig, 1910-1931); *Festschrift für Grünberg zum 70. Geburtstag* (*Symposium Dedicated to Grünberg at his 70th Birthday*) (Leipzig, 1932).

16. Josef Krunzel, *Allgemeine Volkswirtschaftslehre* (*General Economics*) (Wien, 1929).

17. Michael Hainisch, *Die Landflucht* (*Rural Exitus*) (Jena, 1924); *Reden und Abhandlungen* (Speeches and Treatises) (Graz, 1931).

18. Viktor Mataja, *Lehrbuch der Volkswirtschaftspolitik* (*A Course of Economics*) (Wien, 1931).

19. Eugen Schwiedland, *Volkswirtschaftslehre* (*Economics*) (Wien, 1918); *Die Volkswirtschaft unter dem Einfluss der Umwelt* (*The Influence of the Environment on Economic Life*) (Wien, 1918).

20. Friedrich von Wieser, *Theorie der gesellschaftlichen Wirtschaft* (*A Theory of Social Economics*) (Tübingen, 1924); *Das Gesetz der Macht* (*The Law of Power*) (Wien, 1926).

21. Ludwig von Mises, *Die Gemeinwirtschaft* (*Economics of the Community*) (Jena, 1922).

22. Ferdinand von Degenfeld-Schönburg, *Geist und Wissenschaft* (*Mind and Economics*) (Tübingen, 1927).

23. Adolf Menzel, *Friedrich Wieser als Soziologe* (*F. Wieser as Sociologist*) (Wien,

1927) ; *Grundriss der Soziologie (System of Sociology)* (Wien, 1937) ; *Geschichte soziologie des Staates (Sociology of State)* (Wien, 1936).

24. Hans Kelsen, *Sozialismus und Staat (State and Socialism)* (Leipzig, 1920) ; *Der Soziologische und der juristische Staatsbegriff (The Sociological and Juridical Concept of State)* (Tübingen, 1922) ; *Die philosophischen Grundlagen der Natur-rechtslehre (The Philosophical Basis of Natural Law)* (Charlottenburg, 1928).

25. Fritz Sandler, *Algemeine Gesellschaftslehre* (General Sociology) (Jena, 1930).

26. Erwin Voegelin, *Über die Formen des amerikanischen Geistes (On the Forms of the American Mind)* (Tübingen, 1928) ; *Rasse und Staat (Race and State)* (Tübingen, 1933) ; *Die politischen Religionen (The Political Religions)* (Wien, 1938).

27. Wilhelm Jerusalem, *Der Krieg im Lichte der Gesellschaftslehre (The War in the Light of Social Theory)* (Stuttgart, 1915) ; *Einleitung in die Philosophie (Introduction into Philosophy)* (Wien, 1923) ; *Einführung in die Soziologie (Introduction to Sociology)* (Wien, 1926.)

28. Sigmund Freud, *Massenpsychologie und Ich-Analyse (Mass Psychology and Ego-Analysis)* (Wien, 1921) ; *Das Unbehagen in der Kultur (Discontentment with Culture)* *(Wien, 1930)*.

29. Othmar Spann, *Der wahre Staat (The True State)* (Leipzig, 1921) ; *Gesell-schaftslehre (Sociology)* (Leipzig, 1923) ; *Gesellschaftsphilosophie (Social Philoso-phy)* (München, 1928) ; *Soziale Kategorienlehre (The Theory of Social Categories)* (Jena, 1924) : *Geschichtsphilosophie (The Philosophy of History)* (Jena, 1932) ; *Naturphilosophie (The Philosophy of Nature)* (Jena, 1937).

30. Jakob Baxa, *Einführung in die romantische Staatswissenschaft (Introduction into the Romantic Theory of the State)* (Jena, 1923) ; *Adam Müller* (Jena, 1930).

31. Johannes Sauter, *Franz von Baaders Schriften zur Gesellschaftphilosophie (Franz v. Baader's Writings on the Philosophy of Society)* (Jena, 1925) ; *Baader und Kant* (Jena, 1928).

32. Wilhelm Andrea, *Platons Staatsschriften (Plato's Writings on the State)* (Jena 1923-26).

33. Friedrich Schreyvogl, *Ausgewählte Schriften zur Staats- und Wirtschaftslehre des Thomas von Aquino (Selected Writings on the State by Thomas Aquinas)* (Jena, 1923).

34. Hans Riehl, *Fichtes Schriften zur Gesellschaftsphilosophie (Fichte's Writings on the Philosophy of Society)* (Jena, 1928-1929).

35. Karl Faigl, *Ganzheit und Zahl (Totality and Number)* (Jena, 1926)

36. Walter Heinrich, *Grundlagen einer universalistischen Krisenlehre (The Bases of a Universalist Theory of Crisis)* (Jena, 1928).

37. Gustav Seidler-Schmid, *Systemgedanken der sog. klassischen Nationalökonomie (Systematic Thought in So-called Classical Economics)* (Jena 1926).

38. Viktor Gutmann, *Industriepolitik (Industrial Politics)* (Jena, 1932).

39. Ferdinand von Westphalen, *Die theoretischen Grundlagen der Sozialpolitik (The Theoretical Foundations of Social Politics)* (Jena, 1931).

40. Ernst Lagler, *Theorie der Landwirtschaftskrisen (A Theory of Crises in Agri culture)* (Wien, 1935).

41. Ernst Gruenwald, *Das Problem der Soziologie des Wissens (The Problem of the Sociology of Knowledge)* (Wien, 1934).

42. Benedikt Kautsky, *Friedrich Engels' Briefwechsel mit Karl Kautsky (The Exchange of Letters Between F. Engels and K. Kautsky)* (Wien, 1954).

43. Otto Bauer, *Einführung in die Volkswirtschaftslehre* (*Introduction into Economics*) (Wien, 1956).

44. Karl Renner, *Marxismus, Krieg und Internationale* (*Marxism, War and the International*) (Stuttgart, 1918); *Die Wirtschaft als Gesamtprozess und die Sozialisierung* (*Economics as a Total Process and Sozialization*) (Berlin, 1924); *Die Rechtsinstitute des Privatrechts* (*The Institutionalization of Private Law*) (Tübingen, 1929).

45. Max Adler, *Das Soziologische in Kant's Erkenntniskritik* (*The Sociological Element in Kant's Criticism of Knowledge*) (Wien, 1924); *Kant und der Marxismus* (*Kant and Marxism*) (Berlin, 1925).

46. Franz Martin Schindler, *Die soziale Frage der Gegenwart* (*The Social Problems of the Present Age*) (Wien, 1908).

47. Ignaz Seipel, *Die Bedeutung des neuen kirchlichen Rechtsbuches für die Moraltheologie* (*The Implications of the New Ecclesiastic Book of Law for Moral Theology*) (Innsbruck, 1918); *Die österreichische Verfassung* (*The Austrian Constitution*) (Wien, 1930); *August M. Knoll, Ignaz Seipel* (Wien, 1956).

48. Johannes Messner, *Die soziale Frage der Gegenwart* (*The Social Problems of the Present Age*) (Wien, 1934).

49. Anton Orel, *Oeconomia perennis* (Mainz, 1930).

50. Ferdinand Prodl, *Gesellschaftslehre (Sociology)* (Wien, 1936).

51. Franz Arnold, "Wiener Richtungen" ("The Viennese Schools"), in *Staats lexicon* (Freiburg i.B., 1952), pp. 1295-1305.

52. Ernst Karl Winter, *Die Sozialmetaphysik der Scholastik* (*The Social Metaphysics of Scholasticism*) (Wien, 1929); *Platon, das Sociologische in seiner Ideenlehre* (*Plato, the Sociological Element in his Theory of Ideas*) (Wien, 1930),

53. August M. Knoll, "Warum 'scheiterte' der österreichische Ständestaat 1934-1938?" ("Why did the Austrian 'Ständestaat' 1934-1938 Break up?") *Civitas* Monatsschrift des Schweizerischen Studentenvereains, Luzern, 1949).

54. August M. Knoll, *Der Zins in der Scholastik* (*Interests in Scholasticism*) (Wien, 1933).

55. August M. Knoll, *Grande und Zins* (*Grace & Interests*) (Wien, 1933).

56. Alois Dempf, *Selbstkritik der Philosophie* (*Self-Criticism of Philosophy*) (Wien, 1947).

57. Ernst Topitsch & Wilhelm Weber, "Der Wertfreiheitsproblem seit Max Weber" ("The Problem of Value Freedom Since Max Weber"), *Zeitschrift für Nationalökonomie*, XIII, 2 (1951), 158-201 (Wien, 1953).

58. Rudolf Stemberger, *Immanual Kant als Philosoph und Soziologe* (*I. Kant As Philosopher and Sociologist*) (Wien, 1953).

59. Felix Klezl-Norberg, *Die geistigen Grundlagen der Staats-und Wirtschaftsformen* (*Ideas as Foundations of Political and Economic Life*) (Wien, 1950).

60. Albert Mitterer, *Elternschaft und Gattenschaft. Nach dem Weltbild des hl. Thomas von Aquin* (*Parenthood and Marital Relationship According to the World View of Saint Thomas Aquinas*) (Wien, 1949).

61. Albert Nidermeyer, *Handbuch der speziellen Pastoralmedizin* (*Handbook of Special Pastoral Medicine*) (Wien, 1949).

62. Heinrich von Srbik, *Geist und Geschichts vom deutschen Humanismus bis zur Gegenwart* (*Mind and History Since the 18th Century Humanistic Thought*) (Salzburg, 1950).

63. Hans von Plainits, *Die deutsche Stadt im Mittelalter* (*The German Town in the Middle Ages*) (Graz, 1954).

64. Heinrich von Fichtenau, *Das karolingische Imperium. Soziale und geistige Problematik eines Grossreiches (The Carolingian Empire. The Social and Spiritual Problems of a Big Empire)* (Zurich, 1949) (translated as: *The Carolingian Empire,* Oxford: Blackwell, 1957).

65. Otto Brunner, *Adeliges Landleben und Europäischer Geist (Feudal Culture and the European Mind)* (Salzburg, 1949).

66. Leo Santifaller, *Autobiographie (Autobiography)*, vgl. *Oesterreichische Geoschitswissenschaft der Gegenwart in Selbsdarstellungen (Austrian Historiography of Present Days in Autobiographies)* (Wien), II (1951), 163-208.

67. Friedrich Heer, *Aufgang Europas (The Beginning of Modern Europe)* (Wien, 1949); *Tragödie des heiligen Reiches (The Tragedy of the Holy Empire)* (Stuttgart, 1952); *Europäische Geistesgeschichte (European History of Ideas)* (Stuttgart, 1953).

68. Heinrich Benedikt, *Geschichte der Republik Oesterreich (History of the Austrian Republic)* (Wien, 1954).

69. Hugo Hantsch, *Die Geschichte Oesterreichs (The History of Austria)* (Wien-Graz, 1951-1953).

70. Karl Eder, *Der Liberalismus in Altösterreich (Liberalism in Ancient Austria)* (Wien, 1955).

71. Albert Fuchs, *Geistige Strömungen in Österreich 1867-1918) (Intellectual Currents in Austria, 1867-1918)* (Wien, 1949.)

72. Leopold Lentner, *Das Erwachen der modernen katholischen Sozialidee (The Awakening of the Modern Catholic Social Theory and Teaching)* (Wien, 1951).

73. Johann Christoph Allmayer-Beck, *Vogelsand. Vom Feudalismus zur Volksbewegung (Vogelsang: From Feudalism to a Popular Movement)* (Wien, 1952).

74. Rudolf Till, *Hofbauer und sein Kreis (Hofbauer and his Circle)* (Wien, 1951).

75. Kurt Skalnik, *Karl Lueger. Der Mann swischen den Zeiten (K. Lueger, A Man Between Historical Periods)* (Wien, 1954).

76. Robert Endress, *Revolution in Österreich 1848 (Revolution in Austria 1848)* (Wien, 1946).

77. Ernst Fischer, *Österreich 1848 (Austria 1848)* (Wien, 1946).

78. Alexander Novotny, *1848. Österreichs Ringen um Freiheit und Völkerfrieden von 100 Jahren. (Austria's Fight for Freedom and International Peace 100 Years Ago)* (Wien, 1948).

79. August M. Knoll, "Zur Soziologie der Österrechischen Revolution 1848" ("On the Sociology of the Austrian Revolution, 1848"), *im Sammelwerk: Das Jahr 1848 (in the Symposium: The Year 1848)* (Wien, 1948).

80. Jakob Fried, *Nationalsozialismus und katholische Kirche in Österreich (National Socialism and the Catholic Church in Austria)* (Wien, 1947).

81. Karl Rudolf, *Aufbau im Widerstand (Construction During Opposition)* (Salzburg, 1947).

82. Alfred von Verdross, *Grundlinien der antiken Rechts- und Staatsphilosophie (Main Theories of Classical Legal and Political Philosophy)* (Wien, 1946)

83. Otto Weinberger, *Die Wirtschaftsphilosophie des Alten Testament (The Economic Philosophy of the Old Testament)* (Wien, 1946).

84. Rudolf Stanka, *Die politische Philosophie des Altertums (The Political Philosophy of Antiquity)* (Wien, 1951).

85. Gustav Wetter, *Der dialektische Materialismus (Dialectical Materialism)* (Wien, 1952).

86. Robert L. John, *Dante* (Wien, 1946).

87. Ulrich Schöndorfer, *Das philosophische Menschenbild der Gegenwart (The Philosophical Image of Man in Our Present Age)* (Linz, 1947).

88. Otto Storch, *Die Sonderstellung des Menschen (The Special Characteristics of Man)* (Wien, 1948).

89. Wilhelm Koppers, *Der Urmensch und sein Weltbild (Early Man and His World View)* (Wien, 1949).

90. Viktor E. Frankl, *Der unbedingte Mensch (Unconditional Man)* (Wien, 1949); *Homo patients* (Wien, 1950).

91. Hans Thirring, *Homo sapiens* (Wien, 1949).

92. Hubert Rohracher, *Die Arbeitsweise des Gehirns und die Psychischen Vorgänge (The Working of the Brain and Psychic Processes)* (München, 1953).

93. Alexander Mahr, Ed., *Neue Beiträge zur Wirtschaftstheorie, Festgabe für Hans Mayer (New Contributions to Economic Theory, Symposium for Hans Mayer)* (Wien, 1949).

94. Ernst Lagler, Ed., *Wirtschafliche Entwicklung und soziale Ordnung, Festgabe für F. Degenfeld (Economic Development and Social Order, Symposium for F. Degenfeld)* (Wien, 1952).

95. Richard Kerschagl, *Volkswirtschaftslehre (Economics)* (Wien, 1952).

96. Anton Tautscher, *Geschichte der Volkswirtschaftslehere (History of Economics)* (Wien, 1950).

97. Wilhelm Weber, *Wirtschaftswissenschaft und Wirtschaftspolitik in Oesterreich (Economics and Economic Policy in Austria)* (Wien, 1949); *Wirtschaftswissenschaft von heute (Economics of Today)* (Wien, 1953).

98. Hans Bayer, *Sozialisierung und Planwirtschaft (Socialization and Planned Economics)* (Wien, 1952); *Gewinnbeteiligung (Profit Sharing)* (Wien, 1952); *Technik und Gemeinwirtschaft (The Technical System and Economics of the Community)* (Wien, 1956).

99. Theodor Pütz, *Theorie der allgemeinen Wirtschaftspolitik und Wirtschaftslenkung (Theory of General Economic Politics)* (Wien, 1948); *Neue Wege und Ziele der Sozialpolitik (New Ways and Aims of Social Politics)* (Wien, 1954).

100. Othmar Spann, *Religionsphilosophie (The Philosophy of Religion)* (Wien, 1947); Walter Heinrich, Ed., *Festgabe zu Spann's 70. Geburtstag: Die Ganzheit in Philosophie und Wissenschaft (Symposium at Spann's 70th Birthday: The Whole in Philosophy and Science)* (Wien, 1950).

101. Walter Heinrich, *Wirtschaftspolitik (Economic Politics)* (Wien, 1948-1954).

102. Hans Riehl, *Urwissen (Original Knowledge)* (Graz, 1949).

103. Karl Renner, *Mensch und Gesellschaft. Grundriss einer Soziologie (Man and Society, An Outline of Sociology)* (Wien, 1952).

104. Robert Endress, *Staat und Gesellschaft (State & Society)* (Wien, 1952); *Geschichte Europas und des Orients. Das Weden des europäischen Geistes (The History of Europe and the Near East)* (1944-1952).

105. Ernst Glaser, *Mensch und Gesellschaft, Kleine Soziologie und Sozialpsychologie (Man and Society, Brief Sociology and Social Psychology)* (Wien, 1952); *Familie, Beruf, Freizeti (Family, Occupation and Leisure)* (Wien, 1954).

106. Benedikt Kautsky, *Amerikas Arbeiter im Vormarsch (America's Workers Progress)* (Wien, 1951); *Friedrich Engels' Briefwechsel mit Karl Kautsky (F. Engels' Exchange of Letters with K. Kautsky)* (Wien, 1954).

107. Published since 1946.

108. Johannes Messner, *Das Naturrecht, Handbuch der Gesellschafts-, Staats- und*

Wirtschafsethik (*Natural Law, A Handbook of the Ethics of Society, State and Economics*) (Wien, 1950); *Kulturethik* (*Cultural Ethics*) (Wien, 1954).

110. Albert Auer, *Der Mensch hat Recht* (*Man is Right*) (Graz, 1956).

111. Walter Riener, *Katholische Soziallehre und soziale Gerechtigkeit* (*The Catholic Social Doctrine and Social Justice*) (Wien, 1956).

112. Johann Schasching, *Katholische Soziallehre* (*Catholic Social Doctrine*) (Wien, 1956).

113. Josef Dobretsberger, *Katholische Sozialpolitik am Scheideweg* (*Catholic Social Politics Facing a Decision*) (Wien, 1947).

114. August Zechmeister, *Kirche und Sozialismus* (*Church and Socialism*) (Wien 1947); *Die Freiheit des Wortes in der Kirche* (*The Freedom of Speech in the Church*), in der von A. Zechmeister hs., Sammlung *Kirche und Kirchenvolk, Elemente und Gestalten einer theologische Soziologie* (in the series: *The Church and the Christian People, Elements and Configuration of a Theological Sociology*), Heft I (Wien, 1951).

115. Wiard von Klopp, *Die sozialen Lehren des Freiherrn Karl von Vogelsang* (*The Social Teachings of the Baron K. v. Vogelsang*) (Wien, 1938).

116. Karl Kummer, *Der dritte Weg. Grundsätzliche und praktische Vorschlage für eine Sozialreform* (*The Third Way. Basic and Practical Propositions for a Social Reform*) (Wien, 1949,).

117. Anton Burghardt, *Eigentumsethik und Eigentumsrevisionismus* (*Ethics and Control of Property*) (München, 1955).

118. Franz König, *Christus und die Religionen der Erde. Handbuch der Religionsgeschichte. Unter Mitarbeit von 24 Autoren* (*Christ & the Religions of the World. Handbook of the History of Religion, published in collaboration with 25 authors*) (Wein, 1951).

119. Bernhard Häring, *Macht und Ohnmacht der Religion* (*Power and Agony of Religion*) (Salzburg, 1956).

120. Ernst Karl Winter, *Christentum und Zivilisation* (*Christianity and Civilization*) (Wien, 1956).

121. The Catholic Institute for Ecclesiastic Social Research is to be found in Vienna IX, Boltzmanngasse 14.

122. Kurt Blaukopf, *Musiksoziologie* (*The Sociology of Music*) (Wien, 1950).

123. Hans Georg Marek, *Der Schauspieler im Lichts der Soziologie* (*The Actor in the Light of Sociology*) (Wien, 1956).

124. Ernst Topitsch, *Strukturanalyse der Weltanschauungen* (*Structural Analysis of World Views*), im *Erscheinen* (to be published).

125. Friedrich Kainz, *Psychologie der Sprache* (*Psychology of Language*) (Stuttgart, 1954), S. III, S. 485ff. (*Sprachsoziologie*) (*The Sociology of Language*).

126. Rudolf Blüdhorn, *Internationale Beziehungen* (*International Relations*) (Wien, 1956).

127. Johann Mokre, *Grundriss der Arbeiterkunde* (*An Outline of the Sociology of Work and of the Worker*) (Wien, 1950); *Aus der Welt des Arbeiters* (*The World of the Worker*) (Wien, 1955).

128. In the field of industrial sociology have appeared such works as: Max Pietsch, *Wert und Würde des menschlichen Arbeit* (*Value and Dignity of Human Work*) (Wien, 1952); Karl Bednarik, *Der junge Arbeiter von heute—ein neuer Typ* (*The Young Worker of Today—A New Type*) (Stuttgart, 1953); Fritz Klenner, *Das Unbehagen in der Demokratie* (*The Discontentment with Democracy*) (Wien, 1956);

Ludwig Reichhold, *Die europäische Arbeiterbewegung* (*The European Worker's Movement*) (Frankfurt-Main, 1953). Numerous publications of Hans Kraensky deal with this field also.

129. Lagler, with Heinrich Demelius, is editing the *Wiener Studien für Genossenschaftswesen* (*Viennese Studies in Problems of the Cooperative*); so far 4 volumes have appeared. Under the direction of E. Lagler and A. Steden, *Rural Studies* (*Dorfuntersuchugen*) have been undertaken, reported periodically in *Bodenkultur* (published in Vienna since 1955). Lagler is also editing the *Wiener Studien zur Agrarpolitik und Agrarsoziologie* (*Vienna Studies of Rural Politics and Rural Sociology*).

SPAIN

Enrique Gomez Arboleya
University of Madrid

Concrete methods of sociology, when applied to the study of the contemporary reality, explain the historical orientation and slow development of sociological thought in Spain. In a sense, Spanish sociology began with the break-up of the stable, traditional organization of European society and the rise of the middle class. The supremacy of the middle class, comprised largely of uprooted individuals who owed their success to their own efforts, gave free reign to mobility and insured the triumph of a new mentality. To understand the uniqueness of a society which has a vast cultural heritage and an embryonic sociology is to gain fresh insight into what sociology actually is. The application of concrete methods of investigation to the study of Spanish society also reveals the inner tensions of a continuing drama: the evolution of collective forces and living conditions under the stimulus of the contact or conflict between two cultures.

THE STRIVING FOR MODERNITY

Though detailed studies are few, it is easy to define the salient features of Spanish sociology. During the nineteenth century there was an attempt in the direction of self-affirmation on the part of the Spanish middle class. Far from being homogeneous as in other countries, the Spanish middle class comprised forces that differed strikingly in background and economic position: merchants, industrialists, government workers, military men, members of liberal professions and artisans. As the century progressed, the middle class grew not only in numbers but in diversity. Various forces re-inforced its actual position and ideological orientation: (a) the anti-Napoleonic war, which had given social power, in the framework of the army, to men of common birth; (b) industrial progress, especially in certain areas;

(c) the withdrawing of privileges which broke the position and power traditionally ascribed to the nobility and clergy and gave the general public access to certain properties; (d) the ideological heritage of the Enlightenment, which gave the middle class a number of tenets for use against the traditional forces.

Revolution and counterrevolution, the sign of our age, has also characterized the history of Spain, but with this difference: unlike other countries, Spain was not impregnated by the modern spirit through two centuries marked by conflicting forces. The Spanish middle class is faced with an anachronistic economic and political situation. Nor is the enemy wholly external: the middle class itself occupies a wretched position that marks it as somewhat anachronistic. This gives the Spanish liberal the distinction of having much in common with the absolutist, as foreign observers are quick to discern. Further evidence is provided by the historical events of the last century: both forces made effective use of their only weapon, the pronunciamento.

The implicit duality of the position of the new middle class was most obvious in the intellectual sphere. Spain possessed a rich cultural tradition, but specific signs of the modern age had scarcely appeared in her culture: the positive sciences, natural as well as social. Exceptions merely confirmed the rule. The University of Spain was experiencing one of the worst periods in its history; it had not kept in step with the times.

The task was to fill the breach of two centuries and make Spain into a modern nation. The economic and social rise of the middle class had its countereffect on the development of science. Indeed, two figures that merit the highest esteem stand out during the first half of the century: Ramón de la Sagra and Jaime Balmes. The instability of the middle class focused attention on the conquest of power, which seemed to offer the easiest means of reform. The middle class lived by and through politics. Even nascent intellectual reform took on a public character; the Atheneum and its public forum. Oratory, pamphleteering and journalism were used to advance poltical ideas. In a sense, politics was the touchstone of middle-class advances: the organization of institutions of learning and the establishment of contacts with outsiders.

Middle-class politics resulted in changes in the intellectual life of Spain during the last third of the nineteenth century. These changes, with their special character, are still being worked out.

THE INFLUENCE OF KRAUSISM

Krause, almost unknown in his own country, had a profound influence on Spanish thought. Spanish Krausism emphasizes the affirmation of the consciousness and harmonious development of the individual personality. We know that cultural contacts offer numberless examples of the transmission of a trait that functions differently in its new context. His nebulous metaphysics, with its stress on the conscience as the seat of the divinity and its pantheism or panentism, brought unity to a group torn between hostile forces. A number of distinct intellectual values merged with Krausism.

The Krausist group and the Catholic group gave special attention to the social sciences, and to sociology in particular. Both groups enriched the study of Spanish society and the Spanish community. Their activity is attested by a great number of articles in periodicals and by many translations. Within a period of twenty-five years, practically all of the important literature on the historical and social sciences was translated into Spanish. The translations are bad, but they extend from Spencer to Giddings and Ward, and include many second-rate writers. They laid the groundwork for a real science of sociology. The formative period, which lasted until 1914-17, was followed by a new period which lasted until 1940. The new period was characterized by the formalizing of sociological data; in one sense this favored the study of sociology, but in another sense it had the opposite effect.

GINER & COSTA

First in the study of sociology come the names of F. Giner and J. Costa. Giner, who is probably more important as a personality than as a thinker, is a philosopher of law. His philosophy is vitiated by the weakness of Krausism. Law has three sources: the conscience of the individual, the order of the world and the community. Society is a metaphysical organic whole. Every society is made up of a union of individuals who achieve a common life through organic co-operation. Life may be either spontaneous or reflective. The masses make possible an elite; unified life, functions; functions, organs; and organs, ends. These are the metaphysical ends which human life must pursue. In society the intellectual elite are basic.

Opposite Giner stands J. Costa, more exact and more modern. He is a man of modest birth who battles fiercely and never wishes to be drawn away from the solid ground of reality. Law may be a matter of conscience, but can also be something external; both concepts enter into the "life of law," which is usage and custom. Costa is the leading student of Spanish common law. These investigations led him to the study of the concrete structures which originate and support common law. Still of great importance are his studies of the large family in some regions of Spain.

G. Azcarate is a transitional figure in the history of sociology in Spain. He, too, shows the influence of Krausism. He still looks upon sociology as a part of philosophy and an element in mankind's march toward perfection. His study of the problem of the concept, method and system of sociology led to some singular investigations. If sociology is a science, it must have its own object. To say that its object is society conceived as a natural and rational collectivity is to say much and little at the same time. Much because society comprises the data of the historical sciences; little because it has no clearly-defined object. Sociology studies the "essence, nature and structure of society, the total social organism." It is a part of social philosophy. Its unique object is to determine general laws from the data furnished by history. Azcarate's principles are illustrated by his analyses of English and Spanish politics and by his studies of political parties.

FIRST MODERN SOCIOLOGISTS

The first real sociologists, in the modern sense, were Sales y Ferré, A. Posada and S. Aznar.

Sales y Ferré evolved from Krausism to positivism. Sociology is the heir to both philosophy and history. But for the à priori method of the latter it substitutes induction and experimentation. Only in this way can social laws be formulated. Philosophy must be eliminated. Human evolution is marked by phases: Matriarchy, Patriarchy, Tribe, City and Nation. Each phase has its analogical period: branch, territorial, democratic, etc. To support his thesis, he draws from a wide range of modern and classical sources. He knows how to select and interpret. His work stills holds many surprises in store for the reader.

D. Adolfo Posada is an outstanding figure and an excellent sociologist. He displays an exhaustive knowledge of currents and tendencies. In his writings he cites not only all European sociologists from Compte and Spencer to De Greef and Durkheim but also the great teachers representing sociology in the United States: Giddings,

Small and Ward. Posada has been called the second Ward, and rightly so; for him, Ward had carried the scientific study of sociology to its highest point. The formative stage of any science is complex. Posada stresses systematization and is not deterred by his own erudition. Basic to any science are: a concrete object that lends itself to investigation; the relation of subject to object; the rational classing of acquired knowledge; and the interpretation of data assembled. Sociology meets all the requirements of a science, though its initial stages offer many problems.

Posada is not misled by the diversity of terms used to designate the object of sociology: society, collective life, social phenomenon, social process, world, order, superorganic phenomenon, etc. All express the same reality. Only positive, concrete, empirical investigations can reveal the social reality and bring about an understanding of social forces. Working hypotheses must guide investigations, and the comparative and experimental method predominates, though intuition enters into the interpretation of data. Without sociological techniques there can be no data; without data, no reality; hence the capital importance of statistical method in analyzing the structure and functioning of society.

In sharp contrast to Posada, the jurist and theorist, stands a man of action: Severino Aznar. The limitations of Spanish society had an immediate and lasting effect on Aznar, a man of humble birth; the desire to understand and reform society was to shape his powerful personality; as a reformer, he ranks with the pioneers of sociology. Aznar ignores the ultimate basis of society and concentrates on the existing structure; in this sense he is the most positive sociologist of his generation. The advance of specialization and technology encouraged him to perfect his techniques of investigation in order to obtain exact data which would have independent value even though put to practical use in bringing about reform.

Aznar uncovers a complex of causes in his study of the Spanish reality. He finds that a social phenomenon which appears simple on the surface has a whole skein of hidden causes. The sociologist must discover analytical devices. In the social problem of Spain, for example, he sees three basic dimensions that require investigation: the agrarian economic substructure; demography and ecological distribution; and social strata. The plight of the worker, his main concern, is attributable to the economic substructure of Spain. The agricultural poverty of Spain has various causes: physical—lack of forests, mineral-

ization of the land, progressive diminution of rivers; biological—
neo-Malthusianism and a high coefficient of mortality; juridico-legal—
neglect of the agricultural class, which has no technical schools, no
financial help, no sanitary legislation, and the outmoded concept of
property; social—recreation, including bull-fighting and hunting; and
economic—urbanization and concentration of property, together with
absentee ownership. This brief sketch of one of his works points up
his concern over national problems and his ability to bring together
sociographic descriptions of them. Severino Aznar belongs to the
Catholic movement which tries to bring about reform in Spain.

PARASOCIOLOGICAL DISCIPLINES

In historical dynamics, direction of movement is more important
than movement per se. The growth of sociology had its influence on
parasociological disciplines. U. González Serrano was among the first
to point out that psychology and sociology must work together in
explaining the individual's relationship to society. No less important
than early works in the field of psysiological and social psychology
are studies in anthropology, ethnography and folklore. Here, two
names stand out: T. de Aranzadi and L. de Hoyos Sainz.

Both worked closely together in order to accomplish the systematization of the sciences of general and comparative anthropology,
ethnology and ethnography. They used questionnaires and detailed
charts in their monumental investigation of rites, customs, and beliefs concerning birth, marriage and death in Spain. Following the
path of Frazer, they have achieved brilliant results.

Criminal sociology has received its share of attention. The leading
figure in the field of penology is P. Dorado Montero who, though
influenced by posivitism during his Italian schooling, stresses the
relativity of social forces. He holds that no penologist can define crime
and draw up a list of offenses which will be recognized as such at all
times and in all places. Everyone is a criminal and no one is. The
paradox is instructive: it shows the value of convention and of social
forces; every convention is a human fact which owes its origin to the
life of the ruling group. Laws are not based on fundamental principles
of absolute nationality and justice; they are but a social phenomenon
resulting from the converging of numberless forces; conduct toward
others within a group is regulated and limited by the necessities im-

posed by group living, but there are no rules or limitations governing conduct with respect to other groups. Working from such hypotheses, Dorado elaborates a plan for a co-operative State and a system of penal law.

Montero's systematic approach contrasts with the anti-systematic method of R. Salillas, who excels in concrete investigations, which are the result of anthropological methods of inquiry or simple observations made possible by virtue of his position as director of the prison in Madrid. His specialty is the customs and speech of the underworld. His attempt to formulate a basic theory of bio-sociology is unsuccessful because of his unsystematic reasoning. More enlightening is his study of the parasitic or picaresque element in the Spanish culture.

SPANISH SOCIOLOGY AFTER WORLD WAR I

A new period in the history of Spanish sociology began after World War I. Spanish intellectuals began to make their influence felt, here as elsewhere in Europe; these representatives of the middle class began to assume control of the State now looked upon as a national State. The notion of the nation as a metaphysical unit with its own organic rhythm and growth had been spreading across Europe since Herder. The liquidation of the Spanish empire in 1898 had encouraged the affirmation of a national "soul" or the acceptance of the belief that the nation is a storehouse of intangible values that stands up against modern "materialistic" science and technology.

Typical of the new period are two great figures: Angel Ganivet and Miguel Unamuno. Paradoxically, Unamuno, who translated Spencer in his youth, was to vent all his genial irony on sociology in later years. In the same way, his literary genius and humanistic knowledge of European culture was to belie his proposal to set Spain apart from Europe. His remarkable personality and brilliant paradoxical thought are indicative of the high level of Spanish culture (this is the beginning of the second golden age of Spanish literature) and also of his aloofness from pressing contemporary problems.

The stand taken by the intellectual elite was the result of their scientific knowledge, the intellectuals were supposed to have an authentic, excellent education. Only a selected few were accepted; only the best and most timely scientific training was offered. Many students went to Germany, where technology and formalization were the hallmark of university training, to complete their education. There, where the language barrier was like an initiatory rite, society had been dominated until the nineteenth century by small courts and all the other trappings of the middle ages; the result was that the intellectual could be modern only through his thought and scientific training. That Bismarck did not change the archaic system is proven by modern European history. In Spain, too, where the medieval structure and attitude of an agrarian society still prevailed, knowledge alone could up-date the intellectual. For twenty-five years the influence of Germany on Spanish culture was to be decisive.

Along with the rise of the middle class came the affirmation of the *Volksgeist*, the metaphysics of the nation, which might be called the conservative pole. Against this stood the opposite pole, the affirmation of the supremacy of the State over society in the form of a systematic and comprehensive set of norms and techniques. Meusel, in his studies of the European middle class, points up the forces that support the recognition of the supreme worth of the *republica* over and above all else. Formalism triumphed among the technically-skilled middle class from which State functionaries were drawn. Jurisprudence exemplifies purity of method in its study of the norms of legal logic. Society is a kind of natural being which the jurist can hold in contempt. There is a distinction between what the norm is and what it should be. Neo-Kantism exerted a stifling influence in Spain; the only studies in sociology translated into Spanish were those of formalist writers, especially Simmel.

Here we can merely broach the intellectual problems introduced by a second great current of thought that has embraced our whole generation: phenomenology. Its antipositivism, anti-empiricism and unconditional regulation of a world of forces unnecessarily multiplied, threatens the unity of man and reality and entails countless "logical," quietist and utopian consequences. Further, the world of forces embodied in the pure I was to bring about the disappearance of every concrete datum of society (man, worker, employer, urbanite, farmer, etc.); these forces, which reveal the basic structure of life, supplement "I" with "you," "he," and especially a mystical "us," when phenomenology undertakes to formulate a theory of society. A reciprocity of perspectives unites them.

The differentiation between a professional group and the others reinforced the in-group solidarity of the intellectual elite. As their power increased, the professionals aspired to absolute control and

drew a sharp distinction between themselves (the elite) and the masses
(the collectivity which the in-group looked upon with disdain). Closely
related to all the other forces previously mentioned, the attitude of
the intellectuals conditioned the status of sociology during the entire
period. The fact is that during this brilliant stage of Spanish arts,
letters and science, sociology hardly existed. D. Severino Aznar occupied the only chair of sociology in the University of Madrid, directed
the "Semanas Sociales" institution and served as the leader of the
"Grupo de la Democracia Cristiana." Socialists and social Catholics
joined together in support of the institute dedicated to the study of
the social problem, the "Instituto de Reformas Sociales," founded in
1904. But sociology lagged behind the arts and science.

The period does offer, however, a philosophy of society and a general diagnosis of the modern world. The outstanding figure is José
Ortega y Gasset, one of the greatest Spaniards of all time. He merits
the rare title of *Magister hispaniae*, both in his role as teacher, thinker
and writer and in his activities as founder and director of the *Revista
de Occidente* and its Library. The social life of man has a place in
Ortega's philosophy of existence. He stresses the concept of society,
customs, ideas and beliefs. The intellectual fruits of his deep, suggestive social philosophy have not all been harvested. In considering
the dynamics of the modern world, he elaborates his notion of generations and considers studies of the crucial figures of the European world
in a matchless series of interpretations: Galileo, Kant, Goethe, among
others. In his courses at the University of Buenos Aires he tried to
determine the characteristics of the contemporary period. The best
known part of his work, his *The Revolt of the Masses,* has been
translated into every major language. His notion of "mass" calls
upon two divergent elements: from the numerical or quantitative
point of view, the mass is the multitude which has taken over the
positions reserved for the minority; from the qualitative point of
view, the mass-man is the average man whose life lacks purpose and
who sets no value on himself but feels that he wants to be exactly
like everybody else. Our era is characterized by what Rathenau called
the "vertical invasion of the barbarians," accompanied by an absence
of ideas and intervention in public life through "direct action"; the
tendancy toward dissociation in the main is supported by barbaric
psychology: barbaric eras are those in which men break apart into
hostile groups; syndicalism and fascism are contemporary phenomena;
mass-men in revolt jeopardize the very principles of our civilization;

the monstrous growth of the modern State may rule out the possibility of revolution, but the State which society has created may in turn devour its creator in the tragical process of Statism. *The Revolt of the Masses* is a thought-provoking book which directs attention to the historical preoccupation of the elite: the revolt of the masses may open up new vistas to mankind—or it may sound the knell of human destiny.

THE CIVIL WAR PERIOD

The Spanish Civil War is analogous to the revocation of the Edict of Nantes in the history of France: in both instances, an important intellectual minority emigrated and brilliantly developed its latent potentialities in a foreign culture. Like the Huguenots, the intellectual Spanish minority, especially those who had emigrated to Mexico and Argentina, flooded the book market with translation; books on modern sociology included those of Tönnies, von Martin, Alfred Weber, and most important of all, the splendid version of Max Weber's historical-interpretative sociology, *Wirtschaft und Gesellschaft;* to the German flood was added a new stream of contemporary knowledge from North America: English-language history and sociology, including the magnificent *Biblioteca de Sociología (Library of Sociology)*, which is a tribute credit to both its director, J. Medina Echevarría, and Spanish culture. The result was a quantitative outpouring that modified the overall structure of sociology, forcing broad areas of the humanities to shift toward it, and penetrated even deeper strata: a new mentality was in preparation. New sociologists and sociologists reaching maturity had the unique distinction of being sociologists without a society. Society-less sociology had to develop among the exiles in the form of great systematic works which inspired concrete investigations in which their authors were unable to participate.

EXILED SPANISH SOCIOLOGISTS

The three salient figures of Spanish sociology, exiled across the Atlantic, are Francisco Ayala, Luis Recaséns Siches and José Echevarría. Each has a strong personality.

Francisco Ayala combines the subtlety of the political thinker with the rare ability to weld scattered fragments into a plastic and lively whole to produce analytical works that have a double appeal, the intellectual and the artistic. In his three-volume *System of Sociology*, he attempts to solve the social problem. For him, the scientific discipline called sociology is nothing more than a man-made product, a cultural creation that consists of a concerted attempt to acquire knowledge of a fixed order of realities. Social science is beset by a crisis of knowledge. As applied to man, knowledge encounters the resistance of an object, not passive like nature, but active. Strict scientific treatment would yield only peripheral knowledge, making it necessary to search out new routes. This leads the author to retreat to knowledge of the subject in order to discover an order of realities linked to the subject: cultural products, including *social forms*. Exhaustive analysis of initial contacts between men reveals that social class is the "cardinal sociological entity" of community and society. The historico-social process develops along two routes, civilization and cultural processes, like the contradiction between society and community, determines the concrete situation. Ayala's later two-volume *Sociological Treatise* and Posada's work are the two best systematic studies of sociology.

Luis Recaséns Siches was for a long time the guiding light of modern Spanish legal philosophy. He introduced his great knowledge of German thought, especially the neo-Kantian juridical ideas that prevailed under the influence of Ortega. His two handbooks offer a faithful presentation of modern sociological theories and outline a social order based on an analysis of the life of the individual in his relationship to other men with whom he coexists. Society is a composite of individuals that are influenced by other human beings, either near at hand or far away. For Recaséns, law is a form of human life objectivized, and the processes responsible for the forms of the State are also responsible for the integration of its members.

At the time of the exodus, José Medina Echavarría was one of the most promising intellectuals. His finished works include *Sociologia: teoría y técnica* (*Sociology: Theory and Technics*), a text whose length belies its depth. Going back to the ideas of Comte, he seeks to redefine sociology; he denies the impossibility of determining what the social is, but holds that it can not be defined philosophically any more than can life, the object of study of science. The sociologist must go beyond *residual categories* and penetrate the "most terribly concrete themes of the human community." He must study and analyze scientifically the outer, observable data of the social reality of the man of flesh and

bone. Medina's reflections on techniques of investigation are noteworthy. His other contributions include studies on the sociology of
war and the role of intelligence in society.

CONTEMPORARY TRENDS

The war had mobilized the whole social reality in one way or
another, not only physically but structurally and economically. The
havoc and massacres wrought by the war, the scarcity of men in the
traditional professional groups, and the appearance of new groups
of professionals had changed the socioeconomic make-up of postwar
Spain. The complications of social classes, changes of fortune, etc.
created a mobile reality. The new intellectual group, though sometimes lacking the rigid, arcane training of their predecessors, had a
better grasp of real, immediate problems. The social situation was
responsible for the new social orientation of the intellectuals. The
intellectual developments of postwar Spain, still in its initial stages,
is characterized by complexity coupled with the absence of any striking signs of individuality. Sociological studies may be conveniently
grouped around specific centers, the three most important being the
Institute of Political Studies, The Balmes Institute and the Leo XIII
Institute.

The Institute of Political Studies, under the leadership of Javier
Conde, has given a decisive impetus to Spanish sociology. Its review,
Revista de Estudios Políticos, has published some remarkable sociological studies. The Jaime Balmes Institute has an excellent library;
it has shown a special interest in problems of demography and industrial sociology; it publishes the *Revista Internacional de Sociología*.
The Leo XIII Institute is the center of Catholic studies. The work
of these three centers is supplemented by the new Faculty of Political,
Economic and Commercial Sciences.

The plurality of problems dealt with fall loosely into eight categories: (a) social philosophy, (b) history of sociology, (c) contemporary
sociology, (d) anthropological sociology, (e) demography, (f) urban
sociology, (g) rural sociology, (h) studies of the family.

(a) There are two basic problems of the problem of the social being
and the problem of the data that corresponds to it. Among one group
of writers, the influence of phenomenology and Ortega's idea of life
still predominate. A. Perpiña studies the community and society from

the phenomenological point of view. J. Marias, Ortega's disciple, develops his master's ideas in his books on general philosophy and on social structure. The scholastic position is represented by I. M. Alcorta and J. Todolí. Both L. Legas Lacambra and S. Lisarrague, who shows strong signs of Anglo-American influence, are making interesting contributions in the field of legal sociology.

(b) The great value of studies in the *history of sociology* is that they have constructed a new basis for their theoretical positions. The late appearance of sociology in Spain, its slow development, its practical and theoretical poverty and, later, the exile of its theoreticians, had left a partial vacuum in the postwar intellectual arena. The first important contribution is Javier Conde's series of articles on the sociology of sociology; he outlines a formal typology of modern man's community life (competition, communion and subordination) and studies different forms of political organization. A second important contribution is Gómez Arboleya's attempt to demonstrate the successive rationalization of the spheres of life tending toward a society in which mobile situations and social phenomena are basic and lend themselves to positive and scientific treatment. Other contributions to the history of sociology include the works of L. Legas, and M. Fraga and A. Perpiña, whose study of present-day trends won the Luigi Sturzo award.

(c) *Contemporary sociology* makes history a part of the present system. Formalism is rigorously avoided. Social reality is a historical reality; man conforms to social groups and institutions. Sociology is a modern science dealing with contemporary reality: modern scientific mind and present-day society. Gómez Arboleya stresses the role of sociology as the science of phenomena. Since the notion of phenomenon or fact was elaborated by physico-natural science, sociology always runs the risk of confusing truth and error: its scientific character and the objectivity of natural sciences. Fraga insists that every social phenomenon is a part of a structure embodying a series of functions and classes, and that structural systems are the objects of sociology. Putting it another way, sociology studies the historical realization of groups and institutions. The system of sociology is a system of the ties that bind men together, abstracted from the actual historical reality. This accounts for the methodological assumptions that give rise to controversies over the distinction between fact and event, the characteristics of the social structure, the development of the social structure and causality, the difference between sociology and history, the definition of sociological conceptuation, etc. A tendency toward the concrete emphasizes the liberation of Spanish sociology from the German influence. There has been a modest but effective attempt to assimilate and adapt modern techniques of sociographic investigation. Bujeda has made a short study of socio-economic techniques and has applied them in an unpublished series of investigations; Father Iribarren has made a study of modern American techniques; J. L. Pinillos has carried out scientifically controlled investigations of attitudes and opinions; and techniques have, as we shall see, played an important part in demographic studies. These developments have been supplemented by the translation of many American textbooks, including those of Ogburn and Nimkoff.

(d) *Anthropological sociology* manifests the same tendencies as studies of contemporary society. The leading contemporary specialist is Julio Caro Baroja.

(e) *Demography* has attracted a number of scholars. Members of the Academy of Moral and Political Sciences stimulated great interest in demographic problems when it posed the problem of the influence of war on demography in 1940. The Balmes Institute has published a number of important monographs on the subject. Noteworthy also are M. Terán's work with respect to the cartographic representation of population density and L. de Hoyo's recent study of population trends in Spain.

(f) Numerous studies in *urban sociology* have recently been undertaken or completed. M. Terán has prepared several studies on urban life, population statistics, and social cartography; he has mapped the popular streets of Toledo and Alcala on the basis of family relationships. Other noteworthy scholars have patterned their investigations on Terán's program: J. García Fernández, J. Bosque and C. Llorca. The influence of American scholarship is seen in the studies of New York and Madrid made by F. Chueca. A. López Gómez and N. González have published or are in the process of conducting investigations on communications and population density in the suburbs.

(g) Foremost in the field of *rural sociology* stands M. Terán. His studies of rural life and cartography are important contributions to methodology. J. Tortajada and J. García Fernández contributed doctoral theses on the subject of rural sociology; important also are the works of J. M. Casas and A. Floristán.

(h) *Studies of the family* have some tradition in Spain. J. Costa, and the Academy of Moral and Political Sciences, have made im-

portant contributions to the study of family life. From 1947 to 1953
M. Fraga carried out a series of investigations. The sociology department of the University of Madrid is currently carrying out investigations modeled on the familiar monographs of Wurzbacher and
Schelsky. Preliminary results of eighty-one studies were reported to
the International Congress of Sociology which met in Amsterdam
in 1956. Works in progress include a doctoral thesis on the large
family in Aragon, under the sponsorship of I. R. Kuhn, and one on
Catholicism by one of my students, M. Lizcano.

Human relations and industrial psychology have not been neglected.
A new mentality and a new science are developing. Scattered efforts
are being co-ordinated. The new mentality and concerted efforts may
soon result in a significant Spanish contribution to contemporary
sociology.[1]

SELECTED BIBLIOGRAPHY

Harry E. Barnes, *Historical Sociology* (New York: Philosophical
Library, 1948).

Harry E. Barnes & Howard Becker, *Social Thought from Lore to
Science* (Washington, D.C.: Harren Press, 1952), Vol. II: Chapter
XXVIII, "Spain and Portugal," pp. 1102-1119.

Pierre Jobit, *Les éducateurs de l'Espagne contemporaine, I:Les
Krausistes* (Paris: E. de Boccard, 1936).

Rex D. Hopper, "The 'Lester F. Ward' of Spanish Sociology,"
Chapter XXX, 585-602, in Harry E. Barnes, Ed., *An Introduction to
the History of Sociology* (University of Chicago Press, 1948). A systematic study, supported by numerous footnotes and references, pp.
596-599, which also deal with Krause, Giner, Azcárate, and others.
Hopper, "Spain," Chapter III, 79-139 in Max Salvadori, Joseph S.
Roucek, George B. de Huszar & Julia Bond, Eds., *Contemporary Social
Science, Vol. II* (Harrisburg, Penna.: The Stackpole Co., 1954). Supplements Barnes and Becker; bibliography, pp. 136-139.

Alfred Mendizábal, "Spanish Sociology," Chapter XXIII, pp. 653-
670, in Georges Gurvitch & Wilbert E. Moore, Eds., *Twentieth Century Sociology* (New York: Philosophical Library, 1945). A good
survey of the period preceding 1945.

José Ferrater Mora, *Ortega y Gasset, An Outline of his Philosophy*
(New Haven: Yale University Press, 1957). A useful introduction.

Enrique Gomez Arboleya, Professor of Sociology at the University
of Madrid; studied at the University of Berlin where he completed
his doctoral thesis on Herman Heller (published in 1940). LL. D.

Granada. Professor of philosophy of law at University of Granada
(1933-1948). Visiting professor at the Universities of Buenos Aires,
Chile and Uruguay (1948); Returned to Spain to organize and offer
courses in sociology. Strongly influenced by developments in English
and American sociology. His *Historia de la Estructura y del Pensa-
miento Social* is now ready for publication.

NOTES

1. This article is but an abridgment of the larger, original study in Spanish.
The bibliography has been prepared by the editor.

PORTUGAL

Fernando Falcao Machado
Gil Vincente Grammar School (Lisbon)

HISTORY OF SOCIOLOGY IN PORTUGAL

Sociology became known in Portugal through the journal *O Positivismo* in 1878 edited by Teófilo Braga and Júlio de Matos, and in which Vasconcelos Abreu, Teixeira Bastos and Consiglieri Pedroso collaborated; it was influenced by Comte, Stuart Mill, Spencer and Letourneau. In 1881 Oliveira Martins severely criticized the concept of sociology in his *On the Nature and Place of the Social Sciences.*

The difficulties which were encountered in the systematization of sociology in Portugal and the fact that the authors were not specialists led them to divide their researches among various branches of social studies. In 1883 a Library of Social Sciences, covering anthropology, criminology, economics and history, was started. Then followed a period of relapse during which we meet only the descriptive works Teófilo Braga[1] and Rocha Peixoto,[2] none of which are very consistent from a scientific point of view. Sociology was fostered to a certain degree in the Faculty of Law in Coimbra through the influence of José Dória; there it was taught in relation to economics, statistics and the philosophy of law. Quetelet exercised a great influence on the teaching of the subject.

This state of affairs changed in 1909 when Léon Poinsard came to Portugal to make a sociological investigation. A revival took place in the direction of the Soical Science of Le Play. Shortly afterwards, in 1910, the change in the political regime led sociology along the path of social reform. The social reformers produced doctrines of an economic and social nature under the name of sociology. Some of these were utopian, others constructive and political, and others empirical. There still existed a group of scientists, non-specialized sociologists, or, more exactly, philosophers of sociology. Some of these were researchers who, by means of personal observation and methodical

840

and systematic inquiries, took sociology from the descriptive stage to the interpretative one, as befits a science. Apart from the work of L. Poinsard,[3] a study on criminology by Mendes Correia[4] should be noted.

In Coimbra, some university professors, such as Serras e Silva, José Alberto dos Reis, Carneiro Pacheco and Oliveira Salazar, formed a group interested in sociology. Articles by Paul Descamps were published in the Bulletin of the Faculty of Law. On the initiative of J. S. Machado Fontes, the Portuguese Society of Social Science was founded in Oporto in 1918, and the collaborators in its Bulletin included Matos Braamcamp, Alves Espinheira, Costa e Almeida, Bento Carqueja and Alves Pimenta, with regional monographs. Although Fernando Garcia introduced the studies of social geography into Portugal,[5] it is to José Alberto dos Reis that we owe the work of the time that is most clearly sociological in character.[6] Through his influence, Abel Mendoca experimented in the Coimbra Agricultural School with the methods of the École des Roches.

Interest once again began to decline, but the seeds that had been sown bore fruit, as seen from the teaching of law in Coimbra and certain works on archaeology,[7] history,[8] and economics.[9] The idea of social service was defined by Caetano Goncalves.[10] In 1925 the legacy of D. Francisco Barbosa de Andrade was applied by Lino Gameiro to the foundation in Lisbon of the Maria Luisa Barbosa de Carvalho, Institute of Professional Guidance, the purpose of which was to train specialized experts. A special Chair of Sociology was instituted in the course and was the first in Portugal. The professor was Vieira de Almeida. In 1926 Serras e Silva published a work which attracted much attention because of the vast amount of information and theory it provided.[11] From that time on, the number of works with a social or even sociological character greatly increased in the fields of economics,[12] feminism,[13] criminology,[14] social hygiene,[15] the family,[16] nationalism,[17] and ethnography.[18]

On the suggestion of Oliveira Salazar, who was then beginning his political career, Paul Descamps inaugurated a course in sociology at Coimbra (1930 to 1931). With the lectures of Descamps, we can say that the pre-scientific period of sociology in Portugal ended, for around him gathered a small group of scholars with the necessary cultural background, methods and technical knowledge who carried out many tasks, all of which are mentioned in his classic work.[19] Many social studies were published, but not all authors, even though special-

842

ized in various branches of social studies, possessed the necessary methodical systematization. On the other hand, the influence of the environment and the period in which they worked made them restrict their attention to practical application or social claims. Some of these aspects are the following: school health,[20] wages,[21] women's work,[22] human relations[23] and training for social reform.[24]

In 1939 and under the aegis of Carneiro Pacheco, the Social Service Institute was created, where sociology was taught at a higher level with a view to the training of social assistants. Published works of a sociological nature continued to appear. Some of the most noteworthy dealt with geography,[25] abnormalities of behavior,[26] sociological criticism,[27] social problems,[28] economics,[29] élites,[30] history,[31] methodology,[32] social criticism,[33] the family,[34] sociometry[35] and social structure.[36] In 1952 Mme. France Govaerts Marques Pereira gave a series of lectures on sociology in the Higher Colonial School which were later published.[37] In them she discussed not only methods but also some present-day theories.

In 1955 the Minister of Education, Professor Leite Pinto introduced a course in sociology in engineering courses, in order to present the moral and social questions connected with technical science. Dr. Veiga de Macedo, the Minister of the Corporations, decreed a Plan of Social and Corporative Development in 1956 with the creation of an Institute for Training, a Study Centre and the Social Labor Service.

PRESENT STUDIES IN SOCIOLOGY

Teaching. In the Maria Luisa Barbosa de Carvalho Institute, Professor Vieira de Almeda limited his lectures to Comte, Spencer, Durkheim, Gomplowicz, Quetelet and Gustave Le Bon. The Social Service Institute has undergone various influences including those of Bureau and Rousiers, de Greef, Martinet and Mary Richmond. The remaining courses are as yet too recent for us to be able to discern concrete influences. By means of the classes of Mme. Marques Pereira, the work of Giddings, Sorokin, Santayana and Roucek was made known.

The lack of systematic and methodological teaching, with the exception of the courses given by Descamps, has restricted the development of any strictly scientific speculation on sociology.

Published Works. Some novels have a decidedly social, or even sociological stamp. As has been seen above, social studies have been devoted mainly to problems and certain aspects of the family, work, wages, economics, ethnography, hygiene, crime and history in relation to the Portuguese interests. These have almost all been analytical and descriptive studies of Portuguese society and almost all called for social reforms based on the Catholic social doctrine.

As for political and constructive works, we should here mention Cortez Pinto,[38] Sousa Gomez,[39] Vicente Moreira,[40] Raul de Carvalho,[41] E. A. Soveral,[42] Viriato Gouveiva,[43] J. A. Navais,[44] M. Melo,[45] A. A. Pereira Marques,[46] Paul Brandao,[47] Joaquim de Carvalho,[48] Ary dos Santos,[49] and Guardado Lopes.[50] Among the utopians, António Sérgio[51] stands out for his intelligent posing and discussion of problems.

As far as their usefulness and application is concerned, many of these works present ideas and raise problems that have the merit of producing solid material for the use by Portuguese social policy being effected in Portugal under the guidance of Oliveira Salazar. If he is not a follower of the Social Science School of Le Play, Salazar is at least in sympathy with it.

SELECTED BIBLIOGRAPHY

Diogo Pacheco de Amorim, *Princípios fundamentais de sociologia católica* (*Fundamentals of Catholic Sociology*) (Coimbra, 1944). This is a full account, based on the *De Rerum Novarum* and *Quadragésimo Anno* and other Catholic social teaching.

France Govaerts Marques Pereira, *Curso de Sociologia* (*Course of Sociology*) (Lisbon, 1954). A series of lectures which is quite up-to-date, and the most interesting speculative work since Paul Descamps.

Joao Porto, *O Honem e a ordem social* (*Man and the Christian Social Order*) (Coimbra, 1944). An essay based on the modern doctrines of Christian sociology.

José Fontes, *Sciencia Social—O méthodo* (*What is Social Science? Method*) (Oporto, 1918). A systematic account of the doctrines of the Le Play school and the Nomenclature of Henry the Tourville. It was the first work on social systematics and taxonomy to appear in Portuguese.

José Lopes Dias, *Doze licoes sobre servico social* (*Twelve Lectures on Social Service*) (Castelo Branco, 1945). A series of lectures on the application of the inquiry method for social assistants.

Manuel de Melo, *As grandes correntes da sociologia crista* (*The Great Currents of Catholic Sociology*) (Coimbra, 1945). A systematic account.

Paul Descamps, *Le Portugal—La vie sociale actuelle* (*Portugals Present Social Life*) (Paris: Firmin-Didot, 1955). This is the fundamental work on the application of sociology in Portugal, following up Léon Poinsard's book *Portugal Ignorado*; it is the fruit of exhaustive on the spot investigation carried out throughout Portugal and contains many interesting observations and a full bibliography. It is the joint work of many scholars interested in sociology and pupils of Descamps and is to be continued in the *Histoire Sociale du Portugal* which is being written at this time (1957).

Paul Descamps, *Les Repercutions sociales du climat du Portugal (Social Repercussions of the Climate in Portugal)* (Lisbon, 1935). An essay on certain phenomena in social life and customs connected with the variation of climate in various regions.

Rodrígues Ribeiro, *Fundamentos para uma sociologia renovada (Bases for a Renewed Sociology)* (Guimaraes; Gil Vicente, 1956). An account of the teaching based on the concepts of Daniel Rops, attempting to apply it to social reform.

Serras e Silva, *Social Science in Education and History* (Coimbra: Coimbra Editora, 1926). A work of considerable interest, in view of its thorough exposition of doctrine and method and plentiful historical exemplification applying the doctrines of Le Play, Tourville and Descamps.

Fernando Falcao Machado, born in Coimbra (1904); took his degree in Arts in the University there; attended the Higher Training College and specialized in Professional Guidance in the Maria Luisa Barbosa de Carvalho Institute; followed with interest the sociology courses given by Paul Descamps and was entrusted with the editing of his posthumous work *Social History of Portugal* (to be published shortly by Firmin-Didot, Paris); teaches at the Gil Vicente Grammar School in Lisbon and was formerly Lecturer in Sociology in the Police Technical School and to the National Republican Guard. In addition to some studies in geography and archaeology, has published the following sociological works: *Lisbon Enjoys Itself; Oporto Works; Coimbra Studies; Braga Prays—Why?* (Lisbon, 1930); *Talks on Secondary Education* (Aveiro, 1940); *Aspects and Problems of Town-Planning* (Lisbon, 1942); *At the Crossroads of Life* (Faro, 1944); *Considerations on Method in Sociology* (Lisbon, 1948); *The Cabedos of Setúbal* (Lisbon, 1953), an historical and sociometrical study of a family; *The Choice of a Career in Secondary Teaching* (Aveiro, 1956); "The Complex of Adelino Veiga," *O Despertar* (Coimbra, 1956), on the segregation, economic and intellectual, between students and non-students in Coimbra.

NOTES

1. Teófilo Braga, *O Territorio e a Raca* (*The Land and the Race*) (Oporto: Chardron, 1894).

2. Rocha Peixoto, *A Terra Portuguesa* (*The Portuguese Land*) (Oporto: Chardron, 1897).

3. Léon Poinsard, *Portugal Ignorado* (*Unknown Portugal*) (Porto: Magalhaes e Moniz, 1912).

4. Mendes Correa, *Os criminosos portugueses* (*Portuguese Criminals*) (Coimbra: Franca Amado, 1914).

5. Fernando Garcia, *A Fisionomia de Setúbal* (*The Physiognomy of Setubal*) (Setúbal, 1918).

6. José Alberto dos Reis, *A formacao social do inglés a do alemao e a educacao portuguesa* (*The Social Training of the Englishman and the German and Portuguese Education*) (Coimbra: Franca Amado, 1919).

7. Mendes Correa, *Os povos primitivos da Lusitânia* (*The Primitive Peoples of Lusitania*) (Oporto: Tavares Martins, 1924).

8. Mário Saa, *A invasao dos Judeus* (*The Jewish Invasion*) (Lisbon, 1924).

9. António Sérgio, *Antologia dos Economistas Portugueses* (*Anthology of Portuguese Economists*) (Lisbon: National Library, 1924).

10. Caetano Goncalves, *O ideal do servico social e a escolha duma carreira* (*The Ideal of Social Service and the Choice of a Career*) (Coimbra: University Press, 1922).

11. Serras e Silva, *A Ciência Social na Educacao e na História* (*Social Science in Education and History*) (Coimbra: Coimbra Publishing House, 1926).

12. F. Antónia Correa, *A evolucao económica e a crise social* (*Economic Development and the Social Crisis*) (Lisbon, 1927).

13. Emílio Costa, *As mulheres e o feminismo* (*Women and Feminism*) (Lisbon: Seara Nova, 1928).

14. Ferreira Deusdado, *A onda do crime* (*The Crime Wave*) (Lisbon, 1931).

15. Fernando Correia, *Doencas sociais e Higiene* (*Social Diseases and Hygiene*) (Caldas da Rainha, 1932).

16. Alberto Esteves, *A Família* (*The Family*) (Coimbra, 1932).

17. Fran Paxeco, *Portugal naoéibérico* (*Portugal is not Iberian*) (Lisbon: Rodrigues Bookshop, 1932).

18. José Leite de Vasconcelos, *Etnografia Portuguesa* (*Portuguese Ethnography*) (Lisbon: National Press, 1933).

19. Paul Descamps, *Le Portugal Inconnu* (in French) (*Portugal and its Present Social Life*) (Paris: Firmin-Didot, 1935).

20. J. Paiva Boléo, *O valor médico pedagógico dos inquéritos sociais* (*The Medical and Pedagogical Value of Social Inquiries*) (Lisbon: 1937).

21. Serafim Leite, *A retribuicao do trabalho* (*Payment for Work*) (Oporto, 1937)

22. Riba Leca, "A defesa moral da mulher operária" ("The Moral Defence of the Woman Worker"), *Brotéria*, XXIV (Lisbon, 1938).

23. A. Vincente Ferreira, *O Engenheiro, dirigente social* (*The Engineer as a Social Leader*) (Lisbon, 1939).

24. Teotónia Pereira, *A batalha do futuro* (*The Battle of the Future*) (Lisbon, 1937).

25. A. de Amorin Girao, *Geografia de Portugal* (*Geography of Portugal*) (Barcelos, 1940).

26. M. Simoes dos Reis, *A vadiagem e a mendicidade em Portugal* (*Vagrancy and Begging in Portugal*) (Lisbon, 1940).

27. S. Wloszczenski, *Le diagnostique de Poinsard sur le Portugal* (*Poinsard's Diagnosis on Portugal*) (Lisbon, 1941).

28. Manuel Rodrigues, *Problemas Sociais* (*Social Problems*) (Lisbon, 1943).

29. Ezequiel de Cempos, *O enquadramento geo-económico da Populacao Portuguesa através dos séculos* (*The Geo-Economic Moulding of the Portuguese Population through the Centuries*) (Lisbon, 1945).

30. Carlos Selvagem, *O problema das élites no mundo moderno* (*The Problem of the Elites in the Modern World*) (Lisbon, 1945).

31. J. A. Vaz Pinto, *A Chave da História de Portugal* (*The Key to the History of Portugal*) (Lisbon, 1945).

32. Falcao Machado, *Consideracoes sobre o método em Sociologia* (*Considerations on Method in Sociology*) (Lisbon, 1945).

33. Vieira de Almeida, *Paradoxos sociológicos* (*Sociological Paradoxes*) (Coimbra, 1948).

34. José Francisco Rodrigues, *A família, a mulher e o lar* (*The Family, the Wife and the Home*) (Lisbon, 1949).

35. Vasco Fortuna, *Teoria sociométrica do imposto* (*Sociometrical Theory of Taxes*) (Lisbon, 1949).

36. Mendes Corrêa, *Estrutura social do Povo Português* (*Social Structure of the Portuguese People*) (Lisbon, 1942).

37. France Govaerts Marques Pereira, *Curso de Sociologia* (*Course of Sociology*) (Lisbon, 1954).

38. Cortez Pinto, *O problema do desemprego no após guerra* (*The Unemployment Problem after the War*) (Lisbon, 1945).

39. Sousa Gomes, *Uma experiência de accao social familiar* (*A Social Action Experiment in the Family*) (Lisbon, 1945).

40. M. Vincente Moreira, *O problema da habitacao* (*The Housing Problem*) (Lisbon, 1950).

41. Raul de Carvalho, *Doencas evitáveis* (*Avoidable Illnesses*) (Lisbon, 1932).

42. Eduardo Soveral, *O problema do escol* (*The Problem of the Elite*) (Coimbra: Cidade Nova, 1956).

43. Viriato Gouveia, *Missao médica ou profissao médica* (*Medical Mission or Medical Profession*) (Setubal: Simoes, 1942).

44. José A. Navais, *A Psicologia ao servico da Indústria* (*Psychology in the Service of Industry*) (Lisbon: Philosophy III, 1956).

45. Manuel de Melo, *Inquérito à estrutura social do concelho de Espinho* (*Inquiry into the Social Structure of the Espinho District*) (Lisbon, 1943).

46. A. A. Pereira Marques, *O centro de assistência social da Guarda* (*The Social Assistance Centre at Guarda*) (Lisbon, 1945).

47. Raul Brandao, *O sangue—in Vale de Josafat* (*Blood in Vale de Josafat*) (Lisbon, 1956).

48. Joaquim de Carvalho, *A cultura castreja* (*Castle Civilization*) (Lisbon, 1956).

49. Ary Dos Santos, *Como nascem, como vivem e como morrem os criminosos* (*How Criminals are Born, Live and Die*) (Lisbon: Livraria Clássica Editora, 1938).

50. J. Guardado Lopes, *Relatório do Inquérito Estatístico aos Serviços Jurisdicionais de Menores* (*Report of the Statistical Inquiry into the Juvenile Jurisdiction Services*) (Caxias, 1950).

51. António Sérgio, *Cadernos de Antologia Sociológica* (*Notebooks of Sociological Anthology*) (Lisbon, 1956).

SWITZERLAND

Roger Girod
University of Geneva

One of the most important ancestors of scientific social thought J. J. Rousseau, was a citizen of Geneva, now part of Switzerland. The question of the relation between the individual and society is among the main elements of his works: man is modified by social life; social life as presently organized is an artificial and nefarious construction; society therefore, should be reconstructed in such a way that the true nature of man, its original, essential character could fully come into its own.

Other men, such as Necker and Sismondi, contributed to the constitution of modern social science. In the first part of the 19th century there was a great interest among the intellectual and leading social groups for concrete surveys on different aspects of economic and social life, particularly on the condition of the new class of industrial workers. At the same time, these people were able to use and discuss the concepts and systems of the great thinkers of their time.

After this period, there developed, as in the rest of continental Europe, a strong separation between concrete social observation (which became more and more a specialty of administrative statisticians) and sociological thinking (which became more and more speculative). The situation has been changing since World War II. In Geneva at least, the influence of experimental psychology and scientific educational research was one of the most important factors of this change.

Since 1889, very important work was done in this direction by men like Flournoy, Claparède, Bovet, and the other creators and organizers of the different institutions which are now assembled around the Geneva Institute of Educational Sciences (J. J. Rousseau Institute), the laboratories of psychology, and the International Bureau of Education.[1] F. de Saussure, a specialist of linguistics must also be mentioned here, because of the sociological orientation of his system and

848

because of his influence. The research work and theoretical constructions of Jean Piaget are largely based on this ground.

JEAN PIAGET AS A SOCIOLOGIST

Jean Piaget is generally known as a psychologist and as a philosopher of science (epistemology). In fact his sociological contribution
is also very important. He taught sociology at the University of
Geneva from 1939 to 1952 and also at the University of Lausanne
for a few years. But this is only a very secondary aspect of his connection with sociology. In fact, for him, psychology and sociology are
concerned with the same object: the concrete behavior of social (interacting) beings. This point of view is developed particularly in books
like *La psycholgie de l'intelligence*, or *Introduction à l'épistémologie
gànétique* (see specially the final part of the third volume, which
specifically concerns his sociological theories). From the beginning,
the field observations of Piaget were sociological in part, as well as
psychological. They are centred around the processes of socialization
of the intellectual and moral behavior of the child. Social dynamics
are analyzed by him as the factors which produce this adjustment. In
addition, the epistemological work of Piaget is for a large part a
study of the social conditions and social dynamics involved in the
laws of human intellectual operations, in the genesis of our concepts
and in the historical growth of knowledge. The work of Piaget, without doubt, is a very important part of present day sociology in
general.

SOCIOLOGICAL TEACHING AND RESEARCH

It should be stressed from the beginning that it is not really possible
to speak of "Swiss Sociology." Switzerland is composed of different
cultural parts. Sociologists who are thinking and writing in French,
for example, are in direct symbiosis with French and Belgian sociological life. This is true also of the German-speaking Swiss sociologists
with the intellectual life of Germany and Central Europe, but here
the break of 1933 had lasting effects. Consequently, the development
and tendencies of sociological teaching and research are very different
in the various parts of the country.[2]

SOCIOLOGICAL TEACHING AND RESEARCH

Sociology is taught in all universities of Switzerland. But its place in the curriculum differs widely between universities. In certain cases (especially in the German speaking regions) sociology is only a very very marginal branch. In other cases it is one of the standard elements for the preparation of degrees in economics, political science, social sciences or administration. In the University of Geneva, in addition to that function, sociology offers a possibility for specialization (license en sociologie, doctorat en sociologie).

There are different commercial marketing and opinion research offices (particularly "Analyses économiques du marché," also in Lausanne, and "Gesellschaft für Marktforschung" in Zurich). In certain cases, their surveys are contributing to the sociological documentation available in this country. The Federal Bureau of Statistics in Berne, as well as the statistical offices of some cities like Basel, Berne, Zurich, etc. are furnishing general information. In 1952 a Sociological research centre was created in Geneva; its work is reflected in several of the publications.

SELECTED BIBLIOGRAPHY

Howard Becker & Harry Elmer Barnes, *Social Thought from Lore to Science* (Washington, D.C.: Harren Press, 1952), II, Chapter XXII, "France and French Switzerland," 815-866. Only a scanty amount of information.

Roger Girod, *Attitudes collectives et relations humaines dans les sciences sociales américaines* (Preface by Jean Piaget) (Paris: Presses Universitaires de France, 1953); "Sociologie d'aujourd'hui," *Revue suisse d'économie politique et de statistique* (Bâsle, March, 1954); "Couches sociales et secturs économiques en Suisse," in *La Suisse dix ans après la guerre* (Bern: Annuaire de la Nouvelle Société Helvétique, 1956); *Le passage de la description à l'explication dans le cadre de la sociologie concrète* (Paris: P. U. F., 1956, Cahiers internationaux de sociologie, 1956); etc.

Handbuch der schweiz. Volkswirtschaft (Bern: Benteli-Verlag, 1955). Two volumes of encyclopaedic information on the different economic and social aspects of Switzerland.

Jean Piaget, *The Language and Thought of the Child* (New York: Meridian Books, 1935); *Judgment and Reasoning in the Child* (London: Kegan Paul, 1928); *Moral Judgment of the Child* (London:

Kegan Paul, 1950); *The Psychology of Intelligence* (id., 1950); *Intro-duction à l'épistémologie génétique* (Paris: P. U. F., 3 vols., 1950), Vol. III includes a special part on sociological thought; *Pensée égo-centrique et pensée sociocentrique* (Paris: P. U. F., Cahiers inter-nationaux de sociologie, 1951).

G. Solari, *Les salaires annuels dans le bâtiment à Génève en 1955* (Geneva: Document du C.R.S.G., 1957, mimeographed).

Roger Girod (1921–) was born in Geneva; is Professor of Sociology, University of Geneva (1952——); Professor of Research Techniques, University of Lyon (France) (1956——); Director, Geneva Sociological Research Center (1952——).

NOTES

1. Pierre Bovet, *Vingt Ans de vie: L'Institut Rousseau de 1912 à 1932* (Neuchâtel: Delachaux et Niestlé, 1932).

2. See, for instance, the papers by F. Baumgarten and Ph. Muller, on the situation of psychology in Switzerland, in *Bulletin de psychologie*, edited by the "Groupe d'études de psychologie de l'Université de Paris" (17 rue de la Sorbonne, 27 février 1957). The situation of sociology is very similar, but sociology is at a different, earlier stage of development.

ITALY

Camillo Pellizzi
University of Florence

This historical process called "Risorgimento," which brought about the political unity of the Italian peninsula during the middle part of the 19th century, either created or brought into evidence numerous grave social problems; but these had not always been glaringly evident to its originators and promoters. In their fight against the pre-existing political structures, these social leaders had naturally stressed the social and cultural factors which made all Italians feel that they belonged to one nation, while differences and specific local problems remained widely unknown or unexplored. The years between 1870 (the occupation of Rome and the annexation of the Papal State to the Italian kingdom) and the dawn of our Century were largely absorbed by major political and administrative problems: the realization of the deep sociocultural differences between East and West, North and South, dawned upon the majority of Italians as a gradual and, for the most part, unpleasant reawakening from a happy dream. If ever there was a chance for sociologists to prove their worth, it was this one: yet the discipline had hardly begun to exist. There is on record the teaching of it, as a non-compulsory subject, as early as 1875 in a few universities; and it is a sad reflection that even in our day there is only one fully appointed chair (in the University of Florence). The subject is being dealt with in most Universities by junior staff members, or, as a spare-time activity, by professors of other subjects.

This, however, does not imply that the variety of problems which are the habitual concern of the sociologist remained totally unheeded and unexplored. Historians, economists, statisticians, psychologists, ethnologists and others, very often came to grips with essentially sociological issues and, in a number of cases, produced works of outstanding merit. The country's population was increasing impressively, particularly in the poorer areas; industry was making big strides in a few centres, mainly in the North, while agriculture was going through a very uneven process of modernization, and many of the old and renowned arts and crafts were threatened with extinction. Primitive and insanitary conditions still prevailed in many parts; deforestation contributed to the erosion of certain lands and the extension of marshes, which in its turn increased the incidence of that greatest of social scourges, malaria. Temporary and permanent emigration, which had remained but a secondary social fact until then, began to gather momentum in the early 'eighties, and was on the upgrade almost regularly until 1913, when a maximum of about 1,300,000 emigrants (mostly to the Americas) was reached for that single year (nearly 3% of the total population). Money sent home by recently emigrated people began to be one of the financial assets in the economy of the country, but the drawbacks were many, and some of them required careful study before being discovered and analyzed. The extreme variety of cultural and economic conditions in the different regions of the Peninsula and the Islands contributed to focus the attention of scientists on criminology: the strong urge towards unity in legislation sometimes led to grievous local crises where conditions and traditions were too much at variance with the general rules that were being enforced. Education, which was largely in the hands of the State, having to cope in some regions with more than 50% illiterates, in its turn opened up a large chapter of problems and, consequently, of research.

THE EARLY GROWTH OF SOCIOLOGY

This list of problems, which is far from being exhaustive, indicates how much sociology was needed, at a time when the discipline was still in its embryonic phase in most if not in all countries. It also gives some partial explanation of the following facts: that for some decades (ending before or during the first World War) there was a great wave of sociological, or pseudo-sociological studies and initiatives, in which, too often, quantity was far in excess of quality—a fact which contributed to the discouragment of serious students and threw discredit on the discipline; that a great deal of work, sometimes highly valuable, was carried out by specialists and under the name of other disciplines; and that certain outstanding contributions (such as the enquiry on conditions in the South carried out by S. Sonnino and G. Fortunato) (1) which, by their nature and even method of work, should be described as sociological, did not go under this name and did not help strengthen the hands of those few who maintained that these studies should be organized more regularly, to begin with, in the Universities. This was one of the sore points of the whole problem, and one that led to the formation of a "vicious circle," which has not been overcome to these days. The structure of scientific activities in the country was becoming more and more academic, in the sense that an ever larger part of it (in certain subjects, the totality) came to be concentrated in the Universities, which were either run by the State or, in some less important cases, at least closely controlled and regulated by it. Especially in our field, this led to an even greater rigidity than is normally to be found in academic structures and endeavors; budgetary limitations would do the rest. Successive governments would never find the encouragement and the money needed to start specialized chairs and institutes in the subject, and the lack of such chairs and institutes in turn would impede the training of specialized students and research workers. The absence of high-level specialists and researchers was always a good argument in the hands of those who opposed the establishment of chairs and institutes!

The names and thinkers and scholars, however, who did most of their work in the last decades of the XIXth Century, deserve to be mentioned in these notes, for the prestige they acquired in their time and for the fertile seeds of thought they left to subsequent generations. Roberto Ardigò probably was, of them all, the most famous in his time: he started from Comte and worked out some revision of his doctrines; particularly in connection with judicial problems; from the University of Padua, where he was teaching; for a number of years he exercised a considerable influence on the country's culture, although the impact was felt perhaps more in philosophy, and perhaps even in theology and politics (Ardigò came to be a bugbear of conservative circles) than in the method and application of sociological science proper. The philosophical and humanistic traditions of Italian culture, the great impact that the trend of German Idealism (mainly the Hegelian school) had on large sections of Italian thinkers, —all this affected adversely the fertility of Ardigò's work and example.

Important, although occasional and collateral, contributions came from those economists and, generally, social scientists, who had a keener interest in the general principles and foundations of their disciplines: men like Angelo Messedaglia, Antonio Labriola (probably the most eminent student of Marx in Italy), Enrico Leone, Giuseppe Toniolo (who originated a Catholic school of thinking in the subject), and, most important of all, Wilfredo Pareto. The two last mentioned will have to be discussed again in these notes, but we might as well mention here the fact that the positivistic and even Comtean tradition of thought and research has never been completely interrupted to these very days, although, as was to be expected, it has undergone a number of revisions and modifications. The main line of Italian criminology may be considered to have remained within these mental boundaries, and to have been always intensively concerned with the anatomic and physiological variables concerning the criminal, on the lines of thought and research set to it by its principal originator, Cesare Lombroso, and by Eugenio Florian, who gave it a more systematic structure. Almost immediately, however, other students stressed and began to study the psychological and social aspects and conditions of crime: Enrico Ferri, who was also a politician and a lively propagandist, deserves especial mention as a pioneer in Italy on this line of work, which was variously followed by many others, such as Ellero, Garofalo, Niceforo, Marucci, Puglia, Zerboglio Grispigni Altavilla Di Tullio. Mention can be made here of S. Sighele, who worked especially on "crowd criminality."

Among the anthropologists who displayed a particular interest in sociological problems the names of Sergi, Savoragnan and Niceforo should be mentioned, as well as that of Giuseppe Mazzarella, the focus of whose interest was juridical ethnology.

For well over thirty years, beginning early in the Century, probably the most fertile Italian sociologist, and one who would also stress "applied" sociology, was in fact a German, Roberto Michels, who had left his native country mainly for political reasons, and finally became a professor of sociology in Perugia. In his youth Michels was an active socialist, which brought him almost naturally to pay attention to the growth of the Italian socialist party as a sociological phenomenon. He then extended his research on the Western "mass parties" generally, and was able, as early as 1912, to predict developments (concerning the structure and dynamics of those parties, as well as of the regimes they would establish once they came to power) which more than forty years of history have since confirmed in their main lines, as English-speaking readers can see in the recent translation of one

of his works.[1] Criticisms concerning Michels' methods in collecting
data and his working hypotheses (or, sometimes, lack of them), as
well as his style, often diffuse and lacking vigor, seem to be justified,
in terms of the more sophisticated methodology of our days. If we
refer them, however, to the time and country in which this author
did most of his work, we must qualify them by adding that some
of his conclusions are valid to this day, and that, tendentially at least,
he was a forerunner of some of the most recent developments in
sociological work.

THE "NEAPOLITAN" (1906) AND OTHER DISCUSSIONS

Historians of different trends and schools, like Guglielmo Ferrero,
Giuseppe Salvioli, Enrico Loncao, C. Barbagallo; philosophers of the
positivistic orientation, like De Sarlo and Calò; and more especially
philosophers of law (Giuseppe Carle, Icilio Vanno, M. Vaccaro, G.
Solari and others), all in various ways contributed to the discussion
of the general problems of sociology between the end of the last
century and the beginning of our own. Francesco Cosentini introduced in Italy the "genetic school" of sociology of Kovalewsky, and
was perhaps the first among the moderns to claim for G. B. Vico, the
Neapolitan thinker of the XVIIIth Century, the honor of having
been the direct forerunner of sociology as we understand it. Many
other names should be mentioned here from the welter of keen,
though mostly uncoordinated and sometimes unsystematic, Italian
students of sociological problems, particularly in the early years of
our century: those for instance of A. Chiappelli, R. Garfalo, A. Grop-
pali. The latter, in particular, persevered in these studies and publications until recent years. A junior man in comparison with those
mentioned so far is Eugenio Rignano: a deep and rigorous analyst
of epistemological problems connected with the social sciences, who
brought to his work the support of a mathematical skill and competence in general scientific methodology which were not universal
among other writers of the period. If J. M. Robertson could write
"in few countries has there been more of sociological activity than in
Italy," [2] this flattering statement, unfortunately, could only be confirmed in retrospect, with special reference to the period ending with
the first world war. If we take the principal periodical Italy has had
in the field of sociology, the *Rivista Italiana di Sociologia,* we find

that it was born under good auspices in 1897, edited by A. Bosco and G. Cavaglieri, then by F. Fiamingo, but came to an end in 1921. A later revival, under the editorship of S. Rugarli, was of short duration and lesser scientific relevance. Even before 1921, however, the last years of the *Rivista* were characterized by the fact that most of the contributions published by it just bordered on sociological problems, but were mainly concerned with demography, economics, anthropology, criminology, etc.

It seems clear that interest in this discipline was undergoing a deep and pervasive crisis: its object, justification, definition, *raison d'être*, methods of work, were heavily challenged. The attack was tuned to the pitch of a highly sophisticated criticism, and the humble but very real services which had been rendered by some at least of the sociologists in the field found no grace in the eyes of many leaders of the country's thought: these were, for the most, humanists, philosophers, jurists, historians, in a country where higher culture is pervasively humanistic. The economists (with one great exception as we shall see) were hesitant or definitely hostile to the "new" discipline; many stoical statisticians would feel that most of the basic work was done by them and feared duplication and confusion of thought; psychology was going through its teething difficulties and, insofar as there could yet be any talk of a social psychology, it was felt that this discipline might cover at least a good part of the ground claimed by the sociologists as their own; anthropology and ethnology were treated mainly from a descriptive and historical approach, field work on a camparative basis being rather the exception, with the result that sociological research in Italy could hardly rely on the support of these cognate disciplines, as it did at times in France and in Germany.

If sociology was in for a long spell of hard treatment, however, it must be conceded that this was not without objective reasons, some of which are haunting to this day the structure and methodology of the discipline: a great deal was lost, in the knowledge and treatment of burning practical problems, in the many "lean" years of Italian sociology, but at least one positive result was secured: i.e., a keener awareness, among the few serious students of the subject who survived the storm, of the basic difficulties and "trick" inherent in the very conception of sociology. In this connection it should be clearly stated that a "political" explanation of the "lean years" of Italian sociology would be untenable. Neither the dogmatic influence of the Catholic Church, nor the political strictures of the fascist regime, had really anything to do with it. A definable trend of "Catholic" socio-logical thought, as we shall see later, never ceased to make itself felt; on the other hand, sociological studies were on the wane long before fascism got into power, and the main leader and flag-bearer of the anti-sociological approach, Benedetto Croce, was at the same time one of the most prominent anti-fascists. The fact, which seems now gener-ally proved, that sociology ekes out but a meagre life in totalitarian countries, does not by itself explain the origin of this long-protracted crisis of Italian sociology: not only did the crisis originate before fascism, but it was prompted by intellectual factors having no specific connection with it.

A good digest of the main arguments which were put forth for or against sociology in Italy in the early years of our century will be found in Vol. XXXVI of the *Atti della Regia Accademia delle Scienze Morali* of Naples (1906). A small symposium of savants (Igino Petrone, Filippo Masci, A. Chiappelli, R. Garofalo, F. Persico and G. Arcoleo) had discussed at great length the legitimacy of the dis-cipline called "sociology," also in connection with the claim, which was being put forth on many sides, that regular chairs in the subject should be established in the State Universities; and the report of their discussion is exhaustive and widely illustrative.

The case for the prosecution was presented by Petrone in a first contribution, which was mainly a criticism of the Comtean position, and then in a second one, in answer to the "case for the defense" as presented in his long contribution by Masci. Petrone's first attack mainly hinges on Comte's asumption that *consensus* "characterizes and connects the human and social phenomena" (Petrone's words). This, he maintains, denies the legitimacy of psychology, economics, and indeed every science which isolates from the social "whole" one of its phenomena or phases in order to study it in itself and indepen-dently from the others. Sociology and "the particular and concrete social sciences, if the latter must be conceived to be also autonomous," cannot therefore coexist. On the other hand, the pretence of sociology to know the "human and social object" as a whole, independently from the processes of analytical discrimination, which he evidently assumes to be the task of the "special" sciences, is absurd. Taking as example two of Simmel's works, he fails to find in them "the ele-mentary, irreducible *sociological* datum"; the data he finds in them should, in his opinion, be referred back to a variety of other disciplines. Among these, however, he lists some which are historical or philosophical in character, and not observational and empirical; which seems to allow the suspicion that some at least of the possible subject matter of sociology is not absorbed by other *empirical* sciences of social facts. From this Petrone proceeds to a wide and rapid survey of a number of sociological schools, maintaining that each of them founds its system either on some analogy taken from another empirical discipline (e.g., mechanicism, organicism, psychologism, economics, ethno-anthropologism, statics, dynamics, etc.), or on a syncretic criterion somewhat arbitrarily superimposed, from the outside, on the phenomena to be studied. The analogies and metaphors taken from other sciences are not always handled, he says, with full consciousness of what this transposition should involve, and "laws" are looked for, as if we were here dealing with physical facts. "The *law* is the formula of a *repetition* of identical facts, therefore its notion is not applicable to the development of a successive series. . . . Every social fact is . . . itself, i.e., a differentiated individuality, heterogeneous, diverse. . . . In nature unity is typical, whereas in the historical and human world it is individual (Rümelin)."

Leaving aside here the interventions of Chiapelli and Persico, which were less important, the following is a short summary of Masci's riposte to Petrone. He maintains that the laws of history are "laws of trends," and consequently accepts, insofar as this aspect of the problem is concerned, Comte's inversion of the method of the physical sciences in the case of sociology: in physics, experience checks on the results of deduction; in sociology, instead, historical experience finds the laws, and deduction from the biopsychological laws of human nature verifies them. Sociology, therefore, "is far removed from the extreme uncertainty of the laws of history proper," but meets with heavy difficulties because of the very general character of its aim, as it embraces everything that is "historically *institutional*"; this affects the certainty of its laws, but not the importance of the discipline. The attempt to extend to sociological problems the theories or laws of other social or non-social sciences is not in itself inadmissible; why should "the generalizing function, which pervades the whole of the scientific process, stop in the face of social phenomena?" As compared with psychology, which has in any case a basic position in connection with all the sciences of the mind, sociology studies "the attitude of the mind in connection with a new order of objects and conditions of its existence. This *novus ordo*, in fact, is the social life." "The ideal trends, which control the specific areas of socal life, must

be considered as irreducible qualities." Whenever the "specific" social
sciences transfer their attention from the "single groups of social
facts" in order to consider the mutual interdependence of the social
phenomena, they thus apply "a more general science, and the application will be all the more valid in proportion as the principles of
such science are more solidly established." "To deny that human
societies have general laws, because those they have are not so rigid
we find them in physical nature, means to move from an arbitrary
concept of 'law' in order to reach an arbitrary denial of the same."
"The *ego* and the *alter* are but the two poles of the same notion. . . .
That transfer of the consciousness which is the result of the polarity
of the *ego* (failing which there would be no social fact) . . . must
be intellectual; if it were merely emotional or impulsive, it might
give origin to a pre-social group, of a biological character, and not
to a society and a social progress."

Petrone's answer to Masci insists on the "reducibility" of the subject-matter claimed for sociology to that of other "particular" social
disciplines (such as economics, psychology, ethnology, etc.): it being
understood, as Masci himself had conceded, that sociology must exist
as a "general" social science or not at all.

Keeping in mind that this debate was taking place in 1906 one
would conclude that Petrone's indictment, after all, was not much
further removed from our present-day attitudes than Masci's gallant
defense of sociology at it was then understood. Most of us would
find it difficult nowadays, and perhaps even irrelevant, to decide
whether sociology should be described as a "special" or "general"
social science. The operational definition of subjects and disciplines
has largely replaced the old, and heated disputes on "subject matters."
Physical epistemology, in addition to having adopted relativity and
Heisemberger's "uncertainty principle," seems now ready to throw
overboard even such an ancient holy of holies as the principle of
conservation of parity. It would seem ungraceful and anachronistic,
in our days, to demand a more rigidly classical definition of whatever
work one intends to do under the name of sociology than is demanded
of any other program of empirical research: considering that the
number of variables the sociologist normally has to cope with is
admittedly higher than in most other disciplines. What the sociologists
have done in these last fifty years, the world over, is not in itself a
definition of the science, but provides material for it which was not
available in 1906; yet it is perhaps typical of the Italian mind, or at

least of one phase in its history, that such theoretical difficulties stood heavily in the way of any actual development of studies and research, so that for nearly a half century a number of social problems were either forgotten or incorrectly dealt with, unless students of other disciplines (such as statistics, law, economy, etc.) made an effort to face them, mostly from their own particular points of view. Petrone's attitude, which was upheld with greater authority and at a more general philosophical level by Benedetto Croce (not strictly a neo-Hegelian as he is often described) and by his many followers to our own day, had behind it strong emotional values, which were more or less consciously exploited by the anti-sociologists: particularly when he maintained that the sociological attitude would treat the human mind and its freedom as an "epiphenomenon."

All this however, did not pass without bringing some positive result as well. Field research and the general development of the discipline suffered, but Italian students are now more alert than some of their foreign colleagues to the basic difficulties of definition and method which still lurk behind the present-day development of sociology. We are not surprised, for instance, to find that a book published by A. Aliotta early in our century is favorably quoted by modern American students of sociological methodology;[3] but we find it queer that they should describe his position as "idealistic." In fact, Aliotta was a positivist of sorts, and his aim was to save what he could of the tra-ditional methodology of the empirical science (the sciences of man being well included) from the onslaught of Croce and other philos-ophers, generally described as "idealists." But to do this he had to give way on all those grounds on which the traditional positivistic attitude did not prove solid enough.

PARETO AND HIS FOLLOWERS

Vilfredo Pareto was the scion of a noble family from Genoa. He started his active life as an engineer, particularly interested in rail-way problems and undertakings. Italy was then (in the seventies and the eighties of the last century) proceeding to the development of her road and railway system, and having to overcome heavy difficul-ties connected with the geography of the land, scarcity of capital and qualified labor, regional jealousies, etc. Politics and high finance came either to clashes or to doubtful collusions over this knotty problem, and Pareto, whose office was then in Florence, was prompted to delve more and more into the social and economic aspects of the railway industries and of others more or less connected with them. He would occasionally publish the results of his studies, and his sharp, often witty, always unbiased statements, sometimes verging on the paradoxical, would gain him admirers among the intelligent readers, but also enemies among the powerful ones. At the same time his omnivorous mind would explore ancient and modern history and literatures (he was, among other things, a classical scholar and a linguist), collecting episodes and anecdotes which he would then try to fit into the systems that were gradually taking shape in his mind. His strong mathematical training, his professional habit as an engineer, prevented him from being satisfied unless and until he could translate his thoughts into formulas, and his arguments into mathematical demonstrations.

This is how his efforts gradually gave way to an ever deeper interest in economic problems, and to the development of a general theory of economics of his own. His first contributions in this field made him better known in certain specialized circles abroad than at home, and he was finally invited to take up the chair of economics in the University of Lausanne, where he succeeded Walras. As an economist he was one of the founders of the modern mathematical approach, and his works remain among the classics in that discipline. He was never content until he could give a geometrical presentation of the relationships and regularities he was dealing with, and his general picture of the economic world looks like mountainous scenery made of a number of curved lines, each of which represents the movement of a human desire or appetition: there are thus the "hills of desire" and the "valleys of repulsion," divided by a theoretical horizontal "line of indifference."

One of the original points in this conception is the notion of "ofelimity" (the actual appetition or impulse towards the obtaining of a certain good or service), which Pareto takes to be the realistic basis from which the derivative concept of "value" can be obtained. His is thus a general mathematical theory of the working and correlations of human desires: a dynamic of desire. Yet, from the beginning of his studies in economics, he was struck by the fact that people do not seem to act coherently with their desires. While conceding that this all-pervading phenomenon would also admit of the psychological approach, particularly in order to understand individual cases better, he would insist that, taken as a whole in its social implications, the fact required a general study, and was susceptible of conceptualization in a general theory: which, in his mind, would be correctly described as a general theory of sociology. His *Traité de Sociologie* (2 vols., 1906 et seq.), published originally in French like most of his main works, may be described as a general geometrical presentation of the "non-logical" behavior of men. "Logical" behavior, in his conception, would practically consist in economic behavior. Sociology, therefore, is the systematical analysis of men's non-economic conduct in its social implications.

Any attempt to summarize Pareto's sociological system in the short space we have at our disposal would do it an injustice. One other way of describing it would be as a theory of motivations, looked at not from the psychological but from the socio-dynamic point of view: as forces moving in the historical medium, previous to and irrespective of the operation of logical processes. Concepts such as those of "residues," "derivations," "combinations," could not be presented in a short definition without reference to the system as a whole. Taken separately, each of them could be easily criticized in terms of later developments of the human sciences: what remains most valuable in our opinion, is the basic realism of the inspiration and the superb example of a single man trying to work out a general coherent system embracing practically the whole chaotic welter of human deeds.

Pareto could be also a blunt and telling polemist. Most of his life was spent in his lonely villa near Lausanne, with his wife and some twenty Angora cats; his temperament was somewhat morose and bizarre at times, to which much of his writings bear testimony: they are overburdened with anecdotes, quotations and disgressions, often humorous and pointed, but also redundant to the economy of the work. Most of these redundancies were meant by the author to have a polemical or even a directly political effect, and some of them, like the articles which he would sometimes give to the press, would often have an impact on given situations, or affect other, more practical, minds and thus influence future developments. In the radical, sometimes cynical, revision and criticism of conventional notions of social freedom, democracy, socialism, and the like, which had such a deep influence on cultured Italians at the beginning of our century, Pareto was undoubtedly one of the inspiring forces,—which explains, without yet justifying it, the misconception which made of him a "fascist sociologist" (to be found in American sociological manuals in the

late 'thirties). It is only true that in the early years of the fascist regime he was granted a larger measure of recognition in his own
country, and was made a member of the Senate. In fact he was a non-
party realistic analyst of social facts, a "debunker," at times a pungent
commentator of current events. In actual politics he would never
identify himself with any single movement or regime.

He had however, his bogeys. One was "moralism": himself a man
of unimpeachable conduct, he thought that preaching moralists were
always confusing the real issues, both in everyday life and in politics,
and fell heavily on them whenever he could find an opportunity.
"Theoreticism" was another: he would not object to men behaving
"non-logically," provided they did not pretend that they were otherwise; but, of course, "logics" tended to identify itself, in his mind,
with his own engineering method and approach, and philosophers
had on occasion an easy game at finding fault with his conceptualizations. Finally, Pareto was a born enemy of "abstract equalitarianism"
in every form, especially political anarchism or unintegrated democracy) and economic (all brands of socialism). Following a tradition
of Italian social studies which goes back at least to Machiavelli,
Pareto always paid a great deal of attention to social hierarchy and
its dynamics: hence his theory concerning the *élites* and their "circulation," closely parallel to that which a political writer, G. Mosca,
was developing in the same years (before 1914) with even greater
literary success. Pareto's book *I sistemi socialisti* (1921) is one in which
the economist, the sociologist and the political commentator join
forces in a general analysis and criticism of socialism in all its forms,
and to this day may be considered a classic of its kind.

Unfortunately, the trend of both academic and non-academic
thought in Italy during the whole period of Pareto's mature production, was much more oriented towards the type of problems of
which the "Neapolitan debate" givese an example than to his analytical and systematic attitude, so that his teaching and example,
especially in sociology, were not as fertile as they deserved to be, and
did not lead to the growth of a real "school." In this connection, the
name of Guido Sensini deserved to be mentioned in particular, for
his advanced mathematical treatment of sociological problems, with
a special interest in the dynamics of social classes. L. Galvano and
others of the younger generation have also worked on similar lines.
In economics, Luigi Amoroso stands out as Pareto's most prominent
follower in Italy.

A statistician with a keen interest in demographic and sociological studies, Corrado Gini has contributed to the problem of the circulation of the *élites* since the concluding years of the last century, extending his attention to the numerical variations of classes and the processes of the concentration of wealth. In sociology he has always been oriented towards a "biological" interpretation: he would speak of "social metabolism" when dealing with the diffusion of genetic and cultural characters within a social area and its effects on a nation's history. He would recommend that the demographic factor be considered as an independent variable and a *primum movens* of wars and revolutions, though men are so inclined to forget or ignore it (an echo, perhaps, of Pareto's "derivations" and their frequent lack of corespondence with observable facts). Gini upholds a "neo-organicist" interpretation of sociology (in his definition, an organism is "a system . . . endowed with powers of self-preservation and self-balancing"— (which, in our days, might seem to apply to some cybernetic contraptions as well!) In economics, Gini maintains that the classical school expresses a sort of "physiology" of a healthy society, although a "diseased" society has its regularities as well: which justifies an "economic pathology." It was Gini who, working on Pareto's "circulation of the *élites*," concluded an exhaustive range of historical and statistical studies with the statement that a *return* to prominence of decayed layers of the population is a rare exception, and the "circular" image is therefore not quite correct. It is also true, however, that the demographic decadence of a prominent class is often counterbalanced by intermarriages with individuals from other layers and admission into the given *élite* of newcomers endowed with certain characteristics. Two ladies, Levi della Vida and Federici, who belong to Gini's school, have done further work on the circulation theory, and worked out class differentials in fecundity.

Out of the large number of Italian statisticians who have done work of sociological importance one should cite a further name, that of Livio Livi, who, especially in his work on the biological factors of the social structure, manages to keep a delicate balance between the biological interpretation and the sociological one.[5]

THE CATHOLIC SCHOOLS

The encyclic *Rerum novarum*, by which Pope Leo XIII oriented Catholic thought towards social and labor problems as they present themselves in modern society, has been at the origin of various trends of sociological work in Italy. In matters not touching too closely on points of dogma, Italian catholic circles have been often more alert than others to the importance of sociology. The outstanding name in this field, since the last years of the past century, has been that of Giuseppe Toniolo, who was raised to the altars a few years after his death. Working on the foundations of the Thomistic tradition, he faced the dominant "isms" of his time: positivism, evolutionism, economic individualism (or liberalism), Marxism and other socialistic schools. The type of society theorized by St. Thomas and the Church classics was not very similar to the one Toniolo could see in his days: despite all the advantages that industrialism could bring in its wake, the basic character of *stability*, essential to the old social conception, had disappeared. As an economist, Toniolo was well aware, to mention only one thing, of the periodical economic fluctuations and crises in the capitalistic world, and of the sufferings, fears and uncertainty that they brought to the lower stratum of society—the largest ones, and those most exposed, for lack of cultural maturity, to despair, unrest, blind rebellion; and full employment was (as it still is in Italy) a distant dream in the first quarter of this century, when Toniolo was concluding his work.

Catholic thought and action found themselves confronted with two contrasting foes: liberalism on the one side (the ideal of a society mode of totally "free" and independent individuals) and materialistic socialism on the other. The teachings of classical economy, in Toniolo's mind, partly assumed and also partly produced (through the policies inspired by it) a "society of monads": which he considered to be a contradiction in terms. Nor would he, for obvious reasons, accept dialectical materialism as a *social* alternative. He thought that a non-materialistic integrated society must be a "corporate" society: something not too essentially different from what had existed in the middle ages, and had been theorized (sometimes, also, idealized) by the classical writers of the Church. The basic idea of a corporate conception is that a system of super-economic values should provide the common ground for a harmonization of individual and group interests and efforts: and, in the spirit of this school, Christianity as a whole is, potentially at least, such a society (the basic values being transcendental in nature). Seen in this perspective, the study of social problems becomes almost a religious duty. It was in this spirit that the Catholic University of Milan was founded, early in this century, when it was the only University in Italy having a Faculty of Social Sciences. Its founder and, to our day, its Rector, Father Agostino Gemelli, is a physiologist, and a psychologist, whose contributions in these two fields were already well known before he started, in his own University, a Laboratory of applied psychology which was largely devoted to work psychology and to social psychology as applied to industrial problems. Gemelli's early critical studies of the theories of Lombroso and his school, his contributions on the origin of mystical behavior, on the science and philosophy of language, on the origin of the human family, etc., often gave the lead to other work by his school. As a further instance, Gemelli and A. Galli's research on man's adaptation to repetitive machine work may be taken as a good specimen of the production of this group.[6]

On a wider area of scientific interests, the Faculty of Social Sciences of the Catholic University has been the center of a number of initiatives, often of direct interest to sociology. Its periodical, *Rivista Internazionale di Scienza Sociali*, has been for a number of years, especially after the disappearance of the *Rivista Italiana di Sociologia*, the main Italian publication dealing, though not exclusively, with sociological matters. Of the many prominent men who worked in the Milan Faculty we shall mention Mercello Boldrini for his works on social classes and the *élites*, biometry and anthropometry, cultural and demographic statistics; Amintore Fanfani for his works on the history and sociology of labor, the conditions of the poorer classes, the origin of the capitalistic attitude in Italy, catholicism and protestantism in the development of modern capitalism; Luigi Bellini, originally a criminologist, for his two volumes on general sociology (morphology and dynamics); Francesco Vito, an economist, for his important studies on emigration and on the corporate concept of economy.[6a]

IIis answers could be, very inadequately, summarized as follows. The historical process is "open" at the two ends: its origins and its aims. Both of these belong to the sphere of the Divine. In between the two, man is neither abstractly and absolutely free nor mechanically determined; he is endowed with possible freedom in varying measure according to circumstances, and the exercise of his intelligence and his will. The analytical knowledge of circumstances, including those which pertain to social structures and habits, is a necesary part of that understanding, which in its turn is one of the preconditions of the relative freedom of man. The final aims of life are definitely placed by Sturzo in the transcendental, and consequently they are not closely connected with society as such: perfection is the aim of the individual person, not of society, yet the improvement of society is one of the conditions necessary for the achievement of that perfection. It follows that the systematic study of social facts is the sort of exercise which should most directly contribute to man's striving after perfection.

This theory differs in many ways from the type of "ethical" sociology which is dominant in many catholic quarters, and is probably one of the main efforts made in our time to reconcile revealed faith with science and the humanistic approach to social problems. On a number of specific points concerning politics and the economy Sturzo is more of a liberal than a "corporative" thinker; and, generally speaking, the "corporative" formula has lost popularity in these days, largely due to the fact that it had been taken up by fascism (as a formula, at least). Other Catholic students, however, such as Guido Menegazzi, have consistently upheld this approach and the ensuing principles both during and after the fascist period.

Mention must also be made here of the Jesuits' periodical, *Civiltà Cattolica* (Rome), where social problems have always been currently and competently discussed by a number of writers. Father Angelo Brucculeri deserves a special mention among them, as his strict orthodoxy has never obscured a keen and well-informed insight into social events.

THE FASCIST PERIOD

It may take years, and perhaps centuries, before an unbiased critical history of the fascist period in Italy can be written; whatever is said about it at present must remain totally open to discussion. Information on the subject, however, is generally scarce in other countries, except in the very restricted and specialized circles, and we submit that to a better study of the Italian literature of the period dealing with sociological matters would help clarify many points and throw light on general perspective. It would be difficult even now to say in a few sentences what was in fact the impact of the regime on sociological studies. The very fact that the Italian word "fascism" has entered ordinary language everywhere, and refers to ideologies, deeds and situations very different from one another and sometimes having hardly any connection with the Italian model, is one of the elements which add to the general confusion. Another negative factor to a clear understanding is to be found in the number of changes of attitudes and orientations, even on basic items of principle and policy, which Italian fascism underwent during the quarter of a century of its history. Three main characteristics, however, can be said to have been fairly constant in the whole process: first, a stern and militant patriotism, or nationalism; second, a criticism of parliamentary as well as of socialistic forms of democracy, and a tendency (official, though not equally factual) toward a "corporate state"; third, a personal and increasingly autocratic form of government.

Of these three aspects, or elements, of the fascist venture it was the second which mostly aroused the interest of social scientists and gave occasion to a number of studies and debates, while the third (autocracy) did not always stand in the way of such activities, yet in the main had an increasingly negative effect on them. In point of fact, four University Faculties of political sciences were created under the regime in 1934 (in addition to the Catholic one of Milan, which remained non-statal, but applied all the regulations of the statal ones). The "C. Alfieri" Institute of Social Sciences of Florence, which had been in existence for nearly sixty years as a postgraduate institute, became one of the four. Sociology was one of the subjects in their syllabus, but never had a full-time chair allocated to it: this, however, was due to circumstances existing prior to the regime, and to the opposition of such men as Benedetto Croce, who, with some prominent exceptions, were also hostile to the regime. It is practically impossible to establish any positive or negative correlations between the fortunes, or misfortunes, of sociology in Italy and those of the fascist regime.

Those fascist leaders, like the minister G. Bottai, who were particularly interested in social problems and in the establishment of the corporate system, often found it difficult to promote all the studies that would be required, not so much because of political strictures as in consequence of the inexistence or inadequacy of field research work in the social disciplines, and more particularly in sociology: although it remains to be seen whether they themselves saw the problem in these terms. The efforts towards the establishment of a "corporate state" covered a number of years and never achieved a real success;[7] yet it involved a great amount of intellectual and research work, part of which would be of interest even in our own day, provided that certain idiosyncrasies of terminology, which belonged to the obligatory ritual of the regime, are discounted from the beginning.

Officially, national trade unions were established as public institutions, the agreements they reached on work conditions were binding all over the country, a magistrature was established to deal with labor controversies, a Charter of Labor was proclaimed, and National Corporations (including, for each branch of activity, management and labor organizations, and representatives of the state, who were expected to stand for the interests of the consumer) were finally brought into existence. The deadly germ at the heart of all this, however, was the fact that the representativeness of the national committees and offices was largely nominal, and became ever more so as the years went by: too often the central political power had the first and the last word in vital social questions. All the same, a huge number of studies were carried out and the results published,[8] and the assumption that all this was done in bad faith or out of sheer servility would be a somewhat sterile working hypothesis.

Most of the work was done by philosophers (e.g., Ugo Spirito, whose notion of "corporate ownership" created a stir, and something of a scandal, at the Ferrara Congress of 1932), jurists and theoreticians of law (A. Volpicelli and many others), economists and finance specialists (Alberto de' Stefani, L. Amoroso, etc.), specialists in labor legislation and what would now be called industrial relations (Luisa Riva Sanseverino, C. Arena, etc.), statisticians and others. Elements of sociological work in a strict sense could be found everywhere in this large mass of material, and perhaps more particularly in some historical treatises (Nello Quilici's essay on the modern Italian middle classes is an outstanding example of this).

It would be unfair to expect that genuine sociological work could develop, in the years of the regime, among those who were opposed to it, considering the unfavorable circumstances among which many of them had to live and work. In this connection, however, the name of A. Gramsci deserves mention, as of a social philosopher whose work often confronts sociological problems. A militant communist, he died in prison under the fascist regime and had a well-deserved apotheosis after its downfall. Some maintain that his final conclusions would be hard to reconcile with strict communist orthodoxy if he were still alive, but this point need not be discussed here.

TRENDS

The chaotic circumstances in which Italy found herself at the end of the last major war were not completely unfavorable to new developments in sociological studies. Political freedom might be expected to act as a pre-condition, if not as a determinant, for the starting of this type of work on fresh lines, and the importance this science has acquired in other countries certainly spurred many Italian minds to emulation. Yet, it was years after the war before something began to be done. Despite the strong support sociology received from prominent personalities like L. Sturzo, the Universities were still inhibited by old preconceptions and, which was still worse, suffered from almost complete lack of qualified teachers and institutes. It was only in 1949, after a long debate, that a regular chair in sociology was established in the Faculty of Political Sciences of Florence University, and it still remains the only one in the country.

Many signs of a reawakening, however, can be found both within and without the academic world. N. Abbagnano (a philosopher) and F. Ferrarotti (a sociologist) started a quarterly in Turin (*Quaderni di Sociologia*, Ed. Taylor) in 1948. Other periodicals edited by, or under the auspices of, the Faculties of Political Sciences display a keen interest in the subject: such are *Il Politico* of Pavia (edited by Bruno Leoni, it publishes, among other things, a good bibliography of current sociological literature in Italy by F. Barbano) and *Studi politici* of Florence (Ed. Sansoni). A non-academic magazine of Bologna, *Il Mulino*, also shows an interest in the subject, followed in this, more or less regularly, by other publications. Recently, a bimonthly mainly concerned with industrial sociology, *Problemi Umani —Società e Lavoro,* has been started in Rome by V. Lupo, with the cooperation of jurists like G. Del Vecchio, psychologists like M. Ponzo, pedagogists like L. Volpicelli, philosophers like F. Lombardi, and a group of sociologists (L. Palma, C. Pellizzi, L. Potestà, G. Sacco and others).

All this is merely indicative of a trend which still has to prove its worth through actual scientific fertility. In the given circumstances it was to be expected that the rebirth of sociological interest in Italy would manifest itself at first as a discussion of the methodological differences which led to the "crisis" of the discipline in the early years of the century. This is noticeable in the works of Abbagnano, N. Bobbio (a jurist), Ferrarotti, Leoni Lombardi, Pellizzi and others. Franco

Ferrarotti is also responsible for a volume on the trade union movement in the States and a further one on "the workers' revolt."[9] It
is felt on many sides in field-work sociology, and some attempts have
been made already, at the Florence Faculty, in the "Cattolica" of
Milan, and elsewhere, in the teeth of obstacles which are those usual
in similar circumstances: lack of trained researchers, lack of funds,
and, most important of all perhaps, lack of understanding and sympathy for this effort on the part of public authorities, organization
and political interests. The wheel, however, has been set into motion,
and specialists from neighboring disciplines add to its momentum:
as in the case of A. Marzi in Florence, A. Massucco-Costa in Turin,
G. Jacono in Naples, Lidia De Rita in Bari (all of them working in
the field of social psychology), and ethnologists like T. Tentori of
Rome and A. de Martino.

SELECTED BIBLIOGRAPHY

F. Barbano, *La sociologia in Italia, oggi (Italy's Sociology Today)*
(Pavia: El Politico, 1954 et seq.). A mine of information.

Howard Becker & Harry Elmer Barnes, *Social Thought from Lore
to Science* (Washington, D.C.: Harren Press, 1952), II, Chapter XXV,
"Sociology in Italy," 1002-1028. A good synthesis.

W. Rex Crawford "Representative Italian Contributions to Sociology: Pareto, Loria, Vaccaro, Gini, and Sighele," Chapter XXIX, 553-
584 in Harry Elmer Barnes Ed., *An Introduction to the History of
Sociology* (University of Chicago Press, 1948). The best available surveys of these selected sociologists.

Franco Ferrarotti, "Sociology in Italy": *Modern Sociological Theory*
(New York, The Dryden Press, 1957).

B. Magnino, *Sociologia* (Brescia: Motcelliana, 1953). A mine of
bibliographical information.

C. Pellizzi, "Gli studi sociologici in Italia nel nostro secolo"
("Italian Sociological Studies in Our Century"), *Quaderni di Sociologia* (Turin), XX-XXI (1956), to be completed.

Max Salvadori, "Italy," Chapter IV, 140-183, in Max Salvadori,
George B. de Huszar & Julia Bond, Eds., *Contemporary Social Science.
II: Eastern Hemisphere* (Harrisburg, Penna.: The Stackpole Co., 1954);
sociology is covered on pp. 141-148; see the bibliography, 182-183.

Camillo Pellizzi (1896——) was born in Turin (Italy); Dr. J. (Pisa,
1917), D. Lit. (London, 1931); Assistant, Lecturer, Reader, then Professor of Italian, University College University of London (1920-1940);
Professor of Sociology in the Faculty of Political Sciences C. Alfieri,

University of Florence (1949——); Counsellor on Training and Applied Social Sciences of the O.E.E.C., Paris (1955——). Has published numerous works: *Problemi e realtà del Fascismo* (*Problems and Realities of Fascism*) (Florence: Vallecchi, 1924); *Cose d'Inghilterra* (*English Realilities*) (Milan: Alpes, 1925); *Le Lettere Italiane del nostro secolo* (*Italian Literature in Our Century*) (Milan: Nuova Italia, 1929); *The English Theater: The Last Phase* (London: MacMillan Co., 1936); *Romanticism and Regionalism* (London, Acts of the British Academy, 1932); "La struttura elemetare del comporamento sonsapevole" ("The Elementary Structure of Conscious Behavior"), in *Critti di sociologia e politica in enore di L. Sturzo* (Rome, 1954).

NOTES

1. Roberto Michels, *Political Parties* (*Glencoe*, Ill.: Free Press, 1951).

2. J. M. Robertson, *Courses of Study* (3rd Ed., London, 1932) , 217

3. Antonio Aliotta, *The Idealistic Reaction against Science* (English transl., London: MacMillan, 1914).

4. The literature in English on Pareto is more than adequate; see such works as: John Harrington, S. J., "Vilfredo Pareto," Chapter 9, 174-200, in Clement S. Mihanovich, Ed., *Social Theorists* (Milwaukee: The Bruce Publ. Co., 1953) ; Andrew Bon giorno, "A Study of Pareto's Treatise on General Sociology," *American Journal of Sociology*, XXXVI (November, 1930) , 349-370; L. G. Henderson, *Pareto's General Sociology* (Cambridge, Mass.: Harvard University Press, 1935) ; Talcott Parsons, "Pareto's Central Analytical Scheme," *Journal of Social Philosophy*, (April, 1936) 244-262, "Pareto," *Encyclopedia of the Social Sciences* (New York: The MacMillan, Co. 1933) , VI, 576-578, J. A. Schumpeter, "Vilfredo Pareto," *The Quarterly Journal of Economics*, (May, 1949) , 147-172; Pitirim A. Sorokin, *Contemporary Sociological Theories* (New York: Harper, 1928), 37-62; N. Timasheff, "Law in Pareto's Sociology," *The American Journal of Sociology*, XLVI (September, 1940) , 139-149; etc.

5. L. Livi, *I fattori biologici dell'ordinamento sociale* (*The Biological Factors in Social Order*) (Florence, 1923).

6a. In *Bollettino del Laboratorio di Psicologia Applicata* (*Bulletin of the Laboratory in Applied Psychology*) (Milan: Universita Cattolica del S. Cuore, 1930).

7. See: C. Pellizzi, *Una Rivoluzione mancata* (*A Revolution which Failed*) (Milan: Longanesi, 1949).

8. G. Gradilone, *Bibliografia sindacale e corporative* (*Bibliography of Union and Corporate Studies*) (Rome: I. N. C. F., 1939).

9. F. Ferrarotti, *La Rivolta operaia* (Rome: Ed. Comunita, 1956).

LATIN AMERICA*

Robert C. Williamson
Los Angeles City College

It has often been said that the Latin American knows the United States considerably better than we are acquainted with him. The characterization seems particularly to be relevant to the social sciences for there is profound ignorance of Latin American trends. The lack of interest on the part of American students was not surprising in view of the antiquated state of sociology to the south of us. However, there has been marked change in recent years. In San Paulo, Brazil, to mention the most notable example, one observes the development of empirical studies that might well be the envy of *any* American university. This change is all the more significant in that Latin America offers the social scientist a vast laboratory for research with its sharp variations in society and culture. The contrasts featured in travel posters that have lured the traveler south are not without significance for the social scientist as well.

Latin American sociology reflects a striking heterogeneity of people, backgrounds, movements, and philosophical orientations. These variations exist as much within a national culture as from one to another. Although sociology has tended to remain longer in a non-empirical phase than has been true of the United States, there is at the same time conspicuous evidence of change. Namely, a new generation is apparent: For one thing, a man of wealth, with a dilettante interest is no longer the necessary requisite for becoming an academician. University positions are increasingly passing to individuals who are systematically trained in a given discipline.

Latin American sociology has tremendous potentiality as there are rich possibilities for social research, both theoretical and applied. It represents a predominantly Western culture adapted in varying degrees to a complex of indigenous cultures. It is an area where social

* Terms and titles are translated only where necessary to clarify; citations are given for only the most important publications.

873

planning and social reform are urgently needed, as it is plagued with discrepancies that require investigation and adjustment: (1) Latin America is marked by geographic diversity, including the second highest mountain barrier in the world. The range even within one country of latitude, temperature, altitude, and vegetation has changed the cultural pattern sufficiently to make for comparisons of more than routine interest. The primitiveness of transportation has intensified this regionalism and isolation. Frequently communication is more feasible with Europe than with another country in the continent. Individuals in Lima and Santiago are more likely to have contact with Madrid or New York than with the other capitol. This tendency has been further intensified by national rivalries. (2) Perhaps the most exciting changes of the area have been in the structure of the population: a young and rapidly expanding society of Indian, Negro, and European sources. Although the population has remained rural and generally traditional in its behavior, the emergence of industrial and urban life has created new problems of adaptation. (3) Institutional norms, as in marriage and family systems, religious practices, and political preferences, vary sharply among the aboriginal, mestizo, and even the European groups. (4) There is pronounced social and economic stratification with some regions being characterized by the lowest standard of living in the Western world, especially in rural areas. Too, urban areas exhibit a blurring of the middle and lower class. (5) Illiteracy has existed as a major problem and amounts to eighty-five per cent in some countries. Since 1940 there has been a major project of *desanalfabetizacion* in order to remedy this situation. (6) Social disorganization is revealed by a number of symptoms: poverty, alcoholism, illegitimacy, and a relatively high rate of delinquency and crime. Perhaps most serious are the low standards of health and sanitation. (7) There is a kaleidoscope of social and political movements with divergent patterns of democracy, *caudillismo*, and even totalitarianism. It is only in the last generation that the government has been wrested from the military in a number of countries. In addition, there has been the problem of interference, or the reverse, indifference, on the part of larger world powers. Latin America considered herself victimized by the United States as late as the nineteen twenties. On the other hand, since World War II the feeling has been that our country has relegated inter-American interests to a second place position in comparison with our European commitments.

THE DEVELOPMENT OF SOCIOLOGY

Much of what is labelled as sociology, even in the present, includes material that we more frequently refer to as history and philosophy. The antecedents of sociology are found in nineteenth century social thought. And even today much of Latin America sociology is what might be more accurately called social philosophy.

There appear to be four periods in Latin American sociology: (1) The writings of early social and political leaders, such as the Argentines Rivadavia and Sarmiento, structured social thinking and formulated some of the expressed goals of their respective national society. Two, after 1880 there was a positivistic and organistic period in which social philosophies were molded along the traditional European framework of the period. This was characterized by men like Gonzales and Alberdi in Argentina, Romera in Brazil, and Arcaya in Venezuela. There was a strong Comtian cult and positivism was followed even by occasional government leaders. The words "Ordem e Progresso," that appear on the Brazilian flag are a reflection of this late nineteenth century optimism that seemed appropriate to an expanding society in a new world. The writings of certain contemporary sociologists still reflect Comtian and Spencerian idiom. The third era begins shortly after 1900 when sociology became recognized as a separate subject. Furthermore the discipline reflected a broader basis than positivism. Sociology became a synthesis of Le Play, Durkheim, Tönnies, Simmel, and, of course, Comte. Although not as influential as the European sociologists the following Americans were not without an audience: Sumner, Ward, Giddings, Ross, and more recently, Ogburn and Sorokin. Viewpoints had to be flexible. The social forces in Ibero-America —church and state, military and civilian, conservatism and revolution —called for variable ideologies. In some cases, a sociologist made a distinct contribution to theory, still others provided valuable insights into cultural or regional problems.

The fourth period has been developing since 1935, and especially since the end of the war. The emphasis has shifted to the empirical study of specialized problems: of acculturation, culture conflict, the community, stratification, demography, and social disorganization. While this new trend has markedly affected Brazil and Mexico more than the other nations, a new sociology is emerging in other parts of the Americas.

Generally the field has suffered from the lack of recognition from other disciplines and the reluctance in a number of universities to grant a full-time chair. Earlier, sociology was taught in the law school, which was a vestige of the 17th century concept of *derecho natural* (natural law), society being part of the nature of things. As sociology moved from the Escuela de Derecho to the Facultad de Filosofía y Letras (the equivalent of our College of Letters and Science), it was amalgamated with philosophy or history. In fact, *sociologia*, represents a blending of history, geography, and ethnology; hence the many national *sociologias*. *Sociologia argentina* means simply Argentina culture, with emphasis on the ethos of the people.

Recently, in a number of the universities the assignment of sociology to the Facultad de Ciencias Economicas (School of Economics) which includes various social sciences, has provided an orientation toward the applied phases of the discipline. Also, there has been an increasing tendency to bring together sociology and anthropology, as in areas where preliterate populations dominate numerically. Consequently, only an arbitrary distinction can be made between the two fields.

We may now examine some the leading sociologists of the last half century:

Argentina. Argentines have generally regarded their nation as the center of the Hispanic American world. Due to the lack of an Indian population, there has been a minimum of cultural studies, and sociology has remained philosophical and historical in character. After the turn of the century it alternated between the French tradition, Le Play, Comte, and Durkheim on one side, and German influences, particularly neo-Hegelianism, on the other side. Ortega y Gasset has had considerable influence in intellectual circles. Early in the century Jose Ingenieros provided an intuitionist philosophy reflecting such widely distant sources as Marx and Bergson. His proclamation that Argentina held a unique role cultivated an isolationism that has been transformed into political thought and action on more than one occasion.

The best known sociologist has been Raul Orgaz of the University of Cordova (until his removal during the Peron era). In his influential work, *Introduccion a la Sociologia*[1] he emphasizes in a Durkheimian fashion the cultural or institutional aspects of sociology. At the same time he introduces a psychologistic approach à la Tarde to explain social behavior. He is a good example of the syncretism, for which Latin American system builders are famous. Alfredo Povina of the University of Buenos Aires may be described as a neo-Hegelian with leanings toward Max Weber, Max Scheler, and Hans Freyer. He has attempted to synthesize "sociology" (theory) and "sociography" (description and specialization), although apparently his interest has revolved largely about social philosophy.[2]

Among the "younger" sociologists is Gino Germani, also of the University of Buenos Aires. Although he has written widely in theory and methodology, his main contribution is in demography. His *Estructura Social de la Argentina*[3] is probably the most mature work to appear in that country. He employs census material but adds a remarkable amount of original material on stratification, political ecology, and regionalism. The census data was analyzed in terms of sex, age, marital, regional, and occupational subcultures. Not least is his interest in I.Q. differentials as they affect social behavior. His book may be symptomatic of a new trend in Argentine sociology. It appears proper that the country should enjoy a more productive role than has been the case in the past. The country has probably the largest number of universities as well as institutes and periodicals in the social sciences, in Hispanic America.

Brazil. Brazil has the most developed program in sociology, not only in the sophistication of theory and methodology, but in the range of fields under investigation. As the largest country both in area and population in Latin America, it has also been enriched by localism due to diverse geography and the difficulty in internal communication and transportation. It enjoys the most varied culture and population, racially and socially speaking.[4] No other country appears to have experienced such startling change in a generation, and yet the spirit of a frontier still permeates much of the west and northeast regions. It is set off, too, by its Portuguese origin and in the nineteenth century it turned mainly to France for inspiration, whereas the other countries retained in some fashion an allegiance to Spanish. institutions. Perhaps it with Argentina, as one crosses from one border to the other, that one notes the most profound difference. Whether this extends to personality type, as observers have pointed out, remains for some future psychologist to determine.

According to Fernandes, Brazilian sociology may be divided into three periods: (1) There was the preparatory stage of the late nineteenth century when social thought was directed toward the cultural order. Brazil was undergoing a number of changes, most important of which were the establishment of the republic and the abolition of slavery, and the transition to a class system within the framework of

Western culture. (2) The first quarter of the twentieth century was identified with interest in social institutions and regionalism and the attempt to apply "rational methods" to social change. (3) The third phase, which began in the twenties, is marked by increasingly effective use of theory and empirical investigations.[5]

One could mark the beginning of Brazilian sociology in 1902 with Euclydes da Cunha's *Os Sertaos*,[6] a documentation of a cultural isolate in the arid backlands (sertaos) of the northeast. It is a history of cultural and economic conflict—the acculturated population of the coast and the simpler society of the interior. One of the most definitive steps was the publication of *Introdução a Sociologia Geral* by Pontes de Miranda. "General sociology" was stated in positivistic terms, with emphasis on quantitative methods. In the same decade Olivera Viana produced a number of works on population, race, and aspects of social history. Djacir Menezes in the early thirties was providing scientific orientation to sociologists in his country and has specialized in the fields of social mobility and law. His numerous works portray deep understanding of methodology, as well as the theoretical framework of the *Wiener Kreis* and logical positivism.

The most important work to appear since *Os Sertaos* was Gilberto Freyre's *Casa Grande e Senzala*.[7] This work, along with *Sobrados e Mucambos*[8] and *Nordéste*[9] introduced a situationalism in Latin American sociology. He had studied at Columbia University under Giddings and Boas, and was possibly influenced by W. I. Thomas. These works portrayed the evolution of the feudal system and its transition to semi-urban life. The complex set of personal relations between master and slave, white and black, as well as the evolution of political forms, are examined with rare insight.

Among other sociologists who have centered on practical aspects is Delgado de Carvalho with works on education, social processes, and the problem of social disorganization. Like Freyre he was more influenced by American than European training. Carneiro Leao is important for *A Sociedade Rural*,[10] in a country that is over sixty per cent rural and has since reflected some of the reforms he suggested. Artur Ramos, anthropologist and social psychologist, left before his untimely death in 1949 several works, most important of which was *O Negro Brasileiro*[11] (The Negro in Brazil).

Included in the group of sociologists of Rio and northern Brazil, one of the outstanding contemporary ones is Mario Lins. He has been a most able interpreter of semantics, field, theory, and logical positivism. Among his numerous works are *A Evolucao Logico-Conceitual de Ciencia*[12] and *Operations of Sociological Inquiry*.[13] He has introduced a number of writers in methodology and operationalism to an international public.

It is in San Paulo that a sociological renaissance has most clearly taken place. Much of this development is related to the Escola Livre de Sociologia e Politica founded in 1933 and maintained for some years on an independent basis but now part of the Faculdade de Filosofia, Ciencias, e Letras of the University of San Paulo. A number of individuals have played a principal role in the development of this revitalization of sociology and anthropology. One is Fernando de Azevedo, who has been a prolific writer in several fields of sociology. His *Principios de Sociologia*[14] has been in several editions of Portuguese and Spanish. Influenced predominantly by Durkheim, his theory emphasizes the pre-eminence of social facts. Likewise, as a student of Ogburn, he has been concerned with social change, which is reflected in his *Brazil, An Interpretation*.[15] From a practical viewpoint his most influential work is probably *Sociologia Educacional*,[16] based not only on Durkheim, but of a number of others, including John Dewey. De Azevedo, too, has made his contribution to regional sociology, namely, *Un Trem Corre para o Oeste*[17] (A Train Goes West), a study of the effect of a railroad on the frontier. He has furthered sociology in Brazil not only by his voluminous works, but by having founded the Brazilian Sociological Society.

Perhaps the most important figure in developing a well conceived theory and methodology for sociological and anthropological research is Emilio Willems. At present he is principally on the staff of Vanderbilt University but in the years in Brazil he compiled (with Herbert Baldus) a sociological dictionary and studied race relations and the acculturation of immigrants, particularly of Germans in the extreme southern part of the country. Likewise, Donald Pierson, an American, who, after receiving his doctorate joined the staff at San Paulo.[18] Another important immigrant is Roger Bastide who has had a primary influence on the sociological training of Brazilian students. Included in his several interests is the sociology of religion.

Among the younger generation of individuals trained in both sociology and anthropology is Florestan Fernandes, who with Roger Bastide, has made an exhaustive study of white-Negro relations in the city of San Paulo.[19] Probaby Fernandes' most significant work, though, is a functional-historical study of the Tupinamba society, particularly the role of war as an integrative factor in social processes and institutions. Methodologically speaking, the work demonstrates the possibilities and limitations of historical research among an extinct culture. Fernandes, it may be added, represents only one of the many students of social organization and affiliated problems in San Paulo. Even a most fragmentary list would have to include Roger Bastide, Eduardo Galvao, Giocanda Mussolini, Darcy Ribeiro, and Egon Schaden.

Chile. In South America only Uruguay can equal Chile in the strength of its democratic institutions, and certainly no country surpasses it in attractiveness of climate and topography. It is to be hoped that the country may contribute more outstanding sociologists. Looking over the last few decades the principal figure still remains the social historian, Augustin Venturino, whose *Sociologia Chilena*[20] examines the development of Chilean culture largely for its geographic determinants. In this and other volumes he examines the various Latin American aboriginal cultures, the interdependence of flora and fauna, race and class, past and present.

Alexandro Lipschutz, of Lithuanian origin, has provided some important works on both physical and cultural anthropology. Oscar Alvarez Andrews of the University of Santiago has written on various problems, such as stratification and social disorganization. Probably *Las Fuerzas Sociales* represents his most definitive work, a theoretical but incomplete statement of how mathematical, physical, biological, and social constructs are interrelated. Moises Troncoso, as an economist, has been active in the sociology of labor and economic history.

Mexico. Mexico represents certain unique features. As one of three largest Latin American countries in area and population, it has probably had the most violent history, and yet has had political and social stability during the last decade or two. The writer's ethnocentrism might lead him to attribute this progress to the proximity of the United States—and undoubtedly this factor does explain certain developments in Mexico—but probably the answer remains elsewhere. One factor has been the capability of its political and intellectual leadership. In addition to its native talent, there have been since the late thirties, a number of Spanish refugees.

The leaders of social thought over the last generation are best exemplified in two individuals. Jose Vasconcelos has been a prolific writer and has influenced trends in politics, education, and religion. The other, Antonio Caso, particularly set the pattern of Mevican sociology until his death in 1946. Although primarily a social philos-

pher, he introduced such figures as Tarde, Durkheim, Husserl, Tönnies, and Giddings to his country and his impressionistic method is
well represented in his *Sociologia*.[21] His syncretism combined such
diverse ideas as imitation with geographic determinism. Nonetheless,
he offers a considerable degree of originality.

The leader of present day Mexican sociology is Lucio Mendieta y
Nuñez. Besides being editor of the most important Spanish language
journal in sociology. *Revista Mexicana de Sociologia*, over the last
twenty years, he has written a number of distinguished books in the
field. A partial list would include *El Problema Agrario, La Habita-
cion Indigena, Las Clases Sociales, Los Partidos Politicos, Theoria de
los Agrupamientos Sociales, Valor Sociologico del Folklore*.[22] The works
present something more than routine social philosophy and together
with many other of the publications of the *Caudernos*, Mendieta y
Nuñez has provided the Spanish speaking world with a rich library
of eclectic sociology. Other sociologists who have contributed to social
theory in Mexico are Jose Echeverria, Echanove Trujillo, and L.
Recasens Siches.

Mexican sociology, on the whole, has been less influenced by European theorizing and is more related to practical needs. Sociology is
more oriented toward anthropological questions due to the large Indian and mestizo population. Excellent field work has been performed
by such individuals as Manuel Gamio and Alfonso Villa Rojas.

Peru. To many students, especially outside Latin America, the
greatest sociologist of the entire Ibero-American world was Mariano
H. Cornejo. His *Sociologia General* represents an ingenious attempt
to fuse the theories of such diverse origins as Spencer, Frazer, Tarde,
Durkheim, Ward, Comte, Tylor and Giddings. He was attempting to
explain the origin of culture, the psychologistic basis of institutions,
and a general theory of evolution. All of his sources were European
and his interests were in no way related to the contemporary American
scene. Also, the translation of his work into French soon after its
publication assured the work an international audience. As Bernard
points out, although the work suffers from a number of defects, including a Lamarckian viewpoint on heredity, it probably represents
the most comprehensive attempt at systematization in early twentieth
century sociology in Latin America.[23]

The outstanding sociologist in Peru today is Roberto MacLean y
Estenos who has interpreted social change in his country, with *Sociedad
Peruana*[24] and *Sociologia Educacional en el Antiguo Peru*,[25] in addi-

tion to his more general *Sociologia Integral*.[26] As with most Latin American sociologists the theory is predominantly a resume of a hundred years of social thought. There is a considerably larger offering of anthropology and geography than with Cornejo.

These above sociologists are only representative. In Bolivia there is Arturo Urquida. In Columbia (where it is asserted that the first course of sociology in the Americas was offered in 1882) Luis Lopez de Mesa and Luis Nieto Arteta, in addition to certain anthropologists, are at least on the periphery of sociology. In Cuba, among others, Robert Agramonte is active in a number of fields. In Ecuador, from which relatively little has been forthcoming of a sociological nature, we find one of the most exciting community studies ever to appear in Hispanic America, namely, Gonzalo R. Orbe's *Punyaro*,[27] documenting social behavior and institutional life in the small Indian-mestizo suburb of Otovalo. Arcaya and other sociologists in Venezuela, together with the leadership of George Hill, lead one to believe that scientific sociology is being launched.

The basic pattern then is that sociology has remained largely speculative and philosophical. It is not irrelevant that history has remained the leading social "science" in Latin America in comparison to the lower status of the other disciplines: economics, political theory, and sociology. It is only in the last decade or so that social anthropology has become truly respectable.

Although sociology has largely been an eclectic adoption of European and (less frequently) North American theories has not prevented the cultivation of certain national interests. All of these countries have focused to some extent on their own problems, which is not surprising in view of the isolation and regionalism.

It is increasingly apparent that a "new look" has crept into Latin American sociology. It is a diffusional process from the United States and Europe and, more important, from San Paulo and Mexico City. Not only are names like Lundberg, Stouffer, and Parsons now current, but Latin Americans are providing training in empirical methods. There are a number of results from this new orientation which have developed gradually since the mid-thirties.

FIELDS OF SPECIALIZATION

One dominant trend is the necessity of sociology to specialize—a recognition that the subject matter is complex and can no longer be a general treatise, another *Sociologia general*. One distinction that has been clarified is that between what is theoretical and what is applied. Conveniently, the latter term has been employed for every relatively non-philosophical or non-theoretical expression of interest from social history to folklore to the problem of social reform. Today applied sociology is becoming more specifically related to problems of social disorganization and social planning.

We have already mentioned the tendency of "sociologia" to be applied in national terms, as this, "sociologia argentina" or "sociologia colombiana." In some cases, there may have been political necessity at the root of the publication. On the other hand, the term "cultural sociology" refers to the study of a given society, generally aboriginal.

Regional Sociology. Well entrenched in South American sociology are regional and community studies. This trend began with the century in da Cunha's *Os Sertaos* and in Argentina with Juan Garcia's *La Ciudad Indiana*. In contemporary Brazil this tendency has amounted to a passion. It appears that the country may become the most studied area in the world. There has been Freyre in the northeast; Pierson on the Cruz das Almas,[28] together with the San Paulo staff directing a number of investigations in the San Francisco Valley; the farreaching series of studies on Bahia under the direction of Charles Wagley and Thales de Azevedo; Oracy Nogueira on Itapetininga in the state of San Paolo; and Eduardo Galvao with *caboclos* and acculutrated Indians in the Rio Negro area of the Amazon. In Mexico, starting with Robert Redfield's Topozotlan study, there has developed a tradition of community studies: Alfonso Villa Rojas in Yucatan and Chiapas, Alfonso Fabila in the north of Mexico, and a dozen other social anthropological investigations. In this connection one cannot lose sight of the role of foreign sociologists in Latin American regional studies, to mention only a few: Lowry Nelson, *Rural Cuba*; Carl Taylor, *Rural Life in Argentina*; or Sol Tax in Guatemala; Alfred Metraux in Brazil; or Ralph Beals and John Gillin in a number of places. Although rural sociology has been in a more pivotal situation, attention is becoming increasingly focused on urban sociology. Likewise ecology has enjoyed growing interest.

Demography. The study of population has now become meaningful in that statistics are more regularly maintained. Organizations like the Institute Brazileiro de Geografia e Estatistica are communicating their findings to a professional public. The work of Gino Germani in Argentina has already been mentioned. Public health has preoccupied the sociologist, as, for example, Alberto Ramos' study of infant mortality, indicating that it must be viewed according to community stratification, and other social patterns.[29] Again, international teams have been fairly productive in this area of measuring populational statistics.

Family sociology, like most functional courses, is not found in many curricula, however, the subject has become a particularly vital one in Brazil in recent years. Many of the community studies are developing subordinate topics of family organization. Antonio Candido and Levy Cruz, in addition to others already mentioned, are specializing in family systems. At the same time, the field of *culture and personality* is only slowly emerging in Latin America. In part, this may be explained by the extensive amount of ground work to be performed before this area can be a significant one. Furthermore, psychoanalysis does not have the following in most foreign areas (except for a few centers like Buenos Aires) as it has in the United States. In fact, the field of *social psychology* is in its infancy. Undoubtedly the Catholic influence is partly responsible here. Among the several exceptions are Manuel Gamio in Mexico, Luis Lopez de Mesa in Colombia, and Luis Bossano in Ecuador. De Azevedo and others in Brazil have been influential on the positive side in this respect. Also, Brazil, Mexico, Colombia, and Venezuela have established public opinion institutes. *Folklore* is another area of concentration with a number of societies devoted to its study, including a *Revista de Folklore* having been published in at least two countries, Colombia and Venezuela. Again, we are reminded that the division between cultural anthropology and sociology is arbitrary in Latin America, if it exists at all.

Urban sociology has recently become a center of interest, as indicated by two penetrating investigations of Buenos Aires and Caracas, respectively.[30] *Sociology of law* is not infrequently offered in the curriculum, particularly as sociology courses are still offered in the *Facultad de Derecho* (law school) in a number of institutions. Nor is it surprising that in an area where there has been a frantic attempt to attain universal literacy, *educational sociology* is offered in the curriculum.

Some perspective of the field's of interest may be gained from examining some typical courses at the *Escola Livre* of San Paulo: General Anthropology, Introduction to Sociology, Culture and Personality, Brazilian Ethnology, Social Organization and Social Disorganization, Comparative Institutions, Culture and Personality, Human

Geography, Methods of Research in the Social Sciences. In addition, nearly thirty courses are required in biology, psychology, history, economics, political science, education, and statistics. More frequently, in the smaller universities, there exists one or two courses in sociology. More rarely is an applied course offered, say, in marriage and family relations, social welfare, or crime and delinquency. Mexico, on the other hand, has been more interested in the practical type of courses, especially at the National School of Political and Social Sciences, which has a different offering from the Escuela Universitaria or of the National School of Anthropology and History. In most countries these problems are introduced in a general course, if at all. The emphasis in a basic course is almost invariably on sociological systems and theories. If there is a textbook, it generally would be of the nature of a history of social thought.

RESEARCH FACILITIES, PUBLICATIONS AND ORGANIZATIONS

Ibero-America has become considerably more sophisticated methodologically over the last twenty years. For one thing, there has been a translation into Spanish of a number of works dealing with research methods, such as MacIver's *Social Causation*, Kaufman's *Methodology in the Social Sciences*, and Lundberg's *Social Research*. Again, Brazilian students for some years have been deeply concerned with experimental design and the problem of social causation. Fernandes exemplifies this problem in his careful analyses of a host of writers from Spencer to Radcliffe-Brown, from Durkheim to Merton.[31]

In the shift to more scientific research, one factor that has been most important has been the growth of private, governmental, and international institutions (including, of course, those in education) that are more aware of their responsibility than they were a generation earlier. Universities in the advanced areas have been able to secure more adequate financial support. Interamerican organizations, as well as the United Nations, have been advantageous in this respect. For instance, the University of Puerto Rico has been aided by the Social Science Research Council in developing a sound program in demography and the sociology of the family. Similarly, the University of Venezuela has expanded their training program in the social sciences under a plan of "intellectual collaboration" with the University of Wisconsin.

As with other countries, the role of institutes (which may be centers of instruction, research, or publication, or all three) has been critical in developing this empirical orientation. Foremost there is the Centro de Pesquissa (Research Center) in our much cited Escola at San Paulo, where Emilio Willems and Romano Barrato have been publishing since 1938 the quarterly *Sociologia,* the most professional sociological journal of Latin America, or in any romance language for that matter. In Rio de Janeiro there is the Brazilian Institute of Public Opinion and Statistics under the direction of A. Panteado. In Mexico City there is the Instituto Indigenista and the Instituto de Investigaciones Sociales, where Lucio Mendieta y Nunez publishes the quarterly *Revista Mexicana de Sociologia* (which also commenced in 1938) and a most mature series of publications, *Cuadernos de Sociologia.* Laslo Radvanyi also edits *Social Sciences* (apparently replacing the *International Journal of Public Opinion*) which has been more an American publication than a Latin American one. In addition to these publications, there is the *Fondo de Cultura Economica* series. Although the mortality rate for journals is high in Latin America, there is hope for the Instituto Venezolana de Sociologia and its *Revista Internacional de Sociologia.* Certainly Venezuela enjoys a happier economic basis than most other Latin American countries. Argentina, which during the nineteenth century had the leading position in sociology, may yet return to that status in Hispanic America. The University de Buenos Aires publishes the *Boletin de Sociologia,* and at the University of Tucaman appears periodically a *Revista de Sociologia.* The *Revista Internacional de Sociologia* published by the Instituto "Balmes" de Sociologia in Madrid has served as another outlet for Latin American sociologists.

Governmental stability and adequate fiscal systems will continue to determine the extent of research and publication facilities. In Bolivia, for example, economic and political instability may prevent the fulfillment of the ambitious program of the Instituto Boliviano de Sociologia which hopes to study systematically various aboriginal cultures throughout the country. Apparently, there is some investigation already underway regarding the movement of a group of Aymara Indians from the high plateau to the tropical area of Santa Cruz.

Sociological Organizatons. Foremost among the organizations that have continent-wide interest is the Asociacion Latin Americana de Sociologia with its annual meetings. Argentine sociologists, especially Alfred Povina, have been most active in maintaining this organization, which has been generally more interested in history and philosophy than in empirical research. The association is related to national organizations and the International Sociological Society, and the *Boletin de Sociologia* is its organ. Latin Americans appear to be even more *aficionado* for conventions than are other inhabitants of the world, and hence from Monterey to Santiago there are regional or international meetings on folklore, criminology, or social welfare. For instance, the annual meeting of the Mexican Sociological Association produces a worthwhile volume, *Estudios Sociologicos*, generally devoted to one area.[32]

The United Nations Organization (particularly through Unesco) has offered advantages to the development of the social sciences. The Pan-American Union, which publishes the monthly *Ciencias Sociales*, and the Office of Inter-American Affairs are active in promoting communication and in offering scholarships and fellowships for students and research scientists.

FUTURE TRENDS AND NEEDS

This article has presented all too little of Latin American sociology, both past and present—as concerns individuals, publications, and organizations. However, certain long range tendencies are clear, most important of which is the emergence of empirical methods. The "new" centers, like Mexico City and San Paulo, are apparently of the nature of catalyzing agents throughout Latin America. Men like Oscar Alvarez Andrews in Chile and Francisco Ayala in Argentina have turned from philosophical issues to empirical problems. There is a suggestion of more international cooperation throughout Latin America. The articles in the *revista* are more practical in orientation.

Certainly the present author has no right to prescribe the kind of research that Latin American sociologists should follow, but the philosophical tradition of the previous generation hardly appears functional in the nineteen fifties. It would be impossible to predict the direction that sociology to the South will follow in the years ahead. It does appear however, that certain discrepancies should be corrected: (1) As with some other parts of the world, there is need for more full-time chairs in sociology. This would serve to establish sociology as an independent discipline in universities where it is only an adjunct of philosophy, history, or some other discipline. (2) Emphasis should be placed on further specialization in the various fields of sociology, and for the formulation of hypotheses that would be relevant to the problems of Latin American society. (3) Considerably more training should be given in research methods, both statistics and field work. In some of the writings one is appalled by the inability to accumulate valid data and the complete lack of documentation. Courses in methodology have, after all, been offered in only a few of the larger universities. (4) Until Latin American facilities are more adequate, students should be urged to procure advanced training in foreign schools. The San Paulo school has for two decades urged their more hopeful students to secure graduate work in Western Europe and the United States. The United Nations and our own government might assume some of the financial responsibility for this program.

In view of the progress of the last decade, it would not be surprising to find in another decade cities like Havana, Caracas, Lima, Montivideo, and Satiago as vital a sociological center with well-trained personnel as one finds at present in certain more established facilities. A mutitude of problems, both theoretical and applied, await these future researchers.

SELECTED BIBLIOGRAPHY

(Due to the language problem, only sources in English are given, except for a few indispensable references in Spanish. For the few who read Portuguese, there are references contained in the text. It might be added that for one who reads Spanish, acquiring a reading knowledge [not a speaking knowledge!] of Portuguese is fairly simple).

F. Aquilera, *Handbook of Latin American Studies, 1950* (Gainesville: University of Florida Press, 1953). A complete bibliography on Latin American publications; the section on sociology by T. Lynn Smith is useful; see also succeeding years.

American Anthropologist, LVII(June, 1955). This issue is largely devoted to Latin America; however, other issues frequently contain articles or book reviews in that area.

Roger Bastide, "Latin America," 615-637, in George Gurvitch & Wilbert E. Moore, Eds., *Twentieth Century Sociology* (New York: Philosophical Library 1945). An interpretative summary of major trends.

Howard Becker & Harry E. Barnes, *Social Thought from Lore to Science.* (Washington, D. C.: Harren Press, 1952), II, 1119-1134. Although now quite dated, these pages present very adequately some of the earlier sociologists.

L. L. Bernard, "The Systematic Sociology of Mariano H. Cornejo," in Harry E. Barnes, Ed., *An Introduction to the History of Sociology* (The University of Chicago Press), 902-930.

Boletin de Sociologia (Buenos Aires: Instituto de Sociologia, Universidad de Buenos Aires, 1952). This series of articles is a good cross-section of Latin American sociologists from the social historian Ricardo Levene to the logical positivist, Mario Lins. The articles on methodology by Gino Germani are particularly good.

Rex W. Crawford, *A Century of Latin American Thought* (Cambridge, Mass.: Harvard University Press, 1944). An excellent discussion regarding a number of 19th and 20th century *pensadores*.

Harold E. Davis, *Social Science in Latin America* (Washington, D.C.: 1950); "Latin America," Chapter X, 423-500, in Philip L. Harriman, Joseph S. Roucek, & George B. de Huszar, Eds., *Contemporary Social Science*. Vol. I: *Western Hemisphere* (Harrisburg, Penna.: The Stackpole Co., 1953). Valuable summaries.

Fernando De Azevedo, *Brazil, An Interpretation* (New York: The MacMillan Co., 1945). A foremost sociologist summarizes the history, culture, and value orientations of his country.

Gilberto Freyre, *The Masters and the Slaves* (New York: Alfred A. Knopf, 1946). A superb example of descriptive sociology in a historical context.

Ralph Linton, Ed., *Most of the World* (New York: Columbia University Press, 1949). The sections, "Mestizo America," (John Gillin) and "Brazil" (Charles Wagley) introduce the reader to some of the major social problems.

Donald E. Worcester, & Wendell G. Schaeffer, *The Growth and Culture of Latin America* (New York: Oxford University Press, 1956). The stream of Ibero-American history with considerable attention to the social aspects.

Robert C. Williamson is a member of the Psychology and Sociology Departments, the Los Angeles City and State Colleges. In addition to being co-author with S. Stansfeld Sargent of *Social Psychology* (Ronald Press, 1958), he has written numerous articles and book reviews; a partial list includes "Socio-economic Factors in Marital Adjustment in an Urban Setting" (doctoral dissertation) in *Marriage and Family Living* (November, 1952), and *American Sociological Review* (April, 1954); "Race Relations in South Africa," *Sociology and Social Research* (January, 1955); "Sociology in Latin America," *Sociology and Social Research* (October, 1955); "Crime in South Africa: Some Aspects of Causes and Treatment," *Journal of Criminology, Criminal Law, and Police Science* (July, 1957). In addition, he has been a contributor to *Sociological Abstracts*. As a member of the American Sociological Society (and in connection with his extensive travels in Europe, Africa, and South America), he has served on the Committee for Relations with Sociologists in other Countries.

NOTES

1. Raul Orgaz, *Introducción a la Sociologia* (Cordova: Universidad de la Cordova, 1952).

2. Povina reflects Hegel in his not atypical statement: "The State is the political superstructure of society that mediates the legal disposition of the power instinct (la ordenacion juridica del instinto de poderio), satisfies the social and political functions of group life." "El Estado como Concepto Sociologico," in Gorrado Gini, Ed., *Proceedings of the 14th International Congress of Sociology* (Rome: Societa Italiana di Sociologia, 1951), 590-595. In this same period it may be added that Peron himself was something of a social philosopher. Justicialism was coined to represent a middle position between spiritualism and materialism, democracy and communism.

3. (Buenos Aires: Ed. Raigal, 1955).

4. According to Wagley, approximately five different cultural types are identifiable: *Caboclo,* or mixed European and Indian, in other words, mestizo. Frequently in the coastal area and in a variety of occupations; *fazendo,* agricultural workers in the large plantations; *cidade,* or small town; metropolitan lower class; and metropolitan upper class. Charles Wagley, Brazilian Community Studies: A methodological Evaluation, in Florestan Fernandes, Ed., *Symposium Ethno-sociologico sobre Comunidades Humanas no Brazil* (San Paulo: Anais do Congreso Internacional de Americanistas, 1955), pp. 357-376. At the same time there are roughly three racial types, European (the older Portuguese and the more recent immigrants), Negro and mulatto—color is a gradation in Brazil with only vaguely discrete demarcations and *caboclo,* the mixed Amerind and white.

5. F. Fernandes, "Die sozialgeschichtliche Entwicklung der Soziologie in Brasilien," *Sociologus,* VI (1956), 100-115.

6. Translated as *Rebellion in the Backlands* (University of Chicago Press, 1944)

7. (Rio de Janeiro: Mai and Schmidt, 1933); translated into English as *The Masters and the Slaves* (New York: Alfred A. Knopf, 1946).

8. (San Paulo: Editora Nacional, 1933).

9. (Rio de Janeiro: S. Olympia, 1937).

10. (Rio de Janeiro: A. Noîte, 1939).

11. (Rio de Janeiro: Civilização Brasileiro, 1934).

12. (Rio de Janeiro: Jornal do Commercio, 1954).

13. (Rio de Janeiro: Jornal do Commercio, 1956).

14. (San Paulo: Ediçoes Melhoramentos, 1935).

15. (New York: The Macmillan Co., 1945).

16. (San Paulo: Ediçoes Melhoramentos, 1940).

17. (San Paulo: Livraria Martins Editora, S. A., 1950).

18. Possibly Pierson is best known for his study of race relations in Bahia, *Negroes in Brazil* (University of Chicago Press, 1942).

19. *Relaçoes Raciais entre Negros e Brancos em Sao Paulo* (San Paulo: Editora Anhembi, 1955).

20. (Barcelona: Cervantes, 1929).

21. (Mexico City: Editora Porrua, 5th ed., 1948).

22. Most are published in the series *Caudernos de Sociologia* (Mexico City:

Biblioteca de Ensayos Sociologicos, Instituto de Investigaciones Sociales, Universidad Nacional) .

23. L. L. Bernard, "The Systematic Sociology of Mariano H. Cornejo," in Harry E. Barnes, Ed., *An Introduction to the History of Sociology* (The University of Chicago Press, 1948) , 902-930.

24. (Lima: Editora Gil, 1942) .

25. (Mexico City: Caudernos de Sociologia, 1955).

26. (Lima: Editora Gil, 1945) .

27. (Quito: Editorial Casa de la Cultura Ecuartoiana, 1956) .

28. Donald Pierson, *Cruz das Alma: A Brazilian Village* (Washington, D. C.; Institute of Social Anthropology, 1952) .

29. *Sociologia de la Mortalidad Infantil* (Mexico City: Biblioteca de Ensayos Sociologicos, 1955) .

30. Canal-Feijoo, Bernardo, *Theoria de la Ciudad Argentina* (Buenos Aires: Editorial Sudamericana, 1951) Sampiero, José, *La Populacion del Area Metropolitana de Caracas* (Caracas: Cuadernos de Informacion Economicas, 1956) .

31. F. Fernandes, *Ensaio sobre o Metodo de Interpretação Funcionista na Sociologia* (San Paulo: Universidade de Filosofia, Ciencias e Letras, Boletim No. 170, 1953) , *Current Theoretical Trends of Ethnological Research in Brazil* (unpublished manuscript, 1956) .

32. The issue on *Sociologia Economica* (1954) had some especially significant papers.

RUSSIAN SOCIOLOGY AND
"SOCIOLOGY" UNDER COMMUNISM

Joseph S. Roucek
University of Bridgeport

In Communist theory, "bourgeois sociology" rejects the idealistic as well as the naturalistic theories of society as not corresponding to facts. Communism accepts as its working hypothesis the dialectic unity of the subjective elements and the objective environment of society and nature. At the present stage in history, society and not nature leads in the dialectic process of social evolution.

From this point of view, we can even question whether Soviet Russia can boast of sociology, since "the social sciences in Russia present a marked contrast to those of the western world."[1] It is true that the pre-communist sociologists of Russia had made remarkable contributions (as shown by such oustanding names of world-wide reputation as P. A. Sorokin, Nicholas S. Timasheff, and others).[2] But these sociologists have been exiled, making their contributions to American and Western sociological thought; as far as their "Russian sociology" is concerned, here they have made their contributions by offering us their knowledge of the Russian thinkers and by analyzing, sociologically, the past and present conditions in the USSR.[3]

A direct quotation from G. F. Aleksandrov, author of *The History of Western Philosophy*, indicates the difference between Western and Soviet sociology:[4]

> ". . . the foremost difference between the Marxist-Leninist science of society and all sorts of idealistic sociological theories is that Marxist-Leninist science was able to discover the objective, systematic relationship of historical phenomena—was able to recognize and discern, among the thousands and thousands of great and petty events, the single advancing, ascending, progressive line of development of society. At the same time, the Marxist science of society has definitely established the fact that progressive evolution of production—that material foundation of the whole life

of society—lies at the root of this social advance, accomplished despite all the obstacles erected by reactionary forces, despite so frequent and at that time prolonged delays and even retreats and backward steps."

Furthermore,

"The Marxist-Leninist science of society is distinct from all other theories of society's development in that it is capable of correct estimates of contemporary events, as well as past. It judges events accurately in the periods of society's more or less ordinary development; it evaluates them just as accurately in time of abrupt and rapid breakup of the old—in times of the sharpest and most intense class struggle. It can discern the seeds of the future which the present contains; it has a clear perspective of society's development. Marxist-Leninist science is based on historical experience; it generalizes the phenomena of life and applies the rest of reality to theoretical and political deductions and premises." [5]

If we are to present differences between Western and Soviet sociology, it is clear that the first aims to be empirical and causal, the other dialectical and mystifying.

For the Western sociologist, man is the product of society apart from his genetic inheritance; and in that society, all institutional, technological, and cultural factors are dynamic and interdependent in their results; thus also non-economic factors can influence the rest and changes can be inaugurated at any point. But for the Marxian follower, man is the product of society, and society, in turn, is only the product of the methods of production; and this formula must not be tested and modified, since it explains the dialectic tendencies in history "with an iron necessity towards an inevitable goal."

Basically, the Soviet social scientist assumes that a genuine social science can be developed only by Marxism-Leninism, the only possible "scientific" ideology. Philosophy is the chief integrating "ideological science," functioning (1) to clarify "the Marxist foundations of both social and natural sciences," and (2) "guiding" the other sciences in the ideological crusades of the day. Thus the Soviet scientist cannot challenge but must record, cannot theorize but rationalizes, does not inquire but reflects. He studies Soviet society from scientific facts— universally applicable and fully predictable portents of historical materialism. He gathers illustrative material for the formally propounded principles of the workings of various components of Soviet society, giving "scholarly" publicity to the Party's official claims. Thus the Soviet social scientists "has ceased to be a scientist in the true meaning of the term. He has ceased to theorize and has shown remarkable reluctance to generalize on any level."[6] Hence "there is not discipline in the Soviet Union resembling a sociology of knowledge, for the Soviet man of learning . . . studies science ideologically."[7]

In the final analysis, whatever "sociology" Soviet Russia has developed has been directed, since 1929, by the Soviet Academy of Sciences which uses the principle of practical usefulness as the chief criterion in appraising scientific research and requires minute and rigid planning. This highest scientific body in the USSR deals with all the branches of systematized knowledge and trains future scholars.

Instructors in the social sciences for "higher institutions of learning" and theoretical personnel for "scientific-research institutions" and "scientific journals" are also trained by the Academy of the Social Sciences which heads the system of Party schools; it is directed by the Central Committee. The following fields of specialization are recognized: "political economy, economics and politics of foreign countries, theory of state and law, international law, history of the USSR, general history, international relations, history of the Communist Party, dialectical and historical materialism, history of Russian and Western philosophy, logic and psychology, theory and history of literature, theory and history of art, and foreign languages."[8] "Refresher courses" for the instructors degree ("Aspirantura") and a Doctor's degree ("Doktorantura"). "Aspirantura" was founded in 1925, requires three years, numerous written examinations, rigorous training and teaching and research, and a written dissertation; from here come most of the scientific cadres and teachers in the schools of higher and specialized learning. Since 1943, the Doctor's degree has been granted after two years of training to the possessors of a Candidate's degree and who have published a number of works in their respective fields; they must present a thesis making a scientific contribution and thus prove their ability to carry on research work.

Yet, in spite of the domination of the science by Marxist and Stalinist ideology, we must note that "recent years have shown marked advances in many areas of Soviet science and technology and an increasing conformity with the principles of world-wide science."[9] This has been certified to, for instance, by the National Science Foundation which, on January 14, 1957, asserted that the United States' leadership in technology "can no longer be taken for granted" in the light of educational developments within the USSR. In its sixth annual report to President Eisenhower, it stated:

> "We do not wish to be forced into a position of competition with the U.S.S.R. on its own terms; but Russian emphasis on science and mathematics, particularly in secondary schools, lends added weight to the need for scrutinizing our own educational system closely." [10]

SOVIET BRAND OF SOCIOLOGY

There is no Soviet counterpart of Western sociology. The Department of Social Sciences, founded in 1919 at Moscow University, which included a Chair of Sociology, was closed in 1924. Ethnography survived in the new Department of Ethnology until 1930; from then until 1939, when a Chair of Ethnology was founded in the Department of History, there was no academic teaching on topics even distantly related to sociology.[11] The Chair of Anthropology in the Department of Biology worked in the field of Physical Anthropology. The subject-matter of sociological inquiry was removed from academic life and placed under direct Party supervision, subsumed under Marxism-Leninism and taught as Political Economy or Philosophy, or as part of general political education. Several academic institutions occasionally engaged in investigations of a social character (such as surveys of working-class family budgets), but they did not survive the purge of 1930. Today there is no department of sociology or separate institutes of sociology. The Academy of Sciences of the USSR (as pointed out) has a section on social sciences, comprising institutes of philosophy, economics, ethnography, law, and history, but no sociology. Theses for higher degrees in the social sciences (written also at various economic and pedagogical institutes, the Military-Political Academy, the Higher Party schools, etc.) sometimes deal with subjects bordering on sociology, but within the Marxian framework (covering such subjects as: "Defense of Socialist Society— A Sacred Task and Honorable Duty of the Citizens of the USSR," or "Militarization of the Economy and Deterioration of the Condition of the Working-Class in the U.S.A. in the Post-War Period, 1946-54").

That there is no sociology in Soviet Russia as we understand it in the West is due to historical reasons, since nearly, if not all Rus-

sian sociology before 1917 was basically social philosophy, represented
by several ideological movements elaborated in a speculative fashion.[12]
When the Soviet came to power they did not like liberals as Sorokin,
or any ideas of having a separate, independent science, carried on
independently from the ideology of Marxism-Leninism. Yet, on the
other hand, under the Soviets the Soviet scholars have produced
monographs in ethnology, ethnography, folklore, social history and
studies of social processes in connection with social planning which
would be "customarily included in the field of sociology elsewhere." [13]

Thus it is important to remember that the Soviet sociologists know
no such discipline as sociology in its empiric aspects; and that all
social science in the USSR is Marxist science and any research must
be carried on within this ideological framework. Marxism claims to
be the only truly scientific method of seeking truth; it is accordingly
considered as the proper method for use in all fields of social science,
including history, sociology, economics, psychology, and geography.[14]
For instance, S. Kovalyov, published an article in the March, 1947
issue of *Bolshevik*, proclaiming:[15]

> "Leninist-Marxism teaches us that new ideas and theories spring
> up only after the material development of society has placed
> new problems before the community . . . Marxism-Leninism
> theory, the one genuinely scientific theory of the development of
> society, generalizes the experience gained in the struggle of the
> laboring masses, anticipates life, lights the way for the practical
> activity of the people, affords a clarity of perspective, a con-
> fidence in the victory of Communism. The Leninist-Marxian
> concept of life is the cornerstone of Communist education of
> the workers of our country; its diffusion speeds the elimination
> of outdated views and the mass birth of a Communist conscious-
> ness."

Without analyzing this well-known doctrine, let us only note that
the Marxian-Leninist premises, in spite of the ideological battles carried on within the Communist camp, have been propounded and
re-interpreted by Stalin and by his contemporary successors. For instance, proclaimed Stalin in 1938 and 1952:[16]

> "Marxism regards laws of science—whether they be laws of
> natural sciences or laws of political economy—as the reflection
> of objective processes which take place independently of the will
> of man. Man may discover these laws, get to know them, study
> them, reckon with them in his activities and utilize them in the

interests of society, but he cannot change or abolish them. Still less can he form or create new laws of science."

and

"The prime task of historical science is to study and disclose the laws or production, the laws of development of the productive forces and of the relations of production, the laws of economic development of society."

These assumptions, accepted as "the truth," are glaringly different from the assumptions of western sociology and social sciences. History is not the only valid approach to truth and the fundamental laws of relationships which would be universally valid have not been discovered as yet: revolutions help historical changes but there are other processes of change, and economic production is only one of the basic factors in social relationships, and "even the pollsters admit that there are many areas of human relationships which are, in practice, unpredictable."[17]

MARXIAN "SOCIOLOGY" IN RUSSIA

The present Marxian interpretation of "everything" in Soviet Russia, including sociology, has its roots not only directly in Karl Marx,[18] but in several Russian interpreters and followers or critics of Karl Marx.[19]

The theories of Marx attracted many Russian thinkers from the very beginning, since his ideology helped them to get work for the abolition of the stranglehold of autocracy and for the creation of a new social order; especially attractive to them was Marx's idea that changes in the form of production are followed by an inevitable change of social and political institutions.

Two factions arose from these Marxian or Objectivist sociologists: the Orthodox (headed by the "father" of Russian Marxism, Plekhanov and his pupil Lenin) and the heterodox Neo-Marxists and Revisionists (composed of Struve, Tugan-Baranovsky and Bogdanov).[20] They all can be included among the proponents of Historical Sociology.

George Plekhanov (1857-1918), a famed revolutionary, who founded the Marxian wing of Russian Social Democracy, had to go into exile in Switerland; on his return he lived in Russia under several pseudonyms (N. Beltov, Volgin, Valentin, etc.). As a leader of the Menshevik faction (which opposed Bolshevism after the split in the

Russian Socialist Party in 1903, and particularly in the Russian revolution of 1917, as a minority (in Russian "menchinstvo") at the party congress preceding the split), he opposed Lenin, the accepted leader and chief theoretician of Bolshevik Communism, although Lenin paid personal high tribute to his former friend and teacher, long after their political and ideological routes had parted. Plekhanov's fist Marxist study was also the first Marxist sociological study by a Russian: *Toward the Development of a Monistic Conception of History* (1895); for him the economic factors were primary historical factors, and he attacked the subjectivists's idea that society is the product of interaction of social forces or factors. (The "Subjectivists" were headed by Lavrov, Mikhalovsky, Youzhakov and Kareyev; they accepted Comte's classification of the sciences, with minor changes and stressed that the psycho-social factors and activities and leading individuals were the determining factors within organized society). Plekhanov's beliefs formed the theoretical foundation for the socio-democratic movement in Russia, and were expounded in his *Socialism and the Political Struggle* (1883), *Our Differences* (1884), and especially his *Essays in Historical Materialism* (New York: International Publishers, 1940).[21]

Peter Struve (1870-1944) edited a periodical *Emancipation* (together with a famed historian Paul Milyukov), which rejected the class struggle and revolutionary action and wanted to persuade the government, by the pressure of public opinion to grant reform. These were his revised views, since, at the beginning, he used Simmel's and Riehl's sociological and psychological generalizations to support the Marxian sociological assumptions. He ended by propounding that social evolution had to proceed by gradual compromise and reform; finally he changed into a counterrevolutionary and almost a mystic (so that Hecker classified him as belonging to "the subjectivist school of sociology"). Tugan-Baranovsky, formerly Professor of Political Economy in St. Petersburg, authored, among his numerous works, *The Theoretical Basis of Marxism* (1905), propounding the materialistic conception of history, although differing from Marx by recognizing other human interests along with the ecoonmic interests as important social forces. Alexander A. Bogdanov (1873-1928), was educated as a physician and in 1903, joined the Bolshevik faction of the Russian Socialist Democratic Party; but he differed with Lenin on philosophic issues and remained politically inactive until 1917, when the Soviet government granted him subsidies for scientific research.

He differed from Marx by identifying sociability with social consciousness, and in stating that classes would not disappear by capturing social power, not by the worker capturing the means of production, but by the socialization of organizational experience and through the education of the laboring class in "proletarian culture." "The anti-Marxian errors in Bogdanov's theories are now generally recognized by Communist thinkers."[22]

"SOCIOLOGY" UNDER THE SOVIETS

Under the Soviets, "Communist sociology has grown, through the direction given to it by the genius of Lenin, into a magnificent science of socialist planning . . ." claims Hecker, who, today, certainly would have to apologize for his additional claim that this science "is still in its infancy but which has all the promise of delivering humanity from the anarchist chaos into which the capitalist system of production has placed it."[23]

At any rate, Nicholas Bukharin (1888-1938), the author of *Historical Materialism, A System of Sociology* (New York: International Publishers, 1925), is highly appreciated as the most able recent sociologist; he proclaimed that historical materialism was not only a method of research but also a general theory of society which guides the laws of social evolution. For him, sociology provides the way of "scientific prediction" in social processes as any natural science can. This proponent of mechanistic materialism also stressed a socio-psychological analysis of society and developed an occupational psychology in the sense that one's occupation tends to influence the nature of personality; the subtler influences of one's environment are not recognized by the individual, but will be recognized if a person takes the place of society and views the operation of environmental forces objectively. (He was executed with Rykov and Yagoda in March, 1938, on the then commonplace charges of treason and espionage).

Vladimir Ilyitch Lenin (1870-1924), has been the final authority, with Marx, "on everything" in Soviet Russia. One of the most influential figures in contemporary history, we cannot deal with the details about his remarkable careers and his numerous writings; in fact, the literature available on him is growing every day.[24]

Born on April 22, 1870, at Simbirak, this son of a college teacher, became a lawyer, joined the revolutionary labor movement, adopted the alias of Lenin (his actual name being Ulyanoff). A strict Marxist, he led the radical, uncompromising wing in the Russian Socialist Party which broke away from the moderate faction in 1903 under the name of Bolsheviks. Living in exile at Paris, Vienna and Zurich from 1907 to 1917, he advocated a revolutionary course at socialist congresses; and denounced the socialist support of World War I in 1914. During his time, Marx and Engels helped socialism to reach its test-tube maturity; but the man who perfected the bacterial warfare whereby the body of capitalism was to be infected was Lenin. In 1902, he clearly outlined the sociological part of Marxism, especially Marx's analysis of the sociological weaknesses of the bourgeois system. Later, Lenin picked up J. A. Hobson's liberal critique of imperialism and applied it to a Marxist analysis of the weaknesses of the bourgeois system on the international plane, propounding that internally and internationally capitalism is creating the forces of self-destruction, not only because of the economic trends (which are the master cause) but directly through the social and cultural tendencies it generates.

In 1917, Lenin interrupted his writing of *The State and Revolution* with the words: "It is pleasanter and more useful to live through the experience of a revolution than to write about it." He went through it. Under him, socialism ceased to be merely a theory and became a political reality, since Lenin started to master a great state, ruling 170,000,000 people.

Transported by the orders of the German General Staff in a sealed carriage across Germany to Russia, Lenin arrived at Petersburg in April, 1917, took over the Bolshevik Party. Together with Trotsky, he organized a first uprising in July which proved abortive, and a second on November 7, 1919 (October 25 in the Russian calendar) which overthrew the moderate Kerensky government. He became President of the Council of the People's Commissars; under him and Trotsky, the civil war ended in 1921, when the victory of the Bolsheviks (now calling themselves Communists) became a reality. Lenin organized the Communist (the Third) International, which is still combating socialism and has become the first class subversive and spying organization. In 1922, Lenin was shot by a woman member of the anti-Bolshevik social revolutionary party; his health remained weak thereafter. He died on January 21, 1924; his embalmed body has been permanently exhibited at the Lenin Mausoleum in Moscow.

Lenin adopted the Marxian ideas to Russia. He stressed that reality is "independent of human consciousness" and believed in a world whose laws should be studied objectively. The world is an "interpenetration of opposite forces" that approach a unity and then pull apart. The law of change is basically evolutionary, interrupted from time to time by "spontaneous, periodic breaks"—revolutionary outbursts. Lenin also applied the Marxist analysis to the new forms of capitalism which have developed since Marx. Following the inevitable concentration of capital, huge trusts and combines have superseded the small producers of the earlier stages of capitalism. Large capital interests and the state have become inextricably interwoven, and the former drive the governments to imperialistic policies with a view to securing foreign markets and sources of raw materials. The clash of the various imperialisms leads to war in the interests of big capitalists, and to further greater crises and wars until the proletarian revolution overthrows capitalism and organizes socialism instead. He resented the labor aristocracy dominating the socialist parties and propounded that the poorer classes of workers continue to adhere to revolutionary socialism. Lenin, like Marx, defined the state as the instrument of the ruling class; the proletariat must replace it by a new state machinery of its own. The parliamentary state is but a concealed dictatorship of the capitalistic class and must be superseded by the Soviet state, the overt dictatorship of the proletariat.[25]

Joseph Stalin (1879-1953) was a miserable theoretician and his works are clumsy, unoriginal, and full of quotations of Marx and Lenin.[26] He was also quite inconsistent, contradicting orthodox Marxism and especially Trotsky, at one time, on the maxim that the social revolution must take place at once on a world-wide scale. He also pronounced that Russia, representing socialism-in-one-country, cannot at once be completely communistic, and must, for a while, survive in a partially capitalist stage (which he distinguished from communism by calling it socialism).[27]

BRANCHES OF SOVIET "SOCIOLOGY"

Without going into the periodic somersaults taken by the Party in regard to the official interpretations of Marxism-Leninism, let us note that Socialism took Lenin's mixed heritage and developed it to a one-man dictatorship, operating an immense bureaucratic national state, with an increasingly powerful industrial and military base, thus reshaping the Marxist concept of the state to conform to this circumstance. Stalin obviously conceived of the state and of himself as the maker of "historically objective" conditions. While Lenin appreciated state power as a means of accomplishing communism's international, human goals, Stalin's extended the separation of ends and means, and built up the authority of the state in the name of aims which have been receding with each passing year, but whose ultimate achievement is the basic justification for the Soviet dictatorship.[28]

Important to remember is that in the monistic Marxist pattern of reasoning, all sciences are tightly integrated; hence all ramifications: what we would describe as sociology is an all-inclusive science, with the ideology of Marxism-Leninism at its base; furthermore, numerous subjects which are elsewhere treated as belonging to other fields, are treated from the point of view of social aspects (rather than from that of analysis of style and language). If, therefore, we would like to survey the development of sociology in the USSR from the Soviet point of view, we would have to cover all aspects of Soviet life. Since this is impossible, we shall limit ourselves to a few selected areas.

ETHNOGRAPHY

Ethnography in the USSR is perhaps the Soviet academic discipline closest to the western concept of sociology, although it can hardly be compared to Western social or cultural anthropology. It is limited mainly to the material aspects of the culture of various Soviet peoples, to "folklorism," social history, and the investigation of various tribes living on Soviet territory. Most of its products are mixtures of history and archaeology, and the first Professor of the re-established Chair of Ethnography at Moscow University, S. P. Tolstoy, is working on the history of Khorezm, based on excavations in Soviet Central Asia. Most of the works during the Stalinist period were used for patriotic aims; for instance, ethnographic studies of the Scythians were added to the denunciation by the historians of the "Norman theory of the origin of the Russian state," and so to free Soviet historiography from "foreign influences." Several studies of the *kolkhoz* village (*Sovetskaya Etnografiya*, No.3, 1955) have sociological aspects, but cover mainly dress, forms of housing, and patterns of settlement, paying less attention to non-material culture. In general, Soviet ethnographers depend on the conceptual framework of Morgan and Tylor, sticking to the enumerative concept of culture and concentrating on its material aspects.[29] The basic ideology of Sovietism—that history is the scheduled march of humanity from primitive communism to the classless society—cannot be questioned, and the new data made available by Western anthropologists during the last half century are ignored.

EDUCATIONAL SOCIOLOGY

Since Education is one of the most social control weapons of the Soviet society, we might note that there is no Educational Sociology there, but that an elaborate system of Soviet philosophy deals with education in its social aspects. The ultimate aim is to create a perfect society made up of more perfect individuals.[30] These aesthetic and rational aims are completely divorced from "religion." Man is the product of his society and his character is formed by his social environment, and only a socialized society can produce socialized personalities. To provide this proper environment, the authorities have tried to exterminate the capitalist society and to form a classless communist social order in which communist educational methods could be applied.[31] Secondly, according to Lenin's dictum that "culture requires a certain material base," the aim has been to build a prosperous economic base upon which would support the communist building of education; thus the rapid industrialization, the abolition of the old order, and the establishment of a Soviet state are the main goals of Soviet education.

The changes in the educational theories have reflected the ideological somersauts. In the early thirties, the principles of instruction popular before the revolution, were re-introduced. The emphasis upon subject matter replaced that upon the study of the child ("pedology"); coeducation disappeared and discipline was restored. The Dalton Plan and other "progressive" aspects of education were given up in favor of textbooks and the drill methods; such "old-fashioned" subjects as language, arithmetic, geography were restored. When the War broke out, patriotism was the main feature of instruction.

One more feature must be noted: great stress upon extra-curricular education, which hopes to help abolish illiteracy and promote the politico-educational work on all levels; the central theme is the industrial and professional education of the masses, and more stress is now laid on the mastery of technology than on the recitation of socialist principles.[32]

THE SOCIOLOGY OF LAW

As we have pointed out, in the Marxian-Leninist ideology, there is no area of human behavior and control which is not under the influence of the "sociological" approach; the policies of the state toward the family, the treatment of crimes and religion, are but a few selected segments of human relations which are handled according to the ideological interpretations of Marxism-Leninism by the party decisions. For instance, since Marx looked upon law as a weapon of the exploiting classes, at one time the Soviet jurists proclaimed that law was superfluous as a device regulating the relations between the individuals in a socialist society; in conformity with Lenin's doctrine of the withering away of the state and law, the first Soviet constitution (1918) promised the abolition of state authority. Lenin's doctrine dominated Soviet jurisprudence until the thirties. The proletarian state was considered as a temporary instrument of oppression, necessary only for the period of organization of a socialist economy and the creation of a classless society. Krylenko, who had been Prosecutor and thereafter People's Commissar of Justice, denied the necessity for a Criminal Code in the future and offered to leave a free choice of social defense measures to the OGPU. Goibarg, author of the Family Code, asserted that there was no need to have the state interfere in marital affairs and predicted that the family as a juridical entity would disappear. Pshukanis explained the appearance of the Civil Code in the socialist state as a temporary concession to private trade; like, the temporary re-establishment of the commodity exchange and a monetary system, and predicted that the Civil Code would be replaced with regulations of a purely technical character as soon as a socialist economy could be realized.

However, neither state nor law disappeared in the USSR. After 1936, Stalin, Vishinsky, and Yudin attacked severely those who supported the idea of the withering away of the state and law and characterized them as "enemies of the people" and "wreckers" ("vrediteli"); the evolutionary process eventually embraced the disparate phenomena of the new Soviet Constitution and the Great Purge, leaving a large and elastic area where "enemies of the state" may be dealt with outside the law and the courts.[33]

Interesting also is the Soviet interpretation of International Law, as expressed in a new textbook for Soviet law schools, completed in 1955, by the A. Ya. Vyshinsky Institute of Law (a branch of the Soviet Academy of Sciences).[34]

Glaringly, the Soviet Union is, according to Soviet lawyers, the only true federation, which has not only solved "satisfactorily" the problem of self-determination for her numerous component nationalities, but might be willing in the future to offer the same alternative to other ethnic groups which the Russia communists might intend to include within the frontiers of the USSR, favor "peaceful coexistence," "non-interference in the domestic affairs of other countries," etc., etc.

NATIONALISM AND MINORITIES

One of the most discussed problems in pre-Soviet and contemporary Soviet Russia has been the problem of minorities (and thus also of nationalism). The Czarist state had the difficult problem of handling the diverse hostile and separatist national minorities; the policy of "One Czar, one religion, one language," left to the Soviets a heritage of bitterness and resulted in an increase of national minorities' consciousness as well as the development of a national intelligentsia who have remained a key element in the nationality problem down to today.[35]

Lenin's doctrine on the national question upheld the principle of the right of every nation to self-determination, including the right of secession.[36] But, at the same time he upheld the international solidarity of the proletariat and the consequent duty of every working class to prefer the working class of a neighboring nation to the bourgeoisie of its own nation. So far, "the contradictions between these two principles could not be, and has not been, resolved either in theory or in practice."[37]

During the October Revolution, the geopolitical location of each nationality determined their fate. Thus the Poles Finns, Lithuanians, Letts and Esthonians were allowed to form independent states because they were first occupied by the invading Germans and then defended by the victorious Western Powers; the Georgians, Azerbaidjanis, and

Armenians, after enjoying a few years of independence, were conquered because Turkey also was interested in their fate and because
they antagonized the Western Powers. Since the Ukrainians, Volga
Tartars, and Central Asians, were too far from Western Europe to
be helped by Western Europe, they were overrun first by the White
and then by the Red armies.

Once the Bolshevik regime was formed, the official policy was
hinged in the principle of "a culture national in form and socialist
in content." Fundamentally, the Soviet nationality policy was determined by ramifications of Stalin's general policy. During the N.E.P.
policy the Ukrainians were favored with a real measure of self-
government in Transcaucasia, power was controlled by local individuals. But, at the same time, after the disgrace of Sultan-Galiev,
the Volga-Tartars lost most of their autonomy; in Central Asia, power
was focused in the hands of the local Russian minority.

Stalin's second (1929) revolution (featured by collectivization of
agriculture and rapid industrialization) promoted ruthless national
centralization. In 1930, Ukrainization was given up; starvation or
flight of nearly half the Kazakh nation and the Russification of
Kazakhstan was written into history. Then came the purges of
Ukraine, North Caucasus, and Central Asia, including the autonomous republics of Tataria, Bashkiiria, and Buryat Mongolia.

World War II identified patriotism with subservience to Stalin and
the punishment of real or potentially disloyal nations: the Volga
Germans, Crimenal Tatars, Chechens, Karachays, and Kalmyks. World
War II led to raised the status of the USSR and nationalism had
to bow to the current concept of USSR's nationalism. The national
epics of the Moslem peoples were suppressed and the history of North
Caucasians, Kirgiz, Ukrainians, Romanians (of Bessarabia and others),
was falsified. The campaign against "cosmopolitanism" forced, for
instance, Tadjiiks not to compete with the nationalistic pride with
Persians; they had to stress the links between Tadjiik and Russian
cultures. Seton-Watson thinks that in "Georgia and Armenia there
has hitherto been absolutely no Russification." . . . But in the Ukraine
and Azerbaidjan the problem is more complicated."[38] While the
Ukraine is ruled by Ukrainians (though the former Polish provinces
are an exception), in Azerbaidjan most Russians run the government
machinery. On the other hand, the border provinces (Western
Ukraine, the Baltic states, Western White Russia, and Bessarabia,
and then in the Far East—Sakhalin and the Kurile Islands) the stra-

tegic considerations have forced massive deportations and massive colonization. While Russification has taken place in the economically developing regions of Asiatic Russia (peopled by Moslem, Buddhist, and Shamanist nations), colonization of Russians and Ukrainians has influenced the new industrial centers (Tashkent, Izhevsk, Ufa, Ulan Ude). Russian has been taught as a compulsory language and is the only language in secondary and higher education in areas of mixed population; the universities of Central Asia have for the most part Russian as the language of instruction, and the imposition of the cyrillic alphabet for Asian languages and the systematic introduction into those languages of Russian works has been another aspect of Russification. Recently, the systematic falsification of the history of the nationalities has been going on.[39] Russification is used because they are most numerous, "culturally and economically the most advanced," and "because Russians, as Russians, are less likely to be disloyal to the regime." [40]

Basically, however, Seton-Watson claims, "Soviet policy is a war of extermination against the principle of nationality. It can also fairly be described as imperialism. But it is not inspired by the desire to russify the nationalities." [41]

Today we see a strange combination of chauvinistic nationalism and messianic socialism which is as elusive as it is important; and interpretations of Soviet Russian nationalism run a wide gamut; most of these writings are little or no sociology, being mostly arguments over the ideological interpretations of what is the right of self-determination and the definitions of nationalism, an element of reasoning which was carefully considered by Lenin, Stalin and by the geopoliticians of the Kremlin's schemes and formulas to conquer the world.[42] At one extreme are those who think communism has swallowed up Russian nationalism and who view Soviet foreign policy as simply the continuation of Czarist imperialism in more modern guise.[43] At the opposite end are those who stress the social doctrines and worldwide pretensions of communism as the basic ingredients of Soviet patriotism and who regard the regime's manipulations of nationalistic appeals as a mere tactical maneuver to consolidate domestic support.[44] Then there are a few but a growing number of studies presenting calm sociological analyses of the explosive minorities question in various ramifications, which recognize that the problem is complex, that the roots of Soviet patriotism go deep, and that the content of the concept has varied with time and circumstance.[45]

POST-STALINIST DEVELOPMENTS

The post-Stalinist developments have not affected the Marxist-Lenin-Stalin theories too much. The efforts to subordinate science to Party control have continued taking their zig-zag course. But some political relaxation has been felt in economics and vital statistics. After 1930, the blackout on statistics was glaring; the last figures of professional distribution were given in 1937; demographic data ended with the publication of the 1939 Census—and only crude results were given out. The Soviet demographers, headed by Ryabushkin and Kuzminov, who attended the World Population Conference in 1954, "could not even produce figures of the Soviet population." [46] But in 1956, for the first time in almost two decades, a statistical handbook appeared.[47] During that period, the abusive style vis-à-vis Western sociology and anthropology has somewhat weakened. But factual writings still remain rare (an exception being V. S. Semenov's "Sociological Societies and Periodicals in the U.S.A.," Voprosy Filosofii, 3(1956), 246-248). Ethnographic, these still remain propaganda in their nature, but their scope has been widened, and studies on societies outside the USSR, especially Africa, have been more numerous.

Yet, the hostile attitude toward Western sociology remains bitter. George Gurvitch is labeled as a "Machist." Or Ruth Benedict and Margaret Mead are publishing works "openly dictated by the attempts of reactionary circles to stir up hostility among peoples, to facilitate the policy of domination over the Asiatic nations, the policy of colonialism." [48] One Russian author discovered that "bourgeois sociology" has a branch of "atomic sociology," which is "a part of bankrupt atomic propaganda." [49] Jessie Bernard is accused of promoting the "sociology of espionage and subversion," since she "justifies the use of any means, including espionage and subversion, to achieve a goal. She praises Hitler as a practical 'expert in the theory of strategic games'." [50] Professor F. Ogburn represents the group which "prefers not to notice such phenomena in the U.S.A. as the impoverishment of millions of toilers on the one hand, and the increasing fabulous profits of the monopolists on the other." [51]

Nevertheless, Soviet scientists have started in recent years to attend international conferences. Thus, despite the "anti-scientific character of bourgeois sociology," a Soviet delegation was sent to the World Congress of Sociology in Amsterdam (August, 1956); "the fact that sociology as a separate discipline does not exist in the Soviet Union was no obstacle."[52] The representatives were no sociologists, since the delegation was headed by P. Fedoseyev, Director of the Institute of Philosophy; he had been purged from the position of editor of the organ of the Party, *Kommunist*, but reappeared after Stalin's death; other members belonged also to philosophy or were lecturers on Marxism-Leninism. Their papers dealt with internal changes in the USSR and were propaganda of the usual Soviet type. But contrary to the previous international meetings which saw the Soviet representatives abusing the Western colleagues, there was no name calling and the tone of the speeches and private conversations stressed the necessity of international scientific cooperation. But it was also glaringly evident that the Soviet spokesmen still do not know what Western sociology is.

RUSSIAN SOCIOLOGIST ABROAD

Whether a great philosopher of history, Nicholas Berdyayev (1874-1946), can be considered a sociologist is debatable; at any rate Barnes and Becker classify him as a historical sociologist.[53] Kohn states: "Berdyayev belonged to the brilliant young generation of Russian thinkers and poets of the beginning of the century, who, partly under the influence of Vladimir Solovev, fully participated in European intellectual and artistic life."[54] Berdyayev was influenced by Marx and Nietzsche. The failure of the Russian revolution of 1905 disillusioned him so that he began to profess religious nationalism near the Slavophil position.[56] He believed himself to be the herald of the fall of a humanistic civilization due to the spiritual disease of the Western Man, and attacked the "heresies" of racialism and collectivism. He held that cultures have patterns of growth and decay, which repeated in outline, always end in tragedy. What gives man his illusory hope for a better earth is his unquenchable will to free his creative spirit from the natural forces, inside and outside himself, that try to drag him down; what makes him despair is the rigid dialectic of history, by which every human work is "riddled with contradictions and carries the seeds of its own destruction," so that it passes inevitably into its opposite. "Humanism," composed of individualism, liberalism, naturalism, and rationalism, is the keynote of modern history; the doctrine that man is the lord of creation, is sufficient unto himself, needs no master but his own mind. The two instruments man devised to solve his problems—the control of nature and the ordering of society—inevitably turned against him, for man has put all his faith in capitalism and technology. All social theory ultimately becomes economic theory, and economic theory sets no limits to man's instrumentalization of his fellows. Technicism, a product of Humanism, is a symptom of its end; the coming of age will mean the end of Humanism, but then again men will once more embrace Christianity, when they will strive for a new sense of brotherhood and organic unity with each other. In 1937 Berdyayev authored *The Origin of Russian Communism*, tracing the roots of Leninism in the Russian tradition.

Just like Berdyayev, Georgie Petrovich Fedotov (1886-1951) died in Paris and debated to what extent was the communist revolution an outcome of Russian history and how did it relate to the old struggle between Westernizers and Slavophils? While Berdyayev favored the Slavophil ideology, Fedotov represented the Westernizing trend. In fact, the sides taken by Russian intellectuals in the spiritual battle between East and West, has really never been settled.[57]

In the field of historical sociology belongs the thesis of Alexander and Eugen Kulisher propounded in *Weltgeschichte als Volkerbewegung* (1932), that the major movements of history depend on migrations (a theory, incidentally, originating with their father, I. M. Kulisher). In the field of sociological jurisprudence (or juristic sociology), Nikolai Korkunov (1853-1904), depending on Spencer, Fouillée, Kareyev, Gumplowicz, and others, became quite well known outside Russia; he propounded a system of law from sociological principles. Several Russian specialists worked on the relationship between various types of crimes and the related sociological and psychic factors (N. S. Timasheff, now of Fordham University, Kosin, Teranovsky, Chubinsky, and others). Sorokin believes that the work of Leo Petrazycki (1867-1931), a famous Polish-Russian professor of legal philosophy at the University of Petrograd (and later at the University of Warsaw), in the field of logic and psychology is one of the most important contributions in the 20th century. He stressed the role of emotion as an autonomous and truly normative agent in behavior (which can be compared to Pareto's "residues"); he dealt especially exhaustively with legal and political institutions and his influence in Russia can be compared to that of Durkheim in France. The school of psychological sociology arose from the works of Pavlov and Bekhterev (1857-1927), aiming for complete objectivity by excluding all non-quantitative data and by focusing on external social phenomena that are repetitive.

Pitirim A. Sorokin (1889–), one of the most prolific contemporary sociologists, started his sociological career in Russia. As a student, he edited *New Ideas in Sociology*, wrote extensively in criminology, and became active in the Socialist Revolutionary Party during the 1917 revolution.[58] As a young sociology teacher at the University of Petrograd and a bitter opponent of communism, he became secretary to Kerenski during the brief life of the Russian Republic. After Kerenski's downfall, he lectured on sociology, but he was exiled by Lenin for trying to publish a book criticizing the Soviet administration for inducing the Ukrainian famine in 1921.[59] Helped by the sociologically minded government of Masaryk and Benes in Czechoslovakia, he then was invited by S. A. Chapin to come to the University of Minnesota in 1924. Achieving rapid fame with his numerous writings, he became the first head of the Department of Sociology at Harvard University in 1930. Today, retired from the Departmental headship, he is running the Research Center in Creative Altruism of Harvard University (at Winchester, Mass.).

One of the most prolific writers, whose works have been translated in several languages, Sorokin started to make his contribution in 1914, when he published *Crime and Punishment* (1914), which he followed with *Leo Tolstoi as a Philosopher* (1915), *System of Sociology* (1919) and *Elements of Sociology* (1919), and *General Theory of Law* (1920) —all in Russian and published in Petrograd.[60] Since his arrival in the United States, Sorokin has continued his flow of publications, headed by his *Sociology of Revolution* (Philadelphia: Lippincott, 1925); a pioneer work in the field of social structure analysis, *Social Mobility* (New York: Harper, 1924); *Contemporary Sociological Theories* (New York: Harper, 1928), one of the first surveys of this field in English bringing together sociological contributions from all corners of the earth; before going to Harvard C. C. Zimmerman and Charles Galpin collaborated with him on *Principles of Rural-Urban Sociology* (New York: Henry Holt, 1930) and *Systematic Source Book in Rural Sociology* (Minneapolis: University of Minnesota Press, 1930-1932); from Harvard's research came the *Social and Cultural Dynamics* (New York: American Book Co., 1937), summarized in a small, popular *The Crisis of Our Age* (New York: E. P. Dutton, 1941). Other works followed, the best known being *Culture, and Personality: Their Structure and Dynamics* (New York: Harper, 1947), and *Social Philosophies of an Age of Crisis* (Boston: Beacon Press, 1950); his latest book is *The American Sex Revolution* (Boston: Porter Sargent, 1956). Sorokin's basic theories can be best summarized from his *Social and Cultural Dynamics*, which has given rise to more critical book reviews than any other sociological work of the decade.[61] The theme is Western civilization for the past twenty-five centuries, showing how the ascertainable cycles of social and cultural changes in the west are the period occurrences of dominantly ideational, idealistic, and sensate cultures (developing here the theories of Bergson, Spengler, Pareto, Durkheim, Villerme, Quételet, Guerry and Kitchin). Cultures are characterized by a dominant mentality, the key to the integration of the culture; Sorokin's "ideational culture" is characterized by the meanings, values, and norms objectified and socialized in the behavior patterns and predominantly supersensory vehicles, which are even superrational, focused toward the same basic supermeaningful entity, God; examples are provided by ancient Greek culture of the pre-Socratic Age and the medieval European Christian culture. The opposite is offered by sensate culture, which features the ultimate, meaningful sensory value; "the Sensate reality is thought of as a Becoming, Process, Change, Flux, Evolution, Progress, Transformation. Its needs and aims are mainly physical, and maximum satisfaction is sought for these needs. . . . In brief the Sensate culture is the opposite of the Ideational in its major premises."[62] Its cycle is represented by the Graeco-Roman civilization from about 100 B.C. to 400 A.D., and the modern phase of our present civilization from 1600 to the present. Then Sorokin presents the third type of culture; the idealistic pattern combines both elements of the ideational and sensate, but reason is more dominant than religious faith or sense impulses—the Golden Age of Greek philosophy, the period of Scholastic philosophy just before the Renaissance inaugurated by St. Thomas Aquinas. Using these definitions, Sorokin then describes all the rhythms and fluctuations of history by offering a tremendous conglomeration of material describing painting, sculpture, architecture (the ideational-idealistic-visual rhythm), music-drama, literature and art criticism (the ideational-idealistic-sensate rhythm), religion, philosophy, and science (the systems of truth and knowledge). He concludes his third volume by presenting the curves supporting his theory of culture integrate and sociocultural change, and theorizes that there is no other possible change but for the better for the present stage of the contemporary decadent sensate culture, since an idealistic or ideational phase of Western civilization is coming after the downfall of the present phase due to the weight of its own gigantism.[63]

Nicholas S. Timasheff received his LLD from the University of St. Petersburg in 1914. After his arrival in the United States, he was associated with Sorokin at Harvard for a while; today he is Professor of Sociology at Fordham University. Also a prolific writer, he is especially known for his *The Great Retreat* (New York: E. P. Dutton, 1946), evaluating the main social and cultural trends in Russian life before and after the revolution, and his textbooks in the basic field and theory.[64]

AMERICAN AND OTHER SOCIOLOGISTS ON SOVIET RUSSIA

Roughly speaking, the knowledge of Russia in the United States was quite limited before World War I, and the few scholars specializing in this field had an unquestioned monopoly in this area. In fact, Professor T. G. Masaryk of Charles University was "imported" to the University of Chicago, partly because of his reputation as one of the few English-speaking scholars whose reputation was based on his famed book of Russia's history, literature and philosophy, and which had for a long time been considered as a classic on Russian thought of the pre-communist era.[65] World War I produced several anti-communist studies, but as a recognized American subject, Russia remained a *terra incognita;* Professors Samuel Hazzard Cross of Harvard, Robert J. Kerner of the University of Missouri and later of the University of California, with a few other scholars, and Robert W. Seton-Watson of London, had a hard time to arouse American public opinion on behalf of the need to cultivate more systematically the "enigma" Russia (the name used for "Soviet Russia" in the United States). The course of events in World War II gave a powerful impetus to the sudden need to provide specialists in everything Russian. From one point of view the results have been confusing, with the influx of many persons claiming to be experts in that area, simply because they had been refugees from the region and had some knowledge of a Slavic language;[66] on the other hand, Harvard, California and a few other institutions inaugurated a systematic program of the study of Soviet Russia's sociological background and cross-currents, with some definite results which, in some respects, have surpassed the outstanding products from the School of East European and Slavonic Studies of the University of London before World War I and II.[67] In fact, in recent

years there has been an enormous growth of academic literature covering the sociological aspects of Soviet Russia from various angles.[68]
Most of this academic production has been good; but some of it has
aroused considerable criticism due to its pro-Soviet approach.[69]

At any rate, in addition to the valuable sociological studies produced
by the Russian Studies Center of Harvard, at Yale, Columbia, University of California, and a few other places, we should note the contributions made by the Institute for the Study of the History and Culture
of the USSR, founded in July, 1950, "as a free corporation of scholars
and specialists who had left the USSR and had joined in an effort
to present to the Western world an objective picture of what is happening in the Soviet Union."[70] The main publications are the *Bulletin*, an English-language monthly, the *Vestnik*, a Russian quarterly,
the *Dergi*, in Turkish, and other periodicals. In 1956, The Department
of Slavic Studies of the University of Montreal started publishing
Slavic and East-European Studies.

Otherwise, the rising flood of books on numerous sociological
implications of the USSR has been growing. We can mention here,
probably two representative works. W. W. Rostow's *The Dynamics
of Soviet Society* (New York: A Mentor Book, 1954), sponsored by
the Center for International Studies, Massachusetts Institute of Technology, a brilliant analysis concerned mainly with the devices of social
control. Harry Hodgkinson's *The Language of Communism* (New
York: Pitman, 1955) sets out a few trail-markers through the petrify-
ing forest of bolshevized Marxist linguistics. The author has evidently
trampled the great lava beds of Soviet journalism, literature, ukases,
encyclopedias, decrees and polemics, and toiled in the lead mines of
the Marx-Engels-Lenin-Stalin classics. The result is a beginner's handbook of what might be called progressive pidgin, published in England
under the honest title of *Doubletalk*. Peering through the bars of
Hodgkinson's caged semantic monster, we find here such strange animals as the Marxist breed of "equality" ("Ravenstvo"). "By equality
Marxism means, not equalization of individual requirements and
individual life, but the abolition of classes," reported Stalin to the
17th Party Congress (1934). Or the author has fun with the word
"peace" ("mir"), and the bellicose roarings of those who advocate it,
including the Czech miner who promised to "batter the warmongers
to death with peace." From other useful listings, the reader will learn
that "salami tactics," as a term originated in salami-rich Hungary—
meaning slicing away opposition gradually; and that "absolutism"

("absoliutizm") in Russia ended, once and for all, with the overthrow of the Czarist regime. Above all, the volume shows that one word can have different meanings when used by communists in Russia or in the West. According to a Hungarian female communist, for instance, the "informer" ("donoschik") is "the mightiest and most honorable discharger of responsibility." Especially does the book show that international communism has created a linguistic apparatus for a general attack on the whole logical structure of the Western mind—and that includes sociology.

(For SELECTED BIBLIOGRAPHY see the following article on "Ukrainian Sociology")
(For the author's biography, see p. 930.)

NOTES

1. C. J. Fredriksen, "Russia," Chapter X, 358-408, in Max Salvadori, Joseph S. Roucek, George B. de Huszar, & Julia Bond, Eds., *Contemporary Social Science* (Harrisburg, Penna.: The Stackpole Co., 1954), vol. II; *Eastern Hemisphere,* 359.

2. For surveys of pre-Communist Sociology, see: Howard Becker & Harry Elmer Barnes, *Social Thought from Lore to Science* (Washington, D. C.: Harren Press, 2nd ed., 1952), vol. II, Chapter XXVI, "Russian Sociology," 1029-1059, and bibliographical references, xci-xciv; Harry Elmer Barnes, Ed., *An Introduction to the History of Sociology* (University of Chicago Press, 1948), 441-442, 93, 889, and: Harry Elmer Barnes, "The Sociological Doctrines of Jacques Novicow: A Sociological Criticism of War and Militarism," Chapter XXII, 19-440; N. S. Timasheff, "The Sociological Theories of Maksim M. Kovalevsky," Chapter XXIII, 441-457; Hans Speier, "The Sociological Ideas of Pitirim Alexandrovitch Sorokin: 'Integralist' Sociology," Chapter XLVI, 884-901; Fredriksen, *op. cit.,* "Bibliography," 406-408; Clement S. Mihainovich, *Social Theorists* (Milwaukee: The Bruce Publishing Co., 1953), Chapter X, "Pitirim Alexandrovitch Sorokin," 201-215, by Albert S. Foley, S. J., and bibliography, 214-215; James J. Burns, "Marxian Social Theory," Chapter XIII, in *ibid.;* Max M. Laserson, "Russian Sociology," Chapter XXIV, 671-702, in Georges Gurvitch & Wilbert E. Moore, Eds., *Twentieth Century Sociology* (New York: The Philosophical Library, 1945), and bibliography, 701-702; Alfred A. Skerpan, "Russia and Soviet Russia," Chapter XXVI, 351-366, in Matthew A. Fitzsimons, Alfred G. Pundt, & Charles E. Nowell, Eds., *The Development of Historiography* (Harrisburg, Penna.: The Stackpole Co., 1954), and scattered references in the Bibliography, 441-458; Joseph S. Roucek, Ed., *Slavonic Encyclopaedia* (New York: Philosophical Library, 1949), articles under such titles as "History," "Education," names of thinkers, and especially "Sociology: Russia Czarist," by Nicholas S. Timasheff, 1230-1233, and "Ukraine," by M. I. Mandryka, 1233-1234; Yaroslav Chyz & Joseph S. Roucek, "Ukrainian Sociology before 1914," *Journal of Central European Affairs,* I, 1 (April, 1941), 74-87; Joseph S. Roucek, "Ukrainian Sociology after the First World War," *The Ukrainian Quarterly,* I, 2 (1944), 152-163.

3. See: for instance; Nicholas S. Timasheff, *The Great Retreat* (New York: E. P. Dutton, 1946), a sociological analysis of "The Growth and Decline of Communism in Russia," and numerous other studies by this prolific sociologist, now occupying

the chair of sociology at Fordham University; even more prolific has been Sorokin, at Harvard, who incorporated surveys of Russian thinkers in all his numerous books, and especially his *Contemporary Sociological Theories* (New York: Harper, 1928), and applied sociology to the Russian conditions in *Leaves from a Russian Diary*—and *Thirty Years After* (Boston: Beacon Press, 1950), and *The Sociology of Revolution* (Philadelphia: J. B. Lippincott, 1925).

4. G. F. Aleksandrov, *The Pattern of Soviet Democracy* (issued in cooperation with the Russian Translation Program of the American Council of Learned Societies, Washington, D. C.: Public Affairs Press, 1948), trans. by Leo Gruliow, 15.

5. *Ibid.*, 2. Adam Ulam, "Stalin and the Theory of Totalitarianism," 157-171, & Waldemar Gurian, "*Partiinost'* and Knowledge," 298-306, in Ernest J. Simmons, Ed., *Continuity and Change in Russian and Soviet Thought* (Cambridge, Mass.: Harvard University Press, 1955), are good summaries of the Soviet ideological approach to science.

6. Alexander Vucinich, *The Soviet Academy of Sciences* (Stanford University Press, 1956), 45.

7. *Ibid.*, 70.

8. George S. Counts, *The Challenge of Soviet Education* (New York: McGraw-Hill, 1957), 282.

9. John Turkevich, "Soviet Science in the Post-Stalin Era," 139-151, in Philip E. Mosely, Ed., "Russia Since Stalin: Old Trends and New Problems," *The Annals* of the American Academy of Political and Social Science, CCCIII (January, 1956).

10. The report which the President submitted to Congress, said there was evidence of "widespread relaxation" of requirements in American secondary schools for such subjects as language, mathematics and the sciences. It urged a "sober reappraisal of secondary school training in science and mathematics . . . as a guide to the extent this country may fall short of achieving its high potentials."

11. K. I. Kozlova & N. N. Cheboksarov, "Ethnography at the University of Moscow," *Sovetskaya Etnografiya*, 2 (1955), 100-111; "The Social Sciences in the U.S.S.R.," *Soviet Survey*, 10 (November, 1956), 1-19 (published by Congress for Cultural Freedom, 25 Haymarket, London, W. S. 1).

12. Julius F. Hecker, *Russian Sociology* (London: Chapman & Hall, 1934).

13. Theodore Abel, "Sociology in Postwar Poland," *American Sociological Review*, XV, 1 (February, 1950), 104-106.

14. V. D. Kazekevich, "Social Sciences in the Soviet Union," *American Sociological Review*, IX (June, 1944), 314; John Sommerville, *Soviet Philosophy* (New York: Philosophical Library, 1944).

15. S. Kovalyov, *Ideological Conflicts in Soviet Russia* (Washington, D. C.: Public Affairs Press, 1948), "Issued in Cooperation with the Russian Translation Program of the American Council of Learned Societies."

16. U.S. Information Agency, *Soviet World Outlook. A Handbook of Communist Statements* (Washington, D. C.; 1954), 397.

17. Fredriksen, *op. cit.*, 362.

18. Teachers of courses on social stratification, industrial sociology, and social theory have difficulties when they want to refer to the writings of Karl Marx. In spite of the numerous collections of his writings, only one has appeared so far assembling the scattered passages which relate directly to sociology: T. H. Bottomore & Maximilien Rubel, Eds., *Karl Marx: Selected Writings in Sociology and Social Philosophy* (London: Watts & Co., 1956); the Introduction, pp. 1-28, summarizes

Marx's sociology and social philosophy; the remainder is a useful guide to the literature on the influence of Marx's ideology. Another useful collection, often covering sociological thinking of Marx and his interpreters, is: Sidney Hook, *Marx and the Marxists: The Ambiguous Legacy* (Princeton, N. J.: D. Van Nostrand, 1955), which also covers Georgi Plekhanov, 57-61, Lenin, 75-90, Leo Trotsky, 91-99, Stalin, 107-121, with selected readings.

19. See such surveys as: Leopold Schwarzchild, *The Red Prussian: The Life and Legend of Karl Marx* (New York: Scribner, 1947); Max M. Laserson, "Russian Sociology," Chapter XXIV, 671-702, in Georges Gurvitch & Wilbert E. Moore, Eds., *Twentieth Century Sociology* (New York: Philosophical Library, 1945); J. F. Hecker, *op. cit.;* Harry Elmer Barnes & Howard Backer, *op. cit.,* II, Chapter XXVI, "Russian Sociology," and Notes, 33-36; E. S. Bogardus, *op. cit.,* Chapter XVIII, "Mikhalovsky and Russian Social Thought," 261-274; Hare, *op. cit.;* Hecker, *op. cit.,* Part IV, "Communist Sociology and the Revisionists of Marxism," 229-300; Helen Pratt, *Russian, From Tsarist Empire to Socialism* (New York: American, Council, Institute of Pacific Relations, 1937); Sorokin, *op. cit.* Notice, however, that Timasheff, *op. cit.,* does not mention such Marxian interpreters as Plekhanov, Struve and others in his *Sociological Theory.*

20. Hecker, *op. cit.,* 253.

21. Leopold H. Haimson, *The Russian Marxists, and the Origins of Bolshevism* (Cambridge, Mass.: Harvard University Press, 1955), is a valuable interpretive study of the evolution of Bolshevism in Russia in the 19th century, an analysis of Marxist ideology, its factors, interpretations by various groups, acceptance and growth.

22. Hecker, *op. cit.,* 296.

23. *Ibid.,* 297.

24. Hans Kohn, Ed., *The Mind of Modern Russia* (New Brunswick, N. J.: Rutgers University Press, 1955), Chapter XII, "Russia and the Revolution II: Lenin," 232-247; Hook, *op. cit.,* Chapter 5, "Lenin," 75-90; D. Shub, *Lenin* (Garden City, N. Y.: Doubleday, 1948), deals with Lenin, Trotsky and Stalin up to 1914; etc. Edmund Wilson, *To the Finland Station* (New York: Harcourt, Brace, 1940), is an invaluable book, which makes Marxist theory, aims and tactics intelligible to any literate non-Marxist mind; the title is derived from a shabby, grey and pink stucco building where trains from free Finland arrive in Leningrad, and where, on the night of April 16, 1917, arrived Lenin, and here, in the person of Lenin, socialism first issued from the dank sub-cellars of contemporary society and became a political reality.

25. All Lenin's works have been translated and published in "Little Lenin Library" by the International Publishers (381 Fourth Ave., New York), for such ridiculous prices as 15 cents.

26. Most of his works can be also secured from the International Publishers. One of the most prophetic and little known in America, has been *Foundations of Leninism* (International Publishers, 1939) ("Little Lenin Library, vol. XVIII, 35¢), a sort of *Mein Kampf,* since it clearly proclaims the basic aims and devices of the Soviets. For more favorable views of Stalin (than those of the author), see: Alexander Erlich, "Stalin's Views on Soviet Economic Development," 81-99, and Adam Ulau, "Stalin and the Theory of Totalitarianism," 157-171, in Simmons, *op. cit.*

27. Stalin's views have been discussed at length, the controversy focusing mostly around the concept of mechanism in social thought; see: John Sommerville, *Soviet Philosophy* (New York: Philosophical Library, 1946), "Pivotal Controversies," 213-

228. The most current debate has been that dethroning Stalin; see: Russian Institute, Columbia University, Ed., *The Anti-Stalin Campaign and International Communism* (New York: Columbia University Press, 1956).

28. For the analysis of these ideologies, see: W. W. Rostow, *The Dynamics of Soviet Society* (New York: A Mentor Book, 1954), 96-122.

29. P. Tolstoy, "Morgan and Soviet Anthropological Thought," *American Anthropologist, XXXIV* (January-March, 1952), 8-17.

30. Eugene Medynsky, "Schools and Education in the USSR," *American Sociological Review,* IX (1944), 290; Joseph S. Roucek, *Soviet and Russian Educational Imperialism* (1956, reprinted from *Journal of Human Relations,* Fall issue, 1955, and Winter, 1956).

31. A. Pinkevich, *Science and Education in the USSR* (New York: Putnam, 1935), 15-16.

32. Definitely related to the sociological trends in Soviet Russia is the influence of I. P. Pavlov (1849-1936), Bekhterev, Kornilov, and others in the field of reflexology; for details, see: Fredricksen, *op. cit.,* 398-406; H. K. Wells, *Pavlov and Freud* (New York: International Publishers, 1956).

33. H. J. Berman, "Law Reform in the Soviet Union," *The American Slavic and East European Review,* XV, 2 (April, 1956), 179-189; Hans Kelsen, *The Communist Theory of Law* (New York: Praeger, 1954), a comprehensive study of the theory of law based on the "materialistic" or economic interpretation of society inaugurated by Marx; it examines the communist doctrine that the law is an ideological superstructure with the relationships of economic production and shows how Soviet theory has adopted from "bourgeois jurisprudence" the very elements which conventional scholars have rejected because of ideological deficiencies; H. J. Berman, *Justice in Russia* (Cambridge, Mass.: Harvard University Press, 1950); J. Guins, "Soviet Law in the Mirror of Legal Science," *American Slavic and East European Review,* XVIII (February, 1957), 66-73.

34. W. W. Kulski, "The Soviet Interpretation of International Law," *American Journal of International Law,* XLIX, 4 (October, 1955), 518-47.

35. Frederick C. Barghoorn, *Soviet Russian Nationalism* (New York: Oxford University Press, 1956), is a skillful introduction to the meaning, background and purpose of the dangerous combination of contradictory elements making up Soviet Russian nationalism.

36. For an analysis how the Soviet and Nazi doctrines became intertwined for the purpose of conquests, see: Joseph S. Roucek, "Nazi and Soviet Techniques of 'Extended Strategy,'" *Social Science,* XXVIII, 3 (Summer, 1953), 160-170.

37. H. Seton-Watson, "Soviet Nationality Policy," *The Russian Review,* XV, 1 (January, 1956), 3-13: Samad Shaheen, *The Communist (Bolshevist) Theory of National Self-Determination: Its Historical Evolution up to the October Revolution* (New York: Gregory Lenz, 1956).

38. Seton-Watson, *op. cit.,* 6.

39. Seton-Watson, *op. cit.,* does not think that "the Soviet government is in terested in Russian nationalism, the conflict being between these nationalities and a centralized totalitarian regime" (8)

40. *Ibid.,* 8-9.

41. Seton-Watson, *op. cit.,* 9-10; but for the opposite point of view, see: Joseph S. Roucek, "Soviet and Russian Educational Imperialism," *Journal of Human Relations,* IV, 1 (Fall issue, 1955), 26-44, and IV, 2 (Winter, 1956), 35-60, with bibliographical references and direct quotations.

42. Samad Shaheen, *The Communist (Bolshevist) Theory of National Self-Determination: Its Historical Evolution Up to the October Revolution* (New York: Gregory Lenz, 1956).

43. John A. Armstrong, *Ukrainian Nationalism 1939-1945* (New York: Columbia University Press, 1955); Olaf Caroe, *Soviet Empire; The Turks of Central Asia and Stalinism* (New York: St. Martin's Press, 1953); Roman Smal-Stocki, *The Nationality Problem of the Soviet Union* (Milwaukee: Bruce Publishing Co., 1952), stresses the alleged identity of communism and the Russian political tradition, and is involved in heated quasi-political polemics with the opponents of the author's views; etc.

44. Richard Pipes, *The Formation of the Soviet Union: Communism and Nationalism, 1917-1923* (Cambridge: Harvard University Press, 1954), emphasizes the political aspects of the national movements in the borderland areas (although no attention is given to national groups, such as the Finns and the Poles, who were separated from Russia during the period of the Revolution); the story involves the relationships of the Bolsheviks, who were prepared for revolution, and the internally divided and ideologically split nationalist movements.

45. Nicholas P. Vakar, *A Bibliographical Guide to Belorussia, and Belorussia, the Making of a Nation. A Case Study* (Cambridge, Mass.: Harvard University Press, 1956), a history of White Russia, describing the land, people, tradition, and particularly national self-determination; H. Handley Cloutier, "Leontiev on Nationalism," *Review of Politics,* XVII, 2 (April, 1955), 262-272; John S. Reshetar, Jr., *The Ukrainian Revolution* (Princeton University Press, 1952); Rudolf Schlesinger, Ed., *Changing Attitudes in Soviet Russia: The Nationalities Problem and Soviet Administration* (London: Routledge & Kegan Paul, 1955), supplies a selection of original source materials; the editor's personal contribution is restricted to an introduction giving the background of the developments illustrated in the documents, and to a few explanatory notes.

46. "The Social Sciences in the U.S.S.R.," *Soviet Survey,* 10 (November, 1956), 10.

47. *Narodnoe Khozyaistvo SSR* (Moscow: Central Statistical Administration, 1956).

48. E. Bagramov & B. Labrentiev, "Racist Inventions about the Japanese Nation," *Kommunist,* 9 (June, 1956), 113-120.

49. G. L. Episkoposov, *On Some Aspects of Contemporary Reactionary Bourgeois Sociology* (Moscow: All-Union Society for the Dissemination of Political and Scientific Knowledge, July, 1956), 10.

50. *Ibid.,* 38.

51. *Ibid.,* 21.

52. "The Social Sciences in the U.S.S.R.," *Soviet Survey, op. cit.,* 12.

53. O. F. Clarke, *Introduction to Berdyaev* (New York: The Macmillan Co., 1950), reviews the Russian Orthodox background of Berdyaev and the main outline of his philosophy; a similar contribution is George Seaver's *Nicolas Berdyaev: An Introduction to his Thought* (New York: Harper, 1950) (has bibliographical footnotes); among Berdyaev's works, see: *The Realm of Spirit* and *The Realm of Caesar* (New York: Harper, 1953), the last work by him, which summarizes several of his basic ideas on the nature of truth, the role of the Christian in the world and in relation to God, and the contradictions of Marxism.

54. Hans Kohn, Ed., *The Mind of Modern Russia* (New Brunswick, N. J.: Rutgers University Press, 1955), Chapter XIII, "Communism and Russian History: Berdyaev and Fedotov," pp. 248-281.

56. N. V. Riasanovsky, *Russia and the West in the Teaching of the Slavophiles:*

A Study of Romantic Ideology (Cambridge, Mass. Harvard University Press, 1953), the first history of Slavophilism in English. It was a movement propounding Russia's regeneration through a return to the old idea of Russia's civilization as it stood before the western innovations of Peter the Great.

57. Of importance to notice at this point is Thomas G. Masaryk's *The Spirit of Russia* (London: Allen & Unwin, 1919), republished in 1953 in New York: The MacMillan Co., 1953, with two chapters by Jan Slavik. Of importance is also Paul N. Miliukov, 1859-1943, *Outlines of Russian Culture*, ed. by Michael Karpovich (Philadelphia: University of Pennsylvania Press, 3 vols., 1942), a member of the Russian Provisional government, whose book is a mine of valuable historical information; his writings were influential among the intellectuals who saw the main task of the intellectuals in fighting the detailed struggles for the democratic order and to spread education among masses.

58. P. A. Sorokin, *Leaves from a Russian Diary* (New York: E. P. Dutton, 1924), is a valuable human document, covering Sorokin's revolutionary days.

59. *Ibid.*, 298-308.

60. For surveys and evaluations of Sorokin's sociological contributions, see: Clement S. Mihanovich, *Social Theorists* (Milwaukee, Wis.: The Bruce Publ. Co., 1953), "Pitirim Alexandrovitch Sorokin," by A. S. Foley, Chapter 10, 201-215, and bibliography, 214-215; Hecker, *op. cit.*, "P. A. Sorokin's Contribution to Sociology," Chapter IV, 217-226; Hans Speier, "The Sociological Ideas of Pitirim Alexandrovitch Sorokin: 'Integralist' Sociology," Chapter XLVI, 884-901, in Harry Elmer Barnes, Ed., *An Introduction to the History of Sociology* (University of Chicago Press, 1948).

61. A. E. Tibbs, "Book Reviews of *Social and Cultural Dynamics:* A Study in Wissenssoziologie," *Social Forces*, XXI (1942-1943), 473-480.

62. Sorokin, *Social and Cultural Dynamics* (New York: American Book Co., 1937), I, 73.

63. In his latest work, *The American Sex Revolution*, Sorokin deplored the books, cocktail parties, advertisements, and the TV, film, and stage plays, that flaunt sex, insisting they thereby threaten to destroy U.S. civilization. "Our morals have changed so notably that continence, chastity, and faithfulness are increasingly viewed as oddities, as the ossified survival of a prehistoric age. This sex revolution is as important as the most dramatic political or economic upheaval. It is changing the lives of men and women more radically than any other revolution of our time . . ." But in spite of his severe criticism of American morals, the author is still hopeful, and details the approach to a more deeply satisfying and more socially stabilizing sex attitude which is within our power to achieve.

64. Nicholas Timasheff & Paul Facey, *Sociology* (Milwaukee: The Bruce Publ. Co., 1949); Timasheff, *Sociological Theory: Its Nature and Growth* (Garden City, N. Y.: Doubleday & Co., 1955), which surveys the theories of Auguste Comte, Herbert Spencer, and others up to date, including Sorokin, 231-238, and 271-273.

65. T. G. Masaryk, *The Spirit of Russia: Studies in History, Literature and Philosophy* (trans. by Eden & Cedar Paul; additional chapters and bibliographies by Jan Slavik) (New York: The MacMillan Co., 1955).

66. Joseph S. Roucek, "Russlandkunde in den USA," *Jahrbucher fur Oeschichte Oste-europas*, IV, 1 (1956), 64-71 (Munchen); S. H. Cross, "On Teaching Contemporary Russian Civilization," *The Slavonic and East European Review*, XXII (1944), 92-101; Walther Kirchner, "The Place of Russian History in the Curriculum of American Universities," *Bulletin* of the American Association of University Professors, XXXII, 2 (1946), 298-302; J. A. Posin, "Russian Studies in American

Colleges," *The Russian Review,* IV (1948), 62-68; A. P. Coleman, "The Teaching of Russian in the United States," *Ibid.,* IV, 1 (944), 83-88; G. P. Noyes, "Slavic Languages at the University of California," *The Slavonic and East European Review,* XXII, 60 (1944), 53-60; Josef Brozek, "Russian Studies in American Universities," Association of American Colleges *Bulletin,* XXIX, 2 (1943), 241-245.

67. See such recent studies as: Ernest J. Simmons, Ed., *Continuity and Change in Russian and Soviet Thought* (Cambridge, Mass.: Harvard University Press, 1956); Hans Kelsen, *The Political Theory of Bolshevism* (Berkeley, Calif.: University of California Press, 3rd ed., 1954); Leopold Haimson, *Russian Marxists and the Origin of Bolshevism* (Harvard University Press, 1955); Richard Pipes, *The Formation of the Soviet Union: Communism and Nationalism, 1917-1923* (Harvard University Press, 1954); etc.

68. See, for instance: Margaret Mead, *Soviet Attitudes Toward Authority* (New York: W. W. Morrow, 1955); A. G. Mazour, *An Outline of Modern Russian Historiography* (New York: D. Van Nostrand, 1955); Herbert S. Dinerstein, *Two Studies in Soviet Control: Communism and the Russian Peasant* (Glencoe, Ill.: The Free Press, 1955); etc. Specialized studies appear in various American periodicals, and especially in: *American Slavic and East European Review,* quarterly (431 W. 117 St., New York 27); *The Current Digest of the Soviet Press,* weekly (Washington: U.S. Library of Congress); *East European Accessions List,* monthly (Washington: U.S. Library of Congress, since September, 1951); *Monthly Bulletin of the International Peasant Union* (Washington, D. C.: International Peasant Union); *News from Behind the Iron Curtain,* monthly (New York: National Committee for a Free Europe, 4 West 57 St., New York); *The Slavonic and East European Review,* semi-annual (London: School of Slavonic and East European Studies, Senate House, W. C. 1); *Problems of Communism* (edited by U.S. Information Agency, 1776 Pennsylvania Ave., N. W., Washington 25, D. C.), semi-monthly; *Bulletin,* Institute for the Study of the USSR (Augustenstrasse 46, Munich), monthly.

69. See such works as: Corliss Lamont, *Soviet Civilization* (New York: Philosophical Library, 1952); Bernard J. Stern, "Soviet Policy on National Minorities," *American Sociological Review,* I (June, 1944), 229-235, Edgar Snow, *People on Our Side* (New York: Random House, 1945), etc.

70. "The Institute's Fifth Anniversary," *Bulletin* of the Institute for the Study of the History and Culture of the USSR, II, 7 (July, 1955), 59-62.

UKRAINIAN SOCIOLOGY

Joseph S. Roucek
University of Bridgeport

The Ukrainian spokesmen insist that they are a minority in Soviet Russia and that they have a right to national independence; the evidence they have been able to produce on behalf of their cause, especially academically, is rather overwhelming.[1]

At the turn of the 19th century, Ukrainian scientists started collecting ethnological material, folk songs, historical documents and other data in order to disprove the contentions that they were Russians or Poles.[2] Collecting, interpreting, and editing old historical documents and studying Ukrainian folk poetry was the chief preoccupation of the earliest Ukrainian sociologists (influenced by the ideas of Johann G. Herder (1744-1803). Most prominent were Michael Maksimovitch (1805-1873), who published several collections of Ukrainian folk songs, Osip Bodiansky (1808-1876), the editor of numerous Ukrainian historical documents and professor of Slavonic languages in the University of Moscow, and Ismail Sreznewsky (1812-1880), a historian, philologist and collector of folk songs.

This sketchy research furnished some factual basis for romanticism in Ukrainian literature and resulted in a more scientific approach to current political and social problems. This was accomplished mainly by a circle of writers, poets, ethnologists and historians who organized in Kiev in 1847, the short-lived, secret Brotherhood of Sts. Cyril and Methodius, whose initial aim was to secure the abolition of serfdom and to establish a democratic federation of Slavs. The police jailed or exiled its members, but some members continued their scientific activities in their respective fields. The most eminent among them, in addition to the poet Tasar Shevchenko, were the historian Nicholas Kostomarov (1817-1885), and the poet, historian, and literary historian Pantaleymon Kulish (1819-1897); some of their writings contain interesting sociological ideas. For instance, Kostomarov's *Two Russian*

Nationalities (St. Petersburg, 1861-62) tried to explain the cause of the rise of the Ukrainian and Russian nationalities within the framework of geography and history and culture. His conclusions even today form the basis of the less critical discussions of Ukrainian nationalistic claims. Kulish was interested in the social task of literature and tried to establish, on a moral basis, the types of city and village people. The linguistic end of the arguments on behalf of the Ukrainian cause was taken up by Alexander Potebnia (1836-1891), University of Krakov, who, in 1862, laid the foundation for the socio-psychological research of poetry and language by his *The Mind and Language*; in his subsequent works, especially *Language and Nationality* (1895) he described the substance and the social significance of words, legend, poetry, and science. (His contributions are now appreciated in Russia and Ukraine, and belong to the school of V. Humboldt, Lazarus, Steinthal, etc.). Vladimir Antonovich (1834-1909), a historian, anthropologist and archeologist who was active in Kiev, defined nationality as a "totality of characteristics by which one group of people differs from various other groups," and divides them into: (1) those inborn, dependent on race and on the influence of geography, and (2) those acquired by education and appearing in the historical evolution of the social culture. He thought that human personality is composed seventy-five percent of heredity, five to ten per cent of education or the formulation of ideas on the basis of past experiences, and fifteen percent of the physiological and psychological contributions of the individual himself. Antanovich's theories were formulated before the theories of reflexes. He applied them to the national characteristics of the Russians, Poles, and Ukrainians; his scheme but was more elaborate repetition of Stomarov's theory about the absolutism of the Russians, the aristocracism of the Poles, and democratism of the Ukrainians. He is honored as the founder of modern Ukrainian scientific historiography.

Mikhaylo Drahomanov (1841-1895) is the real founder of the sociological schools studying social life of Ukraine. He died as Professor at the University of Sofia (in exile) and made his chief contributions by studying Ukrainian nationality as seen in its folk poetry, history and social structure in relation to world history. Emphasizing the objective method of research, he opposed the Russian school of "subjective sociology," and also disagreed with Marxism, recognizing it in its metaphysical characteristics (calling it "Engelism"). According to him, the history of a nation is determined primarily by geographic, economic, cultural, and moral factors; social ideas are also important moving forces of history.[3]

Nicholas I. Ziber (1841-1888), a leading Ukrainian economist, analyzed the theories of socialist materialism, and contributed considerable research on the beginnings of organized social life, government, family life, ownership and formulation of classes in primitive and peasant groups.

The publications of the Taras Shevchenko Scientific Association of Lviv, especially those of its Statistical and Legal sections, contain many interesting sociological studies, especially Stanislav Dnistryansky's *Man and His Needs in the Legal System* (1899). A very provocative and complete system of sociology was presented by Timfiy Osadchiy (1860-1920) in his *Social Existence* (Paris: *La civilisation et les grands fleuves historiques,* 1889); acquainted with the works of Spencer, Giddings, Ward, Durkheim and Gumplowicz, he was a pluralist in his understanding of social factors, granting preference to the development of consciousness as the fundamental factor; according to him, to know society meant to know its social forces. His work culminated the sociological thinking in Ukraine in the pre-war period.

The year 1918 became the cornerstone in the history of Ukraine; the scientific social thought was promoted, thanks to the pressure of the needs produced by the revolution. The center of sociological research became the Ukrainian Academy of Sciences with its socio-economic and historical-philological sections and its special chair of sociology occupied by Bohdan Kistyakivsky, and later by Professor Semkovsky, a Marxist.[4] The Institute published five volumes on demography, showing the high level of research. The Institute for the History of Ukraine under M. Hrushevsky also included a sociological section (O. Hermaize, P. Klimenko) and a branch on Primitive Culture (under Katherina Hrushevska); interested in the problems of generic sociology it published, since 1926, a special annual on *Primitive Society.* As Hrushevsky and his collaborators belong to the school of Durkheim, the character of their work is explained by that background.

The Ukrainian Institute of Marxism in Kharkov had the following sections: (1) the philosophico-sociological; (2) economic; (3) historical; (4) for nationalities and the racial problems; and (5) preparatory. The main aim of the Institute was the research into social processes and the preparation of Marxists; hence it was divided into sections for research and education. The Ukrainian Research Scientific Institute of Pedagogy in Kharkov specialized in socio-technics; beginning in

1925 the Institute published the *Ukrainian Journal of Experimental Pedagogy and Reflexology,* edited by B. Propopov. The Ukrainian Psycho-Neurological Institute of Kiev had its organ, *The Journal of Psychoneurology,* edited by Professor Hakkebus. The Ethnographical Society, the Geographical Society, and the Anthropological Society produced some direct sociological works, especially the 3 volumes of *Materials of Anthropology of Ukraine,* edited by Nikolayev. Some valuable sociological material can be found also in the first three volumes of *Criminal Anthropology and Court Medicine* (Kharkov, 1926-28).

In Western Ukraine, the center of Ukrainian work in Galicia was the Scientific Society of Shevchenko (*Naukove Tovarystvo im. Shevchenka*), which celebrated its 50th anniversary in 1924; it had published over 225 volumes, its main specialty being the sociography of Ukraine; other works covered the study of languages, religion and of the politico-economic processes. S. Dnistryansky is considered the first lawyer-sociologist who tried to build up his own theory of law as a social product.

UKRAINIAN SOCIOLOGY ABROAD

The first attempt to organize the Ukrainian sociological studies abroad was made in Vienna; Mykhaylo Hrushevsky, the great Ukrainian historian, was sociologically-minded and helped the publication of his *Genetic Sociology* (1921), V. Starosolsky's *Theory of the Nation* (1922), and M. Shrah's *State and Socialist Society* (1923). After his return to Ukraine in 1924, Hrushevsky directed the work of the historical section of the All-Ukrainian Academy of Sciences in Kiev; its cultural-historical committees, with the sections on primitive culture and for historical research, were especially active. Hrushevsky removed from the Academy in 1930 and died in exile in 1934. But his is a great name among the Ukrainians in all walks of life, as the leader of the Ukrainian nationalistic rejuvenation, and the first President of the Ukrainian People's Republic and its Central Council.

Vyacheslav Lypynsky's *Letters to my Fellow Husbandmen* (published in Vienna, 1920-21 in *The Agricultural Ukraine* journal), modernized Plato's idea that a state should be governed by philosophers by seeing a true aristocrat in a common Ukrainian farmer, who, finding his home menaced with destruction at the hands of a bolshevized mob during the last revolution, made haste to save first of all his library and died in defense of cultural values. He exerted a great influence on the formation of sociological thought of the entire Ukrainian anti-socialist camp, especially among the Ukrainian Monarchists, Nationalists, and Catholic Democrats.

The Czechoslovak government of Masaryk and Benes extended considerable help to the Ukrainian Immigrant Committee in Prague, headed by Shapoval, which drew up plans for the foundation of the Ukrainian Agricultural Academy in Podebrady and the Ukrainian Pedagogical Institute of M. Drahomaniv (in Prague). In addition to the two technical faculties, the Agricultural Academy was also given a socio-economic faculty, with chairs of theoretical sociology, social politics, social hygiene, statistics, together with numerous speicalists who lectured on their subject from the sociological standpoint. The Academy published its own *Journal* (*Vistnik*). Sociology was compulsory at the Ukrainian Pedagogical Institute, where Prof. Eichelman lectured; he also lectured for the Ukrainian Free University of Prague. In the fall of 1924, M. J. Shapoval founded the Ukrainian Sociological Institute of Prague, which granted the degree of doctor of sociology after two years of graduate work, the passing of examinations, and the presentation of a thesis.

Before World War II, the sociological thought of the Ukrainians had taken different directions. The representatives of the "materialistic" approach were most numerous. Kiev was the center of the followers of Durkheim, Kharkov of Marxism and reflexology; the emigrants tended to favor reflexology and behaviorism, with a smaller number promoting eclectic idealism. Interesting trends developed among the Catholic Democrats, as represented by Mikola Konrad in his *Sociology*; but this Professor of Sociology and dean of the Philosophical Faculty at the Ukrainian Greek Catholic Theological Academy of Lvov, was executed by the Reds during the first occupation of Western Ukraine in 1941; he applied to the Ukrainian scene the sociological thoughts of Papal Bulls—*Rerum Novarum* of Leo XIII and the *Quadragesimo Anno* of Pius XI. Gabriel Kostelnik developed an original approach to the practical democracy of the common man, criticizing the sociological views of Drahomanov. Ukrainian nationalistic sociology was leaning towards totalitarianism by setting the state above all else, with Mikola Sciborsky dwelling mostly upon agrarian problems and Vikul on the relations between the church and state.

Since World War II, Ukraine's sociology in Soviet Russia has been completely submerged under the Marxist-Leninist stranglehold. Abroad, the sociological research by Ukrainian scholars has been organized around the Free Ukrainian University of Munich, and in America around Professor Nicholas D. Chubaty, editor of *The Ukrainian Quarterly.*

SELECTED BIBLIOGRAPHY

A. A. Baikov, *Twenty-Five Years of the Academy of Sciences of the USSR* (New York: International Publishers, 1944). The Academy of Sciences was originally an institution for geographical exploration, but, under the Soviets, has become the main directing body of all scientific research in Soviet Russia.

B. P. Babkin, *Pavlov: A Biography* (University of Chicago Press, 1949). A biography that makes another one unnecessary. I. P. Pavlov's *Conditioned Reflexes: An Investigation of the Physiological Activity of the Cerebral Cortex* was translated and edited by G. V. Anrep (New York Oxford University Press, 1927).

Frederick C. Barghoorn, *Soviet Russian Nationalism* (New York: Oxford University Pres, 1956). Despite the internationalist elements of Marxist ideology, the USSR is, the author contends, the most integrated and centralized nation-state ever to exist; Soviet nationalism is described as "an often bewildering combination of traditional Great Russian nationalism, Eastern universalist Marxism and a system of rationalizations of the political order which has taken shape since 1917."

Harry Elmer Barnes & Howard Becker, *Social Thought from Lore to Science* (Washington, D.C.: Harren Press, 1952), Vol II: 1029-1059, "Russian Sociology." A systematic survey of the secondary literature.

S. H. Baron, "Plekhanov and the Origins of Russian Marxism," *Russian Review*, XIII (January, 1954), 38-51.

Nicholas Berdyayev (Nicolai Aleksandrovich Berdiaev), *The Realm of Spirit and the Realm of Caesar* (New York: Harper, 1953). The last work written by the exiled Russian philosopher before his death; a summation of several of the basic ideas on the nature of truth, the role of the Christians in the world and in relation to God, and the contradictions of Marxism. Important for his relations of ideas to those of Sorokin.

E. S. Bogardus, *The Development of Social Thought* (New York: Longmans, Green, 1955), Chapter XVIII, "Mikhalovsky and Russian Social Thought," 261-274; bibliography, 274.

H. E. Bowman, *Vissarion Belinski*, 1811-1848: *A Study in the Origins of Social Criticism in Russia* (Cambridge, Mass.: Harvard University Press, 1955). The place in Russian letters held by an influential literary critic of the 19th century whose ultimate belief that literature should perform a utilitarian social function laid the groundwork for contemporary Soviet views on art; he is sometimes called the Father of the Soviet Intelligentsia.

G. S. Counts, "Remaking the Russian Mind," *Asia and the Americans*, (October, 1945), 478-484; George Counts & N. P. Lodge, *The Country of the Blind: The Soviet System of Mind Control* (Boston: Houghton-Mifflin, 1949). A discussion of the methods used to make the arts and sciences, education and the press conform to an official pattern; quotations from Soviet sources are used.

Ruth C. Christman, Ed., *Soviet Science* (Washington: American Association of Science, 1952). A symposium.

B. D. Grekov & E. V. Tarle, "Soviet Historical Research," *Science and Society*, VII(1943), 217-232. A survey of historical research of twenty-five years praising the Soviets and attacking Pokrovsky.

John H. Hazard, "Soviet Textbooks on Law," *Slavonic and East East European Review*, XXI. 56 (March, 1943), 211-222. Good on the changing focus in the field of law that originated in the thirties.

Julius F. Hecker, *Rusian Sociology: A Contribution to the History of Sociological Thought and Theory* (New York: John Wiley, 1934). Shows the relationship of Russian revolutionary movements to the development of the various contending sociological theories.

The Hoover Library Collection on Russia, by Witold S. Sworakowski (Stanford University Press, 1954). A descriptive survey of the 40,000 books and pamphlets forming the Hoover Library Collection on Russia written by the Curator of the Slavic and East European division; the collection is one of the largest in the world, and includes also a comprehensive periodicals library as well as a large collection of manuscripts.

Julian Huxley, *Heredity East and West: Lysenko and World Science* (New York: Henry Schuman, 1949). A good summary how on August 7, 1948, the science of genetics had its throat slit by a decree of the Central Committee of the Communist Party, when it was announced by a Russian plant breeder named Trofim D. Lysenko who had repudiated the historic principles of Gregor Mendel and Thomas Hunt Morgan.

Count Paul N. Ignatiev, Dimitry M. Odinetz & Paul J. Novegorotsev, *Russian Schools and Universities in the World War* (New Haven: Conn.: Yale University Press, 1929). A brilliant analysis of the sociological implications of war to the educational policies.

Alex Inkeles, *Public Opinion in Soviet Russia* (Cambridge, Mass.: Harvard University Press, 1950). An objective, factual description of the Communist system of mass communication in the USSR.

Institute for the Study of the USSR (München 37, Augustenstr. 46), *Report on the Soviet Union in* 1956(Munich, 1956). Contains good summaries in the sections on "Contemporary Social Science," and "Socialist Realism and its Current Approach," 63-98, & 99-126.

V. D. Kazakevich, "Social Sciences in the Soviet Union," *American Sociological Review*, IX (June, 1944), 312-318.

Hans Kohn, Ed., *The Mind of Modern Russia* (New Brunswick, N. J.: Rutgers University Press, 1956). Brings together in one slender and readable volume a representative selection of the Russians' "agonizing reappraisal" of their own place and mission in the world. From Chaadayev and Pogodin, with their completely opposed views of the 1830's, to Lenin and Berdyayev some fifteen passionate and talented spokesmen speak directly to readers of English.

Max Laserson, *"Russian Sociology,"* Chapter XIV, 671-702, in G. Gurvitch & W. E. Moore, Eds., *Twentieth Century Sociology* (New York: Philosophical Library, 1945). Informative, but with a miserable bibliography.

A. G. Mazour, *An Outline of Modern Russian Historiography* (Berkeley, Cal.: University of California Press, 1939). The best available account of this field.

J. F. Normano, *The Spirit of Russian Economics* (New York: John Day, 1945). A valuable survey of economic thought.

A. Pinchevich, *Science and Education in the USSR* (New York: Putnam, 1935). Records the changes of the early 1930's.

G. Plekhanov, *Essays in Historical Materialism* (New York: International Publishers 1940). The ideology of the father of Russian socialism.

Melvin Rader, "Soviet Communism," in Joseph S. Roucek, Ed., *Twentieth Century Political Thought* (New York: Philosophical Library, 1946), chapter II, 18-36. A systematic summary.

Joseph S. Roucek, Ed., *Slavonic Encyclopaedia* (New York: Philosophical Library, 1949). A wealth of references to the sociologists and sociological thought; *Soviet and Russian Educational Imperialism* (Reprinted from *Journal of Human Relations*, Central State College, Wilberforce, Ohio, Fall issue, 1955, and Winter, 1956); for the changes in the education system, see: William H. E. Johnson, "Education in the Soviet Union," chapter 12, 384-413, in Arthur Henry Moehlman & Joseph S. Roucek, *Comparative Education* (New York: The Dryden Press, 1952), and bibliography, 410-413.

S. Rubenstein, "Russian Psychologists," Part VI, 207-278, in Carl Murchison, Ed., *Psychologists of 1930* (Worcester Mass.: Clark University Press, 1930). A good description of various schools of Russian psychological thought by I. P. Pavlov, A. L. Schniermann, and K. N. Kornilov.

Margaret Schlauch, "Folklore in the Soviet Union," *Science and Society*, VIII(1944), 205-222.

E. J. Simmons, Ed., *USSR: A Concise Handbook* (Ithaca, N. Y.: Cornell University, 1947). Especially see: Chapter X, "Soviet Philosophical Thought," by John Sommerville; Chapter XV, "The Development of Social Institutions," by Rose Maurer.

Nicholas Timasheff, *The Great Retreat* (New York: Dutton, 1946).

A widely scattered but valuable material on various aspects of sociology.

John Turkevich, "The Progress of Soviet Science," *Foreign Affairs,* XXXII, 3(April, 1954), 403-439.

A. Varonic, "The History of Belorussia in the Works of Soviet Historiography," *Belorussian Review,* II(1956), 73-97.

Alexander Vucinich, *The Soviet Academy of Sciences* (Stanford University Press, 1956), is the latest examination of how the Academy operates; valuable is the discussion of the extent and limitations of ideological demands upon Soviet scientific inquiry and exploration.

Conway Zirkle, Ed., *The Death of a Science in Russia* (Philadelphia: University of Pennsylvania Press, 1949). A good history of Lysenko's rise and of the maneuvers that culminated in the events of August 7, 1948; contains official and unofficial documents.

Joseph S. Roucek (1902—), was born in Czechoslovakia but naturalized in the United States (1927); B.A. (Occidental College), and M.A. and Ph.D. degrees, New York University (1928, 1937); a member of the Editorial Boards of *Social Science, American Journal of Economics and Sociology, Journal of Human Relations.* The author of numerous works *(Contemporary Roumania and Her Problems,* 1932; *Politics of the Balkans,* 1939, *Balkan Politics,* 1948; *The Development of Educational Sociology,*1956; etc.), he has also edited, co-edited and collaborated on numerous works published in the United States and Abroad *(Slavonic Encyclopaedia,* 1949, *La Sociologie au XXe Siècle,* 1947; *Social Control,* 1956; *Twentieth Century Political Thought,* 1946; *One America,* 1952; *Contemporary Europe,* 1947; *Sociological Foundations of Education,* 1942; *Contemporary World Politics,* 1954; *World Political Geography,* 1954; etc.). Has published articles in the leading academic periodicals in the United States, Canada, South America, Spain, Italy, France, Czechoslovakia, Yugoslavia, Roumania and elsewhere. Has taught in New York University, Pennsylvania State College (now University), Hofstra College, San Francisco State College, University of Washington, College of the Pacific, New Mexico Highlands University, Union of Wyoming, Occidental College, University of Southern California, University of British Columbia, University of Puerto Rico, Portland State College, etc.; in the spring of 1956, lectured under the auspices of the U.S. Information Service in Spain, Austria, Yugoslavia, Germany, Holland and France and also for several universities and learned bodies in these countries. Professor and Chairman of the Departments of Sociology and Political Science, University of Bridgeport (1948—).

NOTES

1. See the publications of the *Ukrainian Committee of America* (303 West 13 St., New York 14) , and especially *The Ukrainian Quarterly* (in its 12th year of publication in 1956); also ; *Ucrania Libre* (Free Ukraine) (a quarterly, Soler 5039, Buenos Aires, Argentina) and the scholarly work of the Free Ukrainian University (Munich 8, Versaillerstr. 4) . In Munich live some 30,000 Ukrainian refugees from communism. For the background and accomplishments of the American Ukrainians, see: Joseph L. Lichten, "Ukrainian Americans," 134-143ff. in Francis J. Brown & Joseph S. Roucek, *One America* (New York: Prentice-Hall, 1952) , and bibliography, 719.

2. Yaroslav Chyz & Joseph S. Roucek, "Ukrainian Sociology: Its Development to 1914," *Journal of Central European Affairs*, I, 1 (April, 1941), 74-87.

3. There is a marked similarity between Drahomanov's influence and that of T. G. Masaryk; both analyzed the historical process from the realistic standpoint but neither represented any sociological system. Their sociological and political writings contributed to the movements for independence.

4. For details, see: Joseph S. Roucek, "Ukrainian Sociology after the First World War," *Ukrainian Quarterly*, I, 2 (1944) , 152-163.

SOVIET RUSSIA'S SATELLITE EUROPE

Joseph S. Roucek*
University of Bridgeport

Prior to 1945, all the Central-Eastern European countries (now known as "People's Democracies") had developed their own cultural and scientific life in harmony with the principles of their national individuality; thus, with the exception of mathematics, natural history and the related branches of science, national heritage played an important role. This fact actually caused different characteristics in the various fields of knowledge—but only to a certain extent, since, in fact, it was easy to ascertain the common source of intellectual activity in the respective countries as regards Western civilization. The overwhelming majority of scientists sincerely believed that Western science, both in spirit and methodology, represented the highest possible level of scientific thinking.[1]

Sociologists also followed the Western (and American) patterns. The only difference among them was that some belonged to the German sphere of influence, most to the American one, and others were influenced by the French, Italian and some other minor cultural movements. But important it is to notice that none of these intellectuals showed any significant Russian or Soviet impact—until after the so-called "liberation" by the Red Army. Up to that time, sociology in all of these Iron Curtain countries had existed as a separate discipline aiming to become as empiric as possible.

After the enthronement of the pro-Soviet consuls, these countries soon started to suffer a tremendous change in their politico-economic-

* In cooperation with Francis S. Wagner, Ph.D., who was born in Krupina (Czechoslovakia), studied at the University of Szeged (Hungary), lectured at the Universities of Budapest and Szeged and has published several books and articles in the field of historiography and dialectical and historical materialism. A Librarian and Assistant in the Department of the University of Szeged (1931-1938) and then Professor in the State Teachers College (Budapest), after World War II, Wagner served as chief consultant on Slavic questions in the Hungarian Ministry of Foreign Affairs and then headed the Hungarian Consulate General in Czechoslovakia (1946-1949); he is now a staff member of the Library of Congress.

social and cultural systems which has eventually led to a sovietization, aiming to imitate the USSR's example.[2] There were and have been some differences in the tempo of these changes and thus also in the cultural changes accompanying them.[3] This relationship between the political changes and cultural orientation also provides the key to a review of the situation in regard to sociological research.

The first phase lasted until 1948-1949, when new Academies of Science were founded in line with the Soviet pattern.[4] But the reorientation did not take place immediately. For instance, even after the memorable Communist seizure of power in February, 1948 in Czechoslovakia, strong "bourgeois" traces influenced university work, and Professors Josef Král, Karel Galla and Antonín Boháč tended to continue sociology (in Charles University, Prague) as an independent science, quite remote from the content of Marxism-Leninism.[5] Similarly, "bourgeois sociology" was propounded in Poland immediately after World War II, when the pro-Communist forces were already dominant; four philosophical and one sociological periodicals were reestablished by the old board of editors.[6] In general, this was the situation in all the other countries of the area. Although the USSR imposed its political domination in this region in varying degrees, Marxism-Leninism lagged behind the conquering design.

CULTURAL REVOLUTION

It did not take long, however, to follow up the political domination by cultural imperialism. By 1950 or so, the human and library resources of the sociological departments had been simply taken over and put to work within the context of the regime; in some cases, the "old" men and organizations have continued to function, in a creaking manner, on behalf of the Soviet-Russian cause, and even adding up to existing knowledge. In the first phase, everything which had anything to do with Western tradition was sharply criticized. Thus, for instance, the sociological concepts and social philosophy of T. G. Masaryk were condemned only in 1953.[7] But, at the same time, the satellite governments started to enforce the directive that dialectical and historical materialism, as formulated by Marx-Lenin-Stalin, was to be the dominant philosophy of all science. Yet, the official attitude toward sociology, as toward all sciences, has been, ever since, a paradoxical one, because on the one hand, the approach to science is to be based upon scientific foundations, while, on the other hand, the anti-dogmatic attitude of all true science must fit into the Marxian view of things. The escape takes the form of a crude ideological explanation of science as merely a means to an end.

Of benefit to the communist spokesmen has been the heritage left by the pre-communist sociologists. The human and library resources of the former Sociological Departments were simply taken over and put to work within the context of the new regimes; in some cases the men and organizations have continued to function, in a creaking manner, on behalf of the Russian cause, and even producing new knowledge. At the same time, the pro-communist regimes have been utilizing the persistent flow of scientific contributions of free societies (since, from the Western point of view, there is no check on the free exchange of scientific knowledge). The result has been that "the contributions of Soviet science to the general progress of science are very limited indeed." [8]

Today, Sociology as such does not exist; its subject matter is investigated chiefly by philosophers (ideologists), historians, economists and jurists. The starting point for investigating social phenomena is the theory of dialectical and historical materialsm, according to which social consciousness is a reflection of social existence. Consequently, social consciousness does not determine social existence as it is conceived by the leading philosophers of Marxism-Leninism-Stalinism.[9] Hence all social research has aimed to stress both the ideological orthodoxy and the importance of using Marxism as the starting point of all inquiries.

HISTORY—AND PARTY-MINDEDNESS

In all People's Democracies, history is sponsored as an extremely important branch of learning, and the application of Marxism-Leninism is the main task of historically-oriented social science methodology. Hence the Budapest Congress of Historians (June 6-13, 1953) was carefully planned and produced important results; it presented the first opportunity for Soviet experts to evolve a workable plan for cooperation and mutual understanding.[10] The Congress has been a milestone as all the subsequent meetings of that kind have been influenced by its decisions, calling for the mobilization of all social scientists in the service of dialectical and historical materialism, with special emphasis upon application of the economic basis and superstructures to historical analysis. In fact, since the Budapest Congress, satellite social sciences depend mainly on historical analysis, and not on the prevalent methods of social research used in the West.

Thereafter satellite experts in all fields of social sciences (including economic and social history, jurisprudence, linguistics, and the philosophy of history) began to reevaluate the past and present events in their countries; these efforts were in full swing on the eve of the October Revolution (1956) in Hungary and resulted, among other things, in the writing of several university textbooks dealing with the economic and social aspects of the satellites.

At the same time, the satellite communist parties set up their own institutions for the analysis of the social conditions of the working people. Today, all scientific workers must produce fresh data on socio-economic phenomena supporting the prevailing Party ideologies in order to investigate the very practical task of building up socialism. These are mainly concerned with the questions of nationalization, collective farming, class warfare, and many other acute problems of the socalled "transition period."

The central idea of the communist hierarchy of principles is "party-mindedness." This becomes clear when analyzing the critique of relativism of Karl Mannheim's "Sociology of Knowledge."[11] Mannheim's assumption is that all ideology is socially conditioned. But, argues Adam Schaff, a noted Polish Academician, Mannheim is guilty of reaching an erroneous conclusion ("perspectivism"),[12] since the social conditioning of an ideology by the interests of a revolutionary class is the basis of its objective character. Schaff then claims that the Marxist theory makes it possible to overcome relativism inherent in the sociology of knowledge. The same method of reasoning is used, for instance, by Schaff's colleague, Marek Fritzhand, when searching for the relationship between elementary moral norms and the all-human elements of morality, as well as for the mutual relation between all-human and class elements; he concludes that the working class is the only rightful heir to all-human moral values, which is the specific combination of all-human and class elements in communist morality.[13]

All satellite social scientists believe that Montesquieu held a unique place in the history of progressive social thought in the period of Enlightenment, since Montesquieu's relativistic and skeptical views of social phenomena testify to the limited vision characteristic of his middle-class origin. But empiricism, rationalism, and materialistic approach should be regarded as permanent values of his social philosophy; his method of investigating social history comprises the generalizaton of empirical data, and includes seeking the determination of opinions and social institutions by objective living conditions; therefore, Montesquieu's doctrine promotes understanding of a social reality and is thus a forerunner of Red-minded progressive social thought. A similar reasoning is provided by the logic about John Hus's ideas. Kalivoda claims that the thoughts of Hus could not be against the interests of the laboring classes and hence the cultural heritage of Hussitism belongs to the communist regime.[14]

The chief product of this new "scientific" approach is a unique concept of the nation and its ideology—socialist patriotism. From the standpoint of the "sociologist," the nation, the people, and even the underdeveloped ethnic groups, are composed of only three valuable elements—the industrial (or the like) workers, the working peasantry, and progressive intelligentsia. All other elements are excluded from this concept. A practical way of forming such a "socialist" nation is through the mobility of the laboring classes, as has occurred in post-war Hungary since the beginning of the occupation by the Red Army.[15]

ORGANIZATIONAL STRUCTURE

Although all the satellite states have to conform to the same ideology and its application, we must note that there are some differences in the organizations handling "sociology." Closest to the Soviet model is the Bulgarian Academy of Sciences, consisting of 7 sections: (1) physics, mathematics, and technical science; (2) geology, geography, and chemistry; (3) biology and medicine; (4) history, archaeology and philosophy; (5) law and economics; (6) linguistics, ethnography, and literary science; and (7) creative arts and history of arts.[16] Sociology is associated with various other fields of learning, especially: philosophy, history, and economics. In Hungary, in contrast to the Bulgarian setup, the second Section of the Hungarian Academy of Sciences is devoted exclusively to the social and historical sciences; but here the Institute of Labor Movement has played the most important role since its foundation (1950). The Institute of History of the Roumanian Academy of Sciences, founded in 1948, is critically evaluated by its members as being unable to incite its experts to work successfully on the relationship between the labor movement and "scientific socialism" and for a general lack of collaboration among the several poorly organized institutes.[17] In Poland, the Institute of Social Sciences of the Central Committee of the Polish United Workers' Party, a center of Marxism-Leninism, organized in 1950, is a dominant factor in training "sociologists."[18] In Czechoslovakia, the situation is also different in many respects. Social studies are scattered throughout various organizations; thus the 7th Section of the Czechoslovak Academy of Sciences is composed of economy and law—and at present time, political economy is the most important of all social sciences in that country, for it has been searching for the laws of economic and social development of People's Democracies since the Great Socialist Revolution in 1917. On June 18, 1956, the Presidium of its Institute of Philosophy had several sections: (1) dialectical materialism; (2) historical materialism; (3) scientific socialism; (4) history of philosophy; etc. In effect, this reorganization concentrated sociological studies into the "most advanced science" of Marxism-Leninism.

POST-STALINIST DEVELOPMENTS

As the revolts in Poland and Hungary in 1956 showed, the pro-Soviet ideological control of the satellites has not been as effective as the satellite governments would have us think. Although the ferments of Poland and Hungary have not reached such a boiling point in other satellites, the fact remains that de-Stalinization has produced concurrent muttered resentments also in East Germany, Czechoslovakia, Rumania and Bulgaria.

Basically, the de-Stalinization policy led very fast to a new interpretation of fundamental doctrines and fact. In Hungary, especially, the cultural and scientific trends began to ignore the political ideology and started formulating a Western-like approach toward social phenomena. Public disputes actually revolutionized the Hungarian attitude toward an appraisal of the People's Democracies' achievements since May 1956. On the eve of Hungary's Fight for Freedom, the Hungarian Writers' Association, on behalf of professional scientists and in cooperation with historians and economists, took the initiative in reevaluating the social and economic order. On October 20, 1956, a noted writer, Domokos Varga, published a vitriolic article, titled: "The Time is Urgent." Proclaiming a new doctrine, Varga states: "All dogmas must be forgotten. Hungary's social and economic system must be reexamined on the basis of reality." [19]

Another element in the growing resistance of the non-Marxian thinkers to the pro-Marxian domination has been the new line in Soviet foreign policy which has resulted in a widening of scientific contacts. Soviet scientists (including social scientists) have started to attend international conferences.[20] Thus, in spite of the "anti-scientific character of bourgeois sociology", the Soviets sent a delegation to the World Congress of Sociology held in Amsterdam in August, 1956.

In contrast to the Soviet delegates (who "simply did not grasp what sociology is about"), the satellite delegates showed individual differences of opinion.[21] Especially the Polish delegates were quite critical of their Soviet colleagues; some of them "were authentic sociologists, who complained at being cut off for such a long time from the West." Others wanted to know more about Western techniques of sociological investigation and statistical analysis and tried to arrange for a few Polish students to study abroad. They also reported on some empirical research (a factory survey, rural investigations, and a study of the cultural integration of Polish settlers).

In summary, sociology, as is known to the Western world, is unknown to the satellites. Yet, the imposition of the Marxist ideology on what has been left of this sociology there has also failed. But it would be too hopeful to expect that the trend against empiric sociology will be reversed (as the repressions against the Hungarian revolutionaries at the turn of 1956-1957 were showing). If anything, it appears that the dominant political ideology of the Soviet-controlled empire will decide the future of the social science principles and methods in the enslaved countries.

ROOTS AND REMNANTS OF SOCIOLOGY IN AND ABOUT CENTRAL-EASTERN-BALKAN EUROPEAN COUNTRIES

The downfall of sociology under the satellite regimes must not obscure the fact that a number of Western-minded sociologists have succeeded, since 1948, in escaping. And these exiles, together with the growing number of the descendants of the immigrants or refugees from this area, have made definite contributions to sociology in America and elsewhere. (For instance, Florian Znaniecki, the greatest

Polish sociologist of the present generation, and at one time President of the American Sociological Society, admits that: "Thanks . . . to Robert MacIver, I lectured at Columbia University in the summer and fall of 1939, and thus escaped a Nazi concentration camp and could join the University of Illinois faculty in 1940").[22]

We shall proceed to summarize the trends in sociological thinking in these satellite countries, summarizing especially the developments from about the end of World War II to the beginning of their conquest by the pro-Soviet forces, and then the main contributions made by the sociologists to sociology abroad.

CZECHOSLOVAKIA

It can be safely stated that, between the two World Wars, Czechoslovakia developed the most successful sociology (next to Poland), thanks to the official and unofficial support given to it by two sociologists, Presidents Thomas G. Masaryk and Eduard Benes.[23]

The efforts to restore Czechoslovakia's sociology to its leading place after 1945 met with scanty successes. Under Gottwald's regime, Bláha, the ardent follower of Masaryk, tried to save the quarterly, *Sociologická Revue*, by devoting one whole issue of "Stalin as a Sociologist" —but in vain; the periodical simply ceased to exist. While Bláha died in his native country, Munk and O. Machotka emigrated to the United States; others went elsewhere; for instance Zděnek Ullrich died in Egypt and I. Gadourek has distinguished himself in Holland with his *A Dutch Community* and *The Political Control of Czechoslovakia*.[24]

Since sociology in pre-communist Czechoslovakia had been sponsored both by Benes and Masaryk, the pro-communist regime has been trying to eradicate the memories of Masaryk and Benes, distorting the past influences of these two men and glorifying all things Russian.[25] What has been happening to Czechoslovakia's sociology can be judged from reading *T. G. Masaryk's Antipopular Policies* (Prague: Orbis, 1953):[26]

"The fiction of the 'Masaryk-Republic's' still being spread and kept alive by the treacherous exiles working on orders of the American oppressors and warmongers . . . The task of this compilation and of further scientific work, on the documents contained therein, as well as on the whole work of T. G. Masaryk, is therefore this: to remove the Masaryk legend from our history and the remnants from the conscience of our people; to show the true face of the false bourgeois prophets, so that our people can with ever increasing vigilance and firmness defend our new popular state against its enemies."

Among the charges levelled against Masaryk is that he was a warmonger and organizer of anti-Soviet and anti-communist campaigns (p. 5), that he masterminded a plot to murder Lenin (p. 15), that he was "the head of the fascist forces in the pre-Munich republic" (p. 5), etc.[27]

Today, all Czechoslovak sociologists abroad are the followers of Masaryk and Benes, and the active ones are living in exile.[30] Among the most active has been K. Absolon,[31] Jiri Kolaja,[32] Jiri Nehněvajsa,[33] Pavel Sěbesta,[34] and others.

In the field of anthropology, international reputation has been won by Jindrich Matiegka (1862-1945), Lubor Niederle (1865-1933), and Ales Hrdlička (1869-1943). Matiegka was a physician and became interested in archaeology and finally specialized in it; he published about 250 works (all of them in Czech), with a few translated into English.[35] As Professor at the Charles University, he founded, with the help of Hrdlička, the Institute of Archaeology, and was the editor of the periodical *Anthropologie* and of the Anthropological Library (published by the Charles University) after 1923. After his retirement, he laid, again with Hrdlička's help, the foundations for a Museum of Man in Prague. Niederle specialized in classical archaeology and under the influence of Masaryk turned to anthropology, after studying at Munich (under Johannes Rank) and in Paris (L. Manouvrier). After travelling in Russia, he specialized in Slavonic anthropology and in 1891 founded (with Zděnek Zíbrt) the *Ethnological Survey* (in Czech). After his appointment as Professor of Anthropology in Charles University, he founded the periodical *Survey of Slavonic Antiquity* (in Czech) (after 1901 titled as *The Survey of Slavonic Philology and Antiquity*).[36]

Ales Hrdlička (1869-1943) was born in Moravia (Czechoslovakia); received his M.D. degree from Eccletic College (1892) and from the New York Home College (1894); Hon.Sc. Doctore from the Charles University (1920) and Comenius University (Brno, 1929). Started his career as Assistant in Anthropology, New York State Pathological Institute (1896-1899), after studying in Paris, and was then in charge of Physical Anthropology of Hyde Expeditions for the American

Museum of Natural History (1899-1903). He was no dull academician, although even on trips to the ends of the earth he wore "gates ajar" collars. In 1903 he was appointed Curator of the Division of Physical Anthropology of the National Museum (Smithsonian Institution). Most active in the academic field of writing, he was Associate Editor of the *American Naturalist* (1901-1908), the founder and editor of the *American Journal of Physical Anthropology* (1918), and Secretary of the Committee on Anthropology of the National Research Council (1917-1918). Among his numerous works (and numberless articles), we can note: *Ancient Man in North America; Ancient Man in South America; Medical and Physiological Studies Among Indians; Anthropology of Florida; Anthropometry; The Old America Skeletal Remains of Early Man; Animal-Like Manifestations in the Human Child; Practical Anthropology; Memoirs and Papers on Man's Evolution; Origins of the American Indian.* Hunting for many summers in Alaska and the Aleutians, he claimed to have provided the proof that aborigines came to America over those steppingstones. He denied that high brows indicate braininess, and dug up an Aleutian skull larger than Daniel Webster's. He did much to disprove Nazi race dogmas, and concluded that United States life had streamlined the European body, that Uncle Sam and the Gibson Girl fairly represented old U.S. white stock in evolution.[37] A collection of 63 of Boas' important papers dealing with fundamental problems of anthropology, forming an integral part of the history of this science, was published as *Race, Language and Culture* (New York: The Macmillan Co., 1940).

POLAND

According to Theodore Abel, before the War "Poland had the most highly organized and productive center of sociology in Europe."[38] Most productive work was carried on by the Sociological Institute of the University of Poznań. *The Polish Sociological Review* (the eighth volume appeared in 1939) was a first-rate scientific periodical. A growing number of sociologists was being trained at three Universities. The government helped substantially research activities, especially in the field of the ecology of the city, rural sociology, rural stratification, and social movements.

The report made by Dr. Znaniecki in 1945 questioned the future of Polish sociology, since most of the older sociologists had died or been executed by the Nazis; the only hope he held was that the few exiled sociologists might form "a nucleus for the future development of Polish Sociology." But, reports Abel, "this prediction has not come true," and "the resurgence of Polish Sociology has been as remarkable as the recovery of Poland from the devastations of war." Today, Poland has departments of sociology at Lódź, Lublin, Warsaw, and Wroclaw; the University of Lódź has three chairs of sociology and ten instructors; the *Sociological Review,* has started to reappear again (as *Przeglad Sociologiczny*). The leading initiative has been taken by Josef Chalasinski, Znaniecki's pupil and a former Rockefeller Fellow, before the war Director of the Institute of Rural Sociology whose reputation was based on his monumental reesarch monograph on the younger generation of Polish peasants (*Mlode Pokolenie Chlopow*, Warsaw, 1993, 4 volumes; an abreviated version, edited by J. Poniatowski & G. Herlinga-Grudzinski, appeared in Rome, 1946). He is head of the Department at the University of Lódź and chief editor of the *Review*; he is also Chairman of the State Commission for Higher Education. The other outstanding Sociologists are Stanislaw Ossowski, the head of the Department and the research organizations of the University of Warsaw, and Tadeusz Szczurkiewicz, the Chairman of the Department at the University of Poznán.[39] While several Polish sociologists were exterminated by the Nazis (W. Okinski, S. Rybiecki, etc.), among those still active are: Nina Assorodobaj, Jan Szezepanski, St. Kowalski, Jan Strelecki, J. Lutynski, etc.

Abel also describes how sociological work is carried on academically. In 1948-1949, the University of Lódź had sociological seminars (two, called proseminars, for the first year students, while the third seminar specialized in the works of Comte, Spencer, Marx, LePlay, Dilthey and Durkheim, and in such topics as Western Liberalism in the Twentieth Century, the Development of Nationalistic Ideologies, Catholic Social Thought, etc.). The fourth seminar was for second year students and considered inter-class mobility, the formation of class-consciousness and occupational "mentality," and the concept of social class in the writings of Marx and Engels. The fifth seminar was designed for students in their third and fourth year, with the general topic being the typology of social movements in relation to socio-economic structures.[40] A sixth seminar specialized in advanced social research.

The general courses offered during that year were: Social Structures in Primitive Society; Systematic Sociology (social groups, social organization, and social factors in personality); Theories of Social Structure;

the Sociology of Work; Sociology in Relation to Social and Intellectual Currents of the Nineteenth and Twentieth Centuries; Sociological Problems of Education; Methodology of Social Research; Social Statistics and Demography. "The structural-functional approach is characteristic for the program as a whole. Theoretical and methodological concepts and problems are developed in conjunction with the systematic analysis of historical types of social organization and of social processes in particular societies. . . ."[41]

Abel rejects the idea that "the development of cultural life in Poland is under compulsion closely to parallel Russian custom," and, referring to his visit, states that "there is no evidence that this condition obtained during my recent visit to Poland." Furthermore, "in my opinion, this view does not consider the important role of scientific research in a planned economy. Even in regard to Soviet Russia, although it is true that Russian Universities have no 'Department of Sociology,' it is not true that there are no researches of a sociolgical nature conducted by Russian scientists."

Abel believes also that sociologists of pre-war Poland had emancipated themselves from social philosophy under Florian Znaniecki and adopted the methods of objective, scientific research. "The fact that sociology, as a science, need not incorporate ideological components, was considered established. Therefore, it is not surprising that a place was found for scientific sociology in the new social order after the National Revolution of 1944-45.[42] Furthermore, it is apparent that such a sociology is an essential instrument for the implementation of a policy of rational social planning." This, in turn, has induced "the makers of Polish socialist policy . . . by the full support given to sociology so far."[43]

Poland's outstanding sociologist has been Florian Znaniecki (1882-1958), born in Swiatniki (now the Russian-dominated part of Poland), was expelled from the University of Warsaw for participation in a student rebellion. After studying in Geneva, Zurich, and Paris, he took his Ph.D. in Philosophy at the University of Cracow (1909). While Director of the Emigrants' Protective Association in Warsaw, he met W. I. Thomas, as whose invitation he came to Chicago (1914), lectured at the University of Chicago (1917-19), and after the formation of the Republic of Poland, was invited to the new University of Poznan as a philosopher, but established the first chair in Sociology in that country. He was Visiting Professor at Columbia University in 1931-33 and in the summer of 1939, thus escaping World War II in Europe.

He returned to Columbia as Julius Beer Lecturer (1939-40) and joined the University of Illinois (1940-1950), when he retired. He collaborated with Thomas on *The Polish Peasant in Europe and America* (originally published in 1918-20 and by A. A. Knopf, 1927), a classic study of the changes in the social attitudes of the immigrants under the impact of "Americanization," and known also for developing a distinct method involved in the detection, description and causal explanation of all the factors entering into the social situation, or determining the behavior of group studies, and of social laws discovered by social analysis which are then valuable for the determination of fundamental policies of social construction.[44] This work has also given a marked stimulation to actual social research and its reputation is even appreciated today in terms of a method of studying personality in terms of four basic wishes (New Experience, Security, Recognition, Response). Znaniecki's later work, *The Laws of Social Psychology* (University of Chicago Press, 1925), is also well known.

Znaniecki founded the *Polish Sociological Review* and the Polish Sociological Institute which conducted many sociological investigations in Poland. Appreciated on both sides of the Atlantic, he was elected President of the American Sociological Society, and has given to sociology many articles and books in various languages, among them: *The Problem of Values* (in Polish, 1910), *Introduction to Sociology* (in Polish, 1922), *The Sociology of Education* (in Polish, 2 vols., 1928-30); his *Social Actions* (New York: Farrar & Rinehart, 1936) is a notable advance over Tarde's initial contribution to this field, based on reading that involved 3000 or more references in several languages. His *The Social Thought of the Man of Knowledge* (New York: Columbia University Press, 1940) is a brilliant contribution to the field of "The Sociology of Knowledge"; the same applies to *Cultural Sciences, Their Origins and Development* (University of Illinois, 1952); his *Modern Nationalities* (University of Illinois, 1952) is a presentation of a comparative analysis of numerous works of historians, biographers, ideologists, men of letters, sociologists, and observers of social life in many countries, showing that nationalities have some degree of distinctive cultures and thus some degree of solidarity and a specific organization irreducible to political structures—and that this organized social unity is steadily growing and gaining influence throughout the world.

Alfred Habdan Korzybski (1880-1950), an early authority on semantics, founded a new school of psycho-philosophical semantics, which he named "general semantics." Widely credited with having expanded semantics from its ordinary concern with only the meaning of words into a new system of understanding human behavior, he had hundreds of followers throughout the world and was consulted by many scientists and scholars. Holding the conviction that "in the old construction of language, you cannot talk sense," he contended that because of Aristotelian thinking habits, which he thought outmoded, men did not properly evaluate the world they talked about and that, in consequence, words had lost their accuracy as expressions of ideas, if ever they had such accuracy. Life was composed of nonverbal facts, each differing from another and each forever changing. Too often, he contended, men got the steps of their thought-speech processes confused, so that they spoke before observing and then reacted to their own remarks as if they were fact itself. Korzybski explained that general semantics had to do with living thinking, speaking and the whole realm of human experience.

His theory was put to practical use in the fields of public, industrial and race relations, and everywhere that misunderstanding among peoples is due to different values and construction of words. In explaining simply what he meant by misleading words, Korzybski said that to say a rose "is" red is a delusion because the red color was only the vibration of light waves.

His *Manhood of Humanity—The Science and Art of Human Engineering* (1921) caused a stir in the intellectual world, as did his second book, *Science and Sanity, An Introduction to Non-Aristotelian Systems and General Semantics* (Harrisburg, Penna.: The Science Press, 1933). In 1946, he moved the Institute of General Semantics (from Chicago, where he had founded it in 1938) to Lakeville, Connecticut.[45]

One of the great names in the field of anthropology has been that of Bronislaw Malinowski (1884-1942), born in Cracow (Poland). He does not belong to the group of recent "exiles," but to the generation known to Western Europe already during and after World War II; yet his influence has been felt even today in all fields of social anthropology. He did research work at the British Museum and the London School of Economics; in 1914 he went with the Robert Mond anthropological expedition to New Guinea and northwestern Melanesia; in 1924 he was appointed a reader in Social Anthropology at the University of London, and came, in 1933, as Messenger Lecturer to Cornell University; later he joined the faculty of Yale University. Among his numerous works we can mention *Crime and Custom in Savage Society* (New York: Harcourt, Brace, 1926), *The Dynamics of Culture Change and a Scientific Theory of Culture* (1947), and others.[46] His *Scientific Theory of Culture* (1949) claims the role of generalizing social science for cultural anthropology and demonstrates the use of functionalism in research. Malinowski thus became, with Radcliffe-Brown the outstanding exponent of functionalism in cultural anthropology, and a strong supporter of a moderate evolutionism.[47] According to this approach, any custom must be treated as a organ of a functionary world, showing its effects on the lives of its moulders and their society. (His works have been translated into French, German, Italian and Spanish).

Among the other works by Polish exiles, we might note Manfred Kridl's *A Survey of Polish Literature and Culture* (New York: Columbia University Press, 1957), a valable summary of varied information. Of sociological orientation is definitely Jerzy Zubrzycki's *Polish Immigrants in Britain: A Study of Adjustment* (New York: S. S. Heimann, 1956), a systematic study of the origin, formation and evolution of the Polish immigrant community in Britain from 1939 to the present. Although there are no specific sociological sections in *Poland*, edited by Bernadotte E, Schmidt (Berkeley, Cal.: University of California Press, 1945), many portions of the treatment are of sociological significance; among the well-known writers we find here Oscar Halecki, an outstanding Polish historian living in America, Jerzy Radwan, former Director of the Agrarian Party, Polish Government in London, Jan K. Kasprzak, former Professor in the Teachers' College of Warsaw, Edmund Zawacki, Head, Department of Polish, University of Wisconsin, and others.[48] Zbigniew Brzezinski, Assistant Professor of Government and Research Associate, Harvard, a Polish born specialist, has written (with Carl J. Freidrich) a provoking study of total dictatorship.[49]

World War II produced a Polish community in Britain, which has been carefully studied by Zubrzycki (inspired by the classic study of the Polish community in the United States by Thomas and Znaniecki).[50] The Polish community in Britain is a political community, the author asserts, again and again, and as such it is conscious of an obligation to keep itself intact for the great end. Naturalization is frowned upon, assimilation is not encouraged. A certain accommodation to British ways is conceded as inevitable, but in the hostels and industrial colonies of Polish composition, even this is often found unnecessary. (Now, as we know from the daily papers, this community is slowly beginning to disintegrate.) The author's conclusions are arrived at by use of primary materials, such as case histories, records of the many Polish associations in Britain, and newspaper reports. He supports his conclusions with lavish use of tables.

One of the most important studies to have appeared to date on Polish history, and offering much more than its promised title, has been the work of Leslie.[51] It gives an excellent account of the social and economic conditions in Poland from the middle of the 18th century to 1830, with particular emphasis on the *szlachta* and peasant problems. Then follows a brief discussion of the impact of romanticism on the younger generation in Congress Poland which resulted in a flowering of Polish artistic genius on the one hand and a growth of radicalism finding its outlet in conspiracy on the other. The author tears away the legend enveloping these conspiratorial activties and the ensuing revolution; brought about "by a handful of youths" in a "haphazard way, almost with no plan," it was a foolhardy action. The concluding chapter contains some penetrating observations on the effects of the revolution on the subsequent Polish national development.

HUNGARIAN SOCIOLOGY

Hungarian sociology has continued its "checkered career."[52] In fact, here whatever sociology existed has been always used for political arguments. The ethnographic arguments over the racial origins of the Hungarians are still alive. In addition, the traditions of legalism have also left their mark, since the privileged of Hungary have used the legalistic approach to sustain their power.

But exiled Hungarian sociologists have certainly made their influence abroad. Oscar Jászi, after finding refuge in Czechoslovakia, settled at Oberlin College; his *The Dissolution of the Hapsburg Monarchy* (University of Chicago Press, 1924) is a masterful analysis of the social, political, and intellectual trends of the monarchy, especially also of Hungary, in the last decades of its existence. Rustem Vambéry, one of the pioneers in the juvenile court movement in Hungary, ended his career by resigning as Ambassador to the United States, disgusted with pro-communist tendencies of his government soon after World War II.[53] But there is no doubt that the most famous Hungarian sociologists is Karl Mannheim (1893-1947); he was born in Budapest, educated for the most part in Germany, and spent his concluding fourteen years in England thanks to his removal from the Chair of Sociology at Frankfurt University in 1933; he lectured at the London School of Economics and edited the International Library of Sociology and Social Reconstruction of London and New York. Illness prevented him from accepting the chairmanship of the European section of the UNESCO, for which he was designated; he also had to decline an offer of a free hand to reorganize Canberra University (Australia). His book, *Diagnosis of Our Time* (New York: Oxford University Press, 1943), was one of the most widely discussed of recent contributions to sociological literature, although his first extensive formulation of the sociology of knowledge had appeared in his *Ideology and Utopia* (New York: Harcourt, Brace, 1936).[54]

The literature surveying and evaluating the Sociology of Knowledge, and thus also Mannheim, is enormous.[55] More specifically, it can be said that this area of sociology is not "history of ideas in their social contexts," "social determinism of thought," "dominance of material over non-material culture"; it is the analysis of the functional inter-relations of social processes and structure on the one hand and the patterns of intellectual life, including the modes of knowing, on the other. The study of this field was given principally by the Chicago school, including such men as Robert E. Park, Louis Wirth (who wrote an Introduction to Mannheim's *Ideology and Utopia*), and others; Howard Becker, in his *Social Thought from Lore to Science*, with Harry Elmer Barnes, helped to bring the subject of the sociology of knowledge—and Mannheim—to the forefront. In addition, many Middle European social scientists have come to this country as refugees, and have participated in this "movement," especially certain sociologists and economists of the Marxian school, or those influenced by Max Weber, Max Scheler, Ernst Troeltsch, etc.[56]

Roughly speaking, Mannheim stresses how the nature of any particular line of thought cannot be fully understood unless its social origins are brought to light; it is essential in doing research concerning the meaning of concepts to investigate "the concrete setting of an historical-social out of which individually differentiated thought only very gradually emerges."[57] All individuals are a part of an intellectual continuum to which he may make modifying contributions. A person belongs to a group not only because he was born into it, but also because he sees life and the world largely in terms of the meanings that have been acquired by or developed in the group in question.

All in all, Mannheim has been "credited with bringing the new fields of the sociology of knowledge into sociological thinking,"[58] and outlined the factors which lead to social change. He also gave a basic, sociological groundwork to social planning for the various civilizations that are now in conflict but that need to be integrated into one human civilization. An English authority credits him with being "more than anyone to arouse the interest of the teaching porfession here (England) in sociological thinking, and his all too brief spell of service in the University of London already stands out as a landmark in recent history of the training of teachers in this country" (England).[59]

In the thirties, in Hungary, where the bulk of the population belongs to or takes its origin from that category, a vigorous movement started exploring the life of the peasantry and showing to the public the grave social conditions it lives in. The invaluable work of Bártok and Kodály of collecting the musical motives of the peasants in the Danube Valley gave the initiative to these groups of enthusiastic young writers, sociologists and religious workers. The methods of sociology were often neglected, emotions were widely used and the presentation was often one-sided, although idealistic. They fulfilled however, the most important task of drawing public attention to the dynamics of social strain in the agricultural masses; they stood up gravely for their ideas in various court-trials and undeniably succeeded in arousing public opinion. The next step was the scientific collection of all the facts of the peasant problem and a systematic study of their history from the beginning. By that time, the tide of war entered the Danube Valley and washed away the possibilities of academic study of the problem.

Probably the most valuable contribution to this field has been Istvan Szábo's contribution.[60] Written by a Professor of Debrecen University and published before the pro-communist rule became all-dominant, it is an important systematic study of the evolution of Hungarian peasantry from the end of the Middle Ages to 1848; the influence of Sombart can be observed all through the book.

During the same year appeared a systematic survey of the Balkan Peninsula by the Balkan Institute.[61] Until quite recently, the Hungarians did not pay much attention to the Balkans, which, in their opinion, was a backward area of poor goat and swine herders. In Mendol's point of view such an attitude is "in many respects erroneous and in its consequences unquestionably damaging." This certainly indicated great changes in at least some Hungarians' attitude towards their neighbors to the south by 1848. (All through the treatment of

Fiume and Voivodina and Transylvania, Mendol never mentions that these were for centuries Hungarian, and neither does he mention Hungarian minorities in Yugoslavia or Rumania). Roughly, this is primarily a study in human geography, which covers the geographical aspects, the problems of land use and economic development, the ethnic question of the main regions of the peninsula, the importance of religion in the question of nationality (especially in the case of the Catholic Croats, the Eastern Orthodox Serbs and the Moslem Bosnians who speak the same language yet write in three different ways and belong to three widely divergent cultural communities); the discussion of the various types of houses founded in the peninsula is especially interesting sociologically, and is related to an analysis of urban and rural communities, with the patterns of villages, towns, cities, and their economic functions.

RUMANIA

In spite of being the most recent book on Rumania, Alexandre Cretzianu, Ed., *Captive Rumania* (New York: Praeger, 1956), written mostly by Rumanian refugees painting the pre-communist regime "white" and everything under communism as being "black," nothing is mentioned here about the considerable advancements in sociology made during the royal regime.[62]

In fact, the roots of a sort of sociology can be traced as far back as the 19th century. Sorokin rates highly the work of A. D. Xenopol (1847-1920) who, as Professor at the University of Iassi tried to provide a link between the relations of the philosophy of history and sociology, and has been evaluated (with Indelband and Rickert) as the founder of the logic of historical sciences; he limited sociology to the study of facts of coexistence and repetition. An exponent of Neo-positivism, D. Draghicescu was rather popular before World War I, with his theory that sociology is directly based on biology, and that psychology is either "subjective sociology" or physiology and there were many other Rumanian sociologists.[63]

The development of Rumanian sociology by Dimitri Gusti reminds us of the work and influence exerted by Florian Znaniecki in Poland.[64] Educated in Leipzig and Berlin, he was appointed Professor of Sociology and Philosophy at the University of Iassy in 1910; he dominated Rumanian sociology after 1921, when appointed Professor of Sociology in Bucharest. He directed the *Institutul Social Român* (Roumanian Social Institute), founded then for research work in the social sciences and to make the results of its efforts known in order to further social reforms; its *Arhiva (Archives)* became a mine of information especially on the research among the peasantry.[65] Gusti specialized in several fields (the sociology of war, social reform, the sociology of political parties, the relation of sociology to ethics, and in the field of educational sociology). He conceived of sociology as a non-normative, autonomous general science of social life, coordinating and systematizing the elements common to all the other social sciences; this science should not be wholly derivative but should provide direct observation of society within the framework of its own reference, utilizing the results in monographic studies prepared according to the most exacting standards of modern methodology. Along this line of reasoning, the Social Institute produced numerous magnificent studies (sponsored in many cases, by Gusti's friend, King Carol, the late ruler of Rumania).

Gusti's followers were many in Rumania.[66] After the coming of World War II, whatever Rumanian sociology might have been carried on—and there is no information available from the Rumanian sources —it is only a servant of Marxism-Leninism.

At the same time, we must note the contributions by an Anglo-American sociologist, whose outstanding contributions, however, are seldom noted by the sociologist, although they are sociology *par excellence*. David Mitrany, D.Sc., Ph.D., Oxford, England, was formerly Professor of the University of Harvard and London and Yale; has served on the editorial staff of the Manchester Guardian and as assistant European Editor of the Carnegie Endowment's Economic and Social History of the World War; and has authored numerous works, the most important, sociologically, being *The Effect of the War in South Eastern Europe* (Yale University Press, 1936), and *The Land and the Peasant in Rumania* (Yale University Press, 1930), the outstanding sociological analysis of the changing world of Rumanian peasantry. Definite contributions to sociology have been made by Dr. Dagobert D. Runes, editor and owner of the Philosophical Library (New York), which has published numerous sociological studies which, otherwise, would not have been made available to the public by commercial publishers.

The Sovietization of Rumania has brought forth numerous studies arguing violently mostly against Communism, and a few still recalling, one way, or the other King Carol's regime. We have noted Cretzianu's book, which is in spite of its weaknesses, a useful but undigested compendium of information on Rumania's life under communism. More valuable is G. Ionescu's *Social Legislation in Rumanian Agriculture* (New York Mid-European Studies Center, 1954), Constantin Iordan's *The Rumanian Oil Industry* (New York University Press, 1955), S. D. Zagoroff & others, *The Agricultural Economy of the Danubian Countries,* (1935-1945 Stanford University Press, 1955). Two American historians have recently tried their hand surveying the available literature (and thus depending extensively on Mitrany) on the Rumanian peasant movement; Henry L. Roberts, *Rumania: Political Problems of an Agrarian State* (Yale University Press, 1951, covers especially the agrarian problem since World War I); Robert Lee Wolff's *The Balkans in Our Time* (Harvard University Press, 1956) has a lot of undigested material in the sections covering Rumania.[67]

THE BALTIC

"Until the beginning of the 19th century there was no Lithuanian (that is Baltic) bibliography in the true meaning, . . . and the first Lithuanian bibliography of publications in Lithuanian was published by Kajetonas Zabitis in 1842."[68] As in the Balkans, the rise of Baltic literature having connection, if any, with sociology, was integrated with the ideological claims to national consciousness and eventually national independence.[69]

This work, however, was definitely handicapped by the opposition of the Czarist government. During their brief period of independence, the Baltic nationalistic writers tried to free themselves from the domination of the field by German historians (interested mainly in the cultural influences of German settlers on the eastern Baltic coast and the Hanseatic League) and the scholars of Denmark, Sweden, Russia and Poland. Especially interested were these Lithuanian, Latvian and Estonian scholars to separate their own national background from that of the other Baltic people.

In Lithuania, this work was the continuation of the ground laid by the Lithuanian Scientific Society (founded in 1907 at Wilno), which promoted the study of the language, folklore and history under the direction of Jonas Basanavicius (1851-1927), the father of the Lithuanian Renaissance, who also edited *The Lithuanian People*, a periodical valuable for studies in many fields. During World War I, the society popularized especially the historical claims of the Lithuanian people. With the formation of the independent state, the government gave most support, naturally, to all studies supporting Lithuania's historical claims to independence. The Kaunas University (founded in 1922 and rechristened Vytautas the Great University in 1930), became the main research center, mainly in the field of history, with many studies bordering on the field of sociology,[70] although most attention was paid to medieval history and much less to contemporary conditions. A. Janulaitis became the author of the studies in political history, law, jurisprudence and economic and social developments. With the Soviet occupation, a policy of cultural persecution followed, and all "more sensible" literary work has been carried on abroad, particularly in the United States[71] (especially promoted by the Lithuanian Legation and the Lithuanian American Information Center); in this respect, most valuable have been the studies by an American scholar, Walther Kirchner (of the University of Delaware), since he can read and utilize so many languages of the area, and whose *The Rise of the Baltic Question* (Newark, Del.: University of Delaware, 1954) is a valuable study of the role which the eastern Baltic region has played in world affairs.[72] Sociologically speaking, however, probably most definitely "sociological" have been several analyses of the immigration aspects of the Baltic peoples.[73]

Esthonia also started to have its past probed by native historians at the end of the 19th century, during the period of national revival. In 1919, the old University of Dorpat was reestablished as Tartu University and the historical studies were directed by Arno Raphael Cederberg, imported from Helsinki; he founded, as the first President, the Academical Historical Society, whose main accomplishment was *Estonian Encyclopaedia* (Tartu, 8 vols.); in 1933 appeared the *Bibliotheca Estoniae Historica*, edited by E. Blumfeldt & T. Loone, covering the books and articles which appeared between 1877-1917; between 1918-1923 and 1929-1930, all writings were listed in the *Estonian Philological and Historical Annual Review* (in Estonian). Many of the writings dealt with the archaeological nature, culture conflicts, ethnography, the subject of domination (colonialism is the term today), and agrarianism.[74]

Russian-German-Soviet occupation has ended Estonia's independence and thus this kind of research. Today several good books on that country are, however, available in English: *Estonia: A Reference*

Book, compiled by Villibald Raud (New York: Nordic Press, 1953) covers the political, economic, and cultural achievements in the interwar period, there are also useful chapters about the conditions in that country under the Soviet rule and the life of Estonian refugees in the Western World; Albert Pullerits' *Estonia, Population, Cultural and Economic Life* (Tallinn: Kirjastus Uhisuse Trukikoda, 1937), if found in any American library, is an extremely useful handbook.

Latvia has gone through the same historical evolution in scholarship as Lithuania and Estonia; there history was used to provide ideological props for the creation and survival of the new state. The groundwork had been laid by the first Latvian history of the 19th century, J. Krueger-Krodznieks (1854-1924), who also promoted the collection of folksongs, legends, tales and riddles, local history and translation of foreign works; in fact ethnology and folklore was featured, while archaeology was handicapped by the supervision by the Russian police. The Latvian State University started, right after its foundation in 1919, to promote historical, archaeological and ethnographic work. F. Balodis, director of the Latvian Historical Museum, was the leader in the field of archaeology trying to reconstruct Lettish life from the 9th to the 12th century. The government-subsidized Latvian Historical Institute works were published in *Journal of the Lavian Historical Institute* (in Latvian, founded in 1937), which also sponsored a series in *Les sources de l'histoire de Lettonie.* After the war, the Latvian cause was especially promoted in the United States by Alfred Bilmanis, the Latvian Minister to the United States.[75]

BULGARIA

There appears to be no systematic survey of sociology in Bulgaria, although traces of some sociological thinking can be found in Bulgaria's historical writings.[76] Influenced by the Russian and Pan-Slavic thought, together with the ideas of France entering Bulgaria via Serbia and Greece, the Bulgarian scholars worked at first on their claim to nationalism and on the attempts to establish the roots of the science of Bulgarian linguistics in the language spoken in the days of Saints Cyril and Methodius (the middle of the 9th century). Under the influence of P. J. Safarik's *Slavonic Antiquities* they also spent a lot of time on ethnographic research, and on the religious and cultural origins of the Bulgarian people. After the turn of the century, most students investigated the field of institutional, ecclesiastical, economic, social and constitutional history. Interestingly enough, the Marxian influence was felt early in Bulgaria (D. Blagoev, Ivan Yankov Sakuzov and others). N. Penev labored a sociological and a philosophical answer to the question concerning the nature of the Bulgarian national tradition, and tried to evaluate the historical place of the educated element or the intelligentsia in Bulgaria's cultural development. The work of St. Romanski was a study of the Bulgarian population in Wallachia and Moldavia, using the methods of contemporary physical anthropology (which in the Balkans has always been tainted with political bias). Anastas Ishkirov (1886-1937) was one of the typical ethnographers, specializing in the social institutions of the typical village in Bulgaria; N. S. Bobchev studied the Bulgarian gentry (*Tschorbajis*) and its role in the social structure, and evaluated the influence of the Ottoman occupation on the character, spirit and structure of Bulgarian society. Dimiter V. Blagoev (1857-1924), the outstanding socialist leader of his country, popularized the teachings of Marx in such works as *A Contribution to the History of Socialism in Bulgaria* (Sofia, 1906). In recent decades, in fact, and especially under the Communist influence, most work in Bulgaria in this field has been built around the conception of the philosophy of history.

Today most definite contributions of sociology of or in Bulgaria are being published abroad. Christ Anastasoff heads the group of the Macedonian emigrés who have been carrying on a hopeless fight on behalf of Macedonia's independence in various books and pamphlets and articles.[77] Roughly, the best available sociological works dealing with Bulgaria are R. H. Markham, *Meet Bulgaria* (Sofia: the Author, 1931), probably unavailable any more, and Irwin T. Sanders, *Bulgarian Village* (Lexington, Ky.: University of Kentucky Press, 1949), an application of the theme of *The Middletown* and *The Middletown in Transition* to a Bulgarian village; the author taught at the American College (1929-1932, 1934-1937) and was an Agricultural Attaché of the United States in Sofia in 1945-46; his intimate knowledge of Bulgaria has led to this work, focused around the peasant family and community life. The bulk details the ways of life of a tranquil rural folk clinging to a Bulgarian mountainside, in the shadow of a 12th century monastery—their history, economic system, courtship and marriage customs, patriarchal family life, and reluctantly yielding to the ways of the western world. Here is depicted the Bulgarian world that the author came to know in the 1930's; the concluding chapters already describe what was happening to the village late in 1945, when the posters in the streets were proclaiming "Welcome to the Heroic Red Army" and "Long Live Stalin."

ALBANIA

Since the first higher educational establishment was opened in Tirana only in 1957, sociology, as an academic subject is unknown in Albania. But in addition to the run of the mill polemical publications mirroring the political differences in Albania, there have been several publications dealing with the various sociological aspects of Albania and with the Albanian emigrants. Sociological observations are scattered in the works of Robinson, Stickney and Swire;[78] the problem of the Albanian immigrant in the United States produced the studies of Federal Writers' Project[79] and Roucek.[80]

Of the most recent publications, the most ambitious is *Albania*, edited by Stavro Skendi (New York: Praeger, 1956), a mass of scattered information on Albania under the Soviets, which would gain a lot by having a sociological framework (although the limited bibliography, pp. 355-370, is useful). A note can be also made of Marcellus D. A. von Redlich, *Albania: Yesterday and Today* (Worcester, Mass., 1936), and UNRRA, *Economic Rehabilitation in Albania* (in *UNRRA Operational Analysis Papers*, 1-53, No. 46 of series; 53 nos. in 6 vols., London: UNRRA European Regional Office, 1947).

In the field of physical and cultural anthropology, good studies are: Carleton S. Coon, *The Mountains of Giants: A Racial and Cultural Study of the North Albanian Mountain Ghegs* (Cambridge, Mass.: Harvard University, Peabody Museum, 1950); Margaret Hasluck, *The Unwritten Law in Albania* (Cambridge, England: University Press, 1954). Albania is also partly covered in Philip E. Mosely, *The Distribution of the Zadruga Within South-Eastern Europe* (reprint from *The Joshua Starr Memorial Volume* (Jewish Social Studies, Publ. Vol. V, New York, 1953), 219-30, and Wilbert Ellis Moore's *Economic Demography of Eastern and Southern Europe* (New York: Columbia University Press, 1946). Stavro Skendi's *Albanian and South Slavic Oral Poetry* (Philadelphia: The American Folklore Society, 1954) is certainly a contribution to a little known field, since sociological studies, even before World War I, were concerned, next to politics, mostly with the "queer" folkways and mores of the Albanians.

YUGOSLAVIA

Before World War II, Yugoslavia had had a rather promising and fruitful development of Sociology.[81] Ethnography, human geography, historical sociology, and the "ideological sociology" had had most promising advancements. Before World War I, Baltazar Bogisic, at one time Professor at the University of Odessa, later Minister of Justice in Montenegro, and at the end of his life a private teacher of sociology, became interested in the "traditional-saturated patriarchal world of the Slavic south" and published an introduction to the study of the customary law of the region which evoked a most enthusiastic approval of Henry Sumner Maine; his subsequent monographs were imitated by the Poles, Russians, Czechs and Rumanians.[82] Jovan Cvijić, head of the Geographical Institute of the University of Belgrade produced a fund of materials covering the forms of settlement, migrations, psychical and cultural differentiation and economic life of the Balkan peoples; his reputation as an outstanding human geographer became known throughout Europe. In the field of historical sociology, Slobodan Jovanovich provided a rich mine of material for a typological psycho-sociology of the Serbs during the period of transition from a simple barter economy to urban capitalism. In the field of ideological movements, Svetozar Marković became the outstanding proponent of Peasant Populism, who tried to apply the Marxist principles to the peculiar problems of Balkan Europe. Tito's regime hailed him as a spiritual forerunner of the Yugoslav Partisan movement and had his works republished.[83] But the sociology of the modern type was expounded by Mirko M. Kosić, a Neo-Simmelian, who eventually continued his career in exile (in Geneva).

According to Dr. Radomir D. Lukić, since 1940 Professor of the Theory of the State and Law and of Sociology in the Faculty of Law in Beograd, the more developments of sociology in Yugoslavia appear to be as follows:

"As in the pre-war years, the post war period saw a relatively more intensive development of the particular cognate social sciences (anthropogeography, history and ethnology) than of theoretical, general sociology. But work was also started in this last direction. Consciousness of the need of sociology for a society engaged in building new social relationships was the foundation of the theoretical framework. The Yugoslav Sociological Society was founded in 1954, with Dr. Oleg Mandić, Professor of Sociology at the University of Zagreb, as its President. Courses in Sociology were introduced at all five of Yugoslavia's universities; in 1957 the Sociological Society, in cooperation with the Philosophical Society, planned to launch in Beograd its *Časopis za filozofiju i sociologiju (Philosophical and Sociological Review)*, intended to be devoted predominantly to theory. Different social problems, including also sociology in considerable measure, are discussed in such current periodicals as *Nasa stvarnost (Our Reality)*, *Statistička revija (Statistical Review)*, *Arhiv za pravne i drustvene nauke (Archive for Jurisprudence and Social Sciences)*, *Anali Pravnog fakulteta u Beogradu (The Annals of the Faculty of Law in Belgrade)* (all published in Belgrade); the *Pregled (The Review*, Sarajevo), *Pogledi (Views*, Zagreb), *Pravnik (The Jurist)*, *Nasa sodobnost (Our Reality)*, and *Delo (The Work)* (the last three published in Ljubljana).

Yugoslavia's sociology of today has taken three directions. (1) There are the sciences cited above and their development is continuing in the same direction and using the same method as before World War II; they tend toward concrete empirical-historical research rather than theoretical generalization. The principal works in anthropogeography have been published in the manual of the Serbian Academy of Science in Beograd, *Vaselja i poreklo stanovnistva (Agglomerations and the Origins of the Population)*, which was founded by Cvijić and to which several new volumes have been added. Valuable ethnological works are being published by the Yugoslav Academy of Sciences and Arts in Zagreb in its *Zbornik za narodni zivot i obicaje Juznih Slavena (Manual of the Folk Life and Customs of the South Slavs)*. (2) The second direction of Yugoslav sociology is represented by the effort to build, on the theoretical basis of historical materialism, a general sociology that would differ from the predominantly formal and static sociological systems in the West, based mainly on an individualistic concept of sociology. The main question being treated is the relationship between historical materialism and sociology and the class structure of society, notably at the transition from capitalism to socialism. The most important works have been written by the most eminent Yugoslav sociologist today: Boris Ziherl, Professor of Sociology in the Faculty of Philosophy of Ljubljana, and then by Dr. Joze Goričar, Professor of Sociology in the Faculty of Law in Ljubljana, and Dr. Oleg Mandić. (3) The third trend in sociological activities is special empirical research into contemporary sociological problems, especially on the basis of the excellent and abundant data of the very well organized Yugoslav statistical service. But this has been underdeveloped and the main effort of those engaged in the furthering of sociology is to promote modern methods of sociological research and create especially trained personnel for the task; plans are afoot to set up a sociological institute to conduct such research. At the moment, all such research is carried on by the Ethnographic Institute of the Serbian Academy of Sciences (Beograd) which also has taken over the main tasks of the former Rural Research Institute of the same Academy and similar institutes at the Zagreb and Ljubljana academies and economic institutes operative in all the major centres.

"The topics which are now investigated cover first of all demography, notably in connection with the structure of labor; the question of the status of the peasantry and its transition to industrial labor (today the most important form of social mobility of the population in Yugoslavia); the study of economic, notably industrial sociology, and particularly within the framework of the Work Productivity Research Institute in Beograd; and the study of the family, with the women's societies and the societies of friends of children and youth as the prime movers. Sreten Vukosavljević is the most distinguished rual sociologist, with numerous studies to his credit (*A History of Peasant Society, I: The Organizing of Peasant Land Tenure*, Beograd: Serbian Academy, 1953); others interested in this field are: Dr. Cvetko Kostić (*Peasant-Industrial Workers*, Beograd: Rad, 1955); Dr. Mijo Mirkovič, (*The Peasants in Capitalism*, Zagreb: Matica Hrvatska, 1952) and Dr. Nikola Vučo (*The Status of the Peasantry, I: Expropriation of Land in the 19th Century*, Beograd: The Economic Institute of the Faculty of Economics, 1955). In the field of economic sociology have appeared the works of Dr. Rudolf Bičanić, (*The Age of Manufacture in Croatia and Slavonia*, 1750-1860, Zagreb: Yugoslav Academy, 1951), and Dr. Milivoje Perović (*Leskovac, a Commercial Industrial Town*) (Leskovac: The People's Museum, 1954)."

Sociological Contributions Abroad. In view of the scanty opportunities for empiric sociology in Yugoslavia, enterprising young sociologists went into exile or were forced to live abroad. Probably the most productive has been Dinko Tomasic, who went to the United States as a Rockefeller Fellow on the basis of his background as a Professor of the University of Zagreb, remained in that country when World War II broke out, and became eventually Professor of Sociology in Indiana University and a Fellow of the Hoover Institute and Library of Stanford University.[85]

The pro-Croat ideological sentiment permeates the work of Clement S. Mihanovich of St. Louis University, although his *Social Theories* (Milwaukee: The Bruce Publ. Co., 1953), is a substantial survey of the development of sociological theory (mainly from the Catholic point of view). But Mihanovich has also lent his name in support of the publications of the "Croatia" Cultural Publishing Center (Chicago 15) which might be a valuable propaganda agency on behalf of the Croat demands against Tito's regime, but academically publishes books which are exercises in "self-justification, extensive recrimination, fantasy history and dubious sociology." [86]

For a while, Louis Adamić was quite a rage in America, popularizing ethnic sociology with his *Native's Return* (New York: Harper, 1933), delightful vignettes of the native customs of Yugoslavia, as seen through the eyes of an "Americanized" Yugoslav. He continued his publications promoting the theme of "cultural pluralism," and stressing on and during World War II that, after World War II, the liberated Europe (and thus also Yugoslavia) could be restored to democratic ways by having it run by the Americans of Yugoslav descent.[87] (It has never been ascertained whether Adamić committed suicide, or was murdered by Soviet agents, resentful of his change from pro-Russian activities to the cause of Titoism.[88]) A similar pro-Russian attitude was taken by Stoyan Pribichevich, whose works, in spite of their bias, had valuable sociological information on the Balkan life.[89]

Before the cause of Tito-ism took over the spotlight of world attention, the ramifications of Yugoslavia's social and political history appeared in a symposium edited by Robert J. Kerner, *Yugoslavia* (Berkeley, California: University of California Press, 1949), dedicated to Dr. Nicholas Mirković, a young Yugoslav sociologist (killed in 1944), with chapters by three American Yugoslavs, who made quite a reputation for themselves in subsequent years: Jozo Tomasevich, Alex. N. Dragnich, and Wayne S. Vucinich. Tomasevich's *Peasants, Politics, and Economic Change in Yugoslavia* (Stanford University Press, 1955) is a systematic presentation of the history of Croatian, Serbian and Slovene agriculture from the Middle Ages up to 1938, based mainly on secondary sources and most of these by native South Slav writers, and permeated with sociological and anthropological interpretations. Dragnich's *Yugoslavia, Tito's Promised Land* (New Brunswick, N. J.: Rutgers University Press, 1954) was prepared on the basis of the author's impressions while a cultural attaché of the United States in Yugoslavia, and, in spite of its bitter criticism of Tito's regime, has numerous sociological comments, especially on the futility of the efforts to separate national communism from Russian communism at the present day. Vicinich has published numerous political and social studies on the Balkans in various periodicals, headed by his volume, *Serbia Between East and West* (Stanford University Press, 1954).

Most of these recent studies belong to the field of Political Sociology, to which Roucek has contributed numerous articles in periodicals and books, especially *The Politics of the Balkans* (New York: McGraw-Hill Book, 1939), and republished in a revised edition as *Balkan Politics* (Stanford University Press, 1948).[90]

Yugoslav scholars have been especially active in the field of human geography, folklore and social anthropology, following in the footsteps (as we have already pointed out) of Jovan Cvijić (whose *La Péninsule balkanique*, 1918, is a mine of information on the forms of settlement, migrations, psychic and cultural differentiation of the Balkan peoples), Baltazar Bogisic, F. Demelic and Tihomir Gjorgjevic. Today, the most productive of this group of specialists is Bozo Skerlj of the University of Llubljana.[91]

Each of the federal republics has at least one or more periodicals publishing historical materials; there are also regular publications by the Academies of Science. *Komunist*, the organ of the Central Committee of the Communist Party often carries the official directives on how to write history, what topics to investigate and general method of approach. *Arhiv za pravne i drustvene nauke (Archives for Legal and Social Studies)*, published by the Association of Lawyers, covers current social and legal problems and institutional history. The *Glasnik Zemaljskog muzeja* (Sarajevo), a bulletin of the Territorial Museum of Bosnia-Herzegovina, is an outstanding periodical dealing with the history, archeology and ethnography of that region. Special attention has been especially granted to Macedonia, a region in the heart of the Balkan Peninsula with a dominant strategic position; but the area included is only vaguely defined and has been claimed by Yugoslavia, Greece, Bulgaria and even Albania.[92] The literature dealing with this concept has been nearly all lost in arguments on behalf of this or that cause, with some sociological facts thrown in in order to strengthen the respective argument. One of the most recent useful studies of this field has been Elizabeth Barker's *Macedonia: Its Place in Balkan Power Politics* (New York: Royal Institute of International Affairs, 1950), and H. R. Wilkinson's *Maps and Politics, A Review of the Ethnographic Cartography of Macedonia* (Liverpool: University of Liverpool Press, 1951).

Tito-ism. The phenomenon of Titoism has produced voluminous literature, which is nearly all polemical, although here and there one can find sociological elements, all belonging to the field of Political Sociology. Among the more sociologically inclined we can include Milla Z. Logan's *Cousins and Commissars* (New York: Scribner's, 1949), rich with valuable observations by a Yugoslav-American revisiting the native country; Harry Hodgkinson's *Challenge to the Kremlin* (New York: Praeger, 1953) takes the Tito-Stalin dispute as a point of departure, examining the strains and contradictions appearing in world communism, and offers some stimulating hypotheses. Or, Hamilton Fish Armstrong's *Tito and Goliath* (New York: The MacMillan Co., 1951) was one of the first good and substantial accounts of the rise of Titoism, followed by another excellent analysis: Adam B. Ulam's *Titoism and The Cominform* (Cambridge, Mass.: Harvard University Press, 1952).

"The break with the Soviet Union and the Cominform in 1948 had a profound effect on Yugoslav social sciences."[93] The Yugoslav scholars were assigned the task of criticizing Soviet propaganda that the Kremlin liberated Yugoslavia and to present to the world the counter-propaganda that Yugoslav leaders were traitors to international communism. Boris Ziherl, and Radovan Lalič especially denounced the aggressive Soviet nationalism, the abolition of several autonomous republics, utter disregard for the national rights, national claim to all scientific and technical discoveries, the claim that Russian is the "language of socialism." Marko Kostrenčić advised Grekov, a leading Soviet historian, how to write history; Fedor Moačanin did the same in regard to Y. V. Gote, and M. N. Tihomirov. In fact, all these ideologists had to stress that they were promoting the cause of Marxism-Leninism, and were denouncing Soviet revisionism and the idea that all the socialist revelations came from Soviet Russia. This was done especially by Edvard Kardelj, who accused Soviet leaders of distorting the basic concepts of Marxism, that the Soviet leaders were trying to apply the specific forms of communist struggle in Russia as general laws, even though the Yugoslav wartime experiences proved the contrary, and that the aid of the Soviet army was unnecessary for the liberation of the "enslaved peoples."

In general, all Yugoslav social scientists are engaged with rewriting their field in the spirit of Marxian materialism and the nationalistic aspirations of the Tito's regime. "An effort is also made to popularize history, to give it an instructive Marxian character, and to make it accessible to the average reader." [94] Also, the "Marxianized" history is being popularized for the masses and the study of regional history is promoted in harmony with the principles of "ethnic democracy" and "cultural autonomy." The principal subjects of investigation are the social and economic past of the Yugoslav peoples, the revolutionary movements, the origin of socialism, and the National Liberation Movement, and "Marxian dogmatism, the unilinear evolutionary theory, an exaggerated reliance on economic determinism, and nationalistic coloring characterized the published materials, reports Vucinich. But the "abundance and high quality of postwar research is impressive." [95]

The main lines of research of the new Yugoslav writers are outlined by Tito, Kardelj, (and until recently by Djilas). Above all, everybody must adhere to the Marx-Lenin ideology, stressing the "international working class," "historical materialism," the only "scientific" method; the role of the masses in history must be stressed. One group of Yugoslavia's people must not be stressed at the expense of others.

The directives for the work of Yugoslav scholars was laid down by the Fifth Congress of the Communist Party: they must strengthen Marxism-Leninism within the party and the workers and must stress historical materialism; all "revisionism" must be exterminated, and "mysticism" and "idealism" taken out of textbooks. The Marxian approach must be applied to the history of Yugoslavia's regions, the Party, workers' movement, the NIM (National Liberation Movement), and the development of postwar Yugoslavia.

Interestingly enough, Marxian historians are willing to acknowledge the contributions of the "progressive" bourgeois historians (Krstić, Novaković, Rački, Mazuranic, Misjuskovic, and from abroad: Maikov, Florinski, Zigelj, Jireček, Kadlec, Hubel)—all legal historians, but they object to the "negative" contributions of the contemporary historians, especially those covering the interwar period, as failing to note the importance of class-struggle and class consciousness and to evaluate properly chauvinism and fascism, and as serving reactionary and ruling classes.[96] The new historians must first revise the old legal historiography, exposing bourgeois historians; then investigate the history of the neglected or insufficiently treated peoples, since too much emphasis had been laid on Serbian and Croat legal and institutional

history and little on Slovene, Bosnian, Macedonian and Montenegrin
history; then they must appreciate properly those bourgeois historians
(Rajic, Kovecevic, Jovanovic, Racic, Nodilo, Smiciklas, Klaic) who
propounded that the history of all Slavs (including Bulgarians) must
be treated as a unit); finally on the basis of historical materialism,
the new historian must study the modes of production, the socio-
economic development of individual states, the role of the working
class, the class struggle, and the conditions bringing new states into
existence.[97]

Although Yugolslavia has several educators who, historically, have
made definite contributions to educational theory in pre-Tito Yugoslavia,[98] the educational reformers have been trying to follow the
Soviet example after 1945; after 1948 they tried to adapt the educational system again to the ideology of national communism, whose
main theoretician has been Edvard Kardelj.[99]

CONTRIBUTIONS BY EXILES

A most systematic effort to "maintain the intellectual and cultural
heritage of the peoples of Central and Eastern Europe now under
Communist control, to assist exiles of scholarly competence to continue their work, and to increase the quantity and to improve the
quality of information available concerning East-Central Europe,"[100]
has been made in recent years by The Mid-European Studies Center,
a unit of the Free Europe Committee (formerly the National Committee for a Free Europe). A glance at Horna's survey shows that
altogether 1214 projects are on the way, covering history, international
relations, politics and government, economics, geography, language,
literature and arts, law, population and religion, either as general or
monographic works, pertaining to the area as a whole or to Albania,
Austria, the three Baltic states, Bulgaria, Czechoslovakia, Eastern
Germany, Hungary, Poland and Yugoslavia. Unfortunately sociology
as such is not listed, although numerous titles are directly or indirectly related to sociology (such as Florian W. Znaniecki's *The Historical Evolution of Social Systems*, Alexander Hertz's *The Problem of
the Intelligentsia*, etc.).

The same organization has now in press books analyzing Communist rule in Albania, Bulgaria, Czechoslovakia, Hungary, Poland,
Romania, and Yugoslavia (New York: Praeger); so far (up to 1956),

two studies have appeared: *Captive Rumania*, edited by Alexandre Cretzianu, and *Albania*, edited by Stavro Skendi. Both have practically the same table of contents: historical background, the land and the people; the political system; the economic system; cultural and social developments; and bibliography. Although both provide valuable sociological material, sociology, as such, for some strange reason does not appear at all; for instance, although the pre-communist Rumania is briefly covered, Dimitri Gusti's name, the leading Rumanian sociologist of world-fame, is not even listed.

Over a hundred collaborators helped to prepare *Slavonic Encyclopaedia*, edited by Joseph S. Roucek (New York: Philosophical Library, 1949), the first book of this type covering this field in English. Although the publication has met with mixed receptions and criticisms (some unjustified, since the volume was the product of "the labor love," prepared on a "shoe-string" budget, and during the period when the pro-Soviet feeling was dominant in America), it contains numerous sections dealing with definite topics, such as: "Sociology: Czechoslovakia," (1223-1234), by M. I. Mandryka, and "Sociology: Yugoslavia," (1223-1239), by the editor; in addition, throughout the work are numerous articles on outstanding Slavic thinkers and scientists, and such related topics as "Historiography," "History," "Jews," "Language," "Nationalism," "Psychology," "Educational Theory," etc.

Feliks Gross, now a Professor of Sociology at Brooklyn College, was an Associate Editor of *Slavonic Encyclopaedia*. A specialist in legal and political sociology, he left the diplomatic service of Poland (after Yalta) and during his academic career has produced numerous articles and books in this field.[101] He is best known for his *European Ideologies* (New York: Philosophical Library, 1948), a systematic survey, in 27 chapters, of the sociological roots of the 20th century political ideas, contributed by such outstanding Slavic specialists as George M. Dimitrov, Secretary-General of the International Peasant Union, Waclav Lednicki, formerly of the University of Cracow and now of the University of California, Vladimir Zenzinov a member of the Russian Provisional Government, and others. His most original work is *Foreign Policy Analysis* (New York: Philosophical Library, 1954), a systematic sociological inquiry into the formulation of foreign policy dynamics. Other sociologists, such as Znaniecki, have been already noted.

SLAVONICA IN POSTWAR GERMANY

In Germany, research concerned with Eastern Europe and the Slavonic areas was particularly hard hit by the outcome of World War II, since most of the related libraries, archives and institutes had been located in the German Eastern territories. After the war, many of the scholars who had been attached to these institutions began carrying on the work in the Federal Republic.[102] Berlin, Tübingen, and Stuttgart each have an Osteuropa Institut, occupied primarily with research on Eastern Europe and particularly with the Soviet Union,[103] while in Göttingen a group called "Göttinger Arbeitskreis" is responsible for a number of publications in this field. In April, 1950, the Johann-Gottfried-Herder Forschungsrat was founded in Marburg; its purpose is the study of "Eastern Central Europe" (Poland, Czechoslovakia, the Balkan countries and the German territories separated from Germany). In taking Herder's name, this group wished to demonstrate its intentions to follow that philosopher and poet in "the breadth and versatility of this thinking, the depth of his concern, his openmindedness and championship of justice among nations." The Herder Forschungsrat has founded an institute of the same name, in which a staff of twelve scholars answers verbal and written inquiries, arranges meetings and lectures and collects international publications in this field of research; it also supervises the work of five groups throughout West Germany which specialize in pre-historic research, political and social science, intellectual history, the history of art and folklore research as well as six further groups for studying the history of the German Eastern territories.

The main work is concentrated on Eastern developments during the last decade. Three publications have attracted the German public: An historical analysis of the Oder-Neisse Line (*Quellen zur Entstehung der Oder-Neisse,* 1956) includes the most important documents on Allied negotiation in this sphere during World War II. In 1955 appeared a handbook on the German Eastern territories, providing information on all aspects of their development before and after World War II; in the economic sector, for instance, this handbook points out that under Polish domination ship and freight traffic in the harbors of those territories has decreased to about half of what it was before World War II. The third noteworthy publication is the beginnnig of a series called "Eastern Europe under Foreign Administration" (*Ostdeutschland unter fremder Verwaltung*). Concerned with East Prussia, it shows how the region around Königsberg has also deteriorated economically and that this is probably due to the Soviet's being interested in the area only from a military point of view; Poland, unexpectedly enlarged by the German territories after World War II, has tended to neglect the area around Allenstein in favor of concentrating her efforts of development on Pomerania and Silesia.

The Herder Institute at Marburg has a library of 33,000 volumes, emphasizing works published in the countries of Eastern Europe since 1945; available is also a catalogue of publications on Eastern and Central Germany, which lists where these 110,000 books can be had in the libraries of West Germany; archives contain more than 100,000 press clippings, 6,500 maps and 23,000 photographs.[104]

SELECTED BIBLIOGRAPHY

Theodore Abel, "Sociology in Postwar Poland," *American Sociological Review*, XV, 1(February, 1950), 104-106. A laudatory account of the accomplishment of sociology under Communism.

C. E. Black, Ed., *Readings on Contemporary Eastern Europe* (New York: Mid-European Studies Center of the National Committee for a Free Europe, 1953). Some pertinent sociological observations in these readings; but the main value of the publication is "Selected Bibliograpy," by Ivo J. Lederer, 317-346, rather well annotated.

Frederick C. Burghorn, *Soviet Russian Nationalism* (New York: Oxford University Press, 1956). Good on the efforts of Great Russian imperialism to impose itself on the satellites.

Anthony F. Czajkowski, chapter 21, "Twentieth Century Tendencies—Poland and Baltic Countries," 286-312, in Matthew A. Fitzsimons, Alfred G. Pundt & Charles E. Nowell, Eds., *The Development of Historiography* (Harrisburg, Penna.: The Stackpole Co., 1954). A valuable survey which is not limited to the works in history and includes those having sociological implications. See, in this book, also: Joseph S. Roucek, "Czechoslovakia," chapter 22, 303-312; Stephen Borsody, "Hungary," chapter 24, 325-334; George S. Waskovich, "Rumania and the Balkans," chapter 25, 335-350.

Feliks Gross, Ed., *European Ideologies* (New York: Philosophical Library, 1948). This "Survey of 20th Century Political Ideas" is loaded with the sociological aspects of the contemporary ideologies; see especially chapter xiii, "Nationalism," 539-584, by Thorsten V. Kalijarvi; Roucek, "Regionalism and Separatism," chapter xiv, 585-612. Waclaw Lednicki, "Panslavism," chapter xxii. 805-912.

Dagmar Horna, Ed., *Current Research on Central and Eastern*

Europe (New York: Mid-European Studies Center, Free Europe Committee, 1956). Surveys the current research on the area; contains the addresses of scholars and teachers interested in this region.

Stephen D. Kertesz, Ed., *The Fate of East Central Europe* (University of Notre Dame Press, 1956). Although the main theme of the work is "Hopes and Failures of American Foreign Policy," Parts Two and Three cover the postwar history of individual countries and show how American foreign policy asserted itself (or failed to assert itself) in the political, economic, and cultural developments within the East Central European states.

P. E. Moseley, "A Roumanian Journal of Rural Sociology," *Rural Sociology*, II(1937), 457-65.

Joseph S. Roucek, Ed., *Slavonic Encyclopaedia* (New York: Philosophical Library, 1949). Contains chapters on sociology and the related fields, including biographies; Roucek & Associates, *Central-Eastern Europe* (New York: Prentice-Hall, 1946). Includes sections dealing with the social and cultural backgrounds of the various countries in the region; Roucek, "Education in Czechoslovakia," chapter 11, 358-383, in Arthur H. Moehlman & Joseph S. Roucek, *Comparative Education* (New York: The Dryden Press, 1952). Surveys also what might be called "Educational Sociology;" see bibliography, 381-383; *Soviet and Russian Educational Imperialism* (reprinted from *Journal of Human Relations* Ohio: Wilberforce, Fall and Winter issues, 1955-1956, III-IV, 26-44, 35-60), with extensive bibliographical references; Roucek, Ed., "A Challenge to Peacemakers" *The Annals of The American Academy of Political and Social Sc*ience, 232(March, 1944), presents the ideological formulations of the nationalistic claims of all the countries in the area (bibliography, 177-181), & "Moscow's European Satellites," *Ibid.*, 271 (September, 1950), a collection of studies by specialists in this area in all sociological ramifications.

W. S. Vucinich, "Postwar Yugoslav Historiography," *Journal of Modern History*, XXXII, 1(March, 1951), 41-57.

George Waskovich, "The Balkans," chapter VI, 250-289, in Max Salvadori, Joseph S. Roucek, George B. de Huszar, & Julia Bond, *Contemporary Social Science, II; Eastern Hemisphere* (Harrisburg, Penna.: The Stackpole Co., 1954). Probably the only more recent survey of the whole field of social sciences. The same applies to Roucek, "Czechoslovakia," *Ibid.*, IX, 339-357. Both studies include bibliographies (288-289, 356-257).

(For the author's *curriculum vitae*, see the previous chapter.)

NOTES

1. Howard Becker & Harry Elmer Barnes, *Social Thought from Lore to Science* (Washington, D. C.: Harren Press, 1952), II, XXVII, "Sociology in Eastern Europe, The Balkans, and Turkey," 1060-1101, and especially: I, "Czechoslovakia" 1060-

1066; II, "Emigre Ukrainian Sociology," 1067-1068; III, "Poland," 1069-1077; IV, "Hungary," 1078-1080; V, "Yugoslavia," 1081-1087; VI, "Roumania," 1088-1093; Georges Gurvitch & Wilbert E. Moore, Eds., *Twentieth Century Sociology* (New York: The Philosophical Library, 1945) , XXV, "Eastern European Sociology," 703-754, and specifically: Eileen Markley Znaniecki, A. "Polish Sociology," 703-717; Joseph S. Roucek, B. "Czechoslovak Sociology," 717-731; A. Manoil, C. "Rumanian Sociology," 732-740; and Joseph S. Roucek, D. "Sociology in Yugoslavia," 740-754.

2. For the changes in the various aspects of life, see: Joseph S. Roucek, Ed., "Moscow's European Satellites," *The Annals* of The American Academy of Political and Social Science, CCLXXI (September, 1950) .

3. J. Gorsky, *Prehled ústavného a politického vyvoja Ludovodemokratickych zemi (A Review of the Constitutional and Political Evolution of the People's Democracies)* (Prague: statní pedagogické nakladatelství, 1945) shows that developments have not been uniform in all these states; this fact must be regarded as a basis for evaluating their cultural and scientific differences.

4. The formula is described in Alexander Vucinich, *The Soviet Academy of Sciences* (Stanford University Press, 1956) .

5. *Seznam prednasek na Universite Karlove v zimnim semestru 1948-1949 (The List of Lectures in Charles University during the Winter Semester 1948-49)* (Prague: Akademicky senat University Karlovy, 1948) , 76.

6. A. Schaff, "Dziesiec lat walki a zwyciestwo filozofii marksistowskiej w Polsce Ludowej" ("Ten Years of Struggle for the Victory of Marxist Philosophy in People's Poland") , *Mysl Filozoficzna,* III (1956), 21.

7. Karel Kosik, "O socialnich korenech a filosoficke podstate masarykismu" ("The Social Roots and Philosophical Bases of Masaryk-ism") , *Filosoficky casopis,* II, 3 (1954) , 196-215.

8. Carl J. Friedrich & Zbigniew K. Brzenzinski, *Totalitarian Dictatorship and Autocracy* (Cambridge, Mass.: Harvard University Press, 1956), 264; see also: Barrington Moore, *Terror and Progress in USSR* (Cambridge, Mass.: Harvard University Press 1954) , Chapter 5.

9. B. Fogarasi, "Tarsadalmi let es tarsadalmi tudat az atmeneti korszakban" ("Social Existence and Social Consciousness in the Transition Period") , *Magyar Tudomanyos Akademia II. Tarsadalmi-Torteneti Tudomanyok Osztalyanak Kozlemenyxei,* I (1950), 3.

10. Source material was gathered in *Magyar Tortenesz Kongresszus 1953 junius 6-13 (Congress of Hungarian Historians)* (Budapest: Akademiai Kiado, 1954), 688.

11. Karl Mannheim, *Ideology and Utopia* (New York: Harcourt, Brace, trans., 1936).

12. A. Schaff, "Mannheima socjologia wiedzy a zagadnienie obiektywnosci prawdy" ("Mannheim's 'Sociology of Knowledge' and the Objective Character of Truth") , *Mysl Filozoficzna,* I (1956), 116-134.

13. M. Fritzhand, "O elementarnych normach noralnych" ("About the Elementary Moral Norms") , *Mysl Fiolozoficzna,* I (1956) , 3-28.

14. R. Kalivoda, "Knekterym otazkam hodnoceni Husova uceni" ("Some Questions about the Evaluation of Hus' Teachings"), *Filosoficky casopis,* III (1955) , 34-62.

15. J. Redei, "A dolgozo Osztalyok aramlasa" ("Migration of Laboring Classes") *Szabad Nep,* XIII, 229 (August 19, 1955) , 2.

16. E. Niederhauser, "A bolgar tortenettudomany fejlodese," *Szazadok,* LXXXIX 2 (1955) , 270-286; A. Hadzhilov's article in *Akademiai Ertesito,* LXII (March, 1955) , 80.

17. V. Cherestesiua, E. Stanescu, I. Ionascu, "A tortenettudomaby tizeves fejlodese Roman Nepkoztarsagagban," *Szazadok*, LXXXIX, 2 (1955) , 262-269.

18. B. Lesnodorski, "Nauka historii w pierwszym dziesiecioleciu Polski Ludowej' *Kwartalnik Historyczny*, LXII, 1 (1955) , 17-58.

19. Gy. Paloczi-Horvath, "Az orszag gondjai," *Irodalmi Ujsag*, VII (October 20 1956) , 1.

20. *Transactions of the Third World Congress of Sociology* (Amsterdam: International Sociological Association, 1956) , Vols. I-III.

21. "The Social Sciences in the U.S.S.R.," *op. cit.*, 13.

22. Florian Znaniecki, *Cultural Sciences: Their Origin and Development* (Urbana, III.: University of Illinois Press, 1952) , "Preface," viii.

23. Joseph S. Roucek, "Sociological Periodicals of Czechoslovakia," *American Sociological Review*, I, 1 (February, 1936) , 168-170; Antonin Obrdlik, "Sociological Activities in Czechoslovakia," *Ibid.*, I, 4 (August, 1936) , 653-656; Roucek, "Czechoslovak Sociology," 717-731, in Georges Gurvitch & Wilbert E. Moore, Ed., *Twentieth Century Sociology* (New York: Philosophical Library, 1945) ; I. A. Bláha, "Contemporary Sociology in Czechoslovakia," *American Sociological Review*, IX (December, 1930) , 167-179; Roucek, "Czechoslovak Journals," *American Sociological Review*, II (April, 1937) , 270-271; Roucek, "Eduard Benes as a Sociologist," *Sociology & Social Research*, XXIII (September-October, 1938) , 18-24, & "Masaryk As Sociologist," *Ibid.*, XX (May-June, 1938) , 412-420; & "The Trends in Educational Sociology Abroad," *The Educational Forum*, III (May, 1939) , 488-494; Howard Becker & Harry Elmer Barnes, *Social Thought from Lore to Science* (Washington, D. C.: Harren Press, 1952) , II, "Czechoslovakia," 1061-1066.

24. I. Gadourek, *The Political Control of Czechoslovakia* (Leiden: H. B. Stenfert Kroese, 1953) , a brilliant study in social control of a Soviet satellite state; *A Dutch Community* (Leiden: H. E. Stenfert Kroese, 1956) , a publication of the Netherlands' Institute of Preventive Medicine, is a systematic study of the social and cultural structure and processes in a bulb-growing region in the Netherlands, especially the place known as Sassenheim; the study is distinguished by utilizing the results and the findings from several culture-areas (especially the United States, as shown in the bibliographical references gathered from far and wide and in several languages) . His second volume (but the first to be published) is a clever application of the social control methods, as studied mostly in the United States, to the Nazi techniques used in Czechoslovakia.

25. See, for instance: *Czechoslovakia on the Road to Socialism* (in Czech) (Prague: Orbis, May, 1949) , 14-18.

26. *Dokumenty o protilidoví a protinàrodní politice T. G. Masaryka* (Prague: Orbis, 1953) .

28. Eduard Benes, *Memoirs of Dr. Eduard Benes* (Boston: Houghton Mifflin, 1955) .

29. See also: "T. G. Masaryk 1850-1950," *Journal of Central European Affairs*, X, 1 (April, 1950), with articles by Oscar Jaszi, W. W. Kulski, Otakar Odlozilik, and S. Harrison Thomson. But politics is the core of Eduard Benes' article, "Postwar Czechoslovakia," *Foreign Affairs*, XXIV, 3 (April, 1946) , 397-410. Judgments of Benes's politics are: Otakar Odlozilik, "Edvard Benes' Memoirs," *Journal of Central European Affairs*, VIII, 4 (January, 1949) , 412-420; Eduard Taborsky, "Benes and Stalin-Moscow, 1943 and 1945," *Ibid.*, XIII, 2 (July, 1953) , 154-181.

30. Periodic surveys of the literature provided by the Czechoslovak exiles, including the sociologists, have been provided by the Czechoslovak Foreign Institute

in Exile, Documentary Centre, *Bibliografie* (Leiden, Holland: Tribuna, Postbus 91).

31. K. Absolon, "Archeological News of Recent Discoveries," *American Journal of Archaeology,* LII (1948), 228-230; "Moravian Paleolithic Times," *Ibid.,* LIII (1949), 19-28.

32. Jiri Kolaja, "A Note on the Spatial and Social Pattern of a Small Discussion Group," *The Journal of Educational Sociology,* XXVII (1954), 222-225; *"Historical Development of Medical Ethics in the United States,"* World Medical Journal, I, 3 (1954), 139-141, 155-157, 174-176; "Polituczne konsekwencje cech narodobych," *Kultura* (Paris), LXI, 1 (L952), 74-76.

33. Jiri Nehnevajsa, "Some Ideas on the Social Psychology of the Czech Radio-Listener under the Present Government," Department of State, *VOA,* (January, 1952), pp. 64; "Eine Bibliographie der Soziometrik," *Kölner Zeitschrift für Soziogie,* VII (March, 1955); "Sociometry: Decades of Growth," *Sociometry,* XIX (December, 1955).

34. Pavel Sebesta, *Les Pygmes du Congo* (Bruxelles, 1952).

35. His chief works were: *Crania bohemica (Bohemian Skulls,* 1891-1893); *General Theory of Races* (1928); *Somatology of Youth* (1928); *Soul and Body* (1918); *Remains and Famous Men and Their Identification* (1912); *Origins and Beginnings of the Czechoslovak Nation* (1918); *Physical Characteristics of the Czechoslovak People* (1917).

36. In spite of his world-wide fame, Niederle's works have been published nearly all in Czech: *Short History of Archaeology* (1899); *Contributions to the Anthropology of the Czech Lands* (1891); *Mankind in Prehistorical Times, With Special Regard to Slavonic Countries* (1895) (also in Russian); *The Origins of the Slavs* (1896); *The Problem of the Origin of the Slavs* (1899) (also in German); *The Beginnings of Czech History* (1900); the monumental *Slavonic Antiquity* (1901-1925) (also in French); *The Slavonic World* (1909) (also in French and Russian); *Manual of Czech Archaeology* (1910); etc. For more details on Niederle's influence, see: "Niederle, Lubor," 894-895, in Roucek, ed., *Slavonic Encyclopaedia* (New York: Philosophical Library, 1949).

37. Today, Hrdlicka is seldom noted by the cultural anthropologists, who dominate the field of anthropology. For more details about his remarkable life and theories, see: "Obituary," *Current Biology* (1943); *School and Society,* LVIII (September 11, 1943), 186; *Science,* SCVIII (September 17, 1943), 254-255, by W. M. Krogman; *Time,* XLII (September 13, 1943), 74; *Wilson Library Bulletin,* XVIII (November, 1943), 198. A. H. Schultz, *Biographical Memoir of Ales Hrdlicka* (Washington, D. C.: National Academy of Sciences, Biographical Memoirs, XXIII, 12th Memoir) (1945).

38. Theodore Abel, "Sociology in Postwar Poland," *American Sociological Review,* XV, 1 (February, 1950), 104-106; we have summarized this survey here. But we disagree with this conclusion, since Czechoslovakia under Masaryk and Benes, both sociologists, was even better "organized." For the best available survey of Poland's pre-war sociology, see: Howard Becker & Harry Elmer Barnes, *Social Thought from Lore to Science* (Washington, D. C.: Harren Press, 1952), XXVII, III, "Poland," 1069-1077, and bibliographical references, xcvii-xcviii.

39. Stanislaw Ossowski, *Historical Laws in Sociology* (Warsaw, 1935); *The Social Bond and Bloodkinship* (Warsaw, 1939). Tadeusz Szczurkiewicz, *Race, Environment and the Family* (Poznam, 1939); *Social Structure and the Process of Individualization* (Poznam, 1939).

40. The base for discussion was R. H. Tawney & P. Hazard, *The Crisis of European Conscience 1680-1715,* and three Soviet monographs: Smirin, *The National*

Reformation of Muntzer and The Great Peasant War (1947); Porshniev, *The National Uprising in France before the Fronde* (1947); and Kan's *Two Uprisings of Silesian Weavers in 1793 and 1844* (1948).

41. Abel, *op. cit.*, 106, then describes the research activities.

42. One could disagree with Abel on the term "the National Revolution." The author would prefer here to classify it as the "Soviet Conquest."

43. *Ibid.*, 106.

44. Herbert Blumer, *Critique of Research in the Social Sciences* : (*1*) *An Appraisal of Thomas and Znaniecki's The Polish Peasant in Europe and America* (New York: Social Science Research Council, 1939); Florian Znaniecki, "William I. Thomas as a Collaborator," *Sociology and Social Research*, XXII (1932), 765-767.

45. Although seldom cited in the sociological literature, Korzybski has had a marked influence on the development of semantics to the sociology of knowledge; see: Stuart Chase, *The Proper Study of Mankind* (New York: Harper, 1956), 286-7, 314; Joseph S. Roucek, Ed., *Social Control* (New York: D. Van Nostrand, 1956), 232-33, 238.

46. See: Max Gluckman, *An Analysis of the Sociological Theories of Bronislaw Malinowski* (New York: Oxford University Press, 1949).

47. B. Malinowski, *A Scientific Theory of Culture* (Chapel Hill, N. C.: North Carolina Press, 1944).

48. For post-war Polish historiography, some of which has relationship to sociology, see: Anthony F. Czajkowski, 21, "Twentieth Century Tendencies—Poland and Baltic Countries," 286-312, in Matthew A. Fitzsimons, Alfred G. Pundt, & Charles E. Nowell, Eds., *The Development of Historiography* (Harrisburg, Penna.: The Stackpole Co., 1954).

49. Carl J. Friedrich & Zbigniew K. Brzezinski, *Totalitarian Dictatorship and Autocracy* (Cambridge: Harvard University Press, 1957).

50. Jerzy Zubrzycki, *Polish Immigrants in Britain: A Study of Adjustment* (The Hague: Martinus Nijhoff, 1956).

51. R. F. Leslie, *Polish Politics and the Revolution of November 1830* (University of London Historical Studies, III, New York: John de Graff, 1956).

52. Howard Becker & Harry Elmer Barnes, *Social Thought from Lore to Science* (Washington, D. C.: Harren Press, 1952), II, 1078-1080.

53. See his *Hungary to Be or Not to Be* (New York: Frederick Ungar, 1946).

54. It must be noted that the concept of the sociology of knowledge had been formulated by Max Scheler, *Versuche zu einer Soziologie des Wissens* (1924), and even before him by Wilhelm Dilthey in the early part of the second half of the 19th century. J. J. Maquet, *The Sociology of Knowledge* (Boston: Beacon Press, 1951), is a good critical analysis of this field and a discussion of the role of Pitirim A. Sorokin in this field; another valuable analysis of the six essays by Mannheim is Paul Kevskemeti, Ed., *Essays on the Sociology of Knowledge*, edited by Karl Mannheim (New York: Oxford University Press, 1952). In addition to the work edited by Kecskemeti, the works by Mannheim are: *Essays on Sociology and Social Psychology*, edited by Paul Kevskemeti (New York: Oxford University Press, 1953); *Ideology and Utopia* (New York: Harcourt, Brace, 1936); *Man and Society in An age of Reconstruction* (New York: Harcourt, Brace, 1940); *Diagnosis of Our Times* (New York: Oxford University Press, 1944); *Freedom, Power, and Democratic Planning* (New York: Oxford University Press, 1950); *Essays on the Sociology of Knowledge* (New York: Oxford University Press, 1952); *Essays on the Sociology of Culture* (New York: Oxford University Press, 1956).

55. See such analyses as: E. S. Bogardus, *The Development of Social Thought* (New York: Longmans, Green, 1955), XXXVIII, "Mannheim & Sociology of Knowledge," 605-619; Gerard L. DeGré, *Society and Ideology* (New York: Columbia University Bookstore, 1943); Robert K. Merton, *The Sociology of Knowledge* (reprinted from ISIS, No. 75, Vol. XXVII, 3, November, 1937), 493-503; Frank E. Hartung, "Problems of the Sociology of Knowledge," *Philosophy of Science*, XIX, 1 (January, 1952), 17-32; Helmut R. Wagner, "Mannheim's Historicism," *Social Research*, XIX, 3 (September, 1952), 300-321, etc.

56. Franz Adler, "The Sociology of Knowledge Since 1918," *Midwest Sociologist*, XVII, 2 (Spring, 1956), 3-12.

57. Mannheim, *Ideology and Utopia*, 3.

58. C. Wright Mills, "Methodological Consequences of the Sociology of Knowledge," *The American Journal of Sociology*, XLVI (1952), 316-330.

59. A. K. C. Ottoway, *Education and Society* (London: Routledge & Kegan Paul, 1953), vii-x.

60. Istvan Szabo, *Tanulmanyok a magyar parasztsag sortenetebol (Studies from The History of the Hungarian Peasantry)* (Budapest: Teleki Institute, 1948).

61. Tibor Mendol, *A Balkan Boldrajza (The Geography of the Balkan Peninsula)* (Budapest: Balkan Institute, 1948): an excellent bibliography included.

62. A. Manoil, "Rumanian Sociology," 732-740, in Georges Gurvitch & Wilbert E. Moore, Eds., *Twentieth Century Sociology* (New York: The Philosophical Library, 1945); Vladescu-Racoasa, "La sociologie en Rumanie," *Revue international de sociologie*, XXXVII (1929), 1-22; Vladescu-Racoasa, *L'Institut Social Roumain, 15 ans d'Activites* (Bucharest, 1933); Hraian Herseni, *Teoria monografiei sociologice; Cu an studiu introductiv: Sociologia monografica stiinta a realitatii sociale de D. Gusti (The Theory of Sociological Monography. With an Introductory Study: Monographic Sociology, Science of Social Reality, by D. Gusti)* (Bucharest: Instituul Social Roman Biblioteca de Sociologie, Etica si politica, Seria A, No. 1, 1934); P. E. Mosely, "The Sociological School of Dimitrie Gusti," *Sociological Review*, XXVIII April, (1936), 149-165; Roucek, "Sociology in Rumania," *American Sociological Review*, III February, (1938), 54-62; N. Petrescu, *The Principles of Comparative Sociology* (London: Watts & Co., 1924), *The Interpretation of National Differentiation* (London: Watts, 1929); Roucek, *Contemporary Roumania* (Stanford University Press, 1932), *passim*, and especially 379: Georges Gurvitch & Wilbert E. Moore, Ed., *La Sociologie au XXe Siècle* (Paris: Presses Universitaires de France, 1947), II: A. Manoil & A. Golopentia, "La Sociologie Roumaine," 735-750, and the numerous bibliographical footnotes were; Howard Becker & Harry Elmer Barnes, *Social Thought from Lore to Science* (Washington, D. C.: Harren Press, 1952), II: VI, "Roumania," 1088-1093.

63. For their names, see: for instance, Becker & Barnes, *op. cit.*, 1091.

64. Most of Gusti's works appeared in Rumania and French; see the list in Manoil & Golopentia, *op. cit.*, 743. In English, it appears he has published only: *Considerations on the Social Service Law in Romania* (New York: Columbia University Press, 1939).

65. Additional information can be found in R. J. Kerner, *Social Sciences in the Balkans and Turkey* (University of California Press, 1930).

66. For the relationship of sociology to other social sciences in Rumania, see: George Waskowich, "Rumania and the Balkans," 25, 335-250, in Matthew A. Fitzsimons, Alfred G. Pundt & Charles E. Nowell, eds., *The Development of Historiography* (Harrisburg, Penna.: The Stackpole Co., 1954); Waskowich, "The Balkans," VI, 250-289, in Max Salvadori, Joseph S. Roucek, George B. de Huszar & Julia Bond,

974 TRENDS ABROAD

Eds., *Contemporary Social Science*, II: *Eastern Hemisphere* (Harrisburg, Penna.: The Stackpole Co., 1954).

67. Robert Lee Wolff, *The Balkans in Our Times* (Harvard University Press, 1956) is a curious volume, loaded with valuable material, but devoting more than one hundred pages to the Balkan history, in spite of its title, and underplaying Greece and Turkey (pp. 7-9), although the modern stress on the geopolitical approach cannot conceive of such a "separatism." More useful, as a general survey, is Hugh Seton-Watson's *The East European Revolution* (New York: Praeger, 1951), in spite of its excessive stress on the "wave of the future"—communism—as being more or less inevitable in that area.

68. Vaclovas Birziska, "Lithuanian Bibliography," *Knygu Lentyna* VIII, 3-4 (March-April, 1955), 9 (published by the Lithuanian Bibliographical Service, 602 Harvey St., Danville, Ill.).

69. For the background of such developments, see: Johannes Kaiv, "Estonian Nationalism," 39-42, Alfred Bilmanis, "Free Latvia in Free Europe," 43-48, P. Zadeikis, "An Aspect of the Lithuanian Record of Independence," 49-51, in Joseph S. Roucek, Ed., "A Challenge to Peacemakers," *The Annals* of The American Academy of Political and Social Science, 232 (March, 1944), and bibliography, 178-179; T. V. Kalijarvi, "Latvia, Lithuania, Estonia up to 1918," VII, 174-192, XXI, "Latvia, Lithuania, Estonia from World War I to World War II" 470-487 in Joseph S. Roucek, *Central-Eastern Europe* (New York: Prentice-Hall, 1946), & bibliography, 487; Mary Estella Bates, *Bulletin of Bibliography*, XVII (Boston: F. W. Faxon, 1943), pages 6-7 gave a workable bibliography in English on Lithuania; should be used in conjunction with "Modern Books on Lithuania," *The Literary Journal*, LVII (October 1, 1932), 816-818; Anthony F. Czajkowski, "Twentieth Century Tendencies—Poland and Baltic Countries," XXI, 286-302, & especially 294ff.; more recent bibliographical surveys can be followed in *Lithuanian Bulletin* (Lithuanian American Council, 233 Broadway, New York 7), and *The Baltic Review*, ed. by Alfreds Berzins (The Committees for a Free Estonia, Latvia and Lithuania, 4 West 57 St., New York 19), since 1954.

70. For more details, see: Czajkowski, *op. cit.*

71. For a survey of the literature between the two Wars, see: Ernst C. Helmreich, "The Baltic States," XXI, 540-565, in Joseph S. Roucek, *Contemporary Europe* (New York: D. Van Nostrand Co., 1947).

72. Among the several other recent studies, we may note: H. Jackson, *The Baltic* (London: Oxford University Press, 1941); William F. Reddaway, *Problems of the Baltic* (New York: The MacMillan Co., 1940); Royal Institute of International Affairs, *The Baltic States* (New York: Oxford University Press, 1938); T. V. Kalijarvi, "Poland and the Baltic States," X, 342-363, in Joseph S. Roucek, Ed., *Governments and Politics Abroad* (New York: Funk & Wagnalls, 1948); H. G. Wanklyn, *The Eastern Marchlands of Europe* (New York: The MacMillan Co., 1942); etc.

73. Joseph S. Roucek, "Latvian Americans," 185-190, "Lithuanian Americans," 190-198, "Estonian Americans," 198-202, and bibliographies, 721-722, in Francis J. Brown & Joseph S. Roucek, Eds., *One America* (New York: Prentice-Hall, 1952); Rev. Casimir Peter Sirvaitis, *Religious Folkways in Lithuania and Their Conservation among the Lithuanian Immigrants in the United States* (Washington, D.C.: Catholic University of America Press, 1952), a study in acculturation; E. J. Harrison, *Lithuania* (London: Hazell, Watson & Viney, 1928), with the chapter by V. K. Rackauskas, "Lithuanians in America," 85-91; F. S. Kemesis, *Co-Operation among the Lithuanians in the United States* (Washington, D. C.: Catholic University of America Press, 1924).

74. For more details, see: Czajkowski, *op. cit.*, 300-301.

75. Alfred Bilmanis, *Latvia and Her Baltic Neighbors* (Washington, D.C.: Latvian Legation, 1942), & *Baltic States in Post-War Europe* (Washington, D. C.: Latvian Legation, 1943), & *Latvia in the Making, 1918-1928* (Riga: Riga Times, 1928). R. O. G. Urch, *Latvia* (London: George Allen & Unwin, 1938) is the best recent work in English; Clarence A. Manning, *The Forgotten Republics* (New York: Philosophical Library, 1952); John A. Swettenham, *The Tragedy of the Baltic States* (London: Hollis & Carter, 1952); Alfred Bilmanis, *A History of Latvia* (Princeton University Press, 1951); Arnolds Spekke, *History of Latvia* (Stockholm, 1951).

76. George Waskowich, Chapter 2, "Rumania and the Balkans," 335-350, in Matthew A. Fitzsimons, Alfred G. Pundt, & Charles E. Nowell, Eds., *The Development of Historiography* (Harrisburg, Penna.: The Stackpole Co., 1954); Waskowich, "The Balkans," VI, 250-289, in Max Salvadori, Joseph S. Roucek, George B. de Huszar & Julia Bond, Eds., *Contemporary Social Science*, II: *Eastern Hemisphere* (Harrisburg, Penna.: The Stackpole Co., 1954); C. E. Black, *The Constitutional Govrnment in Bulgaria* (Princeton University 1943); Robert J. Kerner, *Social Science in the Balkans and Turkey* (Berkeley: University of California Press, 1930); P. E. Moseley, "Post-War Historiography of Modern Bulgaria," *Journal of Modern History*, LX (1937), 348-366.

77. Christ Anastasoff, *The Tragic Peninsula* (St. Louis: Blackwell Wielandy Co., 1936), is a polemical work on behalf of the Macedonian problem; Anastasoff has contributed also numerous articles on Bulgaria and Bulgaria's personalities to the *Slavonic Encyclopedia*.

78. Vandeleur Robinson, *Albania's Road to Freedom* (New York: W. W. Norton, 1942). Edith Pierpont Sstickney, *Southern Albania or Northern Epirus in European International Affairs, 1912-1923* (Stanford University Press, 1926). Joseph Swire, *Albania: The Rise of a Kingdom* (London: Williams & Norgate, 1929).

79. Federal Writers' Project of the Works Progress Administration of Massachusetts, *The Albanian Struggle in the Old World and New* (Boston: The Writer Inc.. 1939).

80. Joseph S. Roucek, "Albanian Americans," 232-239, in Francis J. Brown & Joseph S. Roucek, Ed., *One America* (New York: Prentice-Hall, 1952); Dita Guri, *American-Albanians in Bridgeport* (Bridgeport, Conn.: University of Bridgeport, 1950); Glenn A. McLain's *Albanian Exposé* (Quincy, Mass.: Albanian American Literary Society, 1952), is a description of the current conflicts agitating the Albanian minority in the United States. Roucek has published numerous, widely scattered studies of various aspects of Albania; see his: *Balkan Politics* (Stanford University Press, 1948), V, "Albanians," 125-146; "The Social Character of Albanian Politics," *Social Science*, X, 1 (1935), 71-79; "Social Aspects of Albania," *World Affairs Interpreter*, VII, 1 (April, 1936), 70-76; "The Albanian and Yugoslav Immigrants in America," *Revue Internationale des Études Balkaniques* (Beograd), IIIe annee, II (6) (1938), 499-519; "Recent Albanian Nationalist Educational Policy," *School and Society*, XXXVIII (July, 1933), 467-468; "The Albanian Educational Progress," *Ibid.*, XXXVII (February 4, 1933), 149-151; "Albanian Battle," *World Digest*, III (August, 1936), 78-80; "Economic Conditions in Albania," *Economic Geography*, IX (July, 1933), 256-264; "Trouble and More Trouble in Albania," *World Affairs Interpreter*, XXV, 3 (October, 1954), 315-322; "Albania (up to 1918)," XI, 214-217, and "Albania (1918-1945)," in Roucek, Ed., *Central-Eastern Europe* (New York: Prentice-Hall, 1946), and the bibliography, 537-8; etc.

81. Howard Becker & Harry Elmer Becker, *Social Thought from Lore to Science* (Washington, D. C.: Harren Press, 1952), II, 1081-1088; George Waskowich, "The Balkans," 250-289, in Max Salvadori, Ed., & others, *Contemporary Social Science*

(Harrisburg, Pa.: The Stackpole Co., 1954, II); *Eastern Hemisphere;* **Waskowich,** "Rumania and the Balkans," 25, 335-350, in Matthew A. Fitzsimons, Alfred G. Pundt & Charles E. Nowell, Eds., *The Development of Historiography* (Harrisburg, Penna.: The Stackpole Co., 1954); Joseph S. Roucek, "Sociology in Yugoslavia," 740-754, in Georges Gurvitch & Wilbert E. Moore, Eds., *Twentieth Century Sociology* (New York: Philosophical Library, 1945).

82. For more details, see: Barnes & Becker, *op. cit.,* 1082.

83. For more details on his life and accomplishments, see: *Encyclopaedia Slavonica, op. cit.,* 743-744.

84. Dr. Radomir D. Lukic (1914–), Doctor of Law of the University of Paris (1939); Professor of the Theory of the State and Law and of Sociology at the Faculty of Law, Beograd (1940–); author of *La force obligatoire de la norme juridique* (Paris: Sirey, 1939); *Teorija drzave i prava* (*The Theory of the State and Law,* 2 vols., Beograd: Naucna Knjiga, 1953-54); *Istorija politickih i pravnih teorija,* I: *Od antike do pocetka XVII veks* (*The History of Political and Legal Theories;* I: *From Antiquity to the Beginning of the 17th Century* (Beograd: Naucna Knjiga, 1956). In preparation: *Osnovi sociologije* (*The Bases of Ssociology*).

85. See, for instance, Dinko Tomasic, *Personality and Culture in Eastern European Politics* (New York: George W. Stewart, 1948); but the volume also contains a valuable bibliography of Yugoslav and other sociological works on the Balkans (239-249). *The Impact of Russian Culture on Soviet Communism* (Glencoe, Ill.: Free Press, 1953). propounds the thesis that the "power-seeking" Horsemen of the Steppes and the "power-indifferent" Old Slavonic Plowmen somehow combine to produce not only the Great Russian society but also the expansive power of Bolshevism.

86. J. B. Hoptner, reviewing in *The American Slavic and East European Review,* XV, 4 (December, 1956), 561-2: Basil & Steven Pandzic, *A Review of Croatian History* (1954); George W. Cesarich, *Croatia and Serbia: Is Their Peaceful Separation a European Necessity?* (1954); Antjuj F. Boniface & Clement S. Mihanovich, Eds., *The Croatian Nation In Its Struggle for Freedom and Independence* (Chicago: "Croatia" Cultural Publishing Center, 1955).

87. Louis Adamic, *What's Your Name* (New York: Harper, 1942). *My Native Land* (New York: Harper, 1943), is a pro-Tito tract, highly critical of General Mikhailovitch. *America and Trieste, and God and the Russians* (New York: United Committee of South-Slavic Americans, 1946), is an example of his propaganda techniques.

88. Committee on Un-American Activities, U.S. House of Representatives, *Report on the American Slav Congress and Associated Organizations* (Washington, D. C.: Government Printing Office, June 26, 1949), 30, 39-49, 58, 77, 88-89, 91, 195, 106, 122-125, bluntly accused Adamic of "antagonistic views of the United States, . . . hopes for a Communist revolution, and his completely pro-Russian bias. . . ." (47).

89. Stoyan Pribichevic, *World Without End* (New York: Reynal & Hitchcok, 1930); *Spotlight on the Balkans* (New York: Foreign Policy Association, 1940). F. W. L. Kovacs, *The Untamed Balkans* (New York: Modern Age Books, 1941), is a superficial but interesting introduction to the social aspects of the Balkan peasantry. G. E. Mylonas, *The Balkan States* (St. Louis: Eden Publishing House, 1946), stressed mostly the political aspects of Macedonia. During the war also appeared: Olive Lodge, *Peasant Life in Jugoslavia* (London: Seeley, 1942), a variety of bucolic information on rural Yugoslavia; Robert St. John, *From the Land of Silent People* (Garden City, N. Y.: Doubleday, Doran, 1942), journalistic impressions, but

quite impressive in their penetrations; Rebecca West, *Black Lamb and Grey Falcon* (New York: Viking, 1943), a beautifully written work by a prominent British novelist and essayist, containing sociological observations; etc.

90. See also: Joseph S. Roucek, Ed., *Slavonic Encyclopaedia* (New York: Philosophical Library, 1949); Francis J. Brown & Joseph S. Roucek, Eds., *One America* (New York: Prentice-Hall, 1952), and the chapters therein on "Yugoslav Americans," 168-176, "Bulgarian Americans," 176-184, "Hungarian Americans," 220-26, by Emil Lengyel, "Romanian Americans," 227-231, by Peter Trutza, "Albanian Americans," 232-239, by Roucek, "Polish Americans," 143-157, by Joseph V. Swastek, "Czechoslovak Americans," 168-176, by Roucek, and "Latvian Americans," 185-190, "Lithuanian Americans," 190-198, and "Estonian Americans," 198-202, by Roucek; Roucek Ed., *Twentieth Century Political Thought* (New York: Philosophical Library, 1946), "Central-Eastern Europe," XXIV, 515-552, by W. J. Ehrenpreis; Roucek, "Central-Eastern Europe," VIII, 138-155, in Howard R. Anderson, Ed., *Approaches to an Understanding of World Affairs* (Washington. D. C.: National Council for the Social Studies, 25th Yearbook); Roucek, Ed., *Central-Eastern Europe: Crucible of World Wars* (New York: Prentice-Hall, 1946); Roucek, Ed., *Governments and Politics Abroad* (New York: Funk & Wagnalls, 1948), with chapters on Czechoslovakia. Hungary, Romania, Yugoslavia, Bulgaria and Greece; etc.

91. Bozo Skerl, "Jugoslavia: Anthropological Review for 1952-1954," *Yearbook of Anthropology 1955* (New York: Wenner-Gren Foundation for Anthropological Research, 1955), 651-670. Encyclopaedic information on anthropological and sociological aspects of Yugoslavia is now being published in: *Hrvatska Enciklopedija* (Zagreb: Tisak-Behrotisak-Offset); *Enciklopedija Jugoslavije*, A-Book (Zagreb: Izdanje i naklde Leksikografskog Zavoda FNRJ, 1955, Miroslav Krleza, Director Kelsikoggrafskog Zavoda, Zagreb). A valuable bibliography is: *Books and Periodicals on Yugoslav and Other Balkan Countries* (Rijswijk (Z.H.), Holland: Mouton & Co., n.d.).

92. For more details, see: Roucek, *Balkan Politics*, Chapter VI, "Macedonians," 147-168, and the literature cited therein.

93. Wayne S. Vucinich, "Postwar Yugoslav Historiography," *Journal of Modern History*, XXIII, 1 (March, 1951), 44.

94. Wayne S. Vucinich, *op. cit.*, 41-57.

95. *Ibid.*, 41.

96. For more details, see Vucinich, *op. cit.*, 42.

97. The pre-war Yugoslav historians followed German historiography and idealistic philosophy. The most prominent of the proletarian historians was Edvard Kardelj (who used a pseudonym of "Sperans") who authored *Razvoj slovenskega narodnega vpr asanja* (1939), analyzing the Slovene national development during the past two centuries.

98. Joseph S. Roucek, "Pre-War Educational Theory in Yugoslavia," *Educational Theory*, VI, 1 (January, 1956), 35-46. Ruth Trouton, *Peasant Renaissance in Yugoslavia 1900-1950* (London: Routledge & Kegan Paul, 1952), is a brilliant sociological study which stresses especially the role of education in the peasant movement of the Yugoslav lands.

99. Edvard Kardelj, "Evolution in Jugoslavia," *Foreign Affairs*, XXIV, 4 (July, 1956), 580-602. Cf. also: Joseph S. Roucek, "Tito's Educational Experiences and Experiments," *The Educational Forum*, XXI, 2 (January, 1957), 193-201; & "A Visit to Titoland," *Contemporary Review*, 1093 (January, 1957), 15-19.

100. Robert F. Byrnes, "Preface," to Dagmar Horna, Ed., *Current Research on Central and Eastern Europe* (New York: Mid-European Studies Center, 4 West 57 St., New York).

101. Feliks Gross, *Crossroads of Two Continents* (New York: Columbia University Press, 1945), was a thorough sociological analysis of the possibilities of federation in Central-Eastern Europe and its relation to Europe as a whole; the same year appeared his *The Polish Workers: A Study of a Social Stratum* (New York: Roy, 1945), a history of Polish workers' organizations in recent years, both before and during the Nazi occupation. See also: "Some Social Consequences of Atomic Discovery," *American Sociological Review*, XV, 1 (February, 1950), 43-50; B. J. Vlavianos & Gross, Eds., *Struggle for Tomorrow, Modern Political Ideologies of the Jewish People* (New York: Arts, 1954).

102. "Scrutinizing the East," *The Bulletin* ("A weekly survey of German affairs issued by the Press and Information Office of the German Federal Government," Bonn), V, 2 (January 17, 1957), 5.

103. See: Joseph S. Roucek, "Russlandkunde in den USA," *Jahrbücher für Oeschichte Osteuropas*, IV, 1 (1956), 64-71 (Osteuropa Institut: Munich 22, Maximilianst., 41).

104. The Herder institute plans to carry out specific research in the field of: Polish-German relations during World War I; modern settlement of Eastern Europe; the music of Bohemia; the early history of Pomerania and of the German settlements in the Sudetenland; the events leading up to the Munich Agreement of 1938; German economic policy in Latvia from 1914 to 1945; and the impact of American policy on the Baltic States from 1940 to 1953. While the topics listed indicate the political interest of such research, more academic research is being carried on in Austria: the Forschungsinstitut für Fragen des Donausraumes in Salzburg (Imbergstrasse 22), under the direction of Dr. Peter Berger (formerly of Georgetown University), and the Slavonic Seminar of Professor Josef Matl (Seminar für Slawische Philologie, Graz, Mozartgasses, 3).

JAPAN

Keiichi Chikazawa
Yamaguchi University

and

H. H. Smythe
Brooklyn College

In a very broad sense there were isolated instances of what may be considered sociological study in Japan prior to its opening to the West in the middle of the nineteenth century. Toshiaka Honda brought out his population theory in 1798, and Banri Hoashi projected his *kyuri-tsu or* "The Principles of Philosophy" between 1830-1842, which paralleled in part the positivism of August Comte.[1] Likewise, before the Meiji Revolution (1868) Amane Nishi went to Europe and upon his return to Japan spread the principles of Comte in 1870,[2] but it was the work of Herbert Spencer, introduced by Ernesto Fenollosa and Syoichi Toyama (the latter held the chair of sociology at Tokyo Imperial University from 1893-1896) that really began to influence Japanese sociology beginning around 1878 that laid the groundwork for its development as a full-fledged discipline in the country.[3] From these early beginnings sociology began to move ahead and its development may be conveniently characterized by three distinct periods.[4]

The first or the founding era, the period of what is known as organismic theory (1870-1906) was noted for its synthesis of the sociology of Comte and Spencer, and the work of Tongo Takebe who became professor of sociology at Tokyo Imperial University in 1898; the latter began to systematize sociology upon Comtian philosophical positivism and Confucian thought. The next stage (1908-1929) was the interlude of "scientific" sociology with interest focusing around psychological and formalistic trends. The final period, dating from 1929 to the present, has witnessed the gradual development of sociology as a realistic science; critical implications were felt and cultural and synthetic sociology held forth up until 1945; since then the pragmatism of America has been making inroads,[5] and the contemporary scene reflects this influence in various ways.

FIELDS OF INTEREST

The Family. The study of the family had received some serious attention in prewar Japan but it was concerned mainly with types, relationships, and customs. Since the war interest has concentrated on historical fundamentals related to feudalistic characteristics and patriarchal aspects in terms of their control elements; the rural family has come in for increased attention in this connection, as well as the *dozuku-dan* or the clan-like kinship group. There is interest developing also in the functional approach to family study and factors related to the role of merchant families in urban areas.[6]

Rural Sociology. The interest in the rural family has carried over into the village community study and this trend is understandable, since Japan is yet largely rural in composition and the majority of today's urban population has rural origins. The methodology of American rural sociology is employed in this research and fishing villages are coming in for increasing emphasis with attempts at classification of such communities taking the lead.[7]

Urban Sociology. The War in Japan, as elsewhere, brought demographic shifts and the urban trend enhanced interest in the study of cities and problems connected with them. Although before the war this interest was known and Matataro-Okui analyzed the metropolitan community and an organization for urban research was established in 1933, the postwar period has seen an upward surge in urban area study. Contemporary interest has seen developments of urban community study from the standpoint of its relationship to industrial sociology, while Takeo Yazuki and Seigo Koyano introduced the methodology of human ecology as used in America in making such analyses. However, urban community studies still lack a strong theoretical foundation and are purely of academic interest mainly, although Yazuki and Saburo Yasuda are trying to remedy this through their work on mass society and urban stratification. Community study as such, however, has not yet taken deep root in Japan.[8]

Industrial Sociology. The urban movement naturally created problems connected with labor and industry, and where before the war industrial sociology was a very undeveloped field, today this is one of the aspects of sociology receiving very serious attention, especially through the work of Kunio Odaka, Keizo Yoneyama and others. Increasing attention is being given to research projects dealing with factory laborers, farm workers, employee-management relationships, and the role and function of unions. Although earlier studies seemed largely management-oriented, more recent materials are analyzed with an emphasis on labor.[9]

Population. The postwar shifting of peoples to the city not only enlarged interest in industrial sociology but reemphasized the significance of population study for a nation like Japan with too many people on too little land. Before 1945 population research was carried on in Japan with German and French demographic practices dominant, but currently American methodology holds sway. Major areas of research center around problems concerned with birth rates and village stratification, the influence of birth control, the relationship of later marriage age to size of family, socio-economic class and marriage postponement and its effect on the population, agricultural development and optimum population in rural areas, the influence of feudalistic institutions of family size, and questions of employment and unemployment.[10]

Communications Study. The field of mass media and public opinion was almost unknown in prewar Japan but the concept of "mass communication," an entirely new postwar introduction, has now become one of the most popular terms in sociological development. Receiving impetus from the publication of Ikutaro Shimizu's *Shakai Shinrigaku* (Social Psychology), other sociologists began to devote time to the mass communication field with earlier works trying to probe theoretical relationships involved in the reliability of mass media and the reality of meaning for the masses and validity of opinion as expressed by the public. More recent emphasis is exemplified in Rokuro Hidaka's *Lectures on Mass Communication* stressing the correlation between morphology of mass communication and the structure of society. Research is continually going on in this field with studies being made by Katsuhiko Nishimura, Kotaro Kido, Akira Tsujimura, Atsushi Misaki, and Keizo Yoneyama.

As regards public opinion organizations similar to the mass survey institutes that exist in the United States a number of them were established immediately after the end of the war and the surveys of public opinion were numerous and on almost any conceivable subject. However, the popularity of these soon diminished and today only a few organizations carry on such work, these being largely departments of the larger newspaper publishing firms who make surveys several times a year of important questions felt to be of general public concern. Although a national public opinion was created within the government, once sociologists acquired the know-how of making such surveys they, in general, turned their attention to conducting such studies in rural communities instead of focusing on urban centers which were the main attractions in the early years of public opinion survey popularity.[11]

Legal Sociology. The sociology of law had received very little attention before the end of the war but it was not unknown, for Michitaka Kaino had published in 1943 his *Hoshakaigaku no Shomondai* (Problems of Sociology of the law), dealing with the differences between folk customary law and statutory legal regulations. Interest has grown slowly in this area of sociological study with sociologists giving attention to it focusing on familial associations and legalism as evident in Takenobu Kawashima's *Nippon Shakai no Kazokuteki Kosei* (The Familial Structure of the Society of Japan). Most workers in this field are lawyers and they are looked upon by other members of their profession as belonging to a "reformist" school rather than falling into the traditional pattern of being interpreters of the law. Those interested in the sociology of the law are concentrating on problems dealing with civil law such as family or social legalistic questions, democratic legislation, the methods and purpose of surveys, and the like.[12]

Educational Sociology. Turning to educational sociology, as early as 1915 Tongo Takebe published his *Shakaigaku to Kyoiku* (Sociology of Education), but as a formal field of study this branch of sociology began to develop in the 1920's with the works of Sukeshige Tase, *Bankin Shicho Gakko Kyoiku no Shakaika* (Socialization of School Education), 1921, and Kazuta Kurauchi *Kyoiku Shakaigaku* (Educational Sociology, 1927.) Tase's work was influenced by American trends of the time, while Kurauchi revealed European ideas. But following the war the field began to grow and take on importance as educational sociology assumed a definite place in the curriculum of teachers colleges; and in 1947 the activity of Yuzuru Okada pushed this work into a significant place in Japanese sociological circles which is has maintained up to the present.

As indicated in the 1953 publication, *Kyoiku Shakaigaku Koza* (Lectures on Educational Sociology), the trends in Japanese sociology of education follow patterns found common to the discipline in the United States. There is wide emphasis placed on social studies and on school-community relationships, and the direction in which this aspect of sociological study is moving may be understood from reports

made at recent annual meetings of the educational sociology association which discussed history of education, theory of educational
sociology, methodology, industrial education, social education, culture
and children, professional education and educational conscience, education and community, collective behavior and others. Major concentration in this field is centered on the relationship of education to
other social phenomena, and how to meet the challenge of forces
adversely affecting education.[13]

Social Pathology. In Tokyo and Osaka in prewar times some work
was done on social derelicts of various kinds—vagrants, juvenile delinquents, etc. Since the war, however, approach to these problems has
taken on a more scientific hue and they are being studied empirically
as problems in social disorganization with various types of surveys
being made and a more disciplined and systematized emphasis given
to research here through analysis of the theory of anomie by Keiichi
Sakuda, Shigeru Susato, Shoji Kato among others, while Koyu Iwai
has devoted time to antisocial groups. There is also developing some
real interest in juvenile delinquency and criminology, and efforts are
being put forth to adapt to the Japanese scene American methodology
in the study of these problems. In 1951 a group for the study of
criminal sociology was organized and in 1954 published its first bulletin containing reports of investigations in this field. However, as yet
very little material is available in this aspect of sociology on which
to base any definite trends.[14]

Intergroup Relations. This area of sociology was largely neglected
in Japan until the end of the war, but since then the UNESCO tension study, in which Japan participated, helped to arouse interest and
it is beginning to receive the attention of some sociologists. Japan's
indigenous caste group, the Eta, has come in for study and is now
approached as a minority group worthy of serious research. Groups
interested in the study or research of them, including both Eta and
non-Eta Japanese, are functioning in Waseda, Keio, Ritsumeikan, and
Nara Girls' Educational universities. As regards racial problems,
though students had given some attention to the matter previously,
it was not of scientific nature and there was no connection between
its study and its practical societal implications. Interest here is now
growing, especially as regards the problem of Koreans resident in
Japan.[15]

Sociology of Social Work. As a special discipline this was unknown
in Japan in prewar times, since it is a relatively recent newcomer as

a major discipline even in the West. However, even in the time of the Meiji era (1868-1912) some attention was paid to welfare work and this was followed through in the Taisho period (1912-1926) where courses on the subject were set up in some private higher schools and universities where sociology was an already basic course and social surveys related to the work began to play a significant role in such efforts. But after World War II, with the many and different problems it caused in Japan, a more scientific approach was needed and desired. Consequently, it is now current practice to expect some training in sociology by those who enter the field of social work as a profession, given serious attention sociologically by the research of Takenaka, and the field itself, in terms of its fundamental problems, has been Yokoyama, and Ohashi.[16]

Survey Movement. Prior to the war the survey as a tool of sociology was understood and used even as early as 1883, and even more scientific ones were projected in studies of lower socio-economic groups in Japan by Gennosuke Yokoyama in 1898. Through the first forty years of the twentieth century the survey movement was characterized by study of older patterns of social phenomena, emphasis on structural analysis, lack of dynamic approach, and attempts to show the pragmatic value of surveys. But the postwar period ushered in a confused social era and the survey came into its own as an instrument to collect data useful in finding solutions to social problems and for shedding light on chaotic social relationships, results of the hangover of feudalistic remnants in modern Japanese society, and general living conditions. The Occupation gave emphasis to the valuable utility of surveys through studies of agricultural, mountain, and fishing villages, as well as scientifically inspecting urban communities. With this as a stimulus Japanese took over and numerous surveys of various kind have been made and are still being made. The techniques of interviewing, study of attitudes, and sampling methods are now employed; but little is being done as regards research on individual personalities.

On the whole, the trend in Japan as regards sociological surveying is somewhat mixed. Some sociologists are trying to use survey methods yet are retarded by an inclination to follow well trodden paths of pure abstractionism and theorizing as an academic exercise. This is indicated from a report of the Japanese Sociological Society which questioned its members and found that in 1953, of those who responded 53 were using field survey methods to gather data to test their hypotheses, but in 1955 this number had dwindled to 20. The whole problem of sociological surveying in Japan is held back by the inability of sociologists to come to any agreement as to its use and methodology. Older sociologists today maintain a rigidly critical attitude against its use as a means of research, adhering largely to the German philosophical-theoretical tradition. A second group leans in the Marxian direction and they contend that surveys of sociologists are not historical and include too many details; some anti-Marxians say the Marxian approach is not scientific but politically inspired. Another group, those with more experience in survey method and technique, deplore the carelessness with which surveys are made and results projected, and this last group of sociologists contend that in Japan as yet there is no really scientific methodology and that American practices are not wholly applicable to the Japanese scene.[17]

Small Group Study. Relatively new in America, small group study is even more recent in Japan; yet it has been taken up by a few Japanese sociologists and has provoked some real thought among them. It is not likely to make much headway in the near future, since Japanese sociologists are by tradition against dynamic research and have not been hospitable towards the measurement of attitudes and the probing of individual personality problems. Group dynamics, however, has been introduced by a few teachers in the universities.[18]

Sociological Theory. Although Japanese sociologists have long had a tradition of working largely in a theoretical framework resting on philosophical foundations and using their talents in what appears to be intellectual academic exercise, very little original theory has come from them, for most of their work in the past has relied mainly on foreign importations, especially from Europe. This trend has continued into the postwar period. Immediately after the war Max Weber and Karl Mannheim were looked to as guides, but their influence waned and today the works of the Americans Talcott Parsons, Robert Merton, and Robert M. MacIver have the greatest influence.[19]

ORGANIZATIONS AND PUBLICATIONS

There is in Japan an overall society of sociologists, the Japanese Sociological Society of more than 800 members. It meets annually in various parts of the country and its program is much like that of any similar professional organization in other countries. Papers are given and discussed, new research is brought to the attention of the membership, elections are held and so on. Its official publication is *Shakaigaku Hyoron* (Japanese Sociological Review) which is released quarterly. In addition, there are four regional bodies in the country and these meet generally in annual convention and carry on programs much like the parent society. Various universities publish sociological journals at irregular intervals.

TRAINING AND EMPLOYMENT OF SOCIOLOGISTS

In prewar times there were less than twenty universities in which sociology as a field of study was considered of any importance. But since 1945 the discipline has grown somewhat, aided in no small part by the inclusion of the social studies course in the public school curriculums of the postwar period, and other practices which insure that nearly all students will have some contact with the social sciences. Consequently, practically all the nearly 500 junior and senior higher institutions of learning in Japan have at least an introductory course of sociology or something akin to it; more than thirty universities have it as a major field of study, while a few now offer work leading to a graduate degree in the discipline.

However, in spite of reforms and suggestions made during the Occupation, Japanese universities still follow essentially the plan found in German institutions of higher learning in methods of instruction and departmental structure. Sociology departments still suffer from too much inbreeding, which is a traditional characteristic of university practice in general in the country. The sociology faculty of the nation's leading institution, Tokyo University, is made up entirely of its own graduates. And the permanent departmental staffs are still very small in size, even at the most distinguished schools such as Kyoto and Tokyo universities; currently there is is estimated to be some 200 professional sociologists in Japan, the majority of them being employed as teachers. Sociology is still not classified with other social sciences, but is usually made a subdivision of the faculty of letters and classified with philosophy and literature.

As regards graduates, ordinarily those who have majored in sociology upon graduation have found work in journalism, in business firms as clerks, social workers (especially family case work), and as teachers in elementary or high schools.

EXCHANGE WITH FOREIGN SOCIOLOGISTS

Japanese sociology has historically depended upon foreign developments in the field and as yet has not contributed much that is original. Today there is a tendency among some Japanese sociologists to reflect upon this and to question their deficiency here with the hope that something can be done to improve the situation. This perplexing problem is being met, in part, however, through the stimulation that Japanese sociologists receive through the interchange with visiting scholars from other countries. Since the war this practice has been carried on regularly with foreign teachers serving as visiting professors in Japanese institutions for varying lengths of time, through visits to Japan of such distinguished social scientists as Ginsberg from England, Lundberg, Baber, and Borton from the United States, and Jean Stoetzel from France, among others. The effort has been aided also through the establishment in Okayama of an institute by the University of Michigan. On the other hand, Japanese social scientists, such as Kinnesuke Otsuka, Yuzuru Okada, Jiro Suzuki, Bunshichi Ohata, Takeshiro Kodera, and others, have and continue to visit abroad lecturing, serving as research scholars, working on special projects of the United Nations Educational and Scientific Organization and others, regularly attending meetings of the world congress of sociologists, carrying on correspondence with co-workers in other lands, while a number of younger Japanese sociologists have gone abroad for further study and training.

One outstanding influence of this exchange with foreign sociologists has been the development in Japan of a trend towards more cooperative work among Japanese sociologists themselves. In prewar times this was an almost unheard of practice; but today there is an increasing tendency for two or more scholars to collaborate on studies and research projects, while several organizations have also come together and pooled their efforts to carry out jointly a survey or study problem. In addition, Japanese sociologists are beginning to work cooperatively in cross disciplinary programs associating themselves in studies involving scholars in the field of history, geography, archaeology, economics, and anthropology or ethnology (anthropology alone usually refers to physical anthropology in Japan), the latter with which it is very closely allied. As yet, working relationships with psychology have not developed appreciably.

TEXTBOOKS AND COURSES

Although American influence has been rather widespread in sociological circles in Japan, at this writing no American introductory textbook has yet been translated, and the type commonly used in the United States has not been adapted as the pattern for those that have appeared in Japanese schools. However, a change seems to be in the making, for the newer textbooks now appearing in Japan contain data from field studies which are interwoven in discussion of the traditional concepts. Examples of this are to be found in Yuzuru Okada's *Shakaigaku Gairon* (Outline of Sociology) and in *Shakaigaku: Shakai to Bunka no Kisoriron* (Sociology: Basic Theories of Society and Culture), by Tadashi Fukutake and Rokuro Hidaka. With small staffs the number of courses is still very limited, restricted to more traditional one in general, and emphasis is on narrow specialization.

RESEARCH

Empirical studies were not a common feature of Japanese sociology in prewar times but with the end of hostilities social research began to make some headway in Japan. Younger sociologists began to make studies of rural communities and other areas, and to make investigations whose purpose was to unearth facts on social conditions and problems. Indicative of the trend was that in the 1954 annual meeting of the Japanese Sociological Society 43 out of 76 papers were field study reports dealing with agriculture and fishing villages, industry and labor, the family, morals and religion, delinquency and crime, ethnic groups and population. Empirical work has been and is still being carried on in problems of social tension, political parties, and divorce.

Empirical research is helping to make sociology a more popular and useful field in Japan but it still has to contend with several obstacles. Sociologists specializing in social theory rarely turn to field data to support their conclusions and in general they are very critical of empirical research. Others are simply set against emphasis on the study of Japanese conditions and problems; much of this criticism is against ill-planned and superficial research by incompetents, but the tendency is for many sociologists to be critical of progress made in empirical research. This aspect of sociology is likewise hampered by the lack of funds to finance research projects and practical field studies.[20]

SUMMARY

In general sociology Japan currently is increasing in interest. Although still characterized by elements adapted from earlier European patterns, American influence has been expanding since the war; however, this is largely one-sided because few American sociologists have opportunity to become acquainted with Japanese developments since almost no Japanese sociological material is translated into English; although now the American publication, *Sociological Abstracts* is helping to fill this need through publication of abstracts of material from the official Japanese society journal. The number of sociologists is growing and attendance at annual meetings of the national society is twice its prewar figure.

This overall expansion has seen a widening of the fields of study and an emphasis on empirical research; there is more cooperation on the part of both scholars and organizations in the conduct of investigations and publications of materials. Weak spots are still to be found in the number and variety of courses offered, in the quality and quantity of staff, in the continued practice of faculty inbreeding, and in the shortage of funds for research and further study. Viewed objectively, however, sociology in Japan still occupies a minor niche in academic circles, but there are heartening signs of its growth and development to a place of real significance in the future.

SELECTED BIBLIOGRAPHY

Tetsuo Atoji, "Nippon Shakaigaku Kako to Genzai" ("Japanese Sociology, Past and Present"), in *Nagoya-Daigaku Bungakube Kenkyu Ronshu*, XII.

Y. Atoji, "Nippon ni Okeru Shakaigaku no Hattatsu" ("The Development of Sociology in Japan") in *Shakaigaku no Kiso* (Tokyo: Shakaigaku Kenkyu, Nippon Shoin, 1953).

Akio Baba, "Sengo Junen Shakaigaku no Doko to Genjo" ("The Trend and Present Status of Japanese Sociology Ten Years After the War") in *Shakaigaku Ronso*, 5(Tokyo: Nippon Daigaku Shakaigaku Kenkyushtsu).

Sunao Fukutake, Ed., *Nippon Shakaigaku no Kadai (The Problems of Japanese Sociology)* (Tokyo: Yuhikaku, 1956).

N. Hayashi, "Nippon Shakaigaku no Hattatsu" ("The Development of Japanese Sociology"), in *Kyoyo Koza*, edited by Hayashi and Usui (Tokyo: Yuhikaku, 1954).

Rokuro Hidaka, *Masu Kommunike ishon Koza (Lectures on Mass Communication* (Tokyo: Kawade Shobo, 1951).

Elichi Isomura, *Toshi Shakaigaku (Urban Sociology)* (Tokyo: Yuhikaka, 1953).

K. Kurauchi, "Bakumatsu Meiji ni Shakaigaku ("The Sociology of the Togugawa Era and the Beginning of Meiji Era") in *Gendai Shakaigaku no Shomondai* (Tokyo: Kobundo, 1949).

Kunio Odaka, "Japanese Sociology: Past and Present," *Social Forces*, XXVIII, 4 (May 1950), 400-409.

John C. Pelzel, "Japanese Ethnological and Sociological Research," *American Anthropologist*, L, 1 (January, 1948), 54-72.

Ikutaro Shimizu, *Shakai Shinriigaku (Social Psychology)* (Tokyo: Iwanami Shoten, 1951).

Hugh H. Smythe and Taro Sakata, "Japan," chapter 13 in *Contemporary Social Science*, II, edited by M. Salvadori, J. S. Roucek, G. B. deHuszar, and J. Bond (Harrisburg Pa.: The Stackpole Co., 1954).

Jesse F. Steiner and K. K. Morioka, "Present Trends in Japanese Sociology," *Sociology and Social Research*, XLI. 2 (November-December, 1956), 87-92.

Sonraku Kenkyukai, *Sonraku Kenkyu no Seika to Kadai* (The *Problems and Issues of Rural Research*) (Tokyo: Jichosha, 1954).

(For *curriculum vitae* of H. H. Smythe, see p. 196-197.)

Keiichi Chikazawa was born on Kyushu Island (Japan); his early education was obtained at Kyushugakuin, a Mission school run by the American Lutheran Church, and the Fifth Higher School at Kumamoto. Then entered Tokyo Imperial University (1933) and received his A.B. degree from the faculty of Agriculture and Literature; subsequently enrolled at Kyushu University where he studied sociology. Traveled in Korea (1943); during World War II did military service in China. Prior to going to his present position in 1950 as a member of the sociology faculty of Yamaguchi University, served on the teaching staffs of Kassui-Jogakko, Kyushu Semmongakku, Miyazaki Kogyo-Semmon-gakko, and Miyazaki University; specializes in the study of suicide and rural villages and has carried out field research in the states of Miyazaki in Kyushu and Yamaguchi on the main island of Honshu. Is now engaged in statistical investigations of suicide and the Japanese family, as well as a cooperative project of a rural village with professors of Yamaguchi Women's College. Currently an assistant editor of *Shakaigaku-Hyoron* (Japanese Sociological Review), his publications include materials on Japanese names in early Japan, seasonal variation of suicide rates, and family structure in mountain villages, among others.

NOTES

1. Banri Hoashi, *Hoashi Banri Zenshu (Works of Banri Hoashi)* (Tokyo: Hoashi Kinen Toshokan, 1926).

2. Toshikama Okubo, *Nishi Amane Zenshu (The Works of Amane Nishi)* (Tokyo: Nippon Hyoronsha, 1945).

3. Tetsuji Kada, *Meiji Shoki Shakai-shiso no Kenkyu (The Study of Social Thought in the Meiji Era)* (Tokyo: Shujusha, 1933).

4. See Tetsuo Atoji, "Nipon Shakaigaku Kako to Genzai," (Japanese Sociology, Past and Present), *Nagoya-Daigaku Bungakube Kenkyu-ronshu*, XII.

5. For a more detailed analysis of the overall development of sociology in Japan consult M. Salvadori, J. S. Roucek, G. B. deHuszar, and J. Bond, editors, *Contemporary Social Science*, Vol. II, "Eastern Hemisphere" (Harrisburg, Pa.: The Stackpole Co., 1954), Chap. XIII, "Japan."

6. Takashi Koyama, "The Family" in *Sonraku Kenkyu no Seika to Kadai (The Problems and Issues of Rural Research)*, ed. by Sonraku Kenkyukai (Tokyo: Jichosha, 1954), 56-64; Seiichi Kitano, Shakaigaku *(Sociology), ibid.*, 3-15; Taku Nakano, "Dozokudan Kenkyu no Kiten to Kadai" ("Fundamentals and Problems of Clan-group Studies") in *Nippon Shakaigaku no Kadai (The Problems of Japanese Sociology)*, ed. by Sunao Fukutake (Tokyo: Yuhikaku, 1956), 67-84.

7. Seiichi Kitano, *op. cit.*; Tetsundo Tsukamoto, "Noson Kenkyu no Seika to Kadai" ("The Findings and Problems of Rural Studies") in Sunao Fukutake, *op. cit.*, 85-96.

8. Saburo Yasuda, "Toshi-Shakaigaku no Mondai" ("The Problems of Urban Sociology"), in Sunao Fukutake, *op. cit.*, 99-100; Eiichi Isomura, *Toshi Shakaigaku (Urban Sociology)* (Tokyo: Yuhikaku, 1953).

9. Shizuo Matsushima, "Rodo Shakaigaku no Tomensuru Futatsu no Kadai" (Two Problems Confronting the Sociology of Labor"), in Sunao Fukutake, *op. cit.*, 201-214; Joji Watanuki, "Rodosha Ishiki Kenkyu no Hihan to Kadai" (Criticisms and Problems of the Studies of the Responsibility of Labor") in Sunao Fukutake, *op. cit.*, 247-260.

10. Ryutaro Nakashima, "Jinko" (Population), in Sonraku Kenkyukai, *op. cit.*, 98-114.

11. Akira Tsujimura, "Mass Communication and Journalism" in Sunao Fukutake, *op. cit.*, 179-199; Ikutaro Shimizu, *Shakai Shinrigaku (Social Psychology)* (Tokyo: Iwanami Shoten, 1951); Rokuro Hidaka, "Masu Kommunike ishon Gairon" ("Introduction to Mass Communication"), in his *Masu Kommunike ishon Koza (Lectures on Mass Communication)* (Tokyo: Kawade Shobo, 1951).

12. Michitaka Kaino, *Horitsu Shakaigaku no Shomondai (The Problems of Sociology of the Law)* (Tokyo: Nippon Hyoronsha, 1943); *Hoshakaigaku* (Annual Reports of the Japanese Association of the Sociology of Law, 1951-1956) (Tokyo: 1956); Takenobu Kawashima, *op. cit.* (Tokyo: Gakusei Shobo, 1948).

13. Yoshihiro Shimizu, "Kyoiku Shakaigaku no Kadai" ("Problems of Educational Sociology") in Sunao Fukutake, *op. cit.*, 263-274.

14. Kaoru Ohashi, "Shakai Kaitairon ni Okeru Mondaiten no Shiteki to Sono Kaiketsu no Hoko" ("The Outlining of Problem Areas and Trends Towards Solution in Social Disorganization"), in Sunao Fukutake, *op. cit.*, 351-370; Koyu Iwai, "Kenkyu Hoho" (The Methodology of Antisocial Groups), Sunao Fukutake, *op. cit.*, 371-378.

15. Kozo Iwao, "'Buraku Mondai' Kenkyu no Shosokumen to sono Kadai" ("Aspects and Problems of 'Buraku' or The Eta Community"), in Sunao Fukutake, *op. cit.*, 415-430.

16. Sadao Yokoyama, "Fukushi Shakaigaku no Kadai" ("The Problems of Welfare Sociology"), in Sunao Fukutake, *op. cit.*, 431-447.

17. Minoru Shimasaki, "Shakai Chosa no Doko to sono Mondaiishiki" ("Trends and Problems of Social Surveys"), in Sunao Fukutake, *op. cit.*, 449-472.

18. Masao Hamao, "Nippon Shakaigaku no Genjo" ("The Present Situation of Japanese Sociology") in *Tsukue,* VII, 8, 10-15.

19. Akio Baba, "Sengo Junen Shakaigaku no Doko to Genjo" ("The Trend and Present Status of Japanese Sociology Ten Years After the War"), in *Shakaigaku Ronso,* 5 (published by Nippon Daigaku Shakaigaku Kenkyushitsu), 1-26; Tetsuo Atoji, "Nippon Shakaigaku Kako to Genzai" in *Nagoyadaigaku Bungakubu Kenkyu Ronshu,* XII, 105-131.

20. For further information here and on textbooks and courses see Jesse F. Steiner and K. K. Morioka, "Present Trends in Japanese Sociology," *Sociology and Social Research,* XLI, 2 (November-December, 1956), 87-92.

CHINA

Morton H. Fried
Columbia University

The task of conveying the spirit of and some of the main developments in the fields of anthropology and sociology has special problems
with regard to contemporary China. Not the least of these is the
fact that there are, politically speaking, two Chinas, each of them
associated with a distinct approach to the social sciences. A second
problem arises from the fact that in dealing with China we may not
assume familiarity on the part of the audience with the background
so essential to the comprehension of more recent trends. It is especially desirable that there be clarity as to elements of continuity
between the China of yesterday and that of today since this matter
is of itself a subject of prime interest to our fields. This being the
case, we turn first to a survey of the development of modern sociology
and anthropology in China.

FOUNDATIONS

History, economics and political theory comprise a strong triad of
disciplines in Chinese intellectual history. While the West brought
new and often revolutionary ideas to these studies, they clearly pre-
date such influences. Yet, in a very real sense basic creation is precisely
what is claimed for Western contacts in the matter of sociology and
anthropology. In 1944 Francis L. K. Hsu[1] began a brief article on
the history of sociology in China with the words, "Sociology in China
began with Yen Fu's translation of Herbert Spencer's works, but
true Chinese sociology did not begin until much later." Thus Hsu
places the earliest stirrings at the turn of the present century but
sees the emergence as even more recent. While many Chinese share
the substance of Hsu's view, some qualification is usually added.
This frequently takes the form of paying tribute to specific writers
and works of the classical heritage. A recent article from Taiwan

includes in its introductory remarks a lengthy list of ancient histories, such as *Shang Shu, Shan Hai Ching,* and the works of Sse-ma Ch'ien, to show that Chinese social scientists, despite great reliance upon the West, have an indigenous foundation for their work.[2] The works referred to, however, are generally comparable to such materials in the Western heritage as the books of Herodotus or Tacitus, and are of primary value as sources of data and certainly not as models of method.

The political and economic events which constituted a climate of pressure for technological reform and adaptation at the end of Ch'ing also precipitated the collapse of the traditional Chinese educational system.[3] This, in turn, had serious repercussions in the intellectual areas that were to emerge as sociology and anthropology. By 1903 there was a growing number of translations of books and articles. Some of Herbert Spencer was available, as was Haberlandt's *Völker-kunde* (translated as *Anthropology*) and Jenks, *A History of Politics* (significantly titled *A Commentary on Society* in its translation). In 1903 the failing Ch'ing government took notice of these develop-ments by formally adding anthropology to the list of courses that stood as the officially approved curriculum but no actual teaching of the subject seems to have resulted.

During the course of the next several years translations multiplied. Concomitantly, there was a spate of Western-style texts of the universal knowledge variety produced by Chinese students who apparently read three books and wrote the fourth. There was also great concern for the status of the new knowledge and the efforts that were expended in the complication of simple thoughts continued long enough for Francis L. K. Hsu to comment that[4]:

> some of our sociologists prefer long and obscure terms . . . to short and simple ones. They do so not primarily to clarify their thought (such terms generally being used to disguise muddled thinking), but to augment the aura and respectability of their science.

Perhaps the most important development of the first quarter of this century in Chinese sociology was the establishment and expan-sion in missionary colleges of departments staffed by Americans and devoted to Christian reform. Starting from the premise that China had to be swept clean and rebuilt on a new ethical plane, these sociologists specialized in a kind of generalized social work. Their basic theory, when it was not simply a collection of ethnocentric moral judgments, was largely derived from rural sociology and educational theory. Despite subsequently heavy criticism from Chinese, it may be said that the primary achievement of these sociologists was their extensive use of the social survey. To some degree the surveys have substantive value; perhaps more important, however, was the fact that through working on them, many Chinese students became seriously interested in social science.

The two closely related elements of a reform orientation and the social survey have had lasting effect on Chinese sociology. Becoming linked with certain political and 'cultural' movements of great vitality and strength (though quite discrete genesis), the influence of these elements spread beyond the Christian colleges to invade the intellectual atmosphere of the day and even penetrate official quarters. Students and scholars who had no attachment to Christianity, but who felt great need to modernize and reform China, began to incorporate aspects of missionary college sociology into their own schemes. There was virtually no such thing as pure research; every investigation had as its purpose the supplying of information to the immediate benefit of China. Even Francis L. K. Hsu, whose papers demonstrate his interest in such unapplied fields as kinship terminology and the structural-functional significance of unilateral cross-cousin marriage, wrote that, "Sociological research will, by studying the customs and requirements embodied in the different cultural areas, supplement Dr. Sun [Yat-sen]'s program and by revealing the common people's real grievances and incentives will facilitate the progress of Dr. Sun's wishes." [5] A similar stand was taken earlier, in 1920, when the Folklore Research Society was established in Peking. The purpose of this society was to bring the people to literature and literature to the people but also to gather materials on social protest to help push and direct social reform. This was not merely a programmatic device. Many scholars, including persons of considerable eminence, such as Hu Shih and Tung Tso-pin, began to asemble folk songs for their sociological content. One folklorist, Liu Ching-an, analyzed some 300 Honanese songs, using the data to throw light on the status of women in rural China and expose certain kinds of marital problems.

Thus the early period saw the establishment of themes which persist to the present moment. The reformist character of the social sciences in China can be described both on the mainland and in Taiwan; the association with official and semi-official organs of the government is most pronounced on the mainland but may also be seen in Taiwan. As for the social survey, it remains a major aspect of sociological work in Taiwan,[6] though in Communist China it seems to have undergone total eclipse.

THE "MIDDLE" PERIOD

In line with the convention that everything has a beginning, middle and end, we may distinguish in our subject matter a period of founding, the present situation and the interlude between. Actually, there is some objecive justification for these divisions. In the case of anthropology but not in the case of sociology. The middle period accords with a time of florescence in Chinese anthropology. Whether the present bifurcation represents a decline in either branch depends in part upon the viewer's political beliefs. We shall see below, however, that some concrete things may be said upon this question. At any rate it is beyond cavil that two distinct anthropologies may be distinguished and that most Western social scientists who might contribute to problems at issue can no longer work freely on the mainland.

It is difficult to apply the epithet 'florescent' to Chinese sociology during the period concerned except in a quantitative sense. During the 'twenties and 'thirties there was an exceptional burgeoning of periodicals devoted to or including serious sociological work. Most were in Chinese, such as *Shê-hui k'e-hsüeh ts'a-chih (Journal of Social Sciences)* and *Shê-hui-hsüeh chieh (Sociological World)*. There were also many English-language journals, indicating the particular affinity that existed between Chinese social scientists on the one hand and American and British scholars on the other.

During this period a mass of Marxist literature was translated into Chinese. While the bulk of it was Stalinist, it should be recalled that in the late 'twenties and early 'thirties Trotskyism was a vital contender in the ideological struggles within the Chinese Communist Party and among the larger circle of intellectuals. Among the books that appeared in translation were the first book of *Capital*, the *Critique of Political Economy* and other works of Marx, as well as *The Origin of the Family, Private Property and the State, Anti-Dühring*, and others writings of Engels. Bukharin's *Historical Materialism* appeared in this period, which also saw the publication of Trotsky's

Problems of the Chinese Revolution and lectures on dialectical materialism given at the National Sun Yat Sen University by August Thalheimer.

Among the leading left-wing theorists whose work typifies this period are T'ao Hsi-sheng, Ch'en Tu-hsiu, and Kuo Mo-jo. At the same time, however, a number of illustrious scholars of non-Marxist cant were applying themselves to essentially the same materials with somewhat different results, among them being Li Chi, Ts'ai Yuan-pei, Hu shih and Tung Tso-pin. A famous periodical which carried many of the articles in which these positions, particularly the former, unfolded was *Shih Huo* (*Food & Money*). Specializing in articles devoted to historical reconstruction and social typology, the outlines of the present Chinese Communist position on the developmental stages and classification of Chinese society can be clearly discerned in twenty year old issues of *Shih Huo*.

With some alterations for the ravages of time, the alignment of names given above still represents a functioning dichotomy, that between Peking and Tapai. Kuo Mo-jo is Chairman of the Chinese Academy of Sciences on the mainland while Li Chi and Tung Tso-pin are honored academicians of the Academia Sinica in Taiwan.

During the middle period social surveys flourished, as did the idea of a living laboratory for sociological research. Both of these were quite exciting to Chinese scholars who felt that they were throwing off the heavy, dead hand of armchair speculation. Largest of the projects was that sponsored by the Chinese National Association of the Mass Education Movement. An entire county, Tinghsien, in Hopei province, was the subject of research and controlled reform from 1926 through 1933.[7] The Tinghsien work is exemplary but most other social surveys suffered severe methodological difficulties,[8] and many Chinese social scientists who began their productive careers during the 'thirties took pains to distinguish their work from that of the survey type. Much of their resentment against the survey method stemmed from the feeling that the categories of analysis were being imposed forcibly on the Chinese data, rather than being extracted from Chinese culture itself.

Actually, the most important critics of the social survey method were not the products of missionary sociology but had other roots. In 1928 the Academia Sinica was founded under the direction of Ts'ai Yuan-pei. Dr. Ts'ai took personal control of the section of ethnology within the division of social sciences. While he did not do fieldwork himself, he felt that the scientific nature of ethnology depended upon such work and, therefore, he urged and aided his colleagues and students in getting into the field. According to Ho Lien-kwei,[9] the earliest fieldwork sponsored by the Academia Sinica was done jointly by F. Jaeger, a German, and Shang Ch'eng-tsu, a Chinese ethnographer, who studied the Yao of Lingyün, Kwangsi, in 1928.

Since 1928, the non-Han peoples of China, including the northeastern provinces, adjacent Mongolia and Tibet, have been the subject of fairly intensive fieldwork. Until fairly recently, however, the main focus of these investigations was physical, anthropological, folklorist, or concentrated on material culture. It was really only with the movement of several young scholars with quite modern training into Yunnan during the Sino-Japanese War that emphasis shifted to social organization and even personality and culture. The leader in this movement was Wu Wen-tsao, a man who made a superb impression as teacher and organizer. The teaching of Professor Wu seems to have been thoroughly eclectic; certainly no "school" in the ideological sense developed about him. Indeed, his leading pupils are active today both in Communist China and on Taiwan and even in the United States.

In conjunction with the emphasis on fieldwork, various universities, particularly those in Peking, intensified their efforts to draw prominent Western scholars into the Chinese educational milieu. Thus, during the 'thirties a number of foreign anthropologists lectured at Chinese universities. Among them were Elliot Smith, Seligman, W. Schmidt, B. W. Aginsky, Reo Fortune, Radcliffe-Brown, and Leslie White. Several of these scholars wrote original articles for Chinese periodicals, some of them being translated into Chinese. When the center of Chinese university life shifted from the east China coast to Szechuan and Yunnan three anthropologists whose visits to China were eagerly awaited had to be cancelled. The men in question were Malinowski, Sapir and Raymond Firth. Even if these men did not manage to appear personally in China, their influence was felt. Fei Hsiao-tung was a pupil of Malinowski and translated into Chinese an article of Firth's that has never to my knowledge been published in English.[10] Sapir was a teacher of Li An-che.

It should not be forgotten that at least one non-Chinese anthropologist of note, Sergei Shirokogoroff, resided in China for more than two decades until his death in 1939. This man had great influence on the generation of Chinese anthropologists now in middle age, and the great drive to do fieldwork is in part attributable to his efforts.

The achievements of the "middle period" in Chinese anthropology are considerable. Advances occurred on almost every front. Sensational discoveries of protoanthropic man at Chouk'outien were made by P'ei Wen-chung and various Chinese and non-Chinese scientists. Li Chi, Creel, Teilhard de Chardin, and others, supplied data on neolithic and protohistoric China beyond the dreams of researchers of the preceding generation. Meanwhile cultural anthropologists including Fei Hsiao-tung. Chang Chih-i, Francis L. K. Hsu, and Lin Yueh-hua were employing ethnographic methods to study the Chinese peasantry. The community studies done at that time were diversely oriented and, though few in number, are almost a microcosm of the method. Oddly enough for studies undertaken in a culture so rich in historical sources, few utilize available records and none use the local histories extensively. This seems to be due in large measure to the independent status of sinology as a discipline. Even for Chinese scholars the burden of combining first rate professional talents in Chinese history and modern community analysis is too great. Certainly up to this writing no one has appeared who thoroughly blends the two approaches in a unified work.

The "middle period" was partly shaped by the fortunes of war. Though Chinese ethnographers have applied themselves to the study of the non-Han peoples of China for several decades, this work was given stimulus by the relocation of the core of academic life in Szechuan and Yunnan during World War II. A great increase in the number of studies undertaken among the Miao, Yao, Lolo, Lisu, and other non-Han peoples, as well as a greater weight of published material about these cultures may be noted.

While most Chinese anthropologists were busy in their own Southwest, many Japanese anthropologists and sociologists were at work on problems relating to China. Interest in these problems antedated the situation then existing between the two countries; indeed, with respect to modern sociology and anthropology the usual vectors of diffusion between China and Japan were somewhat reversed; some of the major inspiration for modern developments in the social sciences, though originating in Europe, were mediated to China through Japan, where at the turn of the century, many Chinese were in the universities. After the period of establishment, however, the flow of theory and data between the two countries became somewhat erratic, particularly on the Chinese side. Thus, while Japanese mate-rials are frequently quite thorough in their Chinese documentation, Chinese sources only sporadically refer to Japanese work.[11]

Before moving on to strictly contemporary developments, it is neces-sary to complete the background by referring, albeit briefly, to the work of Western sociologists and anthropologists in China or dealing with that society.

Actually, it is somewhat difficult to draw clear disciplinary boun-daries about the Westerners who have dealt with or in China. Sinology is an areal discipline *par excellence* (and perhaps bears study as such, for the remarkable achievements of this discipline might well equip it to serve as a kind of model for the disciplines now emerging in the study of other areas). As an areal discipline, sinology effectively crosscuts many of the standard academic divisions. This has been true despite sinologist's traditional emphasis on history. As a matter of fact, for several decades the historical study of Chinese society and culture has been particularly oriented toward dynamic interpretations of Chinese development. This orientation has meant that more than usual concern has been shown for the integration of anthropological, sociological, economic, political, legal, and historical data as well as the relevant general theory of each of these fields.

Worthy of special mention is the attention given China by the English classical economists. Though their mentions of China tend to be parenthetical if not marginal, they are sufficiently numerous and complete to project a picture of China that fits neither the stereotype of ancient antiquity, nor that of feudalism, nor that of capitalism. The view that "oriental society" differed from all of these was ac-cepted by Marx, though he did not give a great deal of attention to it. Max Weber made much of the idea. He expanded it and saw the relationship between the vast Chinese bureaucracy and the under-lying requirements for the control of ground water in irrigation and flood prevention. It is perhaps not too much to say that Max Weber's work on China and India cannot be understood unless this prior relationship is grasped.

The theory of oriental or "hydraulic" society is given its clearest and best documented expression in the work of Karl August Wittfogel. This scholar, who refers to himself as an "institutional historian," began his contributions to the highly controversial "hydraulic theory" with the publication of *Wirtschaft und Gesellschaft Chinas.* (Leipzig, 1931) and articles in *Unter den Banner der Marxismus.* Both through his writings and through personal travel in China, Wittfogel influenced many scholars, Chinese and non-Chinese alike. Chi Ch'ao-ting acknowledged Wittfogel's assistance in the introduction and text of his Columbia doctoral dissertation, *Key Economic Areas in Chinese History* (1935) and Owen Lattimore also acknowledged Wittfogel's aid in his magnus opus, *Inner Asian Frontiers of China* (1940, reissued 1954).

The disputation over the hydraulic theory is more than usually acrimonious for what is, to the layman, a scholarly debate over the taxonomy of Chinese socio-political institutions. Paralleling and sometimes overshadowing this part of the debate is another part which has to do with the nature and possible future of Communist China and, even beyond this, the nature and prospects of the Soviet system.[12]

While most of the work on Chinese law has been done from a rather strict legalist viewpoint, consisting of translations and commentaries on specific codes and a few general descriptions of the Chinese legal system at given moments in history, there has been a little work done on the sociology of law in China. Of particular interest is the work of Ch'ü T'ung-tsu,[13] who, during this middle period, was intimately associated with many of the Chinese anthropologists whose work we have cited. Dr. Ch'ü has prepared an English version of his work but the manuscript has yet to be published. Having been privileged to read Dr. Ch'ü's work, this writer looks forward to its prompt appearance.

Legal handling of Chinese family problems has always attracted much attention. An early study was by Pierre Hoang, *Le mariage chinois au point de vue légal* (Shanghai, 1916). Subsequently, some of the most significant work in this field has been done by M. H. Van De Valk[14] who has pursued this topic through the recent years of Communist China.[15]

Foreigners have made great contributions to the study of Chinese society and culture but it is not the intent of this paper to catalogue their names and productions. Sinologists like Otto Franke, Richard and Helmut Wilhelm, and Henri Maspero have contributed masses of data from which sociologists and anthropologists profit and, indeed, these scholars have also offered lucid interpretations of their own. Of special interest to anthropologists and sociologists is the work of Marcel Granet, whose intuitive reconstructions of early Chinese society have stimulated Claude Lévi-Strauss in the field of the theory of social organization.[16]

The "middle period" in Chinese sociology and especially in anthropology was definitely one of dramatic growth and rich promise. Chinese scholars were in the vanguard of every important development but they enjoyed many benefits of international cooperation. While almost all of the mature Chinese sociologists and anthropologists at the end of the period had been trained abroad in part or whole, the increasing number of highly qualified Chinese scientists and the regular flow of foreign scholars indicated that complete graduate training in anthropology was not far off. The collapse of the Nationalist government completely altered the picture. We shall turn now to the picture that has emerged—the past decade of anthropology and sociology in Taiwan and on the mainland.

TAIWAN

As a consequence of the Communist victory, the body of anthropologists and sociologists divided by fission, part remaining and part removing to Taiwan; in every component field some of the leading scholars remained while others fled. Among the prominent fugitives to Taiwan we may list Li Chi and Tung Tso-pin, archeologists and students of the society of Shang and pre-Shang China. Among the ethnographers are Ruey Yih-fu, Ho Lien-kwei, and Ling Shun-sheng. Already on Taiwan, were several social scientists of demonstrated competence, for example the Japanese-trained sociologist and demographer Ch'en Shao-hsing and the ethnographer Ch'en Chi-lu.

The Academia Sinica moved officially to Taiwan in 1949 and since then has been quite actively pursuing field research among the aboriginal inhabitants of Formosa and Botel Tobago and continuing the study of neolithic and Shang culture through the large collections which were thoughtfully transferred to Taiwan before the debacle.

Anthropology fares well at the National Taiwan University where most of the staff of the Academia Sinica are among the instructors. Emphasis in teaching, after basic courses, is either upon ancient Chinese society or local ethnography. While students are reportedly not numerous, their calibre is encouraging.

The publications of Taiwan anthropologists are weighted much more heavily in the direction of material culture studies and comparative mythology than is presently fashionable in the United States, they also show considerable interest in social organization. While much of the data for these publications on problems of social organization derive from contemporary field work in Taiwan, there is a considerable use of data collected in fieldtrips in southwestern China prior to 1949. It is also noteworthy that the theoretical cast of these articles shows considerable familiarity with contemporary American work in the same field, particularly that of George P. Murdock.

The most hesitant extrapolation from fieldwork now being done in Taiwan and its environs clearly calls for the extension of the efforts of the fieldworkers into Southeast Asia. There is, however, no indication that this desideratum is moving toward reality—a reflection, no doubt, of the extreme economic disabilities present in Taiwan; as well as an index of the delicacy and inevitable political complexity of such moves.

From earlier sections of this paper the sociologist-reader may have gathered that there is little basis in Taiwan for a theoretical sociology of proportions similar to our own. The writer has not visited Taiwan since 1948 and therefore cannot speak personally for conditions there except as they are revealed to him in Taiwan publications. (The same *caveat*, of course, applies to later remarks about the mainland.) There is one advantage in the case of Taiwan, however, for a colleague presently teaching in Taiwan has described the situation in personal letters. This correspondent, who prefers to remain anonymous, confirms the writer's impressions. He remarks that, "Theoretical conceptualization is not of any interest here . . . Most Chinese 'sociologists' are in reality social workers." The correspondent specifically omits anthropology from his remarks and explicitly exempts Dr. Ch'en Shao-hsing from his remarks. Dr. Ch'en, he writes:

> is interested in and using 'theory' in our frame of reference . .
> He was trained in Japan (where theory is strong) and has kept
> up. . . with new developments . . . He is interested in the inter-
> disciplinary approach, and is impressed with the work of Parsons
> and Kluckhohn built on the frame of Mannheim, Weber and
> Durkheim.

As for social work, the correspondent from Taiwan remarks that this is "not social work as we know it [in the United States]. Social work is connected with education and it is not unusual for a social worker . . . to be an administrator, to run a kindergarten, etc."

No nation has a larger population than does China; few cultures are as long associated with a tradition of formal census taking as is the Chinese. For these reasons, if no other, it is suitable that Chinese social science be in part dedicated to demography. Modern Chinese interested in this discipline are largely recruited from three divergent specializations. There are those whose interests are largely biological and genetic, those who are primarily historians, and those who work within sociological frameworks similar to those accepted by Western demographers. In the first category I include the life table studies;[17] in the second, all of the various commentaries upon and translations of the census materials of previous dynasties.[18] The main demographic studies, however, are those that may use historical data (as indeed they must) but are focussed upon the present. Many Chinese participated in demographic research during the period between World War I and II; perhaps the foremost was Chen Ta[19] who accepted in 1946 an estimate of the total Chinese population that was but two-thirds of the figure published by the People's Government in 1955.

Considerations above and beyond those relating to scientific objectivity apply to discussions of whether China's tremendous aggregate of citizens constitutes overpopulation. A view very close to that associated with present Comunist government statements on the matter was voiced in 1949 by Chang Chih-i.[20] Chang asserted that a controlled economy and proper, equitable distribution of the nation's food and resources would eliminate whatever problems of overpopulation were said to exist. However, a highly competent rejoinder to Dr. Chang's piece appeared subsequently; this written by George W. Barclay[21] who, unlike Chang Chih-i, was a thorough specialist at demographic problems. Dr. Barclay has subsequently contributed two volumes on the population of Taiwan.[22] Further work on the population of Taiwan has also been done by Ch'en Shao-hsing,[23] mentioned above.

MAINLAND CHINA

In his article, "The New Sociology in China," G. William Skinner,[24] begins with the remark: "The success of the Chinese Communists in defeating their adversaries and consolidating their power is in large measure attributable to their capture of the sympathy and support of students and intelligentsia." Support for this statement is perhaps to be found in the very limited emigration of established social scientists to Taiwan or abroad during and after the Communist achievement of power. While, as stated above, some scholars of prominence removed to Taiwan, the bare fact is that most did not. Indeed, the majority of those known personally to the writer were, in 1948, eagerly awaiting the change of regimes. Some of them, like Fei Hsiao-túng, were personna non grata to the Nationalist government long before the death-throes of 1949. Others, perhaps seeking the phoenix, retained faith in the eleventh-hour appearance of a third camp. Whatever their motivation, a substantial majority of mature social scientists elected to remain in China when the Communists took over their government.

It is too early to compare the dream with reality, but one of the first tasks that confronted the Chinese social scientists who remained behind was to bring their thought into harmony with official doctrine. The example of Fei Hsiao-túng is illuminating. In March, 1950, he wrote "How to Reform Sociology Departments."[25] Earlier, Fei had written an article, "Wo che-i nien" ("That Year of Mine,")[26] which is something of a "confession," since it explains how Fei purged himself of several old "mistakes and bourgeois preconceptions." Fei added further details in a later article, "Chieh-fang yi-lai" ("After Liberation").[27] which describes how long and intensive communal study periods (hsüeh-hsi) had enabled him to conquer his individualism.

Dr. Skinner, who based his brief discussion of the "new sociology in China" in part upon personal observations made in Szechuan after the Communists came to power, has pointed out that the independent status of sociology as a discipline was in considerable jeopardy. Thus he reported that at a Sino-Russian conference held in 1950 "a Russian educational expert pointed out that in the Soviet Union neither sociology departments nor sociology as a separate discipline was a part of university organization and curriculums."[28] The answer of the sociologists was that they could play a vital role in disseminating Party theory. That they could, in fact, do so was already in the process of demonstration. For one thing, there was the matter of public confession. For another, there was a spate of books and pamphlets written for an audience of strikingly divergent degrees of sophistication and largely for use as texts in the hsüeh-hsi (communal study) groups.[29] A common characteristic of these volumes is their uncritical acceptance of the details (not to mention the stages) of Engels' position as described in *The Origin of the Family. . .* , as well as the homage they pay to Engels' classic article on the role of labor in the evolution of the human form. Finally, several social scientists were employed in bettering relations with non-Han peoples.[30]

The basic departmental reforms necessary to the inclusion of sociology among prescribed academic subjects are summarized by Skinner as follows:

> (1) The entire curriculum must be completely "scientific," that is, Marxist-Leninist. Old courses that had previously been influenced by Marxism, such as "History of Social Development," must do away with the remaining non-Marxist elements. Other old courses of some usefulness in the period of new democracy must change their approach entirely, while all other courses should be eliminated outright. (2) The department must do away with all foreign teaching materials [excepting Soviet materials] and relate subject matter to Chinese society. Everything taught must be practical, not excepting Marxist-Leninist theory. (3) The department must cooperate closely with the People's Government and especially arrange its professional training to accord with social needs, which will of course be satisfied by and through the government.[31]

The soundness of Skinner's remarks are confirmed in a recent development of great importance, the so called policy of "Let flowers of many kinds blossom, diverse schools of thought contend." The line was set in a speech of May 26, 1956, by Lu Ting-yi, Director of the Propaganda Department of the Central Committee of the Chinese Communist Party.[32] In its major aspects the new policy applies to both arts and sciences and permits limited discussion and variation in place of the total restrictions which prevailed to that time. The limits, however, are carefully set; no bourgeois deviationism of the type associated with the name of Hu Shih will be tolerated.

How important the gains under the new policy are to Chinese artists and scholars may be gauged from the widespread discussion of the policy which has ensued. Kuo Mo-jo, head of the Academy of Sciences,[33] hailed the new policy in a speech entitled "Long Live the Policy—Let Diverse Schools of Thought Contend."[34] In addition to a slight loosening of intellectual bonds, the policy has also been viewed by Kuo and others as a means of reducing the pressures on social scientists to spend most of their time in practical political work.

While it is impossible to consider the work of mainland sociologists and anthropologists apart from its political context, the broad outlines of scholarly application can be discerned. The three foremost areas are in archeology, linguistics, and the rationalization and interpretation of the historical position of the People's Government.

Archaeological research has been pushed on several fronts. Pei Wen-chung and Yang Chung-chien have specialized in human paleontology as well as associated cultural horizons. The most sensational of the recent discoveries reported from the mainland has been that of a large number, about 40, of *Gigantopilhecus* teeth. Two points should be made about these discoveries. First, Pei announces that three of them were discovered *in situ* in Kwangsi (the area to which they were ascribed by von Keenigswald and he tentatively assigns them a date no older than *Sinanthropus* and perhaps younger!). (This would tend to upset some of Weidenreich's speculations which were based upon the primitive morphology of the Canton-Hong Kong teeth.) Second, the method of popular archaeology which sends hordes of laymen scouting for relics of the past after a few hours of superficial lectures, a technique which we may imagine was eagerly sponsored by scholars seeking the favor of the government and which has been used through-out China during the past several years, has come close to wreaking a disaster. Few laymen understand that the least part of archaeological technique is devoted to *finding* evidences of the past. Far more im-portant—and difficult—is the interpretation and dating of the relic and its site. This is rendered impossible when people, no matter how well meaning, act as scavengers and despoil the context of a find. Towards the close of 1956 there were scattered indications that dam-pers were being put upon popular archaeology.

Neolithic and post-neolithic archaeology has also been given con-siderable attention, largely under the direction of Hsia Nai and his associates. While newspaper and magazine accounts of finds are fre-quent, the present writer has seen no scientific publications based on these announced finds.

Most of the work in linguistics is eminently practical in nature. The former problem has been much discussed in the United States,[34] while the latter has been of primary concern to specialists.

The non-Han peoples of China have been given very extensive con-sideration by the People's Government. While much of this treatment has had to do with literacy and with the political treatment of the areas concerned, removing them from the regular political hierarchy and treating them as special areas, considerable attention has also been paid their cultures. A key institution in this regard is the Central Institute for Nationalities, which has also served, it would seem, as a general employment agency for anthropologists and scholars of closely related disciplines. Thus such well known anthropologists as Fei Hsiao-tung and Li An-che are vice-presidents of this Institute, and the historian Feng Chia-sheng is a staff-member.

To conclude this section let us consider the words of Fang Lienche, a historian of the Hoover Library. In a review of some Chinese works some time ago Fang wrote:

> Scholars in all disciplines who are interested in China, whether in history or philosophy, in sociology or political science, have been watching with keen interest and to some extent speculating on what Chinese cultural traditions are to be accepted or rejected. . . .
>
> The revisions in the 1953 edition [of the *Chung-kuo t'ung-shih chien-pien*] may offer some clues. . . . In the two former editions Confucius was presented in some 2,000 characters, but in this revision Confucius is allotted over 5,000 characters.[35]

Thus Fang sides with those who agree with Herrlee G. Creel that "There would seem to be little doubt that, as time goes on, a great many elements of China's tradition that have been called 'feudal' and 'reactionary' will gradually find their way back into good standing."[36]

CHINESE ABROAD

In addition to the split in social sciences as between the scholars on the mainland and in Taiwan, there are many Chinese who continue to contribute to the field while living abroad. Some of them, like Francis L. K. Hsu, began their careers in China but now have merged without distinction with their colleagues in the new environment. Hsu, incidentally, is one of the few Chinese anthropologists whose interests are in the field of personality and culture.[37] Among other exemplary individuals we can notice C. K. Yang, Theodore Ch'en, and S. C. Lee. The problems which these people deal with are generally dissimilar and they utilize a variety of methods and approaches; there is absolutely no question of a "school" involved.

A second type of overseas Chinese scholar is perhaps what Rose Hum Lee has called the "sojourner"—one who considers his overseas experience as transitory, maintaining basic intellectual ties with home scholars. Such a one is Prof. Huang Wen-shan who, despite long residence in the United States, has a distinguished academic record in China and, moreover, is celebrated by Chinese sociologists, at least those in Taiwan. Huang Wen-shan used the term "culturology" in Chinese during the 'twenties and some years ago published a volume dealing with the theoretical position of the science of culture.[38] At present Prof. Huang is pursuing two studies, one dealing with a reinterpretation of Chinese totemism and the other devoted to the sociology of overseas Chinese. Similarly, Prof. Chang Chung-yuan, though trained primarily in education and psychology, is making studies which combine several disciplinary approaches, the subject being the pivotal conception of *tao* in the Chinese system of values.

CONCLUSION

Sociology and anthropology in the modern disciplinary sense came to China in relatively recent times—one might say almost in the last generation. While there has been great unevenness of development, theoretical sociology, for example, being rather neglected, certain component fields have grown with remarkable speed and today display great vigor. Though practical problems of a political and economic nature restrict intercourse between Taiwan sociologists and western theoreticians, there are indications of growing interest on the part of the former in the achievements of the latter. The immediate political climate at the time of writing does not enable the writer to be so sanguine about mainland China where both sociology and anthropology clearly labor under severe ideological restrictions.

SELECTED BIBLIOGRAPHY

Chao Wei-pang, "Modern Chinese Folklore Investigation," *Folklore Studies* I (1942) 55-76, II (1943) 79-88. An account of twenty years of research in folklore studies, emphasizing sociological content of such research.

Fei Hsiao-tung & Chang Chih-i, *Earthbound China* (University of Chicago Press, 1945) esp. p. 1-18. The introduction briefly surveys the methods and problems of the community study approach in China with references to the literature.

Morton H. Fried, "Community Studies in China," *Far Eastern Quarterly* XIV (1954), 11-36. A survey of the existing social surveys and community studies done in China and published in English or Chinese.

Ho Lien-kwei, "Ssu-shih nien lai chih Chunk-kuo min-tsu-hsüeh" (*Ethnological Study in China during the Past Four Decades*), *Chung-kuo min-tsu-hsüeh pao* (*Bulletin of the Ethnological Society of China, Taiwan*) I (1955), 1-17; English summary 18-24. An interesting but uncritical account that tends to be an annotated bibliography. Weak on contemporary developments in Taiwan, which are probably taken for granted, and almost devoid of reference to the mainland.

Hsu, Francis L. K., "Sociological Research in China," *Quarterly Bulletin of Chinese Bibliography* n.s. 4 (1944), 12-26. Excellent account and commentary on growth of Chinese sociology and anthropology, from the viewpoint of an active participant.

Hsü I-t'ang "Ethnological Research in China," *Quarterly Bulletin of Chinese Bibliography* 4 (1944), 27-33. Very brief, particularistic account of specific research projects.

Shirokogoroff, Sergei M., "Ethnological Investigation of China," *Folklore Studies* I (1942) 1-8. Posthumously published note on the desirability of doing ethnographic research in China and indicating lacunae in research.

Skinner, G. William, "The New Sociology in China," *Far Eastern Quarterly* X (1951) 365-71. Valuable discussion of the fate of academic sociology under the Communists.

Wang Yü-ch'uan, "The Development of Modern Social Science in China," *Pacific Affairs* 11 (1939), 345-62. A memorandum assembled from Wang's notes. A panoramic view of the development of social science in China emphasizing the relations between these developments and broader socio-economic phenomena in China.

Morton H. Fried, Associate Professor of Anthropology, Columbia University and Chairman of the Asia Research Committee of the Division of Psychology and Anthropology of the National Research Council, has done fieldwork in China and South America and is the author of *Fabric of Chinese Society* (New York: Praeger, 1953) and a contributor to various scholarly publications.

NOTES

1. "Sociological Research in China," *Quarterly Bulletin of Chinese Bibliography* (Chungking), N. S. 4 (1944), 12.

2. Ho Lien-kwei, "Ssu-shih nien-lai chih Chung-kuo min-tsu-hsüeh (Ethnological Study in China in the Past Four Decades)," *Chung-kuo min-tsu-hsüeh pao* (*Bulletin of the Ethnological Society of China*), Taipei, 1 (1955), 3-4.

3. Chang Chung-li, *The Chinese Gentry* (Seattle: University of Washington Press, 1955), 205-209.

4. Hsu, *op. cit.*, 16.

5. *Ibid.* 17.

6. See especially the works published through the cooperation of the National Taiwan University, and the U.S. Mutual Security Mission to China, under the auspices of the Joint Commission on Rural Reconstruction: *Rural Taiwan: Problem and Promise* (Taipei, 1953) and *Urban and Industrial Taiwan—Crowded and Resourceful* (Taipei, 1954). Though a large staff was responsible for each of these works, we note in particular the roles of two sociologists in their production: Ch'en Shaohsing and Arthur Raper.

7. The basic publication of this work is by Li Ching-han, *Ting-hsien shê-hui kai-k'uang tiao-ch'a* (1933). Much of that work is available in English through the work of an American who was vitally associated with the project; see Sidney Gamble, *Tinghsien* (New York: Institute of Pacific Relations, 1954).

8. For a critique and partial bibliography of Chinese social surveys see Morton H. Fried, "Community Studies in China," *Far Eastern Quarterly*, XIV (1954) 14-17.

9. Ho Lien-kwei, *op. cit.*, 6.

10. "Chung-kuo nung-ts'un shê-hui t'uan-chieh-hsing ti yen chiu," [English title given as "Social stability in North China village life".] *Shê-hui hsüeh-chieh*, X (1938). Vol. 9 of this journal is dedicated to A. R. Radcliffe-Brown; it contains translations of three articles for which he was famed, and one written specially for the occasion.

11. This may be attributed in part to the linguistic difficulty which is greater by far for Chinese reading Japanese than vice versa. For bibliography on Japanese contributions to sociological and anthropological research in China see M. Honda and E. B. Ceadel, "Post-war Japanese Research on the Far East (excluding Japan)," *Asia-Major*, IV (1954), 103-150, esp. 124-5.

12. Karl A. Wittfogel, "Oriental Despotism," *Sociologus*, III (1953), 96-106; "The Historical Position of Communist China: Doctrine and Reality," *The Review of Politics*, XVI (1954), 463-474; "Oriental Society in Transition," *Far Eastern Quarterly*, XV (1955), 469-478; etc. See also Wittfogel's forthcoming: *Oriental Society and Oriental Despotism* (New Haven: Yale University Press, 1957). Wittfogel's views are challenged by Benjamin Schwartz, "A Marxist Controversy on China," *Far Eastern Quarterly*, XIII (1954), 143-153; Wolfram Eberhard, *Conquerors and Rulers: Social Forces in Medieval China* (Leiden: Brill, 1952); and Wu Ta-k'un, "An Interpretation of Chinese Economic History," *Past and Present*, I (1952).

13. *Chung-kuo fa-lü yü chung-kuo shê-hui* (*Chinese Law and Chinese Society*) (Shanghai: Commercial Press, 1947).

14. *An Outline of Modern Chinese Family Law* (Peking: Monumenta Sercia, Monograph Series No. 2, 1939).

15. M. H. Van Der Valk, *Conservatism in Modern Chinese Family Law*, Studia et Documenta ad Iura Orientis Antiqui Pertinentia, IV (1956).

16. Marcel Granet, *Catégories matrimoniales et relations de la proximité dans la Chine ancienne*, Annales Sociologiques, Série B (1939); Francis L. K. Hsu, "Concerning the question of matrimonial categories and kinship relationship in ancient China," *T'ien Hsia* XI (1940-41), 242-69, 353-62; Claude Lévi-Strauss, *Les structures élémentaires de la parenté* (Paris: Presses Universitaires de France, 1949).

17. For example, H. E. Siefert, "Life Tables for Chinese Farmers," *Milbank Memorial Fund Quarterly*, XI (1933); and J. C. Yuan, "Life Table for a Southern Chinese Family from 1365 to 1849," *Human Biology* (1931); etc.

18. For example, Hans Bielenstein, "The Census of China During the Period 2-742 A.D.," *Bulletin of the Museum of Far Eastern Antiquities*, XIX (1947); Roswell S. Britton, "Census in Ancient China," *Population*, I (1934); and Otto Van der Sprenkel, "Population Statistics of Ming China," *Bulletin of the School of Oriental & African Studies*, XV (1953); etc.

19. *Jên-k'ou wen-t'i (Population Problems)* (Shanghai: Commercial Press, 1934); *Population in Modern China* (University of Chicago Press, 1945).

20. "China's Population Problem: A Closer View," *Pacific Affairs*, XXII (1949).

21. "China's Population Problem: a Closer View," *Pacific Affairs*, XXIII (1950).

22. *Colonial Development and Population in Taiwan* and *A Report on Taiwan's Population* (both published by Princeton University Press, 1954).

23. "Population Growth and Social Change in Taiwan," *Bulletin of the Department of Archaeology and Anthropology* (Taiwan), V (1955) and "Population Change in Taiwan," *idem*, VI (1955); the two articles actually comprise a single lengthy paper and are accompanied by English translations.

24. G. W. Skinner, "The New Sociology in China," *Far Eastern Quarterly*, X (1951), 365-371.

25. Fei Hsiao-tung, "New Reconstruction," in Hsin Chien-shê, cited by Skinner *op. cit.*, 36ff; it contains synopsis of Fei's ideas.

26. *Jên-min jih-pao (People's Daily)* (Peking, January 3, 1950).

27. In Chang Chih-chung, Ed., *Tsên-yang kai-tsao (How to Change and Rebuild)* (Peking: Ho-tso shu-tien, n.d., 1951?), 36-41.

28. Skinner, *op. cit.*, 368.

29. For example, Teng Chu-min, *She-hui k'o-hsüeh ch'ang-shih chiang-hua (Common Sense Lectures in Social Science)* (Peking: Wen-hua kung-ying shê, 1949) ;& Lun Pien-hsieh, Shen-me shih yüan-chih shêh-hui *(What was the Nature of Original Society)* (Shanghai: Hua-tung jen-min ch'u-pan shê, 1953).

30. Cf. Fei Hsiao-tung, *Hsiung-ti min-tsu tsai Kuei-chou* (Brother Tribesmen of Kweichow) (Peking: San-lien shu-tien ch'u pan, 1951).

31. *Loc. cit.*, 368-69.

32. Cf. *Jen Min Jih Pao* (Peking) (June 13, 1956); *People's China* (1956) Supplement to No. 16.

33. The mainland equivalent of the Academia Sinica. On June 1, 1955, the Academy of Sciences established four main departments, the fourth being devoted to philosophy and social sciences.

34. Cf. *People's China* (1956) no. 17, pp. 4-10. Additional discussion appears on pp. 11-15 of this same issue.

34. Cf. Harriet Mills, "Language Reform in China: Some Recent Developments," *Far Eastern Quarterly* XV (1956), 517-40.

35. Fang, "Recent Chinese Publications," *Far Eastern Quarterly*, XIII (1954), 355.

36. H. G. Creel, *Chinese Thought from Confucius to Mao Tse-tung* (New York: Harper, 1953), 257.

37. F. L. K. Hsu, *Under the Ancestor's Shadow* (New York: Columbia University Press, 1945); *Americans and Chinese* (New York: Schuman, 1953); etc.

38. *Wen-hua-hsüeh chi ch'i tsai k'o-hsüeh shen-hsi chung ti wei-chih (Culturology and its Place in the System of Sciences)* (Canton: South West Social & Economics Institute, Lingnan University, 1949).

INDIA

A. K. Saran
Lucknow University

The development of sociological thought in modern India has been, like all modern Indian thought, co-temporaneous with her contact with the West which, in this case, also meant conquest. A systematic history of the development of sociological thought in India will not be attempted in this chapter but some reference to earlier thinkers is necessary for a proper understanding of fundamental trends in contemporary Indian Sociology.

It is not to be supposed that the contact between India and the West was a contact between a traditional and a non-traditional society. Such an encounter is, in fact, excluded by the concept of Tradition. It is always a disintegrating society that the new society encounters, for what appears as the developing, new society is only a stage in the dissolution of the traditional society. The drama of this encounter had already been nearly played out in the West when the Indian contact effectively took place. The difference in the case of India was that whereas in the West a "new" culture was rising in the midst of the disintegrating traditional society—a huge step towards advancement from the emerging modern point of view, a stage in the decay (involution) of the tradition from the traditional point of view—the disintegrating Indian society had thrown up no new culture from within itself. The encounter of India with the West, unlike that of modern with Medieval society on the continent, therefore meant an encounter with a foreign force. This difference and the fact that during this time India was more or less completely conquered by England provide the context in which modern sociological thought of India is to be understood.

To this situation there have been three different responses.[1] In the first place there have been those thinkers who totally reject the Modern Western Civilization and want a return to the traditional principles. Secondly, there are those who would want a synthesis of the two.

Since a synthesis of two cultures can be oriented to one or the other culture, it is of importance to indicate the orientation of those who think in terms of synthesis. A third important line of difference among Indian social thinkers—which is strictly only an aspect of synthesis—concerns the basis of synthesis. In some there has been a marked tendency to interpret—and to justify—traditional concepts and institutions in terms of modern rationalistic-positivistic ideas, while others have endeavored to adopt what they call a value-neutral scientific attitude and have studied the process of acculturation as it has been going on in Indian history. This last represents the most recent trend in Indian social thought. However, as we shall see, it is not value-neutral in the strict sense; for, as is commonly recognized now neutrality like simplicity is a most difficult pose to keep up in the social sciences. This trend is oriented to the construction of a new society—though it stops short of leading to a "Science of Revolution." We shall not begin directly with this trend but with the first response which is neither of very recent origin nor of great influence in contemporary sociology and yet poses the problem which, in somewhat less fundamental form, has continued to occupy Indian sociologists, and its dilemma and failure symbolizes the dilemma and the failure of the thinker in the modern Indian society.

COOMARASWAMY

The only Asian writer of importance who rejects modern civilization and stands for traditional society is Ananda Kentish Coomaraswamy. Among foreigners who adopt this attitude the most stable are René Guénon, and Frithjof Schuon, Joseph Campbell, C. G. Jung and Heinrich Zimmer who are also seriously concerned with tradition but whose attitude is not as uncompromising as that of the former; Jung and Zimmer have their faith in modern science and civilization, though it is seriously qualified.

Coomaraswamy has not written any systematic work in social science as such, but his works contain a fairly systematic exposition of the traditional theory of man and society. It is, however, not an accident that he has mainly written on art for that perhaps is the most convenient way of expounding the (traditional) general theory of symbolism of which the theories of society, art and culture are merely specific aspects.

Coomaraswamy's judgment on modern civilization is uncompromising—it is, he says, a civilization which has been described as "a murderous machine with no conscience and no ideals," "neither human, nor normal, nor Christian" and in fact "an anomaly not to say a monstrosity."[2] Such a severe judgment is by no means confined to traditionalists—in fact, in the above passage Coomaraswamy is quoting from scholars who cannot be described as traditionalists; the specificity of the traditionalist's attack lies in his belief that there is such a thing as a normal civilization based on First Principles—Wisdom uncreate. Accordingly his critique exposes the contradictions of Modern Society at a far deeper level than would be possible for a critic with a modern outlook. Coomaraswamy judges every civilization from the standpoint of a normal society. "The distinctive character of a traditional society," he says, "is order. The life of the community as a whole and that of the individual whatever his special function may conform to recognized patterns, of which no one questions the validity: the criminal is much rather the man who does not know how to behave, than a man who is unwilling to behave. . . ."

"In the unanamious society the way of life is imposed in the sense that 'fate lies in the created causes themselves,' and this is one of the many ways in which the order of the traditional society conforms to the order of nature: it is in the unanimous society that the possibility of transcending the limitations of individuality is best provided for. It is in fact for the sake of such a realization that the tradition itself is perpetuated."[3]

Held by a modern thinker this theory of society obviously poses a serious problem, particularly in the context of Indian society, which has ceased to be traditional without becoming modernized. If, as repeatedly shown by Coomaraswamy, our condition is really so hopeless, if what people think to be progress is only a swift and steady drift towards disaster, what could be the relevance of this "normal" view of man and society for us? Coomaraswamy cannot avoid this question by saying that a thinker is interested in truth for its own sake, for he has himself exposed the contradiction implicit in such doctrines. Should the West follow the East? Or, shall our aim be some kind of synthesis of East and West? Coomaraswamy's answer is clear but superficial. He does not advocate orientalization of the West, nor does he hope for a fusion of the two. Equally clearly he rejects "eclecticism" or "syncretism." Quoting Réné Guénon he says that what the knowledge of the traditional theory of society and culture implies is an effort to bring about the "return of the West to a traditional civilization, that is one in which everything is seen as the application and extension of a doctrine whose essence is purely intellectual and metaphysical." Agreeing further with Réné Guénon, Coomaraswamy continues, ". . . the work must be undertaken by an 'elite' . . . The divergence of the West and East being only accidental the bringing of these two portions of mankind together and the return of the West to a normal civilization are really just one and the same thing." [4]

This "return" does not at all mean that the West should go back to, say, the Middle Ages. All archaism Coomaraswamy regards as the "proof of a deficiency." "In reproduction," he says, "nothing but the accidental appearance of a living culture can be evoked." Replying to the charge that his remedy for the ills of contemporary civilization is some kind of a revivalism or archaism Coomaraswamy points out that what he does suggest is not a "return" to an earlier social organization, but a return to "first principles." Translated from metaphysical into religious terms, this means, "Seek first the Kingdom of God and Righteousness and all these things shall be added unto you. What this can have to do with a sociological archaism or eclecticism I fail to see." [5]

While this leaves no doubt about what Coomaraswamy does not mean by the "return" which he advocates, it is not clear what he means by it in terms of historical possibility. In so far as the First Principles are nontemporal, no departure from, and hence no return to, them is possible; when however we refer to their historical epiphanies a return to them does imply an attempt to move backwards in cultural time. If this return movement is understood in terms of the cyclic theory of socio-cultural dynamics it must be considered a natural movement and, in that case, the "elite" must be *avatáras* or *bodhisattavas,* for if they are less than that wherein would be the essential difference between this theory of re-formation and the Marxian Theory of Revolution? The point is that both René Guénon and Coomaraswamy have not appreciated the predicament of the "modern man," more specifically the misery of the ordinary Hindu thinker in modern India whose consciousness and socio-cultural world are still haunted by the vestiges of a normal civilization and who, now living under the total impact of a civilization that is obviously irrational, finds that all his efforts in consistent thinking and normal living constantly result in an aesthetic form of life and thought—that all his avoidance

of mere ornament keeps on turning into "interior decoration." For
the ordinary intellectual is not a genius and hence does not inhabit
"a world of his own"; "he has neighbors."

This predicament is perhaps the key to the understanding of the
fundamental trends in contemporary social thought in India. It is
not that the misery of this predicament is directly reflected in the
consciousness of contemporary sociologists and colors their work—this
is confined to a very small and rather obscure minority. It is, however,
the context of their major preoccupations and basic attitudes as also
of some socio-political movements of recent origin—like the Rashtriya
Swoayam Sewak Saugh, the Jana Sangha and the Ram Rajya Parishad.

It will also be seen that the failure of Coomaraswamy to suggest a
way out is not confirmed to the traditionalist alone but extends to
those also who do not reject modern civilization—unless they happen
to be Marxists. Perhaps it is not a question of discovering a way out,
but of suffering, which too may come to nothing more than "living
down."[6]

MUKERJEE

The name of Dr. Radhakamal Mukerjee is rather well known in
America. He has been trying to broaden the framework of Modernism
so that the elements of the tradition could also be included therein.
In his earlier works,[7] Mukerjee was concerned himself with a systematic revision of economics—the most typical science of the modern age
—with a view to broadbase it. He shows how economic principles are
founded on physical and psychological principles and how intimately
they are connected in their functioning with the institutional set up.
Since quite early in his intellectual career he has been advocating an
integral interdisciplinary approach to human problems. *The Institutional Theory of Economics* (New York: Macmillan, 1940) carries
this line of thought further. Here he not only joins the American
school led by Veblen, Commons and Mitchell, but gives it a new
orientation by emphasizing the central role of traditions and values.
This has led him to a "sociological" theory of value. In his hands,
economics emerges as a dynamic cultural science, based, however, on
the natural and the psychic orders. This is connected with his regionalism in which field too, his main contribution has been the emphasis
on the cultural dimension of the region. This approach raises the

problem of the continuity of the different orders. Here he utilizes the
ideas of level and *Gestalt*. The increasing emphasis that he, in opposition to the narrowly empiricist trends of the West, came to lay on
traditions, norms and values, led him to make a sociological study of
these concepts in two of his recent books: *The Social Structure of
Values* and the *Dynamics of Morals* (London: Macmillan, 1949 and
1950). Here too his main concepts are those of *Gestalt* and level. He
gives a fourfold typology of groups arranged in a hierarchial series:
the Crowd, the Interest group, the Community and the Commonalty.
These groups have different norms of organization, criteria of evaluation, sanctions and means of control and different ends and values
are viewed in the context of these types of groups, being differently
articulated in each. The resulting relativity of both values and morals
is sought to be overcome by a hierarchial view and by an emphasis
on the supreme value of transcendental love and knowledge—the ideal
of *Home Universus* held up in the *Dynamics of Morals*, is a huge
attempt to overcome the crippling relativity arising from his relativistic anthropology. It is not, however, clear how all this is related
to his evolutionism. It is an important aspect of his attempt to reconcile the relativist and absolutist thought that he has laid increasing
emphasis on myth, language, ritual, art and symbolism in general,
especially in their socially integrative roles. In accordance with his
general approach he views not merely society and culture in terms
of symbolism, but gives in turn a sociological analysis of "myths,
ritual, art and symbols" as well. Largely as an extension of this emphasis, but also as a necessity of the gradual development of his
system, he has devoted one of his latest books (*The Symbolic Life of
Man*) to the general theory of symbolism which too is based on the
ideas of hierarchy, level and *Gestalt*. From the very beginning the
key concept in Dr. Mukerjee's thinking has been what he now calls
Multi-dimensional analysis. It is on this foundation that he has attempted to build a general theory of society in his latest writings
("The General Theory of Society" in *Frontiers of Social Science:
Essays in Honour of Radhakamal Murkerji;* and his book, *The Philosophy of the Social Sciences*).

   In his intellectual career Dr. Mukurjee has tried to meet the challenge of the West almost in all forms in which it has come. In the
theoretical sphere, modern Western outlook is empirical, rationalistic
and antimetaphysical. This Dr. Mukurjee meets in two ways. Firstly,
he has criticized all these attitudes, quoting for his support some of

the eminent thinkers of the West itself. Secondly, he has tried to create an outlook which would combine the virtues of both Eastern and Western outlooks. (Whether such a combination would be coherent is another question). In this way what he has tried to do is to produce a modernized Western edition of the traditional world-view.

In the sphere of practice, this leads him to his strong belief in social meliorism, in social work of the American type, and in empirical research; he advocates the abolition of the traditional caste organization and espouses the ideal of an egalitarian and socialist socio-economic organization. Of course, he adduces support for these ideals from the traditional texts—and it is here that the interest, though not the validity, of such efforts lies.

Except for incidental references, he does not examine the sociological theories of Marx, His acceptance of the socialist ideal of society shows how he would meet the challenge of Marxism. In his opinion, the social content of Marxism can be, and should be adopted by India, without, however, accepting the theory from which it is derived in the Marxian system. As to the mode of bringing about this change, he definitely rejects the theory of revolution and would put his faith in persuasion and conversion through the usual democratic media of communication. In accordance with the theory of groups in which the Commonalty with its spontaneous and universal love stands at the head of the series, he rejects class-struggle and exploitation—two basic concepts in Marxian sociology. Other Marxian theories concerning the individual, the society, human motivation and ideological thinking, he seeks to overcome by his multi-dimensional analysis and a holistic outlook in which the natural, the economic, the political, the psychic, the social and the supra-social appear as successive levels or different dimensions (one is not sure, which) of a single reality, the nature of which is left vague. The belief in a non-cyclic philosophy of history and the ideal of a self-directed humanity common to both the Marxian and the non-Marxian modern traditions, is, however, fully shared by Dr. Mukerjee—though this is quite inconsistent with his acceptance of the transcendental and the supra-human.

The bases of Dr. Mukerjee's synthesis of Traditional and Modern thought are the concepts of level, hierarchy and the theory of symbolism; also the methods of reinterpretation and adaptation. These concepts and methods are all traditional. Dr. Mukerjee has, however, used them in a rather arbitrary way without bothering to understand their meaning and dialectic. Thus he combines the concept of level

with a genetic-evolutionary view of order; analysis in terms of levels
with a multi-dimensional analysis; the concept of hierarchy he combines with a systematic-functionalist analysis; sometimes it is used in
the traditional-transcendent context, at others it is used almost synonymously with functional gradation. Consequently, it never strikes him
that an egalitarian and a hierarchial society are opposed types and the
equality implied by the latter is essentially different from that idolized
by the former.

As we remarked earlier the crucial difficulty of any approach in
terms of levels lies in the problem of their continuity. Dr. Mukerjee
has been aware that this can be solved by a general theory of symbolism. The importance of language and symbolism for the study of
society and culture has been greatly emphasized by a number of
thinkers like Mead, Cassirer, Langer and others, and Dr. Mukerjee
has followed them in his previous works. In *The Symbolic Life of
Man* he now attempts to develop a general theory of symbolism. His
undialectical mode of thinking, however, prevents him from realizing
that if the theory of symbolism is to provide the foundation for the
theories of level and hierarchy, it cannot itself be formulated in terms
of these very concepts. His theory of symbolism as usual seeks to combine the empiricist, psychological, the social and the metaphyical
theories of language, but the result is an eclectic theory which is
unduly elastic and viciously circular. It seems that a general theory
of symbolism must enable sociology to avoid psychologism in its various forms, some of which are extremely subtle, and would also help
it meet the challenge of the neo-Wittgenstenians, more particularly
of Wittgenstein himself. Dr. Mukerjee is aware of the danger of
psychologism and it is particularly remarkable that in spite of strong
American influences, he has rejected Parsons' general theory of society.
His own general theory, however, does not provide any tenable alternative in so far as his attempt to integrate the natural and the psychological and the social into the supra-social fails to meet the problem
of discontinuity. His eclecticism and his anxiety to compromise with
the modern spirit likewise prevent him from realizing that there is
a profound difference between the modern functional and the traditional metaphysical interpretation of myths and symbols. In giving
a functional, socio-psychological reinterpretation of traditional myths
and symbols, Dr. Mukerjee overlooks that cultural reinterpretation
is of two types: through one, original meanings are reactivated;
through the other, the old is used to establish the new and this re-

presents a forgetting of the original meanings. Unfortunately it is the second which we find in his works.

Dr. Mukerjee is not a deep thinker: intellectual seriousness is almost foreign to his mode of thought—but this is a common characteristic of much modern thought. His writings are extraordinarily loose and repetitious and full of undigested ideas. Inconsistencies, confusions, and self-contradictions abound in his works. His main sources have been American and German thinkers, but he does not seem to have felt any serious need of reflecting on the incompatibilities of the different modes of thought on which he has drawn throughout.

And yet his contribution to and place in Indian sociological thought are undoubtedly very important. In economics and sociology both, he has made a big effort to meet the challenge of the West. It may be added however, that the logical foundations of his synthesis are weak.

The tendency to view the impact of the West on India from a sociological point of view—not as a problem but as a process—is represented by Professor D. P. Mukerji. The tendency in his earlier writings, *Basic Concepts in Sociology* and *Personality and the Social Sciences* (London: Routledge, 1932 and 1929) is somewhat different. In these works he seems to be concerned with liberalizing the modern Western outlook. It is the idea of harmony which he emphasizes rather than conflict and competition; he is, however, not unaware of their social role. In these writings understanding between India and the West is sought, so to say, within the Western tradition. In his later thought, of which we may take his *Modern Indian Culture* as a good representative, the theme of East and West has assumed greater prominence in the form of the problem of conservation and change of culture. The specific question of the impact of the West on Indian society is seen as a phase in the social process of cultural assimilation and synthesis that has been going on in Indian history almost from the very beginning. It is a common mistake, he points out, to regard the impact of the West as a unique event in Indian history and to think that it has disintegrated India's traditional culture beyond hope. The mistake arises from our conception of Indian culture as something eternally given. Such a view would be unhistorical and arbitrary. The fact is that Indian culture has grown by a series of responses to the successive challenges of so many races and cultures—it is a synthesis. Western impact is the latest phase in this process and the problem is not one of acceptance or rejection but of understanding the laws of cultural synthesis in the context of Indian history. The impact of the West is viewed by him in the context of the Islamic contact. The process of synthesis which Islam had initiated was interrupted by the English conquest. The conquest and the fact that it also represented a major change in the economy constitute the specificity of this phase of Indian history. An important feature of Professor Mukerji's analysis of Indian culture is his emphasis on economic factors in the processes of culture-formation and culture change. It is here that the influence of Marxian thought is most apparent though his analysis cannot be called orthodox Marxist.[8] Professor Mukerji tries to show that the post-British culture of India is at once the flower and the thorn of the socio-economic maladjustment which was occasioned by the failure of the pre-British social economy to develop along historical lines. The earlier middle class, he goes on to show, was replaced by a new middle class that was fostered by the unrealistic policies of land settlement and education. Indian society ceased to be of the "closed" type without becoming "open," with the result that the older agencies of change ceased to function and the fact of Indian culture as a process of tradition-formation was replaced by the idea of mechanical unity likely to fall apart at the slightest clash of middle class-interests.

And yet he has faith in the emergence of a new, stable culture in India; this is because of the role which he assigns to economic forces. In his later thought, however, his view of tradition has undergone an important change and though he lays his emphasis only upon the study of traditions and insists on social change, the orientation is now different and while his latest views do not by any means imply revivalism, the question of a reformation in one or another does certainly arise. It is to be particularly noted that in unequivocally rejecting Parsons' general theory of action—something in itself important in view of the prompt and uncritical acceptance of this theory and its terminology by a majority of Indian social scientists—he puts forward as the alternative the Hindu theory of man and society and not one conceived either in terms of Marx or the Western liberal tradition which he would perhaps have done in the earlier phase of his thought. If the implications of his latest views are seriously followed up they will lead us far beyond Professor Mukerji's present position, for its direction is towards traditional sociology not far removed from that of Coomaraswamy (and Schuon). That, of course, implies the same crucial problem to which we referred in our discussion of Coomaraswamy. Since, however, he has not formulated the problem, the question of a solution does not arise for him. But the problem is there.

The fact that in Professor Mukerji's thought this problem is not sharply posed is connected with his insistence on analysis. Professor Mukerji's importance in Indian sociological thought can not be appreciated on the basis of his books, which are few, or his articles, which are considerable. It is by his teaching, conversation and personal relationships that he has made a most important contribution to the appreciation of the sociological point of view and has influenced the younger generation of scholars. In his teaching, he emphasizes the importance of institutions and the processes of change. He has always advocated the cultivation of a critical, analytical, open-minded attitude towards social problems, insisting however, that one's thinking and analysis must always be rooted in the realities of the situation. Anyone with as keen a mind as Professor Mukerji cannot but be aware that analysis cannot be enough, that in fact all analysis implies or presupposes a metaphysic. He has, however, never allowed to assume the form of a serious problem; nor has he offered orthodox Marxism as a way out. Here, once again, we come upon the predicament of the modern intellectual (cf. Cambridge analysts and linguistic philosophers today).

INDIAN SOCIAL THOUGHT AS SOCIOLOGY

Though we have devoted a good deal of space to theoretical work by Indian sociologists—and this was necessary in our view for a proper orientation—it should not give the impression that there has been considerable work in the theoretical field. In fact, Indian social thought is largely Indian sociology. For reasons that should be clear from the first section, Indian thinkers, with one or two exceptions, have been too much dependent on the West for their theory and have been promptly accepting the changing theoretical frameworks from the West. In this applied field too, almost all the studies have been concerned with the working of Indian institutions in a society which was coming increasingly under the influence of Western industrial socio-economic system. The caste system of India has attracted the attention of almost every scholar and social reformer. The earlier tendency in this field was to seek the origins of this system and to provide a rational—at any rate, an historical—basis for it. The recent tendency is to study the institution of caste in its functional aspects. Dr. Mukerjee early saw the fruitfulness of this approach and Dr. D. N. Majumdar has also advocated a functional view though he has been concerned with the question of origins as well. It is to be noted that what may be called the sociological theory of the caste (or more properly the Varna system) (or even such versions as those of Heard or Ouspensky) has not found acceptance from well-known sociologists or anthropologists in India. (It is, however, accepted by some members of the Sociology Department at Lucknow). Nor has the distinction between Varna and Jati (that is, the principle of hierarchy and the vocational differentiation of the social system) been usually recognized. Hutton, whose work, *Caste in India* (Cambridge, 1946) has a great influence, is aware of this distinction but does not fully realize its importance. An earlier scholar, Mees, who attempted a synthesis of the traditional and the "scientific" psycho-sociological points of view in his theory, systematically distinguishes the Varna from the Jati. But his work did not have much influence and has been generally neglected. It is an indication of the current climate in Indian sociology that little attention has been paid to the theory of Hocart, who was a professional anthropologist and based his theory on comparative anthropological data (*Caste*, London 1950).

But, as we just now said, interest is no longer focused on the origin of the caste, but has shifted to its actual structure and functioning in contemporary society, the change which it has undergone under the impact of modern industrial civilization and the British rule. Recent studies of caste have, therefore, been occupied with caste and credit, caste occupation and economic status, intercaste relations (tensions and distance), caste attitudes, degrees of intercaste connubium, political relationships and caste structures. Another favorite theme has been the relationship between leadership and caste status and the emergence of new castes. Caste has loomed large in village-studies and social surveys too which are the current fashion in India.

Before, however, passing on to these studies and certain features of sociology in Independent India, we should mention some of the more important work in other fields. The institutions investigated are kinship, family and marriage. Dr. Kapadia has written on both *Hindu Kinship* (Bombay: Popular Book Depot, 1947) and *Marriage and Family in India* (Bombay: Popular Book Depot, 1956), while Dr. Ghurye in *Family and Kin in Indo European Culture* (Oxford,

1955) has made a comparative study of the family institution in West and East. Dr. Kapadia describes the growth of kinship, marriage and family on the basis of ancient sources and generally tries to interpret them in terms of modern thought, though any special attempt to show them to be in full conformity with modern thought is not made. Modern family, too, is studied, changes in its structure and functioning are indicated and a brief study of the effects of recent legislation on marriage, divorce and Hindu women's right to property is also made. Dr. Ghurye makes an historical and comparative study of the family among the Indo-Aryans again based on written sources. Dr. Ghurye has also published a study of sex attitudes of American women, *Sexual Behavior of the American Female* (Bombay: Current Book House, 1950), which is based on empirical data collected by others. His conclusions do not always agree with those of Kinsey. Earlier, Dr. Ghurye had made a study of sex attitudes of some Indian men too, but such studies have rarely been made, probably because of strong inhibitions. He has made another notable departure from current interests in making a study of the Indian Sadhus (*Indian Sadhus,* Bombay: Popular Book Depot, 1953). It is an excellent sociography of the various sects and religious organizations, particularly of the four religious centers established by the great Vendantic philosopher, Shakaracharya. Its orientation is in conformity with the efforts of the Indian government to use the Sadhus and their organizations for social welfare work particularly under the Five-Year Plans.

A general study of Hindu social organization has been made by Dr. P. N. Prabhu. As described by the author himself, it is a "socio-psychological study, and looks at the Hindu institutions from the ideological and valuational point of view; . . . Asrama-institutions provide primarily for the *nurture,* the schooling, the psychological development, and the *Varna* institution provides primarily for the *nature,* the given, the biological characteristics of man." The author has tried to show that the principles of Hindu social organization as a whole and of its main institutions are consistent with modern social psychology. He is an excellent representative of the tendency to reconcile tradition and modernism by rationalizing the former in terms of the latter. It is not surprising that, as the author informs us, some critics considered him to be inadequately loyal to tradition while others thought that he had betrayed modernism.

An account of Hindu social theory which would be based on the traditional general theory of language and would thus incidentally meet the challenge of certain tendencies in modern linguistic philosophy particularly of the thought of later Wittgenstein is an important desideratum both in theoretical and applied sociology. Perhaps no work has been done in this direction, Dr. Mukerjee's *Symbolic Life of Man*, being a work that is mainly psychologically oriented. Mention may, however, be made of Mr. S. P. Nagendra's unpublished dissertation at Lucknow University on the Sociological Theory of Ritual in which ritual is considered as a symbolic form from the viewpoint of the traditional theory of language. The thesis, however, stands in need of much further development.

COMMUNITY STUDIES

Village and other monographic studies to which we must now return represent the third basic trend we mentioned at the beginning, namely that of studying the relation of tradition and modernism from the "scientific" viewpoint. (As was hinted earlier, the standpoint actually is scarcely possible here). Most fruitful studies in this area have focused on the various aspects of the village life. Interestingly enough, most of them have been produced by American scholars and those that have been done by Indians have been made, with a few exceptions, in collaboration with American research projects. The method of study has been mostly ethnographic, the techniques employed being interview, and participation observation; also questionnaires done by paid investigators. It has been the belief of students in this field that intensive studies of a few select villages would yield in course of time certain generalizations, firstly, in the field of Indian rural sociology and secondly, in general social theory. With the second end in view, a few comparative studies have also been made. They, however, do not seem to be making much progress. Besides describing the habits and customs, rituals and ceremonies of the people, and the economic structure of the village, most of the authors are concerned with the social structures of the different villages studied in terms of caste rankings and the social and economic relations of the castes. The aim is to discover the determinants of these intercaste rankings, but so far it has been difficult to discover any consistent set of criteria even for a single village—the chances of discovering general principles applicable to Indian rural society as a whole seem, therefore, very remote. Some students of the villages find a correspondence between caste, status and economic condition but the rule does not consistently hold.

An important process which has been noted in this connection is that of "Saskritization" as Dr. Srinivas calls it. By this he means the gradual adoption of Brahman ritual practices and other traits of ancient Hindu culture by inferior caste with consequential rise in their status. This process usually goes along with improvement in economic condition, or sometimes, in political position.

This is connected with a broader problem namely, the problem of relating folk-culture to urban-culture or—to use the terminology of Redfield and Singer—the relation of primary to secondary civilization. The attempt is made to treat the Indian village as a Little Community which has a culture and a world view of its own—the precise meaning of this idea is, however, not clear to this author. The problem, then is to relate these "Little Communities" to what is called the "great tradition" of "the greater communities." This naturally assumes that the Indian village is an isolable unity—but this is obviously doubtful. In *Village India*, McKim Marriott[9] has sharply posed these problems, but has not insisted on any rigorous solution—a characteristic of much modern thinking. He is content with the suggestion that the village —the Little Community in this latest jargon—be treated as a "small half world!" He has devised two concepts for understanding the mutual relations of little and great tradition—one of them being closely similar to "Sanskritization." They are called "universalization" and "parochialization." The former is used to designate the carrying forward and upward not only of cultural awareness but also of cultural contents. "Parochialization" is "the reverse process of localization, or limitation upon the scope of intelligibility, of deprivation of literary form, of reduction of parochialization constitutes the characteristic creative work of little communities within India's indigenous civilization."

This approach to rural sociology is being accepted by a number of Indian social scientists without critical examination. It represents another attempt—this time from the standpoint of cultural anthropology—to understand the state of traditional society and culture of India in terms of the assumptions of modern thought. Such an attitude implies a refusal to understand tradition in its own terms.

This is not the place to examine this approach in a systematic manner, but it must be pointed out that the distinction is made in the wrong way. The idea of a great and a little tradition is not wholly unwarranted—traditional thought distinguishes between the Greater and the Lesser Mysteries. But there it does not refer to evolutionary-

genetic processes and the relation between the two is essentially typological and only incidentally historical. The distinction between
"parochialization" and "universalization" obscures the vital difference
between processes of decadence and creativity. It is held that parochialization is the reverse to universalization. In terms of the meaning
given to the respective concepts it can only mean that the former is
a devolution and hence no upward movement can be traced from the
little to the great tradition. But the main point of the approach
represented by the author is to show that the Great Traditions have
evolved from the Little Traditions. For this reason the distinction is
formulated in value-neutral terms. The way he uses the concept of
"culture content" suggests that the same culture content could be
"parochialized" and "universalized" alternatively—which would be un-
intelligible unless this "content" were something transcendental.

A trend of thought that is critical of current village studies and
the ethnographical-monographic method in general is, however, slowly
emerging. It has been pointed out that these monographs have not
been confined to describing a specific village alone (not that it could
be done); a number of implicit or explicit generalizations have also
been made, which are unwarranted not only because inducted from
insufficient data but also because evidence to the contrary has been
cited.[11] Most of these studies have been made in a period from 6 to 18
months. It has been pointed out that this is too short a period for a
proper understanding of the region studied—and this is particularly so
in the case of foreign scholars. In the circumstances, distortions, exaggerations and important omissions can hardly be avoided. The only
person who seems to have realized this obvious requirement of empirical study is Mrs. Iravati Karve who has planned a ten-year long
social survey of a single region (see the appended list), otherwise we
seem to have accepted the empirical-individualistic methodology (particularly as developed in America) so completely that any examination
of its logic, presuppositions and requirements is considered morbid.

It is to be noted that most of these village studies and other surveys
(see *Village India* and *India's Villages and Rural Profiles*) have been
undertaken in free India in collaboration with American universities
or learned foundations (with one or two exceptions where English
universities have collaborated with Indian universities). Often it has
been with the concurrence of the Government of India. In fact, some
of them were commissioned by them. This indicates an important
tendency in postwar sociology in India. Independence has brought an

important change in the attitude of the Indian social scientist. While in one sense the problem has continued to be the same, namely the relation between the active (West) and passive (East) modes of disintegration[12] of the Tradition, the difference in orientation is important. In pre-independent India, no sociologist could feel wholly at ease in accepting Western civilization for it was associated with our subjection to Britain.[13] And hence there was a bias in favor of specifically Eastern and Indian values. Though revivalism was never seriously advocated in academic sociology, change was envisaged more in terms of reform and adaptation than in terms of replacement. The danger of strengthening foreign political rule through acceptance of foreign culture being over, the major problem for most of the Indian sociologists is how best to effect the transition of India from a backward society to a fully industrialized, "open" society. The dominant trend accordingly is to make an intensive study of the actual state of affairs both in the villages and the cities with a view to finding out how best the general characteristics, attitudes, habits and means of communication could be utilized for introducing, without too much maladjustment, economic and technological changes and corresponding emergent social relationships.

SOCIOLOGY AND SOCIAL ENGINEERING

India's commitment to planning has given a new turn to sociological research. In the opinion of the Planning Commission, there must be a regular arrangement for gauging the effects of changes introduced in the course of implementing the plans so that better methods of making the changes take root may be found and necessary modifications may be introduced in the plans. For this purpose they have set up a regular research section called the Programme Evaluation Organization. It finances various universities and research centers for undertaking socio-economic surveys and other projects to study the impact and chain effects of changes already introduced —in short to discover scientific devices to help the state in the task of transforming a tradition-haunted (backward) society into one that is *modern* and fully industrialized. Hence the most important topics and areas of research now are—sociological economic surveys of different regions with special reference to family and caste patterns; effects of technological changes and social and economic legislation; group and class

attitudes, media of communications, social stratification and leadership. The Planning Commission having accepted the view that India
is over-populated, family-planning is another area of research which
will be increasingly cultivated.

The role of the social scientist is very differently conceived now—
he is a social engineer rather than a theoretician. The President of
the First Sociological Conference asked the sociologist to study Indian
traditions—of the Second, held in December, 1956, thinks of his goals
and methods in a different way: "If social relations at any stage of
development hinder or hamper the historical productive relations,
that is, the relationship of man to nature, the only way to avert catastrophic cultural blow up is to modify the existing social relations.
Here comes the real role of a sociologist, for, in this sense, his discipline represents an instrument of social policy. With his expert knowledge of social relationships, the sociologist can help predict, control
and direct social change and speed up social progress. . . . It is in the
field of causation and change that the sociologist's role of an engineer
for the community rebuilding is manifest. The academician-sociologist
in his role of social engineer has an important contribution to make
in solving social problems. And it is here that the competence and
ingenuity of the sociologist are put to test."

It is of great significance that while the outgoing President of the
Conference (D. P. Mukerji), long recognized as one of the leading
Marxian scholars of India, pleads for the study of traditions and says
that *the thing changing* is more important than change *per se*, the
present President, never known for Marxism, thinks in terms of historical productive relations. None of them perhaps wants a full-fledged
communist society in India, but while Mukerji's reaction reveals a
Brahmin soul's resigned hope, Majumdar's shows the optimism and
enthusiasm of a modern Indian social scientist under the influence
of the West (particularly America).

Another feature, not unconnected with this, is that social research
is increasingly becoming a huge financial proposition and this, in the
circumstances, means that it should be financed by the State. A vested
interest is thus being created affecting the freedom of the sociologist
—where the financing agency is the Government, the pressures and
compulsives may work on several levels. There would also be a tendency for inferior people to be drawn into research. As the financial
aspects assume increasing importance, the choice of areas and themes
of research will have a tendency to pass out of the social scientist's

hands. In this process fundamental theoretical research and thinking will suffer, affecting adversely the quality of applied and empirical research too.

Interdisciplinary approach to social problems, particularly the ethnographic, is a third feature of recent research in India. It has its dangers.

More important, however, is another feature namely, the collaboration of foreign, mainly American agencies. There has been a growing feeling against it. About two years back, six social scientists of Lucknow University expressed their opposition in a joint letter to the Press.[14] The signatories had their "serious doubts about the theoretical validity of modern methods of empirical research" and hence they failed to see the necessity of associating with our research schemes a large number of Americans and other foreigners who were "supposed to be experts in these methods." They, however made it emphatically clear that they were not advocating anything like Indianization of research; for, in their opinion, this type of patriotism or loyalty was wholly misplaced in the academic world. They go on to say that,

> "Persons familiar with the writings of such thinkers as Sorokin, Voeglin, Wiener, Langer, Coomaraswamy, René Guénon and Schuon will have no hesitation in asserting that in bringing our world to this helpless state the methods, orientation and underlying values of modern social sciences have played an important part. We would like to point out that most of the modern research methods and tools which these foreign experts are using have been implicitly designed to serve commercial purposes and are now being adapted to military objectives. This is why all American research projects in India are concentrating on Communication, Culture Contact, Social Stratification and Public Administration. These fields are strategic for Commercial and military purposes, an awareness of which is reflected in their questionnaires."

This letter did have an effect, but it did not have the type of effect the signatories wanted, one reason was that it raised questions of a fundamental order about the purposes and presuppositions of research in the human social sciences and this has disturbing implications. It may be that an accurate and detailed knowledge of "what is" gives the sociologist power to predict "what will be" and hence also power to direct it.[15] But what is the status and *bonafide* of those who would thus control, and what is the status of those who would be thus controlled? And what about the "new society" in whose birth the social scientist wants to aid? A fusion, or synthesis of tradition and modernism is, as we have shown in the first section of this chapter, a vain hope. The concept of understanding as put forward by Guénon is again not helpful. Do we then accept the values that have brought the world to the brink of utter annihilation? The Indian sociologist, like the Indian economist, is too much preoccupied with his country's "backwardness" to realize the dreadful urgency of these questions. But is there a way out for him, if he did attend to these questions?[16]

SELECTED BIBLIOGRAPHY

Howard Becker & Harry Elmer Barnes, *Social Thought from Lore to Science* (Washington, D.C.: Harren Press, 1952), II, Chapter XXIX, "India," 1135-1147. A good summary, with bibliographical notes.

A. K. Coomaraswamy, *The Dance of Shiva* (Bombay: Asia Publishing House, 1948); *Figures of Speech or Figures of Thought* (London: Lucac & Co., 1948). The author is discussed in this chapter.

Rollin Chambliss, *Social Thought* (New York: The Dryden Press, 1954), Chapter V, "Ancient India," 102-124, good on the roots of India's social theory; bibliography, 448-449.

S. C. Dubey, *Indian Village* (London: Routledge & Kegan Paul, 1955). A good example of community studies.

G. S. Ghurye, *Caste and Class in India* (Bombay: Popular Book Depot, 1950); *Culture and Society* (Oxford, 1947).

J. H. Hutton, *Caste in India* (Cambridge: University Press, 1946 & 1951).

A. M. Hocart, *Caste* (London: Methuen, 1950); *Social Origins* (London: Watts & Co., 1954).

K. M. Kapadia, *Hindu Kinship* (Bombay: Popular Book Depot, 1947); *Marriage and Family in India* (Bombay: Popular Book Depot, Depot, 1955).

R. Mukerjee, *The Social Structure of Values* (London: Macmillan, 1949); *Social Ecology* (London: Macmillan, n.d.); "The Social Conception of Religion," *Sociology and Social Research*, XIII, 517-525; Mukerjee & N. S. Sen-Gupta, *An Introduction to Social Psychology* (Boston: D. C. Heath, 1928). Representative works of the famed Indian thinker.

D. P. Mukerji, *Basic Concepts in Sociology* (London: Paul, Trench, Trubner & Co., 1932); *Modern Indian Culture* (Allahabad: Indian Publishers, 1942); *Views and Counterviews* (Lucknow: Universal Publishers, 1946).

McKim Marriott, Ed., *Village India* (University of Chicago Press, 1955).

D. N. Majumdar, Ed., *Rural Profiles* (Lucknow: Ram Advani, 1955); author: *The Matrix of Indian Culture* (Lucknow, 1946).

P. N. Prabhu, "Indian Sociology and the Dharma Sastras," in *Progress of India Studies*, edited by Poona Dandekar (1942); *Hindu Social Organization* (Bombay: Popular Book Depot, 1954).

Max Weber, *The Hindu Social System*, trans. by Hans Gerth & Don Martindalee (Minneapolis: University of Minnesota Sociology Club Bulletin, No. 1, 1950). Although Weber never visited India, he wrote a classic analysis.

H. Zimmer, *Myths and Symbols in Indian Civilizations* (London: Routledge & Kegan Paul, 1946); *Philosophies of India* (London: Routledge & Kegan Paul, 1952).

A. K. Saran is lecturer in Sociology, University of Lucknow (India).

NOTES

1. This does not necessarily commit the author to a belief in the situational or existential determination of thought. The author maintains that the major problem for modern Indian sociology was set by the situation indicated—that an independent shift in thought might have been an important factor in the genesis of the situation is not thereby denied.

2. A. K. Coomaraswamy, *The Bugbear of Literacy* (London: Dennis Dobson, 1949), 1.

3. Coomaraswamy, *Figures and Speech or Figures of Thought* (London: Luzac & Co., 1946), 218-219.

4. Coomaraswamy, *The Bugbear of Literacy*, 74.

5. A. K. Coomaraswamy, *Why Exhibit Works of Art* (London: Luzac & Co., 1943), 87.

6. Limitations of space do not allow us to discuss even briefly the work of other less recent important sociologists, such as Dr. Bhagavan Das, Aurobindo Ghosh, Sri Aurobindo, etc.

7. Radhakamal Mukerjee, *Principles of Comparative Economics* (London: P. S. King & Co., 1922); *Borderlands of Economics* (London, 1925).

8. Marxist sociology has not developed in India in a systematic manner. Mr. B. N. Dutta's Studies in *Indian Social Polity* is a Marxist interpretation of the caste system in which its origin is traced from the formation of economic classes. It will not stand careful critical examination. Mr. S. A. Dange's *India from Primitive Communism to Slavery* (Bombay: People's Publishing House, 1949) is a Marxist interpretation of Indian history which has, however, been unacceptable to Marxists themselves. Dr. D. Kesambi's essay "The Basis of Ancient Indian History" (*Journal of American Oriental Society*, LVX, 1955) is also an attempt to see Indian history from an economic angle.

9. McKim Marriott, "Little Communities in an Indigenous Civilization," in *Village India* (Chicago: American Anthropological Association, Memoir No. 23, 1955).

10. *Ibid.*, 200.

11. See N. S. Reddy, "Need for Sociological Stepping-stones in Indian Village Studies" (Presidential Address read to the Second All-India Sociological Conference, Patna, 1956). Dr. Majumdar's plea for fundamental research in sociology also implied dissatisfaction with the current emphasis on applied and monographic work.

12. See Frichjof Schuon, *Spiritual Perspectives and Human Facts* (London: Faber and Faber, 1954), 22.

13. Though by no means a revivalist or a believer in sociological archaism—on the contrary a great social innovator—Mahatma Gandhi was fully and rather un-compromisingly aware of the bond between alien culture and alien rule. (See A. J. Toynbee, *A Study of History*, vol. VIII, Oxford, 1954, 546-47). A study of Gandhi's sociological ideas would be valuable but cannot be attempted here.

14. *National Herald* (Lucknow, March 21, 1955). Subsequently this letter was circulated among all the members of the Indian Parliament.

15. For a brief exposition of these points see the present writer's "Methodological Foundations of Empirical Research in Sociology," Paper presented to the First All-India Sociological Conference, Dehra Dun, 1955; published in the *Agra University Research Journal (Letters)* (December, 1955).

16. The author is grateful to Professor D. N. Majumdar for his kind help in the preparation of this chapter.

INDONESIA AND SOUTHEAST ASIA

Justus van der Kroef
University of Bridgeport

The lag in indigenous scientific advancement, so characteristic of all new nation states of Southeast Asia, is in the case of Indonesia particularly evident in the field of the social sciences. Modern Sociology in Indonesia, though showing promise of bearing valuable fruit in the near future, is as yet in its infancy, and insofar as it is the work of Indonesians themselves (as opposed to the labors of various Dutch social scientists in the colonial period), it has hardly begun. This retardation is not only the result of a combination of historical factors, related to the political development of the country, it stems also from certain social structural and cultural problems and inclinations which are conspicuous at present. For purposes of this discussion these two sets of factors may perhaps be analyzed separately under the headings of (1) evolution of Indonesian Sociology and (2) problems of Indonesian Sociology today.

EVOLUTION OF INDONESIAN SOCIOLOGY

Although examples of sociological analysis acceptable to the canons of modern science cannot be dated earlier than the last hundred years or so, Indonesian descriptions of man in relation to his social environment are much older by far. Even if these do not meet the rigorous standards of latter day inquiry they remain valuable sources to the contemporary social scientist. With this in mind we may divide the development of Indonesian sociology into three phases, (1) the pre-colonial era, (2) the colonial period and (3) the stage of national independence, with the additional observation that modern scientific sociology does not make its appearance until late in the second period.

The Pre-Colonial Era. Prior to the sixteenth century and the coming and gradual consolidation of Dutch power over the various parts of the Indonesian archipelago, important and more or less unified

1035

political and social structures had emerged, flourished and perished there. Autonomous harbor principalities, inland states and even empires, had existed side by side with tribal societies of lesser cultural complexity in various degrees of isolation. Most of these political and social units—it is difficult to accord all of them the term "states"—attained a measure of internal stability and structural continuity that came to be reflected in accepted folkways and usages, symbolized by emblems and totemic insignes, as well as by inscriptions, genealogical tables, court histories, and cycles of legends and myths. Particularly in the Western part of Indonesia, where Hindu-Indian cultural influences during the first eight centuries of the Christian era were strong if intermittent, ancient scriptural data have been found of inestimable value to the historian as well as to the social scientist. For example, the body of literature left by the *mandala*, more or less independent estates or communities under priestly-clerical control, as well as guilds of smiths, weavers, and potterers, provide important data and insights into inter-group interaction in some of the major Hinduized principalities, into the structure of society, the division of labor and patterns of social control of pre-colonial Western Indonesia. In the written *çasana* or charters of these various more or less independent communities and associations not only an attempt has been made to describe the different roles and status of each participant with a certain exactitude, but also one may find descriptions of other vocational or clerical associations and their mutual dependence on (and often ill concealed antipathy for) the court center and its aristocracy.[1]

Of equal importance are the court histories and genealogies, the work of a special group of clerics and literati, whose major task was to legitimize new dynasties and new political constellations in terms of established public philosophy and mythology. To that end the historical facts were unquestionably altered and falsified, yet to dismiss them as mere court inspired frauds is to seriously misread their purpose. For these myths and court records cannot be divorced from the concept of literary magic as it prevailed in Indonesian cultural traditions: the written or spoken word of the priest-literatus was believed to possess an actual *creative* function, that is to bring about as truth that which he uttered.[2] Rewriting the records of society meant to recreate the historical and social facts retroactively in accordance with dynastic ambition. The importance of this tendency will be explained later in this essay. Suffice it to mention here the sociological character of such pieces of court literature as the *Nagara-kertagama*, a lengthy narrative poem completed in 1365 by Prapantja, the head of Buddhist clerics in the Java centered kingdom, Madja-pahit. *Nagarakertagama*, notwithstanding its often tortuous lyrical embellishments, provides what in all probability we can accept as a reasonably accurate description of Madjapahit court society, its eco-logical and social structure, its recreations and opulence, its relations with the inhabitants of the kingdom and so on. More directly gene-alogical is the literary pendant to the *Nagarakertagama*, the *Para-raton* or "Books of Kings," setting forth dynastic vicissitudes spanning several centuries. Like other *babad* (chronicles), folk tales and legends, this pre-colonial Indonesian literature is often uninten-tionally sociological in character, in that under the creative magic, literary flourish, religious motive or ontological intent there lies the hard core of a record of the social process, of class interaction and of social control, interpreted in the light of autochthonous tradition.

The Colonial Period. Impelled by the search for commercial pro-fits the early Dutch in Indonesia at first subordinated all interests to economic gain. Consolidating their monopolies in production and trade through the medium of such a semi-political agency as the Dutch East India Company (1602-1800), proved to be impossible, however, without acquisition of territories and entrepots and thereby control-ling portions of the conglomerate inhabitants of the Indian islands. Of necessity, and to a large extent against their will, Dutch traders became administrators, suzerains and judges over an alien population, a knowledge of whose laws and customs in turn became indispensable to a smooth and above all an inexpensive functioning of their com-mercial apparatus. Law was therefore the father of sociology in Indo-nesia, and in later centuries there remained a close connection between ethnological and sociographic inquiry on the one hand and Indonesian law, written or unwritten, on the other. In the period of the Dutch East India Company legal-sociological research was of necessity limited in scope and fraught with error, yet such compila-tions as Fryer's *Compendium* (1754), commissioned to ascertain the nature of Indonesian customs from "native chieftains and priests as well as other Muslim legal scholars," have more than historic value. More generally sociographical is the survey of the Reverend François Valentijn, *Oudt en Nieuw Oost Indien* (East India Old and New), published between 1742-1726, which despite its Calvinistic prejudices and allusions to classical literature still manages to present a lively if not always accurate description of Indonesian customs, history and relations with the Dutch.

Worthy of special mention is the "corporation analysis" of one of the East India Company's own attorneys, Pieter van Dam, whose *Beschrijvinge der Ooost-Indische Compagnie (Description of the East India Company)*, written as a memoir early in the eighteenth century for the benefit of the Company's executive and only later published, provides us with an exhaustive survey of the bureaucratic structure of the Company, its formal and informal means of social control, its political and diplomatic methods, as well as its commercial operations.

With the gradual expansion of Dutch authority in the nineteenth century ethnology and the study of law received new impulses as well. During the Napoleonic period most of the Dutch possessions in Indonesia had fallen into the hands of the English. The English Lieutenant Governor over Java, Thomas Stamford Raffles, published in 1817 a *History of Java*, which for its time delved far and deep into Indonesian concepts of law, landownership and labor, political power and administration, drama as well as the plastic arts. It was to remain a vademecum for Dutch administrators long after the English interregnum. Increasingly, in the first half of the nineteenth century, we note the appearance of published articles and reports, in literary as well as scientific journals published in Indonesia, dealing with ethnological topics. Dutch scientific curiosity in Indonesia was awakening as the Dutch flag was planted more firmly through the remoter parts of the Indonesian archipelago. The second half of the nineteenth century saw the beginnings of that vast range of scientific research which was to bring renown to such pioneers as J. H. Kern in philology, J. L. Brandes in archeology, and C. P. Rouffaer in ethnology. The work of all of these has remained of value to the sociologist in Indonesia today, not the least because of their wide, interdisciplinary interests and approach. Within this era also falls much of the labor of the renowned Islam scholar, C. Snouck Hurgronje, whose monumental study of *The Achinese* (1893-1894) is perhaps the first complete cross cultural area study in Indonesian sociology. Snouck's later contributions to the field of Indonesian Islam are also of lasting importance to the sociology of religion. Painstaking gathering of ethnological fact likewise characterized the work of civil servants like G. A. Wilken, and of missionaries like N.

Adriani and A. C. Kruyt. Adriani's and Kruyt's joint study of the Toradja societies of Sulawesi (Celebes) has still not been superseded. In this connection mention must also be made of the monographs by F. D. van Ossenbruggen and Kleiweg de Zwaan, who were perhaps among the first to apply a cultural anthropological approach to Indonesian mores and social institutions.

Again, however, it was law that provided the chief impetus for further social scientific inquiry. In the annals of discovery and systematic analysis of Indonesian unwritten law and judicial concepts Professor C. Van Vollenhoven towers above all others. The training of the colonial civil service became increasingly important also, and in consequence, the University of Leyden, where until the nineteen thirties most Dutch officials were trained, became the font of a stream of reports and dissertations written by van Vollenhoven's students dealing with the legal process in various Indonesian societies. Of necessity these studies, though from a modern sociological point of view lacking in the requisite theoretical technique and formulations, dealt with the entire social structure of the Indonesian groups whose legal systems they brought under examination, so that even today they are a veritable treasure trove for Indonesian sociology. Later the University of Utrecht and the Law College in Djakarta (then Batavia) contributed to this fund of information. Yet it is noteworthy that Indonesian ethnology and cultural anthropology in the twentieth century under such scholars as H. T. Fischer, J. de Josselin de Jong and J. Duyvendak and their students made gigantic strides forward, but that the field of sociology proper, as distinct also from law, did not reach a comparable level of development. Indeed a separate faculty of the social sciences was absent from Dutch universities and from the higher educational system in Indonesia until after the Second World War; most students wishing to specialize in the social sciences being compelled to take their work under the Faculties of Literature and Philosophy or Law. In consequence the careful accumulation of social scientific data in the dissertations on law, for example, remained unleavened by sociological theory; indeed the development of theory has thus far not been the *forte* of Dutch sociologists in Indonesia or outside of it. In the realm of cultural anthropology the situation was somewhat better: the dissertations written under the mentorship of de Josselin de Jong do exhibit in many instances a broader conceptual base and a familiarity with the current methodological literature.

Finally, it must be noted that such investigations as touched most directly upon sociological field work often occurred under official auspices. A good illustration are the admirable labors of the Statistical Office of the colonial government's Department of Economic Affairs, compiler of, among other data, the results of the general census. Interest in and development of statistical method was not lacking in the activities of the Office or of its predecessors.[3] Primarily sociological in character were also the publications of other governmental departments, surveys by special commissions of inquiry, and welfare reports in the early decades of the present century. Among all these special mention must be made of the exhaustive multivolume analysis of "The Diminishing Welfare of the Native Population of Java and Madura" (1905-1914),[4] the report by the outstanding government sociologist and historian B. O. Schrieke on the processes of social disorganization and the political disturbancees on the West Coast of Sumatra (1928),[5] the study of the tax burden imposed on the Indonesian population on islands beyond Java,[6] the report of the mode of living of coolies of the municipality of Batavia in 1937,[7] and the report of the so-called "Coolie Budget Commission" on the standard of living of plantation workers and peasants in Java (1939-1941).[8]

National Independence. Since officially acquiring her independence from the Netherlands in December, 1949, sociological research in Indonesia has,—at least on paper—taken a larger flight. Both the revolutionary struggle against the Dutch and the character of the Indonesian Republic reflect a popular ideology in which the social function of the state, in the sense of providing equal opportunities to all citizens regardless of sex, race or religion, of taking all such measures as are deemed essential to the public welfare, and of guiding existing social processes to desirable ends in keeping with official national ideology, is stressed very heavily. As a result there is hardly a department of government in Indonesia today, which does not engage, in some form or another, in sociological research and planning, whether it involves community development and the propagation of new settlements for migrants, urban reconstruction, establishment of welfare services for the population, or promulgation of measures to give the Indonesian a greater share in the complex functioning of the national economy. This emphasis on social reconstruction, as part of the general upbuilding of the nation, contrasts sharply with the often haphazard socio-economic planning or, more often, even deliberate refusal to interfere in the social process, of the colonial era.

At the same time, however, Indonesia has such a dearth of qualified technicians, including social scientists, and has experienced such aggravated problems of political and economic stability, that the grandiose plans are many years this side of initial implementation.

As in the colonial era much actual sociological field work is conducted under official or semi-official auspices. At the same time in many of the—state controlled—centers of higher learning, sociological theory and field techniques are being taught for the first time. The University of Indonesia in Djakarta may, at the moment, be said to have something of a lead in this respect over the younger, regional universities and private institutions of higher learning. An illustration is the *Lembaga Penjelidikan Ekonomi dan Masjarakat* (Institute of Economic and Social Research), of the Djakarta School of Economics, University of Indonesia, which has done promising work in a variety of fields, many of them related to the national reconstruction effort. Mention may be made for example of the Institute's Report, drafted with the cooperation of the National Planning Bureau and the Department of Industries, of the present stage of the government's program on industries.[9] After a survey of the aims of the industrial program the report notes in critical fashion why thus far "industrial development in our country is still far from the point of having reached momentum." Of sociological significance are the references in the report to the attempt at organization of production on the basis of central manufacturing and processing units (*induks*) in an effort to improve output, quality, and marketing procedures, to "the desperate conditions of public administration with particular reference to the agencies with industrial development," and to the marketing problems of industrial entrepreneurs in an underdeveloped economy. It cannot be doubted that the Institute's analysis is a major economic, as well as sociological contribution. The *Lembaga* has thus far also published an informative study of social movements and patterns of social change in the capital city of Djakarta, undertaken at the instigation of UNESCO.[10] The government Agricultural College in Bogor (West Java) has conducted useful research into sociological aspects of land tenure and land usage in a number of rural areas in West and Central Java. Yet another illustration of sociological work being carried on by a government agency are the "Economical Development" reports published by the *Biro Perantjang Negara* (Natonal Planning Bureau), reports which also contain useful informaton on recent population trends, the development of education, the work of cooperatives and so on. A recent Bureau report also is a general survey of census problems in Indonesia, a question all the more acute since no general census has been held in the country since 1930.[11] An instance of sociological inquiry being conducted on an interdepartmental basis in the Indonesian government is the recent report on Indonesia's population, prepared by officials in the Health, Agriculture, and Labor Ministries, the Department of Transmigration, the Central Bureau of Statistics and the National Planning Bureau.[12] The official or semi-official character of so much social scientific field work is also for the time being a typical feature of sociology in Indonesia today.

Individual sociological work, though as often as not carried on by government officials or advisors, has tended to follow existing paths or to concentrate upon old questions that usually have some public significance. For example, the recent studies of Kurt Horstmann, formerly affiliated with the National Planning Bureau, suggest new aspects of the population problem,[13] while the concern with law, also in its sociological aspects, is as intense as ever,[14] and interest in the social correlates of economic development[15] is equally in evidence. The heterogenous composition of Indonesia's population and the social interaction and cultural position of various minorities has yielded two recent analyses, both by Indonesians of Chinese descent.[16] Mention should also be made of the work of H. J. Heeren, lecturer in sociology at the University of Indonesia, who has done much to organize the field in the country since the Second World War.[17]

As the Indonesian area has begun to arouse increasing popular as well as scholarly interest in other countries of the world, the number of foreign experts going to the region for their field work may be expected to grow. It would be impossible to mention all of these foreign researchers, not a few of whom are moreover in the employ of the government. Mention has already been made of the work of Kurt Horstmann. The publications of A. M. de Neumann and S. Daniel Neumark, though more particularly concerned with economic problems are not without value for the sociologist.[18] The Canadian demographer N. Keyfitz has published valuable surveys and interpretations of Indonesia's unevenly distributed populations and its problems.[19] Among the American sociologists who have been working in the area mention should be made first of all of Raymond Kennedy, whose tragic death at the hands of assassins in Java in 1950, cut short a long term research project, of which some preliminary field notes have been published.[20] Paul M. Kattenburg's study of a central Javanese village in 1950 continues a type of survey work of which much more is needed for our understanding of social changes at the rural level.[21] In this connection the project of a group of ten Harvard graduate students, who under the direction of the philologist, Rufus Hendon made a socio-economic analysis of a Javanese town is especially commendable.[22] The present author, on the basis of two field trips since the Second World War, has published surveys of the position of ethnic minorities in Indonesia, as well as analyses of various aspects of social and cultural change.[23]

As was the case before the Second World War the contribution of the Dutch to sociology in Indonesia continues to be a majar one, notwithstanding the exodus of Dutch scholars and the worsening relations between Holland and Indonesia. Actual field work by Dutch researchers has tended to diminish somewhat in the last ten years, but worthy of note are the investigations of E. Allard of the social conditions of the Eurasian minority in Bogor and the Minehassa area, the analyses of H. T. Chabot of Makassarese and Buginese society in Sulawesi and of the transmigration of inhabitants of the Sangihe and Talaud islands to South Sulawesi,[24] and lastly the ethnological inquiries of G. J. Held on Sumbawa island, the latter research being prematurely terminated by Held's unexpected death in 1954. In the Netherlands proper sociological studies of Indonesia has received a new impetus with the labors of W. F. Wertheim of the University of Amsterdam,[25] and the publication in the English language of social scientific studies on Indonesia by various Dutch scholars, published for the Royal Tropical Institute of Amsterdam with the assistance of the Dutch Organization for Pure Research.[25]

PROBLEMS OF INDONESIAN SOCIOLOGY

There are, as the Indonesian legal historian G. J. Resink has pointed out, several paths through the dense jungle of Indonesian history, that is several forms of historiography, both Indonesian and "Western," each of which has its own type of literature, and a somewhat different attitude toward reality.[27] The problem is not different in Indonesian sociology, here too, there are different approaches to the manner and purpose of recording and analyzing the social process. To a large extent the fundamental distinction between the tradi-

tional Indonesian and modern Western methods is a difference between assigning a subjective function to the former and an objective
to the latter. To Indonesian tradition, science, including "social"
science, has a magically creative function, the written or spoken
word of those competent to utter it, establishes reality, not merely
reflects or describes it. Historiography in this view is not only a
description of history, but it is a creating of history in conformity
with desired objectives; it is the same with the study of society. The
advent of a modern scientific temper as part of incisive "Western"
acculturation processes has by no means obliterated this tradition.
Words, slogans and reports have a tendency to be regarded in a
"realist" (i.e. in the medieval scholastic sense) light: they are "true,"
or by their very utterance or publication they establish "truth." [28]

One consequence has been an unusual apprehension on the part
of the present public authorities of the power of the printed or
spoken word over the still untutored mass, as evidenced by the
provision of severe penalties for those who utter alleged falsehoods
about or are attempting to bring discredit to the chief state officials.
Indonesia's unstable political condition has undoubtedly been another
factor in the promulgation of such measures. Hence sociological
inquiry is hampered because of its potential critical character; to
report an undesirable condition in society is not only to attack by
implication various leaders and officials, frequently extremely nationally conscious, it is also to establish the truth in the untutored
mind of the situation existing, even if in fact that situation did not
exist before,—and thus it becomes, or can be interpreted by those
influenced by the subjective function of science, as an act of *lèse
majesté,* an attack on state and society and their magic and supernatural foundations as these are believed to prevail in the Indonesian world view. In the opinion, therefore, of one knowledgeable
sociologist teaching at the University of Indonesia, among the reasons why sociology in Indonesia has hardly gained momentum is the
fact that there is "a certain apprehension to publish," so that "the
results of possible research remain *in camera*": [29]

> Inasmuch as every objective social inquiry may be compelled to
> note inadequacies, this is sometimes felt as criticism of persons
> and conditions. It is understandable that this is appreciated the
> less if such criticism is of foreign origin. In order to avoid such
> sensitive spots one chooses either innocent subjects or confines
> the circulation of reports to a small circle, the latter also in

order to prevent that such reports get into the hands of pressure groups.

Unquestionably related to the reluctance of the Indonesian sociologist to publish his findings is the fact that in most cases he is in some kind of government service and must of necessity accept some limitation on his freedom of expression. The relative absence in Indonesia today of a class of specialists and professionally trained *not* dependent in some form or another for their position and livelihood on the government makes its deleterious influence felt also in this connection.[30] Indonesia sadly lacks qualified technicians of all sorts, and in view of the government's ambitious development programs it is understandable that some form of government service is indicated for most of those with special skills. Moreover, there is a steady effort at "Indonesianization" of all faculties in institutions of higher learning, in consequence of which the few available Indonesian specialists must do double duty, in teaching as well as in government service, leaving little time or occasion for research and publication, which as often as not, seem to be relegated to visiting foreign scholars.[31] Even the means of publication, given the presence of available data, are barely developed. Indonesia has no national sociological society, nor any periodical devoted to sociological research. Matter of sociological interest is often published in journals specializing in related social science fields, such as economics, or must be published abroad, or else appear in condensed and popular form in newspapers.[32] On the other hand, the Indonesian scholar usually finds national publishers eager to publish his findings in book form, while a rash of literary and political and cultural periodicals also provide an outlet of sorts.

Yet none of the "technical" problems of bringing Indonesian sociological studies to a level of greater productivity can compare in gravity with the question of the particular political and cultural instability in which Indonesia has found itself since attaining her independence, and which inevitably exercises influence upon all scientific research, including that in the social sciences. There are in the country, it would seem, two more or less opposing trends in political and cultural life, one of which seems most "Western minded," is receptive to the rapid adoption and application of modern Western concepts of scientific research and organization, to highly rationalized principles of administrative efficiency in all phases of public life, and is perhaps the most skeptical toward its own nationalist ideologies. The other is more "tradition" or "history" minded, unshakenly convinced of the mystiques of its own nationalism, frequently favoring ineptitude and incompetence over "Western efficiency" so long as things are done in an "Indonesian way" and abide by near zenophobic standards of social value and utility.[33] The Indonesian sociologist, anxious to apply the criteria and methods of the former trend, may find himself in collision with the latter, he too—as it has by now become a truism to remark— is a prisoner of his country's nationalism. Dispassionate scientific inquiry is not apt to flourish in a climate of extreme political passions, aroused by nameless anxieties and popular frustrations.

It is hoped in many Indonesian quarters that with the development of education not only the volume of scientific research will increase but that popular support and appreciation of the endeavors of national scientists will increase in proportion, so that the intellectual climate of the country will be such as to favor the publication of research results, even if these are critical of existing conditions. Without necessarily dashing this expectation, one is bound to point out several formidable obstacles that lie in the path of its realization. Indonesia inherited from the colonial period a severely inadequate educational system, which left more than 80% of the Indonesians illiterate. Since the attainment of independence popular education, particularly in the sense of promoting literacy, has made giant steps forward, illiteracy having been reduced to about 50%. The primary school system is, moreover, expanding rapidly, but major problems remain. For one thing seasonal factors, so common among a rural population, hamper continued school attendance; for another opportunities to *remain* literate, through the assistance of book lending services, the dissemination of periodicals, papers and other printed media are still few, and as in the colonial period the danger of sliding back into a state of semi-literacy for want of practice is as great as ever. But from the point of view of raising scientific interest and developing the next generation of researchers the chief problem is that secondary schools and qualified teachers for them are still too few, and that, moreover, attendance upon a secondary school is, unlike attendance upon primary schools, not free of cost, indeed, is beyond the means of a majority of Indonesian parents with school age children at present. What is true for secondary education holds true even more for higher education. It is not only the present lack of qualified scientists that is hampering advancement in all branches of scientific inquiry in Indonesia; it is even more the inadequate rate with which the necessary new generation of scientists is being produced that gives cause for alarm.[34] And over all hovers the severe problem of inadequate facilities to accommodate the demand for education. To cite a few instances: (1) in the year 1956-1957 nearly four million students could not attend school for lack of space, (2) in Medan, East Sumatra, students have threatened to set fire to all schools if they are not accommodated and (3) at the present rate only ¼ of the necessary number of secondary school teachers is available.[35] Under such conditions the promotion of sociology, or of any other scientific discipline, is faced with unusually difficult problems. Like so many other aspects of development in Indonesia, it may be said that sociology in Indonesia is as yet decades from the point of reaching momentum. Yet even so, one must hasten to admit that neither the sympathetic assistance from outside scholarly and educational interests, nor the increased numbers of Indonesians obtaining the necessary advanced social scientific training abroad will be and is as great an asset in the laborious struggle to solve these problems as the slowly spreading critical temper among the country's intelligentsia and political leaders.

SOUTHEAST ASIA

To greater or lesser extent the problems confronting the development of sociology in the other countries of Southeast Asia are the same as beset Indonesia. Here too, we note the absence of a modern social scientific tradition, the preponderance of foreign scholars in present day sociological research, the concentration of indigenous research in government reports and surveys, and finally the lack of trained scholars and facilities in the ambitious national development schemes. Again, as in Indonesia governmental needs determine much of the character of official or semi-official sociological inquiry, as e.g. inter-ethnic relations in Malaya, rural government and village society in Burma, and land tenure and the position of the Chinese minority in the distributing trade in the Philippines. Other than the government agencies, it is again the national universities (Rangoon, the universities of Malaya or the Philippines) in which social scientific research is concentrated, usually reflecting the labors of one or two faculty members and a handful of students, many of whom are really preparing for agricultural or community development services or for the law. Developed social scientific curricula are still at a premium and such as would wish to matriculate in them are forced to journey abroad. Yet there can be no question that the need for a broader educational system is recognized, indeed, as a Burmese government publication has it, "Education is the greatest social investment we can make."[36]

Sociology's stake in the development of the social sciences in the countries of Southeast Asia is not merely to be measured in terms of conceivable contributions to standard problems that have already been explored to a considerable extent, such as inter-ethnic relations and discrimination, population trends, social structure and types of land-tenure, but also in terms of the contribution expected in a methodological way. For example the use of opinionnaires and questionnaires, the stock in trade of the sociologist in the Western world, become of doubtful value in the many cultures and societies of Southeast Asia where interpersonal relations are so severely circumscribed by etiquette and status consideration that any direct question calling for opinion or expectation violates propriety and individual conscience. One looks particularly toward the slowly emerging generation of Southeast Asian sociologists for a solution to such problems. May the time be soon.

SELECTED BIBLIOGRAPHY

P. H. Honig and F. Verdoorn, eds., *Science and Scientists in the Netherlands Indies* (New York: Querido, 1943). An exhaustive compilation of the major achievements in the natural and social sciences in Indonesia during the colonial era.

H. J. Heeren, "Sociologie in Indonesie," *Cultureel Nieuws Indonesië* (1955), no. 40, 72-74. A brief survey of major problems and present projects.

William Thomas, ed. *Anthropology Today* (University of Chicago Press, 1951). Contains an informative chapter by the late G. J. Held on Indonesia.

Encyclopedie van Nederlandsch-Indie (The Hague: Martinus Nijhoff, 1918 ff), 8 vols., including supplements; has several useful, if dated articles on ethnology, adat law, and on the work of colonial social scientists.

F. G. Hsien and R. R. McAuliffe, *Social Surveys in Malaya* (University of Malaya, 1949, mimeo). Summary of intra and inter-ethnic relations studies conducted by a team of researchers at the University of Malaya.

H. T. Chabot, "Administration and Sociology in Dutch Indonesia," *British Journal of Sociology*, VII (September, 1956) 253-258. A useful survey of sociology in the service of Dutch colonial public administration.

Chester L. Hunt and associates, *Sociology in the Philippine Setting* (Manila, Alemar's, 1954). A text, the results of collaborative effort of sociologists in the University of the Philippines, focussed on the Philippine setting. Also of value to the specialist.

Justus M. van der Kroef, Assistant Professor of Sociology and Political Science, University of Bridgeport (Bridgeport, Connecticut), born in Indonesia, and largely raised and educated there. Attended the University of Indonesia, the University of Melbourne, Australia, (A.B.), the University of North Carolina (M.A.) and Columbia University, New York (Ph.D.). A specialist on Indonesia he twice returned for extended research trips to his native land since World War II; has served in a number of governmental functions. Among his publications are: *Dutch Policy in Indonesia: A History and A Perspective* (Ann Arbor, 1951); *Indonesia in the Modern World*, 2 Vols. (Bandung, Indonesia, 1954-56), *Indonesian Social Evolution. Some Psychological Considerations* (Amsterdam, 1957); and numerous articles and contributions to scholarly as well as popular journals and symposia.

NOTES

1. On the *mandala* and *çasana* see F. H. van Naerssen, *Cultuurcontacten en Sociale Conflicten in Indonesië* (Amsterdam: J. M. Meulenhoff, 1946), 7-8.

2. C. C. Berg, "Gedachtenwisseling over Javaanse Geschiedschrijving", *Indonesië*, IX (June, 1956) 177-216.

3. E. A. van de Graaff, *De Statistiek in Indonesië* (The Hague: Bandung; W. van Hoeve, 1955), 6.

4. See especially *De Volkswelvaart op Java en Madoera. Eindverhandeling van't Onderzoek naar de Mindere Welvaart der Inlandsche Bevolking*, Xa, deel 1 (Batavia: Ruygrok & Co., 1914).

5. *Rapport van de Commissie van Onderzoek ingesteld bij het Gouvernementsbesluit van 13 Februari 1927, no. la* (Weltevreden: Landsdrukkerij, 1928). An English translation of portions of this report in *Indonesian Sociological Studies. Selected Writings of B. Schrieke. Part One.* (The Hague, Bandung: W. van Hoeve, 1955), 83-166.

6. *Verslag van den Belastingdruk op de Inlandsche Bevolking in de Buitengewesten* (Weltevreden: Landsdrukkerij, 1927). See also J. Meyer Ranneft and W. Huender, *Onderzoek naar de belastingdruk op de Inlandsche Bevolking* (Weltevreden: Landsdrukkerij, 1926).

1050   TRENDS ABROAD

7. *Een Onderzoek naar de Levenswijze der Gemeentekoelies te Batavia in 1937. Mededelingen van het Centraal Kantoor voor Statistiek* (Batavia: Kolff & Co., 1939).

8. *De Levenswijze van de Arbeiders in de Cultures en van de tanis op Java in 1939-1940. Eindrapport van de Koelie Budget Commissie* (Batavia: stencil, 1941).

9. Institute of Economic and Social Research, University of Indonesia (Sumitro Djojohadikusumo, editor), "The Government's Program on Industries", *Ekonomi dan Keuangan Indonesia,* VII (November, 1954), 702-736.

10. H. J. Heeren, ed., "Urbanisasi Djakarta," *Ekonomi dan Keuangan Indonesia,* VIII (March, 1955), 107-152.

11. National Planning Bureau, "Census Tasks and Problems in Indonesia", *Ekonomi dan Keuangan Indonesia,* IX (May, 1956), 280-299.

12. "The Population of Indonesia", *Ekonomi dan Keuangan Indonesia,* IX (February, 1956), 90-115.

13. Kurt Horstmann, "The exceptionally small number of children in Indonesia", *Ekonomi dan Keuangan Indonesia,* IX (April, 1956), 209-212 and the same author's "The household—an important socio-economic unit", *Ekonomi dan Keuangan,* IX (August, 1956), 463-471.

14. See e.g. R. S. P. Atmosoedirdjo, *Vergelijkende Adatrechtelijke studie van Oost Javase Madoerezen en Oesingers* (Amsterdam: Poortpers, 1952); Singgih Praptadihardjo, *Sendi-Sendi Hukum Tanah di Indonesia* (Djakarta: P. T. Pembangunan, 1954); Sukanto, *Menindjau Hukum Adat Indonesia* (Djakarta: P. T. Pembangunan, 1954); Mahadi, *Beberapa Sendi Hukum di Indonesia* (Djakarta: P. T. Pembangunan, 1954); St. K. Malikul Adil, *Pembaharuan Hukum Perdata Kita* (Djakarta: P. T. Pembangunan, 1956).

15. R. A. Sual, "Pengaruh beberapa faktor-faktor sosiologis terhadap tingkat dan pembagian pendapatan nasional Indonesia", *Ekonomi dan Keuangan Indonesia,* IX (July, 1956), 432-443; R. A. Sual dan A. Wattel, *Ke-Ekonomi Berkooperasi* (Djakarta: J. B. Wolters, 1956).

16. Pouw Boen-Giok, *De Kerkrechtelijke Positie van een Ethnisch Bepaalde Kerk in een Ander Ethnisch Bepaald Milieu. Een Ecclesiologische Studie over de Situatie van Chinese Christen Gemeenschappen in Indonesië* (Utrecht: H. J. Smits, 1952) and Gouw Giok Siong, *Segi-Segi hukum peraturan perkawinan tjampuran* (Djakarta: no publ., 1955).

17. By H. J. Heeren (see e.g.), "De Trek der Toradjas naar Makassar", pp. 52-62 in G. H. van der Kolff, ed. *Sticusa Jaarboek 1952* (Amsterdam; no publisher, 1952) and "De Sociale Omstandigheden der Studenten in Djakarta," *Indonesië,* VII (October, 1954), 514-519.

18. S. Daniel Neumark, "The National Income of Indonesia", *Ekonomi dan Keuangan Indonesia,* VII (June, 1954), 345-391; A. M. de Neuman, *Industrial Development in Indonesia* (Djakarta: G. C. T. van Dorp, 1955).

19. N. Keyfitz and Widjojo, *Soal Penduduk dan Pembangunan Indonesia* (Djakarta: P. T. Pembangunan, 1955).

20. Raymond Kennedy, *Field Notes on Indonesia. South Celebes. 1949-1950* (New Haven, Conn. Human Relations Area Files, 1953). Kennedy's earlier contributions include *The Ageless Indies* (New York: John Day, 1942), as well as various bibliographic compilations and essays on the colonial problem of our time.

21. Paul Kattenburg, *A Central Javanese Village in 1950* (Ithaca, N. Y.: Cornell University, Southeast Asia Program Data Paper, 1951).

22. For some preliminary results of this survey see Clifford Geertz, "Religious Belief and Economic Behavior in a Central Javanese Town: some preliminary con-

siderations", *Economic Development and Cultural Change,* IV (January, 1956), 134-158.

23. Justus M. van der Kroef, *Indonesia in the Modern World* (Bandung, Indonesia: Masa Baru, 1954-1956), 2 vols.

24. H. T. Chabot, *Verwantschap, Stand en Sexe in Zuid Celebes* (Groningen, Djakarta: J. B. Wolters, 1950) and the same author's "Jonge Vrouwen in Conflict", *Indonesië,* VIII (February, 1955), 40-47.

25. W. F. Wertheim, *Indonesian Society in Transition. A Study of Social Change* (The Hague, Bandung: W. van Hoeve, 1956).

26. See e.g. *Indonesian Trade and Society. Essays in Asian Social and Economic History by J. C. van Leur* (The Hague, Bandung: W. van Hoeve, 1955); *Indonesian Sociological Studies. Selected Writings of B. Schrieke. Part One.* (The Hague, Bandung: W. van Hoeve, 1955).

27. G. J. Resink, "Alat-alat babad sedjarah Indonesia," *Indonesië,* VII (April, 1954), 330-333.

28. For the cultural, historic and psychological origins of this tendency see the essay "The Realist Convergence" in J. M. van der Kroef, *The Journey from Darmo. Essays in the Changing Character of Indonesian Society* (forthcoming).

29. H. J. Heeren in *Sociologische Gids* (Meppel, Netherlands), October, 1954, reprinted in *Cultureel Nieuws Indonesië* (1955), no. 40, 72-74.

30. Cf. J. M. van der Kroef, "The Changing Class Structure of Indonesia," *American Sociological Review,* XXI (April, 1956), 147.

31. H. J. Heeren in *Cultureel Nieuws Indonesië* (1955), no. 40, 72.

32. As an illustration of the latter see, for example, the article on the position of Indonesian woman from the pen of Professor Pryono in *Merdeka* (Djakarta) (August 28, 1954).

33. Compare Benjamin Higgins, "Indonesia's Development Plans and Problems," *Pacific Affairs,* XXIX (June, 1956), 119.

34. See J. M. van der Kroef, "Educational Development and Social Change in Indonesia," *Harvard Educational Review,* XXIV (Fall, 1954), 239-255 and the same author's "Higher Education in Indonesia," *The Journal of Higher Education,* XXVI (October, 1955), 366-377.

35. *Java Bode* (Djakarta) (July 16, 21, August 7, 27, 29, 1956).

36. Economic and Social Board, Government of the Union of Burma, *Pyidawtha. The New Burma. A Report from the Government to the People of the Union of Burma on our Long-term Program for Economic and Social Development* (London: no publ., 1954), 154. For other statements of sociological importance see also *Conference Papers on Current Economic Problems of Burma* (Rangoon: Government Printing and Stationery Office, 1951) and *The Economic Survey of Burma, 1956* (Rangoon: Government Printing and Stationery Office, 1956).

MIDDLE EAST

Lincoln Armstrong

American University (Beirut, Lebanon)

Within the area known as the Middle East, from Morocco to Pakistan and from Turkey to Yeman, there are many regions and even nations in which sociology has taken a strong and varied hold. A vast amount of sociological research, theory and description is growing in every corner of the Middle East. The sources are indigenous, and the interest in the economic, political, educational, and social developments are shown in research programs sponsored by the United Nations and its affiliated organizations, U.S.O.M. (Point Four) and similar organs of other Western powers, national governments, and private foundations (such as the Near East Foundation, the Middle East Institute, Ford Foundation, Rockefeller Foundation and the major oil companies). Native students from all countries have for several years been pursuing their graduate studies in Europe and the United States and through them Western influences are making themselves strongly felt.

While the Middle East has produced its famous social philosopher in Ibn Khaldoun, he had no indigenous following that could be called a school. Therefore, this makes our task doubly difficult since the sources of sociological influence are almost exclusively external to the Middle East.

In providing a survey of sociological trends in the Middle East a brief summary of local educational centers that are sociologically active will be presented first, followed by a tabular analysis of who is doing what and where it is being done; finally, there will be a content analysis of the products of sociological effort during the past ten years. (We shall not deal here in detail with the growth of Middle Eastern study centers and institutes located in the United States).

CENTERS OF SOCIOLOGICAL ACTIVITY IN THE
MIDDLE EAST[1]

Sociology is distinguished by independent departmental status in few universities in the Middle East. Its most prominent position is in Egypt, with fullfledged departments at Ein Shams University, Cairo University and Alexandria University. These three teach Sociology directly in their Schools of Law as well as Arts. Sociology is dealt with indirectly in their Schools of Commerce and Agriculture. At the American University of Cairo, to which there is attached a Ford Foundation sponsored Social Research Center directed by Dr. John H. Province, Sociology has become one of the major fields of activity; this is by far the most active research center in the Middle East today. There is also in Cairo an Institute of Sudanese Studies, occasionally mentioned in connection with sociological literature and research. In addition, Ford Foundation, Point Four, the Fulbright program and the UNESCO Middle East Science Cooperation Office have been bringing research scholars to Egypt, sending Egyptians abroad and encouraging programs based upon sound research findings. Finally, there is no doubt that the Egyptian government has been the most congenial Arab governmental host to the new trend toward scientific sociology.

While Lebanon is second in terms of total volume of social science activity, having fewer universities than Egypt, it is, nevertheless, able to boast possession of the most active Middle Eastern University in its American University of Beirut. The American University of Beirut has at present a five man Sociology and Anthropology Department which grants B.A. and M.A. degrees; in the latter case it is the only institution in the Arab world so doing. In addition, there is a Psychology Department of similar stature in which the orientation to Social Psychology is very strong and cooperation with sociology very effective. (Both departments have been assisted in research by a Rockefeller Brothers Fund Educational Research Program awarded to the the department of Education).

St. Joseph University in Beirut, while having no Sociology department, has a long tradition of teaching sociology type courses in its schools of Eastern Arts and Law, the French influence is indicated by such course titles as "Islamic sociology," and "Lebanese Folklore." There are two other French sponsored schools in Beirut which offer very little sociology, if any.

There is a Lebanese College and a Lebanese University both of which offer a little general sociology and social psychology; the Presbyterian Mission sponsored Beirut College For Women has a School of Social Work in which the B.A. degree is offered. Some Sociology and Psychology are offered in that curriculum.

In Turkey there are two universities in both of which Sociology has had considerable prominence. At Istanbul, Sociology Departments are connected to schools of Arts, Economics and Law. Until 1945 the University of Ankara had a Sociology Department; but it was nominally abandoned at that time for political reasons. Sociological research of a high quality continues to be produced at both institutions. There, as in Egypt and other countries of the Middle East the sponsoring hand of Point Four, Ford Foundation and other similar organs has been very influential. A Congress of the International Institute of Sociology was held in Istanbul in 1952 under the direction of Turkey's Hilmi Z. Ülken; the 17th Congress of I.I.S. was held in Beirut in September, 1957.

While the University in Syria at Damascus has no Sociology Department, Sociology courses, including general and rural sociology and criminology, are offered; in the School of Education a certificate may be earned in Sociology. In Damascus is also a Census Center for government employees that teaches law, statistics, and population trends.

Iraq has no University, but teaches Sociology in five of its nine colleges: Law, Commerce, Arts (which now has a "Social Relations Center" founded by Dr. Godfrey Lienhart and a "Department of Sociology and Philosophy"), Queen Aliya (which has a Department of Social Sciences organized by Dr. J. B. Adams), and the College of Upper Teachers (which offers a four year program in the social sciences generally).

Teheran University in Iran teaches "social geography" and statistics in its Law School, a general course in Sociology in the School of Arts, and has Institutes of Administrative Science and Criminology in which Anthropology, Sociology, Census Statistics, and Criminal Psychology are taught.

The Sudanese University in Khartum has been very active in ecological and demographic research. There are many French schools of Higher Studies throughout North Africa and the Middle East which are occasionally mentioned in connection with the work of French trained Orientalists. At present leadership goes to American

Universities in Beirut and Cairo, the Egyptian Universities, and the Universities of Istanbul and Ankara.

WHAT IS BEING DONE, WHERE, AND BY WHOM TODAY?

An analysis of current research in the Middle East shows that in the annotated bibliographic source, were listed 1017 items of which less than 200 were considered to qualify within the definition of scientific sociological research.[2]

The following table presents results to the question "What are the target areas of specific fields of sociological research?"

Classification by sociological field of researches going on in the Middle East in 1955.

Field of Sociology	Number	Field of Sociology	Number
Rural and Urban institutions and Relations	43	Social Anthropology	18
Political Sociology, Social Control and Intl. Relations	23	Ethnic & Religious Minorities	18
Demography and Ecology	22	Educational Sociology	18
Socio-economics, Industrialization, & Social Development	19	Social Change & Social Organization	13
Social Psychology & Communication	19	Family & Female emancipation	7
		Total	198

No comment on table 1 is necessary other than that what has previously been said about dominant centers of sociological activity in the Middle East seems to be borne out by these figures.

The next question to be answered briefly and summarily is "Who are doing the research, nationals or foreigners?" The answer is as follows:

Americans	52%
Nationals	35.7%
French	9.5%
English	1.7%
Others	1.1%

Finally, we may ask, "Under what auspices or sponsorship are the various researches being conducted?" The answer may be given tabularly as in table 2.

Table 2

Sponsoring Agencies of Sociological Research In The Middle East

	No. of researches		No. of researches
United States Agencies: *At Home*		**French & Other European Agencies:** *At Home*	
University of California-Berkeley	9	Centre Etudes d'Administrative: Musulmane, Paris	3
University of California-Los Angeles	6	Centre Nationale de la Récherché Scientifique, Paris	3
University of Michigan	6	Other agencies and independents	12
University of Pennsylvania	6	Total	18
University of Princeton	4	**French and Other European:** *Abroad*	
University of Harvard	3		
Rice Institute: "Cross Cultural Research"	8	University St. Joseph: Beirut	4
Ford Foundation	4	Other agencies and independents	5
Other agencies and independents	42	Total	9
Total	88	**Middle Eastern Institutions:**	
United States Agencies: *Abroad*		University of Istanbul & Ankara	12
American University of Beirut	19	University of Cairo, Ein Shams and Alexandria	7
American University of Cairo	7	Other agencies and independents	14
Others	5	Total	33
Total	31	Unidentified	19
U. S. Grand Total	119	Grand Total	198

While table 2 is self explanatory the author wishes to indicate his awareness of the role bias may have played in producing such an overwhelming amount of American influence. First, the bibliographical source may have been unintentionally selective in listing its researches. Second, the analyst was an American sociologist and may have discriminated in selecting the 198 items which seemed to him to coincide with standards of scientific research methodology in sociology. But even if such biases are fully recognized there would remain little doubt that the Middle East has caught the eye of American Sociologists and their sponsors in a very impressive way. Finally, in the on-going competition for leadership in the Middle East, it appears that "orientalist" scholars continue to have a three or four to one advantage over their more empirically oriented contemporaries. It is believed this advantage is decreasing.

THE NATURE AND QUALITY OF SOCIOLOGICAL RESEARCH IN THE MIDDLE EAST TODAY

It is possible to present an overall view of what has been going on in the Middle East during the past ten years by means of a content analysis of an important current bibliography.[3] This bibliography, which is the result of a thorough search of materials printed on the the Middle East in English in the behavioral sciences, is particularly useful for gauging the influence of U.S. sociologists. The summary table presented below shows a ranking in terms of scientific quality of 1115 items classified into fourteen primarily sociological areas. The scale on which items were ranked for scientific rigorousness can be summarized briefly as follows.

Rank No. 1 - Experimental or Quantitative Field Studies involving systematic data collection, census or sample; test of an hypothesis; scientific analysis; and use of controls if possible or applicable.

Rank No. 2 - Theoretically and methodologically sound descriptive analyses and interpretations of relationships based on relatively reliable primary or secondary quantitative data; rigorous content analysis; superior case study and participant observation. (In many instances an anthropologist would wish to reverse the order of ranks No. 1 and 2.)

Rank No. 3 - Semi-scientific descriptive studies; limited in quantification but based on intensive case study or observation or exhaustive library research.

Rank No. 4 - Scholarly and serious but non-objective, non-quantitative descriptions; good journalism, folklore collections, selective library research and good travelogues.

Rank No. 5 - Completely unscientific; poor journalism, propaganda, social reformism, opinion and argument.

Rank No. 6 - Descriptions of projects and programs of social action and miscellaneous: i.e. biographies, bibliographies, etc.

Rank No. 7 - Scientific theoretical analyses and discussions.

Table 3

1115 items representing fourteen sociological fields by scientific quality.

Sociological Fields	Total No. Items in each category	Ranks of Scientific Quality or Rigorousness						
		1	2	3	4	5	6	7
1. Social change and Social Movements	180	—	9	31	68	62	5	5
2. Education	141	4	9	14	8	62	42	2
3. Rural Sociology	133	4	9	46	24	11	37	2
4. Anthropology and Ethnology	111	1	22	35	30	20	—	3
5. Refugees Studies	79	2	—	21	5	16	34	1
6. Family and Kinship	76	3	8	27	14	14	3	7
7. Social Problems	66	—	1	14	9	10	28	4
8. Urban-industrial	64	3	6	25	12	9	9	—
9. Social Factors in Development	61	—	4	24	22	3	—	8
10. Social Control and Communication	60	1	4	19	19	10	2	5
11. Social Structure: General	53	—	8	12	15	12	2	4
12. Social Psychology	37	10	2	3	10	3	1	8
13. Ecology and Demography	36	3	15	—	6	3	4	5
14. Minorities	18		3	6	2	7		
	1115	31	100	277	244	242	167	54

While a bibliographic bias in selection and possible analytical biases undoubtedly caused some of the differences apparent in Table 3, two conclusions may safely be drawn. First there can be little doubt that the "orientalist" tradition is still strong in Middle Eastern studies with its emphasis on historical accounts of political movements and international relations (accounting for more than 75% of the items in "Social Change and Social Movements"), pseudo scientific lay anthropological description, archeology, Islam, and Biblical studies. Second, the modern trend toward scientific studies of specific problems is much more emphatically developing in some areas than in others. This can be demonstrated by comparing the percent of all studies in each area which fall into scientific categories Nos. 1, 2 and 7.

Ecology and Demography	63.8%	Minorities	16.6%
Social Psychology	54.0%	Social Structure: Urban	14.1%
Family and Kinship	23.7%	Social Structure: Rural	11.2%
Anthropology-Ethnology	23.4%	Education	10.6%
Social Structure-General	22.6%	Social Change and Social	
Social Factors in		Movements	7.7%
Development	19.7%	Social Problems	7.5%
Social Control and		Refugee Studies	3.8%
Communication	16.6%		

No disparagement toward studies classified as semi-scientific (Rank No. 3 in Table 3) is intended. The vast majority of materials in this area were as objective and scientific in method as the circumstances under which the research was performed would allow. The Middle East provides very little census or statistical data and nowhere in the Middle East is a scientific approach to problem solving given very much priority.

TRENDS

Brief observations on trends within the areas which underlie the data presented above are in order. Development in the area of Ecological and Demographic Studies has been most urgently awaited by all social scientists in the Middle East. It appears that finally something is beginning to be done to quiet the woeful complaints of researchers who desire a foundation of census-type data. In some areas resistance to "head-counting" is political and religious; in most areas there is resistance resulting from protective isolationism. Serious general studies of population have been attempted by Charles 'Issawi;[4]

William B. Fisher[5] and Alfred Bonné.[6] But it has been in Egypt that
the problem has been attacked most specifically, frequently and boldly,
by Egyptian governmental agencies and by Arab students working for
advanced degrees in sociology and economics at home, in England
and in the United States. The influence of Point Four technical advisors and Prof. Notestein's Princeton group has been strong in Egypt.
In Lebanon at the American University of Beirut some pioneering
census work has been done on a small scale. Charles W. Churchill's
sample census of the city of Beirut[7] as well as his and Lincoln Armstrong's census based studies in rural villages are promising. Point
Four in Lebanon has also sponsored agricultural and infant mortality
censuses. Quite recently the government of Iraq, again influenced by
U. S. technical aid experts, has been conducting some serious special
problem oriented census taking. There remains a great need for intra-
and international migration research throughout the Middle East as
well as an enormous need for the systematic collection of vital statistics. In the meantime the Social Research Center at American University of Cairo and several departments at American University of
Beirut are conducting small scale but penetrating community and
regional demographic, ecological, public health, agricultural, and socio-
economic descriptions and analyses.

Social Psychology is the field showing the most promise in the
Middle East today and this trend has been heavily influenced by
United States scientists. The main dynamics have been the social
psychologists at the American University of Beirut and at Egyptian
universities, including the American University of Cairo. The main
influence recently has come from the Bradford Hudson *Cross Cultural
Research Group*, sponsored by Rice Institute. Membership on this
team includes Mohamed K. Barakat, senior lecturer in Psychology,
Ain Shams University, Cairo; George Gardner, Social Research Center,
American University at Cairo; J. D. Keehn, Assistant Professor of
Psychology, American University at Beirut. Robert B. Macleod, Pro-
fessor of Psychology, Cornell University, Ithaca, N. Y.; Levon Melikian,
Associate Professor of Psychology, American University of Beirut;
George Miller, Dean Aleppo College, Aleppo; Ibrahim A. Muhyi,
Higher Teachers College, Baghdad; Mohamed O. Nagaty, Faculty of
Arts, Cairo University; Pergrouhi Najarian, assistant professor, Amer-
ican University of Beirut, the leading Social Psychologist of the area,
has contributed many papers on attitudes and values to professional
journals. Sociology Professors L. Armstrong and T. A. Matthews of

the American University of Beirut are also doing social-psychological research on value orientations.

An increasing scientific orientation to the study of Family and Kinship is actually much greater than is apparent in the figures presented. Although the literature still has a sizeable portion of journalism on women's rights and the feminist movement, the veil, midwifery, and family and child welfare; there are some first rate empirical studies and many of those classified as semi-scientific entailed as much empiricism as the kind and amount of data available would allow. One of the most significant studies in this area is that of Hamid Mustafa 'Ammar, *Growing up in an Egyptian Village*[8] which employed the usual anthropological field methods plus the cultural historical as well as psychological projective techniques. Equally outstanding have been Hilma Granqvist's and J. W. M. Whiting's studies of socialization,[9] Sarhan's cross-cultural study of children's interests,[10] and John Gulick's penetrating analysis of kinship structure in a Lebanese village.[11] J. H. and K. W. Douglass' study of marriage and family living among Egyptian peasants (fellaheen)[12] and M. Hamza's work on personalities of Egyptian juvenile delinquents[13] may also be mentioned.

The strong showing of Anthropology-Ethnology is not a matter of development. The Middle East has a long tradition of scholarly activity in this field. The change that may be taking place is toward an increasing sociological-quantitative approach and a decreasing preoccupation with exotic culture patterns à la Orientalist tradition. Many anthropologists are today indicating greater concern over the generalizability of their findings and are tackling problems of practical usefulness in a modernizing world. The influence of the A. Radcliffe-Brown and Evans-Pritchard functionalist school is strongly felt particularly in Baghdad where Dr. Godfrey Lienhart and Dr. Kenneth Orr are working, the former having recently organized a department of Anthropology and Sociology in the College of Arts and Sciences. As indicated elsewhere this functionalism was also introduced at Alexandria University. The Ford Foundation and Harvard, Michigan and Pennsylvania Universities through their Middle Eastern departments are currently sponsoring numerous pragmatically and quantitatively oriented studies. Carleton S. Coon's *Caravan: The Story of the Middle East*[14] is a monumental synthesis of social science findings on the Middle East in general. Readers of such journals as the *Southwestern Journal of Anthropology*, the *American Anthropologist* and the *Royal Central Asian Journal* will recognize the names of such prominent researchers as Elizabeth E. Bacon, Raphael Patai, S. F. Nadel, T. Ash-kenazi, Henry Field and W P. Thesiger. Wm. D. Schorger's North African Studies,[15] and John Gulick's work in Lebanon,[16] are other examples of the modern trend. Finally, Hassan el Sa'aty formerly of Alexandria University and the Department of Sociology at American University of Beirut are currently blending anthropological and socio-logical approaches in the study of industrial groups.[17] It is to be hoped that social anthropologists will continue the trend away from studies of exotic isolated culture complexes and patterns, concentrating and coordinating their efforts instead on the urgent problems of social organization and development which until recently have been largely the concern of economists, sociologists, and political philosophers. The establishment of the Institute of Sociology at Alexandria under A. Radcliffe-Brown in 1948 which has developed nicely under the direc-tion of the late Dr. Zdenick Ullrich has been a hopeful sign.

In the category "Urban-industrial," urban and industrial sociology as understood in the U. S. have received little attention while the labor movement from both economic and political points of view have dominated the literature. Hassan el Sa'aty, now at Ein Shams University, Cairo, has completed an ecological study of industrializa-tion and social change in Alexandria[18] under a grant of the Social Research Center of the American University at Cairo. This may prove to be the really pioneering study of its kind since it is based on a stratified sample of 60 out of 484 industrial plants and detailed inter-views of over 2000 workers. Monroe Berger's study of professionalism and bureaucracy in the Egyptian Civil Service and the current urban research of Gerald Breese, both reflecting interests of Princeton Uni-versity, will also help to establish a truly sociological approach in these fields in the Middle East. The Sociology Department at the American University of Beirut is also conducting research in industrial sociology.

General studies of social structure have been relatively rare but Stuart C. Dodd's *Social Relations in the Middle East*[19] perhaps estab-lished a precedent in this worth while direction. S. N. Eisenstadt,[20] Wm. B. Fisher,[21] many UNESCO researches, Isam Ahmad Hassoun's study of migration and settlement in the Gezira,[22] Charles 'Issawis Egyptian socio-economic studies of population, class structure, industry and related economic problems,[23] Afif Tannous's many studies in the Lebanon, "Social Differentiation in Selected Lebanese Villages" by Lincoln Armstrong and G. K. Hirabayashi,[24] and Hashim Jawad's

The Social Structure of Iraq[25] are all examples of a promising trend. An overall review of the literature reveals continuing domination of rather pure economically oriented studies but even the economists are today showing an increasing awareness of social factors and the import of their findings upon social relations. The work that is going on in Sociology at the American University of Beirut and in Egypt clearly reveals the influence of George A. Lundberg and Calvin Schmidt of the University of Washington.

The category titled "Social Factors in Development" is devoted mainly to discussions and arguments about different types of technical aid and which problems should receive priority. Some excellent quantitative surveys have been produced by UNESCO and other U.N. agencies, the British Middle East Office in Beirut and the several Point Four programs in the Middle East. However, as table 3 indicates it is high level theoretical discussion that is outstanding in this area rather than actual experimental and quantitative researches. A few specific studies which deserve mention have been completed by Alfred Bonné,[26] H. V. Cooke,[27] the International Bank for Reconstruction and Development[28] and K. C. Twitchell;[29] the latter two in Iraq and Saudi Arabia, respectively.

Very little has been done in the area of Social Control and Communication and of what there is, there is little evidence of a strong sociological influence. *The climates of Opinion* surveys conducted by the Bureau of Applied Social Research at Columbia University established a precedent in this area. The Sociology Department at the American University of Beirut has completed a few public opinion surveys and the literature reveals a few analyses of press and radio media. Some good communication research is under way today in Lebanon, Egypt and Sudan but largely the work in this area is characterized by political-philosophical discussions of the law and Islamic thought and ideology. In the planning stage today is a Center for Communications Research at the American University of Beirut, jointly conceived by the Sociology and Psychology Departments. One already exists in the Social Research Center at the American University of Cairo to be described later.

The strong racial and biological orientation of Minority Group Study characteristic of the West is not found in the Middle East. In its place on a much less prolific scale we find religious, ethnic and linguistic differentiation. A. H. Hournai's *Minorities in the Arab World*[31] is the best single work in this area. In addition there have been several worth while surveys of Jewish communities and in recent years there has been prolific study of the Palestinian refugees. Much of the latter, however, has been devoted to discussion of difficulties inherent in relief, resettlement, and repatriation programs and proposals. Sigfried Landshut's study of *Jewish Communities in Nine Moslem Countries* is one of the better of its kind.[32]

A vast literature has developed in the field of rural sociology which is being supplemented by urban studies in recent years. It is the opinion of the author that Afif Tannous has led the way in rural sociological research. Other references to his work are cited elsewhere in this paper. His "The Arab Tribal Community in a Nationalistic State,"[33] "Land Ownership in the Middle East,"[34] and "Rural Life in Arab Countries"[35] deserve separate mention here. Doreen Warriner's *Land and Poverty in the Middle East*,[36] and Father H. H. 'Ayrout's *The Fallaheen*,[37] are fine examples of general rural studies conducted in Egypt. Imam Selim's *Planned Rural Community for the Nile Valley*,[38] C. W. Churchill's *The Island of Arwad*[39] and the multivillage study currently underway under the direction of Gordon K. Hirayabashi of the Social Research Center at the American University at Cairo are examples worthy of note. A study related to the latter named one is being directed by L. Armstrong in the Bekaa Valley of Lebanon which when completed should provide some useful cross-national comparisons. Among several studies of rural house-hold economy is one recently published by Dr. Hassan Hussein (University of London) for the Permanent Council of Social Services in Egypt. The studies mentioned above are utilizing random sampling methods and are attempting to solve some of the problems of reliable data collection in these non-census areas. Much emphasis is being placed on scheduled interviewing and careful training of enumerator-interviewers. It remains a fact that a great deal of writing in the rural field is concerned with description of development projects a good example of which is Harold B. Allan's *Rural Reconstruction in Action*.[40] Descriptive studies of urban slum conditions are also to be noted in the literature.

EDUCATIONAL STUDIES

As is evident in table 3 the bulk of educational writing falls in non-scientific categories. Of the little that meets the requirements of science most involves presentation of literacy statistics and trends or the results of measuring intelligence. Much simply consists of descriptions of community educational resources, programs and projects. There are some notable exceptions of which a few can be considered examples of sociology or social psychology of education. Ray Lebkicher has described the process of training Saudi Arabians for Oil work in a truly objective manner and provides an analysis of many of the social factors involved.[41] R. D. Matthew's and Matta 'Akrawi's survey of education in the Near East is very authoritative, comprehensive and objective.[42] William R. Polk's study, *The Student in the Middle East: A Study in Frustration*[43] is interesting politically as well as socio-psychologically. The problems involved in intelligence test construction and standardization are empirically treated in G. C. Scott's "Measuring Sudanese Intelligence."[44] At the American University of Beirut the Department of Education under the direction of Dr. Habib Kurani is turning out M.A. theses based on empirical studies. Through a grant from the Rockefeller Brothers Educational Research program at the American University of Beirut L. Armstrong and G. K. Hirabayashi have published the results of a random sample educational participation study conducted in rural Lebanon.[45] These are a few selected examples of work in the field of education which it is hoped may lead to further development of a scientific approach in that area. The most important educational project in the Middle East is the UNESCO Arab States Fundamental Education Center at Sirs Alayan, Egypt, where a truly technical and experimental approach is being fostered.

SOCIAL CHANGE AND MOVEMENTS

As indicated previously Social Change and Social Movements have had but little development in a sociological direction. Sociological study of social change depends heavily upon statistical records which are scarce in the Middle East. Social movements has barely escaped the level of scholarly political-philosophical treatment. Carleton Coon's, "The Impact of the West on Middle Eastern Social Institutions"[46] successfully makes the break. Charles 'Iswassi,[47] The Middle East Institute in a symposium,[48] Feu'ad Ahmed 'Aly[49] and Raphael Patai[50] are among the few others who have succeeded. The social-economic revolution in Egypt is being treated seriously and the effect of mechanization on agricultural life and technological change in general has been described by social scientists at Ankara and Istanbul Universities in Turkey where Z. F. Findikoglu is doing a factory study and G. C. Helling is applying sociometric techniques in his industrial research. George Lenczowski (University of California) and Fahim I. Qubain (Staff member, Human Relations Area Files) are coping with sociological aspects of the impact of oil industry on the Middle East. Industrialization also is the focus of research activities of G. H. Gardner at the American University at Cairo and R. A. Hicks of the U.S. Education Foundation in Iraq. All in all in no area would extensive sociological research be more fruitful than it shows signs of becoming in the area of social change and industrialization.

Closely related to this subject some notable work is discovered in Egypt on the emerging professional classes. In 1951 Patricia Kendall of the Columbia University Bureau of Applied Social Research completed a study of "The Ambivalent Character of Nationalism Among Egyptian Professionals." The study utilized the case study method involving 110 interviews. In a special study for U.S.I.S. Dr. Chahen Turabian (American University, Cairo) interviewed 600 randomly selected professionals. A report which resulted from this study, "Readership Survey of an Egyptian Magazine among the Elites in Cairo, 1955," is the first scientifically designed readership survey in Egypt, and paved the way for the researcher's appointment to the Social Research Center in 1956 as head of its Laboratory of Surveys and Polls, the only laboratory of its kind in the Arab World. The major activity of this Laboratory in addition to public opinion studies will be marketing surveys.

Also nearing completion is a survey of higher women civil servants in Cairo by Dr. Laila Shukry (Cornell University). This is another of the Social Research Center projects and involves the statistical analysis of some 2000 cases from which a random sample of 100 was selected for intensive case studies.

SOCIAL PROBLEMS

The Social Problems that dominate the literature in the U.S. such as juvenile delinquency, crime, suicide, alcoholism, social discrimination, divorce, prostitution and other sex relations, etc. have rarely been subjected to scientific study in the Middle East. This is largely due to the failure of these societies to define such behavior as societally problematic which in turn may be due to their relative infrequency or social invisibility. In their place the Middle East seems more concerned with broader problems such as illiteracy, social security, community development, public health, etc. It is these topics which have dominated the five Arab States Social Welfare Seminars that have been held to date. Only in Egypt do we find anything that resembles reliable crime statistics a'nd these were utilized by Hasan el Sa'aty in his Ph. D. dissertation on juvenile delinquency, the only study of its kind that has come to light.[51] A great deal of the literature as indicated in table 3 is concerned with descriptions of projects and conferences about social problems.

Sociology has been recognized and accepted in the Middle East. Its continued growth is assured unless all ties with the West are suddenly broken. Even then there are so many U.S. trained Arab sociologists in the Middle East that it is difficult to imagine any reduction of the modern trend toward scientific sociology in this area.

SELECTED BIBLIOGRAPHY

Hamid M. 'Ammar, *Growing up in an Egyptian Village* (London: Routledge and Kegan Paul Ltd., 1954). An anthropological study of an Upper Egyptian village, throroughly documented, with special emphasis on the socialization process; most significant is the introduction of psychological projective techniques into this study.

Alfred Bonné, *State and Economics in the Middle East: A Society in Transition* (London: Kegan Paul, Trench, Trubner, 1948). An attempt to discover the impact of modern civilization on the social and economic fabric of the Middle East; in four parts: evolution of the state, agrarian society, industrial revolution, and problems of a changing society.

Carleton Coon, *Caravan: The Story of the Middle East* (New York: Holt, 1951). An anthropological introduction to the Middle East, including North Africa; social, religious, and economic structure.

Hedley V. Cooke, *Challenge and Response in the Middle East: Quest for Prosperity*, 1919-1951 (New York: Harper, 1952). A close examination of major plans for elevating the living standard in the region: land settlement, village welfare, health improvement, education, Bedouin settlement; background data and some information on the impact of the West on the Middle East.

H. R. P. Dickson, *The Arab of the Desert* (London: Allen and Unwin, 1949). An ethnographic study of the Arabian Bedouin, par-

ticularly the Mutair tribe; includes tales, proverbs, dream interpretations, and a glossary of common Bedouin words; well illustrated.

Richard Ettinghausen, ed., *A Selected and Annotated Bibliography
of Books and Periodicals in Western Languages Dealing with the
Near and Middle East with Special Emphasis on Mediaeval and
Modern Times* (Washington, D.C., 1952); with *Supplement*, 1954.

Sydney N. Fisher, ed., *Social Forces in the Middle East* (Ithaca: Cornell University Press, 1955). A symposium including, among others,
valuable articles by E. A. Speiser, "Cultural Factors in Social Dynamics
in the Near East"; Thomas B. Stauffer, "The Industrial Worker";
Charles 'Issawi, "The Entrepreneur Class"; Dalton Potter, "The Ba-
zaar Merchant"; J. C. Hurwitz, "Minorities in the Political Process";
Raphael Patai, "The Immigrant in Israel"; and D. C. Crary, "The
Villager."

Sydney N. Fisher, ed., *Evolution in the Middle East: Reform, Revolt and Change* (Washington, D.C.: Middle East Institute, 1953).
Papers on Middle Eastern Affairs; changes in education, religion,
literature, economics, politics and social awareness.

W. B. Fisher, *The Middle East: A Physical, Social and Regional
Geography* (New York: E. P. Dutton, 1950). Geographic conditions as
"social forces" and their relationship to some of the basic problems
of the area; human ecology.

John Gulick, *Social Structure and Culture Change in a Lebanese
Village* (New York: Viking Fund Publications in Anthropology, No.
21, 1955). A good example of the best in a traditional anthropological approach to social organization; excellent kinship structural-
functional analysis.

Royal Institute of International Affairs, *The Middle East: A Political and Economic Survey* (New York: 1954). Background data by a
group of experts on the region as a whole: geography, politics, religions, minorities, socal and economic conditions; and more detailed
information for each country; statistics, maps, bibliography; 1954
edition completely revised to include developments since 1950.

Hassan el Sa'ati, *Industrialization and Social Change in Alexandria*
(Cairo: Social Research Center, American University at Cairo, 1956);
(Renaissance Bookstore, Cairo, 1957): Perhaps the first empirical, ob-
jective and quantitative approach to this subject matter in the Middle
East.

Doreen Warriner, *Land and Poverty in the Middle East* (London:
Royal Institute of International Affairs, London, 1948). An analysis
of the causes of poverty in the Middle East and methods of raising
living standards; based on an examination of the land tenure system
and social structure.

T. Cuyler Young, ed., *Near Eastern Culture and Society: A Sym-
posium on the Meeting of East and West* (Princeton, N. J., 1951).
Addresses presented at Princeton Bicentennial, 1947. Part I: "how the
West has met the East and has been enriched in its culture"; Part II:

an analysis of current problems involved in relations of Islamic peoples and states with those of the West and the effects of cultural contact on older societies.

Lincoln Armstrong, B.A., Columbia University, 1941; Ph.D., University of Pennsylvaina 1951; Instructor & Assistant Professor of Sociology, University of Delaware, 1947-1952; Assistant Professor of Sociology University of Washington, 1952-1953; Assistant and Associate Professor of Sociology, Chairman of the Department of Sociology, American University of Beirut (Lebanon), 1953—. Has contributed numerous studies to the field of Social Organization, Social Change and Communication.

NOTES

1. UNESCO; *Round Table on the Teaching of the Social Sciences* (Damascus August, 1954, Middle East Science Cooperation Office, Cairo, Egypt), see also: E. T Prothro, "Psychology in The Arab Near East," *Psychological Bulletin*, LII, 4 (July 1955).

2. The source for this analysis was The Middle East Institute: *Current Research on the Middle East: 1955*, Ed. Harvey, P. Hall and Ann W. Noyes, (Washington D. C., 1956).

3. Jean T. Burke, *An Annotated Bibliography of Books and Periodicals in English Dealing with Human Relations in the Arab States of the Middle East* (American University of Beirut, Lebanon, July, 1956).

4. with C. Dabezies "Population movements and population pressures in Jordan, Lebanon, and Syria," Milbank Memorial Fund (New York), *Quarterly*, XXIX (October, 1951), 385-403.

5. "Population problems of the Middle East," *Royal Central Asian Journal* XXXVI (July-October, 1949), 208-220.

6. "Land and population in the Middle East," *Middle East Journal*, V (Winter 1951), 39-56.

7. Charles W. Churchill, *The city of Beirut: A Socio-Economic Survey* (Beirut: Dar el Kitab, 1954).

8. Hamid Mustafa 'Ammar, *Growing up in an Egyptian Village* (London: Rou: ledge, Kegan Paul, 1954).

9. Granqvist Hilma, *Birth and Childhood among the Arabs: Studies in a Muham madan Village in Palestine* (Helsingfors: Soderstrom, 1947); & *Child Problems Among the Arabs* (Copenhagen: Ejnar Munksgaard, 1951); Irwin L. Child, *Child Training and Personality: A Cross-Cultural Study* (Yale University Press, 1953).

10. *Interests and Culture* (New York: Columbia University Press, 1950).

11. John Gulick, *The Lebanese Village, AA*, LV, 3 (1953), 367-372

12. J. H. & K. W. Douglass, "Aspects of Marriage and Family Living Among Egyptian Peasants," *Marriage and Family Living*, XVI, 1 (1954), 45-48.

13. M. Hamza, "The Dynamic Forces in the Personalities of Juvenile Delinquents

in the Egyptian Environment," *The British Journal of Psychology* (Cambridge) X_1IV (1953) , Part 4, 330-338.

14. C. S. Coon, *Caravan* (New York: Holt, 1951).

15. W. D. Schorger, *The Caravan Trails of North Africa* (Harvard University Peabody Museum Library, Senior honor thesis in Anthropology, unpublished).

16. John Gulick, *Social Structure and Culture Change in a Lebanese Village* (Vol. 21 in the Viking Fund Series, 1956) ; *The Maronites: A Study of the Indigenous Christians of the Lebanon* (Harvard College, A. B. Honors thesis, unpublished).

17. Hassan el Sa'aty, *Industry and Social Change in Alexandria*, with Z. K. Ullrich (Cairo: Social Research Center, American University at Cairo, 1950) . Alfred Zakha:-riya, *Vocational Skill Level and Educational Background in the Printing Industry in Beirut* (American University at Beirut, M. A., thesis under the guidance of Dr Lincoln Armstrong, 1956) .

18. Hassan el Sa'aty, *op. cit.*

19. S. C. Dodd, *Social Relations in the Middle East* (Beirut: American Press, 1946).

20. S. N. Eisenstadt, "Development of Modern Elites in Asia," *Hamizrah Hehadash* (Jerusalem, Israel) , I (July, 1950) , 227-284.

21. Wm. B. Fisher, *The Middle East: A Physical, Social, and Regional Geography* (New York: E. P. Dutton, 19, 1950) .

22. Isam Ahmad Hassoun, "Western Migration and Settlement in Gezira," *Sudan Notes and Records* (Khartoum) , XXXIII (June, 1952) , 60-112.

23. Charles 'Issawis, *Egypt: An Economic and Social Analysis* (New York: Oxford University Press) ; *Egypt at Mid-Century* (New York: Oxford University Press, 1950).

24. Lincoln Armstrong & G. K. Hirabayashi, "Social Differentiation in Selected Lebanese Villages," *American Sociological Review*, XXI, 4 (August, 1956).

25. Hashim Jawad, *The Social Structure of Iraq* (Baghdad: New Publishers, 1945 "Facts and Prospects in Iraq Series," No. 6) .

26. Alfred Bonnée, *The Economic Development of the Middle East* (London: Routledge & Kegan Paul, 1945) .

27. H. V. Cooke, *Challenge and Response in the Middle East: The Quest for Prosperity, 1919-1951* (New York: Harper, 1952).

28. The International Bank for Reconstruction and Development, *The Economic Development of Iraq* (Baltimore: John Hopkins University Press, 1952) .

29. K. C. Twitchell & E. J. Jurji, *Saudi Arabia: An Account of the Development of Its Natural Resources* (Princeton University Press, 1947, 1953) .

30. Edmund de S. Brunner, "Rural Communications Behavior and Attitudes in the Middle East," *Rural Socology*, XVII (1951) , 149-155.

31. A. H. Hournai, *Minorities in the Arab World* (London: Oxford University Press, 1947) .

32. Sigfried Landshut, *Jewish Communities in Nine Moslem Countries* (London: Jewish Chronicle, 1950) ; for rare examples of quantitative studies in the refugee areas, see: F. C. Bruhns, "A Study of Arab Refugee Attitudes," *Middle East Journal* IX, 2 (1955) , & L. Armstrong, "Occupational Changes of Palestinian Refugees," *Proceedings: XVI Congress of International Institute of Sociology*, IX (1954) .

33. Afif Tannous, "The Arab Tribal Community in a Nationalist State," *Middle East Journal*, I, 1 (1947) , 5-17.

34. Tannous, "Land Ownership in the Middle East," *Foreign Agriculture*, XIV (1950) , 263-269.

35. Tannous, "Rural Life in Arab Countries," *Al-Abhath* (Beirut), VI (1953), 175-191; see also his "The Village in the National Life of Lebanon," *Middle East Journal*, III, 2 (1949).

36. Doreen Warriner, *Land and Poverty in the Middle East* (London: Royal Institute of International Affairs, 1948).

37. H. H. 'Ayrout, *The Fallaheen* (Cairo: R. Schnilder, 1945).

38. Imam Selim, *Planned Rural Community in the Nile Valley* (Ph.D. Thesis, unpublished, University of North Carolina, Chapel Hill, N. C., 1951).

39. C. W. Churchill, *The Island of Arwad* (American University of Beirut: Public Health Department, 1956).

40. H. B. Allan, *Rural Reconstruction in Action* (Ithaca, N. Y.: Cornell University Press, 1953).

41. Ray Lebkicher, *The Training of Saudi Arab Employees: Arabian American Oil Company.*

42. R. D. Matthew & Matta 'Akrawi', *Education in Arab Countries of the Near East* (Washington, D. C.: American Council on Education, 1949).

43. W. R. Polk, *The Student in the Middle East: A Study in Frustration* (Cambridge, Mass.: National Student Association, 1950).

44. G. C. Scott, "Measuring Sudene Intelligence," *British Journal of Eudcational Sociology*, XX (1950), 43-54.

45. L. Armstrong & G. K. Hirabayashi, in *Transactions of the Third World Congress of Sociology*, V (1956), 123-132.

46. Carleton Coon, "The Impact of the West on Middle Eastern Social Institutions," *Proceedings*, Academy of Political Science, XXIV, 4 (1952), 443-466.

47. Charles 'Issawi, A note on the conditions of economic progress in the Middle East, *Journal of Economic Development and Cultural Change*, IV (December, 1952) 289-294.

48. Sydney N. Fisher, Ed., *Evolution in the Middle East: Reform, Revolt and Change* (Washington, D. C.: Middle East Institute, 1953).

49. Feu'ad Ahmed 'Aly, *A Proposed Experiment in Community Change by the People of a (Selected) Egyptian Village* (Nashville, Tenn.: Vanderbilt University, Ph.D., thesis, unpublished, 1952).

50. Raphael Patai, *On Culture contact and its working in modern Palestine* (American Anthropological Association, Memoir No. 67, 1947); also: "Religion in Middle Eastern, Far Eastern, and Western Culture," *Southwestern Journal of Anthropology*, X (1954).

51. Hassan el Sa'aty, *Juvenile Delinquency in Egypt* (Ph.D., Thesis, University of London, unpublished, 1946).

ISRAEL

R. Bar-Yoseph
and
Dov Weintraub
Hebrew University (Jerusalem, Israel)

Sociology in Israel is of comparatively recent standing, even for a country whose national and scientific history in the modern era has been so short. It would, in fact, be no exaggeration to say that in many respects, notably the empirical one, it dates no further back than the establishment of the State. For while sociological theory had been a recognized part of the academic curriculum in previous years; and while some of the scientific bodies, to whom studies reference will be made later on, had by then a long record of activity and achievement; the truth, nevertheless, is that research in this field had been almost entirely neglected.

This had certainly been the case with the Department of Sociology of the Hebrew University, the body most closely concerned with the subject; and the other departments or institutions had been characterised by specifically psychological, statistical-demographic, or economic bents, and had not yet included sociological aspects in their work. This, in itself, does not constitute a background unique to Israel, or to other recently established states, as in most countries sociological as distinct from purely anthropological) research gained its great impetus in the forties largely due to objective, external circumstances and necessity. However, the factors which contributed to the development of this sphere of activity in Israel at that particular junction, namely the grave and complex social problems created by the establishment of the State on the one hand, and the new national tools and resources on the other, combined also to determine to a large extent the future of the country's sociological research along certain characteristic and specific lines. This does not mean, of course, that an Israeli "national" Sociology has developed, or, following the recent universal trends in the field, that this country has also endeavored to work in the main stream of international contacts and in accordance with the increasingly unified outlook; at the same time, it seems that some interconnected elements do give sociology in this country a somewhat distinct quality.

The first of these elements may perhaps be described as an extremely close interrelationship between "pure" and "applied" research. The second is the applicability of studies focused on seemingly local question, to problems inherent in other concrete settings as well as to a more comprehensive comparative framework. The third element which seems the culmination of the former two, is the consequent ability to contribute to the bulk of sociological theory without submerging the local aspects on the one hand, and without over-stresssing the particular on the other. In order to illustrate these qualities with greater precision, the particular factors and circumstances which have, as mentioned above, conditioned the direction of the work undertaken, must be given some prominence. The complexity and gravity of social problems created by Statehood as such (the transition from a pioneering society to an organized state is but one example in this connection) as well as by the later trends in the national development (the absorption of immigrants constituting a most prominent feature) needs, it would seem, no elaboration.

The first concrete result of the existence and particular nature of these problems has been the fruitful cooperation of scientific bodies with various public agencies and institutions, which have in many cases initiated, encouraged and helped research oriented towards the solution of concrete problems. This has been especially true of governmental, national and philanthropic institutions (foreign and international as well)[1] so that continuity of work could be ensured on a level which is usually characteristic of countries embarked on an all-out effort. It is probably this state of sustained national endeavor that had allowed Israel to devote to this field more than the share appropriate to and commensurate with its resources. The somewhat austere reality of emergency (legitimately so termed, although for the most part not of a predominantly military nature), necessitating careful planning as well as utmost economy and efficiency in the use of means, contributed thus, among its other benefits, to scientific development.

The situation, however, has been characterized by more than technical facilities and cooperation, or even (though in itself of no mean importance) the creation of a climate, or atmosphere, favorable to the spread, utilization and influence of sociological research. The interesting thing has been that in many of the projects undertaken, basic questions of sociological theory had to be approached together with, or perhaps rather as a condition of, attempting an adequate solution to the concrete problems encountered. This fact may possibly be attributed to the composition and state of the Israeli society: this society (in particular the ever increasing segment of newcomers) has been relatively unintegrated as well as in constant flux. The low common social denominator, no less than the scanty basic data available on the various sections and groups of the population, combined to arouse fundamental questions of theory. (We shall exemplify these statements in the section on the actual projects undertaken). Conversely, this state of affairs has sometimes enabled the sociologist to formulate his studies in such a way as to combine the practical and the theoretical aspects in a wider, more integrated and more complementary way than is often possible. Because of this combination of factors, and the presence of many social forms within the framework of one small country, certain "laboratory" conditions seem to have been created; thus, as many of its problems are similar to those of other settings (in particular many underdeveloped areas, countries which have recently achieved political independence, and immigrant absorbing societies), the studies undertaken and the results obtained (even though often fragmentary and inconclusive) may be of wider direct practical applicability on the one hand, and constitute focal points for more embracing comparative research on the other. (Not all specific projects undertaken fall, of course, within this scheme which embraces some aspects only; these aspects, however, seem to be important as well as characteristic.)

RESEARCH IN HETEROGENEITY

In order to set off more clearly the characteristics of Israeli sociology, as outlined in the opening section, one project will be described in greater detail, with a consequent brevity in the treatment of some studies and the omission of others. The balance of work done in the country in general should not, however, be distorted by this sacrifice for the sake of clarity; similar reasons have dictated also the inclusion in this chapter of various well known theoretical points, introduced in order to emphasize the combination theory and practice, and of "pure" and "applied" research, inherent, it is suggested, in the setting and subject matter of Israeli social investigation.

The project which is to be the central theme of this survey represents indeed the main line of sociological interest in the country. Though specifically carried out by the Department of Sociology of the Hebrew University, under the direction of its chairman, Professor S. N. Eisenstadt, it has, nevertheless, been closely connected with work undertaken by other bodies. The investigation has been focused on the processes through which a democratic society develops out of various heterogeneous elements. Many of these elements, consisting mostly of diverse groups of new immigrants which have come to Israel since 1948, were from backgrounds greatly different from that of the existing Jewish community, whose main social institutions formed the basis of the new state. While the majority of these institutions had followed predominantly Western political (democratic) and economic models (even if with special developments of their own), many of the immigrant groups come from traditional social and cultural settings and from economically underdeveloped countries. The various aspects of the social structure of Israel seemed thus of importance for the understanding of these processes, with concrete local, general, comparative, and theoretical implications.

The execution, as well as the application of this extended study to the country's concrete problems, has been carried out in two sub-projects: (1) Investigation of a sample of local communities inhabited by new immigrants, focused chiefly on internal cohesion, main value-orientation, participation in general associations, identification with the country's types of leaders and leadership selection, and relations between leaders and communities. (2) Investigation of political activities among new immigrants (not described in the survey).

The specific purpose of the first sub-project was to examine the patterns of social relations in various ecological foundations and types of settlement of new immigrants and to analyze the function of these patterns in the immigrants' absorption in actual places of habitation as well as in their integration in the general society. All the main types of immigrant settlements, such as cooperative agricultural settlements (moshavim), transitional work settlements (maabaroth), semi-urban places, and an immigrant town, were included. Two interrelated clusters of factors, one connected with the immigrants' countries of origin, and the other with the type of community in which they settled in Israel, were analyzed. In the study of the first cluster, four major groups of immigrants, taking as a criterion the type of society they had come from, were distinguished: *The Western group*, consisting of immigrants from highly industrialized countries, whose occupational structure and reference group were typically middle class and whose integration, at this stage of the Israeli society's development in which not all their expectations could be met, seemed to depend on their ability to change their occupational and status image.

The "Eastern European" group – here reference is made not to a geographical region but to a type coming from all the countries that are partially industrialized or in the first stages of industrialization.

The "Colonial" group – consisting of persons coming from colonial countries, or countries with a similar economic and social structure, namely non-industrialized and non-democratic, and characterized by an incipient nationalistic trend and, at the same time, a particular kind of western influence.

The "Oriental" group – including immigrants from underdeveloped countries, whose contact with western ideas had been very restricted. This type carried over into Israel its traditional community organization, such as a nearly intact kinship structure based on the extended patriarchal family. The self-image of this group is determined not by class or occupational status, but by traditional and religious values, and successful integration seems thus to be best accomplished when these values are linked to the standards of the absorbing society.

The changes of values implied by the process of absorption was also analyzed. The value-learning process was studied in three aspects: (1) the nature of the value; its concreteness or diffuseness, the degree of verbalization it attained, and its general validity; (2) the distance between the norms to be learned and the normative pattern of the immigrant; and (3) the channels of communication which make the values and the norms available to the immigrant. In this context the importance of elites was given special attention, and conditions were studied in which old and new elites met and were able to fulfill their communicative functions in the concrete settings and in respect to various norms and values.

It seems that the first aspect does not depend directly on the type of immigrant group or on the type of community in which it lives in Israel; the above mentioned factors were nevertheless found to determine sometimes the occurrence of situations necessitating reference to the new value. The second aspect was found to be directly connected with the existing value-patterns of the immigrant types. Here the ecological variable proved fruitful as it made possible a finer analysis of the integrational processes by providing sub-types of the

Israeli value-pattern. Thus a kind of continuum of maximum and minimum distance between each immigrant pattern and the Israeli sub-patterns could be discerned.

Theoretically, the main variables of this project have thus been as follows:

> reference-group behavior
> communication
> norms and values
> social participation and leadership

The juxtaposition of these variables has proved fruitful and, besides explaining the specific Israeli problems discussed above, has thrown some light on general theoretical questions of stability and integration of social systems. Up to the present, studies of reference group behavior have been focused mainly on the influence of these groups on an individual's attitudes and behavior, but there has been almost no systematic exploration of the different types of reference-groups which are "referred to" in a given society and of their relation to the institutional structure of that society. Thus it was the purpose of this research to provide such a systematic exploration, as only in this way could the relation of reference-groups to the status-system and the integration (or disintegration) of a society be analyzed. It was thus possible to enquire why different individuals choose different types of reference-groups, what determines their choice, to what extent it is compatible with orientation to the society's values, and what are its effects on their conformist and deviant tendencies. Regarded as taking place within an organized social system and as related to the main values and norms of society and not only as a segment of individual behavior—reference group behavior is thus clearly related to communication processes. Systematic analysis of communication within society had already shown its two functions of providing the individual with both technical and valuational orientations beyond his immediate surroundings and groups; this project was thus able to extend the knowledge of the problems of effectiveness of communication and of communicative receptivity, i.e. of the predisposition to receive various types of communications, especially in respect to what may be called the "central" channels, namely those concerned with the transmission of values. In this context, the next problem, namely that of leadership, was taken up. Recent studies of communication have emphasized the importance of:

a. – the primary group, and

b. – the "opinion leader,"

as channels of communication, and the relation between the two had been investigated. The scope of this project was extended to include various levels of leadership, formal and informal, and the extent to which they exert communicative influence within the society. In this way the processes through which the institutional structure of a society exerts its influence on the choice of reference-groups by various individuals could be systematically approached. It was possible to analyze the processes of transmission of various goals and values from the bearers of authority, power and influence to various members of the society, and the conditions of their effectiveness or non-effectiveness. The initial problem of the relation of the various reference-groups to the institutional framework of the society thus becomes, as it were, rounded up and, at the same time, closely connected with problems of social consensus, conformity and deviance.

RESEARCH IN SOCIAL AND OCCUPATIONAL MOBILITY

These problems of integration have also been investigated in related fields, notably youth movements and groups. The scheme of this project envisages, in its complete form, a comparative study of immigrant and native youth, connected, on the one hand, with direct problems of immigrant absorption and, on the other, with the continuity of social structure through generations.

The recent appearance on the Israeli scientific scene of the Falk Project for Economic Research in Israel (most of whose researches are purely economic but which has sponsored also an extended sociological study) has enabled the Department to carry out a project on social and occupational mobility. While primarily directed towards an investigation of the institutional sphere of economy in Israeli society, it has also constituted an integral element of the main line of work already described. In this respect, its special interest lies in studying some of the problems, tensions and adjustments brought about by statehood in connection with the transition from an equalitarian, pioneering society to a predominantly bureaucratic structure of the organized state.

Two ocupational categories which seemed of particular significance from this point of view were chosen—the civil servants and administrative employees of the General Federation of Labour in Israel, illustrating the new bureaucratic forms, power and influence, and several groups of industrial workers, exemplifying the recent changes in the Zionist ideology of manual work. (In this study, the industrial aspect was analyzed. The agricultural aspect of the Zionist ideology is being investigated, i.e., in the project on collective settlements referred to further on.) Here mention should be made of the research on the social structure of the professions, a project whose value seems to lie chiefly in analyzing the importance of collective orientations for the shaping of professional organization and ideologies.

While in most of the studies described above greatest prominence was given to structural aspects, recently value patterns have begun to be emphasized. This trend has been evident in the inclusion of various culture-contact studies in the projects under execution, and—more specifically—in the great amount of anthropological work devoted to ethnic groups in concrete ecological settings. (This trend is also present in the work of other bodies, notably of the Henrietta Szold Foundation of Child and Youth Welfare).[2] The new project on social differentiation in collective settlements should also be viewed within this framework.

The collective settlements of Israel are by now well known all over the world; being a unique feature of this country, they are sometimes seen as one of its most characteristic aspects. Several sociological studies have been published about the "Kibbutz" but, unfortunately, none by Israeli sociologists. These studies are based on short observation periods or research done in specific areas only, and it is clear by now that they cannot provide an adequate basis for forming a comprehensive picture of the kibbutz. It is hoped that the new project of the Department of Sociology of the Hebrew University will be able to make important contributions to the understanding of this special type of society as well as to some theoretical problems. Concrete practical questions have not been neglected and even the partial analysis of the data presented to the central organs of the collective settlements was utilized as a guide in taking important organizational and educational decisions.

The central theoretical problem of this project is the functional interrelation between the cultural value patterns and the structural patterns of a society. The collective settlements, while starting with a more or less well defined "pioneering" value pattern of a non-differentiated "bund-type" social organization have, under the impact of different factors (economic growth, population growth, age, etc.), undergone perceptible changes. Using a stratified sample of settlements of different size, age, economic and social stability—the dual process of changing value patterns and changing social structure could be followed. These have been studied as they appear in some of the important institutional activities of the settlement members—family life, work, organizational activity—in their opinions and attitudes and in the informal group relations. The theoretical evaluation of the processed data is not yet accomplished but even so, many stimulating insights have already been obtained.

Especially interesting is the observation of the finer mechanisms which may throw some light on the integration of the individual into the web of social organization and the connections between the general societal value pattern and individual attitudes and opinions.

The Department has also carried out various studies in Jewish social history;[3] these are of interest not only for Jewish traditional history and its importance for studying Jewish society today, but may also contribute to a general knowledge of the processes of disintegration and subsequent recrystallization of societies.

GROUP DYNAMICS

Another line of research has been fruitfully developed over the last two years—namely, group dynamics. The Institute of Group Dynamics of the Hebrew University, though only recently established, has already done sound and illuminating work in developing this approach and applying it to concrete problems in industry, youth groups and other spheres of group management.[4]

PLANNED RESEARCH

The specific projects described above have all been undertaken by the Department of Sociology of the Hebrew University, which, understandably enough, is most concerned with the development of this field of study in the country, especially in its broad theoretical aspects. As has been pointed out, however, many other institutions are also engaged in sociological work—some of them in conjunction with the Department of Sociology or along the lines described above; others in related but more practical fields.

Among these should be mentioned the Henrietta Szold Foundation for Child and Youth Welfare which has carried out valuable work chiefly in the fields of education and socialization in connection with problems of cultural background and change.

The quick growth of population, the diversity of backgrounds and cultures of each successive immigrant wave, and the emergence of new problems, create, of course, also the need for constant basic surveys. Various agencies deal with this problem trying to keep track of all the different stages of the development of Israeli society. Important work is being done by the Central Bureau of Statistics of the Government, survey and research departments of various other governmental bureaus and municipalities, and the Israeli Institute of Applied Social Research.

The Central Bureau of Statistics publishes as part of its routine job a statistical monthly and a statistical year-book which contain extensive census data. Besides this regular statistical information, the Bureau engages from time to time in specific surveys in the field of income tax statistics and cultural and economic statistics, as well as inquiries in the fields of education, public health and social welfare.

The research departments of other governmental bureaus share this work by undertaking special surveys in their respective fields and by tackling some of the specific problems connected with their activity. Fine work is being done by the Ministry of Health and the Ministry of Social Welfare where a group of young sociologists and anthropologists are engaged in finding the most effective ways to teach habits of hygiene, proper feeding and child care, to an immigrant population from underdeveloped countries, as well as in helping the western immigrant to adjust his taste and standards to the possibilities and requirements of a Mediterranean climate and a restricted budget.

The Israel Institute of Applied Social Research is partly responsible for some of the opinion surveys and attitude research studies and job evaluation projects carried out for the above mentioned government offices. The Institute was and is involved in a wide variety of projects which cannot be enumerated here. To mention only a few: a "national survey of radio listening habits and attitudes in Israel"; "Health attitudes and practices of different cultural groups in Israel"; "Factors affecting occupational choice of boys about to graduate from High-School"; "Thumb-sucking habits of Jerusalem school children and their consequences," etc.

The above mentioned projects were designed to give answers to practical problems and are clearly client—and not theory-oriented; nevertheless, apart from their practical importance, they serve as the raw material of important theoretical work.

Census and survey data were analyzed by Professor R. Bachi, the Chairman of the Statistics Department of the Hebrew University and the Director of the Central Bureau of Statistics, in his demographic studies. Taking full advantage of the specific demographic situation in Israel, he concentrated on the demographic problems connected with mass immigration, immigrant absorption, and cultural change. Most important for sociologists is his work on the family patterns in different ethnic and cultural groups, differences in reproductive habits, and the process of change in the demographic pattern of these groups. As Professor Bachi started his demographic work in the pre-state period and continues to this date, he is able to view demographic change in a wide variety of situations.

Professor L. Guttmann of the Hebrew University and Director of the Institute of Applied Social Research, and his associates at the Institute, have made important contributions to the field of methodology. These new developments, grown out of work done at the Institute, have been tested there and later utilized to make applied research more fruitful and more economical.

Professor Guttmann has summarized his work under several headings: (1) Principal Components of Scalable Attitudes—related to the perfect scale. A whole series of components were found as intensity, closure, involution, etc.; (2) Image Analysis—"Images" are items predicted from the rest of items. By analyzing the interrelations of the images, one can discover the latent common structure of a set of items; (3) "Facet Design and Facet Analysis"—useful for "designing the universes of content of research projects"; (4) The "Radex" approach to factor analysis—the "Radex," a combination of the "Simplex" and "circumplex" formation of intercorrelations expresses the simultaneous differentiations in degree and in kind of a set of variables.

It is hoped that this review is not too pretentious. Most of the projects need further elaboration and are in fact still in the process of work. Moreover, the whole field of Sociology in Israel obviously suffers from a two-fold difficulty: on the one hand there is the constant and unrelenting pressure of concrete problems requiring answers to immediate and short-term problems, a fact which may often affect adversely studies with more general theoretical orientation; and on the other hand, there are the country's limited resources—though in this respect a great deal has been done to ease the technical problems of research as well as to train adequate scientific staff for the immense work to be done.

SELECTED BIBLIOGRAPHY

(This bibliography is severely restricted. The reader's attention is drawn to the research reports and to the publication lists of the principal bodies engaged in social research in Israel—the Department of Sociology of the Hebrew University, the Israel Institute of Applied Social Research, and the Henrietta Szold Foundation for Child and Youth Welfare; from these lists and reports an idea can be obtained of projects not mentioned in this survey, as well as of additional publications—in English, French and Hebrew).

R. Bachi, "La Population Juive de l'État d'Israel," *Population* (Juillet-Septembre, 1952), 405-452; "A Statistical Analysis of the Revival of Hebrew in Israel," *Scripta* of the Hebrew University (Jerusalem), III (1956), 179-247.

Y. Ben-David, "Report on the Research Project on Youth Movements in Israel," *Transaction of the Second World Congress of Sociology* (London) (1954), I, 90-95: "Professions and Social Structure in Israel," *Scripta* of the Hebrew University (Jerusalem), III (1956), 126-152.

S. M. Eisenstadt, "Youth Culture and Social Structure in Israel," *British Journal of Sociology*, II (June, 1951), 105-114; *Absorption of Immigrants* (London: Routledge & Kegan Paul, 1954); "Communication Systems and Social Structure. An Exploratory, Comparative Study," *Public Opinion Quarterly*, XIX, 2 (Summer, 1955), 153-157; "The Social Conditions of the Development of Voluntary Association —A Case Study of Israel," *Scripta* of the Hebrew University, III (1956), 104-125; "Political Struggle in Bureaucratic Societies," *World Politics*, IX, 1 (October, 1956), 15-36; *From Generation to Generation* (Glencoe, Ill.: Free Press 1956).

C. Frankenstein, Ed., *Between Past and Future: Essays and Studies on Aspects of Immigrant Absorption in Israel* (Jerusalem: the Henrietta Szold Foundation).

Y. Garber-Talmon, "Social Stratification in Cooperative Settlements," *British Journal of Sociology*, III, 4 (December, 1952), 339-357; "Differentiation in Collective Settlements," *Scripta* of the Hebrew University, III (1956), 153-178.

L. Guttman, "An Outline of Some New Methodology for Social Research," *Public Opinion Quarterly*, XVIII (Winter, 1954-1955), 395-404.

The Hebrew University Department of Sociology, *Report on Research Activities, 1950-1955* (Jerusalem, 1955).

Henrietta Szold Foundation for Child and Youth Welfare, *List of Publications, 1953-1957* (Jerusalem, 1957).

The Israel Institute of Applied Social Research, *Bibliography of Project Reports and Scientific Publications* (Jerusalem: January, 1955-December, 1956).

Rivkah Bar-Yoseph is Research Assistant, Department of Sociology, Hebrew University (Jerusalem). Born in Hungary, she reached Palestine in 1939; received her B.A. and M.A. degrees from the Hebrew University; did post-graduate work, Harvard University.

Dov Weintraub, Research Assistant, Department of Sociology, Hebrew University is in charge of research administration; born in Poland (1926––), came to Palestine (1940); did his graduate and post-graduate work at the Hebrew University.

NOTES

1. Among these, chief mention should be made of UNESCO and the Ford Foundation. The first sponsored a project on "Tensions," as study in the main line of sociological work (described in the next section of the chapter); the second made possible the principal research analyzed in this survey (namely Communication and Leadership, as well as the projects on the demographic and economic aspects of the absorption of new immigrants, undertaken by the Departments of Demography and Economics of the Hebrew University, in cooperation with the Central Bureau of Statistics). See: the UNESCO *International Social Science Bulletin,* VIII, 1 (1956), devoted to Cultural Assimilation and Tensions in Israel.

2. Notably: D. Feitelson, "Changes in Educational Patterns in the Kurdish Community" (in Hebrew), *Megamoth* (Jerusalem), VI (October, 1955), 275-297; D. Willner, "The Field of Anthropology and Certain Anthropological Perspectives on Immigrant Absorption" (in Hebrew), *Ibid.,* VII (January, 1956), 86-92; Willner, "Problems Involved in the Establishment of Cottage Industries in Immigrant Co-operative Settlements" (in Hebrew), *Ibid.,* VII, 3 (July, 1956), 274-285; M. Kols, "Culture Patterns and Adjustment Processes in Moroccan Immigrants from Rural Areas" (in Hebrew), *Ibid.,* VII, 4 (October, 1956), 345-376.

3. Chiefly: J. Katz, "Clarification of the Concept 'Precursors of Zionism'" (in Hebrew), *Shivat Zion* (1950), 91-105; "Rabbi Zvi Kalischer as a Historical Figure" (in Hebrew), Ibid. (1952), 26-41; *An Outline of Jewish History in the Modern Era* (in Hebrew) (mimeographed, 1953); "Religious Tolerance in the Method of Rabbi Menachim Hameiri in Halacha and Philosophy" (in Hebrew), *Zion* (1953), 15-30; *The Disintegration of Traditional Jewish Society* (in Hebrew) (mimeographed, 1954); "Messianism and Nationalism in the Teaching of Rabbi Judah Alkalai" (in Hebrew), *Shivat Zion* (1955), 26-41; "The Concept of Social History and Its Possible Use in Jewish Historical Research," *Scripta* (of the Hebrew University, Jerusalem), III (1956), 292-312; *The Attitudes of Jews Towards Gentiles in Traditional Jewish Society* (in Hebrew, in preparation).

4. Due to its recent standing, the Institute has not, as yet, published the results of its work; however, one of its chief projects, a study on cross-cultural education in respect to American students in Israel—is nearing completion and a report is expected shortly.

AFRICA

Chancellor Williams

Howard University

The impact of the rapid socio-political developments in Africa during the past ten years has influenced both the tone and the trends in sociological literature on the area.[1] From the historical perspective, the social changes in Africa are sudden. They appear to have taken the Western World somewhat by surprise; and social scientists, drawn to troublesome areas as by a magnet, have been confronted with a new challenge.

This challenge is being met in different ways. Some follow the standard procedure of research, supported by direct field studies of a community, a tribe or of a particular institutional phase that is being affected by revolutionary changes; some, while claiming concern with a particular aspect, nevertheless take the broader approach in the actual work and include many related, and often unrelated problems; others confine themselves to the traditional subject matter and methods without reference to the African upheaval; while still others, called upon at last for a more positive leadership in helping to shape the course of the twentieth century, have appeared in public forums and international conferences on Africa, presented scholarly papers which, unlike the usual research paper, generally brought to bear the total professional training and experience of these social scientists upon problems which actually involve the rest of the world.

Perhaps in no other period have social scientists been so called upon, so much relied upon, to help guide the world in the solution of pressing social problems by the use of the results of their investigations of the social structures of these newly aroused societies, their value systems and beliefs, economic life, political objectives—and the interrelations of all these.[2]

"Trends" in sociological literature have already been qualified above in reference to "others (who) confine themselves to the traditional subject matter and methods without reference to the African upheaval."³ This may be regarded as a counter-trend, predominant in French, Belgian and Portuguese Africa, but not at all confined to these colonies. The political philosophy of these countries, in so far as their African possessions are concerned, is reflected in the works of their social scientists: African nationalism is originated, not in Africa or by Africans, but in the West by non-Africans; Africans are being rushed by certain countries (Britain, for example) along political lines which they really neither desire or are prepared for; all the African wants, actually, is economic improvement, not political independence. Hence, the social scientists in these areas are more preoccupied with studies concerned with better housing, wages, accident insurance for workers, family compensation, health, and even programs to increase farm workers income to a level always higher than urban wages.⁴

It is also noteworthy that French and Belgian social scientists appear to be in larger numbers and far more active in these areas than is true of other social scientists in any other part of the continent, or even in all others combined.⁵

The over-all trend, however, is clearly influenced by the African "uprising" which has upset the European time-table for eventual self-government and independence. The effects of the continent's re-awakening on sociological activities are manifest not only in current social science literature, but also, as previously indicated, in the number of international institutes, conferences etc. summoned expressly to deal with the increasingly urgent African problems. These are significant, first because the social scientist, freed from some of the restrictive requirements of the scholarly monograph, can make a more effective contribution toward the solution of these problems, and, secondly, he can reach and influence a larger public through these means.⁷

There runs through much of the current writing a self-condemning criticism of the role of Western civilization in Africa. As has been stated, this is not confined to the French, Belgian and Portuguese possessions. The criticism is often another version of the innate-inferiority—of—Africans theory, for it says in effect that without the Western contact Africans would have remained forever contented (and backward), and would never have aspired to a status of equality with their Western benefactors. As it is, according to this theory, they are, at best, merely children trying to ape or play with the institutions of a higher civilization for which they are, and by a law of nature will always be, unfitted.

The role played by Western culture in upsetting or destroying native customs, beliefs, family life and the institution of chiefdom is therefore bemoaned. Even the Christian missions have been condemned for their undermining and destructive influence.[8]

As of May, 1957, the Belgian program of sufficient economic well being as a counter force to political aspirations on the part of Africans appears, on the surface at least, to be successful. Yet a sharp eye is being kept on educated Africans, and ways and means to keep them relatively contented are being studied, and different plans proposed. One of the latest of these concerns social legislation that will provide a special status for the educated Africans in such a way that the masses will not be disturbed.[9] It would seem to be obvious that this latter expectation can hardly be realized, and time alone will tell whether the educated classes can be kept permanently satisfied by a scheme of preferential treatment.

In contrast with the activities in the colonies which are under rigid French and Belgian control, there are vast areas in central, east and northern Africa which are relatively quiet in so far as sociological investigations are concerned. The few studies which have been made either come under the category of those concerned with the impact of the West on cultural patterns, particularly as regards social disorganization, or those concerned with purely internal problems as they now exist, and without any direct reference to possible Western influence.[10]

The Uganda study, although primarily sociological, is also concerned with the history of economic development, land laws etc.[11] One study in the Sudan compares the tribal religions as a means of determining what behavior patterns make for stability,[12] and another seeks to show the need for a knowledge of the human factors in a society before undertaking development schemes.[13]

It has been observed that most of the countries in north, east and central Africa, such as Ethiopia, Libya, Egypt, Kenya, Morocco and Tanganyika, are notable by the general absence of sociological interest. There are reasons for this, some being political; but this fact does not lessen the great need for the attention of social scientists to these areas.[14]

Reference has been made to the general nature of many of the African studies. These are useful, but we can proceed more safely to the general if we have first a body of foundation materials which only specific areas of study can provide: the family, the village community, recent cultural changes, population, multi-racial aspects, and the impact of recent socio-political movements on these and other aspects of the societies.[15]

West Africa fares better. Here social science seems to have touched most of the areas coming within its province, yet only the surface has been scratched. The impact of rapid social and political changes, as well as the influence of Western culture is reflected rather clearly in the literature on the area. This includes studies of (1) traditions and the cultural pattern, [16] (2) the family system, [17] (3) general social disorganization of an entire country, such as Ghana, where specific aspects, involving such things as the religion or the land system of a typical community or tribe are studied,[18] (4) demography and [19] (5) the strategic importance of Africa as a whole from the viewpoint of Western economic interests and military security.[20] Social geography takes on a new importance as the background environment "for human activities and stock-taking to clear the deck for action," [21] while the political situation appears to be claiming more of the attention of the sociologist than the political scientist, possibly because of the basically sociological phenomena involved in the sudden upsurge of so-called primitive and backward peoples.[22]

Standing like a rock immovable in the very heart of every African problem is the African's religion. It crops up in whatever aspect of the society one may be studying, for it runs through the whole life of the people. It is perhaps the most serious problem that faces the students of society and the agents of social change, for while our respect for all religions is such that a hands-off, non-interference policy is a part of our heritage, here we shall be forced to recognize eventually that the term "religion" is used as a cloak for many evils which cannot continue in any civilized community. Some African religious values will, by any unbiased appraisal, stand co-equal with those of the world's great religions. Encrusted around these wonderful values, however, are beliefs and practices of savagery and ignorance which have become institutionalized as an essential part of the Africans' tradition and culture.

Now both the social scientist and the educator may wish to by-pass this fact, but in doing so they should be well aware of the nature of the force which will set at naught most of their labors. The greatest single obstacle to the African's progress in the modern world is his own religion, and this will remain true until his religion is stripped of its savage increments. [23]

The studies centered around religion, therefore, are of high importance. They generally disclose hidden obstacles to progress in all the other fields, regardless of whether it is the home and family, disease and health, or better living from better use of the land.[24]

The African religions therefore become a matter of major concern to sociologists and other social scientists if their work in other fields in the continent is to be successful. Christianity has done practically nothing that disturbs those basic African beliefs which block progress. This is the same as saying that the Christian education program has failed in fundamental particulars. The reasons are many. Here it can only be pointed out that the Christian African, both educated and uneducated, generally holds fast to his own native religion, and sees no conflict or basic differences between the two, except that Christianity is linked in his mind with colonialism—and for this reason alone cannot be wholeheartedly accepted. Few Africans would agree with Carpenter that "the adoption of Christianity imposes no limitation on the general social evolution of an African individual or group." His premises for such a conclusion are certainly invalid.[25] A "sociology of Christian missions in Africa" might well be a great undertaking which can clear the deck for a more effective program of religious education for the West first, and then Africa. Certain small scale studies have been made. Some include material which would be useful in a more comprehensive study.[26]

The overall picture of the sociological literature on Africa during the last ten years is encouraging. Its chief characteristic is one of helpfulness—a sincere desire to help newly emerging peoples to find their way in a confused and complex modern world. Almost hand in hand with their brothers in the field of anthropology, the sociologists at work in Africa, drawn mostly from the West, have attacked many diverse problems. Many, such as the institution of domestic servitude, which is actually slavery, have been by-passed.

This survey indicates certain other areas requiring study and, in particular, suggests a comprehensive study of the role of both Christianity and "paganism" in contemporary Africa as basic to all other studies. Reference is also made to the over-concentration of social scientists in certain areas, relatively speaking, and the almost total neglect of others. In this connection it was suggested, albeit in a footnote, that our age would be better served if some of the many fellowship grants going to Europe could be diverted to areas of much greater and far more urgent needs—Asia and Africa.

SELECTED BIBLIOGRAPHY

David E. Apter, *The Gold Coast in Transition* (Princeton University Press, 1955). A study of the sociological factors of institutional transfer under impact of rapid political movement; the work "broke at the seams" in many places because it undertook to include too much of what was challenging and interesting, but not really relevant, within the sociological framework which the author set for himself.

G. M. Aulwick, "Social Change in the Gezira Scheme," *Civilizations*, (February, 1955), pp. 173-80, shows how both human and natural resources are needlessly wasted through failure to know human factors before undertaking development schemes.

D. Balandier, "Messianisme et Nationalisme en Afrique Noire," *Cah. Institute Sociale*, (January, 1953), pp. 41-66. A study of the effects of mission activities on the social and economic structure of a society.

W. R. Bascom, "Urbanization Among the Yoruba," *American Journal of Sociology*, LX (March, 1955), pp. 446-454. New factors shown in tribal organization which tend to offset modern trend, e.g., where most of the farmers live in a town, or a chief moves in with his people and keeps them together under traditional rule in a particular area of the city.

H. Baumann, *Les Peuples et les Civilizations de l'Afrique* (Paris: Payot, 1948). One of the best and most comprehensive of the general works on Africa, but general more in the sense of its continental scope rather than its subject matter; for it studies the cultural pattern of Africa as a whole and its relation to constitutional development in the countries which are moving rapidly toward self-government.

K. M. Buchanan & J. C. Pugh, *Land and People in Nigeria* (London: University of London Press, 1955). An excellent contribution in social geography of Nigeria; it seeks to bridge the gap in geographical knowledge as a basis for planning to meet the social changes, particularly those involving economic development.

K. A. Busia, *The Position of the Chief in the Modern Political System of Ashanti* (London: Oxford University Press, 1951). The study of the impact of modern social innovations on a traditional institution.

B. Colson, "The Native and Cultural Patterns of Contemporary Africa," in *Africa Today*, (July, 1956), pp. 69-84. While Baumann and Westermann did manage to do a satisfactory job in their book dealing with the cultural patterns of the entire African continent, the same could hardly be expected of Colson's article of 15 pages;

it does give some of the highlights, and perhaps this is all that was intended.

A. Doucy & P. Feldheim, *Problèmes du Travail et Politique Sociale au Congo Belge* (Bruxelles: Ed. de la Libarie Encyclopedique, 1952). Typical of sociological studies in French and Belgian Africa; the emphasis is economic, and this particular work deals with social legislation to protect African workers, accident compensation, family allowances, etc.

St. Clair Drake, "Prospects for Democracy in the Gold Coast," *The Annals* of the American Academy of Political and Social Science, 306 (July, 1956), pp. 78-87. A sociologist analyzes a political revolution within a democratic framework somewhat alien to the country.

M. Fortes, "Kinship and Marriage Among the Ashanti," in *African Systems of Kinship and Marriage* (London: Oxford University Press, 1950), pp. 252-283. The effects of social change on the family system, especially as regards the matrilineal descent problems; these are intensified, first of all, by the new economic outlook.

M. D. W. Jeffreys, "The Society of Ibibio Women," *African Studies,* XV (January, 1956), pp. 15-29. The most illuminating study shows how certain savage practices persist because they are all mixed up with desirable values.

D. Paulme, "Structure Sociale en Pays Baga," *Ifan,* Ser. B, XVIII (January, 1956), pp. 98-116. One of those studies of family and social structure of a community in transition which was referred to as basic to overall studies of societies; also includes the problem of new-comers in a settled society hitherto dominated by a few "principal" families.

L. Petillon, "Le Probléme de la main d'Ouvre," in *Discours du Governeur Général* (Leopoldville: Conseil de Gouvernement, 1952), pp. 19-29. Social and Economic Improvement of African workers is object of this study as a guide to social legislation.

A. I. Richards, *Economic Development and Tribal Change* (Cambridge: Wm. Heffer & Sons, 1954). A sociological work which, like many others noted in this survey, seems to have been forced by events into history, economics, etc.

L. Dudley Stamp, *Africa* (New York: John Wiley, 1953). A classic work in African social geography, the kind without which the social scientist is handicapped; it evaluates the geographical factors which should be considered in the study of societies or any part of social organization.

A. Sohier, "La Politique d'Integration," *ZAIRE,* V. 9 (November, 1951), pp. 899-928. Studies problem of how to integrate the educated African into colonial system.

Chancellor Williams (1905-   ) was born in South Carolina and attended the elementary school there before moving to Washington, D. C., where he graduated from Howard University, B.A., 1930; M.A., (1935); Ph.D., American University (1940). While Visiting Research Scholar, Lincoln College, Oxford University (1953-1954) he continued studies of sociological and educational problems of Africa; in 1956-1957, attached to the University College of Ghana, he carried out field studies of Howard University (1945-   ), he served as Visiting Professor of Sociology and Education, Tuskegee Institute (summer session, 1951-   ). Author of such works as *The Raven* (historical work on Poe, 1943), *Have You Been to the River* (novelized version of doctoral dissertation: *The Socio-Economic Status of Store-Front Church Movement in the United States*), he edited *The New Challenge*, and *The Principals Analyze Their Task* (a research publication), and has contributed to *Journal of Negro Education*, *The Social Studies*, etc.

NOTES

1. Melville J. Herskovits, "The African Cultural Background in the Modern Scene," in *Africa Today* (Baltimore, Mary.: John Hopkins University Press, 1954), pp. 30-31; E. Colson, "The Native and Cultural Patterns in Contemporary Africa," *Ibid.*, p. 70; William Bascom, "Obstacles to Self-Government," *The Annals* of the American Academy of Political and Social Science, 306 (July, 1956), pp. 62-63; H. R. Rudin, "The International Position of Africa Today," *Ibid.*, p. 50; Daniel F. McCall, "Liberia: An Appraisal," *Ibid.*, p. 88.

2. Herskovits, *op. cit.*, pp. 34-45.

3. Petillon, "Le Problème de la main d'ouvre," in *Discours du Gouvernour Général* (Leopoldville: Conseil de Gouvernement, 1952) pp. 19-29.

4. A. Doucy & P. Feldheim, *Problémes du Travail et Politique Sociale au Congo Belge* (Bruxelles: Editions de Librarie Encyclopedique, 1952); J. Mercier, "An Experimental Investigation into the Occupational and Social Categories in Dakar," in *Social Implications of Industrialization and Urbanization in Africa South of the Sahara* (London: International African Institute, 1956); David Tait, "La position occupée par la libation dans le rituel Konkomba," *Ifan*, Ser. B 17 (January, 1955), pp. 168-172. The first two of these are typical of the new concern with the social and economic welfare of Africans, while the last two proceed according to the traditional pattern, without reference to or any concern with the general ferment in Africa as a whole. These are characteristic of the sociological trend in French, Belgian and Portuguese Africa.

5. These growing activities on the part of the French and Belgian social scientists may well reflect a growing uneasiness over what is happening in the rest of Africa.

6. Examples are the 1954 Conference on Contemporary Africa, sponsored by the John Hopkins University School of Advanced International Studies; the 1956 Hawaii Conference on Africa; and the 1956 sessions on Africa and the Western World, sponsored by the American Academy of Political and Social Science etc.

Reference was made to the scholarly lecture, "freed from some of the restrictive requirements" of the monograph (footnotes etc.). To the established and recognized scholar this "requirement of scholarship" is often a fiction of scholarship. Many examples could be cited, but just now I have before me Dr. Kofi A. Busia's *The*

Position of the Chief in the Modern Political System of Ashanti. (London: Oxford University Press, 1951.) This study is mainly concerned not only with Prof. Busia's own tribe, but also with the very royal family of which he himself is a member. Yet throughout the work he quotes Rattray and others, to meet footnote requirements, on matters which he (Busia) himself is unquestionably the best authority. The work is thereby weakened. On the other hand, he and other social scientists are far more effective when they appear in a public forum. One senses their feeling of more freedom and less inhibition. Cf. K. A. Busia, "The Gold Coast and Nigeria on the Road to Self-Government" in *Africa Today*, pp. 289-304. See also: St. Clair Drake, "Prospects for Democracy in the Gold Coast," *The Annals, op. cit.,* pp. 78-87; W. R. Bascom, "Obstacles to Self-Government," *The Annals,* op. cit., pp. 62-70.

7. The essays are published either in a book form and enjoy world-wide distribution, as in the case of the John Hopkins studies, or in a special magazine edition, as in the case of the *Annals.*

8. G. Balandier, "Messianisme et nationalisme en Afrique noire," *Cah. Institute Sociale,* (January, 1953), pp. 41-66; J. Binet, "Commandement Africain ou Cameroun," *Pennant,* (July, 1954), Pt. II, pp. 67-78.

9. A. Sohier, "La politique d'intégration," *Zaire,* V, 9 (November, 1951), pp. 899-928.

10. D. Paulme, "Structure sociale en pays Baga," *Ifan,* ser. B. 18 (January, 1956), pp. 98-116. This study is exceptional in that it deals with factors in social disorganization which develop naturally without any Western contact. As a matter of fact, the Western influence is much overplayed by many social scientists; for it would seem almost trite to point out that social change and disorganization of one kind or another were going on in various African societies all along before the Europeans came.

11. A. I. Richards, *Economic Development and Tribal Change* (Cambridge: Wm. Heffer & Sons, 1954).

12. S. F. Nadel, "Two Nuba Religions," The *American Anthropologist,* LVII, 4 (August, 1955), pp. 661-679.

13. G. M. Aulwick, "Social Change in the Gezira Scheme," *Civilizations,* (February, 1955), pp. 173-180.

14. One of the greatest contributions toward the advancement of modern civilization and world brotherhood would be made if some of the "army" invading Europe every year with study-grants from various foundations could be diverted to Asia and Africa where the needs are greatest and most urgent.

15. By "general studies" reference is made to the following examples: Edward C. Jandy, "Ethiopia Today," *The Annals, op. cit.,* pp. 106-116; M. Perham, *The Government of Ethiopia* (London: Faber & Faber, 1948); C. G. Rosberg, "The Federation of Rhodesia and Nyasland: Problems in Democratic Government," *The Annals, op. cit.,* pp. 98-105; Rogert Le Tourneau, "North Africa: Rigorism and Bewilderment," in *Unity and Variety in Muslim Civilization,* ed. by G. E. Grunebaum (University of Chicago Press, 1955).

16. Colson, *op. cit.,* pp. 70ff.; Herskovits, *op. cit., passim;* H. Bauman & D. Westermann, *Les Peuples et les civilizations de l'Afrique* (Paris: Payot, 1948).

17. M. Fortes, "Kinship and Marriage Among the Ashanti," in *African Systems of Kinship and Marriage* (London: Oxford University Press, 1950), pp. 252-283.

18. W. R. Bascom, "Urbanization among the Yoruba," *The American Journal of Sociology,* LX (March, 1955), pp. 446-454.

1094 TRENDS ABROAD

19. K. M. Buchanan & J. C. Pugh, *Land and People in Nigeria* (London: University of London Press, 1955).

20. R. L. Conolly, "Africa's Strategic Significance," in *Africa Today,* pp. 55-63.

21. L. Dudley Stamp, *Africa* (New York: John Wiley & Sons, 1953), "Introduction."

22. David E. Apter, *The Gold Coast in Transition* (Princeton University Press, 1955); Drake, *op. cit.,* pp. 78-87; Busia, *op. cit.,* pp. 289-304. (See also Busia's *Position of the Chief in the Modern Political System of Ashanti,* footnote # 6.)

23. The time has come to call for a bill of particulars as to just what the European experts on Africa and many African leaders mean when they insist that "African culture and traditions must be maintained." For they never say which "traditions" or what parts of the culture they would maintain. Domestic slavery? Human sacrifices at the death of a Paramount Chief?

24. J. Harris, "Human Relationship to Land in Southern Nigeria," in *Rural Sociology,* VII, 1 (March, 1942), pp. 91-92; S. K. Akesson, "The Secret of Akom," *African Affairs,* XLIX (July, 1950), pp. 38-49; Nana Kobina Nketsia IV, *A Study of Morality in Selected Primitive Societies* (an unpublished B. Litt. thesis, Lincoln College, Oxford University, 1956); this study, by a highly educated African Chief, seems to advocate the retention of all African customs and traditions, including human sacrifices. At the death of a chief the "chief's retinue is conscripted and sacrifices for service . . . The king must be accompanied thither (the other world) by a retinue . . . and those who are conscripted, as well as those who elect to go voluntarily, all die in duty to king and country" (p. 149). The argument here is that this is as right and civilized as the universal rule for conscripts (draftees) and volunteers who are called upon to die for their country.

25. C. W. Carpenter, "The Role of Christianity and Islam in Contemporary Africa," in *Africa Today,* p. 112.

26. M. D. W. Jeffreys, "The Nyama Society of Ibibio Women," *African Studies,* XV (January, 1956), pp. 15-29; P. C. Lloyd, "Yoruba Myths—a Sociological Interpretation," *Odu,* 2 (1955), pp. 20-28; Akesson, *op. cit.,* pp. 38-49; Tait, *op. cit.,* pp. 168-172; Blandier, *op. cit.,* pp. 41-66; Nadel, *op. cit.,* pp. 661-679.

SOUTH AFRICA

S. Pauw

Principal Vice-Chancellor

University of South Africa (Praetoria)

The publication in 1932 of the report of the Carnegie Commission on the Poor White Question was the first important stimulus to the development of sociology in South Africa. The Commission recommended the establishment of a department of social studies at one of the South African universities. Within a few years all the universities had implemented this recommendation.

Initially the main emphasis fell on the study of poverty, other pathological phenomena and the training of social workers. Sociology and Social Work were embodied in the same courses, and even today the two subjects are taught under the aegis of the same Departments. Since 1940 there have been separate courses in Social Work. The poor white question gradually lost its significance as a major national problem and the accent shifted to other pathological phenomena such as prostitution, alcoholism and crime. Towards 1950 some universities instituted separate courses in Criminology. Even today, several universities focus their attention to a large extent on the study of pathological conditions, and sociology is still influenced by its bearing on the training of social workers. At the University of Pretoria, for example, Social Work is known as Applied Sociology.

The first professors of Sociology had been trained in Holland, Germany and England. Those with a continental training were appointed persons from England. The result was that the strong philosophic character of continental sociology was transplanted to the majority of the Afrikaans universities whereas at the English universities sociology evinced a more empirical character. The training at Cape Town, for example, was strongly directed to the social survey, an influence which had been brought from the London School of Economics.

While the first professors had mainly a European background, there was also the influence of the vast volume of literature from America. From the outset the text-books used were largely of American origin. The American influence was strengthened by personal visits to, and study in that country. In the forties, for example, the American influence at the University of Stellenbosch led to a strong trend towards empirical research with the accent on quantitative techniques. It was especially the influence of G. A. Lundberg that was spread in South Africa in this manner. In the course of time the other universities in South Africa also gave increasing attention to empirical research, and quantitative techniques played an increasingly important role.

This trend was carried so far that in certain circles research was seen as not much more than the collection of facts and the application of the most recent techniques. The theoretical bases of research and the interpretation of results were neglected. A large proportion of the research work was of a descriptive nature and made no permanent contribution to the determination of valid sociological generalizations. In recent years especially under the influence of Talcott Parsons, R. K. Merton and P. A. Sorokin, there has been a marked movement towards more theoretical analysis and a more profound theoretical emphasis in teaching and research. These trends are particularly noticeable at the Universities of Stellenbosch and Natal.

In the meantime the contrast between the English and the Continental approach has largely disappeared owing to the stronger influences from America. Nevertheless there has recently been a revival of influence from Holland at the Universities of Potchefstroom and the Free State. While the Social Survey still remains the main feature of sociology at the University of Cape Town less attention has lately been devoted to comprehensive surveys of the whole community and more attention has been given to surveys of particular social phenomena.

In a country such as South Africa with its strong tensions between the various social groups, one would have expected sociology to have been directed largely to the study of race relations. Actually this has not been the case. It is true that the Universities of Cape Town and Stellenbossch have undertaken considerable research on the economic position and the social conditions of the Cape Coloureds. It is also true that in Natal much attention has been focused on the study of

various communities such as Indians, Coloureds, Bantu and Whites
and that other universities have published works on racial and social
policies. It cannot, however, be said that sociology in South Africa
has devoted itself to any appreciable extent to the study of the relations between the various racial groups. It was rather the departments
of Social Anthropology and African Studies that undertook research
of this nature. They have made their influence felt through the
medium of two opposed bodies, viz. the Institute of Race Relations
which on the whole advocates a policy of racial integration, and the
South African Bureau for Racial Affairs with its policy of the separate
development of the various racial groups. At the University of the
Witwatersrand the Department of Psychology has done important
work on race attitudes.

The rapid urbanization of South Africa is reflected in the importance assigned to the study of urban sociology. Initially the University
of Stellenbosch attempted to concentrate its attention on rural conditions, and Rhodes University is engaged on a comprehensive
regional survey, but apart from that very little has been done in
South Africa in rural sociology. Practically all the universities have
done more in the sphere of urban sociology. The social surveys made
by the University of Cape Town dealt with the city of Cape Town,
while the University of Natal is at present undertaking a promising
series of ecological studies on Durban. The urban pattern in South
Africa seems to be very different from that reported in Europe and
America.

In the course of time a tendency towards specialization has become
increasingly apparent. The University of Pretoria is mainly concentrating on the development of the sociology of the family and on
criminology. At the University of Witwatersrand attention is being
focused on demographic studies, while at Stellenbosch the development of Industrial Sociology is envisaged.

As elsewhere there is a marked tendency in South Africa towards
interdisciplinary research and teaching. This tendency is most clearly
seen in a scheme for the advanced training of social research workers
at the University of Natal. With the aid of Carnegie funds a number
of consultants have been brought from America to give guidance in
connection with the advanced training of research workers. The
training was undertaken through the medium of a number of research
projects at Durban. Various departments of the University took part
in these projects, and conferences were arranged and were attended

also by representatives of other universities and research bodies. At Stellenbosch a comprehensive project covering the position of various racial groups in the Western Cape Province is being undertaken by a team of more than twenty research workers, representing practically all the social sciences and several natural sciences.

The limited vocational possibilities for sociologists has up to recently been a considerable handicap to the development of sociology. Up to the present approximately 50 persons have obtained their doctorates in Sociology at South African universities. About 50 per cent of these persons today occupy academic posts at the universities, while most of the others are employed by churches, welfare organizations and by the State. But the vocational possibilities for social research workers are clearly improving. Already these possibilities have had an adverse effect on the training scheme in Natal. The majority of the advanced students who have so far enrolled for this scheme have interrupted their studies because of attractive offers of employment or scholarships for study overseas.

The number of sociology students at the nine South African universities is probably about 2,000; of these approximately 1,100 are in the first year, 500 in the second year, 300 in the third year, while 100 are post-graduate students.

In South Africa public support for research comes mainly through two channels, viz. the National Council for Educational and Social Research which sponsors research in the sphere of the social sciences and the humanities, and the Council for Scientific and Industrial Research which sponsors research in the sphere of industry and the natural sciences. The latter body has far more funds at its disposal than the former; in fact, research workers in the sphere of this body have found it possible to undertake more research in the sphere of psychology and sociology than the research workers of the National Council for Educational and Social Research. Through its National Institute for Personnel Research it has already accomplished much in the sphere of industrial sociology by the development of psychological tests and the accompanying social research.

Sociologists play an important role in South Africa in the moulding of public policy. Most of the heads of university departments have been members of one or more Government Commissions of Enquiry. In some cases *ad hoc* research has been undertaken by the universities for commissions of this nature.

In the sphere of industry the sociologists of the Council for Scientific and Industrial Research have started undertaking contract research for industry. Sociologists also play a leading part in the work of national and local welfare agencies.

During the past quarter of a century much progress has been made in South Africa. As in other countries we find different approaches and different trends of development. There is a great lack of unity of vision and unity of purpose among South African sociologists. There is as yet no nation-wide association of sociologists, nor is there a sociological journal. But in spite of that, sociology and sociologists enjoy prestige in society, and there are many indications of a promising future.

SELECTED BIBLIOGRAPHY

C. W. de Kiewit, *A History of South Africa* (Oxford: Clarendon Press, 1941). The social and political growth of the Dominion.

W. W. M. Eiselien, "South Africa: Education for Non-Europeans," in *The Year Book of Education,* 1949 (London: Evans Brothers, 1949), 222-234. Treats education for the European, Indian, mixed-blood, and native elements of the South African population. Advocates "full opportunities for the Natives in their own spheres of life."

Ellen Hellman & Quintin Whyte, "Union of South Africa," in *Fundamental Education: Common Ground for All Peoples* (New York: The MacMillan Co., 1947), 63-80. A description of the current status and problems of education by an officer and a staff member of the South African Institute of Race Relations.

Alain Locke & Bernhard J. Stern, Eds., *When Peoples Meet* (New York: Hinds, Hayden & Eldredge, 1946). A collection of articles many of them covering or touching on the race and culture conflicts in South Africa.

Bronislaw Malinowski, "The Pan-African Problem of Culture Contact," *American Journal of Sociology,* XLVIII (1943), 649-665. A discussion of the techniques needed to "make a branch of humanity jump across centuries of development."

The Peoples of South Africa (Pretoria: The State Information Office, n.d.). A systematic factual and systematic survey.

South African Quiz (Pretoria: The State Information Office, 1956). A small handbook, synthesizing information on all aspects of South Africa's culture.

South African Scene—Volume I (Pretoria: State Information Office, n.d.). A valuable collection of photographs and articles, covering especially the field of social anthropology.

South Africa's Heritage (1952-1952) (Pretoria: The State Information Office, 1952). "The story of White Civilization in South Africa from the landing of the first Dutch settlers with Jan van Riebeeck to the present day."

Anson Helps Stokes & Thomas Jesse Jones, & J. D. Sheinalt Jones, & L. A. Roy, *Progress in Negro Status and Race Relations: The Thirty-Five Year Report of the Phelps-Stokes Fund* (New York: Phelps Stokes Fund, 1948). Includes a paper on the racial situation in Africa (and numerous brief statements concerning the activities of the Phelps-Stokes Fund in promoting education in Liberia).

Herbert Tingsten, *The Problem of South Africa* (London: Gollancz, 1955). A Swedish editor's report on a visit to South Africa and the desperate blind alley in race relations there.

UNESCO, *Social Implications of Industrialization and Urbanization in Africa south of the Sahara* (New York: UNESCO publications center, 1956). Pilot studies of the social effects of urbanization in Africa and the determinant factors of the social structure of African urban populations, considered with specific reference to a particular area by a group of authorities on the subject.

Margaret Wrong, "Education in British Central and South Africa," *Journal of Negro Education*, XV (Summer, 1946), 370-381. A systematic presentation of conditions in each of the territories and a fourfold recommendation for improvement.

S. Pauw, the second Principal of the University of South Africa (Since April 1, 1956); spent his youth at Elsburg (near Germiston) where his father was Principal of the Goede Hoop School; continued his studies at the Pretoria Normal College and at the University of Pretoria where he obtained the T.2 diploma and the B.Sc. degree respectively, his major subjects for the latter being Psychology and Chemistry. In the meantime the first courses in Mental Hygiene had been introduced at the Pretoria University which aroused his interest in Social Sciences, this occurring at the time of the Carnegie Inquiry into the poor white problem in South Africa; Pauw was invited to assist the Carnegie Commission for six months in compiling data and statistics. In 1934 the University of South Africa recognized Sociology as a major subject and Pauw, who had taken up teaching, started specializing in this field, receiving his M.A. degree in Sociology from the University (1938); his interest in social work led to his appointment as Employment Officer in Cape Town (1937) where he completed his studies for the M.A. degree with a thesis dealing with post-school youth; temporary lecturer in Sociology, University of Pretoria (1940), serving there 9 years; awarded the D.Phil. degree cum laude for his dissertation: *Die Berepsarbeid van die Afrikaner in die Stad* (1946); appointed, first, Senior Lecturer, Univesity of Pretoria, and (1948) co-professor of Sociology and Social Work; subsequently accepted a Professorship, University of Stellenbosch; appointed Director of the National Bureau of Educational and Social Research, Pretoria (April, 1945).

CANADA

Frederick Elkin
McGill University (Montreal)

Sociology is one of the newer social science disciplines in Canada. Sociology courses of a kind were taught early in the 20th century and MacIver came to teach at the University of Toronto in 1915. However, at the time, MacIver was identified with political science more than sociology and his orientation was more theoretical than empirical. Thus it was not until 1922 when Carl A. Dawson, a student of Robert E. Park and Ellsworth Faris, was appointed to McGill that professional sociology had its real beginnings. Dawson was especially instrumental in promoting sociology through the example of his work on the pioneer country; through encouraging students to do research; and later, through his textbook and activities in the Canadian Social Science Research Council.[1] Since then sociology has grown slowly but steadily, with gradually increasing specialization and acceptance by other disciplines, and is now firmly established in Canada's universities.

The contribution of sociology is perhaps best evidenced by its recognition from other areas of study. Schools of education and several schools of nursing require a basic course in sociology; psychiatrists and architects-in-training at McGill are given series of lectures; home economists at the Universities of Manitoba and British Columbia and divinity students at McMaster University include sociology in their curricula. Sociology plays a role in the Industrial Relations Centers at McGill and Laval Universities and, also at McGill, a joint M.A. degree can be taken in conjunction with the Department of Sociology and the Physical Planning Committee.

Further recognition has come from government agencies, including the Department of Citizenship and Immigration, Defence Research Board, Department of Labour, and Dominion Bureau of Statistics. Increasing numbers of sociologists are being appointed into these agencies and sociologists are often called in as consultants. Relatively little sociological research is done in private industry; however, a few sociologists have recently been employed. In total there are almost 100 persons in Canada who have had training in sociology and are working, fully or partially, as sociologists.

In recent years sociologists in Canada have become increasingly conscious of themselves as a group and in 1956 formed a chapter within the Canadian Political Science Association. This chapter, through representing sociologists to other groups and by means of a proposed newsletter, will undoubtedly strengthen ties among Canadian sociologists.

In discussing the development of sociology in Canada, we must consider two underlying factors, Canada's unique history and the development of sociology in the United States. In many respects, Canada's development has been similar to that of the United States. In both countries there have been pioneer developments, streams of immigration, westward movements of the population, and increasing urbanization. But Canada also has its unique characteristics. Geographically, Canada is a sparsely settled country with distinctive problems of transportation and communication. Secondly, mass immigration and the development of frontier communities have continued in Canada after the second World War. Thirdly, Canada never severed its strong ties with Great Britain, ties which are evident in its government and judiciary, the organization of certain mass media, and religious and educational institutions. And perhaps, most important, Canada's heritage includes a French-Canadian subculture. The French Canadians, who comprise almost one third of the population and live primarily in Quebec, are not immigrants, but "charter members" who have self-consciously sought to maintain their language, cultural heritage and identity.

The second major factor has been the development of sociology in the United States. Many disciplines in Canadian Universities borrowed their patterns of organization from British schools; however there were few English precedents in academic sociology. As a result, the proximity to the United States and similarity of many social problems led to a close association with American sociology. The link is evident in both the content and organization of the field and in personnel. The subdivisions of sociology are similar to those in the United States and almost all sociologists in Canada have had their advanced training in the United States or from Canadians who have studied in American schools. Even now, with only the University of Toronto and Laval offering Ph.D. programs, most Canadians do their advanced graduate work in the United States. The close association between American and Canadian sociologists continues after training with a constant interflow of sociologists and sociological communications and with Canadian affiliations to the American Sociological, and Regional, Societies.

At present sociology is taught in all major universities in Canada. McGill, Laval, and the University of Toronto have the largest and most active departments. Several have recently enlarged their staffs, especially the Universities of Montreal and British Columbia. Since World War II only two students have taken Ph.D.'s in sociology in Canada; however, approximately 85 have received M.A.'s.

In sociology in Canada, as distinct from certain other disciplines, the English and French Canadian Universities have similar orientations. More stress is placed on problems of French Canada at Laval and the University of Montreal, the two leading French-Canadian schools; however there is no difference in basic methods or theoretical interests.

Only a few schools have separate departments of sociology. At the University of Toronto, sociology is a subdivision of the Department of Political Economy. In the smaller universities there are too few sociologists to warrant a separate department and sociology remains either part of a social science division or allied with economics, political science, or psychology. The emerging pattern seems to be that of separate departments of sociology, perhaps joined with anthropology.

FRENCH CANADA

French Canada presents a unique situation in North America and has led to a special literature which covers many fields of sociology. The early impetus to research on French Canada came from Everett C. Hughes, formerly of McGill University. Hughes introduced the framework of a rural-urban axis, hoping to gauge changes in French-Canadian culture and institutions through a series of community studies, taking French village life at one end and Montreal at the other.[2] This plan never materialized; however two community studies were completed, one by anthropologist Horace Miner, of St. Denis, a stable, traditional rural community, and one by Hughes himself of the small industrial city of "Cantonville."[3] "Cantonville" is a French-Canadian community in which major industry was introduced by the

English, a situation not uncommon in Quebec. Hughes elaborates on the division of labor, the service and business enterprises, and the institutions, relating each of these to the two ethnic populations.

Research has continued on various aspects of French Canada, generally focussing on industrialization and its concomitants and following the framework established by Hughes. In a study of the Eastern Townships, a group of communities east of Montreal, Aileen D. Ross of McGill has described the population shifts of the French-Canadians and the effect on the displaced English group. Employing an ecological framework of invasion and succession, Ross indicates how the displacement has led to a readjustment of social and institutional life, with English religious and educational institutions dying out for lack of support and with increasing French participation in commercial enterprises and government.[4]

At Laval University there has been more emphasis on changes among the French Canadians than on English-French relationships. Jean-Charles Falardeau, approaching the parish as a social institution, notes that urban residents now belong to associations organized around secular interests which do not take into account that traditional parish structure and the urban parish must now compete for its clientele. And Falardeau, with M. Lamontagne, in a study in Quebec City, shows that urban famiiles are changing but still tend to be more "rural" than their American counterparts, suggesting the persistence of strong religious and traditional values in family life.[5]

The impact of urbanization is also apparent in a study of differential fertility of rural families by Nathan Keyfitz of the Dominion Bureau of Statistics. Employing census data, Keyfitz notes that the family size of French farms is smaller nearer to the city. The current of diffusion of family size is not from the English to the French, but from the city outward. A broader survey with further elaboration of fertility trends among French Canadians is given by Jacques Henripin, a Paris trained demographer at the University of Montreal.[6]

Miner, following a revisit to St. Denis in 1949, writes of more recent social changes. Miner found that the once largely self-sufficient community had moved towards greater interdependence with the outside world, especially in production and communication technology. Now too there is widespread electrification and a considerable cash income. The only surprise, not in accord with previously noted trends, was an increase in birth rate after 1936.[7]

In a history and analysis of an asbestos strike in 1949, a group of interested laymen and social scientists, including Falardeau and Fernand Dumont of Laval, further discuss the social impact of industrialization in Quebec. The authors tend to view the five month strike, in which the clergy and provincial government played important roles, as a turning point in the industrial, political, and ideological life of French Canada. The union sympathies of some of the authors are often in evidence; yet the research does point up the relationships between many institutional groupings in Quebec and the links between industrialization in French Canada and related developments in the western world.[8]

Philip Garigue has recently challenged the rural-urban framework which underlies much of the work on French Canada. Garigue affirms that too much emphasis has been placed on the traditional rural heritage and that historically, as well as currently, French Canada should be seen as a variant of North American culture. French-Canadian culture, he claims, had its beginnings in the commercial ventures of New France and high proportions of French Canadians have always lived in urban areas. Likewise, following a study of St. Justin, Garigue states that even in farm areas, the inheritance of land as a unit through a single heir, a point stressed by Miner, is not confirmed. Garigue also argues that French Canadians have traditional characteristics which fit them for life in the industrial urban world and there is no breakdown of traditional culture or family ties. He cites a study of kinship among French-Canadian families of urban backgrounds in which he found a wide range of kinship and genealogical knowledge, a high frequency of contact, and considerable interfamily services.[9]

It appears in the light of the various researches that we must be cautious in generalizing about traditional French Canada. However any disagreements that exist are vastly overshadowed by the basic recognition that the significant event in Quebec has been increasing industrialization and the resultant restructuring of ethnic relationships and institutions.[10]

Further research is continuing on various aspects of French-Canadian life. Jacques Brazeau of the Defence Research Board is studying the adaptation of French Canadian volunteers to the Canadian Armed Forces; Stuart M. Jamieson of the University of British Columbia is focusing on relations between French-Canadian workers and English-speaking employers; Andrew Kapos and Julian Blackburn of Queens University are studying attitudes toward bilingualism and cultural pluralism; P. Garigue is continuing his research on rural and small towns; at the University of Montreal, Norbert Lacoste is analyzing Montreal census tract data, J. Henripin is studying social aspects of infant mortality, and Hubert Guindon is doing research on the changing roles within the "Collège Classique"; and at Laval, M. Adelard Tremblay is preparing material on the kinship structure of Acadian communities, Roger Chartier is studying the impact of industrialization on a small community, Guy Rocher is doing research on intergeneration occupational mobility and the sociologists in various collaborative efforts are studying labor mobility in the forest industry, parish religious behavior, and cultural aspects of teaching in Quebec.

ETHNIC RELATIONS

To some degree, the concern with French Canada has overshadowed an interest in Canada's other ethnic groups. As a consequence, although much research has been done, authoritative sociological information on the general pattern of immigrant absorption is lacking.

Among the sectarian groups which settled in Canada and on which Dawson reported in 1936,[11] the Doukhobors have perhaps received the most attention. In recent years, their resistance to government directives led to an interdisciplinary project directed by anthropologist Harry B. Hawthorn of the University of British Columbia and sponsored by the provincial government. The project sought to obtain objective data rather than test specific hypotheses. The authors summarize the history, geographical data, and occupational distribution of the Doukhobors and relate these data to their economic history, familial patterns, religious organization, legal entanglements, and agricultural developments. Of particular importance in understanding the Doukhobors' way of life are their authoritarian parental relationships, the strong religious organization, and the values of the culture which stress both dependence on the community and the right of an individual to decide his own destiny.[12]

Research, primarily of a historical nature, has also been done on the Mennonites of Manitoba by E. K. Francis of the University of Notre Dame. Begininng with the experiences that led the Mennonites to leave Russia, Francis discusses such institutions as the mutual aid system and self government and such problem areas as school conflicts, attitudes towards the outside world, migration to other areas, and current adjustments. Francis notes that currently Mennonite settlements range from extremely conservative village communities to modern urban groups who have accommodated rather thoroughly to the society about them.[13]

The most extensive account of a problem faced by one particular group is given in Forrest E. LaViolette's *Canadian Japanese and World War II.* LaViolette, formerly of McGill University, studied the fate of 24,000 Canadian Japanese who were evacuated from British Columbia Defense Zones during World War II. With a range of source material including legal reports, government documents, statistical data, letters, newspaper reports, and case materials, LaViolette describes and analyzes the original crisis, the evacuation from "Little Tokyo," relocation and resettlement policies, and the general reactions and feelings of both the Canadians and the Japanese.[14]

Among particular immigrant groups studied, the most recently reported research has been by John Kosa, formerly of Sir George Williams College, Montreal. Kosa compares the settlement patterns of Hungarians in the United States and Canada. In both countries the early immigrants established colonies which offered protection and companionship as well as low rent; however, in Canada, the colonies tended to break up sooner. After World War II, the Hungarian immigrants in both countries were of a higher social class level and felt less need to associate with the earlier immigrants. Soon after arrival they took over the residential mobility patterns of the general population.[15]

Considerable statistical data have been compiled about the Jews of Canada by Louis Rosenberg of the Canadian Jewish Congress. Using census materials, Rosenberg has shown the trends for Canadian Jews in occupational distribution, population growth, intermarriage, and related problems, with an especially detailed analysis of the situation in Winnipeg.[16]

Research has also been done on the Chinese, Germans, Negroes, Poles, Ukrainians, and other minority groups in Canada. However, some of these studies are not specifically sociological and some are theses that have never been published.[17]

Reports have also been written on the reactions of Canadians to immigrants. In one article, Frank E. Jones of McMaster University discusses theoretical aspects of immigrant research noting the importance of a group point of reference and the functional significance to the "system" of bringing in new members. In another report, Jones, in collaboration with Wallace E. Lambert of McGill University, used a scalar technique to study the attitudes towards immigrants of a sample population in an Ontario community. In their theoretical framework they viewed each group to which one belongs as a social system moving towards established and valued goals. They found that favorable attitudes to immigrants correlated with high social status and the type and extent of immigrant contacts. Thus unskilled workers, for example, with low status and little control of their contacts, had less favorable attitudes. In general, immigrants were most strongly disapproved of when they were perceived as threatening the means through which native Canadians sought their goals.[18]

Guy Dubreille of the University of Montreal supports this picture in a report on attitudes towards immigration. In a sample of over 1000 persons in Montreal, Dubreille found that lower income groups and French Canadians were most likely to feel threatened and consequently were unfavorably disposed towards mass immigration.[19]

Ethnic and intergroup relations promises to be a major area of research. Projects now under way include a study by Audrey Wipper of the Defence Research Board of the organization of the Hungarian community in a crisis situation; continued research by Rosenberg on intermarriage, occupational trends, and farm settlements of Jews; studies by Kaspar D. Naegele of the University of British Columbia on English and German immigrants; several studies by Frank G. Vallee of the Department of Citizenship and Immigration; and a project by Daniel G. Hill of the Toronto Welfare Council on the Toronto Negro community.

OCCUPATIONS AND PROFESSIONS

There is much interest in the study of occupations and professions although some researchers are still reporting on material gathered in the United States. Most prominent in this field is Oswald Hall, formerly of McGill and now of the University of Toronto, whose main concern has been the medical profession. To Hall, following in the tradition of E. C. Hughes, the medical profession is of primary interest in so far as the knowledge derived therefrom can contribute to an understanding of the sociology of work. Hall points out that the medical organization forms an ordered system with formal and informal controls, established types of career patterns, and distinctive rights and responsibilities for its various members. Of special importance is the "inner fraternity," which functions to organize and, through recruiting and sponsorship, maintain the continuity of the system. Nor can this system be understood apart from the institutions and community in which its activities are carried out. Hall suggests that there is a fruitful approach in the merging of studies of occupations and institutional structures.[20]

Also in this sociology of work tradition is the discussion of the police by William A. Westley of McGill University. Following a study of the police department of a midwestern American city, Westley reports that the occupational experiences and needs of the policeman lead to both illegal use of violence and a strong code of secrecy. The police justify their use of violence by the morality and importance of their ends while the secrecy serves to protect the police against the attacks of a hostile public.[21]

Thelma H. McCormack, Research Associate and Extension Lecturer at McGill, follows this same tradition in a study of pharmacy students. Pharmacy is an occupation marginal to both business and profession and one might expect the students to experience a status dilemma. However, following a study of students in an American school of pharmacy, McCormack suggests that these prospective pharmacists try to avoid any internal conflict. While tending to idealize pharmacy as a profession, most expect to become independent proprietors and fuse the two systems.[22]

K. D. Naegele approaches occupations from a more comparative point of view. Naegele participated in the Wellesley project, in which social scientists and social practitioners collaborated with community leaders in an experiment in preventive psychiatry. Naegele's interest was partly in the roles, perspectives, and relationships of the research and community personnel involved. Following a Parsonian "pattern variables" approach, Naegele discusses similarities and differences between the roles of the psychiatrist, teacher, and minister, illustrating how these different roles imply different values and approaches to problems of common interest.[23]

Several occupation studies are now in progress. David N. Solomon of McGill University is studying the career lines of chemists; A. D. Ross is analyzing the changing status and ideologies of nurses; Elmer Luchterhand of the Aluminum Company of Canada is studying the engineer in large corporation, giving particular atention to the effects of managerial policies and practices; K. D. Naegele is extending his work to include student nurses, dieticians, and salesmen; Maurice

Leznoff of the University of British Columbia is studying the career line of the painter; and Roy E. L. Watson of Acadia University is doing research on the Nova Scotia Teachers Union.

SOCIOLOGY OF RELIGION

The most significant pieces of research on the Sociology of Religion are S. D. Clark's *Church and Sect in Canada* and W. E. Mann's *Sect, Cult, and Church in Alberta*.[24] In an earlier volume,[25] Clark of the University of Toronto had discussed the relationship between areas of economic exploitation in Canada, such as the fur and timber trades, and the social organization, noting how the new demands of economic activity had led to readjustments in the established institutions. In *Church and Sect in Canada*, Clark selects religious institutions for more intensive study. Through an analysis of historical documents, he traces the religious development of Canada from about 1760 to 1900, illustrating how religious institutions relate to developments on the frontier, urbanism, industrialization, and other social changes. With new social demands there developed new sectarian forms of religious organization which inevitably came into conflict with the established forms of church organization.

This historical analysis has been continued into a more recent era in Mann's study, one of a series, edited by Clark, on the background and development of the Social Credit movement in Alberta. Mann is a sociologist and Anglican minister, associated with the Toronto Diocesan Council for Social Service. Mann's analysis of the fundamentalist groups that bypassed the established churches follows the path set by Clark and other writers on sects. Particularly during the periods of depression there were many who felt psychologically as well as economically deprived. The established institutions were unable to meet or resolve the problems experienced by these depressed groups and the result in the religious sphere was the flowering of many sects and cults. In this volume Mann describes not only this historical development, but also the ideologies of the various sects, their techniques of evangelization, and the roles played by particular leaders.

Also worthy of note is the report of Hawthorn who uses his aforementioned Doukhobor material to test Simmel's statements on the operation of a secret religious society. In an analysis of the rebellious Sons of Freedom sect, Hawthorn suggests that the group, in its early years, aptly illustrated Simmel's hypotheses; however now, certain extensions and limitations are necessary.[26]

POLITICAL AND ECONOMIC SOCIOLOGY

The most significant work in Political Sociology is S. M. Lipset's *Agrarian Socialism*, a study of the development of the Socialist Co-operative Commonwealth Federation (C.C.F.) in Saskatchewan. Lipset, formerly of the University of Toronto, focuses especially on the relationship between political participation and organized groups, showing how the C.C.F. had to compromise in order to attain power and then adapt itself to the previously existing bureaucratic structure. Since radical agrarian movements have not been uncommon in North America, the immediate data have a relevance beyond the Canadian West.[27]

Also in this area are reports of S. D. Clark and T. H. McCormack. Clark compares the development of political institutions in Canada and the United States, suggesting that frontier experiences and revolutionary traditions were similar in both countries; however, in Canada, there was a reaction against these forces which led to a more centralized federal control. McCormack gives a general review of studies concerning the motivation of political leaders noting that emphasis has ordinarily been placed on the deviant personality type while the social context in which the radical behavior develops has been ignored.[28]

John Porter of Carleton College, Ottawa, has begun a most significant project on the power position of the Canadian elite, viewing Canada as an example of the Western industrial system. He states his purpose as follows: "If power roles can be satisfactorily identified in the social structure and social characteristics of the incumbents studied, a clearer picture of social mobility and power stratification would emerge."[29] Following the differentiation of elite roles into economic, political, bureaucratic, military, and ideological, Porter presents an analysis of the economic elite showing the high degree of concentration of economic power through an analysis of the multiple directorships of Canada's dominant corporations. Also, by analyzing the backgrounds of the elite, Porter suggests how the group maintains its social and ethnic continuity.

John Meisel of Queens University has discussed the relationship between voting behavior and religious affiliation. On the basis of sample surveys in Kingston, Ontario, following the federal election of 1953, and the provincial election of 1955, Meisel found that Catholics, compared with Protestants, had a much stronger preference for the Liberal Party. However, the relationship is not a simple one since there are variations among Catholics depending on the general political atmosphere and their "closeness to the church."[30]

Research is continuing in these areas: Porter and Meisel are carrying on their studies of the elite and voting behavior; Muni Frumhartz of Carleton College is studying voting patterns in Canada from 1945 to 1953; Leo Zakuta of the University of Toronto is doing further research on the C.C.F., and S. D. Clark is studying Canadian radical political movements in general.

THE FAMILY

The reported research on the family has focused almost entirely on middle class groups. The most intensive study is *Crestwood Heights* a prosperous suburb of a metropolitan city in central Canada and typical in many respects of similarly situated suburbs in the United States. The focus of the research is on the family since child rearing is the primary task to which the community is devoted. The authors discuss the ideologies, institutions, socialization patterns, and way of life of the residents. The ideological climate of the community, which is progressive, democratic, and experimental, is responsible for some of the problems which these families experience for the parents tend to look to child guidance experts for advice, and the experts' advice is variable and inconsistent. The residents seek to mediate some of their own struggles by sending their children to reputable schools, camps, and other institutions hoping to get the children back more mature. Also noteworthy is the authors' affirmation that it is not primarily ethnic, age, or social status differences that divide the community, but the ideological conflict between men and women. By scientific canons, many propositions of the authors are not confirmed, but the report does give a consistent, plausible, and perceptive picture of a suburban community.[31]

A study of a well-to-do suburb of Montreal by Frederick Elkin and William A. Westley of McGill tends to corroborate this picture of "Crestwood Heights." Using a sample of adolescents, Elkin and Westley likewise note the parents' concern with child rearing and the protectiveness of the setting. Their data contradict the oft-stated generalization that adolescence is a period of storm and stress which leads to the formation of rebellious peer groups and a distinctive youth culture. Adolescence in this community, they report, is part of a continuous development and by the time the children are in high school they have already internalized many adult goals and behavior patterns. And the parents on their part rather than upholding definite standards for their children, modify their demands in accord with the changing patterns of the society around them.[32]

K. D. Naegele, reporting on Wellesley project data, likewise discusses middle-class families. Naegele's research suggests that we should be cautious in generalizing about the more subtle aspects of family relationships. In one report, derived from interviews with mothers, Naegele discusses the expression of aggression in the family. The mothers all admit to some hostile feelings, but there is considerable variation in the way these feelings relate to patterns of authority, solidarity, and division of labor. Likewise, in a study of fathers, Naegele and his collaborator Aberle could find no clear cut connections between the particular satisfactions and strains of the father's occupational setting and his behavior at home. The fathers, in general, they report, were most concerned with traits in their sons which they considered to be prognosticators of success in middle class occupational life.[33]

Other research projects on the family are described in the sections on French Canada and social psychiatry. Still others are under way. Oswald Hall is studying family responses to the crisis of illness; A. D. Ross is preparing material for publication on the urban Hindu family; David Kirk of the McGill School of Social Work is carrying through a large scale study of the experiences of adoptive parents and the relationship between community and professional values and substitute family patterns; and C. W. Topping, now of United College in Winnipeg, is testing on Canadian families the hypotheses of Burgess, Cottrell, Terman, et al. on the prediction of marital success.

SOCIAL PSYCHIATRY

Social Psychiatry is one of the newer problem areas with which sociologists in Canada are concerned. The area has come to the fore partly because the presence of certain sects and the isolation of certain communities in Canada have presented good research opportunities. In some instances the research has been both interdisciplinary, involving collaboration with psychiatrists, and international, involving Canadian and American personnel.

The most ambitious project is the Stirling County Study, begun in 1950, and conducted by Cornell University in collaboration with the Department of Health and Welfare of the Province of Nova Scotia. Cooperating Canadian universities include Acadia, Dalhousie, and Laval. A group of sociological and psychiatric researchers, under Director Alexander Leighton and Canadian Deputy Director Alister MacMillan, have been intensively studying a rural area in eastern Canada, an area presumed to be reasonably typical of rural north-eastern North America. The central purpose of the research is to examine the relationship between psychiatric disorders and the social and cultural setting. A psychiatric unit recorded and described the psychiatric cases while a sociological unit under the immediate direction of M. A. Tremblay, studied the socio-cultural situation. As yet there are only scattered reports which describe the frame of reference and the material gathered. Perhaps most striking, sociologically, has been the selection of certain dimensions, including poverty-affluence, migration, English-French acculturation, secularization, broken homes, leisure, and communications which are presumed to have some connection with mental health. A judgment on the success of the authors in integrating these dimensions and relating them to mental health must await the final reports.[34]

John Cumming and Elaine Cumming, the latter now associated with the Committee on Human Relations at the University of Chicago, in another collaborative effort of psychiatry and sociology, studied the impact of a six month program of mental health education on a small relatively isolated community in central Canada. A well planned research design included an interview both before and after the campaign. In this instance the program was not successful in altering the popular attitudes towards the mentally ill; on the contrary, the campaign increased the anxiety and the negative feelings toward psychiatry. The authors interpret this reaction in part as a defense against the threat of unpredictability which is entailed in mental illness.[35]

The study of mental health among the Hutterites by Joseph W. Eaton of Wayne University and Robert J. Weil reports on data gathered in both the United States and Canada. The authors found, contrary to publicized opinion, that the prevalence of mental illness among the Hutterites was not very dissimilar to that found among other reported groups. However the techniques by which the Hutterites handled such illness were distinctive. The Hutterite colonies, in effect, were therapeutic communities which provided an atmosphere within which disturbed persons were encouraged to get well or function within the limits imposed by their illness.[36]

Other projects in the mental health area are in progress. Westley and Elkin are collaborating with psychiatrists at McGill in studying interaction patterns among families that have at least one emotionally healthy child; Bernard R. Blishen of the Dominion Bureau of Statistics is studying the relationship between certain aspects of the social structure and the etiology of mental illness; and Farrell C. Toombs of the University of Toronto is concerned with a program for the education of "practitioners" of psychological medicine.

OTHER AREAS OF RESEARCH

In recent years, researches have been reported in many other subfields of sociology. In the area of *Rural Sociology*, the most significant study is *Next Year Country* by Jean Burnet of the University of Toronto. In this volume, another in the socal credit series, Burnet analyzes conditions in the rural area of Hanna. Hanna was a community with little cohesion and, when drought and depression struck the area in the 1920's and 30's, the rather ineffective formal and informal groups were unable to withstand the crisis. Burnet discusses the resultant disturbances in the social structure, disturbances which were not even resolved with the relief of wartime prosperity. In another report, derived from the same material, Burnet focuses on the rift between Hanna and the surrounding area. She discusses the social and economic manifestations of the rift, especially pointing out the roles played by the town newspaper and the United Farmers of Alberta. In so doing, she convincingly points out the inadequacies of any simple rural-urban typology of communities.[37]

In recent years, Helen C. Abell of the Department of Agriculture, has been directing large survey projects and employing more specialized techniques. Generally reporting in Department of Agriculture bulletins, she has studied various aspects of rural life, including the exchange of farming information, plans of rural youth, and the reasons for the persistence of small farms.[38]

In *Population*, Enid Charles has quite thoroughly analyzed 1941 census data to present a picture of fertility differentials and trends in Canada. Nathan Keyfitz has engaged in various demographic studies, perhaps most notably reconstructing the immigration and emigration statistics in Canada. He estimates that between 1851 and 1951, with a movement of almost 14,000,000 people, the net gain to Canada was only about 600,000. Norman B. Ryder, formerly of the University of Toronto, similarly affirms that the major reason for the growth in the Canadian population has been the high rate of natural increase.[39]

A recent study by William Petersen of the University of California concerns post-war Dutch immigration, in the framework of the Dutch and Canadian cultures and social structures, Petersen discusses the attempts of the Netherlands' government to encourage and control migration to Canada while Canada sought to attract a limited number of immigrants of certain types. Petersen offers evidence that the administrative controls in both countries were established more in response to irrational pressures than as a rational means of solving a social problem.[40]

In the area of *Social Institutions*, A. D. Ross presents significant data on the organization of philanthropic campaigns in an eastern Canadian city. She shows how philanthropic activity is related to the successful business career and points out the importance of the "inner circle" who, through their ability to give or withhold sponsorship and institute positive or negative sanctions, can determine the success or failure of a campaign. Complementing these reports is the forthcoming detailed analysis of a Community Chest campaign by J. R. Seeley of the Alcoholism Research Foundation of Ontario.[41]

The most noteworthy development in the area of *Social Disorganization* was the establishment in 1954 of a program in Criminology at the University of British Columbia for the training of provincial correctional officers and the development of an M.A. course. With the appointment of several specialists and the close collaboration of the Provincial Attorney General, we may look forward to a significant research program. The most recently reported research in social disorganization is the study by Leznoff and Westley of homosexuals. They distinguish between secret and overt groups and describe the means by which homosexuals seek to evade social controls.[42]

In the related field of *Collective Behavior*, W. A. Westley has rather thoroughly reviewed the literature on crowds and has described tech-

*

niques by which the police of certain United States and Canadian cities handle various types of crowd formations.[43]

In *Methodology*, O. Hall demonstrates how role theory in social organization can be used along with sampling procedures; F. Elkin shows how widely experts may disagree in their interpretations of a life history document; M. Leznoff discusses the difficulties of gaining the confidence of homosexuals; and Mary Northway of the University of Toronto, and J. R. Seeley write on sociometric techniques, the latter reporting a method for scoring sociometric matrices and the former, following many years of research, publishing a handbook on the technique.[44]

In *Communications*, Kurt Lang, formerly of the Canadian Broadcasting Corporation, discusses the implications of a pre-television survey in Halifax which indicated that radio was preferred to newspapers as a source of news, F. Elkin comments on the value implications of popular films and analyzes the themes of the "western"; and Albert A. Shea, of CORE, a research organization in Toronto, has conducted a world survey of mass communications for UNESCO.[45]

In *Military Sociology*, D. N. Solomon points out the many areas in which the military may be employed as a laboratory for social study and reports on various studies concerning the socialization of the recruit into the Canadian army; and F. Elkin shows how the language of the soldier manifests his changed self-conception and his attitudes towards authority.[46]

In *Industrial Relations*, Elmer Luchterhand has recently discussed the adjustment of the employees in Kitimat, a northern frontier town built by the Aluminum Company of Canada; and C. W. M. Hart, formerly of the University of Toronto, has pointed out the importance of power groups in Windsor, Ontario, noting especially the union's growing role in the community and the inadequacies of a Mayo-type approach.[47]

CONCLUSIONS

In the past decade sociology has made considerable progress in Canada. Both in the number of sociologists and the amount of research there has been great expansion. Sociology has grown basically because of a demand for its distinctive orientation to problems of society. From an educational point of view, this orientation has broadened the perspective of thousands of students while practically, it has helped many in government, business, and the professional world resolve problems of administration and policy. We may expect sociology to continue to expand both within and without the university since the current growth and societal adjustments in Canada and the world at large demand continuous attention and the contribution of sociology in understanding these changes is becoming increasingly recognized.

Within the field of sociology itself, the current range of interests among Canadian sociologists is extensive and will probably continue to be so. Research has continued in previous areas of study and many formerly neglected areas such as social psychiatry and occupations have become major fields of concern. Within almost all subfields of sociology, as in the United States, there has been a tendency to employ more rigorous techniques of empirical research, a trend which will undoubtedly continue in both research and training.

Perhaps the most notable shortcoming of Canadian sociology, with the exception of work on French Canada and religious institutions, has been the lack of theoretical and substantive continuity in research. However with increasing personnel and with an increasing awareness of the relevance of theory, we may expect this to be less true in the future.

To what degree do Canadian sociologists view themselves as sociologists of Canadian life? Some projects in which sociologists have participated and will continue to participate are essentially of local interest, for example, problems of social agencies or government departments. However most sociologists in Canada view their work as having wider sociological relevance. They are well aware that their concepts and theories are not limited to Canada, that French-English relations are intergroup relations, that the C.C.F. is a political movement, and that suburbanization in Montreal has similar causes and counterparts elsewhere. In this respect, the sociology of Canada, save for its immediate problem selection and illustrative material, should be no different from the sociology of the United States or of any other country.

SELECTED BIBLIOGRAPHY

Jean Burnet, *Next Year Country* (University of Toronto Press, 1951). In this community study of a drought and depression stricken area,

Burnet reveals disturbances within the Alberta social structure which made possible the rise of the Social Credit movement.

S. D. Clark, *Church and Sect in Canada* (University of Toronto Press, 1948). Clark brings to bear his rich knowledge of both Canadian history and sectarian developments in this analysis of the development of religious institutions from about 1760 to 1900.

S. D. Clark, *The Social Development of Canada* (University of Toronto Press, 1942). Clark presents illustrative source material along with his historical analysis; he places particular emphasis on the relationship between the areas of economic enterprise and the development of social institutions.

C. A. Dawson and W. E. Gettys. *An Introduction to Sociology* (New York: Ronald Press, 3rd ed., 1948). This introductory text is noteworthy for its ecological approach and for the inclusion of considerable Canadian data; it has had a strong influence on Canadian students.

Jean-C. Falardeau, (ed.), *Essais sur le Québec contemporain* (Quebec: Presses Universitaires Laval, 1953). A series of papers focusing on changes in the economy and institutional structure of French Canada; the chapters include discussions of industrial growth, population problems, and the changing social structure.

Harry B. Hawthorn (ed.), *The Doukhobors of British Columbia* (Vancouver: J. M. Dent & Sons, 1955). This interdisciplinary project was sponsored by the Province of British Columbia in order to obtain objective data about the Doukhobors; chapters include discussions of religion, family relationships, economic history, and political problems.

Everett C. Hughes, *French Canada in Transition* (University of Chicago Press, 1943). This study of "Cantonville," a small industrial city in Quebec, was most significant in developing an interest in social research in French Canada.

Forrest E. LaViolette, *The Canadian Japanese and World War II* (University of Toronto Press, 1948). The Japanese on the west coast in Canada, as in the United States, were forcibly evacuated to relocation camps. LaViolette describes these developments and their social implications.

S. M. Lipset, *Agrarian Socialism* (Berkeley: University of California Press, 1950). A study of the rise to power and record in office of a Socialist party in Saskatchewan; the author argues that the movement can be understood only in terms of the background of agrarian radicalism in North America.

William E. Mann, *Sect, Cult and Church in Alberta* (University of Toronto Press, 1955). Although Mann is an Anglican minister as well as sociologist, he is notably impartial in reporting on the origins, characteristics, and functions of the splinter and non-conformist religious groups in Alberta.

William Petersen, *Planned Migration* (Berkeley: University of California Press, 1955). For two countries, one "overpopulated," and one "underpopulated," planned migration would seem to be an ideal solution; however Petersen shows that this "rational" solution leads to many complications when the social structures of the countries are considered.

John R. Seeley, R. A. Sim, and E. W. Loosley, *Crestwood Heights* (University of Toronto Press, 1956). This study of a prosperous suburb of a city in central Canada was part of a five year program of research, training, and guidance undertaken by the Canadian Mental Health Association in collaboration with the local university.

Pierre E. Trudeau, (ed), *La Grève de l'Amiante* (Montreal: Les éditions Cité Libre, 1956). Many authors, including social scientists, journalists, union officials, lawyers, and a priest have contributed to this study of the background, development, and implications of one of the most significant strikes in the history of Quebec.

Frederick Elkin, Assistant Professor of Sociology at McGill University, Montreal, Canada, (1952), was born in the United States and took his academic training at the University of Chicago (Ph.D., 1951); has also taught at the University of Southern California and the University of Missouri. Served in the U.S. Army (1942-1945); on the research staff of the Motion Picture Association of America, Hollywood, California (1947-1950). Has participated in research conducted by the National Opinion Research Center and has served as project director and consultant for the Defence Research Board, Canada. A member of the Canadian Political Science Association, American Sociological Society, and Eastern Sociological Society, his articles have appeared in the *American Sociological Review, American Journal of Sociology, Journal of Abnormal and Social Psychology, Social Forces, Journal of Educational Sociology, Sociology and Social Research,* and *Hollywood Quarterly*. Currently he is participating in research projects on persuasion in interpersonal relationships and family interaction patterns relating to mental health.

NOTES

1. C. A. Dawson and W. E. Gettys, *An Introduction to Sociology* (New York: Ronald Press, editions, 1929, 1945, and 1948).

2. E. C. Hughes, *The Natural History of a Research Project* (MS, McGill Library n.d.).

3. H. Miner, *St. Denis: A French Canadian Parish* (Chicago: University of Chicago Press, 1939). E. C. Hughes, *French Canada in Transition* (University of Chicago Press, 1943).

4. A. D. Ross, "French and English Contacts and Institutional Change," *Canadian Journal of Economics and Political Science* XX (August, 1954), 281-95; "Ethnic Group Contacts and Status Dilemma," *Phylon*, XV (Third Quarter), 267-75.

5. J.-C. Falardeau, "The Parish as an Institutional Type," *Canadian Journal of*

Economics and Political Science, XV (August, 1949), 253-69; J.-C. Falardeau and M. Lamontagne, "The Life Cycle of French-Canadian Urban Families," *Canadian Journal of Economics and Political Science*, XIII (May, 1947), 233-47.

6. N. Keyfitz, "Population Problems," chap. IV, in *Essais sur le Québec con temporain*, ed. by Falardeau (Québec: Les Presses Universitaires Laval, 1953); J.Henripin, "From Acceptance of Nature to Control: the Demography of the French Canadians Since the 17th Century," *Canadian Journal of Economics and Political Science* (forthcoming).

7. H. Miner, "A New Epoch in Rural Quebec." *American Journal of Sociology*, LVI (July, 1950), 1-10.

8. P. E. Trudeau, ed., *La Grève de l'Amiante* (Montreal: Les éditions Cité Libre, 1956).

9. P. Garigue, "Mythes et Réalités dans l'Etude du Canada Français," *Contributions à l'Etude des Sciences de l'Homme*, III (1956), 123-32; "St. Justin," *Canadian Journal of Economics and Political Science*, XXII (August, 1956), 301-18; "French Canadian Kinship and Urban Life," *American Anthropologist*, LVIII (December, 1956), 1090-1101. Garigue has also prepared a bibliography of materials on French Canada, *Bibliographical Introduction to the Study of French Canada* (Montreal: Dept. of Sociology and Anthropology, McGill University, 1956).

10. For a broad review of research on the social organization of French Canada, see Falardeau, "The Changing Social Structures," chap. V, in *Essais sur le Québec contemporain*.

11. C. A. Dawson, *Group Settlement: Ethnic Communities in Western Canada* (Toronto: MacClelland and Stuart, 1936).

12. H. B. Hawthorn, ed., *The Doukhobors of British Columbia* (Vancouver: J. M. Dent & Sons, 1955).

13. E. K. Francis, *In Search of Utopia* (Altona, Manitoba: D. W. Friesen & Sons, 1955).

14. F. E. LaViolette, *The Canadian Japanese and World War II* (Toronto: University of Toronto Press, 1948)

15. J. Kosa, "Hungarian Immigrants in North America," *The Canadian Journal of Economics and Political Science*, XXII (August, 1956), 358-370.

16. L. Rosenberg, *The Jewish Population of Canada: A Statistical Summary from 1851-1941* (Montreal: Canadian Jewish Congress, 1947); *A Population Study of the Winnipeg Jewish Community* (Montreal: Canadian Jewish Congress, 1946).

17. See: *Research on Immigrant Adjustment and Ethnic Groups: A Bibliography of Unpublished Theses, 1920-1953* (Ottawa: Department of Citizenship and Immigration, 1955, mimeographed).

18. F. E. Jones, "A Sociological Perspective on Immigrant Adjustment," *Social Forces*, XXXV (October, 1956), 39-47; F. E. Jones and W. E. Lambert, "Attitudes Toward Immigrants in a Canadian Community: 1. The Development of a Questionnaire," *Public Opinion Quarterly* (forthcoming).

19. G. Dubreille, "L'Immigration et les Groupes canadiens," *Contributions à L'Etudes des Sciences de L'Homme*, II (1953), 95-148.

20. O. Hall, "The Informal Organization of the Medical Profession," *Canadian Journal of Economics and Political Science*, XII (February, 1946), 30-44; "Sociological Research in the Field of Medicine: Progress and Prospects," *American Sociological Review*, XVI (October, 1951), 639-44; "Some Problems in the Provision of Medical Services," *Canadian Journal of Economics and Political Science*, XX (November, 1954), 456-66.

21. W. A. Westley, "Violence and the Police," *American Journal of Sociology*, LIX (July, 1953), 34-41; "Secrecy and the Police," *Social Forces*, XXXIV (March, 1956), 254-57.

22. "The Druggists' Dilemma: Problems of a Marginal Occupation," *American Journal of Sociology*, LXI (January, 1956), 308-315.

23. K. D. Naegele, "Clergymen, Teachers and Psychiatrists," *Canadian Journal of Economics and Political Science*, XXII (February, 1956), 46-62.

24. S. D. Clark, *Church and Sect in Canada* (The University of Toronto Press, 1948). W. E. Mann, *Sect, Cult and Church in Alberta* (University of Toronto Press, 1955).

25. S. D. Clark, *The Social Development of Canada* (University of Toronto Press, 1942).

26. H. B. Hawthorn, "A Test of Simmel on the Secret Society: the Doukhobors of British Columbia," *American Journal of Sociology*, LXII (July, 1956), 1-7.

27. S. M. Lipset, *Agrarian Socialism* (Berkeley: University of California Press, 1950).

28. S. D. Clark, "The Frontier and Democratic Theory," *Transactions of the Royal Society of Canada*, XLVIII (June, 1954), 65-75; T. H. McCormack, "The Motivation of Radicals," *American Journal of Sociology*, LVI (July, 1950), 17-24.

29. J. Porter, "Elite Groups: A Scheme for the Study of Power in Canada," *Canadian Journal of Economics and Political Science*, XXI (November, 1955), 506. Also see Porter, "The Concentration of Economic Power in the Economic Elite in Canada," *Ibid.*, XXII (May, 1956), 199-220.

30. J. Meisel, "Religious Affiliation and Electoral Behavior," *Canadian Journal of Economics and Political Science*, XXII (November, 1956), 481-496.

31. J. R. Seeley, R. A. Sim, and E. W. Loosley, *Crestwood Heights* (University of Toronto Press, 1956).

32. F. Elkin and W. A. Westley, "The Myth of Adolescent Culture," *American Sociological Review*, XX (December, 1955), 680-684.

33. K. Naegele, "Some Problems in the Study of Hostility and Aggression in Middle-Class American Families," *Canadian Journal of Economics and Political Science*, XVII (February, 1951), 65-75; K. D. Naegele and D. F. Aberle, "Middle Class Fathers' Occupational Role and Attitudes Towards Children," *American Journal of Orthopsychiatry*, XXII (April, 1952), 366-78.

34. A. H. Leighton, "The Stirling County Study," in *Interrelations between the Social Environment and Psychiatric Disorders*, (New York: Milbank Memorial Fund, 1953), 161-66.

35. E. Cumming and J. Cumming, *The Blackfoot Project: An Experiment in Mental Health Education* (New York: Commonwealth Fund, 1955).

36. J. W. Eaton and R. J. Weil, *Culture and Mental Disorders*, (Glencoe, Ill.: Free Press, 1955).

37. J. Burnet, *Next Year Country* (University of Toronto Press, 1951); "Town Country Relations and the Problem of Rural Leadership," *Canadian Journal of Economics and Political Science*, XIII (August, 1947), 395-409.

38. H. C. Abell, "Some Reasons for the Persistence of Small Farms," *Economic Annalist*, XXVI (October, 1956), 115-120; *The Exchange of Farming Information* (Ottawa: Canada Dept. of Agriculture, August, 1953); Abell and F. Uhlir, *Rural Young People and Their Future Plans* (Ottawa: Canada Dept. of Agriculture, January, 1953).

39. E. Charles, "The Changing Size of the Family in Canada," (Ottawa: Dominion Bureau of Statistics, 1948). N. Keyfitz, "The Growth of Canadian Population," *Population Studies,* IV (June, 1950), 47-63. N. B. Ryder, "Components of Canadian Population Growth," *Population Index,* XX (April, 1954), 71-80.

40. W. Petersen, *Planned Migration* (Berkeley: University of California Press, 1955).

41. A. D. Ross, "Philanthropic Activity and the Business Career," *Social Forces,* XXXII (March, 1954), 274-80; "Organized Philanthropy in an Urban Community," *Canadian Journal of Economics and Political Science,* XVIII (November, 1952), 474-86; "The Social Control of Philanthropy," *American Journal of Sociology,* LVIII (March, 1953), 451-460; J. R. Seeley, *Community Chest: A Case Study in Philanthropy* (University of Toronto Press, forthcoming).

42. M. Leznoff and W. A. Westley, "The Homosexual Community," *Social Problems,* III (April, 1956), 257-263.

43. W. A. Westley, *The Formation, Nature and Control of Crowds* (Ottawa: Directorate of Atomic Research, Defence Research Board) 1955.

44. O. Hall, "Use of Sampling Procedures and Role Theory in Sociological Research," *Canadian Journal of Economics and Political Science,* XV (February, 1949), 1-13; F. Elkin, "Specialists Interpret the Case of Harold Holzer," *The Journal of Abnormal and Social Psychology,* XLII (January, 1947), 99-111; M. Leznoff, "Interviewing Homosexuals," *American Journal of Sociology,* LXII (September, 1956), 202-204; J. R. Seeley, "Net of Reciprocal Influence: A Problem in Treating Sociometric Data," *Canadian Journal of Psychology,* III (December, 1949), 234-40; M. L. Northway, *Primer of Sociometry* (University of Toronto Press, 1953).

45. K. Lang, "Interest in News and the Selection of Sources," *Canadian Journal of Economics and Political Science,* XXII (November, 1956), 535-545; F. Elkin, "The Psychological Appeal of the Hollywood Western," *The Journal of Educational Sociology,* XXIV (October, 1950), 72-86; "The Value Implications of Popular Films," *Sociology and Social Research,* XXXVIII (May-June, 1954), 320-22; A. A. Shea, *World Communications* (UNESCO, 1950).

46. D. N. Solomon, "Civilian to Soldier: Three Sociological Studies of Infantry Recruit Training," *Canadian Journal of Psychology,* VIII (June, 1954), 87-94; "Sociological Research in a Military Organization," *Canadian Journal of Economics and Political Science,* XX (November, 1954), 531-41; F. Elkin, "The Soldier's Language," *American Journal of Sociology,* LI (March, 1946), 414-22.

47. E. Luchterhand, "Social Planning and Adjustment at Kitimat," *Canadian Personnel and Industrial Relations Journal* (October, 1956), 13-20; C. W. M. Hart, "Industrial Relations Research and Social Theory," *Canadian Journal of Economics and Political Science,* XV (February, 1949), 53-73.

V.

SOME CRITICAL COMMENTS

PHYSICALIST AND MECHANISTIC SCHOOL

Pitirim A. Sorokin
Harvard University

During the last few decades, various currents of Physicalistic or Mechanistic interpretations of sociocultural and psychological phenomena continued to be laboriously cultivated, especially in the United States. In this country particularly the period is marked by the intensified invasion and diffusion of the imitative "natural science, sociology, and psychology," "social physics," "social mechanics," "mechanical psychology," "cybernetic sociology," by physicalistic pseudo-mathematical, pseudo-experimental, and operational research of psycho-social phenomena, by proliferation of a legion of mechanical tests applied to all sorts of psycho-social and cultural problems; in brief, the period has been a sort of a Golden Age for physicalistic sociology and psychology. This trend has expressed itself, first of all, in an increased imitation of the terms of physical science, like "valence" instead of "attractiveness," "locomotion" instead of "change" or "transformation," "social atom" in lieu of an "individual," "dimension" in place of "aspect," "field" instead of "class or category of phenomena," "cohesion" in lieu of "solidarity," and so on. Secondly, the trend has manifested itself in an intensified importation and transcription of the formulae, methods, models, and tests of macrophysics, geometry, chemistry and biology. Third, in setting forth a large number of various physicalistic and mechanistic theories of psycho-social phenomena. So far there is no clear sign, as yet, of any recession of this trend. Let us now outline the main currents of the "modern" physicalistic sociology.

RECENT "SOCIAL PHYSICS"

We shall begin our survey of the recent "social physics" with a "manifesto of physicalistic sociology" by P. W. Bridgman.[1] Being an eminent physicist of our time, he unfortunately knows little of sociology or psychology. As a result, his manifesto is marked by the same characteristics which usually stamp a credo of a person who invades a science little known to him; that is, by the traits of incompetence, mistakes and, of course, by the discovery of table of multiplication after it was discovered long ago.

The book opens with a repetitious proclamation of the all too familiar credo of physicalistic sociology.

"It is to be a fundamental thesis of this essay that the same principles which physics have discovered to control any valid reconstruction of its concepts also control any valid reconstruction of social concepts." . . . "The parallelism in situation between physics and society is so close as to constitute more than a mere analogy, for it reveals a logical identity. . . . The physical approach [to social problems] thoroughly justifies itself." Operational method of study of social phenomena is the only reliable method. And so on, and so forth.

The bulk of the book deals with the concepts and methods of physics with an insistent advice to sociologists to follow this approach.

The last part of the book is devoted to a discussion of social concepts and problems such as: duty, rights, morality, politics, and economics.

Our eminent physicist seems to be unaware of the fact that his manifesto of physicalistic sociology is but a repetition of hundreds of such manifestoes promulgated by the partisans of "social physics" and "social mechanics" of the preceding centuries.[2] For this simple reason Bridgman's credo of physicalistic sociology does not have even a fascination of novelty. In his discussion of social problems—duty, rights, morality, "intelligent individual," "society," and so on, Bridgman seems to be unaware of an enormous amount of study of these social and ethical problems done during the preceding centuries. In comparison with the great types of ethical, political, and sociological theories in the field, Bridgman's views appear about as crude as Leucippus-Democritus' atomic theory in comparison with the atomic theories of modern physics. No wonder that Bridgman's reconstruction of sociology along the patterns of physics does not go beyond purely wishful analogies and stops short before it even clears the ground for the aspired magnificent palace of "social physics."

Somewhat further goes the attempt of a group of recent social physicists led by John Q. Stewart, an astrophysicist of Princeton. Like other physicalistic sociologists this group also assumes that sociology must pass through the stages of evolution analogical to those of physics; and that the former must follow the methods and concepts of the latter. In these and other assumptions the group uses the familiar analogical arguments open to criticism at all points of their presentation. Fortunately the group does not stop at these misleading analogies, but tries to discover various uniformities of psycho-social phenomena, and to describe them in terms of physical science. Let us glance at Stewart's social physics, its methods, uniformities, and other results of the group's labor.

> "Our immediate quest is for uniformities in social behavior which can be expressed in mathematical forms more or less corresponding to the known patterns of physical science. Social physics so defined analyses demographic, economic, political, and sociological situations in terms of purely physical factors: time, distance, mass of material, and numbers of people, with recourse also to social factors which can be shown to operate in a similar way to two other physical agents, namely, temperature and electrical charge. . . . Social physics describes mass human relationships in physical terms, treating large aggregations of individuals as though they were composed of 'social molecules'—without attempting to analyze the behavior of each molecule."[3]

His social physics thus views the social universe as six-dimensional or made up of six "social quantities" or "fundamental categories": "distance, time, mass, temperature, electric charge, and number of molecules," whatever social interpretation is given to each of these "dimensions" or "social quantities." We are told further that "this list [of six dimensions] makes social physics in its dimensional structure isomorphic with physical science," that is, "there is a complete and trustworthy analogy between two or more situations" which entitles "to transfer equations from physics to politics."[4]

Having thus outlined the framework of social physics, Stewart proceeds to round up together various social uniformities, and to interpret them in terms of his six-dimensional categories. As the most important example of the uniformities, Stewart takes Zipf's "rank-size rule" (discussed further). He extrapolates it much farther than Zipf did. We shall see further that Zipf's rule is at best purely local, temporal, and in no way is it as general as Zipf and especially Stewart claim. However, when Stewart is confronted with a task of interpretation of the rationale of this "rank-size rule," he completely fails to give any adequate explanation of it. "The rank-size rule is not at present derivable from general principles." Here we have "the widespread mathematical regularity for which no explanation is known."[5]

The failure leaves to Stewart only one way out of the difficulty, namely, issuing a big check for the unknown bank of the future where some day, somehow, by some bank the check of "social physics" will be redeemed "after much more study." This hope for the future banks where all doubtful checks of the present will be fully paid is also very familiar. However, it has nothing to do with a real scientific theory: science does not ask to "believe in its future promises," but, so far as it claims its recogniton at present, it pays its checks any time, anywhere, from its present capital of evidence.

Let us now glance closer at the social meaning of six categories, and at how they work in "scientific cognition" of social phenomena. First, we note that the time-dimension is taken by Stewart in the sense of uniform, evenly flowing, infinitely divisible time of macro-physics ("watch time"). Here he seems to forget that this macrophysical time is not quite applicable even to the microphysical phenomena. And he seems to be unaware that this time is only one of the "socio-cultural times" in no way identical with the variety of "qualitative social times," which are neither uniform, nor infinitely divisible. Being a mere variety of empirical "tempus" tied up with ever-changing sensory phenomena, Stewart's time entirely misses two fundamental forms of time called by the medieval scholastics: *aeternitas* and *aevum*. *Aeternitas* deals with eternal or unchanging forms of being, while *aevum* is category for semi-eternal forms of being like the truth of scientific propositions, which in their potentiality are viewed even by the scientists themselves as tending to be eternal and invariant (otherwise the true propositions would not differ from ever-changing fallacies).[6]

The moral of these remarks is that limiting his "time" to a "clock-time" Stewart cannot "locate" in time-process or to measure in time-units a large part of the sensory-empirical, and especially the "eternal or semi-eternal" values of sociocultural universe.

His other five "dimensions-categories-social quantities" are still worse for cognitive purposes than his "time-dimension." What, for instance, can mean "social mass," or "social electric charge," or "social temperature," or "social distance?" If they mean exactly what "mass," "electric charge," "temperature," distance," etc., signify in physics, then no "social physics," or "social mass," "social distance," etc., are needed. Physical sciences take good care of "mass," "electric charge," "temperature," "distance," etc., whenever and wherever they are found, including the human universe. If they mean something different from these categories of physics, then one has to show what each one of these terms really means, and, if it means something basically different from the meaning of these terms in physics, one has to give a reason why they are called by the terms of physics, and why the whole discipline is called "social physics?"

In Stewart's use these terms mean something quite different from their meanings in physics. Thus, his "electric charge" means really not an electric charge at all, but "desire"; the term "mass" means "the bodies of the people and of their domesticated animals, their stocks of harvested food, their clothing and personal equipment, artificial housing, buildings, and ships, plants of all sorts, the weight of material that had to be moved in constructing trails, roadways, railways, mines, harbor improvements, airports, dams. It includes water being circulated by pumps, and the mass of the tilled soil." Quite a "mass" indeed! After such a meaning of "electric charge" and "mass," we are not surprised at the meaning of "social temperature" which signifies "level of activity" of people and the intensity of their interaction; or by the meaning of "distance" which has very far relation to physics' "distance." On the other hand, several terms of the psycho-social sciences are given no less surprising (though not new) physicalistic meaning; for instance, "the politico-economical concept of liberty" is viewed as a form of "socal enthropy."[7]

The above shows that Stewart's "social physics" has no relation to physics at all. His physicalistic terms are likewise the total strangers to similar terms of physics. The categories of: "desire," "population and material culture" ("social mass"), "intensity of interaction and level of human activity," and so on, are just ordinary notions of traditional psycho-social sciences, and do not make these sciences "physicalistic" at all. For Stewart's sociology the term: "social physics" is a complete misnomer in its "physics" as well as in its "social" parts.

Taking now Stewart's categories in their real meanings: "desire," "level of activity," "the population and its material culture," "time," "distance," etc., we can easily see that this framework of categories is neither adequate logically nor fruitful empirically. It is certainly more clumsy and defective than several conceptual frameworks of general sociology. In addition, it combines together several incommensurable notions like "desire" and "social mass," (in Stewart's letter) "time" and "reason," "distance and authority," and so on. In this respect the framework is an abortive bastard of pseudo-physics and pseudo-sociology.

Unsatisfactory, also, is each of Stewart's dimensional categories. For instance, one can hardly use his category of "social mass" as an instrument of analysis and measurement of psychological and sociocultural phenomena. By itself this "social mass" is made up of so many, so different, and so difficult to measure and partly immeasurable quantities, that it is doomed to be a largely undefined, unmeasurable, and indeterminate variable or category.

One of the components of "the social mass" is "the bodies of the people." Now, suppose we find that one group of 100 individuals has the total weight ("the social mass") of 10,000 pounds (because it has many babies and children), while another group of 100 individuals has the total "social mass" of 16,000 pounds (partly because it has a few babies and the grown-ups are fatter and heavier). What sociological significance may such a difference have in the total weight of these two groups? And why is it important to know this "social mass," especially if we pay no attention to the age-sex-health composition of each group, its somatotypes, its morbidity and intelligence? If we pass from this component of the "social mass" to such components of it as "the mass of tilled soil" (not the acreage), we are confronted at once with the task of how to measure this mass of tilled soil. By acreage of one or two or five feet deep? And why is such a mass more important than the fertility of the soil or the average amount of crop produced per acre? And is not the whole of "social mass" an incomplete, and cumbersome, and very inadequate form of material wealth or capital more easily and accurately measured by economics? Why does Stewart's "social mass" give an importance to merely "weight" and "bulkiness" of plants, buildings, tilled soil, amount of food, clothing, buildings, "roadways," "railways and so on, without any consideration of their quality at all? A ruin of a mediaeval castle would weigh more and is bulkier than a dozen of modern houses; old siege machine weighs more than a small atomic bomb; a haystack weighs more than a bottle of vitamins; assortment of instruments of a jazz band weighs more than one Stradivarius violin; thousands of factory-made pictures weigh more than one sketch of Raphael or El-Greco. Does this mean that the group that possess these heavy "masses" is more advanced, more creative, more civilized than the group which has lighter "masses" of atomic bombs, vitamins, Raphael's picture, one Stradivarius, as Stewart seems to think? Shall we call more cultured a person who has a large library of detective stories, comics, grade-school texts, popular magazines, than a person who has only a few books like Plato's *Dialogues*, Kant's *Critique of Pure Reason*, Homer's *Iliad*, Shakespeare's *Tragedies*, and Dante's *Divine Comedy?*

These questions make clear that Stewart's "social mass" cannot serve either as an index of material wealth and prosperity, or as a measure of standard of living, of cultural and social creativity, or of cultural and civilizational levels, or of hardly any other important sociocultural state of a person or group. Being perfectly useless, it does not justify an astronomical load of work to obtain even its roughest measure. Being an astronomer, and having a meager knowledge of psycho-social sciences, Stewart seemingly assumes they hardly ever studied the problems of his social physics. His paper is interspersed by his semi-satirical remark that "spaces which separate people are airily ignored" (by social sciences); that "demographers had never introduced a term to measure the influence of people at distance"; that "the concept of demographic field" was unknown to social scientists; that they did not study intensively the phenomena of interaction, and so on. I can positively assure the author that not only all psychological and sociocultural phenomena discussed by him have been studied by the psycho-social sciences, but these sciences have investigated these problems with an incomparably greater care, adequacy, objectivity, and quantitative precision than Stewart's amateurish smattering does. Economics has handled and measured "the natural resources," "wealth," and "capital" much more accurately than the "social mass" of Stewart does. Sociology has studied demographic phenomena, the phenomena of interaction, "the influence of people at distance," social migrations and mobility, levels and forms of cultural and social activity, and so on, again so much better that any comparison with Stewart's superficial utterances in these matters becomes superfluous.[8]

If Stewart had seriously studied economics, demography, sociology, psychology, philosophy, and previous attempts to create "social physics" he would have hardly come out with his amateurish "social mass," "social temperature," "desire," and other dimensional categories of his antiquated "social physics." If anything, it is even more primitive than some of the previous "social physics and mechanics" outlined in Chapter I.

What is said of Stewart's "social physics" can be said, with still greater reason, of other modern "social physics," "social mechanics," "topological psychologies," "physicalistic politics," and so on, and so forth. In spite of my criticism of Stewart's endeavor, his social physics is better than most of the other physicalistic speculations of our time.

TRANSCRIPTIVE PHYSICALISTIC IMITATIONS

Here are transcriptive examples of these speculations, coined in the impressive terms of physico-mathematical sciences. T. Parsons and R. F. Bales solemnly announce: "We have found four fundamental generalizations for defining the equilibrium of social system in terms of 'four-dimensional space.'"

> "1. The Principle of Inertia: A given process of action will continue unchanged in rate and direction unless impeded or deflected by opposite motivational forces."
> "2. The Principle of Action and Reaction: If, in a system of action, there is a change in the direction of a process, it will be balanced by a complementary change which is equal in motivational force and opposite in direction."

In similar terms are formulated: "3. The Principle of Effort"; "4. The Principle of System-Integration."[9]

These and similar "fundamental generalizations" merely repeat similar transcriptions of practically all the earlier representatives of "social physics" (C. Berkely, Saint-Simon, H. C. Carey, L. Winiarsky, A. P. y Barcelo, and others, outlined in Chapter One). For this reason Parsons-Bales' contention: "we have found" is somewhat amusing. They did not find anything new. Secondly, if their transcription of Newton's, d'Alambert's, Lagrange's, or Bernoulli's "laws" aims at a mere popularization of these "laws," then they should have been given in the exact formulations of these great physicists and mathematicians, instead of the "home-made" formulations of our authors. Third, if Parsons-Bales' propositions contend to be the basic principles of human or social actions, then they become either meaningless or fallacious. They are meaningless because without the units of time, space, direction, change, force, neither the change of action nor its direction or motivational force, nor "equal" and "opposing" forces can be determined, defined, and measured. Since the authors give none of these units, their propositions become a meaningless imitative verbiage.

If we try to apply these generalizations to empirical social actions, they turn out into the obvious fallacies. According to Parsons-Bales' "principles of inertia," if one starts to eat or to micturate, one will be eating or micturating forever with the same "rate" and in the "direction," if there are no impeding and deflecting motivational forces. According to the "principle of action and reaction" no real change can take place in any system of action, because any tendency to change its direction "will tend to be balanced by a complementary change which is equal in motivational force and opposite in direction." Consequently, all actions will be forever frozen in the form in which they appeared for the first time. If one's primordial prototype action was, say, reading or chopping wood, one will be forever "frozen" in this action, unless some external force interferes. The absurdities of these "amateurish laws" are due: to a misinterpretation of the respective laws of physics by our "home-made physicists," to a clumsy application of the laws of physics to the phenomena to which they are inapplicable, to a vaguest definition of the principle of equilibrium[10] by the authors, and, especially, to their forgetting two basic principles: the principle of immanent change of a system according to which any system or action, as a going concern, cannot avoid change from "within" even in the constant and unchangeable environment; and the principle of limit according to which for any change in a certain direction there always is a limit.[11]

The criticism of Parsons-Bales' transcription and misapplication of the laws and principles of physics can be applied to all other misuses of physical and mathematical sciences.

As a rule knowing poorly these sciences, our "sociological physicists" are so strongly carried by their enthusiasm for the natural sciences that they import their terms without any regard as to whether the terms and their meanings can be applied to, and can be fruitful in a study of, psycho-social phenomena. These sociologists are so obsessed by their desire to create "a natural science of sociology" that fairly often they give gibberish definition and proposition made up of the carelessly thrown together terms of physics. The terms which have in the natural sciences clear and precise meanings are imported into sociology, and are given a meaning quite different from their original sense. In their new meanings they simply replace one of the traditional terms of sociology without adding to it any cognitive value. Instead of making the traditional terms more precise, the imported terms are explained by the traditional ones in order to have any meaning whatsoever. In this way a large number of perfectly parasitic terms have been imported into sociology where they merely litter its field, without rendering any fruitful service. Through this littering these imitators have turned sociological language into an obtuse jargon and sham-scientific slang devoid of clear meaning, precision, and elementary elegance. Thus, "valence" is introduced instead of "attractiveness," "syntality" in place of "the vital performance of group," "synergy" in lieu of "the total energy of group," "locomotion" in place of "change," "cathexis" for "pleasure-seeking and pain-avoiding or contacting," "enthropy" in place of "habit," and so on. The amusing side of these operations is the fact that the importers do not try to clarify the meaning of "attractiveness" by that of "valence," but try to define "valence" through "attractiveness," and so forth.[12]

When these physicalistic terms, emptied of their real meanings in the process of importation, are combined together to give supposedly a precise definition of psycho-social phenomena, they give factually a mere dump of these terms devoid of any clear sense. Here are a few examples of this meaningless verbiage.

> Organism is "a system of energy operating within a field of forces."[13]
> Individual is "both a mechanical system . . . and a semantic self."
> Mind is "an organism's selection of particular kind of material operations to perform upon particular kinds of matter-energy in order to minimize the organism's own probable work."
> Organism "is a movable mathematical point in space-time, in reference to which matter-energy moves in such a way that a physical situation exists in which work is expended in order to preserve a physical system from a final gravitational and electromagnetic equilibrium with the rest of universe."[14]

Sometimes our innovators ponderously define mere platitudes, even tautological platitudes at that.

> "From the definition of promotively and contriently independent goals, it appears that (a) any person, X, who has promotively interdependent goals with persons, A, B, C, will come to have promotively interdependent locomotions in the direction of his goal with persons A, B, C"; or "X has locomoted towards his goal." "Implications of cooperative situations are: 'substitutability,' 'positive cathexis,' 'promotive inductibility.'"[15]

These examples show well the physicalistic obsession of many a modern "natural science sociologist," as well as the cognitive fruit-lessness of their imitative efforts. Let us glance at other varieties of this obsession. About all this "jabberwocky" one can say with Alice: "It seems pretty, but it's rather hard to understand! Somehow, it seems to fill my head with ideas—only I don't exactly know what they are." With Humpty Dumpty we also can say: "There are plenty of hard words there."

RECENT "PSEUDO-MATHEMATICAL IMITATIONS"

K. Lewin's and J. F. Brown's "topological" psychology serves as another example of the meaningless transcription of geometric and physicalistic terms, propositions, and signs. They turn psychology into "psychological field" "as a space construct" where space "is under-stood in its post-Riemannian sense." To this "psychological field" they order all "psychological activities," and then transfer to it the terms of physics and of geometrical space: "direction, vector, sense, magni-tude, distance, force, continuity or discontinuity, liberty or restriction." They add to this assortment their own "home-made" terms like: "purpose," "goal," "striving," "ambition," and so on, entirely alien to any geometric space or science of physics.[16]

These transcriptive operations are instructive only in their errors while they remain sterile in their cognitive fruitlessness. First, they give an example of tautological definition of psychology as "psycho-logical field," or science of "psychological activities." Second, the authors distort the precise meanings of concepts of physics and geom-etry, giving to them psychological meanings entirely alien to the physical sciences. Third, they distort the meanings of psycho-social terms like: "goal," "purpose," "ambition," by interpreting them in spatial sense. For instance, the authors translate the term: "direction" into "goal" or "purpose" into "direction." The term: "direction" in physics or geometry means always "direction in space"; it has nothing to do with "goal" or "purpose" and is never used in this sense. Physics and geometry have "no spaceless goals," "aims to be achieved," "am-bitions to be realized." On the other hand, psycho-social meaning of the terms of: "goal" or "purpose" is rarely spatial; as a rule is does not have any spatial connotation. The goal of Mr. X. to become a millionaire or of Mr. Y. to get his Ph.D. degree has no latitude, altitude, longitude, nor any strictly spatial locus or direction. When these terms are called "spatial directions," the expression becomes meaningless. Fourth, by declaring that "the points in the psychological field . . . may for the present only be nonmetrically defined," the authors make these terms void of any significance: for the nonmetric magnitude, force, direction, distance, vector become the notions of a most indeterminate nature, hardly ever used in the physical sciences in this qualitative vague form. Fifth by mixing together physical and psycho-social terms our authors produce the meaningless bastards of these sciences disserviceable to physical as well as to psychosocial disciplines. Finally, a lack of fruitful cognitive results of these transcribing activities of our authors is an additional evidence of the futility of their imitative efforts. If Lewin, Brown, de Miranda, and others made some contribution to our knowledge of psycho-social phenomena, they made it in their real, non-imitative studies in which these transcriptive operations were absent.

"SHORTHAND" SOCIOLOGIES

Side by side with the imitative pseudo-physical and pseudo-geometric sociological theories, the physicalistic trend of the period has also manifested itself in a veritable proliferation of pseudo-mathematical studies of psycho-social phenomena. Perhaps the most conspicuous examples of these sham-mathematical sociologies are given by the *theories that substitute shorthand symbols and empty formulae for the true mathematical ones.* Here are a few examples of these sham-mathematical imitations.

In his quantitative study of interaction as a specific social energy A. Lysen tells us that: (1) the social ties can be either positive or negative; and, (2) that the interacting agents may be either qualitatively equal (inorganic ties) or unequal (organic ties). Expressing both criteria "mathematically," Lysen denotes the quantities of social energy by the symbols: a, b, c, and its qualities by those of x, y, z. Having obtained his symbols, Lysen proceeds to use them in the following manner: (1) $ax = bx + x$ means a horde or the sum of persons devoid of social consciousness and held together only by instinct; (2) $ax = bx - cx$ means the negative social ties or social conflicts; (3) $ax = by \times cz$ means the positive organic ties or collective consciousness of the interacting individuals; (4) $ax = by : cz$ denotes the

negative-organic ties or the sum of interacting persons aware of subordination, dependency, etc.[17]

No lengthy comments are necessary in order to see, besides a poor
classification and analysis of interaction phenomena and group-
structures, the sham-mathematical nature of the shorthand symbols
hindering rather than helping his verbal definitions of social energy,
positive and negative ties, and the types of groups. His *ax, by, cz,*
etc., do not mean anything clearly defined; neither do they mean
any measureable quantity or definite quality: his signs of: $=, +, -,$
$\times, :$ are perfectly arbitrary and do not mean at all what they mean
in mathematics. Why, for instance, is a group with collective consciousness denoted by the symbol of multiplication ($by \times cz$), while a horde
is denoted by the sign of addition of bx to cz? Or why the group
with domination-subordination is expressed by the equation:
$ax = by : cz$, while the group with social conflicts is defined by the
equation: $ax = bx - cz$? Why division in one case and subtraction
in the other? These formulae, symbols, and equations are nothing
but a logical mess, mathematical nonsense, and empirical rubbish.

Another example of sham-mathematics is given by many shorthand
formulae of K. Lewin, J. F. Brown, and others. For instance, the
notion that "the variety of behavior increases during childhood with
normal development," Lewin expresses by the following formula:
$var(B^{Ch})$ $var(^{Ad})$ "where *var* means variety; B^{Ch} behavior of child;
B^{Ad} behavior of adult." Or, "we call the totality of these factors the
life-space (L Sp) of an individual and write B = F (P, E) = F (S Sp)"
(B means behavior, P-person, E-environment).[18]

Lewin's works are full of these home-made shorthand symbols. Having no relationship whatsoever to mathematics, his cumbersome
hieroglyphics serve no useful purpose whatsoever.

S. C. Dodd supplies another set of sham-mathematical symbols.
Like other formulae of this sort, they do not serve even pedagogical
function of alleviation of understanding of Dodd's verbal statements.
Dodd's basic "S-theory" is the example of his formulae. Here is its
essence.

> "The generalization, 'People's characteristics and environments
> change,' can be more rigorously stated as: 'Any quantitatively re-
> corded societal situation (S) can be expresed as a combination of:
>
> 4 indices [I], namely: of time [T], space [L], a human
> population [P], and indicators [I] of their characteristics; each
> modified by:

4 scripts, namely: the exponent [I^s], and descripts denoting a series of classes [Is], of class-intervals [sI], and of cases [^{s}I]; all combined by:

8 operators (;), i.e.: for adding [+], subtracting [−], multiplying [×], dividing [:], cross-classifying [::], correlating [.], and identifying [!]."

The S-theory is a system of hypotheses which assert that combinations of these basic concepts [in square brackets] will "describe and classify every tabulation, graph, map, formula, prose paragraph, or other set of quantitative data in any of the social sciences."[19]

Here is the master formula of the S-theory: S = s/s (T;L;P;Ipp, Ir)/ss. Here S stands for recorded social situations; T—denotes time; L—distance; F—number of people; Ipp—indices of population's characteristics; Ir—residual characteristics.

We should not be surprised at a sharp reaction of an eminent mathematician to this metrophrenic abracadabra.

"There is no more pathetic misapprehension of the nature and function of mathematics than the trite cliché that mathematics is a shorthand . . . Mere symbolization of any discipline is not even a respectable parody of mathematics . . . For all its symbols, a theory may take the name of mathematics in vain. . . . No reckless abuse of the mathematical vocabulary can [of itself] transform a theory not yet mathematical into anything more substantially mathematical than a feeble mathematical pun . . . [Dodd's] 'Research Suggestions' contain several queries relating to possibilities for mathematical developments, for example, 'Can dimensional analysis of societal situations be used, as dimensional analysis is used in physics?' with a citation of P. W. Bridgman's (sic), *Dimensional Analysis*. Offhand, a mathematician would say, probably not, at least until someone can give a meaningful answer to such exactly analogous questions as, 'How many yards of buttermilk does it take to make a pair of britches for a bull?' Such queries as some of these in 'Research Suggestions' may seem profound to the mathematically uninitiated; to at least one mathematician by trade they seem profoundly pretentious . . . There is no mathematics in the book. As for the 'geometric technique consisting of translating S-theory into terms of vectors with their points, lines, and angles,' it seems to fritter out in a new 'verbalistic nebulousness,' evaporating finally in an unimplemented aspiration for a mathematical theory of human relationship."[20]

CYBERNETIC SOCIOLOGY

One of the most recent varieties of physicalistic sociology is repre-sented by the imitations of cybernetic models in a study of psycho-social phenomena. An eminent mathematician, N. Wiener, who coined the term "cybernetics" means by it a science of "control and commu-nication in the animal and machine," including man and social environment. In his opinion "the operation of living individuals and the operation of some of the newer communication machines are pre-cisely parallel." [22] Another leader in cybernetics, D. M. MacKay asserts, with some reservations, that the computing electronic machines can initiate human behavior on the same principles as the brain works.[23] The Cyberneticists claim that cybernetics not only clarifies the processes of transmission, operation, and control of organism by the messages coming from other agencies and of the agencies by the messages of a given organism, but that cybernetics furnishes "a new frame of reference for solution of such long-standing philosophical problems as: free will, consciousness, teleology, scientific method," etc.

For physicalistic sociologists and psychologists cybernetics has be-come a God sent gift for their mechanistic exploration of socio-cultural and psychological phenomena.

Whatever are the contributions of cybernetics to the problems of communication and control in machines and in physical mechanism of animals, sociological cybernetics has yielded, so far, very meager, now and then even wrong, results. First reason for that meagerness is the old fallacy of similitude of machine and human brain. The theories of similarity, even identity, of man with machine are very old. They already were voiced by several Hindu, Buddhist, Chinese, Greek and Roman thinkers. In Europe these "yarns" were developed by Descartes, T. Hobbes, Pascal, Leibnitz, Malebranche, Spinoza, Condillac, and others. Today's cybernetics notions of this sort are but one of the latest variations of this old theme. These notions are based on an unsound logic of a misleading analogy: "man has two eyes and cat has two eyes; therefore man and cat are identical ani-mals."

When the theory of similarity of man and machine is seriously examined by the foremost authorities in the field, like Sir Charles Sherrington, it is found to be fallacious. "Between the calculating machine and the human brain there is no basic similarity. The brain is a mystery—it has been—and still is. The facts we know concerning the brain . . . all fail to give a key to the mystery of how it creates our thoughts and feelings; that is . . . our mind."[24] The same conclusion is reached by one of the leading cyberneticists, D. M. MacKay. "I believe most seriously that man is 'more than' the physical organism . . . This implies not necessarily that there must be gaps in the physical amount of his activity, but that man has other *aspects*" that are neither revealed by, nor are contained in, the physical man.[25] Exactly the psycho-social aspects of man, his meaningful behavior and the meaningful aspects of social and cultural phenomena[26] cannot be explained, nor can be caught by the cybernetic net: they entirely slip between its meshes.

This cardinal condition explains why fishermen (K. Deutsch, L. K. Deutsch, L. K. Frank, R. D. Luce, A. Rappoport, A. Bavelas, C. M. Churchman, partly S. C. Dodd and others)[27] have not caught any big psychosocial fish in their cybernetic nets. While fishing with the non-cybernetic equipment they have caught a few real fish. Their cybernetic expeditions have given but empty shells, like the painfully elaborated platitudes, tautologies, and "rediscovery" of the physical law of falling bodies long ago discovered by Galileo and precisely formulated by physics. For obtaining these platitudes, tautologies, and "home-made" physical laws no costly and painstaking experiments were needed. A mere exercise of an elementary logic and mathematics, and comfortable reading of the texts of physics, history, sociology, and psychology would have given all the sound results of these cybernetic explorations, and a great deal more. At the same time such a reading would have prevented our cybernetic fishermen from catching several "dead fish" in their nets.[28]

TESTOMANIC SOCIOLOGY

In psychology and psychiatry the physicalistic trend of the period has manifested itself in the development of a "robot psychology," mechanical techniques and tests of personality characteristics, and in other currents of research dispensing largely with "mind," "mentality," "consciousness," "will," "thought," and similar "metaphysical entities" of the old-fashioned psychology. In the words of A. H. Maslow, the psychology of the period has mainly been "the technique-centered" psychology, "playing down the meaningfulness, vitality, and significance of the problem and of creativeness in general." [29] Accordingly, physicalistic psycho-social sciences of the period have "invented" hundreds of mechanical techniques believed to be testing scientifically any and all characteristics of the individual or a group. A veritable plethora of these tests has invaded these sciences and a vast army of "the testers" has succeeded to sell their products to their fellow-scholars, educators, governmental agencies, business and labor managers, and to the public at large. At the present time in the Western countries almost every individual is tested from the cradle to the grave, before and after an important event in his life. We are living in an *age of testocracy*. By their tests of our intelligence, emotional stability, aptitude, character, unconscious drives and of other traits of our personality the testocrats largely decide our vocation, occupation, social position, promotion or demotion, normality or abnormality, in brief, a large part of our life. At the present time, the testocrats have at their disposal a vast battery of supposedly scientific tests of all possible characteristics of personality or group. This ever-growing battery contains: (1) dozens of various intelligence tests; (2) tests of various traits of personality: aggressiveness, submission, caution, conformity, conscientiousness, originality, deception, suggestibility, and so on; (3) tests of instincts, "prepotent reflexes," and emotions; (4) tests of moods, temperament, will-power, extroversion-introversion, etc.; (5) tests of attitudes, interests, preferences; (6) tests of aptitudes, abilities, and leadership; (7) tests of ethical judgments and values; (8) tests of mental and moral normality or abnormality; (9) a legion of specific tests like: potential general and specific criminality, compatibility or incompatibility of prospective bridegroom and bride, loyalty and subversivity, successful or unsuccessful parole, etc.; (10) tests of the "basic type of personality"; (11) projective tests; (12) sociometric tests; and many others.[30]

This sort of "test--centered" psychology and psychiatry are largely responsible for penetration and permeation of the recent sociology with the testomanic fashion. The use and administration of various tests of personality or group have become a sort of preliminary "must" in the bulk of the modern sociological studies. A large portion of this research consists mainly of a statistical summary of various tests given to the persons or groups studied, beginning with their intelligence test and ending with the Rorschach, or the sociometric, or the psycho-dramatic tests.

If these tests were scientific indeed, and if they tested the respective traits of the individuals or groups as accurately as, say, thermometer tests the body temperature or barometer tests the barometric pressure, such tests and researches could only be welcomed. Unfortunately, the real situation is quite different. Almost all of the numerous tests are very far from being adequate, reliable, or scientific tests. About all these tests one can say what one of the pioneers of intelligence tests, E. L. Thorndike, says about mental tests. "Just what they measure is not known; how far it is proper to add, subtract, multiply, divide, and compute ratios with the measures obtained is not known; just what the measures obtained signify concerning the intelligence is not known."[31] When the tests are tested in their testing adequacy, the results often show that they either do not test at all what they are supposed to be testing, or they test a given characteristic in an unreliable, sometimes in a misleading way, or they yield the "quotients," "indexes," and "scores" as enigmatic as some of the utterances of the Pythia of Delphi or of the old tea-leaf tests. Even the most carefully administered intelligence tests like those carried on by L. M. Terman and his associates in their classical selection of 1,070 potential geniuses with I.Q.'s. ranging from 135 to 200 out of some 290,000 California children, did not seem to select the potential geniuses much better than a chance selection of 1,070 children out of a quarter-million of professional and business family children would have done. When Terman and his associates studied what happened to their 1,070 "potential geniuses" twenty-five years after their selection, the net results of this verifying study were fairly similar to a blind selection of 1,070 children of professional and business families, picked up without the battery of tests administered by the Terman group of investigators.[32]

When a competent team of psychologists, psychiatrists, and social scientists thoroughly tested the aptitudes and intelligence of some 5,391 recruits for the Office of Strategic Services and when, one year after the appointment of the testees to the overseas positions for which by the tests they were supposedly most fit, the staff of the experts tried to find out how successfully the testees performed their functions, the results were disappointing. "None of our statistical computations demonstrates that our system of assessment was of great value." The coefficients of correlation between the assessments of job rating (through the battery of tests) and the actual performance of the testees run between .08 and .37, mostly between .1 and .2.[33]

Still less reliable or less testing are other mechanical tests of personality: ascendance-submission, caution, compliance, perseverance, dominant interest, emotionality, will-power, originality, aggressiveness, etc.[34]

The same can be said of the projective tests of the hidden, unconscious regions of personality: drives ,"complexes," "repressions," "basic types of personality," and so on. The thematic apperception test, the free word-association test, the Rorschach test, the dream-interpretation test, the Rosenzweig P-F test, the story-completion test, tests through interpretation of plays, drawings and art-expressions, the doll and puppet test, are the examples of the projective techniques which, according to their adepts, open to us the dark caverns of the unconscious otherwise inaccessible to the non-projective tests. Critically examined the projective tests are full of holes. They are based on unproven theories and doubtful assumptions. The tests' nature is largely indeterminate. Interpretations of their results are quite arbitrary. Their validity is little demonstrated. When they are tested in their testing power, they are shown to be incapable to register even the strongest biological and "unconscious" drives. Thus, for instance, the whole battery of these projective tests hardly registered the strongest and persistent striving for food of 36 conscientious objectors kept on a semi-starvation diet for six months during which they lost about one-quarter of their initial body-weight.[35]

The reasons for the fallibility of all the mechanical tests are at hand. First of these reasons was long ago mentioned by M. de Montaigne: "Man is a marvelous, vain, fickle, and unstable subject, and on whom it is very hard to form certain and uniform judgement."[36] The highly complex, creative, and plastic nature of man is the main obstacle for the validity of the psycho-social tests generally, and of mechanical tests particularly, of persons and groups. This nature is responsible for many a wrong appraisal of the men of genius by capable observers, examiners, and teachers who knew them well. Such men of genius as St. Ignatius Loyola, St. Thomas Aquinas, G. Vico, Isaac Newton, F. Hegel, A. Pushkin, Leo Tolstoi, L. van Beethoven, J. S. Bach, G. Verdi, and others were estimated by some of their contemporary "experts" rather very low as to their creative ability. And *vice versa,* a legion of the "smart Alecs" who did not create anything significant were often evaluated as geniuses.

The second main reason for the fallibility of the modern tests of personality and groups is the perfectly artificial and superficial character of the bulk of these tests. An overwhelming majority of the tests represent either paper-pen or vocal operations and responses of the testees to the written questionnaires and to the vocal interview and quiz-questions. Only rarely the tests consist in an actual performance of the tested activities: violin or piano playing by the tested musician, designing and construction of a new gadget by a prospective inventor, writing a poem or novel by a writer; car-driving by a tested driver, and so on. In contrast to these real tests, the bulk of the contemporary tests are paper-pen and vocal tests, given mostly *ad hoc,* of a short duration, autocratically designed by the testers, assuming that the testees are capable to answer the questions instantaneously, ignoring the individual differences of the individuals, paying no attention to their mental state (moods, indisposition, blocking, etc.) at the moment of testing, favoring the fast and disfavoring the slow test-operations. Often the questions asked are vague; then they frequently ask for wishes, desires, aspirations, and hypothetical responses to imaginary situations and not for a factual knowledge. A large part of the questions do not require a display of logical thought, originality, or real skill, but mainly a memorized informational stuff. For these reasons, the answers to this sort of questions hardly reveal the difference between the competent and incompetent, skillful and skilless, original and "rubber-stamped," talented and untalented persons. Probing questions in psycho-social, ethical, political, economic, philosophical, and artistic fields yield often unreliable results for the reason of existence of divergent theories, approaches, generalizations, and values. As the testers are all too human, they are inclined to regard as correct the answers and values which agree with the testers' "denominational creed," and as wrong the answers different from their own. This daily occurring subjectivity contributes its share of errors to the test-results.

The inadequacy of the tests is notably magnified by the subsequent interpretation and quantification of the test' results. In contrast to the precise and direct indication of body-temperature by thermometer, or of barometric pressure by barometer, the indications that do not need any indirect interpretations, the results of the psycho-social tests, taken *per se,* are neither direct, nor clear, nor diagnostically meaningful. They acquire diagnostic or other meaning only when they are "interpreted" by the tester. And "the interpretations" are usually quite different from the empirical nature of the results as such. Empirically the results of a word-association test are but a number of various words uttered by the testee in response to the words of the tester. Perceptionally, the results of the Rorschach test are but a mass of various images evoked in the testee by an ink-blot of a Rorschach card.

Neither the words nor the images have, *per se*, any diagnostic or other meaning. They acquire such a meaning only through interpretation of these "syndromes" by the tester. Whether he wants it or not, he must *superimpose his interpretation upon the responses of the testee*. And these superimposed interpretations are quite different from the empirical or perceptional nature of the test-results. A patient tells correctly his last-night dream to his psychoanalyst or psychiatrist. He tells that in his dream he was climbing a mountain; that when he was near to its peak he suddenly lost his footing and began to fall down; that this falling down evoked in him a mortal fear, and in this state of trepidation he finally awoke. Such is the empirical content of the dream. By itself it does not have any diagnostic or other meaning. To acquire this meaning, it has to be interpreted by a psychoanalyst or psychiatrist. Is the dream a syndrome of some unconscious processes? If it is, does it manifest the Oedipus complex, or fear of castration, or some other "repressed" wish, or something else? Whatever the interpretation, its diagnostic character is quite different from the content and character of the dream itself.

These interpretations open the royal road for all sorts of arbitrary, fanciful, and subjective misinterpretation of the tests and their results. The very assumption that a dream is a syndrome of this or that subconscious process is already an arbitrary assumption quite different from the dream itself. That a given dream is a syndrome of a certain complex or repressed wish is again an arbitrary conjecture, devoid of a minimum of scientific proof.

When carefully studied most of the interpretations are found to be based not on a proven causal connection between the tests' results and the specific interpretation, but mainly on a dogmatic belief in the results as true syndromes or omens of certain—unconscious or conscious—entities and forces: repressed wishes, instinctive drives, various complexes, "native intelligence," "prepotent reflexes" or dominant interests of a certain variety, and so on. Among other things this is confirmed by fairly frequent discrepancy between the interpretation of the same results by different interpreters. To sum up: the interpretations import a large portion of non-scientific elements into the tests' results, and thereby notably contribute to their invalidity.

Still greater distortion of the tests-results is introduced by *their quantification*. Obsessed by quantomania our testers indefatigably measure their test-data and present them in an "exact," and "objective" form of numerical scores, indexes, statistical tables, marvelously decorated with impressively looking mathematical formulae and other simulacra of a precise quantitative research. A legion of psycho-social researchers sincerely believe that these impressively looking scores, indexes, rows of figures, coefficients of correlations, probable errors, standard deviations, coefficients of reliability, and so on, deliver but the objectively studied and exactly measured "diamonds of a valid knowledge." As a matter of fact, the bulk of these "diamonds" are but arbitrary, subjective, often fantastic, assumptions of the testers dressed up in quantitative costumes and mathematical make-ups.

The bulk of the tests' data is qualitative and, so far, is untranslatable into quantitative units. These data do not have objectively given quantitative points. They neither show how many score-points each test-response has, nor which response has a greater and which a lesser number of score-points. For this simple reason the points of each response cannot be counted: added, subtracted, divided, multiplied, or subjected to other mathematical operations.

This means that these quantitative units or scoring points with all the subsequent quantitative manipulations are largely the arbitrary creations of the quantifiers. They arbitrarily decide how many score-points to be given to each of numerous responses of the testees; which responses are to be given 10, 5, or 99 points. No less arbitrary become their scoring if they decide to give an equal number of points to all responses. If, instead of scoring points, the testers decide to rank the responses into a certain number of ranks, or numerical classes, such a decision remains also arbitrary. The same is true of their placing each response into one of these ranks. If, instead of one tester, the ascription of points, weights, units, or ranks is done by five "expert-testers" (and this subterfuge is frequently used) the quantification of five and five hundred pseudo-experts still remains arbitrary, since none of them has any objective basis for his numerological distribution of points or weights or ranks.

For the present, the totality of the considerations given about the doubtful validity of the artificial psycho-social tests and about the conditions additionally damaging their adequacy are sufficient to justify a strongly sceptical attitude towards the scientific nature of these tests. All in all they are hardly more scientific than the old-fashioned tea-leaves or coffee-grounds tests.[37]

Since the bulk of the modern psychological and sociological research consists in constructing and using all sorts of artificial tests outlined, with subsequent largely arbitrary quantification and interpretation of the tests' results, such a research can hardly contribute much to our understanding of sociocultural and psychological phenomena. In spite of an enormous amount of labor and funds invested in this "testomanic" research for the period considered, it has given to us a disproportionally meager knowledge of psycho-social phenomena. It has hardly disclosed to us any new significant uniformity, any valid causal or probabilistic relationship, and a deeper understanding of these phenomena. It has largely been busy with construction of many test-mirages and then in a quantitative investigation of the relationship between various illusionistic point-variables of these mirages. Living and operating in the world of these artificial mirages the testomanic sociology has largely missed the genuine psychosocial reality, inevitably committed many blunders, and is now lost in the jungle of its own numerous tests, their indexes, scores, coefficients, and arbitrary interpretations. To be sure the vast capital of labor and funds expended by the testomanic psychosocial science has given to us also some modest dividends of real knowledge of mainly insignificant facts, but the bulk of the capital has been rather fruitlessly wasted in its hunt for mechanical tests of the non-mechanical human beings, their properties, their societies, and their creative cultural achievements.

OPERATIONAL AND SO-CALLED EXPERIMENTAL
SOCIOLOGIES

Operationism. Next manifestation of physicalistic trend in the modern psychosocial sciences consists in a rapid spread of operational or/and experimental studies and methods. Though experimental method was widely used in pre- and post-Newtonian physics, P. W. Bridgman gave to it a new name: "operational" and attempted to make it as the only scientific method for physical and other sciences.[38]

> The essential meaning of operationalism in physics is that physical concepts should be defined in terms of actual physical operations. On this view there is no meaning to a concept unless it represents an operation which can be performed in laboratory. Thus the term 'pressure of gas' signifies nothing until an operation is described which constitutes the measurement of pressure [with the description of the apparatus like glass and rubber tubing, mercury, and the operations to get a pointer reading called the pressure of gas].[39]

So heralded by Bridgman and others, operationalism converted a legion of sociologists and psychologists into its followers. Operational method and definitions have become a sort of sociological and psychological "must" for a scientific researcher in these fields. Operational procedures and terms have become magic catchwords ascribed infallibility, precision, objectivity, and other virtues.[40]

When, however, the role of operational (experimental) method is carefully studied, one finds that its role even in the physical sciences has been much more modest than the operationalists claim, while in sociology and psychology operational approaches appear to have been mainly sham-operational and largely unscientific procedures having little in common with a real operational method of the natural sciences. In the natural sciences operational or experimental method has been highly fruitful within certain limits when it worked in cooperation with the logico-mathematical (theoretical) and intuitional methods. In no way, all or most of scientific discoveries have been due exclusively to it. Most of these have been started by intuition, developed by mathematico-logical (theoretical) thought and, at the last stage, tested and verified through an experimental procedure. Without intuitional flash and logico-mathematical reasoning, the operational (experimental) approach alone could hardly discover any of the basic generalizations and formulae of uniformity in these sciences. Bridgman's attempt to make the operational method as the only scientific method has been rejected by most of the natural scientists, and in his latest work Bridgman himself seems to have abandoned his excessive claims.[41]

As a matter of fact, many experimental (operational) discoveries happened to be contradictory and questionable, such as: the Compton effect, the value of the charge on the electron, and so on. The contradictions have been removed only through use of the non-operational (theoretical) logical deductions and mathematical inferences. Then, an experiment performed for the sake of experiment, and not for testing a non-operational hypothesis, conceived before the experiment, is irrelevant and meaningless. Further on, any operational experiment deals always with a narrow range of experience or reality. As such it gives only fragmentary results significant from the standpoint of the operation performed, but irrelevant for, and contradictory to, the results obtained through different operations. There would be as many different results and concepts as different operations are performed in a study of a given problem. None of these operations can give a general formula, concept or uniformity valid for different operational manipulations. For instance, the concept of pressure of gas measured by the ordinary U-tube is different operationally from that measured by ionization gauge; "intelligence," and I.Q. will be different when operations of their testing are different. At its best, operational method can give different, and often contradictory, fragments of knowledge. This explains why practically all basic discoveries, generalizations, formulae, and concepts of the natural sciences have been achieved only through cooperation of the intuitive, logico-mathematical, and experimental methods. In these discoveries the experimental method has ordinarily been not the first, but the last step consisting in testing a theory, conceived intuitionally and developed by logico-mathematical thought.

If such are the limitations of experimental-operational method in the natural sciences, still greater are they in the field of the psychosocial sciences. In sociological research the real operational method has hardly been used at all. Instead, under the name of operationalism its enthusiasts used the procedures which have hardly anything common with the real operational method. For instance, C. Kirkpatrick operationally defines "marital maladjustment" "as that quality in marriage which causes one close friend to classify the couple as maladjusted."[42] Marital adjustment was crudely defined in a similar way. Other operational investigators of happiness in marriage, like E. W. Burgess, L. S. Cottrell, H. J. Lock and L. Terman,[43] ask a lot of questions of the married couple itself, then arbitrarily weigh, score, and tabulate their unchecked answers, and present the results in the form of many statistical tables as an example of operational study of marriage-happiness. A majority of other psychosocial operationalists reduce, in a similar way, this method to a collection of the untested opinions —through questionnaires and interviews—then to a statistical processing this "hearsay stuff" (not admitted as an evidence in any court, not to mention science), and presenting to us a legion of figures, indexes, and coefficients as operational scientific study.

For anyone who knows ABC of a real experimental or operational method, these procedures have no relationship to a real experimental or scientific method generally. A physicist does not measure a barometric pressure by asking the opinion of two or more persons about the pressure. Instead, without asking anybody's opinion, he uses a barometer which gives a fairly precise reading of the barometric pressure. Likewise, a physician desirous to find out the temperature or the blood-pressure of his patient does not find the answer by collecting the opinions of either his friends or even of the patient himself. Instead, he uses thermometer, cardiograph, or other "gadgets" which give the answer to his questions.

Similarly, a physicist, or chemist, or biologist does not solve his problems in the easy ways of going and asking various persons what, in their opinion, is the structure of atom, or composition of a given chemical compound, or the nature and functions of chromosomes. Instead, they set forth an intuitional postulate, then make the deductions and inferences from it through their logico-mathematical analysis, then test the inferences experimentally, without collection of any hearsay stuff from two or more persons. Replacement of this scientific method by gathering untested opinions—through questionnaires or interviews—is an utter distortion of operational-experimental method generally.

Another variety of operational method, used by psychosocial scholars, represents an already familiar transcription of concepts, definitions, and formulae of the physical sciences. Constructed for a study of physical phenomena the conceptual framework of the physical sciences has a definite meaning, preciseness, and measurability. Applied to quite different psychosocial phenomena this framework becomes meaningless and useless. S. C. Dodd's "system of operationally defined concepts for sociology" serves as an example of these meaningless "operational transcriptions." [44] He introduces the concepts of: "time, space, population," and "all characteristics of people or of their environment" as the basic concepts of his operational system of sociology. With the help of these concepts and of their symbols: T, S, P, and so on, he reveals to us that "all static or timeless data may be represented by a zero exponent on the time component, . . $T° = 1$. . . . Acceleration is defined by dividing the speed, by the overall time period. The formula of it is $1/T^2$ or T^{-1}. . . . A societal force may be defined as an acceleration of change in a population and may be measured . . . as the product of acceleration and the population accelerated." Its formula is: $F = T^{-2}$ IP. And so on. In regard to all these transcriptions one can say, first, that none of these concepts are derived by Dodd from any operational procedure of his own, nor they are defined by him in any way; he simply takes them from physics. Second, since Dodd does not give any real unit for the measurement of societal force, or societal change, or acceleration, his definitions become empty and disoperative. Meaningless become also Dodd's statements like:

"the product of the acceleration and the population accelerated" and his "shorthand" symbols like $F=T^{-2}$ IP. Third, there is hardly any old-fashioned empirical study of psychosocial phenomena which does not use the concepts of time, space, population, environment, and other Dodd concepts. Why, therefore, these all too familiar concepts are introduced as "operational" and allegedly new, remains a mystery. To sum up: the whole transcriptive operation of Dodd has no relationship to a real experimental or operational method. It is but an imitative parody of it.

The same is to be said about many other "operational" studies of sociologists and psychologists, including those that identify the meaning of the terms: "operational" and "operationism" with those of: "quantitative" and "measurement." (S. A. Stouffer, D. S. Thomas, and others).[45] If we accept this identification, then the "operational method" in all these different meanings given to it by sociologists and psychologists becomes a sort of money whose real value, even its non-counterfeit nature, remains unknown.

This conclusion is empirically confirmed by H. Hart's study: "Toward Operational Definition of The Term 'Operation.'"[46] Hart shows that in some 140 papers on operationalism the basic term: "operation" is given very different meanings, remains undefined and devoid of any precision. Its leaders seem to have "understood each other" only "a minor fraction of time" and have hardly "achieved, and consistently maintained clearcut, operational concepts at crucial points."[47]

To sum up: in psychosocial sciences the operational method has hardly been used in the sense of a genuine experimental method. A wide variety of its uses represents a distortion of this method and has remote relationship to any scientific method generally. No wonder, therefore, that it has been notably fruitless in its cognitive results.

Sham-Experimental Method. Since the real operational method is experimental method—highly fruitful within its proper limits; and since almost all "operational" studies in psychosocial sciences have been "pseudo-operational," the question arises as to what extent the experimental method is actually used in sociological research? If we have to believe the claims of the texts and research-papers, experimental method seems to be flourishing in modern sociology. If, however, one keeps in mind the very essentials of the real experimental method, one regretfully finds out that almost all the allegedly experimental studies in sociology are in fact sham-experimental. Hardly any of these "experimental" studies meets the canon of inductive inference according to the rules of either agreement, or difference, or concomitant variation, or residue, or others.[48]

If, according to F. S. Chapin, "the fundamental rule of the experimental method is to vary only one condition at a time and to maintain all other conditions rigidly constant," then none of the experiments analyzed in Chapin's and Greenwood's works referred to are real experiments. Likewise, except purely physiological experiments, most of the experimental studies of strictly psychological phenomena are spurious, so far as their experimental character is concerned.

The most common type of a supposedly experimental procedure in psychosocial research consists in matching the experimental and the control groups or persons or situations, or in observation of the same group or person before and after exposing it to the conditions or agencies experimented with. The experimenters seemingly believe that by these matchings they make all the other conditions constant and vary only the condition experimented with. Though there are different degrees of matching, among this sort of studies I hardly ever have met any single study where the matching approaches the real experimental conditions. In practically all matching studies there always are dozens, even hundreds, of variables which are neither constant nor controlled, not even considered. Even the traits in which the experimented and controlled groups or persons are matched, being apparently similar, say, in age, sex, or religion, or political party, or school education these matched traits are as a matter of fact, not identical but very different variables.

The females or the males of the same age and race display all the imaginable difference in beauty, intelligence, somatic type, character, tastes, etc. Roman-Catholicisms of a new Chinese convert, or Jacques Maritain, Dorothy Day and of Cardinal Spellman are again quite different from each other. The Republican party of Senator McCarthy has hardly anything in common with the Republican party of a liberal Republican. And so on. For these obvious reasons "the matching" in such studies is not really matching in the identical traits, but a comparison in different traits fictitiously assumed to be identical. As a result such matching studies are comparing two phenomena different from one another, not only in the unmatched, but also in the matched conditions. For these reasons, if a researcher finds some difference between the experimented and the allegedly controlled groups or persons or situations, he does not have any solid ground to ascribe this difference to his experimental variable.[49] If he does so, he turns into a careless detective who arbitrarily picks up Mr. Jones out of hundreds of possible suspects, having not even any circumstantial evidence for his picking up of Mr. Jones. Such a procedure has evidently no relationship to a real experimental method.

The same can be said of practically all other procedures covered by the term: "experimental" in sociology and psychology. So far they represent mainly a poorest imitation of the real experimental method.[50] The sham-experimental nature of these studies is largely responsible for a comparative poverty of the results yielded by a large bulk of this sort of investigations, as well as often for contradictoriness of their results.[51]

We should cultivate by all means a real experimental method wherever it can be applied, and the more it is used in psychosocial sciences, the better. But we should avoid using its sham-experimental imitations. These cannot contribute to a real knowledge of psychosocial phenomena. If anything, they corrode the experimental studies and psychosocial science itself.

ATOMISTIC AND SMALL GROUP SOCIOLOGIES

Hunt for social atoms. Recent "atomistic" and "small group" sociologies are also, to a large extent, a belated manifestation of the prevalent physicalistic trend in the psychosocial sciences. Since the pre-twentieth century physics dealt with atoms as the simplest units of physical phenomena, our physicalistic sociologists had to find the psychosocial counterpart of atoms. Since the main methodological rule of the bio-physical sciences of the nineteenth century was to proceed from a study of the simplest atoms or organisms to the increasingly complex physical and biological phenomena, the partisans of "the natural science sociology or psychology" had to imitate this rule by assuming that "the small groups" are the simplest social bodies and, as such, should be the starting point for a study of the large and complex social organizations. Hence the contemporary pre-occupation with "social atoms" and "small groups."

Of several recent theories of "social atoms," L. J. Moreno's theory is probably the best. According to Moreno

> The social atom is the nucleus of all individuals toward whom a person is emotionally related, or who are related to him at the

same time [emotional relatedness means attraction or repulsion].
It is the smallest nucleus of an emotionally toned inter-personal
pattern in the social universe. . . . The social atoms are the centers of attraction or rejection. It is the social atom which is the
smallest social unit, not the individual. . . . The social atom is
simply an individual and the people he is emotionally related
to at the time.[52]

The web of emotional relationships between a newly born baby
and his parents and siblings makes ordinarily the earliest social atom
of an individual. Subsequently, "the volume of the social atom is in
continuous expansion as we grow up. These social atoms change from
time to time in their membership."[53]

The shortcomings of this conception of the social atoms are many.
First, it considers only the emotional tone of social relations and
completely ignores the intellectual and the non-emotional aspects of
these relations. The point is, there exists a multitude of social relations which are emotionally neutral and yet very important in their
intellectual and other values for every individual. This means that a
large part of the universe of social relationships is not covered by
Moreno's social atoms. Second, out of a wide variety of emotions,
Moreno takes only attraction and repulsion, and ignores many emotions which cannot be strictly called as attraction or rejection, such
as: compassion, forgiveness, sorrow, apathy, envy, generosity, joy, ec-
stasy, peace of mind, and so on. As a result, his "social atom" does
not cover even a large part of emotional relationship among the individuals or groups. His social atom is not social atom at all for a large
portion of the universe of social relationships. In this point it sharply
differs from the physical structures. Third, Moreno's atom differs
from the physico-chemical atoms also in that some ninety physico-
chemical atoms, like hydrogen, oxygen, iron, gold, uranium, etc.,
differ from each other not by one trait only (like mass or weight),
but by several characteristics, particularly by the number and arrangement of the electrons around the central nucleus. Moreno's social
atoms are distinguished from one another by one trait only: by either
emotional attraction or rejection. In the mentioned three respects the
atom of physics and Moreno's social atom have very little in common
with each other. For this reason there is no basis for Moreno to borrow the term: atom from physics and to give to it an entirely different
meaning devoid of even a superficial similitude.

Fourth, contrary to Moreno's statement, his atom in no way is the simplest and smallest unit of all social relationships. The network of emotional attraction or rejection centered around monarchs, dictators, presidents, popes, patriarch, military leader of vast armies, leaders of large political parties, big captains of finance and industry, and so on, involves thousands, often millions, of individuals whom such leaders attract and reject, and by whom they are admired or hated. The total network of emotional relatedness of such social atoms is not the simplest and smallest unit, but is one of the vastest and most complex webs of social relationships in the whole universe of emotional interactions of human beings. Only euphemistically such networks can be called "the smallest" or "the simplest." Fifth the physical atom of any of the ninety elements, for instance, oxygen or hydrogen remains identical to itself in its essential traits. Moreno's atom incessantly changes, expands and contracts in the number of its social relatednesses and in the kind of the individuals with whom emotional rapport is established. In this point again it is dissimilar from the physical atoms.

Without adding to these defects of the social atom many others,[54] the above criticism warrants the following conclusions: 1) In regard to the social world Moreno's social atom does not play the same role which the physical atom plays in regard to the physical universe; neither does the former resemble the latter in its structure. 2) For this reason the term "social atom" is a misnomer for the network of emotional attraction and repulsions. 3) It is neither "the smallest" nor "the simplest" unit of emotional or social relatedness. 4) It does not cover all social relations; even not all emotionally colored social interactions. It is neither an ultimate nor universal unit out of which all webs of social relationships are built, and to which they can be analytically reduced. 5) It is so diverse in its structure and function, in its volume and properties—now embracing millions of persons, now involving only a few—and at the same time it so incessantly changes, that it is not the same unit in all these diverse forms. The term covers rather a series of different phenomena. For these reasons it cannot perform the functions of a simplest unit of social phenomena. The concept of the network of emotional rapports of an individual is a valuable concept for several purposes; but it cannot serve the tasks of the social atom. In this point it is useless. Such, in brief, are the shortcomings of Moreno's social atom. Still more defective are "the social atoms" discovered by other sociologists.

A *coup de grâce* to Moreno's social atom, as well as to all searches for the social atom as the simplest unit of social relationship, has been given by the modern physics. It ceased to view atom as the simplest unit of physical phenomena, and has replaced it by an ever-increasing number of progressively smaller and smaller "elementary particles." About 1930 the electron and the proton replaced atom as the simplest unit. During subsequent years a number of other elementary particles has been discovered: the "non-material" photon, then the neutron, the positron, two kinds of meson, the neutrino, the antiproton, the antielectron, the antineutron, the antineutrino, and the antiproton. With this increase of the elementary particles, the very terms "elementary" and "ultimate particle" of physical reality have radically changed their meaning. In the words of an eminent physicist, "elementary" now seems to mean "the equivalent of criptic, arcane, perplexing, enigmatic, inscrutable." Since many of these enigmatic partciles do not have most of the characteristics of "mattter," the term "material" has also become inapplicable to them and had to be largely abandoned.[55]

Thus, while the physical science has already abandoned atom as the simplest unit, our "sociological physicists" are still playing with atomic marbles, and still looking for the social atom as the most elementary unit of social phenomena, relationships, and structures. It is high time to drop this playing with the atomic marbles and to terminate the search for the sociological Humpty-Dumpty. In my works I have pointed out many times[56] that there is no elementary "social atom" or the simplest unit of social phenomena. Instead, we should look for the generic model of social phenomena that gives us the traits and relationships common to all social phenomena. Our efforts should be concentrated on a study of this generic model and not at the non-existing social atoms.

Hunt for Elementary, Small Groups. Following the precept of the biology of the nineteenth century that a study of structure and evolution of organisms should begin with their simplest and smallest forms, a number of sociologists and psychologists have "discovered" in recent years "a small group" as the elementary social unit. Accordingly, they started an intense investigation of "the small groups" as the most promising approach for discovery of the generalizations valid for larger groups and for the whole universe of social phenomena. The initial impetus to the study of the small groups was given by Moreno's theory of the social atoms and his "sociometry" and by K. Lewin's pseudo-mathematical schemes of "group dynamics." Under their influence a number of younger researchers—like the members of the "Group Dynamics," R. Bales, A. Bavelas, G. C. Homans, E. F. Borgata, and others[57]—have enthusiastically engaged in the studies of the small groups and made such studies fashionable for the present moment. Parallel with the development of this movement its partisans have increasingly contended the revolutionary character of their discoveries, the exceptionally scientific nature of their studies, up to the claims that they started the scientific—experimental, objective, and quantitative—study of the small groups for the first time in history, and that before their scientific research the psychosocial sciences have been mainly a speculative arm chair philosophy.

When the claims of the partisans of this movement are carefully examined, they are found to be largely baseless. When their research methods are seriously considered, they turn out to be mainly sham-experimental and sham-quantitative procedures; when their discoveries are analyzed they appear to be either a rediscovery of the long ago discovered sociological table of multiplication or insignificant trifles or errors.

To begin with, the researchers of the small groups still do not have a satisfactory definition of a small group which they study. Their definitions stress two *differentia specifica* of the small groups: first, face to face interaction "in which each member receives some impression of each other member distinct enough so that he can give some reaction to each of the others as an individual person, even though it be only to recall that the other was present"; second, a small membership of the group fluctuating from one to some twenty-five or so members. On the basis of these characteristics of the small groups, a face-to-face meeting of some 20 persons previously unknown to each other, where each member does not receive "a clear perception" of many members of the meeting—be it an incidental cocktail party, a spontaneous political gathering, or a religious revival—is not a small group by the definition. On the other hand, a series of meetings of some 600 members of a parliament where each member knows all other members; or the Republican convention with more than 1,000 delegates who interact face to face, and who usually know one another, will be a "small group." In addition, we are told that even one person, when he talks with himself or feels ashamed, is "a small group." Thus, according to the basic characteristics of the definition of a small group, many a large group are "small groups"; while many a small group are not small groups at all. As an additional surprise we can have a small group consisting of one person only. Such a use of the term: "small and large" in the senses almost opposite to what these terms usually mean, does not contribute to the clarity of the definition. It hopelessly confuses the issue, and makes the concept of a small group exceedingly vague and even self-contradictory.

Further on, both characteristics of the small group's definition do not give us any *homogeneous* class of social groups but, instead, deliver to us a veritable motley of the most *dissimilar groups* because either one of the two characteristics is found among most heterogeneous groups or gatherings of persons. Thus face to face interaction takes place in the meeting of two lovers, of executioner and the executed, in the family reunion, in the meetings of the directors of a business corporation, in the interactions of a milling and shouting crowd, in a discussion group, in a platoon on a battle field, in the session of a parliament or political convention; and so on and so forth. The mere face-to-face interaction does not make these and hundreds of other groups similar or belonging to the same species of groups. Likewise, a small membership is found among the most dissimilar groups: in the family, in the board of directors of a corporation, in a group of revolutionary plotters, in a gang of criminals, in "exclusive" clubs of various kinds, and in hundreds of other groups as different from one another as they can be.

Such a unification of the most heterogeneous groups into one class of "the small groups" is contrary to the basic scientific rule of classification of phenomena. It is as anti-scientific as a biological unification into one "nosey" species of such different organisms as insect, fish, dog, bird, and man; or into "taily" species: snakes, ants, horses, and birds. We know well that such a species is not a species at all. For the same reason the class of the small groups is not a class at all. The very attempt of making a specific class of "the small groups" is devoid of any logical, semantic, and empirical grounds. It is about as unscientific as would be an attempt of a botanist to make a special species of "the small plants" out of all plants from 1 to 25 inches tall, or the endeavor of a zoologist to make a new species of "the small organisms" out of all organisms from 1 to 20-pound weight. In biology such taxonomic classes do not exist, and if attempted, they do not have any chance of being accepted by biologists. In sociology, unfortunately, they are still made and have a notable vogue at the present moment.

Since the partisans of the small groups do not have any real class of social groups for their study; and since they do not know exactly what are "the small groups" which they try to investigate, no wonder that this initial "sin" has been responsible for many defects and errors of their industrious research. To this primordial sin is due their false assumption that a small group is the simplest unit of social groups or structures. By face-to-face interaction and by the size of its membership the family is a small group; and yet in its structure and functions it is one of the most complex and most encyclopedic groups among all social organizations.[58] By the size of their membership many national and international associations like the Democratic or the Republican party, the American Federation of Labor, the National Association of Manufacturers not to mention many religious and other bodies, are vast groups with millions of members. Structurally and functionally they are much simpler groups than the family. Structurally their members are bound together by only one or a few bonds or interests—economic, or occupational, or recreational, or religious or scientific, etc.—while the members of the family are bound together by many bonds or interests. Functionally the activities of these vast organizations are also much less encyclopedic, more narrow and specialized, than the "encyclopedic" activities of the family. Generally, many a real community (*Gemeinschaften*) are ordinarily small in size in comparison with many an association (*Gesellschaften*); and yet, structurally and functionally such communities are much more complex than many a vast association. This shows that the small size of a group does not necessarily make it a simple group, and *vice versa*. The partisans of the small groups grossly err in their identification of the small group with the simplest groups. This means that if we want to follow the precept of the study: "from the simplest to the more complex," a study of social groups must not necessarily begin with the smallest groups and then pass to the larger groups. Moreover, the precept itself in no way is a universal methodological principle: in many cases the Aristotelian opposite precept, namely: the properties of an oak can be studied more fruitfully on a full-grown oak than on its acorn, is more advisable to follow.

The preceding blunders are responsible for a half-hazard approach to the study of the small groups and for the kind of the groups selected for a study by the small-group researchers. The bulk of the investigated groups represents an incidental, semi-organized or non-organized collection of students, or soldiers, or workers, or dwellers of an establishment (room, apartment, classroom, factory room, etc.), previously unknown to one another, and hastily gathered together, often by the command of an authority or by a promise of a payment, for the sake of "discussion," "interviewing and questioning," and similar artificial purposes. These incidental gatherings are mainly the "chatterbox groups." Now and then these little organized collections of a few individuals are replaced by a few, quite heterogeneous, organized groups, like the family in Tikopeio, or a metropolitan club or a small religious sect or a political clique. Without any stress of the profound difference between the organized, the unorganized, and the nominal groups, they all are treated as the small groups. No wonder that a study of this "hash of groups" has yielded meager results little applicable either to the organized, or the non-organized or the nominal groups.[59]

The above criticism does not mean that the *specific forms* of small groups cannot or should not be studied. On the contrary, such small groups as "the dyads," and "the tryads," of various kinds; the family, a small aristocracy, small business group, small sect or political party, and so on, have been fruitfully studied. However, each of these collectivities has been investigated not just as a small group generally, but as a specific group whose structural, dynamic, and functional properties cannot be extended over all or many groups with small membership. The basic properties of the family and the relationships of "husband-wife-child" cannot be extrapolated much beyond the family tryad and cannot be applied to all the dyads, the tryads, and the small business-religious-criminal-educational-military-political collectivities; and especially to the non-organized and the nominal groups, and *vice versa*. If the unwarranted extrapolation of the properties of one of these specific groups is extended over the other groups, as it is regularly done by our discoverers of the small groups, the results are bound to be either meaningless, or fallacious, or cognitively insignificant.

These remarks lead us to a rejection of the claim of the recent investigators of the small groups that before their research the small groups were hardly studied at all, and that today's researchers are the discoverers of the small groups. These pretentious claims are baseless. Since Confucius, at least a series of the specific small groups, beginning with the family, were carefully studied by many thinkers of the past centuries. But these thinkers investigated them as the specific groups and wisely abstained from extrapolation of their results far beyond the group studied.

In this respect their procedure was much more scientific than that of the recent researchers of the fictitious class of the small groups generally. The family and the household, the dyads of: teacher-pupil, master-slave, seller-buyer, employer-employee; the tryads of a "judge-accuser-accused," "husband-wife-lover"; small *Bruderschaften*, small guild, caste, village, and many other small collectivities have been well analyzed already by the authors of the *Laws of Hammurabi,* by Confucius, Mo-ti, and Mencius, by the authors of the Indian Puranas, Tantras, Arthasastras, Nitisastras, including such law books as the *Laws of Manu, Institute of Vishnu,* and by such authors as Kautalya; by Plato and Aristotle, and especially by the great Roman Jurists whose work is incorporated into the *Corpus Juris Civilis.* This *Corpus* alone gives so adequate, so detailed, and so well analyzed definitions of the main specific small (and large) in their size-groups, "corporations," and "institutions," that their work still lives not only in today's law-codes, but in the social life of the European and Latin-American West. In comparison with their definitions, formulae, and analyses of the main small groups, those of the recent small-group researchers are but a babytalk. The quicker these researchers drop their childish claims of being the discoverers of the small groups; and the quicker they acquaint themselves with the *Corpus Juris Civilis* and with other ancient studies of the main organized small groups, the better for the researchers and for sociology.

When we carefully examine the alleged experimental, operational, quantitative, and objective *methods* of the recent investigators of small groups, we find an already familiar imitative veneer of these methods applied mainly to the familiar "hearsay-stuff" of the incidental participants of the hastily recruited "discussion" or "problem-solving" or, more exactly, "chatterbox" groups. At the first glance the setting and procedures of these researchers impress as truly instrumental and objective. Their "small group" meets in a special "laboratory-room" equipped with a one-way mirror, and with sound and interaction recorders. These gadgets allegedly permit the investigator to observe, to record, and to place each "unit of speech" of each member into one of his categories. As a typical example of these categories R. F. Bales' classification can serve. He classifies all possible speech-reactions and overt-actions of the members into the following classes: (1) "shows solidarity; (2) shows tension release; (3) agrees; (4) gives suggestions; (5) gives opinion; (6) gives orientation; (7) asks for orientation; (8) asks for opinion; (9) asks for suggestion; (10) disagrees; (11) shows tension; (12) shows antagonism."

Unseen by the participants, and armed with the sound and interaction recorder, seeing and hearing everything that goes on in the one-way mirror room, the investigator-observer records each "speech-unit" of each member, what it is, to whom it is addressed, and simultaneously puts it into one of his categories. At the end of the session he has the record of all the speech-and-action units of each member, to whom each utterance or action is addressed, in what order, and to what category it belongs. These data then are statistically processed and supply us supposedly with the hitherto unknown, scientific knowledge of the interaction-process, structure and dynamics of the small groups of all sorts. The results obtained are usually generalized and applied to many other—small and large—groups. Bales' small groups fluctuated in size from two to ten and from three to six participants. Their members consisted of Harvard undergraduates, obtained through the Harvard employment bureau. The students did not know each other prior to the first meeting. Each group had four meetings for discussion of a "human relations case." [60]

In spite of all this veneer of scientific operations, the whole procedure is in fact highly subjective, arbitrary, and based on exceedingly vague assumptions and doubtful notions. First, the central concepts of the study—"the speech-unit" and "the action-unit" remain practically undefined. Shall we regard as a "speech-unit" every single word? or every proposition consisting of the subject-copula-predicate? or a series propositions dealing with the same subject? or showing the same emotional tone? or addressed to the same member? or what? A very indeterminate and foggy outline of these units does not help at all deciding what is a "speech-unit" or an "action-unit." As a result, which words or actions make a "speech-unit" (or "action-unit") is quite arbitrarily decided by the observer according to his fancy. Since these central concepts are undefined, the whole huge analytical and statistical superstructure, built upon them, remains but a mirage suspended in air.

No less arbitrary is the simultaneous operation of pigeonholing into one of the twelve categories of each "speech- or action-unit" of every member in the incessant and rapidly moving stream of vocal utterances and notions of the participants—sometimes talking and moving simultaneously. In contrast to the electronic mathematical calculators, "the interaction-recorder" does not automatically classify the speech- and action-units into one of the twelve classes. The pigeonholing is done—again in a great rush—by the observer. He has no time to analyze carefully whether the incessantly uttered words belong to the category of the "gives suggestion" or of the "gives opinion" or of the "disagrees" or of the "shows tension" or of the "shows antagonism." Even if the observer had had plenty of time he would have found still difficult, often impossible, an accurate "pigeonholing," because the categories: "gives opinion," "gives orientation," and "gives suggestion" are so similar to each other that only by some "supernatural intuition" one can draw a clear difference between them and in great haste unerringly place each uttered word into one of these categories. The same can be said of the categories: "disagrees," "shows tension" (what are its signs?) and "shows antagonism." Considering that the observer throughout the whole session of his "chatterbox group" has to record: (a) each "speech-unit" (undefined); (b) each "action-unit" (also undefined); (c) by whom it is uttered or done; (d) to whom it is addressed; (e) to which of his poorly defined categories it belongs; (f) often all these simultaneous recordings he has to do in regard to many-voiced utterances and manifold actions of several simultaneously talking and acting members; considering that all these recordings, analyses, and classifications he has to do almost momentarily, in the greatest rush, no observer can perform these impossible tasks accurately and objectively, and any observer can do it only impulsively, arbitrarily, and blunderously. If thus two basic things in the whole study—the units of speech and action and their pigeonholing—are predominantly subjective and arbitrary, most of the other data of the research, most of its statistical superstructure, and the bulk of the conclusions built upon these two bases, become subjective, arbitrary, pseudo-experimental and pseudo-quantitative. No gadgets and one-way mirrors, no long series of figures and indexes can hide the essentially unscientific nature of the whole research-operation.

A number of other important defects vitiate these research-operations. The classification of the twelve categories is haphazard. It does not have any *fundamentum divisionis*. Several of its categories, like the mentioned ones: "gives suggestion," "gives opinion," and so on, are so similar and overlapping with one another that a most careful investigator, with plenty of time, cannot decide to which of these categories this or that "speech-unit" belongs. On the other hand, the classification unites into one category the words and actions notably dissimilar from one another. For instance, the category "gives orientation" embraces: "information, repetition, clarification, confirmation." "Repetition" is obviously not synonymous with "information," and "clarification" means something different from "confirmation." Such a logically and factually clumsy classification is a very poor tool for a study of the vocal and behavioral units, and it makes unavoidable a great deal of arbitrariness and subjectivity in the research operation.

Further on, the categories of the classification aim to describe only the speech-reactions of the participants, and they are unfit to describe their non-vocal actions. Omitting almost entirely the overt behavior of the participants and the real motives of their actions, the studies of our investigators of the small groups merely glide on the vocal surface without touching the overt behavior of the members of the incidental "chatterbox" group. In this sense researches are superficial and almost completely dodge the real problems of social interaction and group phenomena.

Not mentioning other crucial defects of these studies[61] the above criticism makes comprehensible a conspicuous poverty of the results of these researches. Their pretentious "discoveries" are, in fact, either ponderously formulated platitudes, or tautologies screened by statistical tables, or revelations discovered long ago, or distorted transcriptions of the propositions of the physical sciences, or plain errors. Here are typical samples of these "discoveries." If need be, they can be multiplied *ad libitum*.

"Interaction is a process consisting of action followed by reaction." [62] What a marvellous tautology of the type: A is A. [For leadership] "there must be a group with a common task . . . and at least one must have responsibilities which differ from these of the other members." (R. M. Stogdill)[63] How true! and almost as new as the discovery that "after the spring comes the summer, and after the summer, the fall," and so on. However, as it often happens with platitudes, the statement forgets that sometimes the group and its common task are created by a leader.

"Some members [of a group] may be regarded as rating higher than others in leadership" [because they have responsibility of making the decisions.][64]

Extraordinary new discovery, not a bit older than five thousand years.

"A significant aspect of our society is that persons desire membership in groups." (L. Festinger)[65]

What a revelation is this, especially after Aristotle's "man is a naturally political animal" and "there is in all persons a natural impetus to associate with each other." [66]

No less striking are other "discoveries" of L. Festinger about "why people seek membership in groups." The answer is because "Groups frequently [help] the attainment of important individual goals." The activities of the group are frequently attractive to the member. And they are attractive "because people have needs" that can be satisfied only in groups.

And so on. Proclaiming these platitudes, the author forgets to mention several important limitations of these varieties like the fact that millions of persons become the members of a group automatically, regardless of their wishes; e.g., the state citizenship or caste-membership automatically imposed upon all born from the citizens of the state or the parental caste; and sometimes many individuals, like the prisoners of war and criminals, are coerced to belong to the prisoners' group or to the group of the inmates of a prison, contrary to their wishes. And such "automatic" and "undesirable" memberships play a much more important role in the life of hundreds of millions than the voluntary or sought for memberships.

The same conclusion applies to Festinger's "discoveries" about the relationship between friendship (or enmity) and the territorial and "functional" propinquity, to the conditions of successful community action and practically to all Festinger's conclusions, allegedly derived, from his "experimental" studies of the Regent Hill and the Westgate groups. Each of his roughly sound conclusions was incomparably better formulated, developed, and demonstrated by many social investigators of the preceding generations.

Let us now take the discoveries concerning "the cohesiveness" of groups. The term "cohesiveness" means "the total field of forces which act on members to remain in the groups." (John Thibaut)[67] The term, as well as its definition, is a distorted version of propositions of mechanics borrowed from the physical sciences. It is an extremely vague and inadequate statement. Without a preliminary differentiation of the kind of the groups whose "cohesiveness" is studied, no real understanding of the forms and the "forces of cohesiveness" is possible. The point is that there are "voluntary" and "coercive groups" or more exactly the "familistic," the "contractual," and the "compulsory" groups. The basic difference of these groups from one another manifests itself also in a fundamental difference of the "forces of cohesiveness" in each type of these groups. The factors which unite the members of a good family into one unity and which maintain its identity, "cohesiveness," and continuity are quite different from the factors of cohesiveness that coerce the inmates of a prison "to remain in the group." The forces that keep together the employees and the employer of a business firm are again different from those of the family, a prison group, or of the American Sociological Society.

This differentiation of the types of the groups and the types of the bonds that keep together the members of various types of the groups is not done at all in Thibaut's and other studies of the cohesiveness of the small groups. As a result, all their industrious efforts to study scientifically the problems of cohesiveness of the small groups have not yielded literally any new significant discovery. In comparison with the existing body of knowledge in this field, their theories, their "discovered" uniformities, and their total grasp of the problem in all its main ramifications still remains at a primitive stage, long ago passed over by today's psychosocial sciences.[68] Next discovery is: "the attraction to the group is a function of the resultant forces acting on the members." What "resultant forces?" and how do they act on members? In mechanics all these terms are strictly defined and measurable. Here they remain just vague words devoid of any definite meaning and measurement.

Let us continue to discover "the discoveries" of our "pioneers." Here are further examples of the tautologies of our investigators.

> "The term [of group] cohesiveness refers to phenomena which come into existence if, and only if, the group exists." [How wonderful!]

Or

> "The members of a group who are . . . friends . . . are likely to be more interested in one another as persons, perhaps more supportive of each other, more cordial in interpersonal relations." [What a revelation again! and note especially an extreme "scientific" caution in this remarkable "perhaps."]

Until this revelation we naively thought that, without any "perhaps," "friendship" implies mutual interest, cordiality, and support of the friends.[69]

Reading these revelations I am inclined to borrow G. Saintsbury's expressions: "O clichés! O Tickets! O fudge!"[70]

> "An increase in the frequency of interaction between persons may increase the strength of their favorable sentiment toward one another."[71]

So the more frequently German and American soldiers fight (interact), the more favorable sentiment they develop toward one another. Consequently, the fighting and hating interaction is as good a remedy for development of the mutual admiration, sympathy, and altruism as mutual help. Fortunately for Homans, at the end of the paragraph stating and developing this "scientific" generalization, he seems to have grasped its one-sided fallacy and, therefore, added in just four words two other possible consequences of the frequent interaction, namely, development "of respect or, worst, antagonism."

> "Splinter-group formation will disrupt the larger organization when the goals of the smaller group are incompatible with those of the larger."

Again, what a beautiful tautology! Splinter-groups tend to splint or disrupt! But as it happens with many tautologists, the tautological statement in this form is inadequate because instead of disrupting the larger group, the splinter-group more frequently is suppressed by the larger group. Empirically onesided also is the statement that "the tendency to break apart would be more likely, the larger the group."[72] If the generalization were true, no large groups like the great empires, the world religious organizations, or large labor unions could emerge and have a long life-span. As a matter of fact, during historical existence of mankind there always have been the large groups, and they have had much longer life-span than the small groups.[73]

Here are further examples of the "discoveries" discussed. R. F. Bales and associates start their paper with a usual "amnesiac" claim:

> "The frequencies of communication between members in small face-to-face groups show certain striking regularities which

have not previously been described." . . . "The detection of
these regularities represents a significant gain in our knowledge
about the distribution of communication in small groups, and
provides a basic framework of order within which many more
detailed analyses of the interaction process may be made."[74]

Quite a modest claim! Now let us see what are the discovered
"striking and significant regularities?" Here is an example:

> "The findings reported indicate that if participants in a
> small group are ranked by the total number of acts they initiate,
> they will also tend to be ranked: (1) by the number of acts they
> receive; (2) by the number of acts they address to specific other
> individuals; and (3) by the number of acts they address to the
> group as a whole." [75]

In plain words these ponderous "uniformities" mean that in a
discussion group the most talkative members of a group talk more
frequently and are talked back to more frequently by the other less
talkative members. From this beautiful tautology we can derive an
additional "striking and significant uniformity" overlooked by Bales:
the persons who are silent, talk less frequently, and are talked back
to less frequently than the most talkative persons.

However, like many other tautologies, Bales' tautology in no way
can be considered a general empirical rule for all—small and large—
groups. In the court room group: the judge, the accused, the prose-
cuting and the defense attorneys, and the jury, contrary to Bales'
uniformity, most of the talks are addressed to the jury and the judge.
The jury, as a rule, remains silent, instead of talking most; even the
judge ordinarily talks less than the attorneys. A lecturer, a preacher,
a commander of a platoon issuing orders, are the only talking members of the respective groups. And yet, they ordinarily are not talked
back to at all by the other members of the group. In a large number
of various groups, all the talking members address their talk to "Mr.
Chairman!"; and Mr. Chairman often talks the least in the group.
And so on, and so forth.

Bales' "uniformities" are exceptions rather than the rule, from the
standpoint of the real processes of who, to whom, and how frequently
is talking in an overwhelming majority of the small and large groups.
And what is still more important, no painstaking and misleading
research of Bales' type is necessary for discovering the order, frequency, and the kind of talks by various members of almost all

organized groups: all this can easily be found in the constitution of such groups. The laws and by-laws of each organized group supply an incomparably more accurate information on all these points than the vague and largely fictitious uniformities of the investigators of the small groups obtained with an enormous waste of time, energy, and funds invested in their laborious, pseudo-scientific research.

These discoveries are crowned by what appears to be an "epoch-making discovery," achieved by a cooperative effort of an investigator of the small groups and the producers of "theoretical frameworks" for all the "social actions" and all the psychosocial sciences of all times, by the discoveries of the already discussed Principles of Inertia, of Action and Reaction, of Effort, and of System-Integration.[76]

If there were need, one could go, page by page, through the published studies of the recent researchers in the small groups. Almost on each page one would find "the discoveries," concepts, definitions, and the theories represented by the given examples. Carefully reading these works I have not found any single new discovery even of tertiary importance. And I have found a superabundance of the "pseudo-discoveries" illustrated by the above samples. Factually walking in a well-cultivated park, our investigators seemingly imagine themselves as the great pioneer-explorers opening the hitherto unknown land, or as the first climbers of long ago conquered scientific peaks.

With this summary our exploration of the small groups can be concluded.[77]

Pitirim Alexandrovitch Sorokin (1889——), was born in Touria (a village in Russia); educated in the Teachers College, Kostroma Province (1903-1906), Evening School, St. Petersburg (1907-1909), Psycho-Neurological Institute, St. Petersburg (1909-1910), University of St. Petersburg (1910-1914); Magistrant of Criminal Law (1915); Dr. of Sociology (1922); Privatdozent, Psycho-Neurological Institute (1914-1916) and at the University of St. Petersburg (1916-1917): Professor and Chairman of the Department of Sociology, University of St. Petersburg, Agricultural Academy (1919-1922); University of Minnesota (1924-1930); Professor at Harvard since 1930; Chairman of the Department of Sociology (1930-1943); Director of Harvard Research Center in Creative Altruism (1949——). Member of the Executive Committee, All-Russian Peasant Soviet (1917); member, the Council of Russian Republic (1917); Secretary to Prime Minister (1917); member of the Russian Constitutional Assembly (1918); President, International Institute and Congress of Sociology (1937). Author of some

29 books in Sociology (most of which are translated in from one to eleven foreign languages), the best known being: *Social Mobility* (1926), *Contemporary Sociological Theories* (1928), *Social and Cultural Dynamics* (1937-41), *Crisis of Our Age* (1941), *Society, Culture, and Personality* (1947), *Social Philosophies in an Age of Crisis* (1950), *Fads and Foibles in Modern Sociology and Related Sciences* (1956); etc.

NOTES

1. P. W. Bridgman, *The Intelligent Individual and Society* (New York: The MacMillan Co., 1938), 7, 8, 12, *et passim*, see also his "The Task Before Us," *Proceedings of the American Academy of Arts and Sciences*, LXXXIII (1954), 97-112.

2. See: P. A. Sorokin, *Contemporary Sociological Theories* (New York: Harpers, 1928), Chap. I.

3. J. Q. Stewart, "A Basis for Social Physics," *Impact of Science on Society*, III (1952), 110, 118.

4. *Ibid.*, 122-23.

5. *Ibid.*, 116-18.

6. These remarks are probably unclear to most of modern sociologists and psychologists who hardly ever studied the meaning—forms—and function of time and space, and especially of their sociostructural forms. Clarifying analysis of sociocultural time and space can be found in P. Sorokin, *Sociocultural Causality, Space, Time* (Durham, N. C.: Duke University Press, 1943), Chaps. 3-4; *Social and Cultural Dynamics* (New York: American Book Co., 1941), IV, Chaps. 9, 10, 11; see also G. Gurvitch, *Déterminismes sociaux et liberté humaine* (Paris: Press Universitaire, 1955), where another pluralistic theory of time is developed.

7. *Ibid.*, 118-129. In a personal letter to me, Professor Stewart states that "as the point of view of social physics develops further, you would be willing to consider that the dimensions of reason, feeling, and authority offer sufficient description of many sociocultural phenomena. This would leave time, distance, and mass as purely physical." (Letter, May 26, 1953.)

8. Cf. on these matters above. Sorokin, *Social and Cultural Dynamics*, Vol. IV, Chap. 5; P. Sorokin, *Society, Culture, and Personality* (New York: Harpers, 1947), *passim*.

9. T. Parsons, R. F. Bales, and E. A. Shils, *Working Papers in the Theory of Action* (Glencoe: Free Press, 1953), p. 102. Cf. a more detailed criticism of these "generalizations" in P. Sorokin, *Fads and Foibles in Modern Sociology* (Chicago: H. Regnery, 1955).

10. They outline vaguely one of the five different meanings of the term: "equilibrium," none of which is applicable to psychosocial systems and actions. See an analysis and criticism of all five concepts of equilibrium in P. Sorokin, *Social and Cultural Dynamics* (New York: American Book Co., 1937-41), V, IV, 677-693.

11. See about these principles in P. Sorokin, *Dynamics*, quoted V. IV, Chaps. 12-16, and P. Sorokin, *Society, Culture, and Personality*, Chap. 46.

12. See many examples of these terms in D. Cartwright and A. Zander, *Group Dynamics* (Evanston: Row, Peterson, Co., 1953). For a further criticism of this "fashion" see P. Sorokin, *Fads and Foibles in Modern Sociology*, Chaps. 1, 2.

13. G. A. Lundberg, *Foundations of Sociology* (New York: The MacMillan Co., 1939) , 115.

14. G. K. Zipf, *Human Behavior* and the *Principle of Least Effort* (Cambridge: Addison-Wesley Press, 1949) , 327-28, 253, 212.

15. Cartwright and Zanders, *op. cit.*, 320-21.

16. Cf. K. Lewin, *Principles of Topological Psychology* (New York: McGraw-Hill, 1936) ; and Lewin's *Field Theory in Social Sciences: Selected Theoretical Papers* (New York: Harpers, 1951) ; J. F. Brown, "On the Use of Mathematics in Psychological Theory," *Psychometrika*, I (1936) ; Brown, *Psychology and Social Order* (New York: McGraw-Hill, 1936) ; M. Lins, *Espaço-Tempo e relaçoes sociaes* (Rio de Janeiro, 1940) ; Pinto Ferreira, *Teoria do espaço social* (Rio de Janeiro: A. Coelho Bran Co., 1939) ; Pontes de Miranda, *Intruduccao a sociologia geral* (Rio de Janeiro, 1927) . Cf more detailed criticism of these transcriptions in P. Sorokin, *Sociocultural Causality, Space, Time,* Chap. 3.

17. A. Lysen, "Anorganisches und Organisches in den sozialen Erscheinungen," *Kölner Vierteljahrshefte für Soziologie*, XI (1932) , 139-153.

18. Kurt Lewin, *Field Theory in Social Sciences: Selected Theoretical Papers* (New York, 1951) , 100, 239-40.

19. S. C. Dodd, *Dimensions of Society. A Quantitative Systematics for the Social Sciences* (New York: The MacMillan Co., 1942) , frontpiece. S. C. Dodd, *Systematic Social Science (A Dimensional Sociology)* (American University of Beirut, 1947) .

20. E. T. Bell's review of Dodd's "Dimensions of Society," *American Sociological Review*, VII (1942) , 707-9.

21. Cf. for a further criticism in P. Sorokin, *Fads and Foibles,* Ch. 7.

22. N. Wiener, *The Human Use of Human Beings. Cybernetics and Society* (Boston: Houghton Mifflin Co., 1950) , 9, 15, 16. Cf. also N. Wiener, *Cybernetics or Control and Communication in the Animal and Machine* (New York: J. Wiley, 1948) . F. D. Barrett and H. A. Shepard, "A Bibliography of Cybernetics," *Proceedings of the American Academy of Arts and Sciences*, LXXX (1953) , 204-222.

23. D. M. MacKay, "On Comparing the Brain with Machines," *American Scientist*, XLII (1954) , 261-268; J. O. Wisdom, R. L. Spilsbury and D. M. MacKay's paper in the *Symposium on Mentality in Machines,* Proceeedings of Aristotelian Society, Supplement, 1952.

24. Ch. Sherrington, "Mystery of Mysteries: the Human Brain," N. Y. *Times Magazine* (December 4, 1949) , 19-20.

25. D. M. MacKay, *op. cit.*, 259-60.

26. Cf. on the component of meaning as the main component of all psychosocial phenomena different from their physical components, in P. Sorokin, *Society, Culture, and Personality*, Ch. 3.

27. Cf. S. C. Dodd, "Can the Social Scientist Serve Two Masters?" *Research Studies of the State College of Washington*, XXI (1953) , pp. 195-213; A. Bavelas, "Communication Patterns in Task-Oriented Group," *Journal of Acoustical Society of America*, XXII (1950) , pp. 725-30; A. Bavelas and D. Barret, "An Experimental Approach to Organizational Communication," *Personnel* (April, 1951) ; H. J. Leavitt, "Some Effects of Certain Communication Patterns on Group Performance," *Journ. of Abnormal and Social Psychology*, XLVI (1951) , 38-50.

28. Cf. for a more detailed analysis and criticism of the cybernetic psycho-social theories, P. Sorokin, *Fads and Foibles,* quoted, Ch. 9.

29. A. H. Maslow, *Motivation and Personality* (New York: Harpers, 1954) , 13. Cf. on the recent dominant currents in psychology, G. W. Allport, *The Nature of*

Personality (Cambridge: Addison-Wesley Co., 1950) , 48-75; G. W. Allport, *Becoming* (New Haven: Yale University Press, 1955) , *passim.*

30. Cf. for a detailed discussion, analysis, and criticism of these tests in P. Sorokin, *Fads and Foibles,* quoted: Chaps. 4, 5, 6. See there also the literature on these problems.

31. E. L. Thorndike, *The Measurement of Intelligence* (New York: The Mac-Millan Co., 1927) .

32. Cf. L. M. Terman and M. H. Oden, *The Gifted Child Grows Up* (Stanford University Press, 1947) ; L. M. Terman, *Genetic Studies of Genius, Vol. I.* (Stanford University Press, 1925) ; Vol. II, C. M. Cox, *The Early Mental Tests of Three Hundred Geniuses* (Stanford University Press, 1926) ; Vol. III, B. S. Burks, D. W. Jensen and L. M. Terman, *The Promise of Youth: Follow-up Studies of a Thousand Gifted Children* (Stanford University Press, 1930) . Cf. for analysis and substantiation of the above conclusions, P. Sorokin, *Fads and Foibles,* quoted, Chap. 5.

33. Cf. *Assessment of Men. Selection of Personnel for the Office of Strategic Services by the OSS Assessment Staff* (New York: The MacMillan Co., 1948) , 5-8, 392, 423, 425. Cf. for details in P. Sorokin, *op. cit.,* Chap. 5. See also A. W. Heim, *The Appraisal of Intelligence* (London, 1954) .

34. Cf. for details, *Fads and Foibles,* Ch. 6.

35. Cf. J. Brozek, H. Guetzkow, M. D. Baldwin, R. Cranston, "A Quantitative Study of Perception and Association in Experimental Semi-Starvation," *Journal of Personality,* XIX (1951) , 245-64; G. W. Allport, "The Trend in Motivational Theory," *American Journal of Orthopsychiatry,* XXIII (1953) . Cf. for a comprehensive criticism of the projective techniques in P. Sorokin, *Fads and Foibles,* Chap. 6.

36. *The Essays of Michel de Montaigne* (London, 1913) , V. I, p. 5.

37. Cf. for a detailed criticism of the modern tests in P. Sorokin, *Fads and Foibles,* Chaps. 5, 6, 7.

38. Cf. P. W. Bridgman, *The Logic of Modern Physics* (New York: The Mac-Millan Co., 1927) ; and *The Nature of Physical Theory* (New York: The MacMillan Co., 1936) ; and "Some General Principles of Operational Analysis," *Psychological Review,* LII (1945) .

39. R. B. Lindsay, "A Critique of Operationalism in Physics," *Philosophy of Science,* IV (1937) , 456.

40. Cf. E. G. Boring, "The Use of Operational Definitions in Science," *Psychological Review,* LII (1952) ; on rapidly growing operationalism in psychology see G. Allport, *The Nature of Personality* (Cambridge, 1950) , 57-58.

41. Cf. the referred works of Lindsay, Allport. See also H. Margenau, *The Nature of Physical Reality* (New York: The MacMillan Co., 1950) and his "Physical vs. Historical Reality," *Philosophy of Science,* XIX (1952) , 203. About Intuitional and Logico-Mathematical methods see P. Sorokin, *The Ways and Power of Love* (Boston: Beacon Press, 1954) , Chap. 6; R. Ulich, *Man and Reality* (New Haven: Yale University Press, 1948) ; F. S. C. Northrop, *The Meeting of East and West* (New York: The MacMillan Co., 1946) ; E. W. Sinnott, *Two Ways to Truth* (New York: Viking Press, 1953) ; P. W. Bridgman, "The Task Before Us," *Proceedings of the American Academy of Arts and Sciences,* LXXXIII, 3 (1954) .

42. C. Kirkpatrick, "A Methodological Analysis of Feminism," *American Journal of Sociology,* XLIV (1939) , 332.

43. Cf. E. W. Burgess and L. S. Cottrell, Jr., *Predicting Success or Failure in*

Marriage (New York: Prentice-Hall, 1939); E. W. Burgess and H. J. Locke, *The Family* (New York: American Book Co., 1945), 458ff.; L. M. Terman, *Psychological Factors in Marital Happiness* (New York: McGraw-Hill, 1938).

44. S. C. Dodd, "A System of Operationally Defined Concepts for Sociology," *American Sociological Review,* IV (1939).

45. Cf. my criticism of these in P. Sorokin, *Fads and Foibles,* quoted; Ch. 3.

46. *American Sociological Review,* XVIII (1953), 612-17.

47. The same is true of A. Rapoport's attempt to define operationalism, operational definitions and operational philosophy. Instead of giving clear concepts of these, he factually gives a wide variety of different, sometimes even contradictory, notions of operationalism. Cf. A. Rapoport, *Operational Philosophy* (New York: Harpers, 1953).

48. Cf. on this canon in J. S. Mill, *A System of Logic* (London: Longman Co., 1843), Book 3, *et passim;* J. Venn, *The Principles of Empirical and Inductive Logic* (London, 1889); see also F. Znaniecki, *The Method of Sociology* (New York: Farrar and Rinehart, 1934); P. H. Furfey, *The Scope and Method of Sociology* (New York: Harpers, 1953); R. Carnap, "Inductive Logic and Science," in *Proceedings of the American Academy of Arts and Sciences,* LXXX (1953), 189-197; F. S. Chapin, *Experimental Designs in Sociological Research* (New York: Harpers, 1937); E. Greenwood, *Experimental Sociology* (New York: King's Crown Press, 1945); G. and L. B. Murphy, *Experimental Social Psychology* (New York: Harpers, 1931) and later editions.

49. Recent "experimental" studies of S. Schachter, L. Festinger, L. Killian, L. Coch, and other members of the "Group Dynamics," and of C. I. Hovland, A. A. Lumadaine and F. D. Sheffield can serve as examples of this sort of pseudo-experimental research. Cf. D. Cartwright and A. Zander, *Group Dynamics,* quoted; C. I. Hovland and others, *Experiments on Mass Communication* (Princeton: Princeton University Press, 1950).

50. See a development of this criticism in my *Fads and Foibles,* Chap. 9.

51. Compare, for instance, the results obtained in the studies of the relationship between friendship and social distance by P. Sorokin in his *The Ways and Power of Love,* 21ff., by J. B. Maller, in his *Cooperation and Competition* (New York: Columbia University Press, 1929), and by B. A. Wright in her *Selfishness, Guilt-Feeling and Social Distance,* and *Fairness and Generosity* (unpublished theses, University of Iowa, 1940 and 1942).

52. J. L. Moreno, *Psychodrama* (New York: Beacon House, 1946), Vol. I, 184, 229; *Who Shall Survive* (New York: Beacon House, 1953), 77 ff., 96.

53. J. L. Moreno, "The Social Atom and Death," *Sociometry,* X (1947), pp. 80-84.

54. Cf. on these defects P. Sorokin, *Fads and Foibles,* Ch. 10, G. D. Gurvitch, "Microsociology and Sociometry," *Sociometry,* XII (1949), 1-31.

55. Cf. E. Fermi, *Elementary Particles* (New Haven: Yale University Press, 1951); E. Schradinger's article in the *Endeavour,* IX, 35 (1950); H. Margenau, "The Meaning of Elementary Particle," *American Scientist,* XXXIX (1951), 422-431.

56. Cf. P. Sorokin, *Society, Culture, and Personality,* 39-49, *et passim.*

57. As representative samples of the small group studies may serve: P. Hare, E. F. Borgatta, R. F. Bales, Eds., *Small Groups* (New York: A. A. Knopf, 1955); R. F. Bales, *Interaction Process Analysis* (Cambridge: Addison-Wesley, 1950); G. C. Homans, *The Human Group* (New York: Harcourt Brace Co., 1950); Cartwright and Zander, *Group Dynamics,* quoted.

58. Cf. on the complexity of the family in P. Sorokin, *Society, Culture, and Personality*, 246ff.

59. The organized groups so basically differ from the unorganized and both from the nominal plurals, that no competent scholar can ignore this difference and indiscriminately unite them into a fictitious class of the small groups. Cf. on the organized, unorganized, and nominal groups in P. Sorokin, *Society, Culture, and Personality*, Chap. 4, *et passim*.

60. Cf. R. F Bales, "A Set of Categories for the Analysis of Small Group Interaction," *American Sociological Review*, XV (1950), 257-63; R. F. Bales, "The Equilibrium Problem in Small Groups," in T. Parsons, R. F. Bales and E. A. Shils, *Working Papers in The Theory of Action* (Glencoe: Free Press, 1953); R. F. Bales, *Interaction Process Analysis* (Cambridge: Addison-Wesley, 1950).

61. Cf. for a more detailed criticism in P. Sorokin, *Fads and Foibles*, Chap. 10.

62. R. F. Bales, "The Equilibrium Problem in Small Groups," in T. Parsons, R. F. Bales, and E. Shils, *Working Papers in The Theory of Action* (Glencoe: Free Press, 1953), 121.

63. D. Cartwright and A. Zander, *Group Dynamics*, quoted; 42.

64. *Ibid.*, 49.

65. *Ibid.*, 93.

66. Aristotle, *Politics*, 1253a.

67. Cartwright and Zander, *op. cit.*, 103.

68. See the state of this problem in today's sociology and vast literature in P. Sorokin, *Society, Culture, and Personality*, Chaps. 5, 6,7, 8, 21, 22.

69. *Ibid.*, 76-79.

70. G. Saintsbury, *A History of Criticism and Literary Taste of Europe* (London, 1900), Vol. I, 128.

71. G. C. Homans, *The Human Group*, 444.

72. Cartwright and Zanders, *op. cit.*, 86-87.

73. See on the life-span mortality and resurrection of various groups in P. Sorokin, *Society, Culture, and Personality*, Chap. 34.

74 R. F. Bales, F. L. Strodtbeck, T. M. Mills, and M. E. Roseborough, "Channels of Communication in Small Groups," *American Sociological Review*, XVI (1951), 461, 465.

75. *Ibid.*, 468.

76. T. Parsons, R. F. Bales, and E. A. Shils, *Working Papers*, 102.

77. Besides the criticism given in this paper, the basic criticism of previous physicalistic theories analyzed in my *Contemporary Sociological Theories* (Chap. 1) are fully applicable to all these recent theories.

INDEX

1177